PSYCHOLOGY
Fourth Edition

PSYCHOLOGY

FOURTH EDITION

JOHN P. DWORETZKY

Department of Psychology,
Western Washington University,
Bellingham, Washington

WEST PUBLISHING COMPANY

ST. PAUL ■ NEW YORK ■ LOS ANGELES ■ SAN FRANCISCO

Copy editing: Elaine Levin
Technical illustrations: Ayxa Art Studio and Barbara Burnett
Anatomical illustrations: Barbara Burnett
Cartoon drawings: Tom Burnett
Composition: Parkwood Composition Service
Cover: Helen Frankenthaler, *Tutti Fruitti,*
Albright-Knox Art Gallery, Buffalo, New York,
Gift of Seymour H. Knox, 1976.

Photo credits and Acknowledgments follow index.

Library of Congress Cataloging-in-Publication Data

Dworetzky, John.
  Psychology / John P. Dworetzky.—4th ed.
    p.   cm.
  Includes bibliographical references and indexes.
  ISBN 0-314-77462-9
  1. Psychology.   I. Title.
BF121.D96 1991
150—dc20   90-24428
                                                              CIP

CONTENTS IN BRIEF

UNIT 1 PSYCHOLOGICAL FOUNDATION: THE MIND AND THE BODY   1

CHAPTER 1
History, Systems, and Research Methods   3

CHAPTER 2
The Biological Bases of Behavior   35

CHAPTER 3
Sensation   77

CHAPTER 4
Perception   115

CHAPTER 5
State of Consciousness   149

UNIT 2 INTERACTING WITH THE ENVIRONMENT   183

CHAPTER 6
Conditioning and Learning   185

CHAPTER 7
Memory and Information Processing   221

CHAPTER 8
Cognition and Language   253

CHAPTER 9
Motivation   289

CHAPTER 10
Emotion   315

Unit 3 Development and Individual Differences 339

CHAPTER 11
Development Through the Lifespan 341

CHAPTER 12
Intelligence and Creativity 385

CHAPTER 13
Personality 415

Unit 4 Conflict and Adjustment 443

CHAPTER 14
Health Psychology 445

CHAPTER 15
Abnormal Behavior 471

CHAPTER 16
Therapy 515

Unit 5: Relating to One Another 549

CHAPTER 17
Social Behavior 551

CHAPTER 18
Sexuality, Attraction, and Intimacy 591

CHAPTER 19
Applied Psychology 625

APPENDIX A
Statistics 653

APPENDIX B
How to Locate and Read Research Articles in Psychology 667

Glossary   G-1
References   R-1
Name Index   I-1
Subject Index   I-15

CONTENTS

Unit 1 Psychological Foundation: The Mind and the Body   1

CHAPTER 1
History, Systems, and Research Methods   3

PROLOGUE   3
An Introduction to Psychology   4
  Becoming a Psychologist   5
  Areas of Specialization   6
The Beginning of Psychology   7
Philosophical Approaches to the Study of Psychology   9
  Structuralism   9
  Functionalism   10
  Psychoanalysis   11
  Behaviorism   12
  Gestalt Psychology   13
  Humanistic Psychology   14
  The Neurobiological Approach   15
  Cognitive Psychology   15
  Modern Trends and the Emergence of Scientific Psychology   16
Research Methods   16
  Experimental Methods   18
    Selecting Subjects   18
    Interobserver Reliability   19
    The Control   19
    Observer and Subject Bias   20
    The Results of Our Experiment   22
    Replication and Expansion   22
    Single-Subject Experiments   23
CONCEPT REVIEW: THE EXPERIMENT   23
  Nonexperimental Methods   24
    The Correlation Method   24
    Naturalistic Observations   26
    Case Studies   27
    Surveys   27
    Testing   29
AN ENDURING QUESTION: WHAT ARE THE LIMITS OF PSYCHOLOGICAL UNDERSTANDING?   30
EPILOGUE: SCIENCE AND THE SPIRIT OF WORLD   32
Summary   32
Suggestions for Further Reading   33

FOCUS ON RESEARCH: ETHICS AND PSYCHOLOGICAL RESEARCH   25

FOCUS ON RESEARCH: HOW TO GET HONEST ANSWERS   28

CHAPTER 2
The Biological Bases of Behavior   35

PROLOGUE   35
Why Psychologists Study the Nervous System and the Brain   37
The Divisions of the Nervous System   38
Neurons and the Body's Electrochemical System   40
CONCEPT REVIEW: THE ACTION OF THE NERVOUS SYSTEM   40
  Neuron Structure   42
  Neural Transmissions   43
  Synaptic Transmissions   45
    Excitatory Synapses   46
    Inhibitory Synapses   46
  The World of Neurotransmitters   47
    Long-Term Effects   47
    Drugs and Neurotransmitter Receptors   48
    Neuropeptides   49
Hormones and the Endocrine System   52
The Structure of the Brain   54
  The Hindbrain   58
    The Medulla   58
    The Cerebellum   58
    The Pons   59
    The Reticular Activating System   59
  The Midbrain   59
  The Forebrain   59
    The Thalamus   59
    The Hypothalamus   60
    The Limbic System   60
    The Corpus Callosum   61
    The Cerebrum   61
Brain Scanners: PET and MRI   63
The Brain and Behavior   66
  Specialized Areas in the Brain   67
  The Split Brain   70
AN ENDURING QUESTION: WHAT AND WHERE IS THE MIND?   73
EPILOGUE: MR. NIETHOLD'S TOOTHACHE   75
Summary   75
Suggestions for Further Reading   76

FOCUS ON THE FUTURE: BRAIN TRANSPLANTS   50

FOCUS ON RESEARCH: THE MAN WHO MISTOOK HIS WIFE FOR A HAT 68

CHAPTER 3
Sensation   77

PROLOGUE: SYSTEMS CHECK   77
Why Psychologists Study Sensation   78
Sensory Thresholds   79
Vision   80
  The Retina   81
    The Fovea   82
    The Blind Spot   83
    Photoreceptor Cells   85
  Dark Adaptation   88
  Color Vision   88

    The Young-Helmholtz Theory   89
    Color Blindness   90
    The Opponent-Process Theory   92
    Color Constancy Theory   92
    Aftereffects   95
CONCEPT REVIEW: VISUAL CELLS OF THE RETINA   94
  Receptive Fields   95
    Putting it all Together   95
Hearing   98
  How Sound Is Created   98
  The Structure of the Ear   99
  Theories of Hearing   100
AN ENDURING QUESTION: CAN WE LEARN TO FAKE IT?   102
Taste   104
Smell   105
Touch   106
Kinesthetic and Vestibular Senses   108
EPILOGUE: THE READY ROOM   111
Summary   112
Suggestions for Further Reading   113

FOCUS ON RESEARCH: COMPUTER
MODELING   97

FOCUS ON A CONTROVERSY: EXTRA
SENSES   110

CHAPTER 4

Perception   115

PROLOGUE   115
Why Psychologists Study Perception   116
Perceptual Basics   117
  Brain Pathways   117
  Form and Shape Perception   119
AN ENDURING QUESTION: THE NATURE AND NURTURE OF
PERCEPTION   124
Illusions   127
Perceptual Constancies   129
Depth Perception   132
  Monocular Cues   132
CONCEPT REVIEW: MONOCULAR CUES OF DEPTH PERCEPTION   136
  The Moon Illusion   137
  Binocular Cues   138
  The Visual Cliff   142
Motion Perception   142
Other Senses   143
EPILOGUE: "THAT'S HIM!"   145
Summary   146
Suggestions for Further Reading   147

FOCUS ON AN APPLICATION:
SIGHTLESS VISION   118

FOCUS ON THE FUTURE: SEEING IS
BELIEVING   140

CHAPTER 5

State of Consciousness   149

PROLOGUE   149
Why Psychologists Study States of Consciousness   150
States of Consciousness   151
Sleep   151
  Stages of Sleep   151

CONTENTS

REM Sleep   152
Sleep Duration   155
Sleep Deprivation   155
AN ENDURING QUESTION: WHY DO WE SLEEP?   156
The Ciradian Rhythm   159
Sleep Abnormalities and Pathology   160
Insomnia   163
Narcolepsy   163
Sleep Apnea   164
Dreaming   165
Psychoanalytic Theory   165
The Activation-Synthesis Model   165
The Housekeeping Hypothesis   165
The Off-Line Hypothesis   166
Daydreaming   166
Hypnosis   167
Dissociation   168
Memory Enhancement   169
Pain Relief and Changed Emotional States   170
Behaviorial Changes   170
Disinhibition   171
Posthypnotic Suggestion   171
Meditation   171
CONCEPT REVIEW: TYPES OF HYPNOTIC EFFECTS   172
Psychoactive Drugs   173
Central Nervous System Stimulants   173
Amphetamines   173
Cocaine   174
Central Nervous System Depressants   175
Alcohol   175
Benzodiazepines   176
Heroin   176
Designer Drugs   177
Hallucinogens   177
PCP   177
Marijuana   178
EPILOGUE: THE END OF A NIGHTMARE   179
Summary   180
Suggestions for Further Reading   181

■

UNIT 2   INTERACTING WITH THE ENVIRONMENT   183

CHAPTER 6
Conditioning and Learning   185

PROLOGUE   185
Why Psychologists Study Learning   187
The Behavior of Organisms   187
Simple Forms of Learning   188
Habituation   188
Sensitization   188

FOCUS ON APPLICATION: IF THIS IS
TUESDAY, IT MUST BE THE
GRAVEYARD SHIFT   161

FOCUS ON A CONTROVERSY:
HYPNOSIS AND AGE
REGRESSION   173

Classical Conditioning—Does The Name Pavlov Ring a Bell?   189
  Pavlov's Experiments   189
  Higher-Order Conditioning   191
  Classical Conditioning in Everyday Life   191
    Prejudice   192
    Drug Overdose   193
    Fear   194
  Contiguity versus Contingency   195
Operant Conditioning   198
  The Law of Effect   198
  Operants   198
  Reinforcement and Extinction in Operant Conditioning   199
  Operant Conditioning in Everyday Life   200
  Shaping   200
CONCEPT REVIEW   201
  Generalization and Discrimination   202
  Strengthening a Response by Positive or Negative Reinforcement   202
  Weakening a Response by Punishment or Extinction   203
    Punishment   203
    Extinction   205
  Primary and Secondary Reinforcement   205
  Schedules of Reinforcement   205
  Discrimination and Stimulus Control   206
  The Premack Principle   208
Challenges to the Behaviorist View   208
Social Learning—Observation and Imitation   208
  The Importance of Models   208
  Performance versus Acquisition   210
Cognitive Learning   212
Inheritance and the Biology of Behavior   216
  Canalization   216
EPILOGUE: THE NAIL BITES THE DUST   218
Summary   219
Suggestions for Further Reading   220

CHAPTER 7
Memory and Information Processing   221

PROLOGUE   221
Why Psychologists Study Memory   222
AN ENDURING QUESTION: WHAT IS THE BIOLOGY OF MEMORY?   223
Two Memories are Better Than One   227
A Model of Declarative Memory   228
  Sensory Memory   229
  Short-Term Memory   229
    Displacement   230
  Chunking   231
  Long Term Memory   231
CONCEPT REVIEW   232
  Meaning and Memory   233
  Mnemonics   233
Theories of Declarative Memory   233
  The Dual-Code Theory   235
  Propositional Network Theory   236

FOCUS ON RESEARCH: CONDITIONING ON THE CELLULAR LEVEL   197

FOCUS ON APPLICATION: BEHAVIOR MODIFICATION   211

FOCUS ON THE FUTURE: SNIFF—OH, NOW I REMEMBER!   234

CONTENTS

Propositional Networks and the Dual-Code Theory   237
Forgetting   238
  Decay and Loss   238
  Interference Effects   238
    Proactive Interference   238
    Retroactive Interference   239
  The Tip-of-the Tongue Phenomenon   239
  Retrieval Cues   240
  Reconstruction and Retrieval   241
  Failure of Consolidation   241
  Motivated Forgetting   242
  Somatogenic Amnesia   242
Strengthening Memory Through Elaboration   243
Encoding Effects   245
  Locus-Dependent Memory   245
  In the Mood   246
The Spacing Effect   248
EPILOGUE: REMEMBRANCE OF THINGS PAST   249
Summary   250
Suggestions for Further Reading   251

FOCUS ON APPLICATION: TO CRAM
OR NOT TO CRAM?   247

CHAPTER 8
Cognition and Language   253

PROLOGUE   253
Why Psychologists Study Thought and Language   254
Thinking   255
  Subvocal Speech   256
  Thinking Machines   256
Human Performance   257
  Intellectual Skills   257
    Mental Procedures   257
AN ENDURING QUESTION: IS THE BRAIN A MACHINE?   258
    Concepts and Concept Formation   261
  Declarative Knowledge   262
  Cognitive Strategies   262
    Attention   263
    Heuristics Versus Algorithms   264
    Means-End Analysis   266
    Problem Solving   267
  Impediments to Problem Solving   268
    Mental Set   268
    Functional Fixedness   270
  Motor Skills   272
  Attitudes   273
CONCEPT REVIEW: HUMAN COGNITIVE PERFORMANCE   273
Language   274
  Linguistic Relativity   274
  Language Acquisition   275
    The Onset of Language   275
    The One-Word Stage   276
    The Two-Word Stage   277
    Telegraphic Speech   278

Syntactic and Semantic Structure   278
Why Does Language Acquisition Occur?   280
Teaching Language to the Great Apes   280
   Sign Language   280
   Arguments Against Language in Apes   284
EPILOGUE: THE MAN WITH THE MEANS TO REACH HIS ENDS   285
Suggestions for Further Reading   288

CHAPTER 9
Motivation   289

PROLOGUE   289
Why Psychologist Study Motivation   290
The Concept of Motivation   290
Biological Motives   291
   Hunger   292
   Thirst   293
   The Interaction of Hunger and Thirst   294
   Motivation and Individual Differences   295
   Sex Drives   295
Stimulus Motives   298
Learned Motivation   300
Theories of Motivation   301
   Maslow's Hierarchy of Motives   301
   The Need to Achieve   301
   Learned Helplessness   302
   Altruism and Intrinsic Motivation   303
   Solomon's Opponent-Process Theory   306
      Emotional Contrast   307
      Addiction   309
      Critical Decay Duration   309
CONCEPT REVIEW: ADDICTION   310
AN ENDURING QUESTION: WHY DON'T WE ALWAYS DO WHAT'S IN OUR OWN BEST INTEREST?   310
EPILOGUE: GETTING A CHARGE OUT OF LIFE   312
Summary   313
Suggestions for Further Reading   314

CHAPTER 10
Emotion   315

PROLOGUE   315
Why Psychologists Study Emotions   316
The Biology of Emotion   317
Why Emotions Evolved   317
What Makes us Emotional?   320
Judging Emotions   321
Theories of Emotion   322
   The James-Lange Theory   324
   Schachter's Cognitive Appraisal Theory   325
   Facial Feedback Theory   328
   Plutchik's Psychoevolutionary Synthesis of Emotion   332

FOCUS ON RESEARCH: THE PHYSIOLOGY OF GRAMMAR AND SEMANTICS   281

FOCUS ON RESEARCH: ASPECTS OF OBESITY   296

FOCUS ON AN APPLICATION: TEACHING CONFIDENCE AND SUCCESS   304

FOCUS ON A CONTROVERSY: LIE DETECTION   318

FOCUS ON RESEARCH: SUDDEN VIOLENCE   323

CONTENTS

Primary Emotions 333
Functional Aspects of Emotion 333
Emotional Intensities, Similarities, and Differences 335
EPILOGUE: "THEY'LL LET ME GO TOMORROW" 336
Summary 337
Suggestions for Further Reading 337

UNIT 3: DEVELOPMENT AND INDIVIDUAL DIFFERENCES   339

CHAPTER 11
Development Through the Lifespan   341

PROLOGUE 341
Why Psychologists Study Human Development 342
Issues in Development 343
  Nature versus Nurture 343
  Stability versus Change 346
  Continuity versus Discontinuity 346
Beginnings (0 to 1 Year of Age) 346
  Are Babies Passive? 347
  Infant Physical and Motor Development 349
  Infant Personality and Social-Emotional Development 350
    The New York Longitudinal Study 350
    Goodness of Fit 350
    Social Ties 352
    The Dynamics of Human Attachment 353
AN ENDURING QUESTION: WHO SHOULD MIND THE CHILDREN? 355
    Infant Emotional Development 357
Early Childhood: Toddlers and Preschool Children (1 to 6 Years of Age) 358
  Cognitive Development 358
    The Sensorimotor Stage (0 to 2 Years) 358
    The Preoperational Stage (2 to 7 Years) 359
  Personality Development in Early Childhood 360
  Social Relations in Early Childhood 360
    The Development of Sibling Relationships 361
    The Development of Peer Relationships 361
    The Development of Friendships 362
    Play 362
Middle Childhood (6 to 12 Years of Age) 362
  Cognitive Development in Middle Childhood 362
  Social-Emotional Development in Middle Childhood 364
    Peer Relationships 364
    Adult Versus Peer Influence 365
    The Influence of Television 366
Adolescence (12 to 18 Years of Age) 367
  Storm and Stress? 368
  Physical Growth in Adolescence 368
  Cognitive Development in Adolescence 370

FOCUS ON RESEARCH: BREAKING THE CODE 345

FOCUS ON A CONTROVERSY: THE MOTHER-INFANT BOND 354

Alternative Views of Cognitive Development   370
Developmental Tasks of Adolescence   371
   Choosing a Career   371
   Addressing the Crisis of Identity   373
The Peer Group   373
Early Adulthood (18 to 40 Years of Age)   374
   Physical Changes in Early Adulthood   374
   Marriage and Parenthood   374
   Planning for a Career   375
Middle Adulthood (40 to 65 Years of Age)   376
   Physical Changes in Middle Adulthood   376
   Midlife Crisis   376
   The Empty Nest   377
Late Adulthood (65 or More Years of Age)   377
   Physical Changes in Late Adulthood   378
   Sex and the Elderly   378
   When Life Ends   380
EPILOGUE: ALGEBRA AND FORMAL OPERATIONS   381
Summary   382
Suggestions for Further Reading   383

CHAPTER 12
Intelligence and Creativity   385

PROLOGUE   385
Why Psychologists Study Intelligence   386
Defining Intelligence   386
Measuring Intelligence—IQ Tests   387
   Test Validity   388
   Factor Analysis   389
The Triarchic Theory of Intelligence   392
AN ENDURING QUESTION: HOW MUCH OF INTELLIGENCE IS
INHERITED?   393
Birth Order and Intelligence   395
IQ, Race, and Culture   396
   Cultural and Educational Bias   397
   Culture-fair Testing   399
The Effects of Environmental Stimulation   400
Intellectual Changes Over Time   401
   Difficulties in Measuring Intellectual Change   402
   Terman's Study   403
Creativity   406
CONCEPT REVIEW: INTELLIGENCE   406
Some Final Thoughts on Intelligence   410
EPILOGUE: THE GIFTS   410
Summary   412
Suggestions for Further Reading   412

CHAPTER 13
Personality   415

PROLOGUE   415
Why Psychologists Study Personality   416
Theories of Personality   417

FOCUS ON THE FUTURE: WHY DO
WE GROW OLD? CAN AGING BE
PREVENTED?   380

FOCUS ON A CONTROVERSY: THE
PROPER USE OF INTELLIGENCE TESTS
398

FOCUS ON AN APPLICATION:
MAINSTREAMING THE
INTELLECTUALLY
HANDICAPPED   407

CONTENTS

Personality Types   417
The Trait Approach   419
  Allport's Trait Theory   *419*
  Cattell's Trait Theory   *420*
The Psychoanalytic Approach   422
  The Three-Part Personality   *422*
  Instincts and Defense Mechanisms   *423*
  Psychosexual Stages of Development   *424*
  Contemporaries of Freud   *424*
  The Influence of Psychoanalytic Theory   *425*
Behavioral and Social Learning Approaches   425
  Behavior Theory   *426*
  Social Learning Theory   *427*
The Humanistic Approach   428
  Roger's Self Theory   *429*
Personality Assessment   429
CONCEPT REVIEW: COMPARING THEORIES OF PERSONALITY   430
Measuring Personality Traits   430
Predictive Validity and Reliability   434
Psychoanalytic Personality Assessment   437
Behavioral Personality Assessment   438
Humanistic Personality Assessment   439
  Q Sorting   *439*
  Interviews   *439*
EPILOGUE: THE EYE OF THE BEHOLDER   440
Summary   441
Suggestions for Further Reading   442

FOCUS ON A CONTROVERSY: DOES
PERSONALITY THEORY HAVE A
FUTURE?   431

FOCUS ON AN APPLICATION: BEING A
CAREFUL CONSUMER: THE LIMITS OF
PSYCHOLOGICAL TESTING   435

UNIT 4: CONFLICT AND ADJUSTMENT   443

CHAPTER 14
Health Psychology   445

PROLOGUE   445
Why Psychologists Study Health   446
Health Psychology   447
Risk Assessment   447
  Protecting Yourself   447
  Hazard Perception   448
Acute Stress and Chronic Aftermath   450
Reactions to Stress   454
  The Body's Reaction   454
    Stages of the General Adaption Syndrome   *454*
CONCEPT REVIEW: EMOTIONAL PINBALL   455
    Stress and Illness   *456*
    Stress and the Immune System   *456*
  Measuring Susceptibility to Stress and Illness   457
AN ENDURING QUESTION: ARE THERE DISEASE-PRONE
PERSONALITIES?   459

FOCUS ON AN APPLICATION:
STOPPING SMOKING AND
DRINKING   451

Hassles   460
Suicide   461
Ways of Coping with Stress   465
   Psychological Defense Mechanisms   465
   Stress Management   465
      Clinical Stress Mangement   466
      Coping Strategies   466
EPILOGUE: HELP WHEN IT WAS MOST NEEDED   468
Summary   469
Suggestions for Further Reading   470

CHAPTER 15
Abnormal Behavior   471

PROLOGUE   471
Why Psychologists Study Abnormal Behavior   472
Defining Abnormality   473
Models of Psychopathology   474
   The Medical Model   474
   The Learning Model   476
   The Psychoanalytic Model   476
   The Humanistic-Existential Model   476
Classification and Assessment of Abnormal Behavior   476
Anxiety, Somatoform, and Dissociative Disorders   479
   Anxiety Disorders   479
      Simple Phobia   479
CONCEPT REVIEW: THE STRENGTHS AND WEAKNESSES OF CLASSIFYING
MENTAL DISORDERS   480
      Generalized Anxiety Disorder   482
      Panic Disorder   482
      Obsessive-Compulsive Disorder   483
   Somatoform Disorders   486
      Conversion Disorder   486
      Hypochondriasis   487
   Dissociative Disorders   488
      Psychogenic Amnesia   488
      Psychogenic Fugue   488
      Multiple Personality Disorder   489
Mood Disorders   491
   Bipolar Disorder   491
   Major Depression   493
Schizophrenic Disorders   495
   Causes of Schizophrenia   497
      Genetic and Environmental Factors   498
      Biochemical Factors   500
      Structural and Anatomical Factors   501
Delusional (Paranoid) Disorder   502
   Delusional (Paranoid) Disorder   503
   Induced Psychotic Disorder   503
   Causes of Delusional (Paranoid) Disorder   504
Personality Disorders (Axis II)   504
The Assessment of Mental Disorders   506
   Assessment Bias   506

FOCUS ON A CONTROVERSY: IS
THERE A RIGHT TO COMMIT
SUICIDE?   462

FOCUS ON AN APPLICATION: THE
LEGAL MODEL: INSANITY AND THE
LAW   475

FOCUS ON RESEARCH: THE BIOLOGY
OF OBSESSIVE-COMPULSIVE
DISORDER   485

An Enduring Question: Should Mental Disorders be Classified
Before Their Underlying Causes are Understood?   508
    Misdiagnosis   510
    Epilogue: The Trichotillomaniac   512
    Summary   513
    Suggestions for Further Reading   514

CHAPTER 16
Therapy   515

Prologue   515
Why Psychologists Study Therapies   516
The History of Therapy   516
    The Greek and Roman Era (Approximately 400 B.C. to A.D. 476)   517
    The Middle Ages (A.D. 476 to 1453)   517
    The Renaissance (Approximately 1400 to 1600)   517
    After the Renaissance   518
        Mental Institutions   518
        The Era of Psychology   519
Somatic Therapies   520
    Psychopharmacological Therapy   520
        Neuroleptics (Anti-Psychotic Drugs)   521
        Antidepressants   522
        Antimanic Drugs   523
        Antianxiety Drugs   523
    Electroconvulsive Therapy   524
    Psychosurgery   525
        Frontal Lobotomies   525
        The Effectiveness of Modern Psychosurgery   528
Psychotherapy   529
    Psychoanalysis   530
    Humanistic-Existential Therapies   531
        Client-Centered Therapy   531
        Existential Therapy   532
    Rational-Emotive Therapy   532
    Gestalt Therapy   534
    Group Therapies   534
        Sensitivity Training and Encounter Groups   535
        Family Therapy   535
        Transactional Analysis   535
    Behavior Therapy   535
        Classical Conditioning Therapy   536
        Systematic Desensitization   536
        Operant Behavior Therapy   537
        Cognitive Behavior Therapy   539
    Hypnotherapy   540
An Enduring Question: Does Psychotherapy Work?   542
    Brief Therapy   544
Epilogue: A Bird in the Hand   544
Summary   545
Suggestions for Further Reading   546

Focus On A Controversy: The
Deinstitutionalization Of The
Mentally Ill   526

Focus On A Controversy: Recipes
For Treatment?   541

Contents

CHAPTER 17
Social Behavior   551

PROLOGUE   551
Why Psychologists Study Social Behavior   552
Interpersonal Influence   553
  Conformity   553
    Why People Conform   554
    Reference Groups   554
  Obedience   556
    The Milgram Experiment   556
    Variables Influencing Obedience   557
  Conformity and Obedience   559
Helping Others   561
CONCEPT REVIEW: BYSTANDER INTERVENTION   565
Cooperation and Competition   568
The Influence of Groups   571
  Deindividuation   571
  Polarization   573
  Leadership   574
Prejudice and Discrimination   575
  Personality and Prejudice   577
  Overcoming Prejudice   577
Social Cognition and Attitude Change   578
  Forming Social Attitudes   578
    Measuring Attitudes   579
    Attitudes and Self-Awareness   579
  Changing Attitudes: Persuasive Communication   580
    Characteristics of the Communicator   580
    Characteristics of the Communication   581
    Characteristics of the Listener   582
  Cognitive Dissonance and Attitude Change   583
  Attribution   585
EPILOGUE: BRAINWASHED   587
Summary   588
Suggestions for Further Reading   589

FOCUS ON RESEARCH: THE
DEVELOPMENT OF MORALITY   566

CHAPTER 18
Sexuality, Attraction, and Intimacy   591

PROLOGUE   591
Why Psychologists Study Sexuality, Attraction, and Intimacy   593
Biological Aspects of Human Sexuality   593
  Anatomical Characteristics   593
  The Effects of Hormones on Behavior   595

CONTENTS

Gender-Role Acquisition   598
  Social Learning Theory   599
  The Cognitive View   599
    The Development of Gender Understanding   599
    Gender Constancy and Cognitive Theory   600
  Gender Schema Theory   600
AN ENDURING QUESTION: DO MALES AND FEMALES HAVE DIFFERENT "NATURAL" SKILLS OR TRAITS?   601
  Sexual Orientations   604
Attraction   607
  Liking   607
    Closeness   608
    Similarity   609
    Competence   609
  Theories About Liking   610
    Reinforcement Theory   610
    Equity Theory   610
    Exchange Theory   611
    Gain-Loss Theory   614
  Love and Intimacy   614
    Passionate Love   615
    Conjugal Love   616
Sexual Myths and Research   617
  Early "Research"   617
  Modern Research   620
EPILOGUE: THE CONQUEST OF SPERMATORRHEA   621
Summary   622
Suggestions for Further Readings   623

FOCUS ON RESEARCH: THE POWER OF GOOD LOOKS   612

FOCUS ON AN APPLICATION: CHANGING SEXUAL BEHAVIOR   618

CHAPTER 19
Applied Psychology   625

PROLOGUE   625
Why Psychologists are Interested in Applied Psychology   626
Industrial/Organizational Psychology   626
  Organizational Behavior   627
    Leadership and Supervision   627
    Employee Participation, Feedback, and Conflict Resolution   628
  Personnel Selection   629
CONCEPT REVIEW: PERSONNEL SELECTION   629
  Productivity and Personnel Behavior   631
    Job Satisfaction   631
    Absenteeism   632
    Turnover   632
  Motivation and Performance   634
Sports Psychology   635
  The History of Sports Psychology   636
  The Physiology and Personality of the Athlete   636
  The Peak Performance   637
  Psychological Techniques for Achieving Peak Performance   637
  Future Directions for Sports Psychology   639
Environmental Psychology   639
  Illumination   639
  Atmospheric Conditions and Toxic Hazards   640

FOCUS ON THE FUTURE: HOME WORK   633

CONTENTS

Heat   640
    Pollution and Environmental Toxins   640
    Noise   641
  The Structured Environment   641
Consumer Psychology   643
  Consumer Research   643
  The Physiological Approach   645
  Consumer Protection   645
Educational Psychology   646
  The School System   648
  The Teacher   649
  The Successful School   650
EPILOGUE: THE LONGEST THROW   651
Summary   651
Suggestions for Further Reading   652

APPENDIX A
Statistics   653
Descriptive Statistics   654
  Frequency Distributions and Graphs   654
    Regular Frequency Distribution   654
    Grouped Frequency Distribution   654
    Histogram   655
    Frequency Polygon   655
  Central Tendency   656
    Mean   656
    Median   656
    Mode   656
  Variability   657
    Range   657
    Variance and Standard Deviation   657
  Transformed Scores   658
    Percentiles   658
    Standard Scores (Z, T, SAT)   658
  The Normal Bell-Shaped Curve   660
Inferential Statistics   660
  Populations and Samples   660
  Probability   661
  Null Hypothesis (Retain or Reject)   661
Correlation   662
  Correlation Coefficient   662
  Positive, Negative, Perfect, and Zero Correlations   663
  Scatter Diagrams   663
  Correlating Test Scores with TV Viewing   663
  Correlation and Causation   665
Summary   666

APPENDIX B
How to Locate and Read Research Articles in Psychology   667
Research Sources   667
The Research Article   668

FOCUS ON A CONTROVERSY: ARE WE TEACHING IN THE BEST WAY?   647

The Abstract   668
Methodology   668
Results   668
Discussion   668
References   668
Selected Journals in Psychology   669

Glossary   G-1
References   R-1
Name Index   I-1
Subject Index   I-15

PREFACE

Psychology is the study of ourselves, our behavior, our thoughts, our feelings, our lives. We have learned much about human behavior, and we are learning more. Someday, perhaps in the not too distant future, psychologists might be able to apply their knowledge to help reshape the world. Perhaps this power will come from our increasing knowledge of the brain and its chemistry, or from our understanding of aggression and war, or perhaps from a greater comprehension of the factors that motivate us or control our feelings. This textbook contains an introduction to the research and knowledge that psychologists and others have accumulated.

The 19 chapters of the text are divided into five major units. While the text has been designed as an introduction to psychology for undergraduates, it has a strong emphasis on reporting the most recent and important research. The text material is extensive and sometimes detailed, but great efforts have been taken to write every aspect in a way that is clear and easy for a beginner in psychology to understand. This does not mean that the material has been made simple, but that it is understandable. For this, I thank the many students who have given me invaluable feedback in the more than 50 introductory psychology classes that I have taught.

The text is comprehensive, but, like all introductory textbooks, it presents selective rather than inclusive research. Within the text are focus sections in which a particular discussion appears in depth. These sections focus on selective research, applications, controversies, and possible effects that research might have on our future. Almost every chapter begins with a dramatization of a classic experiment, written as though the reader were present. In this way, students are encouraged to feel more like participants than bystanders. In addition, each chapter ends with an epilogue that demonstrates how material in the chapter directly affected the life of just one person.

Most chapters also include a feature that is new to the fourth edition. This feature is known as the enduring question. The Enduring Question section of any chapter addresses important philosophical questions or issues that have been of lasting concern to psychologists. For example, the enduring question addressed in chapter 2, the chapter dealing with the brain and nervous system, asks, "Where is the mind within the brain? This, in turn, leads to a discussion of the mind-body problem, a problem about human consciousness that has fascinated philosophers for centuries and continues to influence psychology to this day. By examining psychology's "enduring questions" students are given an uncommon opportunity to see the big issues that often helped shape and drive psychological research placed side by side with the more traditional material found in introductory textbooks.

Also within each chapter, following a particularly complex or difficult section, is a pedagogical aid known as a concept review. Within the concept review difficult material is addressed once again, but from a different angle or perspective, which helps to make the concept easier to grasp or understand.

Furthermore, a running glossary is provided in the margins. Whenever a new important term is presented, it appears in boldface. Even though it may be defined in text, it is also defined, often in greater detail, in the marginal glossary to help students review and reinforce their learning. This aid emphasizes important terms so that readers may become more familiar with them. Every boldface term also appears in the glossary at the back of the book.

At the end of each chapter are a chapter summary and suggestions for further reading. The suggestions for further reading have been chosen with care, and provide students who are interested in pursuing a particular area more information at a suitable introductory level.

Throughout the text, each important piece of research is referenced. These references generally appear at the end of the sentence to which they pertain and are shown parenthetically. The original sources of the research and statements are listed in full in the reference section at the back of the text so that students may examine particular research in greater detail.

Two appendices are also included. Appendix A provides the student with a brief introduction to the statistics used in psychological research. Appendix B describes a typical research article, lists sources of psychological research, and identifies selected journals that contain articles in psychology.

In addition, there are a number of important supplements to this textbook. A study guide for *Psychology* has been prepared by two of my colleagues, Richard D. Rees and Stephen S. Cooper, to assist students in making full use of the textbook. An instructor's manual, containing suggestions for class and lecture, has been developed by Elizabeth Lynch of Glendale College, Arizona, and myself. It includes a comprehensive test bank, written by Richard D. Rees, along with film suggestions, a capsule summary for each chapter, and behavioral objectives.

No work of this size could ever be accomplished alone, and I owe a great debt to many others. I wish to express my gratitude once again to those colleagues who helped me with the previous editions of *Psychology* and whose ideas and comments are a continuing influence:

J. Whorton Allen
Utah State University

Ellen B. Barker
Bloomsburg State College

Ronald K. Barrett
Loyola Marymount University

D. Thompson Bond
Thomas Nelson Community College

Arthur Brody
Lehigh University

James Butler
James Madison University

Dennis Coon
Santa Barbara City College

Ernest J. Doleys
DePaul University, Illinois

Jack E. Edwards
Illinois Institute of Technology

Donald Elman
Kent State University

Robert B. Graham
East Carolina State University

Michael Grelle
Central Missouri State University

Charles G. Halcomb
Texas Tech University

Robert O. Hansson
University of Tulsa

A. Christine Harris
Chaffey College

Courtland Holdgrafer
Santa Ana College

Ellen C. Huft
Glendale College

Maria Krasnec
University of Idaho

Brian M. Kruger
Wright State University

Barbara Hansen Lemme
College of DuPage, Illinois

Max W. Lewis
University of Arkansas

Svenn Lindskold
Ohio University

Wesley C. Lynch
Montana State University

Spencer A. McWilliams
University of Arizona

Inger Olsen
Vancouver Community College

Gayle H. Olson
University of New Orleans

Robert R. Pagano
University of Washington

John N. Park
Mankato State University

Robert J. Pellegrini
San Jose State University

Janet D. Proctor
Auburn University

Duane Reeder
Glendale College

Robert P. Robison
Everett Community College

Susan A. Schodahl
San Bernardino Valley College

Lee Springer
Glendale College

Laura A. Stephenson
Washburn University of Topeka,
   Kansas

Barbara Streitfeld
University of Hartford, Connecticut

Robert Tilley
Amarillo College

Joe M. Tinnin
Richland College

Donald L. Tollefson
Canisius College

Marcia L. Weinstein
Salem State College

David Wilson
Texas A & M University

Warner Wilson
Wright State University

Carol Woodward
California State University

Rudolph L. Zlody
College of Holy Cross, Massachusetts

I would also like to express my thanks to the following members of the academic community who reviewed the chapters included in this fourth edition, and who provided comments, suggestions, and critiques:

Ann Brandt
Glendale Community College
Glendale, Arizona

Roy E. Cain
Pan American University
Edinburg, Texas

William H. Calhoun
The University of Tennessee
Knoxville, Tennessee

Bruce H. Hinrichs
Lakewood Community College
White Bear Lake, Minnesota

Lela Joscelyn
Mount Mary College
Milwaukee, Wisconsin

Khalil A. Khavari
The University of Wisconsin,
   Milwaukee
Milwaukee, Wisconsin

Raul C. Martinez
Adams State College
Alamosa, Colorado

Charles F. Matter
University of Wisconsin, Green Bay
Green Bay, Wisconsin

Linda Sandham Quinn
Penn State, Wilkes-Barre Campus
Lehman, Pennsylvania

Robyn Rogers
Southwest Texas State University
San Marcos, Texas

I wish especially to thank all of my colleagues at Glendale College for their comments, especially Professors Stephen Cooper and Richard Rees for their advice, collaboration and friendship.

I am especially grateful to Bill Stryker for the excellent design of this textbook, and for his great speed, talent, and encouragement. I also wish to thank Lyn Dupré for her extremely fast and competent copy editing, Barbara Barnett for the beautiful artwork, and Parkwood Composition Service for their skillful typesetting. Finally, I wish to thank my friend and editor, Clyde Perlee, Jr., editor-in-chief of West's College Division, for his skill, ideas, and encouragement. As always, without his friendship and support, this book could never have been written.

John P. Dworetzky

UNIT 1 | Psychological Foundation: The Mind and the Body

Chapter 1
History, Systems and Research Methods

Prologue
An Introduction to Psychology
The Beginning of Psychology
Philosophical Approaches to the Study of Psychology
Research Methods
Epilogue: Science and the Spirit World

Chapter 2
The Biological Bases of Behavior

Prologue
Why Psychologists Study the Nervous System and the Brain
The Divisions of the Nervous System
Neurons and the Body's Electrochemical System
Hormones and the Endocrine System
The Structure of the Brain
Brain Scanners: PET and MRI
The Brain and Behavior
Epilogue: Mr. Niethold's Toothache

Chapter 3
Sensation

Prologue
Why Psychologists Study Sensation

Sensory Thresholds
Vision
Hearing
Taste
Smell
Touch
Kinesthetic and Vestibular Senses
Epilogue: The Ready Room

Chapter 4
Perception

Prologue
Why Psychologists Study Perception
Perceptual Basics
Illusions
Perceptual Constancies
Depth Perception
Motion Perception
Other Senses
Attention
Epilogue: "That's Him!"

Chapter 5
States of Consciousness

Prologue
Why Psychologists Study States of Consciousness
States of Consciousness
Sleep
Sleep Abnormalities and Pathology
Dreaming
Daydreaming
Hypnosis
Meditation
Psychoactive Drugs
Epilogue: The End of a Nightmare

CHAPTER 1 | History, Systems, and Research Methods

Prologue

An Introduction to Psychology
  Becoming a Psychologist
  Areas of Specialization

The Beginning of Psychology

Philosophical Approaches to the Study of Psychology
  Structuralism
  Functionalism
  Psychoanalysis
  Behaviorism
  Gestalt Psychology
  Humanistic Psychology
  The Neurobiological Approach
  Cognitive Psychology
  Modern Trends and the Emergence of
    Scientific Psychology

Research Methods
  Experimental Methods
  Nonexperimental Methods

Epilogue: Science and the Spirit World

PROLOGUE

Some have said that outer space is the final frontier, but it isn't. The final frontier, in the truest sense of the word, is within ourselves. All of our experience, our understanding, and our sense of being, is to be found within us, within the mind. The mind is the key to everything.

Although we have gazed at the stars and looked outward for centuries, it has only been in the last hundred years or so that we have begun a systematic search inward. Inner space, the mind, is the final frontier, and psychology has begun the exploration.

As you join in this journey inward, you will encounter many worlds that may at first seem familiar to you. Among these are senses, memories, thoughts, emotions, and motivations—all of them part of you and every human being. But, as you take a closer look, you will come to acquire a new understanding of yourself and of those around you. Welcome to "psychology," literally, the study of the mind. I hope that you will find it as exciting and as interesting as I have.

In this chapter, we'll read about some of the contributions that researchers made in the early days of psychology. We'll also study what every good psychologist, researcher, or student needs to know—how to study a problem scientifically in order to separate fact from fiction. It is the only way we know to uncover the "truth," or at least get as close to the truth as possible. We'll do this together by conducting a psychological experiment, using the techniques psychologists use. Finally, we will look at the limits to our understanding of psychology.

3

AN INTRODUCTION TO PSYCHOLOGY

■ A group of people who have volunteered for a psychology experiment are being shown a very sad movie. Some of them start to cry. The researcher says, "That's okay, go ahead and cry, let it all out." Then, she and her assistants quickly collect the subject's tears in little glass containers for later chemical analysis to see just what, in fact, her subjects were "letting out." She is wondering if tears serve some purpose. Do tears, for instance, contain some substance that the body must rid itself of to overcome or compensate for the sadness? If so, might it be a chemical that could affect our emotions?

■ A researcher working for NASA asks astronauts to respond to emergency lights on a control board as quickly as possible. When green and red lights are flashed, the astronauts have trouble telling the lights apart when they appear in the periphery of their vision. When the researcher substitutes yellow and blue lights for the red and green ones, the astronauts' errors decrease significantly.

■ In a laboratory, an investigator stays awake all night observing sleeping subjects who are attached to sensors and measuring devices. By watching the sensors, she can tell when the sleepers begin to dream, when they become restless, or when sleep disturbances start. She is trying to find patterns that may help to explain why some people have difficulty sleeping.

■ At a large metropolitan zoo, a scientist places a series of small steel rails along the ground throughout the mountain lion compound. From time to time, a mechanical rabbit runs along one of the rails starting from a tunnel. When a lion catches a rabbit, meat is automatically dispensed from a hopper at the far end of the enclosure. The scientist structures the situation so that the lions quickly learn what to do. The curator of the zoo notes that the big cats are healthier and more active now that they are getting exercise and "hunting game."

■ An investigator observes a 3-month-old infant who is watching a rolling ball. The moment the ball rolls behind a couch, the infant loses all interest in the ball and acts as if it no longer exists. The investigator repeats the process with an older infant. When the ball disappears, the older infant leans to one side and tries to see where the ball went. The investigator wonders whether the younger infant simply doesn't yet understand that objects still exist even though they are out of sight.

■ A therapist in a city hospital interviews a young woman inpatient who wants to go home. Five weeks earlier the woman had suffered a deep depression and had tried to stab her husband and to take her own life. The therapist interviews her carefully, calling on all his skill to make a decision that will represent his best professional judgment. He doesn't want to detain her without cause, but he also doesn't want her to return to a situation she cannot handle.

■ An investigator leaves self-addressed unsealed envelopes containing money in church pews all over the city just before the congregations assemble. She leaves similar envelopes in nonreligious halls just before meetings begin. The envelopes are secretly marked so that they can be distinguished later. The investigator then waits at home to see whether churchgoers are more likely to return the money than other people are.

All the professionals in these examples have one thing in common: They are psychologists. Whether studying the chemistry of tears, an astronaut reacting to an emergency, a sleeping person, a hungry mountain lion, a 3-month-old baby, a depressed woman in a hospital, or churchgoers' honesty, each of the psychologists was studying behavior. Although **psychology** means the study of the mind, it is

PSYCHOLOGY THROUGH THE AGES

Cartoon by Jane Zich

most often defined as the study of the behavior of organisms. At first glance, this definition might seem limited. After all, what about thoughts, feelings, motivations, perceptions—aren't they too part of psychology? The answer is that of course they are. However, if we want psychology to be a scientific study, we must be able to record and validate our observations. We can not observe a thought, an emotion, a motivation, or a perception directly. Rather, we must rely on a behavior (what someone tells us, or the way that he acts) for a clue as to what his thoughts, feeling, perceptions, or motivations might be. So this definition, rather than being narrow, is very broad and includes the study of behavior of all animals, not just human beings.

Look at the table of contents and you will begin to appreciate how diversified and encompassing psychology is. If you were to become a psychologist, as your career developed you might spend your entire time working within an area described by just one of these chapters, perhaps by just one paragraph within one chapter. Psychologists are interested in every aspect of behavior. One nice thing about this for those of you who might consider careers in psychology is that you are almost assured of finding something to do that really interests you, simply because there are so many topics from which to choose. Before we go farther, let's take a moment to examine the requirements for becoming a psychologist.

Becoming a Psychologist

Psychologists receive a doctoral degree (such as a Ph.D.) after 3 to 6 years of further training beyond their bachelor's degree (B.A., B.S.). At this point, they are properly called doctors, although they are not physicians. Most states require that psychologists be licensed before they are permitted to administer psychological tests or to engage in psychological therapy and treatment of clients. Clinical psychologists, who often work at hospitals or clinics, may be required to complete an additional year of psychological internship (which provides them with supervised "hands-on" experience).

Some psychologists have a master's degree (M.A., M.S.) instead of a doctorate, indicating that they have completed 1 to 3 years of postgraduate training. Increasingly, however, a doctoral degree is required for employment as a therapist or research psychologist. Figure 1.1 shows the places in which psychologists work and their specializations. As you can see, a large proportion of psychologists are employed by colleges and universities to conduct research and to teach.

Psychologists are not the same as psychiatrists. Psychiatrists must first complete medical school and receive an M.D. degree. Following medical school, psychiatrists generally complete 4 to 6 additional years of training. Psychiatrists, like clinical psychologists, are trained to diagnose and treat people with mental disorders. Unlike clinical psychologists, psychiatrists, as licensed physicians, are allowed to provide drugs and to perform medical procedures as part of treatment.

Areas of Specialization

There are many areas of specialization in psychology. The field offers something for everybody. In the following paragraphs, we will describe a few of the different kinds of psychologists and their interests.

Experimental psychologists, like most psychologists, rely on scientific methods and experiments to examine the fundamental processes that govern behavior. Their research often is conducted in a laboratory. They investigate areas such as sensation, perception, learning, memory, and motivation in both humans and lower animals.

Neuropsychological and psychobiological psychologists are interested in biological factors and their effects on behavior. Both neuropsychological and psychobiological psychologists study the brain, nervous system, genes, and drugs in relation to behavior. Neuropsychological psychologists also treat disorders related to the central nervous system.

FIGURE 1.1

Places of work and specializations of people in psychology. Data were obtained by using a stratified random sample of members of the American Psychological Association employed full-time as psychologists. (SOURCE: Stapp & Fulcher, 1983; Pion, 1986.)

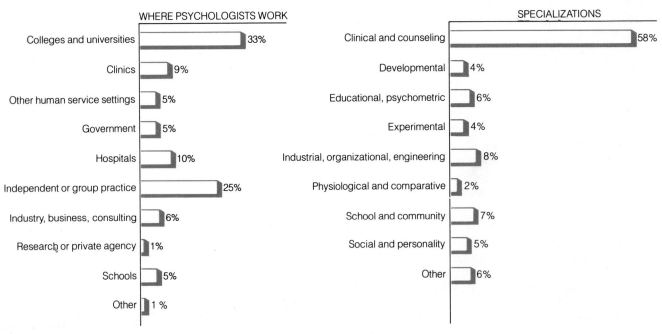

WHERE PSYCHOLOGISTS WORK

Colleges and universities	33%
Clinics	9%
Other human service settings	5%
Government	5%
Hospitals	10%
Independent or group practice	25%
Industry, business, consulting	6%
Research or private agency	1%
Schools	5%
Other	1 %

SPECIALIZATIONS

Clinical and counseling	58%
Developmental	4%
Educational, psychometric	6%
Experimental	4%
Industrial, organizational, engineering	8%
Physiological and comparative	2%
School and community	7%
Social and personality	5%
Other	6%

Developmental psychologists study the way in which behaviors develop and change during a lifespan. Special areas of interest include the development of language, social attachments, emotions, thinking, and perception.

Cognitive psychologists study internal mental processes, which include thinking, memory, concept formation, and processing of information. To the cognitive psychologist, behavior is composed of mental events, internal representations, desires, beliefs, and thoughts.

Social psychologists use scientific techniques to examine the effects that people have on one another. They are interested in topics such as altruism, cooperation, aggression, affection, and group pressure.

Industrial or organizational psychologists generally work with businesses. They are concerned with improving working conditions, raising production rates, and developing decision-making abilities. Many of these I/O psychologists, as they are called, began their work as experimental psychologists and then became consultants for business or industry.

Educational psychologists study educational systems, methods of teaching, curricula, and other factors influencing the learning process. Their goals are to improve education and to make learning easier and more efficient.

Clinical psychologists focus their efforts on understanding, diagnosing, and treating abnormal or deviant behaviors.

Counseling psychologists were traditionally trained to help individuals solve personal, academic, or vocational problems that did not stem from serious mental disorders. However, counseling and clinical psychologists often have similar training and, in reality, the distinction between the two has become practically nonexistent (Fitzgerald & Osipow, 1986).*

Some of these specialized areas may be new to you. When I was first introduced to psychology, for instance, I felt as though I had walked into a strange town where I didn't know anyone and where the buildings, streets, and landmarks were all unfamiliar. Of course, a town isn't strange to the people who have lived there all their lives. They can remember when this building was built, or when that street was named, and they know who lives where and which children belong to which parents. It's easy for long-time residents to make sense of a place; they saw it take shape from the beginning. In the same way, the complex community of psychological interests would no doubt be more familiar to you had you been there from the start. You would know why certain "structures" had been created, why certain "roads" were more important than others, and which ideas were the offspring of which psychological families. If you want to know about modern psychology, the place to begin, then, is the laboratory of Wilhelm Wundt in Leipzig, Germany, a little over a century ago.

THE BEGINNING OF PSYCHOLOGY

Psychology was born of two parents, **philosophy** and **physiology.** For centuries, philosophers had asked questions about human emotions, thoughts, and behavior.

---

*The names enclosed in parentheses are a reference. References are often given after statements made in this text. Their function is to inform you about the sources used to obtain information, in case you wish to know more than is provided directly by the text. The reference also supports the statement with research. In this case, take a moment to turn to the References section at the back of the book. Look up "Fitzgerald and Osipow, 1986" to see the original sources of the information. If you wish to know more about the subject, all you need do is to go to a library and find the May 1986 issue of *American Psychologist*—there you can read everything you're ever likely to want to know about the distinctions between counseling and clinical psychologists (of which there appear to be very few).

PHILOSOPHY
In most general terms, philosophy is "the search for the truth." It encompasses two major branches: epistemology, which includes efforts to comprehend the origins, limits, and nature of knowledge; and metaphysics, in which the reality of existence is examined. Minor branches include esthetics, logic, and ethics.

PHYSIOLOGY
The biological discipline that examines the functions of cells, tissues, and organs within the living organism.

Wilhelm Wundt, the father of experimental psychology (1832–1920).

FIGURE 1.2

The "thought meter" used by Wilhelm Wundt in his early psychological experiments. (SOURCE: *Wundt, 1862, p. 264.*)

They had tried to deduce answers to their questions by applying logic and commonsense reasoning. For example, although people knew that water would not flow through something solid, they observed that, nonetheless, sweat came through the skin. Based on this observation, philosophers deduced that skin must have holes in it—thereby positing the existence of pores centuries before such structures could be seen with a microscope. Philosophers did not always make deductions successfully, however. For instance, the great philosopher Aristotle (382–322 B.C.) believed that thinking occurred in the heart, while the brain served only to help cool the blood. (Aristotle based his deductions on the observations that strongly felt emotions were often sensed in the chest and that the convolutions of the brain would allow a greater surface from which heat could radiate—not bad, I suppose, for an educated guess. Then again, we all have days when our brains don't seem to be doing much other than radiating heat, but that's probably not what Aristotle meant.) Also in error was the famous physician Hippocrates (ca. 460–377 B.C.), who believed that all emotions resulted from different combinations or levels of four bodily humors—black bile, yellow bile, blood, and phlegm—interesting, but wrong.

Although such errors were common, Aristotle's and Hippocrates' ideas about the body and behavior were accepted as fact for almost 2000 years before they were finally challenged by physiologists' experiments during the last few centuries.

Physiologists were especially influential in providing a new understanding of the brain and the nervous system and the ways in which these structures affect behavior. For example, at one time it was a common belief that a person's muscular response occurred the instant the brain requested it. By a series of careful scientific experiments, however, physiologists were able to demonstrate that nerve impulses take time to travel from their place of origin in the brain or spine to the muscles. You can see this for yourself if you assemble about 30 people in a line that forms a complete circle. Ask each person to place a hand on the shoulder of the one in front. State the following rule to the group: "As soon as you feel your shoulder squeezed, squeeze the shoulder of the one in front of you as fast as you can." Someone with a stopwatch can then start the process and stop the watch when he feels his own shoulder squeezed by the one behind him. The nerve impulse has now made the complete circle. Then do it again, only this time, ask each person to place a hand on the ankle of the one in front. By adding the extra distance of ankle to shoulder for everyone in the line, the nerve impulse will take longer to make the circle than it did before!

In addition to the brain and the nerves, physiologists explored the senses and the rest of the body. It was the union between the questions asked by the philosophers and the careful scientific experimentation of the physiologists that led to the field of study we call psychology.

It may surprise you to learn that psychology hasn't always been concerned with mental illness, animal behavior, unconscious thoughts, dreams, IQ tests, personality, or childhood. At the beginning, its objective was to analyze systematically immediate conscious experience. Careful analysis of conscious experience began when a German physician named Wilhelm Wundt (1832–1920), acting on his persistent curiosity concerning matters of the human mind, started his psychological laboratory in 1879. One of the first questions that attracted his interest was the speed of human thought and if this differed from person to person. While considering this idea, Wundt took the bold step of applying scientific methodology to the study of the mind. He built a device he called the thought meter (see Figure 1.2) and began the first truly psychological experiment. The thought meter worked as follows. The pendulum (B in Figure 1.2) swung back and forth. As it did so, the needle (S) attached horizontally to the pendulum would strike the bells (g). The observer's job was to note the exact position of the pendulum when he heard the bell. By adjusting the length of the needle beforehand, Wundt could predetermine the time between bell "dings" and the position of the pendulum at each ding. Wundt discovered that most observers disagreed with the actual time and position by as much as 1/5 second. Wundt's own observations were off by about 1/8 second. Wundt believed that what he had measured was the time of the swiftest thought; that is, the time it took for the person to think about looking at the pendulum from the moment that he heard the bell.* This, Wundt argued, clearly showed that not everyone thought at the same speed!

The very idea that anyone might try to measure the speed of a thought was astounding. Wundt had opened a new area, the scientific investigation of mental processes (Diamond, 1980). He then attempted to build a theory by investigating conscious acts of will and the way in which such acts were related.

Although Wundt's works are of historical interest, the fact is that modern researchers have found most of them to be of limited scientific value. While developing his theories, Wundt often contradicted himself or failed to consider important aspects of his own work. For example, modern researchers now understand that Wundt's thought meter measures not only the speed of thinking but also attention, the speed of muscular responses, and motivation—all now considered under the heading *reaction time*. Still, all psychology owes Wundt a debt of gratitude for doing something no one had done before—setting up a psychological laboratory in which the mind was subjected to scientific scrutiny and measurement.

PHILOSOPHICAL APPROACHES TO THE STUDY OF PSYCHOLOGY

Structuralism

Edward B. Titchener (1867–1927) was an Englishman who taught for a time at Cornell University in New York. He cast himself in the role of Wundt's primary representative and interpreter in the English-speaking world. Titchener wrote and lectured extensively about Wundt's theories. Since many people in the English-speaking world were interested in Wundt's works but couldn't read German, they turned to Titchener for an explanation. Unfortunately, Titchener liked to add and change ideas as he went along, still claiming that he was merely expounding Wundt's theories (Janik & Toulmin, 1973; Blumenthal, 1980). Titchener argued incorrectly that Wundt was trying to discover an exact structure or blueprint of the mind by reducing experience to its elemental components. What developed, then, was a philosophical approach to the study of psychology known as **structuralism,** attributed to Wundt but mostly based on Titchener's ideas and interpretations. Structuralism relied on a self-observation technique known as **introspection.** Trained self-observers, or introspectionists, tried to break down the content of their own conscious experience into all of its component parts. Only persons skilled in the techniques of introspection could, it was argued, provide an objective description of an experience, because only they were trained to describe their immediate perception of an event without adding biased conclusions drawn from expectations or knowledge.

Edward B. Titchener (1867–1927).

---

*The time it takes for the sound of the bell to reach the observer's ears is negligible (about 1/1000 second).

9

William James (1842–1910).

The structural approach taken by Titchener might have remained a powerful force in psychology had it not been for a few critical flaws. The worst of these was the introspective method itself. Have you ever applied introspection to your own conscious experience? For instance, have you ever tried to stop in the middle of a daydream and carefully examine your exact thoughts or sensations? Observing what you are experiencing changes the experience. Psychologists began to discover that the very act of introspection altered many of the conscious experiences they wanted to isolate and examine. It was like trying to grab a handful of water. Even more devastating was the discovery that different researchers independently using the introspective method were getting different results. Nothing could be done to resolve the problem of a disagreement between trained observers. After all, each was describing a personal experience, and who could say which observer was correct? By the 1930s, researchers had begun to abandon structuralism as a way of learning about the mind. Psychologists working with animals were obtaining exciting results without introspection; European psychoanalysts were examining the influence of unconscious mental processes on maladaptive behavior; and many American psychologists were simply more interested in searching for practical solutions to every-day problems.

Still, all psychology owes a debt to the structural approach for three reasons. First, it provided psychology with a strong scientific and research impetus. Second, it gave the introspective method a thorough test, which was worthwhile, because most psychologists now agree that introspection has severe limitations. Third, it provided a body of work against which new schools of psychological thought could rebel.

From what has been said up to this point, it might appear that psychology developed soley from the German scientific tradition, but that is not wholly correct (Buxton, 1985). Along with Wundt's influence, there were many other ideas and forces at work during those early days. These schools of thought included **British empiricism,** the advocates of which argued that all mental thought and activity was the direct result of a person's experiences; French psychiatry, which was making interesting headway using hypnosis (see Chapter 6) to probe the mind; Russian physiology, which, under the guidance of Ivan Pavlov (see Chapter 6), was breaking new ground in the understanding of learning; and evolutionary theory as espoused by Charles Darwin.

Functionalism

Functionalism was the first completely American philosophical approach to the study of psychology. Its founder was William James (1842–1910), who is still regarded by many people as the greatest American psychologist. James received an M.D. from Harvard and was a professor of anatomy. He became interested in psychological inquiry in 1875, and published his famous two-volume work, *Principles of Psychology*, in 1890—it is still fascinating reading. James wasn't an experimentalist, but he had a way of synthesizing psychological principles brilliantly and of getting to the heart of difficult problems. He rejected the idea that the conscious mind had a permanent structure, or blueprint. To him, conscious experience was more like a river that was always changing and flowing. He coined his famous term **stream of consciousness** to express this property.

James was greatly influenced by the work of Charles Darwin (1809–1882), who stated that, through the process of **natural selection,** characteristics in animals that served a valuable function would be favored and carried over from one generation to the next. For example, Darwin argued that sex was pleasurable because only those species that found it so would have survived; a species that didn't like sex would not last more than a generation. Physical characteristics as well—such as eyes, ears, hands, paws, and claws—had all been favored by natural selection because they served a useful function. With this in mind, James concluded that human consciousness must also have a function, or why would it have evolved? He believed that the conscious mind enabled people to make rational choices, which in turn enabled them to survive generation after generation. James considered consciousness to be like "an organ added for the sake of steering a nervous system grown too complex to regulate itself" (James, 1890, p. 144).

Because of this philosophical emphasis, other functionalists who followed in James's footsteps were concerned with why a thought or behavior occurred, rather than with what a thought or behavior was. This was the major distinction between functionalism and structuralism, and it opened the door to many new areas of psychological study by a number of important individuals.

G. Stanley Hall (1844–1924) was perhaps James's most illustrious student. Hall was the first person to receive a Ph.D. in psychology; he was also the founder of the American Psychological Association. Hall's interest in the development of human beings during childhood, adolescence, and adulthood, and his systematic investigations of changes during the lifespan, marked the beginnings of developmental psychology. John Dewey (1859–1952), another functional psychologist and educator, became interested in the problem-solving ability of the conscious mind as a factor in our species' survival (Dewey, 1910). Dewey's interest in problem solving and in ways of improving teaching contributed to the establishment of another new discipline, educational psychology. Also, because animals are capable of learning and because their behavior too serves a purpose or function, the study of animal psychology was born. Industrial psychology also came into being when researchers began making time–motion studies of the value and function of each movement of workers on assembly lines, with the goal of improving efficiency by eliminating wasteful motions. All these psychologies shared the functional philosophy.

Functionalism is no longer a distinct philosophical approach. Even at its peak early in this century, it was a diversified and informal system, a collection of new fields that were linked by the common philosophy that the mind's function was more important than its structure. Today, the areas of psychology to which functionalism gave birth have matured to become fields in their own right.

Psychoanalysis

Psychoanalysis probably has been the most widely publicized of psychological systems, especially among nonpsychologists. Psychoanalytic theory was developed by a Viennese physician, Sigmund Freud (1856–1939). From its beginning in 1895, psychoanalysis created a storm of controversy. Some of its principles and concepts were so shocking that many people regarded them as entirely new. Nonetheless, like all important ideas, it had its antecedents (Sulloway, 1979).

Psychoanalytic theory traces its roots to neurology and medicine. Its goal was to understand and treat abnormal behavior. Freud presented, as one of the major tenets of psychoanalysis, the concept of the unconscious mind. He argued that the mind is like an iceberg in that most of it is hidden beneath the surface. He stated that human beings are controlled primarily not by rational and conscious processes but by drives and urges hidden within the unconscious. To some critics, this was the last of three great blows to human pride. The first was dealt when Copernicus demonstrated that Earth was not the center of the universe; the second, when Darwin showed that humans had evolved from lower species. Now Freud was arguing that we were not even the conscious masters of our behavior.

Freud believed that abnormal behavior and, for that matter, all personality

PSYCHOANALYSIS
A therapy that seeks to bring unconscious desires into consciousness and make it possible to resolve conflicts, which usually date back to early childhood experiences. Psychoanalysis is also the school of psychological thought founded by Sigmund Freud, which emphasizes the study of unconscious mental processes.

could be explained by analyzing the motives and drives of the unconscious. Like the functionalists, Freud had been influenced by Darwin, and he maintained that the unconscious served a function—it kept unacceptable thoughts or desires repressed or hidden from the conscious mind. Because of this, he argued, the unconscious mind was reluctant to give up its knowledge, so special techniques were needed to probe its secrets. Among the techniques Freud used were hypnosis, **free association** (in which the patient is asked to say whatever first comes to mind, regardless of how foolish it may seem), dream interpretation, and analysis of slips of the tongue. In the last technique, for example, a psychoanalyst might conclude that the patient was exhibiting a repressed sexual desire if she answered the question "What is your religion?" by stating, "I'm a prostitute, I mean Protestant." Freud believed that analysis could help resolve unconscious conflicts and correct arrested personality development or abnormal behavior.

Psychoanalysis, however, has been severely criticized for its lack of scientific control and careful experimentation (Rosenzweig, 1985). Many modern psychologists, although agreeing that psychoanalysis is colorful, argue that as a psychology it is unscientific. "The unfortunate truth is that the analysts' statements are so general that they can explain whatever behavior occurs. A genuine scientific explanation cannot do this" (Marx & Hillix, 1963, p. 231). Others point out that psychoanalysis relies on techniques that have never been validated. For instance, no one has found a way to discover whether dreams have important meanings or are simply the brain's attempt to make sense of random electrical activity that occurs during sleep. Yet many conclusions drawn by psychoanalysts rest heavily on dream interpretation.

At the same time, the historical importance of psychoanalysis cannot be denied. Freud's work made a great contribution to psychology because the interest it stimulated in many previously neglected areas—the workings of the unconscious mind, sexuality, emotionality, abnormal behavior, conflict, childhood—proved fruitful.

Behaviorism

Early in this century, an American psychologist, John B. Watson (1878–1958), helped to develop **behaviorism,** a system of psychology he believed to be far more objective than any other. Behaviorism has since become one of the most influential and controversial schools of psychology.

Watson had been trained as a functional psychologist and was especially interested in the purpose and functions of animal behavior. Like psychologists who investigated humans, researchers who studied animal subjects were careful to be scientific in their work. They objectively observed and recorded everything they could. But to Watson's way of thinking, human psychology still had a serious fault: There was no way to observe the conscious mind objectively. No matter how you looked at it, if you wanted to know what people thought, you had to ask them. They alone could tell you. To Watson, this was introspectionism again. He thought that if a purely objective experimental science of psychology was to be developed, psychologists must reject all subjective methods and rely solely on what could be observed and recorded objectively. In Watson's view, psychology had

> made a false start under Wundt . . . because it would not bury its past. It tried to hang on to tradition with one hand and push forward as a science with the other. Before progress could be made in astronomy, it had to bury astrology; neurology had to bury phrenology; and chemistry had to bury alchemy. But the social sciences, psychology, sociology, political science, and economics, will not bury their "medicine men." (Watson, 1929, p. 3)

John B. Watson, the father of behaviorism (1878–1958).

Before Watson, the Russian physiologist Ivan Sechenov had noted that all human behavior might be reduced to the study of muscular movement. In 1863, he stated,

> A child laughing at the sight of a toy, a young girl trembling at the first thought of love . . . Newton discovering and writing down the laws of the universe—everywhere the final act is muscular movement. (Sechenov, 1863/1965)

Watson built on this idea, taking the tremendous philosophical step of rejecting the study of conscious thought and mental activity because they were not directly observable. Instead, he emphasized observable environmental stimuli (for example, a loud noise, a red stoplight, a candy bar, praise from a friend) and the observable behaviors or muscular responses that occurred in the presence of such stimuli. For this reason, behaviorism is known as S–R psychology (for stimulus–response). It is also referred to as black-box psychology because Watson considered the mind to be like a mysterious black box that could never be examined objectively. Of course, Watson also rejected the ideas of psychoanalysis as these too, he argued, dealt with unobservable events, such as dreams (observable only to the dreamer) or the actions of a supposed unconscious mind.

Behaviorism has evolved since Watson's day and remains a powerful force in modern psychology. It has been of great value in demonstrating that much of our behavior is the product of our immediate environment and of our past experiences. Behaviorists have shown that the associations we experience—the pleasant or unpleasant consequences following our actions—and our observations of the actions of those around us often determine our responses. Through behavioral technology, problems such as aggression, phobias, shyness, and poor study habits often can be corrected. In addition, behavioral psychologists have emphasized the need to define terms carefully, to run controlled experiments, and in general to make psychology more of a science. Ironically, this effort has provoked some of the strongest criticism of behaviorism. It has been argued that behaviorists often ignore important but unobservable aspects of human behavior—such as emotion, thought, and unconscious processes—and that they discredit feelings or ideas that don't readily lend themselves to controlled experimentation (Manicas & Secord, 1983).

Gestalt Psychology

At about the same time that behaviorism was becoming the dominant force in American psychology, a different reaction to structuralism was developing in Germany, the Gestalt view. In a strange way, **Gestalt psychology*** owes its inception largely to the motion-picture projector. Structuralists, who wished to break down conscious experience into its simplest elements, had a difficult time trying to explain how a series of still pictures, shown one after another, could seem to move (which is, of course, how a "motion" picture works). The structuralists reasoned that if sensations are elemental, then each picture would be a separate sensation. But that's not what happens. Someone viewing a movie sees one picture that appears to be moving. This false perception of motion is known as the **phi phenomenon.**

In 1912, Max Wertheimer (1880–1943) presented a paper in which he argued that the phi phenomenon needed no explanation. Rather, it was a real phenomenon in its own right, and any attempt to reduce it to simpler sensations would destroy it. At first glance, this argument may not seem revolutionary, but it was. It rejected a fundamental tenet of structuralism, that we can break down all experience into

GESTALT PSYCHOLOGY
The school of psychological thought that emphasizes that wholes are more than the sum of their parts. Gestalt psychologists study forms and patterns and contend that stimuli are perceived as whole images rather than as parts built into images.

PHI PHENOMENON
Specifically, a perceptual illusion brought about by observing two lights placed side by side in a darkened room and flashed alternately. The resulting perception is of one light moving back and forth. Also, often applied to any circumstance in which stationary objects presented in succession appear to be moving, such as occurs when we view a motion picture.

---

*Not to be confused with a more recent innovation, Gestalt therapy.

elemental parts in order to understand it better. Wertheimer, Kohler, and Koffka argued that the whole experience (in German, the *Gestalt*) was not just the sum of its parts; it was more, it was itself. For example, the color white is created by an equal mixture of red, green, and blue. (Although at first it may be difficult to believe, if you take a disk that has been divided like a pie into three equal parts, one part fire-engine red, another part forest green and the third part royal blue, and spin it at high speed, the disk will appear snow white!) Gestalt psychologists emphasized that the experience of white is more than the sum of its parts. Certainly it is red plus green, plus blue, but it is also itself; it is white. Experiencing red, then experiencing green, and finally experiencing blue is obviously not the same as experiencing white.

The Gestalt psychologists weren't the first people to rebel against the idea of reducing consciousness to its supposed constituent parts. Some 22 years before the beginning of Gestalt psychology, William James, whose brilliant mind seems to have been everywhere at once, stated, "The traditional psychologist (structuralist) talks like one who would say a river consists of nothing but pailsful, spoonsful, quartpotsful, barrelsful, and other moulded forms of water. Even were the pails and the pots all actually standing in the same stream, still between them the free water would continue to flow" (1890, p. 279). Had James pursued this line of reasoning a little farther, he might have founded Gestalt psychology as well as functionalism!

Gestalt psychology argues that conscious sensations can be examined but that the whole experience must be taken for what it is. Moreover, the use of specially trained self-observers is unnecessary. To the Gestaltists, the laws of psychology are the laws of *systems*, not of parts, and there is little value in breaking down experiences mechanistically.

The Gestalt philosophy is still prevalent throughout modern psychology (Henle, 1985). It is now well appreciated that many experiences must be analyzed and understood as whole entities and cannot necessarily be broken down into constituent parts.

Humanistic Psychology

Psychologists Abraham Maslow (1908–1970) and Carl Rogers (1902–1987) were both the main developers and leading proponents of **humanistic psychology.**

Humanistic psychologists' understanding of behavior is different from that of psychoanalysts and behaviorists. Humanists don't believe that behavior is governed in an important way either by unconscious drives and motives or by external stimuli and rewards in the environment. Instead, they argue that people are free agents, have free will, are conscious and creative, and are born with an inner motivation to fulfill their potential. Maslow referred to this as **self-actualization.** The humanists view self-actualization as a lifelong process rather than as a goal that a person eventually reaches. The influence of the Gestalt view is also evident—humanists strongly believe that human beings cannot be understood piecemeal; rather, the whole person always must be taken into account if we are to achieve a reasonable understanding of behavior. Furthermore, if we wish to consider the whole person, we can understand behavior only by examining each individual's unique self-perception. In this view, the world is different for all of us, because we all perceive it differently and because each of us, as a whole, is unique.

Some humanistic psychologists, such as Maslow, have developed a concept of personality based on these ideas. Others, such as Carl Rogers, have devised therapies to help people develop their individual potential. These aspects of humanistic psychology are examined in greater detail in Chapters 13 and 16. Like psychoa-

Abraham Maslow (1908–1970).

nalysis, humanistic psychology has been criticized for being based on speculations more often than on evidence obtained from scientific experiments.

The Neurobiological Approach

Learning, remembering, thinking, feeling, perceiving, in fact, all of our abilities and actions, are rooted in our biology. Physiologists and physicians have been interested in the human brain, and the body that supports it, for centuries. But the brain is so complicated that for most of that time even its basic functions remained mysterious and beyond the reach of our understanding.

Until very recently, most of our knowledge of how the brain works came from the study of head injuries. This was especially true during the First World War when improvements in medical care meant that a significant number of brain-damaged people were able to survive their injuries and become objects of study. The neurobiological approach to the study of psychology has expanded rapidly in the last few decades, however, owing to the development of new techniques and instruments that have enabled us to pry loose some of the brain's secrets. And, as we enter the next century, even newer and more sophisticated methods hold the promise of revealing far more than we currently know.

For the first time, we are beginning to look inside the brain and observe how it acts under different circumstances, learning which parts perform which functions, and even seeing how it communicates and talks with itself. We are also beginning to unravel the genetic code and starting to understand in a deeper way how inheritance can influence behavior.

Many researchers believe that unraveling the mysteries of the brain and genetics will give us a profound understanding that will dwarf all previous attempts to explain behavior. In fact, neurobiology is now considered so basic to our overall understanding of psychology, that we will start our exploration into human behavior in Chapter 2 by looking at what has been uncovered by this approach. Some of the things you will read about would have seemed fantastic only a few years ago. The neurobiological approach attempts to understand behavior at the biological level.

Cognitive Psychology

Cognition generally refers to any process that takes an input from the senses and alters, simplifies, expands on, or stores it. Such processes include thinking, remembering, and perceiving. A more informal definition might be "any psychological activity that goes on inside your head."

Although Wilhelm Wundt was interested in mental phenomena, he believed that advanced processes, such as thinking, were so dependent on culture and language that they could not be easily studied. As a result, Wundt limited his investigations to "simpler" matters, such as the perception of objects, until the very end of his career. Because of this, the number of studies that focused on what are now considered to be the traditional topics of cognitive psychology, namely, attention, pattern recognition, memory, language, reading and writing, reasoning, and problem solving (Best, 1989), were relatively few in number until about the time of the Second World War.

At that time, a psychologist named Donald Broadbent became interested in a problem that fighter pilots were having. During combat, pilots discovered that it was especially difficult for them to read all of their gauges and instruments without taking their eyes off the action for a dangerously long time. Broadbent discovered that the pilots had learned to compensate for this by using some gauges more than

SCIENTIFIC METHOD
The principles and processes used to
conduct scientific investigations, including
formation of hypotheses, observation, and
experimentation.

others or by taking shortcuts when trying to get the vital information they needed. To Broadbent, this meant that human beings were much more than passive receivers of environmental stimuli; they actively gathered and interacted with the information in their environments. Human beings were active information processors. This is the keystone concept of cognitive psychology.

Behaviorists continued to criticize strongly those who studied areas such as thought or perception, because there was no way in which to directly observe such things. And yet, cognitive psychology came of age and flourished owing to two events. First, behaviorists were finding some interesting phenomena that seemed impossible to explain without resorting to the concept of thought, and second, scientists were developing computers that held the promise of eventually being able to think.

This second point has had the greatest influence on the upsurge of cognitive psychology. We know what is inside a machine, because we put it there. It is not, as John Watson called the human brain, a black box forever mysterious. As we developed computer technology, we made computers that could "see," "reason," and to a very limited degree, even learn from experience. In an effort to understand better ways to make computers, the cognitive processes of human beings have attracted special interest. In what ways are they like the machine's processes? How are humans different? Can machines be made to work like the human brain? These questions have led to many interesting efforts to understand the human thought process and to the development of many ingenious ways to measure it, albeit indirectly. In Chapter 8, you will have a chance to explore the history and advances in this interesting area of psychology.

Modern Trends and the Emergence of Scientific Psychology

Psychology continues to be influenced by new ideas and philosophical forces. Some of the original systems of psychology, too, have matured and changed. For example, behaviorism and cognitive psychology have both expanded and, to a certain extent, even merged (Kleininna & Kleininna, 1988; Mahoney, 1989). Both have given birth to clinical therapies, social and other learning theories, and theories of motivation. Psychoanalysis has become more diversified and now includes many of Freud's original therapeutic treatments.

Although hundreds of pages could be written about the different psychological groups, subgroups, and offshoots, this doesn't mean that psychology has become a loose amalgam of splinter groups, all going in different directions. All psychologists who rely on the special techniques of the **scientific method** are, philosophically, sharing the same view: They are scientific psychologists. It doesn't matter that one may be a psychobiological psychologist studying a hormone's effects on behavior, or another a cognitive psychologist studying amnesia, or yet another a school psychologist testing a child's academic ability. If they are using or relying on scientific methods, they share a common ground. So that you can fully understand the power and importance of these scientific methods, and why it matters that these methods be used, let's take some time to explore them and even conduct a psychological experiment.

RESEARCH METHODS

All scientific research is based on systematic and objective methods of observing, recording, and describing events. Table 1.1 outlines the six dimensions of psy-

TABLE 1.1 Dimensions of Research

DIMENSION OF RESEARCH	DESCRIPTION
Descriptive versus Explanatory	Descriptive research describes only *what* has occurred, while explanatory research attempts to explain *how* or *why* something has occurred; that is, what caused it. Descriptive research often is a good way to begin, as it is generally less subject to error. A caveman giving a description of what occurred during a thunderstorm might say, "There was a bright flash of light followed by a terrible loud rumble," and he would be accurate. The same caveman attempting an explanation might state, "The Great God Zog throw rock at sky." Not only is he inaccurate, but like all cavemen, his grammar is poor.
	Of course, descriptions can be inaccurate too. The more objective they are, however, the more accurate they are likely to be; for example, you can count objectively the people standing in a given room and not be likely to make an error. The more subjective descriptions become, the more they are open to misinterpretation; for example, how many people on the street would you describe as "happy"? The description of someone as happy is open to personal interpretation and is more likely to be inaccurate. For this reason, psychological researchers often begin with *objective descriptions* and then, through careful experimental research, begin to examine cause-and-effect relationships in the hope that they eventually will explain how and why the events they have described occurred. That is, through scientific experimentation they hope to arrive at a good explanation.
Naturalistic versus Manipulative	When conducting naturalistic research, researchers refrain from interacting with the subjects of their observations in order to examine behavior in a natural setting. They keep careful, detailed records of their observations. During manipulative research, however, researchers purposely manipulate their subjects to observe the effects of the manipulations. Manipulative research can be carefully controlled in a laboratory setting, allowing observation of the limits and parameters of each studied behavior.
Historical versus Ahistorical	If research is fundamentally dependent on past events, it is considered historical research; if not, it is called ahistorical. For example, a study concerned with the effects of a particular therapy for abused children would be historical, because a previous history of child abuse would be an important factor. In contrast, a study concerned with the effects of brightly colored blocks on an infant's vocalizations would be ahistorical, because, in this study, there is no particular interest in the infant's previous experience or history.
Theoretical versus Serendipitous	Research designed to investigate a particular theory is called theoretical research, while research designed simply to investigate phenomena without regard to theoretical speculations is called serendipitous, or sometimes atheoretical.
Basic versus Applied	Basic research advances knowledge; applied research advances technology. Once the basic knowledge has been gathered, applied research is concerned with assembling it for a particular purpose. The Apollo program to send astronauts to the moon is a good example of applied research—most of the basic knowledge about rockets, aerodynamics, and space had been gathered before its inception. The search for a cancer cure, however, is more typically an example of basic research. No one is certain of the fundamental causes of cancer, so our basic knowledge of biology must be expanded before the next major application of technology can occur. Thus, basic research is the foundation on which applied research can be built. Although at first glance some people may think that basic research has no value, because it usually has no immediate application, it is the lifeblood of all science.
Single-Subject versus Group	In single-subject research, the behavior and behavior changes of only one person at a time are of interest; in group research, the researcher looks at group averages, and is not concerned with whether those averages accurately reflect the behavior patterns of any given individual within the group.

EXPERIMENT
A test made to demonstrate the validity of a hypothesis or to determine the predictability of a theory. Variables are manipulated and changes are contrasted with a control that has not been exposed to the variables of interest.

CATHARSIS
In psychoanalytic theory, elimination of a complex by bringing it to consciousness and allowing it to express itself; in general, any emotional releases resulting from a buildup of internal tensions.

SOCIAL LEARNING THEORY
A theory developed by Albert Bandura that stresses learning by observing and imitating others. Social learning is sometimes called observational learning or vicarious conditioning.

HYPOTHESIS
Any statement or assumption that serves as a possible, but tentative, explanation of certain observations. A hypothesis is always formulated in a way that makes it amendable to empirical test.

SAMPLE
A group of subjects who should normally be representative of the population about which an inference is made.

chological research. All the research discussed in this text (and, for that matter, all psychological research) falls into one of each of these pairs of categories. If you become familiar with these dimensions, it will be easier for you to understand the research described in the following chapters.

Experimental Methods

The scientific **experiment** is one of the most powerful research tools that psychologists possess. Perhaps the best way to learn how to conduct an experiment, and how not to conduct one, is to try it yourself.

For the next few pages, let's work on an experiment together.

First, we need an issue that is testable. Some issues are not testable, such as the following:

- Will psychology still be taught 500 years from now?
- How did prehistoric people raise children?
- What will the world be like in 20 years?
- Is there life on Neptune?

Tests cannot be devised for these questions because no one has access to concrete observable information about them. For example, we would need a soil sample for Neptune (assuming Neptune even has "soil"), or child-rearing advice carved in stone by prehistoric people, before we could explore these subjects. Instead, let's examine an issue that can be tested: Do violent programs on television cause aggressive behavior in children who view them?

Sigmund Freud believed that the desire to be violent was instinctive and that viewing violence might satisfy an instinctive urge, acting as a release or a **catharsis**. As a result, the viewer's desire to be violent would be reduced. On the other hand, the contemporary psychologist Albert Bandura has developed a **social learning theory** (which stems from behaviorism) that contradicts Freud's catharsis prediction. Bandura predicts that viewing violence will increase the probability that the viewer will imitate the violence. Clearly, we have a disagreement—and one that can be tested. When researchers make such a prediction, they are, in technical terms, generating an **hypothesis**. Simply put, an hypothesis is an educated guess that can be tested.

To begin our experiment we need some children and some violent programs. We need some observers to watch the children's behavior and to record what happens when the children are exposed to the shows. We also need informed consent in writing from the parents of all the children.

SELECTING SUBJECTS. In selecting the children, we probably should choose children of many ages and backgrounds, because it is always risky to generalize beyond a particular **sample**. If you conduct a study on little boys, for instance, you must be very cautious about applying your findings to little girls. (And, unless you have a sound reason for doing so, you shouldn't even attempt such a generalization.) Psychologists, like all scientists, should not go beyond their data unless they specifically state that they are speculating.

Now that we've assembled the children, let's show them some of those violent Saturday-morning cartoons and see what happens. But first we must solve a problem: How can we tell which cartoons are violent? Moreover, after showing the cartoons, how will we decide whether the children are being aggressive?

DEFINING TERMS. In France, there used to be a platinum–iridium rod that was kept inside a sealed glass case that had been emptied of air. The rod was exactly one meter in length. Whenever a physicist needed to be certain that her meter stick was 1 meter long, she could compare it with the rod. The rod was the *standard*. Nowadays, physicists use an even more precise standard for the length. The point is that everyone agrees on the definition of a meter—but do we all agree on what aggression is? Is a good salesperson aggressive? Are all murderers aggressive? Is it good for a football player to be aggressive? Obviously, aggression has come to mean many different things, and before we can study it, and perhaps conclude that watching TV violence does or does not cause aggression, we must be able to define it. If aggression means something different to everyone who reads our findings, we will have succeeded only in confusing the issue.

If a tree falls in the forest, and no one is there to hear it, does it make a noise? You may have heard this famous philosophical question before, but do you know the answer? There is one. It depends totally on how you define noise. If you define noise as the production of sound waves, the answer to the question is yes. If you define noise as the perception of sound waves by a living creature, the answer is no. The only reason such a question can cause an argument in the first place is that people are often unaware that they are using different definitions.

How shall we define aggression to avoid confusion in our experiment? One definition might be "any act committed with the intention of damaging property or injuring another person." Since this description fits most people's idea of aggression, let's try it, even though intentions aren't easy to observe. We now have what is known as an **operational definition.** We'll also have to define operationally "violent cartoons." One common operational definition is "any act performed by a cartoon character that would be likely to result in injury if it had been carried out by real people." Once we have operationally defined both terms, we can begin the experiment. It will be your job to watch a particular child after the child has viewed a violent cartoon. You will note whether aggression occurs and, if so, how often. Can you be trusted to be accurate in your observations?

INTEROBSERVER RELIABILITY. It may be that our definition allows too much subjectivity. If this is the case, you might consider an event to be an aggressive act according to our definition, whereas another observer applying the same definition to the same event might not record an aggressive act. This could be a serious problem, because different observers would describe the same behavior as both aggressive and nonaggressive. To avoid this problem, we will use two or more people who will independently observe the same child over the same period of time. We can then compare their observations. If they are in fairly good agreement, we can conclude that we have a reliable means of observing and recording the behavior in question. This technique yields a measure of what is known as **interobserver reliability.** If our interobserver reliability turns out to be low, we will have to define aggression more carefully.

THE CONTROL. Now that we will use interobserver reliability to ensure that we agree on definitions of aggression and violent cartoons, shall we show a violent cartoon to the children and observe their behavior? If the children are aggressive after viewing the cartoon, how will we know that it was the violence in the cartoon that provoked the aggression? For that matter, how can we be sure that the children wouldn't have been even more aggressive had they not watched the cartoon? If you ask, "Who won the soccer game?" and all someone tells you is that one team scored five times, you won't know whether that team won or lost. To know, you need the other team's score as a comparison. It's the same with an experiment. You need a comparison, in this case a similar group of children who do not see

A definition derived from a set of operations that will produce what is being defined; for example, human strength = the amount of weight that can be lifted by a person from the floor to a height of 1 foot in 5 seconds. Although such definitions are exact, and work well in scientific studies, they are sometimes considered limited. For example, not everyone would necessarily agree that the definition of human strength is inclusive enough to cover all actions that might be considered to comprise this measure.

INTEROBSERVER RELIABILITY
The degree of disagreement or agreement between two or more observers who simultaneously observe a single event.

CONTROL

Deliberate arrangement of experimental or research conditions so that observed effects can be directly traced to a known variable or variables.

INDEPENDENT VARIABLE

In an experiment, the variable that is manipulated or treated to see what effect differences in it will have on the variables considered to be dependent on it.

DEPENDENT VARIABLE

In an experiment, the variable that may change as a result of changes in the independent variable.

OBSERVER BIAS

An error in observation caused by the expectations of the observer.

The best way to obtain a second group of children who are similar to the first is simply to divide the original group of children in half. Then, in all probability, the two groups will be alike. You must divide the groups randomly, however. *Random* assignment of subjects to study groups means that each child has an equal chance of being placed in either group. For example, you might assign each child to an experimental or a control group by flipping a coin.

The control and experimental groups *must be treated in exactly the same way* except for the one thing you wish to measure, in this case, watching TV violence. If you show the control group no cartoon at all, you fail to control for the effects of simply watching a cartoon. Thus, while the experimental group is watching a violent cartoon, the control group should see a nonviolent cartoon. Ideally, it should be exactly the same cartoon except that the violent acts do not occur. In this way, the effect of violence is isolated from all other effects. Everything that happens to the experimental group is *controlled for* if it also happens to the control group. In our case, everything is controlled except viewing violence, which happens only to the experimental group. If the amount of aggression observed in both groups of children is similar before they see the cartoon but is different afterward, we have isolated the effect of watching violence and probably nothing else. In this way, psychologists are able to separate variables and to observe the variables' effects one at a time. A *variable* is any measurement that may vary, as opposed to a constant, such as the speed of light, which does not vary. Examples of variables include a person's height and weight, the outside temperature or barometric pressure, the miles per gallon obtained by a car, the rainfall in Rangoon, the number of teeth in an audience, or the number of scoops of ice cream dropped on the sidewalks of Detroit each day by consequently upset children.

To repeat, since both groups shared all the variables but one, and since both groups were similar to each other at the beginning of the experiment, any difference between the groups at the end of the experiment can be attributed to the one variable the groups didn't share. Remember, variables shared by both groups are controlled. Or, putting it another way, if it starts to rain on the experimental group, your experiment won't be disrupted as long as it starts to rain on the control group, too. The variable that is manipulated, in our case how much and what kind of TV violence we showed, is called the **independent variable.** The variable that may be influenced by the manipulations, in our case the amount of aggression, is called the **dependent variable.** *

OBSERVER AND SUBJECT BIAS. Before continuing the experiment, we need to examine other problems that might arise. Among these are observer and subject bias. In our experiment, we have used a control group and an experimental group and have treated each in the same manner except for showing violence to the latter. Still, you and those observing the children might be susceptible to an **observer bias.** For example, suppose that all of you are scornful of Freud's theories and certain that Bandura's predictions are accurate. You might all be hoping to see more aggression in the experimental group. Although working independently, you might all consider certain behavior aggressive if it is exhibited by a child from the experimental group, whereas you might consider the same behavior nonaggressive

*If you have trouble recalling which variable is which, just think of freedom and independence. The variable that the experimenter is free to manipulate is the independent variable.

if you observed it in a child from the control group. In this way, your observations could be badly biased even though interobserver reliability might remain high.

Even careful observers can't always avoid such mistakes, since it is very hard not to see what you expect to see. For years, students in psychology labs have been sent by sly professors to observe "bright" rats and "dull" rats running mazes. Even the most careful students have tended to report that the bright rats did better than the dull ones, although the rats have been labeled bright or dull simply by the flip of a coin.

The subjects in experiments also can be biased. **Subject bias** may occur whenever subjects are aware that they are being observed or that particular results are expected from them. Many years ago, the Public Broadcasting System decided to produce a program about a typical American family. The producers of the show decided to follow for a few months all the members of one family, at home, at work, and everywhere they went. A camera crew lived with the family, filming everything the family members did. During the filming, the parents divorced, the eldest son announced he was homosexual, and a younger son started a rock band. Perhaps the family would have behaved the same way if the cameras hadn't been present. However, some family members later said that they felt compelled to put on a show, to do something rather than just sit there, when a camera was pointed at them. In other words, they changed because they knew they were being observed. They may have shown subject bias. People in many situations can act differently simply because they know they are being observed. (Would you be "yourself" while brushing your teeth if TV cameras were taping it for prime time?)

Fortunately, we can easily avoid any bias in our experiment; the observers simply must not know whether the children they are watching are from the ex-

SUBJECT BIAS
Unwanted changes in a subject's behavior owing to her knowledge about the experiment or awareness of being observed.

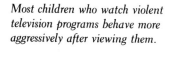
Most children who watch violent television programs behave more aggressively after viewing them.

DOUBLE-BLIND CONTROLLED EXPERIMENT

A research technique in which neither the subjects nor the experimenters know which subjects have been exposed to the independent variable. It is used for controlling biases that may be introduced by either the subjects or the experimenters.

REPLICATION

Repeating an experiment to affirm the reliability of the results.

EXPANSION

An enlargement or extension of initial research efforts.

perimental or the control group (someone else can keep track of that). This will prevent the observers from unconsciously leaning toward one group or the other, because they won't know which is which. Because the children, too, are unaware of which group they are in, subject bias is eliminated. Our study can now be called a **double-blind controlled experiment.** That is, neither the subjects nor the observers know who is in which group. Double-blind controlled experiments are extremely effective as research tools, since they allow us to examine variables one at a time while they eliminate the effects of human biases.

THE RESULTS OF OUR EXPERIMENT. Once we have observed the levels of aggression in the children from both groups, we will statistically analyze the data to determine whether there is a significant difference in observed aggression between the control and the experimental groups.* Let's assume that the results of our hypothetical experiment are similar to those obtained by researchers who have conducted actual experiments examining the effects of TV violence on children. Like them, we find that the experimental group is significantly more aggressive (Hanratty, 1969; Savitsky, Rogers, Izard & Liebert, 1971; Hanratty, O'Neal, & Sulzer, 1972). Our conclusion (and notice how very limited and specific we have to be) is that "viewing cartoon violence increases the probability of immediate post-viewing aggression in grade-school children." In addition, we may note that Albert Bandura's theory fits our observations well, while Sigmund Freud's does not. After we have carried our experiment a bit further, we may even have enough "hard data" to suggest that cartoon violence on children's television be toned down or eliminated.

REPLICATION AND EXPANSION. At the finish of our double-blind controlled experiment, we might want to consider two other valuable procedures, **replication** and **expansion.** An old rule in research states, "If it hasn't happened twice, it hasn't happened." For this reason, it would be a good idea to have someone else, perhaps at another institution, replicate (duplicate) our study to see whether they obtain the same results. If they do, we will feel more confident about our own findings. Such confirmation is important, since there may have been something unusual about our particular sample of children or an important event, unknown to us, that interfered with the treatment or testing. To be honest about it, there isn't enough replication conducted in psychology (Furchtgott, 1984). Perhaps it lacks the glamor of original research, but replicating published studies provides a valuable service. It has been estimated that perhaps as many as 3 percent of all the findings published in the psychology literature aren't real; that is, they are due to statistical quirks or to faults in research methodology. The only way to weed out these errors is to conduct the studies again and to discover that they "fail to replicate."

We also may wish to expand our research. For instance, what would happen if we used live actors instead of cartoons? Would adults become more aggressive in the way that children do? How long does the increased aggression last? Obviously, the answer obtained in an experiment can generate many new questions, all of which may be worth pursuing.

Recalling the division of research methods given in Table 1.1, we can define the dimensions of our own experiment as follows:

▪ Explanatory. We concluded that watching violence was why aggression occurred.
▪ Manipulative. We altered the situation so that the children were exposed to the variable that we wanted them to see.

*The kinds of statistical analyses used by psychologists are outlined in Appendix A.

- ■ Ahistorical. We were not concerned about the children's history.
- ■ Theoretical. We were deciding between Freud's and Bandura's theoretical predictions.
- ■ Basic. We were advancing our knowledge rather than attempting to change the technology of the cartoon industry (although that may eventually be a result of our research).
- ■ Group. We worked with groups of children instead of concentrating on a single subject.

The Concept Review summarizes the concepts concerning psychological experiments that you have learned so far.

SINGLE-SUBJECT EXPERIMENTS. You may wonder about the practicability of conducting an experiment with only one subject, since you would obviously have no control group. But it can be done. In a **single-subject experiment** we use time to allow the subject to serve as her own control; we compare the subject's behavior at one time with that at another. This basis of comparison makes the procedure experimental. To conduct such an experiment, we create a certain condition and note the response, then we observe whether the response continues as long as the condition is maintained. Examine Figure 1.3, the record of an experiment to find the effect of a drug on memory. Since time has been used as a control, we can feel confident that the drug has indeed reduced the subject's ability to recall a list of items. First, the drug was administered and the subject's recall ability declined (condition A). Then, the effect of the drug wore off and recall improved (condition B). To be sure that this result was not just a coincidence, the drug was administered a second time, and once again recall ability decreased (a return to condition A).

SINGLE-SUBJECT EXPERIMENT
An experiment in which only one subject participates. Time is normally used as the control; that is, the subject's behavior changes over time in relation to the presentation and withdrawal of the independent variable.

CONCEPT REVIEW: THE EXPERIMENT

PROCEDURE	PURPOSE
Selecting Subjects	To obtain a sample of subjects that will adequately represent the entire population to which you intend to generalize your findings.
Defining Terms	To set up operational definitions that will help to eliminate confusion concerning what the findings are and what they represent; also helps to remove subjectivity, which may lead to bias.
Measuring Interobserver Reliability	To ensure that independent observers agree about what they are observing. Low reliability implies that the phenomenon being observed is defined too subjectively.
Setting Up the Control	To provide a comparison measure by controlling for all variables to which the experimental group is exposed, except the variable under study.
Using the Double-Blind Method	To eliminate the effects of subject and observer bias.
Performing Statistical Analysis	To determine whether there is a significant difference between the control group and experimental group at the end of the experiment.
Replicating the Experiment	To provide further support for the findings and to help ensure that the findings are valid.

FIGURE 1.3

Example of an A-B-A single-subject experimental design. The purpose of this experiment was to test a drug's effect on immediate recall (memory) by introducing and withholding the drug. In condition A, the drug is active; in condition B, it has worn off.

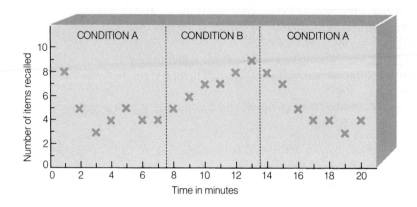

A-B-A SINGLE-SUBJECT EXPERIMENTAL DESIGN

An experimental design in which time is used as a control and only one subject is monitored. The independent variable is given in condition A and withdrawn in condition B. The dependent variable is the subject's behavioral change over time as the independent variable is presented, withdrawn, and finally presented again.

CORRELATION

The relationship between two variables.

CAUSE-EFFECT RELATIONSHIP

A relationship in which one act, of necessity, regularly brings about a particular result.

ETHICS

The study of the general nature of morals and of the specific moral choices to be made by the individual in professional relationships with others.

Since recall ability again diminished when the drug was given, the experimenters could assert with more confidence that the drug was causing a recall deficiency. It seems that by giving the drug, withholding it, and giving it again, the researchers were controlling the subject's ability to recall. This is called an **A-B-A single-subject experimental design.** It can be taken a step further if you wish, by measuring recall once more after the drug has worn off. An A-B-A-B design will thus be created, demonstrating once again the expected behavioral change in the B condition and lending support to the conviction that a cause–effect relationship exists between the administration of the drug and the subsequent decline in recall ability. Be cautious, however, about assuming that what you have discovered about one subject will explain the behavior of any other subject; it may not.

Nonexperimental Methods

THE CORRELATIONAL METHOD. A **correlation** is defined as the relationship between two variables. For example, there is a strong correlation between height and weight. The taller a person is, the heavier he tends to be, and vice versa.

By the late 1800s, army physicians were aware that the best way to stop a malaria outbreak was to move everyone to high, dry ground. Although these physicians were unaware that the disease was carried by mosquitoes, they knew that malaria was well correlated with altitude and moisture. Without knowing the cause of the disease, they were still able to predict the chances of an outbreak.

Sometimes psychologists are unable to conduct experiments or, like the army doctors, they may not know which experiments to conduct. They may then be forced to rely on correlational data. Such data are valuable because they allow us to make predictions. Frequently, too, correlations are scientists' first clue on the path to an important discovery. As you can imagine, doctors soon wondered what it was about damp, warm lowlands that related to malaria.

Nonetheless, when dealing with a correlation you must be extremely careful not to assume that a **cause–effect relationship** exists simply because two variables occur together. For example, if you were to tell me that ice-cream sales in Detroit had increased, I would be able to predict that the number of drownings would also increase—and I'd be correct. But this does not mean that eating ice cream makes you drown or, conversely, that seeing people drown makes you want ice cream! Either of these would be an example of cause and effect. The reason for the correlation between ice cream and drowning is, of course, that in summer both swimming and ice-cream sales increase. Although no one is likely to make this particular cause–effect connection, the difference between a correlation and an apparent cause–effect relationship is not always so clear.

ETHICS AND PSYCHOLOGICAL RESEARCH

Sometimes, a professional group will outline or describe behavior that it considers moral and appropriate for dealing with the specific issues faced by the profession. Such an outline of behavior deemed appropriate for a professional organization and its members defines the **ethics** of that organization and its members. Throughout this text, experiments will be discussed and issues examined that raise questions about ethical procedures and practices. Consider some of the following ethical concerns that I have noticed in the professional literature while gathering data for this text. These are not new problems, but have been concerns for a long time. All raise difficult—and interesting—issues. Space prohibits more than just touching on these topics, but you can see immediately the problems involved with each one.

■ In a nationwide survey it was found that 7.1 percent of male and 3.1 percent of female psychiatrists have had sexual relations with their patients (Gartrell, Herman, Olarte, Feldstein & Localio, 1986). The percentages for psychologists are about the same. This is perhaps the oldest ongoing ethical concern—even the 2500-year-old Hippocratic oath taken by physicians prohibits sexual contact with patients.

■ The National Institute of Mental Health has rebuked a psychologist for "knowingly, willfully, and repeatedly engaging in misleading and deceptive practices in reporting results of research . . . that he did not carry out the described research" (Holden, 1987a). No doubt this psychologist won't be the last researcher who would rather fake his data than do the research—fortunately, however, such practices occur rarely.

■ Although only 5 percent of the American Psychological Association's (APA) members use animals in their research, protests concerning alleged cruelty to animals have sparked nationwide attention (Fisher, 1986). To protect animals from poor conditions or inhumane treatment, the APA has a strict set of guidelines for the care of animal subjects. However, controversy about the use of animals in research continues.

■ Three social psychologists carried out an experiment in which they hoped to measure the tension that people felt when they perceived their psychological space to be invaded. To do this, the researchers placed a hidden periscope overlooking the men's room so that the men who used the urinals could be secretly observed. The researchers wanted to find out whether it would take longer for a subject to begin urinating if someone else were using the adjacent urinal than if the subject were alone. It did take longer, which probably comes as no surprise (Middlemist, Knowles, & Matter, 1976). The subjects, however, were never informed that they were being observed.

These four examples highlight a few of the problems that may occur when people overstep professional bounds. To help prevent such transgressions, the American Psychological Association has compiled a list of ethical principles for psychologists. A general outline of these principles is as follows:

1. In providing services, psychologists maintain the highest standards of their profession. They accept responsibility for the consequences of their acts and make every effort to ensure that their services are used properly.
2. The maintenance of high standards of competence is a responsibility shared by all psychologists in the interest of the public and the profession as a whole. Psychologists recognize the boundaries of their competence and the limitations of their techniques. They only provide services and use techniques for which they are qualified by training and experience. In those areas in which recognized standards do not yet exist, psychologists take whatever precautions are necessary to protect the welfare of their clients. They maintain knowledge of current scientific and professional information related to the services they render.
3. Psychologists' moral and ethical standards of behavior are a personal matter to the same degree as they are for any other citizen, except as they may compromise the fulfillment of their professional responsibility or reduce the public trust in psychology or psychologists. Regarding their own behavior, psychologists are sensitive to prevailing community standards and to the possible impact that conformity to or deviation from these standards may have upon the quality of their performance as psychologists. Psychologists are also aware of the possible impact of their public behavior upon the ability of their colleagues to perform their professional duties.
4. Public statements, announcements of services, advertising, and promotional activities of psychologists serve the purpose of helping the public make informed judgments and choices. Psychologists represent accurately and objectively their professional qualifications, affiliations, and functions, as well as those of the institutions or organizations with which they or the statement may be associated. In public statements providing psychological information or professional opinions or providing information about the availability of psycho-

25

logical products, publications, and services, psychologists base their statements on scientifically acceptable psychological findings and techniques with full recognition of the limits and uncertainties of such evidence.

5. Psychologists have a primary obligation to respect the confidentiality of information obtained from persons in the course of their work as psychologists. They reveal such information to others only with the consent of the person or the person's legal representative, except in those unusual circumstances in which not to do so would result in clear danger to the person or to others. Where appropriate, psychologists inform their clients of the legal limits of confidentiality.

6. Psychologists respect the integrity and protect the welfare of the people and groups with whom they work. When conflicts of interest arise between clients and psychologists' employing institutions, psychologists clarify the direction and nature of their loyalties and responsibilities and keep all parties informed of their commitments. Psychologists fully inform con-

sumers as to the purpose and nature of an evaluative, treatment, educational, or training procedure, and they freely acknowledge that clients, students, and participants in research have freedom of choice with regard to participation.

7. Psychologists act with due regard for the needs, special competencies, and obligations of their colleagues in psychology and other professions. They respect the prerogatives and obligations of the institutions or organizations with which these other colleagues are associated. (From: Ethical Principles of Psychologists. Amended June 2, 1989)

There are also important ethical considerations to take into account before conducting an experiment. We must remember that experimenting on live subjects, especially human beings, is serious business. To protect all subjects, we must respect certain ethical safeguards. To deal with the ethical problems that may arise when researchers conduct experiments, the American Psychological Association has also published

guidelines for psychological research on human subjects. The following is a summary of the major points.

1. All safeguards for the protection of each human research participant must be maintained. The researcher should protect participants from physical or mental discomfort, harm, and danger.

2. Researchers are ultimately responsible for their own ethical practices as well as for those of other people who assist in their research.

3. All research subjects must be informed of any aspect of the research that is likely to affect their willingness to participate.

4. Subjects should be fully debriefed following any concealment or deception.

5. Subjects must be allowed to decline to participate or to terminate participation in research at any time.

6. The investigator must honor all promises and commitments.

7. All information obtained about participants during research must be kept confidential.

NATURALISTIC OBSERVATIONS
Observations in which researchers refrain from interacting directly with the variables being observed.

CASE STUDY
An intensive study of a single case, with all available data, test results, and opinions about that individual. Usually done in more depth than are studies of groups of individuals.

SURVEY
A method of collecting data through the use of interviews and questionnaires.

NATURALISTIC OBSERVATIONS. We noted in Table 1.1, researchers conducting **naturalistic observations** refrain from interacting directly with the variables they are observing. Naturalistic observations can be carried out in an informal or a structured way. The more informal the observations, however, the greater the chance that bias or inaccuracy will affect the results. Part of our experiment with children and TV violence could have been a naturalistic study. Suppose we had simply wanted to observe aggression in a group of children. If we had just watched the children, perhaps from behind one-way glass, and had carefully recorded incidents of aggression (for example, by using the interobserver reliability technique), we would have been performing a naturalistic observation. But once we decided to manipulate variables by showing violent and nonviolent cartoons to randomly chosen experimental and control groups, our study became a manipulative experiment.

Naturalistic observation is most often used to investigate behavior in the natural environment, outside the laboratory. A *natural environment* is defined as any environment that the researcher has not purposely manipulated. The incidence of aggression among gorillas in their natural habitat, the amount of overt affection displayed in a college cafeteria, or the frequency with which vehicles on a particular road exceed the speed limit could all be subjects for naturalistic observation. When collecting data of this kind, observers should be as unobtrusive as possible in order not to change the behavior of the subjects being observed. As you might imagine, information about the incidence of highway speeding might not be too accurate if you collected if from inside a marked, clearly visible police car.

CASE STUDIES.   In a **case study,** researchers report or analyze the behavior, emotions, beliefs, or life history of a single individual in more depth than is usually possible with groups of subjects. The rigorous controls common to the single-subject experimental design are not applied in case studies. Like correlations and naturalistic observations, case studies are not experimental. Still, careful observation of a subject and scrupulous recording of what is observed can yield valuable information.

Sometimes, a case study is the only option available because, for one reason or another, it is impossible for a psychologist to conduct an experiment or to observe a correlation in order to gather data. It would not be ethically proper, for example, to remove part of a healthy individual's brain just to see what would happen afterward. Sometimes, however, such information becomes available through a case study, as in the case of Phineas Gage, who, in 1848, was a workcrew foreman for a railroad. Part of Gage's job was to tamp dynamite with a 13-pound steel rod into holes bored into rock. One unfortunate day, the dynamite charge detonated while Gage was tamping it with the rod. The explosion sent the rod through Gage's face and out the top of his skull (see Figure 1.4), taking with it the front matter of his brain. Incredibly, he survived, but not without undergoing some profound personality changes. As Dr. J. M. Harlow, who reported this case study, stated:

> His physical health is good, and I am inclined to say that he has recovered. Has no pain in head, but says it has a queer feeling which he is not able to describe. Applied for his situation as foreman, but is undecided whether to work or travel. His contractors, who regarded him as the most efficient and capable foreman in their employ previous to his injury, considered the change in his mind so marked that they could not give him his place again. The equilibrium or balance, so to speak, between his intellectual faculties and animal propensities, seems to have been destroyed. He is fitful, irreverent, indulging at times in the grossest profanity (which was not previously his custom), manifesting but little deference for his fellows, impatient of restraint or advice when it conflicts with his desires, at times pertinaciously obstinate, yet capricious and vacillating, devising many plans of future operations, which are no sooner arranged than they are abandoned in turn for others . . . his mind is radically changed, so decidedly that his friends and acquaintances said he was "no longer Gage." (1868, pp. 339–40)

Although such case studies provide valuable data, they cannot by themselves be the basis for solid conclusions. In the Gage case, for instance, it would be impossible to know without further scientific evidence whether Gage's personality changes were due to the loss of brain matter or to the severe shock and facial disfigurement he had suffered.

SURVEYS.   When direct observation is impossible, psychologists must sometimes rely on **survey** techniques, such as conducting interviews or administering questionnaires. Among the best-known national surveys are the Gallup and Roper political polls, the Nielsen television survey, and the U.S. census. Surveys are difficult to conduct properly and to interpret. They are subject to a number of problems. When people answer questions, they often report what they wish were true, or they recall events differently from the way the events actually happened. For example, married couples asked to report how often they engage in sexual relations per month have a tendency to overestimate (maybe "lie" would be a more

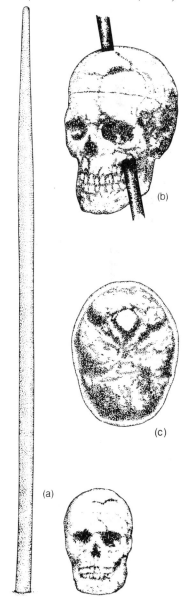

FIGURE 1.4

Harlow's illustrations of the case of Phineas Gage: (a) Comparison of the relative sizes of the tamping iron and Gage's skull. (b) View depicting the trajectory of the iron through Gage's cranium. (c) Upward view of the cranium showing the location and diameter of the hole. (SOURCE: From Harlow, 1868.)

How to Get Honest Answers

Imagine the difficulties that you might have if you were asked to conduct a survey of business people and were required to find out how often, if ever, they committed crimes. Or, suppose you wanted to find out whether people were cheating on their taxes—how would you do it with a survey? How about using a survey to discover how many people are having extramarital affairs? These are the kinds of questions that are not likely to elicit honest answers from the people you are surveying. Researchers interested in surveying people about touchy subjects such as sex, crime, money, religion, politics, or any other sensitive area you might consider run into this problem—people won't answer the questions honestly (can you blame them?).

Sometimes, however, obtaining honest answers can be a matter of life or death. Recently, the medical community has asked psychologists to find out the percentage of people who make condoms a requirement during their sexual activities. The reason for interest in such a question concerns the deadly disease AIDS (acquired immune deficiency syndrome). AIDS is spread by a virus that is passed from one person to another during the exchange of bodily fluids, which may occur as the result of intimate sexual encounters, shared needle use (usually among drug users), or through blood transfusions (although contaminated blood is now less likely to be a hazard owing to the nationwide AIDS antibody blood-screening program). Until the development of a proven vaccine, which may be some years away, there is a way for sexually active individuals to reduce their chances of contracting the virus by engaging in only "safe" sex, which requires the use of a condom. If condom use were sufficiently extensive, the spread of the deadly disease could be checked. Now ask yourself, how would people respond to the following questions on your survey: (1) Are you sexually active? and, (2) Do you require or make use of condoms during your sexual activities? The number of downright lies or refusals to answer will be high because people may strongly believe that such information is personal and therefore is none of your business, or they might not give a true answer because they are afraid to admit that they aren't having "safe" sex, but rather are having either no sex or "stupid" sex. Of course, you could give the questions on paper and require anonymous answers—"no names please"—but even in these circumstances people often are afraid that somehow the researcher will be able to tell which responses were theirs.

It might seem, then, that there is no way to improve greatly the chances that people will tell you the truth when you ask these sorts of questions. There is, however, an ingenious technique called **randomized response** that does just that. It was developed in 1965 by Stanley Warner for, as he said, "no particular reason" (Kolata, 1987a, p. 382). When first introduced, the technique went relatively unnoticed, perhaps because it wasn't immediately applied. But now that honest answers to touchy questions are especially needed for the battle against AIDS, the randomized-response technique, which languished so long in obscurity, has been "rediscovered."

The best way to explain the technique is with an example. Suppose that in your research concerning the spread of AIDS, you wish to know how often men in a given population visit prostitutes. Further, let's assume that you wish to interview 100 men to ask whether they have used the services of a prostitute during the last month. What do you figure your chances are of getting honest answers? Let's be generous and call them slim. But, if you use the randomized-response survey, you should explain to each man whom you survey what it is you are trying to find out, and also show him how he can answer without fear of disclosure. To do this, you give him a coin and turn your back. He flips it and notes whether it is "heads" or "tails." He is instructed that if it comes up "heads," he is to answer your question yes no matter what; if "tails," he should tell the truth. In this way, he can say yes and you'll never know whether it was because he saw a prostitute or simply because he flipped "heads."

For the sake of example, let's say that after you've interviewed 100 men you have a total of 61 yes and 39 no answers. The laws of probability say that 50 of the yes answers are due to "heads," while the remaining 50 are from "truth-tellers." From this, you can deduce that 11 of the "truth-tellers" saw prostitutes. Extrapolating to the whole population, we can now say that 22 percent (give or take the small percent due to fluctuations that may occur in the distribution of heads versus tails in any given 100 tosses of a coin) have been with a prostitute during the last month.

Researchers have conducted even fancier randomized-responses surveys. "How many lovers have you had during the past month?" is the kind of question you can ask using the technique. The surveyor simply provides a "spinner" that has the numbers 0, 1, 2, 3, 4, 5, 6, 7, 8, 9, >10 printed on it. The surveyor gives an explanation of the procedure and asks the respondent to spin the spinner and then to flip a coin. If heads, he reports the number that came up when the spinner was used (which averages out to 5); if tails, he tells the truth (Kolata, 1987a). Again, using the laws of probability, the real number can be deduced with great accuracy (consider how well probability projections work for the TV networks on election night) and the privacy of the individual need never be in jeopardy!

accurate word). This can be a difficult problem for researchers, but there are some ingenious ways to get around it (see Focus on Research).

The way in which questions are worded also can influence the results of a survey. For example, subjects who viewed a traffic accident were more likely to answer "yes" to the question "Did you see the broken headlight?" than they were to the question "Did you see a broken headlight?" Also, surveys often are susceptible to sampling error. The classic case is the 1936 political poll in which a random sample was picked from the telephone book and asked, "For whom will you vote in the presidential election, Landon or Roosevelt?" The majority chose Landon, and the pollsters predicted Landon the winner. Unfortunately for the pollsters and the newspapers that relied on them, in 1936 only more affluent people had telephones—and Roosevelt won easily because he had everybody else's vote.

RANDOMIZED RESPONSE
A data-gathering technique designed to provide anonymity for the respondent by making it impossible to discern the truth from individual answers. In a simple version, subjects are asked to respond "yes" or "no" to a question after privately flipping a coin. If heads resulted, they must answer "yes"; if tails, they must tell the truth. The number of truthful responses may then be deduced by analyzing group data.

TESTING. Some psychological tests, like IQ tests and the Rorschach inkblot test, are so familiar to the public that people can hardly think of psychology without also bringing the tests to mind. Psychologists have hundreds of tests available to them to help in their investigations. Tests can be valuable research instruments. Psychologists use them to measure many aptitudes and abilities. Tests also may make it possible to measure various characteristics of people by measuring large groups of individuals at one time. For this reason, group tests have an important place in education and industry. Tests also may be administered individually, often for the purpose of clinical, intellectual, or personality assessment.

Test construction and use are not simple matters. Psychological tests must be given only by people who are trained to understand their limits and value. Unfortunately, the general public has come to believe that many psychological tests are far more authoritative and accurate than they really are (Snyder, Shenkel, & Lowery, 1977). In Chapters 12 and 13, we will examine some of the problems encountered in developing and interpreting tests, as well as the benefits that can be derived from their proper use.

All the efforts of scientific psychology are aimed at a common goal: to understand, to predict, and to bring under control the behaviors that people wish to change. Many psychologists hope eventually to isolate and understand the variables that have the most important effects on our behavior. Such knowledge would provide us with a better understanding of ourselves and of other people.

Psychological tests may be administered to individuals one-on-one. This may often be done for purposes of assessing personality, intelligence, or mental disorders.

AN ENDURING QUESTION: WHAT ARE THE LIMITS OF PSYCHOLOGICAL UNDERSTANDING?

At first glance, it might seem that we are certain to acquire a complete understanding of human beings if we keep conducting experiments until we have enough knowledge about behavior for us to make very accurate predictions about how a given person will behave in any given set of circumstances. After all, this kind of experimental approach has served physics well. Physicists have studied the fundamental particles and forces, seen how they interact under different conditions, and then made assessments about how these particles and forces may be controlled and manipulated. The development of computers, atomic power, television, and space travel bear witness to the physicists' success.

Psychology, however, is more the study of extremely complex systems (behaving organisms, especially human beings) than it is the study of fundamental particles or forces. Because of this, a psychologist studying variables in a tightly controlled environment might not always obtain results that apply readily to a "real" world of complex interacting systems (Manicas & Secord, 1983). In this sense, psychology has more in common with meteorology (the study of weather) than it does with physics. As an example, consider a meteorologist studying the formation of storms in the laboratory. In the same way that an experimental psychologist might, she too explores how different variables such as air pressure, humidity, and wind interact under carefully controlled conditions. Although this experimental exploration in the laboratory might provide a rough understanding of how real storms develop, it's never going to give her the power to predict, with extreme accuracy, the exact behavior of a real storm. For the physicist, one electron is just like another, but a storm is an evolving system made of many parts, and we can pretty much assume that *no two storms are ever going to be exactly alike.* For a similar reason—that no two people are ever going to be exactly alike—our knowledge derived from experiments will be limited to a degree when applied to the real world (Manicas & Secord, 1983). We simply don't know how thoroughly we will ever be able to understand human behavior.

One area of philosophy and mathematics that is addressing this problem is called **chaos theory** (Pool, 1989). As an example from chaos theory, consider the efforts of scientists to predict where a hurricane will strike along the eastern United States a few days before the storm is due to come ashore. Until the storm is very close to shore, the prediction is extremely difficult because the tiniest change in the storm when it is far out to sea may translate into a difference of hundreds of miles by the time it reaches shore (see Figure 1.5). The same is true for humans. The slightest change in your life today might send you off on a different path that would show up as a major difference years from now. For this reason, to make *long-term* predictions about complex systems like people or storms, we would need to understand the tiniest interactions of all the variables right at the start (because tiny changes, over the long term, can lead to big differences). But, we know now that even at the tiniest level, predictions can't be perfect, because physicists have shown that subatomic particles are, in fact, not exact, but chaotic in their actions, and can only be understood in terms of probability. This subatomic chaos, which appears to be an indisputable part of nature, was not thought to be very relevant when studying large systems like storms or people. But, because the smallest of changes can have huge consequences later, it is now believed that even when studying people, the underlying chaos of matter does, in fact, fundamentally limit our ability to predict behavior, especially over the long term.

Of course, even if our experimental evidence is eventually found to have

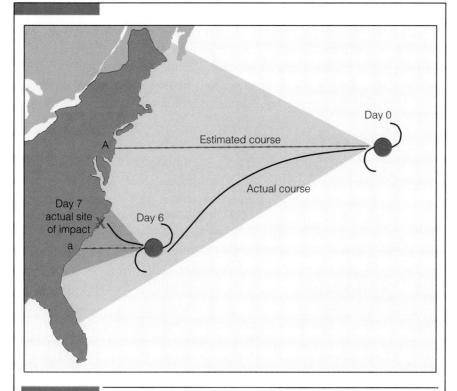

FIGURE 1.5

In the initial state, there is a hurricane 7 days from shore expected to strike point A. In this chaos model, the storm undergoes an undetectable change in barometric pressure and temperature causing a snowball effect of an ever-increasing arcing path for the storm. Seven days later, the storm will come ashore 600 miles south of where it was predicted to strike 7 days earlier. No amount of experimentation or research could have helped to narrow the range of error inherent in the prediction made 7 days beforehand (shaded area). The same effect occurs between days 6 and 7, but with less error because a shorter time frame is involved.

boundaries that cannot be transcended, it is still valuable because it often provides us with enough information to yield an understanding that is sufficient for most purposes.

FOR CRITICAL ANALYSIS

1. As best as we can tell, there is a fundamental limit to human knowledge; research has shown us that we can never be *absolutely* certain of anything.* Science must, therefore, become an investigation of probabilities. But if scientists can never be absolutely certain of their results, why shouldn't anyone's opinion be considered just as valid as findings derived from scientific research?

2. In textbooks such as this one, or in research literature, it is very rare to read that "A proves B," or that "this is proof of that." Instead authors commonly say that "A suggests B," or that "this is an indication of that." Why do you think they do that?

How is this similar to jurors who are instructed to find the defendant innocent unless guilt can be established *beyond a reasonable doubt* (notice that here, too, absolute proof is not mentioned)?

*Except, perhaps, that we can never be absolutely certain of anything.

There is an epilogue at the end of each chapter in this text. These epilogues are not intended to be chapter summaries; they simply illustrate the way in which one person's life was affected by some aspect of the material discussed in this chapter. In this first epilogue, you will see how the scientific method influenced the thinking and behavior of one researcher.

Clark Hull (1884–1952) loved scientific experiments. Early in his career, he earned a reputation for his rigorously controlled experiments on smoking and hypnosis. He eventually applied his scientific work to the creation of a system of theorems and postulates that he hoped would result in a behaviorism as exact as Euclidean geometry. So it came as a surprise to his family and colleagues when he announced one day that he planned to attend a seance to make contact with his dead sister. Hull said that he had heard about a medium who could reach the spirit world, and he wanted to try. At the seance, Hull took a seat and joined hands with the medium and other members of the group. He explained what he wanted, and the medium said she would do her best. The lights dimmed and the medium appeared to enter a trance. She called on the spirit world and suddenly a different voice seemed to come from her throat. "Clark, Clark, it's your sister," the voice said. Hull asked his sister how she was and what the spirit world was like. His sister said that her spirit was at rest and that all was well. She added that someday they would be together and that until then she would keep a protective watch over him. She told him not to worry, that she was all right. Hull began to ask specific questions but suddenly the lights came on again and the medium awoke from her trance. "I'm sorry," she said, "I can only maintain contact for a short time; the strain is too great." Hull was smiling. The medium said, "I see you are happy that you could talk to your sister." Hull's smile became a grin. "I never had a sister," he said. Yes, Clark Hull loved scientific experiments.

SUMMARY

■ Psychology is the study of the behavior of organisms.

■ There are many different areas of specialization or interest within psychology. Among them are experimental, neuropsychological, psychobiological, developmental, social, clinical, industrial, organizational, educational, and counseling psychology.

■ Psychology was born of two parents, philosophy and physiology. It was the union of the philosophers' questions and the physiologists' careful scientific analysis that led to psychological research, which began in a laboratory in Leipzig, Germany, in 1879.

■ The first experimental psychology laboratory was started by Wilhelm Wundt, who was interested in analyzing the mind.

Edward Titchener's subsequent reanalysis of Wundt's work, which became known as structuralism, relied on the technique of introspection. Introspection failed to gain popularity, and by the 1930s structuralism was being abandoned.

■ Functionalism was the first completely American psychology. Its founder was William James. Functionalists, influenced by Charles Darwin, believed human consciousness and behavior must serve a function. Functionalism gave birth to many modern areas of psychological interest.

■ Early in this century, an American psychologist, John B. Watson, developed an objective system of psychology he called behaviorism. Behaviorism remains a powerful force in modern psychology and has been of great value in demonstrating that much of our behavior is determined by our immediate environment and previous history of learning.

■ At about the same time that behaviorism was becoming the dominant force in American psychology, a different reaction to structuralism was developing in Germany—the Gestalt view. Gestalt psychologists argue that conscious sensations can be examined but that the whole experience must be taken for what it is.

■ Psychoanalytic theory was developed by a Viennese physician, Sigmund Freud. It did not develop as a reaction against structuralism but rather had its roots in neurology and medicine. Psychoanalysis has been severely criticized for its lack of scientific control and careful experimentation.

■ Humanistic psychologists' understanding of behavior is different from that of psychoanalysts and behaviorists. Humanists do not believe that people are governed by stimuli or unconscious motives and drives. Rather, they believe that people have free will and a need to achieve self-actualization.

■ The neurobiological approach to the study of psychology has expanded rapidly in the last few decades. It concerns itself with the investigation of the brain, nervous system, genetic inheritance, and biology of the organism as pertains to behavior.

■ Cognitive psychology is the study of internal mental processes, which include thinking, memory, concept formation and the processing of information.

■ All scientific research relies on systematic and objective methods of observing, recording, and describing events. The scientific experiment is one of the most powerful tools that psychologists possess.

■ Ethical considerations in the conduct of research are required to protect the subject from possible abuse or harm.

■ A good experiment makes use of proper procedures for selecting subjects, defining terms, maintaining control, and eliminating biases.

■ Single-subject experiments use time to allow a subject to serve as her own control.

■ A correlation is defined as the relationship between two variables. Data from correlations are valuable because they allow us to make predictions. However, cause–effect relationships cannot be assumed merely because a correlation exists.

■ In naturalistic observations, researchers refrain from directly interacting with the variables they are observing. Naturalistic observation is most often used to investigate behavior in natural environments, in which the researcher refrains from manipulation.

■ Other research tools used by psychologists include case studies, surveys, and testing.

■ All the work in scientific psychology is aimed at a common goal: to predict, to explain, and eventually to control behavior. Psychological research is limited, however, because it is the study of changing complex systems.

SUGGESTIONS FOR FURTHER READING

1. American Psychological Association. (1986). *Careers in psychology*. Washington, D.C.: American Psychological Association. Describes for the student possible career choices in psychology.
2. Greening, T. (1987). *Politics and innocence: A humanistic debate*. New York: Saybrook Publishing. A collection of essays on the past and future of the humanistic movement in psychology. Contains some interesting debates among humanists about the meaning of their movement.
3. Hilgard, E. R. (1987). *Psychology in America: A historical survey*. San Diego: Harcourt Brace. A general survey by an eminent modern psychologist of the history of psychology in America.
4. Pryzwansky, W. B., & Wendt, R. N. (1987). *Psychology as a profession: Foundations of practice*. New York: Pergamon Press. A book designed for the professional psychologist which outlines the future of the profession. Includes sections on ethics, the impact of the legal system, and emerging trends in professional areas.
5. Rieber, R. W., & Salzinger, K. (Eds.). (1980). *Psychology: Theoretical-historical perspectives*. New York: Academic Press. Discusses the theoretical roots of psychology and the men who began the discipline. Helps clear up some of the myths about the early psychologists.
6. Smith, S. (1983). *Ideas of the great psychologists*. New York: Harper & Row. For the student or general reader, an introduction to the principal fields of psychology from a historical perspective. Includes discussions of where the fields currently stand.
7. Wood, G. (1986). *Fundamentals of psychological research* (3rd ed.). Glenview, Ill.: Scott Foresman. A college textbook on the basic methods used in psychological research.

CHAPTER 2 | The Biological Bases of Behavior

Prologue

Why Psychologists Study the Nervous System and the Brain

The Divisions of the Nervous System

Neurons and the Body's Electrochemical System
    Neuron Structure
    Neural Transmissions
    Synaptic Transmissions
    The World of Neurotransmitters

Hormones and the Endocrine System

The Structure of the Brain
    The Hindbrain
    The Midbrain
    The Forebrain
    Brain Scanners: PET and MRI

The Brain and Behavior
    Specialized Areas in the Brain
    The Split Brain

Epilogue: Mr. Niethold's Toothache

Summary

Suggestions for Further Reading

PROLOGUE

You are standing in the laboratory, and Professor James Olds has just handed you a rat, "Here, you can have this one," he says. "We had an accident and put the electrode in the wrong place, but you may as well test him anyway." You look at the electrode. It's a small, short metal rod, and it's sticking directly out of the rat's head. A few days ago you and the other student assistants had watched as the electrodes were inserted into the brains of the anesthetized rats. Their skulls were opened, and the electrodes were pushed into the brains. The bone was then resealed with dental cement. When the rats recovered, the electrodes were attached to small transformers so that a mild electric current could be sent into their brains.

Professor Olds is pursuing work begun by Hebb at McGill University and Delgado, Roberts, and Miller at Yale. They had used the same kind of electrodes, placing them in the lower section of the midline system of rats' brains. They discovered that an exceedingly mild electrical stimulation to the midline caused the rats to avoid from then on whatever they had been doing when they received the electrical impulse. Apparently, the mild current was painful or noxious in some way, and now Professor Olds is investigating further.

Unfortunately, in the rat you're supposed to test, the surgeon missed the midline system entirely, and the electrode ended up along a nerve pathway coming from a different section of the brain. Although other students are having good results obtaining the avoidance response from the rats that have electrodes in the right place, you doubt that you'll be successful. You place your rat in the test area, a large empty box with

35

corners labeled A, B, C, and D. When the rat goes to one of the corners, you will electrically stimulate his brain through the electrode. You will note whether he avoids that corner from then on. The rat goes to corner A. You press a button, administering electrical stimulation to the brain (ESB). The rat moves away from corner A. Is he avoiding that corner? Or did he just happen to walk away? No, it's not working; he's back in corner A. Better give him another ESB. He sniffs around a little bit, moves off, and then returns to corner A. You give him more ESB. For the better part of an hour the rat stays in corner A, even though you keep giving him ESB. Finally, the rat moves to another corner to sleep.

When your rat wakes he immediately goes to corner A. You tell Professor Olds that there is something unusual happening: Your rat acts almost as though he likes the ESB. Everyone comes over to watch. The animal won't leave corner A. "Are you sure you're giving him ESB?" Professor Olds asks. "Is your transformer working?" You answer yes, you had checked that. Olds says, "We can test whether he really likes the ESB by using a technique and apparatus devised by the behaviorist B. F. Skinner."

By the end of the day the apparatus is ready. A lever has been mounted in the rat's box (see Figure 2.1). The lever is set up so that whenever the rat presses it he will close an electrical circuit and administer ESB to himself. Earlier, while Professor Olds was still connecting the wiring, you trained the rat to work the lever by giving him food whenever he pressed it. Now the lever is connected to the electrode. Everyone gathers around. The rat presses the lever, but this time, instead of receiving food, he receives ESB.

Your rat appears excited. He presses the lever again. Soon he is pressing the lever at a rate of 200 times per hour. Is it possible that the misguided electrode has revealed a "pleasure center" in the brain? Could

FIGURE 2.1

The apparatus used in Olds's study of the pleasure center in the brain.

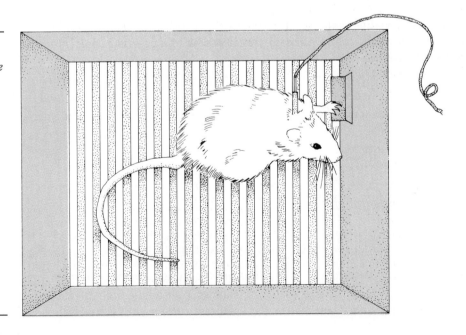

*there actually be a specific place in the brain where good feelings regis-
ter? If there is such an area, how sensitive is it?*

*Professor Olds wonders whether your rat's electrode is square in the
middle of this pleasure center or only near it. In order to find out, he
has more rats implanted with electrodes. Each electrode is placed in the
same general area as the electrode in your rat, but in a slightly different
spot.*

*Some of the new rats, whose electrodes are closer to their brains' mid-
lines, begin to respond. You sit there hour after hour, watching as the
rats press the lever over 30 times per minute for 24 hours, without stopping, until they finally collapse from exhaustion and you feel like joining
them. What must it be like? How could anything feel that good? The
next day you let the rats go hungry. On the day after that you give them
a choice—freely available food or the lever. They ignore the food and run
straight to the levers. They act like people who are hooked on drugs. Is a
similar process at work, you wonder?*

*It has been known for many years that specific places in the brain are
connected with the senses and with the movement of different parts of
the body. But until that day in Professor Olds's laboratory in 1956, no
one had presumed that pleasure was to be found in a particular place.
Since then, many special centers in the brain have been postulated.
Some appear to control hunger or thirst, others to control memory or
emotions or other aspects of a person's psychology. Even other pleasure
centers have been discovered. Many of these areas seem to share control
with one another. Yet the brain remains a largely unknown and un-
charted territory, like darkest Africa two centuries ago.*

There are three major areas of interest among psychologists who study the biological bases of behavior. These are neurology (the study of the brain and nervous system), endocrinology (the study of glands and their internal secretions,
such as hormones) and behavioral genetics (the study of how inheritance influences behavior). Behavioral genetics is covered in detail in Chapter 11. In this
chapter, you will find out about how your endocrine and nervous systems affect your behavior, and you will have a chance to learn about your brain.
Your brain already knows a great deal, so why not give it a chance to learn
something about itself?

WHY PSYCHOLOGISTS STUDY
THE NERVOUS SYSTEM AND THE BRAIN

All human behavior is related, either directly or indirectly, to the functioning of
the nervous system, of which the brain is the central part. In studying behavior,
psychologists are concerned with sensation, perception, consciousness, learning,
memory, thinking, motivation, emotion, intelligence, personality, conflict, love,
and abnormal behavior, to mention some of the most prominent interests. Every
one of these areas of study has a neurobiological base.

NERVES
Bundles of neural fibers that carry impulses from one point in the body to another.

CENTRAL NERVOUS SYSTEM
The brain and spinal cord. All other nerves comprise the peripheral nervous system.

BRAIN
The portion of the central nervous system located in the cranium and responsible for the interpretation of sensory impulses, the coordination and control of body activities, and the exercise of emotion and thought.

SPINAL CORD
The portion of the central nervous system encased in the backbone and serving as a pathway for the conduction of sensory and motor impulses to and from the brain.

PERIPHERAL NERVOUS SYSTEM
The motor and sensory nerves that carry impulses from the sense organs to the central nervous system and from the central nervous system to the muscles and glands of the body.

SOMATIC NERVOUS SYSTEM
The portion of the peripheral nervous system that carries messages inward from the sense organs and outward to the muscles of the skeleton.

AFFERENT NERVES
Nerves that carry messages inward from the sense organs to the central nervous system.

EFFERENT NERVES
Nerves that carry messages outward from the central nervous system to glands or muscles.

REFLEX ARC
The pathway a sensory message travels from an afferent receptor to the spinal cord and back to an effector (the body organ that responds to the stimulation) in order to produce a reflex.

Among neuropsychological and psychobiological psychologists, those psychologists who study the biological bases of behavior, are many people who believe that knowledge of the brain and nervous system will eventually be so complete that the physiological approach will be the predominant means of understanding, predicting, and controlling all behavior. They may be right, but there is a problem with this approach. The problem lies in the fact that there probably isn't anything in this world more complicated than the human brain and nervous system. Next to such a system, nuclear physics is too simple for words. For this reason, many psychologists argue that even thinking about abandoning nonneurobiological approaches is premature and that complete answers from the neurobiological level may be centuries away, assuming that we can ever find them (Peele, 1981). But the work to uncover the secrets of the brain and our biology has begun.

THE DIVISIONS OF THE NERVOUS SYSTEM

Moving, sensing, feeling, thinking, remembering—none of these would be possible without a nervous system. In fact, your entire life, and all of your behavior, depends on the functioning of your nervous system. **Nerves** transmit messages throughout your body, telling you to inhale and exhale and telling your heart to beat. Nerves can bring stored memories to your attention or help your eyes to follow a bird in flight. All your thoughts, hopes, dreams, and desires are there, contained within the most complex system in the human body. Before we can begin to examine behavior from the neurobiological perspective, we will need a map of the nervous system to guide us.

Although the entire nervous system is interrelated, it is often described in parts to make it somewhat more comprehensible. Figure 2.2 shows the nervous system broken into its component parts. We'll introduce the names and functions of these parts in the next few paragraphs and then review them. At first, this might all seem like a lesson in anatomy, but once we get into the workings of the nerve cell you'll find out why drugs can affect behavior and how pain might be controlled, and even get a hint of what thoughts or feelings are made of.

As you can see, the first division is between the central nervous system and the peripheral nervous system. The **central nervous system** is centrally located and comprises all the nerves that are encased within bone. It includes the **brain** and the **spinal cord** (see Figure 2.3). The **peripheral nervous system** is the system of nerves that carries information to and from the central nervous system. The peripheral nervous system is divided into the somatic and the autonomic nervous systems.

The **somatic nervous system** carries messages inward from the sense organs. Light, sound, odor, touch, and taste are among these messages. The somatic nervous system also carries voluntary messages out to the muscles of the skeleton, such as those messages that enable you to move your hands.

Any nerves that carry messages inward to the central nervous system are called **afferent nerves;** any nerves that carry messages outward from the central nervous system are called **efferent nerves.** Afferent and efferent nerves can interact to form one of the simplest arrangements in the nervous system—the **reflex arc,** which doesn't even require the brain's involvement. In a reflex arc, an afferent sensory message travels to the spinal cord and an efferent motor message immediately returns to the muscles. The quick response provided by the reflex arc can be very helpful, for instance, if you place your hand on a hot stove. If you had to wait for the sensory message to travel all the way up your spine to your brain, as most sensory messages do, you'd waste valuable time while your hand cooked. Thanks to the reflex arc, your hand will be off the stove before your brain knows why!

The **autonomic nervous system** carries information to and from organs, glands, and other muscles within the body. Among the muscles controlled by the autonomic nervous system are those responsible for digestion and heartbeat. This system is called autonomic (like automatic) because the glands, internal organs, and muscles it affects are not usually considered to be under voluntary control, as are those directed by the somatic system. They are generally involuntary. The autonomic nervous system is further divided into the sympathetic and parasympathetic systems.

The **sympathetic nervous system** is sometimes referred to as the fight-or-flight system. If you become angry enough to fight, or frightened enough to flee, the sympathetic nervous system is especially active (see Figure 2.4). The functions controlled by the sympathetic nervous system are helpful in preparing you to fight or flee. When you become excited, your pupils dilate, allowing more light to enter. Your heart rate speeds up, causing more oxygen to be sent to the muscles. Your digestion is inhibited, which causes more blood to flow to the muscles. Finally, the sympathetic nervous system orders the release of adrenaline. In a frightening or provoking situation, you will know that your sympathetic nervous system has been engaged when your heart starts to pound, you begin to sweat, your mouth becomes dry, and you feel a fluttering in your stomach.

Once the sympathetic nervous system has become active, there must be a counterbalance to return the organism to its original state. The **parasympathetic nervous system** helps bring about this change. It causes the pupils to constrict, stimulates salivation, inhibits the heart rate, and in a sense undoes the stimulation

AUTONOMIC NERVOUS SYSTEM
The portion of the peripheral nervous system that carries information to and from organs, glands, and smooth muscles within the body.

SYMPATHETIC NERVOUS SYSTEM
The portion of the autonomic nervous system that is primarily concerned with emergencies and emotional states.

PARASYMPATHETIC NERVOUS SYSTEM
The portion of the autonomic nervous system that is most active during the body's quiescent states.

FIGURE 2.2

The divisions of the human nervous system.

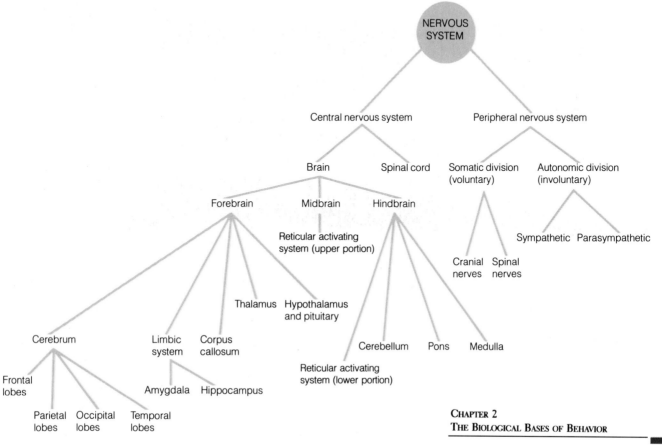

NEURONS
Specialized cells that transmit electrical impulses from one part of the body to another.

resulting from the activation of the sympathetic nervous system (see Figure 2.4). However, these two systems are not always antagonistic. For example, during sexual arousal portions of both systems are stimulated. The Concept Review provides a summary of how the sympathetic and parasympathetic systems can act together.

Interestingly, a prolonged or continuous stimulation of the sympathetic nervous system may result in stress that can, in time, have serious psychological and physical effects on a person's health (see Chapter 14).

NEURONS AND THE BODY'S ELECTROCHEMICAL SYSTEM

As you examine the nervous system and all its parts, you may think that it looks something like a wiring diagram, as if your body were wired so that electrical messages could constantly travel between one place and another. But nerves are distinctly unlike wires. A wire is a single entity stretching a particular length; nerves are not single entities. They are made up of thousands upon thousands of individual nerve cells called **neurons,** which, except in rare circumstances, do not touch one another at their points of communication.

If you broke a wire into thousands of pieces, it's unlikely that a signal would be able to pass through its entire length. Similarly, electrical signals usually cannot pass unaided from neuron to neuron because of the gap between the neurons at

FIGURE 2.3

The central and peripheral nervous systems.

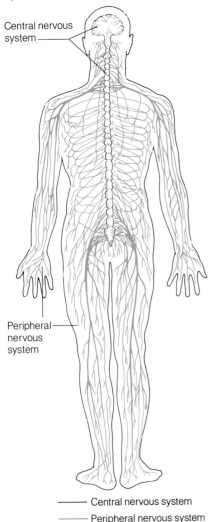

Central nervous system

Peripheral nervous system

—— Central nervous system
—— Peripheral nervous system

CONCEPT REVIEW: THE ACTION OF THE NERVOUS SYSTEM

You're traveling down the highway at a good speed and just a little too close to the vehicle ahead. Suddenly, the driver in front of you brakes hard.

The *afferent* visual nerves of your *somatic system* (part of the *peripheral system*) send messages to your *brain* (part of the central nervous system) about the glow of the brake lights and the apparent increasing size of the other vehicle as you rapidly approach it. Millions of biochemical messages are processed in the part of the brain where vision is received. For each one of these millions of messages received by the visual area of the brain, about 200 messages are sent out to other parts of the brain (Nauta & Feirtag, 1986), making well over one billion messages, all in less than 1/10 second.

At about this time, the *sympathetic division* of the *autonomic nervous system* causes your heart rate to increase, adrenaline to be secreted, your pupils to dilate, and your saliva to stop flowing (why create saliva when you're about to have a crash anyway—you might just as well conserve the energy it takes to make it and put that energy to better use).

You had better do something, or you're going to crash!

A voluntary response is sent from your brain to your *spinal cord* and out along somatic *efferent* nerves, which stimulates the muscles necessary for you to turn the wheel and step on the brake.

After more information has passed from your somatic system into your brain, telling you that the accident has been avoided and that you are safely stopped on the side of the road, your brain sends a message down your spinal cord to the somatic system telling it to relax; this is your signal to release your grip on the steering wheel. Simultaneously, the *parasympathetic* part of the autonomic system begins to fulfill its role of calming you down by slowing the heart rate, making salivation resume (might as well go back to making that stuff now), and constricting the pupils. But since it may take a while for the effects of the secreted adrenaline to wear off, you may remain somewhat shaky for 20 to 30 minutes.

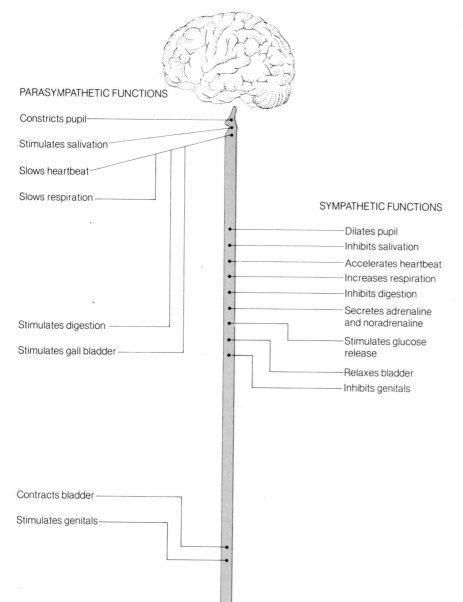

PARASYMPATHETIC FUNCTIONS

Constricts pupil

Stimulates salivation

Slows heartbeat

Slows respiration

Stimulates digestion

Stimulates gall bladder

Contracts bladder

Stimulates genitals

SYMPATHETIC FUNCTIONS

Dilates pupil

Inhibits salivation

Accelerates heartbeat

Increases respiration

Inhibits digestion

Secretes adrenaline and noradrenaline

Stimulates glucose release

Relaxes bladder

Inhibits genitals

FIGURE 2.4

Functions of the autonomic nervous system. Neurons belonging to the sympathetic nervous system originate in the spinal cord (yellow) and are shown on the right side of this diagram. Neurons belonging to the parasympathetic nervous system exit from the medulla region of the brain stem at the very upper end of the spinal cord and also from the lower end of the spinal cord near the organs they affect, which include the bladder and genitals, shown on the left side of this diagram. Almost all organs are enervated by both the sympathetic and parasympathetic systems.

the point of communication. Instead, an electrical signal is sent the length of the neuron, and, when it reaches the end, the neuron secretes a liquid chemical that affects neighboring neurons. The chemical message may stimulate another electrical signal to be sent the length of another neuron, and so on. In this way, electrochemical messages are transmitted throughout the body. Your body is an electrochemical system, not strictly an electrical system, and the brain is the major control center. Interestingly, knowledge of this electrochemical system is the key to understanding much of our psychology, but more about that later.

It's important to realize that the brain, which is part of the nervous system it controls, is more than just a big computer that tells the nerves how to fire. The brain is flexible and can respond to changed conditions. Researchers studying damaged nerves in the hope of helping injured people have conducted many experiments. Let's look at one such experiment that illustrates the living brain's

CHAPTER 2
THE BIOLOGICAL BASES OF BEHAVIOR

SOMA
The cell body.

DENDRITES
The short, branched projections of a neuron that receive impulses from other neurons and conduct them toward the cell body.

AXON
The long projection of a neuron that transmits impulses away from the cell body to the synapse.

NUCLEUS
A central body within a living cell that contains the cell's hereditary material and controls its metabolism, growth, and reproduction.

flexibility. In this experiment, researchers crossed the nerves of monkeys' arms so that the nerves that allowed the monkeys to rotate their arms one way or the other were switched. Unlike the nerves of the central nervous system, peripheral nerves in the arm will regenerate and can be surgically reconnected (Kolata, 1983a). When the monkeys recovered, they were presented with trays on which were bits of their favorite food. At first, the monkeys would find themselves trying to pick up the food with their palms up, which is what you might expect because of the crossed nerves. But almost immediately the animals' brains adjusted and accepted the new arrangement. In short order, the monkeys were able to operate their hands as well as before the surgery (Brinkman, Porter, & Norman, 1983). This research indicates how important learning and experience are for the organization of the nervous system and how flexible, adaptable, and "reprogrammable" the brain can be.

Neuron Structure

The neuron is one of the many individual cells (bone cells, blood cells, skin cells, muscle cells, and so on) that make up your body. No one knows exactly how many cells there are in the average human body—a rough estimate is 60 trillion (60,000,000,000,000, or 6×10^{13}). The neuron is the basic unit of the brain and the rest of the nervous system, and most neurons are located in the brain. No one knows how many neurons are in the average brain. An educated estimate is about 100 billion (100,000,000,000, or 10^{11}) cells. However, other estimates range as high as 1 trillion (Nauta & Feirtag, 1986).

One reason we are unsure as to how many neurons are in the brain is that we cannot simply count the number of neurons in one part of the brain and then extrapolate to the whole brain. The brain differs greatly in the kinds of neurons that are present and in their concentrations from one place to the next.

Not only is it impossible to count neurons, but it is exceedingly difficult to visualize the patterns of neurocircuitry. Because each neuron may receive messages from, or give messages to, as many as 10,000 other neurons, any attempt to comprehend the neurocircuitry of the brain is likely to make you want to turn to something much simpler, such as counting the grains of sand in the Sahara Desert during a windstorm. For this reason, much of our information about neurons has come from studying individual neurons rather than neural systems. In the following pages, we will examine a typical neuron and learn how it functions. The way in which the neuron responds to electrical stimulation and the kinds of chemicals it secretes determine all behavior—which, of course, is what psychologists want to understand.

Neurons come in many sizes and shapes, and they often appear to serve unique and specialized functions. Figure 2.5 depicts a typical neuron. Keep in mind, however, that exceptions to this general description abound. In addition, using new techniques that allow us to follow the development of a single neuron in a living creature, researchers have found that a neuron may undergo many changes during its lifetime, growing, altering its appearance or connections, and even changing its function (Purves, Voyvodic, Magrassi, & Yawo, 1987; Bear, Cooper & Ebner, 1987). This finding helps to emphasize that neurons, unlike transistors or some similar human-made item, are *alive*.

The typical neuron has three distinct structural features: the **soma,** or cell body, the **dendrites,** and the **axon.** The soma contains the **nucleus** of the cell; it manufactures enzymes and molecules essential for maintaining the cell's life. The dendrites generally receive nerve impulses from surrounding neurons. The axon is the mechanism by which the neuron transmits its own nerve impulses. Messages traveling down the axon eventually may stimulate other neurons, muscles, or

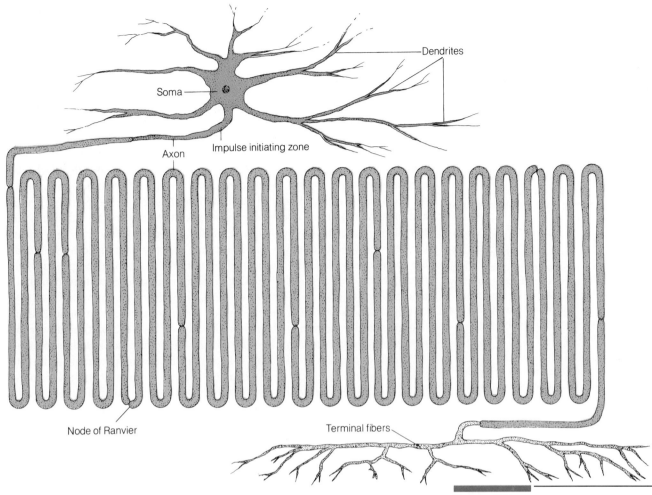

Soma

Dendrites

Impulse initiating zone

Axon

Node of Ranvier

Terminal fibers

FIGURE 2.5

The typical neuron of a vertebrate animal can carry nerve impulses for a considerable distance. The neuron depicted here, with its various parts drawn to scale, is enlarged 250 times. The nerve impulses originate in the cell body and are propagated along the axon, which may have one or more branches. This axon, which is folded for diagrammatic purposes, would be about 2½ inches long at actual size. Some axons are more than a yard long. The axon's terminal branches may communicate with as many as 10,000 other neurons. Similarly the dendrites of the neuron in this diagram might receive incoming signals from tens, hundreds, or even thousands of other neurons. Many axons, such as this one, are insulated by a coating known as myelin, which is interrupted at intervals by the regions known as nodes of Ranvier. (SOURCE: Stevens, 1979, p. 55.)

glands. Some axons are very short, while others are as long as 4 feet—a formidable length given the microscopic size of a neuron.

Surrounding the entire neuron is a thin skin, or membrane. The structure and properties of the membrane directly affect the function and the action of the cell. The membrane acts as a kind of skin, permitting the cell to maintain an internal fluid that is markedly different from the fluid surrounding the cell. This difference is most striking in the concentrations of particular ions (electrically charged atoms), including sodium, potassium, calcium, and chloride ions. You may recognize these elements as essential to your diet. If you don't have enough of any one of them in your system, you will suffer neurological disturbances in conjunction with other health-related problems.

When the neuron is at rest—that is, when it is not sending a message—the ion distribution causes the inside of the cell's axon to be electrically more negative than is the surrounding outside medium. These differing concentrations of ions give the neuron the ability to transmit signals along its entire length.

Neural Transmissions

For the next few pages, let's look at the way in which the neuron transmits messages. You'll soon discover the basic mechanism of *all* behavior—you'll also find out

NEUROTRANSMITTERS

Chemicals secreted by neurons that have an effect on adjacent neurons, muscles, or glands.

ION CHANNELS

Gates or selective openings imbedded within the neuron's membrane that allow charged atoms (called ions) to enter or exit. Such ion exchanges are responsible for neural transmission and communication.

RESTING POTENTIAL

The difference in electrical potential maintained between the outside and the inside of a resting nerve cell, usually about −70 millivolts.

POLARIZED

In reference to the neuron, to have been placed in a state of potential energy release by the resulting electrical forces created by ions on either side of the cell membrane. In the neuron, the polarization results in a resting potential of −70 millivolts across the membrane.

NERVE IMPULSE

The propagation of an electrical impulse down the length of a neural axon once a neuron has fired.

LOCAL EFFECT

The rapid depolarization of a section of the axon in response to the propagation of a neural transmission following the onset of neural firing. It is induced by the rapid depolarization of the soma or of a nearby section of the axon. The local effect results in the rapid depolarization of the next section of axon, thereby maintaining the propagation of the neural transmission.

MICROELECTRODE

An extremely small electric probe capable of monitoring a single cell.

SPIKE

A nerve impulse generated by the neuron reaching action potential.

ACTION POTENTIAL

A localized, rapid change in electrical state that travels across the cell membrane of a neuron at the moment of excitation.

why botulism, cobra venom, and nerve gas are all things to avoid (but you probably already knew that).

When a resting neuron's dendrites are stimulated, an electrical change begins to occur within its soma. If the soma changes enough, a threshold is passed, which causes the neuron to fire and to send a message the whole length of its axon.

The messages that stimulate a particular neuron's dendrites usually are received in the form of chemicals secreted by other neurons that are nearby. These secreted chemicals are called **neurotransmitters,** and will be discussed in more detail later. (Many psychologists believe that all behaviors are linked to the function of neuro-transmitters and that severe mental illness is always tied to some kind of neuro-transmitter mixup or imbalance. The challenge is to figure out exactly what each neurotransmitter is doing!) These neurotransmitters (sent from other neurons) excite the receiving neuron, chemically causing **ion channels** in the neuron's dendrites and soma membrane to open, which allows positive ions (mostly sodium) to enter. Ion channels aren't always opened chemically, however. A few years ago, research-ers were surprised to discover that in the case of some neurons sensitive to touch, the membrane's channels are opened by nothing more than the pressure of the touch, which causes enough stretching in the ion channels of the neuron membrane to allow ions to pour in (Guharay & Sachs, 1985).

Like the dendrites and soma, the inside of the axon is electrically more negative than its outside, measuring about 70 millivolts (70/1000 of a volt) negative relative to the surrounding medium. Because of this, the neuron is said to have a value of −70 millivolts when at rest. This is known as the **resting potential.** In this state, the cell and axon are said to be **polarized** because the outside and inside are like the + and − poles of a tiny battery. By making use of this difference in voltage across the membrane, the neuron can generate a **nerve impulse** down the length of its axon.

When the soma reaches threshold, the membrane at the beginning of the axon undergoes a dramatic change. This is called a **local effect.** Special channels in the axon membrane, like those in the dendrites and the soma, open, allowing positive ions to rush in. This influx causes the beginning of the axon suddenly to become positive relative to the external medium. This process is called depolarization. The first local effect then causes another identical local effect in the next portion of the axon farther along, and so on. This process describes the rapid ion exchange that races down the length of the axon like a flame following a line of black powder. If a **microelectrode** is placed within the axon and attached to a monitor, such as an oscilloscope, the sudden shift from negative to positive as the nerve impulse passes along the axon shows up on the oscilloscope as a sharp **spike** (see Figure 2.6). Whenever enough ions are exchanged to cause a nerve impulse to extend the length of the axon, the neuron is said to have reached its **action potential,** which is another way of saying that the nerve has fired. The amount of stimulation, or voltage change, required to reach action potential differs greatly depending on the type of neuron (Llinas, 1988).

As soon as the spike has passed one area of the axon, the positive ions are forced back out, restoring the original resting potential of −70 millivolts and often even hyperpolarizing the cell (meaning it becomes "very polarized") to about −100 millivolts for a brief time, until everything again equalizes itself at resting potential. Molecular "pumps" within the neuron, often called sodium–potassium pumps, are postulated to be responsible for eventually restoring the original arrangement of −70 millivolts by forcing some ions out and allowing others in.

Nerve impulses produced in this way travel relatively long distances without any loss of strength. The action potential is an all-or-nothing proposition. For the neuron to fire, the dendrites and soma at the head of the axon must be sufficiently stimulated to reach threshold. Otherwise, although some positive ions may flow into the neural soma, not enough will enter to reach threshold and cause an action potential to be reached. An analogy is a fuse that is singed rather than lighted.

You may be wondering how you can feel a great range of intensities of such stimuli as light, sound, and pressure given that a neuron can fire at only one strength. Furthermore, how can you have such a range of motor responses? You can pick something up gently or with a tight grip. These different intensities are achieved in several ways. To express weak intensities, it may be enough for only a few neurons to fire. Strong intensities, on the other hand, may require that thousands upon thousands of neurons fire. Although the strength of each individual impulse is constant, the firing of thousands of neurons can have a cumulative effect. Neurons also can express intensity by how often they fire. A mild intensity may cause a neuron to fire only once or twice per second, whereas an extremely intense stimulation may cause the neuron to fire as often as 1000 times per second!

Synaptic Transmissions

Years ago, researchers debated whether an electric spark actually jumped the gap between neurons. We now know that the secretion of neurotransmitters is responsible for neurons' ability to communicate with one another. The space between neurons, across which communication occurs, is called the **synapse**. Synapses are generally no more than .000005 (5 millionths) inch across. When an electrical spike traveling the length of an axon reaches its end, the spike typically causes neurotransmitters to be secreted into the synapse. If you follow the trunk of a tree upward, you discover that it divides again and again into many individual branches. Similarly, if you follow an axon out to its end, you find that it divides and subdivides into as many as 10,000 end buttons, or **synaptic knobs**. Figure 2.7 is an enlarged drawing showing synaptic transmission at a knob. When a spike reaches a synaptic knob, a change occurs in the knob's membrane. Channels responsive to the positive ion calcium (Ca+) (which is found in the fluid surrounding the neurons), responding in a way that is not fully understood, affect the small vesicles that float within the synaptic knob such that they are attracted to the **presynaptic surface**. The vesicles carry droplets of neurotransmitter, which they spill from the presynaptic membrane into the synapse. Across the synapse, receptors on the **postsynaptic surface** react to the neurotransmitter. If the postsynaptic surface is the membrane of a gland, the neurotransmitter may interact with the receptors and cause the gland to secrete. If the postsynaptic surface is the membrane of a muscle, the neurotransmitter may cause the muscle to contract.

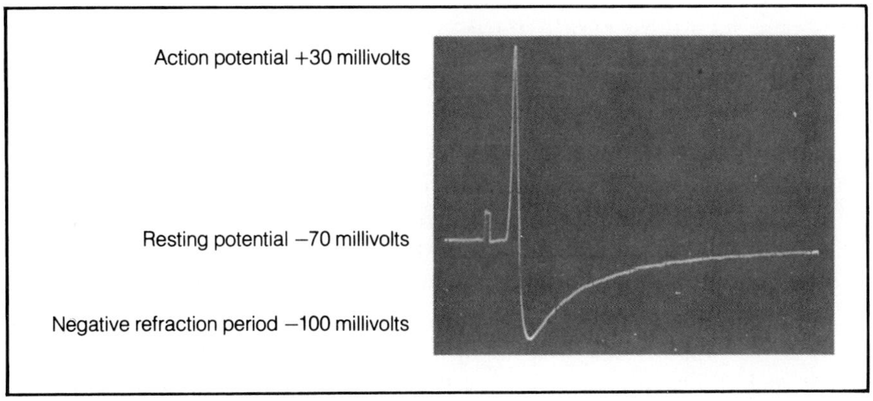

SYNAPSE
The small space between neurons into which neurotransmitter is secreted.

SYNAPTIC KNOBS
The extreme ends of an axon in which neurotransmitter is stored.

PRESYNAPTIC SURFACE
The cell surface from which neurotransmitter is secreted into the synapse.

POSTSYNAPTIC SURFACE
The cell surface receiving neurotransmitter secreted into the synapse.

Action potential +30 millivolts

Resting potential −70 millivolts

Negative refraction period −100 millivolts

FIGURE 2.6

A nerve impulse registers on an oscilloscope as a spike. If an auditory amplifier is attached to the oscilloscope, a click can be heard each time an impulse occurs. Following the spike, there is a negative refractory period during which the difference across the membrane is even greater than resting potential, that is, the cell becomes hyperpolarized. This occurs because, after firing, the neuron's molecular pumps don't stop until the polarization is pushed past resting potential.

45

EXCITATORY SYNAPSES

Synapses associated with depolarization of the receiving cell once neurotransmitter is secreted. If the receiving cell is a neuron, it will become more likely to fire or even to reach action potential.

INHIBITORY SYNAPSES

A synapse associated with hyperpolarization of the receiving cell once neurotransmitter is secreted. If the receiving cell is a neuron, it will become harder to fire, or more difficult to reach action potential.

If the postsynaptic surface belongs to another neuron, as in our earlier example, the neurotransmitter may excite the second neuron, causing it to approach or reach action potential. Once the neurotransmitter has affected the receptors on the postsynaptic membrane, it is either recaptured by the presynaptic membrane, broken down by enzymes, or left to diffuse. Anything that blocks or interferes with this synaptic process will cause extreme, even deadly problems for the organism. Botulin toxin, secreted by the *Clostridium botulinum* bacterium and the cause of botulism food poisoning, keeps neurotransmitter from leaving the presynaptic surface, which is why one of botulism's first symptoms is something such as double vision (because the nerves no longer control the fine muscles that operate the eyes) rather than the stomach pains you might expect from a disorder called "food poisoning." Cobra venom blocks the postsynaptic surface and keeps it from receiving the neurotransmitter. As is the case with botulism, a dose of cobra venom may quickly make it difficult for you to breath, although, for a slightly different reason. Nerve gas, on the other hand, destroys an enzyme that is supposed to break down the neurotransmitter acetylcholine (a muscle activator) after it has been secreted. The gas, therefore, causes the muscles to keep reacting, which leads to a terrible uncontrollable twitching and eventually to death. Enough of this cheery discussion—let's look at the different kinds of synapses.

EXCITATORY SYNAPSES. There are two basic kinds of synapses, excitatory and inhibitory. So far we have discussed only **excitatory synapses,** in which a message from one neuron causes a second neuron to become excited or to fire. However, it would be catastrophic if one neuron in the brain passed on a message stimulating thousands of other neurons, which in turn passed on a stimulating message to millions more. In short order, all or a large portion of the neurons would be firing and the brain would be out of control. This unfortunate event is prevented by the existence of inhibitory synapses.

INHIBITORY SYNAPSES. In an **inhibitory synapse** between two neurons, a neurotransmitter also is secreted from the presynaptic membrane into the synapse, but in this case different ion channels in the postsynaptic membrane open that allow only negative ions to flow in (Harris & Allan, 1985). This produces a negative potential (even greater than the resting potential), hyperpolarizing the cell. In effect, the neural message from the first neuron has made the second neuron less likely to fire than it was before it was stimulated. In addition to preventing an electrical

FIGURE 2.7

When a neural impulse reaches the synaptic knobs at the end of the axon, drops of neurotransmitter carried in the vesicles may be released from the presynaptic surface into the synapse. The neurotransmitter affects receptors on the postsynaptic surface.

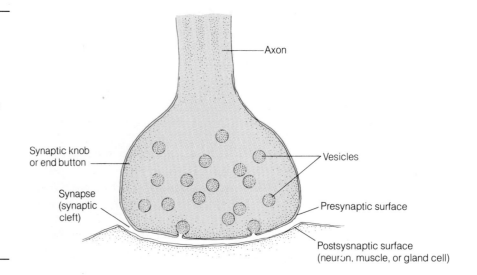

Axon

Synaptic knob
or end button

Synapse
(synaptic
cleft)

Vesicles

Presynaptic surface

Postsysnaptic surface
(neuron, muscle, or gland cell)

brainstorm from following a single stimulation, inhibitory synapses also help to tune and sharpen sensory perception. For instance, while a touch on your finger might cause many neurons in the general area of the touch to fire, the inhibitory synapses will block many of the signals that merely surround the exact point of touch. This will enable you to tell just where on your finger you were touched (Gottlieb, 1988). Without these inhibitory actions, you wouldn't have anywhere near the sensory sensitivity that you do possess.

There are also many inhibitory synapses found within the brain. In fact, in some areas of the brain, inhibitory synapses actually outnumber excitatory synapses (Gottleib, 1988).

The World of Neurotransmitters

Many different substances found within the nervous system are known or are suspected to be neurotransmitters (Panksepp, 1986). These substances are not found randomly in all parts of the nervous system, but rather tend to be localized in specific groups of neurons, the axons of which perform specific functions or send messages to specific areas. Psychologists are interested in neurotransmitters because their effects are directly related to behavior. For example, close examination of concentrations of the neurotransmitter dopamine has led researchers to believe that this substance may be active in some of the brain's pleasure centers (see the Prologue); the exact amount of dopamine secreted there may determine how rewarding we find a particular experience (Wise & Rompre, 1989)! If we ever learn how to control dopamine secretion in the brain, we might be able to alter behaviors that many people wish to stop, such as smoking, drug use, overeating, or gambling, among other things. This might be accomplished by making such behaviors less pleasant while making behaviors people wish to encourage, such as peacefulness, love, or finishing an economics paper, for example, more pleasant (assuming that any amount of neurotransmitter can make economics pleasant). You don't need too much imagination, however, to see the potential for abuse of such knowledge by, for instance, making sure people enjoy the "right" ideas or "proper" behaviors— a chilling thought. How the power to control "pleasure centers" might be used, if it is ever obtained, will certainly form a platform for interesting debates.

Other neurotransmitters also play important roles. The neurotransmitter acetylcholine, for example, is essential for the operation of muscles, and GABA (gamma-aminobutyric acid) is needed, among other things, for the control of inhibitory synapses (Gottlieb, 1988). The same neurotransmitter may often have a different role depending on where it is operating, and many of the neurotransmitters can be classified into subtypes (such as GABA I and GABA II), each subtly different from the other in ways that might have pronounced effects on behavior (Pritchett, Luddens, & Seeburg, 1989). Name a behavior, a feeling, or a thought, and neurotransmitters will be involved at some level.

LONG-TERM EFFECTS. Neurons, synapses, and neurotransmitters change over time. Experience, among other things, changes them. Psychiatrist and neurobiologist Eric Kandel once said, "As I talk to you and you listen to me, the cells in my brain are having a direct effect on the cells in your brain. What's more, the effect could be long-lasting. So don't talk to strangers. It can produce entirely unwanted effects on your synapses" (Herbert, 1987, p. 80). Exactly how these long-term effects occur is not exactly clear, but recent discoveries may give us a hint. Not only do synapses appear and disappear over time, probably as a result of our experiences and how often neurons are required to fire (Bear, Cooper & Ebner, 1987; Kalil, 1989), or our lack of them, but also the kinds and amounts of neurotransmitter secreted by a neuron may vary as an effect of experience. Many neurons secrete more than one kind of neurotransmitter (Nicoll, 1988). Sometimes, when a neuron is stimulated, the effect of the stimulation may last, not for only a millisecond, but for days or even weeks (Marx, 1986), causing the neuron to alter the concentrations of its neurotransmitters. With the alteration of enough neurons, major changes in behavior might be observed over time. If this all seems a bit overwhelming, it's no wonder. Ira Black of the Cornell University Medical College summed it up well when he noted, "In addition to dealing with approximately 100 billion neurons, each of which has on the average 10,000 connections, we now have to realize that the individual neurons may use different signals at different times, depending on the stimuli they receive. The combinatorial power is staggering" (Marx, 1986, p. 1501).

Additional research may even force us to add to this power. For example, the most plentiful cell in the brain is not the neuron, but rather the **glial cell,** which outnumbers the neuron by a ratio of 10 : 1. *Glia* is the Greek word for "glue"; for many years, scientists assumed that glial cells, acting like glue, helped to hold neurons in place. Glial cells also often recover neurotransmitter from the synapse after it has been released there by the neuron and are themselves electrochemically active. Now it has been discovered that glial cells communicate with one another over long distances via changes in electrical potential (Cornell-Bell, Finkbeiner, Cooper, & Smith, 1990). This indicates that glial calls might also modify the electrical activity of the neurons they surround. If this is correct, it may well mean that the nervous system is far more complicated than we thought it was—if it's even possible to imagine something more complicated than we were already contemplating.

Interestingly, Albert Einstein's brain, which has been extensively examined, has been found to be like most other brains with the exception of a very large number of glial cells (Diamond, Scheibel, Murphy & Harvey, 1985). Of course, the human brain is so complex, and we know so little about it, that there are, without doubt, a whole lot of reasons for Einstein's great intelligence other than the number of his glial cells, but that he had plenty of them is an interesting observation nonetheless.

DRUGS AND NEUROTRANSMITTER RECEPTORS. Another important reason for studying neurotransmitters is that drugs that affect behavior appear to do so by modifying or disrupting neural transmissions between brain cells. Solomon Snyder, a renowned researcher in neurotransmission, has stated, "Virtually every drug that alters mental function does so by interacting with a neurotransmitter system in the brain. Many drugs mimic or block the effects of specific neurotransmitters at receptor sites" (1984, p. 23). Hallucinogenic drugs such as mescaline, psilocybin, and lysergic acid diethylamide (LSD) have chemical structures that strongly resemble those of natural brain neurotransmitters. These hallucinogens mimic the natural brain neurotransmitters and stimulate the corresponding natural receptor sites, which can cause an hallucination such as seeing something that isn't there.

Some drugs block, rather than mimic, neurotransmitters. Such a drug is called an **antagonist.** Such a class of drugs are the neuroleptics, which block dopamine receptors (Snyder, 1984). Dopamine, a neurotransmitter, is found in many places in the brain. Neuroleptics often help to control the hallucinations and bizarre thoughts of schizophrenics (people suffering from the serious mental disorder schizophrenia—see Chapter 15), which has led some researchers to conclude that schizophrenics may be producing excess dopamine or have an excess of dopamine receptors in their brains.

Sometimes, drugs work by facilitating or giving a boost to a natural neuro-transmitter. Such a drug is called an **agonist.** The antianxiety drug diazepam (Valium) appears to work by boosting the effectiveness of GABA, the most common neurotransmitter found in inhibitory synapses. By knowing how a drug affects neurotransmitters and their receptor sites, manufacturers can make additional drugs that will mimic, facilitate, or block a neurotransmitter's function. For example, an experimental drug has been developed that counters the effects of GABA, which is the opposite of what diazepam does. When this GABA antagonist is given to human subjects, it causes extreme anxiety, almost a state of panic (Dorow, Horowski, Paschelke, & Braestrup, 1983). By conducting experiments with such compounds, researchers hope to uncover the secrets of brain chemistry and, perhaps, to alleviate mental illness.

There also is evidence that certain neuromuscular disorders may be directly related to dysfunctions in certain brain neurotransmitters. For example, dopamine is concentrated in areas of the brain that control complex movement. If dopamine in these areas degenerates, the result may be **Parkinson's disease,** in which muscular rigidity and tremors occur. One of the great breakthroughs in medicine occurred in the 1970s when a form of dopamine called levodopa was found to help prevent and control the symptoms of Parkinson's disease. Levodopa taken in pill form finds its way into the brain, where it helps to overcome the problem of the missing dopamine. Individuals with Parkinson's disease who were unable even to button a shirt can perform such tasks easily, and will appear to have normal motor and muscular control, within minutes of taking levodopa (see Focus on the Future).

NEUROPEPTIDES. Ever since Susan Leeman at Harvard University purified the first one in 1971 from brain tissue, a whole new class of chemical messengers has been uncovered—the **neuropeptides** (Krieger, 1983). Neuropeptides are small chemicals made from **amino acids.** Well over 50 have been identified and more than 200 are suspected to exist; the actual number may well be higher. The effects of neuropeptides on behavior are wide-ranging. When different neuropeptides are placed in animal's brains, interesting behaviors are triggered, such as yawning, stretching, or grooming (Panksepp, 1986). Neuropeptides have been described as being like "island-hopping cruise ships" that "seem to meander through the brain, glands, and the immune system [making] scheduled stops in the choicest locations, at only those cellular ports with customized receiving docks" (Cordes, 1985, p. 18). By this statement Cordes meant that each neuropeptide has a certain shape that will activate a recipient cell only if it fits a receptor on that cell, like a key in a lock. Sometimes, if the cell it is affecting is a neuron, the neuropeptide may function like a neurotransmitter; that is, it may cause a neuron to be stimulated (making it easier, or less easy, to fire the neuron). Unlike a neurotransmitter, however, neuropeptides travel throughout the body in the bloodstream, eventually joining and affecting neurons far from the neuropeptide's production site. Such a neuropeptide is acting like a **hormone.** Neuropeptides may affect many other types of cells as well.

Although neuropeptides are very small, their effects can be astounding. Let's take a look at one of the neuropeptides, **beta-endorphin.** The story begins in 1971 with Avram Goldstein, who was working with drugs derived from opium, such as morphine. He discovered that when opium was ingested, it tended to concentrate in different areas of the brain, specifically in those areas associated with the perception of pain and with emotion. This made sense to Goldstein, because morphine is known to be a strong pain reliever, and it gives the user a good feeling, a sense of emotional well-being. Goldstein went one step further; he wondered why human

AGONIST
A drug that acts to facilitate or enhance the actions of other drugs or naturally occurring biochemical substances.

PARKINSON'S DISEASE
A progressive nervous disease of the brain characterized by muscle tremor, slowing of movement, peculiarity of gait and posture, and weakness. It is a direct result of dopamine deficiency and can be temporarily treated with a dopamine-like drug, levodopa. The progress of the disease can also be slowed by use of the drug deprenyl.

NEUROPEPTIDES
Extremely small chemical messengers made from short chains of amino acids. Beta-endorphin is a neuropeptide.

AMINO ACIDS
Any of a collection of organic compounds that contain both an amino and a carboxyl group. All life is based on only 20 different amino acids. The neurotransmitter gamma-aminobutyric acid is an example of an amino acid.

HORMONE
A bloodborne secretion of the endocrine glands that specifically affects metabolism and behavior.

BETA-ENDORPHIN
A powerful natural neuropeptide. It means "the morphine within" and is so named because it has properties similar to those of heroin and morphine. It is a powerful painkiller and mood elevator.

BRAIN TRANSPLANTS

If part of your brain becomes damaged or destroyed, there's probably little that anyone can do to repair it. On the other hand, if part of your television set blows up, you can take the set to a repair shop where the broken part can be pulled out and replaced with a new one. Imagine for a moment that the same could be done with the brain. Suppose a damaged brain structure could be pulled out and replaced with a new and functioning one. Perhaps an entire section could be replaced, or maybe the entire brain could be lifted from the body of a person who was dying and placed into the healthy body of someone who was "brain dead" (whose brain was no longer functioning). Mary Shelley suggested such a possibility in her famous novel *Frankenstein*. Of course, that was pure fiction. The very idea of reconnecting delicate brain tissue to the millions of neurons coming up through the spinal column or entering through the eyes or ears is ludicrous. No one could even guess how to begin making such connections. But what about the possibilities of transplanting brain parts, either from animals or from donors, to replace broken brain parts in the living? If that too sounds like science fiction, then you're in for a surprise; it's being done!

These amazing procedures were first performed on mice. The brains of healthy mice were damaged so that the certain cells that produced the neurotransmitter dopamine no longer functioned. The mice rapidly lost their movement and direction control and appeared to have all the symptoms of Parkinson's disease. But these mice were saved by researchers who placed dopamine-producing cells taken from the brains of mouse embryos alongside the destroyed cells in each mouse's damaged brain (Fine,

1986). The foreign tissue was not rejected by the mouse's body because it has been discovered that most areas of the brain are **privileged sites,** places where the immune system cannot attack. A **blood–brain barrier** isolates the brain from the rest of the body; only certain molecules can penetrate this barrier and enter the brain. The attacking cells of the immune system are not able to get through. The complicated nerve connections between the embryo-tissue implant and the real brain grew and began to connect on their own. This occurred because axons of one type typically seek out receptors they recognize, thereby making proper connections (Dodd & Jessell, 1988). The foreign dopamine-producing cells placed in each damaged mouse's brain appeared to help by producing the dopamine that was no longer being supplied to the damaged cells. The mice fully recovered from their Parkinson-like symptoms.

In 1983, at the University of Lund in Sweden, Dr. Anders Bjorklund performed the operation on a human being (Kolata, 1983b). The patient was suffering from Parkinson's disease and was taking the drug levodopa to replace missing dopamine temporarily. Unfortunately, drugs that can cross the blood–brain barrier, such as levodopa, and the newer drug deprenyl, can slow the progression of Parkinson's disease—they cannot cure the disease. The actual neurotransmitter dopamine cannot be given, because it will not cross the blood–brain barrier. Dr. Bjorklund hoped to provide a cure with the new technique. Rather than taking the controversial step of using cells from a human embryo or dying donor, he took dopamine-producing cells from the kidneys of his patient and placed them in her brain. The patient, a 46-

year-old woman who had been so paralyzed by Parkinson's disease that she could do no more than lie in bed, showed substantial improvement (McKean, 1984).

Following on the heels of the Swedish success, Dr. Ignacio Madrazo, of La Raza Hospital in Mexico City, was able to obtain even better results by laying the transplanted tissue from the kidney on top of, rather than deep within, the brains of patients who had Parkinson's disease (Madrazo et al., 1987). Because they were bathed in the cerebrospinal fluid that surrounds the brain, the cells survived better than they would have had they been buried deep within the site of the Parkinson's destruction, as they had been by the Swedish team. How the dopamine was able to get to where it was needed in the Mexican experiment is not clear, but the procedure did work! Some researchers have suggested that these successes show that the transplant couldn't be working by supplying the missing dopamine, but must rather be somehow stimulating the neurons damaged by Parkinson's disease to regrow and thus to make up the loss (Moore, 1987). Similar transplants are now being conducted in the United States, the first of which was performed in Nashville, Tennessee, in 1987.

Interestingly, the new supply of neurotransmitter that these Parkinson patients receive from their brain grafts, may be stimulating parts of the brain that surgeons had not intended to affect. It has been observed that patients, following these brain graft procedures but not following other kinds of brain surgery, often behave in strange ways. For instance, some patients experience real changes in their ability to sense pain, others show odd sleep patterns, some have delusions (for instance, one man firmly believed that a farm store was attached to the hospital; another thought that appliance salesmen were visiting all of the hospital rooms), some show personality changes, and some even have visual or auditory hallucinations (Lewin, 1988). Just as interesting is the fact that all of these strange effects following surgery generally disappear within a month or two. Perhaps the introduction of the neurotransmitter from the graft causes these effects and in some way the brain is eventually able to discount them. No one really knows.

Researchers continuing work on such brain grafts in Sweden and Mexico have discovered that for best results, it may be necessary to implant dopamine-producing tissue taken from aborted fetuses, because such young and immature cells readily make proper neural connections (Madrazo et al., 1988; Lindvall et al.,

1990). This, in turn, has raised ethical concerns in the minds of some who fear that such work might encourage abortions, or even the eventual growing of fetuses in artificial media for the sole intention of providing spare parts for people. Others counter that if an abortion is about to occur anyway, it is a crime to throw away tissue that could otherwise save a life. The legal and ethical considerations of fetal research are receiving increasing notice.

Still, such research is rich with promise, more than helping those who suffer from Parkinson's disease. For instance, researchers have conducted experiments with old rats whose ability to learn certain tasks was quite poor due to their aged brains. Implanting tissue rich in young neurons from rat fetuses into the old rats has improved significantly these older rats' ability to learn (Gage,

Bjorklund, Stenevi, Dunnett, & Kelly, 1984).

Researchers also are excited by a discovery that may help to resolve some of the ethical dilemmas raised by the use of human fetal tissue. William Freed and Richard Wyatt discovered that brain tissue from one species can be successfully transplanted into the brain of another species. They found that mouse tissue easily grafts to a rat brain and will alleviate experimentally induced Parkinson's disease. Again, because the brain is a privileged site, the rat's immune system does not attack the foreign mouse tissue, but instead makes use of the dopamine produced by it. Perhaps someday human brain injury or disease will be cured or alleviated by the transplant of tissue from the brains of beef cattle or other animals that are bred for slaughter. Such experiments are currently being investigated.

---

beings and animals even responded to opium, which, after all, is an extract from a plant. What connection could there be between a human brain and a plant?

Goldstein formed the hypothesis that opiates such as heroin or morphine work because they are mimicking some natural brain substance that binds with the same receptors with which drugs such as heroin or morphine bind. In other words, a natural heroin or morphine must exist in the brain. That substance is beta-endorphin ("the morphine within"), and it was discovered in 1975. Immediately following the discovery, researchers began the attempt to synthesize beta-endorphin; in 1977 the first small amount was manufactured.

The first surprise following this discovery focused on the Chinese technique of **acupuncture**. Acupuncture usually is performed by inserting thin needles into particular places on a person's body and rotating the needles back and forth. When the acupuncturist does this, an anesthetic reaction can be induced—people in China, for example, undergo certain forms of surgery with no anesthesia other than acupuncture, and they do not feel pain. Nothing is injected through the needles.

Many researchers now believe that acupuncture may produce its anesthetic effect by stimulating the secretion of beta-endorphin. Support for this idea comes from the fact that acupuncture is not as effective if **naloxone** (an opiate antagonist and therefore a beta-endorphine blocker) has been administered beforehand (Weiss, 1988).

PRIVILEGED SITE
A location (typically in the brain) in which foreign tissue is safe from attack by the body's immune system. Sites in the brain are generally privileged because cells from the body's immune system cannot penetrate the blood–brain barrier that surrounds and protects the brain.

BLOOD–BRAIN BARRIER
The semipermeable membrane and tissue surrounding most brain structures that allows only limited brain access to substances borne in the blood. Usually, only specific molecules are able to enter. Many drugs as well as the cells from the body's own immune system are typically unable to cross the blood–brain barrier.

ACUPUNCTURE
A traditional Chinese therapeutic technique in which the body is punctured with fine needles. It usually is used as an anesthetic or to relieve pain.

NALOXONE

A heroin antagonist. Naloxone blocks and essentially neutralizes heroin. Naloxone has the same effect on morphine and beta-endorphin.

PLACEBO

An inert substance often given to subjects in a control group in place of the treatment given to subjects in the experimental group.

For years, psychologists have known that, when people who are in pain are given a **placebo** and are told to expect relief, approximately one-third of them will report that their pain has lessened. These people are called placebo reactors. The placebo may be a sugar pill, an injection of water, a magic incantation, or the laying on of hands—anything that usually would not be expected to relieve pain. Why should this power of suggestion work? Research now indicates that placebo reactors in some unconscious way may be activating their body's natural pain-suppression system and causing the release of beta-endorphin (Levine, Gordon, & Fields, 1978). Support for this idea also comes from the finding that naloxone (a beta-endorphin blocker) lessens the pain-killing effect of a placebo. Even in the presence of naloxone, however, placebos can sometimes have a painkilling effect (Gracely, Dudner, Wolskee, & Deeter, 1983), which indicates that other substances not blocked by naloxone may plan an important role, with beta-endorphin, in the perception of pain.

Beta-endorphin also may function as the body's own "tonic against disappointment." It has been discovered that the famous pleasure center found years ago by Professor Olds is loaded with the brain's own natural opiate (Gerner, Catlin, Gorelick, Hui, & Li, 1980).

Vigorous exercise causes the release of beta-endorphin, which may help to explain the "high" associated with regular vigorous activity. Beta-endorphin also is known to dilate blood vessels, which in turn helps to lower blood pressure, a result often associated with regular exercise (Berk, 1981).

The neuropeptides have been implicated in other areas besides pleasure and pain. For instance, research has indicated that beta-endorphin may play an important role in learning and memory (Bolles & Fanselow, 1982). Without question, these chemical substances are opening a new chapter in psychobiology and the surprises have only just begun to appear (Panksepp, 1986).

HORMONES AND THE ENDOCRINE SYSTEM

Hormones are substances that travel throughout the body and have wide-ranging effects on behavior. Hormones are secreted by glands, of which there are two kinds

The Chinese technique of acupuncture produces an analgesic (pain-killing) response from the body by stimulating the production of the body's natural pain reliever, beta-endorphin.

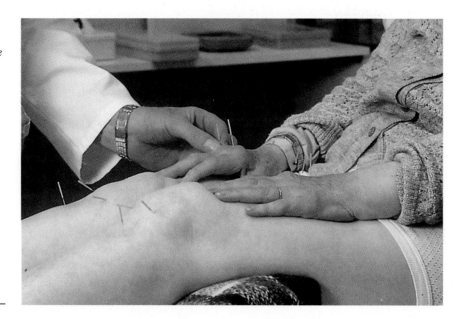

in the body. The **exocrine glands** secrete into ducts that usually lead to the surface of the body; they include tear and sweat glands. The **endocrine glands,** which make up the endocrine system (see Figure 2.8), secrete hormones directly into the bloodstream. Chief among the endocrine glands are the pituitary gland, the adrenal glands, and the gonads. Our basic knowledge of the endocrine system, however, is still growing, as evidenced by the fact that only recently was it discovered that the heart (which was thought to be only a pump) is also an endocrine gland that secretes a hormone that alters the permeability of the ion channels in surrounding neurons and helps to regulate blood pressure (Cantin & Genest, 1986; Sorbera & Morad, 1990). Hormones are messengers, but, unlike neurotransmitters, which are fast-acting and travel the extremely short distance across a synapse, hormones are slow-acting and are carried throughout the body by the bloodstream. Hormones can affect parts of the body distant from the gland that secreted them and also may affect many different parts of the body at once. Some substances, such as noradrenaline and some neuropeptides, do double duty, acting as hormones in some cases and as neurotransmitters in others. One example of the many vital links between the endocrine and nervous systems is the following: We know that if neurons receive no stimulation over a long enough period, they will die. An old saying among neuroscientists is, "Use it, or lose it." If the adrenal glands are removed, and the hormones they produce are not replaced, certain neurons in the brain will die (Sloviter et al., 1989).

Endocrine glands secrete hormones in response to neural messages or in reaction to changes in body chemistry. Hormones are known to have a vital function in physical growth and sexual development. They also are involved in changes of mood, reactions to stress, and levels of activity (Reinisch, 1981).

Some of the hormones released by glands such as the pituitary or by the hypothalamus (the portion of the brain directly above the pituitary) are called **executive hormones** because they, in turn, bring about the release of other hormones in the endocrine system.

The **pituitary gland** often releases its hormones after it receives executive hormones from the hypothalamus. For example, orders from the hypothalamus tell

EXOCRINE GLANDS
Glands that secrete fluids through a duct to the outside of the body or to a specific organ.

ENDOCRINE GLANDS
Ductless glands that pour their secretions directly into the bloodstream. The hormones secreted by the endocrine glands are important regulators of many body activities.

EXECUTIVE HORMONES
Hormones that order or control the secretion of other hormones.

PITUITARY GLAND
A gland located beneath the hypothalamus that controls many hormonal secretions. It often is called the master gland because it appears to control other glands throughout the body.

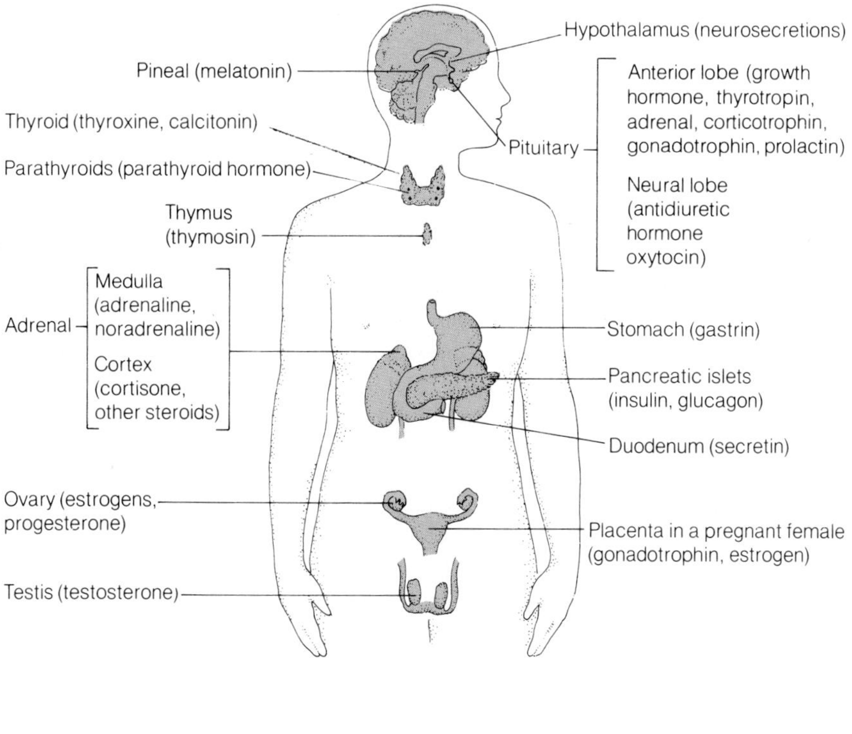

FIGURE 2.8

The glands of the endocrine system and some of the hormones they secrete.

ADRENAL GLANDS
Endocrine glands located above the
kidneys that secrete the hormones
adrenaline, noradrenaline, and steroids.
These hormones influence metabolism and
the body's reaction to stressful situations.

ADRENALINE
A hormone secreted by the adrenal glands
that stimulates the sympathetic nervous
system; also called epinephrine.

NORADRENALINE
A hormone secreted by the adrenal glands
that brings about a number of body
changes, including constriction of the
blood vessels near the body's surface. It
causes the adrenal glands to secrete
steroids, which in turn release sugar so that
energy is available for emergency action. It
is also called norepinephrine.

STEROIDS
Any of a number of organic compounds
that have a 17-atom carbon ring, including
some hormones. Cortical steroids (secreted
from the adrenal glands) help to control
the release of sugar stored for use in
emergencies.

GONADS
The sex glands that regulate sex drive and
the physiological changes that accompany
physical maturity. These glands are the
ovaries in the female and the testes in the
male.

BRAIN MAPPING
A technique neurosurgeons use to pinpoint
the functions of different areas in the brain
so that they don't destroy something vital
during brain surgery.

the pituitary how much growth hormone to secrete. Too little or too much of this hormone can dramatically affect growth, creating either a dwarf or a giant.

The **adrenal glands** are located just above both kidneys. They secrete **adrenaline** and **noradrenaline** (these same substances, when acting within neurons as neurotransmitters, are called, respectively, epinephrine and norepinephrine). Both hormones have much to do with the action of the sympathetic nervous system. They help to prepare an organism for an emergency or for a stressful situation. Adrenaline causes the heart to beat faster and blood vessels to constrict within the stomach and the intestines. Noradrenaline is an executive hormone. When it reaches the pituitary, it stimulates the release of other executive hormones that act on the adrenal glands, causing the adrenals to secrete **steroids**. Steroids are a class of hormones that cause the liver to release stored sugar (glycogen), so that energy can be made available for emergency action. It is this hormone that has been abused by some body builders and other athletes who want to develop large muscles in the hope of improving performance. Overuse of steroids, however, carries with it health risks associated with stressful reactions, including heart disease and high blood pressure. The **gonads,** which secrete sex hormones, are discussed in Chapter 18.

As we have mentioned, some of the same chemical substances may be secreted by glands as hormones or used by neurons as neurotransmitters. Similarly, as we have seen, some neuropeptides do double duty, acting like hormones some of the time and like neurotransmitters at other times. This state of affairs has led some modern researchers to abandon terms such as "hormone," "neuropeptide," and "neurotransmitter," and to use instead the collective term *informational substances* to denote chemicals that carry messages, wherever or however they do.

THE STRUCTURE OF THE BRAIN

Imagine you're looking at a slide under a microscope. On the slide is a tiny speck, a piece of brain. What do you see? The piece of brain resembles a small translucent blob containing thousands of extremely tiny, black, spiderlike specks that have long streaks emanating from them (see Figure 2.9). The spiderlike specks and streaks appear to meander in a chaotic, tangled pattern. What you are seeing are neurons that have been chemically stained for viewing. The spiderlike specks are somas and dendrites, and the streaks are axons. In the background, there seems to be a black haze, caused by the microscope's inability to accommodate the whole depth of the speck at one focus setting. As you turn the focus knob, the neurons you were looking at become blurry and the haze that was in the background becomes clear, showing up more neurons. Beneath are even more neurons, thousands of them, and millions of synapses—and all of this in one small speck of brain.

Exploring the brain at this microscopic level and tracing all of the neurochemical circuits is far beyond the present capacity of our science. The experience of viewing just one small speck can be overwhelming. Even professionals familiar with the brain and its workings sometimes find themselves overcome by a sense of awe. Consider a neurosurgeon mapping the brain of a patient. **Brain mapping** is a technique neurosurgeons use to make certain that they don't cut through or destroy something vital during brain surgery. Throughout the brain-mapping procedure, the patient is alert and awake. Because the surgeon has used a local anesthetic while opening the skull and exposing the brain, the patient feels no pain. As the neurosurgeon touches different places on the surface of the brain with a small electrode through which a tiny current is passed, the patient reports what he senses. For example, when one point on the brain is stimulated, the patient reports that he feels a tingling on his gums; at another point, he reports a ringing in his ears; at another point, the little finger on his left hand twitches. The surgeon then places tiny numbered paper tags directly on the brain at each point identified, and records the function of the point.

If you stop for a moment and think about what is happening, you'll realize that neurosurgeon is, in fact, talking to a body organ and it is answering back!

When you look at a human brain (shown in Figures 2.10 and 2.11), three features are likely to catch your immediate attention. First, the brain appears to be rippled, filled with crevices and folds. Second, a long fissure running the length of the brain appears to separate it into a left and a right half. Third, some portions

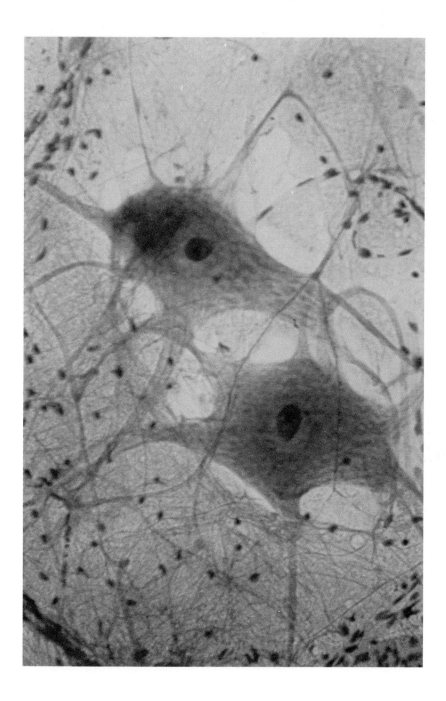

FIGURE 2.9

These cells have been made visible by coloring them with the purple Golgi stain. The dark bodies are the neural somas, and the spidery threads are the axons.

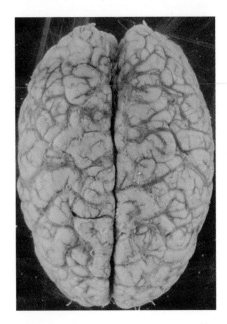

FIGURE 2.10

The human brain. Viewed from this angle, only the cerebral cortex is visible. The cerebral cortex is the largest part of the human brain; it contains 70 percent of the neurons in the nervous system.

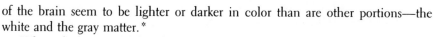

SULCI
The narrow fissures separating adjacent cerebral convolutions.

GYRI
The prominent rounded and elevated convolutions at the surfaces of the cerebral hemispheres.

MYELIN
A white, fatty covering on neural fibers that serves to channel impulses along the fibers and increase their speed.

of the brain seem to be lighter or darker in color than are other portions—the white and the gray matter.*

Why is the brain convoluted and rippled? One good reason may be the advantage of saving space. If you flattened out the human brain, it would fill a 4-square-foot area. Perhaps our brains could have evolved in the shape of a great circuit board, instead of the way they did, but the skull shape necessary to contain such a form would certainly have been unusual, and it would probably have presented aerodynamic problems on a windy day! The best way, then, of fitting a large brain into a reasonably shaped skull is to crumple it up. If you crumple a piece of paper into a ball, you will see that you have created fissures and convolutions. In the brain, the fissures are called **sulci** and the convolutions **gyri.**

The long fissure running the length of the brain does, in fact, divide the brain in half, except for a few important connections. As you will see, it may be more accurate to consider the brain to be two brains, joined and sharing information and controlling different aspects of behavior.

When Agatha Christie's master detective, Hercule Poirot, was deep in thought, he would often tap his forehead and refer to the "little gray cells." These gray cells are neurons without **myelin.** Myelin is a white, fatty sheath that coats the axons of some neurons. It insulates and provides nourishment to the neuron. Myelinated neurons are able to transmit messages faster than nonmyelinated neurons can. Billions of nonmyelinated neurons give the appearance of a grayish mass within the brain—the gray matter. Billions of myelinated neurons create a white, glistening sheen—the white matter—because of the white of their myelin sheaths.

*Actually, the white and gray matter have a pinkish-red hue because of the blood flowing to the brain.

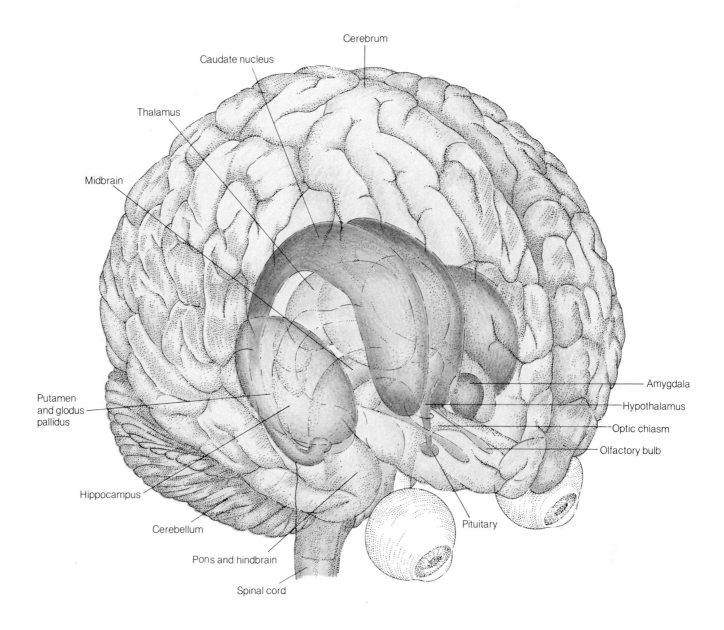

Caudate nucleus

Cerebrum

Thalamus

Midbrain

Amygdala

Hypothalamus

Optic chiasm

Olfactory bulb

Putamen
and glodus
pallidus

Hippocampus

Cerebellum

Pituitary

Pons and hindbrain

Spinal cord

FIGURE 2.11

A human brain, drawn so that its
internal structures are visible through
"transparent" outer layers of the
cerebrum. (Figure 2.12 shows a
generalized mammalian brain in a highly
schematic view. Corresponding structures
in the realistic and schematic models are
the same color.)
The brain and spinal cord of human
beings and other mammals can be
subdivided into smaller regions according
to gross appearance, embryology, or
cellular organization.
The most general way of dividing the
brain is into hindbrain, midbrain, and
forebrain. The hindbrain includes the
cerebellum.
The forebrain is more complex. Its outer
part is the cerebral hemisphere, the
surface of which is the convoluted sheet of
the cerebral cortex. The rest of the
forebrain includes the thalamus (which
has numerous subdivisions) and the
hypothalamus (which connects to the
pituitary complex). Some structures
depicted in this drawing have not been
mentioned in the text because they are
beyond the scope of our discussion. They
are included here, however, to show that
each major structure has a name.
(SOURCE: Nauta & Feirtag, 1979,
p. 102.)

57

CEREBRUM

The large rounded structure of the brain occupying most of the cranial cavity, divided into two cerebral hemispheres by a deep fissure and joined at the bottom by the corpus callosum.

CEREBRAL CORTEX

The extensive outer layer of convoluted gray tissue of the cerebral hemispheres, which is largely responsible for higher nervous functions, including intellectual processes. It is also called the neocortex.

HINDBRAIN

The posterior section of the brain, which includes the cerebellum, pons, and medulla.

MIDBRAIN

The middle section of the brain, which contains the structures responsible for processing and relaying auditory and visual information.

FOREBRAIN

The top portion of the brain, which includes the thalamus, hypothalamus, corpus callosum, limbic system, and cerebrum.

MEDULLA

The oblong structure at the top of the spinal cord that is responsible for many vital life-support functions, including breathing and heartbeat.

CEREBELLUM

A portion of the hindbrain situated just beneath the posterior portion of the cerebrum. Its function is to coordinate muscle tone and fine motor control.

The largest part of the brain, and the part you usually think of when you picture the brain, is the **cerebrum** (see Figures 2.10 and 2.11). No fewer than 70 percent of all the neurons in the central nervous system are contained in the cerebrum (Nauta & Feirtag, 1979). The outer layer of the cerebrum is called the **cerebral cortex.** *Cortex* in Latin means "bark," and, in a way, the sulci and gyri of the cortex do resemble the bark of a tree. The cerebral cortex is also known as the *neocortex,* meaning "new cortex," because in evolutionary terms it is the most recent development. You can trace the evolutionary history and development of your brain by following the lower structures upward to the neocortex. The structures that are deeper and lower in the brain are older in evolutionary terms. For convenience, the brain may be divided into the **hindbrain,** the **midbrain,** and the **forebrain,** and each area may be further subdivided (see Figures 2.2, 2.11, and 2.12).

The Hindbrain

The major components of the hindbrain are the **medulla,** the **cerebellum,** and the **pons.** In evolutionary terms, these portions of the brain are very old. Humans share these brain structures with older and less complex species, such as reptiles. In fact, the hindbrain in humans often is referred to as the "reptilian brain."

THE MEDULLA.   As the spinal column enters the stem of the hindbrain, it begins to widen. This is the location, deep and low within the brain, of the medulla, a small, narrow concentration of millions of neurons perhaps 1 1/2 inches in length. The medulla controls many life-support functions, including breathing and heartbeat. The slightest damage to it can result in death.

THE CEREBELLUM.   Just above the medulla, but in the rear portion of the brain stem, is the cerebellum, which in Greek means "little chamber." Like the cerebral cortex, it has sulci and gyri. The function of the cerebellum appears to be pretty much the same for reptiles, fishes, birds, and mammals, including humans. It coordinates muscle tone and fine motor control. Although the commands for motor movements may originate in higher areas of the brain, it is the cerebellum that controls and fine-tunes the movements (Ito, 1984). The cerebellum also stores highly repetitious procedures that, after a person has mastered them, require little thought and almost seem automatic; skills such as riding a bicycle or typing letters. Damage to the cerebellum causes awkward and uncontrolled movements.

FIGURE 2.12

Schematic drawing of a generalized mammalian brain. (Colors for parts correspond to those in Figure 2.11.) (SOURCE: Nauta & Feirtag, 1979, p. 102.)

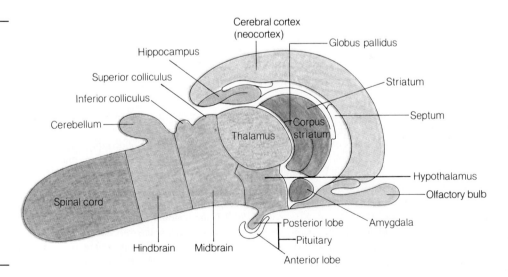

THE PONS. At about the same level as the cerebellum, in the front portion of the brain stem, is the pons. Many important ascending and descending nerve fibers run through the pons, connecting it with other brain areas. The pons regulates motor messages traveling from the higher brain downward through the pons to the cerebellum. It also is thought to regulate some sensory information, since cells involved with vision have been found in the pons (Glickstein & Gibson, 1976). In addition, nuclei (densely packed concentrations of neural dendrites and somas) associated with respiratory regulation have been found in the pons.

THE RETICULAR ACTIVATING SYSTEM. Running upward from the hindbrain toward the midbrain is a complex network of neurons known collectively as the **reticular activating system.** It is made of relatively few neurons that seem to monitor the general level of activity in the hindbrain, maintaining a state of arousal. Wakefulness and sleep are regulated in part by this portion of the brain. Sleeping animals whose reticular systems are stimulated by electrodes usually will awaken. If the reticular system is severely damaged, a permanent state of sleep may result. The reticular system also seems to be important in helping to focus attention or to make an organism alert. As you can see, the hindbrain, which is old in evolutionary terms, contains structures vital to the survival of all animals.

The Midbrain

The upper portions of the reticular formation are found in the midbrain along with important sensory-processing and relay areas. These areas modify visual and auditory messages and also function as sensory amplifiers or suppressors. Have you ever wondered why a subtle motion seen out of the corner of your eye can be so attention grabbing? Part of the reason may be that your midbrain has amplified it (Meredith & Stein, 1983). Such a mechanism is valuable for you or for any animal to possess, considering that what you spot out of the corner of your eye might be a hungry predator or insurance salesman who is sneaking up on you.

The Forebrain

The forebrain includes the thalamus, the hypothalamus, the limbic system, the corpus callosum, and the cerebrum.

THE THALAMUS. Buried beneath the cerebral cortex on top of the brain stem are two structures lying on either side of the brain and shaped something like large eggs. These are the left and right halves of the **thalamus.** We know of two important functions that are served by the millions, or perhaps billions, of neurons that make up the thalamus. Like the reticular activating system, the thalamus seems to be involved in wakefulness and sleep. Perhaps more important, the thalamus is a relay and translation center for sensory information. Before continuing on to higher brain structures, information from the senses passes through the thalamus. There is one exception, however, and that is the sense of smell. Olfactory (smell) messages from the nose bypass the thalamus, traveling directly to the area know as the **olfactory bulb.** The sense of smell may be a very old sense and may have evolved in its own direction, while the newer senses have taken advantage of the relatively newer areas of the brain and have become associated with them (Nauta & Feirtag, 1979). It is assumed that sensory information other than olfactory must be processed by being passed through the synaptic connections in the thalamus, for the messages to be understood at the higher brain levels.

PONS
Part of the brain stem lying just above the medulla and regulating motor messages traveling from the higher brain downward through the pons to the cerebellum. It also regulates sensory information.

RETICULAR ACTIVATING SYSTEM
A complex network of neurons that monitors the general level of activity in the hindbrain, maintaining a state of arousal.

THALAMUS
Part of the forebrain that relays sensory information and is involved in wakefulness and sleep.

OLFACTORY BULB
A mass of cells in the forebrain associated with the sense of smell. The olfactory nerve fibers enter and form a tract leading farther into the brain.

HYPOTHALAMUS
An elongated structure in the forebrain that appears to control an entire range of autonomic functions, including sleep, body temperature, hunger, and thirst.

LIMBIC SYSTEM
An aggregate of brain structures, the two major components of which are the amygdala and the hippocampus. Some of its major functions include attention, memory, emotion, and motivation.

AMYGDALA
A small bulb at the front of the brain that is associated with emotion. It is part of the limbic system.

HIPPOCAMPUS
A small area at the back of the forebrain that is known to be important in the memory process. It is part of the limbic system.

The olfactory sense, or sense of smell, is evolutionarily very old. Olfactory messages are the only sense messages to bypass the thalamus, traveling directly to the olfactory bulb.

THE HYPOTHALAMUS. The **hypothalamus** is an elongated structure located in front of and between the thalamus orbs. Although it is a relatively small structure in the brain, it has been the focus of intense interest because it appears to play many important roles. The hypothalamus apparently controls an entire range of autonomic functions. It takes part in regulating sleep and wakefulness and in controlling body temperature, hunger, and thirst (see Chapter 9 for greater detail). Blood pressure and metabolism also are related to activities within the hypothalamus. At the lower tip of the hypothalamus, and partly under its control, is the pituitary gland, which controls many hormonal secretions. Because the hypothalamus is related to the endocrine (hormonal) system, it has been implicated in the control of sexual behavior and reproductive cycles as well as in aggression and reactions to stress.

THE LIMBIC SYSTEM. The **limbic system** is the portion of the brain most strongly associated with emotional responses. Structures in the limbic system also are associated with learning and memory. Located beneath the cerebral cortex, the limbic system is not a single structure but rather is an aggregation of structures, its two major components being the **amygdala** and the **hippocampus.** The limbic system also is believed to represent one of the first evolutionary developments to break away from fixed, instinctive behavioral patterns. Whereas animals such as reptiles flee, fight, or eat in stereotypical and repetitive ways, animals with limbic systems seem to be better able to modify their inherited behavior patterns to meet new demands.

The amygdala, a small bulb located in the front of the brain, is associated with memory and emotion. In monkeys, if a lesion (such as a cut) is made on one portion of the amygdala, the animal may go into a blind rage, attacking everything within sight. If a lesion is created in another part of the amygdala, the animal may respond to attacks against it without any emotional expression, remaining passive, as if nothing were happening.

The hippocampus, a small area at the back of the forebrain, is also known to be important in the memory process. Damage to either the amygdala or hippocampus can cause memory to be disrupted.

THE CORPUS CALLOSUM.   The **corpus callosum** is the most important connection between the two hemispheres of the brain. The left and right hemispheres, though separate and distinct, share information by passing neural messages back and forth. *Corpus callosum* means "hard or calloused body" in Latin. If you were to insert your fingers between the two soft hemispheres of your brain and press down, you would feel the corpus callosum as a hard surface connecting the surrounding tissue. * Certain rare forms of severe epilepsy can be controlled by cutting the corpus callosum, thereby severing the two hemispheres and creating two independent brains. Patients with such split brains show some amazing qualities, which we will investigate later in this chapter.

THE CEREBRUM.   As mentioned earlier, the cerebrum in humans contains fully 70 percent of all the neurons in the central nervous system; it is a massive portion of the brain. Throughout evolution, the cerebrum has grown larger and has become the brain's most prominent feature (see Figure 2.13).

The folds and shapes of the cerebral cortex lend themselves to a division into four main lobes. These four lobes, appearing in both left and right hemispheres, are the **frontal,** the **parietal,** the **occipital,** and the **temporal lobes** (see Figure 2.14). More than any other part of the brain, our large and complex cerebrum probably is responsible for the unique qualities that we as humans share. It is believed to give us our great capacities for thought, language, memory, and comprehension.

In 1870, while working with dogs as subjects, Gustav Fritsch and Eduard Hitzig made the first attempt at brain mapping and discovered that applying a weak electric current to an area of the cerebral cortex immediately in front of the **central sulcus,** a major fold, caused twitches in muscles on the side of the body *opposite* the brain hemisphere being stimulated. It has since been discovered that as neural fibers from one side of the body ascend through the spinal column, they cross to the opposite side at the hindbrain. As a result, the left hemisphere of the brain controls the right side of the body, and the right hemisphere controls the left side of the body. If a person suffers a stroke that leaves the left side of his body paralyzed, the neurosurgeon knows that the stroke must have occurred in the right cerebral hemisphere, and vice versa.

Further experiments along this line have revealed areas along the cerebral cortex that are responsible for both sensory and motor stimulation. At the back of the frontal lobe, just in front of the central sulcus, lies the **motor area** that controls the body's movement. Electrical stimulation anywhere in this area can produce contractions in particular skeletal muscles. Figure 2.15 shows which muscles are controlled by the different portions of the motor area. As you can see, much of the motor area is reserved for control of the hands, which in our species are extremely important. Another large area is given over to the control of the lips and the mouth—speech is also an important behavior in our species. If you had less brain to control these functions, you might find it impossible to be articulate, that is, to make sounds necessary for language. Similarly, if you had less brain available for hand control, you might find you were clumsy in using your hands and less able to make delicate movements such as writing.

Directly behind the central fissure at the start of the parietal lobe is a section known as the **somatosensory area.** If this area is electrically stimulated, a sensation will be perceived as though a message had been received by the brain from another place in the body. For instance, a subject may feel a tingling on her finger, or

CORPUS CALLOSUM
The structure that connects the two cerebral hemispheres to each other. When it is severed, the two hemispheres can no longer communicate with each other.

FRONTAL LOBES
The portion of each hemisphere of the cerebrum extending from the very front of the cerebrum to the central sulcus. It includes the primary motor association areas, and it is known to be involved with emotion and language.

PARIETAL LOBES
The top portion of each hemisphere of the cerebrum extending from the central sulcus to the beginning of the occipital lobes. The parietal lobes contain the primary somatosensory area as well as association areas, including language areas.

OCCIPITAL LOBES
The hind portion of each hemisphere of the cerebrum. The primary visual areas are contained within the occipital lobes.

TEMPORAL LOBES
The portion of each hemisphere of the cerebrum on either side of the head near the temples. The temporal lobes contain the primary auditory areas, as well as association areas. They have to do with emotion, vision, and language.

CENTRAL SULCUS
A major fissure in the brain, also known as the fissure of Rolando, which separates the frontal from the parietal lobes.

MOTOR AREA
An area of the cerebrum that control body movement. It is located in front of the brain's central sulcus.

SOMATOSENSORY AREA
An area in the cerebrum that controls sensation. It is located behind the central sulcus at the start of the parietal lobe.

---

*Be sure to wash your hands before trying this.

FIGURE 2.13

The progressive increase in the size of the cerebrum in vertebrates is evident in these drawings, which show a representative selection of vertebrate brains, all drawn to the same scale. In vertebrates lower than mammals the cerebrum is small. In carnivores, and particularly in primates, it increases dramatically in both size and complexity. (SOURCE: Hubel, 1979, pp. 46–47.)

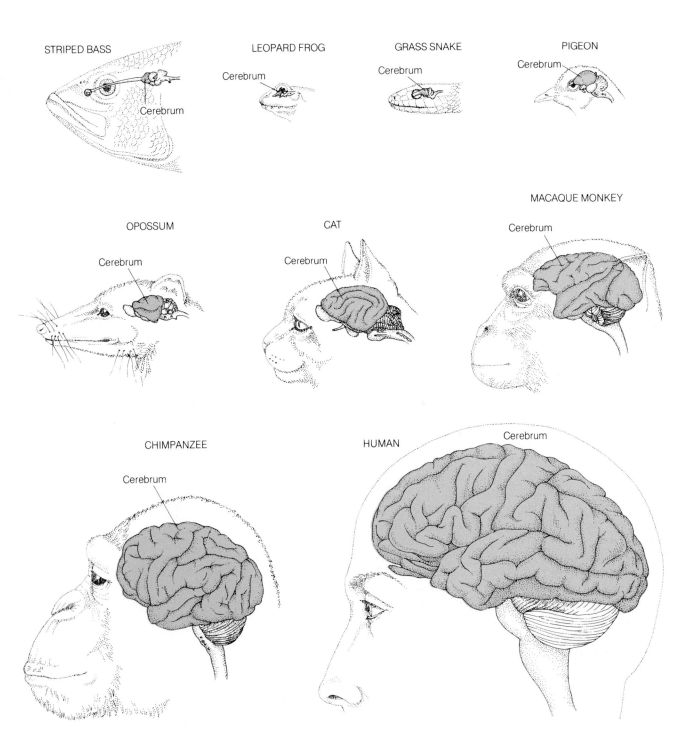

STRIPED BASS
Cerebrum

LEOPARD FROG
Cerebrum

GRASS SNAKE
Cerebrum

PIGEON
Cerebrum

OPOSSUM
Cerebrum

CAT
Cerebrum

MACAQUE MONKEY
Cerebrum

CHIMPANZEE
Cerebrum

HUMAN
Cerebrum

FIGURE 2.14

The four lobes of the cerebral cortex.

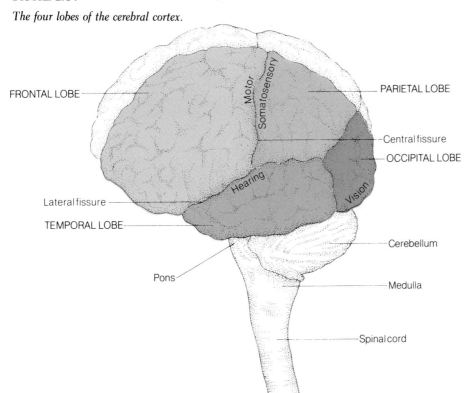

pressure on her lips. Again, a large part of this area is associated with the hands, lips, and tongue (see Figure 2.15).

The occipital lobes form the **visual cortex.** Because the cells in the occipital lobes respond to visual information, if you are struck on the back of the head and the shock causes visual neurons to fire, you will see stars. Or, more exactly, firing will cause you to perceive little points of light. These same points of light can be created by touching the visual cortex with an electrode carrying a mild current.

Most visual information is sent—or, as neuropsychologists say, projected—to the occipital lobes. However, many aspects of vision are also processed by the temporal or parietal lobes. In fact, vision is so important to our species, that fully 50 percent of the cerebral cortex is devoted to processing visual messages (Glickstein, 1988)!

Besides processing visual information, the temporal lobes also receive auditory messages arriving from the ears. If a person's temporal lobes are electrically stimulated, she will perceive sounds. Messages from all of the senses also are integrated in the temporal lobes.

The parts of the cerebral cortex other than the sensory and motor areas are known collectively as **association areas.** Association areas appear to be linked with language, thinking, and memory, and they may even be specialized to control certain scientific or artistic abilities.

VISUAL CORTEX
An area in the brain through which most visual information is processed. It is located in the occipital lobes.

ASSOCIATION AREAS
The parts of the cerebral cortex, other than the sensory and motor areas, that appear to be linked with language, thinking, and memory.

BRAIN SCANNERS: PET AND MRI

Always structure, never function, that's been the problem: Whenever psychologists or neurologists looked at the brain as we have been doing, they saw structure. If

FIGURE 2.15

Somatic sensory and motor regions of the cerebral cortex are specialized; every site in these regions can be associated with some part of the body. In other words, most of the body can be mapped onto the cortex. The distortions come about because the area of the cortex dedicated to *a part of the body is proportional not to that part's actual size but to the precision with which it must be controlled. In humans the motor and somatic sensory regions given over to the face and to the hands are greatly exaggerated. Only one-half of each cortical region is shown: the* *left somatic sensory area (which receives sensations primarily from the right side of the body) and the right motor cortex (which exercises control over movement in the left half of the body). (SOURCE: Geschwind, 1979, p. 182.)*

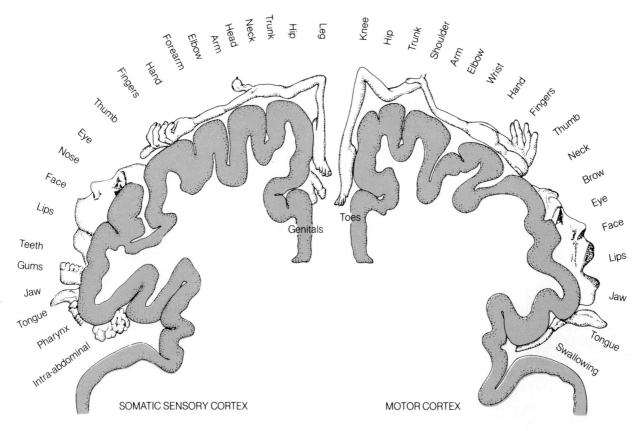

SOMATIC SENSORY CORTEX   MOTOR CORTEX

POSITRON EMISSION TOMOGRAPHY (PET)
A technique by which organ functions, especially brain function, can be directly observed. A scanning device monitors the emission of radiation following the injection of a positron-emitting substance that gathers in specific locations determined by ongoing organ functions.

they opened the skull, they could see the structure. If they cut sections of the brain and put them under slides, they could see the structure. If they scanned the brain with X rays, they could see the structure. Most of our discussion about the brain so far has been related to its parts and structure. No one could actually observe what was going on inside a live brain—at least not with much detail. But it is now possible to observe the brain as it functions, and psychologists and other scientists are seeing the brain in a completely new light (Andreasen, 1988). The breakthrough is the **positron-emission tomography (PET) scan**. Positrons are atomic particles that are emitted by some radioactive substances. If a radioactive substance that emits positrons is placed in the body, sensors can monitor the positrons wherever they go.

Despite what you might have heard about fish being brain food, the brain runs on sugar (glucose). As different parts of the brain become active, they demand more sugar. Consequently, one substance used for the PET scan is a kind of radioactive sugar that emits positrons. When one part of the brain becomes active, the radioactive sugar races to that location, and the machine scanning the brain registers high-positron emissions coming from that area of the brain.

For safety reasons, the radioactive substances used quickly lose their strength (have a short half-life); researchers must therefore rush to administer the injection and to complete the scan before the positron-emitting substance finishes radiating. Once the substance is in the body and on its way to the brain, the functioning of the brain can be observed. If, for example, the patient hears someone speak, or listens to music, or thinks, or remembers, or moves, the portion of the brain that is activated can be observed on the scanner (see Figure 2.16).

Thanks to the PET scan, we are learning that some areas of the brain perform functions we never suspected. One of the PET scan's most exciting potentials is in the diagnosis and investigation of mental illness. Although research results are tentative and are open to some interpretation, early evidence from PET scans indicates that the brains of patients with certain forms of mental illness appear consistently different from the brains of normal subjects (see Chapter 15). Dr. Tibor Farkas, a psychiatrist working the PET scan, has said:

> By the year 2000, this [PET scanning] will be the standard method of psychiatric evaluation. Today, if a man complains to his physician of chest pains, he is routinely sent to have an electrocardiogram. [By the year 2000], if a man complains to his psychiatrist of hallucinations or delusions, he will routinely be sent for diagnosis by the PET scan. (Landis, 1980, p. 28)

Another exciting aspect of the PET scan is its ability to trace neurotransmitters as they travel throughout the brain. Using this technique, researchers can observe with greater accuracy where the neurotransmitters go and with which parts of the brain they interact. Researchers have already used a positron-emitting substance

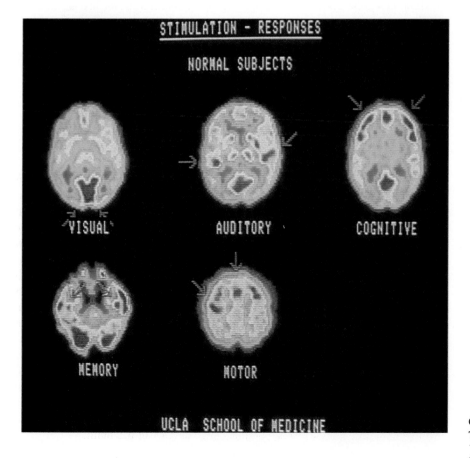

FIGURE 2.16

In these PET scans of the human brain, different areas are seen to respond (red indicates highest intensity) when presented with different stimuli. For example, visual stimulation excites the occipital lobes and auditory stimulation excites the temporal lobes.

known to bind with dopamine receptors to locate and image the dopamine receptors
in a living brain (Wagner et al., 1983). In Figure 2.17 you can observe the red
and yellow areas that highlight where the dopamine receptors are concentrated.
The ability to observe neurotransmitters at work will help to advance our understanding of the brain and perhaps will be useful as a diagnostic tool for people who
have certain mental diseases.

Unlike the PET scanner, the **magnetic-resonance imaging (MRI)** scanner allows
us to visualize structure, not function. But the MRI can image structure inside a
live body in a way that could only have been imagined a few years ago. Unlike an
X-ray machine, the MRI scanner uses harmless radio waves that excite the atoms
of the body. This brief excitation creates a subtle magnetic change that is monitored
by a huge donut-shaped magnet, which surrounds the patient. The shift in magnetic
field is then interpreted by a computer, and a composite image of the inside of the
body is created. Figure 2.18 shows an MRI scan of the brain of a live human. At
first, you may mistake it for an artist's drawing, because it is so detailed. It's the
clearest look anyone has ever had inside the head of a living person. MRI is so
sensitive that it can spot the most minute tumor, it can observe the slightest clog
in an artery, and it can often tell cancerous from noncancerous cells. By using
higher-energy radio waves (also harmless), MRI can be used to analyze fluctuations
among the atoms and to identify all the chemicals that are present (Shulman,
1983). Such a technique may eventually enable researchers to identify the neurotransmitters, neuropeptides, and hormones located in whichever part of the body
they care to look! The MRI is a relatively new tool and scientists are just starting
to use it for research and diagnosis. As you can see, it makes X-ray technology
seem like a stone-age tool.

These new tools and others are opening up the brain as never before. In fact,
new discoveries are coming so quickly owing to such new technologies, and researchers are predicting that many more major discoveries in neuroscience are just
around the corner, that the United States Congress has designated the 1990s as
the "decade of the brain." As you explore this amazing organ further, you will
begin to understand the profound implications of such discoveries.

THE BRAIN AND BEHAVIOR

Scientists and psychologists have known for years that the way in which the brain
functions directly affects behavior. We have learned much about the relationship
between specific parts of the brain and specific behaviors by studying patients with
brain injury and disease. The first comprehensive studies of this kind were conducted
on patients who had received brain injuries during World War I. Researchers
discovered that damage to the left side of the brain brought about changes on the
right side of the body, and vice versa. They also found that damage to the frontal
lobes could cause personality changes (as in the case of Phineas Gage, recounted
in Chapter 1). Damage to the temporal lobes often affected hearing, and damage
to the occipital lobes often affected sight (see Focus on Research). A further discovery was that damage to the left side of the brain more often affected language
ability than did damage to the right side of the brain. Since that time, we have
learned that most adults have specific centers for language in the left side of the
brain. In some people, however, this organization is reversed. Whatever the case,
the halves of the brain are not identical.

FIGURE 2.17

*The neurotransmitter dopamine can be
seen in this PET scan concentrating in
the areas of the brain where it is required.
By attaching positron-emitting substances
to neurotransmitters, researchers hope to
discover their destinations in the brain
and to observe their concentrations when
the brain functions. Such research has
vast potential for providing a better
understanding of the brain and our
behavior.*

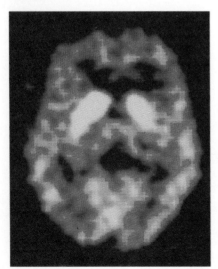

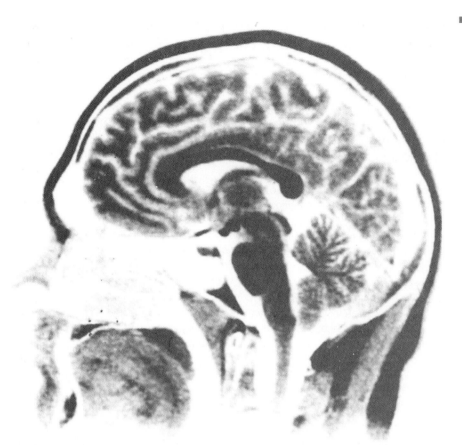

FIGURE 2.18

This MRI scan of a live brain shows structural detail with greater clarity than could ever be produced by an X-ray photograph. In addition, the MRI scan is safer than radiography, as it uses harmless radio waves to produce its pictures. The MRI is also able to identify the chemistry within any given structure of a living system. By looking carefully at this picture, you should be able to identify the parts of the brain highlighted in the color drawing of Figure 2.11 on page 57.

Specialized Areas in the Brain

To show how specialized certain portions of the brain are, we will examine some of the findings that have come about as a result of brain injuries, diseases, or accidents, beginning with the case of Charles Whitman in Texas. One morning in 1966, Whitman, a young man with no previous history of violence, awoke, picked up a rifle and a pistol, and shot and killed his wife and his mother. Then, he calmly gathered up his weapons, food, and water, and went to a university campus, where he climbed to the top of a bell tower, took out his rifle, and proceeded to shoot 38 people. It took police many hours to corner him; he died in a shoot-out.

We've all heard of cases of unexplained violence and aggression, in which someone seems to explode and murders innocent people. In the case of Charles Whitman, however, there may be some clue to the sudden and horrible change in his behavior. During an autopsy of his brain, a malignant tumor was discovered pressing against the amygdala, which, as you may recall, is part of the limbic system. This cancerous tumor eventually would have caused Whitman's death. It had been undetected until the autopsy and, because of its deep location beneath the cerebral cortex, it could not have been operated on even if detected. Was his act the first symptom of the tumor's existence? It is known that the amygdala and the limbic system are involved in emotional response. If this area is stimulated in cats, the cats react with tremendous rage, arching their backs, spitting and hissing, fighting with anything that comes near. Could Charles Whitman's act have been a rage response that he could not comprehend or contain? The rest of his brain was working normally. He was able to think of a plan by which to express his rage,

THE MAN WHO MISTOOK HIS WIFE FOR A HAT

When neurologist Oliver Sacks greeted Dr. P., his new patient, he wasn't sure what to expect. Mrs. P. had asked for help. Her husband, she said, was having severe problems. However, Dr. P., a respected music teacher at a local school, seemed to be all right. Dr. Sacks did discover on testing a slight weakness on Dr. P.'s left side, but nothing exceptional. Other than that, Dr. P. was charming, friendly, intelligent and appeared quite normal. His vision, which some people had seemed to think was poor, was, in fact, quite good.

With the examination completed, Dr. Sacks noticed that his patient hadn't yet put his shoes back on. Dr. Sacks indicated that it was all right for Dr. P. to dress now—to put on his shoes. It was then that Dr. P., indicating his foot, asked, "That is my shoe, yes?" (Sacks, 1985, p. 9). Dr. Sacks, somewhat in a state of shock, said, "No, it is not. That is your foot. There is your shoe." Dr. P. responded, "Ah! I thought it was my foot." Obviously, the examination was not finished! What in the world could be wrong?

Dr. Sacks then showed his patient a picture from a magazine and asked him to tell what he saw. Dr. P.'s eyes darted about, picking up bits and pieces of the scene, but failing to get much of it. Acting as though he had done well on this test, Dr. P., as he prepared to leave, reached over and took hold of the top of his wife's head and tried to lift it onto the top of his own. He had mistaken his wife for his hat! Well that did it. Dr. P. definitely needed to be examined further.

Soon, the real problem became apparent. During a later examination, Dr. Sacks tried one particular test that's worth describing because it highlights Dr. P.'s problem. In Dr. Sacks own words,

"What is this?" I asked, holding up a glove.

"May I examine it?" he asked, and, taking it from me, he proceeded to examine it. . . .

"A continuous surface," he announced at last, "infolded on itself. It appears to have"—he hesitated—"five outpouchings, if this is the word."

"Yes," I said cautiously. "You have given me a description. Now tell me what it is."

"A container of some sort?"

"Yes," I said, "and what would it contain?"

"It would contain its contents!" said Dr. P., with a laugh. "There are many possibilities. It could be a change-purse, for example, for coins of five sizes. It could . . ."

I interrupted the barmy flow. "Does it not look familiar? Do you think it might contain, might fit, a part of your body?"

No light of recognition dawned on his face.

No child would have the power to see and speak of "a continuous surface . . . infolded on itself," but any child, any infant, would immediately know a glove as a glove, see it as familiar, as going with a hand. Dr. P. didn't. (Sacks, 1985, p. 13)

Dr. P., as it turned out, had an inoperable tumor in his right occipital lobe. It had caused his strange problems. Dr. P. could see in the way that a computer might be able to see. He saw lines, angles, details, shapes, but he never could see the "big picture," he couldn't see the "Gestalt," he couldn't see what it was he was looking at. He knew the shapes and angles of his hat (and his wife's head), but he didn't see the wholeness of "wife's head" or "hat." This lost ability apparently was something that his right hemisphere would normally have provided him, had it not been damaged.

Even with this strange problem, Dr. P. was able to function with the help of his wife, who laid out his clothes each day in exactly the same spot and arranged his breakfast and other routines in a set order. In this way, Dr. P. knew he was, in fact, putting on clothes and eating breakfast. He was even able to teach music, which he did until his death brought on by the tumor some months later.

and he had the motor coordination necessary to carry it out. But had something interfered with the portion of his brain that normally enabled him to maintain emotional control? We may never know the answers to these questions, but the autopsy has given us a hint about what may have set off Whitman's rampage.

In our earlier discussion of the hippocampus, we mentioned that part of its function is related to memory. The first indication of this relationship appeared 30 years ago when a neurosurgeon performed a radical surgical procedure on a patient that destroyed much of the hippocampus and several associated areas in both temporal lobes, in order to stop progressively worsening epileptic seizures (Geschwind, 1979). After the operation, the patient's memory seemed to be intact, and he was still able to attend to ongoing events. However, it soon became obvious that he was unable to remember any of these *new* events! Psychologists have long been aware that there are two types of memory, short-term and long-term. Short-term memory holds information for about 30 seconds, and enables you to recall such things as an unfamiliar telephone number long enough to dial it. Long-term memory contains information that you've retained for a long time and are not likely to forget. In the case of this particular patient, the operation had apparently destroyed his long-term memory capacity for acquiring new information, while his short-term memory was unaffected. Consequently, information that had been logged in the long-term memory prior to the operation was intact, but no new information could be stored (with the exception, interestingly, of new motor skills, probably because such skills depend on a different memory system—see chapter 7). If someone came into the room and was introduced to the patient, the patient would reach out, shake hands, introduce himself, and learn the individual's name. The entire introduction would seem completely normal. But if this individual left the room for a couple of minutes and then reentered, the patient would not be able to recall anything about the previous introduction, and he would act as though he were meeting the person for the first time. Horribly, the man now had to live from moment to moment, unable to learn his new address or to remember the location of even the simplest everyday object. And each day he was shocked to see how old he looked in the mirror—which, of course, he forgot about 30 seconds after leaving the mirror.

On the underside of both occipital lobes is a part of the brain that has a special purpose—the recognition of faces. In normal individuals, the ability to recognize people by their faces is truly remarkable. Our brains are well organized to attend to unique features such as head, eye, nose, and mouth shapes, to the sharpness or softness of features. We know about the function of this area of the brain because of what happens to people when the area is damaged. They can no longer recognize faces, a disorder known as **prosopagnosia.** This disorder is accompanied by almost no other neurological or physiological symptoms. Occasionally, there is some loss of vision, but the person continues to be able to perform most tasks, including those that require information processing, without difficulty. The one thing a person with prosopagnosia cannot do is look at another person's face and put a name to it. Even spouses and children may be unfamiliar. It is not that individuals suffering from this disorder don't know who their wives, husbands, or children are; they simply cannot match faces with identities. For instance, a person may not realize that the child she can plainly see is her child until she hears the child's voice. Although she can see and describe the face in fine detail, and even match the face with a photograph, she's unable to form the associations between that particular face and a particular identity (Geschwind, 1979). Researchers have shown that sufferers of prosopagnosia do "know" the faces of familiar people as indicated by their heightened neural responses when viewing familiar faces (Tranel & Damasio, 1985). This finding leads to the conclusion that the disorder is due to a failure of visual and associative memories to get together rather than to a loss of visual memory.

In the left side of the brain are a number of areas that are involved in the production and organization of language. **Broca's area** is one of them. Damage to Broca's area following a stroke or other condition may result in **aphasia,** the absence of ability to speak or severe difficulty in speaking. That the problem is with speech itself, and not with the muscles involved in speaking, is evident because individuals with damage to Broca's area can sing words without difficulty! (A diagram of Broca's area and a more detailed description of the brain and language can be found in Chapter 8, pages 281–282).

PROSOPAGNOSIA
A disorder in which the subject can no longer recognize faces. It is rarely accompanied by other neurological or physiological symptoms.

BROCA'S AREA
An area in the lateral frontal lobe (in the left hemisphere in most cases) that is associated with language production.

APHASIA
Loss of the ability to understand or to use speech; usually the result of brain damage.

Scientists also have found the brain to be somewhat flexible, or plastic. They have known for a long time that if some areas of the brain are damaged, other areas may take over the damaged portion's functions. For instance, when a person has suffered a stroke that has left the language center in her left cerebral hemisphere damaged, she can sometimes regain her lost language ability through the use of nearby portions of her brain. Such **plasticity** is most apparent in young children, especially under the age of 6 or 7 years. If the language center in the left cerebral hemisphere of a young child is destroyed, the right cerebral hemisphere may take over and provide all the lost language function. Plasticity, especially in young children, is probably a result of the way in which the neuronal system develops in the brain (Kolb, 1989). Newborns have many more neurons in their brains than do adults! As the infant grows and gains experiences, neurons are eliminated in a whittling-down process. Some researchers have estimated that neurons in infants die at a rate of about 2 per second (Miller, 1985a). If, during this time, some area is damaged or destroyed, there may be many more neurons ready to take over. By the time a person reaches middle childhood, the number of neurons appears to become stable. Recently, however, it has been discovered that new neurons do appear and grow in the adult brains of birds. It might, therefore, not be unreasonable to assume that the same sort of *neurogenesis* might also be occurring, to a limited degree, in the adult human brain, although it has yet to be proven (Nottebohm, 1989).

No discussion of the brain and behavior would be complete without examining split-brain research—research with subjects who have had the corpus callosum severed and whose left and right hemispheres are now functioning independently. This work has provided some of the most outstanding discoveries in the field.

The Split Brain

Occasionally, when a person suffers from a severe form of **epilepsy** and cannot be treated in any other way, the corpus callosum connecting the two hemispheres of the brain is severed. This prevents the spreading of the epileptic seizure from one hemisphere to the other (Bogen, Fisher, & Vogel, 1965).

In the early 1950s, R. E. Myers and R. W. Sperry made a startling discovery when examining cats in whom the corpus callosum had been cut. They found that the right hemisphere could learn something while the left hemisphere remained ignorant of what had been learned, and vice versa! Over the next three decades Sperry, working at the California Institute of Technology, and M. S. Gazzaniga, working at Cornell University Medical College, added to our knowledge about the divided hemispheres. In sum, in human patients with split brains, the two hemispheres of the brain function differently.

If you were to meet a patient with a split brain, you most likely would not notice anything unusual about him. To find a difference you would have to conduct some tests—for instance, of the seeing process (Gazzaniga, 1970). Figure 2.19 shows how the nerves that carry information from the eyes are organized. Each eye independently sends messages to both hemispheres. The retina (the back part of each eye that contains light-sensitive neurons) has evolved so that the left halves of both retinas send their visual messages to the left hemisphere, while the right halves of both retinas send messages to the right hemisphere.

Even a split-brain patient looking directly at something with only one eye will receive visual messages in both hemispheres. However, if something is glimpsed briefly out of the corners of the eyes, the situation is different. Look again at Figure 2.19; imagine that something has been briefly glimpsed in the far-right field of vision while the eyes were looking straight ahead. Due to the extreme angle, only the left halves of both retinas will see it. Similarly, the left halves of both retinas

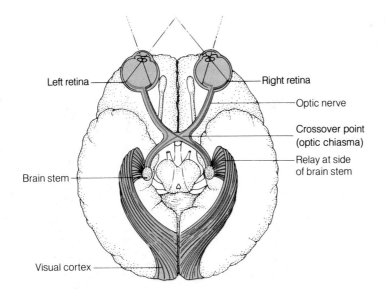

FIGURE 2.19

The left and right eyes send messages to both hemispheres because of the crossover at the optic chiasma. However, the right halves of the retinas of both eyes send messages to only the right hemisphere, while the left halves send messages to only the left hemisphere.

Left retina

Right retina

Optic nerve

Crossover point (optic chiasma)

Relay at side of brain stem

Brain stem

Visual cortex

cannot sense objects far off in the left field of vision. Because of this, in both you and a split-brain patient, something glimpsed out of the corners of the eyes will be projected to only one hemisphere. Unlike you, however, the split-brain patient's receiving hemisphere cannot share this information with the other hemisphere because the connections between the two halves have been cut.

A split-brain person usually has no trouble interpreting such visual messages when they are sent to the *left* hemisphere because that is where the language-capable portions of the brain are typically found. Whatever object or photograph is presented to him, he can tell you what it is. However, if an image is presented off in the *left* visual field, so that it is sent only to the *right* hemisphere, the split-brain person may be unable to tell you what he has seen. This is because the right hemisphere typically has poor language and speech ability compared with the left hemisphere. In most people, the left hemisphere can speak and describe what it has seen, but the right hemisphere, although it too can see, often cannot say what it has seen! But it has seen the object. As proof, consider the following experiment. A number of objects, such as a spoon, a block, a ball, and a toy car, are hidden behind a cloth barrier so that the split-brain patient cannot see them. Then, a photograph of one of the objects is shown off at an angle so that only the right hemisphere registers it and the left brain is ignorant of what has been seen. The split-brain patient will say that she does not know what the picture is (after all, her left brain doesn't know!) In an individual whose corpus callosum has not been severed, the right brain would send the visual information to the left brain and the left brain could then say what had been seen. But, although the split-brain patient usually can't articulate what her right brain saw, she can find the object by reaching behind the curtain *with her left hand* and feeling for it! This is because the right brain, which controls the left hand, knows what the object is and what it should feel like, even though it cannot put this knowledge into words!

It should be noted that some split-brain patients do not show such remarkable differences between hemispheres (Zaidel, 1983; Myers, 1984). This illustrates how variable brain organization can be from one person to the next. Generally, however, it does appear that the left hemisphere of the brain is organized in a way that facilitates language recognition and production (Gazzaniga, 1983; MacKain, Studdert-Kennedy, Spieker, & Stern, 1983).

One of the most striking findings to come from split-brain research is the implication that the brain operates via interconnecting "modules" that are relatively independent. By modules, we mean that each part of the brain has a task to do and works on that task in parallel with other brain modules that are busy working on their tasks. Once each module has done its job, the efforts of each module are combined and integrated. Evidence for this concept of the brain comes from partially split-brained individuals whose corpus callosums were only partly severed (which is often enough to control epileptic seizures) and from stroke victims and others who suffered some form of brain damage. In these individuals integration does not occur. For instance, Michael Gazzaniga has reported a patient who, after some very specific damage, was able to name fruits or red objects, but not red fruits (Gazzaniga, 1989). As another example, consider the partially split-brained patient who *was* able to compare two words when each word was directed to a separate hemisphere, but only if the words looked or sounded alike! Some part of his remaining callosum was able to pass along a comparison of things "looking or sounding alike" but nothing else (Gazzaniga, 1989). This, of course, is an example of a very specific task, probably carried out by one of the brain's many modules.

Split-brain research has also yielded information that indicates the existence of a very special interpreter in the left hemisphere. To illustrate this, let's look at an experiment conducted not long ago by Michael Gazzaniga on a 15-year-old split-brained boy named P.S.

In the laboratory, two pictures were shown to P.S., one to each hemisphere. The left hemisphere was shown a chicken claw, while the right saw a snow scene. P.S. was then shown a number of pictures on cards and asked to pick the one that went with the picture he had seen. His right hand pointed to a picture of a chicken (remember his left hemisphere had seen the chicken claw), but his left hand pointed to a snow shovel (his right hemisphere had seen the snow scene—see Figure 2.20). This was what Gazzaniga had expected. But when P.S. was asked why he had

FIGURE 2.20

Here the left brain sees only the claw, the right brain only the snow scene. The left-brain "interpreter" must generate an hypothesis to explain why one hand is pointing to a snow shovel. (SOURCE: Gazzaniga, 1985, p. 32.)

AN ENDURING QUESTION: WHAT AND WHERE IS THE MIND?

The greatest unanswered question in this chapter may well be the greatest unanswered question of all time. Philosophers have struggled with it for centuries. Perhaps, some day, we will know enough about the brain to find the answer. The question is simply, "Where and what are *you?*"

Somewhere, probably among the cells of your brain, is you. Call it your spirit, your soul, your "youness," your consciousness—whatever—we all feel it, the sense of being alive, looking out of our eyes, hearing with our ears, thinking things over in our minds. But what is "you?"

Visual images enter your eyes, travel from one lobe to the next, but where are you? Where is the conscious person who *sees* the image? If we are just a collection of biological parts, then where is the "ghost in the machine" as philosophers used to ask? This has come to be known as the **mind–body problem** and solving it, if it can be solved, will be one of the greatest accomplishments in all of human history.

With our modern understanding of anatomy and biology, most scientists today argue that conscious experience, the sense of being somewhere inside of your body, is an interesting illusion created by the interaction of the brain's modules, much in the same way as the illusion of white is generated by the equal mixing of red, green, and blue lights. This position is known as the **materialist hypothesis.**

And yet, certain problems remain. Consider the following: You are sitting in a chair. Now pretend that I have a machine that can create an *exact* copy of you, right down to the last atom or electron. The copy appears in the chair next to you. It, of course, looks just like you. It has all of your memories. In fact, its "last" memory is sitting where you are and it is very surprised to find that it has "moved." It *is* you, and yet it isn't, because you aren't *in* that body (at least, I don't think that you would be!). But if you aren't in that body, why aren't you? Is someone else in there? If your bodies are *exactly* the same, *why is there a difference between you?* Maybe you are different from the copy because you each have a different spirit, a spirit that is not made of anything physical that the machine could copy. This view is called the **dualist hypothesis** and is currently unpopular among scientists, probably because the idea of nonmaterial spirits sounds too much like ghosts and phantoms to suit the tastes of anyone holding onto hard science, and also because there is, so far, absolutely no respectable evidence to support the existence of any such energy, force, or entity.

And yet, why are you you, and not someone else? What determines that? Something about conscious existence is obviously very, very peculiar. Whatever conscious awareness actually turns out to be may well be beyond our wildest dreams or anyone's science fiction. Maybe some day we will know.

FOR CRITICAL ANALYSIS

1. How do you know that everyone else has a mind or "spirit?" Couldn't it be that only a few of us do, while the others are merely biological "machines" that will say that they have minds when asked, but are, in fact, empty bodies in which no one is home; much like a movie projector running with the lamp off. Perhaps possessing a mind is like having blue eyes, some do, some don't. Or, perhaps you are the only one with a mind and all of the rest of us are zombies. Or, even more frightening, could the spirit die before the body? If that could happen, then one day "you" might simply cease to exist, and yet, no one else would be aware that anything unusual had happened to you because your body would go right on

THE MIND–BODY PROBLEM
A philosophical issue as yet unresolved centering on the question of whether conscious awareness is a function of the brain, and therefore the body, or whether it is a function of a spirit that is separate from the body.

DUALIST HYPOTHESIS
The philosophical position that the mind is like a disembodied spirit, that it functions independently from the body, and that the mind and body are separate entities functioning parallel to one another.

MATERIALIST HYPOTHESIS
The philosophical position that the mind is part of the body and functions according to the laws of the physical world.

behaving and acting as usual. Can you see that there is no way for you to know whether or not any of these possibilities is true? How might a future brain science, with an advanced command of neuroanatomy, someday attempt to address these dualist dilemmas?

2. If there is no spirit, that is, if the materialist position is correct and the mind is an illusion created by the interaction of the parts of the brain, might this mean that someday machines could be built that, owing to the interaction of their parts, would have consciousness awareness? How would we ever know if they really had consciousness awareness, or were just claiming that they did? Can you see that there would be no way to ever know for sure unless *you* were the machine?

3. The philosopher Rene Descartes said, "I think, therefore I am." How does this comment refer to the idea that you are the only one who can ever know if you are consciously aware and possess a mind?

pointed to these objects, he answered right away, "Oh, that's easy. The chicken claw goes with the chicken, and you need a shovel to clean out the chicken shed" (Gazzaniga, 1985, p. 30).

Stop for a moment to consider what this means. The left hemisphere didn't know why the left hand had pointed to the shovel, so it fished around for a logical reason and came up with one—and was wrong. Based on this work and many other examples gathered over the years, Michael Gazzaniga has come to believe that there is an "interpreter" in the left hemisphere which is independent of the language areas, and which "constructs theories about . . . actions and feelings and tries to bring order and unity to our conscious lives. [It] appears to be unique to the human brain and related to the singular capacity of the brain to make causal inferences" (Gazzaniga, 1989, p. 947).

Could the same error made by P.S. occur to a degree in individuals whose brains are normal and intact? How many times have you acted on a feeling or urge and then tried to come up with the reason for your actions? Did hidden knowledge—that is, information hidden from your left brain—motivate you "unconsciously"? Research shows that these different portions of the brain, or modules, even in an individual with a healthy brain, might not always share knowledge with each other easily (Gazzaniga, 1985). Because of this, Gazzaniga argues that the interpreter may bias its views or interpretations as a result of hidden knowledge contained in other modules. For example, an emotionally neutral event might be interpreted as negative by an individual's left-brain interpreter based on unpleasant emotional experiences maintained in other modules. This hidden emotional content might then cloud or taint the interpretation given neutral experiences by the left-brain interpreter, leading to what clinical psychologists might consider depression (Gazzaniga, 1989).

Wouldn't Sigmund Freud, with his theory of the unconscious mind, have loved these studies! Not that just a few studies could validate Freud's view, but they do strongly imply the existence of motivations beyond the conscious grasp and their ability to affect our conscious thought.

EPILOGUE: MR. NIETHOLD'S TOOTHACHE

This is an account of how one man, among thousands, has directly benefited from the research described in this chapter.

When Charles Niethold walked into the dentist's office to have his tooth filled, he told his dentist that he preferred to have the procedure done without novocaine. His dentist cautioned him that there might be pain, but Niethold said, "No, it won't hurt." With this comment Niethold pulled a small radio transmitter from his pocket, extended the aerial, held the transmitter about 12 inches from his chest, and pressed a button. He then closed the antenna and put the transmitter back in his pocket, and said "OK, doc, go ahead. It won't hurt now." The dentist wasn't sure whether Mr. Niethold needed a psychologist or whether he had been taken in by some quack pushing a piece of phony equipment that was supposed to relieve pain. But the dentist, not wanting to embarrass his patient, proceeded, trying as he filled the tooth not to touch the sensitive nerve. A couple of times, he was sure he had hurt his patient and waited for a reaction, but Mr. Niethold appeared calm, collected, and even somewhat happy.

After the filling the patient said, "See, I told you it wouldn't hurt." The dentist finally broke down and asked for an explanation. Charles Niethold told him the following story.

In 1975, Mr. Niethold had seriously injured his back for the second time in a fall at work. After three operations he still was experiencing chronic pain in his lower extremities. His case was brought to the attention of the University of California Medical Center at San Francisco, and specifically to neurosurgeon Yoshio Hosobuchi. Dr. Hosobuchi operated, but not on Niethold's back, where the injury had occurred, or on his lower extremities, where he felt the pain. Instead, the neurosurgeon operated on Niethold's chest and brain. He placed a radio receiver within the chest cavity and ran wires up through the neck to the brain where he implanted small electrodes in the gray matter. The radio receiver in the chest could be operated by holding a small transmitter close to it and pressing the button on the transmitter. The receiver would then send an electrical message to the electrodes implanted in the brain. Dr. Hosobuchi had discovered that when a certain area of the brain is stimulated, the level of beta-endorphin in the central nervous system becomes two to seven times greater (Hosobuchi, Rossier, Bloom, & Guillemin, 1979). Now, whenever Mr. Niethold feels pain from his accident, he takes out his transmitter, presses the button, and the pain goes away almost magically for hours, sometimes days. Of course, not worrying about the dentist is a bonus.

SUMMARY

■ All human behavior involves, either directly or indirectly, the nervous system, of which the brain is an integral part.

■ The nervous system can be divided into a number of interrelated component parts: the central nervous system, which includes the brain and the spinal column, and the peripheral nervous system, which includes the somatic and autonomic nervous systems.

■ A nerve is made up of thousands upon thousands of individual nerve cells called neurons. Neurons communicate by using electrical impulses and secreting chemicals. The nervous system is therefore considered to be an electrochemical system.

■ Experiments in which nerves have been switched and the organism has adapted demonstrate that the brain can be flexible and adaptable.

■ The typical neuron has three distinct structural features: the soma, the dendrites, and the axon. Messages generally are received by the dendrites and transmitted by the axon. Neurons can communicate with other neurons, with glands, or with muscles when they are stimulated to action potential and discharge an impulse, called a spike, that runs the length of the axon.

■ Messages are carried from a neuron to adjacent cells when neurotransmitters are secreted into the synapse between the cells. Some synapses are excitatory, others are inhibitory. Many substances may function as neurotransmitters. Neurons often secrete more than one neurotransmitter. Stimulation of a neuron can have long-term effects by changing the neuron's membrane or by altering its neurotransmitter emissions.

■ Many drugs that affect behavior appear to mimic or alter the functions of natural body substances. Drugs that block neurotransmitter functioning are known as antagonists; those that facilitate neurotransmitters are known as agonists.

■ Transplanting healthy brain tissue from a donor to help replace damaged tissue in a recipient has proved a useful and valuable technique. Future researchers may be able to incorporate larger and more complex forms of brain transplants into their clinical technique.

■ Neurotransmitters, neuropeptides, and hormones may have long-term, dramatic, and wide-ranging effects on a great many aspects of human behavior. For instance, beta-endorphin, a neuropeptide, has been implicated in control of pain and pleasure.

■ The endocrine system comprises many glands that secrete hormones. Hormones are bloodborne informational substances that can affect neurons, muscles, or glands throughout the body.

■ The brain is extremely complex, and much of its functioning remains a mystery. Using such techniques as brain mapping, scientists are unraveling the complexities of the brain's functions.

■ The brain can be conveniently divided into three areas: the hindbrain, the midbrain, and the forebrain.

■ A massive portion of the forebrain is the cerebrum. The cortex of the cerebrum can be divided into four lobes: frontal, parietal, occipital, and temporal.

■ Modern brain scanners are helping us to explore the brain as never before. The PET (positron-emission tomography) scanner highlights brain functions, while the MRI (magnetic-resonance imaging) scanner highlights structural anatomy and chemistry.

■ We have gathered many clues to the way in which the brain functions by studying patients with brain damage and disease. For example, damage to the limbic system may cause emotional disturbances, and damage to the hippocampus may impair memory functioning. Sometimes brain injuries can result in very unusual behavior, as highlighted by the case of "the man who mistook his wife for a hat," in which Dr. P. manifested the inability to "see" the wholeness of objects, although he was still able to describe them.

■ Research with split-brain patients (in whom the corpus callosum has been severed) indicates that the left and right hemispheres of the brain might best be considered two distinct entities.

■ Research with split-brain patients also indicates that much important knowledge may be stored in the brain out of easy reach of our left hemispheres, where such knowledge could be expressed to ourselves as thoughts. Such hidden knowledge might hold important clues to our motivations for behavior.

SUGGESTIONS FOR FURTHER READING

1. Gazzaniga, Michael S. (1989). *Mind matters: How mind and brain interact to create our conscious lives.* Boston: Houghton Mifflin. For the general reader. A fascinating summary of current brain research.
2. Hooper, J., & Teresi, D. (1986). *The three-pound universe.* New York: Macmillan. Discusses the exploration of the human brain.
3. Klivington, Kenneth A. (1989). *The science of the mind.* Cambridge: MIT Press. The basics of neuroscience for the general reader. Discusses dreams, the senses, language, illness, biological clocks, brain–mind connections and more.
4. Martin, R. (1986). *Matters gray and white: A neurologist, his patients, and the mysteries of the brain.* New York: Holt. A writer follows a neurologist for more than a year and documents all aspects of his practice. Gives an interesting picture of the brain and its diseases.
5. Nauta, W. J. H., & Feirtag, M. (1986). *Fundamental neuroanatomy.* New York: W. H. Freeman. A very comprehensive guide to the brain and nervous system, including its structure and function.
6. Sacks, O. (1985). *The man who mistook his wife for a hat.* New York: Summit Books. A prominent neurologist provides some of his most fascinating case studies concerning brain and nervous system dysfunction.
7. Schneider, A., & Tarshis, B. (1985). *Physiological psychology* (3rd edition). New York: Random House. A college-level introductory textbook on the physiological aspects of psychology.
8. Snyder, Solomon H. (1989). *Brainstorming: The science and politics of opiate research.* Cambridge: Harvard University Press. The codiscoverer of the brain's endorphin receptor discusses the scientific research and political maneuverings that led to the discovery.

CHAPTER 3 | Sensation

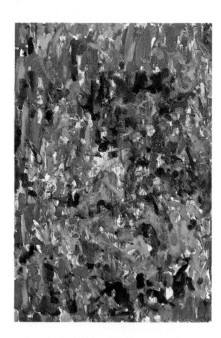

Prologue

Why Psychologists Study Sensation

Sensory Thresholds

Vision
The Retina
Dark Adaptation
Color Vision

Hearing
How Sound Is Created
The Structure of the Ear
Theories of Hearing

Taste

Smell

Touch

Kinesthetic and Vestibular Senses

Epilogue: The Ready Room

Summary

Suggestions for Further Reading

PROLOGUE: SYSTEMS CHECK

Hello. Don't be concerned. We're just conducting a systems check. We need to be sure that the equipment for this experiment is in working order before we continue. If all is going as planned, what you are now reading shouldn't be making any sense to you—but don't worry about it, just keep reading. In order to check the system, however, we will need to tell you the truth. See whether any of what we say seems familiar to you. The following is the truth—the following is what is real.

It is the thirty-fourth century. You are living in the thirty-fourth century. Like us, you have no body. Like us, you are immortal. Like all of us, you long for something new, exciting. We have always wondered what it would be like to live in a body, to be mortal the way we were thousands of years ago. Now we finally have the technology to help us find out first hand what it must have been like. To help us, you, along with many others, volunteered to become a subject in an ongoing experiment. Your mind is now incorporated into the system and all that you are sensing is artificial; that is, nothing that you are currently seeing, hearing, tasting, smelling, or feeling is "real"—it is all being created by artificial input. You are not now on the surface of Earth, and it is not the end of the twentieth century.

The system has just begun to operate. All the memories you have of the days and years gone by, all the memories of your past, your friends, and your family, are artificial and were placed in your mind only a few moments ago. The life you now think you lead, the body you now think you have, were chosen at random only a few moments ago. Is any of this

77

familiar to you, or does it seem as though you really have a body, a life history, and are just reading a textbook? If you sense that you are just reading a textbook, and that you really are who your memory says you are, then the system is functioning correctly.

We have just received information from your mind indicating that you do not believe the truth. Your lack of belief shows that the system is functioning correctly.

This system will continue to artificially input this randomly chosen "life," and end with the input of a randomly chosen "death," giving you experiences much like our forebearers must have had 14 centuries ago. At your "death," the system will terminate and you will again realize who you actually are. You are brave to participate in this experiment. It must be frightening to believe that you are mortal.

All of the words just broadcast to you will now appear in your textbook as though they had been there all along. If it helps, from time to time during your life read our words again. They are the only hint in your "life" that you will encounter as to who you really are. Our best wishes go with you.

...End Systems Check—Continue with "Life"

In this chapter, we will examine the senses, your contact with what you think is real. If this Prologue has unnerved you a little bit, and you're not quite sure anymore who you really are, then you are beginning to realize how much you rely on your senses to tell you about your world. And, oh yes, if you are curious, today's date is March 9, 3518—happy birthday! HAPPY BIRTHDAY MESSAGE IS LAST CONTACT. END CONTACT.

WHY PSYCHOLOGISTS STUDY SENSATION

> We know nothing except by experience, and experience consists of nothing but the information of our senses. Perhaps there is nothing, really, out there to be sensed. All we know is that we sense.—Judson Jerome

What would it be like to be sitting on top of a hydrogen bomb when it exploded? Most people say that whatever the feeling, it would be over quickly. Perhaps a very bright light and a tremendous noise and then nothing. Perhaps a sense of searing heat and of being hurled away. Or perhaps all of that at once, contained within a great roaring explosion, lasting (from your point of view) just a fraction of a second. Obviously, no one could experience this explosion and live to describe it. But we know the answer anyway. Imagine yourself sitting on top of a hydrogen bomb, waiting for it to detonate. You would be looking over your notebook, ready to write down your experiences, feeling the steel casing beneath you, and perhaps listening to the countdown being broadcast over the speakers from the blockhouse miles away. Then suddenly . . . there would be nothing. There would be no light, no sound, no feeling of heat. You would not have sensed anything. How can we be sure? Because we know neural messages have to be translated into electrochemical impulses before they are sent to the brain (see Chapter 2). Consequently, long before your brain had received any of the messages from your nervous system concerning any aspect of the explosion, you would have been vaporized. In fact, the odds are that you would have been vaporized long before visual, auditory, heat, or pressure neurons even had a chance to fire.

This ridiculous, but perhaps memorable, example emphasizes the fact that our senses are our only contact with the world outside our bodies. Students rarely think about the senses when they consider what psychologists might study. But, it does make sense that sensation would be of interest to psychologists when you stop to think that before we can ever experience anything, that is, before any experience can affect our minds, we must wait for sensory messages to make their way into our brains. Without messages from the senses, there could be no experience of external "reality"; without such experience, there could be little in the way of organized behavior.

You may have noticed that I put the word *reality* in quotes. That's because it is not exactly clear what reality is. Our senses determine what is "real," and what we sense as "real" is often different from what scientific experiments might tell us is "real." For instance, consider the fact that the senses are selective. There are many loud sounds that our species cannot hear, many bright lights that we cannot see, and many impacts that we cannot feel. There also are many substances that we cannot taste and many odors that we cannot smell. Our way of organizing and responding to the world depends a great deal on the way in which our senses filter or select from the stimuli, or information, around us. We come to know our world primarily through our senses, and what we sense often affects our behavior. This is perhaps the main reason why psychologists study **sensation.**

SENSORY THRESHOLDS

Your senses can inform you of the presence of a stimulus or of any change in that stimulus. Before energy such as sound or light can be sensed, however, it must satisfy two conditions. First, it must be energy to which your senses can respond. No matter how bright X-ray light is, you cannot see it. Second, the energy must be strong enough to stimulate your senses. Although delicate instruments might be able to sense the light from a match struck on a mountaintop 50 miles away on a dark night, your eyes would not be able to. The amount of energy required to create a noticeable sensation is called the **absolute threshold.** If the match had been struck at a distance of 30 miles on a dark night under the most ideal conditions, you might have been able to detect it, but just barely. This amount of energy would have been within your absolute threshold. The term is misleading, however, because the absolute threshold for any given stimulus can change depending on your physical condition or motivation.

Just as a certain amount of energy is required before you can detect a stimulus, so must the existing energy fluctuate a certain amount before you can detect a *change* in a stimulus. This minimum amount of energy fluctuation is known as the **difference threshold.** Psychologists often refer to difference thresholds as *just noticeable differences,* or JNDs. Difference thresholds also can change depending on the person's physical condition or motivation or qualities of the stimulus being tested.

An interesting aspect of just noticeable differences is that they tend to be fairly constant fractions of the stimulus intensity. For example, if you picked up a 1-pound weight and got used to the feel of it, about half an ounce could be added or subtracted from that weight before you would feel a just noticeable difference. Then, if you became accustomed to a 2-pound weight instead of to the 1-pound weight, the just noticeable difference would be closer to 1 ounce than to half an

SENSATION
Any fundamental experience of events from within or without the body as the result of stimulation of some receptor system. Distinguished from perception in that perception requires the interpretation of a sensation. This distinction is somewhat arbitrary, however, because some perception of a sensation must occur before awareness is possible.

ABSOLUTE THRESHOLD
The minimum intensity a stimulus must have in order to produce a sensation.

DIFFERENCE THRESHOLD
The minimum change that a stimulus must undergo before the change can be reliably detected; it is also called the just noticeable difference (JND).

WEBER'S LAW
The rule that the larger or stronger a stimulus, the larger the change required for an observer to notice a difference. The smallest difference in intensity between two stimuli that can be readily detected is a constant fraction of the original stimulus.

RETINA
The delicate multilayer, light-sensitive membrane lining the inner eyeball. It consists of layers of ganglion and bipolar cells and photoreceptor cells called rods and cones.

ounce. Thus, as the weight you hold is doubled, the just noticeable difference also doubles; that is, the ratio stays the same. This relationship was first described by Ernst Weber in 1834 and has come to be known as **Weber's law.** Perhaps *law* is too strong of a word, however, because although these fractions hold for a fairly wide range of stimulations, they can change drastically when the intensity of the stimulus becomes very great or very small (Carlson, Drury, & Webber, 1977).

Most people consider that there are five ways to sense: seeing, hearing, tasting, smelling, or touching. As you will soon discover, there are more than just those five. But for now, let's begin with seeing—our sense of vision.

VISION

Is the human eye like a camera? Both have a lens that light passes through and that focuses light. In addition, the eye has an iris that opens and closes, allowing more or less light to enter. Most cameras have a mechanical "iris." A camera has light-sensitive film; the eye has a light-sensitive area, the **retina.** Human beings have two retinas, one at the back of each eye, and each is filled with thousands of receptive visual cells. In a sense, the retina works like film. In fact, light-sensitive chemicals taken from the retinas of rabbits have been used successfully on film in cameras!

Once light strikes the retina, neural messages are sent farther into the brain, where cells are either stimulated or not stimulated depending on how the parts of the retina were excited by the light. Film is developed in much the same way. A picture emerges because certain parts of the film have been stimulated by light, while others haven't. When an image enters a camera, it is projected through the lens onto the film upside down. When an image enters the eye, it also is projected onto the retina upside down (see Figure 3.1). At first glance, then, the camera and the eye seem to be very similar.

Actually, nothing could be farther from the truth. Although the "camera theory" of vision is popular among the general public, it provides an extremely limited understanding of vision. There may be many parallels between the camera and the eye, but the two are actually more different than alike. The visual system, unlike a camera, sees things that aren't there and alters things that are there, and in doing so it affects our understanding of the world. Its abilities are strange and amazing.

FIGURE 3.1

Visual images received by the eye are projected onto the retina upside down.

Lens

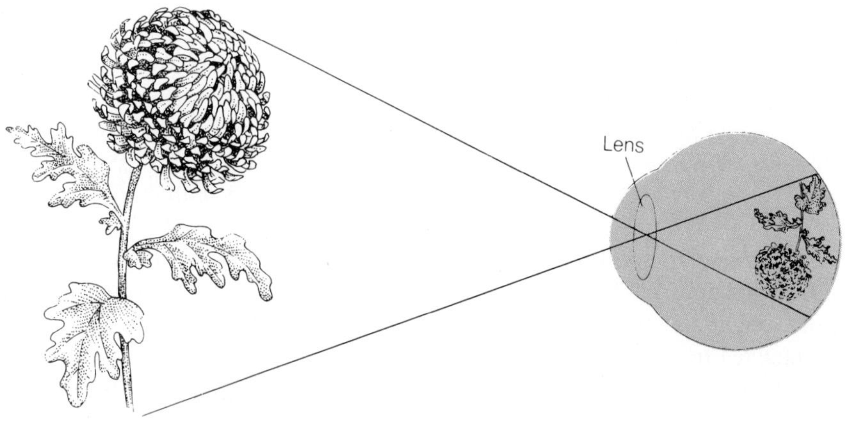

Let's consider the camera for a moment. Have you ever seen a newsreel of a dramatic event during which the photographer who was filming the action had to begin running? What happens to the camera's view of the world when the person who is holding it begins to run? The picture starts to shake violently. It looks as if an earthquake were in progress, and it's almost impossible to see what is happening. To make good movies, you must hold the camera steady, so that light entering strikes each frame of the film in roughly the same place. If you move the camera violently, the light image striking the film also will move violently; when the film is projected onto a screen, everything in the image will seem to be moving and jerking in all directions at once. If our visual system worked in the same way, we all would be walking about as gently as we could to avoid quaking motions in our view of the surrounding world. But this is not the case. You can run down a street and, although the world about you may seem to be moving, it will not be moving with the agitation that you would experience had you been taking movies as you ran. The difference lies in the fact that whereas a frame of film passively records the light that shines on it, the central nervous system interacts with the light. The retina is not a piece of film; it is an outpost of the central nervous system that is closely linked to the brain.

The Retina

Figure 3.2 shows the major parts of the human eye. The outer membrane covering, or white of the eye, is called the **sclera**. The eye itself is not made of a hard substance; its shape is maintained by the fluid within it, which is under pressure. Light entering the eye passes through the transparent **cornea** and enters the **pupil**. The **iris** regulates the amount of light passing through the lens. The **lens** focuses the light onto the retina.

Although the retina consists of ten layers, we will focus our discussion on its three major layers. The first major layer of the retina contains the **ganglion cells,** the axons of which form the **optic nerve.** The second major layer is formed by the

SCLERA
The white, elastic outer covering of the eye.

CORNEA
The transparent outer bulge in the front of the eye through which light waves pass.

PUPIL
The dark circular aperture in the center of the iris of the eye that admits light.

IRIS
The pigmented muscular membrane that controls the aperture in the center of the pupil, which determines the amount of light that enters the eye.

LENS
The transparent biconvex structure of the eye behind the iris and pupil that focuses light rays entering through the pupil to form an image on the retina.

GANGLION CELLS
Nerve cells of the retina, which receive impulses from rods and cones via the bipolar cells and transmit these impulses to the brain.

OPTIC NERVE
The bundle of nerve fibers connecting the retina and the brain.

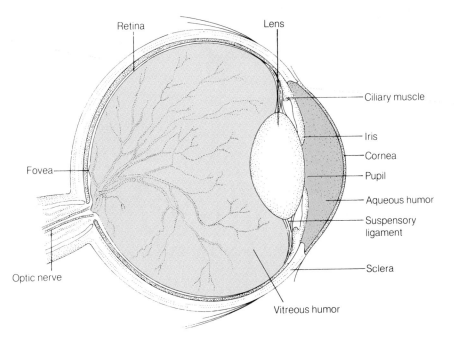

FIGURE 3.2

Structures of the human eye.

CHAPTER 3
SENSATION

81

BIPOLAR CELLS
Nerve cells of the retina, which receive impulses from rods and cones in the retina and transmit these impulses to the ganglion cells.

PHOTORECEPTOR CELLS
Light sensitive cells, called rods and cones, that comprise the third layer of the retina.

RODS
Specialized photoreceptor cells in the retina that are primarily responsive to changes in the intensity of light waves and are therefore important in peripheral vision and night vision.

CONES
Specialized photoreceptor cells in the retina that are primarily responsive to different wavelengths of light and are therefore important in color vision; cones also are associated with high visual acuity.

HORIZONTAL CELLS
Retinal cells with short dendrites and long axons that extend horizontally, linking rods with other rods and cones with other cones. These cells appear to be responsible, in part, for the effects described by the opponent-process theory of color vision.

bipolar cells. The *third* major layer, *nearest the back of the eye*, is made up of **photoreceptor cells** called **rods** and **cones,** which are sensitive to light (see Figure 3.3). When the rods and cones are stimulated by light, their neural messages travel first to the bipolar cells, next to the ganglion cells, and then down the optic nerve to higher parts of the brain. There is also evidence of lateral "cross-talk" between neighboring receptors within the same layer of the retina. These lateral connections are made by the **horizontal cells** and the **amacrine cells,** which comprise some of the retina's minor layers ("minor" in terms of thickness). All the reasons for this lateral circuitry in the retina are not known, but it may be that the lateral connections help to rectify the image and to eliminate visual errors in processing. Whatever is going on, it certainly is not the same process as that happening in a camera! Only a generation ago, people believed that the retina was fairly straightforward. After all, the retina seemed to consist of only five basic cells (ganglion, bipolar, horizontal, amacrine, and photoreceptor). As researchers explored the retina more carefully, you can guess what it turned out to be—that's right, *complicated!* For instance, we now know that in each retina there are at least 30, perhaps 50, different kinds of amacrine cells, each with its own neurotransmitter or neuropeptide (Masland, 1986). What the functions of these cells are is anybody's guess. Also, the retina is a marvel of miniaturization; it is made of perhaps the most densely packed and smallest neurons in the nervous system. In fact, if your retinas were composed of neurons of the size of those typically found in your brain, your eyes would be as big as tangerines—good perhaps for getting bit parts in science fiction films, but for little else.

THE FOVEA. If you stare at a bright white wall or a rich blue sky, you often see outlines of the blood vessels layered within your eye. In addition, many people

FIGURE 3.3

The photoreceptors of the retina. The rods and cones are embedded in a pigmented layer called the choroid. They pass on their messages to the bipolar cells. The axons of the ganglion cells from the optic nerve. Notice that, before light strikes the rods and cones, it must pass through the other layers of the retina.

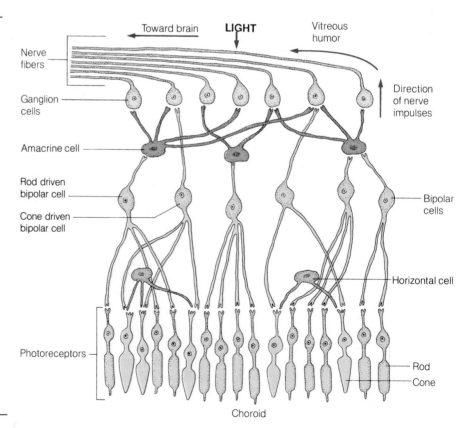

may notice blurry black specks, sometimes with little streamers attached, that seem to pass through their visual field (see Figure 3.4). These objects are called *floaters*.

How is it possible to see something that is inside your own eye? These blood vessels or floating specks interfere with the light image as it passes through the lens on its way to the retina, and, if the light is sufficiently bright and the background is homogeneous, the shadows the objects cast onto the retina become noticeable. Because the objects are inside the eye and cannot be brought into focus by the lens, they are perceived only as shadows cast onto the back of the retina. In normal daylight vision, the most sensitive portion of the eye, and the part onto which these shadows are cast, is the **fovea**. The clarity and acuity of human vision depend a great deal on this area.

Look at a single word on this page. That one word, which is projecting directly onto your fovea, will be very clear. The words around it, however, which are projecting onto peripheral portions of your retina, will be indistinct. If you try to decipher the nearby words without removing your glance from the first word, you'll find you are unable to recognize other words only a short distance away. To see something clearly, you need to focus directly on that object. Then it will be projected onto your fovea.

THE BLIND SPOT.   One portion of the peripheral retina contains no photoreceptors because it is here that the optic nerve passes through the retina on its way to the brain. Because it has no photoreceptors, this area is unable to sense light and is known as the **blind spot**. You can locate your own blind spot by following the

AMACRINE CELLS
Large retinal neurons that connect ganglion cells laterally. There are at least 30 different varieties of amacrine cell. Image rectification appears to be one of their many functions. The functions of most amacrine cells are unknown.

FOVEA
The area in the center of the retina characterized by a great density of cones and an absence of rods. Images focused on the fovea are seen with the highest acuity.

BLIND SPOT
The region of the retina where the optic nerve attaches and where there are no photoreceptors. The fovea also is a blind spot when something is viewed in very dim light.

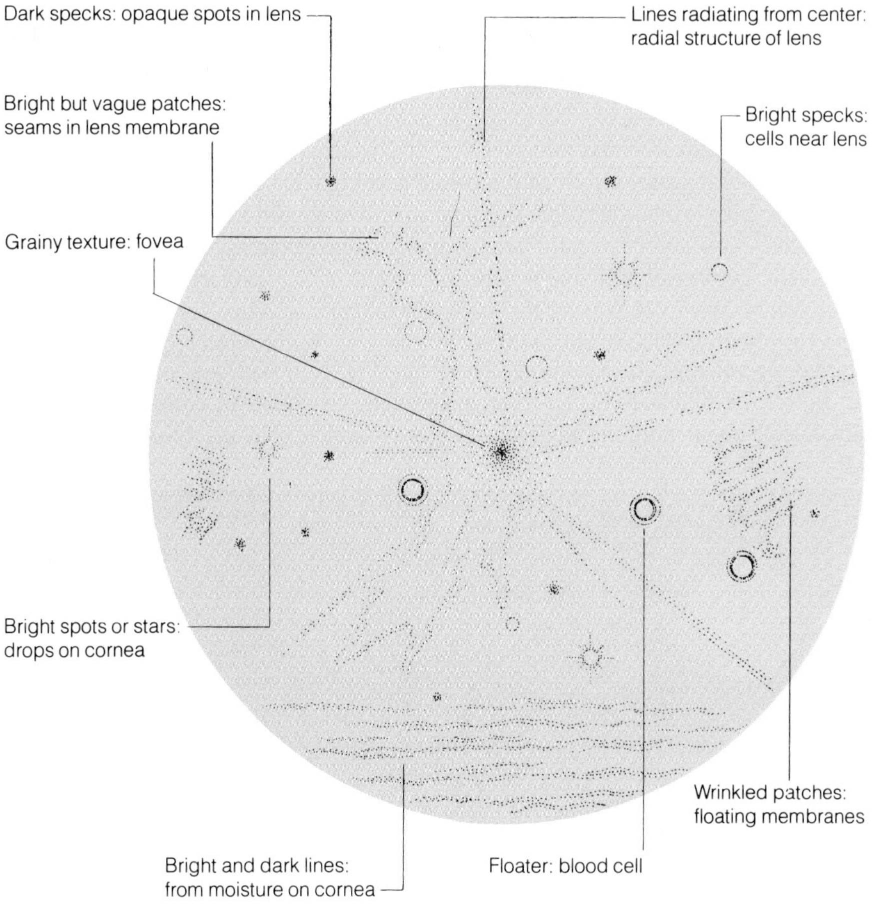

Dark specks: opaque spots in lens

Lines radiating from center: radial structure of lens

Bright but vague patches: seams in lens membrane

Bright specks: cells near lens

Grainy texture: fovea

Bright spots or stars: drops on cornea

Bright and dark lines: from moisture on cornea

Floater: blood cell

Wrinkled patches: floating membranes

FIGURE 3.4

While looking at a homogeneous background, such as a white wall or a blue sky, you may have had a chance to observe shadows of things floating within your eye. You can enhance your view of such objects by making a pinhole through a piece of paper or cardboard and then looking through the pinhole at a homogeneous background. If you've ever wondered what the things that you see floating around are, now's your chance to find out. In this figure, an artist has drawn the things that can be seen and a physiologist has labeled what they are. Try this experiment to see what you find. (SOURCE: Walker, 1982, p. 151.)

The retina is only one-tenth of a millimeter thick making it virtually transparent, which, of course, is why light can pass through all of the layers of the retina and still easily reach and stimulate the photoreceptor cells that make up the third retinal layer. In this photograph of a rabbit's retina, the blood vessels that supply oxygen and nutrition can be seen, but the photoreceptor cells are too small to be seen individually.

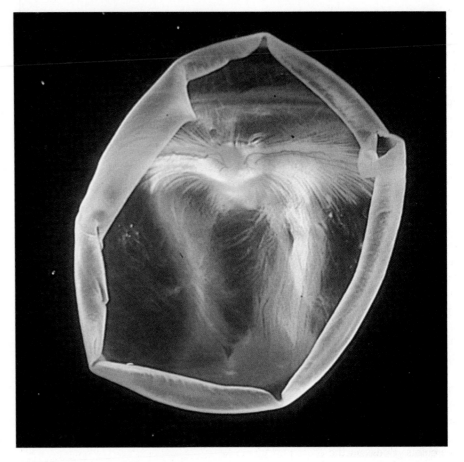

directions in Figure 3.5. As you will see, the white circle completely vanishes. Look at the figure again, but this time, while keeping your eye on the cross, notice what replaces the white spot when it disappears. You should see the red wall. How can this be? You cannot see the white spot because there are no photoreceptor cells on the portion of your retina onto which the spot is projected. But without photoreceptors, how can you see the red wall where the spot had been? The answer is that your brain is lying to you. Unlike the camera, your brain tells you that there is something where there is nothing. These blind spots in each eye are always with you, but rather than let you go through life with two holes in your vision, your brain takes the surrounding material, copies it, and fills in the blind spots with

FIGURE 3.5

Finding the blind spot. With your right eye closed, look at the cross in the upper-right corner. Hold the book up and slowly move it back and forth until the circle disappears (about 1 foot from your eye). This is no small laboratory illusion. Throughout the day, objects disappear in your blind spot. As you walk down the street, whole buildings vanish from your sight—without your awareness. This phenomenon highlights the limitations of our processing system to give us a "real" knowledge of the world (Tollefson, 1984).

similar material. It may be a lie, but it makes life—at least your visual understanding of it—a little less confusing.

PHOTORECEPTOR CELLS.   Interestingly, the photoreceptors that comprise the last layer of the retina are the *first* neurons activated by the incoming light. The retina is so thin that incoming light easily passes *through all the other layers of the retina first* on its way to the photoreceptors. The photoreceptors are the first step in the process by which the brain interprets what it sees. The way in which these receptors work is the key to several interesting phenomena.

As we mentioned earlier, the two main types of photoreceptive neurons are the rods and the cones. As their names imply, the rods have a cylindrical shape, while the cones are more pear-shaped or conical. Each retina contains more than 100 million rods and 6 million cones. These are afferent sensory neurons that are sensitive to particles of light called **photons,** which travel in waves. The distance between waves is called the **wavelength,** and it determines the kind of light. The different kinds of light are shown in the **electromagnetic spectrum** (see Figure 3.6). The human eye is sensitive to only a small portion of this spectrum, known as the **visible spectrum.** X rays and radio waves, which are kinds of light, although you may not have thought of them as such, are found on the spectrum. *Within the visible spectrum* a long wavelength appears red; as the wavelength shortens, the color changes. The middle wavelengths appear green, and the shorter wavelengths blue. The color created by a given wavelength is known as the **hue.** How a color appears to you also may be influenced by its **brightness** or by its **saturation.**

Different rods and cones are stimulated by different wavelengths within the visible light range. The rods are sensitive to all the light within the visual spectrum *except for red.* The cones are not uniform in their response to light. Some are red-sensitive, some are green-sensitive, and some are blue-sensitive (see Figure 3.7). Cone cells are responsible, along with higher areas of the brain, for our ability to see colors. Rods, on the other hand, are not part of the color vision system.

Rods and cones are different in two other important ways as well—sensitivity and acuity, or sharpness of perception. Rods are far more sensitive to light than are cones. For this reason, the rods function best under reduced illumination; they give us our ability to see when there is so little light that objects appear to be no more than black or gray. In fact, rods are so sensitive that a rod cell will respond even if struck by only a single photon of light (Schnapf & Baylor, 1987)! However, many more than one rod cell must respond before absolute threshold can be reached, so although one photon may stimulate a rod cell, it is not enough light for the brain to see. It is just as well that it works this way. Rods are always firing to some extent, if for no other reason than because atoms in a warm body like ours are active (which is why our bodies are warm) and warm atoms will give off a certain number of photons in the range to which rods are sensitive. If our absolute threshold was much lower than it is, our vision might be overwhelmed by this "background noise." Coldblooded creatures like frogs, on the other hand, don't face this problem to the same extent as we warmblooded creatures do. Their atoms aren't as active (which is why they are cold) and their absolute thresholds are much lower than ours, which, of course, gives frogs much better night vision than we humans have (Aho, Donner, Hyden, Larsen, & Reuter, 1988). All this clearly explains why, when it comes to hunting flies at night, frogs will beat you every time.

As light levels increase, rods drastically reduce their function. In fact, as soon as it is bright enough that you become aware of colors, you know that your cones must be responding. When light becomes almost too bright for the rods to handle, it is just dim enough for the cones to begin taking over. For this reason, cones are typically active only during daylight or under indoor illumination.

PHOTONS
Massless particles of light that carry energy. The energy carried is indirectly proportional to the wavelength of the particle: The shorter the wavelength, the greater the energy. Common names for photons depend on the wavelength and include, among others, radio waves, microwaves, visible light, and X rays.

WAVELENGTH
The linear distance from a point on one oscillation of a wave to the corresponding point on the next oscillation of that wave.

ELECTROMAGNETIC SPECTRUM
The entire range of possible wavelengths for light, both visible and invisible (such as X rays and radio waves).

VISIBLE SPECTRUM
The range of wavelengths of light visible to the unaided eye.

HUE
Specifically, the color of a visible light. Hue is determined by the wavelength of the visible light and, depending on the particular wavelength in question, may be called red, yellow, blue, and so on. Perceived hue may also be affected slightly by extreme changes in brightness.

SATURATION
The purity or richness of a color. Highly saturated colors are vivid and striking, while poorly saturated colors appear faded or washed out.

BRIGHTNESS
A property of color determined by the number of photons issuing forth per square unit area. Shifts in brightness are perceived by the observer as changes along a light–dark continuum.

FIGURE 3.6

The electromagnetic spectrum. When a white light is directed through a prism, the visible light spectrum results.

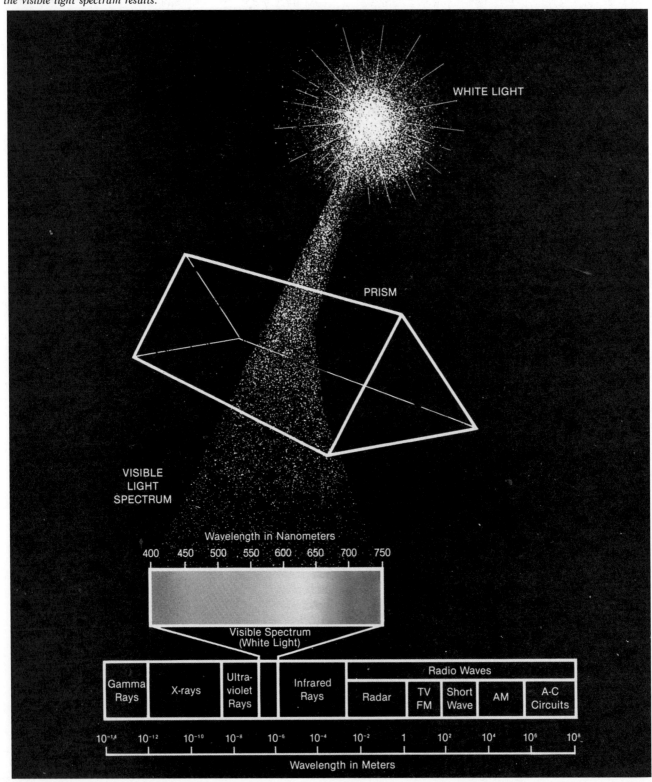

The cones also have far greater acuity than do the rods. One reason that the fovea has such great acuity is that it has no rods, only cones. This explains the clarity with which we see images striking the fovea. There also can be a considerable variation in acuity from individual to individual, depending on how densely cone cells are packed within the fovea (Curcio, Sloan, Packer, Hendrickson, & Kalina, 1987). Rods and cones together make up the periphery of the retina.

Because the fovea has only cones, the eye has a second "blind" spot. If you look *directly at* a dim star on a very dark night, the star may seem to disappear. If you shift your glance a little to one side of the star, however, the star may reappear. This phenomenon occurs because the light from the star, when you look directly at the star, shines on your fovea, which contains only cones, and the cones are not sensitive enough to see such a dim light. When you look to the side, however, the light from the star strikes the periphery of the retina. Rods in the periphery are stimulated by the dim illumination, and the star reappears. This blind spot is distinctly different from the other blind spot we discussed earlier, which is located in an area that has no photoreceptors at all, where the optic nerve exits through the retina.

FIGURE 3.7

Responses of the photoreceptor cells to different wavelengths. Rods and blue-sensitive, green-sensitive, and red-sensitive cones are shown. Although the peak sensitivities of each receptor are located at different wavelengths, there is considerable overlap among cells at many wavelengths. In fact, all four photoreceptors are responsive to the wavelengths of light shown in the gray area of the figure, which corresponds to wavelengths of approximately 460 to 530 nanometers (1 nanometer equals one-billionth of a meter, or 1×10^{-9} meters). For example, if blue light of the *wavelength 450 nanometers strikes the retina, the blue cones will fire at approximately 80 percent of their maximum possible intensity, and the rod cells will fire at approximately 40 percent of their maximum intensity. Unlike the typical neuron that we discussed in Chapter 2, which can fire at only one intensity after reaching action potential, visual neurons are capable of sending messages throughout an entire range of neural intensities, from very weak to maximum strength.* (**SOURCE**: *Adapted from Land, 1977.*)

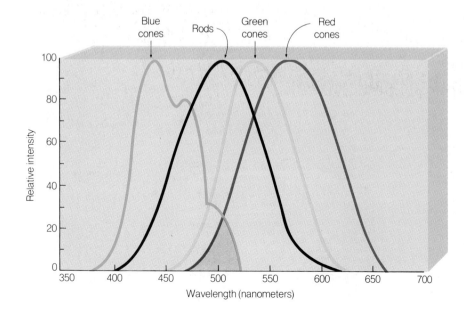

Dark Adaptation

You have no doubt had the experience of going from a lighted room into a dark one. At first, you can't see anything and it's difficult to make out forms or shapes. You are likely to trip over objects or bump into them. Gradually, however, you adapt to the dark. After about 40 minutes, assuming there is a little light, perhaps moonlight or some other dim glow, you are able to see the shapes of objects.

About 30 or 40 minutes after you enter the dark room, your rods reach full sensitivity: They adapt to the dark. This **dark adaptation** is due to a slow chemical change in the rods. To reverse your dark adaptation to **light adaptation,** you need only turn on a bright light; your rods will quickly lose their dark adaptation. When you've been in the light for a few minutes, you become light adapted; then, if you turn out the lights again, your rods will have to become dark adapted again, and this will take some time. Because you have two retinas, you can use a trick to keep your dark adaptation. After you've become dark adapted, tightly close one eye, or even put your hand over it, when you have to turn on a light, so that only the uncovered eye is exposed to the bright light. Use the open eye to work in the light. Of course, when you turn out the lights again you won't be able to see anything with the eye that you've been using, because it will be light adapted. But take your hand off the closed eye and open it. You will find that this eye has remained dark adapted and that you can use it to see your way around in the dark. In the Epilogue, you will learn that there is a way to be in a brightly lighted room without losing dark adaptation, as long as the bright light used is red, because rods are insensitive to that frequency.

Color Vision

Why does a bull charge at a red cape? Whatever the reason, it's certainly not because the cape is red. Bulls do not have color vision and wouldn't know a red cape from a green one. In fact, most animals are totally color-blind and can see only blacks, whites, and grays. Some animals, dogs and cats for instance, have some color vision, but not as rich as ours. In general, color vision is rare in mammals, and even among the primates (humans, apes, monkeys), only some

Some fire departments have painted their trucks a fluorescent yellow-green because this is the color that can best be perceived in dim light when other colors may appear gray or black and white.

have color vision as rich as we humans possess. Color vision is much more common among birds, fish, insects, and reptiles and, especially among insects, may extend to wavelengths beyond those to which human eyes are sensitive.

THE YOUNG–HELMHOLTZ THEORY   Color vision is a complicated phenomenon, and a number of theories have been developed to explain how it operates. A popular theory of color vision developed during the nineteenth century is known as the **Young–Helmholtz theory.** It is based on the work of Thomas Young, an English physicist, and additional work, half a century later, by Hermann von Helmholtz, a German physiologist. It derives from the fact that all colors in the spectrum can be produced from three **primary colors,** red, green, and blue. This odd fact appeared to be explainable only if we assumed that the human visual system was specifically responding only to these three colors (which is why they appeared to be "primary"). The perception of other colors, therefore, must be produced by various mixtures of the three primaries (see Figure 3.8). This idea occurred to Thomas Young in 1802, when he deduced that the retina couldn't possibly hold enough sensors to respond to each of the thousands of different colors that people can discriminate (Nathans, 1989). Instead, he realized that there must be three kinds of primary receptors in the retina.

YOUNG–HELMHOLTZ THEORY
A theory of color vision stating that there are three basic colors (red, green, and blue) and three types of receptors, each of which is receptive to the wavelengths of one of the colors.

PRIMARY COLORS
The three colors from which all other colors can be made, usually considered to be red, green, and blue.

FIGURE 3.8

Additive mixing—*combining beams of light made from the three primaries— gives rise to all possible colors. Where red light and green light intersect, for example, both red and green cones will receive stimulation, creating the sensation of yellow. (If you are curious, a pure yellow light would also stimulate both the red and green cones because both are sensitive to yellow light. This, too, would give rise to the sensation of yellow. Either way, pure yellow light or a red-green mixture, yellow is the resulting sensation.) When equal intensities of red,* green, and blue light are mixed, the result is white. White has no wavelength; it is not a color, but rather it is an experience. In subtractive mixing, pigments that absorb light are blended or, in the case of this example, overlapped with one another. Each time a new pigment is blended or overlapped, more color is subtracted. When equal intensities of the three primaries absorb light, all that remains is black. Purely black objects are completely invisible and are only apparent because they are often surrounded or bordered by visible objects.

COLOR BLINDNESS
The inability to see one or more colors.
The most common kind is green-one color
blindness.

TRICHROMATS
People with normal color vision, who have
all three cone systems functioning
correctly.

DICHROMATS
People with color blindness due to the
defective functioning of one of the three
cone systems.

MONOCHROMATS
People who have color blindness due to the
defective functioning of two of their
three cone systems. Most monochromats
can see no color at all. Interestingly, all
monochromats so far tested have
functioning blue cones. This appears to
occur because the genes for the red and
green cones are located closely together,
making it possible for a single error or
trauma to knock out both red and green
cone systems.

The Young–Helmholtz theory, then, proposes that there are three kinds of color receptors in the retina, one for receiving each of the primary colors. Physiological data have supported this hypothesis, and three different kinds of cones have been discovered—one kind sensitive to red, one to green, and one to blue light (MacNichol, 1964). In fact, investigators have isolated the genes that create the three kinds of cone cells (Nathans 1989), which provides extremely strong support for the theory.

COLOR BLINDNESS.   Some people have an insensitivity to particular color or are unable to see certain colors at all. This condition is known as **color blindness**. Most color blindness is *sex-linked*; it is more common in men than in women. Eight percent of all men and 0.05 percent of all women are afflicted with one form of color blindness or another (see Figure 3.9). The research on color blindness also lends support to the Young–Helmholtz theory that color blindness results from a weakness in a particular cone system or from that system's complete inability to function.

People with normal color vision are called **trichromats;** that is, they use all three color channels. People missing one of the color channels are called **dichromats.** The most extreme form of color blindness exists among **monochromats.** A monochromat has only one functioning cone channel. To date, all monochromats have been found to have a functioning blue channel and defective red and green channels. *Monochromasy* is an extremely rare condition and results in black-and-white vision, not unlike what you would see when observing a black-and-white television set, although not as clear. In such a monochromat, sections of the fovea are filled with many nonfunctioning cones which, to a degree, interferes with the production of normal, clear vision. There are even rare cases of individuals who have no cone channels operating. These people, like monochromats, cannot see color, and they have the additional problem of being "day-blind," because the rods, which don't function under bright illumination, provide their only working visual system. Their visual acuity also is very poor because they have no functioning visual cells in the fovea, since the fovea is packed only with cones and are unable to sense red objects under any illumination (the rods do not respond to red).

The Young–Helmholtz, or three-color, theory argues that there should be three forms of color blindness, one associated with each kind of cone. Three forms do, in fact, exist. People who have defects in their red cones (who are called *red-minus*) are red–green color-blind. To them, both red and green appear yellow. People who have defects in their green cones (who are called *green-minus*) are also red–green color-blind but really have the most trouble discriminating purple from green. Green-minus color blindness is the most common form of color disability. Unlike red-minus or green-minus color-blindness, blue-cone color blindness (known as blue-minus) is not sex-linked, which means that it is just as common in men as in women. Even so, blue-minus color blindness is extremely rare. People who have this disorder are blue–yellow color-blind and cannot tell the difference between those two colors.

We've learned how the world looks to the color-blind, not by deduction, but rather by studying the very rare individuals who have color blindness in one eye but normal vision in the other (Graham & Hsia, 1958). These people look with their color-blind eye at red or green and then match what they see with colors they perceive through their normal eye. The fact that it isn't always easy to simply deduce what a color-blind person should see has led some researchers to conclude that the Young–Helmholtz theory doesn't offer a full explanation of color vision after all.

FIGURE 3.9

A test for color-blindness.

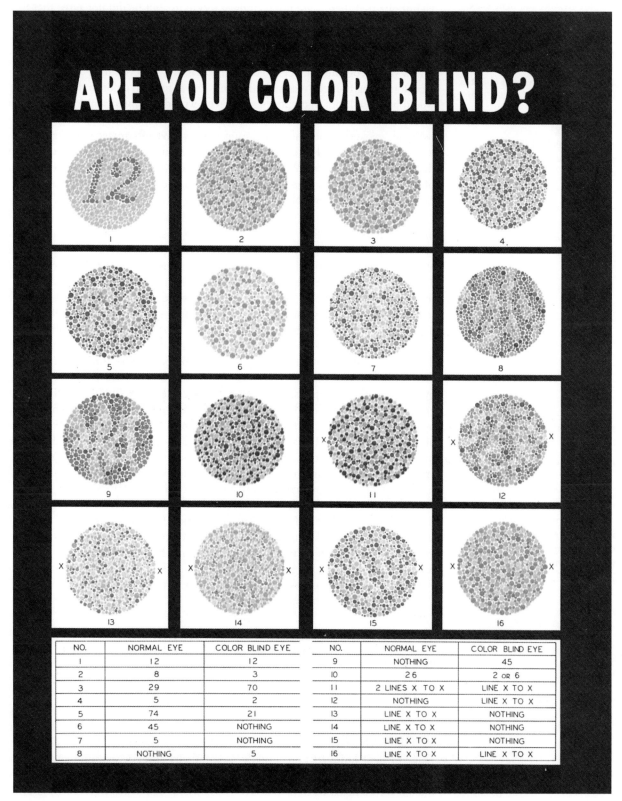

THE OPPONENT-PROCESS THEORY.   The three-color Young–Helmholtz theory was challenged around 1870 by researcher Ewald Hering, who developed what became known as the **opponent-process theory.** Hering believed with Young and Helmholtz that there were three kinds of receptors, but he did not agree that these receptors responded to red, green, and blue. Instead, Hering thought that one kind of receptor responded only to brightness; it was a dark–light receptor. The second kind of receptor responded to a red–green continuum, and the third kind to a yellow–blue continuum (see Figure 3.10). Hering believed that, for example, if receptors along the red–green continuum were at rest, no color in that continuum would be sensed, but that either red or green would be sensed should the receptors be depolarized in one direction or hyperpolarized in the other. This theory, Hering believed, explained the phenomenon of the **negative afterimage** (see Figures 3.11 and 3.12). When a red–green sensitive receptor is looking at red, red is the message that is sent to the brain. When the red message is turned off, the cell leaves one phase and shifts to the other, producing a green afterimage. Hering envisioned the same process for yellow–blue receptors.

The opponent-process view also is supported by evidence at the cellular level. In 1956, researchers first discovered cells that operated in the way Hering had predicted (Svaetichin, 1956). In these experiments, the horizontal cells in the retinas of goldfish were examined with microelectrodes, one at a time. The researchers discovered that some cells became very excited when exposed to a particular color—red, for example. However, when the same cells were exposed to green, they actually responded less than they had been responding before stimulation. Some cells worked the opposite way: Green stimulated them, while red had the opposite effect.

This apparent conflict between the two views has been resolved by modern theories of color vision that include aspects of both. The three-color Young–Helmholtz theory seems to be a good description of the first stage of visual processing by the cone photoreceptors, because cones have been found to be sensitive to red, green, and blue, rather than to light–dark, red–green, and yellow–blue. The opponent-process theory, on the other hand, seems to provide a better explanation of color vision at the horizontal-cell and ganglion-cell levels, where information from the three kinds of cones is not added, but rather is contrasted, as Hering envisioned—by the time the information has reached the optic nerve, it has already undergone opponent-processing in some manner (Haber, 1985).

The three-pigment cone system might even interact in an opponent process at the photoreceptor level. This is one of the more popular possibilities currently under examination. For instance, it has been discovered that in turtles, red and green cones are directly connected to one another in the retina (Normann, Perlman, Kolb, Jones, & Daly, 1984). Similar connections may exist in the human retina. Researchers are making discoveries all the time, and no doubt our view of color vision eventually will be modified further.

COLOR CONSTANCY THEORY.   For many years, Edwin Land, the inventor of the Polaroid camera, had argued that something peculiar was occurring in the color vision system that had not been addressed by either of the theories we have discussed so far. Color film is sensitive to the wavelengths of light that strike the film. Color film acts according to the Young–Helmholtz view in the sense that red, green, and blue light will excite pigments on the film that are sensitive to each of these colors. But have you ever taken a color picture indoors without a flash? Figure 3.13 shows you what can happen. The heavy orange glow from the typical tungsten filament light bulbs that are usually used indoors covers everything and gives an odd cast to the picture. There's nothing wrong with the film—it's "seeing" the orange wavelengths of light that are really there. Land was puzzled by the dis-

FIGURE 3.10

The visual receptor system as Hering believed it might be. Today there is evidence that the cones are receptive to red, green, and blue (MacNichol, 1964) and not to red–green, blue–yellow, and light–dark as Hering thought. However, an opponent-process system somewhat like that Hering envisioned does operate at levels higher than the first layer of the retina.

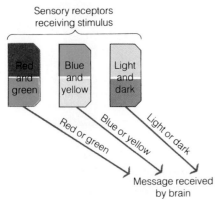

Sensory receptors
receiving stimulus

Red and green | Blue and yellow | Light and dark

Red or green   Blue or yellow   Light or dark

Message received
by brain

crepancy between what we perceive and what the camera records; because if either or both of the theories we have already discussed told the whole story, indoor lighting should look just as orange to us as it does to color film—but it doesn't. Something in our visual system keeps colors looking normal and constant, even under some very great wavelength fluctuations such as those that result in the orange cast caused by indoor light bulbs. Engineers say that a system like ours has *automatic gain control*. In other words, once our visual system has decided that something is "red" in comparison with other colors in the immediate vicinity, it will hold the "redness" constant over an incredible range of lighting conditions, even to the point of eliminating the heavy orange cast created by indoor lighting. This automatic gain control, or **color constancy,** appears to work by measuring ratios of one color to its surrounding color. For example, if you were looking at a yellow canary perched in a green bush, the yellow bird would excite your red cones more than the green bush would. For the sake of argument, let's say your red cones were four times more excited by the bird than by the plant. We can express this as a ratio of 4:1. Now, carry the bird and bush indoors (easier said than done) and look at them in indoor lighting. The orange-ish light from your indoor light bulbs shines on the bird and the bush. Now the bird excites your red cones even more, *but so does the bush!* The 4:1 ratio does not change! Color constancy somehow tells your brain to "keep the canary yellow, the bush green, and discount the orange cast."

Color constancy appears to be one of the functions of a special grouping of cells found far into the occipital lobes (Jameson & Hurvich, 1989). So little is known about these cells that they are currently referred to in the color vision literature as "the blobs" (not exactly a high-tech term, but descriptive nonetheless of both their shape and our bewilderment).

To understand why there is a color constancy system in human vision, we need to examine the reason for the existence of color vision. It appears that color vision evolved because of the advantage it gave primates by enabling them to identify more effectively the useful and dangerous objects in their environments. Considering this possibility, it is reasonable to assume that color vision wouldn't be as useful if the colors of objects constantly altered as lighting conditions changed. So we can further assume that color constancy evolved because of the advantages of keeping the colors of known objects the same. You can readily deduce the value to our arboreal forebears of always sensing a tiger's stripes to be the same orange-ish color whether they were observed in the pink illumination of early dawn, beneath

FIGURE 3.11

To experience a negative afterimage, stare at the yellow circle for about 1 minute. Then glance at a white sheet of paper or a white wall and blink your eyes a few times. A blue circle should appear.

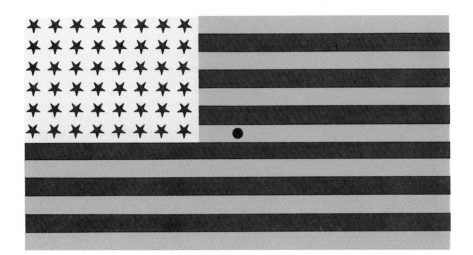

FIGURE 3.12

Another example of negative afterimage. Look at the dot in the middle of the flag for 30 seconds or more. Then look at any white surface, such as a wall or a piece of paper. An American flag in its usual colors should appear.

FIGURE 3.13

A room lighted by typical tungsten filament light bulbs has an **actual** orange cast. The camera sees this. The human eye and brain, through the mechanism of color constancy, will filter out this orange cast, maintaining a perception of the colors as constant under many different lighting conditions.

CONCEPT REVIEW: VISUAL CELLS OF THE RETINA

Rod Cells	The most plentiful of the photoreceptors; not part of the color vision system; supersensitive to light, but unresponsive to red; have poor acuity; not found in the fovea; used for night vision.
Cone Cells	Cells of the color vision system; three kinds: red-, green-, and blue-sensitive; have great acuity; fovea is packed with them; need much more light than rods before they can function.
Bipolar Cells	Cells that collect and consolidate visual information, a particular bipolar cell is either "rod-driven" or "cone-driven," meaning that it receives information from either groups of rods or groups of cones but never from a mixture of the two.
Ganglion Cells	Receive information from bipolar or amacrine cells; operate in an opponent-process fashion; some ganglion cells respond to the direction of motion of an object.
Horizontal Cells	Make lateral connections between cones; influence opposing color processes (such as red and green, blue and yellow) and are probably responsible, in part, for negative afterimages and other opponent-process effects.
Amacrine Cells	Make lateral connections between ganglion cells or between ganglion and rod-driven bipolar cells; modify and control visual messages; sharpen ganglion-cell response; over 30 different kinds, the functions of which are largely unknown.

the bright white light of the noonday sun, or under the blue-gray light of an overcast or foggy sky (Brou, Sciascia, Linden, & Lettvin, 1986).

AFTEREFFECTS. **Aftereffects** are different from afterimages in an important way, and this difference helps to show that specialized cells continue to process visual information further within the brain, beyond the retina. Aftereffects can transfer from one eye to the other (although the transfer effect may be quite weak). Recall the afterimage experiment with the American flag in Figure 3.12. If you look at the flag again, but this time with your left eye only, and then search for the afterimage with your right eye, you won't see any afterimage. This color phenomenon occurs only at the retinal level, and information can't be transferred from one eye to the other. However, if you follow the instructions in Figure 3.14, you'll see an aftereffect that will transfer from one eye to the other. We can infer that the detectors that are fatigued in the aftereffect are not located in the retina, but rather are located at a higher level, where information from both eyes can interact (Favreau & Corballis, 1976). What is happening to the visual information at this higher level is an area of intense interest.

Receptive Fields

The stimulation of the photoreceptor rods and cones is only the first neural step in the visual process. After the millions of photoreceptors are stimulated by incoming light that is focused on the retina, the information is passed to the next layers of the retina, then down the optic nerve, and finally deeper into the brain. As you can imagine, the entire system is unbelievably complicated, and no one is yet certain how it works. Researchers, however, are trying to unravel some of the mysteries. Let's have a look at a few of their ideas.

PUTTING IT ALL TOGETHER. Look again at Figure 3.3, and notice the ganglion cells that make up the last layer of the retina to process visual information. This figure looks complicated enough, but in fact it's far too simple; it doesn't depict the specializations of this layer of the retina. For instance, there are over 20 kinds of specialized ganglion cells (Kolb, Nelson, & Mariani, 1981). Each kind responds to a complex pattern of light created by many rods and cones at a particular location on the retina. Each ganglion cell, then, is responding to what is called a **receptive field** (Westheimer, 1984). For example, one kind of ganglion cell may respond most to a receptive field comprising a red spot on a green background. Another

FIGURE 3.14

A tilt aftereffect. Look at the left drawing. Do not look in one place, but scan your eyes back and forth across the horizontal bar. This provides apparent motion to the object and will help fatigue the complex cells that combine edge detection with motion. Shortly, you will fatigue cells sensitive to the angles in the left diagram. Then quickly look at the right diagram.

Opposing cells will now dominate, and you should see the vertical lines and right angles appear as diagonal lines and acute angles bending in the opposite direction from those in the left drawing. You can prove that this illusion is an aftereffect, not an afterimage, by showing that it transfers from one eye to the other. Look again at the left figure with one eye only. After a sufficient time of scanning the left figure, close that eye and look quickly at the right figure with the other eye. The effect will be very brief, but it should transfer. This demontrates that such edge motion and angle detectors are located at higher levels in the brain, where information from both eyes converges.

95

FEATURE DETECTORS
Innate sensory mechanisms tuned specifically to respond to particular aspects of the environment.

SIMPLE CELLS
Cells in the cerebral cortex that respond to lines of a particular orientation.

COMPLEX CELLS
Cells in the visual cortex that respond to various combinations of motion, orientation, or color. Complex cells usually are associated with large receptive fields.

HYPERCOMPLEX CELLS
Cells in the cerebral cortex that respond to complex combinations of visual stimuli, including width, length, edges, and certain forms.

MODEL
A mathematical, logical, or mechanical replica of a relationship or a system of events so designed that a study of the model can yield some understanding of the real thing.

kind of ganglion cell might respond most to a green spot on a red background. Still another may respond to motion in a certain direction (Poggio & Koch, 1987). In this layer of the retina, then, cells specialized to detect certain kinds of complex stimuli are already in place. But what happens to the message once it leaves the ganglion cells and travels down the optic nerve farther on into the brain? It appears that the visual messages pass through increasingly specialized detectors (cells that respond to unique patterns, forms, or colors), each, it is assumed, with its own receptive field. These are known as **feature detectors.** At each step along the way, feature detector cells help make sense of what you see.

The first important feature detectors in the occipital lobe to receive information from the optic nerve are called **simple cells.** Simple cells are assumed to have receptive fields for information about lines or edges arriving from the visual system. Some simple cells are known to depolarize (fire) when they receive inputs about vertical edges, but hyperpolarize (become harder to fire) when they receive inputs about horizontal edges, and vice versa. Some appear to respond to inputs about diagonal gradations of edges between horizontal and vertical. Some simple cells seem to have receptive fields for information about motion.

Beyond the simple cells are **complex cells.** Complex cells are thought not only to be sensitive to vertical, horizontal, or diagonal edges but also to have receptive fields for the motion of objects. For instance, a particular complex cell may respond most excitedly to combined inputs from feature detectors responding to a diagonal edge *and* a left-to-right motion, while another complex cell may respond most to inputs of horizontal edge *and* an up-to-down motion. At this point, more information about the scene you've glanced at is combined and analyzed. Some complex cells seem to combine color and edges. For instance, certain cells may be responsive to vertical red edges, or to diagonal green ones, or the like. There may be different complex cells for every possible combination.

Information from complex cells then appears to be passed on to **hypercomplex cells.** Hypercomplex cells seem to have receptive fields to inputs about orientation, movement, color, *and* also length or width or even its corners or certain features. Of course, this view of how the brain makes sense of vision leaves us with a distinct problem. There have to be limits to how specialized visual detectors can become, simply because at some point too many cells would be needed to cover all the possible combinations. We can't expect that we will eventually discover super-ultra-hypercomplex cells only responsive to a receptive field of inputs for lavender Oldsmobiles traveling left to right at a distance of five meters. Even hypercomplex cells, then, cannot hope to recognize an entire visual image, but would need to share information with millions of other hypercomplex cells (Hubel & Wiesel, 1979). And therein lies the major problem with this view of vision. It relies on a system that probably requires too many comparisons to be made before a total image could emerge, too many comparisons (billions, perhaps trillions, every fraction of a second as the image changes) for even the brain to make (See Focus on Research).

One solution to the problem we encounter when trying to understand how the brain could possibly make the trillions of comparisons needed for a mental image to emerge from the information gathered by the senses might come from a recent discovery by Barry Richmond and Lance Optican. One day, while measuring the number of firings emitted by visual neurons, Richmond noticed that as he altered the visual stimulus, the number of firings did not change, but the timing and patterns of the firings *did* change. When he pointed out his discovery to others in the lab, they told him to forget it because those patterns were already known and others had wasted years checking them out. The patterns, they said, didn't seem to mean anything, they were just a nuisance. Undaunted, he and Optican began

COMPUTER MODELING

Researchers who study sensation in the brain use many different techniques. One of the most recent involves advanced computers, which can be used to generate a **model** that may yield knowledge about how the brain works. To show you how this is done, let's look at a recent brain model of the occipital lobes, the area of the cerebral cortex most associated with vision.

In the occipital lobes are interesting areas known as ocular dominance columns. When the occipital lobes are stained for viewing under a microscope, these columns, which contain visual receptors, can be seen as swirling stripes throughout the occipital cortex (Constantine-Paton & Law, 1982) (see Figure 3.15). Interestingly, these distinct columns are not present at birth, but develop gradually as we come to experience our visual world. But why should the occipital lobes be organized in this striking fashion? Working with an advanced computer, researchers created a program in which they gave the computer parameters "derived directly from the physiological characteristics of the cells" (Barinaga, 1990, p. 525). In other words, their program incorporated the known actions of the individual visual cells. They then ran the program and waited to see how all of these millions of interactions, which no one could ever have calculated by hand, would eventually organize the cells. The process and results are seen in Figure 3.16; the final form looks strikingly like real ocular columns as pictured in Figure 3.15! Perhaps, then, this com-

FIGURE 3.15

Stripes in the visual cortex of a mammal's brain show the organization of cells responsive to visual information. The stripes are made more visible by a staining procedure. The dark stripes carry information from one eye, while the light stripes carry information from the other. This shows that, while the information from each eye is segregated, it is distributed evenly throughout the visual cortex.

FIGURE 3.16

A computer simulation over time of the action of the visually sensitive cells of the occipital cortex. At first (T = 0), cells respond to information from both eyes. By the end of the program (T = 80), the cells are responding to information from one eye or the other, and have formed structures similar to the ocular dominance columns observed to occur in real brains.

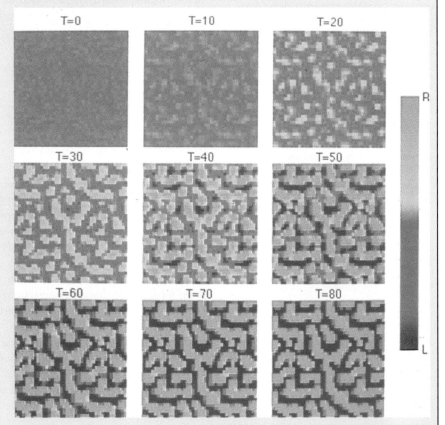

puter program shows us that we already know enough to explain the formation of these columns (Miller, Keller, & Stryker, 1989).

Modeling of the brain with the supercomputers of the future may help us to ask the right questions or lead us directly to new discoveries. For exam-ple, if your program won't mimic the brain unless you add "X" to it, then the next step is to go to the real brain and start looking for something there that is actually doing the job of "X." Conversely, if you discover something in the brain you didn't know existed, then you will want to add that param-eter to your program and see what kind of a difference it makes when you run your model. It is an exciting, interactive way to pursue research and is bound to give us many answers.

MULTIPLEXING
The act of simultaneously sending two or more distinct messages by way of a single transmission carrier.

PITCH
The perception of a tone's frequency. In general, shorter wavelengths (higher frequencies) are perceived as having a higher pitch, while longer wavelengths (lower frequencies) are perceived as having a lower pitch.

FREQUENCY
The number of cycles per unit of time in a periodic vibration. Frequency determines the pitch of a sound. Higher frequencies have shorter wavelengths.

FIGURE 3.17

A sound wave. (a) The compression and rarefaction of air molecules. The wave consists of a pulse of compressed air (X) followed by an area of low density. (b) the wave amplitude that corresponds with the compression and rarefaction in (a). The greater the compression, the higher the amplitude. The distance between compressions, or the distance between waves, is the wavelength.

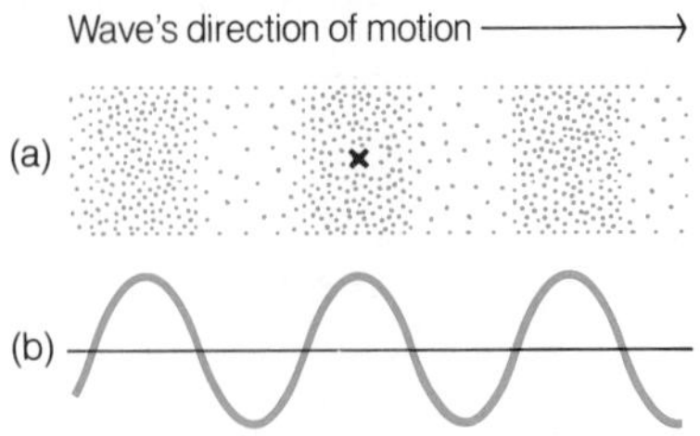

Wave's direction of motion ⟶

(a)

(b)

a very systematic exploration of the different patterns and found that they did indeed go hand and hand with certain stimulations (Optican & Richmond, 1987). This meant that one neuron might be sending two or more bits of information riding on only *one* signal. The different information was contained in the number of firings, spacing, patterning, and so on, of just one neuron. In a way, FM radio works like this. It sends two different sets of information on one signal, which is why you can hear it in stereo (one signal, but each speaker gets a totally different message). Sending two or more bits of information on one signal is called **multiplexing**.

If this is how the brain is working, then all of the comparisons between cells to resolve one image required by the receptive fields theory wouldn't be needed. There would be many fewer comparisons required because individual neurons would already have more than a single bit of information as a result of multiplexing. Engineers have known for years that they can always make a simple transmission system more powerful by multiplexing. Maybe nature already knew that!

HEARING

How Sound Is Created

Just as your eyes are sensitive to a limited range of the electromagnetic spectrum, so your ears are sensitive to a limited range of frequencies caused by the compression and rarefaction of air, which creates sound waves (see Figure 3.17). For something to make a sound, it must disturb the surrounding air, creating air waves that radiate from it. Although light can travel in a vacuum, sound cannot; sound depends on a medium such as air or water. Hollywood movies notwithstanding, real spaceships that went zipping by you in outer space would pass in total silence, without the familiar accompanying whoosh made by objects rushing by in an atmosphere. The moon, for instance, has no atmosphere, and everything that happens on the moon happens in complete silence. When astronauts spoke to one another on the moon, they spoke by means of radio waves, a form of light. Radio waves reaching the astronauts' helmets were converted into sound waves by speakers that caused impacts and compressions within the atmosphere inside the helmets. Had the astronauts removed their helmets and tried to speak to one another, they wouldn't have heard a thing (and they wouldn't have lasted very long, either).

FIGURE 3.18

Loudness is measured in decibels (db). A 10-db sound is 10 times louder than one of 0 db (which is the faintest sound that can be heard); a 20-db sound is 100 times louder than one of 0 db and 10 times louder than one of 10 db. The average loud conversation (60 db) is 1 million times louder than the faintest sound that can be heard.

Sounds above 90 db can permanently injure the ear. Sounds also can combine to cause damage—an air hammer being used amidst loud traffic is more damaging than one operated on an empty street.

Air waves travel out from the source of a sound in much the same way that waves on a pond ripple outward after a rock has been dropped into the water. Sound waves are generated in all directions and, like light waves, they have measurable wavelengths. Wavelength in hearing corresponds to **pitch,** whereas wavelength in vision corresponds to hue. Long sound wavelengths are heard as low pitches. Short wavelengths are heard as high pitches. The human ear can perceive a range between approximately 20 cycles, or waves entering the ear, per second and about 20,000 cycles per second (corresponding to wavelengths of between 17 meters and 17 millimeters).* The number of sound waves per second passing a given point is known as the **frequency.** The **amplitude,** or height, of the wave determines the **loudness** (see Figure 3.18). If you could switch your eyes and ears around in some bizarre way, you might imagine that a bright blue light would sound like a loud high-pitched tone or that a soft low-pitched tone would look like a dim red light.

Some animals are capable of hearing frequencies higher than those humans can distinguish. Dogs, for example, can hear up to 30,000 or 40,000 cycles per second. Dog whistles work in this range. Dogs trained to respond to these whistles can be summoned from blocks away by a very loud blast on the whistle that neither you nor anyone else around can hear. For years, hunters in Africa had wondered about the "sixth sense" that elephants seemed to possess in their apparent ability to communicate silently with one another. Now it has been found that the elephant may be simply relying on one of the familiar five senses—hearing. Elephants, it turns out, are able to make infralow frequency sounds (about 14 cycles per second) that can carry great distances ("Elephant Calls," 1986). Although your ear cannot pick up such low frequencies, the sound is, in fact, very loud (at least to other elephants).

The Structure of the Ear

Figure 3.19 shows a schematic breakdown of the human ear. The **pinna,** or outer ear, helps to capture sound waves that enter through the external auditory canal

---

*Some individuals may have hearing loss in only some of the frequency ranges, often due to overexposure to loud sounds (listening to loud music with earphones is the main hazard among college students). This kind of deafness commonly goes unnoticed until it becomes severe. A quick and easy telephone screening test of your hearing is available in the United States at no charge from Occupational Hearing Services, Inc.; it will work on any telephone of good quality. For the local test number nearest you, call 1-800-222-3277; in Pennsylvania call, 1-800-345-3277.

AMPLITUDE
A measurement of the amount of energy carried by a wave, shown in the height of the oscillation.

LOUDNESS
A measurement of sound intensity that corresponds to the amplitude of the sound waves.

PINNA
The clearly visible outer portion of the ear. It serves to gather sound.

TYMPANIC MEMBRANE
The thin, semitransparent membrane separating the middle ear from the external ear; it is also called the eardrum.

MALLEUS
The largest of the three small bones in the middle ear; it is also called the hammer.

INCUS
One of the three small bones in the middle ear; it is also called the anvil.

STAPES
One of the three small bones in the middle ear; it is also called the stirrup.

COCHLEA
A spiral tube in the inner ear, resembling a snail shell, which contains nerve endings essential for hearing.

and strike the **tympanic membrane,** or eardrum. A subtle vibration of the eardrum sets in motion the three extremely small bones of the middle ear—the **malleus,** the **incus,** and the **stapes.** In fact, these bones are the smallest in the human body. The three bones in turn pass along the vibration, which travels into the **cochlea** within the inner ear. Within the cochlea is the **organ of Corti,** containing approximately 16,000 hairlike cells in four rows. Each hair cell has about 100 **stereocilia,** so there are over 1 million of these little items in each ear, which respond to the different frequencies of sound waves (Hudspeth, 1985). When these superfine stereocilia are bent, they trigger nerve impulses that are sent by the **auditory nerve** to the brain. Perhaps "bent" is too strong a word, because a movement by stereocilia of no greater magnitude than the width of an atom is sufficient to fire the associated nerve cell! Whether these hair cells fire also is determined by nerve impulses they receive from the brain stem area. Researchers assume that these signals have the effect of dampening or amplifying the auditory message. Such dampening and amplification probably give us the abilities to concentrate on only one voice at a loud cocktail party, to pick out the flute in an orchestra, or "to turn a deaf ear" to distracting sounds while we are trying to concentrate.

Theories of Hearing

The cochlea is the size of a pea, yet it allows us to discriminate among thousands of incredibly complex tones. How is this possible? A number of theories have been developed to explain how hearing works. The superfine hairs within the organ of Corti are moved by vibrations sent through the liquid in the cochlea, vibrations made by the eardrum responding to sound waves and hitting against the oval window at the entrance to the inner ear. It is generally agreed that loudness is determined by the total number of nerves that fire and by the activation of **high-threshold fibers.** These fibers are difficult to bend, and only when they are bent by the

FIGURE 3.19

Structure of the human ear.

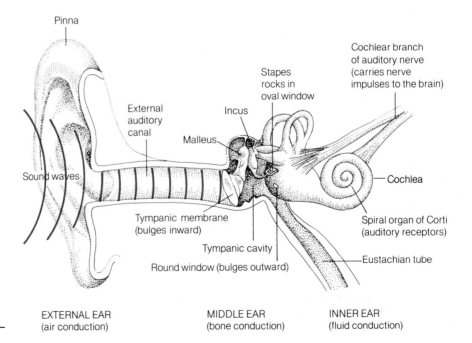

Pinna

External auditory canal

Sound waves

Stapes rocks in oval window

Incus

Malleus

Cochlear branch of auditory nerve (carries nerve impulses to the brain)

Cochlea

Tympanic membrane (bulges inward)

Tympanic cavity

Round window (bulges outward)

Spiral organ of Corti (auditory receptors)

Eustachian tube

EXTERNAL EAR (air conduction)

MIDDLE EAR (bone conduction)

INNER EAR (fluid conduction)

considerable force of a loud noise do the nerves associated with them fire, making you aware of a loud noise.

Interestingly, how loud something sounds is also determined by the fine muscles of your middle ear. Have you ever sat in the front row and heard a great opera star sing or had a baby cry right into your ear? Deafening, isn't it? How come the opera star or baby can stand it, they're even closer to the sound? As it turns out, as soon as you start to vocalize your middle ear muscles dampen down your hearing so that you don't overwhelm yourself with your own noise (Borg & Counter, 1989). Without those muscles, shouting would be deafening for you.[*]

Pitch discrimination is a different matter. The perception of high- and middle-range tones appears to be determined by the *place* within the organ of Corti where hairs are stimulated. Very high-pitched tones stimulate hairs near the oval window, while intermediate-range tones stimulate hairs farther within the cochlea. This explanation of tone perception is known as the **place theory**. The place theory would be adequate to explain hearing, except that lower tones—those below 5000 cycles per second—tend to stimulate hairs throughout the entire organ of Corti.

To explain partially how we are able to hear tones lower than 5000 cycles per second, researchers have developed the **frequency theory**. The frequency of a sound may account for our ability to sense those between 300 and 20 cycles (the lowest that can be registered by the human ear). Because auditory neurons can fire up to 300 times per second, scientists think that auditory neurons may fire in direct relation to the frequency. They have discovered that frequencies between 300 and 20 cycles per second are fairly well correlated with neural firing. Neurons stimulated by very low-frequency sounds within this range fire roughly an equivalent number of times per second, while neurons stimulated by sounds near 300 cycles per second fire at their maximum of 300 times per second.

The frequency theory, however, still leaves unexplained our perception of sounds in the range between 300 and 5000 cycles per second. A proposal that may help to fill this final gap is the **volley theory**. Although 5000 firings per second would be impossible for one neuron, many neurons firing in volleys could generate up to 5000 pulses per second. In other words, if many neurons each fire at their top speed (300 firings per second for auditory neurons), but fire out of sequence with one another so that no two are firing at the same instant, they could produce any number of distinct neutral bursts per second. All that would be needed to make sense of such a volley would be some link or connection between the volleying neurons that would yield a sum total firing rate. Researchers refer to such a neural summing mechanism as a *spatial cross-correlator*. With such a mechanism, many volleying neurons could be analyzed as one, allowing us to perceive sounds in the range between 300 and 5000 cycles per second. There is evidence that the auditory nerve does engage in such a spatial cross-correlation analysis (Loeb, 1985).

Once the auditory information leaves the cochlea, it travels along the auditory nerve to the midbrain and then to the auditory cortex in the temporal lobes. Although the hearing centers in the brain have not been as well examined as the visual centers, scientists believe that different cells, specializing in detecting sounds of different quality, duration, and pitch, help to rectify and organize the information.

---

[*]The "bang" from a gunshot or some other sudden sound might be loud enough to harm your ears. If you can't cover your ears to protect them from a loud sound you know is coming, humming just before the sound occurs *will* help (Borg & Counter, 1989).

ORGAN OF CORTI
The organ located on the basilar membrane in the cochlea, which contains the hearing receptors.

STEREOCILIA
Extremely short hairs extending from the surface of the cells in the inner ear.

AUDITORY NERVE
The nerve leading from the cochlea, which transmits sound impulses to the brain.

HIGH-THRESHOLD FIBERS
Stereocilia in the inner ear that are difficult to bend and thus respond only to loud noises or sounds.

PLACE THEORY
A theory of hearing that attempts to explain the reception of sound waves between 5000 and 20,000 cycles per second. It asserts that different frequencies stimulate stereocilia at different places within the cochlea. High frequencies stimulate stereocilia near the oval window, while intermediate frequencies stimulate stereocilia away from the oval window.

FREQUENCY THEORY
A theory of hearing designed to explain the reception of sound waves between 20 and 300 cycles per second. According to this theory, auditory neurons fire at rates well correlated with the frequency of the sound.

VOLLEY THEORY
A theory of hearing designed to explain the reception of sound waves between 300 and 5000 cycles per second. According to this theory, auditory neurons fire in volleys that are well correlated with the frequency of the sound.

An Enduring Question: Can We Learn To Fake It?

The senses are our window on the world. They bring us information about what is happening. As Yogi Berra once said, "You can observe a whole lot by just watching."* But are our senses telling us the truth? Philosophers have grappled with this question and have come to the conclusion that there is no way to know. Some have even argued that nothing exists until we sense it. But, in truth, no one knows whether our senses create reality or simply register it and, as best as we can tell, there is no way to find out. As the great philosopher René Descartes concluded after asking himself if there were anything about which he could be certain, "I think, therefore I am." By that he meant that he was sure he existed because he could sense, but whether what he sensed was really there was anybody's guess. In fact, he sounds like someone who might have read the chapter preview.

Could we, however, with our growing knowledge about how the senses work, eventually create reality? That is, could we eventually input artificial sensations that could not be discriminated from "real" ones, which would, by definition, make them no less real? Can we someday make any fantasy come true, at least for as long as we are plugged into the "sense machine?" What would such technology do to us as a species; a society?

Perhaps all of this sounds too much like science fiction to consider seriously. If so, you will probably be surprised to learn what has already been done along these lines. Researchers are interested in this kind of work, not because of some far-off chance to create a new reality, but to help those who have lost their vision or hearing. Most of the best work in this area has been accomplished with those who are deaf owing to damage to the inner ear. For example, Donald Eddington, who is a bioengineer, has made an artificial human ear from machine parts in his laboratory with which he has aided individuals who became deaf as a result of disease or injury that damaged the fragile hair cells, or stereocilia, that line the inner ear. Hearing aids, which amplify sound entering the ear, are useless to people who have no stereocilia to turn the amplified sound into auditory nerve signals. Eddington's device is an implant made of tiny platinum electrodes that are placed at different points along the cochlea's inner surface via a thin, surgically implanted plug placed just behind the ear. In this way, Eddington electrically taps into the auditory nerve. Eddington has said, "The implant actually bypasses the damaged ear interior. Our electrodes simply stimulate the nerves directly, not with vibrations, but with minute electrical shocks. The system mimics the electrical patterns received by the brain as speech" (Weintraub, 1980, p. 50). A cable is then connected to the plug behind the ear that runs through a computer to a microphone. The microphone picks up sounds and sends them to the computer, which breaks them down by their frequencies. The computer then stimulates the tiny electrodes inside the cochlea according to the frequencies that have been received (see Figure 3.20). In this way, the auditory nerve is tricked into responding to the implants as if they were stereocilia, and it sends messages to the brain based on the stimulation it receives.

With devices such as Eddington's, patients who had originally been able to hear before becoming deaf are again able to hear voices. Although the voices they hear do sound very "tinny," they are understandable (Tong, Dowell, Blamey, & Clark, 1983; Loeb, 1985).

*Yogi Berra: former baseball great especially known for his unique utterances, such as, "It's like déjàvu all over again," "Nobody goes there—it's too crowded," "He made the wrong mistake," "It ain't over, 'til its over," and so on.

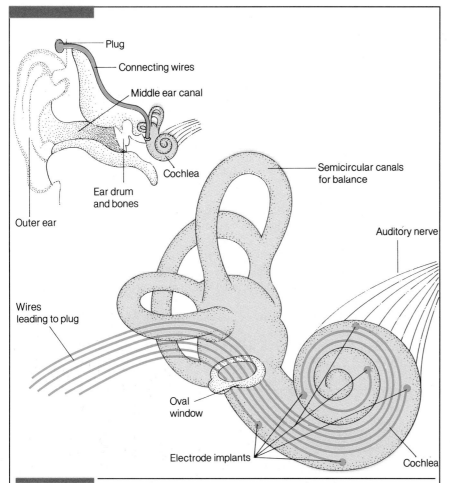

FIGURE 3.20

The original artificial ear. Six platinum electrode implants replace the destroyed cilia. The implants stimulate the auditory nerve by generating small electric shocks in response to different frequencies of sound. (SOURCE: *Weintraub, 1980, p. 51.*)

As computers become more miniaturized and as we learn more about the relationship between places within the inner ear and the kinds of sounds created when these places are stimulated, the artificial ear, no doubt, will be improved further. Researchers are now imagining a pocket-sized computer that could filter incoming sounds and send messages to an artificial ear containing over 5000 platinum implants throughout the inner ear. Perhaps early in the next century, people who had thought they would be deaf for life will be able to hear again as clearly as if their ears had never been damaged.

Similarly, implants of electrodes into occipital lobes that are connected to TV cameras can give rise to the sensation of points of light and colors in individuals who have become totally blind (Dobelle, Mladejovsky, & Girvin, 1974). Suppose someday that such an input could be made to mimic whatever it is that the brain does to the neural image before it reaches the occipital lobes and then input this message directly into the neural structures there. If that could ever be done, there should be no reason why we couldn't make fully functional artificial eyes, perhaps even superior to our own natural eyes.

If we could ever artificially input an entire reality, we could expect a huge demand for it. Think about it—what would you like to experience? But the prospect is also a little depressing. Is this the future of our species—a world of people whose machines and robots do all of the real work so that they can plug their brains into a world of endless excitement and stimulation? Then again, maybe people would use such power judiciously, or as the chapter preview suggested, perhaps they already are.

FOR CRITICAL ANALYSIS

1. Do you see like other people do? If you experience the color red, is that the same experience your friend is having when she looks at something that she, too, has learned to call "red?" How can you know that what she is experiencing isn't an experience you would consider to be "green?" Mightn't you both be experiencing very different colors when looking at the same thing and only think that you are seeing alike because you've both learned to call the experience you are having "red?"

2. Modern computers are becoming so powerful that soon photographs and even videotape will be fakeable beyond the ability of experts to tell. Entire events could be created for the nightly news that never occurred. What could governments do with such power? Consider how strongly the sense of vision controls what you believe. How would such twisting of reality change your view of your own senses?

TASTE

Taste is a fairly limited sense. Most of what we consider to be taste is really smell. If you were blindfolded so that you could not see what you were eating and then had your nose plugged, you could not tell the difference between a piece of raw apple, a piece of raw potato, and a piece of raw onion. Although the three foods smell different, they taste alike. Think of how hard it is to taste foods when you have a cold; it's actually the sense of smell that's being hindered.

The major taste senses are sweet, sour, salty, and bitter. The taste receptors are located primarily on the tongue, and a few are found in the throat. The average **taste bud** is replaced about every 10 days, so that destroying some by burning your tongue is not likely to do any long-term damage. An adult human has approximately 10,000 taste buds. Some are sensitive to only one quality (for instance, sweet); others react to combinations of qualities; and some individual taste buds respond to all four qualities (Arvidson & Friberg, 1980). Most of the taste buds that respond to sweet are found at the tip of the tongue, those responding to salty on the sides and at the tip, those to sour on the sides, and those to bitter toward the back. As you probably realize, the sense of taste is really more complex than this description makes it sound. Some taste buds have up to 40 neurons that may respond to more than one kind of taste, and there is also much "cross-talk" between taste-sensitive neurons, which can greatly modify their responses (Roper, 1989).

Taste senses are quite active early in life. Newborns readily respond to sugar, salt, lemon juice, and quinine, which stimulate the sweet, salty, sour, and bitter senses. Newborns like sweet but increasingly dislike salt, sour, and bitter, in that order. By adulthood, many people have acquired a liking for salty and sour, but

Of the four basic tastes, the taste of sweet is the only one readily preferred by newborns. By adulthood, although many people acquire a liking for salty and sour, sweet remains the favorite.

few people ever acquire a liking for bitter. This probably doesn't surprise you. Most people like sweet candy, salty peanuts, or even sour pickles, but very few, if any, like the bitter taste of dissolved aspirin.

It has been argued that the senses of taste, like other physiological functions, evolved because they were adaptive. We may wonder, for example, why cats have no taste buds sensitive to sweet, while dogs and human beings do. The reason may be that cats, unlike dogs and human beings, have never needed these taste buds. Wild dogs eat meat, roots, or berries, and human beings in the wild eat the same things. Bitter and sour roots and berries are more likely to be poisonous than sweet roots or berries are, so the sense of sweet may have evolved as a protective measure. Animals attracted to sweet would be less likely to be poisoned, and they would pass on their affinity for sweet to their offspring. Cats, on the other hand, are carnivores (meat eaters) in the wild; an affinity for sweet would serve no purpose for them. Supporting the idea that taste evolved because it helped animals to approach or avoid certain foods is the discovery that distinct and separate neural systems are associated with the approach and avoidance of food by taste (Berridge & Fentress, 1985).

SMELL

Smell may be one of the oldest of the senses, and scent messages, unlike information from the other senses, are not relayed through the thalamus but pass to lower areas of the brain that are older in evolutionary terms. The receptors for smell are contained in the **olfactory epithelium** high up within the nose. Receptors in the olfactory epithelium function in a lock and key system. Substances have different odors because they have different molecular shapes. **Molecules** that are shaped alike will fit into receptors that are responsive to them, just as keys of the same cut will fit into a particular lock. Therefore, molecules of similar shape have the same or similar odors.

The olfactory epithelium contains hundreds of different kinds of receptors. Odors are captured within the nasal mucus. There, a special *carrier* molecule picks up the odor and takes it to the receptors (Lee, Wells, & Reed, 1987), where the odor may, in turn, stimulate an individual receptor or combinations of different kinds of receptors to fire. Some molecules, such as carbon dioxide, have a shape that will not stimulate receptors in the olfactory epithelium, and they are therefore odorless. Interestingly, 1.2 percent of the population is smell-blind, that is, they are unable to detect odors of any kind (Smith, 1989).

Many animals have a better sense of smell than humans do. Dogs, for instance, are capable of detecting odors 1000 times weaker than those a human nose could detect. The sense of smell helps animals to recognize objects, locations, and food. Buzzards are an interesting case in point. Because buzzards eat carrion, that is, rotting flesh, they have evolved to find that horrible stink attractive. They have also evolved mechanisms that help protect them from the diseases associated with rotting meat. In fact, in one experiment a researcher injected a buzzard with enough botulism toxin to kill 300,000 guinea pigs—it didn't even slow the buzzard down (Smith, 1989).

In many animals, this sense is especially important for sexual communication. Substances that excite sexual activity, called **pheromones,** may be secreted by an animal and carried downwind, where their reception in the olfactory epithelium of another animal arouses sexual interest. For instance, when dogs in heat secrete pheromones, they can attract male dogs that are downwind at distances as great as

TASTE BUDS
Groups of cells distributed over the tongue that constitute the receptors of the sense of taste.

OLFACTORY EPITHELIUM
Nasal membranes containing receptor cells sensitive to odors.

MOLECULE
A electrically bound grouping of two or more atoms that comprise a chemically distinct entity.

PHEROMONES
Substances that, when secreted, are sexual attractants to receptive organisms via olfactory perception.

Bloodhounds are used for tracking because their acute sense of smell, well over 1000 times more sensitive than our own, enables them to follow a scent trail that may be days old.

1 or 2 miles. But what about human beings? Do we use our sense of smell for sexual identification? Recent discoveries in this area have led to an increased interest in the olfactory sense and to some further surprising discoveries of both a sexual and a nonsexual nature.

At this point, perfume manufacturers and the sexually deprived might wonder if there isn't some substance that people could apply to attract potential sexual partners. In fact, there is a possible substance, called alpha-androstenol. Alpha-androstenol is a strong sexual pheromone for pigs and is found in some human secretions. Researchers have found that if surgical masks are sprayed with alpha-androstenol and given to men and women to wear, those people wearing the treated masks rate people in photographs as more attractive than subjects in a control group do (Kirk-Smith, Booth, Carroll, & Davies, 1978). If you decide to wear perfume or cologne containing alpha-androstenol, however, keep two things in mind. First, human social and sexual behavior is very complicated. Don't think that human beings can be controlled by pheromones as lower animals are. The effect of alpha-androstenol, if any, will undoubtedly be very weak (Rogel, 1978). Second, since it is a very powerful pig pheromone, it might be wise to stay away from farms.

Another area that has generated recent interest is that of *kin recognition*. In mice, it has been discovered that each mouse's genes impart to it a characteristic scent. Animals with similar genes (relatives, for instance) smell somewhat the same. With nothing more to go on than another mouse's scent, mice are able to tell their kin from nonrelatives. Whether this ability has a functional value is not known, but it may aid mice in avoiding mating with kin which, in turn, reduces the chances of genetic disease or defects in the offspring (Beauchamp, Yamazaki, & Boyse, 1985).

There is even evidence that kin recognition by smell occurs in humans. In one study, researcher Richard Porter discovered that 17 out of 18 mothers could distinguish their own child's T-shirt by its aroma from those of other children (McCarthy, 1986). To control for diet and other environmental factors, Porter conducted the same test with husbands and wives (of course, the use of specific detergents, perfumes, and other such substances was controlled). Husbands and wives failed to identify each other's scents. Porter's explanation for this inability is that husbands and wives do not smell "genetically" alike. Researchers are now investigating human kin recognition by scent with an eye on how it might affect the emotional closeness felt between parent and child or how it might influence human sexual behavior. Many neuroscientists now believe that olfaction may be closely tied to such emotional behavior. Their belief is supported by the fact that many nerve fibers leaving the olfactory epithelium detour through the limbic system before traveling to other locations. The limbic system, as you recall from Chapter 2, is a center of memory and emotion. Perhaps in the future we will come to understand better some of these more subtle effects of smell.

TOUCH

The total surface of the skin is about 20 square feet. That is roughly 1000 times more area than that of the retinas. Imbedded within the skin are many receptors for touch. Different touch receptors measure pressure, light touch, vibration, aching pain, sharp pain, cold, and warmth. In addition, there are complex interactions among the touch receptors.

Touch receptors on the skin are not evenly distributed. For example, the lips and the fingertips are far more sensitive than is the back. If someone places two

sharp pencils side by side, holding them so that their tips are only about 1 millimeter apart, and then touches them to your fingertip while your eyes are closed, you will find it easy to tell whether you're being touched with one point or two. This two-point discrimination is simple on the fingertip because of the high concentration of touch receptors there. On the back, however, where there is a lower concentration of touch receptors, pencil points sometimes have to be placed as far as 2 1/2 inches apart before the person being touched can tell whether one or two points are being used!

Touch receptors appear to be distributed over the body in receptive fields, each associated with its own grouping of touch neurons, not unlike the way in which ganglion cells in the visual system are associated with receptive fields of photo-receptor cells. Touch reception is projected to the somatosensory area of the parietal lobes of the brain (see Chapter 2). Different locations in the cerebral cortex receive touch information from different fields on the body. If you wish, you can feel the different locations in the cortex at work by performing Aristotle's illusion (see Figure 3.21).

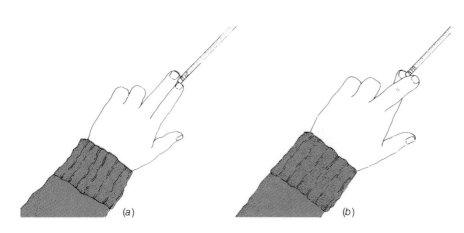

(a)   (b)

FIGURE 3.21

To "feel" a touch at different locations in the cerebral cortex, perform Aristotle's illusion. First, touch the eraser end of a pencil to both fingers, as shown in (a). These locations on your fingertips are close enough together to project to a very similar location on the cerebral cortex, providing you with the sensation of one touch. Now cross your fingers as shown in (b) and touch again. These locations on your fingertips are farther apart and are received at two very different locations on the cerebral cortex, giving you the unexpected sensation of two touches.

Touch also has its emotional and social components, especially when we consider the role of touch in transmitting pain or affection. Pain is perhaps the most feared of the touch senses. Pain is valuable in that it alerts us to bodily damage, but there are times, as we all know, when we desperately want the pain to stop. The best solution would be to stop pain at its source, right at the beginning of the sensation—and we might soon be able to do just that.

In 1949, a Brazilian scientist named Mauricio Rocha e Silva and his student Wilson Beraldo were investigating the reasons for the terrible pain that was associated with the bite of the deadly jararaca snake (see Figure 3.22). Through careful analysis, they discovered that the snake's venom liberated copious amounts of a natural substance in the body of its victims; they called this substance **bradykinin.** We now know that any injury, scrape, or damage to the body causes bradykinin to be formed in the blood—and the pain begins. Bradykinin appears to cause "pain" neurons to reach action potential and to fire. Researcher Solomon Snyder, working with bradykinin, said, "If you take all the known chemicals that collect in tissue after injury and inject them under a person's skin, most of them don't hurt, or don't hurt much. . . . But if you inject bradykinin, the patient goes through the roof" (McKean, 1986, p. 85). Obviously, this is not the kind of research for which it is easy to get volunteers. Researchers are now searching for substances that may be able to block bradykinin.

Touch also has its tender side. Touch obviously plays an important role in affection, and it may have subtle influences as well. People often seem to feel better when they are touched. In one study, researchers even found that restaurant customers who had been lightly touched by their waitress left a bigger tip than other customers did, although most of them said they were unaware of the touch (Crusco & Wetzel, 1984).

KINESTHETIC AND VESTIBULAR SENSES

You may always have considered vision, hearing, smell, taste, and touch to be "the five senses," but there are other senses that are very important in many ways.

FIGURE 3.22

Brazilian scientist Wilson Beraldo with a deadly jararaca snake safely contained in formaldehyde. It was Beraldo who first realized that the snake's bite is so extremely painful because the venom liberates large amounts of bradykinin in the blood of the snake's victims.

The kinesthetic sense is one of these. **Kinesthesis** is the sense that informs you of the position of your body and limbs at any given time. From the feedback you receive when you move or reach for objects, you learn to interpret the weight and pressure on your muscles and joints and to use this information to ascertain your body's orientation in space.

The kinesthetic sense can be altered to some degree, and an interesting experiment demonstrates this. If you were to put on a pair of prism goggles that displaced everything 15 degrees to the right, at first you would find it very difficult to function. If an object was directly in front of you, you would reach for it only to see your hand 15 degrees to the right of its actual position. If you kept the goggles on and continued to reach for the object until your hand finally located it, and you did this many times, your kinesthetic sense would become adjusted fairly quickly to the 15-degree displacement. After that, you would have no trouble reaching for objects if you continued to wear the goggles that displaced everything 15 degrees to the right. If you took off the goggles, however, the world would immediately become a strange place again. There you would be with your goggles off, and you would think everything was normal. You'd see an object directly in front and you'd reach for it, relying on your kinesthetic sense to tell you where to move your hand. Amazingly, your hand would shoot off to the *left* 15 degrees from where you aimed it. Again, a period of adjustment would be required until you learned kinesthetically to position your arms in space. In one fascinating experiment, researchers demonstrated that a person's kinesthetic sense could be tricked by producing certain kinds of vibrations in his wrist tendons. Subjects in the experiment were amazed because the vibrations caused them to experience multiple kinesthetic stimulations simultaneously, which created a sense of impossible limb positions or of having multiple forearms (Craske, 1977).

Most of the kinesthetic information sent to the brain comes from receptors located in the joints (Adams, 1977). In the brain, there appear to be specialized detectors associated with the kinesthetic sense, much as there are specialized detectors for the visual and auditory senses. These specialized kinesthetic detectors appear to be associated with different postures (Costanzo & Gardner, 1981; Gardner & Costanzo, 1981).

The **vestibular sense** is the sense of balance. It tells you the direction in which the force of gravity is operating, or the direction in which you are accelerating (for instance, while you are riding in a car or an elevator). The vestibular sense arises from the functioning of the inner ear, where the **semicircular canals** and **vestibular sacs** are located. The three semicircular canals are roughly perpendicular to one another and lie on three planes, so that body rotation in all three directions can be monitored (refer to Figure 3.19). When stereocilia within the canals are displaced by moving fluid, you know that you have changed position in relation to the field of gravity. In this way, you can sense that you are lying down or standing up at any given moment, even with your eyes shut. If the fluid is disturbed to a great degree, it's difficult to maintain balance. If you ever got on a wound-up swing as a child and spun around and around, you'll recall how you found it absolutely impossible to maintain your balance when you stepped off. The fluid in your semicircular canals continued to move, and it wasn't until the fluid became still again that you regained your orientation. Similarly, diseases and injury to the inner ear can cause an immediate loss of balance.

Researchers have discovered that messages from the visual, kinesthetic, and vestibular senses all come together at specific locations in the cerebral cortex. The fact that these inputs converge is probably what enables us to perform functions such as turning that require all three of these senses (Mergner, Anastosopoulos, Becker, & Deecke, 1981).

KINESTHESIS
An inclusive term for the muscle, tendon, and joint senses that yield information about the position and movement of various parts of the body.

VESTIBULAR SENSE
The sense that keeps an organism in proper balance.

SEMICIRCULAR CANALS
Three small, liquid-filled canals located in the inner ear containing receptors sensitive to changes in spatial orientation.

VESTIBULAR SACS
Two baglike structures at the base of the semicircular canals containing receptors for the sense of balance.

The kinesthetic sense provides us with knowledge about our position in space, and the vestibular sense gives us an idea of the direction in which gravity is operating. Because of the centrifugal force experienced during the loop in a wild ride such as this, the vestibular and kinesthetic senses will not tell you that you are upside down; only your visual sense will. This unusual combination makes the ride thrilling.

We have discussed the five tradition and two other senses, but are there other senses that we haven't covered—"extra" senses? There are words describing such extra senses or powers: *clairvoyance,* sensing events at a distance unhindered by normal physical barriers; *telepathy,* sending thought messages from one person to another; *precognition,* seeing the future; *psychokinesis,* moving solid objects with mental rather than physical power. Although we have words for these senses and powers, does anyone really have any of these faculties? How can we tell? The only way, of course, is to conduct very carefully controlled experiments examining the different powers and senses that individuals claim to possess.

Most researchers believe that no *extrasensory* perception (ESP) has ever been demonstrated under carefully controlled conditions in a manner that could not be explained as chance. Nonetheless, a number of cases are intriguing. Their positive findings may confirm the existence of a weak, but real, phenomenon that is difficult to demonstrate. On the other hand, they may simply confirm that scientists are among the easiest people to fool, especially if an expert magician tries to fool them. People can make a lot of money by claiming they have powers of prediction, for example, and it's difficult, even under what seem to be controlled conditions, to uncover the gimmick they are using to create such an illusion.

These days most scientists, when confronted with discussions of extrasensory perception, reincarnation, UFOs, the Bermuda triangle, or poltergeists, just throw up their hands in disgust and refuse to talk about such matters. But this is a poor attitude,

Uri Geller "bends a spoon" with his "mind power."

because any strange phenomenon probably merits investigation (Child, 1985). With this in mind, a committee of over 40 people has been formed to investigate unusual phenomena, including extrasensory perception. Among its members is a magician, the Amazing Randi (to help show up the tricksters).

Uri Geller was one such trickster. Geller claimed to have a number of extraordinary powers, and he convinced Edgar Mitchell, a scientist and one of the astronauts who walked on the moon, that his powers were real. Mitchell accompanied Geller on a number of talk shows and asserted that Geller's powers were genuine. Geller claimed to be able to bend nails and spoons with the power of his mind and to start watches all over the country whenever he desired, even if the watches were broken. The Amazing Randi was able to duplicate every one of Geller's tricks. Geller had no real powers. In his book *The Magic of Uri Geller,* Randi describes the tricks Geller used to fool the scientists.

More recently, Randi investigated a man who claimed to have the power of psychokinesis. The man stated that he could turn the pages of a tele-

phone book placed on a table by kneeling down to eye level with the table and concentrating. The pages certainly did begin to turn, and viewers were amazed. Randi wasn't. He surrounded the book with styrofoam balls and asked the fellow to try again. This time the power mysteriously failed him. Randi explained that the "psychokinesis" in this case was really a fine jet of air expelled between the lips in pulses in a very subtle way that required some practice. Had the man tried to turn the pages the second time, he would have blown the styrofoam balls all over the place and his trick would have been obvious (Rucker, 1981).

What about researchers from prestigious institutions or universities claiming to have discovered legitimate psychic phenomena? Could such scientists be easily fooled? In 1979, the late James McDonnell, who had been the chairman of the McDonnell–Douglas Corporation, gave half a million dollars to Washington University in St. Louis for the establishment of a laboratory to study extrasensory phenomena. A professor of physics was named the administrator. The laboratory began its work investigating many subjects and by

1982 had found two young men who were considered by researchers at the university to have demonstrated reliable and convincing evidence of paranormal power. Among other things, one had been observed to make a clock slide across a table without touching it, and both were able to make a digital watch suddenly display apparently random numbers. The researchers considered the subjects to be "the most reliable of the people that we've studied" ("Psychic Abscam," 1983, p. 10). Other people stated that what these subjects did was "beyond the usual laws of physics" ("Psychic Abscam," 1983, p. 12).

At this point, the Amazing Randi stepped forward and identified the two young men as assistants of his whom he had sent to the institute. The clock had slid across the table by the means of an extremely thin "magician's wire" attached by one of the subjects when no one was looking; the digital watch read out strange numbers because the subjects bombarded it with microwave radiation that had gone undetected; and so on. Randi's point was clear—some scientists are easy to fool; they don't conduct experiments carefully enough, and they are too eager to find positive results.

Of course, Randi is not the only person hot on the trail of frauds.

Other researchers have found ingenious ways to investigate claims of the paranormal. For instance, one researcher placed $5000 in a sealed box, along with a slip of paper on which he had written a first, middle, and last name of his own choosing. He invited any psychic who makes a living by exercising predictive "powers" (the ones whose startling predictions jump out at you in large black headlines in tabloids at the supermarket checkout stands) simply to state the name he had written on the slip of paper in the box to collect the $5000. So far, no takers.

EPILOGUE: THE READY ROOM

Psychologists who study sensation generally focus on the structure and function of human sensory systems. From this study, they often gain insights that can be applied to the everyday world. The following is an account of how one psychologist used his knowledge of sensation to help the Allied cause in World War II.

In 1940, Hitler launched his Luftwaffe against the British. He had one goal in mind: to destroy the Royal Air Force totally and thus to gain complete command over the English Channel in preparation for Operation Sea Lion, the invasion of Britain. On the other side of the channel facing this aerial onslaught were a few Royal Air Force pilots manning fighter planes. Seriously outnumbered, they took off at all hours of the night to meet the oncoming enemy. Many of them never returned.

Because the pilots had to rush to their planes at a moment's notice in the predawn hours, they had to keep their eyes dark-adapted. They were never sure when they would be called into the air, so they had to avoid light from sunset on, waiting in pitch-black ready rooms. They couldn't play cards, read books, or even see one another's faces. They simply waited, hour after hour in complete darkness, until a call came to take to the air. The loneliness and fear in those ready rooms must have been terrible. Fear has a way of making hours pass very slowly.

In the United States, a psychologist named Walter R. Miles, who was a renowned researcher of the sensory system, heard about the plight

As the sun sets, operators monitoring modern U.S. strategic bombers switch their control room to red light so they will remain dark-adapted throughout the night.

of the British pilots. Miles understood that the fighter pilots had to maintain dark adaptation, but he also realized that it was absolutely unnecessary for them to sit in the dark. Miles knew that the rod photoreceptors, those required for night vision, were not sensitive to the red end of the spectrum, and that red light could therefore not light-adapt the rods. He informed the Royal Air Force of this fact, and red lights were placed in the fighter pilot's ready rooms. Thereafter, pilots waiting for their flights were able to see one another's faces as they played cards or read books. They could pass the time sharing one another's company (Miller, 1980).

Ever since that time, it has been the practice of the military in night operations to use red light in submarines in case the ship has to surface or in aircraft so that the pilots can see when they look out into the dark. Work can go on, because the red-sensitive cones are stimulated by the red light, and dark adaptation is maintained because the rods don't react to that light.

SUMMARY

■ Our ways of organizing the world and of responding to it depend a great deal on how our senses filter the stimuli and information around us. We come to know our world primarily through our senses, and what we sense often affects our behavior.

■ The amount of energy required to create a noticeable sensation is called the absolute threshold. The minimum amount of energy difference necessary before a change in stimulation can be detected is known as the difference threshold.

■ Although there are many parallels between the camera and the eye, the two are actually more different than alike.

■ The retina is composed of layers, containing the ganglion cells, bipolar cells, amacrine cells, horizontal cells, and the photoreceptors—rods and cones.

■ In normal daylight vision, the most sensitive portion of the eye is the fovea.

■ One portion of the peripheral retina contains no photoreceptors; it is here that the optic nerve passes through the retina on its way to the brain. This area is known as the blind spot.

■ Different neural receptors are stimulated by different wavelengths within the visible light range. The rods are sensitive to all light except red. The cones are specialized, some responding to red, some to green, and some to blue wavelengths.

■ The fovea is made up exclusively of cones. For this reason, it is not sensitive to extremely dim illumination.

■ After 30 or 40 minutes in the dark, the rods reach their full sensitivity, a stage called dark adaptation.

■ There are two major theories that explain color vision: the Young–Helmholtz theory and the Hering opponent-process theory. Modern color vision theory incorporates both views. The Young–Helmholtz three-color theory explains the functioning of the cones, while the Hering opponent-process theory helps to explain afterimages.

■ All colors in the spectrum can be produced from three primary colors—red, green, and blue. Using beams of light, all colors can be created by additive mixing (as opposed to subtractive mixing, the process by which pigments are combined).

■ Because most color blindness is sex-linked, it is more common in men than in women. Among dichromats, one of the cone systems is malfunctioning. Green-cone dichromats are the most common. Monochromats have only one functioning cone system and, as a result, are unable to discriminate color.

■ Edwin Land helped to develop color constancy theory, which explains how we continue to sense the same colors under extremely different lighting and illuminations.

■ Ganglion cells in the retina respond to receptive fields created by the photoreceptor rods and cones. From the retina, most visual information passes along the optic nerves through higher areas of the brain to the occipital lobes of the cerebral cortex. There the information is processed by simple, complex, and hypercomplex cells, which are specialized detectors receptive to differences in line orientation, motion, width, length, angle, and color.

■ Aftereffects are visual effects produced by fatigue of one kind of receptor in the higher levels of the visual system. They differ from afterimages in that aftereffects transfer from one eye to the other.

■ Just as the eyes are sensitive to a limited range of the electromagnetic spectrum, so the ears are sensitive to a limited range of frequencies caused by the compression and rarefaction of air.

■ The pitch of a sound is determined by the frequency of the sound wave, and the loudness of a sound is determined by the amplitude of the sound wave.

■ Three theories of hearing have been proposed to explain the range of the human auditory system: the place theory, the frequency theory, and the volley theory.

■ Bioengineers have produced an artificial ear in which platinum implants replace damaged stereocilia in the inner ear and stimulate the auditory nerve by generating small electric shocks in response to different frequencies. Artificial eyes are also under development. Perhaps someday it will be possible to induce a full range of artificial sensory inputs.

■ Taste is a fairly limited sense. Taste buds respond to sweet, sour, salty, and bitter.

■ Smell is one of the oldest senses. The sense of smell works according to the lock and key principle, in which molecules of a particular shape fit into receptors that are responsive to them, allowing a particular odor to be perceived.

■ In many animals, the olfactory sense is especially important for sexual communication.

■ There are many senses of touch. Different sensory systems measure pressure, light touch, vibration, aching pain, sharp pain, warmth, and cold.

■ The kinesthetic sense informs us of the position of our body and limbs at any given time.

■ The vestibular sense helps us to keep our balance.

■ Most researchers believe that no extrasensory perception has ever been demonstrated in a manner that could not be explained as chance.

SUGGESTIONS FOR FURTHER READING

1. Coren, S., & Ward, L. M. (1989). *Sensation and perception* (3rd ed.). New York: Academic Press. A college-level introduction to sensory and perceptual processes.
2. Frisby, J. P. (1980). *Seeing*. Oxford, England: Oxford University Press. An introduction to vision for the general reader. Includes information on visual processing and many full-color illustrations.
3. Goldstein, E. B. (1989). *Sensation and perception* (3rd ed.). Belmont, CA: Wadsworth. A college-level introductory textbook. Includes material on sensation and perception.
4. Hubel, D. H., (1988). *Eye, brain, and vision*. New York: Scientific American Books. A description of the groundbreaking research on vision between the years 1950 and 1980. Written by a Nobel prize-winning scientist.
5. Smith, J. (1989). *Senses & sensibilities*. New York: John Wiley & Sons. An introduction to the senses for the general reader. Very well written and fun to read.
6. Wolfe, J. M. (Ed.). (1986). *The mind's eye: Readings from Scientific American*. New York: W. H. Freeman. A collection of articles from *Scientific American* on visual and perceptual systems.

CHAPTER 4 | Perception

Prologue

Why Psychologists Study Perception

Perceptual Basics
    Brain Pathways
    Form and Shape Perception

Illusions

Perceptual Constancies

Depth Perception
    Monocular Clues
    The Moon Illusion
    Binocular Cues
    The Visual Cliff

Motion Perception

Other Senses

Epilogue: "That's Him!"

Summary

Suggestions for Further Reading

PROLOGUE

You are driving through the dense rain forest of the Congo River valley. You are in a jeep with a native Pygmy named Kenge and an anthropologist named Colin Turnbull. You and Turnbull have been collecting anthropological data, and the native has offered to assist you. The Pygmy has never ridden in a jeep before. He's having a good time. He and his tribe roam exclusively within the rain forest, and this will be the first time he's ventured beyond it. After a few hours of driving, you reach the crest of a great hill where the rain forest ends. Beyond is the wide expanse of the African plain. Visibility is almost 70 miles. In the rain forest, the foliage is so dense that it is hard to see more than 100 yards.

Far away on the plain, in the direction you are traveling, is a herd of water buffalo. You point them out to Turnbull and Kenge. The Pygmy laughs and says, "No, they're insects." Turnbull repeats that they're buffalo, far away. Kenge tells you both to stop telling such stupid lies; he seems insulted. He continues to insist that the water buffalo are obviously insects. Since you are traveling toward the animals, it seems that the argument will be settled in short order. As the distance lessens, the buffalo seem to grow larger and larger until finally it's apparent that what you have been looking at is indeed a large herd of water buffalo.

The Pygmy looks shocked, confused, and frightened. He doesn't say any more and refuses to leave the jeep. It's then that you realize that he is totally unfamiliar with great vistas, because he has spent his life in the rain forest. His perception was different from yours because he never learned that objects appear to be very small when they are far away. Seeing the tiny buffalo, he assumed that they were close at hand and must be insects. On the plain, without a tree or some other measure,

PERCEPTION
The brain's interpretation of the
information processed by the senses.

Kenge is totally unable to judge distance. Later that day, you show him Lake Edward, so large that its opposite shore can't be seen. Kenge can't comprehend this expanse of water, which seems to be a river without banks. Far out on the lake is a wooden boat filled with people. When you tell Kenge what it is, he's amazed. He thought it was a nearby piece of driftwood. All this is too much; he wants to go back to the rain forest (Turnbull, 1961).

In this chapter, we will examine the ways in which you organize your senses to form perceptions of the world around you. Two important theories of perception are presented and the merits of each are discussed. Along the way, you'll learn how moviemakers create special effects, how three-dimensional vision works, what illusions are, and how your biology helps you to organize the complexities of your environment.

WHY PSYCHOLOGISTS STUDY PERCEPTION

Perception refers to the way in which we interpret or understand the messages our sensory systems have processed. Gestalt psychologists helped to develop many of the organizing principles that today form the foundation on which our understanding of perception rests. By knowing about perception, we can better understand how people are organized to deal with their environment and, in turn, understand better why they behave as they do.

Before we venture into this area of study, we must distinguish between sensation and perception. There are a number of surprises in store. Look at Figure 4.1. You

FIGURE 4.1

Fraser's spiral.

will see a spiral curving downward until it reaches the apex. If there were a staircase and you began at the top, you would eventually reach the bottom by walking round and round. At least, that's what your brain tells you (which just shows you how much you can trust your brain). But put your finger at any point on the curves of the design and begin to move down the spiral staircase with your fingertip—see how far you get! Trace very carefully. You will discover there's no spiral at all, only concentric circles, one inside the next.

This design is known as Fraser's "spiral." The spiral that you see is an **illusion;** it doesn't exist. Your brain, however, interpreted this information according to some organizing principle, and you *perceived* a spiral. The illusion is so strong that people tracing the spiral sometimes begin to move inward from one circle to the next, but as long as you trace carefully you'll always come back to your starting point. This example clearly shows the difference between sensation and perception. Sensation refers to the collecting or gathering of sensory information; perception is an active interpretation of that sensory information (see Focus on an Application).

PERCEPTUAL BASICS

Brain Pathways

For many years, researchers have known that whenever we look at any scene, there are three basic tasks required of our perceptual mechanisms. First, we have to distinguish *form* and *shape* from background. In a sense, we are asking, "Is there something there?" If the answer is "yes," then we have to determine the *location* of these forms or shapes in space—"Where are these things I see?" Last, we need to know if they are *moving* or *acting*—"Are these things doing anything?" Once we have perceptually answered these three questions, we can usually comprehend the sensations our eyes are giving us.

Some of the most exciting research of the last few years has been the isolation of distinct and separate pathways in the brain for these different kinds of perception (Livingstone, 1988). The first two tasks, "Is there something there?" and "Where are these things I see?" are both handled by a combination of two different brain pathways. The first pathway is dedicated to color. Because this color information travels from the cones of the retina to the areas of the occipital cortex called "blobs" (see Chapter 3), it has come to be called, believe it or not, the **blob pathway** (see Figure 4.3, p. 119).

The second distinct pathway is dedicated to the high-resolution perception of stationary shape and form outlines. These messages begin in the retina with the stimulation of small ganglion cells (see Chapter 3) and continue on to the midbrain where more small cells are stimulated. From there, the messages travel to areas that surround the blobs in the occipital cortex. The word *parvo*, from the Latin root *parvus*, means "small." Because so many small-sized cells are involved, this pathway has come to be called—are you ready for this?—the **parvo-interblob pathway.**

The third basic perceptual task, *is there motion or action*, is handled by a third distinct pathway that is dedicated to motion and stereoscopic depth perception (the depth vision afforded by the use of both eyes). The messages of this pathway begin in the retina with the stimulation of large ganglion cells (see Chapter 3) and continue on to the midbrain where more large cells are stimulated. From there, the messages are sent to the occipital cortex. This is known as the **magno pathway**, in reference to its many large-sized cells.

The three separate pathways interact in some yet as unknown fashion to produce the complete perception (see Figure 4.4, p. 120).

ILLUSION
A significant and consistent interpretation of sensory information by a given population that is not in agreement with precise and objective measurement.

BLOB PATHWAY
A distinct brain pathway for the transmission of color information. So named because color information is conveyed via a root that travels from the cones of the retina through the midbrain and then to areas of the occipital cortex known as "blobs."

PARVO-INTERBLOB PATHWAY
A distinct brain pathway for the transmission of high-resolution perception of stationary shapes and forms. These messages begin in the retina with the stimulation of small ganglion cells and continue on to the midbrain where more small cells are stimulated. From there, the messages travel to areas that surround the blobs in the occipital cortex.

MAGNO PATHWAY
A distinct brain pathway for the transmission of motion and stereoscopic depth perception. These messages begin in the retina with the stimulation of large ganglion cells and continue on to the midbrain where more large cells are stimulated. From there, the messages are sent to the occipital cortex.

SIGHTLESS VISION

John M. Kennedy and his colleagues have worked with blind children and adults, many of whom have been sightless since birth. Through his research, Kennedy has gathered persuasive evidence that congenitally blind people can picture things in their "mind's eye," even though they've never seen them. Kennedy argues that the blind do this by using an internal understanding of perspective gathered through the sense of touch.

Kennedy has concluded that the principles that underlie visual perception are the same as those used in touch. He argues that vision and touch, unlike hearing, are responsive to dimensions of shape and form. He points out that we do not "see" with our eyes or "feel" with our touch receptors. Instead, both sight and touch are *perceptions* generated by the brain based on incoming stimuli. Because of this, blind people, relying on a sense of touch, may organize and understand their perceptions in ways very similar to those sighted persons use.

That blind people seem to develop a perceptual understanding of the geometry of their world was of interest to biophysicist Carter Collins and other researchers who set out to design a new aid for the blind. The work began with Geldard's 1957 article discussing the possibility that stimulation of the skin could communicate information. Paul Bach-Y-Rita and his colleagues then began developing a system based on this principle (Bach-Y-Rita, Collins, Saunders, White, & Scadden, 1969; White, Saunders, Scadden, Bach-Y-Rita, & Collins, 1970). At the Smith–Kettlewell Institute of Visual Sciences in San Francisco, Collins

impressed televised pictures directly onto a person's back or chest by using a technique called **tactile sensory replacement (TSR)**. A TSR user wears a vest containing a grid on which are hundreds of tiny points that touch the wearer (see Figure 4.2). When the vest is connected to a small black-and-white television camera, the light and dark messages gathered by the camera can be "shone" on the person's back or chest by electrically stimulating the different points and making them vibrate. The entire device weighs only 5 pounds. Blind persons using it have been able to find objects in a room quickly, read meters, and even use an oscilloscope. One blind technician wearing the device was able to assemble something as small as a microcircuit.

What does it feel like to wear the device? The following account was given by a person with normal sight who tried out Collin's TSR device.

I sat blindfolded in the chair, the cones cold against my back. At first I felt only formless waves of sensation. Collins said he was just waving his hand in front of me so that I could get used to the feeling. Suddenly I felt or saw, I wasn't sure which, a black triangle in the lower left corner of a square. The sensation was hard to pinpoint. I felt vibrations on my back, but the triangle appeared in a square frame in my head. There was no color, but there was a light area and a dark area. If you close your eyes and face a light or the sun and pass an object in front of your eyes, a difference appears in the darkness. That difference is approximately what I saw. The image was fuzzy at first, but, even in my ten minutes in the chair, it became clearer. When Collins confirmed that he was holding a triangle, it was clearer still.

For me, believing that there is a difference between sensation and perception

FIGURE 4.2

The TSR device, which allows blind subjects to "feel" what sighted subjects can "see."

has always required an enormous leap of faith. It is hard to believe that I do not see with my eyes or hear with my ears. Although we may learn that there is a difference between sensation and perception, we rarely experience [it]. . . . at the TSR lab I experienced the difference for the first time. The sensation was on my back, the perception was in my head. Feeling is believing. (Hechinger, 1981, p. 43)

Form and Shape Perception

Before we can tell whether there is "anything out there," we need to be able to distinguish the form or shape from its background. This is the ability to distinguish a tree from the background sky or a person from a wall in front of which she might be standing. Technically, it is called the separation of **figure** from **ground**. Figure 4.4 shows two **reversible figures** and demonstrates that separating figure from ground is not due to something inherent in the stimulus, because the same reversible figure may give rise to different perceptual organizations depending on how you look at it. In fact, researchers have isolated cells in the brain that will fire, or not fire, depending on which of the reversible figures you think you are perceiving (whether you perceive the profiles or the vase) (Logothetis & Schall, 1989).

From early in this century, when Gestalt psychologists (see Chapter 1) began to investigate the way in which the mind organizes information provided by the senses, perceptual organization of stimuli has attracted interest. Gestalt psychologists were primarily interested in demonstrating that the structuralist approach of breaking conscious perceptions into component parts was an ineffective way of understanding perception, because humans often organize their perceptions into whole entities. This, the Gestaltists argued, is why you are able to recognize the same melody when it is played at different pitches or by different instruments. The experience of the *relationship* of the parts is as important as the parts themselves, or, as the Gestaltists liked to say, "The whole is greater than the sum of the parts." Another example is that experiencing the perception of "white," which is made from equal amounts of red, green, and blue (see Chapter 3), is not the same as experiencing the colors red, green, and blue one after the other. The whole (white) is something else, something more, than just its parts.

TACTILE SENSORY REPLACEMENT (TSR)
A device to aid the blind. A television camera is connected to a vest worn by the subject. An image is then formed on the viewer's back or chest by means of tactile stimulation. Through practice, the wearer can obtain a perceptual understanding of the visual world.

FIGURE
In perception, a perceptual experience that is characterized by contour, coherence, structure, and solidity. It is typically experienced against a ground (for example, it appears to be in the foreground).

GROUND
In perception, all that is perceived to be background.

REVERSIBLE FIGURES
Any of a class of figures that appear suddenly to change perspective or figure-ground relationship when looked at carefully and steadily.

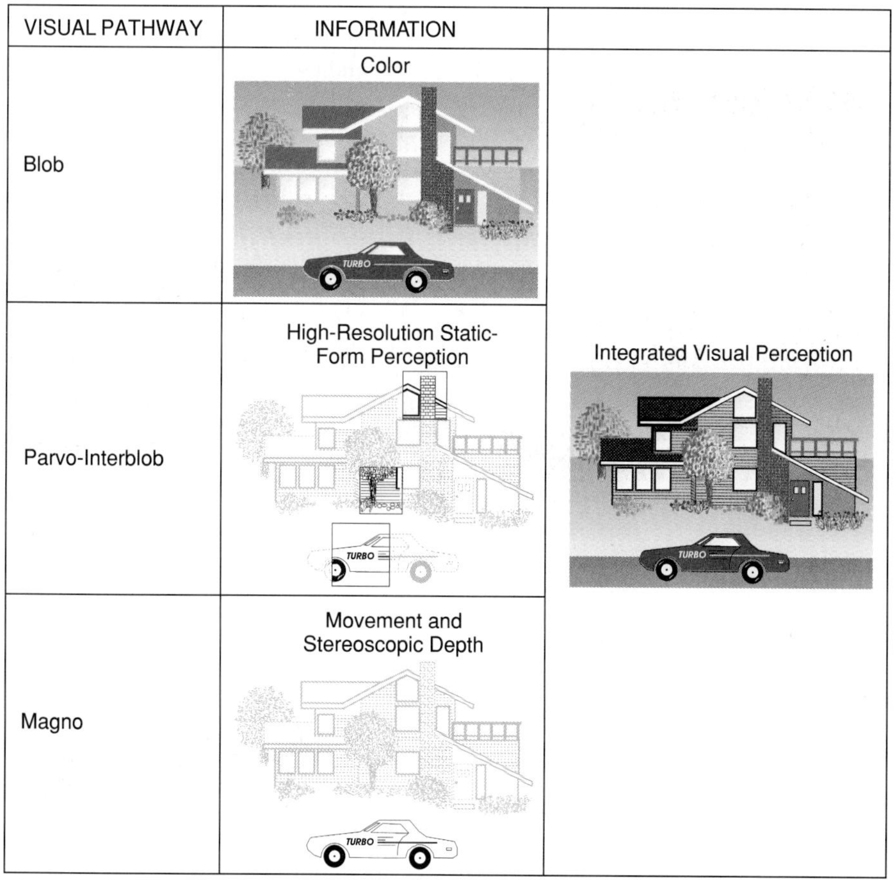

VISUAL PATHWAY	INFORMATION	
	Color	
Blob		
Parvo-Interblob	High-Resolution Static-Form Perception	Integrated Visual Perception
Magno	Movement and Stereoscopic Depth	

FIGURE 4.3

Vision is a system consisting of three parts. The blob pathway is used in color vision; the perception of stationary forms is handled by the parvo-interblob pathway, and the magno pathway handles the perception of movement and depth. When messages from the three pathways are integrated, a unified world in three dimensions is perceived. (After Livingstone, 1988.)

In the course of their research, Gestalt psychologists observed that people tended to organize perceptions in certain ways. The Gestaltists stated a number of principles that expressed this organization, among them *nearness, similarity, continuity, closure* and *simplicity* (see Figure 4.5). Certainly, these examples indicate that a particular organization of all the parts (the sum of the parts) gives rise to different perceptions or "wholes" than do the parts taken separately. We now believe that the brain perceives in "wholes" because of the organization of the different brain pathways described earlier. As an example, let's consider a Gestalt principle called "common fate." **Common fate** occurs when objects or stimuli that would not normally be grouped together are seen as one organization because they share the same movement or "fate" (see Figure 4.6, p. 122). This happens because our perception of movement is so sensitive that even if we see only a part of something move, or only glimpse the direction of its movement, our perceptual mechanisms often will fill in the blanks for us, creating the perception of a single object. This appears to occur because the magno pathway perceives common-fate motions as whole entities and then passes this perception on to the parvo-interblob system, which then organizes its form and shape perception around the wholeness of the common-fate object, suddenly making the moving object stand out (Livingstone, 1988).

These perceptual systems appear to have evolved to work in ways that help us make sense of the world around us. For instance, in Figure 4.7 on page 122, you can see an example of the Phi phenomenon, what the Gestaltists referred to as **apparent motion**. In Figure 4.8 on page 123, however, you can see an interesting twist on apparent motion that has led some researchers to conclude that the perception of apparent motion is "in effect a bag of tricks, one the human visual system has acquired through natural selection during millions of years of evolution" (Ramachandran & Anstis, 1986, p. 102).

What the Gestalt organization principles may be showing us is that we have evolved to perceive the world as it most likely is. If we see part of a leopard in a tree, we may well "fill in" the rest of the leopard, and we probably won't be wrong! In the real world (as opposed to chapters on perception in textbooks), things that look like they are grouped together probably are. In the real world, things with gaps (see the closure example in Figure 4.5) usually *are* whole and are simply partly blocked from view. It makes sense that our perceptual system would evolve to "see" the blocked object in its entirety and to treat it for what it is (see Figure 4.9, p. 123).

According to evolutionary theory, an organism's biological perceptual apparatus *should* have been naturally selected to blend well with the experiences that the

FIGURE 4.4

In the classic reversible figure–ground example, (a) the silhouetted faces can be seen as figures, or as black background for a vase. The reversible figure–ground pattern needn't be two-dimensional. The beautiful vase pictured here (b) was actually created for Queen Elizabeth's Silver Jubilee in 1977. The profiles that can suddenly be seen as "figure" rather than as "ground" are those of Her Majesty and her husband, Prince Philip.

FIGURE 4.5

Principles of organization set forth by Gestalt psychologists.

SIMILARITY

Similar things appear to be grouped together:

```
X X X X X X        X X X X X X
X X X X X X        O O O O O O
X X X X X X        X X X X X X
X X X X X X        O O O O O O
X X X X X X        X X X X X X
X X X X X X        O O O O O O
```

Can be seen as either horizontal *or* vertical rows of X's

Is usually seen as horizontal rows of X's and O's. The similar objects are grouped together.

NEARNESS

Things that are near to each other appear to be grouped together:

```
X X X X X X        XOXOXOXOXOXO
X X X X X X        XOXOXOXOXOXO
X X X X X X        XOXOXOXOXOXO
X X X X X X        XOXOXOXOXOXO
X X X X X X        XOXOXOXOXOXO
X X X X X X        XOXOXOXOXOXO
```

Can be seen as either horizontal *or* vertical rows of X's

Is usually seen as horizontal rows, even though the X's and O's are dissimilar figures.

CONTINUITY

Points or lines interrupted by an overlapping object are seen as belonging together if they result in straight or gently curving lines when connected, and lines tend to be seen as following the smoothest path:

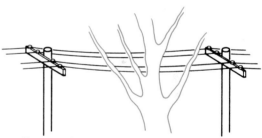

The power lines are seen as *continuous*, despite the fact that they have been segmented by the tree branches.

CLOSURE

Figures that have gaps in them are seen as completed:

Even though there are gaps in the triangle, it is still seen as a triangle.

SIMPLICITY

Every stimulus pattern is perceived in such a way that the resulting structure is as simple as possible:

Is viewed as a triangle and a circle:

It is not seen in a more complicated fashion as a combination of these parts:

 or

121

FIGURE 4.6

This camouflaged fish is difficult to see. If, however, the fish began to move, the animal would clearly stand out from its background. Although it would still look like the background when it was moving, all of its parts would share identical motion, they would share a "common fate." Our perceptual mechanisms quickly unify into a whole anything sharing a common fate.

Frogs perceive their world in a way that makes it easier for them to retrieve bugs from it. Such species-specific perceptual organizations are called affordances.

particular organism is likely to have. An organism's biological mechanisms, therefore, can be said to have been formed by the kinds of experiences its ancestors had (Turvey & Shaw, 1979). This process would favor the perceptions of any properties in the environment (for example, shape, position, or motion) that are directly relevant to survival.

For instance, it has been found that frogs possess perceptual systems that help them to perceive bugs. These "bug detectors" help frogs to organize their perceptual understanding of the world in the most beneficial way. Because frogs eat bugs,

FIGURE 4.7

The Phi phenomenon: When two lights are placed side by side in a darkened room and flashed alternately (between condition a & b), we perceive one light moving back and forth. This probably occurs because our perceptions are geared for the real world, not for a laboratory. In the real world, such an experience would

almost certainly be the result of two consecutive glimpses of one moving object, rather than an unusual consecutive sequence of the illumination and disillumination of two identical objects. Our perceptual mechanisms seem set to provide us with the most likely possibility.

WHAT REALLY OCCURS

a.

b.

WHAT WE PERCEIVE

a.

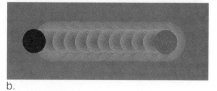

b.

(1)

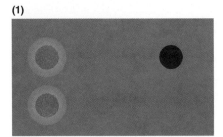

a.

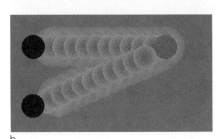

b.

(2)

a.

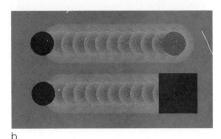

b.

FIGURE 4.8

The following Phi phenomenon supports the notion that we are organized to perceive what is most likely to occur. In (1), two lights flash alternately with one light. Viewers see the two lights appear to travel in the direction of the arrows to fuse to become one. In (2), nothing is altered from condition (1), except that a small square is pasted on the screen in the lower right. Under these circumstances, viewers will now perceive that the lower light travels horizontally and "hides" behind the square. In the real world, hiding is more commonly observed than fusing, and researchers assume that our perceptual mechanisms are choosing to "feed" us the more likely possibility.

there is an obvious value in their perceiving the world in a fashion that makes it easier to retrieve bugs from it. Cats, on the other hand, are highly receptive to motion. They may ignore a stationary object but be immediately fascinated by the same object when it moves. To some degree, this characteristic also is true of humans. J. J. Gibson (1979) used the term **affordance** to describe the interplay between organism and environment that has evolved, whereby each organism is best suited to perceive aspects of the environment that best afford, or offer, the information needed for its particular survival. In this view, how objects or actions are perceived depends on their meaning (relevance) to the organism (Johansson, von Hofsten, & Jansson, 1980).

Although the theory of evolution, as applied to perception, makes sense, its application does not supplant genuine evidence as the final arbiter of the debate concerning how perception comes about. Learning and experience also may play a considerable role in the way we organize perceptions. Psychologists interested in the influence of learning on the perception of shape and form have turned to the study of illusions such as Fraser's spiral, which you saw at the beginning of this chapter.

AFFORDANCE

In J. J. Gibson's theory of perception, the particular properties of an object that offer an organism perceptual information, which often is of unique interest to the organism or which may benefit the organism's survival; for example, a hammer affords a human its graspability.

FIGURE 4.9

The objects on the left appear to have no organization. There is an organization, however. If you could only fill in the missing parts in your mind's eye, you'd see what it is. Filling them in appears impossible, however, but your perceptual mechanisms are so strong that they can do it if we perceive that these same objects are being occluded (covered) by something as shown on the right. In that case, our perceptual mechanisms will "fill in" the parts and we readily see the letter B in a number of places! (SOURCE: Rock, 1984, p. 119.)

123

AN ENDURING QUESTION: THE NATURE AND NURTURE OF PERCEPTION

How do we make perceptual sense of a world as complex as ours? How can we tell whether something is far away or nearby, whether it's large or small, whether *it* is moving or *we* are moving? How do we know when we are about to step off a ledge or walk into a wall? Why are we able to extend our hands just the right distance to grasp something that is directly in front of us? You will probably respond that the reason we can do all these things is that we can see. If you really think about it, however, you will realize that seeing—that is, sensing with your eyes—isn't enough. Not only must we be able to see things but also we must *understand* what we see—we must perceive. The question is, how do we go about doing this? This is not a new question, as questions go, but has endured over the centuries. It has been asked by philosophers both ancient and modern, and only now are we coming close to an answer.

Of the many answers offered, two have come to dominate our understanding of how we come to perceive the space around us and the objects in it. These two views are known as the **image and cue theory** and the **direct perception theory**.

The Image and Cue Theory

The first modern and detailed discussion of the image and cue theory was presented by Hermann von Helmholtz in his book *Treatise on Physical Optics* (Helmholtz, 1866/1924).* Encompassed within that imposing title was an examination of how we are able visually to understand the world in terms of three dimensions when all we have to go on is a flat two-dimensional imagine shining on our retinas. Helmholtz said it was obvious that without experience, learning, or memory, *nothing* that you could see would make any sense. Helmholtz would have argued, for example, that the only reason you know you are looking at a book at this moment is that your visual sensations of books have previously been correlated with the *experience* of touching and manipulating books. Now that you have that experience, you know that the particular shapes and surfaces you are viewing constitute a book. As you might imagine, Helmholtz would have expected Kenge, whom you met in the Prologue, to have trouble distinguishing water buffalo from insects because Kenge lacked the experiences he would have needed to make such a discrimination. After all, based on the Pygmy's experiences, the objects most distant in the dense jungle environment in which he was raised were never more than a few yards away. In fact, according to the image and cue theory, even distinguishing a shape from its background requires experience.

Have you ever seen one of those old Hollywood tearjerkers in which someone who has always been blind finally gets to see? What happens? In the ones I've seen, the person usually looks around and says things like, "Joe, I'd have recognized you anywhere," or "Aren't the flowers and sky beautiful?" Helmholtz would have had a good laugh at such scenes, and would have argued that someone who had always been blind and could suddenly "see" wouldn't have the foggiest idea what he was sensing, let alone be able to recognize good old Joe! Rather, Helmholtz believed that each image to strike the retina must, *through experience*, become a *cue* filled with information for the observer. This, of course, is how the image and cue theory came to be named.

*Sometimes a reference will have two dates as this one does. The first date is when the original paper was published; the second date is when this English translation appeared.

The Direct Perception Theory

Is it really true that nothing we see or hear would make sense until we had *learned* about what we were sensing? Consider the following: Children readily see and understand the distance and shape of objects, but it is very difficult to teach them to play advanced chess. On the other hand, it is fairly easy to "teach" most computers to play advanced chess, but it is incredibly difficult to "teach" any computer to make perceptual sense of a visual image. Furthermore, although some computers are able to "see" in a limited way, none do it nearly as well as even a young child. If, as Helmholtz suggested, learning is the key, we must ask ourselves, "How did little children get to be so smart? How are they able to handle easily the same visual stimulations that overwhelm some of our most powerful computers?" We must also ask, "If Helmholtz's view is correct, how is it that the blind using a TSR device like the one you read about in the focus section, can make quick perceptual sense of what they "see"?

One answer to such questions was supplied by a twentieth-century researcher named James J. Gibson. Gibson argued that we are already organized at birth by our genetics and biology to rapidly mature in a way that will enable us to make some important perceptual sense of our world early in our development. In this view, important characteristics of objects, such as their distances, shapes, or sizes are perceived as the result of the innate ("built-in") mechanisms possessed by all healthy members of the species. Included among such mechanisms would be the cells that appear to be prewired detectors of edges, colors, or movements, which we discussed in Chapter 3.

Gibson also liked to point out that almost any visual experience will have within it observable **invariants** that can yield information about the distance, movement, or shape of objects. One of the invariants to which Gibson often referred was **gradient of texture** (see Figure 4.10). Gradient of texture has to do with differences in detail. Look around you. Regardless of the objects you focus on, you'll be able to see more detail in those that are closer and less detail in

INVARIANTS
In J. J. Gibson's direct perception theory, stimulus features that are unchanging or have proportions that are relatively fixed or constant.

GRADIENT OF TEXTURE
A depth cue. Closer objects show greater detail.

FIGURE 4.10

A texture gradient. The retinal size of the texture elements in this picture increase with nearness and decrease with distance. This feature is found in almost any view of the world, and may provide an invariant from which we innately gather depth information.

those that are distant. If you're sitting on a large lawn, you see the grass that's close to you as individual blades, but on the horizon you see a smooth, uninterrupted green. At intermediate distances, you can't see individual blades of grass, but the green may appear to be somewhat patchy rather than uniform in color. Gibson argued that innate mechanisms sensitive to texture gradient might easily use such an invariant to estimate the size of a novel object without the requirement of prior experience (see Figure 4.11).

The Interactionist View

The modern view of perception, the interactionist view, is that there is clearly evidence to support both explanations of perception—learning and experience are important, but so is neurological organization. Today we know that it isn't necessary to choose one theory over the other, because the two theories need not be mutually exclusive. Important aspects of each could easily be involved in any perceptual organization. Throughout this chapter are examples of how learning and experience interact with underlying biological mechanisms to produce the amazing perceptual abilities that we often take for granted. While it is still true that we don't know how much of our perceptual ability to attribute to our biogenetic organization (nature) and how much to attribute to learning and experience (nurture), we now know that both are very important.

FOR CRITICAL ANALYSIS

1. Our senses act as filters; there are many things to which we are not sensitive. We can't see X rays, hear dog whistles, or smell carbon dioxide. Why do you think our senses are so selective?

2. Cats have color vision; but how do we know this? How would you go about setting up an experiment to tell if a cat knows the difference between red and blue without dissecting its eye to look for cones (an action that, by the way, would not in itself offer proof because you could not be sure that cones in cats worked like they do in humans)? Hints: Use a hungry cat, a lamp that can shine either red or blue light of equal brightness, and a food dispensing lever the cat has learned to work that operates only when, for instance, the red lamp is on. If a cat can see the colors, how will it eventually come to behave? Think of how traffic lights control your actions. How would the animal behave if, in fact, cats were color-blind?

FIGURE 4.11

Although the size of an object might not always be obvious without experience, its relationship to a gradient of texture can immediately place it at a particular distance, which then allows its size to be roughly deduced.

Figure 4.12 contains a number of illusions. Before you look at them, you might want to get a ruler, because some of them are so eerie that you'll want to measure them to see for yourself that the captions are correct.

The Müller–Lyer illusion (d) is a good one to examine in detail. It has been the focus of much controversy. Most people looking at this illusion perceive the horizontal line bordered by the inward-turned arrowheads as shorter than the horizontal line bordered by the outward-turned arrowheads. If you measure the

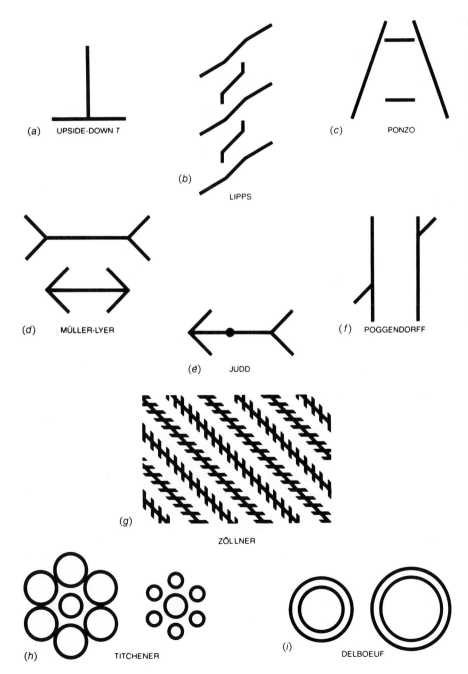

(a) UPSIDE-DOWN T

(b) LIPPS

(c) PONZO

(d) MÜLLER-LYER

(e) JUDD

(f) POGGENDORFF

(g) ZÖLLNER

(h) TITCHENER

(i) DELBOEUF

FIGURE 4.12

Illusions. (a) Both lines are the same length, although the vertical line looks longer. (b) The middle segments of all the lines are parallel to one another. (c) Although the upper horizontal line looks longer, both horizontal lines are the same length. (d) Both horizontal lines are the same length, although the upper one looks longer. (e) A variation of Müller-Lyer. The dot is in the center of the horizontal line. (f) The diagonal lines, if continued toward each other, would join, although it appears that the line on the right would be above the line on the left. (g) The long diagonal lines are parallel and do not converge. (h) The middle circles are the same size. (i) The outer circle on the left has the same diameter as the inner circle on the right.

FIGURE 4.13

The Müller-Lyer illusion can be explained by our experience with floors. (a) If we view a floor from one side of a room, the far side appears foreshortened, although we know that the far side is the same length as the near side. (b) By removing midsections of the floor, we begin to approximate the Müller-Lyer figures. We still assume that the far side is the same length as the near side. (c) The horizontal lines are now made equal, as in the Müller-Lyer figure. We perceive the top figure to be the long far side of a large room and the bottom figure to be the short near side of a small room. By applying our knowledge of three dimensions to a two-dimensional figure, we may be making an assumption that creates the illusion.

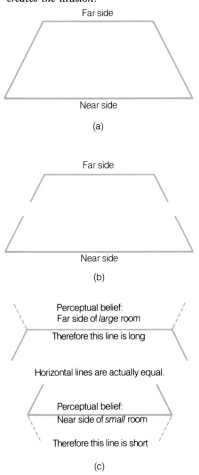

Far side

Near side

(a)

Far side

Near side

(b)

Perceptual belief:
Far side of *large* room

Therefore this line is long

Horizontal lines are actually equal.

Perceptual belief:
Near side of *small* room

Therefore this line is short

(c)

horizontal lines, however, you'll find that they are the same length. Why does the illusion occur?

Knowing that you're being tricked doesn't make much difference; the effect remains. Researchers know that the illusion doesn't take place in the retina. They resolved this issue by an ingenious method. A subject's head and eyes were held very still in an apparatus while the horizontal lines of the Müller–Lyer illusion were flashed into the left eye and the arrowheads were flashed into the right eye. When the subject interpreted the combined sensations in his brain, the illusion was still apparent (Gillam, 1980). This outcome proved that the illusion must be happening at a higher level in the brain than that of the retina.

What explanation could there be for the Müller–Lyer illusion? In Figure 4.13, you see the Müller–Lyer figures in a particular context: a view of the floor of a room or any rectangle lying in front of you with one end more distant than the other. Notice that the horizontal edge that seems to be farther away always has the arrowheads pointing outward, while the horizontal edge that's closer always has the arrowheads pointed inward. According to image and cue theorists, when you look at the Müller–Lyer illusion, you perceive the horizontal line enclosed by the inward-turned arrowheads as being closer than the line with the outward-turned arrowheads. If two objects appear to be the same size but you know that one is closer, then you know—because of your learning and experience—that the one that's farther away must be bigger (see Figure 4.14). And this appears to be what happens when you look at the Müller–Lyer illusion.

We can see the same assumption at work in the Ponzo illusion (refer to Figure 4.12c). That illusion is reproduced every time you look at railroad tracks. The upper and lower horizontal lines in the Ponzo illusion are exactly the same length, but the upper horizontal line looks longer. The upper horizontal line appears to be farther away, and, according to experience and learning, if two objects appear to be the same size but one is farther away, then the one farther away must be bigger.

What about the Poggendorff illusion? (Refer to Figure 4.12f.) Again, scientists argue that our *experiences* with three-dimensional objects cause the illusion. You may never have seen the Poggendorff illusion before, but you've seen something like it, perhaps an overturned chair. The resemblance is obvious in Figure 4.15. Similarly, the Zollner illusion (refer to Figure 4.12g) is caused by our common everyday experience with rectangles. Instead of perceiving the hatched lines as parallelograms, which they are, but which are not common in our daily experience, we perceive them as rectangles viewed from an angle; if these rectangles angle in one direction, we see the long lines leaning in that direction, too.

But what about people from other cultures who aren't familiar with rectangles? Suppose they come from a world where there aren't many buildings with windows. Suppose they haven't been exposed much to railroad tracks or overturned chairs. Researchers who have tested members of such cultures have reported that the people do *not* perceive these illusions. For instance, members of the Zulu tribe in Africa live in round huts and are not exposed to many rectangular shapes and forms. They do not experience the Müller–Lyer illusion when it is shown to them (Deregowski, 1972; Gillam, 1980). Such data concerning illusions imply that learning and experience are extremely important factors in individual perception. However, the cross-cultural studies that have yielded the data have been criticized for a number of reasons, among the most important of which is the possibility that members of other cultures may not have fully understood the comparison the researchers wanted them to make.

Still, there is other evidence that learning might have an important bearing on the perception of illusions. Illusions tend to diminish in effect the more you observe

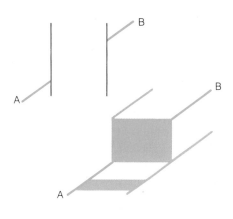

FIGURE 4.14

Objects may cast an image of the same size on the retina, as the bears in this picture do, but if one is perceived to be farther away, it will also be perceived to be larger.

FIGURE 4.15

The Poggendorff illusion in two dimensions makes sense in the three-dimensional world. If this were a real chair, lines A and B could never meet. In two dimensions, however, A and B do meet (use your ruler to prove it).

them. The first time you see the Müller–Lyer illusion, the lines are likely to appear strikingly different; after you've seen it many times, however, the illusion has less impact (Gillam, 1980).

PERCEPTUAL CONSTANCIES
The tendency to perceive objects as yielding the same or similar experiences, even though the viewing conditions may vary widely.

PERCEPTUAL CONSTANCIES

As research with illusions has indicated, learning is an important aspect of perception, just as image and cue theorists had expected. **Perceptual constancies** also offer a good example of the value of learning in perception. If you were to examine

Zulus live in a "round" world and are not exposed to the rectangular angles common in modern cities.

the world solely on the basis of the image projected on your retina, familiar objects would be constantly changing in size and shape depending on the angle from which you viewed them. Yet, in spite of these continual alterations produced by viewing objects from different distances and different angles, you still recognize familiar objects as familiar. This is one of the primary functions of perception. For example, when you look at your parked car as you are walking away from it, your visual sensory system sends a message to your brain. First, the image of the car is projected onto your retina. If you continue looking at your car, the image projected onto your retina gets smaller and smaller as you move farther away. When this happens, do you assume that your car is shrinking? No, you aren't upset at all. Although the *sensory* image of your car is shrinking rapidly, you don't perceive that your car is changing size. Instead, you perceive that your car is becoming more distant. You've learned that its size remains the same. Even when you are 5 blocks from your car and it seems no larger than your fingernail, you perceive that it is still your car and it is still the same size. This learned perception is known as **size constancy.** It is one of a number of such perceptual constancies.

Helping to demonstrate that size constancy is learned is the fact that some people fail to learn it. Mr. S. B. was a 53-year-old cataract patient who had been blind since birth. When his sight was restored by surgery, he had a difficult time adjusting to all the new sensory inputs. One day, he was found trying to crawl out of his hospital window in order to get a better look at the "little" objects, which he believed were close enough to touch. The trouble was that his window was on the fourth floor and some of those "little objects" were full-sized cars in traffic down below (Gregory, 1970).

Even people who have been able to see all their lives may have a limited understanding of size constancy as a result of their particular experience. The Pygmy Kenge was such an individual. As you recall, because of his limited experience, his perception of size constancy did not extend to objects at great distances.

Size constancy does not appear to be present at birth; rather, it develops in infants by about 6 months of age. This was demonstrated in an experiment in which 5- and 7-month-old infants while wearing a patch over one eye (to eliminate the depth cues that the use of both eyes would provide) were simultaneously shown photographs of large and small faces, all of which were presented equidistant from the child. The only distance cue in this case was the size of the face. To adults, who, of course, possess size constancy, only the large face would have looked near enough to touch; the small face would have looked too distant. The 5-month-old infants, however, reached out to touch faces of both sizes equally. The 7-month-old infants, in contrast, reached far more often for the large face, which indicates size constancy, and seemed to react to the small face as though it were beyond reach (Yonas, Pettersen, & Granrud, 1982).

Other constancies also develop through an individual's experience. **Shape constancy** is demonstrated in Figure 4.16. As you can see, objects are perceived to remain constant even though the shape projected onto the retina may change. A door may appear to be rectangular when viewed straight on, or trapezoidal when partially opened, but we do not perceive that the door is changing shape from a rectangle to a trapezoid. Instead, we perceive that the door is opening.

A powerful shape constancy illusion can be created with the aid of the house in Figure 4.17. Make a photocopy of the house or carefully redraw it on heavy paper (notice that the windows aren't quite square). Then follow the instructions in the figure. Once you've created the house, set it on a shelf at eye level where it is lighted so that shadows do not fall on it. Stand about 10 feet away and view it with one eye closed. The shape constancy you possess owing to your experience with houses will soon take over and the house will begin to look like a normal

FIGURE 4.16

Although the shapes of a door's image that are cast on the retina can change drastically, the door is not perceived to have changed shape. Instead, it is perceived to be a rectangular door that is opening.

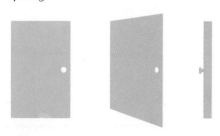

house. Once this happens, begin walking from side to side. Your brain, applying its shape constancy, will try to hang on to what it knows about houses. While trying to accomplish this, the brain creates a strong illusion. Amazingly, the house will seem to rotate all by itself! Finally, hold the base of the house between your thumb and forefinger and extend your arm. Look with only one eye; once it appears to be a normal house, tip it forward or backward or rotate it from side to side. You'll be in for a shock. While your hand turns the house one way, it will actually appear to rotate the other way. As the house appears to turn against the direction of your hand, you will probably expect to feel opposition against your fingers. When no opposition occurs, it will feel very strange. After all, your eyes and hands have been working together for some time now, and, believe me, they're not ready for this.

A perceptual psychologist named Adelbert Ames (1880–1955) demonstrated the power of these perceptual constancies by creating what he called the **Ames room** (see Figure 4.18). Strange things seem to happen in the Ames room. People standing on one side of the room appear to be giants, and people standing on the other side appear to be dwarfs. Individuals crossing the Ames room appear to grow or shrink steadily depending on the direction in which they are walking. The illusion of the Ames room depends on our use of size and shape constancy. In the Ames room, one window is much larger than the other, the windows are trapezoids, the floor is uneven so that one end of the room is higher on the plane than the other, and the floor tiles are diamond-shaped and of different sizes. Because we have not experienced this kind of bizarre arrangement, however, our perceptual constancies try to make different sense of the room. Thus, we perceive the windows as equal in size and rectangular. The room seems to be level and the floor to be made of square tiles. Our desire to perceive the room according to our experience is so strong that when a person walks from one end to the other, our brain prefers to perceive that person as growing or shrinking rather than to give up the idea that the room is regular in shape and size.

Another of the perceptual constancies is known as **brightness constancy**. Because of brightness constancy, objects appear to have the same brightness independent

AMES ROOM
A specially designed room that is perceived as rectangular, even though it is not. Objects of the same size seem to be totally different in size at different points in the room.

BRIGHTNESS CONSTANCY
The perception that objects maintain their brightness independent of lighting.

FIGURE 4.17

The inside-out house. Make a copy and cut it out. Cut line AB. Fold edges toward you along lines BD, BE, and BC. Paste triangular flap ABC to the back of the roof; the front and side of the house should meet in a right angle, and the completed house should be "inside-out." Put the house on a shelf at eye level. From about 10 feet away, observe with one eye. When the house appears "normal," walk to one side. What happens? (SOURCE: Gardner, 1983, p. 64.)

FIGURE 4.18

In the Ames room, people seem to change size as they change location.

of the light in which they are seen. For example, although gray paper in the sun is brighter than white paper in the shade, the white paper appears brighter. We perceive white as bright and gray as dark, regardless of the amount of reflected light actually coming from the surface.

DEPTH PERCEPTION
Perceptual interpretation of visual cues indicating how far away objects are.

DEPTH PERCEPTION

Once you have determined that there is "something there," the next question becomes, "Where is it?" When you're sitting in a room and looking at things, your perceptual abilities enable you to tell how far away they are or how close they are with a fair degree of accuracy. This is called **depth perception.**

Monocular Cues

You may have heard that depth perception is a function of using both eyes and that people who are blind in one eye lose their depth perception. But is this true? Close one eye and look around a room. It may seem that your depth perception is a little impaired, but you can still tell which objects are closest and which are farthest away without much difficulty. Even if you went to a stranger's house with a patch over one eye and sat in a room you've never been in before, you could still judge whether a lamp was closer than a particular chair, the chair was closer than a particular couch, and the couch was closer than a particular wall. You'd still have depth perception.

In this flat, two-dimensional photograph there are many monocular cues that provide a strong perception of depth.

In 1930, film producers came to special-effects expert Willis H. O'Brien with an interesting plot for a movie. In the filmed story, an expedition would be made to a place called Skull Island to capture a huge ape named King Kong and to bring him back to New York, where Kong would escape, kidnap a woman, and climb the Empire State Building, there to be killed by fighter planes. Believe it or not, the producers described this as essentially a love story, with the 50-foot ape in love with the blonde heroine. They said that they would supply the actors. All they wanted from O'Brien was a 50-foot ape, various extinct dinosaurs, and Skull Is-land—all on film. A lesser man might have thrown up his hands in despair, but O'Brien sat back and pondered. How could you make a film such as *King Kong* when no such gorilla or island existed and still fool the audience into perceiving the situation as real? The only way, of course, was to manipulate the cues that people use in their day-to-day lives to gauge such things as size, distance, and motion. O'Brien knew that image and cue theorists had been trying to determine exactly which cues in the two-dimensional image formed on the retina give rise to depth perception. He knew that quite a number of cues had been isolated. The more O'Brien thought about it, the more it seemed that it might be possible to make people believe in the reality of King Kong.

Some of the cues O'Brien made use of probably will be familiar to you, even though you may not know their names. Whether you are conscious of it or not, you've used them all of your life to judge depth.

The first of the **monocular depth cues** is gradient of texture, which we discussed earlier. This cue alone is often enough to yield a strong sense of depth.

The second depth cue is **height on a plane.** We perceive objects that from our point of view are higher on our plane of vision to be farther away than objects lower on the plane. Inside a room, objects that are farthest from you will always appear to be higher on your plane of view. In other words, when you are standing or sitting upright, the farther away an object is, the more you need to raise your gaze to see it.

Another very important depth cue is **linear perspective:** Parallel lines appear to converge on the horizon and to separate when they approach the viewer. Linear perspective is one of the first tricks that any artist learns in order to make a two-dimensional canvas appear three-dimensional. If you look at the railroad tracks in Figure 4.19, you can see the effect of linear perspective and the depth it appears to create on a flat page. Linear perspective is also apparent with just points of light—lines aren't needed. Psychologist E. Lowell Kelly used this knowledge to save lives during World War II. He heard that during night training missions, cadet pilots occasionally crashed into the aircraft directly in front of them because they

MONOCULAR DEPTH CUES
Cues seen with the use of only one eye that give rise to a perception of depth. These cues include an object's height on a plane, linear perspective, overlap, relative size, gradient of texture, aerial perspective, shadowing, and relative motion. On a flat movie screen (with the exception of 3-D movies), only monocular cues give the sensation of depth.

HEIGHT ON A PLANE
A monocular depth cue. Objects higher on a plane are perceived as being farther away.

LINEAR PERSPECTIVE
A monocular depth cue. Parallel lines appear to converge in the distance.

FIGURE 4.19

An example of linear perspective: parallel lines converging at the horizon.

OVERLAP

A monocular depth cue. Objects that are behind (overlapped by) other objects are perceived as being farther away.

RELATIVE SIZE

A monocular depth cue. Familiar objects appear larger than identical objects that are more distant.

AERIAL PERSPECTIVE

A monocular depth cue. Nearby objects are brighter and sharper than distant objects.

SHADOWING

A monocular depth cue. The distribution of light on a curved or angled surface conveys that some parts are closer and some farther away.

RELATIVE MOTION

A monocular depth cue. Objects that are closer appear to move more than distant objects when the viewer's head is moved from side to side.

ACCOMMODATION

In vision, the adjustment of the lens of the eye to bring into focus on the retina objects that are relatively near.

were unable to judge their distance to the tail light of the aircraft directly in front. Kelly got the air corps to use two tail lights on all aircraft mounted a fixed distance apart, which provided linear perspective (the apparent distance between the lights shrank as the lead airplane got further away, and grew as the aircraft drew close to each other) (Fiske, Conley, & Goldberg, 1987).

Overlap is another important cue. We know that if one object appears to overlap another, the object that is overlapped is behind the first object and therefore must be farther away (see Figure 4.20).

Relative size can be a factor in depth perception if we know how large particular objects are. Once we have acquired size constancy, we can then judge an object's distance by how large it appears relative to another object of known size. If you look about a room and see two chairs that you know are the same size, and one appears to be much larger than the other, you will immediately assume, because of size constancy, that the smaller chair is farther away.

If you're outdoors and are viewing objects over a considerable distance, **aerial perspective** lends a sense of depth because, as distance increases, dust and haze in the air tend to reduce clarity. Consequently, the colors of distant objects appear pastel and their outlines are hazy, while nearby objects appear sharp and bright. On very clear days, things at a distance may stand out so sharply that they appear to have moved closer.

The distribution of shadows also can be an important depth cue. **Shadowing** provides information about angles and curves that tells us which parts of an object are closer to us than others are (see Figure 4.21).

O'Brien was unable to make much use of the next depth cue, **relative motion,** because it will not work with a two-dimensional image such as a motion picture, unless the camera is moving. For relative motion to make an impression, a three-dimensional scene is necessary. The idea of relative motion is simple. If you move your head from side to side, you'll immediately notice that nearby objects seem to move a great distance, while distant objects seem to move hardly at all. In fact, relative motion may, to a degree, be an invariant depth cue—the kind that direct perception theorists like to point to. This is because the retina does not simply

FIGURE 4.20

Objects that are overlapped appear farther away than objects that are not.

encompass a flat two-dimensional scene, as image and cue theorists originally believed. Instead, researchers have discovered that the eyes wiggle constantly at a rate of at least three times per second, which yields a continuous depth sense owing to relative motion (MacKay, 1973). The tiny movement of the eyes is all that it takes. To get a sense of how such a tiny motion could be sufficient for the perception of relative motion, hold your head as still as possible, look with one eye, and then make the smallest side to side movements that you can. As you will observe, even with the tiniest of movements you will still obtain relative motion, especially for objects that are near.

The last monocular depth cue, which O'Brien was also unable to use, is the **accommodation** of the lens of the eye to closer objects. As objects draw closer to you (within about 10 feet), your lens must bend to focus on them. Muscles in the eye accomplish this, and the amount of tension these muscles produce can provide feedback concerning distance. To feel the tension on the lens, simply close one eye and look at one finger of your outstretched hand. Then, draw your hand in toward you (bring it very close) and try to keep your finger in focus—can you feel the strain of the muscles bending the lens?

O'Brien took his knowledge of the pictorial depth cues that he could use and proceeded to build a model of King Kong that stood about 30 inches high. He then built models of Skull Island, dinosaurs, and familiar objects such as trees, all of them on the scale of inches. In the famous scene in which King Kong first grabs actress Fay Wray, Kong appears to be his full 50 feet in height. Look at Figure 4.22 and identify the cues on which O'Brien relied. Relative size is one. We know

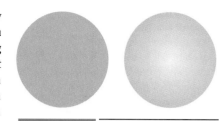

FIGURE 4.21

Two circles with identical diameters. The circle on the left appears flat, two-dimensional. Because of shading, however, the circle on the right looks more like a sphere, indicating that some parts are closer to our eyes, some farther away. The shadowing has replicated the distribution of light and dark that is commonly associated with a sphere.

FIGURE 4.22

King Kong holding Fay Wray. What cues did O'Brien make use of to create the impression of great size?

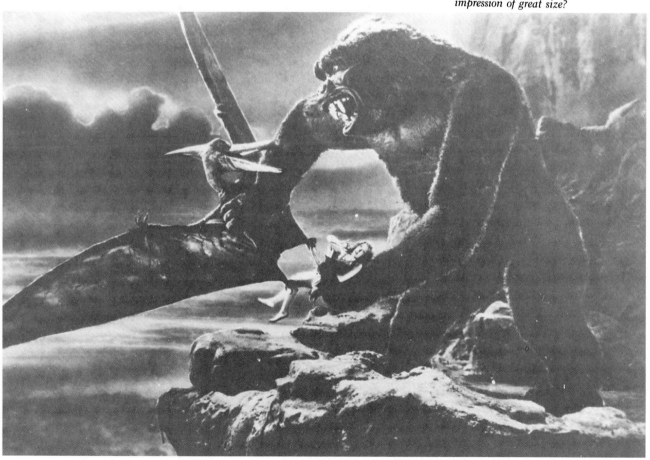

CONCEPT REVIEW: MONOCULAR CUES OF DEPTH PERCEPTION

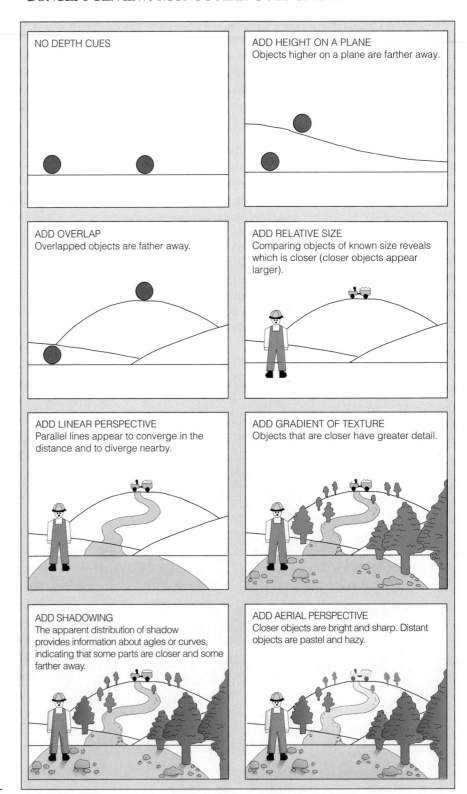

NO DEPTH CUES

ADD HEIGHT ON A PLANE
Objects higher on a plane are farther away.

ADD OVERLAP
Overlapped objects are father away.

ADD RELATIVE SIZE
Comparing objects of known size reveals which is closer (closer objects appear larger).

ADD LINEAR PERSPECTIVE
Parallel lines appear to converge in the distance and to diverge nearby.

ADD GRADIENT OF TEXTURE
Objects that are closer have greater detail.

ADD SHADOWING
The apparent distribution of shadow provides information about agles or curves, indicating that some parts are closer and some farther away.

ADD AERIAL PERSPECTIVE
Closer objects are bright and sharp. Distant objects are pastel and hazy.

how tall the woman should be, and King Kong towers above her. Furthermore, his hand overlaps her, which means that his hand must be closer to us than she is, which adds to the illusion of size. Using a small model and the appropriate cues, O'Brien was able to trick the audience into believing King Kong was gigantic.

The Moon Illusion

Have you ever looked at the full moon when it's just coming up over the horizon? It looks huge. But the same full moon doesn't appear to be so large once it's high in the sky. Have you ever wondered why?

In a series of classic experiments, Kaufman and Rock (1962) demonstrated that the **moon illusion** was due to learned monocular cues, particularly relative size and overlap. They observed that when the moon is directly overhead, it's difficult to judge how large it is. Among the cues for depth perception that you've learned, consider whether any of them would help you determine the size of an object high in the sky. Linear perspective is of no use. Relative size doesn't help much, either, because there is no basis of comparison. Overlap is ineffectual because nothing appears between you and the moon. There is no gradient of texture cue, because there is nothing between you and the moon to show a change in detail. Aerial perspective may give you some clue; if the moon looks fairly hazy, you may realize that it's more than 20 or 30 miles away! Height on the plane is no help, because there is no plane in your line of sight to the moon. There are simply darkness, a few stars, and the round moon.

The situation is different when the moon is first rising, however. Kaufman and Rock noticed that the moon illusion was especially pronounced if a large number of objects separated the observer from the rising moon. For instance, if the moon is rising behind the lights and buildings of a city, the depth cues that have been learned have an immediate effect. One of the most powerful is overlap. The fact that the city is in *front* of the moon means that the moon is farther away, and must be huge. Another cue is relative size. By experience we know that buildings

MOON ILLUSION
A perceptual illusion created by the presence of the monocular cues of relative size and overlap, which make the moon appear 25 percent larger when rising than when overhead.

Because of the existence of the moon illusion, photographers use a telephoto lens when photographing the rising moon so the resulting photograph more closely resembles our perceptual experience.

CHAPTER 4
PERCEPTION

or hills and mountains are fairly large, and yet they are specks compared with the moon globe that is rising behind them. Height on the plane is also informative. Because the just rising moon is highest on the plane that extends from you along the surface of the Earth to the moon, it is obviously farther away than anything else on that plane. All these cues together tell the viewer that the moon coming over the horizon is huge. Because we are not used to dealing with objects bigger than entire cities or the mountains that surround them, the perception created when the moon rises above the horizon is one of awesome size. This perspective, as well as an appreciation of its true size—2160 miles in diameter—is totally lost when the moon is seen directly overhead, without any cues to indicate size.

It's so difficult to believe that the illusion of a giant harvest moon is a result of our learning and experience that most people think it has something to do with the optics of the atmosphere. But it isn't so; the rising moon is not magnified by the atmosphere. If you take a photograph of the moon as it rises, and another photograph of the moon overhead, and then take a pair of scissors and cut out the images of the moon from both pictures, you will see that they fit one on top of the other perfectly; they are the same size. A camera would have recorded an optical magnification had that been the cause of the moon illusion. The camera records no such thing, however; unlike your mind, the camera does not perceive.

Binocular Cues

All the perceptual cues that we have discussed so far have been monocular cues. That is, they are cues that can be sensed even with only one eye. As you may have gathered, you can perceive depth more accurately, up to a distance of about 25 feet, with two eyes than you can with one. Better depth perception with two eyes is the result of **binocular cues,** which can be sensed by both eyes together but not by each eye individually. One such binocular cue is **convergence.** When you look at an object that is closer than approximately 25 feet, your eyes must converge on the object to perceive it as a single object clearly in focus. Figure 4.23 gives an example of convergence. It's an easy thing to test for yourself. Look at a distant object, and while keeping the object clearly in focus, hold your finger in front of your face. As long as you are looking at the distant object you'll see two fingers with blurry outlines. Now look at your finger. You will see a single image clearly in focus. By converging your eyes on your finger, you created tension on the muscles required for this kind of eye movement. Through your learning and experience, you come to understand that a certain amount of muscular tension means that a particular object is a certain distance away. If you must make a very strong effort to converge or cross your eyes to look at a nearby object (such as a fly on the tip of your nose), the muscular feedback lets you know that the object is very close.

Convergence is not a factor when you are looking at objects farther away than 25 feet. In this case, your eyes do not converge; rather, as perceptual psychologists say, your eyes are focused at infinity.

Another powerful binocular cue is **retinal disparity.** Because the eyes are set a certain distance apart in the head, objects closer than 25 feet are sensed on significantly different locations on each retina. Figure 4.24 demonstrates this phenomenon. Retinal disparity also is easy for you to demonstrate. Simply hold the index finger of one hand close to your face and the index finger of the other hand farther away. Line up your fingers. Now look at them with your left eye and then with your right eye, and then with your left again, and keep switching back and forth from one eye to the other. The near finger will seem to leap back and forth a considerable distance, while the other finger will seem to move only slightly. As

FIGURE 4.23

When the eyes focus on a nearby object, they converge. When they focus on a distant object they do not converge.

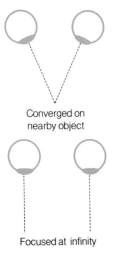

Converged on
nearby object

Focused at infinity

Figure 4.24 shows, an object directly in front of your nose is seen on the far right side of the right retina and on the far left side of the left retina, while an object that is far away is seen on almost the same place on both retinas. Another way of saying this is that objects that are extremely close create great retinal disparity, while objects that are far away produce almost no disparity. At a close distance, retinal disparity, perhaps more than any other cue, gives you a strong perception of depth.

Beginning in the 1950s, a number of films were made in so-called 3-D, or three dimensions. Of course, it's impossible to create real three-dimensional images on a flat two-dimensional screen. By using retinal disparity, however, filmmakers were able to create 3-D movies that were so realistic that the action sometimes seemed to be coming right at the audience. To obtain this effect, two copies of the same movie (that had been filmed by two different cameras set the same distance apart as human eyes) were projected onto the screen at the same time. One of these films was shown in red, the other in blue. By using glasses with different-colored lenses, one red (it washed out the red movie so that that eye could only see the blue version), the other blue (it washed out the blue movie so that that eye could only see the red version), viewers would see a different copy of the film with each eye. The illusion of depth was created by the resulting experience of retinal disparity. Later 3-D movies made use of different polarized light (horizontally versus vertically oriented light waves), which could be differentially filtered by special glasses so that the 3-D movies could then be shown in color. Still, the two versions of the film had to be matched exactly when projected and the 3-D effect ended at the edges of the screen. Modern 3-D, called Imax (see Figure 4.25), incorporates a huge wraparound screen that, unlike a regular movie, includes the audience's peripheral vision. The 3-D effect is created through the use of battery-powered liquid crystal glasses that rapidly (24 times per second) block off vision to first one eye and then the other in direct synchrony with the rapid back and forth projection on the screen of the two different versions of the movie. If you have a chance to attend an Imax 3-D theater like the one I went to in Vancouver, do so. I don't know how exactly to describe the experience other than to point out that sometime during the show I accidentally swallowed my gum. And Imax may just be the beginning! (see Focus on the Future).

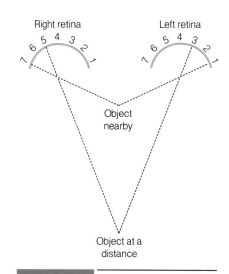

FIGURE 4.24

Viewing objects at a distance creates little retinal disparity; viewing objects that are close creates considerable retinal disparity.

FIGURE 4.25

Viewers in Osaka, Japan, are thrilled by the new Imax 3-D wraparound movie system.

CHAPTER 4
PERCEPTION

SEEING IS BELIEVING

There are two tennis courts in a park about a block away from my house. I'd like to take you over there and show you something. Not now, but 20 years from now. Of course, because this is a book, we won't have to wait—so, let's travel into the future and go 1 block over and 20 years forward.

Well, here we are in the future (quick trip, wasn't it?). As you can see, there are players on both courts. The couple on the far court are playing a typical game of tennis, not at all unusual. Looking at them, you can't even tell that you are 20 years into the future. But what about those two people playing in the near court— what in the world are they doing?! Look at them! They're both wearing some kind of helmet. The helmet appears to be totally solid; it even covers their eyes—how can they see? They're running around swinging their rackets like they're playing tennis. In fact, that one acted like he just hit a ball—but there isn't any ball. And they don't appear to be "playing" tennis with each other; instead, each is playing tennis (if that's what they're doing) alone. They really look weird. Every once in a while, one of them laughs, as though whatever it is she's doing sure is fun.

To understand what is happening (or perhaps I should say what is going to happen), let's take a moment to consider the television or motion picture of today. The pictures produced are flat. We perceive them as real enough, and we are able to make sense of them. But no one would mistake what she saw on television or a movie screen for an image of a real object. When you look at an actor's face on the screen, you know that you are not looking at an actor who is really standing before you. If you

walked behind the screen, you would not expect to see the back of the actor's head! Moreover, if you move your head from side to side, the picture on the screen does not change as it would if you were watching a real, three-dimensional object; that is, you perceive no relative motion.

None of those limitations, however, faces our friends on the tennis court. They are experiencing something called a *virtual environment.* The virtual environment—which, by the way, already exists—was first developed by NASA for training astronauts. The NASA version consists of a 12-pound helmet that fits over the head (see Figure 4.27). Both eyes are covered with clear, full wraparound 3-D images, and the ears receive digital stereo sound. With the optics that are now being developed, researchers hope that the artificial images produced in the helmet will eventually be as sharp and real looking as the "real

world" images your eyes are perceiving at this very moment.

The images and sounds in the helmet are controlled by a computer that takes into account the wearer's motions. If the wearer looks straight ahead, he sees whatever is programmed to be straight ahead. If he looks left, right, down, up, or even behind him, the images move in relation to his actions, just like real images!

Now that we have traveled 20 years into the future, would you like to try on the "tennis game" helmet? OK, walk onto the tennis court. First, you need to wear these special gloves and shoes that will tell the computer what the locations of your limbs are at any given moment. Now, hold this tennis racket and I'll help you on with the helmet—it's a good bit lighter than the old NASA model. Just put it down over your head and . . . YOU'RE AT WIMBLEDON—CENTER COURT— SEE AND HEAR THE CROWD—

FIGURE 4.26

NASA's virtual environment helmet.

LOOK AROUND—SEE ALL THE DIFFERENT PEOPLE? LOOK LEFT, THEN RIGHT—HEAR THE SOUND CHANGE AS YOU MOVE YOUR HEAD? MOVE ABOUT—SENSE THE POWERFUL EFFECT OF RELATIVE MOTION. ISN'T THIS UNBELIEVABLE? HOLD OUT YOUR HAND—THERE IT IS! THERE'S YOUR HAND! AND YOUR RACKET! NOT YOUR REAL HAND AND RACKET, BUT AN EXACT SIMULATION THAT LOOKS AND MOVES IN COMPLETE SYNCHRONY WITH YOUR REAL HAND AND RACKET, AND IT WILL APPEAR WHENEVER YOU MOVE YOUR ARM INTO WHAT WOULD HAVE BEEN YOUR VIEW, HAD YOUR VIEW NOT BEEN BLOCKED BY THE HELMET—OF COURSE, YOU DON'T FEEL THAT YOUR VISION HAS BEEN BLOCKED, BECAUSE YOU CAN SEE "YOUR HANDS"—YOU CAN SEE WIMBLEDON—AND YOU CAN SEE YOUR OPPONENT ON THE OTHER SIDE OF THE NET, WHO, BY THE WAY, IS GETTING READY TO SERVE. BETTER GET TO YOUR PROPER PLACE ON THE COURT—LOOK DOWN—SEE THE LINES MARKING OUT THE COURT? SEE YOUR FEET AS YOU WALK—SEE HOW EVERYTHING MOVES IN RELATION TO YOUR STEPS? TURN TO FACE YOUR OPPONENT. THE HELMET IS SO LIGHT YOU ALMOST FORGET THAT YOU ARE WEARING IT. THIS IS UNREAL! ACTUALLY, IT'S TOO REAL—IT LOOKS JUST LIKE IT'S REALLY HAPPENING! GET READY—HERE COMES THE SERVE—WHAT A BULLET! QUICK! STICK OUT YOUR RACKET! (An air-driven piston in the handle of your racket is fired by the computer at just the right time and strength by radio signal; you feel that a ball has hit the edge of your racket.) YOU WATCH THE BALL BOUNCE AWAY OFF THE COURT—A MIRACLE YOU EVEN GOT A PIECE OF THAT ONE—DID YOU SEE THE SPEED ON THAT BALL! LISTEN TO THE CROWD CHEER—WHO ARE THEY ROOTING FOR ANYWAY? YOU COULD GET KILLED OUT HERE. YOU'D BETTER ASK FOR A LOWER-RANKED OPPONENT. TAKE OFF THE HELMET. ZAP!! You're suddenly back on my neighborhood court. (By the way, the Yankee Stadium baseball program is also fun and don't even ask about X-rated films.)*

As you no doubt noticed, the strangest part about this advanced helmet is that it seemed invisible when you had it on. When you put your hands up to your face, you could feel the solid front plate of the helmet, *but you couldn't see it;* you could see only Wimbledon and all that was happening there—now, that's what I call a high-tech wraparound 3-D optical computer! Of course, it's all ultrahigh resolution and it's digital (would I have taken you 20 years—and 1 block—out of your way to try on a cheap helmet?).

Before such a helmet becomes available for games, however, it probably will have important commercial and professional uses. Such a device, as NASA has shown, would be valuable for training just about anyone who might benefit from learning in a simulated environment—such as airline pilots, emergency room personnel, police officers, tank commanders, or even college students who would rather do laboratory work at home, without the laboratory.

The helmets eventually should become readily available to the public. As one investigator noted, "These will be in homes, much as televisions are today. But you won't watch shows—you'll put on the helmet and go places and experience things" (Rogers, 1987, p. 57). Of course, the experiences might take a little getting used to. No doubt, walking through Paris would be nice, but fighting off an invasion of the giant spiders from Mars right in your own living room might be another thing. (And you can bet that in the same spirit that led to roller coasters after the invention of the train, designers will make "fright" programs—real "helmet-ripper-offers"!)

There are many questions we might ask concerning the effects of such a system: Should young children ever be allowed to wear the family "TV" and shoot it out with "real" bad guys on some apparently real street? Will interacting with simulated violence make viewers indifferent to the real thing? Could children wear the helmets at home instead of going to school and interact with a real teacher who teaches from a TV studio? All of the kids would see one another as though they were sitting in a real class, and they could interact with one another as well as with the teacher. They would perceive the blackboard, the schoolroom, the whole works, only they would all be in their own homes—probably along with their helmet-wearing parents who have "gone to work" without actually having gone anywhere. Such "helmet schools" would save greatly on the expense of maintaining real school buildings, save on commuting, cut down on automobile exhaust, and spell the death of the short-range spitball.

This all makes you wonder. Maybe philosophers who say that reality is in the mind are wrong—maybe it will turn out to be in the software!

*I told you not to ask!

INNATE

Inborn; arising as a hereditary component of a physiological or behavioral trait.

VISUAL CLIFF

An apparatus constructed to study depth perception in animals and human beings. It consists of a center board resting on a glass table. On one side of the board, a checkered surface is visible directly beneath the glass; on the other side, the surface is several feet below the glass, giving the impression of a dropoff.

The Visual Cliff

Because so many of our perceptual abilities appear to be tied, at least in part, to inherited mechanisms, it was only natural for researchers to wonder whether depth perception might not come into being immediately with little or no learning. That is, is depth perception present at birth?—is it **innate?** Let's look at the experimental evidence.

Most animals will avoid a sharp dropoff or cliff, and this tendency can be used to examine aspects of innate perception. Over 20 years ago, Gibson and Walk (1960) constructed a device known as the **visual cliff,** a table with a glass surface marked to simulate a deep dropoff on one side and a shallow dropoff on the other (see Figure 4.27). Infant animals, including humans, can be placed at the center between the shallow and deep sides. Because of the glass, the subject cannot actually fall off the cliff.

Babies of many species were tested on the cliff, and the results demonstrated that they possessed an innate ability to avoid a dropoff, called *cliff avoidance.* Newborn chicks, whose first visual experience was on the cliff, refused to cross over to the deep side. Kittens, puppies, piglets, and various other infant animals also refused to venture onto the deep end. Baby mountain goats (a species that would have an exceptional reason for avoiding cliffs) similarly refused to cross to the deep side and, if pushed in that direction, collapsed their front legs. Gibson and Walk, and many other researchers, also demonstrated that human infants were much more easily coaxed onto the shallow side than onto the deep side, although some infants were willing to crawl onto the deep side. Does this mean that cliff avoidance is innate in humans? Unfortunately, the research conducted on humans was not as clear-cut as was the research conducted on other species.

Unlike baby chicks, kittens, or mountain goats, human infants aren't precocious in terms of motor development. They usually are not able to crawl until they are about 6 months old, and independent movement is a prerequisite for a test of cliff avoidance. Consequently, by the time they can be tested on the cliff, human infants may already have *learned* to avoid dropoffs. This possibility was suggested by the research team of Campos, Hiatt, Ramsay, Henderson, and Svejda (1978), who observed that precrawling infants of 2, 3 1/2, and 5 months of age showed only a decelerated heart rate when placed on the glass over the deep side. Heart-rate deceleration is generally taken to be a sign of interest, not of fear. The implication is that the infants perceived that something was different, but perhaps did not see this difference as a matter of "depth."

Another researcher (Rader, 1979) argued that cliff avoidance is a genetically inherited predisposition but is one that doesn't begin to express itself until it is triggered at about the age of 6 months in humans. The issue has not yet been fully resolved.

FIGURE 4.27

The visual cliff.

MOTION PERCEPTION

After we have determined whether something is there and where that something is, we'll want to know what it is doing, if anything. To know whether some object is moving relative to ourselves, we need to compare it with what does not move. J. J. Gibson believed that our perceptual mechanisms evolved to take a special interest in these invariant stimuli *and to contrast them* with stimuli that were in flux. In other words, once we perceive what's stable, we can pick out what's moving. Gibson said that the terms *persistence* and *change* could describe any environment.

Understanding the perception of motion, however, presents some unusual challenges. For example, when you sense motion, how can you know whether an object has moved or you have moved? If someone playing baseball is running back for a long fly ball, what lets her know the amount of motion to attribute to the ball and the amount of motion to attribute to her own body? Is her knowledge based exclusively on learning?

Physiological evidence indicates that there are special neural mechanisms that allow us to judge motion with some degree of accuracy (Frost & Nakayama, 1983). One of these physiological mechanisms is found within our **peripheral vision,** an area that had been long ignored by researchers. It seems that the fovea of the retina is tuned to respond to local changes in the visual field; that is, to objects moving through the visual field. The periphery of the retina, however, responds to *global* changes in the visual field, the kind that occur whenever *we* move (Johansson, von Hofsten, & Jansson, 1980). If you turn your head from side to side, or get up and walk, you'll notice that there is a tremendous amount of motion in the periphery, which you see out of the corners of your eyes.

You can demonstrate the distinction between foveal and peripheral vision in a rotary-drum room, a very small room contained within a large upright cylinder. The walls inside the cylinder are covered with vertical stripes, and you sit on a chair in the middle of this cylindrical room. While the chair and floor remain stationary, the walls of the room begin to rotate on the vertical axis so that the vertical stripes painted on the cylinder walls pass rapidly in a horizontal direction in front of your eyes. The walls are so close to your face that the spinning surface fills your entire visual field. Because of this, you sense motion in your peripheral vision (as you recall, one of the tricks used in the new 3-D motion picture system Imax). It creates a sickening feeling, and after about 10 seconds, if you're like most subjects, you'll probably grab your chair, swearing that the walls aren't turning but that the chair you're sitting on is spinning! Subjects are often afraid to get up off the chair because they think they'll be thrown to the ground. They sometimes lean as though they are accelerating or yell for help, but all the time the chair stays still and only the cylinder walls are rotating.

The reason that subjects in the rotary-drum room think they are in motion is that their peripheral vision is totally involved (Brandt, Wist, & Dichgans, 1975; Wong & Frost, 1978). This peripheral–foveal distinction suggests that there is a physiological organization to help us perceive motion. In fact, while most of the neurons from the foveal region are projected to the occipital lobes, neural messages from the periphery tend to be projected to the temporal lobes (Dichgans & Brandt, 1978). In addition, neural messages from the semicircular canals, which provide us with a sense of balance and orientation, are projected to areas of the temporal lobes very close to those receiving information from the peripheral vision. It may be that the messages from the semicircular canals function with messages from the peripheral vision to help us maintain our balance, head position, and motion in relation to the world around us.

OTHER SENSES

Research concerning human perception is growing rapidly. Although visual perception dominates the research field, many studies of auditory perception or perception involving the minor senses also have been conducted.

As brief examples of some of this research, consider the following. When you

PERIPHERAL VISION
All visual experiences outside the immediate line of sight; that is, experiences other than those derived from light focused on the fovea. The photoreceptor field on the retina surrounding the fovea gives rise to peripheral vision. Peripheral vision is especially important for determining motion.

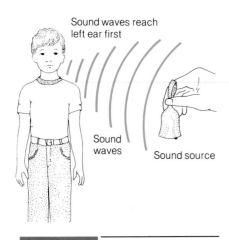

Sound waves reach left ear first

Sound waves

Sound source

FIGURE 4.28

Although this single sound is sensed twice, the child hears, or perceives, it only once, but off to one side.

hear a sound, you actually sense it twice, once in each ear, unless its source is equidistant from both ears. It takes sound slightly less time to reach the ear closer to the origin of the sound than to reach the ear farther away (see Figure 4.28). Even so, you will perceive only one sound but it will seem to be coming from a particular direction. Your brain has somehow used the differences in arrival time between the two sensations to generate an understanding of the sound's location in space—a neat trick! This ability develops early in life. By 6 months of age, a baby can orient its head toward the source of a sound with no more than a 12-degree error, and by 18 months, the error is reduced to a very small angle of only 4 degrees (Morongiello, 1988). This is all the more amazing when you consider that as an infant grows his head size enlarges, making the distance between his ears greater and greater. This means that the infant's brain has to continually recalibrate the meaning of the time delay between receiving a sound in one ear and in the other (Clifton, Gwiazda, Bauer, Clarkson, & Held, 1988).

Another interesting discovery concerning auditory perception is that the auditory cortex is not laid out like the cochlea (see Chapter 3), with many different locations each sensitive to a different frequency of sound, but rather it appears to have different locations, each sensitive to a different fundamental pitch *and to all of its higher frequency harmonic overtones* (Pantev, Hoke, Lutkenhoner, & Lehnertz, 1989). This helps to explain how, when a piano plays a C and a violin plays a C, we can tell that they are both playing the *same note*, even though the instruments sound different. The complex and different sounds made by each instrument stimulated the same "pitch perception" location on the auditory cortex. In fact, some people have such exceptional ability in this area that they are considered to have "perfect pitch," the ability to identify any musical note they hear, regardless of which instrument plays it. They appear to have this ability through an exceptional inborn pitch mechanism and not as a result of experience or exceptional memory (Klein, Coles, & Donchin, 1984). While the frequency of a sound might be a stimulus, its pitch is a *perception*.

Touch perception provides another interesting illustration of research with the "minor" senses. If two pencil tips are touched to your body a small distance apart (at two points on the skin, call them A and B) and the touches are made within a fraction of a second of each other, you will feel as though one pencil tip has touched down at point A and drawn a line along the skin to point B (Geldard & Sherrick, 1986). This is similar to the Phi phenomenon observed in vision (see Chapter 1), in which two stationary lights, when flashed in succession, are perceived as one light in motion. Your brain is filling in the missing information. In the real world, two rapidly close sensations like the pencil touches would *most likely* be caused by one thing moving on your skin (a bug, for instance).

Whichever of the senses is being studied, understanding the processes by which the brain interprets what it senses is fundamental to our knowledge of human perception.

EPILOGUE: "THAT'S HIM!"

Psychologists who study perception have come to appreciate that we cannot always trust our brains to interpret the messages of our senses accurately. In the following account, we see how one man's understanding of perception led him to question the perceptions of other people.

In the mid-1970s, researcher Robert Buckhout was arguing strongly that eyewitness testimony was less trustworthy than most people believed it to be and therefore should not be relied on as heavily as it was. Buckhout pointed out that although such testimony was often challenged, as a rule it was still accepted as conclusive evidence by most juries. Behind this acceptance, Buckhout believed, was a misconception about the way in which the eye functioned. Too many people considered the eye to be like a camera. If an eyewitness saw someone clearly, and then later identified a suspect definitely, there could be little doubt of the suspect's guilt. An eyewitness's testimony was questioned only if the opportunity to observe the suspect had been extremely poor. In cases of face-to-face contact, however, when the victim could pick out the assailant among other people in the courtroom, eyewitness testimony was almost always accepted.

Buckhout knew that perception did not work like photography. He knew that a person's attention might be focused on some cues more than on others, and that the person might later rely on these limited cues for making comparisons. When Buckhout presented his arguments (Buckhout, 1974), his intention was to demonstrate to the legal community, and to others interested in eyewitness testimony, that the way in which we attend to particular cues can affect our assumptions about the innocence or guilt of an individual. He supported his argument by describing, in detail, a not uncommon case of mistaken identity.

It all began when a young man named Larry Berson was arrested for having committed several rapes. Berson pleaded with everyone that he was totally innocent, but the victims had had a good face-to-face look at the rapist under good illumination, and they identified Berson in police lineups as "the one." Some time later, however, the police arrested a man named Richard Carbone, who then confessed to the crimes, clearing Berson. Look at photographs (a) and (b) in Figure 4.29. On which cues do you think the eyewitnesses were focusing their attention when they positively identified Larry Berson as the rapist? Carbone and Berson present several of the same cues, although they are not really look-alikes.

You may argue that this kind of mistaken identification, made by eyewitnesses who were certain about what they had seen, cannot be common. But there was another twist to Buckhout's example. When Carbone was arrested, he confessed not only to the rapes but also to a robbery. The police were surprised to hear the latter confession, since they had arrested George Morales for the robbery on the basis of a positive identification by eyewitnesses. Morales is shown in photograph (c) of Figure 4.29.

(a)

(b)

(c)

FIGURE 4.29

(a) Richard Carbone, (b) Larry Berson, and (c) George Morales.

The eyewitnesses were amazed by their errors; they had been "so sure." Remembering this case, you may have doubts the next time you hear someone say, "That's the man! I could never forget his face!" Like Buckhout, you now know that the eye is not a camera and that recording something with your perception is not the same as recording it on film.

SUMMARY

■ Perception is defined as the way in which we interpret messages processed by our senses.

■ Sightless vision is made possible by tactile feedback that helps the blind to perceive the three-dimensional world.

■ The basic perceptual abilities of the visual system include distinguishing forms from background, determining the location of forms in space, and analyzing whether forms are moving. Unique brain pathways have been associated with these different abilities.

■ Reversible figures demonstrate the influence of learning in distinguishing form from ground.

■ Gestalt psychologists studying perception were interested in demonstrating that the whole was greater than the sum of its parts.

■ Many of the perceptual organizations we make may be the result of perceptual mechanisms that have evolved to provide us with a perception of what is most likely. The Phi phenomenon illustrates this point.

■ J. J. Gibson coined the term *affordance* to denote the perceptual organization possessed by a species that helps to support the species' survival.

■ Among the theories of visual perception, the two that received the most attention were the image and cue theory and the direct perception theory.

■ The image and cue theory proposes that we rely on learned cues for such functions as depth perception. Through learning, we are able to make three-dimensional sense of a two-dimensional image projected on our retinas.

■ Direct perception theorists believe that our genetic and biological organization equips us to make perceptual sense of the world without having to rely much on learning.

■ The interactionist view considers aspects of both the direct perception and the image and cue theories.

■ Research with illusions has indicated that learning is an important aspect of perception. The effects of many illusions can be understood as attempts to bring the illusions into line with our daily experiences.

■ The brightness, size, and shape constancies are perceptual cues that help us to make sense of the world.

■ Depth perception is achieved through monocular cues—that is, through cues sensed with only one eye (such as linear perspective and overlap)—and binocular cues (convergence and retinal disparity). A three-dimensional effect on film is obtained by using retinal disparity.

- Our learning and experience play an important role in size perception. Sometimes, our perception of size can be distorted. The moon illusion, which provides the cues of overlap and relative size, is an example.

- The visual cliff experiment indicates that the ability to perceive dropoffs is innate in some animals. Research also has been conducted on a comparable cliff avoidance mechanism in humans.
- Peripheral vision enables us to differentiate between our own movement and that of our surroundings.

SUGGESTIONS FOR FURTHER READING

1. Coren, S., & Ward, L. M. (1989). *Sensation and perception* (3rd ed.). New York: Academic Press. A college-level introduction to sensory and perceptual processes.
2. Goldstein, E. B. (1989). *Sensation and perception* (3rd ed.). Belmont, CA: Wadsworth. A college-level introductory textbook.
3. Gregory, R. L. (1989). *Odd perceptions*. New York: Routledge & Kegan Paul. A collection of short essays for the general reader on how we perceive color, shape, touch, sound, and other sensations. Some are amusing, some serious. All will make you think.
4. Rock, I. (1984). *Perception*. New York: Scientific American Books. A comprehensive and fascinating exploration of perception and perceptual systems.
5. Wolfe, J. M. (Ed.). (1986). *The mind's eye: Readings from Scientific American*. New York: W. H. Freeman. A collection of articles from *Scientific American* on visual and perceptual systems.

CHAPTER 5 | States of Consciousness

PROLOGUE

It is January 13, 1989. You are with a research team at a cave near Carlsbad, New Mexico. You are watching as a young Italian woman named Stefania Follini enters the cave through an entrance in the ground. She is a volunteer who is helping you investigate the effects of the daily rising and setting of the sun on the human biological clock. She is descending into a 20 × 12 foot subterranean plexiglas module sealed 30 feet below the surface where she has agreed to spend months of

The subterranean chamber Follini occupied during the experiment.

Prologue

Why Psychologists Study States of Consciousness

States of Consciousness

Sleep
Stages of Sleep
REM Sleep
Sleep Duration
Sleep Deprivation
The Circadian Rhythm

Sleep Abnormalities and Pathology
Insomnia
Narcolepsy
Sleep Apnea

Dreaming
Psychoanalytic Theory
The Activation–Synthesis Model
The Housekeeping Hypothesis
The Off-Line Hypothesis

Daydreaming

Hypnosis
Dissociation
Memory Enhancement
Pain Relief and Changed Emotional
  States
Behavioral Changes
Disinhibition
Posthypnotic Suggestion

Meditation

Psychoactive Drugs
Central Nervous System Stimulants
Central Nervous System Depressants
Hallucinogens

Epilogue: The End of a Nightmare

Summary

Suggestions for Further Reading

Stefania Follini exiting the New Mexico cave where she spent four months in an experiment to test the body's reaction to long-term isolation.

time by herself. She is going into a world with no sunrises or sunsets. There are no clocks and she will never be told the time. You will leave messages for her at random intervals on her computer; other than that, she will be cut off from the outside world.

You watch her from up above on a monitor. As the days pass, she unknowingly extends her own day to 25 hours, choosing to go to bed an hour later each night than was her custom before the experiment began. Soon she is staying awake for 40 or more hours straight and then sleeping 14 to 22 hours at one stretch. She also informs you that her menstrual cycle has stopped. After four months, when you ask her to estimate how long she has been underground, she guesses only two months. She thinks it is March when it is May! Her biological clock is completely out of whack.

The experiment ends. When she appears on the surface once again, she is astounded to find how much time has really passed.

In this chapter, we will examine states of consciousness, including sleep and dreaming, hypnosis, meditation, and the effects of drugs. We'll discuss how long dreams last, how self-hypnosis is done, what theories have been developed about why we sleep, why drugs affect us as they do, and how you can alter dreams by taking part in them. You also will discover why Stefania Follini's biological clock began to "free run" once she was cut off from the sun.

WHY PSYCHOLOGISTS STUDY STATES OF CONSCIOUSNESS

Consciousness is the state in which you are aware not only of the external environment but also of internal events such as thinking. Before people act, they often consider things "internally"; that is, they think about them. This fact made the study of consciousness a paramount issue when the science of psychology was first developed. An early definition of psychology was "the description and explanation of states of consciousness and such" (Ladd, 1887). Defining consciousness is not easy, however. When George Trumbull Ladd put forth that less-than-precise definition in 1887, it drew a lot of humorous comment about exactly what should be covered under the umbrella of "and such."

In 1913, John Watson, in his paper "Psychology as the Behaviorist Views It," rejected the study of consciousness as too subjective to be of scientific interest. Although it appeared that objectivity could be preserved by avoiding the issue of consciousness, the concept of consciousness seemed so self-apparent and central to the human experience that it was impossible to ignore for long, and psychologists were drawn to study it (Hilgard, 1980).

Today, thanks to advances in scientific technology, we have some objective ways to measure conscious states. We are able to monitor changes in some conscious experience by using such instruments as the electroencephalograph (which we will discuss shortly) and the PET scan (see Chapter 2).

STATES OF CONSCIOUSNESS

Consciousness is not a fixed, unvarying state, but can be altered. The conscious state is said to be altered any time the content or quality of conscious experience undergoes a significant change. There are many ways to alter conscious experience. Psychoactive drugs can alter your conscious state and your perceptions of the world. Sleeping and dreaming also are considered to be states of consciousness. Hypnosis can alter conscious experience. Other causes are sleep deprivation, religious experiences, mystical or emotional experiences, sensory overload or deprivation, high fever, and prolonged strenuous exercise.

Most research into states of consciousness has concentrated on sleep, hypnosis, meditation, and psychoactive drugs; we'll examine each of these areas.

SLEEP

In the 1920s, a German physician named Hans Berger was the first person to record the brain's electrical activity. Because so many of the neurons and their axons (see Chapter 2) run through the cortex in a parallel direction, their thousands of action potentials add up, giving off an electrical field (just like the kind that surrounds an electric wire) strong enough to be picked up as "brain waves." Berger made readings of this activity with a fairly crude home-made device consisting of a couple of silver electrodes glued to his subject's scalp. When Berger reported his results, they sounded so bizarre that he was either laughed at or ignored for over 10 years. (How would you like to be laughed at or ignored for over 10 years?) "Berger's vindication," however, exists today in the modern form of his crude device, the sophisticated **electroencephalograph (EEG)**. The EEG has a number of applications, among which are those made by sleep researchers who use the EEG to measure the brain waves of sleeping subjects. They have observed that brain waves change dramatically at the onset of sleep and during sleep.

After World War II, electroencephalograms, the tracings made by EEG machines, were routinely incorporated into sleep research. The EEG yielded some interesting findings in the late 1940s and early 1950s. One was that not everyone "drifts off to sleep." Instead, some people go abruptly from a drowsy waking state to sleeping. Researchers also discovered that distinctly different sleep stages occur throughout the sleep period. Each stage is characterized by a different EEG pattern.

Stages of Sleep

When you fall asleep, your body temperature drops slightly, your pulse and breathing rates decrease, and your level of the stress-related hormone **cortisol** drops. Your body seems to be calming down after a busy day; it's becoming quiet. One interesting exception to all this quieting, especially in children, is the sudden increase in the release of growth hormone, which reaches its highest levels during sleep.

As you fall asleep, **alpha waves,** which are associated with a drowsy but awake state, change to small irregular waves. These waves are associated with the first stage of sleep (stage 1). Have you ever caught yourself falling asleep? Sometimes you can, especially if you're very tired and are thinking about something in particular when you fall asleep. As you shift from alpha to small irregular waves, you might,

CONSCIOUSNESS
A state of awareness of sensations, perceptions, or memories. The aspects of mental life of which one is normally aware.

ELECTROENCEPHALOGRAPH (EEG)
An instrument that records the electrical activity of the brain.

CORTISOL
A hormone produced by the cortex of the adrenal glands found just above the kidneys. It is critical for the metabolism of fats, carbohydrates and proteins. It is very similar to cortisone.

ALPHA WAVES
A pattern of brain waves typical of the relaxed, waking state.

just for an instant, realize that your thoughts have become incoherent and illogical. This can happen because a rational train of thought can be lost at the onset of sleep (see Figure 5.1).

Many researchers believe, however, that stage 1 might be better thought of as a transition between wakefulness and real sleep (Borbely, 1986). The typical sleeper will spend only about 5 minutes in stage 1 before descending to stage 2. Stage 2 is considered to be more important because it constitutes about one-half of all our sleep time. As stage 2 begins, the muscles become less tense and the eyes rest quietly. During stage 2, the EEG shows slightly larger waves appearing along with rapid short bursts of brain-wave activity called *sleep spindles*. After about 10 minutes in stage 2, the sleeper descends to stages 3 and 4, which are associated with **delta waves.** Delta-wave sleep is sometimes known as **slow-wave sleep.** The distinction between stages 3 and 4 is somewhat arbitrary. If delta waves constitute less than one-half of the waves recorded during slow-wave sleep, the sleeper is considered to be in stage 3; more than one-half, and he is considered to be in stage 4.

The slow-wave stages of sleep are the deepest. In Figure 5.2 you can see the differences in slow-wave delta activity on a computer-generated visual representation of an EEG. It is most difficult to awaken sleepers from stage 4 (Webb & Cartwright, 1978). As people grow older, they often notice that they become lighter sleepers. The EEG confirms this; it is well documented that slow-wave sleep decreases with age.

After spending time in slow-wave sleep, the sleeper typically returns to stage 2 for some time before entering the first rapid-eye-movement (REM) period (which we will discuss shortly). As Figure 5.3 on page 154 shows, following the REM period, the sleeper usually returns to stage 2 before sinking back into slow-wave sleep. This cycle may occur three or four times in a night before the sleeper finally ascends through stages 2 and 1 and then awakens.

Researchers also have investigated sleeping animals. The stages of sleep appear in all mammals (Borbely, 1986), although the pattern may differ. Other primates—monkeys, gorillas, and orangutans—show sleep patterns on the EEG that are very like the human pattern (Tauber, 1974).

REM Sleep

One of the most astounding discoveries in sleep research occurred in 1953 as a result of the careful observations of a graduate student named Eugene Aserinsky. While watching a subject whose sleep was being monitored by an EEG in the laboratory, Aserinsky noticed that from time to time the subject's eyes appeared to move rapidly back and forth beneath closed eyelids. After awhile, these rapid eye movements stopped, and the subject slept soundly. A little while later, the movements began again. Further investigation revealed that this kind of **rapid eye movement (REM)** occurred in all subjects. Aserinsky wondered whether REM was related to anything in particular. By carefully examining subjects awakened from

FIGURE 5.1

A typical sleep cycle in humans. Sleep becomes progressively less deep throughout the night, and dreams tend to lengthen and intensify. The stages appear as numbers from 1 through 4. The amount of time spent in each stage is read horizontally. REM refers to rapid eye movement. Dreaming is most often associated with REM sleep.

Time of Day

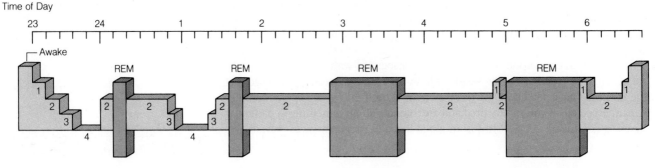

REM sleep and from periods of sleep when they displayed no rapid eye movement, called **NREM sleep** or **orthodox sleep,** Aserinsky and other researchers discovered that a very large proportion of subjects who were awakened from REM sleep had been dreaming! This discovery of a physiological correlate associated with dreaming stimulated researchers to conduct further investigations, and the area of sleep research began to grow rapidly.

In human beings, NREM and REM sleep are considered to be two distinct kinds of sleep. NREM sleep has been divided into the four stages described in Figures 5.1 and 5.2

REM sleep has its own characteristic EEG wave pattern. During REM sleep, an unusual thing happens: The body becomes simultaneously active and inactive (Chase & Morales, 1990). This occurs because both excitatory and inhibitory neural systems are stimulated during REM sleep.

The excitatory aspect of REM sleep can be seen as the sympathetic nervous system becomes active. REM sleep is sometimes referred to as **paradoxical sleep** because the body is excited and brain waves are similar to those of the waking state—blood pressure and heart rate increase, and the body may even act as though it is under attack or is responding to an alarming situation. This heightened activity level doesn't necessarily mean that the sleeper is having a nightmare—she may actually be having a pleasant dream. The excitatory phase of REM sleep certainly appears to argue against the idea that the only reason for sleep is to give our bodies a rest!

At the same time, the inhibitory neural mechanisms occurring during REM sleep cause **atonia,** a loss of muscle tone, resulting in a state of semiparalysis. It becomes almost impossible for the dreaming REM sleeper to move. Some researchers believe that this change protects sleepers from physically responding to or acting out their dreams. (Contrary to what you might have guessed, sleeptalking and sleepwalking have been found to occur mostly during NREM, when the body is better able to move. About 15 percent of all dreams *do* occur during NREM sleep, which may account for the occasional actions of some sleepers, although their dreams appear to be less vivid than those that occur during REM sleep.) The inhibitory neural messages that create the semiparalysis during REM sleep pass through an area of the brain called the *pons.* In cats, when certain small portions of the pons are destroyed, the animals will become *active* during REM sleep. Unlike normal cats, cats with destruction in the pons will stand up during REM sleep, walk, bat at the air with their paws, or even appear to stalk prey, all with their eyes closed (Morrison, 1983). Also, certain drugs that are known to affect the pons can induce REM sleep (Quattrochi, Mamelak, Madison, Macklis, & Hobson, 1989).

Sometimes the excitatory and inhibitory processes occurring during REM sleep spill over into each other's territory. When this happens, semiparalyzed muscle groups may suddenly react. This results in the "nap jerks" or twitches that are commonly observed in sleepers (Chase & Morales, 1983).

The body generally tries to devote a certain portion of its sleeping time to REM sleep each night. During REM sleep, people will often incorporate an unexpected sound into their dreams rather than allow the sound to awaken them. Rather than let a street crew's air hammer wake you up, you might instead dream that you are on a battlefield.

People who are deprived of REM sleep in the laboratory often engage in **REM rebound** when they are finally given a chance to sleep undisturbed. In REM rebound, a person will show an increase in REM sleep after deprivation. Such a REM-sleep-deprived person will lapse into REM very soon after falling asleep, and will engage in more REM than usual. Interestingly, scientists have discovered that

NREM Sleep (Orthodox Sleep)
Non-REM sleep, during which no rapid eye movement takes place. Also called orthodox or quiet sleep because the EEG pattern is markedly different from the waking state.

Paradoxical Sleep
REM sleep. The EEG pattern closely resembles that of a person who is awake, even though the person is still asleep. Most dreaming occurs during this kind of sleep. The sympathetic nervous system shows heightened activity.

Atonia
Loss of muscle tone. During REM sleep, atonia occurs simultaneously with arousal of the sympathetic nervous system. The atonia creates a state of semiparalysis in the REM sleeper.

REM Rebound
An increase in REM sleep demonstrated by a person who has been deprived of it.

Figure 5.2

In these computer-generated visual displays of the brain's electrical activity (a kind of EEG), the red areas indicate the presence of slow-wave, or delta-wave, sleep.

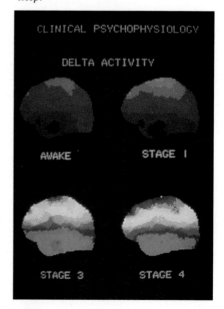

Figure 5.3

EEG patterns clearly show the differences in states of consciousness. Each state is characterized by a different pattern. Notice how similar the patterns are during the drowsy state and REM sleep.

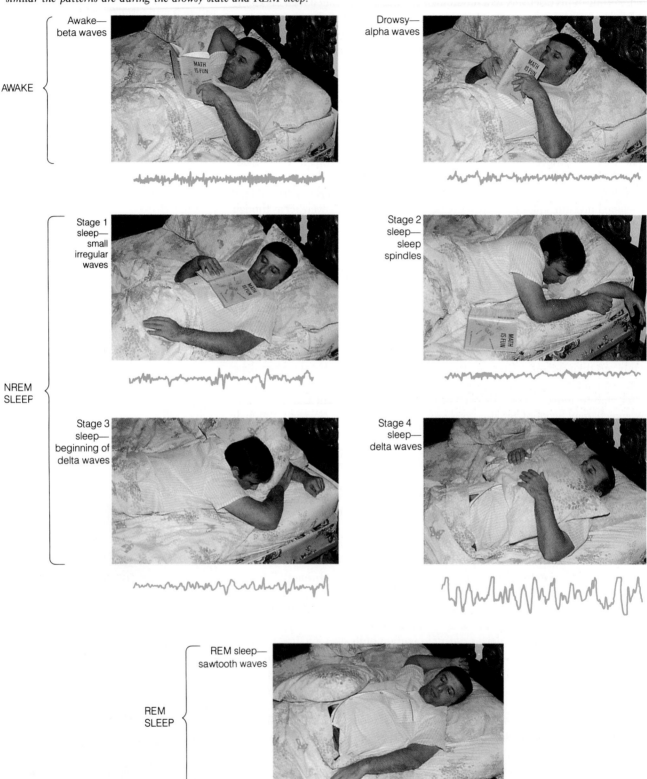

AWAKE

Awake— beta waves

Drowsy— alpha waves

NREM SLEEP

Stage 1 sleep— small irregular waves

Stage 2 sleep— sleep spindles

Stage 3 sleep— beginning of delta waves

Stage 4 sleep— delta waves

REM SLEEP

REM sleep— sawtooth waves

some people may benefit from some REM deprivation. Systematic REM deprivation in the laboratory has been found in some cases to help people overcome *endogenous depression* (Borbely, 1986). Endogenous depression, meaning depression from within, is not triggered by specific events, but is a general sense of sadness that has no apparent cause. REM deprivation is assumed to help the sufferers of such depression by somehow altering the effects of neurotransmitters in the brain.

HEALTHY INSOMNIACS
People who function well with only 3 hours of sleep per night or less, and who do not seem to need more sleep than this.

Sleep Duration

The average young adult needs between 6 1/2 and 8 1/2 hours of sleep a night (Tune, 1969); some people need a little more, some a little less. The most alert individuals are those who sleep until they are simply no longer tired (a luxury to most of us). There is no evidence to support the old notion that "oversleeping" will make you tired (Roehrs, Timms, Zwyghuizen-Doorenbos & Roth, 1989).

On the other hand, some individuals are done with a full night's sleep after significantly less than 8 hours. Such individuals have been carefully monitored in sleep laboratories, and some have been shown to function very well after only 3 hours of sleep (Jones & Oswald, 1968). During the day (and for a good part of the night), they are wide awake and feel fine. When Jones and Oswald reported these findings, they didn't know what to call these people. Should they be considered sleep deprived? The label didn't really apply, because 3 hours of sleep was all they needed. Jones and Oswald finally decided to describe them as **healthy insomniacs.** Some healthy insomniacs even get by with less than 3 hours of sleep per night. A woman who slept 45 minutes a night, day after day, reported that she felt absolutely fine, refreshed, and able to do her work without difficulty. Her claims were carefully documented in a sleep laboratory and found to be true (Meddis, Pearson, & Langford, 1973).

You may be wondering whether these healthy insomniacs eventually burn out. After all, sleep (at least NREM sleep) does apparently give the body a chance to rest, which the body requires—or does it? Many very large animals expend a great deal of energy but sleep only a few hours a night, and do very well. Horses, cows, and elephants usually sleep only 3 to 4 hours every 24. Then again, at the other extreme, opossums and bats sleep 20 hours per day. The range throughout the animal kingdom is considerable. It was even believed for a time that some marine mammals, such as dolphins or porpoises, didn't sleep at all (Webb & Cartwright, 1978), presumably because they would drown if they did. Now, however, through careful observation, we know that such mammals do sleep, but avoid drowning because the two hemispheres of the brain take turns sleeping; while one hemisphere is asleep, the other is awake (Mukhametov, 1984)!

Sleep Deprivation

What would happen if you did not get enough sleep? In one experiment, six couples were asked to reduce their nightly sleep period by 1/2 hour every week until they felt too uncomfortable to continue. All the subjects stopped before they reached less than 4 1/2 hours of sleep per night (Johnson & MacLeod, 1973). No serious inability to perform different tasks occurred with the decreased amount of sleep, but the subjects all reported discomfort. There is no question about it: When you don't get enough sleep, you get sleepy.

What happens when you not only reduce your sleep but also try to stay awake for a long period? The question of how long people can go without sleep has been investigated extensively, with the first studies conducted in 1842 (Patrick & Gilbert, 1896). Most of us have missed one night's sleep, maybe even two nights in a row.

ADAPTIVE THEORY
A theory about why we sleep. It states that for each species a certain amount of waking time is necessary in order to survive, and sleep is nature's way of protecting organisms from getting into trouble during their extra time.

CONSERVING-ENERGY THEORY
A theory about why we sleep. It states that sleep is a good way of conserving energy in the face of sparse food supplies. This theory agrees with the adaptive theory that sleep can be a protective device.

AN ENDURING QUESTION: WHY DO WE SLEEP?

For years, people have assumed that we need to sleep because we must rest. The logic of that conclusion appears undeniable. And yet, when researchers examine sleep closely, sleep is often found to be a time of stress, and physiological and muscular activity (like tossing and turning). Furthermore, quiet resting while awake, no matter how quiet, cannot replace sleep. Also curious are the very differing amounts of sleep needed by different species, although all must sleep some. Why do these differences exist? To this day, the reason for sleep remains one of the most profound mysteries. No one knows the answer, but there are some interesting theories that may help provide an answer.

The first theory advanced about why we sleep, known as the **adaptive theory** (Meddis, 1975; Webb, 1974, 1975), contends that each species needs a certain amount of waking time in order to survive. Large herbivores (plant eaters) such as elephants and cows must consume vast amounts of vegetation to live. Grazing and eating take a lot of time. If elephants slept for 8 hours a day like we humans do, they probably wouldn't have time for the waking activities that maintain their species.

Unlike elephants, humans don't need 21 hours of waking time in order to survive. In examining the Laplanders, a modern tribe in northern Scandinavia that still follows the herds and lives off the land in the same way our ancestors did many thousands of years ago, we find that approximately 15 or 16 hours of daily waking activity are required to sustain human lives and foster the next generation. This leaves 8 hours per day *that aren't needed*. Sleep, then, may be nature's way of telling people to lie down and be quiet during their "extra time." In this view, sleep is a protective mechanism, keeping species out of trouble. If, in your extra 8 hours per day, you wandered about stirring up fights, taking chances, or using up your resources, then you would not be as likely to survive and pass on your genes to your offspring. On the other hand, it would be an adaptive advantage if you, or any species, inherited a predisposition to pass out during your spare time.

The second explanation, known as the **conserving-energy theory**, goes hand in hand with the adaptive theory. Two researchers (Allison & Cicchetti, 1976) observed the sleep patterns in 38 different species and reported that differences in species body weight, which is a good indication of metabolism, and the amount of danger faced by the species in its environment correlate well with the amount of sleep a species needs. The implication is that animals that sleep a great deal and have a high metabolic rate may be sleeping to conserve energy as well as to protect themselves. Human beings, too, may have come to use sleep as a means of conserving energy. You burn fewer calories when you're asleep than when you're awake and active. If food supplies are scarce, going into a kind of hibernation for 8 hours every day is a way of ensuring that your limited food supply won't be consumed too quickly. So perhaps a sleep-promoting factor has become incorporated in our biology because of the value inherent in remaining quiet and conserving energy after a day's tasks.

In fact, natural substances have been found in the body that promote sleep (Krueger, Pappenheimer, & Karnovsky, 1982). One of these, factor S (for sleep) is a small molecule that will induce slow-wave sleep for several hours when it is given to animals. Factor S also stimulates the immune system (Karnovsky, 1986). Researchers note elevated levels of factor S during times of illness, which may explain why we tend to sleep more when we are ill.

The presence or absence of factor S does not completely control whether or not sleep will occur, however. Other sleep factors must also be playing a role. Researchers suspect that there are many additional sleep factors, and they have isolated a few of them (Borbely, 1986). Even so, to this day no one knows exactly why the body produces sleep-inducing chemicals, or why they cause us to become sleepy.

A full and complete understanding of why we sleep may still be decades away. Perhaps someday we will understand the chemistry of sleep, and perhaps even find a way to rid ourselves of the need for it. That might sound unpleasant, but if you never got sleepy, you probably wouldn't want to sleep. Not sleeping would also add 25 to 30 waking years to each person's life.

FOR CRITICAL ANALYSIS

1. If there were a way to safely prevent sleep, and also fix it so that you would never become sleepy, would you want to make use of this discovery and stay awake the rest of your life thereby adding "years" to your existence? If you say no, is it because you imagine yourself becoming tired for some reason? Many people say that under such circumstances they sense that they might develop a need for a quite time like sleep just to get away from stimulation, a need quite apart from the desire to sleep because they are sleepy. Do you also feel that way? Might such feelings also hint at additional reasons for sleep?

2. If people could find a safe way to end the need to sleep, what effect would this have on our environment? Would pollution grow at a faster rate? Would energy resources be used more quickly? Would energy demands remain high throughout each 24 hrs.? How do your answers fit with the idea that sleep is evolutionarily adaptive for the survival of our species?

This scene from the movie They Shoot Horses, Don't They? *depicts an example of marathon dancing, a craze of the 1930s, in which the last couple left dancing on the floor wins the prize. During the Great Depression, couples often danced for days with hardly any sleep in order to win, because they needed the prize money desperately. After about 60 hours of sleep deprivation, hallucinations and delusions become common.*

Some people have stayed awake much longer. In one carefully controlled experiment, six human subjects were kept awake for 205 hours (8 days, 13 hours) straight (Kales et al., 1970). The world record under controlled conditions is 264.2 hours (11 days, 12 minutes) (Gulevich, Dement, and Johnson, 1966). In cases of extended deprivation like the ones just noted, sensory disturbances, hallucinations, and delusions occur after only about 60 sleepless hours:

> The surface of objects begins to waver; the floor appears to be covered with spiderwebs; faces appear and disappear. . . . A participant hears voices in the sound of a running water faucet and thinks they are talking about him. . . . The subject feels a ring of pressure around the forehead, as if he were wearing a hat. (Borbely, 1986, p. 156)

Some research indicates that people deprived of sleep have "micro-sleep" periods, an intrusion of REM during waking, which may account for their hallucinations. Micro-sleep episodes also make it difficult to say how long the subject has truly been awake.

Even after 60 sleepless hours, functions such as heart rate, blood pressure, respiration, and temperature did not show much change. When the subjects were finally allowed to sleep, they slept for about 1 whole day—or even less—awoke, and felt quite good. This seems to indicate that missing a few mights' sleep may not be harmful in the long run to people who are healthy to begin with.

Because of such findings, some researchers began to wonder whether sleep was, in fact, necessary for life. Perhaps sleep was one of nature's big mistakes. Maybe if we could counter whatever it was that made us sleepy, we could get by just fine without sleep. This speculation led researchers to try an experiment in which rats were deprived of sleep to see whether sleep deprivation was harmful to the rats or whether it only made them sleepy. In Figure 5.4 you see the organization of a device used to measure sleep deprivation in rats. Both rats were connected to an EEG that would signal when they fell asleep. One rat was chosen for sleep deprivation; the other rat was used to control for the possible stress effects of just being in the experiment. Whenever the rat to be sleep-deprived fell asleep, the plastic disk the rats were standing on began to rotate. Then the rats would have to walk to keep from falling in the water. The control rat was able to sleep when the other rat was normally awake.

Some of the sleep-deprived rats lasted as long as 33 days! None of the sleep-deprived rats showed any signs of physical abnormalities—that is, until the day before they died. *All* the sleep-deprived rats died; *none* of the control rats did. On

FIGURE 5.4

The experimental apparatus for measuring long-term sleep deprivation in rats. The EEGs of both rats are monitored. When the rat to be sleep deprived falls asleep, the EEG notes the change and closes a circuit, causing the plastic disk that both rats are standing on to begin turning. The rats are called a "yoked" pair, because when the sleep-deprived rat is forced to walk by the turning disk, the control rat must also walk. This arrangement controls for the stress that the rat faces when it is forced to walk in order to keep from falling into the water. A rat who does not walk when the disk turns will be carried to the wall and knocked into the water. With this arrangement, the rat that is not to be sleep deprived is able to sleep when the other rat is normally awake. The sleep-deprived rat can never sleep, because as soon as the rat's EEG senses that the animal is falling asleep, the circuit will close and the disk will start turning. (SOURCE: Rechtschaffen, Gilliland, Bergmann, & Winter, 1983, p. 182.)

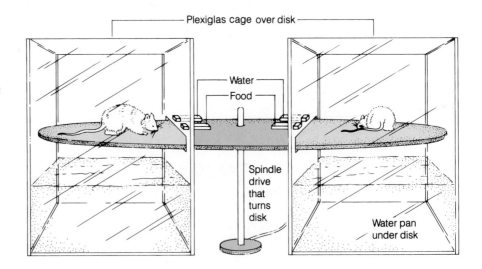

autopsy, the rats who had died were found to have many things wrong with them, including stomach ulcers and internal hemorrhages; in all rats the damage was severe and extensive throughout, although no two rats had exactly the same damage. The researchers concluded that "these results support the view that sleep does serve a vital physiological function" (Rechtschaffen, Gilliland, Bergmann, & Winter, 1983, p. 184).

Of course, the same experiment can't be conducted on humans. However, there has come to light an interesting case study indicating that a fate similar to that experienced by the sleep-deprived rats might await a human subject. In 1986, the case of a 53-year-old man who had a sleep problem was reported (Lugaresi et al., 1986). The man had slept normally until he was 52. At that time, he began to lose the ability to sleep and was soon unable to sleep at all. (Even healthy insomniacs get *some* sleep.) He was admitted to a hospital, but *nothing* given to him would help him to sleep. He finally sank into a vegetative stupor and died. The autopsy revealed that 95 percent of the neurons in an area of the thalamus, which is suspected to be involved with sleep regulation, had somehow been destroyed. Interestingly, one of the man's sisters had died in the same way. Furthermore, sleep researchers have been unable to detect any normal brain-wave sleep patterns in a number of the man's relatives. What causes this fortunately rare sleep failure is unknown.

The Circadian Rhythm

Circadian, from the Latin *circa* (about) and *dies* (day), refers to events that occur in roughly a 24-hour cycle. The sleep–wake cycle occurs daily, and is therefore a **circadian rhythm.** Figure 5.5 shows a typical sleep–wake cycle of a person who is sleeping 8 hours per night. As the circadian rhythm begins its downward trend, the person becomes sleepy, his core temperature drops, and the levels of cortisol in his blood lower. When the circadian rhythm comes back up, the person awakens, and both cortisol levels and temperature increase. During the day, as the circadian rhythm nears its high point (usually in the early evening—but this may vary considerably), body temperature and cortisol levels reach their maximum, and vision, hearing, smell, and taste are at their peak. At this time, the person is most alert.

You can easily sense your own circadian rhythm by staying awake all night. By 2 or 3 A.M., you feel extremely tired, and by 5 or 6 you may be exhausted. But, by 7 or 8, you'll probably begin to feel *less* tired. This resurgence occurs because you are reaching a point in your circadian rhythm where your alertness is beginning to pick up. Interestingly, after missing a night's sleep, you won't need a full 8 hours' extra sleep to make up for it; an additional 1 or 2 hours usually will be enough.

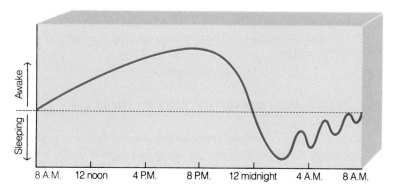

FIGURE 5.5

The circadian sleep cycle of a typical person who sleeps 8 hours per night and who usually awakens at 8 A.M. Notice that the circadian rhythm between midnight and 8 A.M. is similar to that depicted in greater detail in Figure 5.1.

159

JET LAG
An uncomfortable feeling caused by disruption of the sleep–wake cycle that follows an attempt to adjust to a new time zone too quickly. It is called jet lag because long-distance travelers often suffer from it.

SUPERCHIASMATIC NUCLEI (SCN)
Dense clusters of neurons located in the central nervous system close to the hypothalamus just above the optic chiasm where the optic nerves from both eyes intersect. The SCN is known to control the pacing and activation of many circadian rhythms.

FREE RUN
The tendency for the sleep-wake cycle to break away from a 24-hour cycle. This is most likely to occur when day and night cues are reduced or eliminated. Most free running in humans involves a cycle of approximately 25 hours, but many other cycles are possible, most longer than 24 hours, some shorter.

PINEAL GLAND
The pineal gland is located in the brain and it resembles a crude retina. It secretes melatonin, is sensitive to light, and secretes hormones in response to the length of day. The pineal gland is believed to regulate the 24-hour circadian rhythm.

Attempting to change the circadian rhythm abruptly is what causes **jet lag.** That sleepy uncomfortable feeling that you may have after traveling great distances has little to do with being cooped up in jets or the length of the trip. It has to do with adjusting to new time zones. In fact, if you leave an American city to fly, for instance, to Belgium, you can avoid jet lag if you continue to stay on American time. However, if you try to adjust to Belgian time immediately and have breakfast when you would have normally been going to bed back home, you will disrupt your circadian rhythm and you'll find it very difficult to get through the first few days.

For years, researchers tried to find out how the body synchronized its circadian rhythm to the length of the day. After all, how could it know when 24 hours were up? Then, in the early 1970s, scientists discovered that a small cluster of brain neurons alongside of the hypothalamus, called the **superchiasmatic nuclei,** or **SCN,** were mostly responsible for regulating circadian rhythms. In animals, if this area is disrupted, many circadian rhythms will fail or will occur completely out of synchrony with one another and with the 24-hour day. Even stronger evidence supporting the SCN as being the body's timekeeper comes from experiments in which tissue was taken from the SCNs of live hamsters who had 20, 22, or 24-hour cycles and then transplanted into hamsters whose SCNs had been destroyed. The recipient hamsters quickly showed the daily rhythm of the donor hamster, whether 20, 22, or 24 hours long (Ralph, Foster, Davis, & Menaker, 1990). Interestingly, the reason these researchers had hamsters with different circadian rhythms with which to experiment was because they had discovered that different circadian rhythms can be induced through breeding. In fact, Martin Ralph and Michael Menaker were able to trace the differences in the animal's circadian rhythms to differences in a single gene (Ralph & Menaker, 1988). The finding that the body's pacemaker is directly controlled by a heritable, genetic process emphasizes just how deeply ingrained it is.

The SCN isn't bound to a 24-hour day; in fact, the cycle in most people seems to be a little more than 25 hours. The reason for this is unknown, but it may help to explain why it is easy for many people to creep forward in their sleep schedule, going to bed later and later each night (making the morning jolt administered by the alarm clock seem worse and worse—does this sound familiar?). The "creep forward" tendency has been shown in experiments in which subjects have been isolated from all time cues, such as was seen in the Prologue. In these circumstances, subjects **free run;** a circadian rhythm of 25 hours or more is typical (Siffre, 1975).

Synchronizing the SCN to a 24-hour cycle appears to be the job of the **pineal gland** (Czeisler et al., 1986). Surprisingly, recent investigation has shown the pineal gland to resemble a crude retina (Miller, 1985c). In fact, the pineal gland, in evolutionary terms, might have been the first eye. In some species, like the Western fence lizard, the pineal gland even has a lens and cornea associated with it! The pineal gland senses the light and secretes hormones in reaction to the length of day, which, in turn, keeps circadian rhythms on a 24-hour cycle. Sudden changes in this rythm, due to shifts in work schedules, for instance, can be quite disruptive. Psychologists are working on ways to help ease the stress of such changes (see Focus on an Application).

SLEEP ABNORMALITIES AND PATHOLOGY

There are many sleep-related disturbances, among them insomnia, narcolepsy, and sleep apnea. All these disorders are being investigated in the laboratory, and ways of dealing with them are being developed.

IF THIS IS TUESDAY, IT MUST BE THE GRAVEYARD SHIFT

It was 4 A.M. when it happened. The needle on the temperature gauge measuring the heat in the atomic core began to rise. The water-level indicators looked right, but something was obviously very wrong. For the next few hours, workers scrambled to stop what they feared might be happening—a nuclear meltdown.

When the morning-shift workers arrived at the Three Mile Island Nuclear Power Plant, they walked into a control room that was in panic. Within a few minutes, however, the workers from the new shift realized which gauges were not to be trusted and determined what really might be happening at the reactor core. They acted on a guess to stop the rising heat of the core just in time.

In Bhopal, India, an accident occurred at a Union Carbide chemical plant during the night shift; it caused the release of a deadly gas that killed thousands of people (Coleman, 1986).

In the Soviet Union, at the nuclear plant at Chernobyl, the atomic core melted down and exploded, spewing radiation over scattered areas of Europe. No one knows how many cancer deaths eventually may result; some people estimate over 10,000. The failure at Chernobyl occurred during the night shift (Marbach, Carroll, & Miller, 1987).

Was it only a coincidence that graveyard-shift workers were the ones on duty during these accidents, or did the accidents occur because the workers were too tired to think in an emergency?

Many researchers now believe that workers whose schedules are not in synchrony with their circadian rhythms are much less productive and much less safe on the job (Monk et al., 1983; Coleman, 1986). In fact,

when sleep researcher Charles Czeisler interviewed thousands of shift workers, including truck drivers and nuclear power plant operators, he found that more than half admitted to dozing off while working at least once a week (Weiss, 1989).

Such findings may be especially important for industry. Fully 25 percent of American workers have a schedule other than the standard day shift. Furthermore, many of those 25 percent work for companies that rotate shifts in an effort to be fair to all employees. The most common shifting schedule requires workers to take the day shift (8 A.M. to 4 P.M.) one week, the graveyard shift (midnight to 8 A.M.) the next week, and the swing shift (4 P.M. to midnight) the week after that, and then to start the cycle again.

As you now know, when workers suddenly change to the graveyard shift, they are required to be awake

and on the job when their circadian rhythm is telling them to sleep. Then, when they go home at 8 A.M. to sleep, their circadian rhythm is telling them to awaken. No wonder nobody looks forward to the graveyard shift.

In 1980, researchers at the Stanford University Sleep Center were contacted by the operating manager of the Great Lake Minerals and Chemicals Corporation in Utah. The manager was curious about whether the researchers' knowledge of circadian rhythms and sleep cycles could be used to help his workers. For 10 years the corporation had rotated its workers every week to the preceding shift, as described previously; that was common industry practice. In other words, every week, workers would begin their shift 8 hours earlier than the one they had worked the week before.

The Stanford researchers began their experiment by changing the

The control room for Unit II, Three Mile Island, site of the nuclear accident. Workers not in synchrony with their sleep cycles are slower to react in emergencies and less able to think through problems that arise.

schedules of the workers, so that they moved to a later shift (clockwise direction) every 3 weeks (see Figure 5.6). (Various controls comparing nonrotation and different schedules also were incorporated into the study.) The workers were then compared on measures of health, productivity, personnel turnover, and job satisfaction. The results showed that a large majority of the workers who shifted preferred the new forward rotation to the old backward one. To the company's satisfaction, personnel turnover decreased, and productivity increased by 20 percent (Czeisler, Moore-Ede, & Coleman, 1982; Coleman, 1986).

As you may have noticed, there were two major changes made in the schedule. First, there was the change to a clockwise advance in shifts, instead of the traditional counterclockwise direction. As we mentioned, when you are resetting circadian rhythm, it is much easier to go forward than backward—the clockwise direction is in tune with the typical SCN cycle of slightly more than 24 hours. The second change was to a 3-week rotation, instead of a 1-week shift change. The researchers chose this period because it takes from 4 to 14 days for body temperature and hormone secretions to come into synchrony with the new sleep schedule (Coleman, 1986). When the workers were shifted every week, their circadian rhythms (temperature, hormone secretion, and sleep) were desynchronized, leaving them with a generally miserable sense of existence;

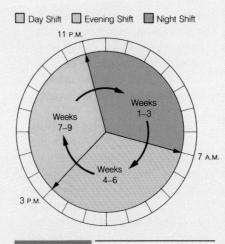

FIGURE 5.6

A 3-week clockwise shift. (SOURCE: *Coleman, 1986, p. 46.*)

never quite awake, never quite asleep.

Even for those workers who shift every 3 weeks, however, there still remain 4 to 14 days that they must endure while their circadian rhythms synchronize to their new sleep schedule. Scientists have discovered, however, that if a person who is going from the swing shift to the graveyard shift sits in front of floodlights like those used on a movie set from early evening until midnight, the pineal gland can be fooled into "thinking" that midnight is really sunset! The pineal gland then rapidly moves the body's temperature and hormone secretions forward, bringing them into line with the new schedule in only 2 days (Czeisler et al., 1986). The shift to a new time schedule can be made to occur even more rapidly by providing a flood of bright light 2 to 3 hours before the individual's usual "dawn" (Czeisler et al., 1989).

Another interesting way in which the circadian rhythm might be reset is by altering the body's hormone levels. Melatonin is a hormone that is secreted by the pineal gland at regular intervals and which affects the circadian rhythm. Researchers have used controlled doses of melatonin to accelerate or decelerate the circadian cycle, restore the cycle to a blind person whose circadian rhythm had become disturbed, and help alleviate the symptoms of jet lag (Reppert, Weaver, Rivkees, & Stopa, 1988). Once the effects of melatonin are better understood, it might eventually be commonly used to help overcome the problems associated with shift work or jet lag.

Organizations such as the Nuclear Regulatory Commission and the Federal Aviation Administration are just beginning to pay attention to sleep cycles and to the possible ways to ease the strain of shift working. In fact, the FAA is now experimenting with allowing "controlled naps" for pilots on long trans-Pacific flights (Palca, 1989), flights that are notorious for causing fatigue. Although no one can say that a particular airline disaster or industrial accident was caused by workers whose various circadian rhythms were unsynchronized, there is no doubt that visual acuity, problem-solving ability, and coordination decrease dramatically when people stay awake at a time when their bodies want to be asleep.

If you have difficulty sleeping—or staying awake—you aren't alone. In just the United States, approximately 50 million people have sleep problems, and about 20 percent of them feel that their difficulty is serious enough to warrant at least one visit to a doctor during any particular year.

Insomnia

People who have **insomnia** find it difficult to fall asleep or, once asleep, to stay asleep. The difficulty may be temporary or long term, mild or severe, and it may be accompanied by one or many symptoms. On the average, 32 percent of American adults report some form of insomnia (Hopson, 1986).

People suffer insomnia for many reasons. The major causes are life-event stressors (upsetting events or circumstances), illnesses, poor sleep habits, or depression (Kales, Caldwell, Preston, Healey, & Kales, 1976), any of which may disrupt the daily sleep–wake rhythm (Coleman, 1986). In fact, such sleep problems can sometimes be an early warning sign of a full-blown depression or anxiety problem (Ford & Kamerow, 1989). Most insomniacs, however, will respond to the simple treatments listed in Table 5.1.

Narcolepsy

Narcolepsy is a peculiar disorder that was poorly understood for many years. It afflicts approximately 250,000 Americans (about one person in every thousand),

INSOMNIA
Difficulty in initiating or maintaining sleep for the necessary amount of time.

NARCOLEPSY
An inherited pathological condition characterized by sudden and uncontrollable lapses into deep sleep.

TABLE 5.1   Ten Things to Do If You Can't Sleep

1. Establish a solid circadian rhythm by always going to bed at a certain time and getting up at a certain time. This is especially important for the getting-up part—no sleeping in on the weekends. If you haven't been doing this, it will take about 2 weeks to "lock in" on a solid rhythm. You'd be surprised how much insomnia this one step can eliminate.

2. If you wake at night, don't get frustrated; rather, find something quiet to do until you are once again sleepy.

3. Cut way down or, better still, eliminate the use of coffee, tea, or other sources of caffeine. Also, avoid alcohol, nicotine, or chocolate in the afternoon or evening, and substitute instead a little of the sleep-inducing amino acid tryptophan (which you can obtain in a glass of milk before bedtime—warm if you like). See, grandma was right!*

4. Keep your bedroom comfortable; avoid excess light and noise and extremes in temperature.

5. Avoid eating heavy meals in the evening.

6. Engage in regular exercise, but not too close to bedtime.

7. In general, avoid napping, especially after a bad night's sleep.

8. Go over your troubles in the morning if you must, but don't take them to bed with you. Instead, when you go to bed, think of something that is repetitive and boring.

9. Avoid using alcohol or sleeping pills (over the counter or prescription) to induce sleep. Such substances usually disrupt the normal sleep cycle and eventually lead to an increase in the severity of the problem.

10. Don't be concerned if, after you've tried to sleep a while, it becomes apparent that you are not going to get 8 hours of sleep. Missing sleep from time to time is not a health hazard; being overly anxious about it, however, might be.

Try each of these suggestions for at least 1 week before giving up. If none of these techniques seems to help, visit a doctor. There might be a medical basis for your insomnia (for example, you may be sensitive to a medication, or you may have difficulty breathing during sleep). Should you need special help beyond what your doctor can provide, you may require help from the more than 150 sleep disorder centers currently accredited by the American Sleep Disorders Association.

*Caution: Some health food stores offer tryptophan in pill form. Recently, some individuals taking such products have contracted a rare and dangerous blood disorder. Although it probably results from a contaminant in the product, to be safe, get your tryptophan the old-fashioned way—have a glass of milk.

SOURCE: Adapted from Hopson, 1986; Borbely, 1986.

both males and females. Although narcolepsy is sometimes called "sleep epilepsy," it appears to have little or nothing to do with actual epilepsy. Narcolepsy is an uncontrollable, recurring, and sudden onset of sleep during the daytime waking hours. The total loss of muscle control during a narcoleptic episode often causes the person to fall. Narcoleptics are most likely to sleep at moments of high anxiety or worry. The disorder appears to occur because there is a sudden onset of REM sleep during the waking state. Narcolepsy most often begins between the ages of 15 and 20 years. At first, it may be very difficult to diagnose, appearing to be nothing more than daytime sleepiness. Onset after age 40 is rare (Matheson, 1986).

Narcolepsy appears to be associated with disturbances in the reticular activating system of the brain stem (see Chapter 2). In general, people who have narcolepsy in their families are 50 times more likely to have the disorder than others.

Researcher William Dement at Stanford University demonstrated, by breeding narcoleptic Doberman pinschers with one another, that narcolepsy is inherited. Whenever these narcoleptic dogs got excited (such as when they were offered their favorite treats), they would all come rushing over, jumping up and down like normal dogs, and then suddenly fall sound asleep. What narcoleptics inherit is an inability to secrete dopamine properly in one particular area of the brain (Mefford et al., 1983). Dopamine is one of the neurotransmitters suspected of playing a role in arousal. Perhaps the kind of brain tissue transplants used to treat Parkinson's disease (see Chapter 2) will eventually be used to help narcoleptics. For the time being, amphetamines, which, are stimulants, are used for this purpose.

Sleep Apnea

Sleep apnea is a syndrome characterized by episodes of cessation of breathing during sleep. An apnea (absence of respiration) may last for only a few seconds or may continue for minutes. Sleep patterns may be severely disturbed because a person who is not breathing begins to wake up, and the sleeper often begins gasping or choking. Severe apnea, which affects about 1 percent of the general adult population, often results in 400 to 500 awakenings a night (Coleman, 1986). In one sleep study, a subject was found to have such severe apnea that he was unable to breathe and to sleep at the same time. He would fall asleep, stop breathing, stay asleep for a minute or two, and awake gasping. When he had taken in enough air, he would fall asleep again, only to stop breathing once more. Although such severe sleep apnea is rare, mild sleep apnea is not uncommon and it is estimated that about 20 million people suffer from the disorder.

Sleep apnea is more likely to occur in men than women, and is especially common among elderly men (Ancoli-Israel, Kripke, Mason, & Kaplan, 1985). Researchers believe this is because the male hormone testosterone is related to sleep apnea. Men who have sleep apnea and are given supplemental testosterone show an increase in apneic episodes. When testosterone levels are lowered, the apneic episodes decrease (Sandblom et al., 1983).

If a person's sleep is sufficiently disrupted by apneas, he or she may experience daytime sleepiness, headaches on awakening, or other uncomfortable symptoms of insufficient oxygen, high levels of carbon dioxide, and a poor night's rest. Some people thought to be senile have been found to be suffering some brain damage each night because of lack of air exchange. Sleep apnea also can cause heart failure, especially if the person takes sleeping pills (Coleman, 1986).

Obstructive apnea, caused by blockage of the airway, can be treated by a number of methods, which include weight loss, changing sleep positions (not sleeping on the back), placing a pillow at the nape of the neck so that the head is tilted backward during sleep, and the use of tongue-restraining devices or special air pressure masks.

Because apnea is sometimes due to collapse of the airway, a *tracheotomy* may be performed in severe cases (Arehart-Treichel, 1977); this procedure creates a hole in a person's throat, through which he breathes.

DREAMING

Typically, a person has three or four dreams nightly, usually associated with REM periods. Moreover, dreams change during the night. Dreams later in the sleep period become progressively longer, more vivid, and more unrealistic. No one knows what dreams are, but there are a number of theories.

Psychoanalytic Theory

The psychoanalytic interpretation of dreams, first described by Sigmund Freud (see Chapter 1), argues that dreams are disguised representations of repressed desires, which appear in symbolic form. This is known as the dream's **latent content.** In this view, the purpose of dreams is to provide unconscious gratification, so that certain desires can be satisfied and thus will not intrude into the sleeper's life when she is awake. Only the surface, or **manifest content,** of dreams is open to straightforward observation (people can tell you what they dreamed) and, according to this theory, without an in-depth *psychoanalysis* the underlying purpose of the dreams is wholly lost. Unfortunately, since this deep interpretation of underlying purpose is not open to experimental investigation, it remains conjecture.

The Activation–Synthesis Model

One of the most interesting dream theories has been proposed by J. Alan Hobson and Robert W. McCarley (1977), based on research conducted into brain activity during REM sleep. Hobson and McCarley called their theory the **activation-synthesis model** of dreams. They had noticed that during sleep a mechanism in an area of the brain called the pons (see Chapter 2) generates neural impulses that stimulate both the oculomotor and the reticular systems. *Oculomotor* refers to motor neurons associated with eye muscles. This stimulation may be the cause of rapid eye movement. The reticular system, as we noted in Chapter 2, is involved in activating the organism. Hobson and McCarley refer to this neural stimulation as the *activation phase* of dreaming.

The signals from the pons are eventually sent to the forebrain. The forebrain is the master integrator of the brain; it relates emotions to thoughts and to planning ahead (Hawkins, 1986). The question is: What happens to all this electrical information heading into the forebrain? Hobson and McCarley believe that a synthesis occurs, in which the forebrain tries to make sense of the messages it is getting, and creates a dream. In this view, dreams are nothing more than a response to random electrical activity and have no particular meanings.

The Housekeeping Hypothesis

Uncomfortable with the notion that all this electrical activity is without purpose, Francis Crick, winner of a Nobel Prize for codiscovery of DNA, and researcher Graeme Mitchison have argued that the brain purposely makes dreams by creating this random electrical activity in order to find and eliminate any senseless or bizarre neural connections that accidentally developed during the course of the previous

LATENT CONTENT
In psychoanalytic theory, the hidden true meaning of a dream. The latent content of a dream, with all of its symbols and concealed meanings, can only be understood, according to this view, through the process of psychoanalysis.

MANIFEST CONTENT
In psychoanalytic theory, the overt, literal, dream content. Usually what is first described or reported by the dreamer.

ACTIVATION–SYNTHESIS MODEL
A physiological model of dreaming that contends that the brain synthesizes random neural activity generated during sleep and organizes this activity into a dream.

day's learning and experience. In this view, dreaming may be a time of "house-keeping" during which nonsensical information or "noise" is brought forth and swept clean. This may help to explain why a person may begin to have bizarre thoughts and perceptions after going without sleep for a long enough period. If Crick is right, remembering your dreams might actually help undo the brain's good work, since you would be strengthening the nonsensical associations the brain is attempting to eliminate (Crick & Mitchison, 1983). The housekeeping hypothesis, however, fails to explain why dreams sometimes have sensical associations or why, if it is a matter of sweeping the brain clean, many people report having the same dream again and again (Brown & Donderi, 1986).

The Off-Line Hypothesis

Animals that have learned a complex task and are then allowed to sleep will forget what they have learned if they are deprived of REM (Hawkins, 1986). Animals deprived of NREM do not show this forgetfulness. These findings imply that REM sleep may be involved in the learning process. It may be that during REM, the new experiences that we have acquired are somehow integrated with our older memories and experiences (Lehmann & Koukkou, 1980). This may explain why many of the events that occur in our lives on a particular day show up again, in one form or another, in our dreams about 3 or 4 days later (Epstein, 1985). REM may be placing these new experiences into our memory in a more profound and lasting way.

All but the very largest computers need **off-line time** to store, sort, and integrate information. Off-line time frees circuits for gathering and sorting new information by consolidating and storing the old information. The same kind of off-line sorting and processing may be occurring in humans during REM sleep (Winson, 1985). In fact, animal studies have shown that during REM, electrical activity occurs that strengthens long term connections in the hippocampus, an area of the brain associated with memory (Winson, 1990).

Switching back and forth between on- and off-line also enables smaller computers to handle loads that would normally require much larger machines. The Australian anteater is the only known mammal that does not engage in REM. Its forebrain is huge in comparison to the rest of its brain (Hawkins, 1986). This may be because its forebrain has to do everything on-line. Perhaps off-line time during REM enables creatures to maintain a smaller and more efficient brain size. If human processing were only on-line, would our powerful brains be the size of basketballs? If so, we certainly have a good reason to go "off-line" and dream!

DAYDREAMING

At the University of Minnesota at Morris, psychology students in Eric Klinger's class took some unusual examinations. During the exams the students were required to respond to loud beeps that were occasionally emitted from a small box on the instructor's desk. They had been told to write down whatever they were thinking about just before the beep occurred. The beep was also used during class lectures; again, the students were to write down exactly what had been on their minds just before they heard the tone.

Klinger says, "It's surprising how little we know about what goes on in people's heads. What I'm hoping to do is find out how much time is spent on different thoughts and how much impact these thoughts have on a person's life" (Bartusiak,

1980, p. 57). During one lecture, Klinger reported, a student wrote down that at the sound of the beep he had been thinking about his church pastor, the Minnesota Vikings football team, and a station wagon. Another man had been fantasizing about being shaved by two women; someone else had been wondering whether to have ham or turkey for dinner. As you can see, Klinger's research indicates that people spend a great deal of time daydreaming about things that are irrelevant to the task at hand.

Daydreaming is often considered to be undirected thought. Amazingly, it appears that the average person spends about one-third of his or her waking conscious time daydreaming. (Doesn't it make you feel better to know you're not the only one?) According to Klinger,

> Daydreaming is so commonplace that we usually think little about what it is, why we do it, how it affects us or what sets off the particular content of our fleeting excursions away from the here and now. But it's an important, intriguing—and for psychologists, challenging—part of our mental life. . . . Daydreams usually start spontaneously when what we are doing requires less than our full attention: Our brains move our conscious attention automatically away from the here and now to work over other concerns. (Klinger, 1987, pp. 37, 44)

Interestingly, the percentage of daydreams that occurs when people are awake and the percentage of night dreaming that occurs when people are asleep is about the same (Foulkes & Fleisher, 1975; Webb & Cartwright, 1978). In each case, about a third of their time is involved in "dreams." Why this is so is unknown.

HYPNOSIS

Altered states of consciousness may be produced by means other than sleep. One of the most interesting and controversial is hypnosis. What we now call hypnosis first received wide attention about 200 years ago, during the eighteenth century. At that time, the Austrian physician Anton Mesmer claimed that he could cure the ill with magnetism. Arguing that living things were influenced by magnetic forces, he coined the term **animal magnetism** to describe the "magnetic" force that people supposedly could exert on one another. Hundreds of Mesmer's patients testified that they were relieved of their pain through Mesmer's efforts. This kind of treatment became known as **mesmerism.**

Mesmer was a faith healer who knew how to make money. To serve the thousands who requested his services, he "magnetized" inanimate objects and claimed that they could heal. The French Academy of Sciences (in consultation with Benjamin Franklin) found no evidence of any curative effects to be derived from magnetism. However, the academy did suggest that Mesmer's personality had influenced his patients' imaginations. Or, to put it another way, Mesmer had the power of suggestion.

What, exactly, this power of suggestion may be or how it works has been explored since the time of Mesmer and continues to be a subject of much interest. Today, the term **hypnosis,** after Hypnos, the Greek god of sleep, is used to describe the effects of suggestion. Hypnosis is not a state of sleep, however. Although a hypnotist may say, "You are falling deeply asleep," EEG readings have shown that hypnotized subjects supposedly in a deep sleep are actually awake, but drowsy. Hypnosis appears to be not a single phenomenon but rather a single word used to describe a number of relatively separate phenomena (Barber, 1969).

Some subjects can be hypnotized; others cannot. Interestingly, whether a person

ANIMAL MAGNETISM
The term coined by Anton Mesmer to describe the supposed magnetic force that people could exert on one another.

MESMERISM
An early term for hypnosis, named after Anton Mesmer, who claimed he could cure the ill with magnetism. In mesmerism, "magnetic" forces were called on to relieve pain.

HYPNOSIS
A state of consciousness characterized by relaxation and suggestibility.

DISSOCIATION
A separation or splitting off of mental processes often associated with the hypnotic state. Subjects can then perform acts that do not register in their conscious memory or can engage in two behaviors while remembering only one of them.

AUTOMATIC WRITING
Writing done by the subject during a dissociated hypnotic state; the subject is not aware of writing.

SELF-HYPNOSIS
A hypnotic state induced by the subject without the aid of a hypnotist.

is hypnotizable tends to remain stable throughout her life (Piccione, Hilgard, & Zimbardo, 1989). In general, individuals who tend to fantasize and daydream are more likely to be hypnotizable (Lynn & Rhue, 1988).

When conducting a hypnosis session, the hypnotist begins by encouraging a subject to relax. The subject is usually asked to fix her gaze on a particular place or point, and then to respond to the hypnotist. Once the subject is relaxed, the hypnotist can test for suggestibility. A scale used to measure suggestibility, or susceptibility, is shown in Table 5.2. People who are highly suggestible will meet many of the criteria on this test. These people are likely to be good subjects for hypnosis. Other people, especially those who are alert and curious about the hypnotic effect and who are waiting for something to "happen" to them are likely not to be susceptible. Some subjects have failed to become hypnotized even after thousands of attempts.

Dissociation

Once the subject is prepared and is showing susceptibility, the hypnotist can aid the subject to create a number of interesting effects. One of the most fascinating is the **dissociation** that can occur in a hypnotized state. The subject can be maneuvered to engage in two things simultaneously, and yet to remember only one clearly. **Automatic writing** is an example of this kind of dissociation. The hypnotist asks the subject to write something, and, while the subject's hand is writing, the hypnotist will draw the subject into discussing or describing something else. Later, the subject may be surprised to learn what his hand has written. At the same time, he will clearly recall the topic he was discussing while the writing was in progress (Hilgard, 1977).

When students first encounter something like automatic writing, they often believe that it's a trick or that the subject was lying and really did know what he was writing. Yet most of us, through **self-hypnosis,** have had a similar dissociating

---

TABLE 5.2 Stanford Hypnotic Susceptibility Scale, Form C

ITEM	CRITERION OF PASSING
0. Eye closure during induction	(Noted, but not scored)
1. Hand lowering (right hand)	Lowers at least 6 inches in 10 seconds
2. Moving hands apart	Hands 6 inches or more apart after 10 seconds
3. Mosquito hallucination	Any acknowledgment of effect
4. Taste hallucination (sweet, sour)	Both tastes experienced and one strong or with overt movements
5. Arm rigidity (right arm)	Less than 2 inches of arm bending in 10 seconds
6. Dream	Dreams well, experience comparable to a dream
7. Age regression (school fifth and second grades)	Clear change in handwriting between present and one regressed age
8. Anosmia to ammonia	Odor of ammonia denied and overt signs absent
9. Arm immobilization (left arm)	Arm rises less than 1 inch in 10 seconds
10. Hallucinated voice	Subject answers voice realistically at least once
11. Negative visual hallucination (sees two of three boxes)	Reports seeing only two boxes
12. Posthypnotic amnesia	Subject recalls three or fewer items before "Now you can remember everything"

SOURCE: Weitzenhoffer and Hilgard (1962).

NOTE: This scale is used in conjunction with a brief attempted induction of hypnosis, during which the subject is observed and rated on performance on the above 12 items. The hypnotist suggests each item and notes whether the subject responds to the suggestion. The highest possible score is 12, and the average score is 5.19.

experience at one time or another. It may actually be easier to hypnotize yourself than to enter hypnosis with a hypnotist's help (Ruch, 1975). If you are by yourself and you fix your gaze on a particular place and begin to daydream, your EEG state may be identical to that of a hypnotized subject. In fact, a very deep daydream may be a perfect example of hypnosis. Unfortunately, some people drive their cars in this state. They fix their gaze, perhaps on the horizon (or worse, on the hood ornament), and begin to daydream. An experience such as this can also have an element of dissociation; that is, while daydreaming they may still manage to arrive at their destination, taking the correct turns and stopping at the stoplights, without remembering a single detail about the trip. This experience, called **highway hypnosis**, is familiar to most drivers. It can happen to drivers very easily at night, when there are few visual distractions and when the broken white line on the highway is going by at a steady rate or at any other time, especially if the road is very familiar. If this has ever happened to you, then you have experienced an effect of dissociation while self-hypnotized.

Memory Enhancement

Another phenomenon of hypnosis is memory enhancement. Although memory itself cannot be directly improved through hypnosis, hypnosis can be used to alleviate anxiety that may be inhibiting memory. The greater the anxiety, the less likely a person is to remember clearly and accurately. Hypnosis has been used effectively by police departments and other agencies to *calm* individuals who are trying to remember something.

There is, however, a danger in using hypnosis to enhance memory. Subjects who are hypnotized often expect their power of recollection to be vastly improved. For instance, in 1981, during a murder trial in Illinois, an eyewitness could not positively identify the murderer he had briefly seen at night from a distance of 100 yards. The witness was placed under hypnosis, and the hypnotist pressed for an answer. He told the witness to zoom in on the murderer's face and to say whose

HIGHWAY HYPNOSIS
A hypnotic state experienced by a person operating a vehicle—often the result of relaxing too much during a long and boring drive.

Susceptibility to hypnosis can be measured by the Stanford Hypnotic Susceptibility Scale. In this instance, if the subject is susceptible, her hand would probably lower at least 6 inches within 10 seconds following the therapist's suggestion that her hand is becoming heavy.

it was. The eyewitness, and the jurors who were listening, believed that under hypnosis this was possible. The eyewitness then identified a classmate of his as the murderer (Orne, 1982). But was this a memory or something his imagination had created under the pressure to come up with something? In experiments, it has been shown that hypnotized subjects who are pressed begin to report "remembering" all kinds of things that are not true (Dywan & Bowers, 1983). Researchers also have shown that when imaginary experiences are provided to hypnotized subjects, the subjects often swear afterward that such experiences really occurred (Laurence & Perry, 1983). Luckily for the classmate accused of murder, an ophthalmologist (a medical doctor who specializes in vision) testified that under the conditions on the night of the murder, it would have been physically impossible to resolve accurately a visual image from a distance of more than 10 yards. Because of the false "memories" that can occur under hypnosis, more and more courts are not allowing hypnotized witnesses to testify (Stark, 1984).

Pain Relief and Changed Emotional States

Hypnosis also has been used to relieve pain and to change emotional states. The possibility that hypnosis can raise the natural endorphin levels in the body enough to relieve pain has excited a great deal of interest (see Chapter 2). But in examinations of hypnotic procedures, endorphin has not been shown to be related in any way to the kind of pain relief obtained under hypnosis. Even when subjects were given naloxone, a drug that blocks the effects of endorphin, hypnosis could still relieve pain (Goldstein & Hilgard, 1975). It is possible that release of some molecule other than endorphin may be responsible for the pain relief achieved through hypnosis, but no one knows.

Hypnosis also can effectively prevent a person from laughing in humorous situations. How can hypnosis bring about such changes? It may be that under hypnosis a person distinguishes between *expected* and *actual* pain or humor. There is a difference. In many cultures, people are taught that certain kinds of pain are more severe than our knowledge of physiology indicates they should be. Any dentist can tell you this. Some patients start screaming before the dentist even touches a tooth. Many dentists have begun using hypnosis to ease such fears. Patients who expect the hypnosis to work, and who are relaxed and comfortable, may then experience only the "real" pain rather than the much more severe "expected" pain.

Certainly, hypnosis has its limits. In cases of extreme pain, no amount of hypnosis is likely to help. Nonetheless, hypnosis has occasionally been successful when anesthetics could not be used, even when general surgery was being performed (Hilgard & Hilgard, 1983). Hypnosis can be especially effective in operations requiring incisions to be made in the back, where there are few pain receptors.

Behavioral Changes

Subjects who are hypnotized frequently behave in strange ways. They may become amnesiac, forgetting specific things, or they may exhibit sensory changes (Kihlstrom, 1985), claiming that they see objects that are not there or denying that they see objects that are in front of them. In the latter case, it is not clear whether the hypnosis causes a real sensory change in the brain. Most researchers attribute such reports to social pressures; that is, participants, in their desire to be good subjects, will go along with the hypnotist, even to the point of lying (Sarbin, 1950). They may swear, for instance, that they see only the hypnotist although they are standing in a crowded room. Of course, it may be that sensory changes are hampering the subject's ability to sense the other people in the room, but the physiology of such changes has not been discovered.

Stage hypnotists frequently entertain their audiences by getting people to act in bizarre ways. A volunteer may begin to imitate a chicken when told that he is one. However, people who volunteer to be chickens may be a little unusual to start with. Perhaps they simply want to be on stage (Sarbin & Coe, 1972). They also may be doing what they think is expected of them. Also, some stage "hypnotists" have a bag of dirty tricks. For example, they may hand a steel ball to a volunteer, saying "I'm going to make you feel as though this steel ball is getting hotter and hotter." Suddenly, the volunteer cries "My hands are burning!" and drops the ball, convinced that it was hypnosis that caused the sensation. In fact, the quack hypnotist has used a steel ball containing two chemicals that, when mixed (when the ball was turned and handed to the subject), caused the ball to become extremely hot—for real.

Disinhibition

Hypnosis can also *disinhibit* subjects; that is, remove their reluctance to do specific things. One of the misconceptions about hypnosis is that a subject will never do something while hypnotized that he or she wouldn't do while "awake" (Orne & Evans, 1965). This is not necessarily true. If a hypnotist tells Sergeant Jones to hit Colonel Brown in the face with a pie, and the sergeant is not hypnotized, the sergeant will wisely say, "No, sir." Once the sergeant is hypnotized, however, and the hypnotist says, "Now hit the colonel in the face with a pie," the sergeant may do as instructed. The difference may be that the sergeant can now attribute responsibility to the hypnotist, especially if the colonel has been watching the whole performance. The sergeant will know that because he was hypnotized, no one can blame him. Furthermore, if the sergeant has always wanted to hit the colonel with a pie, this is a good opportunity. Because responsibility can be transferred to someone else—namely, the hypnotist—subjects may be willing to engage in activities that they had always wanted to do but had never dared to do before.

Posthypnotic Suggestion

Hypnotists can in many instances give **posthypnotic suggestions**; that is, they can tell a subject that later, when the subject sees or hears a particular stimulus, he will get an urge to do something. The hypnotist may say, for example, "The next time you hear a car horn, your shoulder will itch, and you will scratch it." Posthypnotic suggestion may work on the same principle as a memory association; that is, by relaxing and thinking that a car horn goes with an itching shoulder, you may actually be cued (reminded) to scratch your shoulder the next time you hear a car horn.

As you have discovered, *hypnosis* is a word that describes many different phenomena (see Concept Review). Hypnosis is an interesting concept, but is also one that is often misunderstood (see Focus on a Controversy).

MEDITATION

Meditation is a simple technique that can be practiced by anyone. If you sit back, close your eyes, breathe deeply, and, if you wish, concentrate on a particular sound

POSTHYPNOTIC SUGGESTION
A suggestion made to a hypnotized subject to perform some task in response to a particular cue after the hypnotic session is over.

MEDITATION
Deep relaxation brought on by focusing one's attention on a particular sound or image, breathing deeply, and relaxing.

One who practices yoga, a Hindu discipline, the aim of which is to train consciousness to attain a state of perfect spiritual insight and tranquility. Control of body functions and mental states is practiced.

CONCEPT REVIEW: TYPES OF HYPNOTIC EFFECTS

Hypnotic Effect	Possible Reasons for Effect
Dissociation	When conscious attention is distracted, ingrained habits may continue to function without subject's awareness.
Memory enhancement	Anxiety that may interfere with memory retrieval is reduced.
Relief from pain or change in emotional state	Subject expects change; subject reacts only to actual pain or emotional state rather than to expected pain or emotions. Another possibility is that pain is actually blunted by stimulated neurological mechanism.
"Unusual" behavior	Subject feels such behavior is expected or wishes to please hypnotist by being a "good subject" (social pressure).
Sensory or perceptual changes	Perceptual mechanisms may actually change, or subject may lie, either consciously or unconsciously, in order to be a "good subject."
Disinhibition	Subject can now place responsibility for acts elsewhere (on hypnotist).
Posthypnotic suggestion	Subject unconsciously learns association between two events; when one event occurs, the second event is acted out or is brought to mind.

During meditation, a person's heart rate, respiration, and blood pressure decrease dramatically.

or word for about 15 minutes, a number of changes will probably occur: Your heart rate, blood pressure, and oxygen-consumption rate will decrease. The temperature of your extremities will rise. Your muscles will relax.

It's hard for people to realize that meditation can be simple. This is especially true because so many books have been written about different meditation techniques and so many **yogis** have espoused certain ways to meditate and have made dramatic claims. But most research appears to indicate that meditating is the same as resting, and that there is no significant difference between the two states (Holmes, 1984).*

Many researchers over the last years have compared subjects who practiced meditation with subjects who simply rested. No consistent differences were found on measures of heart rate, skin electrical activity, breathing rate, blood pressure, skin temperature, oxygen consumption, muscle tone, blood flow, or any other biochemical factors (Holmes, 1984). Despite all the hype, psychologists have simply been unable to find any physiological differences between meditation and resting, although the issue is debated (Suler, 1985; West, 1985; Shapiro, 1985). This, of course, does not mean that the practice is useless. Taking a nice 15-minute rest twice a day does provide health benefits. It lowers your blood pressure for a short time, calms you, and makes you feel better.

---

*It's important to note that not all kinds of meditation reduce physiological activity. Some kinds—for instance, Maulavi (the kind of dancing practiced by the Whirling Dervishes)—create arousal. The vast majority of meditation techniques, however, reduce arousal.

HYPNOSIS AND AGE REGRESSION

Throughout the years, hypnosis has been credited with many achievements. Some of these claims have received great publicity, although no substantial data are available to support them. One of the most controversial has been age regression. The hypnotist tells the subject to relax and to feel that he is moving back in time to his youth. When asked how old he is, the subject might reply, "Ten," despite the fact that he is obviously an adult. Then, the subject might describe what his life was like when he was 10 years old. He might even be able to recall a language that he spoke then that he can no longer speak with fluency (Fromm, 1970). The hypnotist might ask the subject to regress farther back, to when he was 8, 6, 4, or 1, or even to the time he was in the womb. At this point, the adult might curl up in a fetal position. When asked what he is doing, he might not be able to respond because he is too young to speak. Then

the hypnotist might ask the subject to go back even farther, many years before his birth, and to describe what he perceives or senses. Suddenly, the subject might say that he is a shoemaker in Germany in 1853, and his name is Hans Gunwaldt. "What is life like for you, Hans?" asks the hypnotist, and the subject begins to describe what his earlier life as a shoemaker was like.

What has happened here? Has the subject been sent back to another time, another life? There are ways of testing this phenomenon to see whether it is real (Spanos, Ansari, & Stam, 1979). Adults in the age-regressed state, who are supposedly only 5 years old, often display cognitive abilities far beyond those of a 5-year-old. They answer questions that most adults wrongly believe a 5-year-old could answer but that a real child of that age would never be able to answer (Nash, 1987).

A way of showing the improbability

of the prebirth phenomenon is by demonstrating that hypnotists can impose almost any previous life they wish on their subjects. In such a case, a hypnotist need only be given a fabricated previous-life story to pass on to the hypnotized subject. The subject is then age-regressed back many years before his birth. By subtle cuing, the hypnotist can often elicit the fake previous life from the subject. To date, there appears to be no evidence to support the notion of previous lives. The subject, desiring to comply with the hypnotist's request, has apparently tried to act out what he feels may be expected of him (Sarbin & Coe, 1972). When led back to a time before birth, he will often reenact an earlier life, because this has become part of the hypnosis myth.

PSYCHOACTIVE DRUGS

Any drug that alters conscious awareness or perception is called *psychoactive*. **Psychoactive drugs** often work directly on the brain. The most commonly used psychoactive drugs—including alcohol, nicotine, and caffeine—are so familiar that we rarely think of them as drugs or consider that they have psychological effects. Psychoactive drugs can be classified according to their effects as **stimulants**, **depressants**, and **hallucinogens.** In this chapter we will discuss only the properties of various drugs and their effects on the conscious state. Alcoholism, drug abuse, and addiction are discussed in Chapter 14 (Health Psychology).

Central Nervous System Stimulants

AMPHETAMINES. **Amphetamines** are powerful stimulants originally developed by the military for soldiers who had to stay alert in combat. They are sold under names such as Dexedrine, Benzedrine, and Methedrine. On the street, they are known as uppers, speed, bennies, meth, crystal, or ice. The way in which amphetamines work is not clearly understood, but they are known to facilitate the synaptic secretion

PSYCHOACTIVE DRUGS
Drugs that alter conscious awareness or perception.

STIMULANTS
Drugs that can stimulate or excite the central nervous system. Cocaine and amphetamines are examples.

DEPRESSANTS
Drugs that can depress or slow the central nervous system. Alcohol and tranquilizers are examples.

HALLUCINOGENS
Drugs that cause excitation at synapses associated with sense perception. A person taking these drugs may perceive sensations when there is nothing "real" to see, hear, or feel. LSD and mescaline are examples.

AMPHETAMINES
Drugs that excite the central nervous system and suppress appetite, increase heart rate and blood pressure, and alter sleep patterns. Amphetamines are classified as stimulants.

of dopamine in the brain. If taken in low doses for a limited time, the drugs can help to overcome fatigue and to maintain a high rate of activity, the purpose for which they were developed. Sustained use, however, can result in a number of unpleasant states that can be long-lasting, including paranoia, anger, and prolonged restlessness (Snyder, 1973). Amphetamines also can decrease appetite, and they were widely prescribed as diet pills during the early 1970s. However, people who used the pills for this purpose over an extended period found that they became accustomed to them; as they acquired **tolerance,** they gradually regained their appetite—but they continued to desire the amphetamines. Consequently, the drugs have not been widely accepted as a viable means of controlling weight and have been placed under much stricter federal controls.

COCAINE. **Cocaine** appears to function both as an amphetamine-like stimulant and as a local anesthetic if injected under the skin or rubbed on mucous membrane such as the gum.

One of the leading experts in the study of psychoactive effects of cocaine was Sigmund Freud (1885/1974). Freud initially believed that cocaine was relatively safe, and he encouraged its use. For himself, he found that it increased his alertness, made him feel invigorated, and gave him a sensation of pleasure. Later, however, after observing the visual disturbances experienced by a friend who had taken cocaine, he withdrew his support, realizing that the drug could have dangerous side effects.

Cocaine, in very low dosage, was an ingredient in Coca-Cola until its use in soft drinks was banned by law in 1903. In fact, the drug gave the drink its name. After the law was passed, the Coca-Cola company found that caffeine was an adequate substitute.

Today, cocaine is widely known as a pleasure-inducing drug. To obtain the pleasure-inducing effects of the drug, people usually inhale or snort it, and occasionally inject it into a vein. Cocaine also can be smoked. Taking cocaine in these ways produces euphoria, exhilaration, alertness, confidence, and a high energy level. This reaction may last for 20 minutes to 1 hour, and it is often followed by depression (long-term use may lead to hallucinations or extremely severe mental disorders). During use, the heart accelerates, the pupils dilate, and blood pressure increases, often to dangerous levels. Cocaine not only stimulates the sympathetic

(a) The normal web of the female spider, Araneus diadematus. The irregularity at the right side of the web was caused by the spider's rushing away when the photo was taken. (b) The same spider built this strange web after receiving a high dose of amphetamine. (c) This web, built one day after receiving the amphetamine, shows partial recovery.

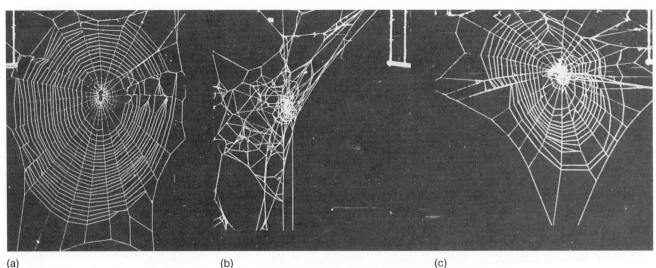

(a)　　　　　　　　　　(b)　　　　　　　　　　(c)

nervous system, but suppresses the parasympathetic nervous system (see Chapter 2). In other words, it not only presses the accelerator, it releases the brake, which may help explain why it can cause enough stress on the heart to kill an otherwise healthy young person with just one use (Cowen, 1990). Use of cocaine can also cause brain atrophy, a form of damage in which the brain actually shrinks (Pascual-Leone, Dhuna, Altafullah, & Anderson, 1990).

In 1985, a very addictive form of cocaine called "crack" (cocaine hydrochloride) appeared. Crack is not snorted, but smoked. Heating the crack, or cocaine rock as it is also called, frees the cocaine for inhalation. When this method of ingestion is used, the drug enters the blood through the lungs very rapidly and goes straight to the brain. Because crack requires fewer steps to process cocaine prices on the street fell dramatically and the drug became readily available. The "high" obtained from crack only lasts about 30 minutes, however, further exacerbating the problem among users, who are driven to take it many times a day. Cocaine is perhaps the most powerful "rewarder" known and may obtain that power by flipping the "main switch" of the brain's reward system, an area rich in receptors for the neurotransmitter dopamine. Once the dopamine is secreted, the cocaine appears to block its reuptake, making the dopamine available to further stimulate the pleasure centers (Wise & Rompre, 1989).

Although cocaine does not *technically* lead to **physical addiction** (Van Dyke & Byck, 1982)—that is, the user does not have to keep increasing the dosage progressively to experience an effect, and full physical withdrawal symptoms from discontinuation of the drugs are not readily apparent—the drug rapidly leads to **psychological addiction** because, as we have noted, it is so powerfully rewarding. It affects the brain's pleasure centers by short-circuiting them—that is, by cutting them off from their natural source of stimulation—such that cocaine users feel that everything is good in their lives no matter how serious their problems may be. Researchers have discovered that heroin activates the same pleasure centers (Goeders & Smith, 1983). Like heroin addicts, cocaine abusers may alter their lives so that every part of life becomes centered around the drug. Friends, associates, and even lovers who do not provide direct access to the drug are dropped. Rapid weight loss also is associated with cocaine use, and this may lead to anemia or to lowering of the body's natural defenses against illness. For these reasons, cocaine is considered to be habit forming and *extremely* dangerous.

Central Nervous System Depressants

ALCOHOL   Alcohol is a depressant that acts on the central nervous system, slowing down its functioning. Owing to differences in the content of stomach enzymes found in men and women, women absorb alcohol into their bloodstreams faster than do men and, consequently, can become impaired at a faster rate than men can (Frezza et al., 1990).

Some alcohol users believe mistakenly that, in limited amounts, alcohol is a stimulant. This belief probably comes from the fact that alcohol does cause an elevation in sex hormones, which may create greater sexual arousal. Alcohol may make you "want to more, but able to less." Alcohol generally makes people less inhibited and may lead them to engage in behavior they later regret (Steele, 1986). Interestingly, part of alcohol's disinhibiting effect may be that, based on what he has heard, the drinker *expects* to be disinhibited after drinking, and may act accordingly (Critchlow, 1986). Alcohol also has been found to affect neurotransmitters in the brain, especially in the region of the hippocampus, an area important in memory consolidation (see Chapter 2), which may help explain the memory losses sometimes associated with drinking (Mancillas, Siggins, & Bloom, 1986).

PHYSICAL ADDICTION
An overwhelming desire for a particular substance due to the mechanisms of tolerance and physical reaction to withdrawal.

PSYCHOLOGICAL ADDICTION
An overwhelming desire for a particular substance due to the immediate sense of pleasure or fear reduction it provides. Psychological addiction often occurs in conjunction with physical addiction. The word *dependence* is often used to characterize either type of addiction and often is specific (for example, drug dependence).

DELIRIUM TREMENS
A state of delirium resulting from
prolonged alcoholism and marked by
extreme confusion, vivid hallucinations,
and body tremors.

BENZODIAZEPINES
An important class of minor tranquilizers
that, since the mid-1950s, has come to
replace the more dangerous barbiturates.
Usually prescribed by physicians to control
anxiety and tension.

TRANQUILIZERS
Any of various drugs that are used to
pacify.

HEROIN
A highly addictive narcotic drug derived
from morphine.

Although behavioral effects vary greatly from one person to the next (Erwin, Plomin, & Wilson, 1984), in general, at concentrations as low as 0.03 percent of alcohol per total volume of blood, users tend to feel relaxed or giddy. At concentrations of 0.1 percent—after about three drinks or three beers—nerve functions in the sensory and motor systems may be impaired to a point at which driving a vehicle would be dangerous. At 0.2 percent, the drinker is severely incapacitated, and levels above 0.4 percent are often lethal. Most state laws define legal intoxication as a blood level above 0.1 percent alcohol; some define it as above .08 percent. Because it is so widely used by people engaged in activities requiring concentration and alertness, especially driving, alcohol is an extremely dangerous drug. Between 30 and 50 percent of all automobile deaths are related to driving while intoxicated (Zylman, 1975). Among pilots, it has been shown that even 14 hours after being legally intoxicated, the pilots' performance had not yet returned to normal (Yesavage & Leirer, 1986).

Although alcohol is not classified as a hallucinogen, excessive use may lead to hallucinations either while it is being consumed or during withdrawal from it. **Delirium tremens** is the term for the hallucinations suffered by alcoholics on withdrawal, during which they often hallucinate about bugs or animals crawling on them. Heavy use of alcohol is also associated with strokes, and accounts for a large portion of strokes in young adults (Taylor & Combs-Orme, 1985).

BENZODIAZEPINES. **Benzodiazepines** are **tranquilizers.** They are the most widely prescribed drugs in the world, administered for the relief of tension or anxiety. Their major effect is to relax muscles by affecting the central nervous system. These drugs are known by such trade names as Librium, Valium, or Xanax.

Benzodiazepines have been found to work hand in hand with GABA (gamma-aminobutyric acid), a neurotransmitter abundant in the brain and associated with inhibitory synapses (see Chapter 2). There appear to be natural receptors in the brain that are particularly sensitive to benzodiazepines. GABA helps the drugs to bind more tightly with these receptors, causing lengthy and increased inhibition at the inhibitory synapses (Guidotti, Baraldi, Schwartz, Toffano, & Costa, 1979). The presence of these natural receptors suggests that the brain may produce its own kind of benzodiazepine and that the drug merely mimics this natural substance.

HEROIN. **Heroin** is indirectly derived from opium, as are the other opiates morphine and codeine. Heroin is made from, but is stronger than, morphine, which in turn is stronger than codeine. Heroin is a powerful narcotic and can quickly result in physical addiction. It works by mimicking the brain's own morphinelike substance, beta-endorphin. Heroin is an excellent painkiller and creates a great sense of well-being in the user. It is usually injected, but recently smoking heroin has become popular. Smokers refer to this activity as "chasing the dragon."

Because heroin is physically addicting, users eventually need to increase their dose to obtain an effect. Sudden discontinuation of the drug causes severe withdrawal symptoms. The sense of pleasure obtained and the physical addiction associated with heroin result from two very separate brain mechanisms. Heroin stimulates the same pleasure centers as cocaine does, but, unlike cocaine, it also stimulates a mechanism at a different part of the brain that causes physical addiction (Bozarth & Wise, 1984; Ling, MacLeod, Lee, Lockhart, & Pasternak, 1984).

If they are very careful about the quality of the drug, use it under sterile conditions, and are lucky, addicts may be able to continue taking heroin for some time without necessarily suffering serious detrimental effects. Their chances of becoming ill, however, increase significantly, because heroin damages the body's natural immune system, which helps ward off disease (McDonough et al., 1980). Heroin deaths also are frequently related to overdose, the dosage being uncertain because heroin is often "cut" (diluted) to make it go farther. Sometimes the heroin is cut with deadly substances. Heroin deaths also may result from unsterile injections, which can transmit diseases such as hepatitis or AIDS. Incorrect injection technique, or simply the accumulated effect of hundreds of injections, may cause serious circulatory disorders. Malnutrition is another factor. Heroin addicts often use their money to buy the drug instead of food; their sense of well-being and the painkilling properties of the drug can render them insensitive to feelings of hunger. As we noted earlier, beta-endorphin appears to be used by the brain to create a natural high when the time is right for feelings of happiness and well-being (Leff, 1978). Heroin users, however, short-circuit their natural reward system. This may explain why addicts often don't care that they may be going to die, or that other people are hurt by their behavior, or that they don't eat or engage in sex. Since the natural pleasure system has been overridden, no external events of significance are likely to have an effect.

DESIGNER DRUGS. In recent years, some unscrupulous chemists have created drugs that are molecularly similar to heroin, but were different enough not to be included under the federal laws that prohibit sale of heroin. These substances have come to be known as **designer drugs.** In general, their effects are unknown, but some of them have proved to be very dangerous (Ricaurte, Bryan, Strauss, Seiden, & Schuster, 1985). One in particular, MPTP, is especially hazardous. Those people who were unfortunate enough to try MPTP almost immediately developed severe and irreversible Parkinson's disease (see Chapter 2). Many of these users were young, and Parkinson's is rare in young people.

The only bright light to come from this sad occurrence is that it provided researchers with some clues as to the cause of Parkinson's disease and enabled them to make a drug that blocks the effects of MPTP. When this new drug, called deprenyl, was given to Parkinson patients, it significantly slowed the rate of progression of the disease by 40–83%, a major advance against the disease (Tetrud & Langston, 1989).

Hallucinogens

Hallucinogens are drugs that cause excitation at the nerve synapses associated with sense perception, producing **hallucinations,** perceptions of lights, sound, and other sensory stimuli when there is nothing "real" to see, hear, or feel. The drugs in this category include mescaline, which is derived from a cactus; psilocybin, derived from mushrooms; and LSD (lysergic acid diethylamide), derived from ergot, a rye mold. As mentioned in Chapter 2, these drugs probably affect us by mimicking neurotransmitters associated with sensation and perception. The effects of some hallucinogens last only a short time; those of others, such as LSD, may last for many hours. Sometimes, after the initial effect of LSD has worn off, the user may experience a **flashback,** such as a burst of color like a sheet of light or mist or other sensory disturbances (Abraham, 1983).

PCP. PCP (phencyclidine hydrochloride), better known as angel dust because it was first given widespread distribution by the Hell's Angels motorcycle club, has unfortunately become a popular drug in the last decades. One of its effects is to cause hallucinations. It has been argued, however, that PCP represents an entirely new class of psychoactive drug (Balster & Chait, 1976), because it gives rise to many serious disorders besides hallucinations. This may be due, in part, to the

DESIGNER DRUGS
Drugs designed in a laboratory by unscrupulous chemists with the intention of creating substances that mimic the effects of a drug while avoiding the federal laws that forbid that specific drug.

HALLUCINATION
A false sense perception for which there is no appropriate external stimulus.

FLASHBACK
A sudden recurrence of a hallucination or sensory disturbance that occurs after the original effect of a hallucinogenic substance has worn off.

PHENCYCLIDINE HYDROCHLORIDE (PCP)
A dangerous hallucinogenic drug that can lead to aggressive or psychotic behavior. It is also known as angel dust.

Marijuana
A hallucinogenic drug derived from the dried flowers and leaves of the cannabis variety of hemp.

Tetrahydrocannabinol (THC)
The active ingredient in marijuana, which in high doses can cause hallucinations.

drug's toxic and damaging effect on the nerve receptors to which it binds (Olney, Labruyere, & Price, 1989). In many cases, a complete loss of contact with reality occurs, accompanied by unpredictably aggressive behavior that can persist for weeks after the drug has been taken. Reviewing more than 100 cases, researchers found that a typical PCP reaction includes three distinct phases: violent, psychotic behavior lasting approximately 5 days, unpredictable and restless behavior lasting about 5 more days, and rapid improvement and personality reintegration during the final 4 days. PCP use should be considered a psychiatric emergency. Even if the drug is not taken again, about one-fourth of people treated after using it suffer serious behavioral disturbances later (Luisada & Brown, 1976). There is also evidence that PCP creates strong psychological dependence (Bolter, Heminger, Martin, & Fry, 1976). Because of the hazards, many drug users are turning away from PCP. Unfortunately, others are not aware of the dangers.

Marijuana.   Marijuana is classified as a hallucinogen because, in sufficient doses, its active ingredient, **THC (tetrahydrocannabinol),** causes hallucinations. Along with its hallucinogenic properties, marijuana can function as both a depressant and a stimulant. The difference appears to be related to dose. At higher doses, the drug acts as a stimulant; at lower doses, it acts as a depressant (Blum, Briggs, Feinglass, Domey, & Wallace, 1977).

A study conducted with female monkeys (whose reproductive cycle is similar to that of human females) found that at moderate dosages (the equivalent of about 15 "joints," or marijuana cigarettes, per week), the animals showed disruption of the menstrual cycle (Smith, Almirez, Berenberg, & Asch, 1983). These doses of marijuana caused failure of ovulation for as long as 4 months, until the monkeys developed a tolerance for the drug. There is also evidence that THC may harm the ova (unfertilized eggs). THC has also been found to interfere with the recall of recently learned material for up to six weeks after use (Schwartz, Gruenewald, Klitzner, & Fedio, 1989). This may be one reason why teenagers who use marijuana do less well in school.

Arguments over the danger of marijuana continue. The amount of danger may be related to dose level and frequency of use. In one study, scientists found that experienced airline pilots working a flight simulator were still significantly impaired 24 hours after smoking only one marijuana cigarette (Yesavage, Leirer, Denari, & Hollister, 1985). The pilots were unaware of their impairment although the simulator clearly recorded their poorer performances.

EPILOGUE: THE END OF A NIGHTMARE

Psychologists who study states of consciousness are aware of the limits of their knowledge, but sometimes they reach a little beyond those boundaries, to a realm not usually within their grasp. Following is the story of one psychologist who tried to step inside his own nightmares.

Nightmares affect millions of people. In fact, depending on the study, between 10 and 25 percent of those surveyed said that they had a nightmare at least once a month (Wood & Bootzin, 1990).

Stephen LaBerge, a psychologist and sleep researcher, has spent many nights at Stanford University Medical School watching and recording the sleep of other people. Early in the morning, when most people would be heading for work, he would be on his way home to bed.

Like most of us, he would have nightmares once in a while. In one, he dreamed that he was drowning; in another, that he was hanging off the edge of a building; and in another, that he was being attacked by someone. Although the dreams were just in his mind, the fear was very real—the pounding heart, the twisting and turning, the struggle to wake up. His dreams made him feel awful, the way nightmares make any of us feel. Unlike the rest of us, though, he decided to do something about them.

He wondered if **lucid dreaming** *would offer a solution. A lucid dream is any dream during which you realize you are dreaming. Such dreams have been known as long as recorded history—Aristotle wrote about them. If LaBerge could interrupt his own nightmares and remind himself that he was dreaming, he thought he might be able to take control of the dream and make it come out any way he wanted.*

He began working on his project. First, he'd note whenever he had a lucid dream. This put him in a frame of mind to think about lucid dreaming. Whenever he went to bed, he'd spend a little time before he fell asleep reminding himself to have a lucid dream. He would also relax and verbalize his intentions. He'd say, "If I'm on the edge of a cliff, I'll do this," or, "If someone attacks me, I'll do that." A few nights later, he had a dream in which he thought he was drowning. Suddenly, it became a lucid dream. He realized he was dreaming and remembered that he had told himself he could breathe under water. The fear melted away, and he began to enjoy his underwater dream.

What he had done, in effect, was to create a state of relaxation, or self-hypnosis, and then to implant a posthypnotic suggestion, such as "If I think I am drowning, I will remind myself it's a dream and that I can breathe under water." Bit by bit, his nightmares came under control, and he was averaging 21.5 lucid dreams per month. The few dreams that started as nightmares now had very different endings:

I am in the middle of a riot in the classroom. Everyone is running around in some sort of struggle. . . . [Someone] has a hold on me—he is huge, with a pock-marked face. I realize that I am dreaming and stop struggling. I look him in the eyes and, while holding his hands, speak to him in a loving way, trusting my intuition to

LUCID DREAMING
The realization by a dreamer that she or he is, in fact, dreaming.

CHAPTER 5
STATE OF CONSCIOUSNESS

179

supply the beautiful words of acceptance that flow out of me. The riot has vanished, the dream fades, and I awaken feeling wonderfully calm. (LaBerge, 1981, p. 48)

In his most recent efforts, LaBerge has helped to make dreams lucid by attaching a red flashing light to a monitor that measures a dreamer's REM onset. When REM starts, the red light begins to flash. The dreamer sees the red flashing light through his closed eyelids and usually does not awaken, but rather incorporates the light into his dream. The dreamer has trained himself to realize that anything that happens while the red light is flashing is just a dream. If a nightmare starts, the dreamer will often see the light and no longer be fearful, causing the nightmare to melt away.

SUMMARY

■ Consciousness is the state in which you are aware not only of the external environment but also of internal events such as thinking.

■ Important advances in scientific technology have provided objective ways to measure conscious states.

■ The conscious mind is said to be altered any time the content or quality of conscious experience undergoes a significant change.

■ The electroencephalograph (EEG) records brain waves as electrical changes and has been used to monitor states of consciousness.

■ There are four stages of sleep. Stages 3 and 4 often are referred to as slow-wave sleep. Rapid-eye-movement (REM) sleep usually is associated with dreaming. REM sleep is also called paradoxical sleep because REM brain waves are similar to those seen during the waking state.

■ Atonia, or loss of muscle tone, occurs during REM sleep, rendering the sleeper semiparalyzed.

■ Sleepwalking and sleeptalking generally occur during non-REM (NREM) sleep.

■ REM rebound, in which more REM than is usual occurs during the sleep cycle, is a result of REM deprivation.

■ The average young adult needs between 6 1/2 and 8 1/2 hours of sleep a night. Some people, known as healthy insomniacs, can get by with much less.

■ Two theories have been suggested to explain why we sleep. The adaptive theory argues that each species requires a certain amount of waking time to survive and that the rest of the time is best spent in a state, such as sleeping, in which there is the least chance of danger or injury. The second theory, known as the conserving-energy theory, argues that sleep is way of conserving energy.

■ Four ideas have been put forth to explain why we dream. First is psychoanalytic theory which argues that dreams are expressions of repressed desire. Second is the activation-synthesis model, which argues that dreams are the brain's attempt to make sense of random electrical activity. Third is the housekeeping hypothesis, which argues that the brain makes dreams to eliminate any senseless or bizarre neural connections developed during the day's learning. Finally, the off-line hypothesis argues that REM sleep enables creatures to maintain a smaller and more efficient brain size by consolidating and storing previously gathered information during sleep.

■ Factor S is a natural sleep-promoting substance that increases slow-wave or delta sleep for a few hours.

■ A limited amount of sleep deprivation may not be physically detrimental to healthy subjects. The most common effects of such deprivation are decreased performance on tasks, hallucinations, and delusions.

■ Animal studies have found that inflicting intensive, long-term sleep deprivation results in death. Some scientists, therefore, think that sleep may serve a vital physiological function.

■ There are many sleep-related disorders, including insomnia, narcolepsy, and sleep apnea.

■ Hypnosis is not a state of sleep. Hypnosis encompasses a number of relatively separate phenomena, including dissociation, memory enhancement, pain relief, changed emotional states, unusual behavior, sensory and perceptual changes, disinhibition, and posthypnotic suggestion.

■ Meditation is a simple phenomenon, very like resting, that can be practiced by anyone.

■ Any drug that alters conscious awareness or perception is called a psychoactive drug. The three major classifications of psychoactive drugs are stimulants, depressants, and hallucinogens.

■ The stimulants include amphetamines and cocaine. The depressants include alcohol, tranquilizers, and heroin. The hallucinogens include LSD, PCP, and marijuana.

■ Designer drugs are chemically similar to psychoactive drugs, and were synthesized to circumvent federal law. Many of them are dangerous and have unpredictable effects.

Suggestions for Further Reading

1. Borbely, A. (1986). *Secrets of sleep*. New York: Basic Books. A book for the student or general reader that contains interesting information about sleep, sleep deprivation, why we need sleep, and sleep as a biological rhythm.

2. Coleman, R. M. (1986). *Wide awake at 3:00 a.m.: By choice or by chance?* New York: W. H. Freeman. A comprehensive book about circadian rhythms with practical suggestions for overcoming insomnia.

3. Hauri, P. & Linde, S. (1990). *No more sleepless nights*. New York: John Wiley & Sons. An excellent drug-free guide to overcoming insomnia. Very detailed and includes a host of techniques and tips.

4. Hobson, J. A. (1988). *The dreaming brain*. New York: Basic Books. Gives an historical review of dream research and discusses the activation–synthesis model of dreams.

5. Hobson, J. A. (1989). *Sleep*. New York: W. H. Freeman. The latest on sleep and dreams from one of the leaders of the field, with many excellent color diagrams to highlight the discussion.

6. Hunt, H. T. (1989). *The multiplicity of dreams: Memory, imagination, and consciousness*. New Haven, CT: Yale University Press. A semitechnical look at dreams from Freud's theory to the work in modern labs. Includes a discussion of lucid dreams and the dreams of animals and children.

7. Julien, R. M. (1985). *A primer of drug action*. New York: W. H. Freeman. Outlines the major classes of drugs and their effects on the body.

8. Langer, E. L. (1989). *Mindfulness*. Reading, Mass: Addison-Wesley. A Harvard psychologist looks at the amusing and serious consequences of daydreaming and failure to pay proper attention in our complex society.

9. Ornstein, R. (1986). *The psychology of consciousness* (rev. ed.). New York: Penguin Books. A revised edition of a classic text on states of consciousness.

10. Quarrick, G. (1989). *Our sweetest hours: Recreation and the mental state of absorption*. Jefferson, NC: McFarland & Co. Provides a look at "hypnosis" in everyday life and explains how to become absorbed in adult play. The link between absorption and hypnosis is examined.

11. Siegel, R. K. (1989). *Intoxication: Life in pursuit of artificial paradise*. New York: E. P. Dutton. A curious but interesting book by a pharmacologist who argues that humans have a natural drive to lose themselves from time to time in an altered conscious state. The author lists a number of healthy alternatives for achieving such a state other than drug intoxication.

12. Weiss, R. D., & Mirin, S. M. (1986). *Cocaine*. Washington, DC: American Psychiatric Association. Two psychiatrists who deal with the treatment and study of drug-dependent individuals discuss the effects of cocaine on the body and treatments for cocaine addiction.

UNIT 2 | Interacting with the Environment

Chapter 6
Conditioning and Learning

Prologue
Why Psychologists Study Learning
Simple Forms of Learning
Classical Conditioning—Does the Name Pavlov Ring a Bell?
Operant Conditioning
Challenges to the Behaviorist View
Social Learning—Observation and Imitation
Cognitive Learning
Inheritance and the Biology of Behavior
Epilogue: The Nail Bites the Dust

Chapter 7
Memory and Information Processing

Prologue
Why Psychologists Study Memory
Two Memories Are Better Than One
A Model of Declarative Memory
Theories of Declarative Memory
Forgetting
Strengthening Memory through Elaboration
Encoding Effects
The Spacing Effect
Epilogue: Remembrance of Things Past

Chapter 8
Cognition and Language

Prologue
Why Psychologists Study Thought and Language
Thinking
Human Performance
Language
Epilogue: The Man with the Means to Reach His Ends

Chapter 9
Motivation

Prologue
Why Psychologists Study Motivation
The Concept of Motivation
Biological Motives
Stimulus Motives
Learned Motivation
Theories of Motivation
Epilogue: Getting a Charge Out of Life

Chapter 10
Emotion

Prologue
Why Psychologists Study Emotions
The Biology of Emotion
Why Emotions Evolved
What Makes Us Emotional?
Judging Emotions
Theories of Emotion
Epilogue: "They'll Let Me Go Tomorrow"

CHAPTER 6 ❙ Conditioning and Learning

Prologue

Why Psychologists Study Learning
The Behavior of Organisms

Simple Forms of Learning
Habituation
Sensitization

Classical Conditioning—Does the Name Pavlov Ring a Bell?
Pavlov's Experiments
Higher-Order Conditioning
Classical Conditioning in
Everyday Life
Contiguity versus Contingency

Operant Conditioning
The Law of Effect
Operants
Reinforcement and Extinction in
Operant Conditioning
Operant Conditioning in
Everyday Life
Shaping
Generalization and Discrimination
Strengthening a Response by Positive
or Negative Reinforcement
Primary and Secondary Reinforcement
Schedules of Reinforcement
Discrimination and Stimulus Control
The Premack Principle

Challenges to the Behaviorist View

Social Learning—Observation and Imitation
The Importance of Models
Performance versus Acquisition

Cognitive Learning

Inheritance and the Biology of Behavior
Canalization

Epilogue: The Nail Bites the Dust

Summary

Suggestions for Further Reading

PROLOGUE

All the pilots who work Coast Guard air–sea rescue realize the difficulties of finding a person who is lost at sea. They know how truly immense the ocean is and what a small speck a person makes upon it. That's why they are interested in the new Project Sea Hunt. Psychologists and biologists worked for a long time to get it ready, and today, using your helicopter and crew, they're going to give it a try.

The researchers have arrived, your crew is ready; you head for the helicopter. Your mission today: Find a pilot in a small raft. You are given as much information as you usually get—a short radio message giving rough coordinates. Only the Coast Guard officers know exactly where he is; they know because he was placed there as part of the experiment.

As you reach the helicopter, you immediately notice something different. Underneath the belly of the chopper, there's a large Plexiglas container. It looks like a big hatbox that has been divided into three sections. Something is moving in one of the sections; you bend down to have a look. It's a pigeon. It's strapped into some kind of a device. There is also a pigeon in each of the other two sections.

You turn to one of the researchers who is going along today; he explains that once the helicopter is airborne, each pigeon will have a 120-degree view of the ocean below. The pigeons have been "conditioned." If they should see a red, orange, or yellow speck on the water below, they'll peck at a button that will sound a buzzer in your helmet. There are three speakers in your helmet, one forward, one left, and one right— each for a different pigeon. That way, you'll know which way to turn to continue the search.

Quickly you start the engines and lift off. Soon you're over the beach and the breakers. A few miles out and you can no longer see the shore.

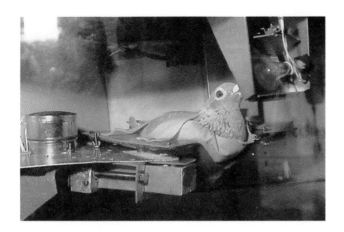 

At left, a pigeon in Project Sea Hunt signals he has detected a red, orange, or yellow speck by pecking at a disk. The entire apparatus is suspended from a helicopter equipped for sea rescue, shown at right.

Now there is only the ocean—white-blown water, rolling blue; huge from horizon to horizon; and you have got to find the tiny orange speck of a life preserver and raft down there somewhere. You and the crew members look at the sea, sometimes searching with binoculars; you calculate how much fuel you have and when it will be dark; you hope you'll get lucky. That's what it's like to look for someone lost "out there."

You start wondering whether to take Project Sea Hunt seriously. As you continue farther out over the ocean, you are mumbling to yourself. Why shouldn't the birds hit the buzzers just any old time? Won't they get bored? Why should they even bother looking? These guys must be crazy. You and your crew scan the ocean with binoculars as usual. You're not going to let some bird beat you. None of you sees anything. Suddenly there's a buzz in your left ear. "Bring her around 120 degrees to port," the researcher says. You swing the chopper around. Now you hear a buzz in front of you. The pigeon in front must have picked it up. "We're on the right track," the researcher says. Neither you nor your crew has seen anything but ocean. You think to yourself, "These birds are goofy, maybe they're airsick—that is, if birds can get airsick?" But then one of your crew members calls out, "There he is!" "Hey, not bad," someone else shouts as the tiny raft comes into view. As soon as you spot the raft, you flip on the radio switch to call in your success to headquarters. You laugh and turn to your copilot, "Hey, Jerry, it just crossed my mind that the birds were trained to hit a switch when they see a raft, and so were we!" "Yeah," he replies, "and we all get paid bird seed."

You turn to the researcher and ask, "Why did you decide to use birds?" He leans forward so you can hear him over the roar of the engine and the buzzing sounds in your helmet. "Birds have much better vision than humans. They have a wider angle of view, and they don't get nearly as bored as people do. Oh, one more thing: They like to fly!"

Over the next few weeks, the experiments continue. You and your crew are able to spot the target victims about 38 percent of the time on your first pass over the target area. The pigeons are averaging 90 percent (Stark, 1981).

In this chapter, we'll examine the different kinds of conditioning and learning that are based on the ideas of behaviorism (see Chapter 1). As you'll discover, many of the special techniques used to train the Project Sea Hunt pigeons can also be used to teach other species, including humans. We will also explore the cognitive and ethological approaches, both of which have added to our understanding of the learning process. Along the way, you'll see how prejudice is learned, how cravings for drugs can occur in abusers, even after complete withdrawal has been achieved, why spanking children is a bad idea, how phobias can be taught, and even how to toilet train a child in less than a day!

LEARNING
A relatively permanent change in behavior as a result of experience.

WHY PSYCHOLOGISTS STUDY LEARNING

Psychology is the study of behavior. Psychologists study **learning** because among most animals, especially humans, many behaviors are learned. Learning may be defined as a relatively permanent change in behavior resulting from experience. We say "relatively permanent change" to exclude the effects of such factors as fatigue. Fatigue, which occurs because of experience, may change behavior, but only temporarily, whereas learning implies a more lasting change.

The Behavior of Organisms

In 1938, a young psychologist named B. F. Skinner, building on the work of many earlier researchers, published a book entitled *The Behavior of Organisms*. In it, he presented many experiments that strongly supported the basic tenets of *behaviorism* (see Table 6.1) and outlined the ways in which the environment might act on an organism to determine what the organism learns and how it behaves.

Because psychology is the study of behavior, any book that expanded on the principles of how behaviors were determined and controlled was obviously important. Some researchers, however, were surprised that the book was entitled *The Behavior of Organisms*, because almost all the work it described was based on studies conducted only with rats. In fact, some people still jokingly define psychology as the study of rats and sophomores (sophomores were added later, once professors discovered that students could be made to "volunteer" for experiments).

Skinner had a ready response for his critics, however. He asserted that because the principles governing learning were so general, research gathered from one

B. F. Skinner (1904–1990). An American behaviorist who championed the idea that the environment controls our behavior more than any other force.

TABLE 6.1 The Basic Tenets of Behaviorism

1. The mechanisms of learning are similar for almost all species. The way you learn to drive a car and the way an elephant learns a circus trick both can be understood by applying the same principles of learning.

2. All learning, no matter how complex, can be understood in terms of two kinds of simple association mechanisms referred to as classical conditioning and operant conditioning.

3. The best way to understand learning is to examine the environment and the observable forces in it and to analyze how these forces affect the responses of the organism in question. Learning is a relatively permanent *observable* change in behavior. Concepts such as the "mind" or "thinking" are best ignored because they can never be directly observed, and are therefore outside of the realm of science.

CHAPTER 6
CONDITIONING AND LEARNING

HABITUATION

A process in which an organism ceases to respond reflexively to an unconditioned stimulus that has been presented repeatedly.

STIMULUS

Any energy or change in energy condition that is sensed.

SENSITIZATION

The process by which a reflexive response is made stronger and more sensitive to stimuli by pairing the eliciting stimulus with a painful or unpleasant stimulus.

CONTIGUOUS ASSOCIATION

The occurrence of two events close enough in time so that they are perceived by the organism as somehow related. Also called temporal association.

species was readily applicable to just about any other species. The same basic principles that explained how rats learned, he argued, applied just as well to dogs, cats, elephants, birds, fish, people, and nearly all other creatures. As you will see in this chapter, many of the learning principles outlined by Skinner and other researchers do seem to characterize a great many animals, including humans.

SIMPLE FORMS OF LEARNING

Habituation

People learn in a number of ways. One of the simplest forms of learning is **habituation,** which takes place when a person becomes accustomed to a **stimulus** because it has been presented repeatedly. If construction work began outside your window, the first ka-BLAM of a pile driver might startle you. This response would be natural because being startled is an inborn, not a learned, response. The stimulus in this case would be the loud noise. If the pile driver continued to make the noise over and over, eventually you would become *habituated* to it; you would learn not to react any more. This is the same reason why pigeons happily eat seed alongside of the freeway while trucks and cars roar past. They have become habituated to the traffic sounds, which, as any urban dweller can tell you, takes only a day or two.

The trouble with applying the definition of learning to the phenomenon of habituation, however, is that although a change has taken place owing to experience, the change is not necessarily "relatively permanent." We can, for example, bring back the natural startle reflex by removing the loud noise for some time and then unexpectedly presenting it again. Nonetheless, a person can be so habituated to a particular stimulus that the change becomes somewhat permanent. Some researchers like to talk in terms of short-term habituation (which ends quickly) and long-term habituation (which may take a very long time to end). There seem to be different brain mechanisms that control each (Leaton & Supple, 1986). So, owing to its relative permanence, long-term habituation might be definable as a form of learning, while short-term isn't.

It's more important, however, to realize that habituation occurs than to argue about whether habituation is or isn't learning. The value of habituation is that we come to ignore a stimulus that has lost its novelty or importance. Habituation frees us to attend to stimuli that are new or that appear suddenly. If you were in the woods picking berries and heard a deep throaty growl nearby, attending to that new stimulus obviously would have survival value.

Sensitization

Sensitization may occur when an animal or a human being is exposed to a stimulus that is accompanied by pain or fear of some kind. As with those of habituation, the effects of sensitization can last from minutes to weeks depending on the amount of training. The effect of sensitization appears to be opposite to that of habituation, and a different biological mechanism within the organism is responsible for it (Marcus, Nolen, Rankin, & Carew, 1988). If you become sensitized to a sound, the next time that sound occurs you may startle more easily than you would have before you were sensitized. A soft clicking sound, for example, would not ordinarily startle anyone. When it has been associated with pain, it can cause you to become sensitized, and you may react by jumping the next time you hear it. Soldiers suffering from battle fatigue often show signs of sensitization. They are jumpy and anxious; the slightest sudden noise may startle them.

CLASSICAL CONDITIONING—DOES THE NAME PAVLOV RING A BELL?

During the 1890s, the Russian physiologist Ivan Pavlov reported an experiment of an associative learning process. He had been investigating digestion (for which he had earlier won a Nobel Prize) and had been trying to understand why his dogs, who were the subjects of his experiment, often began to salivate *before* they received food. This reaction seemed to occur when a **contiguous association** was made between the presentation of food and another stimulus, such as seeing someone in the laboratory open the cupboard where the dog food was kept. Other researchers had observed this phenomenon, but had either considered it a nuisance or had ignored it. Pavlov, however, became seriously interested in this learning process and began to investigate it systematically.

Pavlov's Experiments

In a series of well-known experiments, Pavlov decided to *pair* a stimulus (food) that would elicit an *unlearned* response (salivation), with a stimulus (bell) that did not elicit salivation and was therefore "neutral" at the beginning of the experiment. Because no learning is required to make dogs salivate when they are given meat, meat is referred to as an **unconditioned stimulus (US)**, while the reflex response of salivating is referred to as an **unconditioned response (UR)**.

Pavlov took a stimulus that did not cause salivation in dogs (a bell) and began to pair it systematically with the presentation of food. He would ring the bell, immediately present the food (US), and observe the salivation (UR). After the bell and the food had been paired, or contiguously associated, as psychologists say, Pavlov was able to cause salivation without giving food; ringing the bell was enough. The dogs associated food with the bell, and they would salivate. The bell had become a stimulus to which the dogs responded in a predictable way; they showed that they had learned. For this reason, the bell is referred to as a **conditioned stimulus (CS)**, and the response it elicits is called a **conditioned response (CR)** (see Figure 6.1). The process by which the bell obtains the power to elicit the CR is called **reinforcement**. The more the meat and bell were paired, the more the *bond* between them was strengthened, or *reinforced*, and the more the bell came to easily and successfully elicit the CR (salivation). This procedure is referred to as **classical conditioning**. Conditioning means learning. Figure 6.2 shows the

UNCONDITIONED STIMULUS (US)
The stimulus that normally elicits an unconditioned response, such as the food that caused Pavlov's dog to respond with salivation.

UNCONDITIONED RESPONSE (UR)
The response made to an unconditioned stimulus, such as salivation in response to food.

CONDITIONED STIMULUS (CS)
In classical conditioning, a previously neutral stimulus that is reinforced by being paired with an unconditioned stimulus, so that it acquires the ability to produce a conditioned response.

CONDITIONED RESPONSE (CR)
A learned response elicited by a conditioned stimulus, owing to previous reinforcement of the conditioned stimulus through association with an unconditioned stimulus.

REINFORCEMENT
In classical conditioning, any increase in the ability of a conditioned stimulus to elicit a conditioned response owing to the association of the conditioned stimulus with another stimulus (typically an unconditioned stimulus).

CLASSICAL CONDITIONING
A learning procedure in which a stimulus that normally evokes a given reflex is associated with a stimulus that does not usually evoke that reflex, with the result that the latter stimulus will eventually evoke the reflex when presented by itself.

ACQUISITION
The time during the learning process when there is a consistent increase in responsiveness; a time when learning is occurring.

Ivan Pavlov (1849–1936) is shown (center, white beard) demonstrating his classical conditioning experiment.

FIGURE 6.1

The paradigm used by Pavlov to condition a dog to salivate at the sound of a bell.

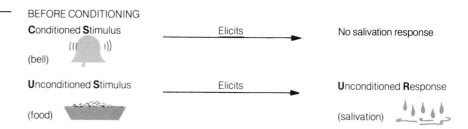

BEFORE CONDITIONING

Conditioned **S**timulus ———— Elicits ————▶ No salivation response

(bell)

Unconditioned **S**timulus ———— Elicits ————▶ **U**nconditioned **R**esponse

(food)   (salivation)

DURING CONDITIONING

Conditioned Stimulus (bell) is followed by presentation of Unconditioned Stimulus (food), which elicits Unconditioned Response (salivation).

AFTER CONDITIONING

Conditioned **S**timulus ———————— Elicits ————————▶ **C**onditioned **R**esponse

(bell)   (salivation)

FIGURE 6.2

The acquisition and extinction of a classically conditioned response. When the CS (bell) and US (food) are paired, the power of the CS to elicit the CR (salivation) increases. The CS, however, rapidly loses its power to elicit the CR each time that it is presented without the reinforcement of the US. This decrease in eliciting power shows the process of extinction. (SOURCE: After Pavlov, 1927.)

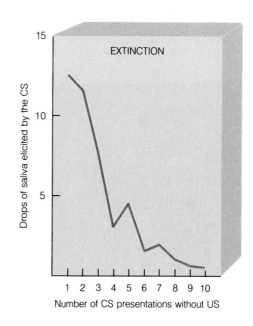

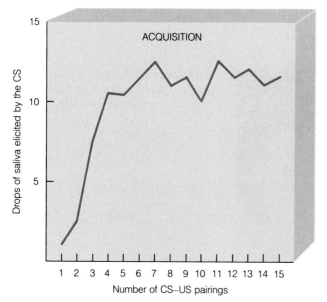

ACQUISITION

Drops of saliva elicited by the CS

Number of CS–US pairings

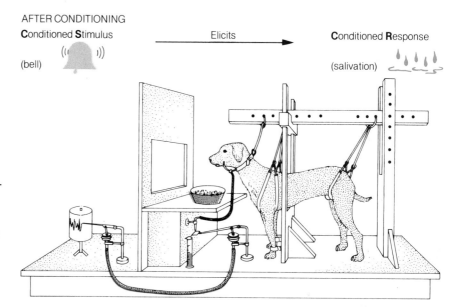

EXTINCTION

Drops of saliva elicited by the CS

Number of CS presentations without US

reinforcement process in classical conditioning and its diminishment as the bond between the CS and US first undergoes **acquisition** and then **extinction**. Figure 6.3 shows the important processes of **generalization** and **discrimination** as they pertain to classical conditioning.

Higher-Order Conditioning

Once the CS has the power to elicit the CR, owing to the reinforcement of the CS–US bond by their contiguous pairing, it is possible to use the CS all by itself to create a *higher-order* CS_2 (see Figure 6.4). In experiments, CS_2s have been used to create even higher-orders CS_3s and CS_4s, but these CSs are very weak. Higher-order conditioning greatly expands the range and influence of associative experiences, however, and may play a role in the creation of the emotional feelings we acquire toward particular things.

Classical Conditioning in Everyday Life

It was at about this point when I was first studying conditioning, having learned and committed to memory the US-UR-CS-CR alphabet, and the assorted bold-faced terms in the previous pages, that I somehow lost sight of what it was all about. Maybe you are starting to feel the same way. To acquire a full understanding

EXTINCTION
In classical conditioning, the elimination of the power of the conditioned stimulus to elicit a conditioned response. Classical extinction will occur if the conditioned stimulus is repeatedly presented without being reinforced through further association with the unconditioned stimulus.

GENERALIZATION
Responding to a stimulus other than the training stimulus as though it were the training stimulus. In classical conditioning, the response tends to diminish the more the other stimulus differs from the training stimulus, thereby creating a "gradient of generalization."

DISCRIMINATION
Differentially responding to two or more stimuli. The responding occurs in such a way that it is obvious that the organism can tell that the stimuli have certain properties that distinguish them from one another.

FIGURE 6.3

In the example of generalization, a dog has been conditioned to salivate to a tone with a frequency of 5000 cycles per second. After the conditioning, tones of different frequencies are sounded. The result shown is known as a gradient of generalization. The gradient is created because the dog will respond to other tones, only less so. Also notice that the closer the new tone is to the training stimulus, the stronger is the response.

In the example of discrimination, our dog has again been trained to respond to a CS tone of 5000 cycles. Next (bar graph A) we present a 3000-cycle tone; the dog also responds, but with less saliva drops, which is what we would expect according to the gradient of generalization. If, however, we keep presenting the 5000-cycle tone with the US, as we had during training, but continue to present the 3000-cycle tone

(which never accompanies a US), the dog will come to discriminate between the two tones. The result is shown in bar graph B. The response to the 3000-cycle tone is almost gone, while the response to the 5000-cycle tone has increased. The dog has learned to discriminate between the two tones and only responds to one of them with any significant degree of strength.

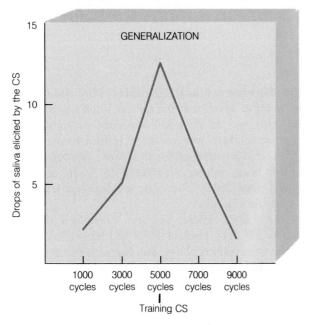

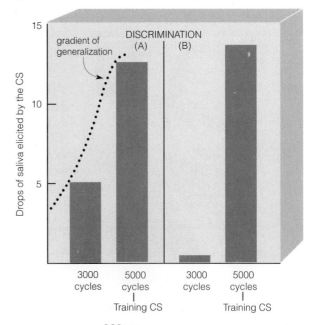

FIGURE 6.4

An example of higher-order conditioning—in this case, second order. Higher-order conditioning tends to be weak, probably because, while the CS_2–CS bond is being reinforced, the power of the CS is decreasing owing to extinction—which, in turn, is occurring because the US is no longer present to reinforce the CS–US bond.

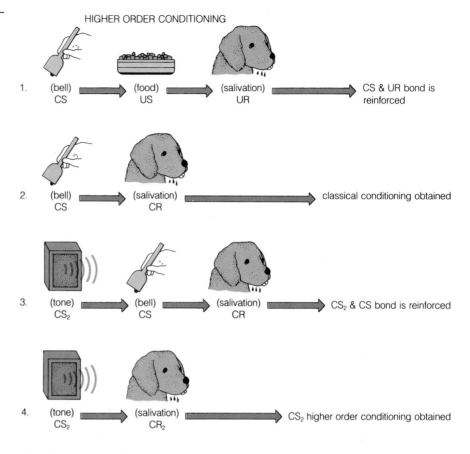

1. (bell) CS → (food) US → (salivation) UR → CS & UR bond is reinforced

2. (bell) CS → (salivation) CR → classical conditioning obtained

3. (tone) CS_2 → (bell) CS → (salivation) CR → CS_2 & CS bond is reinforced

4. (tone) CS_2 → (salivation) CR_2 → CS_2 higher order conditioning obtained

of conditioning, of course, it is necessary to know all these technical terms and definitions, but it would be better to learn what they really *mean*, that is, how they describe people. Let's stop for a moment and take a random assortment of examples of classical conditioning from everyday life—that should be a little more interesting!

In 1947, Dr. Kenneth Clark conducted research on the nature of prejudice. His findings helped establish the fact that children were being affectively conditioned to continue the prejudices of their society.

PREJUDICE. In the mid-1940s, psychologist Kenneth Clark held a black doll and a white doll in his hands and asked the following questions of young white children living in the South:

> "Which doll looks like you?"
> "Now tell me which doll is the good doll?"
> "Which doll is the bad doll?"

These children knew that the white doll looked like them. Most children also indicated that the white doll was the "good" doll and the black doll was the "bad" one, that the white doll was "nice" and the black doll was "dirty" or "ugly" (Clark & Clark, 1947). How had these southern white children learned to make such associations? During decades of racial prejudice in America, darker skin had become *associated* with poverty and with being "inferior," not just in the South, of course, but generally throughout the United States. The white children had learned to attribute these characteristics to black people.

This racist attitude is what the white children had been taught; it is also what the black children had been taught. The black children had been raised in the same general environment, the same country. They, too, had seen that the whites had better and they had worse. And, as the Clarks discovered in further research, a majority of black children *also* chose the white doll as the good one and the

192

black doll as the bad one! This highlights one of the most hateful aspects of prejudice, namely, when those discriminated against come to really believe that they are, in fact, somehow inferior.

A conditioning experiment conducted by researchers Staats and Staats (1958) helped to show how an association process could be responsible for the prejudice Dr. Clark observed. In their experiment, college students were asked to look at one word while pronouncing another. Without being aware of the purpose of the experiment, the students were maneuvered into pairing pleasant words or unpleasant words with a particular name (Tom or Bill) or a certain nationality (Swedish or Dutch). In a short time, subjects revealed obvious differences in attitudes toward these names and nationalities, simply because those words had been paired with positive or negative words. Advertisers, politicians, movie makers, and just about everyone tries to use this kind of conditioning to affect our emotions. When a politician associates himself with a positive symbol such as the flag, or when a movie maker uses dramatic music, or when someone dresses well for a job interview, each is invoking the same process: Each is attempting to render something—the politician, the movie, or the job seeker—more appealing through association with positive stimuli.

What appears to be occurring in instances of association like those just described, is a kind of higher-order conditioning (see Figure 6.5).

DRUG OVERDOSE.   As was apparent in the case of the college students conditioned to like or dislike a certain nationality, classical conditioning often occurs without the conditioned person being aware of it. For example, researchers have found that drug users often unwittingly condition themselves to the stimuli that occur immediately before the administration of drugs (Siegel, 1975). The body has a natural mechanism of building up what is called a drug *tolerance*. In some way not yet fully understood, after enough exposures to a drug the body will require more of that drug before an effect can be achieved. The tolerance mechanism appears to be a natural defense by the body. The buildup of tolerance (UR) may then, be a typical reaction to a sudden influx of an opiate drug (see Chapter 5) such as heroin (US) (Snyder, 1984). Notice how such a case is similar to that of Pavlov's dogs. In the case of Pavlov's dogs, the US (meat) produced salivation (UR). In the case of the heroin addicts, the US (injection of heroin) is believed to produce a certain tolerance reaction (UR).

The immediate environmental surroundings of the drug user (for example, the room he is in, the objects in the room) can become, through associative pairing, conditioned stimuli. After sufficient pairings, whenever the heroin addict enters that same room (CS), his body may respond by producing a tolerance reaction

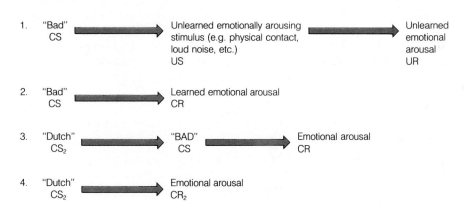

1.   "Bad"   Unlearned emotionally arousing   Unlearned
     CS   stimulus (e.g. physical contact,   emotional
                  loud noise, etc.)   arousal
                  US   UR

2.   "Bad"   Learned emotional arousal
     CS   CR

3.   "Dutch"   "BAD"   Emotional arousal
     CS₂   CS   CR

4.   "Dutch"   Emotional arousal
     CS₂   CR₂

FIGURE 6.5

One possible mechanism to help explain the findings of Staats and Staats, in their study of induced prejudice among college students, might be higher-order conditioning.

(CR), *even though no heroin has been injected*. This may explain why drug-overdose deaths from injecting heroin occur much more commonly in a *new* environment. A user who takes drugs in, say, a strange house may inject into a body that has not produced the usually expected tolerance reaction beforehand (CR), because the usual CS (the old familiar environment) was diminished or absent (Siegel, Hinson, Krank, & McCully, 1982). Now, because his body isn't ready for the size of the dose he is used to injecting, the user is more likely to misjudge how much heroin he needs and overdose.

FEAR.   Fear often is the result of classical conditioning. The case of Little Albert is an example of the classical conditioning of an irrational fear in a child. Although the 1920 study suffered from certain methodological flaws, it is still interesting because it was conducted by one of the founders of behaviorism, John Watson.

Watson and Rayner tested Albert B., a healthy 11-month-old boy, by systematically exposing him to a white rat, a rabbit, a dog, a monkey, various masks, cotton wool, and even a burning newspaper. As Watson noted, "At no time did this infant ever show fear in any situation" (Watson & Rayner, 1920, p. 2). The two researchers found, however, that making a very loud noise by striking a steel rod with a hammer (US) startled baby Albert and made him cry (UR). Next, the researchers paired the loud gong with the white rat that Albert had previously seen. Whenever Albert touched the rat (CS), the loud gong would be struck (US), which would startle Albert and cause him to cry (UR) (see Figure 6.6). Eventually, Albert would start to cry as soon as he saw the rat. In Watson's words,

> The instant the rat was shown, the baby began to cry. Almost instantly he turned sharply to the left, fell over on the left side, raised himself on all fours and began to crawl away so rapidly that he was caught with difficulty before reaching the edge of the table. (Watson & Rayner, 1920, p. 5)

In addition, Albert's fears generalized to related objects, such as a rabbit, a dog, a white cotton ball, and even a Santa Claus mask (probably because of the white beard), but not to dissimilar objects, such as blocks. This probably occurred because Albert had associated the loud noise with characteristics possessed by the rat—

An extremely rare photograph of John Watson (in mask) and Rosalie Rayner, as they prepared to condition Little Albert.

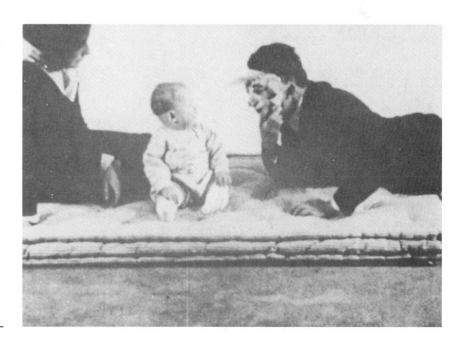

BEFORE CONDITIONING

Conditioned **S**timulus

(white rat)

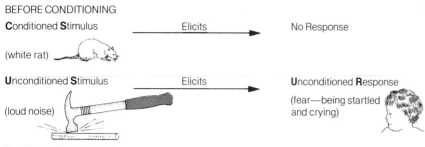

Elicits →

No Response

Unconditioned **S**timulus

(loud noise)

Elicits →

Unconditioned **R**esponse

(fear—being startled
and crying)

DURING CONDITIONING

Conditioned Stimulus (white rat) is followed by presentation of Unconditioned Stimulus (loud noise),
which elicits Unconditioned Response (being startled and crying).

AFTER CONDITIONING

Conditioned **S**timulus

(white rat)

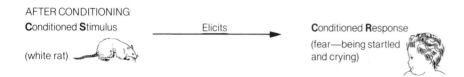

Elicits →

Conditioned **R**esponse

(fear—being startled
and crying)

FIGURE 6.6

*The paradigm used by Watson and
Rayner to condition Little Albert to fear
a rat.*

white, live, legged, and furry—which he subsequently saw in some of the other
objects as well.

The experiment with Little Albert has notable ethical implications. Was it
ethical to create what amounted to a phobia in the child? By today's standards,
this experiment would clearly have violated ethical procedures. To make matters
worse, it appears that before Watson ever began his experiment, he knew that Albert
was going to have to leave the home for invalid children where his mother was
working and that the researchers probably would never have a chance to undo any
learned fear response that they might produce. Yet they went ahead and conducted
the experiment anyway (Harris, 1979). Of course, Albert was not the only human
ever to be classically conditioned; millions of people are daily conditioned in this
way as they come in contact with their environment. Any pediatrician who has
given a child an injection can attest to this fact. The child's screaming fit the next
time she just enters the office is a good indication that classical conditioning plays
a role in fear responses. In fact, most phobias appear to be related to this kind of
conditioning. Later in this chapter, we will discuss the kind of therapy often best
suited to help people overcome phobias, and you will see that it relies on conditioning techniques to help phobia sufferers unlearn their fears.*

Contiguity versus Contingency

We have seen that a conditioned stimulus may gain power to elicit a response by
being associated in some fashion with an unconditioned stimulus. But we haven't
asked *why* this occurs. Is it just the result of two stimuli being paired in time—
that is, contiguously paired? Since the discovery of classical conditioning, there
have been thousands of investigations of this phenomenon. All sorts of different
ways to pair, or contiguously associate, the CS and US have been tried; some have

---

*Note that classical conditioning, while playing a role in the formation of prejudice, fears, or drug use,
is *not* the only kind of learning likely to be involved. A person would also be more likely to show these
behaviors if he were rewarded for emitting them, or if he observed other people, especially those whom
he respected, demonstrating such behaviors. These kinds of learning (operant conditioning and social
learning) are covered later in this chapter.

CONTINGENCY DETECTION

The process by which an organism makes a discrimination between stimuli that are only present when the US is presented and other stimuli that not only happen to be present when the US is presented but also when the US is not presented. The result is that the organism can rely on the sensing of the stimulus that is only present when the US is presented to predict that the US will soon appear.

been shown to create stronger CRs than others do (see Figure 6.7). Interestingly, the strongest associations occur when the CS precedes the US by about 1/2 second. This has led some researchers to wonder whether, indeed, contiguous association is all that accounts for the effect. If it is, why isn't backward conditioning (in which the US is presented before the CS) as effective as trace conditioning (in which the stimuli are presented in the reverse order)? After all, aren't both types of conditioning examples of contiguous association?

In Pavlov's day, people thought that simply contiguously associating two stimuli would cause conditioning to occur. We now know that this is not necessarily the case. Consider that in the experiment with Pavlov's dogs, many other stimuli besides the bell also were associated with the food: the harness to which the dogs were attached, the leather straps that held their front legs, the scaffolding that held the harness, the elevated table on which the dogs stood, the tube used to collect their saliva, and so on. Not one of these stimuli, however, when presented to the dogs, caused salivation the way that the bell did, although each of them had also been contiguously associated with food many times. There was something special about the bell. As it turns out, the reason the bell was special in Pavlov's experiment is that the presentation of the food was *contingent* (dependent) on the presentation of the bell. Unlike the bell, the other stimuli (the harness, table, and so on) also were present when no food was given. The bell, on the other hand, *never* rang when food was not presented. The fact that the animal learned to associate the bell with the food implies that the animal *was using the bell to predict when food would arrive* (smart animal).

As a result of these observations, learning theorists now believe that such **contingency detection** by an organism is at least as important as, and probably more important than, the contiguous association of stimuli in explaining why conditioning occurs (Rescorla, 1988).

FIGURE 6.7

Different kinds of classical conditioning arrangements. The US is presented for a brief time. The CS can be presented in many ways, as the series of examples shows—it even can be presented "backward," after the US.

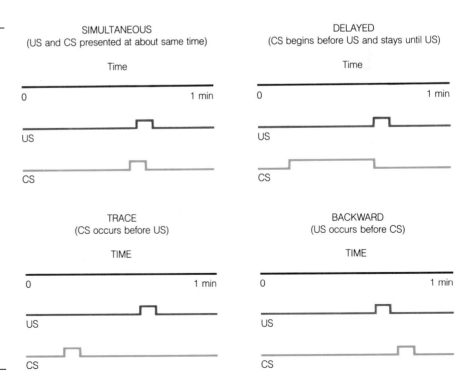

SIMULTANEOUS
(US and CS presented at about same time)

DELAYED
(CS begins before US and stays until US)

TRACE
(CS occurs before US)

BACKWARD
(US occurs before CS)

CONDITIONING ON THE CELLULAR LEVEL

Since the days of Pavlov and Watson, researchers have conducted many classical-conditioning experiments with animals and humans. Many different conditioned stimuli have been paired with unconditioned stimuli. During all those years and experiments, people assumed, of course, that somewhere in the brain a change had to occur during conditioning that placed the conditioning experience into memory. There had to be some mechanism to record and keep the experience, or else how could an organism change its behavior owing to experience? Exactly how such a mechanism might work, however, was anybody's guess. Some people believed that special groups of cells in certain brain areas might control learning. Others argued that learning might be a diffuse general ability, found to occur fairly evenly among cell groups throughout the entire brain. Practically no one expected or suggested that learning might occur at the level of single cells. Now, however, research has indicated that individual neurons have the ability to be conditioned!

In one single-cell conditioning experiment, researchers classically conditioned a single photoreceptor cell by using a bright light (US) paired with a current passed through a microelectrode into the cell (CS). Afterward, when the cell received the current (CS), it behaved as though it had been exposed to light (CR). This surprising result demonstrated classical conditioning at the most basic level (Farley, Richards, Ling, Liman, & Alkon, 1983).

Further research along these lines has shown that an individual cell not only can be conditioned but also can display the processes of extinction and higher-order conditioning (Barnes, 1987a). Of course, this discovery doesn't tell us whether particular locations in the brain contain or hold experiences or how large these areas might be.

Another interesting study, however, provided a hint as to where some conditioned experiences might reside. In this study, rats were trained to fear a soft sound (CS) that had been paired with a shock (US). At first glance, this may not seem particularly special; in fact, it seems similar to many common classical conditioning studies such as the one conducted with Little Albert. But in this experiment, the animal was conditioned after it was made unconscious by an anesthetic. Even when the animal was anesthetized, classical conditioning still occurred (Weinberger, Gold, & Sternberg, 1984). This result gave strength to the idea that areas of the brain deeper than the cerebral cortex (the cortex is where the anesthetic has its most pronounced effect) play an important role in classical conditioning.

Then, in 1984, researchers David McCormick and Richard Thompson discovered and isolated the location of a specific conditioning experience in the brain. In their experiment, they conditioned an eyeblink response in a rabbit. They used a tone as a conditioned stimulus and paired it with a puff of air to the rabbit's eye, which was the unconditioned stimulus. The puff of air made the rabbit blink. After sufficient pairings, the tone alone came to elicit the blink response. This, of course, is an example of classical conditioning. By producing a small cut or lesion in one extremely small area of the rabbit's cerebellum (see Chapter 2), the researchers eliminated the learned response. After the lesion was created, the rabbit was still able to blink its eyes when it wished, and the air puff still elicited the blink, but the tone, which the rabbit could still easily hear, no longer had an effect. The conditioning had been wiped out! It seems that the experience of the conditioning had existed in a tiny piece of cerebellar tissue no larger than a cubic millimeter (McCormick & Thompson, 1984).

Of course, while McCormick and Thompson's study shows us that some conditioning experiences reside in small and specific locations within the brain, it by no means implies that all, or even the major portion of conditioning experiences, reside in the cerebellum. In fact, more research has isolated conditioning experiences in the hippocampus as well, an area of the brain especially tied to certain memory functions (Kelso & Brown, 1986). As you might imagine, on the heels of these discoveries, researchers have been scrambling to uncover what might be one of the brain's most closely guarded secrets—namely, *where does it store what it knows?* Perhaps some day we will have the answers.

OPERANT CONDITIONING

In classical conditioning, a particular stimulus elicits a response that is already in an organism's repertoire (in Pavlov's experiments a bell elicited salivation). For instance, after conditioning, the rat made Albert cry, but Albert already had the ability to cry as evidenced by his reaction to the loud gong. Crying was not a new response brought on by conditioning.

Suppose, however, you wished to teach a new response, something that the organism had not previously shown? We all have acquired such behaviors; the ability to read this book is one of them—you weren't born with the ability to read. The acquisition of novel behaviors is the result of a different kind of conditioning called **operant conditioning**. Much of what you've learned in life has been acquired through operant conditioning. To understand how such conditioning occurs, let's look at a famous series of experiments conducted at the turn of the century by a psychologist named E. L. Thorndike.

The Law of Effect

About the time that Pavlov was studying behavior in dogs, an American psychologist, E. L. Thorndike, was observing the behavior of cats. Thorndike would deprive a cat of food for some time and then place it inside a puzzle box, a container from which it is possible for the animal to escape if it happens to trip a latch that opens the door (see Figure 6.8). Food was placed outside the box in plain view of the cat. Eventually, the cat would accidentally hook a claw onto the wire loop or step on the treadle that pulled the latch, and the door to the box would open, enabling the cat to secure the food. As the cats came to appreciate this way of escaping, each time they were put into the box, they usually released themselves sooner (see Figure 6.9).

Thorndike's observations of such trial-and-error learning led him to consider that the consequences of an act were an important factor in determining the probability that the action would occur. His thesis was that

> any act which in a given situation produces satisfaction becomes associated with that situation, so that when the situation recurs, the act is more likely than ever before to recur also. Conversely, any act which in a given situation produces discomfort becomes disassociated from that situation, so that when the situation recurs, the act is less likely than before to recur. (Thorndike, 1905, p. 202)

Thorndike referred to such learning as **instrumental learning**, and his explanation of this kind of learning, known as the **law of effect**, is one of the cornerstones of operant conditioning. Because this kind of learning is maintained or changed depending on the consequences that *follow a response*, when you respond to something, your response is strengthened if the consequence is pleasant and weakened if the consequence is aversive. In this way you, and members of hundreds of other species, learn because of the outcomes of your behavior.

Operants

In Thorndike's day, behaviorists were concerned with analyzing the muscular responses that constituted behaviors, the way physicists might analyze a billiard shot, to determine exactly which event led to or caused the next one. Because of this, it was quite natural in the case of instrumental learning to ask, "What elicits the initial instrumental response?" For example, what made Thorndike's cats step

E. L. Thorndike (1874–1949).

on the escape treadle? Which stimulus triggered it? Was it the sight of the treadle, or the view of the cage bars, or something else in the cage? The cause is not at all clear, the way it is in classical conditioning (for example, the bell caused the salivation). To make matters more confusing, Thorndike's cats didn't always use exactly the same response in order to escape. Sometimes they'd press the treadle with their left paw, sometimes with the right. Sometimes they'd just rub against it. Should each of these be considered a different response? Did each have its own eliciting stimulus?

Partly to steer clear of the complexities of building a theory of instrumental learning on a convoluted maze of stimulus–response connections, B. F. Skinner argued that *any* lever press, whether with the left paw, right paw, or body, could be considered the *same* response because it *had the same effect on the environment*: It provided the cat with an escape from the box. Skinner introduced the term *operant conditioning* to refer to the learning of instrumental responses that shared the same effect on the environment rather than ones that consisted of exactly the same muscular motions. These **operants,** Skinner argued, can be made stronger if they are followed (as Thorndike had originally suggested in the law of effect) by a reinforcing consequence. In this view, a response is initially emitted for unknown reasons. The *probability* that the response will be emitted, however, can be predicted by the organism's past experience with the effect of that response on the environment. Responses that had pleasant consequences are more likely to be repeated in similar circumstances, while responses that were followed by unpleasant consequences are less likely to be repeated. For our purposes, then, we will consider instrumental learning and operant conditioning to be equivalent terms.

Reinforcement and Extinction in Operant Conditioning

The strength of an operant response can be measured by its resistance to **extinction;** that is, by how long it takes for the behavior to return to its original rate once the pleasant consequence following the behavior no longer occurs (see Figure 6.10). It is correct generally to say that for an operant response to be strengthened, the response should be rewarded. But *reward* in ordinary language denotes *things* such as money, candy, or praise, and something commonly considered a reward will not always work as one. For this reason, psychologists prefer the term **reinforcement** rather than *reward*, because reinforcement is a process of strengthening behavior, it is not a thing.

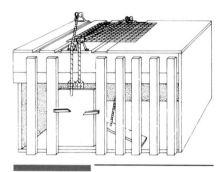

FIGURE 6.8

A puzzle box similar to that used by Thorndike in 1898. (SOURCE: Bitterman, 1969, p. 445.)

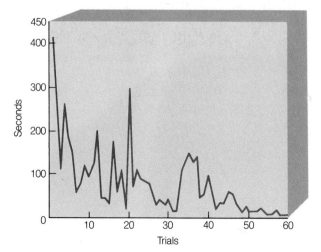

FIGURE 6.9

The graph shows the gradual decline in the amount of time necessary for one animal to release itself from the Thordikian puzzle box in successive trials. This is one of the earliest learning curves in the experimental study of conditioning. Notice, however, that the curve is not completely smooth but has marked fluctuations. Smooth learning curves usually result when many learning curves are averaged out. (SOURCE: Bitterman, 1969, p. 446.)

199

Operant Conditioning in Everyday Life

Operant conditioning is responsible for learned skills that you have acquired since your birth. Learning to play the piano, write a letter, ride a bicycle, open a door, work a screwdriver, cook a dinner, or pitch a tent are all acquired, in great part, through operant conditioning. Any behavior that can be shaped by the pleasant or unpleasant consequences that might follow it can be affected by operant conditioning. In fact, operant conditioning is so prevalent that the best way to give you good examples from everyday life is to let them present themselves during the following discussion of the different aspects of operant conditioning. In this first example, we will investigate the concept of shaping and observe the operant conditioning of a child.

Shaping

In operant conditioning, a response must occur before it can be reinforced. It is impossible to strengthen a behavior that, in fact, never occurs, and forgetting this can sometimes lead to difficulty. I once observed a father trying to get his 2-year-old son to "hand Daddy the newspaper." The child's response was, "No!" This particular father was, however, a psychology graduate student, and he decided to obtain his newspaper by using the principle of **shaping**, also known as the principle of reinforcing successive approximations toward a particular final response.

The father began by dividing the child's future paper-fetching response into a series of substeps:

1. Looking at the paper
2. Walking toward the paper
3. Grasping the paper
4. Carrying the paper toward the father
5. Releasing the paper once it is in the father's hand

Because the child occasionally looked at the paper (a behavior must first occur before it can be reinforced), the first step in the shaping sequence could be reinforced. The father took a fairly safe gamble and assumed that his praise would

Animals are taught to perform tricks through the use of operant conditioning.

FIGURE 6.10

Once an operant response is no longer reinforced, it will undergo extinction. Slowly, over time, the response occurs less and less often until it reaches the level it had prior to reinforcement.

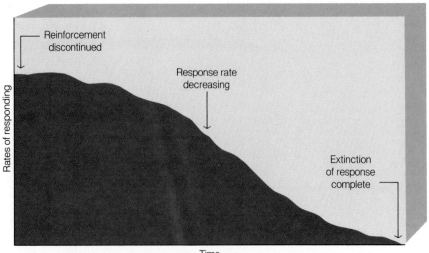

Reinforcement discontinued

Response rate decreasing

Extinction of response complete

Rates of responding

Time

function as a reinforcer for his son. The following events illustrate the shaping of the child's response.*

Father:	Jimmy, please bring me the paper.
Jimmy:	(*Glances about, does not look at the paper*) No.
Father:	(*Looking at paper*) Jimmy, please bring me the paper.
Jimmy:	(*Looking at the paper*) No.
Father:	(*Hugging Jimmy*) Good boy, Jimmy! You looked at the paper. Now bring me the paper.
Jimmy:	(*Seems confused at first, smiles, looks at paper*) No.
Father:	Please bring me the paper, Jimmy.
Jimmy:	(*Looking at paper*) No.
Father:	(*Withholding affection from voice, calmly repeats request*) Jimmy, please bring me the paper.

*Parents sometimes get nervous when their actions are to be described in a textbook. This father was no exception. He asked that if I used this example (I have), I include his statement (I am) that he was only curious about shaping when he did this. He assured me that he has no intention of training his child to be a compliant slave and that he (the father) really does fetch his own paper and stuff most of the time—honest!

CONCEPT REVIEW:

Is crying an unlearned reflex, a classically conditioned response, or an operantly conditioned response? You've probably learned enough by now to realize that it may be any of the three (see below). If a baby cries (UR) when stuck with a pin (US), the crying has not been learned and is therefore considered a reflex. If a child cries (CR) at seeing a dentist's chair (CS), the crying may result because the chair has been associated with pain in the past, and the crying can therefore be said to be classically conditioned. (Notice, too, that this kind of crying is not operant because it does not help the child to obtain or avoid the chair.) Finally, if a child cries because last time in the same circumstances she received ice cream or avoided homework by crying, the crying has been operantly conditioned. The reinforcing stimulus consequence is depicted as S^{R+}.

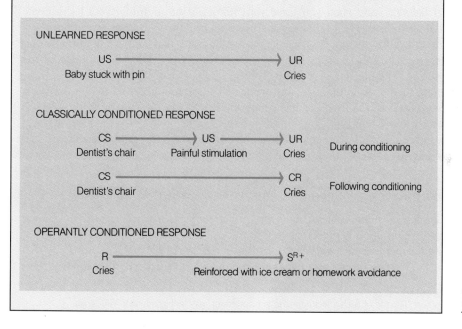

UNLEARNED RESPONSE

US ⟶ UR
Baby stuck with pin   Cries

CLASSICALLY CONDITIONED RESPONSE

CS ⟶ US ⟶ UR   During conditioning
Dentist's chair   Painful stimulation   Cries

CS ⟶ CR   Following conditioning
Dentist's chair   Cries

OPERANTLY CONDITIONED RESPONSE

R ⟶ S^{R+}
Cries   Reinforced with ice cream or homework avoidance

POSITIVE REINFORCEMENT
The process by which an organism encounters a stimulus (following a response) that has the effect of increasing the probability that the response will be emitted again.

NEGATIVE REINFORCEMENT
The process of removing or escaping from an aversive stimulus (following a response) that has the effect of increasing the probability that the response will be emitted again.

Jimmy:	(*Looks at paper, seems confused, walks away from it; then, looking at it takes a few steps toward it*) No.
Father:	(*Hugging Jimmy*) Good boy! You looked at it and you walked toward it. Now get the paper.
Jimmy:	(*Smiles, walks over to the paper, touches it*) No.
Father:	(*Again hugs Jimmy*) Good boy. You touched the paper. Now bring it to me.
Jimmy:	(*Picks up the paper, carries it to his father*) No.

Notice that Jimmy persisted in saying "No" even as he complied with his father's request. To an adult, a "No" following a request is a refusal, a negation. To Jimmy, apparently, the word was a sound he had learned to make following a request. He knew that the sound brought him attention, but the complete meaning of it was obviously unclear to him.

As you can see, shaping is a powerful way to teach a complicated behavior. Animal trainers use if effectively. It also works well with human adults, as can be demonstrated by a simple experiment. A particular teacher may never lecture from the corner of a room, and so this response cannot be reinforced. But 10 well-trained students scattered about a large class may be able to use shaping to alter the teacher's behavior. These students should be careful to pay attention, smile, and take notes when the teacher makes any move toward a chosen corner of the room, but to appear bored or uninterested when the teacher heads in any other direction. Some instructors will change their behavior without any awareness of what's happening and will end up lecturing from the corner.*

Generalization and Discrimination

In our newspaper-fetching example, after the child has been shaped to get the paper, he may start fetching all sorts of things. Such a response is called a *generalization*, because he is responding in the *same* way to different stimuli. If his father does not reinforce him with praise for doing this, the child may soon learn to make a *discrimination* by responding in a *different* way to different stimuli. In this way, he will learn which things his father believes are appropriate to fetch.

You make hundreds of generalizations and discriminations every day. For instance, you generalize shaking hands to a new stimulus (someone you've never met before), and, when you leave your home in the morning, you discriminate the door from the wall (allowing the morning of January 1 as an exception).

Most of the techniques for operant conditioning that we have discussed so far were used by the scientists in Project Sea Hunt, which you encountered in the Prologue. The pigeons were gradually shaped to peck a disk for reinforcement (food pellet); then a discrimination was created. The pigeons received food following a peck only if a small red, orange, or yellow speck was present. Soon the pigeons learned not to bother pecking unless the speck of color was present, since that was the only time reinforcement was available. Now they were ready to search the seas for downed pilots.

Strengthening a Response by Positive or Negative Reinforcement

Although *all reinforcement, by definition, strengthens the response that it follows,* a distinction often is made between positive and negative reinforcement. **Positive reinforcement** occurs when an organism is reinforced for behaving in a way that leads to the occurrence of a pleasant consequence. **Negative reinforcement** occurs

*Caution: The use of such a technique on your professor may be hazardous to your grade.

when an organism is reinforced for behaving in a way that leads to the termination or avoidance of an aversive consequence. This distinction can be summarized as follows:

Positive Reinforcement
Behavior leads to the occurrence of a pleasant consequence.
Behavior is strengthened.

Negative Reinforcement
Behavior leads to the avoidance or termination of something unpleasant.
Behavior is strengthened.

For example, if an animal successfully avoids a shock by pressing a lever, the lever-pressing response is strengthened, and we say the response has been negatively reinforced. Similarly, if someone changes the oil in her car to avoid the car's breaking down, her actions are negatively reinforced because the car continues to run. Remember, when a response is negatively reinforced, the response becomes *stronger*.

Note that positive and negative reinforcement may occur simultaneously. By eating, for example, we may realize a positive outcome (feeling full and satisfied) and may simultaneously reduce a negative state (hunger).

Interestingly, a response and a consequent stimulus don't have to be connected in a cause-and-effect sequence to have a reinforcing effect. If a ball player taps home plate with the tip of his bat just before hitting a home run, the plate-tapping behavior may well be reinforced. Since there is no logical connection between tapping the plate and hitting a home run, acquiring such a response is said to result from **superstitious learning**.

Weakening a Response by Punishment or Extinction

The following paragraphs describe two ways of weakening the strength of a response.

PUNISHMENT. **Punishment** occurs when a response is followed by an aversive stimulus that *decreases* the strength of the response or maintains the response at a lower level than it occurred originally. Like reinforcement, punishment is something that affects behavior. Remember, people aren't reinforced or punished, behaviors are! The following story illustrates the meaning of this statement:

> At 11 o'clock on a Wednesday morning, an alert neighbor spotted a stranger breaking through the front window of the home across the street, and she called the police. Shortly thereafter, two squad cars arrived. Four armed officers stepped from the vehicles. The officers positioned themselves at the front and the back of the house. A few minutes later, the unsuspecting burglar walked out of the front door lugging a color television. He was greeted by two of the officers leveling shotguns at him and he promptly surrendered. By making it obvious that fighting or running away was likely to lead to unpleasant consequences, the officers had practically ensured that the burglar would make this choice.
>
> The burglar was brought to trial and, not surprisingly, was found guilty. The judge pronounced a 3-year prison sentence. Later that night, the burglar awaited transportation from the city jail to the state prison. He was depressed and miserable. Pondering his hapless condition, he vowed to turn over a new leaf. He swore on everything that was dear to him that he would never, never again break into a house—through a front window.

In this story, a behavior was punished, but not the one that society had hoped to alter. Instead of teaching the burglar not to steal, his arrest taught him not to

SUPERSTITIOUS LEARNING
Behavior learned simply by virtue of the fact that it happened to be followed by a reinforcer or punisher, even though this behavior was not the cause of the stimulus that followed the response.

PUNISHMENT
An aversive stimulus consequence that has the effect of decreasing the strength of an emitted response.

Seeing-eye dogs are trained through the use of positive reinforcement, shaping, and discrimination. Punishment is rarely, if ever, used.

steal stupidly. As you can see, before you employ reinforcement and punishment techniques, you should ascertain which behavior will be strengthened or weakened.

Punishment can be extremely powerful, however, and it can control behavior. Some researchers have argued that punishment is the most effective means of stopping a behavior (Azrin & Holz, 1966). This outcome is especially certain if the punishment is severe. Anyone who has ever tried to cook bacon while naked will tell you that the adverse consequences of that behavior diminished the probability of doing it again. The distinction between negative reinforcement and punishment can be summarized as follows:

Negative Reinforcement
Behavior leads to the avoidance or termination of something unpleasant
Behavior is *strengthened*

Punishment
Behavior leads to something aversive or unpleasant
Behavior is *weakened*

Although punishment can be an effective way of terminating or suppressing a behavior, it can have serious drawbacks. When a behavior is punished, especially if it is punished severely, there is often a general suppression of other behaviors. The person or animal may then become withdrawn and less active. Punishment also can lead to hostility and aggression, especially if it is accompanied by pain.

Operant conditioning is essential in training seeing-eye dogs, but the trainers almost never use punishment. If a dog walks forward when it should have stayed, beating it to punish the inappropriate move could lead to a general suppression of behaviors, and the animal might cower in a corner and no longer respond to commands. Or the dog might react aggressively and counterattack. Because of these potential drawbacks, trainers use techniques other than punishment to teach the dog and to correct mistakes. If the dog walks when it shouldn't, the trainer will bring the dog back and try again. If the dog stays the next time, the trainer will reinforce the dog for staying with love and praise. In this way, the dog learns to stay, and the inappropriate behavior is eliminated *without punishment*. The more the animal is taught to respond appropriately, the less chance it has to respond inappropriately.

Unfortunately, the same can't always be said for the way in which we treat our children. The use of spanking to control children's behavior seems to be growing in popularity. A number of people advocate spanking in the schools in order to maintain discipline. Many psychologists, however, are concerned about the growing use of spanking. Based on what you have learned about learning in the chapter, you should be able to appreciate the following arguments against spanking as a technique for controlling children's behavior:

1. Through the process of classical conditioning, the parent or teacher becomes paired with pain, so that the adult comes to elicit a fear response from the child, even without inflicting punishment.
2. Through operant conditioning, the child often is reinforced in such a way that he or she may avoid the adult, lie to the adult, or run away from home.
3. According to research on punishment, mild spankings usually have only a temporary effect; this, in turn, shapes some adults into eventually administering severe and physically dangerous spankings.
4. Additional research on operant conditioning has demonstrated that many non-physical techniques are highly successful in controlling and modifying children's behavior. Supporting this assertion is the fact that many well-behaved children and

adults have never been spanked or hit by either of their parents—I never was (so much for spare the rod, spoil the child).

5. Last, and perhaps most compelling, when parents or other adults spank a child, the child may be learning more than the adult intended. By watching parents who choose to spank, children who are spanked apparently learn that physical force is an appropriate early response to select when they are frustrated with someone; that it's all right to choose to hit people; and that spanking is something that parents are supposed to do (which may help to explain why so many child abusers were themselves abused as children) (Fairchild & Erwin, 1977).

EXTINCTION.   Another way of weakening a response is through extinction. As we discussed earlier, extinction in operant conditioning is the weakening or elimination of a response by removal of a reinforcer that maintained the response. If you like to buy a cup of hot coffee from a particular machine every day, but suddenly discover that the machine has begun to give you the coffee first *and then the cup,* your "coffee-machine patronizing behavior" will eventually stop because the reinforcement has been discontinued.

Even after a response has been eliminated through extinction, however, it may briefly reappear. Perhaps the following Friday you'll give the coffee machine another try. Other creatures also show this behavior (not buying coffee—but rather, once again checking out the situation sometime after extinction has been in effect). It's almost as though the organism had forgotten that the response no longer served its purpose, or as though the organism were checking whether the response would work at a later time. This brief recurrence of a response following extinction is called **spontaneous recovery.** Spontaneous recovery also occurs in classical conditioning. Following extinction, a CS may briefly regain the power to elicit a CR.

Primary and Secondary Reinforcement

You learn because your experiences, in conjunction with your physical needs and genetic tendencies, affect you in some meaningful way. Stimuli necessary for sustaining life can obtain the power to reinforce simply by being withheld for a time; you do not have to learn to need or want them. The stimuli in this category include water, food, and air, as well as proper temperature and barometric pressure. Such stimuli are known as **primary reinforcers.** Other reinforcers, such as money, status, attention, green traffic lights, or even bottle caps (if you would be willing to work for one), are known as acquired or **secondary reinforcers.** You have learned that these things are reinforcers because of their association with primary or other secondary reinforcers. In this sense, primary reinforcers are built in, and secondary reinforcers are learned.

Schedules of Reinforcement

You aren't reinforced for everything you do, but you do receive reinforcement every once in a while. Oddly, once a behavior is learned, reinforcing it less often may cause it to persist. To demonstrate this phenomenon, we can shape a hungry rat to press a lever by feeding the rat whenever it successfully presses the lever. In the beginning, the rat is reinforced for each correct press. This is known as **continuous reinforcement.** Although continuous reinforcement will lead to the highest rate of responding (Nevin, 1988), once reinforcement is discontinued, the lever pressing behavior will extinguish rapidly. If, however, we begin reinforcing every fifth press instead of withholding reinforcement entirely, the behavior will not

SPONTANEOUS RECOVERY
In operant conditioning, the brief recurrence of a response following extinction. In classical conditioning, the brief recurrence of eliciting power of a CS after extinction.

PRIMARY REINFORCER
A stimulus that can be innately reinforcing, such as food or sleep.

SECONDARY REINFORCER
A reinforcer whose value is learned through its association with primary reinforcers or other secondary reinforcers. It is also called an acquired reinforcer.

CONTINUOUS REINFORCEMENT
Reinforcement of a particular response each time it occurs.

Intermittent schedules of reinforcement are a powerful means of controlling behavior. Such schedules strengthen responses by making them resistant to extinction. Here a human subject is operating a lever on an intermittent schedule of reinforcement, just like the rat discussed in the text. By carefully manipulating the schedule of reinforcement, casino operators are able to take in more money than they are forced to give out in reinforcement.

extinguish rapidly. Instead, the rat will learn to persist, at least for as long as five presses. Once the rat becomes used to five presses per reinforcer, the behavior is easily maintained. If we gradually increase the number of presses required for reinforcement, the rat may eventually make as many as 500 presses in order to receive one reinforcer (a miserable, but persistent, rat). Such a reinforcement schedule, in which not every response is reinforced, is called an **intermittent schedule,** and it can lead to persistent responding. For instance, if we placed our rat on an extinction schedule after it had become accustomed to 500 presses per reinforcer, it might press several thousand times before it finally gave up, because it had become used to giving 500 presses. Table 6.2 presents four different schedules of reinforcement. Although there are many complex schedules, these four are often considered basic. It is very rare that behavior is reinforced continuously. Most reinforcement occurs according to intermittent schedules. No doubt, once you have learned these four, you will see how much of the reinforcement in your life is on one or more of these schedules. By manipulating or changing schedules of reinforcement, psychologists often are able to control or change behavior.

Discrimination and Stimulus Control

It would be a chaotic world if operant responses were likely to occur at any time or in any place. This does not happen, because your learning has been such that your operant responses are controlled by various stimuli or cues, called **discriminative stimuli.** In the presence of a discriminative stimulus, a particular behavior is more likely to occur. Experience has taught you the meaning of these cues, and

you have come to rely on them for assessing which actions or behaviors are likely to yield satisfactory results. For example, what cues should be present to increase the probability that you will undress? A comfortable bed, sleepiness, and a clock that reads midnight? The privacy of a bathroom and the sound of running water? Or perhaps a drumroll and a spotlight? People may discriminate stimuli differently. A stimulus that functions as a cue for you may not be a cue for someone else. Once these cues are well learned, they come to control the times and places in which certain behaviors are likely to occur. This result is known as **stimulus control.** How do red traffic lights, ringing telephones, and timepieces "control" your behavior?

You do not need to be aware of discriminative stimuli for them to affect your behavior. Smokers often find themselves unconsciously lighting up at the same places and at the same times. This is probably an example of stimulus control. Furthermore, one cue can lead directly to another, creating a whole series of cues, responses, and reinforcements known collectively as a **habit.**

STIMULUS CONTROL
From learning theory, the idea that discriminative stimuli come to control the behavior they cue.

HABIT
A series of cues, responses, and reinforcers linked together in such a way that each stimulus consequence reinforces the person's previous response and cues the next response.

TABLE 6.2 Four Basic Intermittent Reinforcement Schedules

TYPE	DEFINITION	EXAMPLE	RESULT
Determined by the number of responses			
Fixed ratio (FR)	Reinforcement is given after every *x* number of responses; e.g., FR 4 = every fourth response is reinforced	A worker is paid for every 20 widgets she makes (FR 20)	Produces fairly regular responses as long as fixed ratio isn't set so high that extinction occurs before first reinforcement
Variable ratio (VR)	Reinforcement is given after every *x* number of responses *on the average*; e.g., VR 4 = on the average, every fourth response is reinforced, but reinforcement may follow any response	Old man Crabtree is reinforced with a dead fly for every third swing of his swatter, on the average (VR 3)	Produces high and stable rate of responses
Determined by the passage of time before a response can be reinforced			
Fixed interval (FI)	Reinforcement is given following *first* response to occur after a fixed amount of time has passed; e.g., FI 1 minute = first response to occur after 1 minute has passed is reinforced	A cook waits for a pie to be done (FI 30 minutes) before taking it out of the oven and serving it	Produces very low rate of responses until interval approaches or is passed, then response probability rises rapidly
Variable interval (VI)	Reinforcement is given following *first* response to occur after a certain amount of time, *on the average*, has passed; e.g., VI 10 minutes = on the average, reinforcement follows first response to occur after 10 minutes (it may be 6 minutes, 13 minutes, and so on, but the average is 10 minutes)	A resident checks his mailbox occasionally throughout the day while waiting for the postal carrier	Produces very stable and uniform rate of responses

PREMACK PRINCIPLE
The concept developed by David Premack that reinforcement is relative, not absolute, so that if two behaviors differ in their probability of occurrence at any given time, the chance to engage in the probable will serve to reinforce engaging in the less probable.

SOCIAL LEARNING
Learning by observing the actions of others. It is also called vicarious conditioning or observational learning.

MODEL
In social learning theory, anyone who demonstrates a behavior that others observe.

The Premack Principle

We have seen how different reinforcers and stimuli can control behavior. But behavior itself—that is, the opportunity to engage in a particular behavior—also can control our actions. Psychologist David Premack has demonstrated that the behaviors an organism is more likely to emit can be used to reinforce the behaviors an organism is less likely to emit (Premack, 1959). This observation became known as the **Premack principle.** The Premack principle is sometimes referred to as "grandma's principle" (although parents, no doubt, use it more often) because it is embodied in statements like "Eat your green beans and you may have some pie." In such an instance, engaging in the less likely behavior (eating green beans) becomes more likely because it leads to a chance to engage in a behavior that the organism is more likely to emit (pie eating).

Initially, psychologists studying operant conditioning were interested in how reinforcers strengthened behaviors. Premack, however, showed that organisms, including humans, appear to have a hierarchy of behaviors, ordered according to which are more or less reinforcing, and that the environment structures how and when any of the behaviors in the hierarchy may be allowed. Also, depending on how recently certain behaviors have been allowed to occur, the positions of behaviors on the hierarchy can change (Timberlake & Allison, 1974); that is, once you're sick of pie, you might actually prefer the green beans.

CHALLENGES TO THE BEHAVIORIST VIEW

Both classical and operant conditioning are today considered to play important roles in the development of behavior. They are not, however, the only forces. Other people have added to the view of learning presented by the behaviorists, not so much by attempting to show that the experimental results obtained in behavioral research are wrong, but rather by showing that there is more to learning than the behaviorists have proposed. The two fields of psychological research that have most expanded our understanding of learning are the views provided by the social–cognitive and the ethological perspectives. Let's examine them in turn.

SOCIAL LEARNING—OBSERVATION AND IMITATION

You have seen that an organism can learn as the result of classical or operant conditioning. Now we will investigate a third possible way to learn—by observing another organism's behavior. This is known as **social learning.**

The Importance of Models

Albert Bandura and several of his colleagues at Stanford University have argued that social learning is a distinct kind of learning that requires new principles in order to understand it. Bandura, Ross, and Ross demonstrated their thesis in 1963 in an experiment now considered by many to be a classic. They asked nursery-school children to observe an adult **model** striking a large inflated Bobo doll with a mallet. The model also hit, kicked, and sat on the doll. *Neither the model nor the observing children was directly reinforced at any time during the session.* Later, after the model had gone, the children were secretly observed as they played in a toy-filled room with the Bobo doll. For comparison, other children who had not seen the model's behavior were also allowed to interact with the doll. The results of the experiment clearly demonstrated that the children who had observed the model were far more likely to be aggressive, in imitation of the model's behavior, than were the other children. These results would not have been predicted by classical or operant conditioning theories, since the imitation seemed to be occurring without reinforcement.

If you consider that learning by trial and error can be very time consuming, and even dangerous, you will readily see the value of learning by imitating the behavior someone else has already learned or acquired. If our learning were restricted to what we could gain through classical and operant conditioning, our ability to master our world would be severely limited. Bandura emphasizes this point in the following description of an instructor attempting to teach a driving student to operate a car strictly by using the principles of reinforcement:

> As a first step our trainer, who has been carefully programmed to produce head nods, resonant hm-hms, and other verbal reinforcers, loads up with an ample supply of candy, chewing gum and filter-tip cigarettes. A semi-willing subject, who has never observed a person driving an automobile, and a parked car complete the picture. Our trainer might have to wait a long time before the subject emits an orienting response toward the vehicle. At the moment the subject does look even in the general direction of the car, this response is immediately reinforced and gradually he begins to gaze longingly at the stationary automobile. Similarly, approach responses in the desired direction are promptly reinforced in order to bring the subject in proximity to the car. Eventually, through the skillful use of differential reinforcement, the trainer will teach the subject to open and close the car door. With perseverance he will move the subject from the back seat or any other inappropriate location chosen in this trial-and-error ramble until

Both boys and girls who watched a live actor model violence were more likely to imitate the violence than children who had not seen the model.

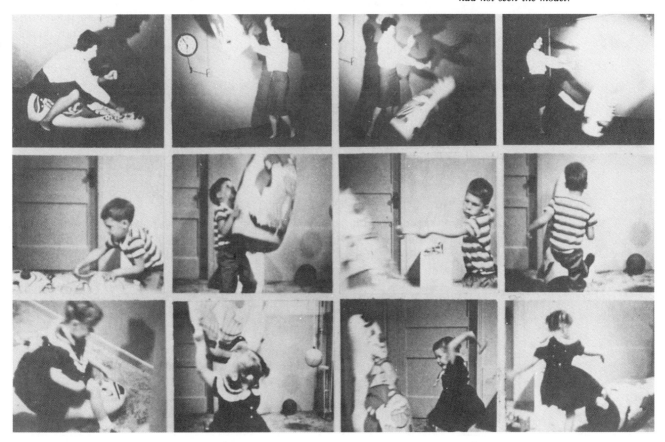

Social learning through imitation may often occur without the need for direct reinforcement.

BEHAVIOR MODIFICATION
A set of procedures for changing human behavior, especially by using behavior therapy and operant conditioning techniques.

at length the subject is shaped up behind the steering wheel. It is unnecessary to depict the remainder of the training procedure beyond noting that it will likely prove an exceedingly tedious, not to mention an expensive and hazardous enterprise. (Bandura, 1962, pp. 212–213)

Social learning can be observed in other species as well. Dachshund puppies learned to pull a food cart sooner when they saw other puppies doing it than when they didn't observe such behavior (Adler & Adler, 1977). Bottle-nosed dolphins learned to pull a rope into their pool by watching other dolphins (Adler & Adler, 1978). Three sea lions learned to pull a rope into the center of their cage after they had watched a fourth learn the task by the shaping method (Adler & Adler, 1977). Rats learned by observing rat leaders who were the first to discover the best route through a cage door (Konopasky & Telegdy, 1977). Another study demonstrated that naive mice learned to copulate sooner by watching other mice do it (Hayashi & Kimura, 1976). Many studies have demonstrated this kind of observational learning in other species.

Performance versus Acquisition

Although learning can apparently take place simply through observation of another person's behavior, reinforcement can be an important supplement in social learning. Consider a second experiment conducted by Bandura in 1965. On one occasion, a group of young children watched as a model was rewarded with juice and candy for being aggressive, and on another occasion a different group of children watched as the same model was scolded for the same aggression. The results of the experiment indicated that the consequences of the model's behavior were very important in determining whether the children would imitate the model. The children who had observed the model receiving juice and candy for aggressive behavior became more aggressive. The children who had observed the model being scolded for aggressive behavior rarely imitated the aggression.

At first glance this experiment may seem to indicate that reinforcement is necessary for social learning. We can resolve this problem by distinguishing between performing a behavior and acquiring it. Reinforcing or punishing the model's

Albert Bandura and his colleagues at Stanford once placed an advertisement in a newspaper offering free aid to anyone with a snake phobia (an unrealistic fear of snakes). Many people answered the ad. As it turned out, the majority of respondents were men who held outdoor jobs and were deathly afraid of encountering a snake. It was hoped that a behavior-modification program could help these volunteers to overcome their phobia. **Behavior modification** is an application of learning theory. By arranging particular associations between stimuli or particular consequences for behavior, or by modeling the behavior that is desired, it is possible to change a subject's behavior; that is, the environment and the experiences of the subject are purposely manipulated in order to change behavior.

In the first part of the behavior-modification program, Bandura made certain that his volunteers did indeed have a snake phobia. He asked each subject to handle a snake, but not one was willing to do so under any circumstances. Next, Bandura used models to help his subjects overcome their phobia. The models did not have a snake phobia. They approached and handled the snakes while the subjects watched. For any male subjects who so desired, Bandura even enlisted the aid of a striptease artist who worked with a boa constrictor named Squeezer (Bandura, 1977). Many of the men found themselves sitting in the middle rows, wanting to be close to the show but far away from the snake.

The results of this experiment in behavior modification demonstrated, as have many similar experiments, the power of modeling as a behavior-modification technique. Within 48 hours, the subjects were able comfortably to handle the snake that they had so feared at the beginning of the experiment. In addition, no recurrences of phobia were reported when the subjects were interviewed a month later.

Use of a model is usually incorporated into a more comprehensive behavior-modification program that includes both classical and operant conditioning. A good example of such a comprehensive program is described in the book *Toilet Training in Less than a Day* by Nathan Azrin and Richard Foxx (1974).

Toilet training doesn't have to be a 3-year trial. It can be accomplished in under 24 hours using the learning principles that have been described in this chapter. To see how this is possible, let's examine some of the techniques used in the toilet training program developed by Azrin and Foxx. As you'll discover, this program takes account of both the child's physical abilities and his or her environment.

1. The authors recommend that no attempt be made to train children who are much younger than 24 months. Children younger than this do not usually have the muscle development necessary for bladder and bowel control.

2. A learning environment should be created in which the child and parent are together without distraction, for the whole day. In this way, all their energy can be devoted to learning and strengthening the new behavior.

3. The steps in the desired behavior sequence are as follows: The child will go to the potty chair when the need arises, lower his or her training pants, urinate or defecate, wipe where appropriate, raise the training pants, remove the plastic pot from the potty chair, empty its contents into the toilet, flush the toilet, and return the plastic pot to the potty chair.

4. The authors give a number of tips for accomplishing these behaviors more easily. They suggest, for example, using large, loose training pants, which are easier to raise and lower.

5. Instrument learning is achieved as the child's appropriate behaviors are reinforced through lavish praise and the administration of large amounts of juice or soda. Drinking liquids makes urination more likely, giving the child more chances to learn the desired response; remember, a behavior must occur before it can be reinforced.

6. The technique of modeling is incorporated in an ingenious way by making use of a doll that wets. At the beginning of the Azrin and Foxx program, before anything else, the child helps the parent "toilet train" the doll. The child watches as the doll models the desired behavior and then sees that the doll is immediately rewarded for its good behavior with praise and juice (administered to the doll in a special baby bottle that refills its reservoir). This is an effective technique because an observer is more likely to imitate a model, even if it is a doll, if she sees that the model's behavior is reinforced.

behavior did affect whether the children imitated the model. Nonetheless, the children who had seen the model disciplined for aggression were quite able, when offered reinforcers for demonstrating what the model had done, to recall and demonstrate the model's behavior, even though they had not spontaneously imitated the model before. This experiment showed that children who observed a model being disciplined for aggressive behavior were unlikely to imitate (perform) the behavior, but that they did learn (acquire) the behavior, and could imitate it at a later time if the reinforcing and punishing contingencies changed.

The term **latent learning** is sometimes used to describe this kind of incidental learning, when the learning may not be apparent from an animal's or a person's behavior. This kind of learning often occurs in the absence of reward. Rats placed in a maze and allowed to wander for a time without reinforcement will later, when reinforced, learn to find the goal box (where there is food) faster than will rats who are new to the maze. Latent learning apparently occurs in the animals as they wander about in the maze. Although no direct reinforcement was given, just the experience of walking through the maze apparently taught the rats to find their way through it.

Other factors besides reinforcement and punishment of a model's behavior can affect the likelihood that imitation will occur. For instance, the perceived status of the model can be important. Some of the earliest social learning studies demonstrated that the behavior of an entire group of people can best be altered by having the individuals with the highest status (as perceived by the group) model the desired behavior, rather than by attempting to influence each group member singly (Lippitt, Polansky, & Rosen, 1952; Polansky, Lippitt, & Redl, 1950). Such prominent models can have a powerful effect, especially when presented to large numbers of observers by mass media (such as newspapers, movies, or television). In addition, a behavior is more likely to be imitated when the models are nurturant, aggressive, or similar to the observers. Imitation also is more likely when a person can already perform the component subskills of the behavior that has been modeled and when the person's usual environment is similar to that in which the model was originally observed.

Of course, whether a particular model will be perceived as a person of high status, or whether a model's behavior will appear worthy of imitation, depends largely on the thoughts of the observer. For this reason, social learning theorists have become interested in the thinking process and its role in the formation of beliefs and attitudes.

COGNITIVE LEARNING

Cognition refers to thinking. Philosophically, social learning is considered to be an interaction between environment and thought, rather than mainly a function of environmental input. As Albert Bandura stated, to exclude thinking from any theory of learning would be like attributing "Shakespeare's masterpieces to his prior instruction in the mechanics of writing" (Bandura, 1978). Because of this philosophical viewpoint, social learning theory cannot rightly be considered to come under the classification of "behaviorism."

Human beings think, and thinking affects behavior. Traditional behaviorists, especially in Watson's day, were unwilling to examine the mind or thought processes because these phenomena were not directly observable. Since then, learning theorists have devoted increasing time to exploring thought processes, problem solving, and the internal understanding we have of our world. As a result, most of them

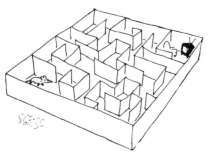

Drawing S. Gross; © 1978 The New Yorker Magazine, Inc.

212

are no longer "strict behaviorists." The study of thinking and its influence on our behavior is known as **cognitive psychology.** *

We respond to the world not just through our conditioned responses but also through our knowledge of it. Does a dog do the same? Do dogs think? Most dog owners assume that they do. Suppose you come home and make a sound as you unlock the door; your dog will be waiting to greet you on the other side (assuming you have a dog—if you don't have a dog, there probably won't be one waiting for you—but I digress). Why was your dog waiting there (assuming you have a dog)? Did it have a mental image of you on the other side of the door? Did it know from the sounds you made that it was *you?* Or did it simply hear a series of cues, or discriminative stimuli, and run for the door because that response in the presence of those cues had previously been reinforced? Moreover, did the dog become excited and wag its tail because it had been classically conditioned, so that the sounds of the door being unlocked aroused its autonomic nervous system—a conditioned arousal? If the dog merely responded to cues and classical conditioning, then it ran to the door, became excited, and wagged its tail without having any "idea" why it acted in this way. The question whether dogs or other animals rely on mental representations of their world is debatable. All we know for sure is that humans often use mental or cognitive abilities when they interact with their environment.

A cognitive representation of the world is a valuable asset. With it, you can manipulate, alter, or change things mentally to examine possible outcomes before you actually do anything. You use your cognitive understanding to orient yourself to particular problems or situations. A rat running a maze in search of food has to learn which turns to make in order to find the food. After a number of trials, it learns that at a certain corner it should turn right, and at another corner it should turn right again, and soon it will come to the food. When you enter a strange town or go to a new neighborhood, you may similarly have to find your way around by trial and error, or by memorizing certain details. Eventually, however, you become oriented, and you acquire what is known as a **cognitive map,** an internal understanding of the locations of things in relation to one another.

In the late 1940s, psychologist Edward Tolman came to the conclusion that rats weren't as stupid as everyone thought, and that they too, had cognitive maps. Working with rats that had learned their way through a maze (see Figure 6.11), he found that, if a particular path was blocked, the rats would attempt to find another path, one never used before but *lying in the same general direction as the food* (see Figure 6.12) (Tolman, Ritchie, & Kalish, 1964). Tolman referred to this

*The topic of cognitive psychology is covered in depth in Chapter 8.

COGNITIVE PSYCHOLOGY
The study of behavior as it relates to perceiving, thinking, remembering, or problem solving.

COGNITIVE MAP
A mental representation of the location of things in relation to each other in a given environment.

FIGURE 6.11

A maze like that used by Tolman to train rats. The rats had to learn their way through the maze, traveling along in the order of the numbers 1 through 6 to reach food at location 6.

tendency as **place learning.** Interestingly, place learning is not limited to mammals or even vertebrates. Honey bees have also been found to rely on place learning to find food and return home (Gould, 1986).

Imagine that you've just entered the living room of a place in which you used to live. Stand there for a moment. Now point in the direction of your bedroom. You've just used a cognitive map.

Researcher Emil Menzel conducted an experiment in which he examined the cognitive maps of chimpanzees. While carrying a chimpanzee with him around a large field, Menzel hid food in 18 locations, usually in clumps of grass or behind other natural cover. Then, returning to a starting point at the edge of the field, he let loose the chimp who had seen the food hidden and five other chimpanzee companions. As you might guess, the knowledgeable chimp was the one who found almost all the food. What interested the researchers most was that the knowledgeable chimp took the most efficient route to the food, a route that had no obvious relationship to the path along which he had originally been carried (Menzel, as cited by Miller, 1984b). The chimp clearly had not simply learned mechanically where to go, but instead had a grasp of the relationship between his own location and other important locations in the field. This enabled the chimp to take shortcuts; that is, to cover ground he'd never been across before. Another way of saying this is that he *knew* where he was going (something we can't always say about ourselves). The chimp did not have a perfect score, however—he did not find all the food. But the researchers began laughing when they tried to find the food that the chimp has missed. They, too, had forgotten some of the hiding places and ended up doing some detailed searching!

Although cognitive maps are mental representations, some geographers and map makers have actually attempted to draw them. By asking many people who

FIGURE 6.12

In this experiment, Tolman presented the rats with a new maze of many corridors, but with the standard route learned by the rats shown in Figure 6.11 blocked. According to behavior theory, an operant gradient of generalization should be in effect, making corridors I and H the most likely choices (they are closest to the blocked corridor). Surprisingly, corridor E was the prime choice! Corridor E leads in the general direction of position 6, where the food is located (who said rats weren't smart?). Tolman called the rats' ability "place learning" because the rats seemed to have a general idea about where they wanted to go.

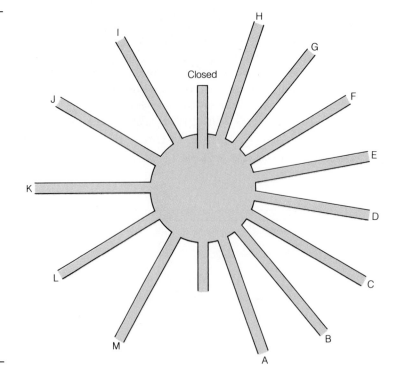

Rats running mazes have demonstrated that they have a cognitive map, or mental representation, of the placement of locations in space.

live in a city to indicate where they think major landmarks and important places are, map makers have been able to regroup locations statistically to represent a mental map that people have of their city. This kind of work is known as **behavioral geography** (Parfit, 1984). Behavioral geographers have discovered that the places people like to go to are often thought to be closer than they actually are, while the places people don't like to go to are thought to be farther away. Dangerous neighborhoods, which people often avoid, are thought to be farther away and smaller than they actually are. Poorer people generally think that places are farther away than wealthier people do, and, since they often cannot afford transportation, places really are farther away for them in a sense (see Figure 6.13). These data indicate that different life experiences influence place learning.

In Chapter 8, we'll examine cognitive psychology in greater detail. We'll see that a new cognitive view of learning has been built on the foundation created by our knowledge of classical conditioning, operant conditioning, and social learning. This new understanding of learning considers how mental processes influence what and how we learn.

FIGURE 6.13

The streets on this map are from downtown Columbus, Ohio. The buildings on this map represent a low-income resident's cognitive understanding of where the buildings are located. The dots associated with each building show their actual locations in Columbus. In the low-income resident's cognitive map, the buildings are farther away from one another than they are in reality.
(**SOURCE:** *Parfit, 1984, p. 129.*)

INHERITANCE AND THE BIOLOGY OF BEHAVIOR

You have seen how social learning theorists and cognitive psychologists have challenged a basic assumption of behaviorism by opening the mind and thought processes to experimental study. Another significant challenge to behaviorism has been mounted from a different quarter. In the many decades since the publication of Skinner's work, we have come to realize that it is also important to know the specific abilities, limitations, and tendencies to learn of any given species. Although Skinner readily admitted that there were differences among species' abilities to learn, he did not believe these were very important differences. Now researchers aren't so sure. Certain animals, including humans, learn certain things readily and do not learn other things. For instance, you have learned a full, rich language based on a grammar; a dog or cat never will. These specific species differences appear to be due to the forces of evolution (see Figure 6.14).

Throughout this century, research on inherited behaviors has attracted great interest, especially in Europe. People who specialize in this area of research are called ethologists, and their field of study is **ethology** (Hess, 1970). Ethologists usually conduct naturalistic observations, and they also are interested in learned behavior. Ethologists have strongly argued that no two organisms have exactly the same behavioral capacities and that many of the differences among organisms are due to genetically inherited biological attributes and predispositions.

Research in this field began to grow significantly after Konrad Lorenz published a paper in 1937 describing the *following response*. At one time, Lorenz made certain that he was the first moving object that some newborn goslings saw. From that time on, the goslings followed him everywhere he went, even swimming! It seemed to Lorenz that the first object to move past these goslings was "stamped into" the animals' brains as the object to be followed. Lorenz called this phenomenon **imprinting.** He also observed that imprinting could occur only during a *critical period* lasting from hatching until about 2 days later. The most effective imprinting occurred approximately 14 hours after hatching. Through the efforts of ethologists, researchers have a fuller appreciation of the fact that the tendency to behave in certain ways can be inherited (Gould & Marler, 1987).

Canalization

To what degree do inherited behaviors exist in humans? While it is true that we do possess a number of simple inherited reflexes, such as coughing and blinking, human beings show their behavioral inheritance more in terms of *tendencies* to learn some things more easily than others. This is the phenomenon of **canalization.*** A behavior is said to be canalized if there is an inherited predisposition within the nervous system to learn the behavior. Canalization occurs not only in human beings but also in most species. Unlike simple reflexes such as sneezing or coughing, canalized behaviors must be learned; it's just that the "prewired" organization of a given species' nervous system makes certain behaviors very easy to learn. Washburn and Hamburg (1965) described the phenomenon as follows:

> What is inherited is ease of learning rather than fixed instinctive patterns. The species easily, almost inevitably, learns the essential behaviors for its survival. So, although it is true that monkeys learn to be social, they are so constructed that under normal circumstances this learning always takes place. Similarly, human beings learn to talk, but they inherit structures that make this inevitable, except under the most peculiar circumstances. (Washburn & Hamburg, 1965, p. 5–6)

*Some researchers prefer to use the term *preparedness* (Seligman, 1970).

Highly canalized behaviors are not only almost inevitable but also highly resistant to the effects of experience. Conversely, weakly canalized behaviors are highly susceptible to change due to experience.

Canalization means, then, that certain kinds of learning are more or less likely to occur because of our biologically inherited predispositions. For example, if a loud noise scared you while you were eating a hot dog, the experience probably wouldn't affect your fondness for that food even if you had been very scared. If, however, you ate a hot dog and coincidentally caught the flu, which caused you to become extremely sick to your stomach, your desire for that food might be gone forever, and it probably wouldn't help much to realize that the food hadn't caused the nausea. Researchers have found that animals make associations between food and nausea very easily (Garcia & Koelling, 1966), whereas they do not easily make associations between food and a loud sound. From an evolutionary standpoint, a built-in or canalized tendency for the nervous system to make such associations is sensible. If an animal was startled while eating a certain food, there would be no survival benefit in thereafter avoiding that food. But if the animal became sick after eating a certain food, there would be a good reason to avoid that food in the future.

Even the seemingly inherited behaviors of a robin building a nest, a cat cleaning itself, or a salmon returning upstream to spawn are really examples of canalization. The behaviors themselves aren't simply "in the genes"; robins have to *learn* to build nests (they're pretty clumsy at fist), cats *learn* to clean themselves, and salmon *learn* to swim upstream to spawn. What the animals have inherited, then, is a very strong tendency, or "drive," to learn these behaviors (Gould & Marler, 1987). Being carried in the genes, the inherited drives to learn these behaviors are passed from one generation to the next (Scheller & Axel, 1984).

ETHOLOGY
The study of human and animal behavior from a biological point of view; it is characterized by the study of animals in their natural environments.

IMPRINTING
As used by ethologists, a species-specific bonding that occurs within a limited period early in the life of the organism and that is relatively unmodifiable thereafter.

CANALIZATION
The process by which behaviors, due to genetic predisposition, are learned extremely easily, almost inevitably. The more canalized a behavior is, the more difficult it is to change or alter.

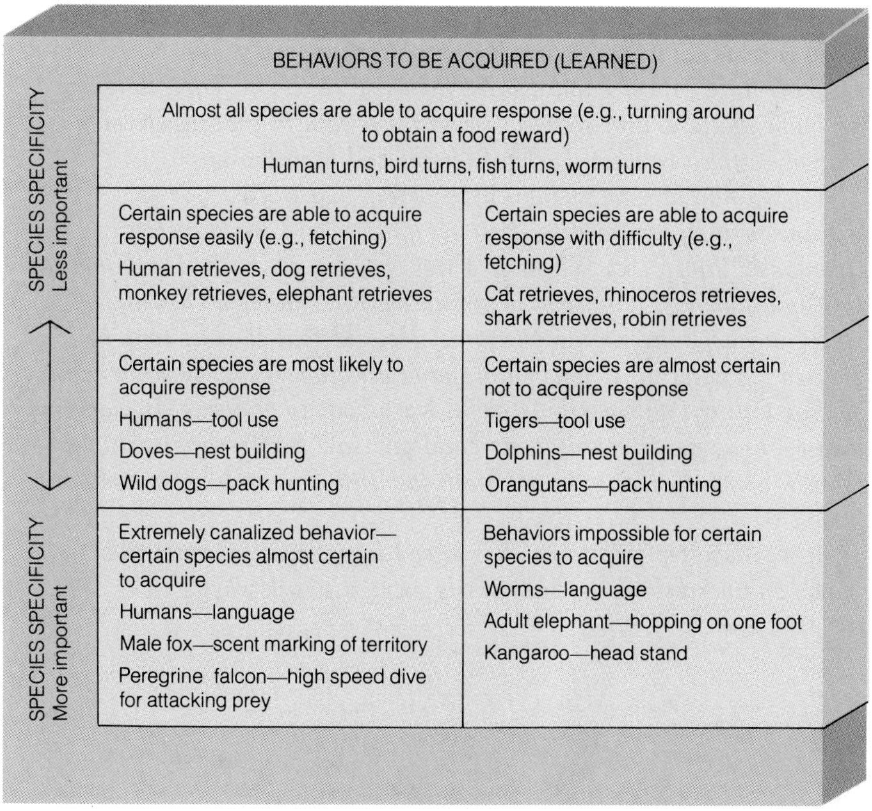

BEHAVIORS TO BE ACQUIRED (LEARNED)	
Almost all species are able to acquire response (e.g., turning around to obtain a food reward) Human turns, bird turns, fish turns, worm turns	
Certain species are able to acquire response easily (e.g., fetching) Human retrieves, dog retrieves, monkey retrieves, elephant retrieves	Certain species are able to acquire response with difficulty (e.g., fetching) Cat retrieves, rhinoceros retrieves, shark retrieves, robin retrieves
Certain species are most likely to acquire response Humans—tool use Doves—nest building Wild dogs—pack hunting	Certain species are almost certain not to acquire response Tigers—tool use Dolphins—nest building Orangutans—pack hunting
Extremely canalized behavior—certain species almost certain to acquire Humans—language Male fox—scent marking of territory Peregrine falcon—high speed dive for attacking prey	Behaviors impossible for certain species to acquire Worms—language Adult elephant—hopping on one foot Kangaroo—head stand

(Left axis, top: SPECIES SPECIFICITY — Less important; bottom: SPECIES SPECIFICITY — More important)

FIGURE 6.14

Species specificity can play an important role in determining which behaviors can be acquired. Many behaviors, as Skinner suggested, can be acquired by a vast number of species according to the same basic learning principles. Other behaviors, however, are acquired either easily or with great difficulty depending on the unique characteristics of a given species. In some instances, species specificity is so important that it determines whether a behavior is either almost certain to be acquired or impossible to acquire.

EPILOGUE: THE NAIL BITES THE DUST

The following account should probably come under the heading "Strange but True." It describes a psychologist's use of self-administered punishment to change a socially unacceptable behavior.

I once knew a psychologist who, for reasons you will shortly discover, shall remain anonymous. For the sake of the story, let's call him Richard. Richard had a bad habit. He chewed his nails. Well, that's not actually correct; he chewed his nails off and then spit them out, usually while he was lecturing. Once in a great while, this practice was called to his attention, and it always embarrassed him. He said that he wasn't aware that he was doing it. It had become such an ingrained habit that he could chew off all ten nails, spit them in all directions, and still be totally unconscious of what he was doing.

Richard was a respected learning theorist, and he decided that if anyone could devise a behavior-modification technique to eliminate his habit, he could. The next day he arrived, all smiles, and said he had a request: If any of us should see him biting his nails, we should let him know about it. It wasn't long before someone said, "Uh, Richard, you're doing it." He stopped and looked at his nails and said, "So I am." Then, as everyone watched, he pulled up his shirtsleeve, grabbed hold of a heavy-duty rubber band that he had wrapped around his wrist, stretched it out a distance of about 10 inches, and let it go. There was a vicious snap. He yelled, cursed, and shook his hand. Everyone looked on in amazement. Surely learning theorists were all a little insane. "Punishment," he said. "Punishment is the answer!"

What happened to the people around Richard was interesting. Some took relish in pointing out that he was biting his nails, just to see him snap the huge rubber band against his wrist; others preferred to ignore his habit, because they couldn't stand to see him in that much pain. Happily, after two days, Richard's habit had been broken.

I asked him how he thought his program had worked. He said, "Well, if I unconsciously learned to chew my nails, then I could certainly unconsciously unlearn it. Whenever I was chewing my nails, I administered this punishment. Pretty soon my brain learned that nail chewing resulted in something very unpleasant." He said that the last time he reached his hand up to his mouth (quite unconsciously), he got a terrible sinking feeling that something awful was about to happen. "It made me aware," he said. "I looked at my hand and saw it was approaching my mouth. Somewhere deep in my brain the little gray cells were screaming, 'Don't do it!'"

It was reported that some days later Richard was wearing rubber bands around his ankles, but nobody wanted to ask why.

Summary

■ Learning may be defined as a relatively permanent change in behavior that results from experience.

■ In his book *The Behavior of Organisms*, B. F. Skinner argued that there are general principles of learning that are applicable to almost all species.

■ During the 1890s, the Russian physiologist Pavlov reported an experiment with an associative learning process. By systematically associating the presentation of a bell with the presentation of food, Pavlov was able to classically condition dogs to respond to the bell by salivating.

■ Once the CS has the power to elicit the CR, owing to the reinforcement of the CS–US bond by their contiguous pairing, it is possible to use the CS all by itself to create a "higher-order" CS_2. This process is known as higher-order conditioning.

■ Associative experiences also can lead to the formation of beliefs and attitudes, and they can influence behaviors as diverse as prejudice, drug use, and fear.

■ Watson and Rayner's experiment with Little Albert demonstrated that classical conditioning also can occur in humans.

■ Originally, scientists assumed that classical conditioning occurred because the CS and US were contiguously associated. Now they recognize that contingency detection plays an important role.

■ Conditioning has been shown to occur in individual neurons.

■ The basic premise of instrumental learning was formulated by E. L. Thorndike at the turn of the century. It is known as the law of effect.

■ In instrumental conditioning, behaviors are learned because of the reinforcing or punishing consequences that follow them.

■ Skinner uses the term *operant conditioning* to describe responses that operate on the environment. Operants are classified not according to the particular muscular motions that constitute a response but rather according to their similar effect on the environment.

■ Reinforcement occurs when a pleasant consequence follows a response, making it more likely that the response will be repeated.

■ An instrumental behavior can occasionally be built up piecemeal through a process known as shaping. Shaping consists of reinforcing successive approximations toward the final response.

■ An organism's responses can become highly selective or more general through the processes of discrimination and generalization. When an organism discriminates, it responds differentially to two or more stimuli. When it generalizes, similar stimuli evoke the same response.

■ Positive and negative reinforcement are both ways of strengthening a response. Positive reinforcement occurs when a behavior leads to a pleasant or reinforcing consequence. Negative reinforcement occurs when a behavior successfully leads to avoidance of, or escape from, an aversive situation.

■ Punishment and extinction are ways of weakening a response.

■ Punishment is an extremely effective way of decreasing a behavior's strength, but its use may have serious drawbacks; for example, it may cause withdrawal, suppression of other behaviors, hostility, or aggression.

■ Stimuli necessary for sustaining life can obtain the power to reinforce simply by being withheld for a time; such stimuli are called primary reinforcers. Other stimuli, known as acquired or secondary reinforcers, are effective because of their association with primary or other secondary reinforcers.

■ Operant behavior may be maintained by various schedules of reinforcement.

■ Through learning, different stimuli come to cue specific responses. Such cues are known as discriminative stimuli.

■ Psychologist David Premack has demonstrated that the behaviors an organism is more likely to display can be used to reinforce the behaviors an organism is less likely to display. This observation became known as the Premack principle.

■ The behaviorist view has been challenged by social learning, cognitive, and ethological theorists.

■ Learning through observation of another organism's behavior is called social learning.

■ Albert Bandura has argued that social learning is a distinct kind of learning because it does not depend on reinforcement.

■ Social learning theorists draw a distinction between performing (imitating) a behavior and learning (acquiring) it. Latent learning is the term used to describe the kind of incidental learning that may not be apparent from an animal's or a person's behavior.

■ Models are most likely to be imitated if they have high status, are nurturant, are aggressive, or are similar to the observer.

■ The study of learning has led to an applied technology called behavior modification.

■ Cognition refers to thinking. Cognitive learning theorists believe that thought processes have an important effect on learning.

■ Cognitive aspects of learning can be seen by studying cognitive maps. A cognitive map is an organism's mental representation of the location of objects in relation to one another and to the organism.

■ Learning is important because it has survival value. Human beings show their behavioral inheritance more in terms of tendencies to learn some behaviors more easily than others. This is the phenomenon of canalization.

Suggestions for Further Reading

1. Domjan, M. P., & Burkhard, B. (1985). The principles of learning and behavior (2nd ed.). Monterey, CA: Brooks/Cole. A college-level textbook on the principles of learning and conditioning.
2. Hulse, S. H., Egeth, H., & Deese, J. (1980). The psychology of learning (5th ed.). New York: McGraw-Hill. A college-level textbook that introduces theories of learning and includes current views on the interaction between types of learning.
3. Pavlov, I. (1927). Conditioned reflexes. New York: Oxford University Press. Describes Pavlov's classic experiments in associative learning.
4. Reynolds, G. S. (1975). A primer of operant conditioning (2nd ed.). Glenview, IL: Scott Foresman. A college-level textbook that describes the principles of operant conditioning, including reinforcement.
5. Skinner, B. F. (1971). Beyond freedom and dignity. New York: Knopf. A book for the general reader in which Skinner outlines his theory of operant conditioning and attempts to apply it to improve social situations.

CHAPTER 7 | Memory and Information Processing

Prologue

Why Psychologists Study Memory

Two Memories Are Better Than One

A Model of Declarative Memory
Sensory Memory
Short-Term Memory
Chunking
Long-Term Memory

Theories of Declarative Memory
The Dual-Code Theory
Propositional Network Theory
Propositional Networks and the Dual-
Code Theory

Forgetting
Decay and Loss
Interference Effects
The Tip-of-the-Tongue Phenomenon
Retrieval Cues
Reconstruction and Retrieval
Failure of Consolidation
Motivated Forgetting
Somatogenic Amnesia

**Strengthening Memory through
Elaboration**

Encoding Effects
Locus-Dependent Memory
In the Mood

The Shaping Effect

Epilogue: Remembrance of Things Past

Summary

Suggestions for Further Reading

PROLOGUE

The year is 1983 and you are working at the Johns Hopkins medical center in Maryland with Dr. John Hart, a neurologist. Today, Dr. Hart wants you to observe a patient who is being tested. "He had a stroke a couple of years ago," Hart explains, "and something very unusual happened to him."

As you enter the testing room, you are introduced to the patient (known only as Mr. M. D. in order to protect his privacy). As you watch M. D., he seems perfectly normal. There is no sign that he has recently had a stroke. His movements are coordinated and his speech appears unaffected. His conversation and emotions seem fine. You ask M. D. whether he is now fully recovered. "Not really," he says, "things are still about the same as before." You wonder what is wrong.

Dr. Hart begins testing. First, he shows M. D. pictures of different things—toys, tools, kitchen objects, colors, clothing, animals, vehicles, food products, and other odds and ends—and asks him to name what he sees. As M. D. zips right through the list you think to yourself, "He's doing as well as I could do." Suddenly, M. D. stops. He is looking at a picture of a peach. Maybe he's just taking a break. Dr. Hart asks him, "What is this?" M. D. shakes his head, "I don't know."

"How about this one?" (a picture of broccoli). M. D. shrugs, "I couldn't say." The remaining pictures are of different fruits and vegetables; whether he is looking at cherries, lettuce, tomatoes, or cucumbers the response is always the same—M. D. recognizes none of them! Dr. Hart points out, "If it grew in a garden or an orchard, he probably can't name it."

Next, a row of pictures of different fruit is placed before M. D. Dr. Hart asks, "Which is the apple?" Immediately, M. D. points to the ap-

221

MEMORY
The complex mental function of recalling
what has been learned or experienced.

ple. "Now, show me the orange?" M. D. points to it unhesitatingly. "Tell me what an orange is." Without difficulty, M. D. describes the kinds of things we all know about oranges.

When the testing is over and M. D. has left, you ask Dr. Hart for an explanation of M. D.'s responses. "Well," he begins, "as you've seen, it's as though a page in his mind containing the names of only fruits and vegetables has been ripped out. It must the the result of the stroke that occurred in the frontal lobe of the cortex and in the areas just below, known as the basal ganglia. It's just that we've never seen such a clear-cut example of this kind of memory loss. M. D. has shown us, for the first time, that a sort of filing system for words exists within our memories and that the system isn't alphabetical or chronological or based on the frequency of words used, but rather is listed according to meaning, like a thesaurus, a mental encyclopedia of categories. Perhaps all of the 75,000 words that the average person commands are categorized in this way."

Curious about the rest of the test results, you ask, "But M. D. hadn't lost the meanings. I mean, he knew what an orange was when you asked, didn't he?"

"Yes, that's right," Dr. Hart continues, "the meanings hadn't been lost, just his access to them. He couldn't name an apple when he saw it, because without the name he was lost. It was the name that gave him the key to the memories of apples and what they were. That's why, if I provide the name of the object, he knows the answer. He had lost the key to that part of the thesaurus, not its contents" (Hart, Berndt, & Caramazza, 1987).

In this chapter, we'll examine how memory works: You will see how you put information into your memory, store it, and retrieve it. We'll also examine how you can improve your memory and use it more successfully. And we will see what investigators have learned from other interesting cases like that of Mr. M. D.

■ WHY PSYCHOLOGISTS STUDY MEMORY

You rely on your **memory** every moment of the day. Without it, you would have no sense of continuity, no realization of the past; and you couldn't benefit from any learning or experience. Without memory, it would be impossible for you to function. All images and materials not immediately available to your senses must be drawn from your memory. Your very sense of self-awareness requires that you remember you had a "self" yesterday—or 5 minutes ago. Without a memory, you would be lost.

Yet memory is not perfect. The mind does not make a record, the way a camera or a tape recorder does; our memories shift. Some memories are forgotten, others are hidden in hard-to-reach places. How well we use our memories influences our ability to think and to understand. Before we can understand human behavior and capability, we must understand how the memory works and what its limitations and potentials are.

An Enduring Question: What Is the Biology of Memory?

Your memory is one of the most remarkable capabilities you have. Although it may take only a fraction of a second to learn something, the resulting memory may stay with you for the rest of your life. Somewhere, somehow, memories are stored away in your brain. But where and how? That's the question.

In 1917, neurophysiologist Karl Lashley began a search for what he called the brain's **engram,** the hypothetical biochemical structure of a single memory. Lashley systematically removed sections from the brains of trained rats, searching for the portion that held the elusive memory, or engram. In his book *In Search of the Engram,* published in 1950, he reported that his studies had yielded information about where the engrams didn't exist, but not about where they did. In fact, he had been unable to find any. He therefore concluded that each memory was not held in a specific place in the brain, but rather was, in some mysterious way, distributed evenly throughout the brain—a theory he referred to as **equipotentiality.**

The biochemical structure of an engram, or memory, is still debated, but evidence is mounting that Lashley's view about equipotentiality was wrong, although, as you will soon see, not totally without merit.

In 1959, neurosurgeon Wilder Penfield discovered, while conducting brain mapping during surgery (see Chapter 2), that he was causing memories to come to his patients' minds when he stimulated certain parts of their temporal lobes with an electrical probe (Penfield & Roberts, 1959). In fact, when he touched a certain part of one woman's brain, she heard a particular song. The "music" would stop whenever Penfield removed the probe. This discovery clearly implied that certain memories, at least, were being stored at particular locations and were not equally spread throughout the brain. However, this effect was only observed on a few occasions; the great majority of memories did not seem to be accessible by this method.

Then, in 1970, researcher Georges Ungar isolated what he believed was one of Lashley's long-sought-after engrams.

Rats are nocturnal creatures who generally prefer to avoid the light. But Ungar trained rats to avoid a darkened corner of a maze by electrifying that portion of the floor (see Figure 7.1). After the training, he examined extracts from the rats' brains and found a new protein he called *scotophobin,* whose name is derived from the Greek words *skotos,* meaning "darkness," and *phobos,* meaning "fear."

If untrained rats were injected with scotophobin, they too avoided the darkened corner of the maze as though they had also received training. It seemed to Ungar

ENGRAM
A lasting trace or impression formed in living tissue responsible for memory.

EQUIPOTENTIALITY
Karl Lashley's concept that memory and learning are not localized in one particular area of the brain, but rather the entire brain is responsible for handling these functions.

Figure 7.1

A device similar to that used by Ungar and his colleagues to isolate scotophobin. A rat (which is nocturnal) naturally seeks the darkened box, but the floor is electrified, conditioning the rat to avoid the dark box. Other untrained rats that are injected with scotophobin from the conditioned rat's brain, will also avoid the darkened box.

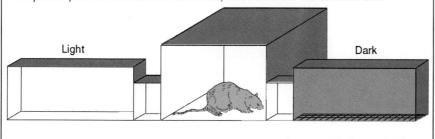

Light   Dark

that he had discovered the chemical responsible for a specific memory, that is, he had found an engram (Ungar, Galvan, & Clark, 1968; Ungar, Desiderio, & Parr, 1972).

And yet most memories and their locations remain elusive. Some even act as Lashley described them by seeming to be many places at once. How can such differences be explained?

Modern researchers generally believe that memories can be held at different neural levels within the brain, perhaps depending on the complexity of the memory. Figure 7.2 shows the current accepted terminology for these different levels of neural organization (Churchland & Churchland, 1990). A simple memory, such as one based on scotophobin, might be held at the level of *molecules* or *synapses* and perhaps at a very particular location in the brain, a location where scotophobin will have an effect, whereas the complex recollection of your high school sweetheart might be spread throughout an entire neural *map* or *system* and be scattered across many areas of your brain. "Recollection," then, may be an aptly descriptive word, because recollecting such a memory might require you to re-collect it from thousands of different locations and activate an entire map or

FIGURE 7.2

The organization of the central nervous system (brain and spinal cord) can be studied at different scales. Perhaps memories can be stored as whole entities at each of these levels depending on the complexity of the memory. SOURCE: *Churchland & Churchland, 1990, p. 36.*

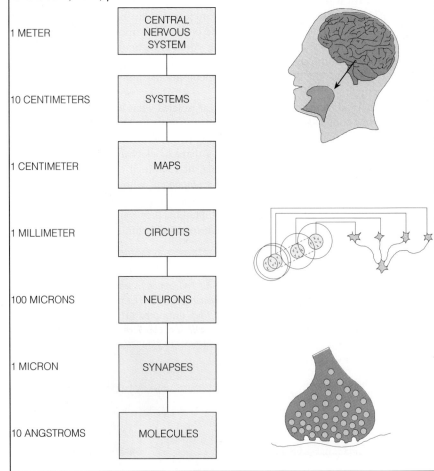

1 METER	CENTRAL NERVOUS SYSTEM
10 CENTIMETERS	SYSTEMS
1 CENTIMETER	MAPS
1 MILLIMETER	CIRCUITS
100 MICRONS	NEURONS
1 MICRON	SYNAPSES
10 ANGSTROMS	MOLECULES

system in order to bring the entire memory together. In this sense, such a complex memory wouldn't be in one place, but would almost seem, as Lashley described it, to be "everywhere at once."

Experimental indications of the existence of single memories held within *circuits*, *maps*, or *systems* come from interesting research in which it has been discovered that when a list of words is memorized and then recalled, certain neurons associated with the memory will fire more when one specific word on the list, such as "luck," is remembered, while other neurons will fire more when a different word, such as "woe," is remembered (Heit, Smith & Halgren, 1988). Only a few neurons were monitored in this experiment, so this probably does not mean that specific neurons were storing certain words, but rather that the different neurons tapped by the experiments were probably involved with different neural *circuits*, *maps*, or *systems*, each of which was, in fact, storing a different word.

We also know from other research that certain neural groupings do play an important part in organizing and controlling memories (Alkon, 1989). One of the researchers who is most involved with the examinations of memories at this level is Mortimer Mishkin. Mishkin has been examining the effects of specific forms of brain damage on memory (Mishkin & Appenzeller, 1987). Mishkin chose the New World monkey as his research subject because its brain is similar to that of humans. He also chose to concentrate on certain brain structures in the limbic system known to be associated with memory, including the amygdala and the hippocampus (see Chapter 2).

In Mishkin's experiment, the monkeys were required to remember from among many little toys and objects the ones they had seen before. Monkeys are very good at this task and usually are right 90 percent of the time. At first, Mishkin's results were similar to Lashley's, in the sense that the destruction of either the amygdala or the hippocampus seemed to have little or no effect on the subject's ability to remember. As you recall, similar discoveries had led Lashley to the idea of equipotentiality. But then Mishkin examined monkeys in which both the amygdala and hippocampus were destroyed on both sides of the brain—and the memory loss was profound. Monkeys missing both limbic structures following surgery could remember nothing new that researchers tried to teach them. These results weren't limited to visual memories. Monkeys trained to remember objects only by feel in the dark also lost this ability following the removal of both of their amygdalae and hippocampi. Mishkin had apparently destroyed an entire memory circuit.

Further examination by Mishkin and his colleagues has shown that the limbic system is the place where messages stored by the senses are compared. Without the amygdala, for instance, the brain can store sensory messages but can't compare them. Mishkin points out that "without your amygdala you could remember what your hometown looked like, but seeing the town might not evoke the fond remembrances connected with living there" (Alper, 1986, p. 46).

Destroying just the hippocampus appears to eliminate the ability to remember how objects are related spatially. Mishkin has said, "If you lost the function of your hippocampus, you could remember what the houses on your block looked like, but you might not remember which houses were next to one another" (Alper, 1986, p. 46).

After sensory messages leave the limbic system, they dive even deeper in the brain down to the basal forebrain. What happens there is not well understood, but it is assumed that the memory circuits join with other circuits to form entire maps.

Another approach to the question of memories and what they are has been

In Mortimer Mishkin's experiment, monkeys were required to remember from among many little toys and objects the ones they had seen before. After both the amygdala and hippocampus were destroyed, this ability was profoundly impaired.

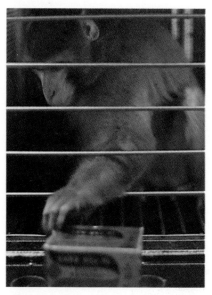

taken by Eric Kandel and Daniel Alkon. They are working at the level of circuits and smaller. Both researchers have been examining simple sea creatures in an effort to understand learning and memory. Kandel, for instance, chose to study sea snails because they have the largest neurons in the animal kingdom. One researcher has noted that the sea snail "is built like an old Philco radio, with simple circuits and large, easily identifiable components" (Hall, 1985, pp. 33–34).

Both Kandel and Alkon have found lasting changes in the neurons of such creatures following learning. Certain stimulation, they discovered, can make neurons more sensitive to later stimulation for up to weeks at a time. They argue that such long-term changes in neurons are an important aspect of memory.

Following these discoveries, researcher Gary Lynch searched for a mechanism within the neuron that might be responsible for the long-term changes observed by Kandel and Alkon (Lynch, 1986). When he stimulated neurons with electrical pulses, Lynch found that there was a great rush of calcium ions into the neurons, which then activated a dormant substance called calpain.

Calpain is an enzyme, which means that it can break down proteins. One important protein called fodrin is a major component of the coating of dendrites (the portion of the neuron that typically receives messages, often in the form of neurotransmitters secreted by other nearby neurons; see Chapter 2). Lynch believes that when calpain breaks down the fodrin coating, additional receptors for neurotransmitters on the dendrites' surfaces are exposed, making the neuron more sensitive to later stimulation. Each nerve stimulation, then, may release more calpain, which, in turn, breaks down more fodrin—and each time, the sensitivity of the neuron to stimulation is further increased. Lynch believes that when enough fodrin is broken down, memory development can progress even further, because the "skeleton" of the neuron becomes so loose that the neuron can change shape and spread, making new connections with other neurons as it does so. These are long-term, perhaps permanent, changes to stimulation, and may play an important role in the formation of memories at the synaptic and neuronal level, which, as we noted before, can last a lifetime.

To test his theory, Lynch gave rats a substance that prevents calpain from breaking down fodrin, and the result was similar to that obtained when both the amygdalae and hippocampi are removed. The rats were unable to remember anything new that the researchers tried to teach them. Control rats had no trouble remembering.

Many more studies must be carried out before any firm conclusions are drawn. But if researchers could ever uncover the secrets of memory and understand fully how it operates, this knowledge would greatly alter the way we do things, including, to consider just a few, educating our children, helping people with learning or memory disabilities, and designing computer "intelligence" (Thompson, 1986). Perhaps, someday, memory will give up its secrets. That day will have been well worth waiting for.

For Critical Analysis

1. Once the biology of memory is understood, do you think that it might someday be possible to add mini-computer chips directly to our brains so that they interacted with our biology and boosted our intelligence beyond anything that we might imagine? Would you like your mind altered in such a way (consider the possibility of being given the knowledge and reasoning of a Ph.D. with just one

surgical operation)? How might the surgical implantation of preprogrammed memory chips into human brains be a grave concern for societies of the future?

2. Sometimes I play a game with my class. It goes like this: Starting with the last row and working forward, each person in class is required to say his or her full name (first & last) out loud while the other students watch. However, before each student can say his or her name, that student must repeat the first and last names of everyone who has gone before, and do it in correct order. As it turns out, just about every student is successful (except when trying to remember the last few names of the sequence, the names that they have only heard once or twice). In the short space of an hour class, almost everyone will easily learn 50 first and last names and will also know each person by name, even if after the game all the students move to different seats and sit in a different order. Everyone is typically very surprised by this amazing, hitherto unknown memory power that they have discovered. What does this tell you about people's knowledge about how their memories work? How might this little game have changed your view of yourself and your potential to be a good student? What does this game tell you about the effect of repetition on the biology of long-term memory?

TWO MEMORIES ARE BETTER THAN ONE

As we discussed in Chapter 6, behaviorists argue that we can understand human behavior as the result of numerous conditioned responses. Cognitive theorists, on the other hand, emphasize that people and some animals think; that is, they act on (behave according to) their mental images and understandings of the world.

As memory researchers worked to uncover the different areas of the brain involved in memories, a startling possibility began to emerge. Although the research is just beginning, it appears that there are at least two distinct kinds of memory, which provides support for *both* the behavioral and cognitive views. They are referred to as **procedural memory** and **declarative memory,** or, more commonly, skill and fact memory (see Figure 7.3).

Procedural memory "is accessible only through performance, by engaging in the skills or operations in which the knowledge is embedded" (Squire, 1986, p. 1614). Procedural memory, then, appears to be acquired according to the principles of classical and operant conditioning described in Chapter 6, that is, through practice and reinforcement.

Declarative memory, on the other hand, is "accessible to conscious awareness, and it includes the facts, episodes, lists, and routes of everyday life. It can be declared, that is, brought to mind verbally . . . or nonverbally as an image" (Squire, 1986, p. 1614). Cognitive knowledge such as mental maps (see Chapter 6) or the kinds of abilities needed for thinking and problem solving (discussed in Chapter 8) are thought to be held in declarative memory. Procedural memory may develop before declarative memory, which would help to explain why we are able to learn or be conditioned as infants, but as adults do not have memories of faces or events from our infancy (Herbert, 1983a).

Perhaps the distinction between the two memories doesn't surprise you. After all, it does seem reasonable that separate memory systems might be involved in such different memories as (1) the amount of tension to place on the lenses of your eyes in order to focus an image and (2) the fact that George Washington is dead.

PROCEDURAL MEMORY
The memory associated with recall of muscular or glandular responses that have been conditioned. Procedural memories are acquired slowly with practice. This memory is required to recall the skills necessary for object manipulation and learned physical activity. It is sometimes called skill or motor memory. Such skills as playing billiards, reading mirror writing, and playing the piano require procedural memory.

DECLARATIVE MEMORY
The memory associated with cognitive skills not directly attributable to muscular or glandular responses. The complete memory may be acquired through a single exposure, but practice is beneficial. Declarative memory is required to recall factual information, and it is sometimes called fact memory. The ability to recognize a face, recall a number, or recall any verbal or sensory information requires declarative memory.

SEMANTIC MEMORY
Memory of meanings, including all factual information of a general nature such as knowledge that the English alphabet contains twenty-six letters.

EPISODIC MEMORY
Memories stored with mental "tags" about where, when and how you acquired the information. It mostly contains personal information, but also includes "flashbulb memories."

FIGURE 7.3

The two kinds of memory.

A MODEL OF DECLARATIVE MEMORY

Unlike a theory, a model is never considered right or wrong. It is simply a picture or a depiction used to clarify an idea. Figure 7.4 is a model of human declarative memory; its only purpose is to help you organize your thinking about memory. In fact, it is not clearly agreed that this is the proper way to describe memory. Some researchers argue that declarative memory should really be considered to be two distinctly different memory systems called **semantic** and **episodic memory**. Semantic memory would include basic factual knowledge, such as George Washington is dead, while episodic memory would encompass personal knowledge about

DECLARATIVE (FACT) MEMORY

Brain Pathways Involved

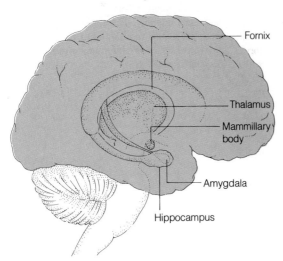

- Fornix
- Thalamus
- Mammillary body
- Amygdala
- Hippocampus

Information Involved

Remembering telephone numbers

Remembering faces

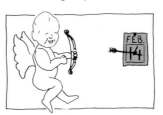

Remembering special dates

Visualizing maps and locations

PROCEDURAL (SKILL) MEMORY

Brain Pathways Involved

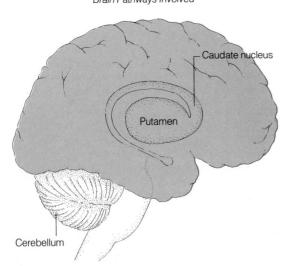

- Caudate nucleus
- Putamen
- Cerebellum

Skills Involved

Playing a musical instrument

Reading mirror-reversed words

Doing physical activities and sports

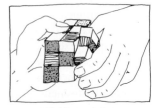

Solving puzzles

228

yourself, your family, and your experiences. The rationale for dividing declarative memory into these two types comes from the fact that in some forms of amnesia, all of a person's personal knowledge is lost (Who am I?) while basic knowledge of things such as the alphabet is maintained. This implies that two distinct kinds of declarative memory may exist.

Furthermore, some amnesiacs who totally lose great blocks of memory may have near normal recall if they are given little hints or partial images about what they can't remember. This has led some researchers to argue that there is yet another kind of distinct memory, called **priming memory,** which helps us remember from little prompts, whereas a different kind of declarative memory works to recall information when there are no hints or prompts available (Tulving & Schacter, 1990). As you can see, the field of memory is still wide open with many differing opinions and views.

For our part in this text, we will stick to the basic outline of declarative memory shown in Figure 7.4. Declarative memory is believed to be composed of three major parts: sensory memory, short-term memory, and long-term memory. We will examine each in turn.

Sensory Memory

The world is filled with sights, sounds, and many other kinds of sensory stimulation, but you don't remember all of them. When you first receive a particular stimulus, it is held for only a fraction of a second in what is known as the **sensory memory,** or sensory register. Unless you pay attention to the sensation and encode (store) it successfully into your short-term memory, the sensation will decay and be lost. Decay can occur within just one-fourth of a second after a sensation is registered in the sensory memory. In other words, if you don't pay attention to a sensation, it is lost almost immediately (Sperling, 1960).

Short-Term Memory

Short-term memory (STM) is the working, active memory. In fact, many researchers prefer the term *working memory* to STM, because it gives a better picture of what is really going on at that level. Using a computer model for a moment, you

PRIMING MEMORY
A hypothetical memory thought possibly to exist as a distinct entity because in certain cases of amnesia, a form of declarative memory appears to yield access via small prompts, thereby giving it its name "priming" memory.

SENSORY MEMORY
The first stage in the declarative memory process. New information is held in the sensory memory for less than one second and will decay unless it is attended to, that is, encoded and placed in the short-term memory. Sensory memory is also called the sensory register.

SHORT-TERM MEMORY
Declarative memory that has a limited storage capacity and a short duration. It is often called working memory because it must call up items from long-term memory so that the items can be examined. Information encoded from the sensory memory is held in the short-term memory and will decay unless the information is rehearsed or stored in the long-term memory.

FIGURE 7.4

A model of human declarative memory. In the first stage of memory, sensory input registers in the sensory memory. Sensory memories decay within a fraction of a second unless they are attended to. Paying attention to sensory memories encodes them into the short-term memory, where they can be held by rehearsal or lost through decay or displacement. To enter the long-term memory, short-term memories must be stored. These stored long-term memories can be retrieved to the short-term memory for examination. After examination, the memories then return to long-term memory. Memories can also be lost through retrieval failure and perhaps through decay.

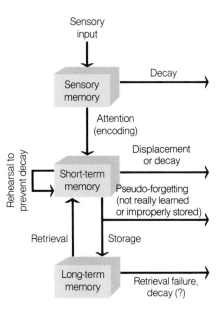

REHEARSAL

A process by which memories can be held in the short-term memory for relatively long periods. In rehearsal, an item is repeated over and over so that it is not lost. This technique may eventually result in storage of the item in the long-term memory.

LONG-TERM MEMORY

Memory with virtually unlimited storage capacity, in which short-term memories may be stored for long periods, even a lifetime.

SERIAL POSITION EFFECT

A phenomenon in verbal learning. Items at the beginning or at the end of a long series are more easily remembered; items in the middle are the hardest to recall.

might think of the STM as the material that can be retrieved onto the computer's display screen at a given time. Information held in STM is active information—information to which you are paying attention. As its name suggests, however, this memory is limited: If the information is new, it can be held in STM for only a brief time, and whether the information is new (that is, coming from the sensory memory) or old (that is, retrieved from long-term memory for examination), only a certain amount of it can be held in your mind at any given time. Most people's STM can hold about seven "items," give or take two.

For example, consider what happens when you look up a new number in the telephone book. As you close the book, you must remember all seven digits in order to dial the telephone. As you can see by looking at the model of human memory in Figure 7.4, there is only one way you can keep the information in STM for longer than approximately 30 seconds. This is by using **rehearsal**—by saying the number over and over again to yourself, constantly restoring it in your STM.

Has the following ever happened to you? You repeat a telephone number to yourself again and again until you dial it. Once you've dialed the number, you no longer rehearse it. But the line is busy. Guess what? Back to the telephone book to look it up again! Typically, the new information in STM was lost because it is no longer being rehearsed or was not stored in **long-term memory** (LTM), that is, it was not memorized.

Perhaps it's good that we forget new information that we need to use only once. How would you like to store everything you have ever known—every telephone number, every street address, every new acquaintance's name? Interestingly, some people have a poor ability to forget information once they are exposed to it. They easily transfer any information held in their STM into their LTM for storage. This is not a happy state of affairs. Such individuals find their minds cluttered with large amounts of useless information that obscure more timely and important facts (Luria, 1968).

DISPLACEMENT.   What happens if you overload your short-term memory by trying to place 20 items into it? You are likely to remember a few of the first and a few of the last items of the list, about seven altogether. The middle items, however, whether meaningful or not, are difficult to recall (see Figure 7.5). The first few items may be easier to recall because you tried to rehearse them, knowing that many more were on the way. But soon you became overwhelmed by the large number of items and lost most of them. When you reached the end of the list, you remembered the last few items because you had just recently been exposed to them. This sequence of remembering is known as the **serial position effect**. The

FIGURE 7.5

Middle items in a series, whether meaningful or not, are the most difficult to recall. This phenomenon is known as the serial position effect. (SOURCE: *Adapted from Postman & Rau, 1957.*)

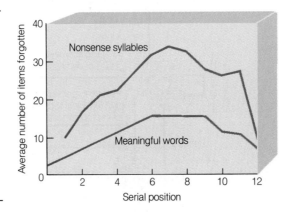

items that you lose undergo **displacement** as other items are retained. The serial position effect also has been observed in other species. For instance, one group of researchers observed the effect among pigeons and monkeys that were reinforced for recalling a series of travel slides (some researcher appears finally to have found a captive audience for his family's trip to the Grand Canyon) (Wright, Santiago, Sands, Kendrick, & Cook, 1985).

Just as material in the sensory memory must be encoded into STM to be retained, material from STM must be stored in LTM in such a way that it can later be retrieved; otherwise the information will be lost, and lost rapidly. Because of this, you can fall into a trap without realizing it, thinking that you have learned much more information than you really have. It's like putting items into a sack without knowing that there is a hole in the bottom. Unbeknownst to you, as you are putting some things in, others are falling out. This is why it's important to go back and test yourself on material after some time has passed. In this way, you can be certain that the material has settled into LTM and that you can retrieve it—that it has not simply been held for a moment in STM and then lost without your knowledge.

Chunking

In 1956, George Miller used the term **chunk** to describe a unit of memory. He agreed that the STM could hold only about seven *meaningless* items of information—such as the digits of a telephone number—but he also argued that more information could be held in STM at one time if many "items" were chunked together. The basis of his argument was that about 7 *meanings* could be held in the STM at once, regardless of how many items were involved in each meaning (Miller, 1956).

Interestingly, chunking isn't a special skill possessed only by humans. Other species can chunk. Consider the fact that a pigeon's STM can hold about five items (human STM has a greater capacity than pigeon STM by a whole two, count 'em, *two*, items). Psychologist Herbert Terrace reported that pigeons were able to remember about five colors or five shapes. However, the birds were able to recall both five colors and five shapes if the colors and shapes were chunked by presenting them together as five colored shapes (such as an orange circle or a blue square) (Terrace, 1987). It is not known, however, whether animals ever chunk items that haven't been especially arranged for them by a researcher.

Long-Term Memory

To store information for days, weeks, years, or a lifetime, we must store it in long-term memory (LTM). It is estimated that the LTM can store about 100 trillion bits of information, which would make a large computer's mere billions appear practically amnesiac.

To examine an item stored in LTM, we must first **retrieve** it into the STM, or working memory. There, approximately seven chunks of stored LTM items can be examined at any one time. Chunks displaced from working memory (by new chunks called up from LTM) return to LTM storage and can be retrieved again.

A memory held in STM can be stored in LTM in various ways. Rehearsing an item (such as a telephone number) many times may cause it to be stored in LTM, but generally items that have the most meaning are the most likely to be stored. Sensations that encompass low levels of information are not as likely to be remembered. For example, once you have finished reading a novel, you are likely to recall the gist of it, but it would be rare for you to recall the exact wording of particular sentences. Things with low levels of information, such as the exact

DISPLACEMENT
The loss of an item of information from short-term memory because of the addition of a new item of information.

CHUNK
A bit of information that can be held in short-term memory. Chunks are not defined by the number of items they contain, such as letters or syllables, but rather by their meaning and organization. One number can be a chunk, but so can an entire sentence if it has a single meaning.

RETRIEVE
To bring material from the long-term memory to the working memory so that it can be examined.

CONCEPT REVIEW

Chunking is a difficult concept to grasp until you've tried it for yourself.

Look at the four "items" shown below in capital letters. They are called nonsense syllables because they have no meaning. STM should be able to hold roughly seven of these meaningless "items," give or take two. Say them to yourself, then close your eyes and try to repeat them.

DAK   GIR   JOP   FID

You should have had no difficulty. Now, try six nonsense syllables:

DIT   LON   KIF   JAT   WUB   BIP

Some people are able to remember six nonsense syllables, but most can't. It's hard to hold that much information in STM. Or is it? Although you may have had some trouble holding six meaningless syllables, you're not going to have any trouble repeating six *meaningful* one-syllable words:

STONE   BRIDGE   PATH   HOP   CUBE   LINE

Why are six one-word syllables easier than six nonsense syllables? It's because they have a meaning and meanings are easier to remember.

How far can the STM memory be pushed? Try nine one-syllable words:

SHOE   MONK   BLADE   JUMP   PLAY
HATE   RUST   SOUP   POND

It's likely that nine one-syllable words have pushed your STM too far. So that's the limit of STM. Or is it? Now, let's *chunk* 12 syllables (12 items) by placing them into three words (three meanings, or chunks).

CANADIAN   TESTIMONY   PSYCHOLOGY

It's easy because you are holding on to three chunks (meanings), rather than 12 syllables (items). Not too difficult. But if you try eight four-syllable words, you're likely to have a little trouble:

DECLARATION   MINORITY   PESSIMISTIC   CONDITIONAL
INFURIATE   AMERICAN   SYMBOLISM   CONSTERNATION

How about 19 words in your STM! Easy, if you break a 19-word sentence into five chunks:

MARTIN   LUTHER   KING,   WINNER   OF   THE   NOBEL
PEACE   PRIZE,   GAVE   A   SPEECH   AT
THE   LINCOLN   MEMORIAL   ABOUT   CIVIL   RIGHTS.

You could do it because your STM was holding five chunks (man's name, kind of prize, what he gave, where he gave it, and subject of speech), not 19 items (Anderson, 1980).

---

wording of sentences, or which style of typeface was used, are useful for processing the information, but are then typically discarded from the memory.

Of course, there are techniques you can master that will facilitate both storage and retrieval. And, interestingly, some storing may occur automatically without any particular effort on our part. Usually, **automatic storage** occurs for meaningful and important experiences, but sometimes not. No doubt you have clear memories of odds and ends from years ago that are of little interest and that may have led you to wonder, "Why in the world do I remember that?"

To store many of the things we wish to remember, however, we must make a concerted effort. In making such an effort, a number of memory techniques can be useful. Let's take a look at some of these.

MEANING AND MEMORY. Most of us complain about forgetting from time to time, but we can learn strategies to improve memory. You have seen that the STM can hold about seven chunks of information and, as you have experienced, the more meaningful a chunk is, the more easily the information can be stored. It seems, then, that our memories rely on meaning. Remember Mr. M. D. from the Prologue, and you will recall that the brain appears to prefer an organization with meaning, even to the point of storing items with like meanings together, as one might find entries organized in a thesaurus.

Without a meaning, an item is difficult to remember. Unfortunately, we're bombarded with the meaningless each and every day. For instance, although the number eight means something—it means eight objects, or two units of four, or four units of two, what does it mean when it's used in a telephone number, such as 831-9011? Eight in this instance is merely a place holder. It may just as well be a nonsense syllable. No wonder it's hard to remember telephone numbers.

Look at Figure 7.6. When people simply study this figure and later try to redraw it, their drawings are not very accurate. That's because, like the number eight in a telephone number, this drawing is meaningless. But suppose I told you that this was a midget playing a trombone in a telephone booth? As soon as I told you this, the figure would take on a meaning. Individuals who have such an image in mind are much better able to recall the item when tested later than are those who simply look at it and try to memorize it (Bower, Karlin, & Dueck, 1975).

MNEMONICS. A memory aid such as the one just used in known as a **mnemonic**. A mnemonic is any kind of remembering system or memory aid. There are many popular mnemonic devices. One of the oldest is known as the **method of loci**, which works well for lists of 10 to 15 items and is very easy to use. Think of a familiar pathway, perhaps the entrance to your home, and then think of 10 or 15 items that appear in a certain order along that path. Associate each item on your list with one of the familiar things along that path. If you are going grocery shopping, imagine bread in your mailbox, broken eggs on the walkway, an orange where the doorknob is, and so on. You'll find, after you have made the associations, that it's relatively easy to recall your whole shopping list just by walking down that path again in your mind's eye and stopping at the different loci to recall the associations made at each.

Mnemonics may not be totally new to you. Did you ever have to memorize the colors of the rainbow in the right order—red, orange, yellow, green, blue, indigo, and violet? You may have been taught the mnemonic aid Roy G. Biv. Budding musicians learn "Every Good Boy Does Fine" (EGBDF) to represent the lines of the treble musical staff. William James once said that there were three ways to remember things: mechanical methods, which require intensive study and repetition, such as the way children learn the alphabet; judicious methods, which are based on logic, classification, and analysis; and ingenious methods, which include the mnemonic devices we've been discussing and which give meaning to the abstract. Other interesting ways of improving memory also have been developed (see Focus on the Future).

THEORIES OF DECLARATIVE MEMORY

Memory is a term that acts like an umbrella—it covers a lot. Although we have said that there are two major memory systems (procedural and declarative), the

AUTOMATIC STORAGE
The spontaneous placement of a sensation or experience into the long-term memory without effort or intent.

MNEMONIC
Any device or technique for improving memory.

METHOD OF LOCI
A mnemonic technique in which items are associated with positions or things along a familiar route in order to make them more easily remembered.

FIGURE 7.6

This figure is easier to remember if it's made meaningful.

SNIFF—OH, NOW I REMEMBER!

In 1976, researcher David de Wied accidentally discovered something that seemed to come from the pages of science fiction—a "memory pill." He injected some rats with the hormone **vasopressin** and found to his surprise that they became easier to train and had better memories (de Wied, van Wimersma Greidanus, Bohus, Urban, & Gispen, 1976). Further research has shown that injections aren't necessary. Vasopressin can be put into a nasal spray and sniffed.

In 1978, a Belgian and Swiss team compared experimental and placebo groups of men between the ages of 50 and 65 years who were suffering from memory loss. The experimental group received three exposures to vasopressin in nasal spray each day, and the control group received three exposures to a placebo nasal spray. The experimental group clearly did better on tests that measured attention, recognition, learning, concentration, and immediate memory (Legros et al., 1978). Later in 1978, four amnesiac patients in Spain—three car-accident victims and one suffering the effects of alcoholism—were treated with vasopressin. All four were reported to have regained their memories within 5 to 9 days, which is much faster than would have been thought possible. Following is a brief account of one of these patients:

The third patient, a man aged 21, presented with severe retrograde amnesia [loss of recent memories often brought on by a traumatic event] after a car accident 6 months previously (coma for 15 days). He could remember nothing of the 3 months before the accident and the 3 1/2 months after it. Vasopressin was given by nasal spray (5 puffs or about 13.5 I.U. [international units] daily). After 1 day the patient could recall several features of the accident, and his memory rapidly im-

proved. By the fourth day of treatment he was even **hypermnesic.** Improvement progressed continuously, and by day 7 he had completely recovered his memory. His mood had improved, he became self-confident and slept well. When placebo was given in place of vasopressin, after 7 days, no change occurred, and his condition has remained satisfactory. (Oliveros et al., 1978, p. 42)

Herbert Weingartner and his colleagues at the National Institute of Mental Health went on to test vasopressin on healthy subjects, depressed subjects, and senile subjects. Some of the subjects received vasopressin; others were given a placebo. All took sniffs daily for 2 to 3 weeks, and every day they were tested for their ability to remember and learn. All three groups of volunteers given vasopressin significantly improved their learning and memory, while those who received the placebo did not (Weingartner et al., 1981).

Vasopressin stimulates the sympathetic nervous system, increases blood pressure, and inhibits kidney functioning. In fact, following the initial reports of vasopressin's effectiveness, some researchers argued that it was not really a specific memory-boosting agent but rather was simply a stimulant to the nervous system, which helped people to remember better, as any stimulant might (Koob, LeMoal, & Bloom, 1981).

In 1983, however, investigators discovered that vasopressin could be broken down into a number of constituents. Some of these building blocks of vasopressin were found to facilitate learning and memory in animals but did not have the stimulating effect on the nervous system and blood pressure that the entire vasopressin molecule did (Burbach, Kovacs, de Wied, van Nispen, & Greven, 1983). This

finding demonstrated that the memory-boosting ability of vasopressin was independent of its stimulating effect on the nervous system.

How vasopressin works to help people remember is not understood. There may be some very important applications for memory-boosting substances, however. Among the latest candidates is a drug called vinpocetine (Begley, Springen, Katz, Hager, & Jones, 1986). Vinpocetine has been able to help victims of strokes recover their memories faster than might otherwise be possible.

Perhaps even more striking is the ability to boost memory through the use of transplanted brain tissue. In one study, researchers gave rats alcohol as their only liquid in an otherwise normal diet. After some time, these rats began to suffer the same kinds of memory loss observed to occur among human alcoholics. To put it bluntly, their brains had been pickled. But by taking tissue from a healthy rat fetus, tissue rich in the neurotransmitter acetylcholine, and transplanting it into the damaged rat brains, these "pickled rats" were once again able to recall new information, and do it as well as control rats could (Arendt, Allen, Sinden, & Schugens, 1988).

Some scientists are already calling for a serious evaluation of the effects of such substances and techniques on society. They argue that memory enhancement, once perfected, should be made widely available, because if only the privileged have access to it, this may exacerbate the differences between social classes or between wealthy and less-developed nations (Rosenzweig, 1984). How do you think memory-boosting chemicals or techniques should be used? (Do you have a test coming up soon?)

truth is that no one really knows how many distinct memory systems there might be (Tulving, 1985). The following discussion highlights efforts to understand this concept we call declarative memory. Keep in mind that the ancient Greeks believed that there were only four elements: earth, water, air, and fire. Modern chemists find that idea "quaint." No doubt, future researchers will also find our current understanding of memory similarly quaint.

The Dual-Code Theory

One popular theory of memory, the **dual-code theory,** argues that declarative memories contain both sensory and verbal information (Paivio, 1971). The basis of this idea is that people can often remember pictures better than they can remember words. Try the test in Figure 7.7. People with good visual memory will remember most or all of the items. In fact, for about 1 percent of adults, the recollection of the image will be so strong that the memory will seem almost as sharp as if they were still looking at the picture. Such an unusual and powerful picture in the mind's eye is known as an **eidetic image.** An eidetic image may last up to 4 minutes with crystal clarity (Haber, 1969). The ability to use eidetic imagery is known informally as photographic memory and, interestingly, is more common in children, although no one knows why.

Now look at the following three-syllable nonsense word; you may store it as a visual image, but you are more likely to break it down into syllables and store it verbally.

KARNOBLIK

You probably remember it as KAR-NO-BLIK, using a verbal as opposed to a visual image. The dual-code theory argues that, instead of using sensory codes, you also can use verbal codes (language) for storing memories (Paivio & Desrochers, 1980; Paivio & Lambert, 1981). In this way, you can store information either as sensory experience or as words.

VASOPRESSIN
A neuropeptide known to affect memory. Vasopressin nasal spray has been used clinically to improve memory.

HYPERMNESIC
Having an unusually exact or vivid memory.

DUAL-CODE THEORY
A theory of memory holding that memories contain both sensory and verbal information and that this information is stored directly, without being transformed.

EIDETIC IMAGE
The formation and reproduction of accurate mental images of objects not currently present. Possessors of these images are said to have photographic memories.

FIGURE 7.7

How good is your photographic memory? Look at this photograph for 30 seconds (don't name the objects), close the book, and see how many objects you can remember.

PROPOSITIONS

The smallest units of information about which it makes sense to render a judgment of true or false. For example, "red apple" is not a proposition. However, "The apple is red" is a proposition, since the statement is either true or false.

PROPOSITIONAL NETWORK THEORY

The memory theory holding that sensory information and words are transformed into propositions in order to be stored in memory.

NODES

In the propositional network theory of memory, the individual parts of the proposition. Nodes serve as junctions and access points in the memory.

LINKS

In the propositional network theory of memory, the pathways between the nodes of the proposition. If two nodes are not directly linked, then recalling the information at one of the nodes will not lead directly to recalling the information at the other node.

FIGURE 7.8

Proposition 1: Jack gave a Chevrolet to Mary. This proposition contains five nodes. A node is a concept or an item of information. Each node is connected to the proposition by different kinds of links. (Links are italicized; nodes are in roman print.) Thinking about any of the nodes (Jack, Mary, Chevrolet, something that happened in the past, or giving) may bring to mind the entire proposition. The arrows do not imply the direction in which thoughts must flow (links are usually two-way streets), but only show the propositions to which nodes belong when propositions are combined in a complex elaboration, as you will see later.

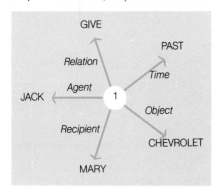

It also may be that both images and words are stored together and are interconnected in some yet-to-be-discovered generic memory (Marschark, Richman, Yuille, & Hunt, 1987).

Keep dual-code theory in mind; we will return to it later. First, however, let's examine propositional network theory, which is rapidly becoming the most accepted explanation for how declarative memories are organized and represented in the brain.

Propositional Network Theory

Although there is evidence that some memories may be stored separately as images or words, it appears that much of our memory is based on a network of abstract representations that we have tied to meanings, rather than to sensory or verbal information. For example, suppose a friend of yours came up to you on the street and told you a long-winded story about what happened the day before. If someone else asked you to explain what your friend told you, what would you say? Would you repeat everything your friend said, word for word? No, you would use your own words. In such instances, your memory stores *meaning*, not words or sensations (Wanner, 1968).

The concept of a memory network of meanings is not new. The physiological foundations of such a network were described by Donald Hebb in 1949. He argued that memories must somehow be fixed directly within the nerve pathways of the brain. Hebb believed that synapses in the brain were altered by the continuous flow of electrical impulses and that when the impulses died down the changes in the synapses remained, creating a network of neurons that stored specific memories. He argued that activating one or two of the neurons in the network could trigger others, thereby bringing stored memories back to mind. As you have read, modern researchers are still pursuing that rich line of thought—with results.

The most popular theory about how meaning is represented in memory is based on **propositions** (Anderson, 1983; Anderson & Bower, 1973; Clark, 1974; Fredericksen, 1975; Kintsch, 1974; Norman & Rumelhart, 1975; Oden, 1987). The word *proposition* is borrowed from logic theory. A proposition is "the smallest unit about which it makes sense to make the judgment true or false" (Anderson, 1980, p. 102). For example, consider the following sentence: "Jack gave a new Chevrolet to Mary, who is his fiancee." This sentence can be broken into a number of simpler ideas, all of which are implied by the original sentence. These include: "Jack gave the Chevrolet to Mary;" "The Chevrolet was new;" "Mary is Jack's fiancee." These are considered propositions because they are either true or false, whereas just "the Chevrolet" could not be a proposition.

Storing something by what it *means*, rather than by how it is stated or by how it looks, requires a propositional representation rather than a visual or verbal representation. **Propositional network theory** argues that if we wish to recall how something looked or was stated, we must first locate (recall) its meaning and from there reconstruct the actual sensory or verbal representation.

If the LTM is filled with many propositions—that is, bits of simple meaning—then there must be a way in which the bits can interact. In a propositional network, each proposition is represented by a circle that is connected to the components of the proposition by arrows. The components are called **nodes,** and the arrows connecting the nodes are called **links.** Each arrow is labeled to indicate what kind of link it is. In Figure 7.8 you see the proposition "Jack gave a Chevrolet to Mary" as it might appear in the LTM, with the different nodes (components) connected by links (relationships). Perhaps this arrangement approximates the biochemical organization of this memory.

In Figure 7.9 are two other propositions, "The Chevrolet is new" and "Mary is Jack's fiancee." In Figure 7.10 the three propositions are joined. By starting at the node "Mary," that is, at one of the places in your memory where you have stored the name "Mary," you can "travel" in many directions, for instance, to the nodes "fiancee," "Jack," or "Chevrolet," because they are all linked to "Mary." Once you reach the node "Chevrolet," you can then travel down a link to the node "new." If information is organized like this in your LTM, then thinking of Mary may remind you that she is Jack's fiancee and that she received a Chevrolet, and thinking of Chevrolet may then trigger the recollection that the Chevrolet was new. To recall a particular node, you may need to "travel" to a number of other nodes; one recollection is likely to trigger another.

Memories seem to be linked in different ways. Some nodes are very close and strongly linked to other nodes, so if you remember one, you are likely to remember the others. Then again, some nodes may be far away from others or poorly linked, in which case remembering one node helps you very little in recalling the other ones. For instance, recalling that the Soviet flag is red, may not be of much help if you are trying to remember where you left your car keys, because the proposition "The soviet flag is red" is probably not closely linked to the location of your keys, whereas recalling the furniture in your kitchen might tip you off, assuming that you left your keys in or near it.

Digging into your memory is much like parachuting into a city. If you land near your target, you can reach it quickly. Otherwise, it may take you a long time, by way of a number of complex routes, to get where you want to be. Memory, of course, is bound to be even more complex in its terrain than are the streets of a city, because it is most likely laid out within the brain in three dimensions.

Propositional Networks and the Dual-Code Theory

So far, all the propositions that have been described to explain the organization of declarative memory have dealt with verbal information. What about visual or other sensory information? Is it organized as the dual-code theory argues, in some unique or special way that is distinct from the organization of verbal information? To examine this question, researcher John Anderson had artists construct faces that were combinations of different eyes, chins, hair, and mouths. Mixing and matching the facial parts, they created a number of different faces. By carefully investigating the way subjects' knowledge about each face portion was stored in the subjects' memories, and by carefully testing how they retrieved this information, Anderson was able to show that "the same retrieval processes that have been documented with verbal material also extend to pictorial material" (Anderson, 1983, p. 28). In other words, visual images also appear to be stored in three-dimensional network form.

There is other experimental evidence that visual memories may be laid out in a three-dimensional arrangement. For instance, when subjects were asked to create an imaginary space around themselves and then to fill that space with various imaginary objects, it was discovered that items imagined to be in front of them could be recalled faster than items imagined as being behind them (Franklin & Tversky, 1990). This research implies the existence of a mental representation connected and linked in a way that is similar to the real personal space around us. Even in our imaginations, then, it takes longer to see something "behind" us than to look at something right in "front" of us.

So, while sensory and verbal information may be stored in different locations in the brain, the underlying storage mechanism may be very similar. They both appear to be assembled in complex three-dimensional networks. Should other sensory mem-

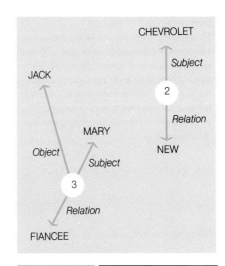

FIGURE 7.9

Proposition 2: The Chevrolet is new.
Proposition 3: Mary is Jack's fiancée.

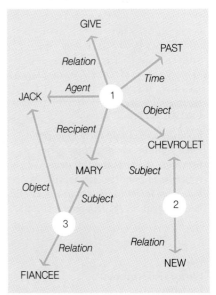

FIGURE 7.10

The three propositions combined.

237

ories (such as acoustic or tactile) be demonstrated to be stored in network form, it would certainly indicate that this format is the brain's major way of organizing memory information, regardless of whether the information is verbal or sensory. The dual-code theory may turn out to be not so "dual" after all (Babbitt, 1982).

FORGETTING

You are not always able to retrieve information that you put into your LTM. Why not? If it's there, why can't you get to it?

Decay and Loss

The first reason for forgetting is a simple one: The information may no longer be in your LTM. Although some researchers believe that LTM items are permanent (Anderson, 1980), others have concluded that some of them may decay and be lost (Loftus & Loftus, 1980). To date, all the biochemical theories of memory support the idea that LTM items can decay, if for no other reason than that any chemical arrangement might, under certain circumstances, break down or become rearranged. Perhaps the LTM items most likely to be lost are chemically weak; that is, they were not extremely important or were not well rehearsed.

A good example of the loss of unimportant information can be found in the first memory experiment conducted by Hermann von Ebbinghaus in 1885. Ebbinghaus memorized a list of things and then retested his recollection at different intervals. What he obtained is known as a forgetting curve (see Figure 7.11). For fun, you might repeat his experiment on yourself and observe the results. You should find that Ebbinghaus's forgetting curve is as accurate today as ever, because your own score is not likely to be much different than his was.

Hermann Ebbinghaus (1850–1909)

Interference Effects

Sometimes, when we try to retrieve a memory from LTM, certain experiences can interfere with the retrieval. The influences of these experiences are known collectively as **interference effects.**

PROACTIVE INTERFERENCE. What happens if the nodes you choose as an entry point into your memory network lead you in the wrong direction? Suppose you

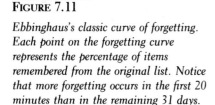

FIGURE 7.11

Ebbinghaus's classic curve of forgetting. Each point on the forgetting curve represents the percentage of items remembered from the original list. Notice that more forgetting occurs in the first 20 minutes than in the remaining 31 days.

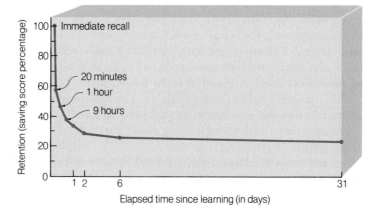

have a new telephone number. Whenever you want to think of your new telephone number, you begin a search in the memory network for the node that holds the number. This old search pattern (looking for your telephone number) has been activated so many times that the search for your new number may lead you to your old number. You know that you have a new telephone number, but you can remember only the old one. What you are experiencing is **proactive interference.** Think of the LTM as a network of streets running through a city to different locations—streets that crisscross each other. If you are used to driving down three or four streets to get to a particular place but now have to get to another place by using the same streets, it's easy, if you're not thinking, to take the wrong turn near the end of your route and go to the old location. Previously learned material is somehow interfering with your ability to retain or recall something new. A similar interference effect also can occur for procedural memory. In that case, it is called *negative transfer of learning;* an example might be trying to learn a new arrangement of letters on a typewriter keyboard *after* you had mastered the regular keyboard. You can imagine the problems you'd face!

PROACTIVE INTERFERENCE
The process by which previously learned material interferes with the ability to learn something new.

RETROACTIVE INTERFERENCE
The process by which learning something new interferes with the ability to recall previously learned information.

TIP-OF-THE-TONGUE PHENOMENON
The experience of being almost able to recall a certain bit of information. You sense that the information is there, you can almost "feel" it, and yet you cannot grasp it.

RETROACTIVE INTERFERENCE. If you practice your new number often enough and are required to recall it under many different circumstances, you will rearrange your memory network so that the new number is now associated with many nodes. Eventually, the links to the new number will be *stronger* than those to the old one, and you'll tend to retrieve the new number when you try to recall your telephone exchange. Once you have thoroughly learned your new number, it's often hard to retrieve your old one again. This is known as **retroactive interference**; that is, learning something new interferes with the recall of old memories (see Figure 7.12).

The Tip-of-the-Tongue Phenomenon

Besides proactive and retroactive interference, other things can get in the way of LTM retrieval. Sometimes, we can't seem to retrieve a bit of information that we're sure we have stored because we can't find a path through the network to the information. This frustration has been known for many years as the **tip-of-the-tongue phenomenon.** William James described the experience in this way:

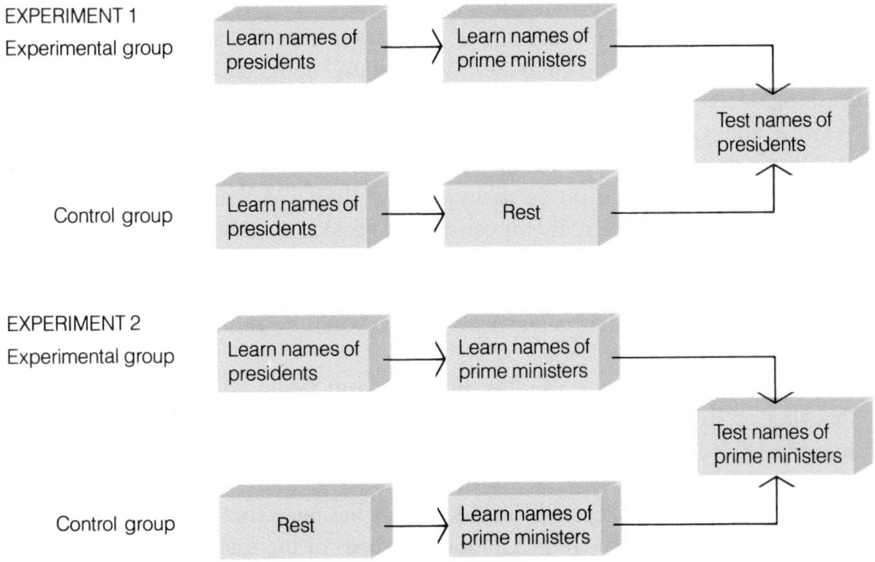

EXPERIMENT 1
Experimental group
Learn names of presidents
Learn names of prime ministers
Test names of presidents
Control group
Learn names of presidents
Rest
EXPERIMENT 2
Experimental group
Learn names of presidents
Learn names of prime ministers
Test names of prime ministers
Control group
Rest
Learn names of prime ministers

FIGURE 7.12

Experimental arrangements designed to test interference effects. Experiment 1 tests for retroactive interference, while experiment 2 tests for proactive interference. If interference effects occur, the experimental groups will have lower test scores than the control groups have.

RETRIEVAL CUE
Any stimulus that can help you gain access to a memory.

Suppose we try to recall a forgotten name. The state of our consciousness is peculiar: There is a gap therein; but no mere gap. It is a gap that is intensively active. A sort of wraith of the name is in it, beckoning us in a given direction, making us at moments tingle with the sense of our closeness and then letting us sink back without the longed-for term. If wrong names are proposed to us, this singularly defined gap acts immediately so as to negate them. They do not fit into this mold. And the gap of one word does not feel like the gap of another, all empty of content as both might seem necessarily to be when described as gaps. (James, 1890)

The tip-of-the-tongue experience is particularly frustrating because we feel so close to the information sought. We even seem to know things about what we can't remember. We seem to be actively searching through our LTM network for an association or link that will take us to the right node.

There are some specific methods we can use to make the needed association. Suppose you can't remember the name of a particular person, but it's on the tip of your tongue. How might you find the path that leads to the correct node containing the name? One way is to travel to related nodes to see whether there is a direct link from any of them to the node for which you are searching. For instance, you might reflect on a picture of that person or on the sound of that person's voice. Or you might proceed through the alphabet sounding out letters to see whether any of those sounds suddenly triggers the recall of the name. By selectively searching all the different accesses you might have to the necessary node, you may eventually find a retrieval cue or direct link.

Retrieval Cues

A **retrieval cue** can be a great help in getting at something that you can almost remember. This is why multiple-choice tests are easier than tests that require strict recall; the former are loaded with retrieval cues. Let's take a look at the difference between a recall versus a recognition test.

Here is a recall question: "Who was the president after Washington?" To answer this question, you need to activate the "Washington" node in your memory and travel from that point to the associations you have made with Washington. You may have many associations with Washington. But can you activate the link that will lead you to the node that holds the answer? Perhaps not. That link may be too weak or nonexistent.

How about a question that encompasses two points of memory access: "Was Adams the president after Washington?" Now you have two places from which to begin your search. You can go to the "Washington" node, check associations about Washington, and try to find a link that leads to Adams. Or you can start with the "Adams" node. If one of the things you know about Adams is that he came directly after Washington, then you can answer the question correctly.

Curiously, there seem to be many links in the LTM that are stronger in one direction than in the other. If you can't get from Washington to Adams, you may be able to get from Adams to Washington. By making the latter association, however, you strengthen the link from Washington to Adams; if you are asked again who was the next president after Washington, you'll be more likely to recall that Adams was.

Many things determine whether links between nodes will be strong or weak. Shocking or surprising events, either pleasant or unpleasant, usually create very strong links. If the event is powerful enough, a strong link will be created between nearly every associated event and the event itself. Whatever the powerful news (that Pearl Harbor has been attacked, John Kennedy has been shot, Neil Armstrong has just stepped on the moon, John Lennon has died, or the space shuttle Challenger has exploded), or whatever the personal shock, people probably can remember where they were standing, who and what were around them, and what others said. This effect is sometimes called **flashbulb memory** (Brown & Kulik, 1977).

Flashbulb memories may be particularly vivid because the hormone ACTH is secreted at times of stress; ACTH has been found to enhance memory formation by increasing attention (Sandman, George, Nolan, Van Riezen, & Kastin, 1975). Other substances, such as vasopressin and beta-endorphin, acting as hormones, may play an important role with ACTH in the creation of vivid memories (McGaugh, 1983; Bohus, Conti, Kovacs, & Versteeg, 1982). One of these is called cholecystokinin, or CCK. CCK is secreted during eating and has been found to act directly on nerve fibers associated with memory (Flood, Smith, & Morley, 1987). This mechanism may have evolved to help boost memories about where food was located, something that is obviously important to any species.

Flashbulb memories also may be vivid because we often bring them to mind (simply because they are so meaningful to us) and thereby rehearse them. Recalling them also links them to other events, which makes the flashbulb memories easier to find later; that is, they become less forgettable. Flashbulb memory, however, doesn't appear to be a special kind of memory. Flashbulb memories can fade over time, and in all other ways they behave like normal memories (Cohen, McCloskey, & Wible, 1988). They are considered exceptional only because they tend to be so vivid and because they are clearer than are our recollections of everyday events.

Reconstruction and Retrieval

Another way of "forgetting" LTM items isn't really forgetting; it just seems like it.

Sometimes we add our own inventions to our original store of *real* memories without realizing it. Such an addition is known as a **reconstruction.** One of the primary ways in which we create reconstructions is through the use of **scripts.** A script is a hypothetical memory organization that encompasses people's knowledge of the *typical* events in everyday experience (Abelson, 1981).

If an LTM item is not complete, we often fill it in with our script knowledge. If you have ever attended a wedding, you no doubt remember the bride being asked, "Do you take this man to be your lawfully wedded husband?" But think about it. Do you really *remember* that particular question, or are you using a script of weddings to fill in your recollection?

Look at Figure 7.13. You've certainly placed the visual image of a penny into your LTM. Or have you? Psychologist Elizabeth Loftus argues that our LTMs are filled with many errors and mistakes. Do you know which of the pennies in Figure 7.13 is the real one? A great number of people don't. If you're not sure, get a penny and check. If you were wrong, why were you wrong? Is it because you had "forgotten" what a penny looked like? More likely, it is because you never really knew. Just because you have a lot of experience with something doesn't mean that the whole experience was stored in long term memory.

Failure of Consolidation

Long-term memories may be lost through the failure of **consolidation.** Consolidation is a dynamic feature of LTM and is not well understood; it seems that after information is first put into the LTM, a certain amount of time is necessary for it to consolidate or to take its place in the memory (John, 1967); that is, information

FLASHBULB MEMORY
The vivid impression left on the memory by all of the stimuli associated with a shocking or surprising event.

RECONSTRUCTION
In memory, the placement into memory of an unconscious deduction or assumption of what one believes must have happened. Such created memories are often recalled as though they were recollections of actual events.

SCRIPT
In cognitive study, one's knowledge of the appropriate events that should occur in a particular social setting and of how one might carry them out. This comprises knowledge of who is expected to do what to whom as well as when, where, and why. A script would include such typical behaviors as those expected of a person visiting a restaurant or going to a movie.

CONSOLIDATION
The strengthening process through which memory traces, or engrams, must go before they can become a fixed part of the long-term memory.

RETROGRADE AMNESIA
An amnesia brought on by a sudden shock or trauma that causes events to be forgotten.

MOTIVATED FORGETTING
Purposeful forgetting in which memories are suppressed or repressed in order to fulfill unconscious desires to avoid the memories.

REPRESSION
A psychological process in which memories and motives are not permitted to enter consciousness but are operative at an unconscious level.

PSYCHOGENIC AMNESIA
A disorder involving selective memory loss for psychological reasons. The individual forgets, partially or totally, his or her past identity, but remembers nonthreatening aspects of life.

SOMATOGENIC AMNESIA
Disorders involving selective memory loss for physical reasons such as brain trauma, disease, or toxic exposure. The kind of memory loss depends on the type of injury or illness.

new to the LTM is somewhat fragile. It may even take as long as several years before the memory is firmly and totally implanted (consolidated) (Squire, 1986).

A number of things can interfere with the consolidation process. For instance, cigarette smoking is known to affect it. The active agent involved appears to be nicotine (Houston, Schneider, & Jarvik, 1978), but exactly how nicotine interferes is unknown. A sudden shock or trauma can interfere with consolidation to an extensive degree, causing complete loss of very recent memories. It's not uncommon for a person who has been involved in a terrifying incident, such as a severe car crash, to forget everything that occurred within half an hour to an hour before the accident. Such loss of memory is known as **retrograde amnesia**, and it may be a permanent loss. If LTM memories are jarred very early in the consolidation process, they may be as forgotten as if they had been lost from the STM. Some victims of car crashes find it particularly upsetting that they can't even remember why they were on a particular road or where they had been planning to go when their accident occurred.

Motivated Forgetting

Motivated forgetting is another way in which LTM items can seem to be lost. This sort of forgetting is an active and purposeful one that people use to keep themselves from recalling threatening, painful, or embarrassing memories. Clinical psychologists often use the term **repression** when referring to the process through which memories are forced from conscious awareness. Repressed memories are not available for active recall.

Under severe psychological stress, repression can become so extensive that many memories can be kept from retrieval. Such a condition is referred to as **psychogenic amnesia.** The lost memories usually are of a personal nature, such as the person's name or address, rather than the letters in the alphabet or how to operate a car. Psychogenic amnesia is discussed in greater detail in Chapter 15.

Somatogenic Amnesia

Somatogenic amnesia is the kind old Hollywood movies tried to depict: The victim would be suddenly thumped on the head and then would forget everything. The

FIGURE 7.13

Which drawing shows the real penny?
(SOURCE: *Nickerson and Adams, 1979,*
p. 297.)

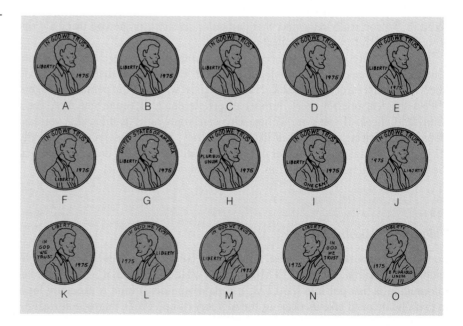

old Hollywood solution to this amnesia, of course, was to thump the victim on the head one more time, setting everything right (a solution that, as you may have guessed, doesn't work very well). In reality, physically induced amnesia is far more complicated and varied. The kind of amnesia produced may vary greatly, depending on the type of injury or disease.

Two of the most interesting cases of somatogenic amnesia, from which researchers have gathered much information, are the cases of H. M. and N. A. We discussed H. M.'s case in Chapter 2. He was operated on in 1953 in an effort to control his seizures. Portions of his limbic system closely associated with memory function were destroyed. After the surgery, H. M. was no longer able to store memories in LTM. He had to get by on what he had learned before 1953. All events since that time faded from his mind moments after they happened. This disorder is called **anterograde amnesia.**

H. M.'s injury also has helped researchers to make further distinctions between declarative and procedural memory. Although H. M. is unable to place facts into LTM, his procedural memory seems unaffected. For example, he can learn new motor skills—playing tennis, reading words backward in a mirror, or solving puzzles. And, although he doesn't remember learning to do puzzles, the more he practices them, the better he gets (Alper, 1986).

N. A. was a college student who one day entered his dormitory room just in time to be pierced by a miniature fencing foil with which his roommate was practicing. The roommate accidentally thrust the tip of the fencing foil into N. A.'s right nostril and upward, piercing the middle of N. A.'s brain. With the precision of a surgeon's knife, the foil cut into the left side of the thalamus. Since N. A.'s injury was on the left side of the brain, he lost many verbal memories, but his memory of images was unharmed. As you may recall from Chapter 2, verbal skills are more often controlled by the left hemisphere of the brain, while spatial representations are more often maintained in the right hemisphere.

As you can see, the kinds of amnesia suffered by H. M. and N. A. are very different from each other, and each has helped to illuminate our understanding of memory.

▌ STRENGTHENING MEMORY THROUGH ELABORATION

Elaboration is the process of linking related memories to create greater access to stored information. In his book *Cognitive Psychology and Its Implications*, John R. Anderson uses propositional networks to demonstrate how elaboration works to improve memory. He begins his demonstration with the simple sentence "The doctor hates the lawyer." Figure 7.14 shows the sentence as a propositional network: Smith hates Jones. Smith is connected by a separate link "is a" to the node "doctor." Similarly, Jones is a lawyer. So we have Smith, who is a doctor, hating Jones, who is a lawyer. This is proposition 1.

If you learn this sentence, but only this sentence, you may eventually have a hard time recalling it. But you may have an easy time if you associate this memory with others. Consider, then, proposition 2: "I studied proposition 1 in the psychology laboratory one dreary morning." By adding to proposition 1 the fact that you were studying it one dreary morning in the psychology laboratory, you have linked two propositions, which is the beginning of elaboration.

Now add proposition 3: "The lawyer had sued the doctor for malpractice." Add to this proposition 4: "The malpractice suit was the source of the doctor's hatred of the lawyer." Tack on the fact that all this hating and suing is unpleasant (prop-

ANTEROGRADE AMNESIA
The inability to recall experiences or events that occur after an amnesia-causing trauma.

ELABORATION
The process of building upon one memory by making many associations with it. Elaborated memories are easier to recall because items in the memory can be reached by many different routes.

FIGURE 7.14

Proposition 1: Smith, who is a doctor, hates Jones, who is a lawyer. (SOURCE: Anderson, 1980, p. 195.)

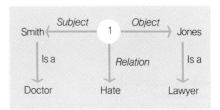

243

osition 5), and add the general knowledge that lawyers sue doctors for malpractice (proposition 6). Now you have an elaborated memory, as pictured in Figure 7.15.

At this point, your memory for the fact that the doctor hates the lawyer is greatly improved because you have many different routes for recalling that fact. Suppose the first proposition had not been elaborated on (as pictured in Figure 7.15), and suppose the link from node "Smith" to the rest of proposition 1 were so weak that when you thought of "Smith" (who is the doctor) you could not recall his relationship to "Jones" (who is the lawyer). If that were the case, there would be no way at all for you to recall the relationship, since you had only one link to the rest of the proposition. But with the kind of elaboration that appears in Figure 7.15, you could go on from "Smith" to recall all of proposition 1, even if the link from "Smith" to proposition 1 were too weak, because other routes could lead you to proposition 1.

If this doesn't seem clear to you, just think for a moment about how your memory seems to work. When you think of one thing, doesn't that often remind you of another, which in turn triggers thoughts of a third thing? Look again at Figure 7.15, the elaborated memory. Suppose you realize that it's a dreary morning. Suddenly that "dreary morning" node might lead you to proposition 2, and you might remember, "Oh, yes, I was studying one dreary morning in the psychology laboratory," which might lead you to proposition 1: "I was studying about the doctor hating the lawyer." That memory might lead you to proposition 5 (that it was unpleasant) or to proposition 4 (that the doctor hated the lawyer because the lawyer had sued him for malpractice), and so on. Because of this, elaborated memories are easier to recall than unelaborated memories.

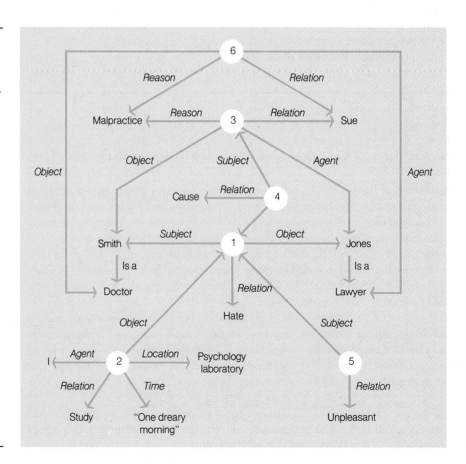

FIGURE 7.15

Nodes are unified into clusters (propositions) according to the meanings they provide. As you can see, a node may be connected to more than one proposition. Arrows indicate the propositions to which different nodes belong. The propositions depicted are:

1. Smith, who is a doctor, hates Jones, who is a lawyer.
2. I studied proposition 1 one dreary morning in the psychology laboratory.
3. Jones sued Smith for malpractice.
4. Proposition 3 is the cause of proposition 1.
5. It is unpleasant that Smith, who is a doctor, hates Jones, who is a lawyer.
6. Lawyers sue doctors for malpractice.
(SOURCE: Anderson, 1980, p. 195.)

ENCODING EFFECTS

LOCUS-DEPENDENT MEMORY
A memory that has been associated with a particular location so that it is easier to recall when you are in that location.

Certain circumstances can influence how memories are encoded (placed) into long-term memory. This, in turn can affect the conditions under which memories can be best retrieved. Two important encoding effects are locus-dependent memory and mood, or state-dependent learning.

Locus-Dependent Memory

The elaborated network in Figure 7.15 suggests that some very interesting things may be going on in human memory. For instance, if you were trying to recall that the doctor hated the lawyer, do you think it would be easier if you happened to be sitting in the psychology laboratory on a dreary morning, just as you were when you first studied the proposition? The familiar atmosphere might jog to memory the proper node for retrieving the information you wanted. If you were sitting on the beach on a sunny day, it might be much harder to remember that the doctor hated the lawyer. This illustrates the phenomenon of **locus-dependent memory**.

Two researchers, Godden and Baddeley, demonstrated this phenomenon in 1975. They had people learn 40 unrelated words either on the beach or, using scuba equipment, 20 feet under the sea. Half the people in each group were then asked to switch locations before everyone tried to recall the words. Table 7.1 shows the results of the study. As you can see, people who learned the list on the beach were able to recall it better on the beach than beneath the water, while those who learned beneath the water could recall better under water. This indicates that during learning, elements in the environment become associated in the memory with the items to be remembered, so that reexposure to the same elements may facilitate recall of those items.*

In another study conducted at the University of Michigan, students memorized lists of paired items one day in a large, windowless room with an instructor who was dressed in a suit and tie. On the second day, another group of subjects learned paired items in a small room filled with daylight, and this time the instructor was dressed casually in jeans and a flannel shirt. In both cases, the items to be learned were presented on a tape recorder. On the third day, subjects were placed in one setting or the other and asked to recall what they had learned. Those who had learned the list in the setting where they were tested were successful in recalling

TABLE 7.1 Relationship Between Recall and Environment

Group	Location to Learn Material	Location to Recall Material	Mean Recall Score
A	dry	dry	13.5
B	dry	wet	8.6
C	wet	wet	11.4
D	wet	dry	8.4

NOTE: Subjects recall material studied in one location more accurately when they are in that same location.
SOURCE: Adapted from Godden & Baddeley, 1975, p. 328.

STATE-DEPENDENT LEARNING
The phenomenon that memories are recalled with greater ease when you are in the same or similar mood or physical state as when you first acquired the memory.

MASSED PRACTICE
A study method that does not create a spacing effect and is therefore not likely to lead to long-term retention. Material is studied in a single session without any interruption. The method is also known as cramming.

59 percent of the list on the average, but subjects who had learned the list in a different setting could remember only 46 percent of the list on average (Smith, Glenberg, & Bjork, 1978).

Subjects also have been found to remember more accurately if the same sounds are present during recall as were present during learning (Smith, 1985).

In the Mood

Figure 7.15 indicates that in addition to your surroundings, your emotional state may have an affect on your ability to remember particular items. As you see, proposition 5 is related to the node "unpleasant," reminding you that the doctor's hating the lawyer is an unpleasant thing. To reach proposition 1, "The doctor hates the lawyer," you might go through proposition 5; to reach proposition 5, you must begin at the node "unpleasant." Does this mean that if you were in an unpleasant mood or felt that something was unpleasant, you would remember proposition 1 more easily? Evidence suggests so.

This phenomenon is called **state-dependent learning.** If people can return to the same emotional or physical state that they were in when they learned information, they find it easier to remember. In Charlie Chaplin's classic comedy *City Lights*, Chaplin plays a character he made famous, the Little Tramp. In the film, Chaplin saves a drunken man from leaping to his death. As it turns out, the drunk is a millionaire and becomes Chaplin's friend. The two spend the evening together, having a good time and becoming drinking buddies. The next day, however, the

Because of contextual overlap, the student who studies in the library will be more likely to recall the information during the test, unless, of course, the test is given outdoors!

millionaire is sober and, not recognizing Chaplin, refuses even to speak to him. Later, the millionaire becomes drunk once more, and the moment he sees Chaplin he reacts as though he had found a long-lost friend. Interestingly, evidence for this effect exists. People who learn something when they are under the influence of alcohol may find that they cannot recall what they learned when they are sober, but can remember it if they once again become drunk (Overton, 1972).

THE SPACING EFFECT

Researcher S. A. Madigan once asked subjects to repeat as many items as they could remember from a list of 48 words that had been presented to them at the rate of one word every 1 1/2 seconds. Most subjects were able to recall about 28 percent of the words. Madigan discovered, however, that if some of the words were repeated, subjects were more likely to remember those words. Specifically, he found that although the subjects could recall only 28 percent of the words they had heard once, they could recall 47 percent of the words they had heard twice (Madigan, 1969).

This discovery should hardly come as a surprise to anyone. After all, the more familiar you become with something, the more likely you are to remember it. But Madigan discovered something else that was a surprise: Among words heard twice, a word was more likely to be remembered if the interval between the first and second presentation had been a long one. If the word had been said twice in a row, it was least likely to be remembered. Madigan's finding is known as the **spacing effect.** As far as anyone can tell, there seems to be no limit to the amount of spacing (additional time between first and second presentations) that will bring further improvement of memory (Anderson, 1980).

Why does this spacing effect occur? One researcher has argued that if you study something for the second time immediately after you have studied it the first time, you may think of the second study session as unnecessary and redundant and pay little attention to it. If you study something a second time after considerable delay, however, you might think of it as a more valuable experience and pay stricter attention to it (Rundus, 1971).

Another possibility is that if you let enough time pass before you study something a second time, your emotional state and the context of your environment will be different on the second occasion. If the contextual variables—that is, the physical environment and your emotional state at the time you study—are important to your recall of information, then it might be valuable to study in as many different physical contexts as possible. This change of time and place provides what is known as **encoding variability,** and it helps to enlarge the elaboration network of a particular memory. In other words:

> The greater the difference between the two study contexts [the first and second time you study the same material], the greater is the probability that one of the contexts will overlap with the test context. On the other hand, at short lags the two study contexts will be more similar, and the probability of study context matching test context will be not much greater than in the single-presentation condition. (Anderson, 1980, p. 214)

The message to the student couldn't be more obvious. If you want to study, study the material, wait some time, and then restudy the material in a different context; and, if possible, study it a third time, after another delay. This procedure is known as **spaced practice,** and it can greatly improve test scores (see Focus on an Application).

SPACING EFFECT
The fact that repeated items are learned better and are more easily recalled the greater the amount of time between the first and the second exposure to the items.

ENCODING VARIABILITY
Acquisition of the same information in different moods, states, or circumstances. Greater encoding variability tends to improve test performance by increasing the chances that the test situation will resemble the learning environment.

SPACED PRACTICE
A study method that creates the spacing effect. Studying is accomplished over time with gaps between study sessions. The method is also known as distributed practice.

In this scene from the movie City Lights, *the drunken millionaire is Charlie's good friend. But whenever the millionaire is sober he can't recall who Charlie is and has him thrown out. This is an example of state-dependent learning.*

TO CRAM OR NOT TO CRAM?

It is a rare and lucky student who loves to study. Most students, although they may enjoy reading assigned material, find that they must make a concentrated effort to recall it during a test. And since studying can be a strenuous process, students commonly put it off until the last possible moment—and then find that they must learn a great deal of material in the few hours remaining before the examination. This concentrated learning is called **massed practice,** or cramming. Is cramming the best way to study?

Of course it isn't, you say. Everybody knows it's a stupid thing to do—a sign of procrastination and poor study habits. The good student will study material regularly as it is assigned. Conversely, a bad student will cram. Therefore, it must be better not to cram. Sounds logical, but is it true?

The spacing effect has shown that information is recalled more accurately if it is learned more than once, especially if there is a large gap in time between the first and the second exposure to the material. The spacing effect, therefore, certainly argues against cramming. But why does the spacing effect work? There is some evidence that if a significant amount of time has elapsed between the first and the second exposure to the same material, it's likely that the material will be learned in different contexts and moods. Thus, the chances are better that the mood and physical surroundings at the time of the test will be similar to at least one of the study sessions. If you are in the same mood, feel about the same way, and have similar physical surroundings when you take your test as you did when you studied the material, you'll have more access to the memory networks containing the information.

For the same reasons, cramming can work well if you know exactly when you are due to take a particular test. If you cram within limits, so that you don't become excessively fatigued, there is a good chance that you will be in the same mood and mental set during testing. If you study thoroughly for many hours before a test and then walk straight into the testing situation feeling much as you did while you studied, you're likely to do well (Glenberg, 1976; Anderson, 1980). If, however, you have to study long in advance of the test, you're likely to be in a different mood, physical condition, and setting when you finally take the test. In that case, spaced practice is best.

Cramming has both weaknesses and strengths. It is not an effective way to learn material permanently. It might get you through one test, but it's a poor way to study for long-term gain or for comprehensive examinations. For lasting comprehension, spaced practice in many different moods and contexts works better. Or, as memory researcher John Anderson has stated,

> Although I hate to admit this, if one's purpose is to pass an exam, concentrating a lot of study the night before the exam should be advantageous; in other words, it's best to cram. Of course, cramming will lead to poor long-term retention, as frequently noted by students a year after a course. Studying throughout the term does have some benefit, though this method is just not as efficient as cramming. The strategy that will result in the best grade combines the techniques of studying during the term and cramming the night before. (Anderson, 1980, pp. 216–217)

When massed and spaced practice are combined, people can remember a surprising amount of material, often for as long as 50 years, without the need of rehearsal. In one study, researchers found that students who 50 years ago had taken 3 years of Spanish and engaged in both massed and spaced practice retained about 72 percent of the Spanish vocabulary that they had originally learned (Bahrick, 1984). Amazingly, these students had not practiced their Spanish or used it since their last Spanish class. The 28 percent of Spanish vocabulary they had forgotten had been lost within 6 years of taking their last class. Following that, their long-term memory of Spanish vocabulary remained stable. A very different result usually is found among students who rely only on cramming at the last minute to pass their tests. Years later, such students typically retain less than 10 percent of what they originally learned.

In a more recent study of language students, spaced practice was found to account for almost all long-term retention (Bahrick & Phelps, 1987). These results argue for widely spaced language sessions throughout one's education if long-term retention is desired. This is not the common practice in college language courses, which usually are offered within one specific period, such as a semester.

EPILOGUE: REMEMBRANCE OF THINGS PAST

The following is an account of how the sudden recollection of a distant childhood memory tore one woman's family apart and how it may yet lead to the resolution of a 20-year-old mystery.

One day, 28-year-old Eileen Franklin-Lipsker of Redwood City, California, was watching her 6-year-old daughter drawing with some crayons. The little girl looked up, caught her mother's eye, and asked about her drawing, "Isn't that right, Mommy?"

Eileen Franklin-Lipsker saw the imploring look in her child's eyes and was thunder-struck as she suddenly recalled having seen that look before. In a shocking, onrushing instant, she remembered something that had been completely hidden from her conscious mind for almost two decades—that her father was a killer. What she had seen in her daughter's expression was the same questioning look she had seen on the face of her childhood friend Susan Nason, just before Susan was murdered by Eileen's father, George Franklin, over 20 years ago.

Once she had recalled that repressed childhood memory, many other memories began to rush back. She remembered "her father and Susan at the bottom of a wooded hill and her father raising a rock above his head" (Carlson, 1990, p. 56). She recalled seeing a smashed ring on her friend's blood-covered finger. And she remembered her father raping Susan and then telling Eileen that it was all her fault for inviting her friend into their van and that if she ever told anyone, he wouldn't be above killing his own daughter. Numbed by the shock of her recollection, Eileen knew that she had to go to the police.

Is what Eileen Franklin-Lipsker said true? There is some evidence to support her claim. Susan Nason did disappear near their home 20 years earlier. The body of the child was found in an area like that described by Eileen, and her skull was smashed in the same way that a rock might have caused it to be. Eileen's older sister, Janice, told authorities six years ago that she too had her suspicions about her father, but nothing could be done at that time without an eyewitness.

The question given to the jury was whether Eileen was to be believed. Could she be making this up to get some sort of revenge on an innocent father, or could her memory have worked as she said it did?

From what has been learned about memory, we know that it is indeed possible for Eileen to be telling the truth. Such a horrible experience might well have led to motivated forgetting. If the incident was never brought to mind, the network holding those memories would not be readily linked with other parts of Eileen's memory. For that reason, any of the nodes within the network holding memories of the murder would be very difficult to access, unless something triggered one of them into consciousness. The look on her daughter's face could be exactly the kind of stimulus needed to activate one of the nodes tucked away in the forbidden part of her memory. Then, once activated, other nodes linked to that one would be accessible, bringing back many of the forbidden memories.

The jury found George Franklin guilty, in part because we know, from years of memory research, that what Eileen Franklin-Lipsker claims occurred to her is well within the bounds of normal memory functioning. It is possible to bury a nightmare for 20 years and then have it come rushing back because of nothing more than a fateful glance from an innocent child.

SUMMARY

■ All the images and sensations not immediately available to your senses must be drawn from your memory. Plans for the future, recollections of the past—all require a functioning memory.

■ In 1917, Karl Lashley began a search for the brain's engram. Engrams are the hypothetical biochemical structures that contain memories.

■ Researchers conducting experiments on animals are beginning to uncover the architecture of memory. Portions of the brain, especially in the limbic system, have been found to be essential for the storage of long-term memories.

■ There appear to be two distinct types of memory, each of which relies on different neural circuitry in the brain. The two types are declarative and procedural memory, often referred to as fact and skill memory.

■ Declarative memory is composed of three major parts: sensory memory, short-term memory, and long-term memory.

■ When you first receive a particular visual stimulus, the image is held for only a fraction of a second in what is known as the sensory memory, or sensory register. Unless you pay attention to the image and encode it successfully into your short-term memory, it will decay and be lost.

■ Short-term memory is also known as working memory. It holds active information—information to which you are paying attention—but it can hold this information for only a brief time. Maintaining information in short-term memory for more than 30 seconds requires rehearsal. The information can be lost through displacement or decay.

■ A chunk is a unit of memory. Chunks are determined not by the numbers of things they contain, such as letters or syllables, but by the meaning and organization they hold. They are the items used for memory storage.

■ The short-term memory is generally limited to a capacity of seven chunks, give or take two. If the short-term memory tries to acquire more chunks than it can hold, some of them (generally the middle items—those acquired neither most nor least recently) will be displaced. This displacement pattern is known as the serial position effect.

■ To store information for days, weeks, years, or even a lifetime, you must store short-term memories in long-term memory, which has a virtually unlimited storage capacity.

■ Meaningful items are stored in long-term memory more easily than meaningless items are.

■ A mnemonic is any kind of remembering system or memory aid. One of the oldest is known as the method of loci, which is the technique of remembering items by associating them in your mind with points along a familiar pathway.

■ Vasopressin is a brain neuropeptide that has the ability to improve memory.

■ The two theories of memory most prominent today are the dual-code theory, which argues that information can be stored as sensory experience or as words, and the propositional network theory, which argues that how information is stored depends on its meaning.

■ In propositional network theory, the bits of information that make up the propositions are called nodes, and the connections between the nodes are called links.

■ Dual-code theory contends that sensory and verbal memories are processed separately. Although different areas of the brain do appear to be responsible for visual and verbal information, both kinds of information appear to be organized in the form of memory networks.

■ Forgetting may occur for a number of reasons, such as decay, interference effects, motivated forgetting, failure of consolidation, and amnesia.

■ A number of interference effects can obstruct long-term memory retrieval. Among these are proactive interference, by which previously learned material interferes with the ability to learn something new, and retroactive interference, by which learning something new interferes with the ability to retrieve an old memory.

■ The tip-of-the-tongue phenomenon describes a situation in which a memory is almost, but not quite, available.

■ A retrieval cue may provide access to a memory that is difficult to find. Such cues may be a great help in getting at tip-of-the-tongue memories.

■ Elaboration helps to strengthen memory retrieval because it provides multiple access paths to specific memories.

■ Both your physical location and your emotional state can affect your ability to recall information. This phenomenon is known as state-dependent learning.

■ The longer the time that passes between the first and the second exposure to information, the more likely a person is to remember the information. This observation is known as the spacing effect.

■ The spacing effect may occur as the result of encoding variability—the learning of information in different moods and environments. Changing the circumstances in which a person learns can facilitate recall, because it increases the chance that the recall situation will be similar to the circumstances in which the material was first learned.

Suggestions for Further Reading

1. Higbee, K. L. (1988). *Your memory: How it works and how to improve it* (2nd ed.). Englewood Cliffs, NJ: Prentice-Hall. A book for the general reader that outlines how memory works and also includes some suggestions for making memory more effective.

2. Klatzky, R. L. (1984). *Memory and awareness: An information-processing approach*. New York: W. H. Freeman. Describes how memory functions and debunks many myths associated with memory. Includes discussions on issues such as eyewitness testimony and advertising.

3. Loftus, E. F. (1979). *Eyewitness testimony*. Cambridge, MA: Harvard University Press. Discusses how eyewitnesses reconstruct what they have seen and the inherent unreliability of such reconstructions. Applies this to everyday problems of memory and the ability of people to recall past events accurately.

4. Norman, D. A. (1982). *Learning and memory*. New York: W. H. Freeman. A college-level introduction to modern concepts in memory and cognitive psychology. Gives interesting examples and relates them to problems in retention, retrieval, and reconstruction of information.

CHAPTER 8 | Cognition and Language

Prologue

Why Psychologists Study Thought and Language

Thinking
Subvocal Speech
Thinking Machines

Human Performance
Intellectual Skills
Declarative Knowledge
Cognitive Strategies
Impediments to Problem Solving
Motor Skills
Attitudes

Language
Linguistic Relativity
Language Acquisition
Syntactic and Semantic Structure
Why Does Language Acquisition
    Occur?
Teaching Language to the Great Apes

Epilogue: The Man with the Means to Reach His Ends

PROLOGUE

It is 1917. The Americans have declared war on Germany, and the whole North Atlantic has become a battleground. A short time earlier, you and Wolfgang Kohler had left Germany to travel to the Canary Islands, 200 miles off the coast of North Africa, where you have been assigned to care for the local chimpanzee colony. It was to have been a limited stay, but now German U-boats and British and American men-of-war prowl the sea, and it's not safe to leave. So you are stuck here—who knows for how long.

Kohler was never one to sit around, however. He's been studying the colony of captive chimpanzees on one of the islands, and he says it's an interesting pastime. He watches them almost every day and invites you to join him.

As you soon discover, Kohler isn't just watching the chimps; he's giving them things to do. One of the chimpanzees, named Sultan, is particularly glad to see Kohler. Sultan has learned that he often can get bananas when he solves Kohler's problems. Kohler places a banana outside Sultan's cage beyond the animal's reach, but provides Sultan with a stick. Sultan grabs the stick and reaches outside the cage, catches the edge of the banana, and begins to pull it toward him. When the banana is within reach, Sultan grabs it.

"That's interesting, isn't it?" says Kohler.

"Oh sure," you reply, looking out at the ocean, and wishing that the island were bigger than 20 square miles.

"Let's try something different," Kohler says. He puts the banana out of reach of a single stick and places two sticks inside Sultan's cage. You wonder what's going on. You notice that one stick is larger than the

other and has a hollow opening into which the smaller stick can be inserted. Now you understand: Mentally, you imagine the smaller stick being inserted into the larger one, so that together the two form one very long stick. With the long stick, Sultan might be able to reach the banana.

"Has he done this one before?" you ask Kohler.

"No," he says, "He's never seen it, I just wonder what he'll do."

"He'll probably throw them at you," you say, as you put your hands in your pockets and watch the chimp futilely try to reach the banana with just one of the sticks.

Sultan seems moody and angry; he pulls the stick back, then tries again, and puts the stick down. "I know how he feels," you say, again looking out over the ocean while trying to think of a way to get off the island. You're watching the ocean, Kohler is watching Sultan, and Sultan is watching the sticks. Sometimes the chimp seems to have human expressions; at the moment he looks as though he's thinking. "What are you thinking about, Sultan?" you wonder. "Why doesn't your stick work any more? Who is the strange man who keeps giving you bananas and sticks?" Suddenly, Sultan's expression seems to change. He stands up and slowly approaches the sticks. He picks up the larger one on his left hand and turns the hollow end toward him. He picks up the smaller stick and inserts it into the larger one to make one long stick (see Figure 8.1). "I don't believe it," you whisper. "He just figured it out." Sultan goes to the end of the cage and extends his new extra-long stick toward the banana.

"He thought it through just as you or I might have," says Kohler, as Sultan reaches the banana with the stick and pulls it toward him.

Based on this observation and a number of later ones, Kohler came to believe that chimpanzees could engage in creative problem solving by

FIGURE 8.1

Sultan used insight to solve the two-stick problem.

using insight. Insight, Kohler says, comes when you have mentally been manipulating different operations toward a goal solution. Suddenly, your mental operations strike on the solution that will work. Then you approach the real situation and put your plan into effect. This, he argues, is very different from a trial-and-error ramble that might occur without thinking. In Sultan's case, the chimpanzee thought about the problem, came up with the solution, and applied it. In other words, the animal relied on insight—he was thinking. (Kohler, 1927).

In this chapter, we'll examine thinking and problem solving and the relationship between cognition and language. We'll learn how language emerges and what language is. In addition, we'll consider whether language is unique to human beings. Other topics will include computers that can "think" and puzzles that require considerable mental dexterity and insight. We'll also look at how different areas of the brain can directly affect the understanding of language and the ability to speak.

WHY PSYCHOLOGISTS STUDY THOUGHT AND LANGUAGE

Perhaps more than any other aspects of our nature, thought and language make us unique. Although apes such as Sultan may think, their thinking is limited— they may acquire the rudiments of language, as you will see, but they do not use it naturally. Our abilities to think and speak are the cornerstones on which modern civilization is built. The generations before us found solutions to many problems and communicated these solutions to us through language. We have built on their knowledge; as we solve our own problems, we will communicate the answers to the next generation. More than any other species, we have the power to control our world and perhaps to make it a better place in which to live. Ironically, these same extraordinary abilities to think and communicate could be our undoing, because we have used them to develop weapons of devastating potential. Perhaps the same powers of thought and speech can help us to overcome the danger in which we have placed ourselves.

Whatever the future holds, our abilities to think and speak have placed us in a situation that is fundamentally different from the situations of all other species. Psychologists study thinking, problem solving, and language because these aspects of our psychology are the essence of the human experience.

THINKING

What is thought? *Thinking* or, more broadly, **cognition,** refers to the use of perceptions, mental combinations, and internal representations of symbols, objects, or concepts. When you imagine something, or solve problems mentally, or use language internally, you are said to be thinking. Not surprisingly, like Sultan the ape, you too can mentally manipulate objects without actually having to move or handle them. There have probably been times when, instead of actually moving furniture about, you mentally pictured the appearance of a room with the furniture rearranged. Such mental manipulations are independent of physical muscular actions.

INSIGHT
In problem solving, the sudden perception of relationships leading to a solution. A solution arrived at in this way can be repeated promptly when the same or a similar problem is confronted.

COGNITION
The process that occurs between the sensing of a stimulus and the emergence of an overt response. It involves the interplay of concepts, symbols, and mediating responses.

SUBVOCAL SPEECH
In learning theory, Watson's concept of
thinking as a series of muscular responses.

Subvocal Speech

John Watson, the father of behaviorism, argued that there was no such thing as an internal mental activity (Watson, 1930). Watson said that humans didn't think; they simply emitted responses that had been conditioned to various stimuli. You might wonder how anyone could believe that humans didn't think, but Watson had an intriguing answer. He said that thinking was not a "mental" activity, but **subvocal speech,** that is, a muscular activity! In other words, people didn't think, they talked to themselves, but so quietly that it wasn't apparent. Measurements taken of the muscles, tongue, and throat disclosed that some people did register very subtle muscular motions when they were "thinking" to themselves. Was it possible, then, that Watson was right, and that we only believe we think when we are actually engaging in subvocal speech, a muscular response? Watson argued that even a person who was mute might make subtle muscular responses in the form of hand signing or other gestures that would be muscular representations of what was assumed to be internal thinking. This idea appealed to behaviorists, because they wished to avoid the concepts of *mind* or *mental*.

One way to test Watson's hypothesis might be to paralyze a subject completely, to the point at which he could no longer breathe, or even blink, and find out whether thinking continued while no muscle could be moved. Believe it or not, such a test was actually carried out using a derivative of curare, a substance used by Amazonian tribes to poison their darts (Smith, Brown, Toman, & Goodman, 1947). The subject—Smith—was one of the researchers. An artificial respirator was used to keep him alive (the things people do for science!). After the experiment, when Smith could move again, he reported that, although paralyzed totally, he was easily able to think, and had understood everything that had been going on around him. These results indicate that thinking is an internal mental activity, independent of muscular responses, and that Watson's hypothesis was wrong. Perhaps it was good to discover that Watson hadn't, as Herbert Reigl once said, "made up his voice box that he had no mind" (Anderson, 1980, p. 383). As it is, thinking is difficult enough to comprehend.

The debate still continues, however. The behaviorist position remains that feelings and thoughts are only accessible to science through direct observation, and while advances in brain science may someday allow us to dissect exactly what emotions or thoughts are in terms of observable cells and circuits, until then, it is hopeless to try and do so with a psychology that is limited to references dealing with unobservable "thoughts" or "feelings," (Skinner, 1989).

And yet, because we can sense our own thoughts and because they are so important to us, the concept of thought and thinking remains so compelling that it is very difficult to keep from trying to explore this area, even if it must be done in an indirect fashion.

Thinking Machines

Some of the earliest researchers to appreciate just how difficult it is to explore thinking, even indirectly, were the computer programmers and designers who first tried to create an intelligent thinking machine. Their early efforts produced simple, weak, mechanical so-called brains that could, in an extremely limited way, process some of the symbolic information with which our own brains are able to work.

As soon as psychologists became aware, through these early projects, that computers were information processors and not just high-speed "number crunchers," they couldn't help but wonder whether the unknowable "black box"—as Watson had called the mind—might be accessible to observation after all, albeit in a roundabout way. If we could build computers that "think," psychologists reasoned, these machines might provide us with many hints about how our own minds worked. Never mind that the one is made of electronic parts and the other of living tissue; steam shovels and human arms can work in much the same way regardless of their composition. Computers, then, just might show us how our minds operate!

Today, cognitive psychologists and computer designers are working hand in hand. When psychologists discover some aspect of the brain that hints at how mental information is processed, computer designers try to make a computer that incorporates a similar feature; when computer scientists discover electronic processes that mimic human thinking, psychologists look within the brain for evidence of similar "wiring." Although the model may be limited, the advent of the computer has revolutionized cognitive psychology. Still, no one has yet created a machine that can think, reason, or perform intellectual tasks as well as people do. But who knows—perhaps someday? (See An Enduring Question.)

▌ HUMAN PERFORMANCE

Cognitive psychologists try to find out what people do when they think, reason, and perform intellectual tasks. Although there are many views on this subject and many disagreements among researchers (Oden, 1987), a sense of what these special abilities might be is beginning to emerge.

Although a few researchers argue that all thinking, reasoning, and performance in human beings is probably controlled by one major set of cognitive abilities (Anderson, 1983), it is more commonly accepted that there probably are five separate categories of human cognitive performance (Gagné, 1984). These five categories are (1) intellectual skills, (2) declarative knowledge, (3) cognitive strategies, (4) motor skills, and (5) attitudes. Each of these categories includes a broad range of human behavior. Many artificial intelligence researchers have argued that if these five broad categories could be mastered by a computer, the machine would indeed exhibit behavior and reasoning ability similar to that of a human being. Let's look at each of the five categories in turn.

Intellectual Skills

Intellectual skills form a general category that includes all the mental procedures, rules, and concepts you have learned.*

MENTAL PROCEDURES.   Think of the different procedures you have acquired about how to do things. Most likely you know the procedure for driving a car, operating a television set, making a telephone call, or shopping at a store. Some jobs, of course, require complex intellectual skills: Think of the procedures a surgeon or a jet fighter pilot must know.

As you master such procedures, it takes you less and less time to carry them out. A medical student might have to think through her mental procedures for some time in order to remove an appendix, but once she has become a seasoned surgeon, her knowledge of the procedures probably will become so rapid and automatic that she doesn't think about each step before she knows what to do. This

---

*Some researchers prefer the term *procedural knowledge* (Anderson, 1980) or *production systems* (Newell & Simon, 1972) to intellectual skills.

For centuries, philosophers have argued about whether the brain was a "machine" or if a spirit of some sort resided there. As you recall from our discussion of the mind–body problem (see Chapter 2), they wondered if there were a ghost in the machine.

If the brain is like a machine, a very complex machine, that senses, stores, analyzes, retrieves, and processes data, then, in theory at least, it should be possible to build a real machine that can do what the brain does and perhaps even surpass the brain's ability. That is, it should be possible to create an artificial intelligence.

Efforts along these lines have begun, but to date we are a long way from such an accomplishment. For instance, just consider what the human mind can do that a computer cannot do:

> We can, for example, recognize our mother. Right after she's had her hair cut. Or permed. We can understand the speech of a cabbie from Boston or a tugboat captain from Baton Rouge. We can recognize something as a chair, whether it is a Chippendale, a bean bag, or a throne. Wee con undrestin wrds efen wen theh ar missspld. Or fill in the blanks when lt rs are missing. Many of us can recognize right away what [Figure 8.2] is: And if we can't, once we are told there is a dog in the center we usually can't help seeing it whenever we look. When we hear "Shall I compare thee to a summer's day?" we don't expect a weather report. When someone asks us if we know Bob Thompson, who plays the trumpet in the school band and lives on Maple Street, we answer yes, but his name is Bill, not Bob, and he plays the trombone, and he moved away six months ago. When given the sentences "The fly buzzed irritatingly on the window. The man picked up the newspaper," we know what is about to happen.
>
> We take this kind of mental work for granted, but computers can't even come close to doing it. (Allman, 1986, p. 25)

The question, of course, is why can't computers come close to "doing it"; that is, why can't they think more like people? Although no one knows the answer, some possible reasons for the computer's failure to "think" like a human are being actively considered. Two of the most important possibilities involve the computer's understanding of meaning and the computer's mode of processing.

Understanding of Meaning. In his book *The Hitchhiker's Guide to the Galaxy* (1979), Douglas Adams describes a fictional event that occurred on another planet. It seems that there once was a world with people much like us who pondered the great questions of their existence, much as we do. Their solution was to build Deep Thought, the greatest computer mind in the galaxy. They asked Deep Thought for the answer to the great question: What is the meaning of life, the universe, and everything?

Deep Thought said that answering this question would be "tricky," but that it could be done. To the dismay of the inhabitants of this world, however, Deep Thought said that such a calculation would take 7.5 million years! The people told Deep Thought to go ahead anyway.

Thousands of generations came and went until the time finally arrived. Two inhabitants were selected to approach Deep Thought and ask for the answer to the question—the meaning of life, the universe, and everything. A humming sound came from inside Deep Thought, and the great computer announced that the answer was . . . *Forty-two.*

In this funny example, it's obvious that there was a failure to communicate. Either the people weren't able to understand the meaning of Deep Thought's an-

FIGURE 8.2

What do you see?

swer, or perhaps Deep Thought didn't understand the meaning of their question. Somewhere along the line, the *meaning* was lost. Oddly enough, this is one of the problems commonly faced by modern researchers who are trying to create **artificial intelligence.**

A good example of this problem comes from early attempts at artificial intelligence back in the 1950s when researchers first tried to use computers to make translations from one language to another. It seemed reasonable to suppose that a computer would be able to translate anything quickly by simply comparing words between any two languages and by following set rules of grammar. Few researchers stopped to think that words weren't just symbols embedded in a formal logic but that words have various meanings that depend on context and experience.

In one famous story from this endeavor, a researcher decided to test his English–Russian translation program. He placed an English sentence, "The spirit is willing, but the flesh is weak," into the computer and had it translated into Russian. He then instructed the computer to translate the new Russian sentence back into English. What the computer gave him was, "The vodka is good, but the meat is rotten" (Waldrop, 1984, p. 372). Some simple translation programs do exist today, but the problem of meaning in translation remains. This is why human translators are still needed; they understand the meaning as well as the symbols.

Developing an artificial intelligence, therefore, first requires that we know what it means to "understand" something. If you consider the following, you will see the computer's problem when it comes to understanding. "If just one person steps onto the rickety footbridge, it will collapse." A computer's literal solution might be to always make sure that two or more people are on the bridge! Even though our memories are filled with millions of facts, our understanding of what the facts mean often gives us an edge and enables us to concentrate on only the relevant ones and to compare them with one another. It may be that before a computer can think like a human (and, ultimately, think beyond a human's ability), it will have to know what it means to be a human. The trouble is, of course, that no one knows how to put such an experience into the formal logic that a digital computer uses. After all, what is the meaning of life? (Yes, I know—42!). If computers could learn from experience, rather than by being given information, perhaps their understanding of what things *mean* would approach our understanding. But for a computer to learn from experience, it would have to process information in a very different way than most computers do now—it would require a totally different mode of processing.

Mode of Processing. The brain doesn't work like a simple computer. It doesn't quickly examine every fact related to a particular problem until an answer is reached. If it did, each time you learned a new face it would take you that much longer to recognize your father the next time you saw him. Instead, the brain appears to process millions of bits of information slowly and at the same time. This is known as **parallel processing.** Some people have compared the simple computer to a bank with only one teller and the parallel computer to a bank in which many tellers are working at the same time. In fact, 20 small personal computers—the kind you can buy in your local department store—when hooked together in parallel so that each performs a small part of a problem, can often process information faster than a large mainframe computer costing many hundreds of thousands of dollars. How to integrate the 20 parts of answers you'll get from these little computers into a sensible whole answer, however, is another problem. The brain does it, somehow, and computer designers are still trying to figure out how best to do it. Until they do, ultrapowerful full parallel-processing computers must remain a dream.

ARTIFICIAL INTELLIGENCE
A computer simulation of human cognitive ability and performance.

PARALLEL PROCESSING
In computer science or neuroanatomy, the handling of information in a manner so that many aspects of a particular problem are manipulated simultaneously, thereby saving time over serial methods in which each aspect of a problem is examined in sequence.

In computer science, computer hardware or circuits that alter their composition or connections in response to experience.

Some computers, however, are able to do some of their work in parallel fashion. This has led to a significant new area of exploration in which computers are being developed that can and do learn from experience. These computers rely on a new kind of internal organization called, interestingly enough, a **neural network.** The organization is based on the idea of computer chips sharing information simultaneously (parallel processing) in a way that mimics the neural processing in the human brain. In a computer based on a neural network system, there is no separate area for memory—memory is spread throughout the system. There are no programs to enter, no rules to begin with. The machine creates its own pathways to solve problems.

Such systems may mark the beginning of computers that can *acquire* their own experience rather than simply being the passive recipient of a programmer's instructions. John McCarthy, who coined the term *artificial intelligence*, believes that some day machines will learn on their own what the world means, and will become not just as intelligent as people, but even more intelligent. In such a world, for instance, scientists might conduct experiments ordered up by a computer and then give the results to the machine. The computer may then ask for more experiments, and then for more, until finally it announces what the "answer" is (hopefully, not "42"). When researchers ask the computer how it came to the answer, the computer may even respond that it's "beyond the ability of human minds to comprehend." Such a machine may be of great benefit to us as it solves some of our most difficult problems, uncovers the secrets of nature, and perhaps figures out how to build an even better computer. Of course, if for some reason we find the machine too frightening or if it gets out of hand, we can always pull the plug (assuming, of course, that it runs on electricity!).

Of course, these advances in artificial intelligence haven't yet answered the question, "Is the brain a machine?" Parallel processing may be only one of the brain's many tricks, and it is unlikely to be the major factor that distinguishes the brain from a computer. Brain scientists have commonly observed that if you think of five ways that the brain might work, you'll soon discover that it uses all five of those ways plus five more that you didn't think of. Some researchers speculate that the brain may be so unique that no machine will ever duplicate it. If this is true, the brain is not a machine, but something unto itself.

Roger Penrose is acknowledged to be one of the greatest physicists alive. He believes that the human mind, that is, the ghost in the machine, will turn out to be so special that it will be discovered to be operating according to a whole new set of physical laws that are unheard of today. Accordingly, Penrose argues, no digital computer will ever duplicate the human brain (Penrose, 1989). Penrose even believes that such experiences as insight may be based on sudden "quantum" shifts at the atomic level that can somehow affect large areas of the brain. Of course, he is speculating, and Penrose admits that the truth is anybody's guess. But it is interesting, nonetheless, that such a fertile mind as his might seriously consider the creation of an artificial intelligence equivalent to our own as a theoretical impossibility. Who knows, he may be right.

FOR CRITICAL ANALYSIS

1. How would life be different if each of us had a computer in our home that not only could understand what we said, but which could also carry on conversations with us and be our friend (keeping us company and providing us with the latest stories and ideas for our enjoyment), and also be an expert in every field from medicine to law; from auto repair to home finance; from psychology to gourmet cooking?

2. If machines become more intelligent than people, should society defer to them when making decisions?

process is called **automatization** (Gagné, 1984). It is the acquisition of significant amounts of automatization that distinguishes the expert from the novice.

The basis of such an intellectual skill as mental procedures is the *if–then* system. In other words, you have learned that *if* this occurs, *then* you should do that. Robinson Crusoe, lost on his desert island, had the mental procedure, "*If* I should see a boat, *then* I should light the signal fire." Your total knowledge of procedures appears to be made of thousands, perhaps millions, of such *if–then* connections.

Computers often have a tough time with *if–then* connections, because of meaning. Of course, you can put into a computer rules about if this, then that; that's what most computer programs contain. You could put the Robinson Crusoe example—*If I see a boat, then I light the fire*—into a computer. But what does *boat* mean to the computer? If you describe the *Queen Elizabeth II* as a boat, the computer might not recognize that a canoe or an aircraft carrier can also be a boat. Telling a computer what a boat is so that it will recognize any boat is not at all easy! Humans might have this same difficulty, except they possess extremely important intellectual skill: Along with the acquisition of mental procedures, they have developed the use of concepts.

CONCEPTS AND CONCEPT FORMATION. One of the most valuable ways in which we can organize thinking is by forming concepts. A **concept** can be defined as the relationship between, or the properties shared by, the objects or ideas in a given group. For example, if you have the concept of boat, you can recognize something as a boat even though it may look different from all the other boats you've ever seen. A new boat can be included within the concept because it has qualities that are common to the entire class of objects we call boats. It has a hull; it floats in water; and it is used for transport. Boats belong to an even larger conceptual category, *vehicles of transportation*. Possessing a concept such as *boat*, *dog*, or *building* is very useful. Most of the ideas we come across each day belong to familiar categories, although they may appear to be different. By applying concepts, we can develop an immediate understanding of new objects or ideas, because we can relate them to a general class of similar objects and ideas with which we are familiar. We know what to expect from an object, even though we're encountering it for the first time. In this way, we save a tremendous amount of effort, which we would otherwise have to expend learning what each new thing is.

Some concepts are very well defined; that is, the rules that classify them are stated explicitly. Among such explicit concepts are *registered voters*, *diamonds*, and

AUTOMATIZATION
A process that occurs after a mental procedure is practiced sufficiently so that the number of if–then connections is reduced to the barest required minimum. Once automatization has occurred, the mental procedure can be called on with a minimum of thought or effort. The mental procedures used by skilled experts tend to be highly automatized.

CONCEPT
An abstract idea based on grouping objects or qualities by common properties.

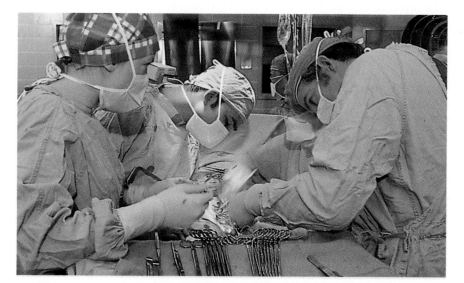

A surgeon must learn many complicated mental procedures in order to perform surgery. After sufficient training many of these procedures become automatized.

CHAPTER 8
COGNITION AND LANGUAGE

hours. These concepts are exclusive: You either are a registered voter or you are not, something either is a diamond or it isn't, and so on. Some concepts, however, appear fuzzy to many people. For instance, consider the concept *bird.* Robins and sparrows are considered highly typical examples of this concept. But turkeys and chickens are not as readily accepted into the concept, especially by children, and penguins are even less likely to be considered birds (Rosch, 1977). Human experience and context also play an important role in concept formation. For instance, "what counts as a bird (and to what degree) is very different in the context of 'The bird crossed the barnyard' than in the context of 'The hunter shot the bird overhead.' " (Oden, 1987, p. 213). In this sense, then, objects that best fit the most common examples of a concept are most likely to be included in that concept.

This kind of contextual difference poses problems for computers when machines must deal with concepts. Even more troublesome for a computer is the additional fact that many conceptual categories are based on human imagination. For instance, Australian aborigine men include both *fire* and *women* under the conceptual heading of *dangerous things* (Lakoff, 1987).

We develop concepts, in part, by classifying objects according to their similarity to other objects, and the classification may occur even when the similarities are very abstract. Further, we tend to classify objects and ideas that appear to be similar under one conceptual heading until a difference becomes apparent. The same objects also may share many different conceptual categories, all of which are based on the person's knowledge of the similarities and differences between objects. For example, is gray more like white or more like black? Well, gray hair is judged to be more like white hair than black hair because of our *knowledge* of aging. But gray clouds are judged to be more like black clouds than white clouds, owing to our *knowledge* of storms (Medin & Shoben, 1988). Because we have knowledge about the world and how it operates, we adjust our conceptual categories accordingly (Medin, 1989). Until computers have human knowledge and experience, their categorizations will simply not be like ours.

Declarative Knowledge

The second important cognitive category is declarative knowledge.* Declarative knowledge includes all the things you might be able to declare or state. The names of people, the words to a poem, an important date in history, the name of a nation's capital—all are considered declarative knowledge. Many researchers believe that such information is stored in declarative, or fact, memory as a network of propositions (see Chapter 7).

One important reason why researchers have distinguished intellectual skills from declarative knowledge is because of the differing effects of experience on each. In the case of mental procedures—an intellectual skill—an expert with much experience will reduce the number of *if–then* steps involved in each procedure as automatization occurs. On the other hand, an expert with much experience in declarative knowledge will *elaborate* the propositional networks of this information, so that they become more and more complex and expanded, rather than reduced.

Cognitive Strategies

Cognitive strategies,** the third important cognitive category, include the abilities you acquire that let you know how best to use your previously learned intellectual

---

*Declarative knowledge is sometimes referred to as *verbal information.*
**These are sometimes referred to as *executive control processes* (Atkinson & Shiffrin, 1968) or *strategic knowledge* (Greeno, 1978).

skills and declarative information for problem solving, remembering, and learning. Cognitive strategies are not well understood, but researchers assume they exist because of the way humans behave. You can pack a digital computer with procedures, even some rudimentary concepts, and certainly a great deal of declarative knowledge. But when you try to get it to think, it will become overwhelmed by the tremendous amount of data you've given it. This occurrence is sometimes called *combinatorial explosion*. It is assumed that we humans have and use cognitive strategies because it is apparent that we somehow avoid being similarly overwhelmed, each time we engage in thought, by the vast amount of information we have stored.

The lack of a cognitive strategy system has prevented parallel-processing computers from becoming the computer world's mainstay, even though these machines can handle vast amounts of information. As you recall, it was the lack of a cognitive strategy system that prevented us from integrating the 20 answer parts we obtained so quickly from our example of 20 home computers linked in parallel series.

ATTENTION.   One of the most important cognitive strategies we possess is the ability to focus our attention on what is relevant while we ignore what is not. Think about the following: You are sitting in a chair. You are relaxed. You feel the pressure of the chair against your body. You feel the pressure of the floor against your feet. You feel the weight of your clothes against your skin. You feel a large spider crawling along your arm. All this tactile (touch) sensory information has converged on you. You probably will not perceive all the inputs equally. Which one will attract the most attention? You probably won't even take notice of the pressure of your clothes or of the floor or of the chair, but the spider crawling on your arm—that will probably get your attention!

Because of our biological heritage and our experiences, some stimuli are more important to us than others. Our cognitive–perceptual system has evolved in a way that enables us to be selective about all the stimuli that we receive, to suppress some while attending to others. Attention is the cognitive strategy that enables you to listen to a particular conversation at a dinner party, even though everyone is speaking; it also informs you about large (or small) spiders on your arm. Since the days of William James, psychologists have wondered what attention is and how it operates.

Scientists once believed that the attention process heightened our awareness of a particular stimulus, but now we know that attention acts as a filter, toning down or eliminating uninteresting stimuli (Moran & Desimone, 1985). As information from the senses progresses through the nervous system higher and higher into the cortex, receptive fields (the amount of sensory information each neural group has to process) become larger and larger. In fact, by the time sensory messages reach the back surfaces of the parietal lobes of the cerebral cortex, which process visual stimuli, the receptive fields are so large that each constitutes half of the visual field (Wurtz, Goldberg, & Robinson, 1982). An interesting demonstration of this fact can be seen by examining the case of the German artist Anton Raderscheidt, who suffered a stroke in the parietal cortex on the right side of his brain. The stroke did not affect his vision; he could see fully everything on both the right and the left sides of his visual field. An artist, however, needs to pay attention to what he's painting in order to put it down on canvas, and Raderscheidt was at first unable to concentrate or to pay close attention to anything in the left half of his world. In Figure 8.3 you can see his attempts at a self-portrait as he slowly recovered from the stroke damage.

Exactly how the cognitive strategy of attention works is still a mystery, but experiments have shown that when attention is required for concentration on one

FIGURE 8.3

These four self-portraits (redrawn) were originally made by the German artist Anton Raderscheidt following a stroke in his posterior right parietal lobe. Although able to see, the artist was not able to attend to the left half of his world. The first self-portrait (a) was painted 2 months after his stroke. The artist was able to paint only what was in his right visual field, as that was all he could concentrate on. The self-portrait (b) was made 3 1/2 months after the stroke, and his ability to attend to the left half of his visual field was returning. Six months later, he painted the self-portrait in (c), and 9 months after the stroke he painted the self-portrait in (d), which shows full attention recovery of the left visual field.

(a) (b)

(c) (d)

of two stimuli, both of which are encompassed in the same receptive field, the receptive field will actually narrow, eliminating the unwanted stimulus (Moran & Desimone, 1985). The mechanism of attention, then, somehow controls the expanding and shrinking of receptive fields, which, in turn, filters out what is unwanted. The mechanism that controls how large a given receptive field will be at any moment in time appears to be under the control of inhibitory synapses within the receptive field itself (see Chapter 2). When these inhibitory synapses are active, they are able to limit a receptive field's response to a narrower area than might otherwise be the case (Gottlieb, 1988). Whatever is going on, there is nothing yet like it in a computer.

HEURISTICS VERSUS ALGORITHMS.   In combination with our ability to attend, we can also integrate the parallel processes of our brain. Exactly how we do this is one of the great cognitive secrets to which researchers would love to have an answer. This ability, however, gives us certain problem-solving skills that allow us to outperform any computer.

Consider the following: Checkers, backgammon, chess, or any other game of strategy require that the player engage in problem solving. People have programmed computers to solve problems and to play games. Computers can play chess, checkers, backgammon, and a number of other games. Have you ever played a game of chess with a computer? You might be surprised to learn that there is not a computer in the world—yet—that can consistently beat the world champion (Hsu, Anantharaman, Campbell, & Nowatzyk, 1990).

What goes on inside the computer's "mind" when it's deciding on a move, and how is the process different from that used by human beings to solve problems? Computers generally work according to **algorithms.** An algorithm is defined as a method guaranteed to lead to a solution if one is possible. Solving a problem by algorithms requires a systematic search of every possible avenue or approach to the solution. Computers can apply this method because they can calculate so quickly. An algorithmic chess computer will examine first every possible move and then the possible moves that might follow any of the first possible moves. The computer will even consider very stupid moves that no experienced human player would bother to investigate. As you can imagine, this computer strategy can encompass an almost infinite number of possible moves. And even though the computer is very fast, it might take 2 or 6 years just to "think" five or six moves ahead in a complicated game situation. For this reason, an algorithm guaranteed to win any game of chess could lead to games that would take centuries to play—not unlike Deep Thought's 7.5-million-year requirement to ponder the great question, "What is the meaning of life, the universe, and everything?" In other words, in a complicated situation, a computer that relies on algorithms will soon be overwhelmed by data. Because it's not practical for a chess computer to take more than a couple of hours for its longest move when playing against a human, any algorithmic method it uses is limited by a clock.

Human beings obviously don't think in that fashion. We generally attempt to solve problems by a cognitive strategy of **heuristics.** Heuristic methods aren't guaranteed to reach a solution, and they aren't as systematic as algorithmic methods. But sometimes they can produce solutions considerably faster. Unlike the computer, which will be trying out every possible solution, the human will be working only with those that seem the most reasonable. He doesn't know how the sequences

ALGORITHMS
Mathematical premises. In computer usage, an algorithm is a program that will search for an answer by examining every possibility.

HEURISTICS
Methods for discovering the correct solution to a problem by exploring the possibilities that seem to offer the most reasonable approach to the goal, rather than all possibilities. Heuristics also involve obtaining successive approximations to the correct answer by means of analogies and other search techniques.

Very commonly, problems are too complex to solve with an algorithm. Chess is an example. In a game of chess, it is impossible to calculate all the possible moves in the game within the given time limits. Even the most powerful computers are unable to do this. As a result, chess requires heuristic methods of play.

CHAPTER 8
COGNITION AND LANGUAGE

MEANS–END ANALYSIS
A problem-solving process in which the difference between the current situation and the desired situation is defined and then a series of steps is taken to reduce, and finally eliminate, the difference. This process is applicable whenever there is a clearly specifiable problem and a clearly specifiable solution.

may lead to the solution; he simply takes the first steps toward the apparent direction of the goal, hoping that as he gets closer, he'll see the further steps that will lead him to his final goal.

MEANS–END ANALYSIS. Searching heuristically for the next right step toward the final goal can be very difficult, because the necessary move is not always obvious. Sometimes, however, it's possible to use a plan or general strategy to organize problem solving. Two researchers, Newell and Simon, developed a computer-planning and strategy program some time ago that they called the general problem solver (GPS), which achieved some limited success (Newell & Simon, 1972). The GPS was one of the first computer programs not to use an algorithm; it relied instead on the heuristic of **means-end analysis.**

Means–end analysis may be one of the important cognitive strategies that people use to control and organize the combination of mental procedures (an intellectual skill) and facts (declarative knowledge). In the following example, you can see how the cognitive strategy of means–end analysis is used to organize a series of procedures based on factual knowledge about things such as cars, repair shops, and telephones.

> I want to take my son to nursery school. What's the difference between what I have and what I want? One of distance. What changes distance? My automobile. My automobile won't work. What is needed to make it work? A new battery. What has new batteries? An auto repair shop. I want the repair shop to put in a new battery; but the shop doesn't know I need one. What is the difficulty? One of communication. What allows communication? A telephone . . . and so on.
>
> If is profitable, therefore, to try to eliminate "difficult" differences, even at the cost of introducing new differences of lesser difficulty. This process can be repeated as long as progress is being made toward eliminating the more difficult differences. (Newell & Simon, 1972, p. 416)

In this example, the major difficulty (taking your son to nursery school) can be solved only by overcoming lesser difficulties (obtaining a battery, making a telephone call). In means–end analysis, you must proceed from where you are (the initial state) to where you want to be (the goal) by a series of intermediate steps. Each step is accomplished by particular means until the major goal is reached, assuming that it is reachable.

Students studying this kind of cognitive strategy for the first time sometimes question its usefulness. If you begin to apply it, however, you may be amazed by how much it can affect your thinking. In fact, you may be surprised at how inventive you become. The following passage is an example of how means–end analysis can affect your thinking.

Problem: People often are injured in the shower or bath. Your goal is to reduce or eliminate such injuries.

Question: Why are people hurt in the shower or bathtub? They often fall. (At this point, the solution may appear to be to suspend gravity or to stop people from falling—except that in posing the problem, you've made a classic error. You must always be careful in defining the problem. People are not hurt in the shower or bathtub because they fall. No one is hurt by falling. It's landing that causes the trouble. Just remember the man who fell out of a 10-story building and was heard to say as he passed each floor, "So far, so good." So let's start over.) People are hurt in the bathtub because they land on something hard when they fall. What is the difference between what you have (initial state) and what you want (end state)? Hardness. What determines hardness? The manufacturing materials. What you need, then, is soft material for the bathtub and shower stall. But soft material is porous. What's the difference between what you have and what you want? Porosity (there really is such a word, but it doesn't seem to come up in conversations very often). Therefore, you need a soft *nonporous* material. Is there such a material? What is the difference between what you have and what you want? Information. Where can information be found? In a library. If you find that there is such a material, you are set. If not, then what is the difference between what is available and what you need, and can you develop a soft nonporous material? As it turns out, there are many soft, fairly rigid, nonporous materials. And there is the answer to your problem, a soft bathtub or soft shower stall. In fact, such tubs and showers have recently been developed. They keep their form, they hold water well, and they are very comfortable. As a bonus, soft materials produce a lot of friction, and they are very difficult to slip on. If a person should fall, however, the original problem of a body landing on a hard surface is eliminated.

The idea of a soft bathtub is so unusual that it might not have occurred to you had you not gone through the means–end analysis in order to eliminate collision with hard objects. As you shall discover in the Epilogue, people who are good at this kind of general problem solving or means–end analysis may invent some fascinating things. Any time you have a problem, state the problem carefully and ask yourself, What is the difference between what I have now and what I want? Then break the problem down into as many subgoals as you require and see where it leads you. The next good invention may be yours!

PROBLEM SOLVING.   Cognitive strategies such as heuristics or means–end analysis help people to solve problems. *Problem solving* is defined as a sequence of cognitive operations directed toward achieving a particular goal. If problem solving makes use of intellectual skills, declarative knowledge, and cognitive strategies that you have already acquired, it is called **routine problem solving.** Evidence indicates that routine problem solving is often so routine that the cognitive operations involved in carrying it out are frequently executed without our awareness. That is, the routine becomes unconscious, requiring little or no directed thought or attention on our part (Kihlstrom, 1987). Creative problem solving, on the other hand, requires attention and directed thought. To give you a good example of that, let's try a little creative problem solving.

You are said to be in the initial state of creative problem solving when you are first presented with a problem. You must then find a way to go from the initial state to the goal. For example, Figure 8.4 shows the cheap-necklace problem. Think about the steps you must go through to find a solution. Here are the instructions:

> You are given four separate pieces of chain that are each three links in length. It costs 2 cents to open a link, 3 cents to close a link. All links are closed at the beginning of the problem. Your goal is to join all 12 links of a chain into a single circle at a cost of no more than 15 cents. (Silveira, 1971)

You are now in the initial state. Your goal, of course, is to make the necklace cheaply; that is, for no more than 15 cents. If you approach the problem with a straightforward sequence of operations and link each segment of chain to the next one, finally closing up the chain entirely, it will cost 20 cents, 5 cents over budget. Most people initially attack the problem in this way.

When the cheap-necklace problem was first used in an experiment, the subjects were divided into three different groups. The first group worked with the problem for 1/2 hour; during that time, 50 percent of the group was able to solve the problem. Members of the second group also worked on the problem for 1/2 hour; however, they were told during the problem-solving session to take a 1/2 hour break, in which they did some unrelated activities. Interestingly, after returning,

ROUTINE PROBLEM SOLVING
Problem solving that requires concepts, thoughts, actions, and understandings that are already in your repertoire.

FIGURE 8.4

The cheap-necklace problem. It costs 2 cents to open a link and 3 cents to close a link. Put chains A, B, C, and D together to form a necklace for no more than 15 cents.

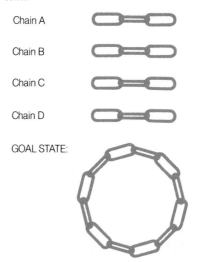

Chain A

Chain B

Chain C

Chain D

GOAL STATE:

64 percent of these subjects were able to solve the problem. A third group also worked for about 1/2 hour on the problem, but was given a 4-hour break during the work period. In this group, 85 percent of the subjects solved the problem when they returned. The subjects in the second and third groups had been kept busy during their breaks and didn't have a chance to think about the cheap-necklace problem. Why should a break be beneficial, and why the longer the better? Although subjects rarely came back after their break with the solution at hand, they often came back with a fresh approach to the problem (Silveira, 1971).

Improving your chances of solving a problem by leaving it awhile and then coming back to it is known as an **incubation effect.** However, if you're on the right track in the first place, taking a break can be disruptive rather than helpful. The most likely time to expect a good incubation effect is when you start out with an inappropriate strategy. If you haven't been able to solve the cheap-necklace problem yet, rather than looking ahead to see what the answer is, take a break and try again later.

The cheap-necklace problem also gives you a good opportunity to experience insight. Many subjects have reported working on the problem for up to 1 hour and then, suddenly, knowing what to do. If this happens to you, you will experience the insight all at once: The answer suddenly will be clear, and you will wonder why you didn't see it before. On the other hand, if you can't stand it anymore, here is the solution:

> Open all three links of chain A at a cost of 6 cents, then use the three links to connect chains B, C, and D with each other, at a cost of 9 cents. In this way you can close the entire necklace, spending only 15 cents (devastatingly simple, isn't it?).

The chimp Sultan's insight about putting the sticks together (see Prologue) or the insight you may have experienced in solving the cheap-necklace problem provides further evidence for the existence of cognitive strategies. The solutions to the problems were achieved through a strategy of manipulating mental procedures and declarative knowledge, rather than through a physical trial-and-error process.

Impediments to Problem Solving

Cognitive strategies also can be helpful in *overriding* acquired procedures and declarative knowledge that may be getting in the way of problem solving. Examples of such impediments to problem solving are mental sets and functional fixedness.

MENTAL SET. Mental procedures usually are very effective in problem solving, especially if they're used for routine problem solving. Sometimes, however, if procedures become too automatized, they may get in the way of a solution that requires creative problem solving. Consider the following example.

In 1942, Luchins formulated a series of water jug problems. In these problems, subjects were given three jugs, each jug having an absolute maximum capacity. They were required to use the jugs to obtain an exact amount of liquid. Table 8.1 sets out 10 of these problems. In the first problem, the jugs can hold 21, 127, and 3 ounces of liquid, respectively. The desired amount is 100 ounces. How could you measure exactly 100 ounces using only these three jugs? The answer is to fill jug B to capacity, then pour liquid into jug C, filling it once, dump that liquid out, fill jug C again, dump that liquid out again (this leaves 121 ounces in jug B), and fill jug A once. You will be left with exactly 100 ounces in jug B.

Working on your own, solve the problems for the remaining nine groups of jugs. By the time you are finished, you may have noticed something interesting.

All the problems but number 8 can be solved in the same way: jug B − 2C jugs − jug A = desired amount. Problems 7 and 9, however, can be solved more simply: A + C = desired amount. Problem 8 cannot be solved by the B − 2C − A method, but it can be solved by the simpler formula A − C. Problems 6 and 10 can be solved by B − 2C − A and also by the simpler A − C.

When Luchins conducted this experiment, he discovered that 83 percent of his subjects used the B − 2C − A method on problems 6 and 7, even though these could have been solved by the easier solutions (A − C and A + C, respectively). This tendency is known as **mental set.** After solving the first five problems by B − 2C − A, the subjects were so used to applying this formula that they used it in problems 6 and 7 as well, even though there were simpler solutions. Subjects who skipped the first five problems and began with 6 and 7 discovered the easier solutions immediately. Interestingly, in Luchins' experiment, 64 percent of the subjects failed altogether to solve problem 8, although it required only A − C; the subjects tried to apply the B − 2C − A method that they had used successfully for the first seven problems. Unable to use a strategy on which they had come to rely, a majority of these subjects said problem 8 couldn't be solved! And 79 percent of the subjects used the B − 2C − A method to solve problems 9 and 10, which are easily solved by other means. If we use the same method to solve similar problems, we may overlook better approaches. A mental set can even cause us to ignore the obvious solution.

Studying the effects of mental sets—in fact, just being aware that they exist—can help you to avoid the problems they cause. Luchins discovered that subjects whom he had advised to pay careful attention were often able to overcome their mental set.

In 1986, about 300,000 sixth graders in California were asked the following question on a statewide test:

If 130 schoolchildren are going on a picnic, and 50 can ride on each school bus, how many buses are needed to carry them all?
(a) 2 (b) 2 and a remainder of 30 (c) 23/5 (d) 3

Fifty-three percent chose either (b) or (c) as the correct answer. Of course, the answer has to be (d), as otherwise the extra 30 children would have to ride in three-fifths of a bus. Some people who viewed these results decried the failings of our

MENTAL SET
A tendency to continue to use a particular approach or type of solution to a problem based on previously learned mental procedures.

TABLE 8.1 Luchin's Water-Jug Problems

CAPACITY OF JUG A	CAPACITY OF JUG B	CAPACITY OF JUG C	DESIRED QUANTITY
1. 21	127	3	100
2. 14	163	25	99
3. 18	43	10	5
4. 9	42	6	21
5. 20	59	4	31
6. 23	49	3	20
7. 15	39	3	18
8. 28	76	3	25
9. 18	48	4	22
10. 14	36	8	6

FUNCTIONAL FIXEDNESS
A mental set in which you are unable to
see beyond an object's customary function
to its other possible uses because you have
relied on too narrowly defined declarative
information.

educational system (Murray, 1986). Many educators argued, instead, that the children's failure to see the obvious answer was simply the result of a mental set—after doing long-division problems for a whole year, a sixth grader understandably might see the school bus problem as nothing more than just another straightforward long division problem, and might solve it blindly. You can bet that if these same children had just solved 100 school-bus-type problems, they would have rounded off the answer to the next highest whole number.

FUNCTIONAL FIXEDNESS.   The declarative information we have also is usually helpful for solving problems. It provides us with the facts we need to find solutions. Sometimes, however, our declarative information can be too tied to specific facts. Once this happens, we may begin to think that objects that have a specific function can function only in the intended way. This inclination is known as **functional fixedness.** Recall for a moment the soft bathtub that you derived from means–end analysis.

The idea of a soft bathtub is so reasonable that it's hard to believe no one thought of it sooner. New inventions often seem obvious—after they've been invented. The problem with the tub is that experience has taught us to think that only hard objects are suitable containers for large amounts of water. This obviously isn't the case. When we link a particular item or material with one particular function, we may find it difficult to imagine other possibilities. In Figure 8.5 you'll see a table on which there are matches, a candle, and a box of tacks. The task is

FIGURE 8.5

Using only these materials, attach the candle to the middle of the door in an upright position, so that it can burn naturally.

to use these materials to attach the candle to the door in an upright position so that the candle can burn normally (Duncker, 1945). Can you think of a good way to do this? Figure 8.6 poses another problem. The two strings must be tied together, but they are so far apart that one person alone can't grasp them simultaneously. Suppose you were this person, and you had to solve the problem with only the materials shown in the picture. What would you do (Maier, 1931)?

If you have trouble with either problem, you may be suffering from functional fixedness. To solve these problems, it is necessary to use the materials differently from the way in which they're normally used. In the first problem (Figure 8.5), most people think of the box as a container for the tacks. The answer, however, is to empty the box of tacks, affix the candle to the middle of the box by pushing a thumbtack up through the bottom, and then fasten the box to the door by pushing thumbtacks through the side of the box into the door. In this way, the box becomes a platform for the candle. The matches aren't needed except to light the candle.

The solution to the second problem (Figure 8.6) requires that the pliers be used as a weight. We typically think of pliers, not as a weight, but rather as a grasping tool. If you tie the pliers to one of the strings, however, you can start the string swinging. Then you can go over and grab the other string, come back, and retrieve the swinging string as it nears you. In this way, you'll be able to hold both strings at once, bring them together, and tie them.

If you're used to using items in unique ways, or if you're aware of unique properties of particular items, functional fixedness is easier to overcome. In one study, the solution required that a screwdriver blade be used as a conductor of electricity in a circuit (Glucksberg & Danks, 1968). The subjects had a great deal of difficulty finding the solution because they were not accustomed to thinking of the screwdriver in this fashion. Functional fixedness had struck again. In a follow-up study, however, a researcher gave subjects practice ahead of time in classifying objects such as paper clips and crayons according to their ability to conduct electricity (Teborg, 1968). These subjects were able to transcend their functional fixedness and to realize immediately that the screwdriver blade could be used in an

FIGURE 8.6

How can you tie the strings together?

CHAPTER 8
COGNITION AND LANGUAGE

electric circuit. This experiment indicates that the more practice a person has solving problems, the more likely it is that the person will be able to solve future problems.

Mental set and functional fixedness don't always interfere with problem solving. In fact, routine problem solving is facilitated by mental sets and functional fixedness, because old methods usually work and using an object as it was intended to be used is normally good strategy. If mental set or functional fixedness does cause a problem, it's likely to be during creative problem solving, when finding a solution may entail breaking away from old ideas and methods. When engaging in creative problem solving, then, be careful not to begin with too many preconceived procedures or facts.

Motor Skills

The fourth important cognitive category is motor skills. These are skills that require muscular motions, such as those needed for riding a bicycle, playing tennis, or using tools. Motor skills are maintained in the procedural memory (see Chapter 7) and are acquired slowly through conditioning and practice (see Chapter 6). Intellectual skills, on the other hand, are sometimes acquired abruptly through insight. Practicing a motor skill requires that the same muscular movements be repeated again and again. To practice intellectual or verbal skills, however, you should apply them in different ways in many circumstances.

Another important distinction between motor skills and intellectual or verbal skills is that we can better remember newly acquired motor skills for a great length

Unlike intellectual or verbal skills, motor skills are not easily forgotten. It is easy to forget, for example, that Quito is the capital of Ecuador, but not easy to forget how to ride a bicycle, even if you haven't been on one for a long time.

of time, whereas we can rapidly forget newly acquired intellectual or verbal skills if we don't practice them. It is easy to forget that Quito is the capital of Ecuador, but not easy to forget how to ride a bicycle, even if you haven't been on one in quite some time (see Figure 8.7). These different rates of forgetting further highlight an important difference between procedural and declarative memory (see Chapter 7). The motor skill, held in the procedural memory, is forgotten much more slowly than the declarative information, held in the declarative memory.

Attitudes

Attitudes comprise the fifth important cognitive category. Many cognitive researchers believe that attitudes are a distinct entity that influence our thinking, reasoning, and performance. Attitudes are thought to be acquired through classical and higher-order conditioning (see Chapter 6) and may also be acquired through other, yet unknown ways. Attitudes appear to be maintained in the long-term memory (see Chapter 7) and influence behavior in important ways (Tourangeau & Rasinski, 1988). They do not determine our performance in the way that intellectual skills or declarative information do. For instance, a positive attitude toward dogs may influence your behavior so that you choose to pet a dog if one is present, but attitudes do not provide you with the skills to know what a dog is or how you can interact with one. Of all our cognitive aspects, attitudes are most closely tied to our emotions.

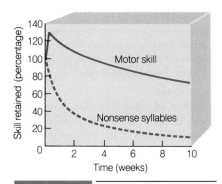

FIGURE 8.7

These curves represent the rate at which particular skills are forgotten and the percentage decrease in skills over time. Subjects were trained, retrained (their motor skill increased 30 percent from the retraining), and then tested over 10 weeks' time. Declarative information (especially of meaningless nonsense syllables) is lost far more quickly than is a motor skill. (SOURCE: Leavitt and Schlosberg, 1944, p. 412.)

CONCEPT REVIEW: HUMAN COGNITIVE PERFORMANCE

1. Intellectual skills: Procedural and categorical knowledge probably held in the declarative memory, including:

Mental procedures: *If–then* connections. As a person becomes expert, the *if–then* connections become automatized and are reduced in number.

Concepts: concrete and abstract ideas grouped according to common qualities or properties. Enable a person's understanding to be greatly expanded beyond her limited experience. Many new objects or ideas can be understood in terms of previously learned concepts.

2. Declarative knowledge: All knowledge that can be declared or stated. Declarative knowledge is maintained in the declarative memory. As a person becomes expert, the propositional networks (see Chapter 7) of declarative knowledge are elaborated and expanded.

3. Cognitive strategies: Higher-level control strategies that enable a person to use intellectual skills and verbal knowledge efficiently. Not well understood. Examples may include:

Heuristics: Methods that offer good solutions through the exploration of what appear to be the most reasonable approaches toward a goal, rather than via the exploration of every possible approach.

Means-end analysis: A problem-solving process that reduces the difference between the initial state and the final goal state into a large number of substeps that can be solved more easily.

4. Motor skills: Knowledge of muscular operations that is maintained in the procedural memory. Motor skills are forgotten at a much slower rate than is verbal knowledge.

5. Attitudes: Perhaps acquired through classical or higher-order conditioning (see Chapter 6). Attitudes influence performance by providing an emotional dimension, but they do not determine performance in the way that intellectual skills, declarative knowledge, cognitive strategies, or motor skills do. Attitudes may be the most difficult aspect of human cognitive performance to teach.

LANGUAGE
Any means of communication that uses signs, symbols, or gestures within a grammar and through which novel constructions can be created.

GRAMMAR
A set of rules that determines how sounds may be put together to make words and how words may be put together to make sentences.

LINGUISTIC RELATIVITY
Whorf's hypothesis that thought is structured according to the language spoken, so that those who speak different languages have different thinking patterns.

Attitudes are also considered distinct because they appear to be the most difficult of the five kinds of cognitive performance to teach. Although schools and training centers are able to teach intellectual skills, declarative information, some cognitive strategies, and motor skills, deliberate attempts to shape attitudes more often meet with failure (McGuire, 1969). Like motor skills, attitudes appear to persist over a great length of time even if they are not practiced. Then again, exactly how an attitude is "practiced" is not clear (Gagné, 1984).

Research to create artificial intelligence also illustrates that the role of attitudes is unique. Scientists hope that computers will eventually contain vast amounts of intellectual skills and declarative information controlled by cognitive strategies. As we mentioned, computers may even need to venture out of the laboratory to experience the world, much the way a human being does, so they can "understand" in the way humans do. For this reason, computers may require motor skills too. But attitudes? How would you program a computer to have "feelings" or "hunches" about the information it is processing? In fact, the presence of such attitudes is one of the reasons physicist Roger Penrose gives for his argument that computers can never be intelligent like humans. Penrose points to certain conclusions from mathematics that are obviously true, but which cannot be proved through calculation. For that reason, he argues, no computer will ever understand them in the way that we do (Penrose, 1989).

Attitudes permeate the atmosphere in which our thinking, reasoning, and performance occur. They may distinguish us from machines more than any of the other categories we have discussed, and yet they remain among the most mysterious of our cognitive abilities.

LANGUAGE

No one knows where **language** fits into the cognitive scheme of things. Some people have argued that language is derived from one general all-purpose cognitive ability (Anderson, 1983). Others have argued that language is the result of a combination of cognitive abilities that include intellectual skills (the procedures for creating a **grammar**), declarative knowledge (the meanings of words), cognitive strategies (putting grammar and meaning together to form sentences), motor skills (operating the mouth, lips, and tongue while speaking), and attitudes (which give emotional content to the meanings of words) (Gagné, 1984). Some researchers believe that language is a special and distinct skill, separate from all the other cognitive skills, and uniquely human (Wanner & Gleitman, 1982). Whichever is the case, it is obvious that speaking a language is a powerful human ability.

Perhaps the view that cognitive researchers have taken toward language has been stated best by Steven Pinker:

> Language acquisition is the jewel of the crown of cognition. It is what everyone wants to explain. . . . In a sense, language acquisition defines what it is to be an intelligent human being. (Kolata, 1987b, p. 133)

Linguistic Relativity

No one knows just how tied together language and thought are. It has been argued that language influences thinking so strongly that thinking itself is actually modified or limited by the words and concepts available in the language. In other words, the fact that you speak the language you do may make it more or less difficult for you to have particular thoughts or ideas than if you spoke another language. Benjamin Lee Whorf called this effect **linguistic relativity** (Whorf, 1956).

Linguistic relativity is an interesting idea. Many people who are bilingual claim that they are able to think and express certain thoughts in one language much better than in the other. But is it true that our thinking, viewpoint, and perceptions are directly influenced by the words we have in our language? To test this hypothesis, one researcher compared the Dani, a Stone Age agricultural people who live in New Guinea, with persons who spoke English (Rosch, 1973). In the Dani language, there are just two terms for color, *mola* for bright, warm colors and *mili* for dark, cold colors. If Whorf's suggestion that words facilitate perception and understanding were true, the Dani should not have understood that many different colors shown to them were different, because their language distinguished between colors in only two ways. Rosch found, however, that the Dani could easily tell many colors apart, even though they had no words for the different colors in their language. This result indicated that the Dani perceived color distinctions independently of the language they spoke.

Still, the Whorf hypothesis is hard to test fully, and it may well be that the kind of language people speak facilitates the way in which they approach problems or make discriminations. What do you think?

Language Acquisition

A language is based on the use of signs or symbols within a grammar; that is, within a structure of rules that determines how the various signs or symbols are to be arranged. Newborn infants don't possess language. Of this we are sure. As infants grow, they develop language in a step-by-step sequence. Interestingly, the sequence of language acquisition is similar among children all over the world.

THE ONSET OF LANGUAGE. The English language consists of more than 100,000 words, 26 letters, and approximately 53 **phonemes**. At first, infants make little vowel-like "comfort sounds." By 2 to 4 months of age, these comfort sounds start to sound a little more languagelike. During this time, a languagelike sound might include "goo" or something similar, which is why this time is known as the **gooing stage.**

By the time infants are 4 to 7 months old, they generally produce a great number of phonetic sounds, often many more than they will require for the language they will eventually speak. This process is called phonetic expansion, and this time is called the **expansion stage.** The new sounds made during the expansion stage include yells, whispers, growls, squeals, and, every parent's favorite, the **raspberry.** Also during this time, the first fully formed vowels appear. Although mature syllables during the expansion stage are rare, as the infant's repertoire of sounds grows, parents will become aware that their infant has begun to "babble."

Between the ages of 7 and 10 months the infant's babbling greatly increases as she begins to produce mature syllables and duplicated sequences such as "dadada" or "mamama." This is known as the **cononical stage** of language acquisition. Interestingly, babies who can hear soon begin to babble cononical syllables, whereas deaf babies, who also babble, do not (Oller & Eilers, 1988). This finding tells us that even early on, experience with sound affects the language acquisition of hearing infants.

Between 10 and 14 months of age, infants narrow their use of phonemes mainly to the ones they will be using in the language they will eventually learn. This process is called phonetic contraction, and this time is called the **contraction stage.** By this time, infants also are beginning to acquire the pacing and rhythm of the language. Sometimes, an infant joins phonemes with a rhythm, pacing, and length

PHONEMES
The most basic distinctive sounds in any given language. Phonemes are combined into words.

GOOING STAGE
A stage of language acquisition that typically occurs between the ages of 2 and 4 months. During this stage, infants combine the vowel-like comfort sounds made earlier with harder sounds that are the precursors of consonants. An example, is "goo."

EXPANSION STAGE
A stage of language acquisition that typically occurs between the ages of 4 and 7 months. During this stage, infants produce many new sounds giving rise to babbling. The onset of the expansion stage does not appear to require feedback because deaf babies also babble. Toward the end of the stage, however, the effects of hearing experience begin to be discernible.

RASPBERRY
In foodstuffs: a rather tasty fruit; a type of berry. In social discourse: an explosive sound owing to the rapid expulsion of air from the mouth that vigorously vibrates the lips (especially the lower lip), which, as required for the effect, have been deliberately placed in a configuration so as to make contact with, and surround, the protruded tongue. Considered unrequired in most social circumstances. (For an exception to this rule, see "Sporting events.")

CONONICAL STAGE
A stage of language acquisition that typically occurs between the ages of 7 and 10 months typified by an increase in babbling and the production of cononical syllables (syllables made of consonant and vowel sounds of certain intensities). Duplicated sequences such as "dadada" or "mamama" also mark this stage.

CONTRACTION STAGE
A stage of language acquisition that typically occurs between the ages of 10 and 14 months. So named because during this time the infant will begin to narrow her production of language sounds until it includes mostly the sounds that are common to the language to which she has been exposed. During this stage, infants also acquire the pacing and rhythm of their language.

that is so similar to actual language (except that real words are not spoken) that parents swear that their baby has just spoken a totally intelligible sentence but they somehow missed what he said.

For infants to acquire the specific phonemes of their language, feedback appears to be necessary. That is, infants have to be able to imitate what they hear before phonetic contraction can begin. This brings up the first of many linguistic problems. If infants imitate what they hear, why don't they speak in sentences? After all, they hear language, not babbling.

The reason that infants babble rather than imitate full sentences may be that individual words can be discriminated or recognized *only* after they have been associated with particular objects, actions, or circumstances (Miller & Gildea, 1987). This process of recognition takes place through experience, as infants grow. Until these associations have been made—that is, until these different sounds have a *meaning*—any of us can discern only the phonemes. Suppose you were suddenly transported to a foreign land where everyone spoke an unfamiliar language. You wouldn't be aware of distinct words. Everything that was said would sound like gibberish to you. After a short time, however, you might become aware of some aspects of the language. Perhaps you'd become aware of the spacing—when sounds began and when they ended. You also might become aware of the rhythm and tonal changes or differences in phonetic sounds. Unfortunately, your sensitivity to these aspects of language wouldn't enable you to communicate. On the other hand, you could be learning to imitate the sounds of the language so well that you might appear to be a native speaker to someone who didn't know the language, even though you couldn't say a single word. This sort of imitation is easy for many people to do; you've probably heard it done many times. Comedians such as Robin Williams or Benny Hill are able in this way to "speak" many languages without having any idea of what they are saying, if anything. But unlike a comedian who learns to "speak" a language phonetically without understanding it, or a computer that can teach itself to mimic a language (also without understanding), children learn their native languages through experience and meaning. As humans, meaning is so important to us that it may well be the core of all cognition. You can "teach" a computer the dictionary definitions of a "warm sunny day" or of "a holiday dinner with the family," but it doesn't learn by feeling the warm sun on its skin or by having a wonderful dinner and sharing the experiences of the day with its family. It is through such experiences, however, that children come to develop meanings.

Infants show an attentiveness to language even before they speak their first words.

THE ONE-WORD STAGE.   Children usually speak their first word sometime between 10 and 17 months of age, with the average age being 13.6 months (Bloom & Capatides, 1987). At this point, they enter what predictably is referred to as the **one-word stage.** Typically, children's first words relate directly to certain objects or actions that are within their own experience. Although it is often difficult to generalize from an adult's experience to that of a child, you might again imagine yourself living in the foreign land we spoke of earlier. Like a child, you might first acquire words that you could pair directly with some tangible object or obvious action. Children seem to acquire concrete nouns and verbs first, such as *mama, go,* or *wa-wa* (water); they learn more abstract words later.*

The first basic nouns that children use tend to follow the *three-bears rule.* The

*The moment when infants first say a duplicated-syllable word such as "mama," "dada," or "wa-wa" generally coincides with the very first occurrence of a preference for using one hand over the other (Ramsay, 1984). This discovery emphasizes how much language may be tied to the development of the brain and nervous system, because both language and handedness are known to be related to the development of the hemispheres of the brain (see Chapter 2).

rule states that a child is most likely to learn a basic noun such as "dog" before she learns a subordinate noun such as "collie" or a superordinate noun such as "mammal." It's called the three-bears rule because, like the story of "Goldilocks and the Three Bears," the category "mammal" is *too large* and the category "collie" is *too small*, while the category "dog" is *just right* (Gleitman & Wanner, 1984). A concept such as "dog" is clearly tied to the simple, basic, and tangible object that is a dog. Such a basic and nonabstract concept is often referred to as **protoconcept** and is especially easy for children to conceptualize (Roberts, 1988). For instance, whereas a "dog" is easy to imagine, imagining the subordinate "collie" requires specialized knowledge about dogs, and imagining the superordinant "mammal" (not a dog, or cow, or whale, or rabbit—just a "mammal") is impossible because the concept is too abstract.

Subordinants appear to be acquired when children are given a new name for something that *they already know by name*. In one study, two different toy dogs were shown to 2-year-olds who already knew that both animals were dogs. One dog was then labeled a "fep." Rather than deciding that both animals were now "feps" or that one should now be called by the proper name "Fep," the children appeared to conclude that the one given a new name was a "fep" kind of dog (Taylor & Gelman, 1989).

Abstract words are acquired after basic nouns and verbs. The first abstract words tend to be adjectives, such as "red," "tall," or "big." Later, terms that are more abstract are acquired, such as the spatial referents "in," "on," and "between." Finally, children acquire very abstract words such as "freedom," "tangential," or the superordinate "mammal," items philosopher Bertrand Russell called "dictionary words" because we learn their definitions verbally rather than by their relationships to real objects. Use of dictionary words among children younger than 5 years is rare. You can imagine the shock one father received when his 3-year-old daughter, while looking at the clouds lazily drifting by, sighed and said, "When I'm older, I'll be free." He recovered from his shock when she added, "I mean four" (Whitehurst, 1982, p. 379).

THE TWO-WORD STAGE.   Children between 18 and 20 months of age usually have begun to utter two-word statements. During this stage (brilliantly referred to as the **two-word stage**), children rapidly learn the value of language for expressing concepts, especially for communicating their desires to other people. During this time, it is not unusual for more than a thousand new two-word statements to appear monthly (Braine, 1963). This rate is not surprising when you stop to consider that the average English-speaking high school graduate has a vocabulary of about 40,000 words. If you add to that all of the names of people and places that he knows, as well as idiomatic expressions, the number doubles to 80,000 (Miller & Gildea, 1987). If you figure that he has been learning words for about 16 years (since the age of 1), that comes out to about 5,000 words a year, or about *13 new words each and every day of his life!* Children with large vocabularies may acquire words at twice that rate. When you think of it that way, language acquisition can be seen for the formidable task that it is.

Once two-word utterances begin, children are able to make use of many of the descriptive forms found in language—nominative ("that house"), possessive ("Daddy book"), and action ("kitty go"). Throughout the two-word stage, children have a chance to practice these language forms before attempting to expand them. The two-word stage is a universal phenomenon (Slobin, 1970). Behavior theory (see Chapter 6) has never been able to explain adequately these two qualities: universality of language acquisition and the incredible speed at which children acquire language (Lenneberg, 1966, 1967).

PROTOCONCEPT
A primary concept of the simplest form usually related directly to a tangible object and exemplifying a general category (such as dog, house, boat).

TWO-WORD STAGE
The universal stage of language development in which children's expressions are limited to two-word sentences.

FIGURE 8.8

An example of the "wugs" used by Berko in her study of the acquisition of language rules (SOURCE: Berko, 1958, p. 154.)

THIS IS A WUG.

NOW THERE IS ANOTHER ONE.
THERE ARE TWO OF THEM.
THERE ARE TWO _____ .

TELEGRAPHIC SPEECH.   Children do not enter a three-word stage. Instead, following the two-word stage, they spend the next few years creating many short sentences. Roger Brown has referred to children's sentences during the two-word stage and after as **telegraphic speech.**

Telegraphic speech is an apt term. When people send telegrams, at so many cents per word, they want to be brief and to the point; unnecessary words are excluded. Children's telegraphic speech is similar. A famous example of telegraphic speech can be found in old Tarzan films. Johnny Weismuller believed that since Tarzan was just getting the hang of English after having lived with the apes for so long, he would speak in a certain way. The speech pattern Weismuller chose in portraying Tarzan was a telegraphic one; it was rich in important words such as nouns and verbs ("Jane go now," "Boy here soon," "Tarzan help Cheetah"). In these instances, certain items called **grammatical morphemes** are missing; that is, there are no tenses, plurals, conjunctions, articles, prepositions, and so on. This structure is typical of telegraphic speech.

Findings indicate that children throughout the world acquire grammatical morphemes in the same general order, although at different rates (deVilliers & de-Villiers, 1973). This sequence of acquisition is so pervasive that even children who have language disorders acquire these grammatical morphemes in the same order (Khan & James, 1983; Brown, 1984).

Researchers aren't certain why children acquire morphemes in a particular order, although the order may have to do with the complexity of each task. Return for a moment to that foreign land to which you were sent earlier in this chapter. Once you had acquired single words and then two-word phrases, and had begun to string the phrases together in a clipped, telegraphic manner, you too would slowly begin to acquire grammatical morphemes—but in what order? Perhaps you would learn the simplest and most obvious ones first. This may be exactly what children do. They learn the easiest and most obvious rule first, and then simply begin to apply it.

Other researchers have argued that it's not complexity, but rather functionality, that determines the order of acquisition (MacWhinney, 1978). In other words, the order of acquisition is determined by how much function each grammatical morpheme serves; the ones providing the child with the most value or function are learned first.

Children eventually acquire the grammar rules that adults use. For instance, children soon learn that adding an "s" after a word such as dog means more than one dog. That children understand the rules they are using and are not simply repeating the word *dogs*, for instance, has been demonstrated in an experiment by Berko (1958). Children were asked to answer the question posed in Figure 8.8. They correctly answered, "Wugs," a clear demonstration that they had learned the plural rule, since they had never before heard the word *wug*.

Syntactic and Semantic Structure

Once they have acquired language competence, how do people learn to express themselves by means of language? Can you recall how you learned to express what you wanted to say? In fact, are you even aware of the process you go through in deciding how to express yourself? **Psycholinguists** examine human language to discover how we "decide to say what we say." As you will see, the process is not simple.

Suppose you are working in the hot sun and are becoming thirsty. How do you express a desire for a glass of water? How do you tell your friend on the job that you think it's time to take a break and get a drink? How do you express your meaning in a structured sentence? You may say simply, "Let's take a break and get a drink of water." But was it that simple? How did you come up with that sentence? Did you just string the words together? Were some words more important than others? Could you have strung them together differently?

In formulating that sentence, you probably didn't begin by searching your entire vocabulary until you struck the word *let's*, which you then decided was the best first word. Although a computer programmed for language might perform in this way—choosing each word in sequence before uttering it—people don't. People sort out entire sentences before they say them. They build the **syntax** of a sentence so that it expresses a meaning, and they do this before they begin to speak. The syntax of a language comprises the rules that describe how words may be put together to form sentences. *Grammar* is a broader term than *syntax*; it includes both syntax and **phonetics**. Phonetics includes the study of how sounds (phonemes) are put together to make words.

Spoonerisms give us a clue to the way in which people organize their syntax to express their meaning. Spoonerisms are interesting transpositions named after William A. Spooner (1844–1930), an English clergyman known for accidentally making such rearrangements. You've probably committed a spoonerism or two yourself. Think of a theater usher who asked a group of people, "Would you like me to sew you to your sheets?" when he had meant to say, "Would you like me to show you to your seats?" What this spoonerism demonstrates is that the usher had to have had the word *seats* in mind (the tenth word in the sentence) before he ever said *show* (the sixth word). Otherwise, how could he have gotten these words confused? People work out their syntax before they say the sentence; they don't simply link one word to the next (Motley, 1985).

Some words in a sentence are more important than others, while other words are systematically arranged around the main words to help express the meaning. Like children in the two-word stage, older children and adults stress nouns and verbs. Unlike children in the two-word stage, however, older children and adults build on the nouns and verbs. In one interesting experiment, adults were classically conditioned to salivate when they heard certain sentences. Later, the individual words of the sentence were spoken to them and the amount of salivation was recorded. Although articles, adjectives, and prepositions were as much a part of the sentence as the nouns and verbs, it was the nouns and verbs that generated the greatest salivary response (Razran, 1961).

How we choose a starting place for building a sentence, however, remains unknown, even though language theorists have debated and wondered about this topic for years. There are researchers who believe we use some as-yet-unknown deep cognitive processing strategy to go from the meaning that we wish to express to the syntax we use. Noam Chomsky (1957), a well-known and respected linguist, has proposed the existence of a **language acquisition device,** or LAD, that has evolved in our species to handle the interaction between syntax and semantics. Others believe that the initial focus of a sentence is tied to the topic at hand and that certain aspects of grammar structure derive from the need to emphasize that topic.

To understand what people mean when they argue that grammar rules may have derived from efforts to express a topic, let's consider the sentence, "The cat followed Ann," and the same idea expressed in the passive voice, "Ann was followed by the cat." Both sentences really say the same thing, which may make you wonder why our grammar has a passive voice. What's the point of having two ways of saying the same thing?

Researcher Henrietta Lempert believes that the passive voice may have gotten started because of our need to select a particular focus, to express a particular

SYNTAX
The body of linguistic rules that makes it possible to relate a series of words in a sentence to the underlying meaning of that sentence, that is, the rules governing word order in a language (sentence structure).

PHONETICS
The study and classification of speech sounds and their production, transmission, and perception.

SPOONERISMS
Unintentional transpositions of sounds in a sentence, as in "people in glass houses shouldn't stow thrones." The phenomenon is named for an English clergyman, William A. Spooner, who was well known for such errors.

LANGUAGE ACQUISITION DEVICE (LAD)
Developed by Noam Chomsky: An hypothesized neural structure inborn in every healthy individual that is preprogrammed with the underlying rules of a universal form of grammar. Once the child is exposed to a particular language, he will select from the complete sets of rules with which he was born, the ones required by the language he is speaking. Most psychologists and linguists currently find the idea to be interesting but agree that a proof is doubtful because it is so difficult to find ways to demonstrate the existence of such an hypothesized device.

topic—and not because somebody one day thought that what we all needed was another rule of grammar.

To understand what Lempert means, consider the following incident: "The bus hit the dog." If it was your dog, and you wanted to talk about what happened to your dog, *your* dog would be the topic of concern; you would focus your thoughts on your dog. Therefore, you would begin your sentence with "My dog." But then where do you go? My dog—what? You can't say, "My dog hit the bus"; that's not what happened. Instead, you are forced to say, "My dog *was hit by the bus*"—the passive voice. Lempert demonstrated in experiments that children of 2 to 5 years could acquire such forms of expression as the passive voice, *especially* if the topic was, like the dog in our example, animate and live (Lempert, 1989). Perhaps our grammar works that way. We start with a central topic and then try to build from it. This, in turn, may lead to a series of complicated grammatical forms, all of which have a use; namely, to support the topic. Such an assumption, however, is incredibly difficult to demonstrate, and no one knows for sure whether it's correct.

Why Does Language Acquisition Occur?

Although some theories have been developed to explain why language is acquired, no one theory has been proven superior at explaining or predicting language development (Bloom, 1983). We do have many hints, however. For instance, not all people acquire the same language, so it is obvious that learning plays an important role. At the same time, it is known that deaf babies will enter the babbling stage (Stoel-Gammon & Otomo, 1986) and that all healthy humans will acquire language except under the most unusual circumstances. These two facts are evidence for a natural predisposition in our species to acquire language. An additional finding in support of natural language acquisition is that specific areas in the human brain appear to be "prewired" for language (see Focus on Research).

Teaching Language to the Great Apes

As we noted earlier, some researchers think that our language ability is not like our other cognitive skills, but that it is separate and unique (Wanner & Gleitman, 1982). Learning theorists, in contrast, have argued that language might be acquired by any organism, as long as the organism had the basic learning power necessary. If the first view is correct, language should be uniquely human. If the second view is correct, it may be possible to teach language to a very bright animal who doesn't normally use it. This is one of the reasons that researchers turned their attention to the great apes.

In the early 1950s, two psychologists attempted to get a chimpanzee named Viki to speak English. After many months of trying, Viki could say "cup" and "up" (and, less convincingly, "mama" and "papa") (Hayes & Hayes, 1952). Many people believe that the chimp's vocal apparatus is unsuited for making English phonemes.

SIGN LANGUAGE.   In 1966, Beatrice and Allen Gardner began to investigate this question. They speculated that chimps might be able to learn to speak if they were taught sign language, specifically the American Sign Language (ASL) used by the deaf (Gardner & Gardner, 1969). This was an ingenious idea; after all, chimps are extremely competent with their hands. They can pick up dimes, work screwdrivers, wind watches, and even thread needles.

The Gardners' first attempt was with a female chimp named Washoe (after Washoe County, Nevada, where the Gardners lived). Their experiment had interesting results. By the age of 12 years, Washoe had acquired over 180 signs (Fouts,

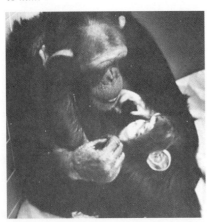
Washoe with her adopted son, Loulis. Loulis acquired a number of signs from Washoe, who often spontaneously signed to him.

In Chapter 2, you learned that there were specialized regions in the brain that appear to be directly involved with language. **Broca's area** was named after Paul Broca, a French physician who during the 1860s discovered that damage to a particular region in the cerebral cortex causes aphasia, a speech disorder. Broca's area is located on the side of the frontal lobe (see Figure 8.9). Broca discovered that aphasia occurs only when this area is damaged on the left side of the brain. If the same area is damaged on the right side of the brain, speech remains intact. Over the last 130 years, this finding has been repeatedly confirmed, and studies continue to shed light on this special area of the brain. The following case studies provide some interesting new findings concerning the left hemisphere and language.

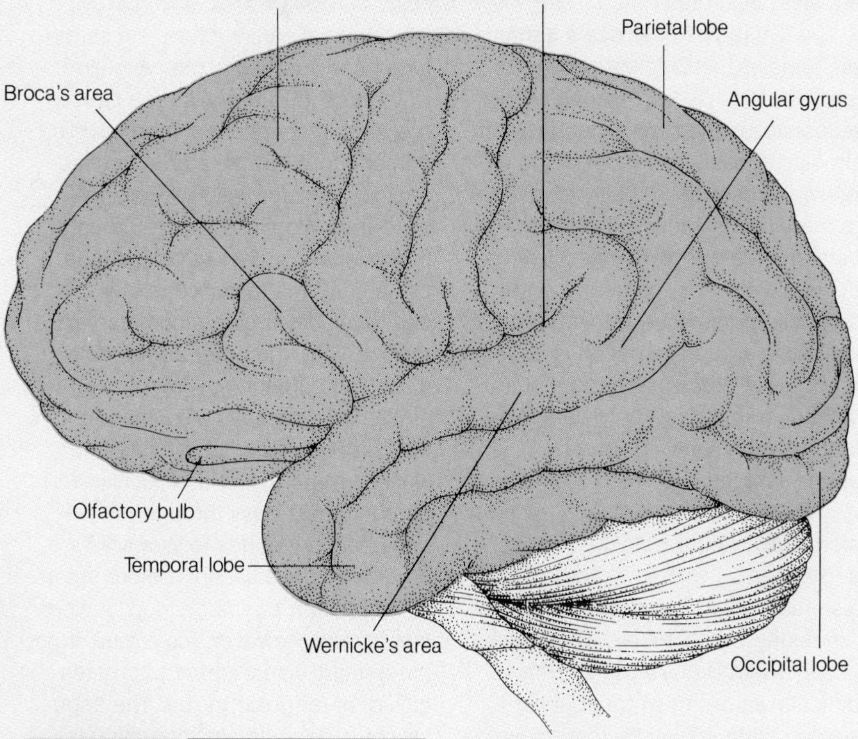

FIGURE 8.9

Major areas of the brain, including portions specialized for language.

The Case of Sarah M.

Sarah M. was born deaf; she communicated with her hands through sign language. She had been a successful artist for much of her life and was expert at painting delicate scenes and designs on eggshells as well as on canvas. Then, at the age of 71 years, she suffered a severe stroke in the right hemisphere of her brain. The stroke destroyed her ability to paint. She could only make a few haphazard lines and disorganized figures. Her doctors had expected this, because the right hemisphere is known to be very involved in spatial perception (see Chapter 2). The left side of her vision also was disrupted and, like the artist Anton Raderscheidt who also had a stroke, and whom you met earlier this chapter, Sarah tended to leave the left side of her attempted drawings blank. To the astonishment of researchers, however, her sign language ability was unaffected! The spatial skills that the right hemisphere controls to such a strong degree, and that scientists had assumed were needed to organize both hands into forming signs, were not required (Poizner, Klima, & Bellugi, 1987).

In stark contrast, but offering further support for the power of the left hemisphere to control all language functions, is the case of Gail D. who, like Sarah, was also deaf from birth and was fluent in sign language.

The Case of Gail D.

At the age of 38 years, Gail had a left-hemisphere stroke. Although she was not an artist, she could draw and copy as accurately after her stroke as she could before. After the stroke, however, she found herself able to sign only a few nouns or verbs and was often unable to place even these few words into a proper grammar (Poizner, Klima, Bellugi, 1987).

Case studies like these help to show that parts of the left hemisphere in humans appear to control language no matter how the language is expressed. Most studies, however, focus on damage to the left hemisphere among people who were previously able to speak language. Such studies are also revealing. Among the kinds of problems that have been observed are Broca's aphasia and Wernicke's aphasia, as well as a host of other interesting disorders.

The symptoms of **Broca's aphasia** are impaired articulation and slow and labored speech. Although their responses make sense, people with Broca's aphasia find it difficult to express themselves in a fully formed or grammatical sentence. They also have trouble with verb inflections, connective words, pronouns, and complex grammatical constructions. Halting telegraphic speech in an adult is a sign of Broca's aphasia. For instance, in referring to a visit from friends, a person with Broca's aphasia might say, "Yes . . . Friday . . . No . . . Joe and Susan . . . Sunday morning . . . eight o'clock . . . Joe . . . and Susan . . . visit. . . ." They might also make word substitutions such as "someday" for "Sunday." Because patients with Broca's aphasia have difficulty speaking words, but not singing them, it may be that singing is controlled by a different area in the brain.

In 1874, Carl Wernicke, a German researcher, identified another kind of aphasia associated with damage to another part of the cortex in the left hemisphere. **Wernicke's area** is in the left temporal and parietal lobes (see Figure 8.9). Wernicke's area is connected to Broca's area by a bundle of nerve fibers called the **arcuate fasciculus.**

The speech of people with **Wernicke's aphasia** is phonetically and grammatically normal, but its semantic content is bizarre. They can string together words with the proper inflections and grammar, but the "sentences" make no sense whatsoever, such as, "The green odor ran concurrently without a day." It may be that semantic content is generated in Wernicke's area, but it is not structured in a suitable grammar until it has passed by way of the arcuate fasciculus to Broca's area, which provides the grammatical structure. These different specializations may explain why damage to Broca's area causes one kind of speech disruption, while damage to Wernicke's area causes another. As information travels forward from Wernicke's area through Broca's area, it passes on to the facial area of the motor cortex, which can then activate the mouth, larynx, tongue, lips, and other appropriate muscles for speech.

Wernicke's area is also important in the comprehension of reading and writing. When a sound is initially heard, it must pass through the primary auditory cortex to Wernicke's area, which is adjacent, before the message can be understood. A word that is read, however, must pass from the primary visual cortex to an area called the **angular gyrus.** The angular gyrus does an amazing thing to the visual image of the word: It transforms it into an auditory form so that it enters Wernicke's area in the same way as a spoken word does. This is why some people seem to hear the words they are reading.

If the arcuate fasciculus, which connects Wernicke's area to Broca's area, is destroyed or disconnected, speech will remain well articulated and fluent. But semantics may be lost, because Broca's area is operating without receiving any information from Wernicke's area. This disorder may seem at first glance to be no different from Wernicke's aphasia but, because other pathways into Wernicke's area are undisturbed, a patient who has had the connection destroyed will appear completely normal when trying to comprehend spoken or written words. This kind of brain damage is especially frustrating because the patient can understand everything that is being said but cannot say anything that makes sense, although the nonsense she may say is likely to be quite grammatical.

A patient who has suffered damage to the angular gyrus may be able to understand speech, but unable to write at all. Damage to the angular gyrus does not affect the spoken word, only the written word. It may be responsible for some cases of **dyslexia,** a "difficulty in reading." Such damage also may explain the apparent limitation of the many children who are alert, intelligent, and able to understand anything—as long as it's not in written form. (People who have difficulty with written material may be considered learning disabled. On the other hand, this assessment must be made with great caution, because many children in today's educational system are very bad at word recognition and comprehension, not because of brain damage, but because they've never been adequately taught to read.) As you can see, the distinction between semantic and syntactic structure appears to have a physiological basis in the brain.

As our understanding of the physiology of language continues to grow, we also begin to see how little we really know. For instance, one interesting discovery, made with new computerized tools that allow us to examine the brain more closely, has shown us that these different language-related areas we've been discussing are really all different sections of one brain area (Gazzaniga, 1989), and only seemed to be distinct and separate to researchers like Broca or Wernicke because of the way that the brain is folded and convoluted. It appears that even our ideas of the basics are changing.

as cited by Zimbardo, 1979). She had learned some syntax and could put signs together in multiword fashion. For example, before she could be taught the sign for *duck*, she spontaneously placed the signs for *water* and *bird* together. It was also clear that Washoe understood the concepts represented by her words. When she saw a door, she would sign open, and she would be let inside. You might argue that this wasn't proof that Washoe really knew the meaning of *open*. Her gesture might simply have been a learned instrumental response (see Chapter 6) to the sight of the door, reinforced by the door being opened. Later, however, when Washoe was first exposed to a car door and a satchel (both of which look very different from a regular door), she immediately signed open and seemed anxious to look inside—evidence that she understood the concept of open. Washoe was also quite aware of the abilities of those around her. When speaking to a visitor whose ASL signing was a bit rusty, Washoe would slow her signing down. Some visitors confessed to feeling embarrassed at being signed to slowly by an ape.

An even more impressive example of language acquisition among the great apes is the progress of Koko, a lowland female gorilla who was studied by Francine Patterson. Koko has mastered over 500 signs, and she understands many equivalent English words for these signs. She has developed syntax and a number of novel constructions like Washoe's "waterbird."

Speaking to a gorilla is like taking a glimpse into the mind of an alien, who sees some things in a different way, sometimes a metaphorically beautiful way. Consider some of Koko's fabulous terms for objects with which we are all familiar:

OBJECT	KOKO'S SIGNS
cigarette lighter	bottle match
zebra	white tiger
hide and seek	quiet chase
pomegranate seeds	red corn drink
viewmaster	look mask
nose	false mouth
Pinocchio doll	elephant baby
mask	eye hat

Koko's ability to understand meanings at more than one level has also been reported. When she was asked, "What can you think of that's hard?" Koko answered, "Rock . . . work" (Patterson, Patterson & Brentari, 1987).

While work with Washoe and Koko was going on, some researchers expressed concern that, although it was true that apes could learn some signs and syntax, they would not naturally communicate with one another using this newly acquired ability. In 1978, however, Savage-Rumbaugh, Rumbaugh, and Boysen at the Yerkes Center reported the first instance of symbolic communication between nonhuman primates. They arranged an experiment in which each chimp had to depend on the other in order to obtain containers of food filled with their favorite items—peanut butter and jelly sandwiches and orange drink. To get the food, each chimp had to choose the correct sign and to flash it on a projector for the other chimp to view. The requested item could then be passed through a hole in the glass from one chimp to the other. The chimp team was accurate between 70 and 100 percent of the time.

BROCA'S APHASIA
A disorder caused by damage to Broca's area. Individuals with this disorder have impaired articulation, labored speech, and difficulty in forming a grammatical sentence, but the semantic content of their speech is usually clear.

WERNICKE'S AREA
An area in the temporal and parietal lobes of the brain associated with speech control.

ARCUATE FASCICULUS
The bundle of nerve fibers in the brain that connects Wernicke's area with Broca's area.

WERNICKE'S APHASIA
The inability to understand spoken language because of damage to Wernicke's area. Individuals with this disorder generally speak normally in terms of phonetics and grammar content, but their speech is semantically bizarre.

ANGULAR GYRUS
A portion of the brain in the parietal lobe adjacent to Wernicke's area. The angular gyrus is involved with reading and appears to "translate" visual word images received by the primary visual cortex into auditory form before passing the information on to Wernicke's area.

DYSLEXIA
An impairment of reading ability, in which little sense can be made of what is read and letters or words often appear transposed.

ARGUMENTS AGAINST LANGUAGE IN APES. Although the evidence for language acquisition in the great apes is appealing, some researchers have presented arguments against the phenomenon. After working for 5 years with his own chimp, Nimchimpsky, psychologist Herbert S. Terrace has concluded that, although chimpanzees can acquire a large vocabulary, they are not capable of producing original sentences or of spontaneously naming things, as children do, without being directly reinforced with food or praise (Terrace, 1979). Terrace argues that language production is still a phenomenon unique to human beings. He believes that the great apes have been instrumentally conditioned to make certain signs in order to get what they want and that they are often inadvertently cued by their owners to produce these signs in sequence. He contends that the apes aren't aware of what the signs mean. In support of this position, B. F. Skinner demonstrated the same kind of communication as the Rumbaughs had produced between chimps—but this time using pigeons!

Savage-Rumbaugh, however, does not accept this argument. She states:

> The difference between a chimpanzee and a pigeon is that the chimpanzee is aware of the content of the intended message and he will seek to amplify and clarify a symbolic request by a glance, gesture or whatever other means are at his disposal. . . . If a pigeon who saw a color and pecked a key was asked, "What do you mean—green?" he would not readily amplify or restate. By contrast, when a chimpanzee asks for an M&M, he looks you directly in the eye and points to it. If a chimpanzee says, "Go outdoors" and you say, "What do you mean?" he finds a collar, puts it around his neck and leads you to the door. (Greenberg, 1980a, p. 300)

Furthermore, in counterarguments produced by a number of researchers, Terrace has been criticized for overlooking the conversations of signing apes in natural circumstances and for leaning too heavily on an analysis of the records of repetitious training sessions (Patterson, Patterson, & Brentari, 1987). These people argue that apes often spontaneously name things to one another without being directly reinforced for doing so and that they often form sentences during more open and less-structured conversations. The debate continues.

Many great apes other than those whom you have met in this chapter have been taught some language, and researchers have had a certain amount of success in getting dolphins to understand a number of signs and signed sentences (Turkington, 1986). Although these creatures do not have abilities at a human's level of complexity, they have demonstrated that they can acquire some of the rudiments of language despite the fact that their brains appear to lack the language areas in the cerebral cortex that exist in our species. Perhaps apes and dolphins do not naturally acquire language because they lack these areas.

The relative success that researchers have achieved in teaching apes some language gives a certain amount of support to the view that language acquisition may be simply an interesting application of our immense general ability to learn. The existence of specific areas in the brain associated with language acquisition and the fact that all healthy humans will acquire language, however, give strength to the view of the *nativists*—that language acquisition is special and uniquely human. Some theorists take an *interactionist position* on the subject of language, believing that both learning theorists and nativists may be partly correct. Many aspects of both viewpoints have merit, and there's no reason why we couldn't have been naturally selected for language acquisition *and* for a very powerful learning brain, and have developed language as a result of both predispositions.

EPILOGUE: THE MAN WITH THE MEANS TO REACH HIS ENDS

The following account describes a man who was especially proficient in using means–end analysis to solve problems. His efforts have touched all our lives.

Solving problems requires a particular attitude. Peter Goldmark had that attitude. He came from a family that believed that if you didn't like things the way they were and wanted them to be different, then you should make them different. His uncle, Karl Goldmark, wanted opera to be different, and so he wrote his own successful operas. Another uncle, Joseph Goldmark, invented kitchen matches.

As a child, Peter Goldmark also was encouraged to create new things. When he was only 12 years old, he built a motion-picture projector from parts that he had obtained. In the 1920s, he wrote away for a primitive television kit and built it, even though the picture was no larger than a postage stamp and could hardly be seen. He enjoyed making things.

In the 1930s, still interested in television, he came to the United States and got a job with CBS. He liked working there, and he liked solving problems. By 1938, CBS had developed a small but practical black-and-white television set. Goldmark and other researchers had worked on it for many months, and it was an exciting new development that had promise for the future.

Then Goldmark went to see the technicolor movie Gone with the Wind. *He was so stunned by the color and the beauty that he came away with what he described as "an inferiority feeling about television in black and white" (Manchester, 1974, p. 1192). Goldmark went back to his laboratory, took a look at what he had, and thought about what he wanted. He had black-and-white television; he wanted color. He began a means–end analysis.*

How could he color light? He knew that a television screen was made up of many different lines composed of many different dots, and that the dots could be either white, black, or various shades of gray. He wanted red, green, and blue, with which he knew he could make any color.

He knew that he could color a beam of light by passing it through a color filter. So he built a wheel with red, green, and blue windows, which spun in front of the ray that projected on the television screen. He then synchronized the ray with the passing red, green, and blue windows in the same way that warplanes had their propellers synchronized with the bullets that were fired forward, so that each shot went between the propeller blades and not into them. If he wanted a particular point on the screen to be green, the ray would fire only when the green window of the spinning wheel was in front of it. Three months after seeing Gone with the Wind, *and after outlining hundreds of substeps toward his goal, Peter Goldmark had built the first color television set.*

The CBS executives were awed. The television picture was perfect—the brightest, clearest color they had ever imagined. World War II inter-

Peter Goldmark

285

rupted further work on color television, so it wasn't until 1960 that television receivers were advanced enough to make the color process economically feasible for introduction on the market.

Goldmark had not been idle in the interim. Back in 1950, he recalled, he was sitting with friends listening to a recording of Vladimir Horowitz playing Brahms on the piano, when "suddenly there was a click. The most horrible sound man ever invented, right in the middle of the music. Somebody rushed to change records. The mood was broken. I knew right there and then I had to stop that sort of thing" (Manchester, 1974, p. 1192). In those days the 78-rpm disk was the only kind of record available, and it played no longer than a few minutes. Goldmark wanted to hear music uninterrupted. He defined the difference between what he had and what he wanted. He found out that 78-rpm records had from 85 to 100 grooves to each inch, and that the number of grooves per inch determined the duration of a record. The next thing Goldmark wanted to know was whether it was possible to put more grooves per inch on a record. By proceeding carefully, breaking his steps into subgoals, he was able to get from 224 to 300 grooves per inch. The speed of play also was an important variable. Was it possible to slow down the record and yet maintain quality? What kinds of distortions occurred when the record slowed down, and how could they be corrected? Bit by bit, Goldmark was able to drop the speed of the record until finally he found a comfortable point, 33 1/3 rpm. Peter Goldmark wouldn't have to have his music interrupted anymore. He had just invented the first long-playing record.

Goldmark continued his work, advocating the development of cable television and satellite networks, until his tragic death in an automobile accident. His ability to solve problems was legendary, and he held well over a hundred patents. Perhaps his power as a problem solver was best expressed by William Manchester when he said about Goldmark:

Once in the late 1960s a radio interviewer asked him whether he thought mental telepathy would ever replace TV. Peter paused, adjusted his glasses, and said it was conceivable that undiscovered radiation from the brain might be used someday. He added: "But that's a long way off." There was a protracted silence in the studio. With Peter you couldn't be sure. (Manchester, 1974, p. 1194)

SUMMARY

■ Thought, or cognition, makes humans unique, perhaps more than any other aspect of their nature.

■ By definition, thinking refers to the use of mental combinations and internal representations of symbols, objects, or concepts.

■ John Watson, the father of behaviorism, argued that all mental activity was really subvocal speech (a muscular activity). An experiment using a powerful paralyzing agent, however, demonstrated that the thought process can continue even when the body is fully paralyzed.

■ Researchers in artificial intelligence hope eventually to create a computer that will perform thinking, reasoning, and intellectual skills in a way that is equal or superior to human performance.

■ Cognitive psychologists try to find out what people do when they think, reason, and perform intellectual tasks. Most cognitive psychologists believe that there are probably five distinct categories of human cognitive performance: intellectual skills, declarative knowledge, cognitive strategies, motor skills, and attitudes.

■ Intellectual skills comprise a general category that includes all the mental procedures, rules, and concepts we have learned.

■ Mental procedures are based on if–then connections. Once

an expert has mastered certain mental procedures, he can call them up with almost no effort, a process called automatization.

■ One of the most valuable ways in which we organize our thinking is by forming concepts. A concept is defined as the relationship between, or the properties shared by, the objects or ideas in a group. We acquire concepts by learning which attributes define each particular category.

■ Declarative knowledge includes all the things you might be able to declare or state, such as the names of people, the words to a poem, or important dates in history. Declarative knowledge is believed to be held in the declarative memory in propositional networks.

■ Cognitive strategies are the abilities you acquire that let you know how best to use previously learned intellectual skills and declarative information. Algorithms, heuristics, and means–end analysis are three valuable cognitive strategies.

■ Computers generally work according to algorithms, whereas human beings typically attempt to solve problems using heuristics. An algorithm is defined as a method guaranteed to lead to a solution if one is possible. Heuristic methods, although not guaranteed to reach a solution, sometimes are able to produce solutions faster. A person using heuristic methods takes the steps that seem most reasonable in order to approach a goal.

■ Means–end analysis is one way to proceed from the initial state to the goal. In means–end analysis, a series of intermediate steps are accomplished by particular means until the final goal is reached.

■ Problem solving is defined as a sequence of cognitive operations directed toward achieving a particular goal.

■ A mental set is a strategy gained from previously learned mental procedures that is applied to similar situations.

■ Functional fixedness may occur when declarative knowledge is too narrowly defined, so a person tends to think that objects that have a specific function can function only in the intended way.

■ Both mental sets and functional fixedness may facilitate problem solving, because old methods usually work and using an object as it was intended is normally a good strategy. If a mental set or functional fixedness does interfere with finding solutions, it's likely to be during creative problem solving, when the solution requires the application of new ideas or methods.

■ Motor skills are skills that require muscular motions, such as those needed for riding a bicycle, playing tennis, or using tools. Whereas intellectual skills may be acquired abruptly through insight, motor skills are acquired slowly through practice. Motor skills are also likely to be remembered for great lengths of time, even if they are not practiced.

■ Attitudes influence behavior, but they do not determine performance in the sense that intellectual skills or declarative information do. Attitudes are thought to be acquired through conditioning.

■ Whorf's hypothesis of linguistic relativity argues that a person's language affects the way in which he thinks about and perceives his world.

■ A language is based on the use of signs and symbols within a grammar.

■ By the time infants are 4 to 7 months old, they generally produce a great number of phonetic sounds; between 10 and 14 months of age, infants narrow their use of phonemes mainly to the ones they will be using in the language they will eventually learn.

■ By 14 months of age, children have typically begun to speak their first word. This is known as the one-word stage.

■ Children's first words are often protoconcepts typically acquired according to the three-bears rule (not too large, not too small, but just right).

■ After the one-word stage, children enter the two-word stage. Both the one-word and the two-word stages appear to be universal among children.

■ Children don't enter a three-word stage; instead, they expand their use of telegraphic speech.

■ The syntax of a language comprises the rules that describe how words may be put together to form sentences. Phonetics is the study of how sounds are put together to make words.

■ Some researchers believe that people use some as-yet-unknown deep cognitive-processing strategy to go from the meaning that they wish to express to the syntax they use. Others believe that the initial focus of a sentence is tied to the topic at hand and that certain aspects of grammar structure derive from the need to emphasize that topic.

■ There are many theories of language development. Among the most debated are the nature–nurture arguments posed, on the one hand, by nativists who believe that humans are prewired for language acquisition and, on the other hand, by learning theorists who think that we use our general learning ability to invent and maintain language. Many researchers take an interactionist view, arguing that, although learning is important for the acquisition of language, the advanced forms of language demonstrated by humans may be the result of innate language-acquisition devices.

■ Human beings appear to have a specialized region in the brain that is directly involved with language. Within this region are Broca's area, Wernicke's area, and the angular gyrus.

■ The symptoms of Broca's aphasia include impaired articulation and slow and labored speech. In Wernicke's aphasia, semantic content is bizarre, but speech is phonetically and grammatically normal.

■ Attempts to teach sign language to the great apes have been somewhat successful. These projects lend support to the interactionist view of language acquisition.

Suggestions for Further Reading

1. Bruner, J. (1983). *Child's talk: Learning to use language.* New York: Norton. Describes how children acquire language and how they use it to advance cognitively.
2. Carroll, D. W. (1985). *Psychology of language.* Monterey, CA: Brooks/Cole. A standard introductory textbook dealing with language.
3. Johnson, R. C., & Brown, C. (1988). *Cognizers: Neural networks and machines that think.* New York: Wiley. For the general reader. A description of neural networks and how they differ from traditional computers. It focuses on machines designed to work like the brain, "cognizers," and how they can recognize objects and understand speech.
4. Lloyd, D. (1989). *Simple minds.* Cambridge: MIT Press. A philosopher addresses the prime question of cognitive science, namely, how can a mind develop from brain matter. His goal is to understand how simple a system can be and still be able to think.
5. Mayer, R. E. (1983). *Thinking, problem solving, cognition.* New York: W. H. Freeman. An introduction to the psychology of thinking, including current research and theories of cognition. Includes applications on solving everyday problems and on teaching problem solving.
6. Norman, D. A. (1988). *The psychology of everyday things.* New York: Basic Books. Do you push when it says pull, or turn on the wrong burner on your stove, or start the windshield wipers when you mean to turn on the headlights? The author argues that designers of everything from simple assembly instructions to power plants are to blame because they disregard the principles of cognitive psychology when they make things with which people will interact.
7. Penrose, R. (1989). *The emperor's new mind: Concerning computers, minds & the laws of physics.* New York: Oxford University Press. A brilliant physicist argues that the human mind is so special that no machine will ever be able to duplicate it.
8. Premack, D., & Premack, A. J. (1984). *The mind of an ape.* New York: Norton. Tells the story of a project begun in 1964 to determine whether apes could be taught to communicate symbolically with one another. Main emphasis is on an African-born chimpanzee, Sarah, and her language progress.
9. Wickelgren, W. A. (1974). *How to solve problems.* New York: W. H. Freeman. A book for the general reader that analyzes and systematically outlines the basic methods for solving problems encountered in everyday life. Includes discussions on chess problems, logic puzzles, and other frequently encountered problems in science and engineering.

CHAPTER 9 | Motivation

Prologue

Why Psychologists Study Motivation

The Concept of Motivation

Biological Motives
   Hunger
   Thirst
   The Interaction of Hunger and Thirst
   Motivation and Individual Differences
   Sex Drives

Stimulus Motives

Learned Motivation

Theories of Motivation
   Maslow's Hierarchy of Motives
   The Need to Achieve
   Learned Helplessness
   Altruism and Intrinsic Motivation
   Solomon's Opponent-Process Theory

Epilogue: Getting a Charge Out of Life

PROLOGUE

It is 1950, and you are working for Professor Harry Harlow in his monkey lab at the University of Wisconsin, helping to conduct experiments in which rhesus monkeys are subjects. When you arrived, Dr. Harlow asked you to give the monkeys in your group some of the puzzles used at the Primate Center and to observe how the monkeys behaved toward the puzzles. The puzzles are of the simple mechanical kind that 2- and 3-year-old children might enjoy playing with (see Figure 9.1). You notice that the monkeys like to take the puzzles apart. They also put the puzzles together quite readily and seem pleased when they are finished.

Harlow wonders whether the monkeys will learn to work the puzzles faster if they are offered reinforcers for doing so. He thinks they will. So you give the monkeys raisins whenever they work with the puzzles. The monkeys love raisins, and they work harder than ever, proving Harlow's hypothesis.

Later, because you like to watch the monkeys put the puzzles together, you give them a puzzle, even though the experiment is over and you don't happen to have any raisins. But they behave differently from the way they did before the experiment. They put out their hands; they want raisins—payment. They appear to become angry when they don't receive any raisins. From that day on, no matter how often the puzzles are presented to them, they won't work them without payment. You wonder how their motivation could have changed. Before raisins were offered, they liked to work the puzzles, apparently just for enjoyment. But once they knew they would be rewarded for working the puzzles, they refused to do it for nothing (Harlow, 1950). They even acted as though

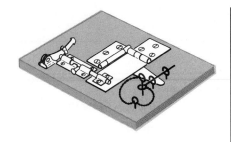

FIGURE 9.1

A *puzzle similar to those used by Harlow in his 1950 experiment.* (SOURCE: *Harlow, 1950, p. 290.*)

the puzzles weren't fun any more (deCharms, 1968). What had changed?

In this chapter we will explore the biology and learning that can influence our drives, needs, and motives. We'll examine specific areas of motivational research and investigate two theories that attempt to account for motives. Along the way, you'll find out why you can tell when you're hungry and thirsty, why some people are motivated to succeed, and why others find a thrill in harrowing experiences.

WHY PSYCHOLOGISTS STUDY MOTIVATION

Psychologists study motivation because they want to know *why* a behavior occurs. They want to understand the underlying processes that activate or maintain behaviors. Of course, psychologists aren't the only ones with an interest in motivation. The study of history, art, religion, theater, literature, and practically every other area of human endeavor is marked by attempts to understand the motivations behind actions. What are the forces behind love and hate? What drives some people to seek power? Why do some people find it easy to share and others not? Why do some people use drugs? Which motivations are learned or taught, and which are innate? How do motives such as hunger, thirst, or sex affect our behavior?

These questions are not new to psychology or to the human experience. Practically every question ever asked about a human action has, in one way or another, addressed the issue of motivation.

THE CONCEPT OF MOTIVATION

In Latin, the word *motivum* refers to the reason something has moved. The English word *motivation* has been derived from *motivum*. Early behaviorists, such as John Watson, hoped to explain behavior in terms of stimulus–response learning without the necessity of discussing concepts such as motivation that were not directly observable. But even the early behaviorists were aware that an animal, when presented with food in identical circumstances, might eat at some times and not at others. Because the external conditions were exactly the same in both circumstances, the only obvious reason had to be some change in internal state. We say that the first time the animal was hungry, whereas the second time it was not. Hunger, then, becomes a handy motivational concept. It helps explain why an animal will or will not eat. Of course, the behaviorists were correct: The motivator hunger is not directly observable. Hunger can only be inferred from the animal's observed eating behavior. For this reason, many researchers prefer to say that they are studying motivated behavior, which is observable, rather than motivation, which is not (Whalen & Simon, 1984).

In the psychological community, there has never been complete agreement on exactly what the word *motivation* means (Kleinginna & Kleinginna, 1981). Some psychologists have preferred a very narrow definition of motivation, which is limited to the internal events that are the immediate and direct cause of an action. Using this definition, many researchers have concentrated on biological or physiological occurrences, such as hormone levels or changes in neurotransmitters that occur just prior to the activation of a motor sequence or action. Other researchers prefer a far broader definition of motivation, which would include any state or condition that might eventually move the organism to act—whether cognitive or physiological. In this view, for instance, a person's beliefs or thoughts could be considered motivators in a given set of circumstances. For the purposes of our discussion, because we want to include the full scope of motivational research, we shall define **motivation** as any state or condition that causes an organism to produce, inhibit, or maintain a motor response or action.

BIOLOGICAL MOTIVES

Perhaps the most obvious kinds of motivations are those that result directly from physical needs. If your water supply were suddenly cut off, your **need** for water would eventually increase. As the need intensified and you became more thirsty, the motivation, or **drive,** to satisfy the need would grow. Your actions would increasingly be directed to filling the need. Similarly, if you went without food or sleep, your motivation to satisfy those needs would also increase. These experiences are so common to the human condition that it seems strange to spend time discussing them. After all, who doesn't know that when you are without water and become thirsty, you are driven to get a drink? We can infer these drives or motives just by watching a person's behavior. If we watch someone searching desperately for food, we immediately assume that the person is hungry; if someone is looking for water, we assume that the person is thirsty. Actually, the only way to observe motivations is to watch the behavior that stems from them. The same thing is true of learning. We assume that learning has occurred because of changes in *performance.* Likewise, we assume that motivation exists because of changes in behavior. Unlike learning, which is a relatively permanent change in behavior due to experience, motivations come and go depending on the needs and drives that are present at a given moment.

Biological motivations such as hunger and thirst are assumed to be "built in," meaning that they exist from birth. You don't have to learn to feel thirsty or hungry. If you go without food or water for a sufficient time, the motivation to obtain those substances occurs automatically. You then want a certain amount of food or water until the condition is alleviated, bringing you back to your original stable point. Psychologists refer to this built-in tendency to maintain stability as **homeostasis.** Homeostatic mechanisms are regulatory; they attempt to maintain an optimal level (Cannon, 1939). Any deviation from the optimal level will create a need (Hull, 1943). The need usually will produce a drive, which is the motivational force for action.

A thermostat in a home is a homeostatic mechanism analogous to the biological ones that exist in humans. Suppose you set a thermostat in a fully temperature-controlled house to 70 degrees Fahrenheit. If it becomes warmer than that, the air conditioning turns on, cooling the house; it if becomes colder than 70 degrees, the furnace turns on, warming the air. In both cases, the temperature of the house will be returned to an optimal level.

Eating food satisfies a primary biological need. Too little food will result in starvation; too much food will eventually result in obesity. The homeostatic mechanism for food intake in most of us is extremely sensitive. For most people, just the small addition of an extra pat of butter or margarine a day will result in a weight gain of 5 pounds per year (Logue, 1986). Yet our homeostatic mechanism

MOTIVATION
Any state or condition that causes an organism to produce, maintain, or inhibit a motor response or action.

NEED
A condition whose satisfaction is necessary for the maintenance of homeostasis.

DRIVE
The psychological representation of a need; a complex of internal conditions, resulting from the loss of homeostasis, that impels an organism to seek a goal.

HOMEOSTASIS
An internal environment in which such body components as blood pressure, blood chemistry, breathing, digestion, and temperature are kept at levels optimal for the survival of the organism through the creation of drives in the presence of needs.

for food intake is so sensitive that most people don't need to keep track of the number of calories they take in during the day in order to maintain a stable weight.

Presumably, other homeostatic mechanisms exist besides those that regulate food and water intake. Our need for an optimal temperature, for example, appears to be homeostatically controlled as well. For such mechanisms to work, there must be sensors in the body to detect deviations from the optimal state. For instance, as far as we know, there are no mechanisms sensitive to the levels of particular vitamins in the human body, and drives to obtain these necessary substances do not occur. Researchers are currently busy trying to uncover the homeostatic detectors that do exist and to learn how these detectors can alter motivation.

Hunger

How do you know when you're hungry? It seems a simple enough question, but the more you examine it, the more you will see that it's really a complicated matter. Perhaps you feel the hunger in your stomach. Your stomach may growl, or it may feel as though it has shrunk. Conversely, your stomach feels full when you have had enough to eat. It may be the pressure of the food against the walls of your stomach that signals you to stop eating. This seems a reasonable assumption—until it is tested. Experiments have been conducted in which a hungry person is asked to swallow a small balloon attached to a tube. The balloon is then inflated so that it exerts pressure. Interestingly, although the person might not be able to eat as much because the balloon is taking up space (Seligmann & Gosnell, 1986), the hunger doesn't go away (Janowitz & Grossman, 1949). Even more striking, patients who have had their stomachs removed because of cancer or other conditions continue to feel hunger and satiation. So the sensor for the homeostatic mechanisms of hunger and satiation can't be located solely in the stomach. Where, then, might a "hunger center" be situated?

In 1954, Eliot Stellar presented a strong argument that such a center existed in the hypothalamus of the brain. His theory became known as the **hypothalamocentric hypothesis.** Excitement grew as more data began to support the idea that the hypothalamus controlled food intake, and perhaps water intake as well (Grossman, 1972; 1975).

In one study with rats, researchers found that if the ventromedial hypothalamus (VMH)—the underside-middle of the hypothalamus—was stimulated, the hungry animal showed immediate signs of loss of appetite, then resumed eating, but at a very slow pace. If, instead of stimulating the VMH, scientists made lesions (cuts) in it, the result was overeating and obesity (see Figure 9.2) (Brobeck, Tepperman, & Long, 1943).

An animal whose VMH has been cut won't continue eating until it explodes. Instead, the homeostatic mechanism is apparently reset at a higher optimal **set point.** An animal's set point is the weight the body tends to maintain by monitoring stored fat. The animal will eat and gain weight until it reaches a certain level beyond its previous capacity, and then it will maintain its weight at that new point.

The idea that the hypothalamus contains centers that activate or inhibit hunger and thirst was popular during the early 1970s. But there were some voices of dissent. For instance, one researcher found that lesions in *other* areas of the brain also could drastically affect eating and drinking (Morgane, as cited by deCharms & Muir, 1978).

Then, different researchers began to discover that organs far from the brain directly affected hunger. For example, signals from the duodenum below the stomach appear to influence food intake. Injections of glucose (sugar) into the duodenum will suppress food intake in rabbits (Novin, 1976). The liver, too, gives

FIGURE 9.2

This rat's "weight problem" was caused by lesions in the ventromedial hypothalamus.

292

signals of both hunger and satiation (Novin, 1976; Vanderweele & Sanderson, 1976). The liver contains receptors for glucose that transmit information along the vagus nerve to the hypothalamus. If that nerve is cut, the normal preference that animals show for the flavors associated with high-calorie foods is lost (Tordoff & Friedman, 1989). Furthermore, the rate of metabolism in the liver is an extremely good predictor of how hungry an individual will be (Friedman & Stricker, 1976). (The metabolic rate determines how quickly food or other biological matter is broken down.) In a sense, the liver acts as a calorie counter and signals us to like the flavors that go with high-calorie foods. In one fascinating experiment, rats were given high-calorie foods directly into their stomach, bypassing the mouth, while flavors usually associated with low-calorie foods were placed on their tongues. Soon the rats came to prefer the "low-calorie" flavors (Tordoff & Friedman, 1989). This would mean that the only reason you like the taste of cake more than spinach is because the spinach leaves you feeling less full than does the cake. What does this finding say about the idea of making yummy desserts with new low-calorie fat substitutes that supposedly taste like the real thing? Once your liver finds out the little trick that you've pulled, it may convince you that you don't like such desserts anymore. It will be interesting to see if that happens.

The most recent view of hunger, then, is that the hypothalamus is not *the* hunger and thirst center, but rather is *a* hunger and thirst monitoring and sensing area (Olds & Fobes, 1981; Logue, 1986). In this view, the hypothalamus works in conjunction with other sensing and regulating mechanisms located elsewhere in the brain and in peripheral organs such as the stomach, the duodenum, the intestines, and the liver. One of the most exciting developments to highlight this interaction is our new understanding of the role of **cholecystokinin,** or **CCK.** CCK is a neuropeptide (see Chapter 2) that is secreted by the intestine and which can stimulate receptors in the brain. For some time CCK was suspected of playing a major role in the creation of feelings of satiety, that is, feelings that let you know that you are full and don't want to eat anymore. By developing antagonists to CCK (other substances that block CCK's effectiveness) and then placing them in animal's brains, researchers were able to weaken feelings of satiety and cause animals to overeat (Dourish, Rycroft, & Iversen, 1989). Following this discovery, it was shown that by stimulating the secretion of CCK in animals, satiety was strengthened, causing animals to eat less (Weller, Smith, & Gibbs, 1990). In other words, CCK stimulants work as natural appetite suppressors. As you can imagine, pharmaceutical companies are spending fortunes investigating a host of CCK stimulants, as well as CCK itself, hoping finally to develop a safe and effective diet pill sometime in this decade.

Thirst

Thirst, like hunger, is controlled by homeostatic mechanisms. Again we might ask, How do we know when we're thirsty? A common answer is that the mouth becomes dry, but, as you may have guessed, a dry mouth alone cannot account for the motivation to drink water (Fitzsimons, 1973).

The desire to drink appears to be controlled by the way in which water is distributed throughout the body, and at least two separate mechanisms appear to control the body's water balance. To begin with, water in the body is not distributed evenly. About 65 percent of it is contained in the cells, about 25 percent is found in the spaces between cells, and roughly 10 percent is contained in the blood. Both intracellular and extracellular mechanisms appear to be involved in thirst regulation. *Intracellular mechanisms* are based on sensor recordings of the amount of water within cells, whereas *extracellular mechanisms* are based on sensor recordings

CHOLECYSTOKININ (CCK)
Cholecystokinin is a nueropeptide that is secreted by the intestine and which can stimulate receptors for satiation in the brain.

OSMOSIS
OSMOSIS
The diffusion of fluid through a semipermeable membrane, such as that surrounding a living cell, until the concentrations of fluid on either side of the membrane are equal.

SCHEDULE-INDUCED POLYDIPSIA (SIP)
Polydipsia means excessive drinking. Schedule-induced polydipsia refers to an increase in the drive to drink as a result of receiving little bits of food on an intermittent schedule.

of the amount of fluid surrounding cells.

Several things can change intracellular and extracellular fluid levels. The two needn't be affected simultaneously. Extracellular fluid, for instance, can be directly affected by loss of blood or diarrhea, while intracellular fluid may not be influenced by these events at all. Cholera, which killed millions of people throughout the world until it was controlled, is accompanied by incessant diarrhea, which causes a massive loss of fluid that cannot be replaced quickly enough. In this sense, many cholera victims die from thirst or dehydration. Blood loss also results in rapid dehydration. In battle, wounded soldiers sometimes cry out for water because of the loss of extracellular fluid.

One way in which the fluid balance might be detected by the brain is through receptors that are sensitive to concentrations of sodium. Sodium does not pass into cells, but rather draws water from cells by a process known as **osmosis.** (For the same reason, salting a steak before you cook it—salt is *sodium* chloride—draws out the juices.) Certain brain cells, then, might be able to regulate the body's water balance by being sensitive to the amount of water being drawn from those brain cells themselves by sodium. These receptors could signal thirst when the volume of water within their cell walls decreased. In fact, salt solutions injected directly into the lateral hypothalamus have been found to produce drinking (Andersson, 1971). Apparently, the injections tricked the osmotic receptors at the location into believing that the cells throughout the body lacked water, when in fact only those in the area of the hypothalamus were dehydrated.

Hormones produced by the pituitary gland, the liver, and the kidneys can affect the amount of water eliminated by the kidneys (Carlson, 1977). Clearly, thirst, like hunger, is controlled by the brain, hormones, and the peripheral action of organs far from the brain. Like hunger, it is complex and is not fully understood.

The Interaction of Hunger and Thirst

In the early 1960s, scientists discovered that, when food-deprived animals were given only little bits of food on an intermittent schedule of reinforcement (see Chapter 6), the animals would consume large amounts of water. In some circumstances, the animals would drink as much as half their body weight in just 3 hours (Falk, 1961)! This phenomenon is known as **schedule-induced polydipsia,** or **SIP.** Researchers later discovered that giving a very hungry animal only little bits of food intermittently excited the animal, so that it was not only likely to drink more water if water was provided but was also more likely to engage in aggression, running,

The need for water and the drive to drink are common to all animal species.

or even the ingestion of nonnutritive substances such as sawdust (Falk, 1971). Researchers refer to SIP as a "displacement" behavior, because it is more likely to occur when what is really wanted (in this case, food) is unobtainable (Wayner, Barone, & Loullis, 1981).

The phenomenon of SIP shows us that motivated behaviors such as eating and drinking are related and may share similar homeostatic mechanisms, because the motivation for one behavior may help to drive other behaviors.

Motivation and Individual Differences

Individual differences exist among animals in terms of readiness to eat or drink or of likelihood to respond to such stimuli as electrical stimulation of the hypothalamus (Mittleman & Valenstein, 1984). Individuals within a given species are different enough from one another in their motivations and needs to make research into biological motives especially complex and difficult. Some of these complexities can be observed in efforts to determine the causes of obesity, in which biological, environmental, social, and cultural factors all intertwine to affect each person in a different way (see Focus on Research).

Sex Drives

For the great majority of people, sex feels good. We have evolved biologically to feel this way. In fact, all species seem to like sex, and for a good reason. Can you imagine an entire species that disliked sex? It wouldn't last long; it would be gone in one generation. Nature has in this way favored animals that enjoy sex. It would seem reasonable, then, to assume that there might be a biological drive or need for sex. But unlike food and water, sex is not necessary to keep an individual alive; it is needed only to maintain the species. For this reason, a drive to engage in sexual activity may not be as obvious in an individual as is the drive to satisfy hunger or thirst.

Research over the years has indicated that the more physiologically advanced the species, the less its sexual behavior appears to be governed directly by chemical and hormonal forces. Even in humans, however, these forces may play a role. (Hormones and human sexual behavior are discussed more fully in Chapter 18.)

The hypothalamus appears to also be involved in regulating the sex drive. It has detectors that are sensitive to different levels of hormones, and these detectors also seem to be able to regulate hormonal output by stimulating the pituitary gland. How these regulatory mechanisms work and exactly how hormones affect sexual behavior are not clearly understood, but there does appear to be some relationship. For example, John Money and his colleagues have found that by administering the drug medroxyprogesterone acetate (Depo-Provera) to male sex offenders, they were able to inhibit the release of **testosterone** and also to reduce the sex drive (Money, Berlin, Falck, & Stein, 1983). These findings imply that sexual activity and testosterone probably are linked in some fashion.

In lower species, numerous data implicate hormones in the direct control of sexual behavior. For instance, in lower mammals, mating occurs only during ovulation, and females typically must be receptive, in terms of hormone levels, before they will engage in sexual intercourse with males. During these receptive periods, the female often secretes a pheromone (see Chapter 3), the smell of which can be picked up by males some distance away. The scent of the pheromone stimulates the males to engage in sexual behavior. As any owner of a female dog in heat can testify, every male dog in the neighborhood shows up at the front door wanting a place on her dance card.

TESTOSTERONE
The male sex hormone produced by the testes. It controls the development of secondary sex characteristics, such as the growth of a beard, and may influence the sexual activity of the individual.

Technically, an individual is obese if his body weight is more than 20 percent above his ideal weight. Over the last decade, researchers have found that obesity usually can't be traced to simple gluttony. Although weight gain is sometimes related to "overeating," fatness is also linked to genetics, to the body's natural regulatory mechanisms, and to the social environment. Yale psychologist Judith Rodin has said, "Today, we see that obesity, like other behavioral disorders, is really determined by biological factors interacting with psychological and sociocultural factors. Behavior can alter biological factors which, in turn, change our behavior again" (Hall, 1984, p. 42).

Set Points

In 1964, Ethan Sims conducted an overeating experiment at the Vermont State Prison. Volunteer prisoners were given extra food and were required to gain 25 percent beyond their starting weight. To Sims's surprise, this was extremely difficult for many of the prisoners. One prisoner, who went from 110 pounds to 143, found that during the last few months of the experiment, just to maintain his newly acquired weight, he had to consume 7,000 calories a day—more than twice what he normally needed (Bennett & Gurin, 1982). After the experiment, without any conscious effort to do so, most of the prisoners returned to their original weights. Their bodies appeared to demand a certain weight.

This finding and others like it have led some researchers to conclude that the body has a particular set point. In this view, a homeostatic mechanism that is extremely sensitive creates hunger or satiation depending on the body-fat levels.

Furthermore, set points are believed to be genetically determined. Evidence for this comes from the fact that individuals who have no obese parent have only about a 10-percent chance of being obese themselves. These odds increase, however, to 40 percent if one parent is obese and to 70 percent if both parents are obese (Logue, 1986). Experiments with different strains of rats bred for obesity indicate that these percentages may well be more the result of genetic inheritance than of eating habits learned in the home (Zucker & Zucker, 1961; Bray & York, 1971). And, data from the most comprehensive human population study so far have led researchers to believe that there may be one major "obesity gene" that, if inherited from both parents, will almost guarantee obesity in the offspring. Indications are that 61 percent of the population does not carry this gene, 34 percent are carriers (that is, they have one such gene inherited from one parent, which in itself will not make them be genetically obese, but does make it possible for them to pass the gene on to their children), and 5 percent have inherited such a gene from both parents and are therefore practically destined to become obese (Burns, Moll & Lauer, 1989). This would not, of course, mean that those without an "obesity gene" from each parent couldn't become obese by overeating and failing to exercise, but only that 5 percent of the population has probably inherited the predisposition to readily store much of what they eat. Such a mechanism would be an advantage in an environment that vacillated between feast and famine, enabling people to store whatever they can in order to carry around their own food in the form of fat so that they could survive once food became scarce. This arrangement, however, is not an advantage in modern industrial societies, in which high-calorie foods are plentiful for most people.

Nonhomeostatic Mechanisms

Thus far in our discussion of hunger and thirst, we have considered only homeostatic mechanisms. However, many researchers believe that **nonhomeostatic mechanisms** play an even greater role in obesity. In a classic experiment conducted by H. P. Weingarten (1983), a tone and light were paired with each meal given to hungry rats. Later, the rats were given free access to food whenever they wanted it and, presumably, ate their fill as they felt the need. However, even when they had all they wanted to eat, the rats would eat still more if the light and tone were turned on! The rats obviously were not satisfying a homeostatic need for food. What does this study suggest about human consumption? It indicates that there are times when we don't need food but are conditioned by the environmental cues to eat. Such times might seem familiar to us all (for example, being at the movies or at a party or sitting in front of the TV set).

Another interesting experiment highlights a different point. In this experiment, subjects were divided into two groups and told that they would participate in a food taste test. One group was told that they would have to miss lunch. Both groups were then given all the snacks they wished to eat. Those who thought that they would have to miss lunch ate considerably more (Lowe, 1982). This is called **anticipatory eating,** another example of nonhomeostatic consumption. Anticipatory eating also may account for the odd fact that so many obese people who try to diet actually end up gaining weight. Almost every dieter at one time or another has said, "I'll try again tomorrow." This allows the dieter to avoid hunger today and also to avoid the guilt of failure by promising success tomorrow. Because she believes that "tomorrow" will be a day without much food, however, the dieter is likely to eat excessively in anticipation of dieting. After 3 or 4 weeks of failed starts, the dieter actually may be heavier than if she had not attempted to diet in the first place.

Some researchers take an even broader view of the power of nonhomeostatio forces to control our eating. They suggest that the way in which food is associated with other events in our lives, especially during childhood when we often may be given food as a reward or to make us feel better, determines to a great extent

how much we eat. Such experiences may condition some of us to eat whenever we need to feel loved or comforted or as a palliative for fear or loneliness (Logue, 1986).

Outlook

Because there are many aesthetic and medical reasons why obese people wish to lose weight, the research on obesity might seem particularly depressing. In fact, it seems to support what psychologists first reported back in the 1950s. "Most obese persons will not stay in treatment of obesity. Of those who stay in treatment most will not lose weight and of those who do lose weight, most will regain it" (Stunkard, 1958, p. 79). More recently, however, it has been suggested that weight loss might be accomplished more easily than this view suggests. Since Stunkard relied on information about people who had specifically sought help for obesity,

researcher Stanley Schachter questioned Stunkard's depressing conclusion. Could it be that those people who sought help were having an especially difficult problem and that other people, who did not seek help, were better able to lick the problem on their own (so researchers never heard about it)? In a survey of people who either were currently or had once been obese, Schachter discovered that a great many indeed had lost a significant amount of weight on their own and had kept it off (Schachter, 1982). This encouraging news indicates that there may be successful dieters out there who generally don't come to the attention of researchers.

Of course, a large number of people who are overweight fail to lose weight. Why some succeed while others fail is still not well understood, and remains a challenge for researchers.

Among primates (which includes human beings, of course), sexual receptivity in the female does not appear to be rigidly tied to being in heat. Nonetheless, evidence gathered indicates that primates may prefer sex during a particular time, especially when the female is ovulating, and may engage in sex partly in response to hormones secreted by the female.

Researchers Richard P. Michael and R. W. Bonsall (1977), who studied rhesus monkeys, reported a preference for sex during the ovulation period of the female's menstrual cycle. This was difficult to observe because the male rhesus monkey is twice the size of the female and usually threatens to assault the female unless she capitulates. Under such circumstances, it is hard to tell when the female wants sexual intercourse. In their studies, Michael and Bonsall developed a unique way of testing the female monkey's desire. They used a cage divided by a door, placing the male on one side and the female on the other. The only way to open the door was by a handle on the female's side. When the male monkey was on the female's side of the partition, therefore, the experimenters could assume that the female was receptive.

As it turned out, the female rhesus let the male in primarily when she was ovulating. Blood samples taken from the female showed that her desire for sexual relations was closely tied to the level of sex hormones in her body. An important question not answered by this research is how the female's desire for sexual inter-

NONHOMEOSTATIC MECHANISMS
In motivation, a motivating system that regulates a drive or an impetus to act, but that is not counterbalanced by an opposing regulatory process that would reestablish the initial condition.

ANTICIPATORY EATING
Nonhomeostatic consumption of food owing to an awareness that food will soon be scarce or unavailable.

CHAPTER 9
MOTIVATION

course stimulates the male to want to engage in sex, too. Michael and Bonsall have isolated vaginal substances from rhesus females that appear to have the properties of pheromones. These substances, which are secreted at the time of ovulation, may help to stimulate the male to engage in sex. From an evolutionary standpoint, such an effect would make sense, because it would be most valuable to engage in sexual intercourse when the female was most likely to become pregnant.

You may be wondering whether these findings apply to humans. Human females appear to be receptive depending on social circumstances rather than biological triggers, and it is generally assumed that mating is likely to occur at any time during the female's menstrual cycle. But there is some evidence that women's sexual drives do fluctuate throughout their menstrual cycle. Is it possible that women secrete sexual attractants at the time of ovulation that might help to stimulate sexual activity in men? Although pheromones have not been conclusively identified in humans, in 1975, Michael and his colleagues found vaginal secretions in women that were identical to the sex attractants found in monkeys. They discovered that more of these particular acids are present at the time of ovulation than at other points during the menstrual cycle. Then, in another study, conducted by Richard L. Doty and his colleagues, men were found to consider women's vaginal odors more agreeable and more intense just before and just after ovulation than at any other time during the menstrual cycle (Doty, Ford, Preti, & Huggins, 1975). These results indicate that there may be biological forces at work that fluctuate during a woman's monthly cycle and that not only influence her desire for sexual intercourse but also encourage potential partners who are within scent range of her.

There also may be times when the desire to engage in sexual intercourse noticeably diminishes. Healthy, active human partners sometimes become sexually bored with each other. Richard Michael and his colleague Doris Zumpe have noticed similar reactions among rhesus monkeys. Adult male monkeys, after being with particular females for a significant time, appear to tire of them. In Michael and Zumpe's studies, four adult male monkeys were paired for 2 1/2 years with four females. After 2 years, the males' sexual interest had decreased by two-thirds, and they avoided sex twice as often. When four new females were introduced into the cages, the males' interest and intercourse rates immediately doubled, and the attempts to avoid sex were cut in half. Some time later, the original four females were returned to the cages, and the males immediately showed a loss of interest. This result implies that the attraction between the sexes is dependent not so much on hormones or other biological influences but, as the researchers have said, "on the nature of the bond between partners." Of course, research in this area is incomplete, because the female monkeys' responses have not been studied.

Michael and Zumpe have noted that the same kinds of behavior are reported by human subjects. That new partners tend to renew a person's sexual interest may, in the researchers' view, have something to do with a tendency to break and remake sexual bonds. The researchers argue that maintaining sexual interest in a monogamous society may necessitate wearing alluring colognes, clothing, and hairstyles, and, particularly, that both sexes refrain from sexual intercourse at times (Michael & Zumpe, 1978).

■ STIMULUS MOTIVES

The biological or physiological drives such as hunger and thirst are not the only ones that do not need to be learned. In addition, both human beings and animals seem to require a certain amount of stimulation. The needs to obtain sensory stimulation, to be active, and to explore and manipulate the environment produce motivations that are referred to collectively as **stimulus motives.**

The motivation to experience a certain amount of stimulation appears to have evolved because of its survival value. By manipulating and exploring the environment and by actively sensing it, every organism learns about it and learns what to expect from it. If you own pets and have ever moved to a new home, you will have observed the need to explore, not just in yourself, but in your pets as well. Animals in a new environment are motivated to learn every aspect of it, to investigate its perimeters, and, in general, to know which parts of it are safe and which may be dangerous.

The need for stimulation is apparent among animal subjects who have been placed in boring and uninteresting environments. In such cases, animals often will work for the chance to engage in something more interesting, even if it is nothing more than looking out a window. No doubt, there have been many times in your life when stimulation levels were too low and you became bored and wished you could do something else. On the other hand, people in highly stimulating situations often seek quiet and solitude, as though they have had too much stimulation. Following overstimulation, such as might be encountered in a stressful job, isolating someone from stimulation can be therapeutic and relaxing (Suedfeld & Kristeller, 1982; Suedfeld, Ballard & Murphy, 1983).

One of the most restful forms of **sensory isolation** uses tanks of warm water in which the subject may comfortably float in darkness and silence. Years ago, when such "sensory deprivation" research was begun, it was thought that depriving someone of sensory input might be harmful. Subjects placed in such restricted environments were given "panic buttons" to signal if they needed to get out fast. There were even some exaggerated reports of hallucinations caused by sensory isolation and they became reported in many textbooks as the norm. Since then, however, much research has shown that the restricted environmental stimulation technique, or REST as it is called, gives most people a profound sense of relaxation and may even have some health benefits (Suedfeld & Coren, 1989).

Perhaps there is an optimal level of arousal somewhere between too little and too much, depending on what you are doing. If you're not sufficiently aroused, your performance is likely to be poor. As you know, you're not at your best if you're exhausted when you have to take a complex test. Too much arousal can also be disruptive: It's difficult to be efficient when you're in a state of terror. In 1908, Yerkes and Dodson discovered that mice were better able to learn a simple task in order to avoid a *painful* shock, and better able to learn a complex task when doing so to avoid a *mild* shock (Yerkes & Dodson, 1908). Later researchers interpreted these findings more broadly, arguing that there was an optimum level of arousal associated with the difficulty of each task in which an animal might engage. Historically, for some odd reason, this broader interpretation became known as the *Yerkes–Dodson law*, making it sound quite formidable, although it really was little more than supposition (Winton, 1987). Although there is no justification for referring to this concept as a "law," it is true that, in the most recent terms, a certain level of arousal is needed to produce the best performance, and the best level of arousal depends to some degree on the difficulty of the task.

Even so, the issue remains clouded by the effects of cognition on arousal. For instance, if you were physiologically aroused before performing in an athletic competition because you were scared of failing, you might not do as well as if you were *equally aroused* because you were all psyched up to succeed in the competition (Neiss, 1988).

STIMULUS MOTIVES
Drives or motives that appear to satisfy a need for certain amounts of sensory stimulation.

SENSORY ISOLATION
Lack of a stimulus input needed for maintaining homeostasis. Prolonged reduction of external stimulation, in either intensity or variety, may produce boredom or restlessness, but is often experienced as profoundly relaxing.

SOCIAL MOTIVATION
Learned motivational states that result from the individual's interaction with his or her social environment or culture.

LEARNED MOTIVATION

Certain motivations can be learned. No one is born desiring a Chevrolet Corvette. Learned motives can be powerful forces. They are often related to incentives; that is, to particular things that we want to possess. When these incentives (sometimes called secondary reinforcers) are present, the motivation to acquire them becomes much stronger, especially if we know what we must do to obtain them.

The term **social motivation** often is used to refer to motives acquired through learning and culture. Theories of social motivation attempt to account for all kinds of impulses or deliberate actions that are not the direct result of biological needs (Pittman & Heller, 1987).

Learned motivations can also imitate biological ones. For example, it's possible to learn to become hungry. Researcher Judith Rodin has shown that one way to bring this about is through classical conditioning (see Chapter 6). Consider what happens when you eat sugar. The sugar (an unconditioned stimulus) triggers the pancreas to secrete insulin (an unconditioned response), and the insulin metabolizes the sugar. Before swallowing the sugar, however, you probably looked at the sweet food, tasted it, and noted its texture, all of which can become conditioned stimuli. If the relationship between these stimuli and the ingestion of sugar is strongly enough established, you can teach your pancreas to secrete insulin. All you need to do is to see or think about the food (a conditioned stimulus), and the pancreas will sometimes secrete insulin (a conditioned response), although no sugar has been swallowed (see Figure 9.3). When insulin is secreted without sugar intake, blood sugar may drop, or oxidative metabolism change, which in turn can lead directly to an increase in hunger. In this way, you can learn to create a genuine biological drive to eat, even when the *need* may not be present (Booth, 1977).

Drinking also can be affected by learning. We frequently take a drink for social reasons or other learned reasons, without really requiring the liquid. As was mentioned earlier, these are examples of nonhomeostatic processes. The interplay between learned motives and biological drives can be so complex that it's almost impossible to isolate one from the other (Rodin, 1981). Some researchers have argued that of the two kinds of motivation, learned motives are more responsible for the complex aspects of human behavior.

FIGURE 9.3

Classical conditioning of the pancreas. After sufficient pairing between the sight of sweet foods and the ingestion of sugar, the sight of the foods alone can result in the secretion of insulin.

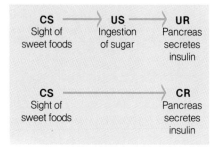

CS	→	US	→	UR
Sight of sweet foods		Ingestion of sugar		Pancreas secretes insulin

CS	→	CR
Sight of sweet foods		Pancreas secretes insulin

Some motivations can be learned; no one is born desiring a brand new sports car.

UNIT 2
INTERACTING WITH THE ENVIRONMENT

THEORIES OF MOTIVATION

Maslow's Hierarchy of Motives

In the past, "grand theories" of motivation were popular—grand in that they attempted to explain most of human motivation. One of the most interesting and frequently cited theories was the **hierarchy of motives** postulated by the humanistic psychologist Abraham Maslow (Maslow, 1970) as part of his research on self-actualization (see Chapter 13). By a hierarchy of motives, Maslow meant that some needs were more powerful than others, depending on an individual's circumstances. The hierarchy is shown in Figure 9.4. As you can see, physiological needs form its base. In other words, to a starving person, the motivation to find food is more powerful and basic than are the motivations to find love, a sense of belonging, and self-esteem. A starving person will be motivated to find food even more than to find safety.

Maslow argued that the higher motivations can come into play only when the basic needs have been satisfied. Before a person can be free to engage in self-actualization—that is, free to continue fulfilling her potential—that person has to meet the physiological needs for safety and security, to find love and belonging, and to have self-esteem and the esteem of others. Accordingly, Maslow placed self-actualization at the top of the hierarchy. Thus, the motivation to realize one's full potential is a fragile thing, easily interfered with by disturbances at the lower levels.

You can see how this hierarchy might explain many of your own motives. Imagine that you arrived in a strange town, hungry and broke. According to Maslow, you would be motivated first to ensure a supply of food and water to satisfy your physiological needs. Then, perhaps, you would look for a job to obtain money for shelter and security. Only after you had a secure base of operations would you begin to make connections to the community to develop a sense of belonging, perhaps by forming relationships. Once you felt that you belonged and that you shared love with other people, your sense of self-esteem could develop as your loved ones and friends held you in esteem. At that point, as a fulfilled member of a community, you might begin to develop your full potential.

Maslow's motivational theory has not always been supported by research, and many questions can be raised about it. For instance, how would you explain someone who throws himself on a hand grenade to protect friends, or someone such as Gandhi, who fasted to attain social and political change? Maslow's theory, like most grand theories of motivation, often fails to predict the complex patterns of human behavior and motivation in unusual circumstances. Still, it does provide a generally valid outline of motivation.

The Need to Achieve

Over 35 years ago, David McClelland described the **need for achievement (n-Ach)** as an acquired motivating force (see Figure 9.5), and used it to make predictions about motivation (McClelland, Atkinson, Clark & Lowell, 1953). Like Maslow, he attempted to expand his motivational theory to encompass as much of human behavior as possible.

At some level, of course, the need to achieve must also have an unlearned component, if for no other reason than that, simply to survive, human beings must obtain a certain degree of mastery over their environment (Spence, 1985).

To measure the degree of n-Ach in his subjects, McClelland showed them

HEIRARCHY OF MOTIVES
A theory of motivation developed by Abraham Maslow in which more basic needs must be met before needs of a higher order can come into play.

NEED FOR ACHIEVEMENT (N-ACH)
A learned motivation, described by researcher David McClelland. Those who score high in n-Ach often behave in different ways from those who score low in n-Ach.

FIGURE 9.4

Maslow's hierarchy of motives.

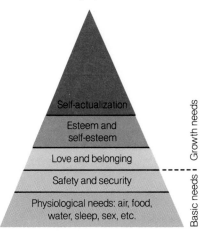

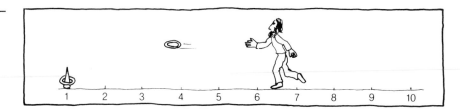

FIGURE 9.5

McClelland used this ring-toss game to illustrate the way in which people are motivated to obtain an optimal level of achievement satisfaction. Most subjects preferred to stand at distance markers 6 or 7 when throwing the ring, because doing so provided the greatest sense of achievement. At marker 1, it's easy to get a ringer, but achievement satisfaction is minimized because it's too easy. At marker 10, it's too hard to succeed, and achievement satisfaction also is lowered.

David McClelland

different drawings from the Thematic Apperception Test (see Chapter 13) and asked them to tell him stories about what they saw. McClelland was able to isolate themes from these stories that he believed demonstrated a high or low need to achieve, and he used these findings to make predictions about how the subjects would behave. For instance, people with a high need to achieve tended to perform better in school than did those with a low need.

McClelland then attempted to generalize his findings to whole cultures and nations. He argued in 1961 that among the nations in which citizens scored low in n-Ach on his tests, the economic standards and gross national product were lower than they were in nations in which the citizens scored high in n-Ach. This assertion came to be known as McClelland's **achieving society theory**. While McClelland's tests for n-Ach have been fairly successful at predicting a person's desire to seek challenges, to set high goals, to delay gratification until the goal is achieved, and to take reasonable risks (Atkinson & Raynor, 1974), they have proved somewhat more limited than originally hoped. For instance, data since 1961 concerning economic standards and gross national products of nations have not given much support to McClelland's achieving society theory (Mazur & Rosa, 1977).

Although it would be very useful to produce a theory of motivation that could explain most of human behavior, most researchers now believe that humans are just too complex to be understood in such a global and all encompassing way. For this reason, modern motivational theory generally is built on highly detailed investigations of many separate areas and limited generalizations, rather than on sweeping hypotheses.

Some fascinating specific areas of research are developing and they tell us a lot about why people behave in the ways that they do. Let's take a few minutes and look at some of them.

Learned Helplessness

Some people aren't motivated to help themselves when they could easily do so. If they have lost this motivation because of their experiences with failure, they may be suffering from what researchers call **learned helplessness.**

It's possible to teach an animal to become helpless. In the classic experiment that first demonstrated this phenomenon, two groups of dogs were given electric shocks. The dogs from both groups were yoked together in an experimental sense: Whenever dogs in one group received a shock, so did the dogs in the other group. The dogs in the first group, however, were able to press a lever and turn off a shock when it began. They had some control over their situation. The dogs in the second group had no such control. What was most interesting about this experiment was the effect that lack of control had on the dogs in the second group. When dogs from both groups were tested in an environment from which they could not escape shocks, the dogs from the first group barked and ran about trying *actively* to do something. Dogs from the second group, however, lay down and *passively* took the shocks as they came (Seligman & Maier, 1967).

Learned helplessness has also been observed in human infants. Two researchers (Watson & Ramey, 1969; 1972) positioned rotating mobiles above the heads of three groups of infants. A pressure-sensitive pillow was placed beneath the heads of the infants in the first group. By moving their heads, these infants could open and close circuits that made their mobiles turn, so they had control over this aspect of their environment. The infants in the second group were given no control; their pillows were not connected to the mobiles. As a result, their mobiles remained stationary. The third group of infants also was given no control; in this case, the mobiles turned randomly. (The purpose of the third variation was to ensure that the infants who learned to move their heads against their pillow were doing so because they had *control* over their environment, not simply because they were watching a turning object). After being exposed to the mobiles for 10 minutes per day for a period of 14 weeks, the infants in the first group learned to turn their heads to make the mobiles move. This is what you might expect an infant to be able to do through simple learning. But there's more.

As in the experiments with dogs, the most interesting aspect of these experiments was how *lack of control* affected the later behavior of the second and third groups of infants. Once again, researchers presented the second and third groups with the mobiles, but this time these groups were given control over the mobiles' movements. Even after extensive training, these infants failed to learn to operate the mobiles. Like the dogs who gave up trying to escape because of their earlier lack of control, the second and third groups of infants had learned to be helpless; they had learned not to expect their behavior to have any effect on their mobiles. As a result, they never seemed to appreciate the link between their head movements and the mobiles' turning that the first group of infants had been able to discern. Like the dogs in Seligman's experiment, infants also can transfer such learned helplessness to new situations (Finkelstein & Ramey, 1977).

Not surprisingly, individuals in institutions and other situations in which they are given little opportunity to manipulate their environments, or in which things are always being done to them or for them, may quickly learn not to try. The U.S. Office of Education issued one of the first reports to lend support to this idea. They found that members of minority groups who believed they were controlled by their environment—rather than the other way around—were more likely to fail in school (Coleman et al., 1966). It's ironic that certain life experiences may be helping children to learn not to learn (see Focus on an Application).

Altruism and Intrinsic Motivation

People often are motivated to help one another. Sometimes, the act of giving help may appear to be particularly selfless. We often use the word **altruism** to describe the motivation for such selfless acts. An altruistic act is the opposite of one motivated by self-interest. Psychologists think that altruistic behaviors are controlled by internalized systems for self-reward and morality. Such **intrinsic motivation** has been found in many cases to be superior to extrinsic (external) motivation in creating and maintaining behavior. In one experiment, researchers tried to teach fifth graders not to litter and to clean up after other children. The children were divided into two groups. The children in the first group were told each day for 8 days that they should be neat and tidy, and the reasons this behavior would be good for them were explained. The children in the second group were told, for the same number of days, that they were neat and tidy. Littering and cleanliness were measured on the tenth and fourteenth days. The differences were considerable. The children in the first group, who were motivated extrinsically, were far less likely to have helped to clean up than were the children in the second group, who had begun to think of themselves as neat and tidy and who wanted to maintain this positive self-image (intrinsic motivation) (Miller, Brickman, & Bolen, 1975).

ACHIEVING SOCIETY THEORY
McClelland's theory that nations whose members show the lowest need for achievement also tend to have the lowest gross national product, whereas nations whose members show the highest need for achievement have the highest gross national product.

LEARNED HELPLESSNESS
Giving up, even though success is possible, because of previous experience with situations in which success was impossible.

ALTRUISM
Behavior that benefits someone other than the actor, with little or no apparent benefit for the actor.

INTRINSIC MOTIVATION
A drive to engage in a behavior for its own sake in the absence of any obvious external reward or reinforcer.

People suffering from learned helplessness aren't motivated to help themselves, even when they could easily do so.

303

Whether a person will show learned helplessness depends a great deal on how he or she perceives the chances of being successful in any given situation. Psychologists refer to this perception as **self-efficacy** (Bandura, 1982). If you have self-efficacy in a certain situation, it means you believe that you can have an effect, that you can make a difference. In a sense, self-efficacy is the same as self-confidence.

High self-efficacy will help an individual to cope. In fact, it is self-efficacy, not fear, that determines whether a person with a phobia will approach what it is that he fears. A person who believes that he has control over the thing that frightens him will usually be willing to approach that thing in spite of his fear. With low self-efficacy, the same person would be unlikely to approach the feared object (Bandura, 1986).

If helplessness can be taught, it would stand to reason that its opposite, a sense of self-efficacy, could also be taught. Researchers have, in fact, discovered that there appear to be four major ways to raise perceptions of self-efficacy (Bandura, 1982): (1) through direct action, (2) by observing others, (3) through the use of verbal persuasion, and (4) by altering how one perceives one's own physical state.

Direct action refers to the actual experience you have in a particular situation. Learning through direct experience that what you do can be successful and that you are capable will enhance self-efficacy. Nothing will boost your confidence like success. Failure, especially as a first experience, can lower self-efficacy. For this reason, when teaching a new task, it is best to structure the first experiences to ensure success before

going on to more difficult parts of the task. In this way, the person builds confidence bit by bit.

By observing other people who are *similar* to you be successful at a task, you are also likely to raise your self-efficacy—it makes you more confident that you, too, could do it. For this reason it is often helpful to team someone new to a job with a successful person who is perceived to be similar to the new worker. Of course, watching someone similar to yourself fail at a task can lower your self-efficacy.

Verbal persuasion, in the form of logical arguments in favor of one's ability to succeed, sometimes can raise self-efficacy, but only if the person's self-efficacy is fairly high to begin with.

Finally, there are the physiological factors, such as fatigue, exhaustion, or fear, which individuals often use as an indication of self-efficacy. Your exact state itself isn't important; it's your cognitive appraisal of the state that matters. For example, trembling might lower an inexperienced soldier's self-efficacy if he perceives this physiological reaction to be an indication of fear, whereas the same trembling in an experienced actor might actually raise self-efficacy if she interprets it as the opening night jitters that will give her first performance more excitement.

High self-efficacy works as a motivator. If you believe that you can succeed, you are likely to try hard. People who try hard enough and long enough will often succeed, further strengthening their confidence. When people use the techniques we have described to help build someone up, psychologists say that they are teaching **mastery.**

When attempting to teach mastery,

it is also important to consider the cognitive factors that play a role in determining how broad a person's newly won confidence and desire to succeed will be. There are three important cognitive dimensions to consider: (1) internal versus external reasons for control, (2) stable versus unstable circumstances, and (3) global versus specific applications (Abramson, Seligman, & Teasdale, 1978; Miller & Norman, 1979). Let's look at each of these.

Internal versus External Reasons

If you think that the control over events resides in the environment rather than in yourself ("There's nothing I can do about it, things just happen to me"), then this perceived locus of control may lead you to believe that what you do doesn't matter. If, on the other hand, you believe that control resides within you and not in the environment ("The reason things went right was because of what I did"), then you may feel more confident about taking on new tasks. A school-aged child, for example, who has an external sense of control typically will believe that he failed because the teacher didn't like him or because the tests were unfair, while a child with an internal sense of control typically will attribute her failure to not trying hard enough. Obviously, such learned helplessness is less likely to occur if a person perceives the reason for lack of control to be internal; that is, believes he is failing because he isn't trying hard enough, rather failing because of forces over which he has no control.

Stable versus Unstable Circumstances

As you might guess, if you believe that whatever bad thing that might be happening to you is going to be long lasting or permanent, you're more likely to demonstrate learned helplessness than if you think it is temporary. For example, someone in a hospital bed who can't walk is less likely to show signs of learned helplessness if he is aware that he will soon be better than if he believes that he'll never walk again. With this in mind, we would predict that the people of what was once East Germany will strive hard and succeed in spite of the hardships they face while transferring to a market economy because, by and large, they view their economic troubles as temporary. Someone without job skills, who is on welfare, and who has a large family to raise in a decaying inner city environment, however, may view her situation as relatively permanent, which will weaken her self-efficacy and greatly reduce her motivation to succeed.

Global versus Specific Applications

Finally, learned helplessness is more likely to occur if you perceive the cause of your loss of control or failure as being applicable in many or all situations (global), rather than being applicable in only a few circumstances (specific). For this reason, self-efficacy and motivation to succeed are not usually too adversely affected by failures that are viewed as isolated or fluky. We would predict that, although the space shuttle *Challenger* disaster was very upsetting, it alone would not deter the United States from continuing its space program. However, if one disaster followed on another until the *whole* program seemed a mess, confidence and mastery could be so undermined that the public might turn away from further efforts as they come to believe that we just can't do it anymore. This could occur in spite of our many great space successes

in the past—learned helplessness is often irrational.

We might, therefore, assume that to develop mastery, it would be best to have an internal, stable, and potentially global sense of mastery (Mineka & Hendersen, 1985). Furthermore, if we consider operant-learning theory (see Chapter 6), we might add that persistence is more likely to occur if success comes intermittently—not with every effort (Jones, Nation, & Massad, 1977). In other words, occasional failures interspersed with successes can teach you that you can "bounce back" from failure, which is an important contributor to a sense of mastery.

As you recall from the Prologue, Harlow's rhesus monkeys enjoyed working with puzzles. They found them intrinsically interesting. Their motivation changed, however, when they were given raisins for working the puzzles. The reward created an extrinsic motive for solving the puzzles, and the monkeys lost interest in the puzzles when they were not offered a raisin.

One of the classic studies that highlights this same problem with humans was conducted with children who were drawing (Lepper, Greene, & Nisbett, 1973). After a time, the researchers gave some of the children a good-player certificate as a reward for having drawn. Interestingly, these children were less likely to draw after that than were the children who had not been rewarded. In this case, the reward actually seemed to undermine the intrinsic motivation behind the drawing.

Since the Harlow experiments, many motivational theorists have become interested in discovering the circumstances under which extrinsic reinforcement will undermine behavior that is intrinsically motivated. This area of research is of special interest to behavioral theorists. In many schools and institutions, people who are not motivated to work often are stimulated to do so through the use of "token economies." That is, when the people behave appropriately, they are given a token that can be traded in for something of value. Some observers have argued that token economies, while effective, can have drawbacks and that researchers and therapists must determine at the outset whether the behavior they want to encourage isn't already intrinsically motivated. If it is, then giving tokens as rewards may undermine the intrinsic motivation, such that, instead of doing something because it's fun or has its own value, people will do it only if there is something "in it for

SELF-EFFICACY

How effective a person is in a particular situation. Perceived self-efficacy can be a powerful cognitive motivator.

MASTERY

In motivation, the opposite of learned helplessness; the acquisition of skills or attitudes that enable one to persist in adversity and that help to "psychologically inoculate" one against giving up or feeling helpless.

CHAPTER 9
MOTIVATION

Monkeys find manipulating these locks to be intrinsically motivating.

them." Imagine the poverty of a world in which no positive behaviors occurred unless obvious extrinsic reinforcement were immediately available. The internal motivations behind love, empathy, charity, and humanity would be gone; there would be no more selflessness (Greene, Sternberg, & Lepper, 1976).

Some researchers believe that altruism and other intrinsic motivations also may have important unlearned components and therefore could never come completely under the control of extrinsic motivators. This view has been best developed by the proponents of **sociobiology,** a theory of behavior first proposed by Harvard zoologist Edward O. Wilson (Wilson, 1975).

To sociobiologists, altruism can, in a manner of speaking, have a "selfish" component that serves a genetic purpose. They believe that one of the reasons a person often is willing to make a sacrifice for other people may be that such an act may promote the general survival of "his kind." Such behavior is common in the animal kingdom. Many animals have been observed even to give up their lives (for instance, by deliberately distracting a predator while the other members of the group flee to safety). Such "altruism" can be very selective. For example, in Chapter 4, we discussed how animals often are able to recognize kin by smell, and researchers have observed that many animals would rather share with or protect a blood relative than an unrelated member of their species (Lewin, 1984). In the mid-1950s, British biologist J. B. S. Haldane anticipated this view when he jokingly announced that he would lay down his life for two brothers or eight cousins. His reasoning was that each brother would have one-half of his genes and each cousin about one-eighth of his genes, which made the decision acceptable in terms of genetic survivability.

The sociobiological view that many seemingly learned motives have important inherited components has given rise to areas of study such as behavioral genetics, which examines questions of nature and nature (see Chapter 12).

The opponent-process theory of motivation helps explain why anyone would actually go out of his way to do this.

Solomon's Opponent-Process Theory

Over the last 15 years, researcher Richard L. Solomon has developed a powerful theory to explain acquired or learned motivation on a relatively grand scale—the **opponent-process theory.** This theory addresses many of the motivational questions that we have discussed so far. Its startling central theme is that most learned motivations are addictions. As Solomon has said,

> The theory attempts to account for such diverse acquired motives as drug addiction, love, affection, and social attachment, and cravings for sensory and aesthetic experiences (cases in which the initial reinforcers are positive) and for such acquired motives as parachuting, jogging, "marathoning," sauna bathing, and a variety of self-administered, aversive stimuli like electric shocks (cases in which the initial reinforcers are negative).
>
> Acquired motives can be as powerful as innate ones. They can become the focus for the major behaviors of an organism, even at the expense of innate needs. A heroin addict, for example, may spend the better part of each day in drug-seeking behavior, may ignore food, liquid, and sexual incentives, and may abandon normal societal obligations. The heroin motive is acquired only because certain experiences have occurred; it is not innate. We tend to think of such addictions as pathological, but they are not. . . . Most acquired motives, such as love, social attachments, food-taste cravings, thrill seeking, and needs for achievement, power, and affiliation, obey the empirical laws for the addictions. (Solomon, 1980, p. 691)

In other words, acquired behaviors—loving, jogging, sauna bathing, parachute jumping, and so on—can become addictions. Even cravings for certain aesthetic experiences can become addicting.

Consider parachute jumping. What actually happens? The first parachuting experience usually is frightening. Fear builds as the jump time nears, reaching a peak when the "ready" signal goes on (see Figure 9.6). Parachutists report that the moment of stepping out of the airplane door is truly a terrifying one. Until the last second, many people think that they won't be able to jump. If they do jump, they discover that the sensation of falling, while slight for one or two seconds after jumping, increases very, very rapidly. There is a sickening feeling in the stomach. What started as a gentle descent through the air quickly becomes a brutal plunge in which winds between 120 and 180 miles per hour batter the parachutist. The winds are surprisingly cold and ripping. The sense of time is distorted: It seems that the parachute should have opened by now, which adds to the terror. Suddenly, there is the upward jerk of the parachute unfurling, and fear recedes as the reassuring brightly colored canopy appears overhead.

EMOTIONAL CONTRAST. When the first-time jumpers land, they usually walk about in a stony-faced silence for a while, slowly recovering from their terror. Then

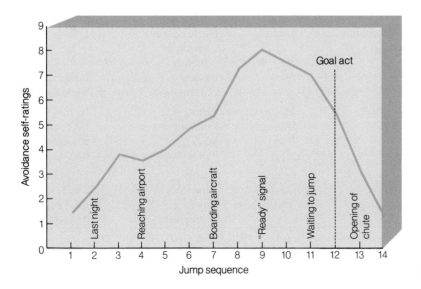

SOCIOBIOLOGY
A theory of motivation and behavior stating that many human behaviors are influenced by inherited biological predispositions. In this view, morality, love, kindness, aggression, anger, hatred, and most other aspects of human behavior are partly viewed in terms of their functional value for ensuring the survival of a person's genes.

OPPONENT-PROCESS THEORY
A theory of motivation by Richard Solomon proposing that many acquired motives, such as drug addiction, love, affection, social attachment, cravings for sensory and aesthetic experiences, skydiving, jogging, sauna bathing, and even self-administered aversive stimuli, seem to follow the laws of addiction.

FIGURE 9.6

The parachute jumper's fear is at the highest level just before the jump, and it lessens significantly when the parachute opens. (SOURCE: Epstein & Fenz, 1965, p. 2.)

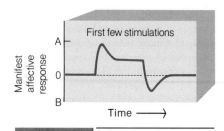

FIGURE 9.7

Emotional contrast. Initially, during the first few stimulations, there is an intense affective (emotional) reaction. Then the person adapts to the reaction, and it remains steady for a time. This state is followed by a strong affective afterreaction that eventually decays, returning the person to the initial state. (SOURCE: *Solomon, 1980, p. 700.*)

an interesting thing happens, which Solomon calls affective or **emotional contrast.** The parachutists begin to smile at one another. They are elated. They run toward each other laughing, shaking hands, and slapping one another on the back. They make jokes, laugh some more—a sense of great relief abounds. This intense feeling can last for several hours. You can imagine it easily even if you haven't watched parachutists, because it is such a natural human reaction.

Solomon first noticed this effect when he went into a hospital where 1-day-old infants were resting. The infants weren't hungry yet, but Solomon gave them milk to drink. They enjoyed it, drinking it readily when he placed the nipple in their mouths. Then he removed the nipple, and the babies began to cry. They had been happy without the milk before he showed up, but now they were crying. After a while the crying subsided, and the babies returned to their initial peaceful state. This kind of effect, Solomon realized, was an example of emotional contrast. Emotional contrast is interesting because it shows us that surviving a terrifying or painful experience, as our parachutists did, can lead to feelings of exhilaration. Conversely a pleasurable experience, such as drinking milk, can lead to feelings of depression. In this way, pleasure can lead to sadness, and pain to happiness!

Solomon has examined many emotional contrasts. As you can see in Figure 9.7, there is an initial primary effect (toward A, in the illustration). With the parachutists, it was one of terror. It peaks, declines a little, remains steady for a time, and then is followed by an intense emotional contrast (toward B), during which the emotions swing in the opposite direction. After a time that, too, wears off, and there is a return to the middle.

Table 9.1 shows Solomon's examples of emotional contrast in four different conditions. The first is injecting heroin for the first time; the second, social attachment, ducklings on their first exposure to a moving mother duck (imprinting;

TABLE 9.1 Emotional Contrast (Changes in Affect) in Four Conditions

CONDITION	PERIOD	AFTER FIRST FEW EXPERIENCES	AFTER MANY EXPERIENCES
I. Self-dosing with opiates	Before	Resting state	Craving
	During	Rush, euphoria	Contentment
	After	Craving	Abstinence-agony
		Resting state	Craving
II. Social attachment in ducklings	Before	Contentment	Some distress
	During	Excitement at seeing the mother	Following the mother
	After	Distress	Intense distress
		Contentment	Some distress
III. Suana bathing	Before	Resting state	Resting state
	During	Pain, burning	Heat, excitement
	After	Relief	Exhilaration
		Resting state	Resting state
IV. Free-fall in military parachuting	Before	Anxiety	Eagerness
	During	Terror	Thrill
	After	Relief	Exhilaration
		Resting state	Resting state

SOURCE: Adapted from Solomon, 1980, pp. 696–697.
NOTE: The emotions in the "After Many" column are those associated with addictive effects.

see Chapter 6); the third, people's first experience of sauna bathing, which is very hot; and the fourth, military parachutists' first experience of free-fall. As you can see, there is an initial state (before). Then comes what Solomon has called the A process, or the first affective peak (during). Then comes the B process, which is the emotional contrast (after), and then a return to the resting state. If the A process is extremely stimulating, the B process is likely to be extremely stimulating *in the opposite direction.*

One of the most remarkable examples of emotional contrast was described by David H. Rosen. The Golden Gate Bridge, which connects San Francisco and Sausalito, California, is one of the longest suspension bridges in the world, and its roadway is hundreds of feet above the strong currents of San Francisco Bay. Unfortunately, over the years the bridge has attracted many suicidal people, and more than 500 of them have died jumping from it. Incredibly, 10 people have survived the jump. This fact is remarkable because at a speed of over 120 miles per hour, the water would feel like concrete on impact—and, after that, assuming the person were still conscious, he or she would have to swim in the strong, cold currents to reach safety. In 1976, David Rosen interviewed seven of the survivors. All of them, he found, had undergone a "spiritual rebirth." They were happy, enjoyed their lives, and felt better than they ever had. Consider these individuals in the light of the emotional contrast phenomenon for a moment. Is it possible that the A process was so intense, the terror and certain realization of imminent death so overwhelming, that surviving the jump called up an opposing B process of such intense exhilaration that the people were left with a happier outlook even after the feeling of excitement had subsided?

ADDICTION. Solomon has gone on to say that emotional contrast can lead to addictions because of two changes that take place in the A and B processes over time. He noticed that when people engage in the same kind of emotional contrast again and again, the initial A state *becomes less potent.* People adapt to it. The B state, on the other hand, *becomes stronger;* it starts sooner and lasts longer (see Figure 9.8). Once these changes have begun to occur, following emotional contrast, a person will not always return to the original state. A weak A process, caused by repeating the experience many times, followed by a strong B process may leave the person in the B state (see Figure 9.9). A person left in the B state may easily become addicted to the activity that resulted in achieving the B state because he will either like the B state (if it is pleasant) and try to maintain it, or he will dislike the B state (if it is aversive) and try to return to the opposing A state—which, ironically, only leads to an even stronger B state. In either case, the addiction is set.

CRITICAL DECAY DURATION. Another important part of the opponent-process theory is the **critical decay duration** of the opponent process. If you experience an emotional contrast, the A process will become weaker and the B process stronger only if you engage in the behavior that produces the contrast again and again. The changes won't happen if you wait too long between experiences. After the critical decay duration, the addicting effect won't occur. In other words, if you wait too long before parachuting again, the terror of the A process may be just as great as it was originally, and the elation of the B process no more than it was before. However, if you immediately jump again and do it a number of times, the A process will weaken and the B process will strengthen, thus slowly beginning an addiction (Starr, 1978).

More research is needed to demonstrate the power of the opponent-process theory of motivation and to investigate the prevalence of its effect. Still, the theory helps to explain how people can come to enjoy danger or pain and why pleasure

EMOTIONAL CONTRAST
An emotional effect that plays an important part in Solomon's opponent-process theory of motivation. Following any emotional arousal (pleasant or aversive), there is often an opposite emotional state. This contrasting emotional state will last for a time and then diminish or end.

CRITICAL DECAY DURATION
From the opponent-process theory of motivation, a time of sufficient length between the onset of an affective A process and its repetition so that no decrease in A process intensity or increase in B process intensity is noted.

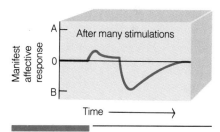

FIGURE 9.8

Changes in the A and B processes after repeated emotional contrasts. The initial A state becomes weaker, and the B state becomes stronger. (SOURCE: Solomon, 1980, p. 700.)

FIGURE 9.9

After many stimulations, the A process may become so weak and the B process so strong that an emotional contrast can leave the individual in the B state.

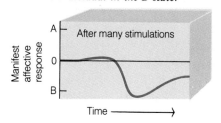

CONCEPT REVIEW: ADDICTION

Take another look at Table 9.1, and you'll see the kinds of changes that occur if a particular emotional contrast is engaged in often enough. In cases I and II (heroin use, duckling attachment) the A process during the first few exposures is pleasant. The contrasting B process that follows is aversive. At first the organism is left in a fairly neutral state, $[A - B] = 0$, because the A and B processes are equal in strength. After many exposures, however, the A process weakens, (for example, the heroin high is mild; the duckling follows the mother but is not excited by her). The B process simultaneously becomes stronger. This change eventually will leave the organism in the B state: [weak A − strong B] = B>A. The B state is aversive in cases I and II.

If the B state is aversive, as in cases I and II, the urge to return to the A state will be great; such a return will, ironically, lead only to a further weakening of the A state and further strengthening of the B state. As you can see, this is the beginning of an addiction. The organism will strongly desire to return to the A state but in so doing will only make the A state weaker still and the B state even stronger. The addiction is complete, the hook is set. This is why long-term heroin addicts don't enjoy their heroin; they simply shoot up to *avoid* withdrawal—making the addiction worse.

In cases III and IV (sauna bathing, parachuting), the A process during the first few exposures is not pleasurable, but aversive. People may have tried such an aversive thing for the first time because of military orders or social pressure. After a few times, however, the aversive A process weakens and the opposing pleasant B process grows: Once again, [weak A − strong B] = B>A. As a result, the stronger B process, which in cases III and IV is pleasant, is sought more and more often (especially because the A process is no longer scary), and, once again, addiction is underway, although for slightly different reasons (reasons of approach rather than escape).

and happiness can be so fleeting. It might also help to answer a number of other questions. For instance, why do people who diet and who find the initial experiences painful sometimes come to enjoy being hungry? Why do soldiers initially terrified of war sometimes reenlist for combat when their enlistment time is up? Why does a job that is initially exciting sometimes become dull and tedious? We also may learn from research into the opponent-process theory how to avoid these kinds of emotional shifts, perhaps by building in critical decay durations at the appropriate times. We may come to understand motivations that at first seem bizarre or unusual. And we may find a better explanation for thrill seeking than George Mallory's for attempting to climb Mount Everest—"Because it's there."

"Because it's there," and because $|A - B|$ *= B > A.*

AN ENDURING QUESTION: WHY DON'T WE ALWAYS DO WHAT'S IN OUR OWN BEST INTEREST?

Have you ever noticed that even though you may know that doing some particular thing will be in your own best interest, you still don't do it? Why is that?

For years, researchers have argued that people will make rational choices unless they are confused by the choice or fail to understand its significance in some way. The gist of this argument is that any rational person will make the smart choice if he fully understands all of the variables involved and their importance. And yet, we know that rational choices aren't always the ones that we'll choose even if we fully understand the options. For example, taking smokers on a tour of a cancer ward will scare them into not smoking, but only for about a day. To explain this discrepancy, we turn to concepts such as addiction. But however you look at it, we are dealing with irrationality.

To demonstrate that irrationality can occur even when choices are obvious, researcher R. J. Herrnstein asked people if they would prefer $100 now or $115 in a week. The hypothetical question was stated in a way so that it was understood that the money would be held in escrow in a bank and that there would be no worry about it being there a week later. Most people said that they wanted the $100 now (Herrnstein, 1990)! Is that a rational choice? Well you might say that they didn't feel that waiting a week for $15 was worth it. So Herrnstein asked another question. He asked them if they would prefer $100 in 52 weeks or $115 in 53 weeks. This time they wanted the $115. What had changed?

From this and many other studies, Herrnstein has concluded that there are certain factors common to human motivation that preclude our always making the rational choice, even when we fully understand the choice.

The first of these factors is the immediacy of an event. For some reason, events some time away are discounted more than are events happening right now. Things happening now seem to be magnified. Something attractive looks even more attractive if it is right in front of us than if it is down the road, and, conversely, unattractive things look worse if they are about to happen now than later. The effect is so powerful that it often overwhelms rationality. Impulse buying is a good example of this principle at work. A car salesman knows that he mustn't let you out of the showroom without getting you to buy, because once you leave the car won't seem quite as desirable.

Let's consider another example. If you are on a diet, it can be very hard to pass up some treat that is right in front of you because the pleasure it offers is magnified out of proportion. As proof, ask yourself what dieter who passed up a treat has ever said *the next day*, "Boy, I wish I had eaten that fattening food yesterday when I had the chance, I really missed something." It's not very likely, because a piece of cake just isn't that important in retrospect—it's only important if you're hungry and it's right in front of you. As Herrnstein has pointed out,

> Imagine, for example, that we could always select meals for tomorrow, rather than for right now. Would we not all eat better than we do? We may find it possible to forgo tomorrow's chocolate cake or second helping of pasta or third martini, but not the one at hand. (Herrnstein, 1990, p. 359)

This effect helps explain how a cigarette *now* can seem a fair trade for heart disease later, or how the threat of a five-second shock of cold water *now* can keep someone from enjoying a day of swimming (no, it doesn't work as well just to inch into the water a little at a time, but people make this irrational choice because the threat of cold water is magnified by its immediacy).

Another reason for the failure to make the best choices is the tendency to engage in **melioration.** We, and most other organisms, allocate our behaviors so that we try to maintain the same *rate* of reward for each of our actions. No one knows why we do this, but we do. However, if you consider what Richard Solomon showed us, that the A process weakens the more we do something, and if you consider that for each activity the A process may weaken at a different rate, you make an interesting discovery. Even though melioration sounds reasonable, it may not lead to maximum happiness (Herrnstein, 1990).

By meliorating, we level our experiences, even the most desirable experiences, down to a common denominator by engaging in them freely. In other words, getting more of something good can actually devalue it so that we get less *total pleasure* from it than if we had it less often! This may explain why multimillion-

MELIORATION
In psychology, the tendency of organisms to shift behavioral allocations toward more lucrative alternatives.

aires usually say that getting their first million was the most fun. Backing that up is research that shows that increasing wealth does not go hand in hand with increasing happiness (Murray, 1988). Similarly, someone who has many sexual partners and often engages in sexual activity may find it becomes progressively more and more difficult to discover sexual experiences that are as exciting as the first ones were. Herrnstein's findings may also explain why many older couples often recall their early years of struggling to get by as some of their happiest. More isn't necessarily better.

As another example, consider my great uncle who grew up in Russia and never saw an orange until he came to this country. He still remembers the first orange my grandfather gave him to eat back in 1921. But most Americans like myself may never know what my great uncle's orange tasted like, because in a land of plenty melioration is the normal mode of action. In fact, I bought some oranges a few weeks ago and then forgot about them. They stayed in the refrigerator until some old fuzz grew on them and then I threw them out. Oranges just aren't special anymore.

If you want to be rational about obtaining happiness—if you want to maximize it—perhaps you should, as the phrase goes, "stay hungry." That is, dole out treats to yourself sparingly. This is another way of saying that you should observe the critical decay duration. In spite of what *Lifestyles of the Rich and Famous* may have us believe, by "staying hungry" to some extent, we may have more total fun than someone who has all the treats all of the time!

After Walter Bonatti became the first person ever to climb the north wall of the Matterhorn alone during winter, an effort that took days and almost cost him his life, he was asked what the greatest part of that experience had been. He said, with a look of ecstasy on his face, that it had been the bath he took in his hotel afterward. Everyone laughed, but Bonatti swore that he wasn't joking. Of course, I'm not suggesting that you search for the critical decay duration for your bath. Although "stay hungry" has its applications, "stay smelly" may be something else again, but you get the idea.

FOR CRITICAL ANALYSIS

1. How might you restructure your own environment to increase pleasure by reducing melioration? What sorts of problems do you immediately encounter?
2. Why do you think people meliorate? In terms of natural selection, what advantages might there be in melioration? (Consider the purpose of pleasure as a motivator and the species survival value of food and sexual activity.)

EPILOGUE: GETTING A CHARGE OUT OF LIFE

The following observation by one researcher added impetus to another researcher's investigations and eventually helped to give birth to a theory of motivation.

H. B. Taussig had been interested in motivation for many years. Like all of us, she pondered on the reasons behind people's actions. In 1969, Taussig became especially curious about what some researchers were calling emotional contrast. Her curiosity stemmed from an incident involving her neighbor's son.

The young man had been playing golf when a storm began. He packed up his clubs and started to leave the golf course. Suddenly, as he was walking away, he began to feel a strange tingling all about him. Then there was a tremendous flash of light. The ground seemed to rush at him. A gigantic BOOM almost broke his eardrums. He lay there, shocked. His shorts were torn to shreds, and he was burned across his thighs. His companions realized that he had been struck by lightning. As they ran up to him, they could hear him screaming, "I'm dead, I'm dead!" (Taussig, 1969, p. 306). An ambulance was called. By the time it arrived, the young man's legs were numb and blue and he was unable to move.

He was rushed to the hospital emergency room. But as he was wheeled in, he was laughing happily. In fact, he was euphoric, talking to everyone, telling them what had happened, showing them his tattered shorts, and smiling broadly from ear to ear.

The more Taussig thought about it, the more incredible it seemed. The young man hadn't been that happy before the lightning hit him. What a strange cause for elation, being slammed to the ground by over a million volts of electricity. Taussig wondered how terror could turn into joy.

Taussig later related this story to Richard Solomon. It convinced Solomon that such extreme emotional switches needed to be investigated more closely, and he eventually developed the opponent-process theory of motivation.

SUMMARY

■ Psychologists study motivation because they want a fuller explanation of why a behavior occurs.

■ The word *motivation* is derived from the Greek word *motivum*, which refers to the reason that something has moved.

■ Scientists assume that biological motivations such as hunger and thirst are built in—they exist from birth.

■ Homeostasis refers to built-in regulatory systems for maintaining the status quo. Any deviation from an optimal state creates a need that usually produces a drive that is the motivational force for action.

■ The hypothalamocentric hypothesis argues that hunger and thirst centers located in the hypothalamus monitor deviations from optimal states. Lesions in the ventromedial hypothalamus result in overeating and obesity.

■ Hunger and thirst also seem to be regulated by sensors distant from the brain.

■ The most recent view is that the hypothalamus is not the hunger and thirst center, but rather is one of a number of hunger and thirst monitoring and sensing areas.

■ The homeostatic mechanism that monitors thirst appears to depend on sodium levels in the intracellular and extracellular fluids.

■ Hunger and thirst have been shown to interact. Providing food to a hungry animal on an intermittent schedule often produces schedule-induced polydipsia by increasing the drive to drink.

■ The homeostatic mechanisms controlling hunger and thirst, as well as other homeostatic mechanisms, may differ considerably from one member of a species to the next as a result of individual inheritance.

■ Although some people gain weight because of overeating or because of defects in regulators in the brain and elsewhere in the body, nonhomeostatic mechanisms also play an important role in obesity.

■ Research has indicated that the more physiologically advanced a species is, the less its sexual behavior appears to be governed directly by chemical or hormonal forces. Even in humans, however, chemical and hormonal factors may play a role.

■ The sex drive in humans may have something to do with sensors in the hypothalamus that are sensitive to different levels of hormones.

■ Human beings and animals seem to have a need for a certain amount of stimulation. Motivations generated by these needs are referred to as stimulus motives.

■ Certain motivations can be learned. Learned motives often

are related to incentives, which are particular things that we want to possess.

■ Learned motivations can imitate biological ones. For instance, it's possible to learn to become hungry through classical conditioning.

■ Abraham Maslow, a humanistic psychologist, developed a theory based on a hierarchy of motives, in which some needs were more powerful than others. Modern motivational theory, however, usually is limited to highly detailed investigations of specific areas.

■ Over the last 25 years, researchers have investigated the need for achievement that is evident in some individuals. Scientists believe that this need is learned as the result of experience.

■ It is possible to learn to become helpless, although this type of learning usually doesn't occur suddenly.

■ When we are faced with a new situation, one of the most important determinants of our behavior is perceived self-efficacy; that is, our belief about how effective we might be. Our performance tends to vary as a function of our perceived efficacy.

■ There are four basic ways to change our self-efficacy. These include direct action, observing other people, verbal persuasion, and our perception of our own physical states.

■ In many cases, intrinsic motivation has been found to be superior to extrinsic motivation in creating and maintaining behavior.

■ Sociobiologists argue that motivated actions, including altruistic ones, may have important genetic components and biological foundations.

■ Richard Solomon has developed a theory of acquired motivation called the opponent-process theory. His theory explains many motivational phenomena as a function of addictions. The theory may help to explain why some people come to enjoy danger or pain and why pleasure and happiness can be so fleeting.

■ Often we do not act in our own best interest. Interfering with our rational choices are the facts that immediate events are magnified—they are seen as better or worse than later events— and that we tend to meliorate, or try to maintain the same rate of reward for each of our actions.

SUGGESTIONS FOR FURTHER READING

1. Arkes, H. R., & Garske, J. P. (1981). *Psychological theories of motivation* (2nd ed.). Monterey, CA: Brooks/Cole. A college-level introduction to some of the theories of motivation discussed in the chapter.
2. Lepper, M. R., & Greene, D. (Eds.). (1978). *The hidden costs of reward.* Hillsdale, NJ: Erlbaum. Discusses some of the problems inherent in any system that uses extrinsic rewards as motivators.
3. Logue, A. W. (1985). *The psychology of eating and drinking.* New York: W. H. Freeman. A discussion of the biological motivations behind eating and drinking behavior. Includes interesting personal experiences of the author.
4. Lyman, B. (1988). *The psychology of food: More than a matter of taste.* New York: Van Nostrand Reinhold. Technical yet readable book about why we eat what we eat. Discusses food texture, color, odor, and appearance, as well as the social and psychological influences that lead us to make food choices.
5. Mitchell, R. G. (1983). *Mountain experience: The psychology and sociology of adventure.* Chicago: University of Chicago Press. A book for the general reader that discusses the motivations of people who climb mountains. Includes a discussion of how groups can motivate people.
6. Petri, H. (1990). *Motivation: Theory and research* (3rd ed.). Belmont, CA: Wadsworth. A college-level textbook covering all aspects of motivational research.

CHAPTER 10 | Emotion

Prologue

Why Psychologists Study Emotions

The Biology of Emotion

Why Emotions Evolved

What Makes Us Emotional?

Judging Emotions

Theories of Emotion
   The James-Lange Theory
   Schachter's Cognitive Appraisal
     Theory
   Facial Feedback Theory
   Plutchik Psychoevolutionary Synthesis
     of Emotions

Epilogue: "They'll Let Me Go
Tomorrow"

PROLOGUE

You are standing in a small observation area looking through one-way glass into a darkened room at your volunteer subject who is seated in a chair. A microphone has been placed over his heart. A wire from the microphone runs back to a recorder. You've told your subject that you are going to monitor his heart rate during the experiment. In front of him is a screen on which slides will be shown. The young man sits in his chair quite comfortably. He's interested in the experiment, since you've told him that he's going to be seeing slides of Playboy magazine centerfolds. You throw a switch to begin the experiment, and the first slide, Miss January, shines on the screen.

The subject says, "I think I'm going to like this." You ask him to refrain from speaking during the experiment. The sound of his heartbeat can be heard as the recorder collects the data. The heartbeat sound is loud enough so that the subject can hear it—you rigged it that way. After a time, Miss February comes on the screen. The man's heartbeat accelerates and becomes louder. Then Miss March, and his heartbeat slows to its earlier rate.

You're trying not to smile or laugh, since you know the secret. Your colleague, Stuart Valins, wanted to test the effect that thinking has on emotion, and so he designed this study. The microphone is a fake; the subject can't really hear his own heartbeat. Instead, the sound of a false heartbeat fills the room. You control the heartbeat and can make it go faster or slower by turning a dial. Earlier, you chose at random the playmates of the month who were going to be associated with a rapid heartbeat—Miss February, Miss August, and Miss November. The sub-

ject is now watching Miss April, so you don't touch the dial. You'll have to wait until Miss August and then Miss November before accelerating the heartbeat again. The whole time, the subject will think he's listening to the sound of his own heart. How will this belief affect him?

At the end of the experiment you thank the subject. He smiles and thanks you! Then you tell him that he can choose any three of the centerfold photographs to take home with him. Little does he know that this is the dependent variable you want to measure. You show him all 12 photographs, and watch as he picks out February, then November, and then after a little thought, September. That makes two out of the three—in statistical terms, significant. As the experiment continues, the results from other subjects support this initial finding (Valins, 1966).

Apparently, the subject in this experiment thought that he had become emotionally aroused while watching particular slides, and he used the false emotional feedback to make a judgment about his preferences and feelings. Valins likes to say that even in the absence of specific physiological reactions, the cognitive or thought component of an emotion can still have an effect. In other words, how you assess your feelings is part of your emotional makeup (Lazarus, 1984).

How many times during the day do you rely on cognitive assessments in order to know what your emotional state is, and how many times might you have been fooled by circumstances in a way similar to what the subjects in the experiment experienced? In other words, how can you be sure how you really feel about things?

In this chapter we'll examine what has been, to date, one of the most difficult and all-consuming tasks in psychology: finding out what emotions are. Although we deal with emotions every day, and although they are an integral part of human interaction and behavior, nobody really knows what they are. Still, some recent theories have brought us closer to an understanding of emotion, and the implications for our understanding of behavior are significant.

WHY PSYCHOLOGISTS STUDY EMOTIONS

It has been said that our emotions are what make us seem most human. We rage, we laugh, we cry, we fear, and we love. To be without emotions is to be unfeeling, perhaps "inhuman."

Everyone has emotions, even infants a few weeks old. Babies demonstrate striking emotional behaviors. They smile and laugh, they form loving attachments, and they show fear. Parents often report that the first smile from their baby is a magical moment that seems instantly to create a closer and more meaningful bond. As adults, we pay close attention to other people in order to discern their attitudes and emotional reactions. Even in the absence of any other cues, emotional monitoring can provide vital information about the people around us. At the same time, we often look to our own feelings to understand why we behave the way we do. Emotions pervade our existence, affecting every moment, and no study of human behavior would be complete without an attempt to understand the power and value of our emotional experiences.

THE BIOLOGY OF EMOTION

During the first year of life, a central emotional system develops within the human brain in a small area called the amygdala (see Chapter 2). There, sensory information about whether to approach or withdraw from an object, person, or situation is evaluated (Fox, 1989). This basic neural decision about whether to approach or withdraw appears to be the first use of **emotion** as a motivator of behavior in the infant.

As the infant grows, emotions continue to develop along "approach or avoid" lines, lines that appear to be distinctly separate in their neural organization. For instance, when the two hemispheres of the infant's brain are monitored, it has been observed that positive emotions such as joy are associated with a surge of electrical activity in the left hemisphere, while the right hemisphere shows increased electrical activity when negative emotions such as sadness are elicited (Fox & Davidson, 1988).

Complex emotions emerge once a greater information exchange between the amygdala and the frontal lobes of the brain becomes possible. This occurs when neural connections form between these areas as the infant develops into a child.

The central nervous system, of which the brain is the primary part, integrates its emotional reactions with the autonomic nervous system (see Chapter 2). During intense emotional reactions, such as fear, rage, or sexual arousal, the sympathetic nervous system becomes more active, resulting in several physical changes (see Table 10.1). The heart rate, for instance, may climb to 140 beats per minute or more, strictly as a result of emotional arousal. The fact that strong, measurable, physiological changes occur in direct relationship with emotional changes is the basis for the **polygraph,** or lie detector (see Focus on a Controversy).

EMOTION
A complex feeling-state involving conscious experience and internal and overt physical responses that tend to facilitate or inhibit motivated behavior.

POLYGRAPH
A lie detector. This device measures physiological changes regulated by the autonomic nervous system (heartbeat, blood pressure, galvanic skin response, and breathing rate). The assumption is that deliberate lying will produce detectable physical reactions.

WHY EMOTIONS EVOLVED

Emotions appear to be common throughout the animal kingdom. Along with anatomical forms and physiological systems, emotions too have evolved. They are an integral part of us as human beings. But why should our nervous system have developed the complex system of reactions we call our emotions? The reason appears

TABLE 10.1 Physiological Reactions Associated with Emotional Arousal

REACTION	DIVISION OF AUTONOMIC NERVOUS SYSTEM CONTROLLING REACTION
Pupils dilate	Sympathetic
Mouth becomes dry	Sympathetic
Heartbeat increases	Sympathetic
Tears are produced	Parasympathetic
Adrenaline is secreted	Sympathetic
Sweating increases	Sympathetic
Bladder relaxes	Sympathetic
Genitals are stimulated	Parasympathetic

LIE DETECTION

A polygraph, also called a lie detector, is designed to measure physiological changes that occur in conjunction with emotional states. It is called a polygraph because it measures several different physiological states. One "graph" monitors respiratory rate, another heart rate, a third blood pressure, and a fourth electrical changes on the surface of the skin—the last is known as a GSR (galvanic skin response) measuring device.

A subject connected to a polygraph is asked questions. Many of the initial questions are routine, such as, "What is your name?" or "What is your address?" These routine questions help to establish a baseline against which to measure changes associated with strong emotions.

A person suspected of having broken into a store the night before might be asked such questions as, "Where were you last night?" If the person lies and answers, "I stayed home all night watching television," the fear the person feels when lying may register as a change in the physiological mechanisms measured by the polygraph. In this way, the machine might be able to detect a lie.

By investigating the polygraph, we can see the interaction of both cognitive processes and autonomic arousal in the evocation of emotion. By doing so, we'll also come to appreciate the difficulties inherent in trying to use a polygraph as a "lie detector."

The Italian psychiatrist Cesare Lombroso was the first person to make similar claims to those of modern proponents of the polygraph when he concluded that he could tell whether someone was lying by noting changes in that person's blood pressure. (Lombroso also believed, by the way, that he could identify a criminal by the shape of the person's skull.)

The first modern machine to rely on the greater sensitivity of all four physiological measures was developed in 1906. Interestingly, this first polygraph was designed as a medical instrument. It wasn't until 1932 that Harvard-trained psychologist William Marston began to champion the device as a "lie detector."*

At first glance, the lie detector may appear to have been a marvelous breakthrough in criminology, because it is supposedly able to determine when someone is lying. Lie detectors, however, have become controversial because they don't detect lies. They do, however, detect nervousness, and there is a very important difference.

Are you the kind of person who becomes nervous when you are accused of having done something wrong, even though you are innocent? People who tend to be nervous when questioned, especially if they are aware which questions are the serious ones, may easily register high rates of nervousness although they have done nothing wrong. Although less common, some people can remain absolutely calm and not be the least bit upset after committing some heinous act. For this reason, many courts do not admit lie detector evidence unless both the prosecution and the defense have agreed to allow its admission. This control alone may

*William Marston had an interesting career. After making a name for himself by offering the new "lie detector" for use during the famous Lindbergh kidnapping trial, he then went on to embarrass serious advocates of the polygraph by suggesting that it be used by husbands to discover whether their wives enjoyed their kisses more than they did someone else's! Following this, Marston entered the world of comic books and created the well-known superhero Wonder Woman (Biddle, 1986). People familiar with Wonder Woman will recall that she possessed a lariat that forced anyone she lassoed to tell the truth—you can guess where Marston got that idea.

Lie detectors don't measure lies but rather a person's physiological level of arousal or anxiety.

not offer sufficient safeguards, however, because the great majority of lie detector tests are given not by law enforcement agencies by by employers to employees, transactions that are not under the control of the criminal justice system.

To better understand the problem, consider the fact that in Los Angeles, a supermarket clerk was fired after failing the lie detector test on the question, "Have you ever checked out groceries at a discount to your mother?" It turned out that her mother had died 5 years earlier (Beach, 1980, p. 44). The opportunity for abuse is great, because businesses, especially banking and retail outlets, administer tens of thousands of tests each year to employees and managers who are under suspicion of some kind and as a routine personnel screening device (Meyer, 1982; Biddle, 1986).

The most commonly used lie detector tests are accurate in no more than two-thirds of cases—and, when they do make a mistake, which is often, they are most likely to indicate that an honest person is telling a lie (Lykken, 1981; Brett, Phillips, & Beary, 1986). In fact, in a population in which about 5 percent of the subjects tested are lying—as we might suspect could be the case when, for instance, a supermarket tests its employees—it turns out that about 90 percent of those testing positive will, in fact, be innocent (Brett, Phillips, & Beary, 1986). During the Reagan presidency, Secretary of State George Schultz refused to submit to a lie detector test that the president wished to make mandatory for government employees. Since that time, the U.S. Government Office of Technology Assessment, after an intensive study of the issue, has concluded that no lie detection method is foolproof and that the polygraph is generally not valid for lie detection because the chances for error are far too high (Saxe, Dougherty, & Cross, 1985; Brooks, 1985).

One of the reasons for the poor performance of the polygraph as a lie detector may be a function of the people who administer the tests. Joseph Buckley, who heads one of the largest testing firms, has said, "Like an X ray, a polygraph records data that take a lot of expertise to inter-

pret. In the wrong hands, it's worse than nothing" (Beach, 1980, p. 44). Other researchers have found that even in the hands of experts, the analysis of lie detector results is still subject to too much error (Szucko & Kleinmuntz, 1981; Kleinmuntz & Szucko, 1984). Yet, in most states, lie detector operators don't even have to be licensed.

To make matters worse, it's quite easy to fool a lie detector. If a subject is agitated when answering the initial baseline questions, perhaps because she or he has purposely thought of something frightening or arousing, or even if the person just bites her tongue or flexes her toes, the lie detector will register a strong reaction to her *truthful* statements (Honts, Hodes, & Raskin, 1985). The baseline thus is recorded as very high in physiological arousal, and later lies will go undetected—when compared with the high baseline. Obviously, any machine that can be so easily tricked should not be relied on extensively; rather, its use should be limited to special circumstances.

One set of circumstances in which the polygraph might be effective is known as the **concealed information test.** In a criminal investigation, for instance, a suspect is given information that only the perpetrator of

the crime could know. For example, he might be told, "The color of the getaway car was red . . . green . . . white . . . blue," "The house was broken into through the back door . . . the front door . . . a window . . . a skylight." The idea here is to see whether the subject will have a pronounced reaction only when he hears the correct answer (such as red car; window), providing strong evidence that he is the real criminal. After enough "correct" reactions, testers can conclude that the person is probably guilty of the crime because he has shown that he has knowledge that only the criminal could have. Innocence, of course, cannot be proved by this method—a person who doesn't react may be guilty, but unemotional.

The American Psychological Association has stated that "the polygraph's validity is 'unsatisfactory,' [and that] there is no physiological response pattern associated uniquely with deception" (Bales, 1988, p. 5). In response to these findings, in 1988, President Reagan signed into law a bill passed by the U.S. Congress that, with few exceptions, forbids the use of the polygraph by private business as a preemployment screening device.

---

to be because emotions help us to survive. When emotions first began to appear in evolving animals, those with better-developed emotions were more likely to pass on their genes to the next generation, which, in turn, furthered the evolution of emotions.

Perhaps we often use the word *feeling* interchangeably with *emotion* because we can feel, or sense, an emotion. Most people find it difficult to express exactly what they feel, because the way in which they experience emotion is very subjective. Writers sometimes try to express these subjective sensations with phrases such as "She was walking on air" (happiness), "He shrank into insignificance" (humiliation), "Her blood boiled" (anger), "He gagged" (disgust). In fact, these phrases are so descriptive that their overuse has made them trite. Still, such descriptions can give us clues to what people feel in certain emotional states. These states function

CONCEALED INFORMATION TEST
In polygraph administration, a method of examining suspects by providing them with specific information to which only someone with guilty knowledge could consistently react.

SOCIAL REFERENCING
The use of emotional signals or cues from others as a guide for one's own behavior in ambiguous situations.

as motivators. The fact that emotions motivate us appears to be one of the main reasons why emotions evolved.

We also use emotion to communicate, which appears to be their other major function. The expression on the face of another person often can tell us a great deal about how she is feeling. Sometimes, if we are not certain about the meaning of the situation in which we find ourselves, we will look at the emotional reactions of other people for information. This checking of others' emotions is called **social referencing.**

Social referencing begins early. In one interesting experiment, a special version of the visual cliff (see Figure 4.28, p. 142) was used. This version of the cliff had only one side, which was neither shallow or deep, but somewhere in between. The subjects were one-year-old infants. In this study, researchers found that the emotional expression on a mother's face could control whether her infant would attempt to go beyond the cliff edge. If the mother looked fearful, her infant was very unlikely to attempt a crossing. On the other hand, if she looked happy, her infant was likely to cross over the edge (Sorce, Emde, Campos, & Klinnert, 1985). Further experiments showed that infants will actively search for emotional cues, not just from their mothers, but also from any familiar adult who happens to be present (Klinnert, Emde, Butterfield, & Campos, 1986).

WHAT MAKES US EMOTIONAL?

Although we have inherited the capacity to experience emotion, whether we will experience emotion depends on many factors. For many years, researchers have gathered data about which circumstances are most likely to arouse emotions (Frijda, 1988). Let's consider some of these.

Emotions arise in situations that are *meaningful* to the individual. Events that satisfy goals, or that offer the promise of doing so, tend to elicit positive emotions. Events that harm or frustrate evoke negative emotions.

Emotions will be more intense if they concern events that are real and if they are perceived in a vivid way. This explains why one photograph of a burned child

Everyone has emotions, even infants only a few weeks old.

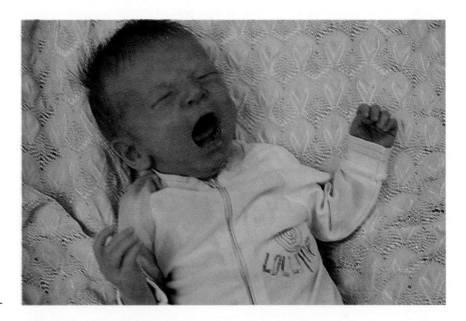

running from a village in Vietnam can have a more powerful emotional effect than cold statistical reports of thousands killed. This is why the presence of television at an event can make the event so memorable. It engages our emotions more effectively because of its visual impact. This statement about emotion also helps explain why, for example, warnings of distant dangers don't deter cigarette smokers. They're not real (in this case, immediate) or vivid enough. If, on the other hand, the number of deaths from smoking were due to the fact that every once in a while a cigarette exploded, it might be a different matter.

Emotions are also aroused more by *changes* in conditions, rather than by conditions that remain constant. Another way of saying this is, "Continued pleasures wear off; continued hardships lose their poignancy" (Frijda, 1988, p. 353). This, of course, is what Richard Solomon discovered when he investigated the effect of repeated emotional contrast (see Chapter 9).

For these reasons, real, meaningful, vivid, change will evoke the strongest emotions. If you are driving along and, as you crest a hill, you see a truck coming toward you in your lane, it will be real, personally meaningful, vivid, and a change—the event will likely arouse your emotions to a high pitch. Take away any of these factors, for example, see the same vivid change in a movie so that it is not real and less meaningful in a personal way, and your emotions will diminish accordingly.

You can also use your cognitive skills to think of experiences in a way that makes them seem more or less real or more or less meaningful, and thereby greatly affect their emotional impact on you. When, in the famous Aesop fable, the fox decided that the grapes he couldn't reach were probably sour anyway, he was reducing the personal meaning of the grapes because he wanted sweet ones, and thereby reduced his emotional stress. In similar ways, our emotions can distort our views of reality, affect our judgment, and motivate us.

JUDGING EMOTIONS

As you saw in the Prologue, people's perceptions of their own emotional states can be altered with false physiological feedback and can thus influence their judgments. Because our own judgments can affect the way in which we perceive our emotional state, subjective reports we may give others are not always a reliable basis for assessing emotion. For this reason, psychologists often prefer to rely on observations of overt behavior when assessing emotions.

Observing overt behavior for clues about a person's emotional state is such a common activity that we have all learned to recognize behavioral cues and their emotional content to some degree. Some of the observations that we make can be quite subtle. Interestingly, back in the days of silent films, actors relied heavily on body and facial cues to show emotion because they believed that without sound to help them, the audience would not pick up emotional meanings. It was thought necessary to overact. Consequently, a heroine in trouble would put the back of her hand to her forehead, assume a look of horror, pant, and lean backward as though she were about to fall (a series of behaviors more in line with food poisoning than fear). These contortions weren't really necessary, however, because people are so responsive to facial expressions and body cues that the actors could have succeeded in conveying emotional states by much subtler means. Today, some actors still have difficulty going from the screen to the stage and vice versa. On the stage, the audience is farther away, and body cues and emotional expressions must be exaggerated. On the screen, during a closeup, a very slight change in facial expression can carry a tremendous impact. For this reason, many actors practice

FRUSTRATION–AGGRESSION HYPOTHESIS
The idea that if one is blocked or prevented from reaching a desired goal, some form of aggression will be an inevitable result.

PAIN-ELICITED AGGRESSION
The desire to harm or defeat another, brought on by pain or anguish. It is common to many species, including humans. Cognitive interpretations can often control or mediate the aggression in spite of the pain or anguish.

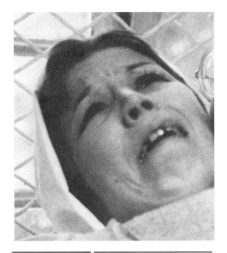

FIGURE 10.1

What emotion is this person feeling?

for hours with videotape equipment and mirrors to learn to change their expressions to reflect subtle changes in mood.

This discussion of actors brings up a problem with relying exclusively on overt behavior to understand emotions. Suppose the hero in a play bares his teeth, shouts, and yells, clenches his fists, makes menacing gestures, glares, and speaks in a deep and threatening voice. You assume he isn't *really* angry. (In fact, he may be happy because the play in which he is acting is about to end and he can get some dinner.) Actors are trained to pretend. But when you see these same behaviors in other people, how do you know these people are really angry and are not pretending? Perhaps you look at the situation they're in and deduce that they're not acting. Of course, this requires a subjective assessment on your part, based on the overt behavior you are viewing, and so subjectivity enters in once more.

Look at the picture in Figure 10.1. Is this person happy or sad? It's not hard to tell, is it? She's obviously sad. In fact, she looks as though some great tragedy has befallen her. A child may have died, or her home burned down. We know what emotions feel like, and we can usually tell by looking at other people what those people must be feeling. Or can we? Now, turn to page 326 to see the entire photograph.

Some tragedy! These people are participating in a joyous reunion. What you see on their faces is an intense emotional response, easy to mislabel. Emotions can be confusing. When we're extremely happy, we sometimes cry—and when we're extremely distraught, we sometimes laugh. Understanding emotion can be a lifelong pursuit; we all engage in it, whether or not we're psychologists.

Currently, most researchers believe that human emotion, although rooted in our biology, is strongly influenced by learning and cognitive processes (Eron, 1987). In other words, although our capacity to be emotional is inborn, the situations that make us emotional often depend a great deal on our thoughts, learning, and experiences (see Focus on Research).

THEORIES OF EMOTION

So far in this chapter, we've discussed what makes us emotional, we've looked at the evolutionary benefits of emotions for motivating us and helping us to communicate, and we've examined some of the biological underpinnings of emotions, but we haven't addressed the central question, namely, what are emotions? Over the years, researchers have attempted to develop theories of emotion that help to explain what emotions are. This task is anything but easy.

From what you've read so far, it is apparent that any theory of emotion must deal with a series of events and feelings. Common sense tells us that an emotion is the result of some specific event and that we react to emotions once they occur. This sequence is shown in Figure 10.2. However, as you learned from the Prologue,

FIGURE 10.2

The commonsense concept of emotion.

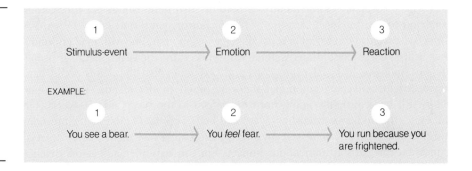

1	2	3
Stimulus-event →	Emotion →	Reaction

EXAMPLE:

1	2	3
You see a bear. →	You *feel* fear. →	You run because you are frightened.

SUDDEN VIOLENCE

In July 1984, in a suburb of San Diego, California, an unemployed security guard named James Huberty walked into a McDonald's restaurant carrying a shotgun, a semiautomatic rifle, and a pistol. Without any apparent reason, he began shooting everyone. When the carnage was over, 22 people, including Huberty, were dead, and many others were injured. It was the worst mass murder in United States history. What would make someone do such a thing? Psychologists believe that they have part of the answer.

One possible result of significant emotional arousal is violence or aggression. Although people who become emotionally aroused usually are not violent and aggressive, those behaviors almost never occur unless emotional arousal has preceded them. For this reason, psychologists who study emotional arousal are concerned with this phenomenon.

Over the years, many people have attempted to explain aggression and violence. One of the oldest explanations (and at one time the most popular) suggested that aggression and violence were the inevitable result of being blocked or frustrated in an attempt to achieve a desired goal (Dollard, Doob, Miller, Mowrer, & Sears, 1939). This became known as the **frustration-aggression hypothesis.**

The frustration-aggression hypothesis has since been modified. We now know that some people react to frustration by becoming aggressive, but aggression isn't an inevitable response to frustration (Berkowitz, 1965). Frustrated people also have been known to respond by trying harder, by crying, and by giving up. Reactions to frustration appear to depend on the individual and on the specific situation. To be frustrated—that is, to be unable to attain your

goal—is aversive and can result in psychological pain or depression. Scientists now realize that people who are anguished or depressed in this way are more likely to become violent. In this sense, frustration, as one of many causes of psychological anguish, can lead to aggression (Berkowitz, 1983).

For years, hunters have known that there is no more dangerous situation than confronting a wounded animal whose back is to a wall. They know that animals who are in pain and unable to flee often will attack. Decades ago, psychologists in laboratories carefully investigated this phenomenon, which came to be known as **pain-elicited aggression.**

When an animal, such as a rat, is placed in a cage and given a painful electric shock, the rat will attack any other animals that happen to be nearby. At first, researchers believed this attack response was a fairly simple, uncomplicated behavior with the purpose of ending the animal's pain. Researchers reasoned that it might be normal for an animal in its natural environment to "assume" that any sudden pain was caused by an attack from a nearby animal. In this view, aggression by the animal in pain is seen as an attempt to stop an attacker. The discovery that rats given electric shocks will attack other small animals but will never attack inanimate objects supported this view (Ulrich & Azrin, 1962).

As the research on pain-elicited aggression continued, it became obvious that the phenomenon wasn't so simple after all. In one study, researchers found that a mouse who had been interrupted during a fight with another mouse would actually cross a painful electrically charged grid to resume his attack (Lagerspetz, as cited by Berkowitz, 1965). The

finding that animals in pain would endure even more pain to attack a victim made researchers believe that the pained animal's greatest inclination is not just to stop pain but rather to do harm to another animal and to gain a victory (Berkowitz, Cochran, & Embree, 1981; Berkowitz, 1983).

When researchers first examined pain-elicited aggression in animals, they did not believe the phenomenon included human beings. After all, if pain-elicited aggression was obvious in human beings, it wouldn't be safe to be a dentist. But once the simple notion that an animal in pain will bite had evolved into the more sophisticated view that an animal who suffers will want to harm another animal, the idea that humans might engage in pain-elicited aggression began to emerge. In short order, studies began to confirm that humans were not immune from becoming more aggressive when they were uncomfortable or suffering. For example, in one experiment, researchers found that subjects were more likely to make a hostile judgment about a stranger if the subjects were asked to express their views while sitting in a hot room (Griffitt & Veitch, 1971). Subjects also were found to be more willing to punish a stranger in an experimental situation if the subjects were irritated by cigarette smoke (Jones & Bogat, 1978) or if they were in a hot room (Baron & Bell, 1975). These findings indicate that people who are in pain or suffering are more likely to lash out aggressively than are contented people (Berkowitz, 1983). For instance, some researchers have argued that the urban riots in American cities during the late 1960s were made worse by the summer heat (Baron & Ransberger, 1978).

People who are hurting often become depressed over their state of affairs. And depressed people often show a substantial amount of aggressiveness (Kendell, 1970; Poznanski & Zrull, 1970). It is also known that depressed people often are apathetic and are unable to engage in the prolonged purposeful action necessary to resolve their problems. For this reason, when depressed people attack, they tend to "attack someone impulsively, revealing their instigation to aggression in a quick outburst of temper not requiring planned and sustained behavior" (Berkowitz, 1983, p. 1142).

This is what psychologists believe may have happened to James Huberty. He was deeply depressed and had even attempted suicide. His mother had left him when he was a young boy. As an adult, he had failed at work and had lost a great deal of money in unsuccessful real-estate

ventures. He moved out west to find employment, but ended up losing a series of jobs. He was suffering and in anguish. Like members of most species, he was more likely to lash out and to try to harm people who were nearby because of his pain. Aggression from such a depressed person was likely to be sudden and impulsive (Berkowitz, 1990). His aggression was particularly deadly because guns were part of his life and were readily available to him. It had been reported that he often sat on his porch with a shotgun on his lap. Had the guns not been readily available, his sudden impulse might not have resulted in so many deaths. But the guns were in his hands, McDonald's was across the street, and there were people nearby on whom he could vent his anger.

Why Huberty attacked so violently,

while other people who are in similar pain (and who also have ready access to firearms) do not, remains a mystery. Perhaps like the dentist's patients, most people are able to cope with their pain cognitively and to understand that they must deal with it without inflicting harm on other people. In the words of one researcher, "This aggressive instigation need not be translated into open attacks on others. We can learn to restrain our aggressive dispositions, be led not to think of others as sources of displeasure, and turn our thoughts away from aggression-promoting ideas" (Berkowitz, 1983, p. 1143). As our society attempts to understand horrors such as this one, we hope to find ways to reach those people who suffer so that we can help them learn to cope with their pain without turning on those around them.

a subjective assessment of an emotional state can influence a person's behavior. When researcher Stuart Valins played false heartbeats as feedback, subjects were influenced by what they thought to be real emotional arousal, inappropriately labeled their "arousal" as sexual interest, and acted accordingly. This kind of occurrence seems to argue against our commonsense understanding, which tells us that an emotion must be felt before we react to it. Many years before Valin's research, this problem was examined by William James, whose brilliant mind was probing psychological issues before most people had ever heard of psychology.

The James–Lange Theory

In 1890, William James argued that the commonsense explanation of emotions—that environmental events create an emotion that in turn gives rise to responses—might be incorrect. Instead, James asserted that environmental experiences give rise to different visceral and muscular responses and that these responses are themselves the emotional state.

According to James, emotion doesn't produce the behavior but rather the emotion *is* the behavior. James believed that encountering something dangerous, such as a bear in the woods, would immediately cause bodily changes associated through experience with danger, and you would run (or freeze or do something to avoid the danger). Only *while* reacting could you create the emotion. The unique body changes that trigger a behavior are *not*, according to James, the emotion. The emotion is the feeling that you experience *when you act* (see Figure 10.3). For example, if you are walking down the street and you trip and start to fall, immediate changes occur in your body, and you thrust out your hands to protect yourself. According to James, you don't "feel fear" until you extend your hands. James believed that this view was correct because some behaviors seemed to occur so fast that there appeared to be no time in which to feel an emotion before acting. A Danish researcher named Carl Lange wrote along similar lines, emphasizing the physical changes that lead to immediate responses. Ever since, the theory has been known as the **James-Lange theory of emotion** (Lange & James, 1922).

The James–Lange theory was developed toward the end of the nineteenth century. It remained undisputed for over 30 years, until strongly challenged by the American physiologist Walter Cannon. In 1927, Cannon and his student Philip Bard took issue with the James–Lange assertion that visceral and muscular responses could be considered to be themselves emotions. Cannon and Bard believed that separate areas of the brain were responsible for the different aspects of what was considered to be emotion. Specifically, they argued that the thalamus of the brain coordinated the perceptions that lead to feelings of arousal, while the hypothalamus governed behavior (Cannon, 1927). Although we now know the particulars of their theory to be incorrect, it was the first effort to point out that there are distinctly separate mechanisms in the central nervous system that are called into action when an emotion and a behavior occur. In disagreement with the James-Lange hypothesis, most modern researchers do, in fact, consider that there is an organization in the brain devoted to emotion that is distinct from the neural pathways involved in the generation of most muscular or visceral actions.

Schachter's Cognitive Appraisal Theory

In 1962, psychologist Stanley Schachter developed a theory of emotion that was a refinement of the James–Lange theory. Schachter was aware that most research at the time had shown that the physiology of emotional arousal was very similar, even for very different emotions. For instance, during intense anger, happiness, and sadness, adrenaline is secreted, heartbeat accelerates, respiration increases, and pupils dilate. How, then, can a person tell which emotion she is feeling from only attending to her physiological arousal? Schachter wondered whether James and Lange might still be correct in proposing that the emotion itself was determined by the behavioral response. If only a very general arousal state exists for each emotion, Schachter argued, then the cognitive (thinking and perceptual) processes must be playing a central role in determining which emotional state we perceive ourselves to be experiencing when we become aroused (see Figure 10.4).

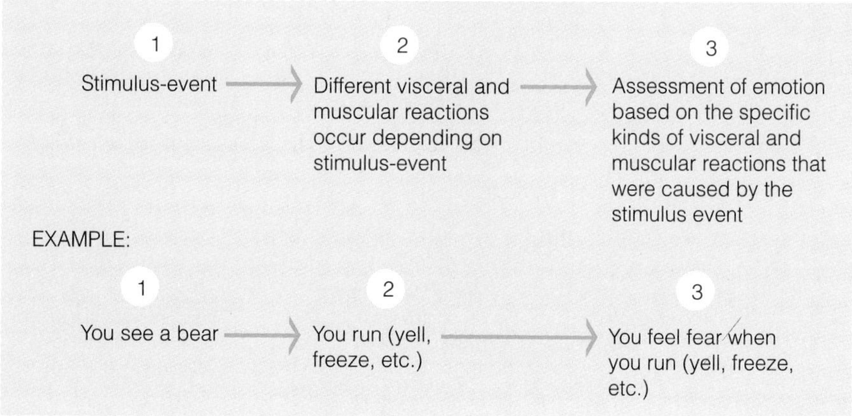

JAMES–LANGE THEORY OF EMOTION
A classical theory of emotion named for William James and Carl Lange, who independently proposed it. The theory posits that a stimulus first leads to visceral and motor responses and that the following awareness of these responses constitutes the experience of the emotion. According to this theory, for instance, we are sad because we cry, rather than we cry because we are sad.

FIGURE 10.3

The James–Lange theory of emotion.

1	2	3
Stimulus-event	→ Different visceral and muscular reactions occur depending on stimulus-event	→ Assessment of emotion based on the specific kinds of visceral and muscular reactions that were caused by the stimulus event

EXAMPLE:

1	2	3
You see a bear	→ You run (yell, freeze, etc.)	→ You feel fear when you run (yell, freeze, etc.)

Imagine, for example, that someone walking through a desert comes on a 6-foot-long rattlesnake. She freezes, she gasps, and her eyes open wide. How would you assess her emotional state? If you think about how you would feel, you might call it terror. As for her physiological state, her pupils would probably be dilated, her heart would be beating faster, her respiratory rate would have increased, and her adrenaline level would be high—all indications of an aroused sympathetic nervous system. However, these signs alone wouldn't enable you to define her emotional state, according to Schachter. She, too, might have trouble labeling her emotion if she relied only on her *general* physical arousal. Rather, she must make a mental or cognitive assessment of the situation. When she does so, she comes to the conclusion that what she feels is happiness, because she has now found her

FIGURE 10.4

Schachter's theory of emotion. Different levels may be placed on similar states of arousal depending on how the situation is assessed.

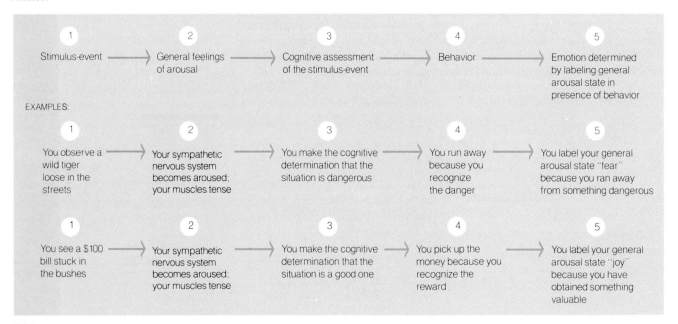

lost rattlesnake Buffy, which escaped from her snake farm just down the road. Her excitement was due not to terror but to her happy surprise, since she had just about given up the search. Yet her initial physiological reaction seems the same as a hiker's would have been, had he simply wandered off the road to look for a tumbleweed and stumbled across a deadly snake by accident. In that case, however, his subjective assessment would have been that he was in big trouble and was likely to be severely injured. He would have assessed his similar arousal as fear.

To test his theory, Schachter designed an ingenious experiment in which his subjects were secretly given a dose of adrenaline, which caused them to feel a certain amount of physiological arousal. Initially, Schachter had planned to spray the subjects' waiting room with adrenaline so that it would be inhaled, but this method turned out to be too expensive. Instead, he invited the subjects into a room and told them that they were going to take part in a vision experiment. They were given an injection of adrenaline, believing it to be a substance that would improve their vision.

By today's standards, such an experiment might not be considered ethical, since injecting a person with a potent substance could be harmful. Nevertheless, the research results were intriguing, and consent for injection of such a substance was not obtained.

The subjects were divided into two groups. One group was told to expect the symptoms they would be feeling (faster heartbeat, sweating, jitters, fluttering stomach, and so on), while the second group was told to expect symptoms unrelated to the true effects of adrenaline (such as itching feet).

The subjects from each group were given a form to fill out and were placed, one at a time, in a waiting room. In the waiting room was another "subject," who was really an actor working for Schachter. The actor behaved in either one of two planned ways—very happy or very angry. In the happy condition, the actor laughed, told jokes, and played with a hula hoop that was in the waiting room. In the angry condition, the actor became furious about the form he had to fill out, which asked personal questions such as, "With how many men has your mother had extramarital relationships? Four and under ____; five to nine ____; ten and over ____."

The subjects who had been told to expect the symptoms that they began to feel attributed their physical arousal to the injection rather than to the actor's behavior, whereas those who were expecting different symptoms attributed their physical arousal to an emotional reaction brought on by the actor's behavior. The second group of subjects, therefore, began to believe that they were feeling what the actor was feeling, either happiness or anger. In the angry condition, for example, the actor became more and more incensed at the questions as he filled out the form, finally crumpling it up, swearing that he would never answer such personal questions, and storming out of the room. Subjects who attributed their physical arousal to emotion, rather than to the injection, were much more likely to become angry, too, in this circumstance (see Figure 10.5). This result indicates that the presence of a physiological arousal may cue a person to search for the reason behind the arousal. Then, by examining the immediate circumstance, the person may come to the conclusion "I must be angry" or "I must be happy." The same general physical arousal, then, can lead to different emotions based on a subjective labeling of the immediate situation (Schachter & Singer, 1962).

Schachter's ideas are known as the **cognitive appraisal theory of emotion.** Consider the following study.

Spanning the Capilano River in British Columbia are two bridges. One is a sturdy, cedar bridge 10 feet above a shallow part of the river. The other is a narrow, wooden footbridge with low, wire cable handrails. It wobbles and sways 200 feet above some rocky rapids.

The Capilano River footbridge created high levels of arousal in those who crossed it (you can see why).

FIGURE 10.5

In Schachter's experiment, the subjects were placed in one of four different conditions. Only the subjects who did not expect the symptoms from the injection showed emotions similar to those of the actor.

		Subjects expect symptoms (attribute arousal to injection)	Subjects do not expect symptoms (attribute arousal to actor)
ACTOR'S STATE WHEN SUBJECT ENTERED ROOM	Actor angry	Subjects generally unaffected by actor's behavior	Subjects became angry
	Actor happy	Subjects generally unaffected by actor's behavior	Subjects became happy

One day, an attractive female researcher stopped men as they came off these bridges, and told them she was investigating how beautiful scenery affects creative expression. She asked them to fill out a questionnaire, which included writing a short story. Most of the men readily complied. Whey they finished, she gave each her name and phone number, using as an excuse, ". . . in case you want to know more about the research." Half the men who crossed the scary bridge called, compared with only 12 percent of those who crossed the safer bridge. And the stories told by the former group contained significantly more sexual imagery than did those of the latter group (Dutton and Aron, 1974)!

The researchers concluded that the fear generated by crossing the rickety bridge was translated into sexual attraction. The men were in a heightened state of arousal when they saw an attractive woman and instantaneously mislabeled some of their heightened arousal as stemming from her!

Although cognitive processes may affect our emotions, our physiology still plays an important role in many aspects of our emotional makeup. Emotions aren't always a strictly cognitive matter (Leventhal & Tomarken, 1986). Think especially of the facial expressions of people who are happy, angry, or sad. Are these expressions learned? Are they part of a cognitive assessment of emotion? Or are they derived from inherited patterns of behavior? The next important work in the field of emotion came from the study of facial expressions.

Facial Feedback Theory

Are facial expressions of emotions universal? Except in extreme cases, such as the reunion example, we can usually guess people's moods by their expressions. If you traveled to a foreign land—Malaysia, for instance—you would be able to recognize facial expressions and would know which emotion the person was feeling (Ekman, 1973; Ekman, Sorenson, & Friesen, 1969; Izard, 1971; Boucher, 1973). This ability to recognize facial expressions and corresponding emotions also is found among tribes that have had little contact with the West or with mass media (Ekman, 1973; Ekman & Friesen, 1974). Except in cultures in which people are taught not to display certain emotional expressions, people universally show the same expressions when experiencing the same emotions (Ekman & Oster, 1979). Six facial expressions have been found to be universal—that is, they are clear to almost all people who see them: happiness, anger, disgust, sadness, fear, and surprise.* (see Figure 10.6).

*The facial expressions for fear and surprise can be distinguished more easily if viewed in a motion picture: The fear expression lasts longer than does the surprise expression.

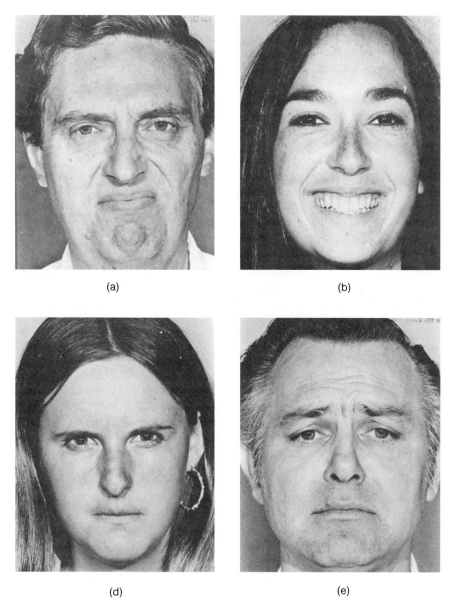

(a)

(b)

(c)

(d)

(e)

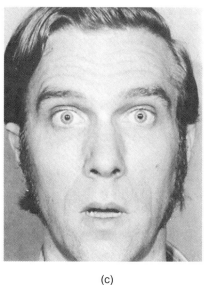

FIGURE 10.6

Can you match each photograph with its proper emotion?

(Answers: (a) disgust; (b) happiness; (c) fear or surprise; (d) anger; (e) sadness.)

No one knows why certain facial muscles become active when particular emotions are being experienced. Why, for instance, should the corners of the mouth turn down when someone is sad? Many researchers feel that these expressions are tied to an innate, genetically predetermined organization that activates certain facial muscles during a particular emotional state (Redican, 1975; Eibl-Eibesfeldt, 1972). Even individuals blind since birth, who could never have seen facial expressions, tend to show them (Charlesworth & Kreutzer, 1973).

Of course, just because our facial expressions may be based on genetic organization doesn't mean that we can't control them. Who hasn't tried to keep a straight face when something funny happens at a time when it is inappropriate to laugh? In fact, attempts to mask feelings by controlling facial expressions have been observed in children as young as three years of age who, in one experiment, were observed trying to "look innocent" after being caught doing something they had been told not to do (Lewis, Stanger, & Sullivan, 1989).

FACIAL FEEDBACK THEORY
A theory of emotion put forth by S. S. Tomkins stating that emotions are determined by feedback from our facial expressions, which are innate, universal responses to specific events.

FIGURE 10.7

In an experiment (Ekman, Friesen, & O'Sullivan, 1988), student nurses were asked to convince an interviewer that the film they had just seen was a pleasant experience. In one case the movie was a nice nature film, in the other, a film about burns and amputations. Smiles that show real enjoyment (photo on the bottom) involve more activity of the muscles that circle the eyes, while the facial actions of a lying smile (on the top) are often quite different.

Researchers have wondered whether feedback from our own facial expressions could tell us which emotion to experience. S. S. Tomkins has argued that such feedback may be the muscular precursor of emotion. Like James and Lange, Tomkins believes that different kinds of muscular actions may be creating different emotions (Tomkins, 1962; 1963).

To test **facial feedback theory**, researchers asked subjects to produce different facial expressions as they carried out certain tasks. They then measured the subjects' self-reported feelings afterward. The purpose was to find out whether deliberately altering facial expressions would directly affect emotions (Laird, 1974). Initial results were inconclusive; by the mid-1980s, however, some surprising results had begun to emerge (Adelmann & Zajonc, 1989).

The surprises started when researcher Paul Ekman examined exactly which muscles were involved in each of the six universal facial expressions (surprise, disgust, sadness, anger, fear, and happiness). Ekman then measured the physiological changes that were associated with the creation of each expression. These measures included heart rate and hand temperature. The subjects Ekman studied were not asked to produce an emotional expression, but were instead told exactly which muscles they were to contract. This was done because people are generally not very good at faking an emotional expression* (Ekman, Friesen, & O'Sullivan, 1988) (see Figure 10.7).

As an experimental control measure, some subjects were asked to contract facial muscles that were not involved with the expression of a particular emotion. To almost everyone's surprise, not only did the building of a facial expression lead to a physiological arousal but also the kinds of physiological arousals associated with each of the six facial expressions were distinctly different from one another (Ekman, Levenson, & Friesen, 1983). To verify that the distinct physiological states created by the facial expressions were associated with each of the six emotions represented by the expressions, Ekman and his colleagues instructed the subjects to relive emotional experiences that would create each of the six emotions. For example, a subject might think of something that was very sad and then rate how sad she felt on a scale from 0 to 8. Relived experiences with high ratings created the same physiological arousals associated with the facial expressions. Again, each emotional experience was associated with the same distinct physiological "fingerprint" created by a particular facial expression (see Figure 10.8).

Later, Ekman and his colleagues traveled to western Sumatra, Indonesia, and conducted the same tests again, only this time on members of the Minangkabau culture. The results were much the same, indicating that people probably share a biological heritage of emotion that is relatively independent of culture (Ekman, et al., 1987).

These data strongly support the original James–Lange view of emotion, for two reasons: They suggest that (1) distinctly different visceral and muscular reactions give rise to each emotion, and (2) emotions may be created by muscular reactions.

If sensitive modern instruments can show that autonomic nervous system activity can distinguish among the emotions, this must also change our view of Schachter's cognitive appraisal theory (Leventhal & Tomarken, 1986). Schachter argued that autonomic arousal did not distinguish among the emotions and that it was our cognitive assessment of a situation that gave rise to an emotion. As we noted, some research has supported that view. More recently, however, acceptance of Schachter's view has declined (Averill, 1983; Marshall & Zimbardo, 1979; Maslach, 1979;

---

*Actors, of course, make their living faking true emotional expressions, so it is possible to do; it's just that most people aren't very good at it. As the great actor John Barrymore once supposedly said, "The key to acting is honesty—once you've learned to fake that, you can do anything!"

Zajonc, 1980), and researchers have begun to look for alternative interpretations of the research results. Perhaps the subjects in Schachter's original experiments were confused about their feelings because they had been aroused in an "unnatural" way through an injection of adrenaline. Perhaps the men who crossed the swinging rickety bridge were more alert because of their fear and took more notice of the woman's beauty. Perhaps, after they had calmed down, their memories of her attractiveness were clearer than were those of the men who crossed the safe bridge, and this prompted more of them to call her for a date. Perhaps the subjects in Stuart Valins's false-feedback experiment were *actually* aroused through classical conditioning by the sound of the false accelerated heartbeat, and so on.

Alternative views such as these are being proposed by researchers who wonder just how important cognitive appraisal is for the creation of an emotion. The issue is not yet settled. Certainly, we know that cognition is important and that our thoughts can create feelings in us, but this is not the same as saying that our cognitions or thoughts are necessary before an emotion can exist. Some researchers believe that in many instances our emotions are separate from our thoughts (Zajonc, 1984). In this view, sensory information may be channeled directly into neural circuits that give rise to an emotion. Other researchers, however, believe that emotions cannot exist until some mental processing or cognitive activity has first occurred that helps to interpret sensations and give them meaning, which then generates an emotional state (Lazarus, 1984). Further research undoubtedly will be required before the debate is resolved.

FIGURE 10.8

The average physiological responses that occurred when researcher Paul Ekman had subjects recreate facial expressions. The results were consistent across subjects. As you can see, by comparing heart-rate change and temperature change, you can distinguish the six emotions from one another in terms of autonomic activity. For instance, although anger, fear, and sadness all have similar heart-rate changes (an increase of 7 to 8 beats per minute), they show quite different temperature changes. With anger, there is a significant increase in hand temperature; with fear, there is a slight decrease; with sadness, there is a slight increase. Ekman argues that since these sensitive changes are consistent, they distinguish the emotions from one another; he believes that his data refute Cannon's and Schachter's contention that there is only a general and indistinguishable arousal state during emotion. (SOURCE: Adapted from Ekman, Levenson, & Friesen, 1983, p. 1209.)

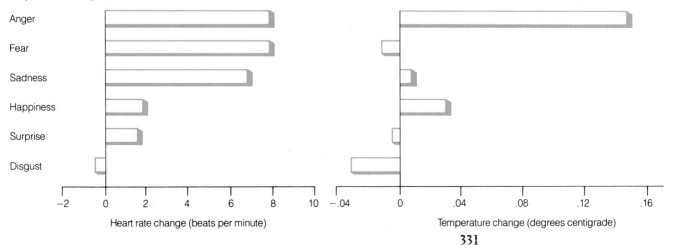

PSYCHOEVOLUTIONARY SYNTHESIS OF EMOTION
Robert Plutchik's theory that emotions evolved because they help a species to survive. In his theory, cognitive assessments of stimulus-events may give rise to innate emotional patterns, which in turn motivate behaviors that ultimately have survival value.

Plutchik's Psychoevolutionary Synthesis of Emotion

Although much of what is considered emotional behavior may be the result of learning and cognitive processes, undoubtedly some of it is innate. The existence of similar facial expressions and emotional reactions in all members of our species is evidence of this. These expressions of emotion are conspicuous in other species as well (see Figure 10.9). The kinds of emotions that we see in our species and in others may have evolved because they help ensure survival. As we suggested earlier, emotions may exist because they serve a function.

Researcher Robert Plutchik has outlined a theory of the **psychoevolutionary synthesis of emotion** (Plutchik, 1980), in which he argues that emotions are inherited behavioral patterns that have important functions and that can be modified by experience. Plutchik's theory begins where others have left off. He defines emotion as "a complex sequence of events having elements of cognitive appraisal, feeling, impulses to action, and overt behavior—all of which are designed to deal with a stimulus that triggered the chain in the first place" (Plutchik, 1980, p. 68).

FIGURE 10.9

Many species of animals display emotions. Such expressions of emotion often are very similar to those displayed by human beings.

PRIMARY EMOTIONS. According to Plutchik, emotions can be thought of in the same terms as colors. Some are fundamental, or primary, and others are mixtures of the primaries (see Figure 10.10). Plutchik has deduced from his research that there are eight primary emotions: sadness, fear, surprise, anger, disgust, anticipation, joy, and acceptance (in the form of sexual receptivity). He has found that these eight emotions are consistent across a wide range of situations. We may have hundreds of words for emotions, but all of them describe either one of the eight emotions or some combination of them (Plutchik, 1980).

FUNCTIONAL ASPECTS OF EMOTION. Plutchik's theory includes not only behavioral aspects of emotion, such as hitting, running away, crying, and laughing, but functional aspects as well—those aspects that help an organism to ensure management of the environment and survival. Charles Darwin assumed that emotions evolved because of the function they fulfilled. He published his arguments on this topic in *The Expression of the Emotions in Man and Animals* (Darwin, 1872/1967).

Table 10.2 outlines the eight basic behavioral patterns of animals and human beings according to Plutchik. Each category is functional—that is, it serves a purpose—which is why it was selected by the evolutionary process. The functional aspects of the eight primary emotions are depicted in the table, alongside each primary emotion. For example, Plutchik argues in the first instance that the reason the emotion *fear* exists is that it affords an organism protection.

According to this view, an emotion has five components: a stimulus-event, cognition of that event, an assessment of feeling, a behavior guided by innate mechanisms and based on that assessment, and the function served by the behavior. Figure 10.11 gives examples of this kind of emotional sequence. The difference

FIGURE 10.10

Plutchik's wheel of emotion. Some emotions are primary (within the wheel), while others are secondary (composites or dyads) made from two primaries (outside the wheel). For instance, disappointment, a secondary emotion, is a combination of two primary emotions, surprise and sadness. (SOURCE: Plutchik, 1980, p. 75.)

FIGURE 10.11

Plutchik's psychoevolutionary synthesis of emotion. Plutchik's theory has elements of both the commonsense view and Schachter's cognitive theory. It meshes with more recent findings by Ekman, and it incorporates Darwin's idea of adaptive function through natural selection. It is like the commonsense view because the emotion stimulates the behavior. It resembles Schachter's theory because a cognitive assessment must be made before *primary emotion can be generated from what would be only a general state of physiological arousal. It also is in agreement with Ekman's findings that there are different arousal states associated with the primary emotions. Finally, Darwin's ideas are expressed by the argument that primary emotional states exist because they serve a valuable function.*

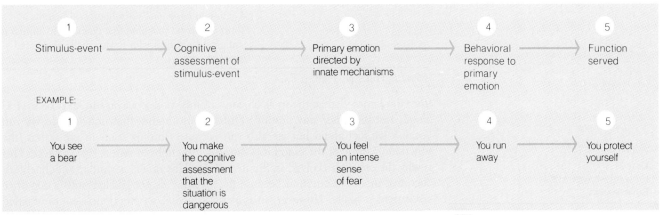

TABLE 10.2 Functional Aspects of the Eight Primary Emotions

PRIMARY EMOTION	FUNCTION	FUNCTIONAL DESCRIPTION
Fear	Protection	Behavior designed to avoid danger or harm, such as running away or any action that puts distance between an organism and the source of danger.
Anger	Destruction	Behavior designed to eliminate a barrier to satisfaction of an important need. This includes biting, striking, or various symbolic acts of destruction, such as cursing or threatening.
Joy	Incorporation	Behavior that involves accepting a beneficial stimulus from the outside world, as in eating, grooming, mating, or affiliation with members of one's own social group. Such actions have the effect of nurturing the individual.
Disgust	Rejection	Behavior designed to expel something harmful that has been ingested, such as vomiting or, at times, defecation. This behavior is believed to be associated with feelings of contempt and hostility and with sarcasm, all of which are essentially a rejection of other people or their ideas.
Acceptance	Reproduction	Behavior designed to provide contact with sex for the purpose of perpetuating one's gene pool. Expressions of this function include sexual signaling, courtship rituals, and sexual intercourse.
Sadness	Reintegration	Behavior associated with the loss of someone who has provided important nurturance in the past. In such circumstances, the individual sends signals that serve to encourage the return of the lost individual or to attract a substitute. Expressions of this function include crying, emission of distress signals, and "babyish" behavior.
Surprise	Orientation	Behavior reactions to make contact with a new, unfamiliar stimulus: a loud noise, a strange animal, or a new territory, for example. The organism must quickly reorient the body and stop what it is doing so that the sense organs can take in information about the novel stimulus.
Anticipation	Exploration	Behavior designed to bring the organism into contact with many aspects of its environment. Getting to know one's neighborhood permits a form of mental mapping that enables the animal to anticipate and deal with future challenges to its survival.

SOURCE: Plutchik, 1980, p.73.

from the James–Lange theory is obvious: In this model, we *do* run because we feel afraid, not the other way around. Plutchik also argues that not only do we run because we feel afraid but we also run because running leads to protection (the function or value of the emotion). Running functions to ensure our survival. This is why the emotion evolved in the first place. This model is similar to Schachter's cognitive model of emotion because the "feeling" is not labeled until a cognitive assessment is made. However, in Plutchik's theory, an emotion is not only based on a cognitive assessment but it is also tied to distinct, innate, physiological mechanisms that guide our responses to serve a valuable function. As we discussed, more recent research (Ekman, Levenson, & Friesen, 1983) has indicated that there are distinct autonomic states associated with primary emotions. Plutchik's theory encompasses this concept.

Plutchik has taken the interesting viewpoint that our cognitive abilities have grown and advanced largely to serve emotion! With a powerful brain that can make rapid calculations and evaluate many situations, we find it easier to interpret what our feelings mean and then to react in a way that's most functional. This idea is unusual; many people think that emotions can get in the way of clear, rational thinking. Plutchik views rational thinking as something that can help us to develop and perfect the emotional experience.

EMOTIONAL INTENSITIES, SIMILARITIES, AND DIFFERENCES. Emotions, as we all know, can vary in intensity. Compare annoyance and rage or apprehension and terror—the difference is one of intensity. Furthermore, some emotions have elements in common, such as rage and loathing, whereas other emotions are distinctly opposites, such as grief and ecstasy. Plutchik has developed a model that maps emotional intensities. In Figure 10.12, you see a three-dimensional figure that resembles a top. Similar emotions are placed close to one another; those that are opposite appear across from one another. The figure is shaped like a top to represent the fact that intense emotions are more definable. Less intense emotions are more alike, which is indicated by their nearness to one another at the bottom of the figure. As you have discovered, emotion is a complex area including aspects of physiology, cognition, and innate mechanisms. No one theory of emotion gives us a complete explanation. No doubt, future research will help us to understand emotion more fully.

MAPPING EMOTIONAL INTENSITIES

More intense

Less intense

FIGURE 10.12

Plutchik's model for depicting the relative similarities and intensities of the primary emotions. Each lengthwise slice of the figure represents a primary emotion, from its most intense to its mildest expression (for example, grief–sadness–pensiveness). Emotions that most resemble one another are adjacent; those most unlike are far apart or are opposite one another. All positions on the figure are plotted from ratings by subjects in a number of studies. At mild intensities, the emotions aren't labeled, because it often is too difficult to discriminate them. The adrenaline injection used in Schachter's experiment may have created an arousal in this range, allowing subjects to misinterpret their emotional state more easily. Confusing loathing with adoration, or ecstasy with grief, would be much less likely. (SOURCE: Plutchik, 1980, p. 74.)

Epilogue: "They'll Let Me Go Tomorrow"

Psychologists who study emotion know that a person can become physiologically aroused for many reasons. They also know that the polygraph, or lie detector, is based on the assumption that emotional arousal can signal when a person lies. The following story helps us to examine this assumption.

In the late 1970s, Floyd "Buzz" Fay was happily going about his business, never expecting that the world was about to fall in on him. On what seemed like an average day to Buzz, a man named Fred Ery was shot and mortally wounded by a holdup man during a robbery attempt. Ery knew Buzz Fay, and as he was dying he said, "It looked like Buzz, but it couldn't have been" (Kleinmuntz & Szucko, 1984, p. 774). After losing a great deal of blood and being given large doses of drugs, Fred Ery began to mumble, "Buzz did it." Although Fred Ery had been incoherent when he made the accusation, the police quickly arrested Buzz Fay at gunpoint the following morning. Fay was amazed. He couldn't bring himself to take the arrest seriously, believing that "they'll let me go tomorrow."

The prosecution realized that they had a weak case, as they had no other evidence of Fay's guilt. They offered him a deal. They would give him two polygraph tests, one to be administered by the Bureau of Criminal Identification and the other to be privately administered. If he passed either test, the charges would be dropped, but, if he failed them both, he'd be charged with aggravated murder and the lie detector test would be admitted as evidence.

Fay thought that the offer was good and accepted it. To his horror, both lie detector tests indicated he was guilty. Fay was quickly convicted of murder and was given a sentence of life in prison. Fortunately for him, the death sentence, which had been in effect in his state (Ohio) until just a few weeks before his trial, was no longer being used.

Adrian Cimmerman, a dedicated county public defender, continued to believe that Fay was innocent. After 2 1/2 years of exhaustive work by Cimmerman to find the truth, while Fay was cooped up in his prison cell, the police finally received a tip by an informant, and Fred Ery's real killer was tracked down and convicted. Buzz Fay was released.

Needless to say, Buzz Fay no longer puts any faith in lie detector tests. As a matter of fact, when Fay was in prison he became something of an expert on the polygraph. He discovered that not only was it based on an implausible theory but also it was easy to beat (Cimmerman, 1981). The polygraph test was commonly used in prisons to get to the bottom of charges against prisoners, such as drug abuse. While Fay was in prison, he coached 27 inmates who were going to take a lie detector test. All the inmates had told him outright that they were guilty of the charges (usually drug offenses). After less than half an hour of training, 23 of the 27 found that they were able to beat the lie detector test (Lykken, 1981).

The next time people tell you that a lie detector test is almost infallible, have them get in touch with Buzz Fay. He has a different opinion.

SUMMARY

■ Everyone has emotions; even infants a few weeks after birth exhibit them. Emotions pervade our existence, and no study of human behavior would be complete without an attempt to understand the power and value of emotional experiences.

■ The word *feeling* often is used interchangeably with the word *emotion* because we feel, or sense, an emotion. We become most emotional when confronted by circumstances that are personally meaningful, vivid, real, and changing.

■ Because subjective reports are not always a reliable guide in assessing emotion, many psychologists prefer to rely on observations of overt behavior.

■ Emotional reactions often are associated with an arousal of the autonomic nervous system. During intense emotional reactions such as fear, rage, sexual arousal, and love, the sympathetic branch of the autonomic nervous system becomes quite active. The strong, measurable physiological changes that occur are the basis on which the polygraph, or lie detector, purports to assess truth telling.

■ As the infant develops into a child, electrical measures of the brain show that positive and negative emotions are associated with the different brain hemispheres.

■ The frustration-aggression hypothesis was once a popular way to explain aggression. Currently, most researchers believe that aggression is a response that derives from our biological heritage, but the things that make us aggressive appear to derive mostly from experience and learning.

■ Pain-elicited aggression may occur in animals, including humans, who are suffering or in anguish. Cognition, especially in humans, may control or mediate the painful experience so that aggression need not be the result.

■ Common sense tells us that an emotion is the result of a specific event and that we react to emotions once they occur.

■ The James–Lange theory of emotion argues that environmental experiences give rise to different visceral and muscular responses, which are themselves the emotional states. In this view, emotion is the behavior, not the producer of it.

■ Schachter developed a cognitive appraisal theory of emotion that was a refinement of the James–Lange theory. Schachter demonstrated that it was possible for cognitive (perceptual and thinking) processes to create an emotion that depended on behavior for its existence.

■ Six different facial expressions have been found to be universal: happiness, anger, disgust, sadness, fear, and surprise. Tomkins has argued that feedback from our own facial expressions tells us which emotion to experience. Data from tests of facial feedback theory strongly support the James–Lange theory.

■ Ekman has shown that distinct and different autonomic arousal states are associated across cultures with each of the emotions created by the six universal facial expressions.

■ Plutchik's psychoevolutionary synthesis of emotion is an attempt to trace the origin of emotions. Plutchik argues that emotions are inherited behavior patterns that have important functions and that can be modified by experience. Plutchik considers emotions to be like colors: Some are fundamental or primary, and others are mixtures of the primaries.

■ According to Plutchik, emotion has five components: a stimulus-event, cognition of that event, an assessment of feeling, a behavior guided by innate mechanisms and based on that assessment, and the function served by the behavior.

■ Plutchik contends that our cognitive abilities have grown and advanced largely to serve emotion.

■ Emotions vary in intensity and in their similarity to other emotions.

SUGGESTIONS FOR FURTHER READING

1. Ekman, P. (Ed.). (1983). Emotion in the human face. New York: Cambridge University Press. An interesting book on facial expressions and their effects on emotions.
2. Lykken, D. T. (1980). A tremor in the blood: Uses and abuses of the lie detector. New York: McGraw-Hill. A book by one of the foremost researchers on lie detection, discussing its valid uses and giving cases where it has been abused in the past.
3. Plutchik, R. (1980). Emotion: A psychoevolutionary synthesis. New York: Harper & Row. Outlines Plutchik's theory of emotion, including its roots in Darwin's theory of evolution. Discusses the survival functions that emotions serve.

UNIT 3 | Development and Individual Differences

Chapter 11
Development Through the Lifespan

Prologue
Why Psychologists Study Human Development
Issues in Development
Beginnings (0 to 1 Year of Age)
Early Childhood: Toddlers and Preschool Children (1 to 6 Years of Age)
Middle Childhood (6 to 12 Years of Age)
Adolescence (12 to 18 Years of Age)
Early Adulthood (18 to 40 Years of Age)
Middle Adulthood (40 to 65 Years of Age)
Late Adulthood (65 or More Years of Age)
Epilogue: Algebra and Formal Operations

Chapter 12
Intelligence and Individual Differences

Prologue
Why Psychologists Study Intelligence
Defining Intelligence
Measuring Intelligence—IQ Tests
The Triarchic Theory of Intelligence
Birth Order and Intelligence
IQ and Race
The Effects of Environmental Stimulation
Intellectual Changes over Time
Creativity
Some Final Thoughts on Individual Differences
Epilogue: The Gifts

Chapter 13
Personality

Prologue
Why Psychologists Study Personality
Theories of Personality
Personality Assessment
Epilogue: The Eye of the Beholder

CHAPTER 11 | Development Through the Lifespan

PROLOGUE

You are in a laboratory with Dr. Anthony DeCasper. You help him place a set of headphones over a baby's ears. "She'll be able to hear Dr. Seuss stories through the headphones," he says. "We'll see which one she likes." You look at the baby. She's very tiny, only 3 days old. What meaning could Dr. Seuss stories have to a 3-day-old baby? How could she possibly tell you whether she liked one better than the other?

Dr. DeCasper places in the baby's mouth a special nipple that is connected to the tape deck. "I've got two tapes here," he says. "They both have the same Dr. Seuss story on them and they'll run at the same time. One of the tapes is read by the baby's mother, the other by a stranger. If this baby sucks quickly on the nipple, she'll hear her mother reading the story. If she sucks slowly, she'll hear the stranger's voice."

After listening for a short time, the baby sucks faster on the nipple. Throughout the day, the experiment continues. Many different infant subjects come and go, brought in by their mothers, who are curious about what Dr. DeCasper is investigating. Sometimes, a slow sucking rate will bring on the mother's voice, sometimes a fast rate. "That way we can control for preferred rates of sucking," DeCasper adds. Regardless of whether the selected rate was fast or slow, at least 85 percent of the infants showed a preference for their mother's voice over that of a stranger and adjusted their sucking rate to maintain their mother's voice on the earphones.

"What are you trying to discover?" you ask.

"Well," he says, "I think babies hear their mothers' voices when they are still in the womb, and they learn to recognize their mothers' voices,

Prologue

Why Psychologists Study Human Development

Issues in Development
  Nature versus Nurture
  Stability versus Change
  Continuity versus Discontinuity

Beginnings (0 to 1 Year)
  Are Babies Passive?
  Infant Physical and Motor Development
  Infant Personality and Social–Emotional Development

Early Childhood: Toddlers and Preschool Children (1 to 6 Years)
  Cognitive Development
  Personality Development in Early Childhood
  Social Relations in Early Childhood

Middle Childhood (6 to 12 Years)
  Cognitive Development in Middle Childhood
  Social–Emotional Development in Middle Childhood

Adolescence (12 to 18 Years)
  Storm and Stress
  Physical Growth in Adolescence
  Cognitive Development in Adolescence
  Alternative Views of Cognitive Development
  Developmental Tasks of Adolescence
  The Peer Group

Early Adulthood (18 to 40 Years)
  Physical Changes in Early Adulthood
  Marriage and Parenthood
  Planning for a Career

Middle Adulthood (40 to 65 Years)
  Physical Changes in Middle Adulthood
  Midlife Crisis?
  The Empty Nest

Late Adulthood (65 or More Years)
  Physical Changes in Late Adulthood
  Sex and the Elderly
  When Life Ends

Epilogue: Algebra and Formal Operations

so I want to see whether, at an early age, they prefer her voice to that of a stranger" (DeCasper & Fifer, 1980).

You think about the idea. You can't help but ask, "Even though they are only 3 days old, couldn't they have learned their mother's voice after they were born?"

"That's possible," he agrees. "That's why we've got this next test."

You watch Dr. DeCasper run the experiment again, this time with fathers. All the fathers in the experiment were presented with their babies at birth and talked to them as often as possible, sometimes for as much as 10 hours. Since birth, these babies have heard no other male voice. The babies, only 2 or 3 days old, are once again equipped with the earphones and the special nipple to hear their father or a stranger read Dr. Seuss. They show no preference for one voice over the other (Kolata, 1984). "Why do they prefer their mother's voice to their father's?" you ask.

"I think it's because they have more experience with their mother's voice. They hear it when they are in the womb. After a few weeks of listening to their father's voice, they will prefer their father's voice to that of a stranger," DeCasper says.

During the final week of the experiments, you are amazed to see that Dr. DeCasper is having 16 pregnant women read Dr. Seuss's book The Cat in the Hat twice a day to their unborn fetuses! Dr. DeCasper says, "By the time they are born, these babies will have heard that story for at least 5 hours." Once born, these babies are given the earphones and a choice of hearing their mothers read either The Cat in the Hat or The King, the Mice and the Cheese, which also is a poem but has a very different beat and meter. The babies suck at rates that allow them to hear The Cat in the Hat.

"Do you really think they're learning from what they hear while they're in the womb?" you ask.

Dr. DeCasper leans back in his laboratory chair, smiles at you, and says, "It's sure beginning to look that way."

In this chapter, we'll examine the behaviors of newborn children and the effects of genetic heritage and learning on important developmental changes during childhood. We'll learn how human attachments are formed. We'll explore cognitive development and the social changes that may be important during childhood. And we'll look at the developmental changes that occur during adolescence and adulthood, examining the development of human behavior throughout the lifespan.

WHY PSYCHOLOGISTS STUDY HUMAN DEVELOPMENT

When should children be expected to walk? How "normal" is it for young children to be strongly attached to their mothers? When do children start to speak, and how much of what is said to them do they understand? How do children acquire a sense of right and wrong? Is adolescence usually a time of stress? Does intelligence decline with age?

Through careful research, developmental psychologists try to find the answers to these and other questions. **Developmental psychology** is the study of age-related changes in human behavior during the lifespan. By understanding human development, psychologists know what to expect at different developmental stages, and they learn the parameters of human growth and achievement.

Modern development psychology places the greatest emphasis on the years of infancy and childhood, the time when changes are the most apparent. After all, the difference between an infant of 2 years and a child of 9 years is far greater than that between adults of 52 and 59 years. Nonetheless, in the last decades, interest in adult development has grown rapidly as well.

Much of the modern interest in developmental psychology stemmed from lectures given at Clark University by Sigmund Freud in 1908. In those lectures, Freud stressed the first 6 years of a child's development as formative. What happened to the child after the age of 6 was thought by Freud to be far less important.

One of the first people to examine the entire lifespan was the psychoanalyst Erik Erikson. Although few developmental psychologists are **psychoanalysts,** all of them owe a debt to Erikson for emphasizing the importance of the lifespan and the social forces that shape it. He views human development as a progression through eight **psychosocial stages,** each of which is characterized by conflicts that must be resolved for healthy development to occur (see Table 11.1).

Erikson does not consider the psychosocial stages to be dichotomies—that is, conflicts are not always resolved so that a person will be fully on one side or the other. Rather, there is a range between the opposing positions at each psychosocial stage. For example, Erikson would not expect an adolescent to have either a complete identity or total role confusion, but rather to be somewhere in between, leaning more, it is hoped, toward the positive identity formation than the negative role confusion. Similarly, in later adulthood, some despair would be normal and natural for persons with healthy personality development. As Erikson has said, "During old age the life crisis involves the conflict between integrity and despair. How could anybody have integrity and not also despair about certain things in his own life, about the human condition?" (Hall, 1983, p. 27).

Most modern researchers believe that Erikson's theory fits well the informal observations obtained from many sources and that his theory may have much to contribute as a general outline for healthy socialization and personality development. Hard scientific proof for Erikson's theory is not easy to come by, however, because of the difficulty of examining each of Erikson's stages under controlled conditions in a laboratory or by other scientific methods.

ISSUES IN DEVELOPMENT

Nature versus Nurture

As you sit now, reading this book, you are presenting an excellent example of the interaction of **nature** (the effects of heredity) and **nurture** (the effects of the environment). Your human brain allows you to process and recall vast amounts of information. If you had inherited the brain of a dog or cat, no amount of training would have enabled you to comprehend this chapter.

However, if this chapter were written in Turkish, you would be unable to understand it (unless, through experience or nurturance, you had come to learn

DEVELOPMENTAL PSYCHOLOGY
The study of age-related changes in human behavior during the lifespan.

PSYCHOANALYST
A practitioner who generally adheres to the school of psychological thought founded by Sigmund Freud that emphasizes the study of unconscious processes.

PSYCHOSOCIAL STAGES
The eight stages of ego development as postulated by Erik Erikson. The stages incorporate both sexual and social aspects and include the entire lifespan.

NATURE
In developmental research, the hereditary component of an organism's development.

NURTURE
In developmental research, the environmental component of an organism's development.

Erik Erikson (1902–).

CHROMOSOMES

A thread-shaped body contained within the nucleus of a body cell that determines the characteristics that will be passed on to the offspring of an organism. Chromosomes carry the genes; humans have 23 pairs of them.

DNA

Deoxyribonucleic acid. A chemical constituent of cell nuclei, consisting of two long chemical chains of alternating phosphate and deoxyribose units twisted into a double helix and joined by bonds between the complementary chemical bases adenine, thymine, cytosine, and guanine. It is the substance that enables cells to copy themselves; it is the essence of all life.

Turkish). So, it is a combination of your inherited brain and your experience with reading the English language, as well as the experience you've gathered in the world up to this point, that enables you to understand and make use of the information in this text. All human development can be understood as an interaction of nature and nurture (Weisfeld, 1982).

There are some behaviors in the developing person that seem to be mainly a function of the genetic component, such as growing physically or acquiring the ability to walk. Others seem to be shaped primarily by the environment, such as driving a car or reading a book. It is important to remember, however, that nature versus nurture isn't a pure dichotomy. Without proper nutrition, a child's growth may be stunted or he may walk much later than he would have; without the inherited physical capacity, driving a car or even reading might be impossible. It is always the interaction between the two that determines our behavior. We hope that someday we will know enough about the biology of human beings to be able to separate the contributions of nature and nurture. To do that, we will need to have a full understanding of our genetic inheritance. This is a tall order, but it may be forthcoming (see Focus on Research).

TABLE 11.1 Erikson's Psychosocial Stages

PERIOD OF TIME	CONFLICT	DESCRIPTION
1. Infancy	Basic trust versus mistrust	Parents must maintain an adequate environment—supportive, nurturing, and loving—so that the child develops basic trust.
2. Years 1–3	Autonomy versus shame or doubt	As the child develops bowel and bladder control, she should also develop a healthy attitude toward being independent and somewhat self-sufficient. If the child is made to feel that independent efforts are wrong, then shame and self-doubt develop instead of autonomy.
3. Years 3–5½	Initiative versus guilt	The child must discover ways to initiate actions on his own. If such initiatives are successful, guilt will be avoided.
4. Years 5½–12	Industry versus inferiority	The child must learn to feel competent, especially when competing with peers. Failure results in feelings of inferiority.
5. Adolescence	Identity versus role confusion	The young person must develop a sense of role identity, especially in terms of selecting a vocation and future career.
6. Early adulthood	Intimacy versus isolation	The adult's formation of close friendships and relationships with the opposite sex is vital to healthy development
7. Middle adulthood	Generativity versus stagnation	Adults need to develop useful lives by helping and guiding children. Childless adults must fill this need through adoption or other close relationships with children.
8. Later adulthood	Ego integrity versus despair	Adults eventually review their lives. A life well spent will result in a sense of well-being and integrity.

Within each of the approximately 60 trillion cells of your body lie 46 tiny microscopic objects called **chromosomes.*** Within each of the chromosomes is the master molecule **DNA.** Certain sections of DNA are called genes. Your genes determine the part of you that we say is owing to nature; genes are your inheritance.

These genes are in the form of a code. Different codes will result in different people or, if different enough from the human code, will result in other animals or plants. All life as we know it (with the possible exception of a few viruses) is based on DNA. Roses, sparrows, people—all share a DNA genetic heritage.

DNA wasn't discovered until 1953 when James Watson, Francis Crick, and Maurice Wilkins determined its structure. Now James Watson has yet another chance to make history. He was chosen to head the team reaching for the next great goal in biology—mapping the human *genome,* that is, mapping the location and chemical composition of every single one of the millions of genes that exist on each of the human chromosomes!

In 1986, when the project was first seriously considered, it was estimated that it might take the better part of 50 years to complete. By 1989, however, new breakthroughs in mapping techniques allowed work that used to take months to be completed in a single day. Watson then asked Congress for more funds saying, "I have stuck my reputation on getting it [an initial general map of all the genes on the chromosomes] done in five years [1994]" (Roberts, 1989, p. 424).

It is now expected that the entire

---

*Sex cells, sperm or egg, are an exception. They carry 23 chromosomes each, which prevents the doubling of chromosome number each generation when the sperm and egg join to create a new human being.

code for a human being, the *complete* sequence and *exact* order of the tens of millions of genes, will be completed before 2005 at a cost of about $3 billion. And success may come even sooner. The United States is not the only nation in the race for the gene technology sure to come from the discoveries. Japan and Great Britain are also making a national effort, and many other labs in countries throughout the world are helping as well. In fact, in order to avoid overlapping research efforts, Watson has suggested that individual countries be given the responsibility for breaking the codes on different chromosomes (Dickson, 1989).

Breaking the human code will offer tremendous benefits. From early on in the project, researchers talked about uncovering the causes of a number of genetic diseases such as cystic fibrosis, Huntington's disease, and muscular dystrophy. There, efforts have already been rewarded. A Canadian team discovered the gene responsible for cystic fibrosis, which kills thousands of children each year. As a result of this work, it is hoped that someday a screening test will be developed that can let people know if they are carriers of the gene before they decide to have children. Breaking the code will also enable scientists to fully resolve the long-argued issue of nature versus nurture because we will be able to discover what, in fact, the genes do control or influence. We might finally learn, for instance, how much of our intelligence, personality, or temperament is attributable to inheritance and how much to upbringing, or nurture.

But there will also be perils in this "brave new world." Consider the following imaginary scenarios:

Ellen spent four years completing her

Ph.D. in industrial and chemical engineering. Today, although wincing as a company doctor draws a few drops of blood for her preemployment physical, she can hardly contain her excitement about the job she's been offered at one of the country's foremost metallurgical institutes.

Two days later the phone call comes. You are perfectly healthy, the young doctor says. But tests have revealed you harbor a gene that can result in decreased levels of a blood enzyme, glucose-6-phosphate dehydrogenase. Without the enzyme's protection, you have a slightly increased risk of developing a red blood cell disease if you come into contact with certain chemicals in our laboratory.

I'm sorry, he says. The job has been offered to someone else.

When Frank married at age 31 he decided to take out a life insurance policy. A swimmer and avid racquetball player with no previous hospitalization, he felt certain his low premiums would be a worthy investment for his family. Weeks later, after a routine physical exam, he was shocked by the insurance company's response. Sophisticated DNA testing had revealed in Frank's tissues a single missing copy of a so-called RB antioncogene and minor variations in two other genes. Computer analysis showed the molecular misprints more than tripled his risk of getting small-cell lung cancer by age 55. His application was rejected (Weiss, 1989, p. 40).

As you can see, bit by bit, as scientists break the code, lawmakers will come face to face with a distinctly twenty-first century problem, *genetic discrimination.* Now is the time to begin thinking about this and other social problems that might be created by our new-found knowledge instead of waiting until the problems are upon us. If we do, the transition into the next century might be considerably smoother.

345

LONGITUDINAL STUDIES
Research studies that are designed to
investigate an individual over time, asking
measurements at periodic intervals.

LINEAR PROGRESSION
Development that progresses steadily and
continuously (as would a straight line). In
this process, each development is
dependent on those that came before.

NEONATES
Newborn infants.

Stability versus Change

There is much evidence to demonstrate that shortly after birth, babies are different from one another (Eisenberg & Marmarou, 1981). Some cry and fret, some sleep, some are quietly active. Workers on obstetrics wards are familiar with the great range of personalities noticeable within the first few days of life. Although newborns may behave very differently from one another, their own individual rates of activity and crying are quite stable and consistent during those first days of life (Korner, Hutchinson, Koperski, Kraemer, & Schneider, 1981).

Longitudinal studies have suggested that there is stability and consistency over time of some personality characteristics (Costa & McCrae, 1980; Thomas, Chess, & Birch, 1970). For instance, infants who are passive during their first bath at age 1–2 months are also likely to sleep well in strange surroundings when they are 1 year old and also to enjoy their first weeks at camp when they are 10 (Thomas, Chess, & Birch, 1968). In other ways, however, people do change during their lives, sometimes dramatically.

As with the nature–nurture issue, it is important to realize that stability and change are not a dichotomy—not an "either–or" situation; both may be involved. Some characteristics may change greatly over a person's lifetime; others may remain stable.

Continuity versus Discontinuity

Developmental psychologists have debated over the years whether human development could be viewed as a natural orderly progression or whether it occurs in a series of stages with abrupt changes occurring from one stage to the next. People often think that human development, and development in general, follows a fairly **linear progression**—one that proceeds at a fairly stable and steady rate and in which each new development is built on all the developments that came before.

This is not usually the case, however. Human development may occur rapidly *and* slowly *and* reach a plateau *and* even appear to reverse, all at the same time, depending on which developmental aspect you consider (see Figure 11.1). Furthermore, some developments appear to be dependent on one another, while others seem to occur in parallel without being directly dependent on one another. In a word, human development is complex. Although some behaviors seem to be acquired in an orderly progression, others may appear in an abrupt way.

The Concept Review summarizes the three developmental issues we have discussed so far in this chapter. Not one of these issues is simple; neither side of an issue completely explains any aspect of human development. Nature is meaningless without nurture; it is impossible to study development without seeing *both* change and stability in the process; and, although certain behaviors appear to be acquired in a relatively orderly progression, many others are not. Throughout the rest of this chapter, you will see how these issues and others apply as the child is born, grows older, and ages.

BEGINNINGS (0 TO 1 YEAR OF AGE)

If you are among the many people who are unfamiliar with **neonates** (newborn infants); if your first reaction to a woman's labor pains is to boil some water; or if you've never thought it odd that in old Hollywood movies the delivery-room nurse always handed the mother a 40-pound "newborn" possessing a full set of teeth, then you probably would be surprised by the appearance of a real newborn baby.

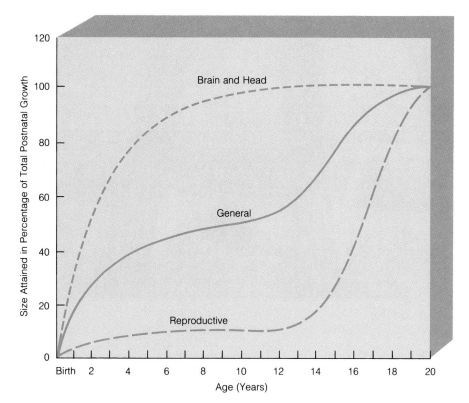

FIGURE 11.1

Different aspects of development proceed at greatly differing rates. As you can see, human development doesn't proceed in a linear fashion. (Source: Adapted from Harris, Jackson, Patterson, & Scammon, 1930.)

Real newborn infants (as opposed to the old Hollywood variety) have skin that is soft, dry, and wrinkled. They typically weigh between 6 and 9 pounds and are about 20 inches in length. The newborn's head may seem huge in proportion to the rest of its body, as it is responsible for fully one-fourth of the baby's length. In addition, the neonate's forehead is high and its nose is flat. And, although the eyes may eventually be brown, most neonates' eyes are steely blue.

Are Babies Passive?

From the turn of the century until the 1950s, most researchers considered the newborn to be a helpless creature who was handed to the world like a lump of clay ready to be molded and shaped. They did not think of the newborn as being competent in any sense of the word. They considered babies in general to be helpless and passive. Babies cried, they wet, they ate, they slept, they possessed some simple reflexes, and that was about it.

CONCEPT REVIEW: DEVELOPMENTAL ISSUES

Nature-Nurture	Are certain behavioral characteristics more influenced by heredity or by the environment?
Stability-Change	Are certain behavioral characteristics relatively stable over time, or do changes occur throughout the lifespan?
Continuity-Discontinuity	Can development be characterized as a steady progression, or does it appear to occur in abrupt shifts?

CHAPTER 11
DEVELOPMENT THROUGH THE LIFESPAN

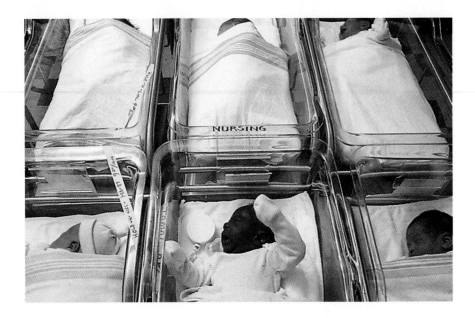

Human newborns have soft, dry, and wrinkled skin. They usually weigh between 6 and 9 pounds and are about 20 inches in length. The neonate's head accounts for one-quarter of its entire length. In addition, the neonate's forehead is high and its nose is flat.

During the 1960s and 1970s, however, there was a sudden surge of research concerning the capabilities of infants. Researchers found, for instance, that throughout infancy babies will initiate social interactions and play an active role in maintaining and developing their parents' responses (Restak, 1982).

This sociability begins only moments after the infant is out of the womb. Newborns will look about, and they will turn their heads in response to a voice as though they are searching for its source. Newborns seem especially attracted to faces and show an interest in them. This behavior, in turn, helps to initiate reciprocal interest from the one receiving the infant's gaze; other attributes that are present at or shortly after birth help to facilitate the social attachment of the infant to its caregiver (see Figure 11.2). As you read more about newborns, you may be surprised to find how many interesting abilities and competencies they have.

Researchers have found that newborns are capable of fairly complex cognitive, learning, and memory tasks. For example, in the chapter Prologue we discussed the fact that the infant not only heard his mother's voice before he was born but also that his memory was developed enough so that he "recognized" her voice again after birth! Soon after birth, infants actively attend and begin the process of encoding information from the environment, placing it into their memories for later retrieval.

Habituation (see Chapter 6) in newborns and young infants also shows their capacity for learning. When a stimulus, such as a sight or sound, is presented repeatedly to the infant often enough, the baby begins to pay less and less attention to it. This suggests that the baby can remember the stimulus and has become, in effect, bored with it. If another, different stimulus is then presented to the infant, the infant often pays attention to it, which shows that the infant has discriminated between the two stimuli. According to psychologist Robert Trotter,

> Habituation is now considered a primary indication of brain and nervous-system functioning and . . . is seen as a good predictor of later intelligence. Habituation, which becomes increasingly acute over the first 10 weeks of life, is commonly assessed as a measure of an infant's maturity and well-being. Infants who have brain damage or have suffered birth traumas, such as lack of oxygen, do not habituate well, and may go on to have developmental and learning problems. (Trotter, 1987, p. 38)

Infant Physical and Motor Development

The term used to describe a genetically determined biological plan of development, one relatively independent of experience, is **maturation**. Human growth seems to be mainly a function of maturation, and, to a large extent, so is motor development. Physical growth and motor development are among the most commonly discussed aspects of infant development among parents, simply because they are so readily observable.

As you can see by examining Table 11.2, the rate of physical growth is incredibly rapid immediately following conception, and *decelerates* quickly thereafter. Although you may have thought of human growth as a fairly linear progression, if the rate of human growth during the first 3 months following your conception were maintained, by the time you were 20 you'd weigh considerably more than all the planets of the solar system combined, with the sun thrown in for good measure!*

Changes in the relative size of different body parts also take place during growth. The change in the ratio of head to body length is an interesting example of this aspect of growth (see Figure 11.3).

In Figure 11.4 you can see how aspects of an infant's motor development also appear to follow a maturational plan. Just as individual babies differ, so too do individual rates of motor development. Some infants proceed quickly; others lag behind. Some develop rapidly in one area and simultaneously are slow in another.

---

*Based on a rate of each cell becoming 25 billion cells every 3 months.

MATURATION
A genetically programmed biological plan of development that is relatively independent of experience.

INFANT ATTRIBUTE	EFFECT
Infant cries	Basic needs are met
Infant is sensitive to touch (Lamper & Eisdorfer, 1971; Yang & Douthitt, 1974)	Promotes close physical contact
Infant attracted to faces (Fantz, 1961)	Facilitates mutual interest, involvement
Infant possesses features innately attractive to adults (Alley, 1981; Lorenz, 1943)	Encourages adults to spend time with infant
Infant engages in "conversations" with caregiver (Rosenthal, 1982)	
Infant vocalizes more when eye contact is made (Keller & Scholmerich, 1987)	Facilitates social communication
Infant appears to be specifically reactive to human voices (Hutt, Hutt, Lenard, Bernuth, & Muntjewerff, 1968)	

ATTACHMENT (protection, nurturance)

FIGURE 11.2

Attributes present at or shortly after birth that facilitate infants' social attachments.

Like the tortoise and the hare, some infants may race ahead of their peers only to be equaled or overtaken later.

Infant Personality and Social–Emotional Development

Although the human infant doesn't appear to possess a fully integrated personality in its first few days of life, it has been observed that newborns do exhibit considerable differences in temperament shortly after birth. Some babies seem "fussy," some have a high activity level, and some seem to do nothing but sleep. **Temperament theories** are based on the fact that these early infant personalities or traits may be consistent or stable over great lengths of time (Goldsmith, 1983).

THE NEW YORK LONGITUDINAL STUDY. In the late 1950s, two physicians, Alexander Thomas and Stella Chess, began what came to be called the New York Longitudinal Study. With their colleagues, they followed 140 children from birth to adolescence. They were initially interested in infant reactivity, but soon came to believe that they were, in fact, empirically documenting differences in temperament. In 1968, they first described their subjects in terms of "easy" or "difficult" temperaments (Thomas, Chess, & Birch, 1968; 1970).

These personality dimensions were obtained through interviews with parents, observation of infants and children, and other measures. According to the study's classification system, *easy* infants adapted readily to new situations, were approachable, responded with low or mild intensity, exhibited pleasant moods, and had regular body rhythms. *Difficult* children, on the other hand, were slowly adaptable to new situations, tended to withdraw from their caregivers, responded with high intensity, and exhibited unpleasant moods. Some children fell in between the dimensions of easy and difficult. Such infants often are referred to as *slow-to-warm-up* babies. Other infants were too inconsistent to categorize, exhibiting "mixtures of traits that did not add up to a general characterization" (Thomas, Chess, & Birch, 1970, p. 105). Among the infants studied, researchers found that 40 percent were easy, 15 percent slow-to-warm-up, 10 percent difficult, and 35 percent inconsistent. What makes these findings most interesting is that these temperaments often appear to be stable over time. In such a case, a child who doesn't cry much with wet diapers at 2 months of age also is less likely to fuss when a shirt is pulled over her head at 1 year of age. Follow-up studies at 5 and 10 years showed certain stability of these traits.

GOODNESS OF FIT. Interestingly, "easy" children aren't always at an advantage. Among the Masai children in Africa, for example, it was discovered that the children

TABLE 11.2 The Deceleration of Growth during Prenatal Development

AGE	WEIGHT (in ounces)	PERCENTAGE INCREASE
Conception	0.00000002	
4 weeks	0.0007	3,499,900
8 weeks	0.035	4,900
12 weeks	0.6	1,614
16 weeks	3	400
20 weeks	8	166
24 weeks	22	175
28 weeks	28	27
32 weeks	34	21

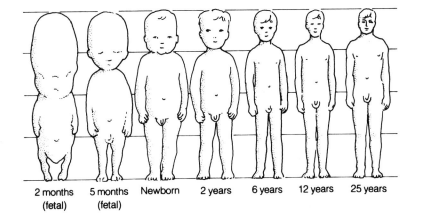

FIGURE 11.3

Changes in body form associated with age. (Source: Jackson, 1929, p. 118.)

2 months (fetal)   5 months (fetal)   Newborn   2 years   6 years   12 years   25 years

with easy temperaments were the ones who most often died during times of famine, probably because they were fed less often than were difficult children who acted more aggressively (deVries, 1984)—a case of the squeaky wheel getting the grease, or milk in this case. Even in Western culture, it has been found that difficult infants from upper- and middle-class families, when tested at the age of 4, obtained intelligence test scores that were 20 IQ points higher than their matched easy counterparts (Maziade, Cote, Boutin, & Thivierge, 1988). This appears to be due to the fact that parents of difficult children find they have to spend more time with their difficult children, whereas the easy children can be more readily left to themselves. Of course, an easy child may yet have the advantage when she enters school and finds herself having to deal with tasks that take time and require concentration (Palisin, 1986). For reasons such as these, psychologists don't auto-

FIGURE 11.4

Some motor milestones from the Denver Developmental Screening Test. The bottom of the bar represents the age at which 25 percent of the sample could perform the task; the top represents the age at which 90 percent had achieved it. (Source: Adapted from Frankenburg & Dodds, 1967, p. 186.)

Months of age

Rolls over	Sits without support	Stands holding on	Pulls self to stand	Stands alone well	Walks well
4.7 mo. / 2.3 mo.	7.8 mo. / 4.8 mo.	10.0 mo. / 5.0 mo.	10.0 mo. / 6.0 mo.	13.9 mo. / 9.8 mo.	14.3 mo. / 11.3 mo.

matically assume that an easy temperament is superior, but rather they talk of **goodness of fit,** when referring to how well suited a given temperament is to a particular environment.

It should be noted, however, that not all temperament researchers agree that temperamental characteristics are stable over time, as the New York Longitudinal Study would suggest (Goldsmith et al., 1987).

SOCIAL TIES.   We humans are social creatures. We live within communities and families; we form social and emotional ties with one another. As was shown in Figure 11.2, the infant seems innately predisposed to form these ties—for one thing, because such ties are essential for newborns who must rely on their parents or others for basic needs. During this time of helplessness, the infant comes to know his parents socially and forms attachments to them.

The mechanism of **attachment,** especially between the infant and his mother, has been intensely debated and investigated by developmental theorists (Bretherton, 1985), and the theoretical orientation taken by most researchers over the years has changed (Lamb, 1984). During the first decades of this century, both Freud and the behaviorists (see Chapter 1) argued that the infant became attached because attachment was associated with the fulfillment of primary biological needs. For this reason, they believed that nursing led to the formation of strong attachments between infant and mother. But research with rhesus monkeys, conducted by Harry Harlow and his associates, cast doubt on this speculation.

In a series of widely publicized experiments begun about 35 years ago, Harlow and his colleagues separated rhesus monkeys from their mothers at an early age and placed them with artificial surrogate mothers (see Figure 11.5). One surrogate was made of wire; the other was covered with terry cloth and possessed a more rhesus-looking face (Harlow & Zimmerman, 1959). Both "mothers" could be equipped with baby bottles placed through a hole in the chest, which allowed nursing to take place. *Regardless of which mother provided food*, the baby rhesus spent as much time as possible cuddling and hugging the cloth mother. Even rhesus

Parents or adult caregivers are seen as intrinsically attractive to an infant. Research indicates that infants are also intrinsically attractive to adults (Lorenz, 1943).

FIGURE 11.5

The cloth and the wire surrogate mothers used by Harlow in experiments with rhesus monkeys. Even if the only food available was from the wire mother, the infants preferred the cloth mother.

monkeys fed by only the wire mother formed strong attachments to the cloth mother and spent most of their time hugging it. A simple piece of soft cloth did not have the same effect; to function as a surrogate, the cloth had to be shaped like a real mother.

Other researchers also have shown that attachment is more than just dependence on someone who fulfills biological needs. For instance, infants may become attached to other infants their own age (Schaffer & Emerson, 1964). Attachment may develop even if an infant is seriously mistreated by the one to whom she is becoming attached (Rosenblum & Harlow, 1963). Infants also respond readily to others in social situations in which they have never received food or contact comfort (Brackbill, 1958; Rheingold, Gewirtz, & Ross, 1959). Furthermore, infants do not become passive and unresponsive once all their biological needs are taken care of; they continue to be social and to show attachment.

In recent years, the most accepted theoretical orientation concerning the development of attachment has been toward an **intraorganismic perspective** (Brazelton, Koslowski, & Main, 1974). In this view, intraorganismic organization means that the infant is biologically organized or ready to form attachments to caregivers (again, see Figure 11.2).

John Bowlby, one of the most important proponents of the intraorganismic perspective, believes there is an innate drive in humans to form attachments that is as strong as the motivational forces of mating or eating (Bowlby, 1982a). His paper "The Nature of the Child's Tie to His Mother" (Bowlby, 1958) has been considered by many researchers to mark the beginning of contemporary attachment theory. Attachment remains an area of considerable interest (see Focus on a Controversy).

THE DYNAMICS OF HUMAN ATTACHMENT. Mary Ainsworth, who trained with John Bowlby, has investigated the parameters of human attachment. Ainsworth's studies are superior to most others in their scope. They have included a 1-year longitudinal investigation of infant attachments in the home; a 20-minute laboratory test known as the **strange situation**, which demonstrates individual differences in the quality of attachment; and an assessment of the variables that determine the quality of infant attachment. By using a number of observational techniques, Ainsworth and her colleagues were able to identify three attachment reactions of differing quality. The first, **secure attachment**, was the most common, accounting for about 65 to 75 percent of children studied. Babies exhibiting this response gave mothers returning from an absence of a few minutes during which the child was left with a stranger a happy greeting and approached them or stayed near them for a time. The second kind of reaction, **anxious/resistant attachment**, accounted for about 10 to 15 percent of children. Infants who responded in this way approached their mothers, cried to be picked up, and then squirmed or fought to get free, as though they weren't sure what they wanted. The third kind, **anxious/avoidant attachment**, accounted for about 20 to 25 percent of children; it was demonstrated by infants who didn't approach their returning mothers or who actively avoided them (Aisnworth, 1973).

Subsequent research has found that securely attached infants are more likely to explore their environments (Joffe, 1980) and to tolerate a moderate amount of separation from their mothers (Jacobson & Wille, 1984). Because of this, securely attached infants also feel more comfortable exploring and, when faced with something new such as a toy or game, will persist in examining it. This persistence often helps them to master the new thing they have encountered (Frodi, Bridges, & Grolnick, 1985). Not surprisingly, children who exhibit such mastery in infancy tend to show greater competence in early childhood (Sroufe, 1983; Messer et al.,

---

GOODNESS OF FIT
From temperament theory, referring to how well suited a certain temperament is to a particular environment. Temperaments well matched with their environments are said to show "goodness of fit."

ATTACHMENT
An especially close affectional bond formed between a living creature and another living creature or object.

INTRAORGANISMIC PERSPECTIVE
The view of attachment asserting that the infant has innate mechanisms that foster and promote the development of attachment. Such mechanisms are believed to have been naturally selected because they have survival value.

STRANGE SITUATION
A laboratory test designed by Mary Ainsworth to demonstrate individual differences in the quality of attachment.

SECURE ATTACHMENT
The most common form of attachment observed by Ainsworth in her research. Securely attached children respond happily to their mothers' return, greet them, and stay near them for a while.

ANXIOUS/RESISTANT ATTACHMENT
A form of attachment observed by Ainsworth in her research. Children who show anxious/resistant attachment approach their returning mothers, cry to be picked up, and then struggle to be free. Their behavior is ambivalent; they appear to wish to approach and to avoid their mothers simultaneously.

ANXIOUS/AVOIDANT ATTACHMENT
A form of attachment observed by Ainsworth in her research. Children who show anxious/avoidant attachment do not approach—and actively avoid—their returning mothers.

In 1972, John Kennell and Marshall Klaus proposed that there might be a period immediately following birth when a special bond formed between the infant and his mother during skin-to-skin contact. Such a bond wouldn't be obvious, but still would be one that fostered a special relationship and, if disrupted, might leave the infant at a lasting disadvantage (Klaus et al., 1972).

Kennell and Klaus investigated the importance of these first few minutes or hours of contact between a mother and her infant. Twenty-eight healthy mothers with normal full-term infants were divided into two groups. The first group was given 16 more hours of contact with their infants during the first 3 days after birth than was the second group (Kennell et al., 1974). A significant difference was noted between the two groups of mothers when they returned to the hospital 1 month later. During feeding, the extra-contact mothers cuddled and soothed their babies more and had more eye contact with them.

After 2 years, five mothers randomly selected from each group were reexamined. The extra-contact mothers still showed differences when compared with the less-contact mothers. The researchers concluded that the 16 extra hours of contact during the first 3 days of life was still having an effect on the mothers' behavior 2 years after the birth! How the mothers reacted to their infants, in turn, affected the way in which the infants responded to their mothers.

These findings, many of which are contained in Kennell and Klaus's *Maternal–Infant Bonding* (1976), led many researchers to conclude that this bond should be encouraged (Klaus & Kennell, 1976; Kennell, Voos, & Klaus, 1979). As a result,

many hospitals began changing their procedures. In fact, such procedures as giving the baby to the mother immediately after birth while encouraging her to hold and stroke the infant can be traced to the research of Kennell and Klaus.

Kennell and Klaus's findings did not go unchallenged, however. The first major criticism of the bonding research was a fairly obvious one; namely, that parents of adopted children feel as close to their kids as does a birth parent. This last observation led researchers to conclude that

> the initial post delivery bonding, as described by Klaus and Kennell (1976) and others, which is obviously not part of the adoption experience, does not appear to be necessary for the formation of a healthy family relationship. (Singer, Brodzinsky, Ramsay, Steir, & Waters, 1985, p. 1550)

These authors argued, therefore, that whatever the early mother–infant bond was, missing it was something that could be overcome easily.

Intrigued by this observation, researchers Chess and Thomas, whom you may recall for their temperament work, decided to examine the bonding research on their own. They concluded that Kennell and Klaus's research design had methodological flaws and that the idea of a unique relationship between mother and child due to skin-to-skin contact immediately after birth was unfounded (Chess & Thomas, 1982, 1986b).

Following this, researchers looking at other cultures discovered that motherly affection wasn't any greater in societies that encouraged early mother–infant contact, that a father's involvement with his child was no greater if he was allowed to attend the child's birth, and that maternal affection or bonding was not greater in

societies that encouraged early nursing (Lozoff, 1983).

In light of these findings, Kennell and Klaus agreed that it would be unlikely for the life-sustaining mother–infant relationship to be dependent on any one process such as bonding (although they still believed the bonding effect to be a real one) and that there probably were many other "fail-safe" routes to attachment (Kennell & Klaus, 1984).

The bonding issue continues to flourish, however, because so many hospitals still encourage what they believe to be bonding behavior despite the fact that research has failed to show a real benefit to be derived from immediate skin-to-skin contact between mother and infant. Because of this attitude among hospitals, problems may arise if, owing to a medical emergency or for some other valid reason, the infant and mother can't be brought together directly following birth. The mother, if she knows about the supposed importance of bonding, may then feel that she has missed something crucial when she is unable to "bond" with her baby (Chess & Thomas, 1986b). Still, a number of welcome humanitarian hospital reforms were brought about by this research; these days, parents are encouraged to participate fully in the birth and to become involved with their newborn, which is something that most parents enjoy and appreciate.

1986). Thus, one of the advantages of a secure attachment relationship is that it can help to foster further social competencies in the infant.

It should be kept in mind, however, that these findings may be limited to certain middle-class American cultures (Lamb, 1988). Among Japanese children, for example, 77 percent are found to show secure attachment and none were found to be anxious/avoidant, probably because part of the strange situation in which the testing is done, requires that the mother leave her infant alone with a stranger for a short time, which is something that Japanese mothers never do. Israeli infants raised on a kibbutz (a collective farm) respond differently, too. They don't find the strange situation to be so strange, probably because they are used to being looked after by strangers. We need to learn much more about these kinds of attachments before we can properly generalize our findings to a broad range of children (van IJzendoorn & Kroonenberg, 1988).

AN ENDURING QUESTION: WHO SHOULD MIND THE CHILDREN?

For as long as our species has existed and in every society, there have been instances when infants had to be left in the care of someone other than their mothers or fathers. In most of these situations, other family members, often a grandparent, functioned as caregiver. Strangers were rarely required to look after the children of others.

Sometimes large-scale infant care by strangers was required because of social disruptions such as war, famine, or plague. From a research perspective, however, if such children were observed to have problems with their development, it was impossible to say how much resulted from nonparental care and how much from the social upheaval that made such care necessary.

Although many societies have questioned the wisdom of nonparental care, its use was usually unavoidable. An exception to this was the "nanny system" common among many aristocracies throughout the ages, so-named after the child caregiver in the nineteenth-century British version of the system. Many writers and scholars argued that being raised by hired help, so that wealthy parents were free to be uninvolved with their children, was harmful. Again, from a research perspective, it is hard to really know just how "uninvolved" such parents really were and how much of the child's eventual development was influenced by factors of being privileged, rather than by the effects of a nanny. It is also difficult to find evidence of real harm owing to this system, but because we lack carefully gathered data, no one is certain.

In the United States during the 1940s, being raised in homes for orphans was shown to result in severe developmental setbacks for children (Spitz, 1945). This discovery led to the use of foster homes. But the care in the orphanages in question was closer to no care than it was to nonparental care, so the question of nonparental care versus care by strangers remained unanswered.

The question about the effects of nonparental care continues today in the United States and in many industrial nations, because so many women who were traditionally charged with raising the children are now entering the work force. In the United States alone, more than 50 percent of mothers are employed outside of the home, and more than 8 million American preschoolers require some form of nonparental care (see Figure 11.6). A number of organizations involved in child care services have estimated that by 1995, two-thirds of mothers with preschool children will be in the job force. In other industrialized nations, a large

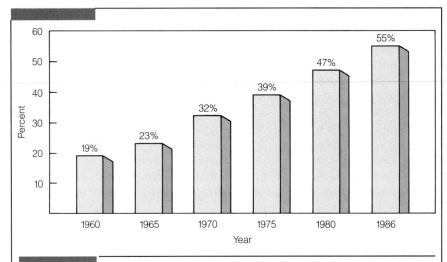

FIGURE 11.6

The percentage of working mothers of children under 6 years of age has been increasing steadily. As a result, many more preschoolers require some form of nonparental care. (Source: Adapted from Wallis, Hull, Ludtke, & Taylor, 1987, p. 59.)

portion of married women with preschool children are also working, even in countries such as Japan where mothers traditionally stayed home with their children. A great number of infants around the world are therefore affected. With modern research techniques and the widespread use of day-care, we are now better able to address the age-old question about the possible harm of nonparental care.

By the late 1970s, an extensive review of the data available indicated that "high-quality nonmaternal care does not appear to have adverse effects on the young child's maternal attachment, intellectual development, or social-emotional behavior" (Etaugh, 1980, p. 309). Most of these studies, however, were conducted in high-quality day-care centers, usually at universities. This is not the day-care setting that most infants encounter. Psychologist Jay Belsky examined infants in more typical day-care settings. He concluded that babies who spent more than 20 hours per week with nonparental care during the first year of life were more likely to show anxious/avoidant attachment to their mothers than were other babies (Belsky, 1986). Other researchers have made similar observations, and have suggested that infants left in day-care might be showing anxious/avoidant attachment because they perceive the mothers' daily abandonment as rejection (Barglow, Vaughn, & Molitor, 1987). As you recall, insecure attachment is associated with problems as the infant matures.

Some researchers have questioned Belsky's findings, however. One of the main criticisms is that he used the strange situation to measure infant attachment. Infants in day-care have much more experience with separations and strangers than do those who aren't in day-care, which could influence how they behave in the strange situation. Perhaps other measures should be used to study the infant's emotional and social well-being. Other critics have found that the quality of day-care makes much more difference than the age at which the child is enrolled in it (Wallis & Ludtke, 1987).

What we can feel comfortable saying today is that high-quality day-care for children over one year of age appears not be a detriment, and, despite parents' fears, the day-care workers do not become substitutes for parents in the eyes of the child (Farran & Ramey, 1977). In many instances, high-quality day-care has even been associated with benefits. Young children in high-quality programs have superior language skills (McCartney & Scarr, 1984) and are more likely to regulate their own behavior (Howes & Olenick, 1986). One study showed that disadvantaged children in particular can benefit from high-quality day-care (McCartney, Scarr, Phillips, & Grajek, 1985). The effect on infants younger than 1 year, however, is still debated and more research needs to be done.

Unfortunately, not all day-care programs are of high quality. Research has consistently shown that there is a difference between children who receive high-quality versus low-quality nonparental care. As yet, day-care arrangements that are informal or unlicensed have not been studied as extensively as have licensed ones. One study, however, indicated that there may not be significant differences as long as the caregivers have experience, interact with the children, and provide them with some structure by giving them things to do (Stith & Davis, 1984). Of course, the results of this limited study do not mean that unlicensed day-care centers are as good as licensed ones. Unlicensed centers may run the range from acceptable to dangerous. (The same may be true of licensed centers; but, presumably, this is less likely.)

Finally, there is no question that a child will fare better spending part of the day with a high-quality caregiver (an educated, trained person in a safe environment, who has few children to care for, and who interacts with the children while giving them structured things to do) than a whole day with a depressed or frustrated parent. So don't be afraid to use day-care if you are a parent or plan to become one. Just use a good dose of common sense when choosing a facility.

For Critical Analysis

1. Should the Federal Government require the establishment of uniform standards for day-care centers? Should governments in other countries do the same? How might such standards be helpful? What should those standards be?
2. How might a second income producing parent provide dividends for his or her children that might offset the possibly disruptive influences of day-care?

INFANT EMOTIONAL DEVELOPMENT.   The facial musculature of both full-term and premature newborns is fully developed and functional at birth (Ekman & Oster, 1979), so infants can make many of the same expressions that an adult can (Oster & Ekman, 1978). Newborns can smile slightly, knit their brows, or appear to pout and cry (Josse, Leonard, Lezine, Robinot, & Rouchouse, 1973; Oster, 1978; Oster & Ekman, 1978). And, if you give them something that tastes awful, they look disgusted (Steiner, 1973).

Researchers used to argue that infants younger than about 6 months of age showed only pleasure, wariness, or rage. In older infants, it was believed, emotions become more differentiated and obvious. Most researchers now believe that *all* the basic emotions are present in newborns and that what occurs as the infant ages is that he becomes better able to express these emotions in a way that others see clearly (Campos, Barrett, Lamb, Stenberg, & Goldsmith, 1983). Supporting this assertion is a study that shows that infants only 10 weeks old can discriminate their mothers' different emotional facial expressions. In this study, an infant's mother would face her baby and say, "You make me (happy, sad, angry)," and match her voice to her facial expression. The infant typically acted as though his mother's expression had meaning, and he too would react. Happy mothers produced happiness in their infants. Babies exposed to angry expressions eventually turned away and stopped looking. Those exposed to sad expressions appeared to suck their lips and tried to soothe themselves (Haviland & Lelwica, 1987).

EARLY CHILDHOOD: TODDLERS AND PRESCHOOL CHILDREN (1 TO 6 YEARS OF AGE)

Cognitive Development

During early childhood, besides physically increasing in size, children show increased motor competence. But some of the most apparent and interesting changes that take place in the first 6 years of the child's life are cognitive in nature. For a long time, psychologists ignored infants' minds. Some psychologists believed that ignoring an infant's mind wasn't a very hard thing to do, because whatever infants thought about, if anything, couldn't be too complex (Pines, 1966). Since that time, however, largely owing to the work of the Swiss researcher Jean Piaget, psychologists have become increasingly interested in the development of cognitive processes in infants and children.

In Piaget's view, cognitive development is the combined result of the development of the brain and nervous system and of experiences that help the individual adapt to his or her environment. Piaget believed that because humans are genetically similar and share many of the same environmental experiences, they can be expected to exhibit considerable uniformity in their cognitive development. In fact, he argued, four predictable stages of cognitive development will occur during specific periods of a child's life. The first two of these stages—the sensorimotor (0 to 2 years) and the preoperational (2 to 7)—take place during infancy and early childhood (see Table 11.3). We discuss these two stages now; later, in the sections on middle childhood and adolescence, we examine Piaget's last two stages.

Piaget argued that children are not simply adults who know less, and, conversely, adults are not simply knowledgeable children. Rather, Piaget believed that older children have more extensive cognitive development. On the one hand, they have broader experiences; on the other, they can process the information in more sophisticated ways because of the more advanced biological and adaptive development of their underlying cognitive structures.

THE SENSORIMOTOR STAGE (0 TO 2 YEARS). The first of Piaget's four stages of cognitive development is the sensorimotor stage, which is characterized by a lack of fully developed **object permanence**. Object permanence refers to the ability to represent an object, whether or not it is actually present. Piaget believed that object permanence is necessary before problem solving or thinking can be carried out internally—that is, carried out by using mental symbols or images.

Look around you—do you see a redwood tree? Unless you live in a scenic Northern California setting and are sitting next to a window, you probably don't. But can you mentally represent the redwood tree to yourself, even though one isn't

The Swiss researcher Jean Piaget (1896–1980) believed that children's thinking is qualitatively different from adults'. He developed a theory of cognitive development that outlined children's cognitive progression through a series of stages, the sensorimotor, preoperational, concrete operational, and formal operational.

TABLE 11.3 Piaget's First Two Stages of Cognitive Development

Sensorimotor Stage (0–2 years)
Characterized by a lack of fully developed object permanence, or realization that objects continue to exist even though they are not presently sensed

Preoperational Stage (2–7 years)
Characterized by the beginning of internalized thought processes; called preoperational because children haven't yet acquired the logical operations or rules of thought characteristic of later periods of cognitive development; beginning of a sense of self

actually present? You can do this in a number of ways. You can picture a redwood tree in your "mind's eye" (if you know what the tree looks like). Or you can think of the letter symbols R-E-D-W-O-O-D T-R-E-E. Or you might actually shape a depiction of a redwood tree with your hands to hold on to that object mentally, even though it's out of sight. The point is, you can keep any object "permanent," even when it is absent, by using these techniques. Without mental images, symbols, or depictions to represent an object, you would be unable to think of it, because you would have no internal way of representing it. In other words, without object permanence, "out of sight, out of mind."

Piaget argued that at the beginning of the sensorimotor stage, an infant may be unable to think. Later on, however, when object permanence becomes fully developed, the child leaves the sensorimotor stage.

THE PREOPERATIONAL STAGE (2 TO 7 YEARS).

The major distinction between the sensorimotor and preoperational stages is the degree of development and use of internal images and symbols. The development of thought, as represented by the establishment of object permanence, marks the dividing line between the sensorimotor and preoperational stages. This internalized thought may be the precursor of a sense of self-awareness.

As the preoperational stage sets in, the child demonstrates greater and greater use of symbolic functions. Language development increases dramatically and imaginative play becomes apparent as children spend much of their time engaging in make-believe. Another difference seen during this stage is that children can imitate another person's behavior after some time has passed, implying that they now have a way of symbolically remembering behavior originally observed in a model. All these actions suggest an internal cognitive mediation between incoming stimuli and later responses.

The reasoning of children in the preoperational stage is limited, however, because these children tend to be egocentric or self-centered (Gzesh & Surber, 1985). By **egocentrism,** Piaget did not mean that children are selfish; he meant that they generally perceive the world only in terms of their own perspective.

Egocentric thinking is only one of the cognitive limitations faced by children in the preoperational stage. An additional limitation is the inability to comprehend more than one aspect of a problem at a time. Piaget referred to this cognitive limitation as the *failure to decenter,* because such children tend to center on only single aspects of problems. This **centration** leads preoperational children to solutions

Some of Piaget's most interesting experiments and observations concerned the onset and development of object permanence during the sensorimotor stage. If, during the first four months of the sensorimotor stage, you show an infant an object that attracts attention and then block the baby's view of it with a screen, the child will act as if the object has simply vanished. By the middle of the sensorimotor stage, a child will try to regain visual contact with an object that has disappeared from view. This attempt may indicate the beginning of object permanence, since the infant may be searching for the hidden object. She or he seems to have some internal representation that the thing was once in view and is now gone. Even at this point, however, object permanence is weak.

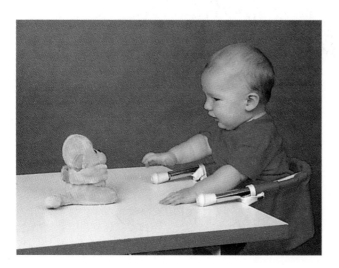

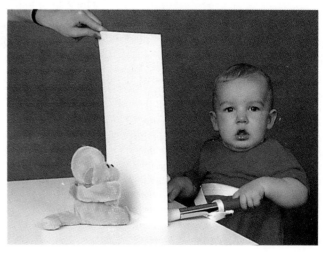

Research has shown that children become attached to their fathers as well as to their mothers. They especially appreciate the father's role as playmate.

that seem more intuitive than logical. For example, a preoperational child presented with two identical glasses of water will realize that they are equally full. But suppose we pour the water from one of the glasses into a dish while the child watches. He most likely will believe, when comparing the dish of water with the remaining glass, that there is now less water in the dish because it is at a lower level than is the water in the glass (see Figure 11.7). Of course, you and I know that there is still the same amount of water. We know that no water has been added or taken away (excluding residue remaining in the glass and evaporation due to pouring). We've *conserved* quantity (one aspect), although the shape has altered (another aspect). Because we can avoid centration, we can comprehend more than one aspect at a time. Children in the preoperational stage don't seem able to do this.

Personality Development in Early Childhood

One of the major achievements of young children is the ability to begin to regulate their own behavior. Regulation of children's behavior usually becomes necessary during the child's second year, because this is when the child begins to display sufficient autonomy to interfere occasionally with parental desires. For this reason, parents may wish to instill in the child an understanding of what is acceptable.

Longitudinal studies have shown that throughout the second year of life, a child's social behavior becomes more consistent and predictable (Bronson, 1985). This increased stability of social behavior may indicate that by the age of 2 years, children are beginning to regulate their own behavior internally in a consistent way.

When children begin to regulate their own behavior, they come to appear to rely on internalized value and reward systems. They can behave appropriately without being forced by external pressures, they can ignore immediate gratification in favor of long-term goals, and they may adhere to personal standards of moral behavior in the face of opposition. Consistency of behavior in different situations marks the beginning of what psychologists call *personality*. By 2 years of age, a social person is emerging; the child has a unique personality.

Social Relations in Early Childhood

All parents have desires and hopes for their children. The way parents achieve these ends can differ greatly from family to family. Researchers do not agree on which of the many childrearing practices is best. It is known, however, that parents provide role models for their children and that children rely on their parents to teach them about the world.

FIGURE 11.7

Testing a child for the ability to conserve. (a) The child agrees that the two glasses contain the same amount of water; (b) water from one of the glasses is poured into a dish. The child doesn't agree that the dish and the remaining glass contain the same amount of water, because the child is unable to conserve one aspect (amount) while another aspect (height) changes. Another way to say this is that the child centers attention on only one obvious aspect (height), whereas an adult would decenter and consider all aspects.

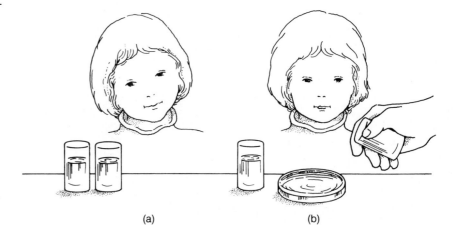

(a)   (b)

360

Mothers and fathers who have assumed the traditional gender roles behave differently toward their children (McHale & Huston, 1984). From the time the child is born, mothers are more likely to assume caregiving responsibilities, even if the fathers are home and are free to help. Fathers, on the other hand, are more likely to engage the infant in active and stimulating play (Parke & O'Leary, 1976; Yogman, Dixon, Tronick, & Brazelton, 1976). As the child grows older, the mother's role of primary caregiver and the father's role of playmate generally continue (Lamb, 1978). Because mothers and fathers behave in this distinctive way, they come to represent different types of experiences for their babies (Lamb, 1979). Both parents, however, transmit and enforce the rules and expectations of society.

THE DEVELOPMENT OF SIBLING RELATIONSHIPS. Although parents usually are considered to be the primary agents of socialization for the young child, in most families the child has a relationship with one or more siblings. Siblings can have a powerful effect on one another. Research indicates that siblings spend a great deal of time together, that they interact on many different levels, and that they often are deeply emotionally involved with one another (Abramovitch, Pepler, & Corter, 1982). This important effect that siblings have on one another, which continues over their lifespans, occurs because siblings are of the same generation, have a common genetic heritage, and share many of the same early experiences (Cicirelli, 1982). Strong sibling relationships have been shown to exist across the lifespan and throughout the world.

Although it was traditionally thought that conflict was the inevitable outcome of a sibling relationship, research has shown that rivalry and conflict are not necessarily the norm. In fact, the most common mode of sibling interaction is that of cooperation and helping (Abramovitch, Pepler, & Corter, 1982).

THE DEVELOPMENT OF PEER RELATIONSHIPS. Although parents and siblings seem to be the major influences on young children's social development, peers begin to have an increasing effect as the child grows older. Strictly speaking, **peers** are equals. Nonetheless, children often have playmates who are 3 or 4 years older or younger than they are. Many researchers therefore consider children who are interacting at about the same behavior level to be peers, regardless of age (Lewis & Rosenblum, 1975). Even so, explorations of peer relationships usually concentrate on children of approximately the same age, because these children are most likely to be interacting with one another (Roopnarine, 1981).

Between the ages of 1 and 2 years, children's social skills and peer interactions remain at a rudimentary level (Hartup, 1983), although the complexity and amount of peer interaction is greater than during infancy (Eckerman, Whatley, & Kutz, 1975). By the age of 2 years, however, many complex social interchanges occur. Imitation becomes more likely, and positive social interactions often are accompanied by appropriate emotional responses, such as smiling or laughter (Mueller & Brenner, 1977).

Cognitive changes during the second year also play an important role in social interaction. Six-month-old infants rarely show distress when a peer takes a toy away; such an interaction between children 20 months of age or older, on the other hand, is likely to start a fight. This occurs because children of this age have reached a cognitive milestone, the beginning of self-awareness (Amsterdam, 1972), or a consciousness of being distinct creatures. In one study, researchers found that as children develop this sense of self-awareness and are able to see themselves as distinct from others, they begin to claim toys and other items as "mine" (Levine, 1983). Once they've defined "mine," they are more likely to become possessive.

As children become older, they spend more and more time with other children, especially close friends. Children who form friendships do many things together, but most important, they form emotional ties with one another.

THE DEVELOPMENT OF FRIENDSHIPS. Most interactions among children between the ages of 2 and 6 years have been studied in day-care centers or in nursery schools. During the preschool years, both friendly and, less commonly, antagonistic social interactions emerge. One of the most apparent is the development of **friendships.**

When children first meet, they are more likely to become friends if they are able to exchange information successfully, to establish a common-ground activity, and to manage conflicts (see Table 11.4). After this initial relationship has been established, other processes become important. As children grow older, they improve their acquaintanceship abilities. They become more successful at exchanging information, establishing common-ground activities, resolving conflicts, and exploring differences. These characteristics, along with the emotional exchanges, become the most important aspects of the friendship (Diaz & Berndt, 1982; Furman & Bierman, 1983).

PLAY. One of the most striking occurrences during the preschool years is the development of **play.** Although children often may play alone, as they grow older play becomes more of a social phenomenon (Cooper, 1977; Hartup, 1983). Playing can be simple and unstructured, as in a game of hide-and-seek, or it can be more complex and structured, as in a school basketball game.

Social scientists generally believe that play has evolved because it has a function (Vandenberg, 1978). It may be that playing with objects, playing make-believe, or playing together at various games helps children to become skilled at manipulating objects (Cheyne & Rubin, 1983), to learn adult roles, or, once they are grown, to cooperate while dealing with serious and complex tasks. Some ethologists have argued that there is an **exploration-play-application sequence** found in humans and in the more advanced animals (Vandenberg, 1978; Wilson, 1975).

When children are confronted with an extremely novel toy, they tend to explore it before playing with it (Belsky & Most, 1981; Vandenberg, 1984). It's as though they want to be sure that it is safe before they play (Weisler & McCall, 1976). This same kind of exploration-before-play sequence has also been observed in chimpanzees (Loizos, 1967; Mason, 1965).

During play, the skills necessary for serious application are acquired. For example, it has been found that chimpanzees need to spend time playing with sticks before they can use sticks for purposeful applications such as food gathering (Birch, 1945; Schiller, 1957). Researchers have found similar play-before-application sequences while investigating human children (Sylva, Bruner, & Genova, 1976; Vandenberg, 1978).

MIDDLE CHILDHOOD (6 TO 12 YEARS OF AGE)

Middle childhood is a time of continued physical growth and motor development. Until school-aged children reach puberty, their rate of growth is relatively steady. Both sexes gain an average of about 7 pounds in weight and about 2 to 3 inches in height each year. On average, girls and boys perform physically at about the same level, at least until the beginning of puberty.

Cognitive Development in Middle Childhood

According to Jean Piaget, at about the time children enter school, they develop the ability to rely on logic or logical operations to form their conclusions. This is known as the *concrete operations stage.* Children in this period are able to use logical rules to deal with problems. How children acquire a logical understanding of the world is not clear, but they seem to do it rather abruptly. During the stage of concrete operations, children's thought processes become more competent, flexible, and powerful, as the children come to understand and apply the concept of **conservation.**

Children are able to conserve when they grasp that the amount of a material does not change unless something is added or taken away, even though its form or distribution may change. For this reason, conserving children will not be fooled by apparent changes in the amount of water when the water is transferred from a container of one shape to one of another shape. They will understand that during these transfers, no water has been added or taken away and that therefore the amount of water remains the same. The amount is conserved despite the change in shape.

CONSERVATION
The principle that quantities such as mass, weight, and volume remain constant regardless of changes in the appearance of these quantities, so long as nothing has been added or taken away.

TABLE 11.4 How Children Establish an Initial Relationship

CATEGORY	EXAMPLE
Information exhange:	
Success	A: What's this?
	B: This is my room righ here. This is my farm here. Look how very, very large.
Failure	A: How come we can't get this off?
	B: You know, I'm gonna get the rolling pin so we can roll this.
Common-ground activity:	
Success: A joint activity is successfully initiated.	A: And you make those for after we get in together, okay?
	B: 'Kay.
	A: Have to make those.
	B: Pretend like those little roll cookies, I mean.
	A: And make, um, make a, um, pancake too.
	B: Oh, rats, this is a little pancake.
	A: Yeah, let's play house.
	B: Okay, play house.
Failure: Initiation is ignored, or disagreed with; activity does not develop	A: Let's play house.
	B: Nope, nope, nope, nope, nope, nope.
	A: Because you're coloring that brick wall?
	B: Yep.
Conflict	A: This is stretchy.
	B: No, it's not.
	A: Uh huh.
	B: Yes.
	A: Uh huh.
	B: It's dirty.
	A: Uh uh.
	B: Uh huh.
	A: Uh uh.
	B: Uh huh.
	A: Uh uh.
	B: Uh huh.
	A: Uh uh. It's not dirty.

SOURCE: Adapted from Gottman, 1983, pp. 27, 53–54.

Piaget stated that the ability to conserve marks the end of the preoperational stage and the beginning of concrete operations. The major difference between the preoperational and concrete stages is not that children can no longer be tricked by problems that require conservation but that children are beginning to use logical operations and rules rather than intuition. This change is viewed as a shift from reliance on perception to a reliance on logic, and it is a giant leap.

Social–Emotional Development in Middle Childhood

During middle childhood, many institutions have an influence on a child's socialization. Among them are the family, peers, schools, and even nonpersonal institutions, such as the media, including television. While the preschool-aged child relies mostly on her parents for information about the world, the school-aged child has much wider and varied social interactions, partly as a result of increased autonomy, and partly because of increased competencies. Figure 11.8 outlines the amount of time spent by school-aged children in various tasks. As you can see, the most common activities in this age group are sleeping, going to school, and watching television.

PEER RELATIONSHIPS.   For the school-aged child, peer relationships both in and out of school become extremely important. Being accepted by one's peers and belonging to peer groups are major concerns.

Between the ages of 7 and 9 years, children generally form close friendships with peers of the same sex and age (Roopnarine & Johnson, 1984). School-aged children have, on the average, about five best friends (Hartup, 1984). After the eighth grade, however, it is not uncommon for adolescents to have a friend of the opposite sex (Buhrmester & Furman, 1987). The older children become, the more they are likely to share with friends (Berndt, Hawkins, & Hoyle, 1986) and the more they come to value friends by personal attributes. For instance, one study found that whereas 5 1/2-year-old children might be more interested in making friends with another child who had a new game or toy, 9-year-old children were more interested in making friends with another child because "he's real nice" (Boggiano, Klinger, & Main, 1986).

Throughout the school years, children also rely on their peers as important sources of information and may use peers as standards by which to measure themselves. By the age of 7 or 8 years, children tend to look to their peers as models of behavior and for social reinforcement as often as they look to their own families. Research has also shown that by the fourth grade, children have come to rely on friends as an important source of social and moral support (Berndt & Perry, 1986).

ADULT VERSUS PEER INFLUENCE. The desire to interact with peers grows throughout childhood. By the age of 10 or 11 years, children view peer friendships as extremely important. If a child's peers exhibit values and behaviors that conflict with those espoused by the child's family, challenges to parental authority and serious family arguments may occur (Elkind, 1971). Generally, however, there is remarkable agreement between a child's peers and family members in terms of accepted values and behaviors (Douvan & Adelson, 1966; Hartup, 1970). This is probably because children are socialized first by their families, and they later choose playmates and friends who hold values similar to those they have been taught.

Parents face two problems when trying to control peer influence. First, as children grow older and spend less time at home, parents may find that they have less influence and that any attempts to control only drive the child toward a greater peer orientation. In fact, by adolescence, the average child will spend more than twice as much time with peers as with parents (Condry, Siman, & Bronfenbrenner, 1968).

The second problem faced by parents who wish to control the influence of peers is that of overcontrol. Overcontrolling children by limiting their social contacts may inadvertently keep them from developing adequate social skills or the confidence to interact in groups. Children who are unable to interact with peers and

FIGURE 11.8

Amount of time per week spent by school-aged children in various tasks. (Source: Adapted from Collins, 1984, p. 18.)

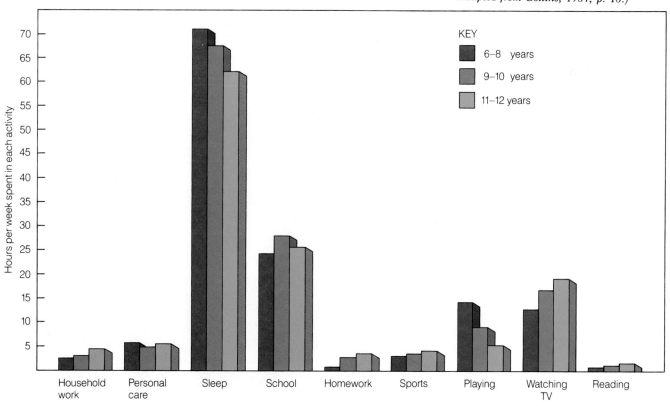

who are not well liked by them often show signs of emotional maladjustment (Hartup, 1970), and they are more likely to suffer from mental disorders as adults (Roff, 1963). It should be noted, however, that these last two observations are correlational and that children who are emotionally maladjusted may have trouble forming friendships in the first place. Consequently, it cannot be said that there is proof that being unpopular with peers or finding it hard to interact with peers *causes* emotional maladjustment.

THE INFLUENCE OF TELEVISION.   Television has been shown to have a great influence on the development of school-age children. American children between the ages of 5 and 13 years spend more time watching television than they spend in any other waking leisure activity! (again, see Figure 11.8) (Liebert & Sprafkin, 1988). These findings may not be quite as alarming as they may seem, because careful analysis shows that of the time that school-age children spend in front of the television, only about two-thirds is actually spent watching. The rest of the time is devoted to other activities (Anderson et al., 1986). Still, television is so wide ranging in its content that it probably has both a detrimental and a beneficial effect on children (Singer & Singer, 1983a; Liebert & Sprafkin, 1988).

Television has changed the way we live and the way we carry on our family life. Just having a television set in the house affects family interaction patterns (Parke, 1978). Although families spend time together watching television, they spend less time directly engaging in activities with one another than they used to (Lyle, 1971). Some people have joked that you can spot a television-oriented family because none of the conversations family members have with one another ever lasts longer than the average commercial. Children, especially, can isolate themselves in front of the tube for hours.

Heavy viewing of violent television programs has been consistently associated with aggression in both children and adults (Liebert & Sprafkin, 1988). In general, heavy television viewing is associated with poor school achievement (Rubinstein, 1983). Heavy viewing also is associated with poorer reading comprehension (Singer & Singer, 1983a). Interestingly, for children of lower socioeconomic status, heavy television viewing has been associated with *higher* reading comprehension and higher scholastic achievement. Television viewing, therefore, appears to have a

Television is so wide ranging in its content that it probably has both a detrimental and a beneficial effect on children.

leveling effect, often raising the abilities of disadvantaged children, while lowering the abilities of children of higher socioeconomic status (Morgan & Gross, 1982; Gerbner, Gross, Morgan, & Signorielli, 1980). Heavy television viewing also is associated with poorer language usage (Singer & Singer, 1983b) and appears to inhibit the development of imagination.

Television also influences children's concepts of gender roles. Children who watch more television tend to view the male and female roles in a more sterotypic fashion (Williams, 1986). Television also shapes what is called "world knowledge." By being exposed to television, children form attitudes and beliefs about their world. This is a good thing insofar as television reflects reality. To the extent that it doesn't, this exposure can cause problems. For example, children who are heavy viewers of television, especially of realistic action shows such as police dramas, tend to view the world as a mean and scary place and as more dangerous than it really is (Rubinstein, 1983). Television instills a certain paranoia in these children and may make them more fearful and less trusting of other people.

On the other hand, television has the real potential for having a positive influence on children. Television may be providing a great deal of *good* information and exposure to ideas and events. For the first time children, no matter how distant from major centers their homes are, are growing up learning about events on the entire planet. Television may thus broaden horizons and stimulate the curiosity of millions of children who would not otherwise have known what the world might hold for them. Also, certain educational goals can be pursued through programs particularly designed for children.

Studies have shown that children can acquire good nutritional habits from television programs designed to teach such habits (Campbell, 1982), and that children can learn to help other people or to give to charity from watching such behavior modeled on television. They can also learn to cooperate, to share, and to be imaginative under certain conditions, all from being exposed to particular television shows (Pearl, Bouthilet, & Lazar, 1982). Appropriate television programming can enhance friendliness and generosity. It can help children learn to delay immediate gratification as well as to overcome fears of strange and unusual situations (Rubinstein, 1983). So, television certainly has its "good side."

ADOLESCENCE (12 TO 18 YEARS OF AGE)

In some cultures there is no social period of adolescence. There are only childhood and adulthood. In such cultures, when a child enters puberty, it is a sign that he or she has become an adult. In many groups and tribes throughout the world, the social change from childhood to adulthood happens in a single day. For instance, a boy might be summoned by his elders, along with other children his age, and taken to a place where a ceremony is conducted that marks his passage into adulthood. Such a ceremony is called a *rite of passage*.

For American children, the transition to adulthood is slow, marked by many separate changes over the period of adolescence. A 12-year-old girl may be allowed to wear nylons and makeup, a 16-year-old person may be allowed a driver's license, an 18-year-old person may marry or vote, and in many states individuals must be 21 years old to drink alcoholic beverages. For this reason, adolescents often count smoking, drinking, driving, and sexual activities as indications of adult status. The physical changes that occur during adolescence also mark an important transition from childhood to adulthood.

PUBERTY
The stage of maturation in which the individual becomes physiologically capable of sexual reproduction.

Storm and Stress?

In 1904, G. Stanley Hall published the first scientific study of adolescence in a two-volume work titled *Adolescence,* and they had a tremendous influence on subsequent thought on the subject. Hall saw adolescence as a period of *storm and stress,* of many changes in direction and swings in mood, of turbulence and turmoil. There are many changes that adolescents must face, and these experiences may alter considerably their self-concept and attitudes (McKinney & Moore, 1982). Adolescents must deal for the first time with sexual relationships, the choice of a career, political decisions, economic alternatives, and a host of other "adult" tasks.

Modern researchers, even though they recognize that there are many tasks and changes taking place in adolescents' lives, have come to the conclusion that adolescence isn't necessarily a time of unusual turbulence and conflict. The conclusion of an 8-year nationwide study conducted at the University of Michigan of 2000 adolescent males as they went from tenth grade to the age of 20 years was that adolescence was fairly benign. The study revealed that self-concept, outlook on life, and a number of other attitudes were well formed by the time adolescents entered tenth grade. Moreover, when the subjects were retested at age 20 years, their attitudes were found not to have undergone the dramatic changes that might be expected following a turbulent adolescence (Bachman, O'Malley, & Johnston, 1978). Other studies have confirmed these findings (Offer, Ostrov, & Howard, 1981; Petersen, 1987). According to one group of researchers,

> The most dramatic . . . findings are those that permit us to characterize the model American teenager as feeling confident, happy, and self-satisfied—a portrait of the American adolescent that contrasts sharply with that drawn by many theorists of adolescent development, who contend that adolescence is pervaded with turmoil, dramatic mood swings, and rebellion. (Offer, Ostrov, & Howard, 1981, pp. 83–84)

Physical Growth in Adolescence

Behind each maturational change lies the development of essential cells within the brain and body. Every aspect of a child—her emotions, skills, and aptitudes—is related either directly or indirectly to her body structure. Feelings about body image underlie many social interactions. This is especially true during adolescence, when many obvious physical changes occur (Chumlea, 1982). Psychologists need to be aware of this physical growth and development and especially of the effects these changes may have on a person's emotions or behavior. In fact, everyone should have a better understanding of the physical changes that take place during adolescence, to understand better an adolescent's feelings and behavior. For instance, although most people know that girls mature earlier than boys, few people give much thought to the fact that adolescents of the same age and sex may vary from completely prepubescent to completely physically mature (see Figure 11.9). Yet the timing of physical development can profoundly affect adolescents and their interactions with peers and the school environment.

At the beginning of adolescence, a number of physical changes occur. These changes are controlled by genetics and hormones. One change is the development of sexual maturity, which occurs during a period called **puberty.** Researchers have found that the hormone melatonin, which is secreted by the pineal gland, is responsible for the onset of puberty. As puberty nears, melatonin concentrations show a marked decrease (Waldhauser et al., 1984).

At the onset of puberty, the testes or ovaries enlarge. During puberty, the reproductive system matures, and secondary sexual characteristics such as facial hair or breast development emerge. Growth also undergoes a marked acceleration.

FIGURE 11.9

Differing degrees of pubertal development in children of the same sex at the same chronological age (in years). (Source: Adapted from Tanner, 1969.)

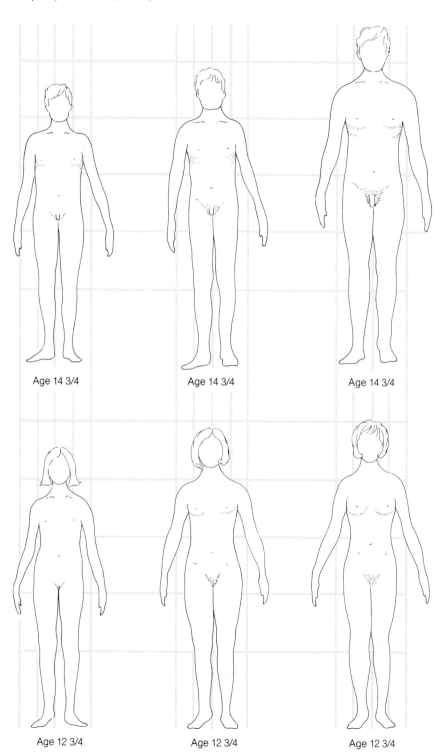

Age 14 3/4   Age 14 3/4   Age 14 3/4

Age 12 3/4   Age 12 3/4   Age 12 3/4

Height and weight increase dramatically, and body proportions change. These changes are known as the **growth spurt.** It begins in girls about 2 years earlier than it does in boys, and it lasts for 2 to 3 years.

Cognitive Development in Adolescence

In most individuals, the ability to reason and to think becomes fully developed during adolescence. Erik Erikson (1968) has described adolescence as a time of identity crisis when the questions "Who am I?" and "What is my role in life?" become dominant themes. Without the cognitive changes that occur, it would not be possible for adolescents to consider such complex philosophical questions.

The adolescent first becomes capable of dealing with the logic of combinations, which requires the simultaneous manipulation of many factors, either singly or in conjunction with one another. Second, the adolescent becomes able to use abstract concepts to make thought more flexible. Third, the adolescent becomes able to deal with the hypothetical as well as the real (Piaget & Inhelder, 1969). According to Piaget, this last step is the most advanced form of cognition, and it defines the *formal operations stage.*

Preadolescent thinking appears to depend substantially on concrete perceptions. Adolescents can analyze the logic of a statement without becoming tied to its concrete properties. In a series of experiments, adolescents and preadolescents were asked to judge whether certain statements were true, false, or impossible to know (Osherson & Markman, 1974–75). The subjects were told that the experimenter had hidden a poker chip in his hand, and that "either this chip is green, or it is not green." Most of the preadolescents thought that it was impossible to judge because they could not see the hidden chip. The adolescents, however, were able to deal with the concept of green abstractly. They realized that something must either be a particular color or not be that color. The adolescents realized that the statement had to be true. For that matter, everything in the universe is either green or not green. Preadolescents have trouble comprehending such an abstraction. This is one of the reasons why educators usually wait until children reach adolescence before they seriously present them with abstractions such as algebra.

Alternative Views of Cognitive Development

Without a doubt, Jean Piaget contributed immeasurably to our knowledge of cognitive development in children. His theories have had a wide influence on education and psychology. Throughout the years, however, people have proposed some strong arguments against Piaget's view—especially researchers in the United States.

In the mid-twentieth century, the learning theorists' view was paramount among American psychologists. Proponents of behaviorism, such as John Watson and B. F. Skinner, took a different approach from Piaget's to explain a child's cognitive development. In their view, development was not driven from *within* by the biological development of the child as she interacted with her surroundings, but rather was added to from *without.* In other words, behaviorists believe that cognitive development is the result of *learning.* They argued forcefully that there were no stages of cognitive development, but rather that cognitive development was a gradual and continuous process.

Researchers also have criticized specific aspects of Piaget's theory. For example, many studies have indicated that supposedly egocentric preoperational children are often quite able to deal with another person's viewpoint (Hart & Goldin-Meadow, 1984; Mossler, Marvin, & Greenberg, 1976; Shatz, 1973). Also, with careful study, object permanence has been observed in infants as young as 3 1/2 months old

(Baillargeon, 1987), and infants of only 14 months of age have shown that they can imitate something unusual that they saw an adult do a full week after having seen it (Meltzoff, 1988). These findings are at some odds with Piaget's assertion that the sensorimotor period is a time in which object permanence is absent. Keep in mind, however, that although Piaget is dead, his theory isn't necessarily complete. During his lifetime, Piaget was his own greatest revisionist (Block, 1982). He changed old ideas for new and reorganized his thinking many times. No doubt this theory will continue to be developed and changed by the work of today's researchers and of future ones.

Currently, the issue remains unresolved, but many theorists have concluded that there is some merit to both Piaget's view and learning theory (Fischer & Silvern, 1985). Piaget may have demonstrated what is *typical* under usual environmental and developmental conditions—that is, what, is *probable*. When modern theorists talk about stages of cognitive development, they often use the term **probabilistic epigenesis** (Gottlieb, 1983) to refer to the fact that stages describe only the typical or most likely development. In fact, researchers currently like to use the word *level* instead of *stage*, when referring to a child's cognitive development, because *stage* has a rigid, inflexible connotation. Table 11.5 outlines the levels of cognitive development that best represent a consensus among most researchers (Fischer & Silvern, 1985).

Developmental Tasks of Adolescence

As their cognitive skills develop, adolescents are confronted for the first time with the overwhelming complexities and abstract qualities of the world. Suddenly, nothing is simple. Religious values, political values, social concepts, and questions about personal identity seem to raise endless hypothetical possibilities from which the adolescent is expected by parents and society to draw conclusions and to adopt a life philosophy. During our adult years, we have time to organize and make sense of this confusion. We adopt a philosophy. We take political, social, and moral positions and incorporate them into our identity. In this sense, adulthood has a stability that is not immediately available to the adolescent.

Our culture demands that adolescents handle a number of developmental tasks. They must come to terms with their physical development. They must face sexual relationships. They must exhibit social maturity in dealings with both sexes. They must realize and adjust satisfactorily to their masculine and feminine role. They must achieve emotional independence from parents and other adults. Decisions about whether to marry or to have children become more immediate. Adolescents are expected, therefore, to develop a philosophy and moral ideology, and to achieve socially responsible behavior (Havighurst, 1972). Sometimes they feel as though all these demands are pressing in on them at the same time, which can be particularly stressful.

CHOOSING A CAREER. Pursuing a career choice is an essential part of adolescent development. "The adolescent becomes an adult when he undertakes a real job" (Inhelder & Piaget, 1958, p. 346). To cognitive researchers such as Piaget, adulthood meant serious training for work and the beginning of an occupation.

Piaget argued that once adolescents enter the formal operations stage, their newly acquired ability to form hypotheses allows them to create representations that are too ideal. The existence of such ideals, without the tempering of the reality of a job or profession, leads adolescents rapidly to become intolerant of the non-idealistic world and to press for reform and change in a characteristically idealistic and adolescent way. Piaget said:

Adolescents often discover that the ideal representations of the world they have developed through formal operational thinking are tempered by the realities of their first real job.

True adaptation to society comes automatically when the adolescent reformer attempts to put his ideas to work. Just as experience reconciles formal thought with the reality of things, so does effective and enduring work, undertaken in concrete and well-defined situations, cure dreams. (Piaget, 1967, pp. 68–69)

Of course, youthful idealism is often courageous and true, and no one likes to give up dreams. Perhaps, taken slightly out of context, as it is here, Piaget's quote seems harsh. What he was emphasizing, however, is the way reality can modify and shape idealistic views. Some people refer to such modification as maturity. Piaget argued that attaining and accepting a vocation is one of the best ways to modify idealized views and to mature.

As careers and vocations become less available during times of recession, lowered productivity, or rising unemployment, adolescents may be especially hard hit. Such difficult economic times may leave many adolescents confused about their roles in society. For this reason, community interventions and government job programs that offer summer and vacation work are not only economically beneficial but also,

---

TABLE 11.5 A General Consensus of the Levels of Cognitive Development

COGNITIVE LEVEL	DESCRIPTION	AVERAGE AGE OF CHILD AT FIRST APPEARANCE
1. Sensorimotor actions	Adaptation of single action (child looks at a face; grasps a rattle).	2–4 months
2. Sensorimotor relations	Differentiation of a means from an end (child moves object aside in order to reach for toy).	7–8 months
3. Sensorimotor systems	Organization of schemes into a cognitive system—actions and events no longer are treated as unrelated or isolated (child knows that a rattle will make the same noise regardless of which action is used to shake it); actions also unified to make first words.	11–13 months
4. Representations	Symbolization of objects, events, and people independent of any particular action by the child (child displays rapid growth of language; pretend play.)	18–24 months
5. Simple relations of representations	Coordination of two or more ideas in a single skill (child can take the perspective of another and relate it to her own; can perform simplified versions of Piaget's concrete operations tasks).	4–5 years
6. Concrete operations	Combination of multiple representations to form complex constructs (child understands the constructs of conservation, seriation, classification, and numeration and is able to complete Piaget's standard tasks for concrete operations).	6–8 years
7. Early formal operations	Generalization from the concrete to construct abstract or hypothetical ideas (child is able to understand the concepts of justice, liberty, personality, conformity).	10–12 years
8. Relations of abstract generalizations	Coordination of abstractions (child can deal with relational concepts, such as liberal or conservative; she can create new abstract ideas; she is able to complete most of Piaget's formal operations tasks).	14–16 years
9. ???	Continuation of cognitive development clearly continues after the age of 16 years (Kitchener, 1982), but it is not yet certain that such development meets the criteria for a new level or levels of cognitive development.	

SOURCE: Adapted from Fischer & Silvern, 1985, pp. 633–636.

in the view of the many developmental psychologists, help to stimulate adolescent ego development (Vondracek & Lerner, 1982).

ADDRESSING THE CRISIS OF IDENTITY.   According to Erik Erikson, the adolescent's main task is to develop an acceptable, functional, and stable self-concept. Those who succeed, Erikson argues, will establish a sense of identity, and those who fail will suffer **role confusion.** Erikson believes that the adolescent needs to maintain a meaningful connection with the past, establish relatively stable goals for the future, and keep up adequate interpersonal relationships in the present in order to feel a sense of personal identity. "The adolescent needs to integrate a conscious sense of individual uniqueness" with "an unconscious striving for a continuity of experience" (Erikson, 1968, p. 165).

Other psychologists have found the concept of identity a valuable tool for understanding adolescent psychosocial development. Research and case studies have indicated that resolution of the identity crisis depends greatly on the adolescent's society, family, and peer groups. Ideally, adolescents achieve their new identity by abandoning some of the values and aspirations set for them by their parents and society, while accepting those that they choose to accept.

The Peer Group

Peer groups provide an important social structure for most adolescents (Brown, Eicher, & Petrie, 1986). Adolescent peer groups vary in size and interests, and adolescents often belong to more than one group at a time. Peer groups may consist of a few close friends of the same sex or a large group of both sexes who hang out together. Such groups can be sources of ready companionship, adventure, and standards against which adolescents compare themselves. As a result, a peer group can have a powerful effect. Its influence on adolescents is a worldwide phenomenon (B. M. Newman, 1982).

To become or stay a member of a desired peer group, an adolescent needs a certain amount of social skill or desirability. Adolescents who lack social skills or who are deemed socially undesirable by their peers may find themselves living a lonely or isolated existence, and eventually they may be adversely affected by the experience. To avoid such rejection, adolescents may go to extremes to please a group. They may radically change their dress, appearance, behavior, or jargon. Adolescents who attempt to adjust to a group that has views opposed to those held by their families may face considerable conflict and stress (P. R. Newman, 1982).

A peer group may function as a reference against which adolescents compare themselves (Petersen & Taylor, 1980). Quite often, differences between an individual and the group are resolved by the person's decision to change behavior to match the group's norms. The group can influence susceptible teenagers either to perform or to avoid misconduct (Brown, Clasen, & Eicher, 1986). It has been shown, however, that peers are less likely to encourage misconduct than they are other types of behavior (Brown, Lohr, & McClenahan, 1986).

Adolescents' evaluations of themselves may have a great bearing on which peer group or group behaviors they find most important and desirable (Eisert & Kahle, 1982). One study discovered that college students (mean age 18.95 years) who evaluated themselves as having high self-esteem chose groups to join and emulate that were composed of students of high socioeconomic status (Filsinger & Anderson, 1982). This is not a one-way street, however; the groups with whom adolescents choose to compare themselves can, in turn, directly affect an adolescent's self-evaluation. No doubt, the students who associated and became friends with high-status peers further enhanced their own self-esteem.

ROLE CONFUSION
An individual's confusion about his or her role in society as a consequence, according to Erikson, of the failure to establish a sense of identity during the fifth psychosocial stage. Without a sense of identity, a person has difficulty forming a life philosophy or creating a stable basis on which to build a career or have a family.

EARLY ADULTHOOD (18 TO 40 YEARS OF AGE)

Young adults face many choices and predicaments in our society. They have to make decisions about sexuality, marriage, children, career, friendships, social and civic interactions, and much more. They undergo changes in cognitive and intellectual functioning that may affect this decision-making process.

Physical Changes in Early Adulthood

By the time people reach early adulthood, their growth typically is completed, but their potential for greater strength increases during early adulthood and reaches a plateau at about age 30 years (Troll, 1975). Yet life experiences are more important than age in this respect, because very few people reach their peak strength potential by age 30 years or at any other time. Between the ages of 20 and 30 years, strength usually reflects lifestyle rather than age. Many men and women are stronger than their age-mates because of exercise. On the average, by age 60 years, a person has lost about 10 percent of muscle strength relative to the peak potential at 30 (Bischof, 1976). But because most people are never at their peak, this loss usually goes unnoticed.

Peoples' speed of reaction, which increases throughout childhood and adolescence, reaches a plateau at about age 20 years, where it remains until it begins a gradual decline at age 26 years (Hodgkins, 1962).

At 30 years of age, people also may experience a sensory decline, resulting in slightly poorer vision and hearing than they had as adolescents, but these differences do not have a significant effect on quality of life (Marshall, 1973). In fact, many of the physical changes that occur during early adulthood are of this small magnitude.

Marriage and Parenthood

Today, the structure of relationships between many young adults is markedly different from that in their parents' day. Significant numbers of these young adults are postponing marriage or are planning to remain single. However, the data suggest that over 90 percent of American adults marry at some point in their lives (Glick, 1977). Marriage is therefore still an extremely important social institution, although more young adults tend to live together or cohabit before marriage than did people in previous times.

Many more men and women in their twenties today express the desire not to have children. This decision appears easier for people to reach in their twenties, because they have plenty of time to change their minds. As they reach their mid-thirties, couples without children often review the decision more seriously.

Like marriage, parenthood has undergone changes with time. The most impressive trend has been a reduction of the number of children per couple, rather than a choice to have no children at all (Doherty & Jacobson, 1982). Young adults who married in the 1970s have an average of only two children, whereas couples who married in the 1950s have an average of three or four children (Glick, 1979).

New parents may face a number of surprises that can lead to stress or difficulty. Our society provides little formal training for parenthood. The average person is given more training in how to handle a new car than in how to handle a new baby, even though the baby is infinitely more complex than the car (and can't be left unattended for long periods in the family garage). Training for parenthood usually is limited to informal family discussions or to information obtained from local libraries. Such information is useful, but it really doesn't prepare a couple for the stark reality of a newborn baby. With the joy comes the realization that parents are on call 24 hours a day for their completely helpless infant. Their ability to adjust to these new demands is highly personal and may depend on many circumstances. If the infant cries often and disrupts the parents' sleep, if the parents are unable to adjust to sleep loss, if they hadn't planned on the child in the first place, or if they feel that "three's a crowd," serious problems may arise, as you can well imagine (Blood, 1972).

Most parents, however, succeed in making the transition to parenthood, handle the stress, and obtain both joy and a sense of pride and accomplishment from their parental duties (Clayton, 1975). It is a good idea for young adults to examine in detail what parenthood requires. If the negative aspects don't come as a surprise and are accepted as a reasonable trade for the happiness that parenthood can bring, the transition from two to three members of the family can be fairly smooth and enjoyable.

Planning for a Career

One of the most important tasks facing young adults is choosing a career. In the last few decades, career planning has become a more complex task (Shertzer & Stone, 1976). There are more careers for men and women now because new fields of specialization are constantly emerging. The reason choices are more complex and difficult these days is that almost everyone now has an opportunity to try a hand at almost any career. Careers have become more accessible than ever before. Gone are the days when only the rich could apply to college, or when a son was certain to learn his father's trade, or when careers were determined by which nearby tradesman happened to need an apprentice-helper. Just consider the number of careers open to those people who graduate from high school each year, especially if they have good grades. Sometimes the possibilities are overwhelming, and people aren't sure what they want to do. In fact, trying out different jobs is becoming more common (Bernard & Fullmer, 1977).

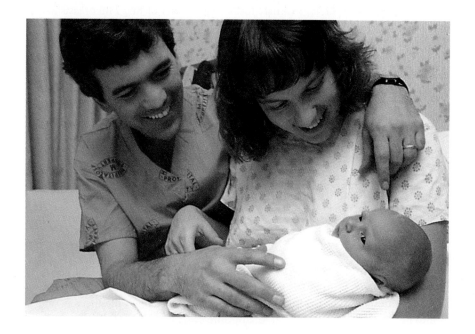

Most young parents succeed in making the transition to parenthood and obtain both joy and a sense of pride and accomplishment from their parental duties.

MIDDLE ADULTHOOD (40 TO 65 YEARS OF AGE)

Youth is idolized by the media and the public as a representation of vitality, health, and sexual viability. But middle age is often a time when the rewards of power, money, and prestige are more apparent. Although it's not uncommon for people to report some depression on their fortieth birthday, since culture reveres youth, it's the middle-aged who have the power.

This chapter defines middle age as 40 to 65 years of age, but the term is defined differently by different groups and by men and women. Social class can influence a person's definition of middle age. Blue-collar workers, whose jobs often are more physical than those of white-collar workers, consider middle age to begin at about 35 years of age, whereas white-collar workers, especially those pursuing an executive career, may think of middle age as beginning at 50 years of age (Neugarten & Peterson, 1957). Men may measure the passage of time by their careers, whereas women may measure middle age by when their children are grown and leave the family (Neugarten, 1968). Of course, these perceptions are based on the social-sexual role assigned to or chosen by individual men and women in our culture. Based on statistics of the average lifespan divided into thirds, middle age includes the time between the ages of 25 and 50 years (B. M. Newman, 1982).

Physical Changes in Middle Adulthood

In our culture, youth is most admired. As middle age progresses, many adults look back wistfully at their lost youth (Nowak, 1977). Most of their sense of loss is the result of changes in appearance rather than physical decline. Deeper, longer lines appear on the face and gray hairs become more numerous. Although some changes in speed, strength, and endurance do occur, they usually aren't obvious unless the adult is an athlete (Belbin, 1967).

Middle-aged women pass through menopause between the ages of 45 and 55. The sudden decrease in sex hormone levels may cause physical changes during this time. For example, women may have hot flashes—sudden episodes of an overheated, shaky, faint feeling, similar to the rapid onset of flu. The breasts and genitals may undergo changes because of lost fluid, moisture, or elasticity.

The amount of anxiety that a woman may feel concerning menopause depends on her desire to have more children, her attitude about growing older, and her concern about changes in her health as a result of menopause (B. M. Newman, 1982). If she has sufficient medical information, is no longer concerned about having children, and believes she is leading an active life with the support of those around her, then anxiety associated with menopause may be minimal or non-existent. In fact, younger women generally are more concerned about menopause than are older women who have passed through it (Neugarten, Wood, Kraines, & Loomis, 1963). There is no similar, rapid decrease in sex hormone levels in men. Instead, testosterone decreases gradually with age.

Midlife Crisis

During middle age, most adults become acutely aware that they have less time left to live than they have already lived. The question "What will I do when I'm grown up?" which may have been posed for 30 years or more, is replaced by a concern that time is running out or that there's less time left to make one's life the way one wants it to be. Such feelings may lead to a **midlife crisis** in which adults reevaluate their lives in the light of a time limit. They may no longer tolerate unsatisfactory conditions. Marriages that have lasted 20 years suddenly may dissolve; careers may be abandoned; and social relationships may be drastically altered. A person's fear of illness or death may become so acute that health problems actually occur. Or the desire to have "one last fling" may cause an adult to embark on an extramarital affair that she or he might never have considered earlier.

Although the notion of a midlife crisis is popular, most middle-aged adults do not have one, and instead express feelings of self-confidence and achievement. Nearly every adult becomes anxious, at one time or another, about the approach of old age or children "leaving the nest." But such realizations needn't precipitate a life crisis.

The Empty Nest

Many studies have examined issues that women may face during middle age. Among these is the belief that once children are grown and leave home, a mother is likely to become depressed at "the empty nest." This belief is rooted in the idea that a woman's role is mother and caregiver for the "nest." Once the nest is empty, it would seem natural for depression to follow.

In a study of 160 middle-aged women, Lillian Rubin investigated the **empty nest syndrome.** All women in the study had children who were leaving or had left home, all the women had given up jobs for at least 10 years following the birth of a child, and a majority were still homemakers. Rubin reported that "except for one, none of these women suffers from the classical symptoms of empty nest syndrome. In fact, just about all of them responded to the departure of the children with a decided sense of relief . . . although a few were ambivalent when the time of departure came close" (Rubin, cited in Greenberg, 1978b, p. 75).

The virtual disappearance of the empty nest syndrome (if it ever existed significantly in the first place) is probably due to the opportunities afforded today's women once they have finished raising children. A large number of women in Rubin's study returned to work or school after their children had left home. In a study of over 300 women between the ages of 40 and 59, those who worked out of the home reported having higher self-esteem, less psychological anxiety, and better health than did those who did not work outside (Coleman & Antonucci, 1983).

LATE ADULTHOOD (65 OR MORE YEARS OF AGE)

Late adulthood is a period of highly personal adjustment. People must adjust to physical changes that begin to interfere with daily activities and to retirement or reduced income. Perhaps most difficult of all is adjustment to the inevitable death of friends, relatives, or a spouse. A survey conducted for the National Council on Aging, however, showed that the American public's expectations of problems associated with aging were much worse than were the actual problems experienced by older Americans (see Figure 11.10). Like menopause, old age is consistently viewed more negatively by people who have not yet achieved it than by those who have (Kogan & Shelton, 1962; Kastenbaum & Durkee, 1964; Serock, Seefeldt, Jantz, & Galper, 1977).

Other misconceptions that finally are beginning to collapse include the view that the elderly are "childlike" and should be treated as such, that people past the retirement age can no longer contribute to society, and that age and illness are synonymous.

EMPTY NEST SYNDROME
Depression generally in women, brought on at the time their grown children leave home.

INTELLECTUAL DEGENERATiON
A permanent and serious loss of
intellectual functioning because of illness
or trauma, often referred to as senility. It is
not the normal result of the aging process.

ALZHEIMER'S DISEASE
An incurable disease of unknown cause,
more common among the aged, that
results in severe brain degeneration and
death; it is characterized by increasing
distortion and disruption of intellectual
and motor functions as the disease
progresses.

In general, the more older adults can find satisfaction within a family or social group, and, the more they can obtain a sense of continuity with the past, the more enjoyable and rewarding they are likely to find later years.

Physical Changes in Late Adulthood

As people reach their later years, their skin loses elasticity and moisture, and wrinkling increases. Bone structure changes; bones become brittle, and older persons actually may get shorter. The body slows down. The kidneys don't filter the blood as well, the lungs have less capacity, the nerves conduct impulses at a slower velocity, the basal metabolic rate decreases, and the cardiac output at rest is less efficient (see Table 11.6). The senses also react to aging by becoming less acute.

Some cognitive and intellectual abilities may decline irreversibly owing to **intellectual degeneration,** but this occurs only in a minority of the elderly. Intellectual degeneration is a term used to describe the severe breakdown of intellectual functioning that may occur among the aged for a number of reasons. This breakdown used to be referred to as *senility,* but senility too often was misunderstood to be a single disease, whereas, in fact, it is a catchall term for many different problems that may result in intellectual degeneration.

Alzheimer's disease probably is the most common reason for severe intellectual degeneration and is one of the leading causes of death. This serious disease should not be confused with the small memory loss and forgetfulness that may occur with advancing age. Or, as someone once said, Alzheimer's isn't forgetting where your keys are, it's forgetting what keys are for. Alzheimer's disease is neither a normal occurrence, nor the natural result of aging. The majority of older adults never suffer from it. The disease may also strike younger people, even teenagers, although this is quite rare.

Sex and the Elderly

Besides the idea that age typically brings on intellectual degeneration, there are other myths associated with aging. One is that sexuality wanes to such a degree

FIGURE 11.10

In a Harris poll taken among the general American public and among the elderly, the general public's expectations of serious problems in old age were much worse than were the actual problems experienced by the elderly. (Source: Derived from National Council on Aging, 1981.)

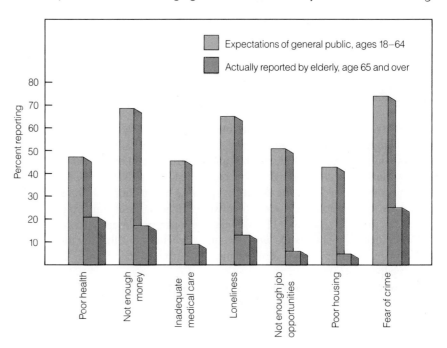

The more older adults can find satisfaction within a family or social group and the more they can obtain a sense of continuity with the past, the more enjoyable and rewarding they are likely to find their later years.

that sex among older adults is rare or unnatural. This myth is beginning to fade with education.

In a sense, the twentieth century can be considered an age of sexual enlightenment because of the scientific research into human sexuality conducted by such investigators as Kinsey, and Masters and Johnson. Before their studies, many people were taught by church, family, and peers that sex was proper only for procreation. Obviously, in light of such a belief, both a woman who was past menopause and her husband were considered immoral if they still engaged in sex.

Add to these views the emphasis on youth in our culture, which has made many younger adults see sexual relations among the elderly as unesthetic, and you can see how such a myth might be fostered. Ironically, many elderly people have accepted these assumptions and have "unnaturally" curtailed their sexual activities in order to do the "right thing."

Attitudes are changing, however, with clear evidence that sexual attraction and activity do not stop with old age and that there is no psychological or biological reason why they should.

TABLE 11.6 Average Percentage of Functions Remaining at Each Decade of Adulthood

BODY FUNCTION	AGE (YEARS)					
	30	40	50	60	70	80
Cardiac output at rest	100	94	83	77	70	—
Vital capacity of lungs	100	88	79	70	59	56
Nerve conduction velocity	100	99	97	94	93	89
Filtration rate of kidney	—	99	91	82	76	58
Basal metabolic rate	100	97	94	92	87	86

SOURCE: Based on data from Shock, 1962.

WHY DO WE GROW OLD? CAN AGING BE PREVENTED?

Why does aging occur? We seem to take this change for granted, because it appears to be common to every living thing. But why does it happen? Why, if you eat properly and obtain the necessary raw materials, doesn't your body reach young adulthood and then, physically, stay there—looking and feeling like the body of a 20-year-old person until you finally succumb to disease or trauma?

One popular theory dealing with this issue concerns **mutation.** Mutations may be caused by ultraviolet and X rays, ingested and inhaled chemicals, heat, viruses, and other mutagens. Scientists think that as the lifespan of humans has increased, mutations in the genetic codes found in every body cell may occur faster than they can be repaired. What happens then may be like a page in a book in which random new letters are substituted for the ones originally there: It doesn't take long before the whole page no longer makes sense. Genes cease to direct the "raw materials" we eat to the right locations. Pigment no longer gets sent to the hair, and the hair appears gray. Skin cells fail to be repaired, so the skin is no longer supple. Other parts of the body also are abandoned bit by bit, owing to the growing number of scrambled codes.

Our bodies have never been naturally selected for immortality—only for a life long enough to pass on our genes to the next generation. There may not even be any genes with codes evolved to maintain any body part for very long.

Between mutations and accumulating damage (such as progressive hardening of the arteries caused by buildup of cholesterol), it becomes a race to see which vital body part will break or be impeded first. This process is called aging.

In the last few years, there has been much excitement about the finding that living creatures may be genetically programmed to age and die. At the cellular level, cells seem to be finite in terms of the number of times they can divide. However, cancer cells and sex cells (egg and sperm) appear to be immortal, without limits to their division. Perhaps when egg and sperm fuse at conception, they reset the genetic death clock, and perhaps cancer cells reshuffle their genetic information in a similar way (Hayflick, 1980).

Can aging be prevented or slowed? There are perhaps four ways in which aging could be prevented or slowed, and scientists are investigating all of them.

First, it may be possible eventually to replace many of the vital parts that fail as we age. Artificial kidneys, hearts, eyes, ears, and joints are being perfected. In this way, longevity may be increased.

Second, it has been observed that longevity tends to run in families. One possible reason may be that some individuals are less susceptible to genetic mutation than others are. The causes of such resistance eventually may be discovered and implanted into our children (perhaps before birth) (Begley & Carey, 1981).

A third approach involves genetic engineering. This eventually may enable us to replace or repair genes in a developed organism. If mutations are responsible for aging, it may be possible to undo such mutations as they occur. Or perhaps there is a way to reset the death clock in body cells. We may be one of the last generations not to live for a few hundred years.

Finally, a fourth method, unlike the others, is within the reach of all of us. Proper diet and exercise have been shown in many cases to help extend life and to improve the quality of life.

When Life Ends

Death can happen to anyone at any time; it doesn't happen to only the elderly. Sometimes death occurs unexpectedly; sometimes there is time to prepare. The latter is especially true of the elderly, who often are aware of their deteriorating health preceding death.

Lifespan varies from culture to culture depending on lifestyle and health. In our culture, most people live into their seventies. Longevity has increased greatly over the years, mostly because of improved health care, which saves many infants and children from death. The increase also is partly due to better health care for the aged.

As far as creatures go, humans are fairly long-lived. The oldest documented age for a human being is 120 (McWhirter, 1986). Some animals, such as tortoises, may live longer, perhaps to 150 years, whereas others, such as dogs and cats, typically live to only 15 years. The longevity of animals and humans appears directly related to the number of times their body cells are able to divide (Hayflick, 1980) (see Focus on the Future). Even though research into the psychology of death has expanded greatly in recent years, we need to learn much more before we truly understand death and dying. Today, dying remains the most personal of acts (Kastenbaum & Costa, 1977).

MUTATION
Any heritable alteration of the genes or chromosomes of an organism.

EPILOGUE: ALGEBRA AND FORMAL OPERATIONS

Our knowledge of the development process has many practical applications. For instance, school systems, to be effective, must take into account a child's developing cognitive abilities. The following is an account of how this affected my own schooling.

When I was in the eighth grade, my cognitive development must have been coming along a little slowly. At the age of 13 years, before I was far enough into the stage of formal operations to deal with abstractions, I had the misfortune of running into algebra. I remembered the previous year seeing older kids in the hallway with math books that had covers showing letters being multiplied by numbers. I remembered wondering how that was possible. I asked my father whether this kind of math was hard, and he asked me, "How many numbers are there?" I said there must be a zillion. He said "Well, how hard can letters be, if there are only 26 of them?" A solid picture of a small group of finite letters seemed simple enough to deal with, so I entered algebra class with confidence.

The instructor began by placing an x on the board. It seemed to me that he had passed up a lot of the alphabet and hadn't very far to go, but that was all right. I raised my hand and asked him what "x" was. I wanted something concrete to hang my hat on. He said, "x is an unknown." In my notebook I wrote, "x = ?". I liked that. I decided that, whenever he used an x, I would use a question mark, because it would make everything easier. After awhile, he wrote a y on the board. I raised my hand and asked what "y" was. He replied that it, too, was an unknown. So I wrote in my notebook, "y = ?". It didn't take Einstein to figure out that if x = ? and y = ?, then x must be equal to y because they were both question marks. So I raised my hand and volunteered, "Then x is equal to y!" The instructor said, "Well, that can happen sometimes, but it usually doesn't." I don't remember much more about that instructor, but I do remember my friend John who sat next to me in class. He and I spent the rest of that year talking about less confusing things.

The second time I took algebra, I think I had the same instructor; at least he looked familiar. This time when he said that x was an unknown and y was an unknown, the meaning was clear to me: They could be anything, equal to each other or not equal to each other. Fortunately, abstract thinking didn't seem so foreign to me anymore. I didn't know it at the time, but I was slowly entering what Piaget called the stage of formal operations and was beginning to handle abstract concepts.

SUMMARY

■ Developmental psychology is the study of age-related changes in human behavior during the lifespan. By understanding human development, psychologists know what to expect at different developmental stages, and they learn the parameters of human growth and development.

■ One of the first researchers to emphasize the entire lifespan was the psychoanalyst Erik Erikson. He views human development as a progression through eight psychosocial stages, during which we are faced with conflicts that must be resolved for healthy development to occur.

■ Three issues have played a great role in developmental psychology. They are nature versus nurture, stability versus change, and continuity versus discontinuity.

■ The purpose of Human Genome Project is to map the position of every gene on human chromosomes and ascertain its function. It has the potential of eventually enabling us to fully understand the contribution of nature to the nature–nurture equation.

■ From the turn of the century until the 1950s, most researchers considered the newborn to be a helpless creature who was not competent in any sense of the word. Subsequent research has demonstrated that newborn infants possess remarkable capacities, including the ability to learn from a very early age.

■ The term used to describe a genetically determined biological plan of development that is relatively independent of experience is maturation. Human growth seems to be mainly a function of maturation, and, to a large extent, so is motor development.

■ Although the human infant doesn't appear to possess a fully integrated personality in its first few days of life, scientists have observed that newborns do exhibit considerable differences in temperament shortly after birth. The New York Longitudinal Study examined 140 children from birth to adolescence and classified them as having easy or difficult temperaments.

■ The mechanism of attachment, especially between the infant and its mother, has been intensely debated and investigated by developmental theorists, and the theoretical orientation taken by most researchers over the years has changed.

■ In a series of widely publicized experiments, psychologist Harry Harlow and his colleagues separated rhesus monkeys from their mothers at an early age and placed them with artificial wire and cloth surrogate mothers. Even rhesus monkeys fed by only the wire mother formed strong attachments to the cloth mother and spent most of their time hugging it.

■ In recent years, the most accepted theoretical orientation concerning the development of attachment has been toward an intraorganismic perspective.

■ John Kennell and Marshall Klaus investigated mother–infant bonding that may occur immediately after birth. They believe that early skin-to-skin contact is beneficial for infant attachment, although other researchers do not agree with their hypothesis.

■ Mary Ainsworth investigated the parameters of human attachment. Her studies have included a 1-year longitudinal investigation of infant attachments in the home; a 20-minute laboratory test known as the strange situation; and an assessment of the variables that determine the quality of infant attachment.

■ The full range of human emotion appears to be present at birth, but it isn't until the infant becomes older that emotional expressions become more differentiated and obvious.

■ During early childhood, the deceleration of growth rate that began just after conception continues. Besides physically increasing in size, children show increased motor competence during this time period.

■ Some of the most apparent and interesting changes that take place in the first 6 years of life are cognitive in nature. In Piaget's view, cognitive development is the combined result of the development of the brain and nervous system and of experiences that help the individual to adapt to her environment.

■ The first two of Piaget's stages—the sensorimotor (0 to 2 years) and the preoperational (2 to 7 years)—take place during infancy and early childhood.

■ The sensorimotor stage is characterized by a lack of fully developed object permanence, whereas the preoperational stage is characterized by the beginning of internalized thought processes.

■ One of the major achievements of young children is the ability to begin to regulate their own behavior. To achieve this ability, children appear to rely on internalized value and reward systems.

■ Mothers and fathers who have assumed the traditional gender roles behave differently toward their children. From the time the child was born, mothers are more likely to assume caregiving responsibilities, even if the fathers are home and are free to help.

■ Although parents usually are considered to be the primary agents of socialization for the young child, in most families the child has a relationship with one or more siblings.

■ Peers begin to have an increasing effect as children grow older. Longitudinal studies have shown that throughout the second year of life, a child's social behavior becomes more consistent and predictable.

■ When children first meet, they are more likely to become friends if they are able to exchange information successfully, to establish a common-ground activity, and to manage conflicts.

■ One of the most obvious occurrences during the preschool years is the development of play. Playing can be simple and unstructured, as in a game of hide-and-seek, or it can be more complex and structured, as in a school basketball game. Social scientists generally believe that play has evolved because it has a function.

■ Middle childhood is a time of continued physical growth and motor development. On average, girls and boys perform physically at about the same level, at least until the beginning of puberty.

■ According to Jean Piaget, at about the time children enter school, they develop the ability to rely on logical operations to form their conclusions. This is known as the state of concrete operations.

■ During middle childhood, many institutions have an influence on a child's socialization. Among them are the family, peers, schools, and even nonpersonal institutions, such as the media, including television.

■ Throughout their school years, children rely on their peers as important sources of information and may use peers as standards by which to measure themselves.

■ Television has been shown to have a great influence on the development of school-aged children. Television programs have such wide-ranging content that they probably have both a detrimental and a beneficial effect on children.

■ For American children, the transition to adulthood is slow, marked by many separate changes over the period of adolescence.

■ Modern researchers have come to the conclusion that adolescence isn't necessarily a time of unusual turbulence and conflict.

■ Adolescents are expected to develop a philosophy and moral ideology and to achieve socially responsible behavior.

■ Piaget has been criticized on a number of points. The debate over whether cognitive development is continuous or stagelike is ongoing. A general consensus has emerged, however, advocating aspects of both approaches.

■ An extensive review of the day-care literature has indicated that high-quality nonparental care does not seem to have a negative effect on young children. The data concerning infants younger than one year of age are unclear.

■ Young adults face many choices and predicaments in our society. They must make decisions about sexuality, marriage, children, career, friendships, social and civic interactions, and much more.

■ Most middle-aged adults express feelings of self-confidence and achievement. Researchers have examined a number of phenomena associated with middle adulthood, including the midlife crisis and the empty-nest syndrome.

■ Later adulthood is a period of highly personal adjustment. Older adults must adjust to physical changes that interfere with daily activities, retirement, reduced income, and, most difficult of all, the inevitable death of friends, relatives, or a spouse.

■ The more older adults can find satisfaction within a family or social group, and the more they can obtain a sense of continuity with the past, the more enjoyable and rewarding they are likely to find their later years.

SUGGESTIONS FOR FURTHER READING

1. Aiken, L. R. (1989). *Later life* (3rd ed.). New York: Holt. A book that outlines the biological and social factors affecting aging. Includes discussions of sexual behavior, mental disorders, retirement, health care, and death and bereavement.

2. Dworetzky, J. P. (1990). *Introduction to child development* (4th ed.). St. Paul, MN: West. A college-level introduction to child and adolescent development.

3. Dworetzky, J. P., & Davis, N. J. (1988). *Human development: A lifespan approach*. St. Paul, MN: West. A college-level introduction to development across the lifespan.

4. Lamb, M. E. (Ed.). (1981). *The role of the father in child development* (2nd ed.). New York: John Wiley. Includes discussions of the father's effect on children and the changing role of the father in American society.

5. Liebert, R. M., & Sprafkin, J. (1988). *The early window: Effects of television on children and youth* (3rd ed.) New York: Pergamon Press.

6. Maurer, D., & Maurer, C. (1988). *The world of the newborn*. New York: Basic Books.

7. Offer, D., Ostrov, E., Howard, K. I., & Atkinson, R. (1988). *The teenage world: Adolescents' self-image in ten countries*. New York: Plenum.

8. Santrock, J. W. (1989). *Adolescence* (4th ed.). Dubuque, IA: William C. Brown. A college-level text that discusses development during the adolescent years.

9. Wolman, B. B. (Ed.). (1982). *Handbook of developmental psychology*. Englewood Cliffs, NJ: Prentice-Hall. A comprehensive handbook that includes issues in developmental psychology and follows development from the prenatal period through old age.

CHAPTER 12 | Intelligence and Creativity

Prologue

Why Psychologists Study Intelligence

Defining Intelligence

Measuring Intelligence—IQ Tests
Test Validity
Factor Analysis

The Triarchic Theory of Intelligence

Birth Order and Intelligence

IQ and Race
Cultural and Educational Bias
Culture-fair Testing

The Effects of Environmental Stimulation

Intellectual Changes over Time
Difficulties in Measuring Intellectual Change
Terman's Study

Creativity

Some Final Thoughts on Intelligence

Epilogue: The Gifts

PROLOGUE

You are working for Thomas Edison in his laboratory at Menlo Park, New Jersey. Your area of expertise is photographic emulsions, and you've been working since early afternoon. It's now 4:00 A.M. You're not alone in the lab, however. A lot of people are working, including "the old man." Edison doesn't sleep much; he catnaps now and then. He likes to keep the lab going 24 hours a day. The building is large and so dimly lighted that it's easy to mistake the time. Still, you enjoy the work and the fact of collaborating with one of the world's foremost intellects, Thomas Edison.

You decide to take a break and get a cup of coffee. You join a man named L. L. Thurstone. He's a mathematician. You ask him what he's doing, since he seems to be working as he sips his coffee.

"The old man's math," he replies.

You nod. "Too busy to do it himself, huh?"

Thurstone looks at you. "Nope, he couldn't do this if he wanted to."

"What do you mean?" you ask. "What kind of math is it?"

"Just algebra," Thurstone says, "but he can't do it. He even has trouble with long division."

"You've got to be kidding," you say.

Thurstone shakes his head. "If I were, I wouldn't be working here. I need this job. He needs me."

You think about this for a moment. Then you say to Thurstone, "Edison must be one of the great geniuses of all time. I'm sure he could do algebra if he wanted to. He just doesn't care to, that's all."

"I've been wondering about that, too," Thurstone says. "And you know what? I don't think there is such a thing as intelligence, at least

not in any general sense. Watching Edison makes me think that there are many different kinds of intelligence. He's a mechanical genius, for instance; he's great at putting things together. But in other areas he's just not that bright. Believe me, when it comes to mathematical ability, you're probably more intelligent than he is."

In this chapter, we'll examine L. L. Thurstone's idea. We'll discuss how a person's intelligence can change owing to experiences. We'll also look at tests that measure intelligence and creativity, and see how such tests are designed. Finally, we'll examine mental retardation, exceptionality, and giftedness and look at the contributions of both nature and nurture to intelligence.

WHY PSYCHOLOGISTS STUDY INTELLIGENCE

People within every group or society are aware that some of their members have superior abilities to analyze problems, to find solutions, to comprehend ideas, and to accumulate information. Such people are valued because they can help the society to reach its goals. They are considered intelligent.

We revere those people whose insights, gifts, and knowledge have enabled them to make brilliant deductions or to see things as no one has seen them before. We know their names—Galileo, Einstein, Newton, Michelangelo, Darwin, and Beethoven, to name a few. But why do some people have these abilities, and others not? Are their gifts present at birth, or are they acquired through experience and learning? Can **intelligence** be taught? Can intellectual potential be found and cultivated? Can we prevent it from being lost or wasted? Does intelligence change over time, or does it remain stable? Is there a general kind of intelligence, applicable in all situations, or are there many kinds of intelligence, as Thurstone suggested? Psychologists are interested in all these questions. In fact, intelligence is such an intriguing subject that nearly everyone takes an interest in it.

DEFINING INTELLIGENCE

What is intelligence? Is it the ability to do well in school or to figure things out? Is it having the skills to find happiness or knowing when to come in out of the rain? Think about the following people and ask yourself if they are intelligent:

The physician who smokes three packs of cigarettes per day?
The Nobel prize winner whose marriage and personal life are in ruins?
The corporate executive who has worked to reach the top and has earned a heart attack for the effort?
The brilliant and successful composer who handled his money so poorly that he was always running from his creditors? (Incidentally, his name was Mozart.)

Examine any of these paradoxes, or consider the lives of your own friends or even your own life, and it will probably be clear to you that intelligence is not an easy thing to define.

The first scientific interest in defining and measuring intelligence testing can be traced to the nineteenth-century inheritance theories of Sir Francis Galton (1822–1911). Galton was interested in the success that English dog breeders had

had in creating so many varieties of dog. He wondered if it wouldn't be possible to also breed humans for desirable characteristics, intelligence being one of them. Galton founded a **eugenics** movement that advocated mating the best men and women for the purpose of producing superior offspring.

The movement never went very far, mostly because people preferred to marry for love rather than genes. Still, Galton's studies of supposedly superior and inferior qualities of people marked the start of the entire psychological testing movement, and people began to think about differences in mental abilities in a way they never had before. By 1900, the public had come to accept the idea that science could measure psychological differences in order to identify superior and inferior abilities. Clouding serious scientific research, however, were numerous nonsensical but popular theories, which were often the product of charlatans or pseudoscientists who purported to be able to measure "inherited traits." One such theory, for example, was **phrenology.** Phrenology is the study of personality based on the contours and bumps of the head. It works about as well as trying to figure out how much money someone has by feeling the outside of his safe. Another idea was the notion that criminal tendencies were mostly inherited and were directly related to such physical features as a low forehead or "shifty" eyes. We now know that this idea is foolish. Among thousands of counterexamples is the fact Australia was settled two centuries ago mostly by criminals banished from England. Many of today's Australians can trace their genetic roots back to these criminals, and yet Australia has a low crime rate. The list of foolish beliefs about inherited characteristics is long. Nevertheless, as the twentieth century dawned it was a common public belief that most human characteristics were the result of heredity; the influence of learning or experience was discounted.

More recently, however, the contributions of experience and environment have been widely investigated, and the more modern view of a characteristic such as intelligence is that it must be viewed as an interaction between inherited capacity and environmental influence.

■ MEASURING INTELLIGENCE—IQ TESTS

In 1905, Alfred Binet (1857–1911) and Theodore Simon (1873–1961) developed the precursor to the modern intelligence test. Its purpose was to determine which Parisian schoolchildren would benefit from regular classes and which should receive special education.

To create the test, Binet established which tasks or questions could be solved easily by children in each of the school grades and which were difficult. Carrying his research further, he developed a concept of **mental age (MA).** For example, a 5-year-old child who performed as well on the test as an average 6-year-old child would be said to have a mental age of 6. A 10-year-old child who performed only as well as an average 5-year-old child would be said to have a mental age of 5. Binet used the term **chronological age (CA)** to represent the actual age of the child.

A few years later, the German psychologist L. William Stern developed a formula to avoid fractions when comparing MA and CA. It yielded a score he called the **intelligence quotient,** or **IQ.** Stern's formula, MA ÷ CA × 100 = IQ, gave a rough index of how bright or dull any child was in comparison with his or her school peers. In the case of the 5-year-old child (CA = 60 months) with an MA of 72 months, the IQ is 120 more than sufficient for schoolwork. But the 10-year-old child (CA = 120 months) with an MA of only 60 months has an IQ of 50, which would be defined as developmentally retarded—not sufficient for schoolwork.

EUGENICS
Term coined by Sir Francis Galton referring to the science of improving the genetic characteristics of humans through breeding.

PHRENOLOGY
A system developed by Franz Joseph Gall for identifying types of people by examining their physical features, especially the configuration of the skull.

MENTAL AGE (MA)
A concept developed by Alfred Binet that was subsequently incorporated in the formula mental age ÷ chronological age × 100 = IQ. The mental age of a person is derived by comparing his or her score with the average scores of others within specific age groups.

CHRONOLOGICAL AGE (CA)
A concept developed by Alfred Binet that was subsequently incorporated in the formula mental age ÷ chronological age × 100 = IQ. The chronological age of a person is his or her actual age.

INTELLIGENCE QUOTIENT (IQ)
A quotient derived from the formula MA/CA × 100, where MA is mental age and CA is chronological age. The intelligence quotient was devised by German psychologist L. William Stern and introduced in the United States by Lewis Terman.

VALIDITY
The capacity of an instrument to measure
what it purports to measure.

In 1916, Lewis Terman (1877–1956) and his colleagues at Stanford University in California revised the original Binet–Simon intelligence scale and incorporated Stern's idea of the IQ. Their revision, known as the Stanford–Binet, became the first of the modern IQ tests. Using the Stanford–Binet test, most IQ scores in a normal population fall between 85 and 115, although some are higher or lower. Figure 12.1 depicts the distribution of scores.

Test Validity

Although we now have IQ tests, intelligence itself has never been adequately defined, and there is some question about the **validity** of these tests. A test is said to be valid if it measures what it claims to measure. Do IQ tests measure intelligence, as most people use the term? Generally, IQ tests measure common skills and abilities, many of which are acquired in school. Consider the areas covered in a widely used intelligence test, the revised Wechsler Adult Intelligence Scale (WAIS-R), shown in Figure 12.2 on pages 390–391. Does the ability to answer the example questions correctly coincide with most people's understanding of intelligence?

Many people think that intelligence also includes such attributes as creativity, persistent curiosity, and striving for success. IQ test scores aren't always good indicators of a person's abilities in these areas. For instance, two researchers worked with a number of bright mathematicians whose IQ test scores were very similar, who were all about the same age, and who all had Ph.D.s from prestigious universities. They found that these subjects had remarkable differences in creative output, as measured by other mathematicians (Helson & Crutchfield, 1970). IQ test scores, then, are not generally a valid measure of creativity.

IQ tests, however, have been found to predict other behaviors. They are generally able to predict success in school with a fairly high degree of certainty—not surprisingly, perhaps, since this is what they were originally designed to do. IQ tests also are sometimes valid for clinical assessments of people who have mental disorders or neurological and perceptual deficiencies.

Whether an IQ test will be a valid predictor often depends on the particular situation and the population being considered. For example, although people have attempted to use IQ tests to predict the likelihood of success on the job (Cronbach,

---

FIGURE 12.1

The standard distribution of IQ scores within the general population. The most common IQ score is 100. Approximately two-thirds of all scores fall within the IQ range of 84 to 116. (Source: Data from Stanford–Binet Intelligence Scale (4th ed.), Technical Manual, 1986, p. 129. The average score for the standardization population was 99.7.)

*Percentage of individuals from a normal population scoring above or below a given score.

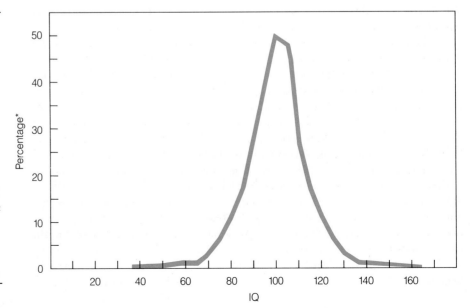

1970), the tests are fairly inaccurate at making such predictions (McClelland, 1973). If the job in question requires the academic skills most often learned in school, however, the IQ test will be a better predictor of success. This again shows the relationship between IQ scores and the ability to do well in school. In one study (Ghiselli, 1966), IQ test scores moderately predicted job success among stockbrokers (a more academic job) but poorly predicted job success among police officers (a less academically oriented job). As you can see, IQ tests may be useful predictors of success in some situations, but they don't necessarily measure the great number of abilities that might be included under the term *intelligence*.

Factor Analysis

Some IQ tests are given individually, one on one, such as the Stanford–Binet or the WAIS-R, while others are given to groups. Some IQ tests are designed to be taken by infants exclusively, or by children, or by adults. All the IQ tests ask different questions, and, although they are all called intelligence tests and they all yield an IQ score, they may measure different abilities. Furthermore, some tests measure the same ability more than once and thereby give that one ability more weight in the final score. The amount of weight or emphasis given to any one ability is known as a **factor load.**

To understand factor load better, let's look at an example from athletics. Think of an Olympic decathlon athlete who must compete in the following 10 events:

- pole vault (requires running start)
- 100-meter dash
- javelin (requires running start)
- 110-meter high hurdles
- pole vault (requires running start)
- 400-meter run
- high jump (requires running start)
- 1500-meter run
- discus
- running long jump
- shot put

As you can see, one ability is measured more than once; that is, it has a heavy factor load. This ability is running. The idea of trying to balance tests—including IQ tests—for factors, so that each ability is tested only once, was advocated by L. L. Thurstone in 1938. To accomplish this, Thurstone relied on a technique known as **factor analysis.** Of course, who's to say that a test equally weighted for all factors is the best indicator of what we call intelligence? Perhaps, intelligence is defined better by tests that have more weight for some factors than for others. Factor analysis is still valuable, however, because, if the factors can be isolated, the value of each factor and the weight it should be given can be determined more accurately. Although the factor analysis approach has been challenged, there is no doubt that some IQ tests are loaded in favor of particular factors. For instance, I do fairly well on the Stanford-Binet test; this test is heavily loaded in favor of verbal skills, and I enjoy talking and writing. But when I take the WAIS-R, my IQ is 15 points lower. The Wechsler includes many tasks that require eye-hand coordination, and it turns out that I am a clod with blocks. Both tests give me an IQ score, however. People often assume that an IQ is an absolute value regardless of the test; as you can see, they are mistaken.

As you learned at the beginning of the chapter, Thurstone was a mathematician who worked in Edison's laboratory, solving the mathematical equations that Edison

FACTOR LOAD
The weight or emphasis given to any factor or ability.

FACTOR ANALYSIS
A statistical procedure aimed at discovering the constituent traits within a complex system of personality or intelligence. The method enables the investigator to compute the minimum number of factors required to account for intercorrelations of the scores on the tests.

VERBAL SCALE

1. INFORMATION: Twenty-nine questions covering a wide range of general knowledge that people have presumably had an opportunity to gain simply by being exposed to the culture.

   EXAMPLE: How many zeros are there in 1 billion?

2. DIGIT SPAN: Fourteen groups of from two to nine digits presented orally, one group at a time. After hearing a group, subjects must repeat it from memory. Some exercises require repetition forward, others backward.

3. VOCABULARY: Thirty-five vocabulary words of increasing difficulty presented visually and orally. Subjects must define each word.

   EXAMPLE: "What does *parsimony* mean?"

4. ARITHMETIC: Fourteen problems similar to those encountered in elementary school. The problems must be solved without paper or pencil.

   EXAMPLE: "How much would three cigars cost if each cigar was $1.80 and the store was offering a 10 percent discount on all purchases?"

5. COMPREHENSION: Sixteen questions that ask subjects to indicate the correct thing to do under varied circumstances, what certain proverbs mean, or why certain practices are followed.

   EXAMPLE: "What is meant by 'too many cooks spoil the broth'?"

6. SIMILARITIES: Fourteen items requiring that subjects explain the similarity between two things.

   EXAMPLE: "In what way are red and hot alike?" (ANS.: Both can be sensed; both are stimuli.)

PERFORMANCE SCALE

7. PICTURE COMPLETION: Twenty pictures. In each picture something is missing. Subjects must identify the missing part.

   EXAMPLE:

8. PICTURE ARRANGEMENT: Ten sets of cards. Each set contains cartoon characters performing an action. If the set of cards is placed in the proper sequence, it will depict a sensible story. Subjects must place cards from each set in the proper order.

   EXAMPLE: "Place the cards in the proper sequence so that they depict a sensible story." (ANS.: Correct order should be 3, 1, 4, 2.)

Figure 12.2

Continued

9. BLOCK DESIGN: Nine designs of increasing complexity must be made using four to nine blocks having sides that are white, red, or half white and half red.

EXAMPLE:

10. OBJECT ASSEMBLY: Subjects are provided with pieces of a puzzle. The pieces are made of hardened cardboard. Subjects must decide what the pieces represent and assemble them correctly.

EXAMPLE:

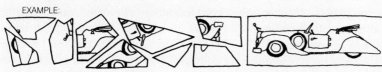

11. DIGIT SYMBOL: Nine symbols paired with nine digits are shown. Subjects must then pair the appropriate symbol with the correct digit in a long list of digits. The test is timed. Subjects who forget and have to look back at the pairings take longer to complete the test.

EXAMPLE:

1	2	3	4	5	6	7	8	9
//	△	□	○	◇	☆	▭	⊙	∿

5	3	8	6	7	2	9	4	1	6	9	5	7	8	4
—	—	—	—	—	—	—	—	—	—	—	—	—	—	—

seemed completely unable to comprehend. Edison's inability in this area led Thurstone to conclude that rather than a single quality called general intelligence, there must be many, perhaps unrelated, kinds of intelligence. One of Thurstone's hopes was that it would eventually be possible to distinguish social from nonsocial intelligence, academic from nonacademic intelligence, and mechanical from abstract intelligence.

Since Thurstone's day, many people have attempted to isolate different kinds of intelligence. One of the most exhaustive efforts was made by J. P. Guilford. He developed a model of intelligence based on factor analysis of the human intellect. In his most recent version of the model, Guilford proposed that there are as many as 150 different factors, of kinds, of intelligence (Guilford, 1982). Other researchers agree with Guilford that there are different kinds of intelligence, but disagree as to the number. Psychologist Howard Gardner, for example, has proposed that there are seven different kinds of intelligence (Gardner, 1983). Gardner's categories are quite broad in their definition of intelligence, including such aspects as social grace and athletic skill.

The view that there are different kinds of intelligence lies in direct contradiction to an idea proposed early in this century by Charles Spearman (1863–1945). Spearman argued that there was only one kind of general intelligence (*g*) and that *g* represented the amount of mental energy that a person could bring to bear on any given mental task (Spearman, 1927). A number of modern researchers also hold this view. Of course, because no one has been able to define intelligence adequately, no one is sure how many kinds of intelligence there may be—a state of affairs that plainly illustrates the difficulty of measuring intelligence (Weinberg, 1989).

Currently, this issue is unresolved. Two camps remain. There are the *lumpers*, who believe that all intelligence stems from one general ability, and the *splitters* who argue in favor of many separate kinds of relatively independent intelligence

COMPONENTIAL INTELLIGENCE
From Sternberg's triarchic theory of intelligence: that aspect of intelligence encompassing the cognitive problem-solving and information-processing skills measured by most IQ tests.

CONTEXTUAL INTELLIGENCE
From Sternberg's triarchic theory of intelligence: that aspect of intelligence encompassing the ability of the individual to adapt to her environment or culture.

EXPERIENTIAL INTELLIGENCE
From Sternberg's triarchic theory of intelligence: that aspect of intelligence encompassing the ability to take a newly learned skill and make it routine.

(Mayr, 1982). There are even some who take a middle ground, arguing in favor of a hierarchical organization of specific skills stemming from only one or two factors (Horn, 1986).

▌ THE TRIARCHIC THEORY OF INTELLIGENCE

After having studied the issues of intelligence and intelligence testing for many years, psychologist Robert J. Sternberg reached a conclusion: Intelligence tests are simply too narrow. "Most psychologists and others who have studied intelligence have attempted to 'look inside the head' in order to understand the nature of intelligence" (Sternberg, 1985, p. 1111). By this, he means that most intelligence tests rely solely on problem-solving skills and cognitive abilities, which is true. In fact, if the tests commonly used by Piaget to test children's cognitive development (see Chapter 11) are assembled and given as an "intelligence" test, they correlate quite well with the Wechsler Intelligence Test (Humphreys, Rich, & Davey, 1985).

In his book *Beyond IQ* (1984), Sternberg proposed an information-processing approach (see Chapter 8) to the study of intelligence, one that would encourage a step-by-step analysis of cognitive processes and be *applicable in any sociocultural context*. Toward this aim, Sternberg developed a triarchic theory of intelligence that would account for what he argues are the two missing legs necessary to support the concept we call intelligence. This triarchic view of intelligence is far broader than the perspective that psychologists have traditionally accepted, and it may be more in line with what most people believe intelligence to be.

The first leg of the theory, of course, includes the cognitive problem-solving and information-processing skills measured by most IQ tests. This is what Sternberg calls **componential intelligence**, which the layperson might call "book smart" or "school smart."

The second leg concerns the ability of the individual to adapt to her environment or culture. This is known as **contextual intelligence**. For years, people have referred to this as "street smart"; knowing the ins and outs, the angles, knowing how to get by in a given situation. Learning how to survive and do well in your cultural and social environment is important and, after all, is an intelligent thing to do. In fact, when Sternberg teaches his psychology graduate students, he likes to include contextual training such as how to compete for a top job, or how to obtain the biggest financial grants, or how to publish in the journals that have the biggest circulation (and why it's smart to do so). Some of Sternberg's colleagues have argued that by discussing the "inside" ways to get ahead, he is covering the seedier side of office politics and that it is inappropriate. Sternberg argues that such inside contextual knowledge is important, that contextual intelligence can be learned, and that it's about time we recognize this fact.

The third leg is **experiential intelligence**. Sternberg argues that an important part of intelligence is the ability to take a newly learned skill and make it routine. We have phrases to describe this kind of intelligence, such as "learning from your mistakes" and "capitalizing on your experiences." People with this intelligence quickly develop expertise by making their newly acquired skills routine. By so doing, the mental tasks that once required thought become almost effortless or automatic.

Sternberg has developed a test to measure these three components (the Sternberg Multidimensional Abilities Test). Perhaps this new test will be better able to predict performance and to help individuals discover their weaknesses and identify ways to correct them than standard IQ tests can (Weinberg, 1989).

For Sternberg, as for almost all modern psychologists, intelligence is understood to be a series of skills, *not* strictly something that you're born with, something that you either have or do not have. These skills, admittedly influenced by heredity, can be nurtured and developed as well. For this reason, correcting weaknesses in intelligence may well become an important part of applied psychology. Sternberg's book *Intelligence Applied* (1986) even provides a training program, based on the author's theory, to help individuals strengthen any or all of the three forms of intelligence he identifies.

An Enduring Question: How Much of Intelligence is Inherited?

Your brain, your nervous system, indeed, your entire body, is made according to instructions received from the genes you inherited from your parents. It would seem reasonable that superior genes would endow a child with superior intellectual capacity. And, in fact, researchers have discovered that parents with high IQs tend to have children with high IQs, while parents with low IQs tend to have children with low IQs.

This finding might appear to prove that intelligence is inherited. But does it really? Rich parents tend to have rich children, and parents who like tostadas and enchiladas tend to have children who like tostadas and enchiladas; it doesn't necessarily follow that these characteristics are carried by genes. Environment also can play an important role. Perhaps being raised by intelligent parents in a stimulating or intellectual home tends to increase a child's IQ.

Nature and Nurture

Genetics determines brain structure to an important degree and differences within that structure—and, obviously, brain structure is related to intellectual functioning. [Individual brain sizes, however, are *not* related to intelligence: A larger brain does not mean a higher IQ (Scott, 1983)]. Psychologists often debate the importance of genetics in determining IQ. What you should remember is that intelligence is an attribute greatly determined by *interactions* among genetic inheritance, culture, and experience.

Also, it is important to understand that if some aspect of intelligence is inherited, it doesn't necessarily mean that that aspect, whatever it might be, is fixed and unchangeable from birth on. Because intelligence is influenced by more than one gene, unlike the determination of eye color, and because it is also a complex response to the environment, it doesn't follow the simple laws for the inheritance of traits. As Richard Weinberg said, "There is a myth that if a behavior or characteristic is genetic, it cannot be changed. Genes do not fix behavior. Rather, they establish a range of possible reactions to the range of possible experiences that environments can provide" (Weinberg, 1989, p. 101).

Methods of Behavioral Genetics

A particular branch of psychological research, known as **behavioral genetics,** is especially concerned with how the interaction of nature and nurture affects behavior.

There are two basic ways to study the inheritance of human intelligence. The first is the **twin design** in which a characteristic or behavior is compared between identical twins (twins born from one egg that splits; they are genetically identical)

BEHAVIORAL GENETICS
The interdisciplinary science that focuses on the relationship of nature and nurture, that is, on the interaction of what is inherited and what is acquired and how that interaction affects behavior.

TWIN DESIGN
A research design used for sorting the influence of nurture from nature. A characteristic or behavior is compared between identical twins; then the same characteristic or behavior is compared between fraternal twins.

ADOPTION DESIGN
A research design used for sorting the
influence of nurture from nature.
Genetically related individuals who are
reared apart from one another or
genetically unrelated individuals who are
reared together are studied.

and then between fraternal twins (twins born from two separate eggs, who are no more genetically alike than regular siblings). The second method is the **adoption design**. Researchers who use this design to study genetically related individuals who are reared apart from one another or genetically unrelated individuals who are reared together. As you can see, this arrangement allows the effects of nature and nurture to be separately examined. It is not uncommon for both designs to be incorporated into a single study.

Let's examine some behavioral genetic research concerning intelligence. To begin, consider the fact that relatives share many of the same genes, whereas unrelated people do not. In Table 12.1, you will see categories of related and unrelated people, with a correlational coefficient next to each. These correlations represent the relationship between the IQ scores of pairs of individuals within each category (the scores of two first cousins, of a parent and child, and so forth).

We can look at parents and their children to see how the correlations are derived. Each parent and his or her child are given an IQ test. Then a computation is made that allows these test scores to be compared with each other; each parent's score is compared with his or her child's score. The more alike these compared scores are, the closer to +1.00 the correlation coefficient will be.* A high positive correlation means that the test scores of the parents and their respective children are similar. We can infer from this that if a parent's IQ is high, his or her child's is likely to be high, or that if a parent's IQ is low, his or her child's is likely to be low also. A correlation of zero, or near zero, indicates no relationship between the two scores. If such were the case, the parent's score would tell us nothing about the child's probable score. A correlation approaching −1.00 indicates an inverse relationship; that is, if one score is high, the other is likely to be low, and vice versa. As you can see, the actual correlation between parents and their children is +.40, a moderate positive correlation.

*For a more detailed discussion of correlation coefficients, see the Statistics Appendix (Appendix A).

TABLE 12.1 **Correlations of Intelligence Test Scores***

CORRELATIONS BETWEEN INDIVIDUALS	MEDIAN VALUE
Genetically Related Persons	
Identical twins reared together	.86
Identical twins reared apart	.72
Parent—child	.40
Fraternal twins reared together	.60
Siblings reared together	.47
Siblings reared apart	.24
Half-siblings	.31
Cousins	.15
Unrelated Persons	
Nonbiological sibling pairs (adopted/adopted pairings)	.34
Adopting parent—offspring	.19

*Based on a study of 111 studies which reported on familial resemblances in intelligence.

SOURCE: Adapted from the Bouchard & McGue, 1981, p. 1056.

One of the areas of greatest interest is the "twins reared apart" category. It is rare for identical twins to be reared apart, but when they are, they give us an ideal chance to study the IQs of two people sharing the same genes *but having different upbringing and experiences*. As you an see from the table, identical twins reared apart have an even higher correlation than do siblings reared together (Segal, 1985). In the most extensive study of identical twins reared apart to date, T. J. Bouchard and his colleagues at the University of Minnesota found that the heritability is around +.75, a strong positive correlation (Lykken, 1987; Plomin, 1989).

Note that even though these data indicate that there is a genetic component to intelligence, other variables also affect intelligence. These variables may have to do with the environment, with cultural variations in upbringing, or with other factors.

FOR CRITICAL ANALYSIS

1. How might poor prenatal care cause environmental damage to a child's intelligence? How might such effects look as though they were due to genetic causes?
2. If it were your job to select people for an intelligence breeding experiment, which aspects of intelligence would you emphasize and why? How could you know if these aspects were under any genetic control before you began to breed subjects?

BIRTH ORDER AND INTELLIGENCE

In 1896, Galton observed something intriguing about the effect of the order in which children were born. He noticed that an exceedingly large number of prominent British scientists were firstborn children. Since Galton's time, a number of studies have indicated that firstborn children have a distinct advantage over other children in certain areas of development (Koch, 1955). Firstborns are more articulate and tend to score higher on intelligence tests than children born later. First-

Psychologists are especially interested in studying identical twins, because intellectual differences between them cannot be the result of inheritance. These identical twins have inherited the same genes.

borns also tend to be more reflective, whereas later children are more impulsive. When dealing with important choices, reflective children tend to examine a number of options and to delay decisions so that they can minimize their errors. Impulsive children, on the other hand, are eager to rush to a solution when dealing with problems (Kagan, 1966). Firstborns also appear to have a greater need to achieve (Sampson, 1962), to be more active (Eaton, Chipperfield, & Singbeil, 1989), and to perform better academically (Altus, 1967). Firstborns are more likely to attend college (Bayer, 1966) and to have high educational aspirations (Falbo, 1981). Interestingly, 21 of the first 23 astronauts to travel into space were firstborn children.

The meaning of these birth-order data is not clear. It may have something to do with the size of the family into which children are born. Perhaps firstborns enjoy a more stimulating environment than do later children, because firstborns have the undivided attention of both parents. Supporting this interpretation is that firstborns develop language rapidly, while twins develop language at a slower rate, and triplets more slowly still (Davis, 1937). Research has shown that twins tend to be shortchanged in this regard by their parents, because parents don't like to repeat themselves. In other words, a twin is likely to be spoken to less often because parents treat the twins as a unit and do not double their verbal interactions (Lytton, Conway, & Suave, 1977). Because IQ scores reflect verbal skills to a considerable degree, it is not surprising, then, that firstborns tend to have higher IQ scores than second children, second children also tend to have higher scores than third children, third than fourth, and so on (Zajonc & Markus, 1975), or that children from families with many siblings tend to have lesser verbal skills (Blake, 1989).

Perhaps parents could mitigate these differences if they paid extra attention to their younger children. Still, there may not be great cause for concern, since the differences between firstborns and later children on IQ tests is generally only three or four points, which in practical terms is not very significant. In addition, the fact that firstborns tend to be more successful may be related to many factors other than extra parental attention or stimulation. Larger families, for example, are often of lower socioeconomic status, and later children, on the average, are more likely to be at an economic disadvantage compared with earlier children, in that fewer opportunities can be made available to them. For example, an eighth-born child is far more likely to be a member of a poor family than a rich one, and by a much larger degree than would a firstborn child.

Finally, not all scientists agree that there is a real or significant birth-order effect (Grotevant, Scarr, & Weinberg, 1975). Some researchers have reported finding no birth-order effect (Galbraith, 1982; McCall & Johnson, 1972). Nonetheless, studies that include large samples of subjects generally support the theory that birth order is related to achievement motivation and to IQ test scores (Belmont & Marolla, 1973; Berbaum, Markus, & Zajonc, 1982; Berbaum & Moreland, 1985).

As you can see, the birth-order effect is small—although it is interesting. Unfortunately, in just about any bookstore, you can find books claiming all sorts of fantastic things about birth order, treating it as though it were destiny itself. The birth order effects described in this text are subtle, and, as best we know, these are all that there are (Ernst & Angst, 1983). Books claiming to tell how any individual child will develop based solely on birth order are nonsense.

IQ, RACE, AND CULTURE

A serious controversy concerning the heritable aspects of intelligence developed immediately after researcher Arthur Jensen published an article in the 1969 *Harvard*

Educational Review. Jensen suggested that the reason whites scored higher than blacks on IQ tests by an average of 15–18 points was probably related more to genetic variables than to the effects of experience. In other words, Jensen was saying that whites were naturally intellectually superior to blacks. The ensuing debates on radio, on television, and in the press were stormy, usually generating more heat than light. In the middle of all this controversy entered William Shockley, a Nobel prize winner (for coinventing the transistor, not for work related to genetics or psychology), who advocated that blacks be prevented from having too many children so that they would not pass on their inferior genes.

Cultural and Educational Bias

No one disputes that whites score higher than blacks do on IQ tests. But this fact does not necessarily mean that Jensen was right. There are other interpretations. The kinds of observations that Jensen made were not new. In 1912, the U.S. Public Health Service gave the then-new IQ tests to immigrants arriving in New York. It was discovered that 87 percent of Russians, 83 percent of Jews, 80 percent of Hungarians, and 79 percent of Italians were feebleminded. It didn't matter to the supervisor of the testing, Henry Goddard, that many of the immigrants couldn't speak English. He was convinced that the tests were adequately translated to suit the immigrants.

If translated versions of the intelligence tests were administered to the immigrants, why did they score so poorly? Unfortunately, a considerable knowledge of American culture was necessary to score well; 79 percent of the Italians tested were not feebleminded, but rather were ignorant of the answers to culturally biased questions.

When the United States entered World War I, the army administered the same IQ tests to all inductees. It was at this time that blacks were first tested in large numbers. Their average mental age was only 10.41, just behind recently emigrated Poles (10.74), Italians (11.01), and Russians (11.34). Of all those who were tested, including the recently naturalized immigrants, blacks were the poorest financially and were the least educated. In other words, educational bias may have influenced

When black Americans enlisted in the first World War to fight for their country, many were given IQ tests for the first time. Those who interpreted the test results often failed to account for differences in education owing to years of racial discrimination.

THE PROPER USE OF INTELLIGENCE TESTS

Ever since Alfred Binet first began to use intelligence tests to differentiate between normal and dull students in the Paris school system, there has been controversy over whether IQ tests are a valid measure of intelligence:

Intelligence tests have been under attack practically since their inception (Cronbach, 1975; Haney, 1981). Critics have claimed, among other things, that intelligence and aptitude tests measure nothing but test-taking skills, have little predictive power, are biased against certain racial and economic groups, are used to stigmatize low scorers, and are tools developed and fostered by those in power in order to maintain the status quo. . . . Though perhaps not as apparent as 10 (or 60) years ago, such criticisms remain prevalent (e.g., Gould, 1981; Lewontin, Rose, & Kamin, 1984; Owen, 1985). (Snyderman & Rothman, 1987, p. 137)

The following case study illustrates

the problem: Some time ago, when Gregory Ochoa was a high-school student in California, he and his classmates, most of whom also had Spanish surnames, were given an IQ test. The result of the testing was that Gregory was placed in a special class. Gregory didn't fully realize what then followed. All he knew was that his special class didn't do regular schoolwork. Any class member interested in intellectual pursuits, such as going to the school library, was told that such activities were out of bounds.

Gregory soon dropped out of school. He was sent to reform school, where he received some remedial reading. After finishing reform school, he joined the navy. There Gregory earned high-school credits, which eventually enabled him to attend college as a student on probation. In college, he received high grades and graduated with honors—while *still* on probation! He believes this occurred

because the college never stopped thinking of him as "retarded." By the time he was 40, *Doctor* Gregory Ochoa was an assistant professor at the University of Washington in Seattle, where he taught classes in social case work.

Ochoa's problems in school had started when he was given his first IQ test and was placed in a special class for no other reason than that his IQ test score was low. No one considered that cultural differences might have played a role in his low score. He was lucky to have received remedial training—other children with low IQ scores were not so lucky.

This ongoing problem finally reached the courts in the 1970s. Larry P., like Gregory Ochoa, was a student in California who had been placed in a special class as a result of his low score on an IQ test. In the court case *Larry P. vs. Wilson Riles,* it was argued that IQ tests should no longer

test scores. Because of inferior schooling, black children may have been less likely than were white children to be exposed to the kinds of strategies and knowledge required by IQ tests. This interpretation, however, was not considered at the time. Instead, the army findings were commonly used to support unfounded racist beliefs that blacks were intellectually inferior. A similar kind of educational bias may explain the fact that Japanese children tend to outscore white American children on IQ tests by about 7 points (Mohs, 1982). Although a few researchers believe that this, too, may be due to genetic differences, most point to the possible effects of the superior Japanese school system.

In an effort to shed some light on this issue, psychologist Sandra Scarr gathered data on the IQ scores of black children adopted and raised by white families. Scarr discovered that the younger the black children were at the time of adoption, the closer their scores were to the white IQ averages (Scarr & Weinberg, 1976). Similarly, the IQs of poor children increased when they were adopted by affluent families (Schiff, Duyme, Dumaret, & Tomkiewicz, 1982).

These results strongly suggest that background, experience, and culture can influence a person's knowledge and thought processes as measured by any particular intelligence test. Different cultures teach not only different things but also different ways to think about things. And different cultures require their children to meet different educational standards. As Jerome Kagan once said in reference to two of the best-known IQ tests, "If the Wechsler and Binet scales were translated into be used to assign students to such "special" classes. The prosecutor maintained that a disproportionate number of blacks such as Larry P. had been wrongly assigned to special classes for the mentally retarded because of nothing more than their IQ scores. In these classes, they were taught little. Furthermore, assignment to such classes stigmatized them. A federal appeals court agreed, and IQ tests were no longer allowed to be used for this purpose.

The case of Larry P. has been somewhat offset by the ruling of a federal district judge in 1980 in *PASE vs. Hannon.* In that case, a federal district court judge in Illinois ruled that IQ tests could still be used to place minority students in special education classes *as long as other factors were considered* when placing the students. That ruling applies to only federal law, however. The states are still free to ban IQ testing based on their

own laws or constitutions, and California is one of those states where IQ tests cannot be administered to students for identifying or placing them in special education (Landers, 1986). This, of course, has left the schools with a problem—to find alternative assessment devices that are valid and can indicate the need for special help. These include assessments of the pupil's past personal history, adaptive behavior, classroom performance, past academic achievement, and use of instruments designed to point out specific deficits in specific skill areas.

Unfortunately, these assessment devices have been shown to be even less valid indicators of future academic achievement than are IQ tests, and psychologists and educators are therefore left with the requirement of identifying pupils in need of special help but with few valid ways of doing so.

In a survey of over 1000 profes-

sionals with expertise in intelligence testing, most were found to favor the continued use of intelligence tests at their present level (Snyderman & Rothman, 1987). But the question remains, can the tests be used without being misused? In the words of Gregory Ochoa:

I think first of all, one would have to ask why you want to know what this person's intellectual capacity is. Are you using it in order to make sure that every horizon available to him is reached, or are you using it to diminish his opportunities or to prove to him, or to oneself, that Blacks, or Chicanos, or other minorities are inherently inferior to others. I think that is the critical issue—what is it being used for? ("The IQ Myth," 1975)

Spanish, Swahili, and Chinese and given to every ten-year-old child in Latin America, East Africa, and China, the majority would obtain IQ scores in the mentally retarded range" (1973, p. 89). Of course, these children wouldn't be mentally retarded in the commonly understood sense of the term, but they would be at a disadvantage in taking the tests until they learned to adapt to our culture. In this case, a low IQ score would represent cultural ignorance or lack of education, not lack of intelligence. Any of us would be at the same disadvantage if we took a test developed in another culture. (See Focus on a Controversy.)

Culture-fair Testing

Any intelligence test that makes use of language is likely to be culturally biased. Consequently, people have attempted to produce language-free, **culture-fair tests** that would be equally difficult for members of any culture. The first such tests generally relied on pictures and nonverbal instructions, but these still tended to favor some cultures. Children in these cultures were simply more familiar with pictures or the requirements of certain tasks (Vernon, 1965). Still, some tests are self-explanatory and do not require pictures of familiar objects. One of the most widely used culture-fair tests is the Raven Progressive Matrices Test. In Figure 12.3, you'll see a sample question from the Raven test. Even without instructions

CULTURE-FAIR TEST
A test that is supposed to be free of cultural biases, usually constructed so that language differences and other cultural effects are minimized.

CHAPTER 12
INTELLIGENCE AND CREATIVITY

you can understand what is required. But in this test, too, people from cultures in which fill-in or matching exercises are more common may be more likely to do well than people from other cultures. To date, no one test has been developed that is completely culture-fair.

Over the years, however, researchers have tried to eliminate some cultural bias from tests that are given to large and diverse populations. Still, the concept of intelligence remains fairly mysterious. For instance, researcher James Flynn examined IQ scores obtained from 14 nations around the world, all the way from the Netherlands to New Zealand, and discovered that there had been a significant jump in IQ scores from the last generation to the current one, an increase ranging from 5 to 25 points (Flynn, 1987).

No one knows why there should be such an increase. It obviously can't be genetic, because the forces of **natural selection** couldn't have worked such a genetic change in only 30 years. The real surprise was that the greatest gains occurred on the Raven culture-fair test, which is purported to measure intellectual *aptitude* that is free of cultural bias. The reason this occurred is probably because culture-fair tests aren't culture-fair. One researcher trying to solve this dilemma has argued that so-called culture-fair tests become easier if your culture has provided you with training, as many modern schools do, emphasizing intelligent guessing (which modern students exposed to multiple-choice testing often raise to an art form) and speed of thought (Brand, 1987).

As you can see, although we have learned a great deal, the factors that influence IQ or intelligence are still far from understood.

THE EFFECTS OF ENVIRONMENTAL STIMULATION

One way to assess environmental influences on intellectual development is to alter the environment on purpose and then to observe the effect on IQ scores. Ethically, of course, it's proper to create only a stimulating environment in the hopes of raising IQ scores.

Project Head Start was designed in the 1960s to help disadvantaged preschool children do better in school as they grew older. At first, research results from the Westinghouse Learning Corporation and researchers at Ohio State University indicated that Head Start was making little difference in the long-term intellectual development of children enrolled in it. However, researchers David P. Weikart and Lawrence J. Schweinhart released an interim report in 1980 on an 18-year study of the progress of 123 children at Perry Elementary School in Ypsilanti, Michigan, which indicated that good-quality preschool education programs do benefit the disadvantaged. The Ypsilanti Project offered 12½ hours per week of education at ages 3 and 4 years, plus 90-minute weekly home visits. Children in the enrichment program scored higher on reading, math, and language achievement tests than did those in the control group. They also showed fewer antisocial and delinquent tendencies (Williams & King, 1980a).

An executive report released in 1986 noted that although it was not known whether all Head Start programs in the United States were producing beneficial results, such results could be achieved if the programs were adequately funded and the teachers were well trained and competent (Schweinhart & Weikart, 1986). Among the benefits are "improved intellectual performance during early childhood; better scholastic placement and improved scholastic achievement during the elementary school years; and, during adolescence, a lower rate of delinquency and higher rates of both graduation from high school and employment at age 19" (Schweinhart & Weikart, 1985, p. 547).

FIGURE 12.3

Sample item from the Raven Progressive Matrices Test.

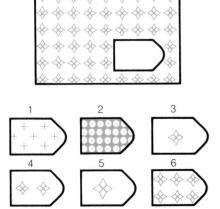

Psychologists hope that by providing stimulating environments for children during their early years, handicaps associated with being raised in underprivileged or unstimulating environments might be overcome.

There have been other programs like the Ypsilanti Project that have been effective (Gray & Ruttle, 1980; van Doorninck, Caldwell, Wright, & Frankenburg, 1981). A notable example of institutional enrichment can be found in Israel, where children of European Jewish heritage have an average IQ of 105, while those of a Middle Eastern Jewish heritage have an average IQ of only 85. Yet when raised on a **kibbutz,** children from both groups have an average IQ of 115.

Early intervention projects have not been uniformly successful. Depending on the program, how it is implemented, and the population that receives the intervention, early intervention may produce many different outcomes. Programs with a high academic content are generally the most successful in producing increases in IQ and achievement (Miller & Dyer, 1975; Stallings, 1975). Special programs aren't always required to give an intellectual boost, however. For example, good-quality day-care has been found to improve the intellectual development of socioeconomically disadvantaged children (Burchinal, Lee, & Ramey, 1989).

In summary, there is no clear-cut way to predict whether early intervention will be effective. Many programs claim success, but their work is often hard to assess because the criteria they use to define success and to define which children are needy often differ (Scarr & McCartney, 1988). The general consensus appears to be that early intervention can have lasting and valuable effects (Lazar & Darlington, 1982; Casto & Mastropieri, 1986), but there is no guarantee for any given program with any given group of children (Ramey, 1982; Woodhead, 1988).

INTELLECTUAL CHANGES OVER TIME

Problems arise when IQ tests are used to measure intellectual changes during the lifespan. In the 1930s, Nancy Bayley developed a test called the Bayley Mental and Motor Scale to evaluate infants' intellectual and motor skills. Interestingly, the 91 subjects who were measured by the Bayley test when they were 9 months of age often had very different IQs when they were retested at 5 years of age by the Stanford–Binet IQ test. In fact, the correlation between the two IQ scores was zero (Anderson, 1939), indicating that the infants' IQ scores at 9 months were totally unrelated to their scores at 5 years. This result is shown in Table 12.2,

KIBBUTZ
An Israeli farm or collective where children are often reared in groups and receive nurturance and guidance from many different adults and older children.

TABLE 12.2 Correlation Between Infant's IQ Scores at Various Ages with Their Scores at 5 Years

AGE (IN MONTHS)	CORRELATION COEFFICIENT BETWEEN SCORES FOR THE SAME SUBJECTS AT 5 YEARS OF AGE
3	.008
6	−.065
9	−.001
12	.055
18	.231
24	.450

SOURCE: Adapted from Anderson, 1939.

401

along with the correlations obtained for the infants when they were younger and older. The correlation at 9 months was zero because tests given at different ages often measure different abilities (McCall, Hogarty, & Hurlburt, 1972). Tests for very young children and infants generally emphasize motor skills, while tests for older children tend to emphasize verbal and cognitive skills. Yet both are said to measure intelligence.

IQ tests for infants were initially devised because researchers hoped that a person's intelligence could be determined early in life. Although such tests have some utility for describing the infant's current state, they simply cannot predict intellectual changes over a long time.

Difficulties in Measuring Intellectual Change

The problem of predicting intelligence can be highlighted by considering what appears, at first glance, to be an extraordinary fact. When Koko, the gorilla who learned sign language (see Chapter 8), was 7 years old, she was given the Stanford–Binet IQ test. Her score was 90, an average IQ for humans! Of course, this doesn't mean that Koko is as intelligent as the average human. Rather, the questions younger children are asked on the Stanford–Binet test contain a heavy motor-skill factor loading, and gorillas develop motor skills faster than humans do. A gorilla baby can climb a tree at an age when a human baby is still having trouble crawling. As a result, Koko's MA was inflated on the human test, and her IQ was relatively high. At a later age, when the questions concentrate more on verbal and cognitive skills, Koko's IQ will probably fall to about 35. This result won't indicate a decline in her intelligence; rather, the questions for older children tap different skills, skills that Koko's species does not develop fully. For the same reason, the "intelligence" measured in younger children usually is not well related to the "intelligence" measured in older children. This lack of correlation makes it especially difficult to measure intellectual change over time during childhood. As Figure 12.4 shows, IQ scores don't tend to become consistent over time (or *reliable*, as psychologists say) until about age 10 years (Bloom, 1964). This means that IQ scores obtained from children younger than 10 years may change considerably as the children grow up.

Finding an early measure of intelligence that is reliable would give us the ability to better predict a child's future performance. Researchers have tried to find a skill that could be measured in infancy that would have a relationship to later intellectual functioning. For example, in one study, 4-month-old infants were given both

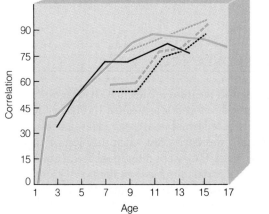

FIGURE 12.4

Correlations between children's IQ scores at various ages and their IQ scores at maturity, according to several studies. (SOURCE: *Bloom, 1964.*)

repetitive and new sounds to listen to. An intelligence score was developed based on how easily they recognized a new stimulus (measured by change in heart rate) and by how quickly they came to recognize a repeated stimulus as familiar. The children were followed until they were 5 years old and were then given the Stanford–Binet IQ test. The correlation was an impressive +.60 (O'Connor, Cohen, & Parmelee, 1984). The researchers assumed that, in this instance, a basic memory skill had been tapped.

Similar results have been obtained with the use of a visual habituation test developed by Joseph Fagan (see Figure 12.5) (Rose, Feldman, & Wallace, 1988). When using this test on 128 infants between 3 and 7 months of age, who were then retested with the Stanford–Binet IQ test at age 3 years, Fagan discovered that he was able to correctly predict 101 of the 104 children whose IQs would be within the normal range by age 3 and also predict fully half of the infants whose scores would be within the retarded range by that age (Bower, 1988).

These tests also appear to be **aptitude tests,** which is what many people perceive an IQ test should be, rather than **achievement tests.**

Regarding the stability of intelligence in adults, many psychologists believe that we have to specify which of two types of intelligence, fluid or crystallized, we are talking about. **Fluid intelligence** reflects our ability to solve novel problems in creative ways. Tests of abstract thinking, reasoning, creativity, and problem solving are considered to be examples of fluid intelligence. Researchers have found that fluid intelligence peaks between 20 and 30 years of age and declines thereafter (Horn & Donaldson, 1980).

The other type of intelligence is **crystallized intelligence,** which is based on the facts that we have stored and on our ability to use those facts. Formal education, reading, traveling, and being with intelligent, stimulating people are considered to be ways of increasing our crystallized intelligence. It is believed that unlike fluid intelligence, crystallized intelligence generally increases as we age and is most likely responsible for what we call wisdom (see Figure 12.6).

Terman's Study

In 1921, psychologist Lewis Terman received a grant from New York City to conduct an extended longitudinal study of children with IQs above 140. Terman

FIGURE 12.5

The baby in this photograph is looking at pictures of two faces. One of those faces he has seen before; the other is new. The researcher is measuring how long the baby looks at each of the faces. Babies who spend less time looking at the familiar face tend to have higher scores on intelligence tests when they reach school age.

CHAPTER 12
INTELLIGENCE AND CREATIVITY

FIGURE 12.6

Smoothed curves summarizing several studies indicating aging changes for fluid and crystallized intelligence abilities. (SOURCE: Horn & Donaldson, 1980, pp. 469, 471.)

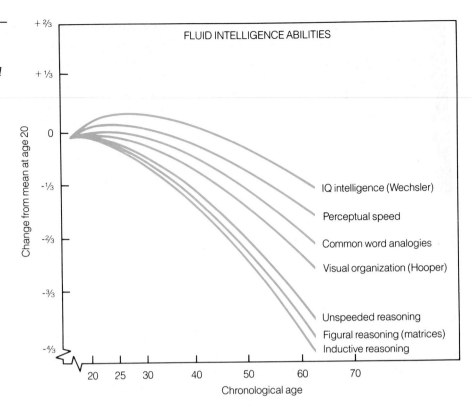

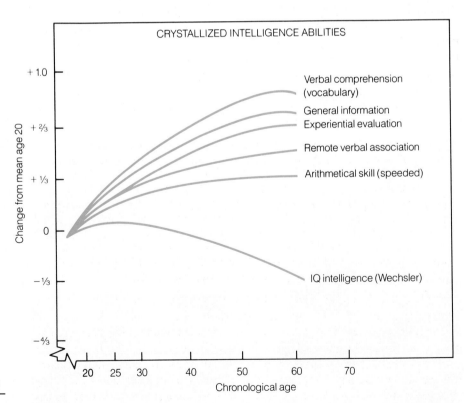

selected his 1528 subjects from grade schools in California. Their average IQ was 150, and 80 of them possessed IQs of 170 or higher (Terman, 1925). Follow-up studies were conducted in 1922, 1927–28, 1939–40, 1951–52, 1960, 1972, 1977, and 1982.

Because few women were encouraged during the 1920s to seek professions, most of the follow-up studies of professional accomplishments concentrated on the approximately 800 men in the original selection. This is not to say that the Terman women didn't choose professions; many of them did, but there were few professional women in the average general population with whom to compare them. By 1950, at an average age of 40 years, the men had written and published 67 books, over 1400 articles, and 200 plays and short stories; they had obtained over 150 patents; 78 of them had received a Ph.D., 48 an M.D., and 85 an L.L.B.; 74 were university professors, and 47 were listed in *American Men of Science*. As Terman noted, "The number who became research scientists, engineers, physicians, lawyers, or college teachers, or who were highly successful in business and other fields, is in each case many times the number a random group would have provided" (1954, p. 41).

Among the Terman women there were also some surprises. According to Pauline Sears, who reviewed the data, the Terman women

> were way ahead of several trends that have only lately become true for the nation as a whole. They were quicker to join the work force. They took longer to marry and have children, and more were childless. A high proportion were in managerial positions; I suspect that because they were bright, they got ahead faster. Their brightness made another intriguing difference: the divorced women among them were happier than most, at least on our measure of satisfaction with their work pattern. Almost all divorced women worked full time, and their work was satisfying to them. The same was true of the women who remained single. All of them worked, and they were much happier with their work than most women are. Their satisfaction wasn't from income, either, but from the work itself. (Sears quoted in Goleman, 1980, p. 44)

Pauline Sears's late husband, Robert Sears, was in charge of overseeing the Terman study. Robert Sears was formerly head of the psychology department at Harvard, and was dean of Stanford University. He was also one of the 1528 children in Terman's original study (Goleman, 1980).

The Terman "kids" are now in their late 70s and early 80s, and, compared with the average person of that age, they are healthier, happier, and richer; they have had a far lower incidence of suicide, alcoholism, and divorce. These studies also dispel the myth that genius is next to insanity, since few of the Terman subjects have suffered from serious behavioral disorders compared with the average populace.

A possible reason for correlations between high IQ scores, happiness, and wealth, or the low incidence of alcoholism or divorce, may be that the subjects in Terman's study stayed in school (probably because they were good at it, which is what a high IQ would indicate). If you stay in school long enough, and do well, you're likely to obtain an advanced degree. And generally, if you have an advanced degree, you'll earn more money. People who are richer tend to be happier (perhaps that doesn't surprise you). If you are better educated, wealthier, and happier, you probably can afford better medical care, are more aware of how to take good care of yourself, and are under less stress. Finally, happier people get divorced less often.

CREATIVITY

Individual differences in intellectual capacity are not the only characteristics that have attracted interest in recent years. Psychologists are also concerned about the development of **creativity**. One researcher pointed out:

> Some of the controversy about the concept of creativity surrounds the question of the extent to which it is a personality trait, a specific cognitive ability, or a type of problem-

CONCEPT REVIEW: INTELLIGENCE

What the Lay Public often Believes:

1. An IQ does not change. Intelligence is something that you either have or don't have.

2. An IQ test tells how intelligent you are.

3. All IQ tests will give you roughly the same score.

4. An IQ test given to a child will tell you how smart he will be when he grows up.

5. IQ tests are good instruments for placing children in special programs.

What the Professionals Know:

1. A person's IQ score may change considerably during her lifetime. Intelligence isn't just something you are born with. The behaviors that we consider to be indicative of intelligence often can be taught or improved through experience.

2. "Intelligence" is a poorly defined term. IQ tests are limited and generally test for the kinds of skills that are helpful for school achievement. They often fail to measure creativity and other important skills that we usually consider to be signs of intelligence (for example, although someone might receive a very low IQ test score, she might show impressive survival skills in her own environment—she might be "street smart").

3. One person's IQ test scores may vary, sometimes widely, from one test to the next, depending on the skills and attributes tested.

4. IQ tests given to people when they are children generally are unreliable predictors of the people's scores as adults.

5. IQ tests are valuable instruments for placing children in special classes. However, the tests are sometimes poorly administered or interpreted; cultural or environmental circumstances might yield a low score in a child who has normal potential. For this reason, a score on an IQ test should never be the sole reason for placing a child in a special class.

MAINSTREAMING THE INTELLECTUALLY HANDICAPPED

If we consider intelligence not as a quality solely the result of inheritance but rather as a fluid and changing group of abilities sensitive to environmental effects, then our understanding of bright and dull, superior or retarded, must change (see Table 12.3).

How many times have you tangled with your own intellect? Sometimes it lets you down, sometimes it doesn't. Does this make you bright, average, dull? At one time or another, every child and adult faces some failure of intellect. Occasionally, incapable adults are left to fend for themselves (which may have unfortunate consequences). But what should we do with incapable children? If they can't match their school peers, should we label them "learning disabled" or "mentally handicapped" and send them for "special" education?

TABLE 12.3 IQ Scores and Their Respective Category Labels*

SCORE	CATEGORY
130+	Very superior
120–129	Superior
110–119	Bright normal
90–109	Average
80–89	Dull normal
70–79	Borderline retarded**
50–69	Mildly retarded (educable)
35–49	Moderately retarded (trainable)
20–34	Severely retarded
below 20	Profoundly retarded (custodial)

*Based on category labels in the Wechsler Adult Intelligence Scale and the American Psychiatric Association's *Diagnostic and Statistical Manual—IIIR.*

**Scores that determine retardation categories may vary from state to state.

How many Gregory Ochoas have been improperly labeled, have dropped out of school, and, unlike Gregory, have been unable to save themselves? On the other hand, some children do have serious problems that are more than occasional and that clearly require special help; we certainly can't abandon all testing and ignore them.

In 1975, Public Law 94-142 was enacted by the United States Congress to deal, in part, with the fact that too many children were not being given the education to which they were entitled; instead, they were being labeled and isolated, usually as a result of a single test or because they had a physical or social-emotional handicap.

In an attempt to change this unfortunate trend, Public Law 94-142 stipulated that the least restrictive educational environment be provided to meet all handicapped children's needs. This is sometimes referred to as **mainstreaming,** because every effort is made to keep the child within the regular academic class.

The results of this law aren't as clear-cut as its language. As with early intervention programs, the outcome seems to depend on the type of mainstreaming program used. In some cases, students who have been exposed to both mainstreaming and special education perform at about the same level in both environments (Semmel, Gottlieb, & Robinson, 1979). But in cases where mainstreaming is supported by the school district, the teachers, and the parents, and where careful planning has gone into selection of students for mainstreaming, then mainstreaming can be successful (Madden & Slavin, 1983).

A good example of the effects of mainstreaming on the intellectually

handicapped can be found in children with **Down syndrome.** Down syndrome is one of the most common birth defects, and is the leading cause of mental retardation in the United States. Children born with Down syndrome often are severely mentally handicapped. They are also commonly born with a constellation of other physical defects. In the past, many physicians told parents there was little hope of an intellectual life for these children. In some cases, physicians have even shown considerable ignorance:

> When Mindie Crutcher was born, physicians said she would always be hopelessly retarded, that she would never sit up, never walk, never speak. "She will never know you're her mother," they told 25-year-old Diane Crutcher. "Tell relatives you baby is dead." Today, the child who would never sit up is a lively seventh-grader. The child who would never walk is the star of dance recitals. The child who would never talk or know her own mother told a symposium of physicians she was "glad Mom and Dad gave me a chance" (Turkington, 1987, p. 42)

Mainstreaming has posed a particular challenge for children with Down syndrome, perhaps because it was so commonly believed that these children were capable of very little, but this challenge has been met by some successful mainstreaming programs. Earlier, many children born with Down syndrome were institutionalized because many physicians and parents often believed that education could not possibly help. But after Public Law 94-142 was passed, many Down syndrome children were given educational opportunities for the first time. One institutionalized girl (with a rarer and less severe form of Down syndrome), who began educational training as a result of the law, received a 2-year associate's degree in early childhood education from the University of Maine (Turkington, 1987).

Researchers now believe that the *majority* of children born with Down syndrome "who are reared at home in middle- or upper-middle class families can be expected to be educable when they enter school" (Turkington, 1987, p. 44). Psychologist John Rynders and his colleagues at the University of Minnesota designed Project EDGE to improve communication skills in children with Down syndrome. The children with Down syndrome entered Project EDGE when they were 30 months old. Seven of the 13 children in the project are currently in educable classes or in a combination of regular and educable classes. In 1984, a follow-up study of 13 EDGE children found that 11 of them were

reading with comprehension at or above second-grade level (Turkington, 1987), a far cry from being "hopelessly retarded, never able to sit up, never able to walk, never able to speak." In 1986, the U.S. Congress passed Public Law 99-457, which was designed to provide early intervention for handicapped children. This extention to Public Law 94-142 encouraged states to begin helping handicapped children from birth, perhaps preparing these children for future regular schooling, as did Project EDGE.

The main concern about mainstreaming has centered around whether handicapped children will be accepted by the normal children in the regular classroom. Two Australian studies, carried out to examine both the academic and the social progress of children with Down syndrome in

the regular classroom, demonstrated that most of the children were well accepted by their peers (Hudson & Clunies-Ross, 1984; Pieterse & Center, 1984). All the handicapped children in these studies had attended some form of early intervention program, such as Project EDGE, and then had been mainstreamed into the regular classroom. These studies emphasize that even though children with mental handicaps may require some form of special intervention or help, they also can do well, if given the chance—and mainstreaming is one way to help them fulfill their potential. Mainstreaming also gives children in the regular classroom the opportunity to learn compassion, tolerance, and understanding, and, even more important, to learn about the special potentials of handicapped children.

CONVERGENT PRODUCTION
In J. P. Guilford's model of intelligence, a type of thinking in which an individual searches through his or her knowledge and uses all that can be found to converge upon one correct answer.

DIVERGENT PRODUCTION
In Guilford's model of intelligence, a type of thinking in which a person searches for multiple ideas or solutions to a problem. It is characteristic of the creative thought process.

FIGURE 12.7

What do you see?

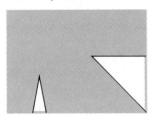

solving strategy that might be learned (Michael, 1977). If it is the latter, there is less need to search for those who know the process than to teach the process to everyone. (Fox, 1981, p. 1108)

Defining *creativity* is difficult, but we all seem to have some idea of what it means. Look at the picture in Figure 12.7 and decide what it is. A fairly common but rather uncreative answer is that it looks like a broken window. But what if someone told you that it was a boat arriving too late to save a drowning witch? That's a more creative response.

One way of defining creativity is to apply the four criteria of *novelty, appropriateness, transcendence of constraints,* and *coalescence of meaning* (Jackson & Messick, 1968). Novel, of course, means new. Something creative should be new. However, spelling *cat* Q-R-S would be new but it wouldn't be appropriate. Jackson and Messick therefore included appropriateness as a necessary dimension. Something transcends constraints when it goes beyond the traditional. A creative idea may transcend constraints by lending a new perspective to something with which we are all familiar. Finally, the most creative ideas have meanings that coalesce over time. In other words, the depth and value of an extremely creative idea often are not apparent at first, but become more obvious as time passes. When Thomas Edison first developed the motion-picture projector, many people wondered why the great genius was wasting his time on something of so little value. It was only after some time that the full significance of the invention became apparent.

High creative ability is poorly predicted by IQ tests. Individuals with very similar IQs often differ considerably in their creativity (Torrance & Wu, 1981). This failure of IQ tests to predict creativity was investigated by Guilford and his colleagues in 1957. They believed that IQ tests typically measure a kind of intelligence different from that required for creativity. Two of the factors Guilford mentioned in his model of the intellect were **convergent production** and **divergent production.** Guilford argued that most IQ tests rely heavily on convergent production, in which people search their knowledge for all that they can find to help them converge on one correct answer. In divergent production, they use their knowledge to develop as many solutions as possible to a given problem. Figure 12.8 illustrates the difference between these two thought processes. Creativity, Guilford believes, relies more on divergent production (Guilford, 1983). If Guilford's view is accurate, then the ability to see many solutions to one problem is very different from the ability to develop one correct answer from a store of information.

Both thinking skills appear to be acquired, at least in part, through experience. In one study, 3- and 4-year-old children were given convergent games to play: blocks that had to be inserted into particular forms cut from a board. These children spent two-thirds of their time placing the pieces into the forms on the board. Another group of children, the divergent group, played with blocks only. Using the different block pieces, they engaged in a wide variety of activities. A third group, a control group, did not partake in either the convergent or the divergent games. After the play period, the divergent group performed better than did the other two groups on new divergent tasks, whereas the convergent group performed better than the other two on new convergent tasks (Pepler & Ross, 1981).

Some tests have been designed to predict creativity by measuring divergent production. One such test, described by Michael Wallach (1970), employs the

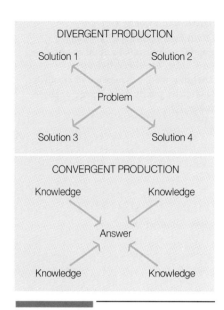

FIGURE 12.8

Illustrations of divergent and convergent production.

Artistic creativity is not measured by IQ tests. Individuals with very similar IQs often differ considerably in their creativity.

concept of **ideational fluency.** Ideational fluency is the ability to develop a large number of ideas appropriate to a particular task. To measure ideational fluency, researchers might ask someone to name as many uses as possible for a common object such as a cork or a shoe or to point out all the similarities between a train and a tractor. People with high ideational fluency produce many answers (Wallach & Kogan, 1965). Divergent production tests such as this one are much more accurate in their predictions of creativity than are IQ tests. In a study of almost 500 college students (Wallach & Wing, 1969), researchers found that ideational fluency correlated well with creative attainments such as receiving prizes in science contests, publishing original writing, or exhibiting artwork. Like IQ test scores, ideational fluency scores among older children appear to be fairly stable over time (Kogan & Pankove, 1972).

SOME FINAL THOUGHTS ON INTELLIGENCE

Biology is not democratic. Some of us are tall, some of us are short, and some of us are no doubt better biologically organized to develop skills considered indicators of intelligence. Inheritance is important. Yet, as the Ypsilanti Project showed, intelligence (or whatever it is that our "intelligence" tests measure) can be dramatically affected by the environment. Intelligence might best be considered a complex interaction between genetic heritage and experience. The Terman subjects probably did well in school, and therefore did well on IQ tests, which ask academic types of questions, both because they inherited excellent brains and nervous systems and also because they were stimulated at home and school to learn and to develop their cognitive and intellectual skills.

EPILOGUE: THE GIFTS

Frank Lloyd Wright (1867–1959) was the greatest architect of his generation. His influence on the shape and structure of the homes and buildings of America continues to this day. There can be no question that he was a creative genius.

The following is an account of how his mother's desires may have fueled that genius.

In 1876, Frank Lloyd Wright's strong-willed mother decided that something had to be done to better her son's primary education. With this in mind, she traveled to Philadelphia to the Centennial Exhibition to see the Froebel gifts.

The "gifts used for art building," as they were called by their creator, Friederich Froebel, were designed to teach creativity to young children. Froebel's methods for using the gifts were involved and complex and predated many of the activities now common to most kindergartens, such as paper folding, wood carving, and clay and sand construction. Froebel advocated that each day the gifts be used for structured, semistructured, and free play activities.

Mrs. Wright, who had already decided that she wanted her son to become an architect, came away from the exhibition convinced that these gifts, most of which consisted of sets of wooden blocks of ever-increasing geometric complexity and which were to be used for "artistic construction, to teach order, exactness, and variations, and predispose the child's mind for his later study in geometry, algebra, and trigonometry" (Clements, 1981, p. 119), would be useful for teaching young Frank.

She began by giving her child the first gift, a set of beautifully colored balls of woolen yarn to teach "concepts of color, roundness, softness, up, down, around, come and go, and near and far" (Clements, 1981, p. 119). Thereafter, every week Mrs. Wright commuted to Boston to take lessons from one of Froebel's disciples on how to best use all the gifts. She even covered the walls of her son's room with blueprints.

Every day, after "her housework was done and providing ample time, she and her seven-year-old son would sit quietly by a low mahogany table and work with the blocks" (Clements, 1981, p. 120). In accordance with Froebel's instructions, after building something interesting with the blocks, young Frank was not encouraged to give in to his natural childish inclination to tear it all down and to build something new. Instead, he was instructed to modify what he had done at least 20 different ways. Froebel wanted his method to encourage divergent thinking.

Did these early experiences influence Frank Lloyd Wright? In 1957, the great architect was asked when he had first begun his profession. He said,

> *Back to the Froebel kindergarten blocks. Presented by my teacher mother with the Froebel "Gifts," then actually as a child I began to be an architect. For several years, I sat at the little kindergarten table ruled by lines about four inches wide. The smooth cardboard triangles and maplewood blocks were important. All are in my fingers to this day. (Wright, 1957, p. 19)*

Of course, many children who used the gifts did not become great architects. Perhaps it was only a coincidence that Frank Lloyd Wright did, or perhaps the desires of Wright's mother shaped him in a particular occupational direction and then his genius took it from there. There is no way to know from the outcome of just one individual—admittedly a very special individual—what effect particular early experiences might, or might not, have had. But we do know that a certain amount of creativity can be taught. Did Mrs. Wright find some combination of love, interaction, play, and work that did the job better than anyone might guess? What did she do? What power did she give him? At the age of 91 years, during the very last interview he ever gave, in the fleeting hours before his death, Frank Lloyd Wright's thoughts returned to the "first gift" and he urged its use: "Let the child hold a sphere, a ball, and get a sense of God. Put blocks in the child's hands" (Farr, 1961, p. 6–9).

SUMMARY

■ The first scientific interest in intelligence and intelligence testing can be traced to the inheritance theories of Sir Francis Galton.

■ In the modern view, intelligence is an interaction between inherited capacity and environmental influences.

■ In 1905, Alfred Binet and Theodore Simon developed the precursor to the modern intelligence test. Its purpose was to determine which Parisian schoolchildren should receive special education.

■ Binet developed the concept of mental age, or MA. By comparing mental age with chronological age, CA, Binet was able to make comparisons among children. The German psychologist L. William Stern developed the formula MA ÷ CA × 100 = IQ, which yielded a rough index of how bright or dull any child was compared with school peers.

■ Although we have IQ tests, intelligence itself has never been defined adequately, and there is controversy over whether these tests measure intelligence as most people use the term.

■ A test is said to be valid if it measures what it claims to measure. IQ tests have been found to be valid for predicting school performance and as tools in clinical assessment.

■ The amount of weight or emphasis given to any one ability measured on a test is called a factor load. Some IQ tests measure particular factors more than others do. For this reason, the same individual may score differently on different IQ tests.

■ To balance a test for factors so that each ability is tested only once, L. L. Thurstone advocated use of a technique called factor analysis.

■ According to Thurstone and other factor analysts, there is no general ability called intelligence; rather, there are many different kinds of intelligence. The debate over this issue continues today.

■ Psychologist Robert J. Sternberg has developed a triarchic theory of intelligence that includes componential intelligence (the cognitive problem-solving and information-processing skills measured by most IQ tests), contextual intelligence (the individual's ability to adapt to her environment) and experiential intelligence (how quickly one can make a newly learned skill routine).

■ Psychologists have studied the heritability of human intelligence and other characteristics by examining people who are related to one another. Based on current data, many psychologists agree that heredity does play a role in determining individual differences and intelligence. How important it is in comparison with environmental experiences has yet to be determined.

■ In 1896, Sir Francis Galton observed that firstborn children appear to have a distinct advantage over other children in certain areas of development. Firstborns are more articulate, tend to score higher on intelligence tests, and are more reflective than children born later. However, not all scientists agree that there is a significant birth-order effect.

■ According to researcher Arthur Jensen, the fact that whites average 15–18 points higher than blacks on IQ tests was mainly the result of genetic variables. Other people argue that cultural bias on the tests accounts for the discrepancy.

■ In one study, Scarr and Weinberg gathered data on the IQ scores of black children adopted by white families. They discovered that the younger the black children were at the time of adoption, the closer their IQs were to white IQ averages.

■ Attempts have been made to devise a culture-fair test, one that contains no cultural bias. However, even on tests that do not use language, an advantage will go to people from cultures incorporating any types of skills or activities required by the test.

■ The Ypsilanti Project and home-based early-intervention projects have generally been successful in raising the intellectual levels of the children who participated.

■ Intellectual changes are difficult to measure over time. Tests measure different skills in subjects of different ages, and as a result reliability is not always high.

■ Lewis Terman conducted a study that has surveyed gifted children for over 60 years and is still in progress. The Terman kids are now in their seventies, and, compared with the average person of that age, they are healthier, happier, and richer, and they have a far lower incidence of suicide, alcoholism, and divorce.

■ Jackson and Messick have judged creativity by four criteria—novelty, appropriateness, transcendence of constraints, and coalescence of meaning. High creativity correlates poorly with high IQ scores.

■ Some tests have been designed to predict creativity by measuring divergent production, the search for multiple solutions to a problem. One such test, described by Michael Wallach, employs the concept of ideational fluency, or an individual's ability to produce many ideas.

SUGGESTIONS FOR FURTHER READING

1. Anastasi, A. (1988). *Psychological testing* (6th ed.). New York: Macmillan. A college-level text that evaluates psychological tests, including intelligence tests.

2. Chapman, P. D. (1988). *Schools as sorters: Lewis M. Terman, applied psychology, and the intelligence testing movement. 1890–1930.* New York: New York University Press.

This book helps describe the age into which Terman's ideas so neatly fit. It also deals with Terman's student, Kimball Young, and how he encountered the misuse of intelligence tests to improperly label Hispanic children as retarded, an experience that led him to reject Galton's idea of inherited intelligence, which had been embraced by Terman.

3. Fancher, R. E. (1985). *The intelligence men: Makers of the I.Q. controversy*. New York: Norton. A discussion of the history and controversies involved in intelligence testing.

4. Lazar, I., & Darlington, R. (1982). *Lasting effects of early education: A report from the Consortium for Longitudinal Studies*. Monographs of the Society for Research in Child Development, 47(2-3, Serial No. 195). A monograph that evaluates the effects of early childhood education on children at risk for learning problems.

5. Lewontin, R. C., Rose, S., & Kamin, L. J. (1984). *Not in our genes*. New York: Pantheon Books. A politically motivated discussion of the genetic determinants of traits, including intelligence. Presents the view that IQ is largely determined by environmental variables.

6. Minton, H. L. (1988). *Lewis M. Terman: Pioneer in psychological testing*. New York: New York University Press. An interesting book that chronicles the personal circumstances surrounding the emergence of Terman's work.

7. Sternberg, R. J. (1986). *Intelligence applied: Understanding and increasing your intellectual skills*. New York: Harcourt Brace Jovanovich. Provides a general overview of the ways in which people can be intelligent and how that intelligence can be increased.

8. Terman, L. M., & Oden, M. H. (1959). *The gifted group at midlife*. Palo Alto, CA: Stanford University Press. Reports on Terman's longitudinal study of gifted children, including their achievements and adjustments.

CHAPTER 13 | Personality

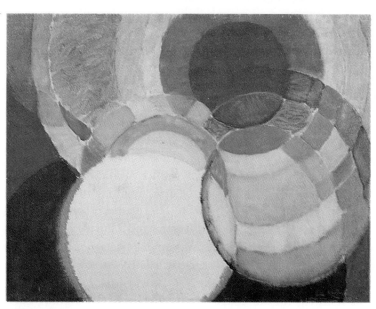

Prologue

Why Psychologists Study Personality

Theories of Personality
   Personality Types
   The Trait Approach
   The Psychoanalytic Approach
   Behavioral and Social Learning
       Approaches
   The Humanistic Approach

Personality Assessment
   Measuring Personality Traits
   Predictive Validity and Reliability
   Psychoanalytic Personality Assessment
   Behavioral Personality Assessment
   Humanistic Personality Assessment

Epilogue: The Eye of the Beholder

PROLOGUE

As the Second World War entered its final months in Asia, thousands of Japanese living in a captured part of China called Manchuria were forced to flee from the advancing Russian army. Attacked by angry Chinese, suffering from extreme hunger and cold weather, Japanese parents were often forced to leave their children behind. They did this to save the children from the hardships of the escape or because the adults could not flee quickly enough with the children in tow. As a result, over 2,500 Japanese children were left behind, usually with childless Chinese couples who offered to adopt them and raise them as their own.

After the war, the Japanese parents were unable to try to find their children because of the Chinese civil war and the closing off of contact with Japan following the rise of Mao-tse Tung. It wasn't until 1981, 36 years after the war ended, that the Japanese government was able to persuade the Chinese government to facilitate contact between the war orphans and their parents.

By this time, most of the "orphans" were middle-aged, had Chinese spouses, and had teenage children of their own. Still, almost all of them took the opportunity to travel with their families to Japan to find their Japanese parents and relatives. Relying mostly on memories of their family names and locations, they began the search. Of those who were older than 9 at the time of separation, 77.5 percent were reunited with their families. Of those who were younger than 5, whose memories were less complete, only 31.3 percent were successful (Tseng, Ebata, Miguchi, Egawa, & McLaughlin, 1990).

As the orphans' search became news, both Japanese researchers in Tokyo and American researchers in Hawaii realized that it presented the chance of a lifetime for anyone interested in studying personality and its formation. These researchers were interested because they knew that distinct cultures encourage different characteristics or personality traits in their members. There are well-described differences between Japanese and Chinese (Yang, 1986; Doi, 1962; Lebra, 1976). The researchers wondered if the orphans would be likely to have retained a higher proportion of the traits most encouraged by Japanese culture, such as those concerned with interpersonal relations, temperament, attitudes toward work, manners, and habits, than would be expected to be found among the Chinese. Or would having lived in China for all those years have lessened the acquisition of traits more typical of Japanese culture? In other words, they were asking an old question, "How much of personality is formed in childhood?" This was a unique chance to find out.

To their surprise, the "orphans" retained many of the attitudes and personality characteristics more common to the Japanese, even though many had been exposed to Japanese culture for less than 7 years of their 40 plus years of life. This finding does suggest that personality traits may be acquired early in life and then remain fairly resistant to change thereafter (Tseng, Ebata, Miguchi, Egawa, & McLaughlin, 1990). Because of this research, the old adage "As the twig is bent, so grows the tree" takes on greater importance.

Although the researchers didn't rule out genetic influences (especially where temperament was concerned—see Chapter 11), many studies of adopted infants from other cultures show the environment to be a forceful molder of personality. This study, however, was the first chance to investigate a large group of children raised for a few years in one culture and then transferred to another for the remainder of their childhoods and many years of their adulthoods. To be able to see the initial effect of the first culture so clearly tells us something about childhood as a special time of personality formation.

In this chapter, we'll examine what personality is and how it is assessed. We'll look at personality from the viewpoint of trait theorists, psychoanalysts, behaviorists, and humanists. Each position has made an important contribution to our understanding of personality, and each takes a different view of personality.

WHY PSYCHOLOGISTS STUDY PERSONALITY

Psychology is the study of behavior. If any behavior were as likely as any other to occur at any given time, it would not be possible to develop a science of psychology. Behavior would be so random that it could not be predicted. But behavior isn't that way. People often are consistent; they reveal qualities in their behavior that can be relied on. You already know this about yourself, your friends, and your family. You know that some people are almost sure to be shy in a particular circumstance, while others probably will be aggressive or outgoing and warm. You've learned to count on certain behaviors from certain people. To a psychologist, this means that the behaviors have predictability, which is the essence of any science.

By assuming that an individual will act in a certain way, we are implying that we know something about that individual's **personality**. Personality is a certain consistency in a person's behavior that remains fairly stable under varying conditions. In fact, when someone does something inconsistent, we often say, "He acted like a different person."

Psychologists wonder whether personality is internally or externally governed or perhaps is controlled by a combination of factors. Is personality shaped primarily by environmental (external) forces? If it is, it will change drastically if the environment changes drastically. If, on the other hand, personality is subject to internal controls, then altering the environment drastically may have less effect. Psychologists want to find out how stable personalities are and what controls them.

PERSONALITY
The organization of relatively enduring characteristics unique to an individual, as revealed by the individual's interaction with his or her environment.

■ THEORIES OF PERSONALITY

To a psychologist, the word *personality* refers to the whole person, not just to a part. Personality encompasses intelligence, motivation, emotion, learning, abnormality, cognition, and even social interactions. In describing someone's personality, you might refer to any of these areas. You might say that someone is intelligent, friendly, good humored, and eager to learn. Although these are different aspects of one person, they add up to a description of personality.

There are many theories of personality, each with a different emphasis and explanation of why certain personalities develop. Like all theories, personality theories should be testable, so that we can create a science of personality. A solid theory of personality would be valuable, because it could be used to assess people and to guide them toward the endeavors to which they are suited. Certain personalities may be suited for certain kinds of work. Other personalities may signal future trouble in the same work. Haven't you ever questioned whether your personality was right for a particular job or was well matched with another person's for a successful marriage, business relationship, or friendship? All of us have wondered at one time or another whether we wouldn't benefit from a change in personality. Imagine how useful it would be if personality could be measured, so that we could choose the lifestyles for which we were best suited and that would enable us to lead the most productive lives. This is the applied goal of all personality theory.

Historically, investigators of personality have attempted to group people into types. This seems a straightforward approach. Other sciences began in the same way. Chemistry has classified the elements according to type, and physics has classified matter and energy according to type. Similarly, personality researchers have been interested in grouping people according to their behavioral differences.

Personality Types

One of the earliest endeavors to categorize people by type of personality was made by the Greek physician Hippocrates (460–377 B.C.). Hippocrates classified four types: *melancholic* (sad), *phlegmatic* (listless and tired), *sanguine* (content or optimistic), and *choleric* (easy to anger). With his limited understanding of biology, he believed that these different personality types were caused by one or more of four body fluids he called *humors*. He concluded that a melancholic temperament was the result of too much black bile, a phlegmatic temperament was the result of too much phlegm, a sanguine temperament was the result of too much blood, and a

ENDOMORPH

One of Sheldon's three body types. An endomorph is broad and thick in proportion to height, is round, and has fairly weak muscles and bones. The corresponding temperament is viscerotonic.

MESOMORPH

One of Sheldon's three body types. A mesomorph is characterized by a predominance of muscle and bone, as in an athlete. The corresponding temperament is somatotonic.

ECTOMORPH

One of Sheldon's three body types. An ectomorph is relatively thin and physically weak. The corresponding temperament is cerebrotonic.

INTROVERT

One of Jung's personality types. An introvert is socially withdrawn, emotionally reserved, and self-absorbed.

EXTROVERT

One of Jung's personality types. An extrovert is gregarious, focuses on external events, is not introspective, and likes to be with others.

TRAITS

Distinguishing qualities, properties, or attributes of a person that are consistently displayed. According to Allport, a trait is a predisposition to respond to many types of stimuli in the same manner.

FIGURE 13.1

Sheldon's body types.

choleric temperament was the result of too much yellow bile. Of course, modern medicine has disproved these ideas, but they are interesting attempts to correlate behavior and physical state.

Among the modern theories of personality types, one developed by the American physician William Sheldon has received considerable attention. Sheldon found a moderate correlation between physique (body type) and personality (Sheldon 1940; 1944). Figure 13.1 illustrates the three physiques—**endomorph, mesomorph,** and **ectomorph.** Sheldon measured subjects according to 7-point scales for each of the three dimensions. For instance, a person who rated 2, 5, and 7 would be low on endomorphy, moderate on mesomorphy, and extremely high on ectomorphy. Table 13.1 outlines the kinds of personality characteristics that Sheldon believed were correlated with the three body types.

Why should different personalities have been found to be associated with different body types? Some researchers, in an effort to explain Sheldon's findings, have argued that physique and personality may be correlated simply because of the kinds of experiences different people have. Because of his body type, an endomorph may find vigorous sports uncomfortable and thus may avoid them. A mesomorph may excel at sports and therefore take part in them frequently. An ectomorph may learn at an early age that she is weaker than other children and consequently may become fearful and introverted. These correlations even may have been due to biases among observers and raters. Because many people think of fat individuals as jolly, thin individuals as restrained, and muscular individuals as athletic, raters may have emphasized these characteristics regardless of subjects' actual behavior (Tyler, 1956). So far, no cause–effect relationship has been established between Sheldon's body types and certain personalities.

As another example, there is Carl Jung (1875–1961), a Swiss psychiatrist and psychoanalyst, who developed a personality theory that separated individuals into two types he called **introverts** and **extroverts** (Jung, 1933). Introverts are withdrawn and tend to avoid social contact, while extroverts are outgoing and try to interact with people as often as possible. Because interaction with other people is an important dimension of personality, as well as an important part of our lives, whether we are introverted or extroverted can have a powerful effect on our existence.

Categorizing individuals according to type is appealing because it appears so simple and reasonable. Yet is it this simplicity that limits the value of any typing system. People are complex, and they behave in many different ways under different circumstances. Researchers have therefore found it extremely difficult to type individuals. More often, they prefer to consider people to have certain traits in less or greater degrees.

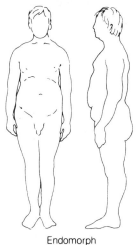
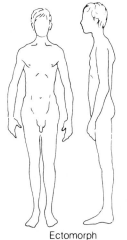
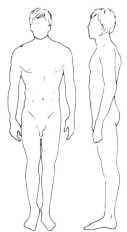

Endomorph   Ectomorph   Mesomorph

The Trait Approach

Traits are important underlying and enduring qualities of a person. We use trait words all the time to describe ourselves and others, Look at the following list of common trait words. Which are most descriptive of your personality?

moody   rigid   pessimistic   unsociable
passive   thoughtful   controlled   even-tempered
sociable   talkative   easygoing   carefree
touchy   aggressive   changeable   optimistic
anxious   sober   reserved   quiet
careful   peaceful   reliable   calm
outgoing   responsive   lively   active
restless   excitable   impulsive

As you can see, many of these trait words may be descriptive of you, but to greater or lesser degrees.

ALLPORT'S TRAIT THEORY.   One of the best-known advocates of the trait approach was Gordon Allport (1897–1967). Allport recognized that each person has certain consistent aspects or, as Allport put it, "predispositions to respond to environmental stimuli in certain ways." What might make one person angry might make another person laugh because of the way the two people are predisposed to respond or, as you or I might say, because of their personalities.

Allport considered traits to be enduring and also general—that is, likely to occur under many different circumstances (Allport, 1937). He recognized that some traits are more enduring and general than others are. Consequently, he drew distinctions among **cardinal traits, central traits,** and **secondary traits** (Allport & Odbert, 1936). Cardinal traits are the most general and enduring. Allport argued that some people have no cardinal traits. For a trait to be cardinal, it must be the overriding factor in a person's life. For example, hatred may have been a cardinal trait of Adolf Hitler, and reverence for every living thing may have been a cardinal trait of Albert Schweitzer.

Central traits are far more common. They are less enduring and less general than are cardinal traits, but they are nonetheless important to us all. According to Allport, central traits are the basic units that make up personality. Surprisingly few central traits are enough to capture the essence of a person. Allport found that when college students were asked to write a description of a person whom they knew well, they tended to mention on an average only 7.2 central traits (Allport, 1961).

Secondary traits are far less enduring and less general than are central traits. In fact, Allport often used the term *attitudes* rather than secondary traits. Examples of secondary traits might be liking to watch old movies, attending baseball games frequently, and putting off work until almost too late.

CARDINAL TRAITS
In Allport's theory, an encompassing trait that seems to influence almost every act of a person who possesses the trait. Cardinal traits are uncommon, observed in only a few people.

CENTRAL TRAITS
In Allport's theory, behavioral or personality tendencies that are highly characteristic of a given individual and easy to infer. Allport argues that surprisingly few central traits, perhaps five or ten, can give a fairly accurate description of an individual's personality.

SECONDARY TRAITS
In Allport's theory, traits that are not as crucial as central traits for describing personality. Secondary traits are not demonstrated often because they are related to only a few stimuli and a few responses.

Gordon Allport (1897–1967).

PHYSIQUE	TEMPERAMENT
TABLE 13.1 Personalities Corresponding to Sheldon's Body Types	
Endomorphic: soft, round, overdeveloped digestive viscera	Viscerotonic: relaxed, loves to eat, sociable
Mesomorphic: muscular, rectangular, strong	Somatotonic: energetic, assertive, courageous
Ectomorphic: long, fragile, large brain, sensitive nervous system	Cerebrotonic: restrained, fearful, introversive, artistic

SURFACE TRAITS

From Cattell's theory of personality, a cluster or group of behaviors that are overt and appear to go together. Inferring the existence of a surface trait makes it possible to classify similar behaviors under one term; for example, constant fighting, yelling, and making angry facial expressions can be categorized under the surface trait term *aggressive*.

SOURCE TRAITS

From Cattell's theory of personality, traits that can be identified only through factor analysis and that are more important than surface traits. Cattell argues that personality can be reduced to 16 source traits and that, although surface traits may appear to be more valid to the common-sense observer, source traits have greater utility in accounting for behavior.

Allport felt that no two people have exactly the same traits, and as a result every personality is unique. Still, many people have traits that are similar, and these traits manifest themselves in the way people interact with the environment (see Figure 13.2).

CATTELL'S TRAIT THEORY.   Some trait theorists have emphasized the need for statistical analysis, such as factor analysis (see Chapter 12), to isolate different traits. After all, you wouldn't expect to find a separate and distinct trait for every trait word in the English language. There would be many overlaps. Raymond Cattell (1950) held this view. He was not satisfied with simply classifying traits; he wanted to know how traits were organized and how they were related to one another.

Cattell began his work by examining the visible or apparent portions of a personality. He referred to the obvious traits that we can all see as **surface traits.** He used questionnaires and direct observation to compile data about surface traits from many people. His subsequent statistical analysis turned up certain surface traits that seemed to come in clusters. To Cattell, such groupings indicated a single underlying trait. Cattell referred to these more basic traits as **source traits.** In Fig. 13.3 you can see results from the 16 personality factor questionnaire developed by Cattell (Cattell, Saunders, & Stice, 1950). In this example, the questionnaire was given to three groups of subjects: airline pilots, creative artists, and writers. As the results show, members of different professions can have similar or different personality profiles. In this case, creative artists and writers have more in common than either group has with airline pilots (Cattell, 1973). Cattell points out that this kind of personality profile can help psychologists to predict behavior. For example, Cattell has shown that a person who scores very high on factor Q3 tends to be accident-prone. A low score on Q means the person is conservative, and scale Q2 helps predict success in school. People with the most stable marriages were similar on factor A, which indicates whether a person was aloof or warm; factor L, the dimension of trusting versus suspicious; and factor Q1, whether a person is group-dependent or self-sufficient. Factor E also is important. Husbands from stable marriages tend to be a little more dominant than their wives were, but husbands who were much more dominant than their wives tend to have unstable marriages.

Trait theory has been criticized for a number of reasons. It is not yet clear which traits are the most enduring and general. Many personality "traits" may be situationally dependent (Bem & Allen, 1974; Endler & Magnusson, 1976). A person who is dominant in one situation may be submissive in another, and a person who is forthright in one circumstance may be sly in another (Becker, 1960). Another problem has to do with how traits are ascribed (Rorer & Widiger, 1982). Sometimes traits are ascribed only after a considerable amount of behavior has been consistently observed; at other times, a few isolated behaviors are used to delineate a trait (Pervin, 1985). For example, before we said that someone has the trait of honesty, she

FIGURE 13.2

Allport viewed traits as intervening variables that help to relate stimuli and responses that at first may not appear related.

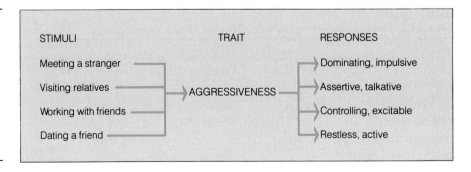

STIMULI	TRAIT	RESPONSES
Meeting a stranger		Dominating, impulsive
Visiting relatives	AGGRESSIVENESS	Assertive, talkative
Working with friends		Controlling, excitable
Dating a friend		Restless, active

might need to show her honesty in many different situations and circumstances. On the other hand, someone who commits one or two murders in his lifetime may be ascribed the trait of homicidal, even though an exceedingly small percentage of his entire behavioral repertoire resulted in murder (Rorer & Widiger, 1983). Traits often are assigned in this fairly arbitrary fashion. Still, research continues to indicate that there are characteristics, uniquely combined in each individual, that appear to endure in a significant enough way to make it difficult to dispense with the idea of traits (Buss, 1989). The concept of traits continues to play an important role in our understanding of personality.

Trait researchers recognize the criticisms of trait theory. They do not argue that all of human personality can be explained by traits, and they agree that the immediate forces in a given situation will always have some effect on behavior and that traits sometimes are ascribed in an arbitrary manner (Pervin, 1985). For a science of personality to be broad enough to predict behavior adequately, environmental aspects and the problem of ascription have to be considered as well. In this sense, there are probably no strict trait theorists; that is, no psychologist sees the entire personality as the result of traits alone. As researchers Jackson and Paunonen have humorously pointed out,

> one encounters the term "trait theorist," with its connotations, in the writings of several authors. Like witches of 300 years ago, there is confidence about their existence, and even possibly their sinister properties, although one is hard pressed to find one in the flesh or even meet someone who has. Similarly, few theorists can be found who take the opposite extreme position that variables associated with the person play no role in behavior. What one can identify are different sets of investigators, some of whom prefer to focus on the stability or continuity of personality across situations, and others who seek to isolate variables in the environment which, for example, arouse motives. There is a third set, those who argue that it is the person–situation interaction that is of crucial importance (Endler & Magnusson, 1976; Magnusson & Endler, 1977; Mischel, 1977). (Jackson & Paunonen, 1980, p. 523)

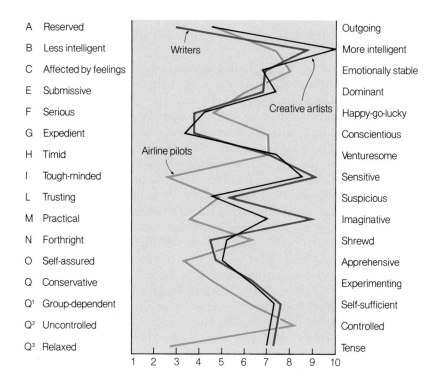

A	Reserved	Outgoing
B	Less intelligent	More intelligent
C	Affected by feelings	Emotionally stable
E	Submissive	Dominant
F	Serious	Happy-go-lucky
G	Expedient	Conscientious
H	Timid	Venturesome
I	Tough-minded	Sensitive
L	Trusting	Suspicious
M	Practical	Imaginative
N	Forthright	Shrewd
O	Self-assured	Apprehensive
Q	Conservative	Experimenting
Q¹	Group-dependent	Self-sufficient
Q²	Uncontrolled	Controlled
Q³	Relaxed	Tense

FIGURE 13.3

The 16 personality factor profiles developed by Cattell for three groups of subjects: airline pilots, creative artists, and writers. (SOURCE: Adapted from the Handbook for the 16PF, 1970.)

ID

In psychoanalytic theory, the reservoir of instinctive drives; the most inaccessible and primitive portion of the mind.

EGO

In psychoanalytic theory, the part of the personality that regulates the impulses of the id in order to meet the demands of reality and maintain social approval and self-esteem.

SUPEREGO

In psychoanalytic theory, the part of the personality that incorporates parental and social standards of morality.

PLEASURE PRINCIPLE

The psychoanalytic postulate that an organism seeks immediate pleasure and avoids pain. The id functions according to the pleasure principle.

REALITY PRINCIPLE

According to Freud, the principle on which the conscious ego operates as it tries to mediate between the demands of the unconscious id and the realities of the environment.

LIBIDO

According to Freud, the psychological energy driving the individual to seek gratification—principally sexual gratification, but also food, comfort, and happiness.

OEDIPUS COMPLEX

A Freudian term representing the sexual attachment of a boy to his mother. This desire is repressed and disguised in various ways. The child expresses jealousy and hatred of his father because the father can have relations with the mother that the son is denied.

DEFENSE MECHANISMS

Reactions to the anxiety caused by conflict that serve to protect and improve the self-image. The mechanisms are not deliberately chosen. They are common to everyone and raise serious problems for adjustment only when they are used excessively and prevent the person from coping realistically with difficulties.

Although the trait approach enjoys a certain popular appeal, it remains, after many years, a descriptive rather than an explanatory (see Table 1.1, page 17) approach, and it has not done a good job of predicting the wide ranges of human behaviors encountered in different situations (Pervin, 1985).

The Psychoanalytic Approach

One of the names most associated with psychology in the minds of people is Sigmund Freud, the founder of *psychoanalytic theory* (see Chapter 1). Freud opened a new era of investigation when he derived a model of personality based on his observations of many patients.

Freud studied human personality with the aid of techniques he developed for probing what he believed were the hidden or unconscious thoughts or desires of his patients. One such technique was the interpretation of dreams by analyzing their symbolic content (Freud, 1900/1953). Another was the analysis of slips of the tongue, which, like dreams, Freud believed revealed hidden desires and unconscious processes.

We use the term *psychoanalyst* to describe practitioners who have accepted Freud's theory either totally or to a considerable degree. Because Freud's theory of personality attempts to explain most of human behavior (Freud, 1940/1964), it is often considered to be a grand explanatory theory.

THE THREE-PART PERSONALITY. Freud relied on his knowledge of biology, psychology, and social experience to create a model—a picture of the personality—divided into three parts: the **id,** the **ego,** and the **superego** (see Figure 13.4). According to Freud, the id and ego are present at birth, while the superego develops through experience with the culture.

The id has no objective knowledge of reality. It ruthlessly and relentlessly drives the organism toward pleasure; it is therefore said to follow a **pleasure principle.**

The ego is the part of the personality that must deal with reality if the id's desires are to be met. The ego therefore functions according to a **reality principle.** For instance, the id may insist on possessing all the money in the bank, but it is the ego that must open the safe, disable the guards, and deal with the other realities of the situation.

On the other hand, we are taught that stealing is wrong, and this is where the superego comes in. Freud considered the superego to be the internal representation of an ideal expressed in terms of social and traditional values.

These hypothetical constructs (id, ego, and superego) were designed to create a picture of the biological (id), psychological (ego), and social (superego) aspects of personality. Freud believed that the dynamics of personality involve a continual conflict among the id, the ego, and the superego (Freud, 1917/1963). He thought that each person has a certain amount of psychological energy, or **libido,** and that conflicts among the three parts of the personality drain this energy. In particular, the instinctive pleasure drive often comes into conflict with acquired social inhibitions about expressing instinctive desires, with the consequent repression of such desires (Freud, 1905/1953). This antagonism is well illustrated in the classic unconscious conflict that Freud called the **Oedipus complex.**

In Freud's view, the major determinants of the personality come from this unconscious reservoir of repressed desires, which are basically irrational. The major theme of all Freudian psychodynamic personality theory is that people are constantly driven by unreasonable demands resulting from unconscious desires and that these desires must be brought to consciousness and resolved before a healthy personality can develop.

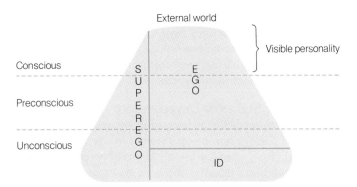

FIGURE 13.4

Freud's concept of the three-part personality.

INSTINCTS AND DEFENSE MECHANISMS. Freud considered sexual behavior and aggression to be instinctive drives. Throughout the animal kingdom, he argued, aggression helps animals to obtain needed food and territory, and sexual behavior maintains species; as such, both are necessary for survival. In our species, however, these aggressive tendencies and sexual desires run head on into cultural taboos against explicit sexual actions and uncontrolled violence.

According to Freud, this struggle between biological drives and social inhibitions produces anxiety, and the ego relies on what he called **defense mechanisms** to control and handle the anxiety effectively. Table 13.2 lists some of the more common psychological defense mechanisms. Freud argued that it was necessary for individuals to distort reality in some way to protect themselves from unacceptable

TABLE 13.2 Some Psychological Defense Mechanisms

Denial

The refusal to admit the existence of events that are unpleasant or that have produced anxiety.

> *Examples:* Someone who continues to buy on credit or to spend more than she has in a checking account may be denying that eventually there'll be a deficit of funds. Someone who continues to speed even after witnessing a terrible traffic accident is denying that such a thing could happen to him.

Rationalization

The justification of irrational, impulsive action, or even failure, to oneself or other people by substituting acceptable explanations for the real but unacceptable reasons.

> *Examples:* A thief rationalizes his stealing by pointing out that he was abused as a child. A doctor deals with his error in judgment by noting that "no one's perfect."

Reaction Formation

When an individual exhibits, and at the conscious level believes she possesses, feelings opposite to those possessed at the unconscious level.

> *Examples:* A parent who hates his child conceals this unwanted and stressful emotion by being overly protective or indulgent. A person is boastful and bellicose to hide feelings of inferiority.

Projection

The attribution of one's own undesirable thoughts or characteristics to other people.

> *Examples:* Someone who flirts with other people's spouses and who then inaccurately views ordinary social contacts by other people with his own spouse as flirtatious. Someone who steals and incorrectly assumes other people cannot be trusted.

In psychoanalytic theory, inordinate persistence in a particular psychosexual stage of development because the id has received either too much or too little satisfaction.

ANAL RETENTIVE PERSONALITY
According to Freud, a personality type formed by fixation at the anal stage. Its characteristics include stinginess, selfishness, and withholding.

Sigmund Freud (1856–1939), the founder of psychoanalysis.

unconscious thoughts and unwanted realities. At first, defense mechanisms may seem to be bad, because they twist the truth; some misrepresentation seems to be necessary, however, for our psychological well-being. In general, psychologists don't consider our use of defense mechanisms inappropriate or unhealthy unless we rely on these mechanisms to an extreme.

PSYCHOSEXUAL STAGES OF DEVELOPMENT.   In Freud's view, child development is an important predictor of later adult personality. According to Freud, during development each person passes through five psychosexual stages. The first three stages—oral, anal, and phallic—are centered on physical satisfaction derived from the erogenous zones (areas of the body that when stimulated, give rise to sexual pleasure, such as the lips or genitalia). They take place during the first 6 years of life. The later stages—latency and genital—occur between ages 6 years and adulthood, and Freud emphasized them less than the first three stages. In summary the stages are as follows:

■ *The Oral Stage (birth to approximately 1 year):* During this time, a child obtains the greatest satisfaction from stimulation of the lips, mouth, tongue, and gums. Freud noted that sucking and chewing are the chief sources of an infant's pleasure.
■ *The Anal Stage (approximately 1 to 3 years):* During this time, the child gains the greatest satisfaction from exercising control over the anus during elimination and retention. Freud believed that the anal stage reaches its peak once toilet training is successful.
■ *The Phallic Stage (approximately 4 to 6 years):* During this stage, the child derives the greatest pleasure from stimulating the genitals. The child also comes to identify with the same-sex parent, a critical step toward developing into a healthy, mature adult.
■ *The Latency Stage (approximately 6 years to puberty):* Freud called this the latency stage because he believed that the sexual drive becomes dormant at about the age of 6 years and remains so until the onset of puberty. During this time, children are supposedly free of erotic feelings and instead expend their efforts on acquiring cultural and social skills.
■ *The Genital Stage (puberty to adulthood):* Freud believed that heterosexual desire awakens during this time and that as long as no strong fixations have occurred, the child is on her way toward a "normal" life.

If the transition through these stages doesn't go smoothly, Freud argued, developmental problems can arise. **Fixation** may occur at any stage. For example, if a child's id doesn't receive enough satisfaction during the oral stage, the child may be reluctant to leave that stage until he feels fully satisfied. A *negative fixation* can result, according to Freud, in a manifestation of oral-stage processes later in adult life. Conversely, a person may want to retain oral-stage satisfaction in later life— a condition Freud called *positive fixation*. Both kinds of fixation result in similar behaviors, but for different reasons.

As an example of fixation, a person might remain immature in his social relations and engage excessively in oral activities, such as eating, talking, and smoking. Such behavior in adult life, Freud believed, might result from negative or positive fixation during the oral stage. Any fixation can lead to problems. If a child's id was not satisfied during toilet training because of the demands made by parents, the child might seek satisfaction through undue retention—an anal fixation. Freud believed that such an **anal retentive personality** would be expressed later in life in stinginess, selfishness, and the like.

CONTEMPORARIES OF FREUD.   Many prominent psychoanalysts who were students and colleagues of Freud broke with him and developed their own theories when their observations of their patients led them to different conclusions. Carl Jung, whom we mentioned earlier for his concepts of introversion and extroversion, for instance, believed that we possess two unconscious minds—a personal one, not unlike that envisioned by Freud, and a species-specific one inherited from our ancestors (Jung, 1936/1959). Jung called the latter concept the **collective unconscious.** He spent much of his life gathering religious and totemic artifacts from different cultures and comparing them in order to demonstrate that similar unconscious symbols have played a role in the psychology of all members of our species (Jung, 1955/1959).

Alfred Adler (1870–1937), a Viennese psychiatrist, was one of Freud's colleagues. Adler believed that people were more motivated by their hopes for the future than they were by their experiences of the past. He saw humankind in a much more benevolent light than did Freud, believing, in contradiction to Freud's view, that underlying biological drives and forces did not predestine humankind to follow a path of conflict and turmoil.

One of Adler's most important principles, which he believed to be a prime motivator in humans, was what he called *striving for superiority*. By this term, Adler was referring to a drive to fulfill one's potential and not, as the phrase might imply, to a wish to dominate other people. Adler's concept of striving for superiority is not unlike Maslow's concept of self-actualization (see Chapter 9); in fact, the humanist concept of self-actualization was derived, to a great degree, from Adler's ideas. Adler also believed that no matter how much we may have accomplished at any point in our lives, if we do not continue to grow and strive upward, feelings of inferiority will result. In this way, we are "pushed" by fears of inferiority and "pulled" by desires for superiority to fulfill our potential, each in our own unique way. Adlerian psychotherapy focuses on these ideas in the treatment of patients.

THE INFLUENCE OF PSYCHOANALYTIC THEORY. Freud's view of personality development has had a powerful influence on the history of psychology. A number of his concepts have been supported by modern research, including the existence of unconscious thoughts and motivations (Kihlstrom, 1987), that is, an individual's unawareness of forces that make him feel and behave as he does. However, it has proved difficult to test many of Freud's ideas by the scientific method (Hook, 1960). For example, to this day, no one has conclusively demonstrated that dreams necessarily mean anything or that there is any special content hidden in them. Furthermore, many of Freud's other ideas have not been well supported (Erwin, 1980). For instance, modern research indicates that the first 6 years of a person's life, while important and formative, are not as crucial to the development of adult personality as Freud believed they were. Then again, Freud's view shouldn't be considered complete just because Freud died. If Freud were alive today, Freudian theory might undergo considerable renovation at the hands of its creator.

Whether or not one agrees with Freud's theory of human personality, or with the views proposed by the other prominent psychoanalysts, their work is regarded as valuable because it has stimulated so much research. Its full value will remain uncertain until we can devise more ways to test it. In the interim, we owe Freud and his colleagues a historic debt of gratitude for their insights and for the impetus they provided to research into human personality.

Behavioral and Social Learning Approaches

Behavioral and social learning theories of personality have developed from the work of the behaviorists, beginning with John B. Watson early in this century (see Chapter 1).

COLLECTIVE UNCONSCIOUS
Jung's concept that a portion of the unconscious contains certain shared experiences, predispositions, and symbols that are inherited and found in all members of a given race or species.

BEHAVIOR THEORY. Following in the footsteps of Watson and others, psychologist B. F. Skinner put forward a view of behavior that implies that personality is controlled by processes fundamentally different from those envisioned by trait theorists or psychoanalysts (Skinner, 1953; 1969). Skinner and the behaviorists refuse to consider drives or other internal motivational factors. As we noted in Chapters 1 and 6, a fundamental aspect of their position is that anything not directly observable, such as drives or thoughts, has no place in an objective science.

Behaviorists believe that conditioning (see Chapter 6) is mostly responsible for the development of personality. They argue that complex social interactions and aspects of personality are due to the history of conditioning unique to each individual.

In addition, behaviorists do not consider traits to have roots within the person, but rather believe they are the products of environmental forces and learning. The reason some traits seem stable is that the environments in which individuals live often are stable for long periods. Skinner and other behaviorists contend that if the environment is sufficiently manipulated, then aspects of personality that have appeared to endure will disappear and quickly will be replaced by others. In this view, then, behavior is controlled by stimulus conditions, and it is not necessary to form hypotheses about internal motives, traits, or conflicts.

Consider the following example. Suppose you knocked on someone's door and asked for a contribution to a worthy charity. If the person gave you money, would you say that this was evidence of the trait of generosity? Or would you say that underlying motivational factors in the person's unconscious mind prompted the gift? Behaviorists argue that whether a person gives is determined by the immediate environment and the person's past history of reinforcement for giving. Furthermore, by manipulating the environment, it is possible to increase or decrease a person's willingness to be generous. In fact, you could do several things to increase the amount of money that people gave as you went door to door for charity (Cialdini & Schroeder, 1976; Kleinke, 1977; Bandura, 1969):

1. Dress well, but don't overdo it.
2. Carry identification that officially associates you with the charity.
3. Carry a see-through collection container; this allows the giver to see that other people have made donations.
   a. Make sure the container is always one-third full (so that it looks as though people have been giving but you still have a way to go).
   b. Remove all pennies (donors will believe that other people have been giving bills and silver—their cue to what they should give).
4. Travel with a colleague (more people will give if more people ask. Just imagine what you'd give if 100 people showed up at your place all at once to ask for a donation!).
5. If the donor is reluctant, use the phrase, "Even a penny will help" (very few people will give only a penny, and few will say that they don't have a penny).

Although the behaviorist arguments seem persuasive, and the theory is very popular in the United States—perhaps because of our democratic institutions and professed desire to view all people as equal at birth—there is evidence of individual differences in personality just after birth, too early for the environment to have had a significant effect. In Chapter 11, we discussed the findings of Thomas, Chess, and Birch that babies have noticeably different personalities just after birth and that these temperaments are long lasting. These data argue somewhat against the idea that personality is solely the result of environmental experience.

Other critics of the idea that situations determine behavior and personality have stated,

We have never met anyone who, from a behavioral viewpoint, was not a trait theorist. If one really believes that situations determine behavior, then there is no reason to test or interview prospective employees for jobs such as police officer; it is only necessary to structure the job situation properly. Picking a mate would simply be a matter of finding someone whose physical characteristics appeal to you. In a properly managed class all students would work up to their abilities. Do you know anyone who believes these things? Obviously not. (Rorer & Widiger, 1983, p. 445)

Trait theorists have further argued that just because situations may often determine behavior, this is not proof that traits don't exist.

The argument as to whether enduring internal qualities or environmental influences are the primary drive behind a person's behavior is known as the **person–situation debate**. In general, most researchers now agree that there is no way currently to assess which may have the most influence on a person and that most studies indicate that which one is stronger may be a function of the particular situation in which a person finds herself. As a rule, then, personality is understood as an *interaction* between a person's unique characteristics and the environmental forces that impinge on her (Kenrick & Funder, 1988; Carson, 1989).

SOCIAL LEARNING THEORY. Social learning theorists, such as Albert Bandura, argue that personality is shaped not only by environmental influences on the person but also by the person's ability to influence the environment (Bandura, 1978). As we discussed in Chapter 6, social learning theory states that thinking is an important determinant of behavior. The inclusion of cognitive viewpoints within a behavioral framework has been a relatively recent trend; an example is the work of personality learning theorist J. B. Rotter (1972). Rotter believes that the most important variables in determining personality are the person's expectations concerning future outcomes and the values of different reinforcements that might occur in a particular situation. In other words, a person's behavior depends on what she expects the outcome of any particular action to be and what those outcomes are worth. The likelihood that someone will be aggressive when trying to return merchandise to a department store would depend, then, on that person's expectations about whether aggression will work.

Rotter doesn't care for the term *trait*, preferring instead the term *generalized expectancy*. The implication is that your behavior or "trait" is really the result of your belief that the behavior will serve you well. Moreover, if traits—the stable aspect of a personality—are actually generalized expectancies, then changing the environment and giving you new experiences may lead to behavioral changes and differences in your personality. This potential is not consistent with the connotation

PERSON–SITUATION DEBATE
From personality theory, the argument concerning whether the primary drive behind a person's behavior is due to enduring internal qualities or environmental influences.

Actors are able to convince us that they have different traits and personalities when, in fact, they are only responding to direction from an external source. Behaviorists wonder if we aren't all actors.

of the word *trait*, which is that the qualities of personality are relatively enduring and unchangeable, even if the environment alters drastically.

Another reason for the apparent existence of consistent behavior in individuals may be the result of a social expectancy that encourages people to view other people as consistent. To make this idea clear, let's consider a truly ingenious experiment designed by the late social psychologist Stanley Milgram (1933–1984), who, sadly, had little time to develop this work fully.

Milgram recalled the story of the great swordsman and writer Cyrano de Bergerac, who, because his large nose made him too shy to pursue Roxane, the woman he loved, lent his words in love letters to his foolish friend Christian, so that he, Cyrano, might still court his beloved Roxane by proxy.

With this in mind, Milgram "created" people he called Cyranoids. A Cyranoid is anyone who, like Christian, speaks the words of another. In one variation of his work, Milgram recruited high-school teachers to interview an 11-year-old boy, asking them to determine the boy's level of general intellectual ability and achievement in areas of science and literature. Unbeknownst to the teachers on the interview panel, the only response that the boy would give to their questions would be to repeat what he was hearing in a concealed earpiece. Whose words was he hearing? The words of Stanley Milgram (the Cyrano of this experiment), who was answering the teacher's questions from a hidden location—the boy merely reported what Milgram said! Milgram, a Ph.D. and prominent social scientist, provided the teachers with the best and most intelligent answers that he could muster.

When the teachers graded the boy, they were way off. For example, in the area of social science, Milgram's specialty, the teachers compared the boy's answers to those of a typical tenth grader, although the boy had been giving the answers of a distinguished professor of social psychology (Herbert, 1985).

Milgram also conducted other experiments in which one Cyranoid would answer many questions or have a conversation, while the real hidden speakers changed off with one another every minute. Even when giving the answers of scores of different people, the speaker was viewed as consistent by the rater, not, as one might expect, as an individual with a fragmented personality. This work implies that there may be a strong bias at work among people to view another person, and her "personality," as unified.

As you can see, in behavioral and social learning theories, the individual's personality is considered to be situationally dependent (Bandura, 1969), or dependent on the expectations of other people. In trait theories and psychoanalytic theories, the personality is believed to be stable across many situations and shaped by underlying motivations and predispositional forces.

The Humanistic Approach

The central focus of all humanistic theories of personality is the concept of self. *Self* refers to the individual's internal experiences and subjective evaluations. Humanistic theories are quite varied, but they share a number of basic themes. They reject the notion that underlying traits or unconscious motivations and conflicts are important forces in the development of personality, arguing instead that human beings are endowed with free will and free choice. Similarly, they reject the idea that environmental forces are the major determinants of personality. Instead, individuals are seen as aware beings capable of unique experiences based on their own view of the world and self.

Most humanistic theories stress that people have a positive drive to grow as human beings and to realize their potential to the fullest. Humanistic approaches are sometimes *phenomenological*. This means that for each of us, there is no objective world; there is only our subjective or personal experience of the world, which depends on our self-concept, attitudes, and beliefs. Humanists argue that to understand anyone's personality, you must know how he perceives the world. You must find a way to "stand in the other person's shoes," even if only for a moment.

That people move in the direction of fully developing their personal potential, especially their emotional potential, is called self-actualization (Maslow, 1954). This concept, as you recall, was derived, in part, from the work of Alfred Adler. Adler's work, in many ways, is viewed as a transition from the psychoanalytic theories predominant in Freud's day to the modern humanistic view.

According to the humanistic view of personality development, there is no simple way to have a more creative and fulfilled life. Knowing the qualities of those people who have fulfilled their potential or imitating them is no guarantee of realizing one's own potential. Self-actualization, therefore, is more of a journey, an exploration, or a way of life than it is a final goal. By observing and interviewing many people, humanists have gained some insight into ways to help foster self-actualization (Maslow, 1968).

ROGERS'S SELF THEORY.   To humanistic psychologist Carl Rogers (1902–1987), a person's unique subjective experience of reality and self was central to any dynamic understanding of personality (Rogers, 1961). Rogers's personality theory often is referred to as a "self" theory because it focused on the individual's self-perception and personal view of the world. Rogers argued that we develop a self-concept through our experience with the world, our interactions with other people, and what other people tell us. We build our own lives, and we are all free to choose for ourselves rather than being at the mercy of learned stimuli or unconscious forces. Rogers stressed that each person is purposeful in his behavior and is positively striving to reach self-fulfillment. The major cause of maladjustment is an individual's perception that his sense of self is in opposition to personal expectations or goals (Rogers, 1951).

Carl Rogers (1905–1987).

The humanistic approach has been criticized on a number of grounds. First, people have argued that concentrating on self-perception and subjective assessment does not bring us any closer to explaining the causes of an individual's behavior (Smith, 1950). Second, they have criticized humanists for concentrating too heavily on the individual and ignoring the environmental problems that may be causing discomfort or disharmony. Third, critics note, the humanist viewpoint has not been demonstrated by rigorous experimentation. There is little evidence, for instance, to support the humanist assertion that human beings are positively striving toward self-fulfillment and possess free will. Finally, the humanistic personality theory has not been very successful at predicting human behavior over a wide range of circumstances or situations, a problem that it shares with other theories of personality (see Focus on a Controversy).

PERSONALITY ASSESSMENT

We study personality in the hope of providing people with insights into their behavior that will help them lead happier lives. For this reason, psychologists have been interested in assessing personality and have developed a number of measures and tests for doing so.

In cognitive study, one's knowledge of the appropriate events that should occur in a particular social setting and of how one might carry them out. This comprises knowledge of who is expected to do what to whom as well as when, where, and why. A script would include such typical behaviors as those expected of a person visiting a restaurant or going to a movie.

CONCEPT REVIEW: COMPARING THEORIES OF PERSONALITY

Type (Hippocrates, Sheldon)
There is little concern with the "self" as the source of motivation. Unconscious processes are considered to be less important than are conscious ones, if they are even considered. Early experience is thought to have little role in the formation of later personality development. Biology and inheritance are seen as important and, to a high degree, are believed to determine personality.

Trait (Allport, Cattell)
Strong emphasis is placed on the "self" as the source of motivation. Unconscious processes are deemphasized. Early experience is thought to have only a slight role in the formation of later personality development. Biology and inheritance are seen as important and, to a degree, are believed to determine the traits that define personality.

Psychoanalytic (Freud, Jung)
Strong emphasis is placed on the "self" as the source of motivation. Unconscious processes are strongly emphasized. Personality determinants are thought not to be directly accessible to the individual without the use of therapeutic techniques for tapping the unconscious. Early experience is strongly emphasized as the primary foundation for later personality development. Biology and inheritance are seen as important and, to a degree, are believed to determine personality development.

Behavioral (Skinner, Bandura)
Strong emphasis is placed on the environment, rather than on the "self," as the source of motivation. Unconscious processes are not considered to be important. Early experience (past history of reinforcement) is thought to have a moderate role in the formation of later personality development (competing with current reinforcement contingencies). Biology and inheritance are deemphasized and are considered to play little role in the development of personality.

Humanistic (Maslow, Rogers)
Strong emphasis is placed on the "self" as the source of motivation. Unconscious processes are deemphasized. Early experience is thought to have only a slight role in the formation of later personality development. Biology and inheritance are deemphasized and are considered to play little role in the development of personality.

	Emphasis			
Theory	**"Self"**	**Unconscious**	**Early Experience**	**Biology**
Type	− −	=	− −	+ +
Trait	+ +	−	−	+ +
Psychoanalytic	+ +	+ +	+ +	+ +
Behavioral	− −	− −	=	− −
Humanistic	+ +	− −	− −	− −

KEY: + + Very Strong, + Strong, = Moderate, − Weak, − − Very Weak.

Measuring Personality Traits

Trait theorists would like to know which traits predominate and how these traits are likely to influence behavior. Perhaps the best known of the instruments used to measure abnormal patterns of personality traits is the Minnesota Multiphasic Personality Inventory (MMPI). The MMPI is the most widely used psychological test in the world (Lubin, Larsen, Matarazzo, & Seever, 1985). Research with the MMPI has been extensive; well over 100 studies are published every year, and the total body of MMPI literature encompasses over 8000 books and articles. The

During the last 15 years, prominent researchers have reviewed the progress of personality theory, and many have come to a pessimistic conclusion:

> Sechrest (1976) suggests that personality theory is in sad shape and Phares & Lamiell (1977) suggest that the field is in a period of crisis. . . . Loevinger and Knoll (1983) appear to take a dim view of how much the field has advanced and, following Meehl (1978), question whether a really impressive theory of personality is possible." (Pervin, 1985, pp. 83–84)

Further concern has been expressed over the way personality is currently presented in textbooks such as the one you are now reading:

> One continues to wonder why personality is still so widely taught as a "procession through the graveyard" in the pungent phrase of a prominent personality researcher. It is true that the lives and insights of Freud, Jung, Adler, Sullivan, Rogers, Maslow, etc., make extremely interesting reading and their historical contributions highlight some of the issues of human relationships that must continue at the center of personality research. But we may well ask why no one teaches cognition, social psychology, developmental psychology, or abnormal psychology by using the views of famous people as the centerpiece for the entire course" (Singer & Kolligan, 1987, p. 535).

These are interesting concerns. Why would researchers believe that the field of personality is "in sad shape," and why is personality so commonly taught by reviewing the major works of historical figures? To answer these questions, we need to consider the term *personality* and what it encompasses. Personality is a *big* term. There is very little behavior in which a human might engage that couldn't be considered an aspect of personality. In short, "personality," as a field of study, covers just about everything.

Early in the history of psychology, behavior was thought to be somewhat less complicated than we now know it to be. During that time, it was not uncommon for an individual such as Freud or Adler to attempt what are called "grand theories" of personality—grand in that they attempt to explain most of human behavior. Unfortunately, grand theories of personality, like most psychological grand theories, often failed to predict complex patterns of human behavior. Consequently, modern personality theory has generally limited itself to highly detailed investigations of many separate areas, rather than attempting to develop grand theories. "Current work in [personality] centers around a few hot topics in the field, a few theoretical points of view, a wide variety of rather unrelated topics and concerns, and major concern with a few controversies and issues" (Pervin, 1985, p. 84–85).

The topics that are currently "hot" in the field of personality include *learned helplessness* (see Chapter 9), *memory organization* (see Chapter 7), *social attribution* (see Chapter 17), *self-efficacy* (see Chapter 9), *cognitive information processing* (see Chapter 8), and a considerable number of others (also found under various chapters and headings in this text). But if these are the current hot topics in personality research, why, then, aren't these topics covered here in the personality chapter? Why, instead, are the grand theories reviewed? There are two reasons for this. First, it is always useful to have some background in the grand historical theories; they still have an influence on our thinking. Second, and more important, is that the term *personality,* by its very nature, implies a grand encompassing view, the kind of view that could not be represented by a collection of, as Pervin calls them, "rather unrelated topics and concerns." Although, as we have noted, grand theories have thus far proven to be of limited value, such theories *are* required if we are to create a field of study as broad as "personality." This, of course, is why so many researchers believe that personality, as an endeavor, is in "sad shape"; there don't seem to be any viable or powerful grand theories that can encompass it.

Could this situation change? Is a really impressive theory of personality possible? Some people believe that it is, and that it may be emerging from the work of cognitive psychologists who have begun to apply information-processing theory to the area of personality (Carson, 1989). Their work, although just beginning, is a significant departure from the theories we have discussed in this chapter. Unlike traditional personality theory, which emphasizes the consistency of the self across situations and circumstances, the cognitive information-processing view looks at the self as a collection of many different cognitive **scripts** that enable the person to change and to be flexible across many circumstances.

Perhaps a grand theory of personality based on how we think and process information will eventually prove its power and utility. Its proponents argue that there is still life in personality theory, and one day hope to show that cognition, learning, motivation, and emotion can all be understood as an interaction based primarily on the way our thinking is organized. Further, they believe that this understanding will, in turn, lead to a powerful new ability to predict human behavior across many diverse situations and circumstances. If the future proves them right, the only heading broad enough to encompass their collected research would be *personality*.

MMPI is more popular now than ever. It has been translated into 124 languages and is regularly used in 46 countries. Even the Russians have used it to test applicants to their cosmonaut program (Holden, 1986b).

The MMPI contains 550 phrases to which the subject taking the test can answer "true," "false," or "cannot say." The phrases tap emotional reactions, psychological symptoms, and beliefs (Hathaway & McKinley, 1940). The following are examples of the kinds of statements made on the MMPI:

■ There have been times when I've considered killing myself.
■ I am my own worst enemy.
■ Most lawyers are honest.
■ I find it difficult to fall asleep.
■ If given a chance, I would do something to benefit the world.

The MMPI is broken down into 10 basic scales. Each measures a different trait (see Table 13.3). In addition, there are three validity (control) scales. The L scale, or lie scale, attempts to spot individuals who are trying to fake a good self-image. People who score high on this scale say that they do a number of commendable daily activities that almost no one engages in, such as never telling a lie or never putting off something they'd rather not do. The K scale, another control, reflects on how defensive or open the subject is being. The F scale, the third control, tests whether the subject is trying to present an exaggerated impression of a personal problem. Throughout the MMPI, a number of statements are made more than once, with only slightly different wording. Responding differently each time will result in an invalid score. Another scale, the Question scale (?), is a measure of the total number of items put into the "cannot say" category.

The MMPI is called a **standardized instrument** because it has been administered to thousands of people from whom profiles have been obtained. If you were to take the MMPI, your profile could be compared with the standards that have already been gathered (Marks & Seeman, 1963). In this way, your personality could be assessed in terms of that of other people whose behavior is known and whose personalities have already been examined.

Problems can arise with even the best personality gauges, however. Sometimes subjects are unwilling to declare how they really feel, and, although the MMPI is considered an objective instrument, one subject's understanding of a statement can differ considerably from another subject's. For example, how would you respond to this sentence?

■ Sometimes I see things that aren't really there.

You might think to yourself, "This question is asking whether I have hallucinations, and the answer is definitely no." Or you might think, "The question is asking whether I see illusions, which is a perfectly normal phenomenon. As a matter of fact, a couple of days ago I was driving down the highway and I thought I saw water on the road up ahead. But when I got there, no water was there. I'll check yes." Different interpretations of a statement's intent can lead to different answers, which can be a problem.

Each person's MMPI scores are recorded on a profile (see Figure 13.5). An atlas that accompanies the MMPI outlines average reactions to situations by people with different profiles. A subject can be given a "code-type" comparing him with these other people, and psychologists administering the test then may predict the degree to which this subject's behavior will be similar to that of other people who have a like score.

Policemen, for example, are often given MMPIs as part of promotion decisions to screen out overly rigid and suspicious personalities, proneness to anxiety or indecisiveness, or a penchant for impulsive use of weapons. Nuclear power plant personnel are screened for factors such as hostility to authority, poor reactions to stress, and substance abuse (which has its own suggestive code-types and subscales). (Holden, 1986b, p. 1250)

STANDARDIZED INSTRUMENT
In psychological testing, a test or measure that has been administered to a wide sample of the population for which it is intended, so that the range and probabilities of responses from that population to the test or measure are known.

TABLE 13.3 The MMPI Scales

SCALE	TRAIT MEASURED
Validity Scales 1. Lie scale (L)	A high score identifies subjects who have stated they possess socially desirable characteristics and behaviors that are in fact very rare. This happens when subjects attempt to fake a good response and do not provide adequate data.
2. Frequency scale (F)	A high score identifies subjects who have checked items that are rarely marked true except by those who are trying to present an exaggerated impression of their problems or by those who are extremely deviant.
3. Correction scale (K)	These items reflect how defensive or honest the subject is being. The scale measures attitudes more subtle than those measured by the L scale. A high score indicates that a subject may not be deliberately lying but is keeping a close check on other true feelings and is not being as open as could be desired.
Clinical Scales 1. Hypochondriasis (Hs)	A high score indicates a subject who is overconcerned with body functions in the absence of any real physical illness.
2. Depression (D)	A high score indicates pessimism about the future, a sense of helplessness and hopelessness, and a concern with death and suicide.
3. Hysteria (Hy)	These items discriminate people who use physical symptoms to control other people, to solve their problems, or to avoid responsibilities.
4. Psychopathic deviate (Pd)	A high score indicates that the subject has a disregard for social customs and mores, is unable to benefit from punishing experiences, and lacks emotional commitment to other people, particularly in terms of sex and love.
5. Masculinity—feminity (Mf)	These items identify men who prefer homosexual relations to heterosexual ones. Women tend to score low on this scale, and the scale for women cannot be used as a mirror image of the scale for men.
6. Paranoia (Pa)	This scale distinguishes people who feel that they are being persecuted and victimized by other people or who believe undue attention is being paid to them by other people.
7. Psychasthenia (Pt)	A high score indicates the existence of obsessive thoughts, compulsive behaviors, and a high degree of fear or guilt, insecurity, and anxiety.
8. Schizophrenia (Sc)	These items identify those people who are aloof, remote, and cold, and who may have bizarre emotional feelings, delusions, or hallucinations.
9. Hypomania (Ma)	A high score indicates emotional excitability, hyperactivity, and a tendency to rush from one thing to the next without finishing anything.
10. Social introversion (Si)	These items pinpoint subjects who are withdrawn, have few social contacts, and have little interest in being with other people.

FIGURE 13.5

An MMPI profile. This one was scored by a computer. Since the instrument has been standardized, the computer compares the responses against those in a large data bank obtained from the standardized group. Personal biases on the part of the person administering the profile are thus eliminated. (SOURCE: Minnesota Multiphasic Personality Inventory Manual, 1970.)

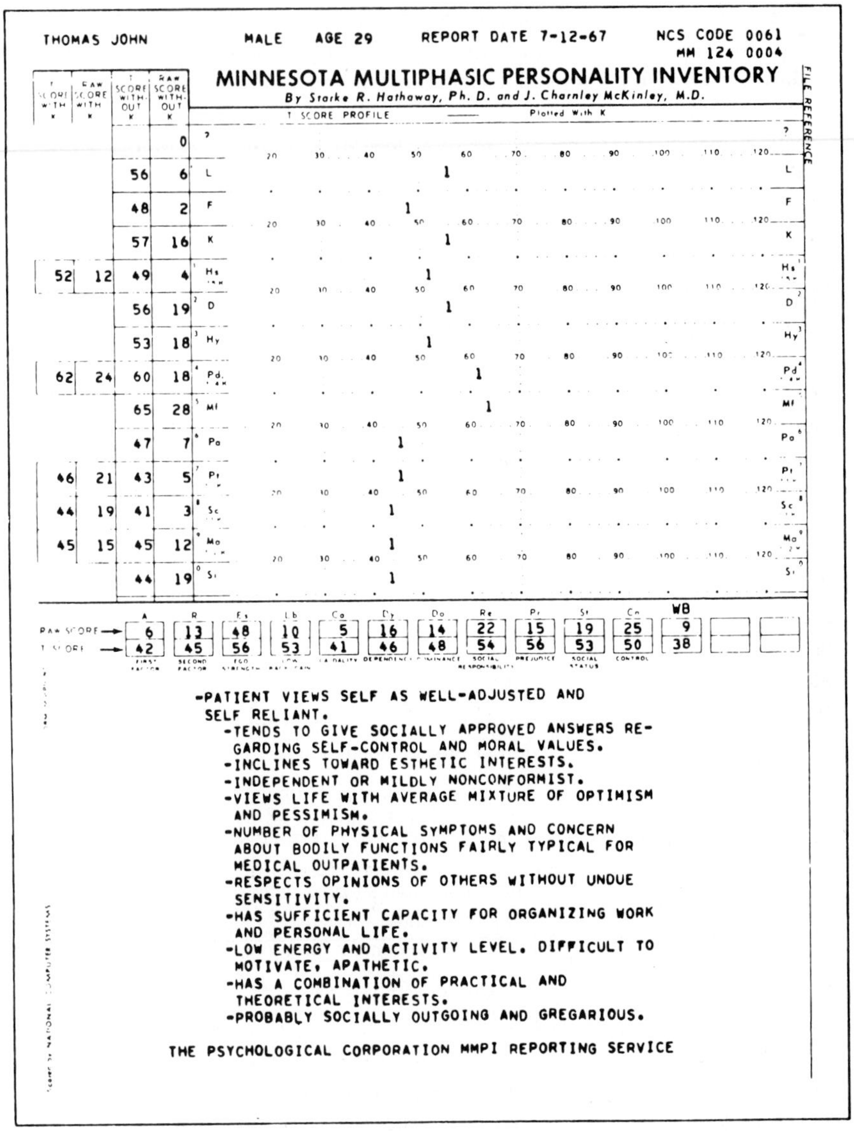

The MMPI can be a valuable instrument if it is used for making general assessments. It usually is not effective for predicting highly specific responses in extraordinary circumstances, but, as in the examples of the police officers or nuclear plant operators, it might give some indication of the behavior patterns a person is likely to exhibit.

Other instruments have been designed to measure attitudes and preferences along certain dimensions, but the MMPI remains the most widely used of these tests. (See Focus on an Application.)

Predictive Validity and Reliability

The results obtained from trait instruments such as the MMPI usually are considered in the light of a subject's actual behavior. In other words, a correlation is obtained between the subject's behavior and the score. In this way investigators can say with some confidence that someone who scored high on the social introversion scale of

BEING A CAREFUL CONSUMER: THE LIMITS OF PSYCHOLOGICAL TESTING

There are hundreds of psychological tests on the market today. The results of these tests can affect what decisions are made concerning hiring and promotion, the way students are handled in school, the outcomes of legal proceedings, and the kinds of medical and psychological treatment people receive. The odds are good that sometime in your life, in connection with school, a job, or health matters, you will be given a psychological test. If interpreted by qualified professionals who understand the use and *limitations* of the test results, many of these tests can be valuable. Unfortunately, some tests either are of dubious quality or are administered by people who have little experience with or understanding of the meaning of the test scores (Matarazzo, 1986). Practically all the tests in existence provide royalties and remuneration for their creators; testing is a business.

Because such testing may have a direct effect on your life, it is important that you be an informed consumer and take an active part in the testing process. The purpose of this focus is to familiarize you with the limits of testing and to help you make intelligent decisions concerning tests you may encounter.

The Barnum Effect

Most psychological tests look official. They come in a handsome case, ask questions that seem important, and are given by testers in a setting of authority. This combination tends to give the average layperson a sense of security that the test is valid and good. In such contexts, psychologists talk of the Barnum effect. The Barnum effect (named for showman P. T. Barnum, who allegedly said, "There's a sucker born every minute") refers to the fact

that people generally believe that personality testing is more accurate than it actually is (Synder, Shenkel, & Lowery, 1977). Psychologists and the informed layperson know, of course, that good packaging and advertising do not necessarily make a test valid or reliable.

Further heightening the Barnum effect is that many personality tests are now scored and interpreted by computer. Even MMPI results may be scored by a computer and a published dissection of the subject's personality may be printed out by the machine. Computers, of course, simply help to score tests quickly. They do not ensure that the test is either valid or accurate. Unfortunately, many people believe that computers are somehow objective and infallible, and personality tests graded by computers tend to be given more credence (Matarazzo, 1983).

Even the very best personality tests available to psychologists provide only a limited amount of information and can be interpreted within only a limited range. For psychologists, the fact remains that if those you wish to test understand what you want to know, have the information you seek, and are not trying to lie, the simplest and most accurate way to find out about them is probably just to ask them rather than to give them a test (Shrauger & Osberg, 1981; Rorer & Widiger, 1983).

The MMPI-2

The Minnesota Multiphasic Personality Inventory (MMPI), the most widely used psychological test in the world, has its limitations, like other tests. For instance, psychologist Robert Colligan argues that the MMPI is based on outdated information about "nor-

mal" personality (Colligan, Osborne, Swenson, & Offord, 1983). To understand this assertion, you need to know how the test was originally developed. In the 1930s, psychologist Starke Hathaway and neurologist John McKinley at the University of Minnesota collected answers to their questions from a group of "normal" people. But where did they get this sample of normal people? As it turns out, a very large portion of their sample was found at the University of Minnesota hospital. The researchers stopped hospital visitors walking in the halls and asked them to take the test. They also sampled some workers on a federal Depression-relief project and some high-school graduates who were coming in for job counseling. As a result, their average normal person was 35 years old, was married, lived in a little town or farming community, and had schooling only through the eighth grade. Colligan has pointed out that "whoever takes the MMPI today is being compared with the way a man or woman from Minnesota endorsed those items in the 1930s or early 1940s" (Herbert, 1983c, p. 228).

To meet these objections to the original test and to satisfy the requests by many clinicians to update it, the MMPI has been revised. The new test, the MMPI-2, was standardized on 2600 people from around the nation and reflects the national percentages of men and women and of minorities as described by the 1980 census.

The new test is different from the old MMPI in a number of ways. Gone are the sexist wording, outmoded expressions, and questions about religion (such as whether the respondent believes in the Second Coming of Christ) that many found offensive.

Added are 15 new content scales of special interest to clinicians that assess such things as suicidal behavior, anger, repression, cynicism, low self-esteem, family problems, job functioning, substance abuse, type-A personality (see Chapter 14), and eating disorders.

The new MMPI-2 is not without its critics, however. The first concern is that the new population on which the test was standardized is not average because it is highly educated: 45 percent were college graduates (as opposed to the national average of 16.5 percent). Only 5 percent were high school dropouts (the national average is 33.5 percent). This appears to have occurred because volunteers were used to standardize the new test and poor readers weren't very interested in wading through the hundreds of questions required by the test (Adler, 1990). As a result, it is feared that the MMPI-2 might not be very applicable

in state hospitals, veterans hospitals, or state-funded treatment centers where clients are often less educated than the sample on which the MMPI-2 was standardized. Furthermore, the code-types from the MMPI-2 often don't match the old MMPI atlas used to predict behaviors. In the old system, someone who scored high on a particular scale on the MMPI could be matched with thousands of others with similar scores, which often helped to predict his behavior. But the same person with a high score on the same scale on the MMPI-2, often doesn't seem to fit the pattern for those with the same scale score on the old MMPI. Because the questions were changed on the new test, the scores on the scales, even though they are the same scales, appear to mean something different.

As you can see, even the most widely used test in the world is open to interpretation. As an informed con-

sumer of psychological testing, you should feel free to ask questions about the tests you may be asked to take. Find out why you are being tested. Find out the name of the test and the publisher. Feel free to consult a professional about how that test was used in your case. This will help you to determine whether the test was valid and reliable in the circumstances in which it was used.

Human beings are extremely complicated. It should come as no surprise that tests that attempt to quantify and qualify an individual's personality are limited in their power and utility. In the right hands, in the right circumstances, they can furnish valuable information. But no test ever devised, or likely to be devised, is going to reduce something as complex as you to a set of test scores and descriptive paragraphs that are totally valid.

PREDICTIVE VALIDITY
The degree to which a score or assessment correlates with a specific outcome. A test with high predictive validity allows fairly accurate predictions to be made about certain future behaviors.

the MMPI is very likely to be withdrawn, shy, and somewhat introverted. Behaviors should reflect scores. If they do, then the instrument is said to have **predictive validity,** sometimes called *criterion validity;* that is, it measures what it purports to measure. To determine the predictive validity, researchers correlate the test score with predicted behavior patterns. A device that has high predictive validity will yield a score from which accurate predictions about behavior can be made. This is exactly what personality theorists want—instruments that will tell them ahead of time what kinds of behavior people with different scores will exhibit. Conversely, if the device indicates that certain behaviors should occur and they don't occur, then the device's predictive validity is low.

Many personality assessment instruments have established useful levels of validity. For example, they often can measure and predict a young couple's marital adjustment by assessing the similarity of the spouses' needs: the more similar, the better the adjustment (Meyer & Pepper, 1977). They can assess the likelihood that someone will graduate from a military training program (Alker & Owen, 1977). These measures aren't accurate all the time—far from it—but they can often help psychologists to make predictions with more accuracy than would have been possible had the instruments not been used.

Unfortunately, assessment instruments don't always work. Quite often they yield an inaccurate description of an individual's personality. There are several reasons for this. One is that people frequently distort their beliefs, attributes, and attitudes when giving information (Edwards, 1961). What they say they are like and what they are really like may be quite different. Subjects may exaggerate some traits and overlook others. People who do this are not necessarily trying to lie. Part of the problem may be that normal human memory is imperfect. For instance, a person who reports feeling anxious most of the time may actually not feel anxious often, but rather may remember occasional moments of anxiety so vividly that anxiety seems an important part of her personality. Other people may profess to be honest because they like to think of themselves as being honest, when in fact they cheat on their income taxes, keep extra change when a cashier gives it to them, and make up lies to excuse lateness to work.

A trait-measuring device or personality assessment instrument must be reliable as well as valid. **Reliability** refers to the instrument's consistency. Does the score remain fairly stable over time? An instrument would not be very valuable if a subject's score changed drastically from day to day. Any measuring device purporting to disclose underlying traits should show reliability, because traits by their very nature are considered enduring and general. They should be there day after day, month after month, and the instrument should reflect this fact.

Psychoanalytic Personality Assessment

Psychoanalysts have developed measures designed to probe the personality in depth, break through the defenses of the subject, and uncover hidden, unconscious motivations. The subject's early history is the focal point of these investigations, especially the way in which the subject dealt with the sexual and aggressive instincts outlined in Freud's hypothesis.

Historically, the two assessment devices most often used for probing the unconscious have been the Rorschach ink-blot test and the Thematic Apperception Test (TAT) (see Figure 13.6). The Rorschach ink-blot test is the fourth most commonly given psychological test, following only the MMPI, the Wechsler Adult Intelligence Test, and the Bender–Gestalt Visual-Motor Test (Lubin, Larsen, Matarazzo & Seever, 1985). It has become so associated with psychology that most students picture psychologists with their ink blots just as they picture physicians with their stethoscopes.

Both the Rorschach and the TAT are considered *projective* tests in that they contain ambiguous stimuli that can be interpreted by subjects in many different ways. The Rorschach consists of ink blots in which a subject can see any number of different things. The TAT contains a series of ambiguous pictures; subjects are asked to make up a story about each. The story should describe what is happening in the picture, but because the picture is open to so many interpretations, subjects are free to *project* onto the picture their own unconscious feelings and desires. Similarly, subjects can project onto an ink blot unconscious images and sensations. The test results are interpreted by a clinician.

Clearly, the clinician is a major factor in psychoanalytic assessment. In empirical tests of the validity of clinical assessment, however, clinical judgments often have been shown to be inaccurate and inconsistent. Research also has indicated that a clinician's assessment of a particular person is not generally improved by the use of projective assessment techniques (Golden, 1964; Soskin, 1959). It is not uncommon for different clinicians to view the same responses to projective tests quite differently. Some people have argued that the problem with projective tests is that they are too projective: Not only is the subject expected to project, but the clinician also may be free to see whatever she wants to in the score (Goldberg & Werts, 1966).

In general, the view of psychoanalytic assessment among psychologists has been split. On one side of the issue are psychologists who support the tenets of Freudian

RELIABILITY
The extent to which a test, rating scale, classification system, or other measure is consistent, that is, produces the same results each time it is applied to the same thing in the same way.

theory and believe that projective tests are a useful way to tap unconscious processes. On the other side are psychologists who argue that projective testing as it is now used is invalid and unreliable.

Behavioral Personality Assessment

As you recall, the behavioral approach to personality is radically different from that of trait theorists or psychoanalysts. For behaviorists, the assessment of personality is the assessment of behavior, and behavior can be assessed only if it has been carefully defined and directly observed. A behavior is counted or timed—in other words, monitored. In this way, a rate or frequency of the behavior can be obtained. A behavioral assessment of personality includes an examination of the stimuli in the individual's environment and of the behaviors that these stimuli control and

FIGURE 13.6

Sample items from the Rorschach and the TAT.

reinforce (see Chapter 6). Attempts to change the individual's personality are made by altering or restructuring the environment. Behaviorists refer to such shaping of the personality as *behavior modification*. The application of behavioral technology to the modification of personality through therapy will be examined in detail in Chapter 16.

The value and importance of different stimuli in a person's life can be assessed by examining the person's behavior in real situations, by investigating the person's preferences, and by knowing which reinforcers or rewards are most effective and important to the person. Behaviorists understand that each person is unique and that stimuli that are reinforcing for some people may not be for others.

Behaviorists rely extensively on experimental methods. Because they deal with only the observable aspects of behavior in a given person, they tend to avoid concepts or constructs that rely on internal qualities or motivations such as traits or unconscious desires. Behavioral assessment often is criticized for avoiding what many people consider to be important aspects of personality, such as emotion and thought.

Humanistic Personality Assessment

The humanistic approach to personality assessment differs greatly from the psychoanalytic, behavioral, or trait approaches. Humanists study personality by examining each person's subjective experience. Subjective experience is difficult to assess, but humanists hope to find objective ways of doing this. Several specific techniques for studying and uncovering a person's subjective experience have been devised.

Q SORTING.   The **Q sort** is one of the techniques that humanists have developed to examine an individual's subjective experience. A Q sort is conducted by presenting a large number of cards to a subject. Each card shows a different statement. The subject must choose whether the statement describes himself (Block, 1961). The Q sort cards may contain statements such as the following:

- I am a reasonable person.
- Most people like me.
- I get frightened easily.
- I have a good sense of humor.
- I am successful at my work.

The subject's selection of cards gives an impression of the subject's self-image. The subject often is asked to sort the cards a second time, according to his *ideal* self.

It is possible to obtain a correlation between people's Q sorts and their likely behaviors. In this way, a personality can be appraised objectively based on the person's subjective self-appraisal (Bem & Funder, 1978).

INTERVIEWS.   Humanists often use personal interviews to facilitate personality assessment. The interviewer gently explores the subject's self-concept and emotional feelings, trying through empathy to see the world as the subject sees it (Jourard, 1967). The interviewer is careful to avoid interjecting her world view and opinions. Carl Rogers based a client-centered therapy on this technique, which will be discussed in detail in Chapter 16.

In recent years, scientists have become increasingly interested in assessing nonverbal cues. Many humanists believe that much about a person's subjective self-appraisal and world view can be learned by examining expressions, posture, gestures, and movement. Some researchers argue that self-concepts such as submissiveness

Q SORT
A personality assessment technique based on a series of statements and traits that the test subject is required to sort into categories from "most like me" to "least like me."

or dominance can be assessed by observing a person's "body language" during an interview.

Humanistic assessment methods have been criticized for their lack of rigor. Some people have argued that many clinical assessments derived from the interview method reflect the clinician's subjective appraisals rather than a true understanding of the subject.

In the end, all personality assessment has the common goal of finding out more about the individual, discovering his enduring characteristics, and uncovering the forces that have created and maintained them.

EPILOGUE: THE EYE OF THE BEHOLDER

For several years, researchers have shown a growing interest in the extent to which individual biases can influence one person's assessment of another's personality (Jackson & Paunonen, 1980). The following is an account of how one researcher uncovered the biases in the personality of another researcher and how these biases influenced some important research.

In 1976, psychologist Molly Harrower obtained some personality profiles that had been derived from the responses of certain subjects to the Rorschach ink-blot test. What made these Rorschach results so interesting was the subjects who had been tested—among them Albert Speer, Hermann Goering, and Rudolf Hess, some of the top leaders of Hitler's Nazi Reich. The profiles Harrower had obtained were the results of the Rorschach tests given at the Nuremberg trials in 1946. At that time, Gustav Gilbert, a prison psychologist, had been assigned to test the captured Nazi leaders (Maile & Selzer, 1975).

Harrower read in Gilbert's assessments of the Nazis' personalities that they were hostile, violent, and concerned with death, that they needed status, and that they lacked any real human feeling. Gilbert wrote, "In general, these appear to be individuals who are undeveloped, manipulative, and hostile in their relationships with others" (Maile & Selzer, 1975, p. 278).

There were 16 Nazi files in all. Harrower wondered how much Gilbert's assessment could have been the result of his own personality. After all, he was testing the most hated men on Earth. Couldn't that knowledge have influenced his feelings and thoughts?

To test this, Harrower took the Rorschach scores from which Gilbert had derived his assessments and mixed them with Rorschach scores from normal healthy people. Then she asked a panel of experts in personality assessment to look through all the scores and to sort normal responses from abnormal ones. Amazingly, none of the experts found anything unusual about any of the test scores (Harrower, 1976).

Gilbert had obviously interpreted the test scores according to his own biases. The test results tell us something about personality, but not about the personality of the Nazi leaders. Instead, they tell us about Gustav Gilbert.

SUMMARY

■ Personality is the sum total of the ways in which an individual characteristically reacts. Personality refers to the consistency in a person's behavior under varying conditions.

■ To a psychologist, the word *personality* refers to the whole person, not just to a part.

■ Historically, investigations of personality have classified people according to certain types. Hippocrates, William Sheldon, and Carl Jung are among those who attempted to classify personality in this way.

■ Instead of categorizing individuals according to type, modern trait theorists generally believe that people possess certain traits, in lesser or greater degree.

■ One of the best-known advocates of the trait approach was Gordon Allport. Allport recognized that some traits were more enduring and general than others, and he drew distinctions among cardinal traits, central traits, and secondary traits.

■ Some trait theorists have emphasized the need for statistical analysis to isolate traits. Raymond Cattell is one such theorist. Cattell has developed the 16 personality factor questionnaire, which makes use of factor analysis.

■ Sigmund Freud was the founder of psychoanalytic theory. Freud divided the personality into three parts: the id, the ego, and the superego. He believed that the dynamics of the personality involved continual conflict among these elements. Freud considered sexual behavior and aggression to be instinctive.

■ Freud believed that this struggle between biological drives and social inhibitions produces anxiety, and that the ego often relies on defense mechanisms to control and handle the anxiety.

■ According to Freud, as a person develops, he or she passes through several psychosexual stages. These stages—the oral, anal, phallic, latency, and genital—mark important points in the development of healthy personality.

■ Many prominent psychoanalysts broke with Freud to develop their own theories of personality. Among them were Carl Jung, who developed the concepts of introversion and extroversion, and Alfred Adler, who defined striving for superiority as a prime motivator of behavior.

■ B. F. Skinner and other behaviorists do not consider drives or other internal motivational factors in their approach to personality. Instead, they believe that learning and environmental forces impinging on the organism shape personality.

■ In contrast to the behaviorist approach, research on infants' temperaments argues against the idea that personality is solely the result of environmental experiences.

■ Social learning theorists such as Albert Bandura argue that personality is shaped not solely by environmental influences on the person but also by the person's effect on the environment.

■ Research by Milgram indicates that people may have a bias to view as consistent diverse behavior from the same individual.

■ The focus of all humanistic theories of personality is the concept of self. Self refers to the individual's personal internal experiences and subjective evaluations.

■ Carl Rogers has developed a humanistic self theory of personality that focuses on the individual's self-perception and personal view of the world.

■ By their nature, personality theories are grand, in that they attempt to explain most of human behavior.

■ Trait theorists are interested in measuring which traits are predominant and how these traits are likely to influence behavior. The best-known instrument for this purpose is the Minnesota Multiphasic Personality Inventory, or MMPI.

■ Everyone should be familiar with the limits of psychological testing and should become a careful consumer. People tend to be too trusting in assessing the power of personality testing. This trust is known as the Barnum effect.

■ Although many personality assessment instruments have useful levels of validity, they often fail to yield an accurate description of an individual's personality.

■ Validity refers to an instrument's success in measuring what it claims to measure. Reliability refers to an instrument's consistency when used repeatedly.

■ Psychoanalysts have developed measures to probe the personality in depth, to break through the defenses of the subject, and to uncover hidden unconscious motivations. The best-known devices for tapping unconscious aspects of personality are the Rorschach ink-blot test and the Thematic Apperception Test (TAT).

■ For behaviorists, the assessment of personality is the assessment of behavior. Behaviorists assess personality by examining the stimuli in the individual's environment and the behaviors that these stimuli control and reinforce.

■ Humanists assess personality by examining people's subjective experiences. One method is the Q sort technique, which asks subjects to choose from an assortment of statements the particular statements that best apply to themselves. In this way, an impression of a subject's self-image is obtained.

■ All personality assessment has the common goal of finding out more about the individual, discovering the person's enduring characteristics, and uncovering the forces that have created and maintained these characteristics.

Suggestions for Further Reading

1. Eagle, M. N. (1984). *Recent developments in psychoanalysis: A critical evaluation.* New York: McGraw-Hill. Analyzes the traditional concepts of psychoanalysis, and discusses the new changes in psychoanalytic theory.
2. Hall, C. S., Lindzey, G., Loehlin, J. C., Manosevitz, M., & Locke, V. O. (1985). *Introduction to theories of personality.* New York: John Wiley. A college-level textbook on personality theory.
3. Mischel, W. (1986). *Introduction to personality: A new look* (4th ed.). New York: Holt, Rinehart, & Winston. A college-level textbook that introduces major personality theories and assessment techniques.
4. Pervin, L. A. (1984). *Current controversies and issues in personality* (2nd ed.). New York: John Wiley. Discusses the issues important to those who study personality, including the interactionist position.
5. Pervin, L. A. (Ed.). (1990). *Handbook of personality: Theory and research.* New York: Guilford Press. A high level, comprehensive compendium of the most recent theory and research in personality.

UNIT 4 | Conflict and Adjustment

Chapter 14
Health
Psychology

Prologue
Why Psychologists Study Health
Health Psychology
Risk Assessment
Acute Stress and Chronic Aftermath
Reactions to Stress
Ways of Coping with Stress
Epilogue: Help When It Was Most Needed

Chapter 16
Therapy

Prologue
Why Psychologists Study Therapies
The History of Therapy
Somatic Therapies
Psychotherapy
Epilogue: A Bird in the Hand

Chapter 15
Abnormal
Behavior

Prologue
Why Psychologists Study Abnormal Behavior
Defining Abnormality
Models of Psychopathology
Classification and Assessment of Abnormal Behavior
Anxiety, Somatoform, and Dissociative Disorders
Mood Disorders
Schizophrenic Disorders
Delusional (Paranoid) Disorders
Personality Disorders (Axis II)
The Assessment of Mental Disorders
Epilogue: The Trichotillomaniac

CHAPTER 14 | Health Psychology

Prologue

Why Psychologists Study Health

Health Psychology

Risk Assessment
  Protecting Yourself
  Hazard Perception

Acute Stress and Chronic Aftermath

Reactions to Stress
  The Body's Reaction
  Measuring Susceptibility to Stress and
    Illness
  Hassles
  Suicide

Ways of Coping with Stress
  Psychological Defense Mechanisms
  Stress Management

**Epilogue: Help When It Was Most
Needed**

PROLOGUE

It's a cold morning in 1983. You and psychologist Andrew Baum approach the first house on the list. He knocks on the door. A voice answers, "Just a minute."

You look around. It's a quiet residential street. The sky is overcast; it looks as though it might rain. You notice that some people down the street are leaving for work. Looking in the other direction, you see where the street dead ends and the weeds begin. The weeds are too high for you to see the river beyond, but you can judge where the river must be by the three huge cooling towers of the Three Mile Island nuclear power reactor looming just beyond in the morning mist. You feel uncomfortable being so close to them.

The door opens; a middle-aged man and woman have answered. "Yes?" says the man.

"Hi, I'm Dr. Baum. I'm here to take the information we discussed on the phone."

"Oh yes, come right in, please."

You both enter the small home. Along with a short checklist of questions, Dr. Baum collects urine specimens that the couple have made available according to previous instructions. He is interested in how much stress local residents near the atomic reactor have been under since the Three Mile Island nuclear accident in 1979.

After collecting the information, you and Dr. Baum depart for the next house. There, the data-collection process is repeated. When you've helped him to collect all his information, you go with him to the laboratory where it is analyzed. Dr. Baum studies the results. "It seems the

STRESS
A psychological state associated with physiological and hormonal changes caused by conflict, trauma, or other disquieting or disruptive influences.

HEALTH PSYCHOLOGY
Any aspect of psychology that bears on the experience of health and illness and the behavior that affects health status.

PRIMARY PREVENTION
Efforts aimed at preventing an illness or pathological condition, mental or physical, from occurring. The focus in on optimizing health. As opposed to secondary prevention in which a pathological condition is treated after it has appeared in hopes of preventing it from becoming worse.

local residents of Three Mile Island have unusually high levels of cate-cholamines in their urine."

"What are catecholamines?" you ask.

"These are substances," he explains, "that are secreted in response to nervous arousal. When there is only a short period of stress, very little of one of the catecholamines—epinephrine—is secreted, while a large amount of another—norepinephrine—is secreted. In the subjects that we have interviewed, the urine levels of both catecholamines are high, which implies that these people's anxiety is due to long-term stress rather than to some immediate fear" (Baum, Gatchel, & Schaeffer, 1983).

"Three Mile Island is different from other disasters," he says. "When a tornado or earthquake occurs, the worst is usually over quickly. At TMI there is no clear sign that the worst is over. For all they know, the worst is yet to come" (Herbert, 1982a, p. 308).

You think about what he has said, and you easily understand why the local residents might be experiencing long-term stress. The radioactive spill, still on the floor of the reactor, probably can never be cleaned up. The government has been considering encasing the entire reactor in concrete as a kind of tomb for hundreds of future generations to ponder. From time to time, radiation either leaks, or is vented from the plant; radiation has been associated with cancer and other disorders. You know you wouldn't live near there unless you had to.

In October 1985, the reactor at Three Mile Island was restarted. Following the restart, the levels of stress and stress-related symptoms among the local residents were observed to increase (Dew, Bromet, Schulberg, Dunn, & Parkinson, 1987). The long-term effects of this stress on the local population remain unknown.

In this chapter, we'll investigate the stress caused by disasters such as Three Mile Island and look at the effects of stress on health. We'll also examine how our behavior influences our health and how psychologists hope to change behavior to better our health and adjustment. On a positive note, we'll explore ways to reduce stress and to promote better health.

WHY PSYCHOLOGISTS STUDY HEALTH

Every year, researchers provide more evidence that our well-being and physical health are directly linked to our behavior. For example, smoking and overeating are both *behaviors*; they are also associated with major killers like heart disease and cancer. How we behave when interacting with the environment, therefore, can be a matter of life and death.

Smoking and overeating are obvious examples of behaviors that may be detrimental to health. There are many other such behaviors, some quite subtle. For instance, just the way we behave when we try to cope with the stresses of our daily lives can have an important effect on our health and well-being. Sometimes, if we fail to deal properly with **stress,** real physical damage may result.

If psychologists can learn how to help people control the behaviors that are detrimental to health, or how to acquire the behaviors that are beneficial, millions of lives could be significantly extended and improved.

HEALTH PSYCHOLOGY

Health psychology has been defined as "any aspect of psychology that bears upon the experience of health and illness and the behavior that affects health status" (Rodin & Stone, 1987, pp. 15–16). As you might imagine, that definition covers a lot of ground. Interestingly, although some early psychologists such as William James and G. Stanley Hall dealt with health-related issues from time to time, health was generally considered to be solely a matter for physicians. However, in 1964, a presidential commission took note of the fact that the leading causes of death were no longer the terrible diseases of the past such as plague, diphtheria, typhoid, or cholera. These scourges can now be prevented or controlled by inoculation, sanitation, or antibiotics. Instead, the report noted that every year hundreds of thousands of Americans and others around the world were dying prematurely as a result of their own detrimental *behavior*, from preventable diseases, incidents, or accidents (Fisher, 1986; Taylor, 1990). As a result, much of health psychology is oriented toward **primary prevention,** that is, toward efforts to preventing illnesses before they happen by optimizing health.

RISK ASSESSMENT

One of the important emerging areas in health psychology is the study of these detrimental behaviors. Detrimental behaviors are those behaviors that pose a risk to human health and well-being. One of the problems faced by health psychologists is to make people aware of which of their behaviors are the most dangerous and preventable. Consider the following two people. One worries about smoking his pipe—a behavior that could cause lip cancer—and talks about stopping. At the same time, he thinks nothing of riding his bicycle through heavy traffic to work. The other friend is concerned about consuming the local water ever since some of the wells in his area were shut down because of pesticide contamination. He is careful to drink only bottled water, and even puts off taking a drink at work until he can get home to his "safe water," as he calls it. As he drives home, however, he doesn't wear his seat belt. What's most likely to kill either of these people is neither lip cancer nor pesticide poisoning, but rather traffic accidents, which are more probable by a factor greater than 1000 to 1. In fact, one out of every 140 Americans will die in a car accident (Allman, 1985). Cars are deadly (and bicycles are 15 times more deadly than cars per mile driven), and yet it seems that it's often the long shots such as the dangers of artificial sweeteners, food coloring, or strangers who might kidnap our children that we most worry about (Weinstein, 1989). It's the *real* dangers, however, on which we must focus most of our efforts (see Table 14.1).

Protecting Yourself

Table 14.2 is a guide that describes the behavior changes you can make to improve your health and well-being. These changes focus on the major threats to the lives of individual's living in industrialized nations* (based on things that kill 10,000 or more Americans each year). If everyone made these changes in his or her behavior,

---

*In the nonindustrialized world, the leading cause of death is malaria.

TABLE 14.1 How We Die (Fatalities per year in the U.S. Population from Selected Causes)

738,000	Heart disease
328,000	Cancer
209,100	Stroke
55,350	Motor vehicle accidents
38,950	Diabetes
24,600	Suicide
23,200	Homicide
21,771	AIDS
21,730	Emphysema
7,380	Drowning
7,380	Fire
3,690	Tuberculosis
2,563	Poison
2,255	Firearm accident
1,886	Asthma
1,517	Motor vehicle collisions with trains
1,025	Electrocution
902	Appendicitis
677	Infectious hepatitis
451	Pregnancy, birth, and abortion
410	Syphilis
334	Excess cold
205	Flood
129	Nonvenomous animal
107	Lightning
90	Tornado
48	Venomous bite or sting
18	Measles
17	Polio
15	Whooping Cough
8	Smallpox vaccination
5	Fireworks
2	Botulism
1	Poisoning by vitamins
0	Smallpox

SOURCE: Allman, 1985, p. 38, Centers for Disease Control, 1990.

millions of lives worldwide would be saved each year. Deaths resulting from causes relatively unrelated to behavior, such as Alzheimer's disease, the fourth leading cause of death in the United States, are not included in the list.

Hazard Perception

Behaviors such as smoking and excessive drinking are extremely dangerous, but they often are not readily perceived to be (Jeffery, 1989). People tend to be more optimistic about their chances than statistics would indicate they should be (Wein-

---

TABLE 14.2 Threats to Your Life (Presented in Order of Actual Danger)

THREAT	DEFENSIVE ACTION YOU SHOULD TAKE
1. Heart disease	It is now known that cholesterol is a major factor in promoting heart disease. See your doctor *now* and discover your blood serum cholesterol level—you may need to have it checked a number of times to obtain a valid average level (Roberts, 1987). Heart disease is the number one cause of death, and yet less than 10 percent of Americans know their cholesterol level. Avoid cholesterol and keep your cholesterol levels low by eating less fatty and fat-saturated foods. Don't smoke. Know your blood pressure. Exercise regularly. Control your weight. Have the entire family learn cardiopulmonary resuscitation (CPR).
2. Cancer	Don't smoke. Know the levels of radioactive radon gas in your home (see the July 1987 issue of *Consumer Reports*, pages 440–447, at your local or college library for a discussion of this hazard and what to do about it). Know your family history and take special care to watch for kinds of cancers that run in your family (especially cancers of the colon or breast). Avoid ever getting a sunburn. Avoid the sun in general; wear sunblock. See your doctor for complete and regular checkups, learn how to check yourself (how to do a self examination of your skin from a dermatologist; for women—learn how to do a self-examination of your breasts from your family physician or gynecologist). For women—obtain a mammogram (if over age 35), obtain a Pap smear on a regular basis. Avoid excessive alcohol consumption. See your doctor about anything unusual that doesn't go away.
3. Stroke	(All those behaviors listed for heart disease.) Avoid excessive alcohol consumption.
4. Motor vehicle accidents	Wear a seat belt with shoulder harness (use proper protective seats for infants). Avoid alcohol consumption before driving. Obey speed limits. Drive a large car. Don't ride a motorcycle.
5. AIDS	Avoid sharing needles if taking drugs. Avoid intimate sexual contact with an infected partner. If in doubt, make use of a condom to reduce chances of infection; practice abstinence for complete protection. If possible, prepare for transfusions in advance of surgery by "stockpiling" your own blood.
6. Diabetes	Have your doctor regularly check your urine for sugar (glucose). Know your family history. Avoid obesity.
7. Suicide	Seek immediately professional help for depression or suicidal thoughts. Know your family history.
8. Homicide	Don't keep a gun in your home. If possible, avoid dangerous neighborhoods or jobs.
9. Emphysema	Don't smoke. Get regular checkups. Get early and regular help for asthma.

stein, 1989). This problem of hazard perception—or, to be more precise, the lack of it—is common. For example, many people believe that it is good to keep a firearm in the home for protection. It generally isn't. In a study conducted between 1978 and 1983, researchers examined all the gun-related deaths in King County, Washington (Kellermann & Reay, 1986), and found that a gun in the home was 6 times more likely to result in a death by accident or in the murder of one family member by another than it was to save a person from an intruder.*

Some hazards get heavy press coverage, which increases people's worry about them. Let's look at a few of them and the real risks they involve. Consider flying. Your chances of being killed in a commercial jet are one in a million for every 1000 miles flown. You are *far* more likely to die falling down the stairs (something we probably don't think much about). What about drinking saccharine-sweetened soda? Couldn't that give you cancer? Perhaps—the data with humans aren't very clear. However, the odds couldn't be greater than about one in 100 million for each soda you drank—which would mean that you were 50 times more likely to be killed by lightning. What about a chest X-ray examination? There is a one in a million chance it will cause a cancer. Asbestos contamination might also cause lung cancer, but, other than for asbestos workers, the chances are very remote. And yet, millions of dollars are being spent to clean up asbestos in the environment. Not that we shouldn't clean up asbestos, but with our limited funds, health psychologists point out, many more lives could be saved if we used the money to buy more police to enforce the speed limits on our highways. And yet, people generally feel safe in their cars. Why is that? Perhaps because we see cars all of the time and are used to them. We control them and feel as though we could avoid an accident

Curiously, people are often more concerned with remote threats to their health such as the potential danger of drinking artificially sweetened beverages than they are with major risks such as riding a bicycle in traffic.

---

*A number of these gun deaths were suicides, but such deaths appear not to be related to the presence of guns in the home. It has been found that when guns are removed from a population (as was the case in Toronto, Canada, when strict gun control was enacted, and in San Diego when laws kept certain troubled individuals from buying guns), the suicide *rate* remained unchanged, only the means of suicide changed (Rich, Young, Fowler, Wagner, & Black, 1990).

CHEMICAL DEPENDENCE
The strong and compelling desire to continue taking a chemical substance because of its physical or psychological effects.

PSYCHOTHERAPY
A category of methods for treating psychological disorders. The primary technique is conversation between the patient and the therapist.

if only we are careful. Asbestos, on the other hand, is out of our control and we often don't know where it is; it may be lurking about waiting to get us. As you can see, hazard perception is an interesting area to investigate.

Health psychology is concerned with not only sorting real from perceived risk but also discovering why people don't change their behavior even after they have been given the kind of information we've been discussing (Krantz, Grunberg, & Baum, 1985). This is the reason health psychologists investigate such problems as why a person won't stay on her blood-pressure medication, or why people have such a difficult time when they try to stop smoking or drinking (see Focus on an Application).

People are most likely to engage in health promoting behavior if they (1) view the threat to their health as severe, (2) see themselves as vulnerable, (3) have self-efficacy, that is, if they believe that they can change their behavior, and (4) believe that their action will make a difference (Taylor, 1990). Much of health psychology is devoted to promoting these four qualities in people.

Health psychologists are not only concerned with behaviors that can promote good health, they are also interested in *any* experience or circumstance that might affect health or well-being. The following sections give examples of such experiences—the kinds of experiences we all hope never to encounter.

ACUTE STRESS AND CHRONIC AFTERMATH

Sometimes, a stressful experience can be strong enough, or last long enough, to result in direct physical consequences that are harmful to good health. The following are examples of such experiences. Even though the experience may be relatively short-lived, it can be so intense that the memory of it can linger for years.

On Sunday morning, May 18, 1980, Mount Saint Helens, a volcano in the Cascade mountain range in the state of Washington, exploded with the force of a large hydrogen bomb. The entire top of the mountain blew off. A towering column of ash and debris rose thousands of feet into the air. Although there had been warnings beforehand, over 50 people lost their lives, some of them more than 20 miles from the explosion.

The wind carried the ash in a predominantly northeastern direction. Over the next few days, ash fell from the sky. One of the unfortunate towns in the path of the ash was Othello, Washington, a town of less than 5000 people, 137 miles away from Mount Saint Helens. There, the ash covered everything. It formed drifts like snow, only it was powdery, hot, and smelled of sulfur. The small agricultural community was completely disrupted by this unpredictable event. No one knew how to deal with the ash. No one knew what effects it would have on health or if it could ever be cleaned up. Worst of all was the fear that this might be only the first of many such eruptions.

Psychologists, concerned about the effects of stress in the community, found that many residents of Othello were afflicted by the symptoms of stress. Hospital and emergency room visits increased 21 percent. The death rate increased 18.6 percent. According to physicians' records, stress-aggravated illnesses, psychosomatic conditions, and mental illnesses more than doubled. Child abuse and divorce increased substantially. According to measures from the community alcohol center, the police, and the courts, alcohol abuse, aggression, and violence also increased (Adams & Adams, 1984). Other nearby communities also showed similar increases in stress-related disorders, increases that were in direct relation to the distance from the explosion. The nearer people were to the explosion, the more likely they were

When the ash fall from the Mt. St. Helens eruption covered the town of Othello, Washington, 137 miles away, the residents soon began to show symptoms of stress.

In this focus, we'll examine the two most serious (in terms of damage to health or lives lost) kinds of **chemical dependence:** dependence on alcohol and on nicotine.

Alcohol Dependence (Alcoholism)

Excessive use of alcohol is deadly. It is a major contributor to death by cancer, stroke, cirrhosis of the liver, and motor vehicles. It often is a contributing factor in high blood pressure, pneumonia, diabetes, suicide, accidents, and homicide. Approximately 9 percent of all Americans drink to excess (more than 20 million people). Loss of health or life owing to excessive alcohol consumption far exceeds similar losses from all other drug abuse combined, except for nicotine use. Only about 3 percent of those alcohol-addicted people who need help are currently receiving treatment, and yet the cost of treating alcoholism and alcohol-related disorders is already approaching 15 percent of the national health bill (Holden, 1987c)! Alcohol abuse is a huge problem.

Whether someone will become an alcoholic is closely related to the number of alcoholics in the family. Studies of adopted individuals suggest that a genetic predisposition for alcoholism exists. Children adopted by nonalcoholics are much more likely than are other adopted children to become alcoholics if either or both of their biological parents were alcoholics. This is true even if these children had never known or lived with their biological parents (Cadoret, Cain, & Grove, 1980). The exact way in which this genetic predisposition works is unknown, but relatives of alcoholics have been found to react to alcohol in a chemically different way from people who have no close alcoholic relatives (Schuckit, Gold, &

Risch, 1987). It has also been shown that mice can be bred to produce offspring that are genetically more susceptible to alcohol than are other mice (Wafford, Burnett, Dunwiddie, & Harris, 1990). The susceptible mice have been found to have significant differences associated with certain neurotransmitters and their actions (see Chapter 2). The same may be occurring in humans who have inherited a genetic susceptibility to become alcoholic, but it has not yet been proven.

Stress also appears to play an important role in alcoholism. Sober individuals with a higher genetic risk for alcoholism have been found to show a greater heart rate and blood pressure increase in response to stress than do people who have a low genetic risk for alcoholism (Finn & Pihl, 1987).

Treatment

The first step in treating alcohol abuse is to detoxify the abuser and to take steps toward physical recovery by providing good food and shelter. Detoxification requires that a person's intake of alcohol be curtailed under supervision. During this time, mild or severe withdrawal symptoms may appear. In severe cases, delirium tremens (see Chapter 5) and convulsions may occur. In modern hospitals and clinics, certain drugs have been found to be helpful in reducing the severity of withdrawal symptoms. Detoxification is only the first step, however. The individual must be taught to take control of his craving for liquor and, if necessary, to abstain from all drinking.

The drug disulfiram (Antabuse) has helped some alcoholics to avoid an immediate return to drinking. A person who has received it will experience extreme discomfort if she then

ingests alcohol. Antabuse given without additional supportive therapy is insufficient, however, since once out of the hospital the person must self-administer the drug. Antabuse is most effective in keeping the alcohol abuser from drinking for a certain time, during which other therapies can be tried.

Psychotherapy focuses on the individual's need to learn to cope with the problems he has been trying to escape and to live without depending on alcohol. Although there is strong genetic evidence that some people have a greater affinity for alcohol than do others, it is possible to learn to avoid alcohol altogether regardless of one's inheritance.

Alcoholism may be treated by psychotherapeutic techniques, but the most effective treatment is one that was begun, and is still run, by nonpsychologists. In 1935, Bill W. and Dr. Bob in Akron, Ohio, started an organization known as Alcoholics Anonymous, or AA. Bill W. had recovered from his alcoholism through a spiritual change. He, in turn, was able to help Dr. Bob stop drinking. The two of them formed a group to help other alcoholics. There are now over 10,000 AA groups with over 1 million members in the United States. AA is a nonprofessional counseling program run by alcoholics for alcoholics. AA argues that an alcoholic is an alcoholic for life and that total abstinence is the only cure. Members support one another at group meetings and can call on one another at a moment's notice in time of need. Often, members discuss in front of the group how their lives are now and how their lives were before they stopped drinking. They discuss ways of living without using alcohol. A similar group, Al-Anon, has been established for the families of alcoholics.

451

With modern therapeutic approaches, social support, and good aftercare, reported recovery rates from alcoholism run as high as 75 percent, but such high rates are rare. Alcoholism can have such a damaging effect on individuals and their lives that it is inaccurate to equate recovery with simply giving up drinking. For an alcoholic to recover, not only must the person cease drinking, but also she must often regain physical health, family relationships, social functioning, vocational functioning, and emotional stability, and she must resolve any legal problems brought on during the days of drinking (Emrick & Hansen, 1983). Recovery is an encompassing process (Holden, 1987b), not just the cessation of a particular detrimental behavior. Fortunately, per capita alcohol consumption in the United States has dropped 4 percent since 1980, the year during which it reached its peak (Holden, 1987c). This decline may be due to the increased awareness among the populace of alcohol's dangers, especially as they pertain to drinking and driving.

If you have a drinking problem, call the National Council on Alcoholism at 1-800-622-2255. They can help you.

Nicotine Dependence

Smoking is even more deadly than drinking, and yet it is more accepted, perhaps because it doesn't change behavior like drinking does. Smoking causes heart disease, cancer, stroke, and emphysema, four of the nine great killers listed in Table 14.2. It is estimated that smoking kills 350,000 Americans each year, the equivalent of seven commercial jetliner crashes every day (Edwards, 1986). In the United States, costs to life and health from smoking, as well as costs to productivity, approach $100 billion per year.

Nicotine is powerfully addictive and many smokers who quit suffer from strong withdrawal cravings that are not just psychological, but also are based on a real physical dependence (Hughes & Hatsukami, 1986). Stanley Schachter is a well-known social psychologist who has published a series of carefully controlled experiments that demonstrate the addictive power of nicotine. Schachter found that blood nicotine levels correlated well with urinary pH (a measurement of acidity). High levels of acid in the blood caused nicotine levels to fall by washing nicotine from the blood. High levels of acid in the urine also indicated the presence of high levels of stomach and blood acid. Schachter formed the hypothesis that when nicotine was washed from the blood, a craving for a cigarette would develop in a person who had become addicted to nicotine through smoking. In his experiments, he demonstrated that the use of antacids such as Rolaids, Tums, or bicarbonate of soda could reduce the craving for cigarettes. Moreover, individuals who smoked cigarettes tended to smoke less when they used antacids to the limit directed on the antacid package. Further studies have shown that the use of antacids can help smokers quit: An addict's desire for a cigarette is lessened because the nicotine he is used to is washed from the blood more slowly when the acid levels are low, enabling him to withdraw from the nicotine gradually. Schachter also discovered that when a person is under stress, blood acid and stomach acid levels rise, washing out some nicotine, which may explain why people get the desire for a cigarette when they become nervous (Schachter, 1977; Schachter, Kozlowski, & Silver-stein, 1977; Silverstein, Kozlowski, & Schachter, 1977; Schachter, Silverstein, & Perlick, 1977).

Treatment

To date, professional methods offered for breaking the smoking habit include psychotherapy, record keeping (so that people become aware of how much they are smoking), group pressure, positive reinforcement, hypnosis, aversive conditioning, the use of antacids, muscle relaxation, assertiveness training, cancer films, and thought stopping (learning to stop your thoughts each time you think of a cigarette), among others. Increased public awareness as well as growing social pressure against smoking has had a good effect. In September 1987, the Centers for Disease Control published a report that smoking in the United States was at that time, at the lowest levels ever recorded; only 26.5 percent of Americans were found to be smokers.

Attempting to quit on your own can work, too. Self-quitters can do as well as those in formal treatment (Cohen et al., 1989). Light smokers (less than 20 cigarettes per day) are 2.2 times more likely to succeed than heavier smokers; 24 percent relapse even after 6 months of abstinence; and it is common for a few long-term quitters to occasionally have a few (Cohen et al., 1989). Data such as these show that quitting is rarely a one time thing, but rather a dynamic process occurring over time.

If you need help to stop smoking call the American Cancer Society at 1-800-227-2345. They have specific information and techniques that can help you to quit on your own. If that doesn't work, you can try a formal program. Many are available—check with your state's psychological association or referral service.

to have stress-related problems (Shore, Tatum, & Vollmer, 1986). Like the community near Three Mile Island that we discussed in the Prologue, the communities near Mount Saint Helens were also suffering.

Some terrible experiences may encompass many months of exposure. For many, the Vietnam war was such an experience. Over the past few years, it has come to light that approximately 15 percent of Vietnam veterans are suffering psychological problems (Kaylor, King, & King, 1987; Goldberg, True, Eisen & Henderson, 1990). Symptoms associated with long-term stress among the vets were not found to be linked to their personalities or behavioral characteristics, but rather to their exposure to combat (Goldberg, True, Eisen & Henderson, 1990). These symptoms, including dizziness, headaches, memory loss, anxiety, intestinal problems, depression, and nightmares, were especially prevalent among combat soldiers who had participated in atrocities, such as torture and murder of prisoners (Yager, Laufer, & Gallops, 1984; Breslau & Davis, 1987). Approximately 35 percent of the veterans who had had heavy combat experience fit the profile for **post-traumatic stress disorder** (PTSD). In addition, many of the veterans had found readjustments to civilian life extremely difficult. Like their World War II and Korean war counterparts, Vietnam combat veterans also suffered an approximately 45 percent higher death rate (due mainly to automobile accident, suicide, and drug overdose) for the first 5 years following their return to civilian life, compared with soldiers assigned to noncombat duty during a similar time period (Bower, 1987). The popular rumor that 50,000 vets have committed suicide since the war is a wild exaggeration, however (Pollock, Rhodes, Boyle, Decoufle, & McGee, 1990). But the vets do have a suicide rate 1 1/2 times more than for a similar population. Vietnam veterans are also twice as likely to have low sperm counts (The Centers for Disease Control, 1988). No one knows why that has happened as most of the vets were not exposed to defoliants or other chemical agents; long-term stress is suspected to have played a role.

Clearly, a traumatic experience can have long-term effects even though the immediate danger has been removed (Hefez, Metz, & Lavie, 1987). How long will stress of this sort last? Perhaps as long as the events are remembered.

Is it possible to prepare yourself for acute trauma, to harden yourself psychologically, so that once the event is over the stress won't continue? Perhaps, but if the stress is severe enough, even the toughest individuals may suffer. Police officers and fire fighters working in large cities often experience stressful events. They become somewhat hardened, but can still be overwhelmed by events. For instance, in San Diego in September 1979, a Pacific Southwest airliner collided with a small plane and plunged into a downtown area killing 144 people. The first police and fire fighters to arrive on the scene were faced with a dreadful scene of human carnage. There was extensive dismemberment among the victims, making the crash more horrifying than most accidents. Parts of bodies were found all over lawns, houses, and roads. Some police said they couldn't walk down the street without stepping on human tissue. Many of the officers who helped to identify and label the bodies had seen death before, but after this they experienced stress symptoms—nightmares, insomnia, headaches, gastrointestinal problems, memory loss. Some actually found themselves paralyzed when they attempted to put on the uniform that they had been wearing the day of the accident. Alan Davidson, president of the Academy of San Diego Psychologists, said, "This has had an impact on the human psyche beyond what we can humanly know" ("Crash Trauma," 1979, p. 61). Police who did not have to deal directly with the carnage, but rather helped with crowd control or arrests, fared much better. It was clearly direct contact with the victims that caused the acute stress and left the memories that resulted in chronic stress.

POST-TRAUMATIC STRESS DISORDER
A disorder characterized by the recurrence of a particular traumatic event in the mind of the individual who experienced it, a numbness or lack of responsiveness to external stimuli, and two or more symptoms associated with depression and anxiety, such as sleep disturbances, low threshold for startling, impairment of memory, and guilt about having participated in the event.

GENERAL ADAPTATION SYNDROME
Physiologist Hans Selye's description of the body's physiological-hormonal reaction to stressors. The reaction consists of three stages, the alarm reaction stage, the resistance stage, and the exhaustion stage.

ALARM REACTION STAGE
The first stage of the general adaptation syndrome, during which cortical hormone levels rise and emotional arousal and tension increase.

RESISTANCE STAGE
The second stage of the general adaptation syndrome, during which cortical hormones maintain high levels, physiological efforts to deal with stress reach full capacity, and resistance by means of defense mechanisms and coping strategies intensifies.

EXHAUSTION STAGE
The final stage of the general adaptation syndrome, during which resistance to the continuing stress begins to fail. Brain functioning may be hindered by metabolic changes; the immune system becomes much less efficient; and serious illness or disease becomes likely as the body begins to break down.

HYPOTHALAMIC-PITUITARY-ADRENAL AXIS
The glands and neural-hormonal complexes of the hypothalamus, the pituitary gland, and the adrenal glands of the kidneys, which together comprise an important stress reaction system.

CORTICOSTEROID HORMONES
Any of the steroid hormones of the cortex of the adrenal glands.

Hans Selye was one of the first to research the effects of stress.

REACTIONS TO STRESS

Conflicts and traumas can cause stress, and stress can lead to illness. But how does all this come about? How can stress make you ill?

The Body's Reaction

Over 45 years ago, the Austrian physiologist Hans Selye called attention to the body's reaction to stress and stressful situations. Selye called the physical reaction to stress the **general adaptation syndrome.** This syndrome consists of three different stages: the **alarm reaction stage,** the **resistance stage,** and the **exhaustion stage** (Selye, 1976).

STAGES OF THE GENERAL ADAPTION SYNDROME. During the alarm reaction stage, the person becomes alerted to the stress, and the body's resources mobilize to help cope with the stress. For many years, scientists knew that one way in which stress could affect the body was via the glands that comprised the **hypothalamic-pituitary-adrenal axis.** In response to stress, the hypothalamus (see Chapter 2) produces a certain hormone (corticotropin-releasing factor) that triggers the secretion of another hormone, adrenocorticotropic hormone (also called ACTH, because no one wants to have to say *adrenocorticotropic* any more often than is absolutely necessary). ACTH then acts on the adrenal glands above the kidneys to cause the secretion of **corticosteroid hormones.**

Corticosteroids have pronounced effects. Some of these hormones act like strong tranquilizers by boosting the effects of inhibitory neurotransmitters (see Chapter 2), which causes the person to become lethargic or depressed (Barnes, 1986). Others have excitatory effects leading to emotional arousal and increased tension, causing the person to become more sensitive and alert to his surroundings (Barnes, 1986). (See Concept Review.) Individuals who believe that they have little or no control over the cause of the stress show an especially heightened alarm response (Breier et al., 1987).

At this early point in the stress reaction, the person often attempts to cope, sometimes by using psychological defense mechanisms (see Chapter 13) and sometimes by attempting to alleviate the stress through direct action. If the stress persists, however, symptoms of maladjustment such as rash, gastrointestinal upset, hives, and sleep disruption may occur, and the person may enter the next stage, the stage of resistance.

The stage of resistance can be characterized as a "full war effort," whereas the alarm reaction was merely an alert. The attempts at defense have reached full capacity now. The individual must find some way of dealing with the stress to prevent complete psychological disintegration. A temporary resistance may be achieved by intensifying the use of psychological defense mechanisms or by taking actions directed at eliminating the stressful situation. During the stage of resistance, a person tends to become fixed in her pattern of dealing with the stress rather than reevaluating the situation and finding a new way to cope.

Unfortunately, the stress response that we have inherited may be old-fashioned when it comes to dealing with modern stressors. Our stress reaction system seems to have evolved to best deal with immediate threats, such as an attacking predator, rather than long-lasting emotional stresses that are often only partially resolved and which have become common in today's society. Such unresolved stress can lead to the exhaustion stage, when all the person's resources are at an end, and the

CONCEPT REVIEW: EMOTIONAL PINBALL

Novel or dangerous situations or disturbing thoughts that cause a person to feel frightened, angry, anxious, grief-stricken or depressed can set the body pinging and flashing like a pinball machine with a dozen balls in play. The chemicals that trigger the uproar can affect the entire body almost simultaneously. For clarity, the process is shown numbered sequentially here, from the brain to the kidneys and the heart and then throughout the upper body.

Electrochemical activity in the brain causes the hypothalamus to trigger the release of adrenocorticotropin (ACTH) (1) from the pituitary gland.

ACTH, a hormone, travels in the blood stream (2), Reaching the kidneys (3), ACTH ultimately prompts the adrenal glands to release hormones like cortisol and epinephrine, which can affect virtually every organ.

Epinephrine signals the heart (4) to beat faster, speeding up the response to a crisis—fighting or fleeing from an enemy, for example.

The stomach (5) starts producing the hormone gastrin as part of a general acceleration of metabolism. Breakdown and synthesis of vital proteins quickens in cells throughout the body (6).

Hormones released in response to crisis may interfere with the complicated reproductive cycle in women, and upset the balance of sex hormones (7).

The kidneys (8) begin to produce renin, provoking the constriction of blood vessels.

High cortisol levels may harm organs vital to the production of white blood cells. The spleen (9) and thymus (10) may shrink, weakening the immune system.

Under certain conditions, the brain may also release endogenous opiates, hormones that usually dampen pain. High levels of opiates may impair the body's response to disease by making some kinds of white blood cells (11) ineffectual. SOURCE: Maranto, 1984, p. 37

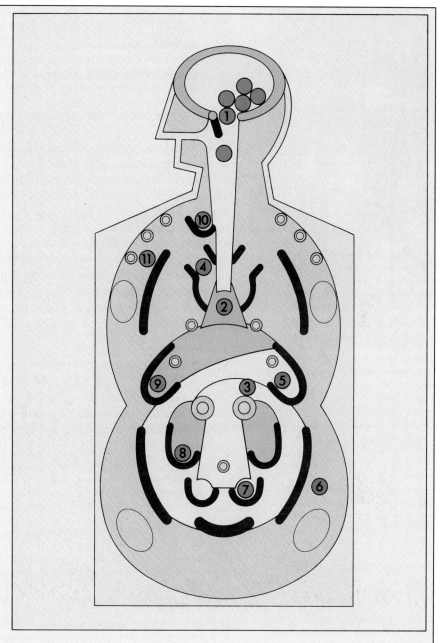

Continued and chronic stress will eventually take its toll on the body.

patterns of coping attempted during the stage of resistance begin to collapse. During the stage of exhaustion, psychological defenses may become inappropriate and exaggerated. Metabolic changes may occur that inhibit normal brain functioning, and eventually a complete psychological disorganization may result. Resistance becomes weaker until, finally, the body begins to break down and to suffer the diseases that can accompany stress. Depression is a likely outcome (Gold, Goodwin & Chrousos, 1988a; Gold, Goodwin & Chrousos, 1988b).

STRESS AND ILLNESS.   Among the most common early symptoms of chronic stress are headaches from muscle tension, gastrointestinal disturbances, skin rashes and hives, dizziness, and fatigue. Chronic stress can also lead to high blood pressure, which is referred to as *hypertension*.

During stressful situations, the kidneys react by retaining sodium and fluid. This increased retention is believed to be the direct cause of stress-induced hypertension (Light, Koepke, Obrist, & Willis, 1983). Hypertension, in turn, can bring on a heart attack, stroke, or kidney failure (Benson, 1975). Chronic stress also can aggravate arthritis, colitis (an inflammation of the colon, or large intestine), asthma, hypoglycemia (low blood sugar), ulcers, and diabetes. Although chronic stress has not been found to be clearly associated with the onset of cancer, it does appear to accelerate the disease in those who have it (Persky Kempthorne-Rawson, & Shekelle, 1987). Chronic stress is related to an increased chance of succumbing to contagious diseases.

STRESS AND THE IMMUNE SYSTEM.   How can stress be related to so many different kinds of illness? For one thing, stress can have a direct effect on the body's immune system. For many years, researchers suspected that there was some kind of direct link between the nervous and immune systems that did not depend on the actions of hormones such as those involved in the hypothalamic-pituitary-adrenal axis, but no one knew what that link might be. In the last few years, however, researchers have begun to uncover the mystery.

Scientists can measure the immune system's proper functioning by examining the effectiveness of the body's lymphocytes (white blood cells). Lymphocytes are the body's means of attacking and destroying foreign or invading organisms. One of the most important discoveries linking the nervous and immune system was the finding that lymphocytes are covered with receptors for neuropeptides (Ruff, Wahl, Mergenhagen, & Pert, 1985). Neuropeptides are messenger chemicals created by nerve cells (see Chapter 2). This finding strongly implies a nervous system–immune system connection.

Researchers have suspected such a link for years, not only because stress was known to have an effect on health, but also because of some direct evidence of this effect on the body's ability to fight disease (Weber & Pert, 1989). For instance, in one study conducted at the Mount Sinai School of Medicine in New York, researcher Steven J. Schleifer and his colleagues examined the lymphocyte counts of men who were married to women dying of cancer. The average age of the men was 65 years. Within 10 months, the wives of all the men died. The white blood count of these men became lower and lower as the stress continued. Schleifer discovered that their lymphocyte counts were significantly depressed after bereavement (Schleifer, Keller, Camerino, Thornton, & Stein, 1983). It is assumed that lower lymphocyte levels make people more susceptible to disease. In fact, after the death of a spouse, it's not uncommon for the remaining partner to become seriously ill or to die within 2 years. This higher rate of illness and death is much more common among survivors than among similar individuals of the same age who have not suffered the loss of a loved one (Glick, Weiss, & Parkes, 1974; Parkes, 1972).

Natural killer cells are a special kind of lymphocyte and are an important component of our immune system. They help to destroy invading disease agents. How severely these important cells are impaired has been found to vary directly with the amount of stress reported by people who are not able to cope effectively with their situations. The more stress the people were experiencing, the more severely their killer cells were impaired (Irwin, Daniels, Bloom, Smith, & Weiner, 1987).

Since the work in this area—known as *psychoneuroimmunology*—began, many direct nervous system–immune system connections have been uncovered; so many, in fact, that researchers now think of the immune system as a *sensory system*, not unlike vision or hearing, because it collects information (about the state of the body's health) and sends the information to the central nervous system for processing—all without your awareness (Marx, 1985).

Because of the discovery of the connections between the two systems, we are in a better position to understand how shocks to the nervous system, such as are caused by stress, bereavement, or depression, are capable of compromising the immune system (Calabrese, Kling, & Gold, 1987).

Stress is relative, however. To understand better what is meant by this statement, consider the following study. Researcher Steven Locke randomly selected 117 students at Boston University and evaluated how much stress they suffered by having them complete a stress survey that measured their symptoms, such as poor sleep or feelings of anxiety. In addition, Locke asked his subjects how each thought he or she was coping with stress. Then blood samples drawn from each subject were exposed to human leukemia cells. Locke's aim was to discover how well the natural killer cells in the blood samples could attack the leukemia cells. He found some notable differences among blood samples—and something else, too. The ability of the body's immune system to attack effectively was less related to *how much* stress each subject faced but instead to *how well* that person was coping with the stress. In other words, a person who can cope with stress may have a better chance of staying healthy than a person who cannot cope (Sapolsky, 1990). This could explain why two individuals in the same stressful job might show totally different bodily reactions to the stress they face (Locke, Furst, Heisel, & Williams, 1978; Locke et al., 1984).

Measuring Susceptibility to Stress and Illness

Is there any way to measure how much stress you may be facing from day to day? In Table 14.3, you'll see a scale for rating life changes, developed by Holmes and Rahe in 1967. Each of these life events is assigned a value, a certain number of stress points. In their study, Holmes and Rahe found that individuals who had more than 300 stress points within 1 year were two or three times as likely to have illness and other stress-related problems than were individuals who had fewer stress points.

One interesting detail you may notice while reading the table is that some very nice things seem to be stressful. Among these often pleasant events or circumstances are marriage, gaining a new family member, a change in financial state (which could mean for the better as well as for the worse), an outstanding personal achievement, the beginning of school, family get-togethers, and even a vacation.

There also are several major points to keep in mind. First, these data are correlational, and do not necessarily imply cause and effect. For example, people of lower socioeconomic status (who are also more likely to have poorer health care) lead lives in which more changes take place, often due to financial problems. Stressful changes in the lives of such people may be only correlated with poor health, not the cause of it. If so, then adding up stress points may not be a valid way to explain future problems. Similarly, the stress points should be used solely as a general guideline. Although the numbers give them the appearance of being highly specific, they aren't; they're only general. For example, it's highly doubtful that one pregnancy, one Christmas, and four vacations would be more stressful than the death of a spouse. So read the table with an open mind.

TABLE 14.3 Social Readjustment Rating Scale

RANK	LIFE EVENT	MEAN VALUE	RANK	LIFE EVENT	MEAN VALUE
1.	Death of spouse	100	24.	Trouble with in-laws	29
2.	Divorce	73	25.	Outstanding personal achievement	28
3.	Marital separation from mate	65	26.	Wife beginning or ceasing work outside the home	26
4.	Detention in jail or other institution	63	27.	Beginning or ceasing formal schooling	26
5.	Death of a close family member	63	28.	Major change in living conditions (building a new home, remodeling, deterioration of home or neighborhood)	25
6.	Major personal injury or illness	53			
7.	Marriage	50	29.	Revision of personal habits (dress, manners, associations, etc.)	24
8.	Being fired at work	47			
9.	Marital reconciliation with mate	45	30.	Trouble with the boss	23
10.	Retirement from work	45	31.	Major change in working hours or conditions	20
11.	Major change in the health or behavior of a family member	44	32.	Change in residence	20
			33.	Changing to a new school	20
12.	Pregnancy	40	34.	Major change in usual type and/or amount of recreation	19
13.	Sexual difficulties	39			
14.	Gaining a new family member (through birth, adoption, oldster moving in, etc.)	39	35.	Major change in church activities (a lot more or a lot less than usual)	19
15.	Major business readjustment (merger, reorganization, bankruptcy, etc.)	39	36.	Major change in social activities (clubs, dancing, movies, visiting, etc.)	18
16.	Major change in financial stage (a lot worse off or a lot better off than usual)	38	37.	Taking out a mortgage or loan for a lesser purchase (for a car, TV, freezer, etc.)	17
17.	Death of a close friend	37			
18.	Changing to a different line of work	36	38.	Major change in sleeping habits (a lot more or a lot less sleep, or change in part of day when asleep)	16
19.	Major change in the number of arguments with spouse (either a lot more or a lot less than usual regarding child rearing, personal habits, etc.)	35	39.	Major change in number of family get-togethers (a lot more or a lot less than usual)	15
20.	Taking out a mortgage or loan for a major purchase (for a home, business, etc.)	31	40.	Major change in eating habits (a lot more or a lot less food intake, or very different meal hours or surroundings)	15
21.	Foreclosure on a mortgage or loan	30	41.	Vacation	13
22.	Major change in responsibilities at work (promotion, demotion, lateral transfer)	29	42.	Christmas	12
23.	Son or daughter leaving home (marriage, attending college, etc.)	29	43.	Minor violation of the law (traffic tickets, jaywalking, disturbing the peace, etc.)	11

SOURCE: Holmes & Rahe, 1967.

Most research dealing with stress and illness begins with an examination of a population suffering from illness; the objective is to determine how much stress that group was under before the illness. But this kind of research can be biased, in that the researchers often know ahead of time that the people they are dealing with are suffering from stress-related illnesses. When time and funds permit, researchers prefer to conduct prospective research, in which they find a healthy population, study the subjects' stress patterns, and observe the long-term effects on health.

The largest study of this kind has been conducted by George E. Vaillant (1979). He selected 204 men who were in the sophomore class at Harvard from 1942 to 1944. For over 4 decades, he kept in touch with 185 of them. During these years, Vaillant and other researchers conducted many psychological and physical tests on, as well as interviews with, the subjects. Stress predictors included how often the subjects visited a psychiatrist or psychologist, whether they were failing to make progress in their job, whether they were dissatisfied with their job, whether their marriage was unhappy, whether they received little vacation or recreation time, and whether they had a poor outlook on life.

The findings of this study generally support the notion that people who have the ability to cope well with stress are likely to be healthier. Of the 59 men in this study who coped well with stress and who had the best mental health, only two became extremely ill or died by the time they were 53 years of age. Of the 48 men who were found to have the worst mental health, 18 became chronically ill or died. The men in this group had shown themselves to be less able to deal with stress. The men in both groups came from very similar backgrounds. Clearly, their ability to cope with stress was directly related to their physical health.

By 1990, Vaillant could report that one of the strongest predictors of mental and physical health after age 65 was the extent of tranquilizer use before age 50 (Vaillant & Vaillant, 1990). It is assumed that those who were in need of tranquilizers were either under more stress or coping less well.

AN ENDURING QUESTION: ARE THERE DISEASE-PRONE PERSONALITIES?

For centuries, philosophers and scientists have wondered about the role of personality in the onset of disease (Taylor, 1990). In the 1930s and 1940s, specific personality profiles were developed along with the claim that they were able to predict the likelihood of hypertension, cancer, heart disease, ulcers, arthritis, and other diseases (Dunbar, 1943; Alexander, 1950). Convincing evidence to support these claims, however, was lacking.

Yet common sense tells us that we shouldn't be too surprised to discover that individuals exposed to prolonged stress differed in their vulnerabilities to serious disease. In 1959, researchers Meyer Friedman and Ray Rosenman separated male personalities into two categories, type A and type B, and linked them to coronary artery disease. Men with type A personalities are intense, alert, competitive, and striving, while those with type B are relaxed, easygoing, and unpressured (Friedman & Rosenman, 1959).

Since that time, much research has indicated that type A males have a greater chance than do type B males of incurring heart disease (Suinn, 1977). This research implies that certain personality types are more prone to specific stress-related illnesses. In fact, the idea of type A personality and its relationship to heart disease became so well established that efforts to change personality with the hope of lessening heart disease have become commonplace.

More recently, however, support for the idea of a heart-attack-prone personality has not been forthcoming. The problems with the concept were brought to light when cardiologist Robert Case analyzed the personalities of 516 heart-attack victims and discovered that type As were no more likely to have heart attacks than were the type Bs (Case, Heller, Case, & Moss, 1985). To avoid possible bias, another physician, Richard Shekelle, conducted a prospective study with 3,110 men who had never had a heart attack. He classified their personality types according to the recognized methods of sorting type A from type B; then he waited to see what would happen. After a few years, the subjects had had a total of 129 heart attacks, divided evenly between type As and type Bs (Shekelle et al., 1985). These new findings have led some researchers to conclude that the earlier positive results linking type A personality to heart disease may have been due to interviewer bias (see Chapter 1) or other confounding measures (Lazarus, DeLongis, Folkman & Gruen, 1985). These findings then prompted two psychologists, Howard Friedman and Stephanie Booth-Kewley, carefully to analyze and compare 101 studies conducted between 1945 and 1984 on disease and personality. This approach is called a **meta-analysis**. Their conclusion was that there does appear to be a link between type A behavior and heart attack (Friedman & Booth-Kewley, 1987). But others conducting meta-analysis of these studies have come to the opposite conclusion, that type A behavior is not related to heart attack (Matthews, 1988). The cause of all this confusion may be that "type A" has never been clearly defined (Friedman & Booth-Kewley, 1988; Rodin & Salovey, 1989), and is often assessed differently from one study to the next.

It may well be that certain personalities make people more prone to illness in general, although perhaps not to *specific* illnesses, but further research is needed before we can say which personalities might be at higher risk.

FOR CRITICAL ANALYSIS

1. It was once believed that stress caused ulcers. We now know that, although stress may exacerbate an ulcer, it cannot cause one. This discovery has reduced the guilt commonly felt by the ulcer patient concerning his condition. Why?
2. If certain personalities are eventually linked to specific illnesses, how might guilt and blame reemerge in patients with physical illnesses? Why might they come to feel this way?

Hassles

Sometimes we know the exact cause of our stress and have an idea about how to handle the problem. Much of the time, however, we can't put our finger on what's wrong when we feel under stress. Stress doesn't have to be only the result of an extreme trauma such as a plane crash or volcanic eruption. Instead, over days and weeks a number of what people call "hassles" can add up, resulting in stress. Hassles include getting stuck in a traffic jam, receiving a personal insult from someone, not being appreciated enough on the job, receiving a parking ticket, having to rush to get to work, burning the dinner, watching a favorite television show get preempted, being $2 short at the supermarket, spilling ink on your clothes, and sleeping through the alarm. How many irritations like these occur each day, none of them significant by itself? They can accumulate and create an overall feeling of stress that we can't blame on any one thing (Kanner, Coyne, Schaefer, & Lazarus, 1981). Enough of these little irritations can lead to a general adaptation syndrome.

If we allow ourselves to be subjected to these kinds of stressors often enough, the reaction can last a long time. We can begin to feel fearful about our very existence. This feeling is known as **anxiety.** Anxiety is different from fear. If you are fearful, you know why you're afraid. If you are anxious, by definition, you don't know the specific cause. Anxiety is not object-related. The American Psychiatric Association has defined anxiety as "apprehension, tension, or uneasiness that stems from the anticipation of danger, the source of which is largely unknown or unrecognized."

Anxiety levels are generally found to be higher among people who handle stress poorly. Such people go through the day with a feeling of dread that's just below the surface, a constant tenseness. They're steeled for the next insult. Why do some people become anxious when facing hassles while others remain calm and relaxed? Recent evidence indicates that there may be a biological or genetic difference in people most susceptible to life's hassles.

Evidence of a genetic factor was gathered by researcher Gregory Carey (Carey, Goldsmith, Tellegen & Gottesman, 1978), who reported that identical twins are much more likely to react similarly to stress than are fraternal (nonidentical twins). Other evidence (Jemerin & Boyce, 1990) indicates that there may be biochemical differences among people that influence how they handle stress. Specific brain cells that seek out benzodiazepines have been discovered. Benzodiazepines are tranquilizers such as Valium or Xanax. The existence of such natural receptors implies that the brain must be manufacturing its own natural benzodiazepine, or else why would there be brain cells ready to receive it (see Chapter 2)? This finding indicates that the brain relies on neurochemistry to mediate how much anxiety people feel in the face of stress. If we discover that people with different levels of anxiety have significantly different brain chemistry, then we might find a biological reason to explain why some people are better able to handle stress than others are. In addition, it may eventually be possible to develop totally safe and effective drugs that enlarge our capacity to endure stress. If such drugs are used judiciously, people could be "tuned" to an optimal level for handling stress without exhausting their psychological and physiological resources.

Suicide

In the throes of a conflict, or under intense stress, some people may consider suicide to be a reasonable solution. Many such people apparently look on suicide as a decision to stop participating in a stressful life. Over the last 15 years, there has been an alarming increase in suicide, especially among adolescents. For those 15 to 19 years old, suicide is the third-ranking cause of death, just behind accidents and murders. The rate of suicide among many of the aged also is alarmingly high (Turkington, 1987).

While it's obvious that anyone would be susceptible to the stress associated with a trauma such as a plane crash or a war, it's also true that many people, even those who appear to have everything they need, live in situations that they appraise as stressful. Stress is highly personal, and each individual reacts to it differently. Some people may suffer severe stress in situations in which others wouldn't experience stress at all or even see the reason for it.

Think of stressful times in your life when you were much younger. Suppose you could play the game "If I only knew then what I know now." Suppose you could bring your current maturity and knowledge to bear in an earlier stressful situation. Conflicts with parents might seem foolish or needless. Concerns over

ANXIETY
A state of apprehension in which the source is usually not specific, as it is in fear. There is a vague but persistent feeling that some future danger is in store, such as punishment or threat to self-esteem. Anxiety typically leads to defensive reactions.

IS THERE A RIGHT TO COMMIT SUICIDE?

A 10,000-word booklet entitled *A Guide to Self-Deliverance* was published by a London society called Exit—the Society for the Right to Die with Dignity.

The society was formed about 50 years ago. Its members believe that suicide is acceptable for people who are painfully or incurably ill. Because they believe this, they think that they are doing society a service by providing a pamphlet that describes the simplest, easiest, and least painful way of committing the act. The pamphlet even lists lethal doses of easy-to-obtain prescription and nonprescription drugs. The *Guide* does, however, counsel against committing suicide if the person's motivation is strictly psychological, which the writers consider may be a temporary state, or if there is even the remotest chance that a cure might exist.

The announcement of the pamphlet's publication alarmed a great many people. The British Medical Association expressed the fear that the booklet might make people feel that suicide was something to be treated lightly. The association added, "There is no reason to assume that a terminally ill patient has no more to contribute or gain in the last months" (Leo & White, 1980, p. 49). Other people think that the information in the *Guide* may be used to commit homicide or that people who are old or sick may feel under pressure to kill themselves once they have the information and hear that other people are using it.

A similar organization, the National Hemlock Society, exists in the United States, and also makes available information for those who wish to know how to kill themselves.

The arguments about the acceptability of suicide among the terminally ill have grown since Janet Adkins, a member of the Oregon chapter of the National Hemlock Society who had recently received a diagnosis of Alzheimer's disease, asked Dr. Jack Kevorkian, a Michigan pathologist, for help to commit suicide. Dr. Kevorkian was known to have developed a "suicide machine." The device was an intravenous drip bottle with a lethal poison that could be self-administered by pushing a button that would activate the flow of the poison. Ms. Adkins traveled to Michigan to see Dr. Kevorkian. He set up his device in a van and then left Ms. Adkins alone after placing the needle in her vein. She administered the poison, which killed her painlessly and instantly. Derik Humphry, the founder of the society, backs her decision, but points out the need for national standards and greater availability of suicide assistance. He adds, "She had to go 2,300 miles to die in a camper in a parking lot. That's not my idea of death with dignity" (Rarick, 1990).

Planned suicide is a highly emotional issue, and there are strong feelings on both sides. Some people think that helping suicide, even in the way that Dr. Kevorkian did, is a heinous act. Other people argue that a prolonged and agonizing death in a hospital, surrounded most of the time by strangers and without any control, is the last insult and one that should not be borne. Still other people think that terminally ill individuals should have the right to die if they want to, but that a book such as the *Guide* will change things so that "committing suicide will no longer be seen as a right. It will fast become a duty" (Seligmann & Donosky, 1980, p. 77).

One side of the controversy finds perhaps its clearest expression in psychiatrist Thomas Szasz's 1986 article in which he argued against suicide prevention, even if the suicide

Dr. Jack Kevorkian, shown here with his "suicide machine."

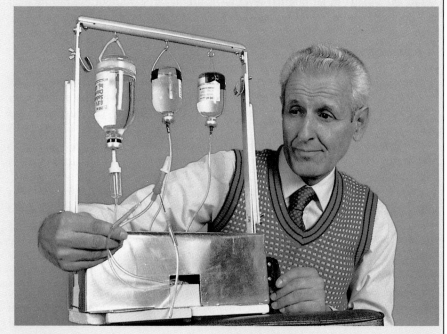

was for psychological reasons (Szasz, 1986). Szasz believes that there should be no *involuntary* suicide prevention treatment, because to administer such treatment requires that professionals be given the power to deny someone her liberty or dignity.

The counterarguments include the observation that court protections are in place to prevent abuse of liberty; that many people who were about to commit suicide, but were forcibly prevented, are now very grateful that they were helped when they needed it; that to ignore the danger of suicide is to shirk professional responsibility; that the victims often are under legal age of consent and should not be left to choose between life and death for themselves; and that many other people are harmed by a suicide than just the one taking his life (Clum, 1987; Holmes, 1987; Mather, 1987).

The issue of suicide and suicide prevention continues to be fraught with ethical and moral dilemmas to which black-and-white answers are not likely to apply.

---

your complexion or your treatment at the hands of certain classmates might seem trivial. The point of this exercise is to show that people who are under stress may be lacking important information. Their view of their situation may not be the only possible view. They may see themselves trapped in a horrible conflict with no way out, when someone with a different knowledge or understanding may not even see a conflict.

Suicide is a final solution, and one from which there can be no return. Many people who have seriously attempted suicide but failed have later found other ways of coping with their stress. Unfortunately, as suicide rates increase and more attention is given to it by the media and the public, it is on the minds of more people and is thought of more often as an alternative. One interviewer discovered that 65 percent of all college students had at one time or another thought of suicide with sufficient intensity to contemplate the means (Mishara, 1975).

Suicide must always be viewed as a possibility among people who are under considerable stress. One of the goals of psychologists is to be aware of the hazard and to make sure that potential suicides are given a chance to obtain help.

Several signs may warn of a potential suicide. First, any attempts at suicide, however mild, or jokes about suicide, however lightly made, must be taken seriously. The person should be offered help in the form of family support or professional counseling. Previous attempts at suicide also are significant, because of those people who commit suicide, 30 to 40 percent have attempted it previously. Furthermore, about 10 percent of people who attempt suicide will kill themselves within 10 years of the attempt (Grinspoon, 1986).

Among adolescents, a population with a high suicide rate, an important warning sign is the perceived failure to achieve in school—a sign that should be especially heeded in students who have superior or better-than-average ability. Of those adolescents who have committed suicide because of perceived failure at school, only 11 percent were actually in serious academic trouble (which again shows how often stress is in the eye of the beholder) (Jacobs, 1971).

Another important sign for members of all age groups is withdrawal from social relationships. Such withdrawal may occur because the person feels unwanted by his family (Rosenkrantz, 1978). Rejection by friends and peers also can contribute to withdrawal. Another indication may be the termination or failure of a love relationship. And any recent loss, even the eviction from an apartment, can tilt a person toward suicide if she has a serious drug or alcohol problem (Rich, Fowler, Fogarty & Young, 1988).

Another possible reason for suicide concerns brain chemistry. In 1975, Swedish researchers were attempting to measure levels of serotonin in the human brain. Serotonin, a neurotransmitter that had been discovered not long before, was known to be involved with mood and emotion. Because brain serotonin cannot be measured directly without destroying the brain itself, the researchers took samples of cerebrospinal fluid from the spines of human subjects and measured the levels of a substance known as 5HIAA, which is known to be a good indicator of the level of brain serotonin. Psychiatrist Marie Asberg still remembers the day in June 1975 when one of her staff psychiatrists happened to notice something, and commented, "All these low-5HIAA patients kill themselves" (Pines, 1983, p. 56). Dr. Asberg recalls, "I thought, my God, what is she saying?" (p. 56). What the staff psychiatrist had in fact inadvertently discovered was a biological marker that might be related directly to the incidence of suicide. Following that discovery, researchers linked low levels of serotonin and 5HIAA with depression, aggression, and impulsivity. As you can imagine, the combination of these three attributes is an obvious formula for violent suicide. In fact, the lower the levels, the more impulsive and aggressive the suicide (see Figure 14.1).

Building on this work, researchers in Finland have studied violent criminals. They discovered that men who committed impulsive unpremeditated murders had the lowest levels of 5HIAA. Among this group, it was also discovered that men who had killed more than once had levels of 5HIAA that were lower than those in men who had only killed once (Roy, DeJong & Linnoila, 1989). Low levels of 5HIAA almost assuredly mean impulsive, aggressive behavior, whether directed at oneself or others.

Researchers also have discovered that the ratio of two other important neurotransmitters, norepinephrine and epinephrine, plays a role in suicide. People who have too much epinephrine, relative to their levels of norepinephrine, have been found to be more likely to kill themselves (Ostroff, Giller, Harkness, & Mason, 1985).

Although more research is needed, these findings indicate that psychologists may be on their way to developing valid screening tests for potential suicides and other violent, impulsive behavior.

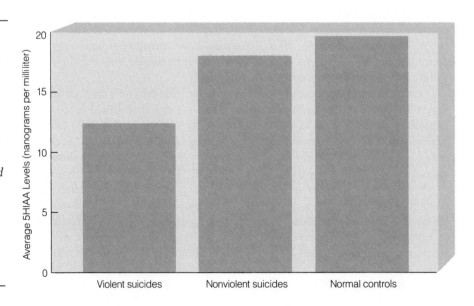

FIGURE 14.1

Marie Asberg's comparison of the 5HIAA levels of 46 patients who had attempted suicide with 45 healthy volunteers. The average 5HIAA level for the suicidal group was 16.3 nanograms per milliliter compared to 19.8 for the controls. More striking was the very low 5HIAA of those who made violent attempts—hanging or drowning, for example. Six patients killed themselves within the year. (SOURCE: Adapted from Pines, 1983.)

Ways of Coping with Stress

If you stop for a moment to think about some of the conflicts or traumas that people face, you may wonder how these people ever adjust. But there are ways, some of which people turn to almost automatically.

Psychological Defense Mechanisms

Sometimes, we're able to handle conflict and stress by using defense mechanisms. These are ways of handling information to make it appear more agreeable; we see a conflict or a trauma in light that renders it less disturbing. Among these mechanisms are **denial, rationalization, reaction formation,** and **projection** (see Chapter 13). Such defenses are normal and healthy. They help us to survive stress. Without them, we would be prey to the full intensity of every conflict or trauma. As we noted in Chapter 13, in general, psychologists don't consider the use of defense mechanisms inappropriate or unhealthy unless we rely on these mechanisms to an extreme.

Stress Management

In contrast to defense mechanisms, which can alter your view of the stressors in your life, **direct coping strategies** help you either to eliminate the stressor or to harden yourself to the hassles that occur every day and the big ones that occur once in a while.

There is no way to avoid stress—but avoiding it may not be necessary. Remember, the amount of stress you face isn't nearly as important as how you deal with it. If you can learn to treat stress in the right way you can defuse it. Psychologists have concentrated much of their effort on training people to cope directly with their stress. Coping does not always come naturally. It must be learned and honed like any other skill.

DENIAL
A defense mechanism in which the individual simply denies the existence of the events that have produced the anxiety.

RATIONALIZATION
A defense mechanism in which irrational, impulsive action, or even failure, is justified to others and to oneself by substituting acceptable explanations for the real, but unacceptable reasons.

REACTION FORMATION
A defense mechanism in which the individual exhibits, and at the conscious level believes he or she possesses, feelings opposite to those possessed at the unconscious level.

PROJECTION
A defense mechanism in which the individual attributes his or her own motives or thoughts to others, especially when these motives or thoughts are considered undesirable.

DIRECT COPING STRATEGIES
Active rational strategies intended to alleviate stress either by eliminating the stressor or by reducing the psychological effects of stress.

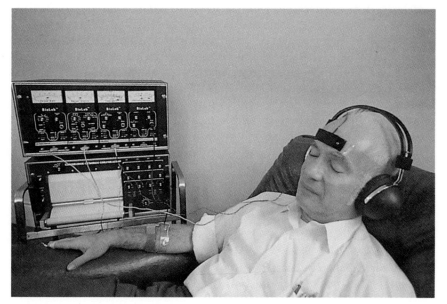

Techniques such as biofeedback have been helpful for training people to relax.

PROGRESSIVE RELAXATION
A technique in which deep relaxation is achieved through the progressive relaxation of one muscle group at a time, usually beginning with the feet and legs. The subject breathes deeply and focuses attention on each muscle group as it is relaxed.

CLINICAL STRESS MANAGEMENT.   In 1921, Edmund Jacobson, at a meeting of the American Medical Association, introduced the concept of psychosomatic illness—physical illness brought on by stress and tension. His interest in this area continued, and in 1938 he developed a treatment for neuromuscular tension, called **progressive relaxation** (Jacobson, 1938). This marked the first serious effort to develop a clinical technique that could be applied to reduce and alleviate stress. Since that time, many different stress-management techniques have been developed. Unfortunately, because modern stress-management technology has become a growth industry and many wildly exaggerated claims have been made by various groups and individuals purporting to alleviate stress, it's not always easy to be a knowledgeable consumer. Many serious scientists, however, have carefully evaluated stress-reduction techniques, and psychologists now have a general idea of how effective each of these techniques is. Some of the techniques that often have been found beneficial are listed in Table 14.4. A word of caution is in order, however. Applying these techniques to the problem of reducing human stress requires a certain amount of therapeutic art. For this reason, the techniques often vary in their effectiveness, depending on the skill and wisdom of the clinician who is applying them (Woolfolk & Lehrer, 1984).

COPING STRATEGIES.   Besides using clinical interventions to alleviate stress, you can use some personal coping strategies:

1. If you find yourself in a conflict, you're probably going to be uncomfortable. No one likes to be uncomfortable. As a result, people have a tendency to get the conflict over with as quickly as possible and thus to end the discomfort. This can lead to a rushed judgment that may in the long run cause even greater problems— you might make the wrong choice. One of the best ways to cope with a conflict is to gather as much information as possible. Say to yourself, "All right, I'm uncomfortable and I'll be uncomfortable for awhile, but it's more important to gather information to help me with my choice than to rush to a conclusion I might not be satisfied with." As you gather information, you usually will find that your view of the conflict begins to change, and the choice becomes obvious. Suddenly, the conflict will be over because you have enough information to make the right decision.

2. Trust in time. Many stressful events can be very painful. Divorce is a good example. After a divorce, many people feel that their lives have been ruined. Even months after a divorce, depression and stress are likely to be severe or even to increase. New stressors must be faced, such as dating again, adjusting to a lower income, or raising children as a single parent. It can seem that the anguish will never end. But, although time may not heal all wounds, it often helps. Mavis Hetherington has found that among divorced couples, the stress is often much lower 2 years after the divorce (Hetherington, 1979). In other words, the pain is likely to decrease significantly. People make new friends, form new bonds, and often remarry. This is true, not only of divorce, but also of other stressful situations. If you find yourself in extreme anguish, feeling that all of your plans are collapsing or that your career is being ruined, trust in time. There is a good possibility that within a year or two after your current world has collapsed, you will find yourself in another one that is fulfilling.

3. Try not to be alone too much of the time. Maintain friendships and contacts. The lonely and the isolated suffer stress more and have poorer health than do those who have company (House, Landis, & Umberson, 1988; Taylor, 1990). Other people can function to distract you by making you interested in things they find exciting. When you're by yourself, to keep yourself company you tend to discuss

personal issues with yourself. But when you're with other people and are involved in doing things with them, it's difficult to engage in self-reflection. Often, the good ideas and moods of other people can have a relaxing and comforting effect. In addition, it is helpful to have a pet with whom to share your time alone. Pets help to keep away loneliness, and their presence has been shown to reduce stress, high blood pressure, and depression (Culliton, 1987).

4. People who have a pessimistic outlook on life are more likely to develop poor health (Peterson, Seligman, & Vaillant, 1988), so try to think positively and rationally. Keep a sense of humor. Enjoy laughter. If someone doesn't like you, there are other people in the world. If you've planned to be a lawyer ever since you were 6 years old and you didn't make it, you've now learned that you can't trust a 6-year-old child to decide your future. You're an adult; pick again. There are hundreds

TABLE 14.4 Stress-Management Techniques

TECHNIQUE	PROCEDURE	THERAPEUTIC BENEFIT
Progressive relaxation	Over many sessions, a subject is taught to pay attention to individual muscles until she is able to recognize levels of tension in each muscle.	Subjects become aware of which muscles are tense at any given time. They can then eliminate unnecessary tension by relaxing and thereby reduce or eliminate headache, neuralgia, excessive physiological arousal, or other stress-related disorders.
Modified progressive relaxation	Deep muscle relaxation is taught by use of a relaxing environment, deep breathing, and cycles of tensing and relaxing muscles. (The emphasis is on learning to relax rather than on learning the tension level of each muscle.)	This technique takes less time than the original form of progressive relaxation. It reduces muscle tension and induces relaxation, which may help stem the general adaptation syndrome.
Yogic therapy	Typically, progressive relaxation is combined with meditation and the body postures associated with yoga. The technique often contains elements of the Hindu religion.	The therapy helps alleviate muscle tension, excessive autonomic arousal, and hypertension. People who like the yoga exercises especially enjoy it.
Meditation	Subjects learn relaxation, deep breathing, and concentration on one particular sound or idea.	This technique reduces blood pressure and may help reduce anxiety, fatigue, insomnia, mild depression, and irritability.
Hypnosis	Hypnotic induction is described in Chapter 5. It is especially useful for subjects who are susceptible to suggestion or feel comfortable with the idea of hypnosis.	Subjects may respond to suggestion by developing greater relaxation and a more positive attitude concerning stressful situations.
Biofeedback	Equipment that amplifies body temperature, muscle tension, or other physiological measures provides subjects with feedback about their biological activity.	In conjunction with therapy and proper assessment, biofeedback can aid subjects to regulate their biological activity. Control of muscle tension and autonomic arousal often is the focal point.
Cognitive therapy	Therapy focuses on the individual's own cognitive appraisals. Stressful ideas, thoughts, and perceptions are directly examined and tested to determine their validity.	The subject's thinking may be restructured, so that situations or circumstances that were once perceived as extremely stressful are viewed in a less stressful, often more realistic, light.
Psychopharmacology	Medications are used to alter psychological or physiological reactions to stress.	In conjunction with psychotherapy, people suffering from acute stress may benefit from temporary use of drugs to control anxiety, depression, and other stress-related disorders such as muscle tension.

of other ways to be happy. And remember that not everything that seems to be a catastrophe really is one. Not every goal is worth having. In fact, you may have been very lucky that you didn't achieve some of your goals. Remember the old saying, "Beware of what you want. You might get it."

5. Begin to think of yourself as a relaxed person. Move and speak more slowly. Eat slowly. Take deep breaths. Stop from time to time to relax your muscles. Watch how hectic the lives of other people seem, and let this remind you to slow down more. Don't schedule your life so that you need to rush from place to place. If you find yourself in a traffic jam, don't think about the future and how the traffic is keeping you from being someplace. Instead, take a deep breath, turn on the radio, listen to the music, and relax. Look at the tense faces and angry expressions of the people around you, and take pleasure in the fact that you are a relaxed person.

These ideas may seem simple; in fact, they are. Nonetheless, relying on them can make a powerful difference. One final thought—remember that stress is not always a bad thing. A small amount of stress may serve to move you to action. Stress is likely to be detrimental only if it is unresolved and long lasting and, especially, if you are prone to deal poorly with it. In one of the Chinese languages, the characters for *stress* mean *pressure* and also *opportunity*. The Chinese have realized that a small amount of stress can motivate people to take action that may eventually provide them with something good, and for this reason their word for stress has both a positive and a negative component.

EPILOGUE: HELP WHEN IT WAS MOST NEEDED

Psychologists who study the effects of sudden and severe stress know how debilitating the condition can be. Sometimes, the speed at which help and intervention can be made available to a person under stress can make the difference between his being able to cope with the stress or becoming one of its victims. The following is the story of how one man quickly delivered help when it was most needed.

In August 1987, Northwest flight 255 from Detroit to Phoenix crashed on takeoff, killing 153 people. The airline company was in shock—it was their first accident in about 25 years. They were suddenly faced with terrible dilemmas. What should they tell the families waiting in Phoenix or the families who were still in Detroit when the jetliner crashed? What could they say to family members throughout the country who would soon be calling in? How could they help their staff to handle the wrenching emotional experience of dealing with the victims' families and the press? How could they get help to the flight crews and personnel, scattered among six "hub" cities, who were suffering because they might have had friends on the flight or who would soon be functioning poorly because they were harboring a secret dread of flying?

The vice president of the airline decided to place a call to psychologist James Butcher, who is known for his work in disaster crisis management. The vice president asked Butcher if he would put together a walk-in mental health counseling program for employees and victims' families in six cities—and do it within 24 hours! James Butcher recalled, "I gulped and said yes" (Bales, 1987, p. 26).

The first thing Butcher did was to pick up the telephone and to arrange for psychologists to staff five of the six cities; Butcher took Detroit for himself, where he could be closest to the problem. The program Butcher set up consisted of three parts: (1) immediate personnel and victims' families; (2) a hotline, also staffed by mental health professionals, who could refer people in need to psychologists in locations other than the six cities; and (3) a special crisis intervention program aimed at those people who were at high risk for emotional problems. Among this latter group were about 150 airline employees who had been asked to care for the victims' families just after the crash (Bales, 1987).

For 2 weeks, the psychologists led by Butcher worked 14 to 16 hours per day. Of course, there was no way to undo the tragedy, but many family members and employees needed help to come to grips with their depression, grief, and anger. They needed professional assurance that their feelings of guilt ("I never should have let her fly by herself, I should have been with her") were normal and were part of grieving. Other people, too numb to feel anything, were counseled that such numbness, too, was a normal reaction following the sudden death of someone loved and that they were neither unfeeling people nor "crazy." They were also told what to expect later, when the sadness and grief would come.

Other psychologists discovered that some people needed help to overcome a new and strong fear of flying. Desensitization techniques (see Chapters 6 and 16) were helpful in these instances.

Finally, employees were "debriefed"; they talked about their experiences and sorted out what had happened in a group setting, after which each employee was able to spend some time alone with a psychologist.

Butcher believes that, although some of the people helped through the trauma may require further aid, the number needing professional assistance will be much lower than it would have been if no one had been there to help. Judging by all the experience gained by psychologists over the years with stress and crisis management, there is little doubt that James Butcher is right.

SUMMARY

■ Health psychology has been defined as "any aspect of psychology that bears upon the experience of health and illness and the behavior that affects health status" (Rodin & Stone, 1987, pp. 15–16). Every year, researchers offer more evidence that our well-being and physical health are directly linked to our behavior.

■ One of the important and emerging areas in health psychology is the study of detrimental behaviors. Detrimental behaviors are those behaviors that pose a risk to human health and well-being.

■ Health psychology is involved with sorting real from perceived risk. It also is concerned with why people don't change their

behavior even after they become aware of which of their behaviors are the most dangerous.

■ The two most serious kinds of chemical dependence in terms of damage to health or lives lost are dependence on alcohol and nicotine.

■ Sometimes, acutely stressful situations arise that did not derive from a conflict. Even though the stressful event may be of relatively short duration, it can be so intense that the memory of it can linger for years, resulting in chronic stress.

■ Stress can lead to illness. Hans Selye has referred to the physical reaction to stress as the general adaptation syndrome, which occurs in three stages. During the alarm reaction stage, the person becomes alerted to the stress. During the resistance stage, the stress continues and the individual engages in a full war effort against it. During the stage of exhaustion, all of the person's resources are gone, and the patterns of coping begin to collapse.

■ Chronic stress can lead to high blood pressure, heart attack, stroke, and kidney failure. It also can aggravate arthritis, colitis, asthma, hypoglycemia, diabetes, and other disorders. Ulcers also are known to be affected by stress.

■ One way of measuring the immune system's effectiveness is to count lymphocytes (white blood cells). A person's lymphocyte count often is lower following stressful situations. Stress also can have an effect on the immune system at the cellular level.

■ The new field of psychoneuroimmunology includes investigations of the many direct nervous system–immune system connections that have been discovered and of their effects.

■ Because of the discovery of the connections between the nervous and immune systems, researchers are better able to understand how shocks to the nervous system—such as those caused by stress, bereavement, or depression—are capable of compromising the immune system's effectiveness.

■ Stress is relative; people differ in their vulnerability to serious disease caused by prolonged exposure to stress.

■ There may not be a link between *specific* diseases—such as heart attack, ulcer, or headache—and certain personality traits. People with certain personalities, however, may be generally more prone to illness than are others.

■ Stress doesn't have to be the result of an extreme trauma such as a plane crash or volcanic eruption. Instead, over days and weeks, a number of "hassles" can add up, resulting in stress.

■ A new picture of anxiety is beginning to emerge. Psychological factors are important, but some people may be biologically more susceptible to anxiety.

■ Over the last decade there has been an alarming increase in suicide. Although suicide may sometimes seem to be the only way out of a conflict, many people who have made serious attempts at suicide but failed have later found other ways of coping with their stress. The possibility of suicide by people who are under considerable stress must always be taken seriously. Such individuals should be offered help in the form of family support or professional counseling.

■ Researchers have shown that increased suicide is related to lower levels of serotonin, an important brain neurotransmitter.

■ People sometimes are able to handle conflict and stress by using defense mechanisms.

■ A number of stress-management techniques have been developed for clinical use. These include progressive relaxation, yogic therapy, meditation, hypnosis, biofeedback, cognitive therapy, and psychopharmacology.

■ Direct coping strategies can help you to eliminate stressors or to harden yourself to the stress. Among direct methods of coping are gathering as much information as possible, trusting in the healing effects of time, keeping a sense of humor, spending time with other people, realizing that all goals needn't be obtained, and learning to relax.

SUGGESTIONS FOR FURTHER READING

1. Friedman, M., & Rosenman, R. H. (1974). *Type A behavior and your heart*. New York: Knopf. Discusses the relationship between personality type, stress, and heart disease.

2. Kutash, I. L., & Schlesinger, L. B. (Eds.) (1980). *Handbook on stress and anxiety*. San Francisco: Jossey-Bass. A comprehensive handbook on the sources and treatment of stress.

3. Meichenbaum, D. (1985). *Stress inoculation training*. New York: Pergamon. A cognitive behavior modification approach to stress and stress reduction.

4. Ornstein, R., & Sobel, D. (1989). *Healthy pleasures*. Reading, MA: Addison-Wesley. Describes ways to achieve good exercise, sleep, nutrition and education, with the aim of improving health in ways that are natural and fun, rather

than via strict regimens. Has lots of practical suggestions.

5. Selye, H. (1976). *The stress of life* (2nd ed.). New York: McGraw-Hill. Outlines Selye's theory on the body's reactions to stress and how to help control these reactions.

6. Stone, G. C., et al. (Eds.) (1987). *Health psychology: A discipline and a profession*. Chicago: University of Chicago Press. A comprehensive treatment of the field of health, psychology, including professional issues, applications, and the training of health psychologists.

7. Woolfolk, R. L., & Lehrer, P. M. (Eds.) (1984). *Principles and practice of stress management*. New York: Guilford Press. Outlines the current techniques in management of stress and their effectiveness.

CHAPTER 15 | Abnormal Behavior

Prologue

Why Psychologists Study Abnormal Behavior

Defining Abnormality

Models of Psychopathology
  The Medical Model
  The Learning Model
  The Psychoanalytic Model
  The Humanistic–Existential Model

Classification and Assessment of Abnormal Behavior

Anxiety, Somatoform, and Dissociative Disorders
  Anxiety Disorders
  Somatoform Disorders
  Dissociative Disorders

Mood Disorders
  Bipolar Disorder
  Major Depression

Schizophrenic Disorders
  Causes of Schizophrenia

Delusional (Paranoid) Disorders
  Delusional (Paranoid) Disorder
  Induced Psychotic Disorder
  Causes of Delusional (Paranoid) Disorder

Personality Disorders (Axis II)

The Assessment of Mental Disorders
  Assessment Bias
  Misdiagnosis

Epilogue: The Trichotillomaniac

PROLOGUE

You have come to the offices of Drs. Elaine Walker and Richard Lewine, who have asked you to be one of the observers in their experiment designed to look for early warning signs that might place an individual at risk for schizophrenia. Schizophrenia is a severe mental disorder. Those who suffer from it commonly experience serious disturbances of emotion and thought. They often become withdrawn, show inappropriate emotional responses, suffer from hallucinations, or express strange thoughts and beliefs. The disease commonly makes its first appearance during early adulthood.

The doctors invite you and 18 other observers into a room where you are to watch some home movies. Dr. Walker gives you your instructions.

"In each of these movies," she says, "you will see a family interacting with one another. These films were made more than 25 years ago and are typical of the kind that most families take. Each family—there are 5 altogether—will have either two or three children, and each film spans a time of at least 5 years in their lives. In each family, one of the children later became schizophrenic. None of the parents has schizophrenia, nor do any of the siblings, who are now at least 25 years old and healthy. No schizophrenia was reported in any of these 5 children until they reached early adulthood. In fact, throughout their childhoods, none of the parents reported seeing any sign of the impending disaster. But I want you to watch these children. I want you to try to guess which child in each family is the preschizophrenic. To avoid biases, we will give you

no criteria for judging; you simply will make a forced choice and pick one of the children from each family."

You wonder how that will be possible if the children were normal until adulthood and even the parents had suspected nothing. What should you look for?

As the room darkens and the first film begins, you see a family with 3 children. They seem so cheerful. It is awful to realize that one of these happy children later suffered from severe mental illness. But which child is it? They all seem normal. But you have to choose, so you watch carefully.

As you watch the children interact, you notice that one of the boys, while looking at nothing in particular, seemed to grin for just a moment in a peculiar way. Was that important? Was that supposed to mean something? You can't imagine that anyone would think so. You also notice that the way he is moving about and swinging his arms seems a little goofy—of course, all kids act like that sometimes, so what? He also seems to make less eye contact with the other family members; still, he seems normal enough. But because you are forced to choose, you decide to pick him. You then make similar judgments while you watch the remaining 4 films.

When it is over, you are given the results. Of the 5 preschizophrenic children, you correctly picked 4 of them, which is about the same success rate that the other observers had (Walker & Lewine, 1990), a success rate far greater than chance would predict.

The two psychologists caution you that whatever it is that you observed in the preschizophrenic children, it isn't enough to enable us to go among a population of healthy children and pick which ones will eventually develop schizophrenia. There are simply too many children who are in some way slightly different or who sometimes behave oddly, but who then grow up to be perfectly normal, healthy adults. But it does indicate that something was wrong with this group of schizophrenics many years before their illnesses appeared, something wrong enough to be seen by you from just watching home movies.

In this chapter, we will examine mental disorders, the differences between normal and abnormal behaviors, how abnormal behaviors are assessed, and the issues that are raised by assessment.

WHY PSYCHOLOGISTS STUDY ABNORMAL BEHAVIOR

We are social beings who live in groups called societies; we depend on one another. We have come to trust one another's behavior. Consequently, abnormal or deviant behavior often is viewed as frightening, puzzling, or disruptive. In a humane society, people ought to help one another; the hungry should be fed, the homeless should be sheltered, the needy should be cared for. When people's behavior becomes so aberrant that they are unable to survive on their own, or so deviant that it is harmful to themselves or to other people, the members of a humane society will want to help change or prevent the behavior.

Psychology is the study of all behavior, normal and abnormal. Psychologists study abnormal behavior to learn more about behavior and to help those in need.

■ DEFINING ABNORMALITY

If we want to assess, treat, or possibly prevent **abnormal behavior,** it would be helpful to begin with a clear definition of the term. Many students are surprised, however, to discover that the distinction between normal and abnormal is not always clear.

Although people often picture someone who is mentally ill as ranting and raving uncontrollably, that kind of behavior is actually quite rare, and is at the extreme of what most psychologists consider abnormal. Most abnormality is more subtle than the stereotype of the "raving lunatic." For this reason, professionals must be careful when assessing behavior; they must try to keep their own beliefs about what is acceptable personal or societal behavior from biasing their assessment and leading them to an unwarranted view of some behavior as a mental disorder. In the Soviet Union, before reforms, the social and political outlook greatly influenced the judgments of Soviet psychiatrists and psychologists. Anyone who went against the party line was generally considered to be mentally or emotionally abnormal and in need of help. As a result, Soviet dissidents often were placed in mental institutions where their so-called abnormal behaviors could be "treated" (Faraone, 1982). More recently, under Gorbachev and his policy of greater openness, the Soviet mental-health system has been transferred from the Department of Security to the Department of Health, and the Soviets have reported that they are making efforts to curtail the abuses that they admit have been common to the system. Time will tell.

Although no one in the United States is likely to be judged to have a mental disorder for official political reasons, there may be certain biases against particular groups. For instance, poorer persons are more likely to be labeled psychotic than are others (Eron & Peterson, 1982; Redlich & Kellert, 1978). Of course, it may well be that the pressures of living at the lower end of the socioeconomic spectrum predispose a person to more serious illness (Wills & Langner, 1980). Conversely, mental disorder may lead to economic loss resulting in poverty (Harkey, Miles, & Rushing, 1976). But it also may be that evaluators expect poverty and mental illness to go hand in hand, which may bias their judgment and create a self-fulfilling prophecy. The elimination of bias and prejudgment in clinical practice is crucial.

How would you define abnormal? The word *abnormal* means "different from the normal or away from normal." In usage, however, the term implies more than just deviating from the norm. Skydiving is certainly a deviation from the norm, in that the average person doesn't do it. In fact, few people do. *Statistically,* then, those who skydive are *ab*normal. But does this mean that they should be helped or be stopped from engaging in their sport?

In the clinical sense, for a behavior to be considered abnormal, it must be not only different from the norm but also *maladaptive* or *self-defeating.* Maladaptive means that the behavior interferes with the person's functioning and development or with the activities of society. A self-defeating behavior is one that will eventually undermine the person's well-being or personal success. Of course, these tests hardly settle the issue. You may have already thought, "Maladaptive or self-defeating by whose standards?" According to this definition, psychiatrists in a police state could consider to be abnormal someone who disagreed vehemently with the government, since this behavior would be different and, in terms of what the state deems

MODEL
A mathematical, logical, or mechanical replica of a relationship or a system of events so designed that a study of the model can yield some understanding of the real thing.

ETIOLOGY
The cause of a disease or disorder as determined by psychological or medical diagnosis.

INSANE
A legal term for those with a mental disorder, implying that they lack responsibility for their acts and are unable to manage their behavior.

appropriate, maladaptive and self-defeating for both the individual and society. Whenever we use such terms as maladaptive or self-defeating, we must consider the context. Almost any behavior might be considered normal under the right circumstances. For instance, yelling, shouting, and undressing in front of other people, which would be considered abnormal at the public library, would be considered quite normal in a locker room before a football game. Subtle distinctions between normal and abnormal require value judgments and careful assessment. Abnormal behavior is not absolutely distinct from normal; rather, there is a continuum from normal to abnormal.

Because of this, there is no completely satisfactory definition of abnormal behavior (Gorenstein, 1984). Some people believe that if psychology was as exacting as medicine, with its diagnoses and diseases, the problem of defining abnormality would be solved (Gorenstein, 1984). But even in medicine there are shades of gray. Try to conceive of an absolute definition of "physically sick" and you will find yourself in the same situation as when you try to define abnormal behavior. Judgments are pretty clear-cut at the extremes, but distinctions in the middle ground are difficult to make.

MODELS OF PSYCHOPATHOLOGY

In evaluating the abnormal behavior of another person, psychologists may use different models to provide an understanding or explanation of the underlying mechanisms that may be contributing to the disorder. A **model** is a depiction or representation that helps to organize knowledge. Several different models may be used to depict the mechanisms that may underlie psychopathology. The model preferred depends on the professional's training and background. In addition, different therapies or treatments are preferred depending on the approach and the model used. Each model has some value. In some circumstances, some models may be more applicable than others. Many mental-health professionals rely on more than one model. For example, most people who rely on the humanistic–existential model would not deny that abnormal behavior occasionally may be caused by biological dysfunction. Nor is someone who relies heavily on the medical model likely to deny that abnormal behaviors can be learned. Instead, each model helps us to understand that abnormal behavior may be the result of many different factors (see Focus on an Application).

The Medical Model

The medical model assumes that the underlying cause, or **etiology,** of a mental disorder is a biological dysfunction. In other words, something has gone wrong biologically, owing to genetics, hormones, biochemical imbalances, trauma, viruses, poisoning, or a host of other events that can disrupt the organism's biology, especially the brain and nervous system. The medical model views abnormal behaviors as analogous to physical illness and as symptoms of an underlying disease. People suffering from mental disorders are referred to as patients, and emphasis is placed on diagnosis and treatment, often incorporating drugs or such other medical therapies as electroshock or psychosurgery. The medical model is becoming one of the most popular models owing to the rapid growth of neuroscience and the resulting expansion of our knowledge of the brain and neurochemistry (Pardes, 1986).

THE LEGAL MODEL: INSANITY AND THE LAW

If someone commits a crime and there is some question about that person's mental state, mental-health professionals may be called on to assess his condition. Such an assessment is often important to a person's criminal defense—because if it could be proved that he hadn't known right from wrong at the time he committed the crime, he might, if convicted, be sent to a mental institution for treatment rather than to a prison for punishment.

Whether the so-called **insane** can be held criminally responsible for their actions is a legal issue, not a psychological one. The legal standards for determining whether someone is insane often are different from those applied by psychiatrists and psychologists.

In the middle of the thirteenth century, madness, or insanity, was defined as a condition in which those afflicted didn't know what they were doing, lacked mind and reason, and were "not far removed from brutes." By the sixteenth century, the generally accepted definition was more precise: those who couldn't count, couldn't recognize their parents, and couldn't understand profit and loss (Amarilio, 1979). This definition, too, was obviously inadequate, and a modern standard was sought.

The development of the insanity defense began in England in 1843 when Daniel M'Naghten shot and killed Edward Drummond, the secretary to Robert Peel, then prime minister of England. M'Naghten was tried for murder, and in his defense he pleaded insanity. Medical testimony was given indicating that M'Naghten was driving by strong delusions to commit the murder and that he didn't

understand the difference between right and wrong. The jury verdict was not guilty, on the ground of insanity (*M'Naghten's Case*, 1843). The M'Naghten rule is still used as the test for legal insanity in several states in the United States.

The M'Naghten rule has been criticized because only those who appeared *severely* disturbed could be classified as insane under its stringent standard. It "does nothing for the person, if he exists, who knows the conduct to be wrong but as a result of mental defect or disease is powerless to control that conduct" (Spring, 1979, p. 26). In many states, therefore, and in the federal court system, further tests of insanity have been developed that attempt to deal with these criticisms (see Table 15.1). However, none of these tests has addressed the most pressing issue: whether insanity should be a defense at all, whether those whom society calls "mad" should be treated differently from others who commit crimes. Some people have recommended that the insanity defense be abolished (Menninger, 1968; Dershowitz, 1973; Spring, 1979), and in a few states, including Montana, Idaho, and Utah, it has been (Bower, 1984). Interestingly, in states where it has been banned, such as Montana, judges have been found more likely than they used to be to rule a defendant incompetent to stand trial, so that the overall number of insanity acquittals has remained about the same (Steadman, Callahan, Robbins, & Morrissey, 1989).

Others have recommended that a defendant's sanity should be considered only during the sentencing phase of a trial and not during establishment of guilt or innocence (Stan-

fiel, 1981). This issue has become more heated since, some years ago, John W. Hinckley, Jr., was found not guilty by reason of insanity of shooting President Reagan (Rogers, 1987). Hinckley very clearly committed the act with which he was charged. In his controversial trial, however, the jury found that the federal prosecution had failed to prove that Hinckley was *sane* when he committed that act. Many states still have this standard, placing the burden on the prosecution to prove that the defendant was sane at the time the act was committed, rather than placing the burden on the defense to prove that the defendant was insane, but this is changing rapidly.

The American Psychological Association has advocated that the insanity defense not be determined or altered by social or political pressures, but rather be based on a valid scientific understanding of human behaviors (Rogers, 1987). A *complete* scientific understanding of abnormality, however, may be a hundred years away. In the meantime, the defense of insanity in criminal trials is likely to remain subject to such pressures, especially the public's feelings about responsibility and punishment.

TABLE 15.1 Legal Standards for Determining Insanity

TEST*	SOURCE AND YEAR	RULE
M'Naghten rule	*M'Naghten's Case* (1843)	Defendant is relieved from criminal responsibility if he either (1) was prevented by his mental disease from knowing the nature and quality of his act or (2) was unable to distinguish between right and wrong.
Irresistible impulse	*Parsons v. State* (1887)	Used as an adjunct to M'Naghten. Defendant is relieved from criminal responsibility if he meets either of the two criteria above or if he had a mental disease or defect that kept him from controlling his conduct (a so-called "Irresistible impulse").
Durham rule	*Durham v. United States* (1954)	"The rule . . . is simply that an accused is not criminally responsible if his unlawful act was the product of mental disease or defect" (*Durham v. United States*, 1954, pp. 874–875).
ALI Model Penal Code	American Law Institute (1955)	"A person is not responsible for criminal conduct if at the time of such conduct, as a result of mental disease or defect, he lacked substantial capacity either to appreciate the criminality (or wrongfulness) of his conduct or to conform his conduct to the requirements of the law" (Amarilio, 1979, p. 362).

*These tests are listed in order from the most stringent and difficult to prove in court to the least stringent and easiest to prove.

The Learning Model

According to the learning model, abnormal behaviors are acquired in the same way as normal behaviors—that is, they are learned through the processes of conditioning and social learning (see Chapter 6). In this model, the behaviors are not considered symptoms of an underlying disease; rather, the behaviors themselves are thought to be the problem. Because the person exhibiting the abnormal behavior is not considered medically sick, she is referred to as a client, not a patient. The abnormal behaviors are eliminated through retraining and conditioning.

The Psychoanalytic Model

In the psychoanalytic model, abnormal behaviors are viewed as evidence of unresolved unconscious conflicts among the id, the ego, and the superego (see Chapter 13). Treatment usually involves psychoanalysis and a detailed investigation of the desires and conflicts in the unconscious.

The Humanistic–Existential Model

The humanistic–existential model depicts abnormal behaviors as the result of a failure to fulfill self-potential, owing to family and cultural influences. Such failure may occur when people lose contact with their real thoughts and emotions or become isolated from other people; eventually, they may view their lives as meaningless and useless.

CLASSIFICATION AND ASSESSMENT OF ABNORMAL BEHAVIOR

Table 15.2 outlines the prevalence of maladjustment estimated to exist in the United States. As you can see, the figures in many instances are very large, indicating that great segments of the population may be in need of help. And yet, the public seems generally unaware of the magnitude of the problem. In a poll, only 1 percent of the respondents thought of mental health as a major health problem (Holden, 1986c).

Before clinicians can consider treatment for a mental disorder, they must make an assessment to determine the nature of the problem. The disorder also must be identified so that it can be adequately explained to others. For this reason, classification systems attempt to organize mental disorders systematically.

Although a number of such classification schemes have been developed, to date none has been completely satisfactory. In 1952, the American Psychiatric Association developed the *Diagnostic and Statistical Manual of Mental Disorders* (DSM), which classified mental disorders according to a format that had been developed by the army during World War II. In 1968, the DSM was modified to bring it into line with different classifications used by the World Health Organization. The new manual, known as DSM-II, was used for a number of years, but eventually its limitations became apparent as new information became available. As a result, a special task force to formulate a revised classification system was assembled; by 1977, their work was complete, and a new classification scheme, DSM-III, was presented for extensive testing and field trials.

DSM-III was new in a number of ways. It described mental disorders in greater detail and made distinctions among disorders that had previously been unified under one heading (Robins & Helzer, 1986).

By 1983, it had become obvious that psychological knowledge was expanding so rapidly that it would be useful to clarify, update, and revise DSM-III while awaiting the publication of the fully revised DSM-IV, which is scheduled to be released in 1992. This new version is **DSM-III-R** (*Diagnostic and Statistical Manual of Mental Disorders*, third edition, revised).

DSM-III-R
The third edition of the *Diagnostic and Statistical Manual,* revised, published by the American Psychiatric Association in 1987. The manual provides clinicians with the most current diagnostic and classification criteria for mental disorders.

TABLE 15.2 Comparison of Lifetime Prevalence Rates* of Mental Disorders of Persons 18 Years and Older

DISORDER	PERCENTAGE EXHIBITING THE DISORDER DURING THEIR LIFETIME
Any Disorder	32.2
Any Disorder Except Substance Abuse	12.6
Substance Use Disorders	16.4
Alcohol Abuse/Dependence	13.3
Drug Abuse/Dependence	5.9
Schizophrenic Disorders	1.5
Affective Disorders	8.3
Anxiety Disorders	14.6
Phobia	12.5
Panic	1.6
Obsessive-Compulsive	2.5
Somatization Disorders	0.1
Personality Disorder, Antisocial Personality	2.5
Cognitive Impairment (severe)	1.3

*Based on a total sample of 18,571 persons in five epidemiological catchment areas of the United States: New Haven, Connecticut, Baltimore, Maryland, St. Louis, Missouri, Durham, North Carolina, and Los Angeles, California.
SOURCE: Adapted from Regier et al., 1988.

In the next few pages, we explore some of the important classifications of DSM-III-R and examine selected types of mental disorders. We describe examples of the behaviors associated with each disorder, and in certain instances provide case studies.

DSM-III-R evaluates each individual according to five dimensions, or axes (see Table 15.3). The first three axes are used to assess the immediate condition of the individual. The fourth and fifth axes rate the stress that the individual faces and offer an overall assessment of her ability to function. These last two axes are valuable because they include in the description of the disorder the kinds of stressors the individual has been facing in her environment and how well she is able to function psychologically, socially, and occupationally.

Before we examine these disorders, it should be pointed out once again that mental disorders usually are extremes of normal behaviors. If you think that some

TABLE 15.3 DSM-III-R Classifications*

AXIS I (ANY MENTAL DISORDERS THAT MAY BE PRESENT)	AXIS II (ANY PERSONALITY DISORDER THAT MAY BE PRESENT)
1. *Organic mental disorders*	*Personality disorders* Paranoid
2. *Schizophrenia* Disorganized Catatonic Paranoid Undifferentiated Residual	Schizoid Schizotypal Histrionic Narcissistic Antisocial Borderline Avoidant

3. *Delusional (paranoid) disorders*
 Delusional (paranoid) disorder
     Erotomanic type
     Grandiose type
     Jealous type
     Persecutory type
     Somatic type
 Induced psychotic disorder
	Dependent
	 Obsessive compulsive
	 Passive aggressive
	
	 AXIS III
	 Any medical or physical disorder that may also be present
	
	 AXIS IV
	 A 6-point scale rating the severity of psychological and social factors that may have placed the individual under stress, ranging from 1 (none) to 6 (catastrophe)

4. *Mood disorders* Bipolar disorder Major depression	
5. *Anxiety disorders* Simple phobia Generalized anxiety disorder Panic disorder without agoraphobia Obsessive–compulsive disorder	AXIS V A 90-point global assessment of functioning scale which allows the clinician to state his or her overall judgment as to the person's psychological, social, and occupational functioning for two time periods; current and past year.
6. *Somatoform disorders* Conversion disorder Hypochondriasis	
7. *Dissociative disorders* Psychogenic amnesia Psychogenic fugue Multiple personality disorder	

*The classifications of Axes I and II have been significantly limited to include only those categories discussed in the text.

of these descriptions fit you a little bit, don't worry. It's not likely to be the first sign that you're on your way to a mental disorder; it probably just means that you're normal. Everyone has little eccentricities, and these are not considered problems unless they become extreme and interfere with the person's life.

As we discuss the disorders listed in DSM-III-R, you may be surprised to discover that very few of them have a known etiology. Many are simply *descriptions* of behavior patterns that have been found to often occur together and, therefore, appear to be a **syndrome.** Don't assume that because certain behaviors are classified under one label they are necessarily due to the same cause. For example, you should not infer that people who are said to have schizophrenia all have one particular "disease." Instead, you should understand that they generally exhibit a similar series or constellation of abnormal behaviors. This also is true for the **organic mental disorders.** Organic disorders are those in which the cause is physical or is strongly suspected to be physical. Neurosyphilis, severe head wounds, and senility are examples of organic disorders that may affect behavior. In each case, brain or nerve damage is likely to have occurred. Although the etiology sometimes is known, more often it is not understood how the organic damage occurred. In these cases, the organic mental disorder may be described only as delirium, senility, dementia, or the like—all terms describing mental disorganization or incoherence, not terms denoting well-defined diseases.

It may be difficult at first for you to realize that many of these disorders are merely descriptive terms. It's like referring to someone as an "accident victim." Accident victims often have a lot in common, such as broken bones, bruises, cuts, concussions. But all kinds of accidents can happen for all kinds of reasons, and just because two people are labeled accident victims doesn't mean that they are suffering from exactly the same damage. When it comes to illness, we're so used to discussing true diseases that have understood etiologies (such as tuberculosis) that we think a term such as schizophrenia must refer to some particular disease, too. Someday, we may uncover a single cause of schizophrenia, or we may find that there are many causes. For many of the disorders classified in DSM-III-R, a common denominator remains to be discovered.

ANXIETY, SOMATOFORM, AND DISSOCIATIVE DISORDERS

Anxiety Disorders

Anxiety disorders are maladaptive syndromes that have severe anxiety as their central feature. Included among these are phobia, generalized anxiety, panic, obsession, and compulsion.

SIMPLE PHOBIA.   Almost everyone has heard of the word *phobia*. Phobia is more than just a fear, however; it is a specific and *unrealistic* fear. Different terms have been used to describe different kinds of **simple phobias.** Perhaps you're familiar with some, such as acrophobia (fear of heights), claustrophobia (fear of closed-in spaces), nyctophobia (fear of the night), arachnophobia (fear of spiders), and *Arachnophobia*-phobia (fear of the movie *Arachnophobia*).

If you were in a tall building that caught fire and you had to go out onto the ledge of the tenth floor, you'd be bound to feel a little fearful (to say the least). Such behavior is not referred to as a phobia; instead, it is called normal! If you had acrophobia, however, you probably wouldn't be able to go two steps up a ladder, and you would avoid going even to the second floor of a building if you

SYNDROME
A number of features, characteristics, events, or behaviors that appear to go with each other, or which are thought to be coordinated or interrelated in some way.

ORGANIC MENTAL DISORDER
A severe behavioral disturbance usually requiring hospitalization and resulting from some organic malfunctioning of the body.

SIMPLE PHOBIA
A person's pathological fear of an object or situation. The individual may realize that the fear is irrational but, being unable to control it, avoids the object or situation. Relatively easy to treat.

Concept Review: The Strengths and Weaknesses of Classifying Mental Disorders

Strengths

DSM-III-R is the result of many years of input by hundreds of professionals. It provides a catalogue of the human mental disorders that comprise behavior patterns that have been deemed to be of clinical significance. The categories are fairly reliable; that is, if many different professionals use DSM-III-R when diagnosing the same individual, they are likely to be in good agreement as to which disorder they have observed (Spitzer & Williams, 1987). DSM-III-R is a system for collective grouping of individuals who behave in the same way, perhaps because they share the same underlying problem. In other words, DSM-III-R defines unified groups who can be studied for similarities in the hope that some common denominator can be discovered among them that could explain their disorder, which, in turn, might facilitate treatment (Hayes, Nelson, & Jarrett, 1987).

Weaknesses

DSM-III-R is a descriptive, not explanatory (and it makes no claim to be explanatory, an effort that at this time would be premature). As a result, there can be "no assumption that each mental disorder is a discrete entity with sharp boundaries (discontinuity) between it and other mental disorders, or between it and no mental disorder" (Spitzer & Williams, 1987, p. xxii). Therefore, some of its definitions may be too narrow and thus omit individuals who should be included, while other categories may be too broad and thus admit individuals who should be excluded.

Without solid underlying explanations for the disorders included in DSM-III-R, some of the disorders may not be "real" mental disorders, but may simply comprise groupings of undesirable behaviors (behaviors simply deemed socially undesirable). For example, one axis II classification in DSM-III-R is called "dependent personality disorder" and is composed of behaviors such as a "pervasive pattern of dependent and submissive behavior" (Spitzer & Williams, 1987, p. 353). Psychologist Marcie Kaplan has argued that including this disorder reflects the bias of the *men* who developed the manual. Kaplan believes that women are more likely to be considered to have dependent personality disorder than men are, because our society has more often taught them to be dependent (Kaplan, 1983). Kaplan further states that, to be fair, there should be a category called *independent personality disorder,* which includes typical *male* traits carried to excess. As you can see, what is "normal" is not always agreed on or determined easily.

General Consensus

DSM-III-R is useful in the hands of people who know and understand its limitations (which are considerable). With our limited knowledge of an extremely complex area of study, DSM-III-R is probably the best catalogue that we are currently able to assemble.

had to be anywhere near a window. People with phobic disorders are well aware that their fear is *unrealistic.* They often are the first to admit, "This is foolish, but I can't help how I feel."

Like all behavior that might be considered abnormal, such fear comes in varying degrees. When you stand near a sheer edge, do you get a feeling that some magnetic force is starting to pull you over? That's a common perception, but people with acrophobia experience a very intense version of this sensation.

Most people deal with their phobias by avoiding the thing they are frightened of. Someone with herpetophobia (fear of snakes) would probably go out of his way to avoid a job that required working in the country.

In general, simple phobias are believed to be learned. In Chapter 6, we discussed the case of Little Albert, in which a phobic disorder was produced in the child by associating a rat with a very loud noise. Little Albert eventually came to fear the rat. Similar occurrences have happened outside the laboratory. The following case study illustrates how a phobia might develop as a result of one's experience.

PHOBIC DISORDER: THE CASE OF JUDY R.

Judy R., a 27-year-old college senior, came to the University Counseling Center because of an intense fear of birds. She had been frightened of birds since she was 9 years old. She was functioning well socially and academically, but she felt that her phobia was beginning to interfere with her plans to become a teacher. Judy had begun student teaching, and several incidents had triggered a fear reaction. On four separate occasions, she suffered severe and almost incapacitating terror: on a class visit to the bird section of a museum, seeing pictures of birds in textbooks, being offered a feather by a student, and being near a baby chick on animal day.

How Judy became afraid of birds is not completely clear. Before the age of 9 years, she had a duck and chick as pets. Between the ages of 10 and 15 years, however, she had a few frightening experiences that may have helped to create the phobia. Once playmates warned her that there was an owl near her home that attacked people; she once saw her friend's parakeet escape and fly wildly about a room; she was once scared by her brothers with a toy bird; and she had seen Alfred Hitchcock's film *The Birds*, in which birds viciously attacked people. But she cold not attribute her fear directly to any one of these incidents.

Judy structured her entire life so that she could avoid birds. Whenever she walked anywhere, she selected routes with minimal foliage and less chance to encounter a bird, even if they took her far out of her way. She would run between her car and entrances to buildings, and she always kept her car windows rolled up to keep birds out. She could not sunbathe, hike, or go on picnics. She didn't dare visit the beach or go to the zoo. She had frequent nightmares about birds and often thought that noises in her house were caused by birds who had somehow gotten in. She was so frightened of birds that she was careful when she backed out of her driveway not to run over or injure a bird for fear that the "word" might get out among the bird community and the birds would get her. She realized that such actions were far beyond the capability of birds and that her fear was irrational, but the thought persisted (Lassen & McConnell, 1977).

Many phobias do not seem to have one specific cause or beginning. This fact has led some medical researchers to speculate that some phobias may be attributable to underlying changes in brain chemistry that predispose the individual to become easily fearful. Psychoanalysts, on the other hand, have argued that phobias are symptoms of an underlying conflict and that the phobia cannot be adequately resolved unless the underlying conflict is resolved through psychoanalysis. Still, psychoanalysis generally has not been effective in treating phobias.

The most commonly used treatments for phobia involve behavior modification and, occasionally, drugs. These techniques have been highly successful, and simple phobias are perhaps the most easily treatable of the mental disorders. There are other phobias, however, that don't appear to be "simple" and that sometimes do not respond so easily to treatment. DSM-III-R treats these phobias separately. They include agoraphobia (fear of being outside the home) and social phobia (fear of social situations in which one might be scrutinized). For reasons not yet understood, these two phobias seem to be special cases in which the unrealistic fear is of a more general nature and is less specifically focused than are the simple phobias. Most simple phobias, however, readily loosen their grip with treatment. In Chapter 16, we'll see how Judy R. overcame her phobia through behavior modification.

GENERALIZED ANXIETY DISORDER. People suffering a **generalized anxiety disorder** are in a continued state of apparently pointless apprehension, worry, and dread over a number of life's circumstances (Barlow, Blanchard, Vermilyea, Vermilyea, & DiNardo, 1986). They will typically show an unrealistic fear concerning unforeseen circumstances (for example, worry about a child who is in no danger, worry about finances for no good reason). As a result, they often are unable to make decisions or to enjoy life. Because their anxiety is not tied to a specific object, it often is called **free-floating anxiety.** The following case study illustrates this kind of anxiety.

GENERALIZED ANXIETY DISORDER: THE MECHANIC'S CASE

The patient, a 31-year-old mechanic, had been referred for psychotherapy by his physician, whom he had consulted because of dizziness and difficulty in falling asleep. He was quite visibly distressed during the entire interview, gulping before he spoke, sweating, and continually fidgeting in his chair. His repeated requests for water to slake a seemingly unquenchable thirst were another indication of this extreme nervousness. Although he first related his physical concerns, a more general picture of pervasive anxiety soon emerged. He reported that he nearly always felt tense and that "if anything can go wrong, it will." He was apprehensive of possible disasters that could befall him as he worked and interacted with other people. He reported a long history of difficulties in interpersonal relationships, which had led to his being fired from several jobs. As he put it, "I really like people and try to get along with them, but it seems like I fly off the handle too easily. Little things they do upset me too much. I just can't cope unless everything is going exactly right." (Davison & Neale, 1978, p. 150)

Although no one knows what causes a person to suffer from generalized anxiety disorder, there may be both environmental and genetic causes. For instance, it is known that people who have experienced real, unexpected, and very stressful events in their lives are at least three times more likely to develop generalized anxiety disorder than are other people (Blazer, Hughes, & George, 1987). It is also known, however, that someone showing generalized anxiety disorder is more likely to have close relatives who also suffer from the disorder than would be expected by chance alone (Noyes, Clarkson, Crowe, Yates, & McChesney, 1987).

PANIC DISORDER. Panic disorder is probably the most common mental-health reason for a person to come to a doctor or hospital for help (Boyd, 1986). When a **panic attack** occurs, the person may be suddenly overwhelmed by fear, and yet he can't think of any real reason to be frightened. Even so, panic attacks are strong and debilitating, so much so, that those suffering from the disorder are at higher risk for attempting suicide (Weissman, Klerman, Markowitz & Ouellette, 1989). The feeling of terror can be overpowering, almost as if the person were having a heart attack. Chest pains, heart palpitations, breathing difficulty, and fainting may occur.

As is the case with generalized anxiety disorder, people who have suffered from real, negative, and stressful events are at greater risk for developing panic disorder than are other people (Roy-Byrne, Geraci, & Uhde, 1986), especially if they have recently lost someone they love (Faravelli & Pallanti, 1989). Unlike those who suffer from generalized anxiety disorder, however, people who show panic disorder do not appear to be more likely to have relatives who have panic disorder than one would expect to find among the average population (Noyes, Clarkson, Crowe, Yates, & McChesney, 1987). This does not mean that biology plays no role in panic disorder; rather, the disorder may not be very strongly tied to *inheritance*. In fact, there are some intriguing data linking panic attack to biology. For instance, among people who have panic disorder, an intravenous injection of sodium lactate will almost always quickly bring on a full-blown panic attack, although it has no effect on other people! Somehow, the lactate must be interacting with the panic mechanism in people who suffer from the disorder (Liebowitz et al., 1985). Interestingly, when lactate-induced panic attack was studied, it was discovered that a few members of control groups (people who did not suffer from panic disorder) did have a panic attack when given a lactate infusion. Further research showed that these individuals were far more likely to have close family members who had anxiety disorders than members of control groups who did not react to the lactate infusion (Balon, Jordan, Pohl, & Yeragani, 1989). Furthermore, PET scans (see Chapter 2) of the brains of people who do react to lactate-infusion generally show an ongoing overactivity in specific areas of the brain that is quite abnormal (Reiman et al., 1986).

Researchers also have noted that caffeine can greatly exacerbate a panic attack (Charney, Heninger, & Jatlow, 1985). This does not seem to be because caffeine can make a person jittery, but rather that use of caffeine over a number of months somehow alters the effects of certain neurotransmitters in the brain, most notably serotonin. In fact, one of the first treatment steps now taken for people who suffer from panic attacks is to get them to abstain from caffeine consumption.

Findings such as these have led researchers to hope that sometime soon the entire mechanism of panic, and perhaps anxiety in general, will be understood sufficiently for the development of medications that will enable us to control problems of anxiety when they arise (Ballenger, 1986).

OBSESSIVE–COMPULSIVE DISORDER. One of the most interesting anxiety disorders is the **obsessive–compulsive disorder,** or OCD. In this disorder, the sufferer typically feels a need to go over unwanted thoughts again and again or to engage in certain actions or rituals repetitively, perhaps as a way of coping with anxiety. From time to time, all of us have had ideas or thoughts that we couldn't seem to get out of our minds. And sometimes we feel better if we carefully organize our daily activities in almost a ritualistic manner. In the obsessive–compulsive disorder, this behavior is taken to the extreme, but it is an ineffective way of coping.

The obsessions and compulsions represent the different properties of OCD. **Obsessions** are thoughts that continue to enter a person's mind unwanted and that become impossible to ignore. For example, a person may have the constant obsession that someone is breaking into the house whenever she is away. This idea could interfere with life, making every minute away from home uncomfortable because of the persistent thoughts about intruders. Some people are obsessed with thoughts about committing violent acts. The guilt and revulsion that accompany these thoughts only seem to bring them to mind more often, although the person

OBSESSIVE–COMPULSIVE DISORDER
An abnormal reaction characterized by anxiety, persistent unwanted thoughts, or the compulsion to repeat ritualistic acts over and over.

OBSESSION
A persistent idea or thought that the individual recognizes as irrational but feels compelled to dwell on.

has no intention of acting them out. Such obsessions, although never realized, may still result in extremely high levels of anxiety.

Compulsions are needs to perform ritualistic acts, and can take many forms. The need to read every license plate on the highway, the need to wear certain clothes on a certain day, the need to avoid stepping on a crack on the sidewalk, or the need to wash one's hands every 15 minutes are examples of compulsions that can, when carried to extremes, interfere with life.

Although it's possible to have obsessions without engaging in ritualistic acts or to have compulsions without obsessive thoughts, the two often coexist, which is why the disorder is referred to as obsessive–compulsive. In fact, the obsession can often be the cause of the compulsion. The person who is obsessed with the fear that there is a stranger in the house may ritually and compulsively check in all the closets and under all the beds before retiring.

It is common for people to have minor obsessions or minor rituals. The point at which such manifestations become serious enough to require help is not always clear-cut. As a rule, it's a good idea for people to seek professional advice any time such behaviors begin to interfere seriously with their lives or functioning. An obsessive–compulsive disorder is described in the following case study.

OBSESSIVE–COMPULSIVE DISORDER: THE CASE OF S. K.

S. K. was admitted to a mental hospital at the age of 29 . . . Soon after the patient's admission to the hospital, his wife was asked to give a history of the patient's illness. She reported that he had exhibited a compulsive handwashing for several months but that it became more serious. "He used to wash his hands and keep the water running for 15 minutes at a time. After he had washed them, he would turn off the spigot with his elbow. He had to count and wash and rinse his hands a certain number of times. If he had touched the door or door knob, he would go back and wash his hands again. One time he began to wash his hands at 1 o'clock in the morning. After we moved into our own house, he refused to use the front door or to turn the knob on the door for fear there might be germs. He used to go to the back window and call me to go to the front door and open it for him. He reached the point where he would climb in and out of windows so that he wouldn't have to enter the doors at all." The wife described also the following compulsion: "He also had the idea that when he walked there was something under his shoe. He would stop and look on the sole of his shoe, but there would be nothing there. He also worried as to whether or not his shoe laces were tied. He would pick up his foot and look to make sure. He had to do that a certain number of times before he was absolutely sure they were tied. When he walked down a street, if he kicked a stone he felt that he should put it back in the same place. If he walked on a line, then he would have to walk on all the cracks in the sidewalk." (Kolb, 1973, pp. 427–428)

Why anxiety disorders occur is not well known. According to the psychoanalytic model, anxiety disorders result from an unresolved clash among the id, the ego, and the superego. According to the learning model, anxiety disorders are learned. According to the humanistic–existential model, anxiety disorders are attributable to a failure to fulfill one's life potential. By this logic, societal pressures or a person's own inaccurate self-images create a sense of terror that the person can alleviate by coming to grips with herself in society. Researchers using the medical model as a guideline are searching for differences in brain chemistry in people who suffer from anxiety disorders; this approach currently is seen by many, if not most, researchers as the one holding the most promise (see Focus on Research). Of course, even if

Obsessive–compulsive disorder is an especially fascinating disorder for us to discuss because we may now be on the verge of truly understanding it. In the mid-seventies, a new antidepressive drug was developed called clomipramine. A number of psychiatrists gave this drug to their OCD patients to help them cope with the depression commonly associated with their disorder. Soon afterward, however, reports began to come in from all over the world that clomipramine was *curing* OCD in about two-thirds of all cases! Other antidepressants, even those very similar in chemical structure to clomipramine, had no such effect.

Quickly, there was a rush to discover how the drug might be working its magic. And, as you might imagine, OCD was converted almost overnight into a biological disorder in the minds of most professionals. As reports of the drug's success were spread by the media, thousands of OCD sufferers began to come forth, people who until then had been too ashamed to admit to their affliction. It was soon discovered that as many as 5 million Americans might be suffering from OCD, many more than had been previously thought (Rapoport, 1989).

Judith Rapoport, a child psychiatrist, is one of the leading researchers in the search for the cause of OCD. She believes that the obsessions and compulsions of OCD are linked to the kinds of subroutines that most animals have, such as those related to territorality and grooming (for example, a cat bathing itself). Such behaviors are repetitive and stereotyped. These subroutines appear to arise in an area of the brain called the basal ganglia. Interestingly, brain scans of OCD patients show that there are consistent abnormalities in the basal ganglia (Luxenberg et al., 1988).

In a normal organism, when the subroutine is completed, the frontal lobes of the brain signal that the routine is done. Rapoport believes that a failure occurs when the frontal lobe signal is somehow dampened or ignored by the basal ganglia. The neurotransmitters involved in this important communication appear to be serotonin and dopamine, two of the most prominent neurotransmitters in the brain. It is believed that clomipramine might work by boosting the effect of serotonin or in some other way influencing the serotonin–dopamine interaction so that the signal from the frontal lobes can function properly once again.

As further evidence, Rapoport has looked at a problem in dogs called *acralick dermatitis*. Dogs that acquire this disorder won't stop licking their paws. Eventually, the problem can get so bad that the hair and skin of the paws are licked away until the bones show through. The usual treatment is to wrap the dog's paws in bandages that it can't lick through, but something else also works—clomipramine! In fact, Rapoport says that she is now "the world's only child psychiatrist making house calls on dogs on a regular basis" (Trotter, 1990, p. 27).

Think about the many routines of your daily life that you have learned to the point of habit. You check to see if your hands are dirty. If they are, you wash them. When you leave the house, you check to make sure that things are right before you go. If they are, you leave. Throughout the day you check and you act, you check and you act, what could be more normal? But suppose your brain couldn't get the "we're done, everything is okay" signal to where it was needed

to break your subroutines? Your hands are now clean, and you know it, but an important part of your brain says "wash!" You know that it makes no sense, but you are forced to wash again, and again. You can't stop. How does it really feel to have that happen? One patient summed it up this way:

> Ninety-five percent of me is rational, and there's five percent of me that's out of control. And I can almost feel where it is in my brain, because I constantly talk to that part and say: "Shut up, and leave me alone. I don't want to do that." (Trotter, 1990, p. 27)

After taking clomipramine, the patient said,

> That part of my brain finally listened and did shut up. It let the other ninety-five percent regain the control it always should have had. (Trotter, 1990, p. 27)

It might well be, then, that OCD should not be classified as an anxiety disorder. Anxiety may not be its root cause or its most important feature. Instead, we may actually be looking at the biochemistry of belief and doubt, that is, the brain chemistry that tells us when something is finished or when it needs to go on, the chemistry that informs us when it is time to leave a certain action to forgo a certain thought—the chemistry that says, "Stop licking your paws!"

such biochemical etiologies are found to be the best explanation, this will not necessarily mean that the other approaches were wrong, because underlying conflict, learning, or inaccurate self-image may cause changes in brain chemistry that may in turn cause an anxiety disorder.

Somatoform Disorders

Soma means body, and **somatoform disorders** are patterns of behavior in which an individual complains about physical symptoms when no physical illness can be found. Somatoform disorders are found in roughly one person in 300, making them about ten times less common than anxiety disorders (Swartz, Blazer, George, & Landerman, 1986), but they may account for as many as 20 percent of those on whom expensive medical tests are conducted each year, making somatoform disorders an important contributor to the high cost of health care (Lipowski, 1988). Unlike anxiety disorders, which are fairly evenly divided between the sexes, somatoform disorders are slightly more common among women than men (Cloninger, Martin, Guze, & Clayton, 1986). The two major somatoform disorders are conversion disorder and hypochondriasis.

CONVERSION DISORDER. **Conversion disorder** gets its name from the fact that the anxiety and stress faced by the person are thought to be converted into physical symptoms. These symptoms may be wide ranging. For example, people may go blind or become deaf although there's nothing wrong with their eyes or ears. Motor symptoms, such as wobbling, shaking, twitching, and collapsing, are not uncommon; again, there's nothing physically wrong that should cause these symptoms. Visceral symptoms such as headache, choking, coughing, and nausea may occur. The visceral symptoms of a conversion disorder can look like a very real physical disease. Cases of conversion disorder have been known to mimic acute appendicitis, malaria, and tuberculosis, although no organic pathology was present. Cases of pseudopregnancy have even been reported, in which the menstrual cycle ceases, the abdomen appears to swell, and morning sickness begins. No actual pregnancy is involved; the symptoms are the result of the conversion disorder.

The reasons a conversion disorder develops usually are fairly clear. Conversion disorders typically serve the purpose of helping people to avoid doing something they would rather not do. For example, conversion disorders were common among pilots during World War II. Pilots who flew night missions often had a conversion disorder of night blindness, while pilots who flew day missions often had other kinds of visual disturbances that caused them to be grounded. Most people who suffer from conversion disorders have at one time or another expressed the wish to become sick to avoid what they had to do. This wish usually is repressed, and when the conversion disorder symptoms begin, the sufferer is *genuinely unaware* that this is not a real physical disease.

Since conversion disorder can mimic so many real illnesses, it's often difficult for physicians to distinguish it from physical illness. Nonetheless, there are some general guidelines for identifying conversion disorder. In Figure 15.1a, you see an example of "glove anesthesia." The entire hand has become paralyzed and immobile, numb all over. However, if you've ever had novocaine at a dentist's office, you know how one side of your lip can be numb while the other side is not. This localized numbness occurs because the nerve beds are laid down lengthwise, not crosswise. Consequently, real neural damage to the hand typically results in paralysis of only one lateral portion (see Figure 15.1b). To a neurologist, glove anesthesia is a dead giveaway of conversion disorder.

FIGURE 15.1

Because of the organization of the human nervous system, a full glove anesthesia (a) is impossible as a function of only physiological causes. Real nerve damage is more likely to result in a loss of feeling similar to that shown in (b). For this reason, a symptom such as glove anesthesia is an indication of psychological problems.

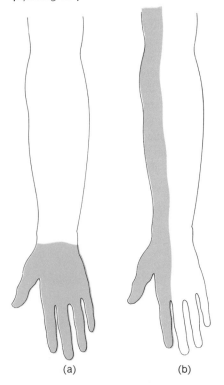

(a)   (b)

About one-third of people suffering from conversion disorder express indifference about their symptoms. Instead of being terrified that they can no longer see or that their arm is paralyzed, they often describe their symptom in a matter-of-fact way, without emotion. It's as though they are relieved to have the symptoms. Often, the symptoms are selective. A person who is blind as a result of conversion disorder is not likely to bump into people or objects. Someone who is actually blind and not yet used to it will typically have a number of accidents. Furthermore, the conversion disorder often can be eliminated or altered under hypnosis, and during sleep a "paralyzed" limb may be seen to move or a "deaf" sleeper may respond to sounds.

Generally, all the models of psychopathology view conversion disorder as an unconscious attempt to avoid danger. Some scientists have argued that the right hemisphere of the brain is more likely to use this defense than is the left hemisphere. This interesting assertion is derived from the fact that, especially in cases of conversion paralysis such as glove anesthesia, conversion disorder is much more likely to occur on the left side of the body than on the right side (Stern, 1977; Galin, Diamond, & Braff, 1977).

HYPOCHONDRIASIS. Hypochondriacs believe themselves to be ill although there is no physical illness present. Unlike people suffering a conversion disorder, hypochondriacs are intensely interested in body functions and illness, and they will avidly seek medical attention in a search for some dread disease that they are sure is present. Approximately 5 percent of all medical outpatients (patients treated at hospital, but who usually don't stay overnight) are not physically ill, but rather suffer from **hypochondriasis** (Barsky & Klerman, 1985). Researchers assume that hypochondriacs use their supposed disability to gain attention, avoid something unpleasant, or feel important.

It is a classic sign of hypochondriasis when people become upset at a physician's reassurances that the tests show no organic pathology and that nothing is wrong. Instead, they hope for some proof that they can hold up to others to maintain their maladaptive behavior pattern. Hypochondriacs are different from malingerers; they are sincere in their belief that they are ill, whereas malingerers knowingly fake a disorder to serve their purposes. Hypochondriasis is difficult to treat, because sufferers often leave a physician or psychologist who will not give them attention for their supposed illness and to seek the services of someone who will. A hypochondriac is described in the following account.

HYPOCHONDRIASIS: THE CASE OF GRACE H.

Grace H. catalogued in excruciating anatomical detail a full range of symptoms—past, present, and future—to which she was heir. She had "almost" had a series of exotic diseases, had suffered for years from a strange collection of symptoms that fit no known malady in humans, and was about to come down with something certain to be nearly fatal . . . Probably the most startling aspect of the scene was the obvious and absolutely noncontroversial fact that Grace H. looked as healthy as a horse. The fact that she was 72 years old had to be some kind of testimony to her hardiness in the face of plague, pestilence, and, as she viewed it, the perversity of the medical profession . . . According to the children, Grace's histrionics had been in evidence for at least the last 40 years. The eldest son, who was 50 years old, recalled that his mother had been ailing when he was just a child. As he said, "Sometimes when I was in school, I would get worried that mother would be dead by the time I got home. I knew she was sick when I went to school and I was sure it would be all over by the time I got home. I had a hard time concentrating on my school work because I was always worried about her health." The mother was an artful specialist in hypochondriasis who had practiced all the arts of being sick while staggeringly well. She seemed to be totally free of anxiety until asked about her health, and at that point she disintegrated into a mass of nervous energy. (McNeil, 1967, pp. 47–49)

Hypochondriasis, however, must be assessed very carefully, because *real* illness can sometimes be extremely elusive. Just because an underlying physical reason can't be found does not guarantee that there isn't one. Before classifying a person as a hypochondriac, psychologists prefer to see clearly how the person is exploiting her "illness." The existence of physical complaints without an apparent cause is not sufficient reason to make the classification.

Dissociative Disorders

Like somatoform disorders, **dissociative disorders** help individuals to obtain gratification and simultaneously to avoid stress. They also provide a means of denying responsibility for behavior that might otherwise be deemed unacceptable. Individuals with dissociative disorders separate themselves from the core of their personality. The effects of dissociative disorders can be very striking. Psychogenic amnesia, psychogenic fugue, and multiple personality are classified as dissociative disorders.

PSYCHOGENIC AMNESIA. **Psychogenic amnesia** is a memory loss, either partial or total; it can last for a few hours or many years. Amnesia can be caused by many things, including psychosis, brain damage, and alcoholic delirium. Psychogenic amnesia, however, has no underlying physical cause, and appears to be the result of stress. People suffering from this disorder usually forget personal material such as who they are, as well as events and other names associated with personal experience. Rarely would someone with psychogenic amnesia forget the name of his country or how to do such things as operate an automobile or read a book.

PSYCHOGENIC FUGUE. **Fugue** comes from the Latin word meaning "to flee." This disorder is an amnesia in which the sufferer leaves home and surroundings and wanders off. In extreme cases, the person may even begin a new life in another city without any recollection of personal events prior to the fugue. Occasionally, the fugue comes to a sudden end, and the person is left in a strange city, unable to recall his new identity but again able to remember his original identity. As you can imagine, it would be a little strange to wake up in a different bed and to find out that 8 years have passed, you are known by a different name, and you are selling ties in St. Louis! The following case study describes a 4-day fugue experienced by a famous American author, Sherwood Anderson.

PSYCHOGENIC FUGUE: THE CASE OF SHERWOOD ANDERSON

Anderson was better known as a paint manufacturer than as a writer in his home town of Elyria, Ohio. He would daydream to escape the boredom of a routine workday and found relaxation in writing short stories. On November 27, 1912, the 36-year-old Anderson suddenly got up from his desk while dictating a letter to his secretary. He stopped in the middle of a sentence, walked out of the room, and was not seen again until four days later, when he was found in a Cleveland drugstore. Anderson was taken to Huron Road Hospital, where experts agreed that he had succumbed to mental strain and was the victim of amnesia. He reportedly told the story of the missing days for the rest of his life, each time with different details. He simply couldn't remember what really happened. (Wallace, Wallenchinsky, Wallace, & Wallace, 1980, pp. 434–435)

MULTIPLE PERSONALITY DISORDER.   In **multiple personality disorder,** an individual develops more than one personality. These personalities rarely appear simultaneously; instead, they seem to vie for consciousness. Often one personality is totally unaware of another. The two most celebrated cases of multiple personality were described in the books *The Three Faces of Eve* and *Sybil.*

MULTIPLE PERSONALITY DISORDER: THE CASE OF SYBIL DORSETT

Sybil Dorsett was a college graduate who was leading what seemed to be a normal healthy existence as a schoolteacher. In 1954, she began work on a master's degree at Columbia University. She came to the attention of psychiatrist Cornelia Wilbur because she was having blackouts and periods of amnesia that were becoming progressively longer, and no physical cause for her ailment could be discerned. It was during a therapy session with Dr. Wilbur that there was a sudden and radical change in Sybil's personality. Her voice changed, her manner changed, and she began to act like a little girl; she even threw a temper tantrum. A short time later, a third personality emerged, who called herself Vicki. Sybil was unaware of the other personalities, but Vicki knew about them. In the course of several therapy sessions, Vicki revealed that throughout her childhood many personalities had been created for Sybil, 16 in all. Some of the personalities were children, some were adults, and some were even male. In Figure 15.2 you can see pictures drawn by Sybil as different personalities were in control.

During the therapy, Dr. Wilbur discovered that Sybil had been systematically abused and tortured by her schizophrenic mother from as early as 3. Apparently, whenever Sybil encountered a situation that she could not handle, a new personality was created to deal with the stress. Over a period of several years, Dr. Wilbur worked with all 16 personalities, attempting to solve the problems of each and eventually integrating them into a seventeenth new and whole personality.

Compared with the disorders we've discussed so far, multiple personality is one of the most complex and difficult to understand (Loewenstein, Hamilton, Alagna, Reid, & deVries, 1987). In the past, researchers thought it was an extremely rare disorder, but because of its complexity, it may have been often confused with the more severe psychotic disorders such as schizophrenia and, as a result, overlooked

Actress Joanne Woodward portraying the personalities of Eve White and Eve Black in the motion picture The Three Faces of Eve, *a case history of a multiple personality.*

for what it really was. With use of the current DSM classification system, however, careful screening has shown that as many as 10 percent of all psychiatric inpatients may have multiple personality (Bliss & Jeppsen, 1985).

No one is sure what the cause of multiple personality is, but there are some interesting possibilities under investigation. One such possibility involves the development of memory. In Chapter 7, we discussed propositional network theory,

FIGURE 15.2

Some of Sybil's 16 personalities were artists, and their paintings helped Sybil to recover. Each personality had a different artistic style. A painting by "Marcia" (a) depicts a grim self-portrait and highlights Marcia's depressed nature. At the right (b) is a painting by an angry, fearful "Peggy." The dark shadow in the foreground represents her sadistic mother. At bottom (c) is a painting of a warm home and family environment by "Mary," who liked to recall her childhood friends. (From Sybil paintings, courtesy of Dr. Cornelia B. Wilbur.)

(a)

(b)

(c)

in which memory is envisioned as a series of nodes of information that are linked to one another. Interestingly, researchers have found that about 98 percent of people with multiple personality were abused as children (Chance, 1986). It may be that these individuals, through fear and anxiety, repressed and isolated their childhood experiences. This in turn may have resulted in their memories developing in a fragmented way, with whole sections of memory cordoned off from other sections, linked together poorly or not at all. If this is the case, when a particular node or memory is activated, a person with multiple personality disorder is trapped within a limited fraction of her memory, with each fraction holding different and limited "knowledge" about herself. Such limited and enclosed areas of memory might easily seem to be separate and distinct personalities. Of course, no one knows the real cause for sure, but this hypothesis is interesting. If it is correct, future researchers will view multiple personality as a developmental failure to integrate memory.

▌ MOOD DISORDERS

Mood disorders are disorders of affect, or emotion. The two most serious types are bipolar disorder and major depression.

Bipolar Disorder

Bipolar disorder is characterized by drastic changes in mood. All of us are happy some of the time and sad some of the time, and mood swings are not abnormal in most instances. But in bipolar disorder the mood change is dramatic. People with bipolar disorder may suddenly have feelings of great elation and extreme agitation. They may become very impatient, show poor judgment, and try to initiate a number of endeavors simultaneously. Occasionally, they become violent.

At other times, the same person may go through periods of intense depression, bordering on suicide. The depressive phase may last for hours or even days. This is what is meant by bipolar disorder—swinging repeatedly back and forth between two poles, the manic and the depressed. Sometimes, the moods and accompanying behaviors are severe enough to classify as a **psychosis.** Scientists have estimated that between 0.4 and 1.2 percent of the adult population have had bipolar disorder (Spitzer & Williams, 1987). The following case study illustrates this fluctuating behavior.

BIPOLAR DISORDER: THE CASE OF M. M.

M. M. was first admitted to a state hospital at the age of 38, although since childhood she had been characterized by swings of mood, some of which had been so extreme that they had been psychotic in degree. At 17 she suffered from a depression that rendered her unable to work for several months, although she was not hospitalized. At 33, shortly before the birth of her first child, the patient was greatly depressed. For a period of four days she appeared in coma. About a month after the birth of the baby she "became excited" and was entered as a patient in an institution. . . . As she began to improve, she was sent to a shore hotel for a brief vacation. The patient remained at the hotel for one night and on the following day signed a year's lease on an apartment, bought furniture, and became heavily involved in debt. Shortly thereafter Mrs. M. became depressed and returned to the hospital in which she had previously been a patient . . . In a little less than a year Mrs. M. again became overactive, played her

MOOD DISORDERS
A group of disorders characterized by extremes of mood and emotion.

BIPOLAR DISORDER
A mood disorder characterized by severe cyclical mood swings. Formerly called manic–depression psychosis, bipolar disorder can often be controlled with lithium-based drugs.

PSYCHOSIS
Any of a group of disorders involving extensive and severe psychological disintegration, disruption of all forms of adaptive behavior, and loss of contact with reality. Psychotic individuals may show bizarre motor behavior, extreme emotional states, absence of emotional responsiveness, withdrawal, delusions, hallucinations, and cognitive distortions. Psychosis often requires institutionalization.

radio until late in the night, smoked excessively, took out insurance on a car that she had not yet bought. Contrary to her usual habits, she swore frequently and loudly, created a disturbance in a club to which she did not belong, and instituted divorce proceedings. On the day prior to her second admission to the hospital, she purchased 57 hats. (Kolb, 1973, p. 376)

In bipolar disorder, the timing of the mood swings is rarely related to external events. This fact has led researchers to believe that there may be important genetic or biological factors directly affecting bipolar disorder.

Evidence for this belief comes from a number of sources. First, as we will discuss in Chapter 16, bipolar disorder often responds well to the drugs based on the metal lithium. Also, bipolar disorder has been shown to run in families (see Figure 15.3). This observation has led geneticists to search for possible clues as to the ways in which bipolar disorder might be inherited. Research so far has indicated that bipolar disorder probably is not related to a single gene but is more likely to have a complex genetic basis (Faraone, Kremen, & Tsuang, 1990). So far, although there have been many research efforts using genetic studies, brain scans, and blood analyses, no reliable biological common denominator associated with bipolar disorder has yet been uncovered (Depue & Iacono, 1989).

Detailed efforts designed to examine possible environmental causes have also been undertaken. One area of special interest has been the examination of interactions among family members in which one or more members has bipolar disorder. It is still too early to say if certain types of family interactions or stresses predispose a person to bipolar disorder (Goldstein, 1988), but some interesting discoveries have been made. One such discovery was that bipolar disorder was more common among those who had demonstrated creative accomplishments, such as writers. The assumption was that the stress of creativity might increase a person's chances of acquiring bipolar disorder. But that bit of information is now considered to be an indication of a biological cause since it was discovered that creative achievements are also more common among blood relatives (but not relatives by marriage) of

FIGURE 15.3

Family trees of two families showing the incidence of psychiatric problems, especially bipolar disorder, for three generations. The oldest generations are at the top of the figure. The first generation couple on the left had nine offspring, eight daughters and one son. The grandmother of this family has bipolar disorder and so do three of her living daughters. The third daughter from the left married twice. The first generation couple on the right had one daughter, who married the only son of the other first generation couple. In this family, the grandfather has bipolar disorder. The numbers represent the individual's age at the time of the study or the person's death. An X indicates that the subject has died. The family tree makes the unusually high incidence of mental disorder in these families apparent. (SOURCE: Elliot Gershon, National Institute of Mental Health.)

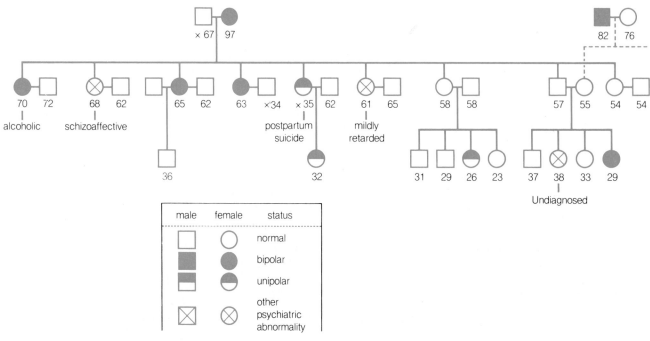

492

those who suffer from bipolar disorder than they are among the general populace (Richards, Kinney, Lunde, Benet, & Merzel, 1988) and that no such relationship exists between creativity and other mood disorders, only bipolar disorder (Coryell et al., 1989).

Major Depression

The term **depression** describes a wide range of emotional lows, from sadness to a severe and suicidal state. Each of us has felt unhappy at one time or another, and sadness can be quite natural as long as there is an obvious cause. **Major depression,** however, is a lasting and continuous state of depression without an obvious organic or environmental cause. A mood of unhappiness and apathy prevails. Major depression is twice as likely to occur among females as among males. Scientists estimate that between 5 and 9 percent of all women will suffer at least one major depressive episode sometime during their lives (Spitzer & Williams, 1987).

Persons with major depression usually regard themselves in a negative way and blame themselves for things that have gone wrong. They typically experience a decrease in drives such as hunger and sex and an increase in insomnia. Their favorite activities bore them, and they feel hopeless about the future (Beck, 1972). The onset of depression often is foreshadowed by a sense of losing control over one's life and environment (Hyland, 1987).

Major depression may include psychotic features such as delusions, hallucinations, or a depressive stupor (in which the patient does not speak or respond); it often occurs, however, without such behavior.

Another form of depression is **dysthymia.** It is far more common than major depression and less severe, but also requires treatment. Some have described dysthemia as the "walking wounded" version of major depression.

Depression may begin at an early age. In one comprehensive study, almost 1 percent of all *preschoolers* were found to be suffering from major depression (Kashani & Carlson, 1987). Among grade schoolers, the percentage rises to about 2 percent. Yet very few parents or professionals who deal with children ever consider such a possibility when attempting to explain a child's withdrawn or listless behavior.

DEPRESSION
A feeling of sadness and sometimes total apathy. Guilt or inability to cope with problems, frustration, or conflict is often behind depression. It may be influenced by chemical imbalances in the brain as well.

MAJOR DEPRESSION
A lasting and continuous state of depression without any apparent cause. It is also known as unipolar depression. Major depression may include psychotic features such as hallucinations, delusions, or a depressive stupor.

DYSTHEMIA
A common form of depression defined by a depressed mood for more days than not, lasting for at least 2 years with no respite from depression for more than 2 months at a time, and associated with some disruption or loss of sleep, appetite, energy, self-esteem, or concentration. Often accompanied by feelings of hopelessness.

It is normal for people to have changes of mood, highs and lows.

ENDOGENOUS DEPRESSION

The suspected inherited form of major depression. Endogenous depression occurs without any apparent external cause. It is marked by long-term despair, dejection, and feelings of apprehension, gloom, and worthlessness.

DEXAMETHASONE SUPPRESSION TEST (DST)

A blood test used to indicate the presence of endogenous depression. Dexamethasone is administered and the suppression of cortisol is measured. Failure to suppress cortisol is an indication of endogenous depression.

DOUBLE DEPRESSION

Severe depression brought about by a combination of endogenous and environmental causes, either of which would have been sufficient in and by itself to create a serious depressive state.

SEASONAL AFFECTIVE DISORDER (SAD)

Depression associated with either a longer or shorter day. It commonly affects individuals in either the winter or summer months and typically passes once the season is over.

Interestingly, individuals who develop major depression before the age of 20 years are more likely to have close relatives with the disorder (Weissman et al., 1984; Hammen et al., 1987). This implies that, as with bipolar disorder, major depression may be partly the result of inherited factors.

The idea that there may be an inherited component of major depression was first investigated systematically in 1962. At that time, psychiatrist Seymour S. Kety studied 85 adoptees with mood disorder, primarily major depression. These individuals had not been reared by their biological parents. Kety reported a significant concentration of depression in the adoptees' *biological* relatives, finding that they were three times more likely to suffer from depression than were members of the adopted families (Kety, Rosenthal, Wender, Schulsinger & Jacobsen, 1978). Among all the family members in the study, both biological and adopted, there were 18 reported suicides. The fact that 15 of these suicides were among the biological relatives of the depressed group suggests the possibility of a genetic factor in depression and suicide. The suspected inherited form of major depression is called **endogenous depression.**

Individuals who have endogenous depression appear to be biologically different from other people. This often can be demonstrated by the use of a diagnostic tool called the **dexamethasone suppression test,** or **DST.** In almost all individuals who do not have endogenous depression, an injection of the drug dexamethasone interacts with the hypothalamic-pituitary-adrenal axis (see Chapter 14) and causes the levels of cortisol to be suppressed or reduced. Among those diagnosed as having endogenous depression, slightly over 50 percent will show no such reduction (70 percent in cases in which the endogenous depression is severe) (APA Task Force, 1987). These results appear to be due to the specific existence of endogenous depression and not simply to the effects of being sad or depressed, because lack of suppression is not commonly observed among people suffering from acute grief (Shuchter, Zisook, Kirkorowicz, & Risch, 1986). It is not known why lack of suppression is seen among so many of those diagnosed as having endogenous depression, but it does emphasize that there are some underlying biological events correlated with the condition.

There are even instances of individuals who have endogenous depression and also have an obvious (environmental) reason to be depressed. Such individuals are said to suffer from **double depression** and show greater impairment and more severe depression than is usually observed in either endogenous depression or environmentally induced depression (Klein, Taylor, Harding, & Dickstein, 1988).

Some sufferers of major depression seem to be affected by the season. Their depression comes on either in the winter or the summer months. This is sometimes called **seasonal affective disorder** or **SAD.** Physicians have been aware of this interesting disorder for well over 2000 years (Wehr & Rosenthal, 1989).

Seasonal affective disorder is different from other forms of depression in some provocative ways that may eventually furnish important clues to the underlying cause of the disorder. For instance, sufferers from SAD typically crave extra sleep and they are especially drawn to consume large amounts of carbohydrates (Garvey, Wesner, & Godes, 1988). This has led researchers to wonder if there isn't some link between SAD in humans and hibernation, a pattern of behavior most markedly observed in bears. So far, no one knows. What we do know, however, is that winter SAD can usually be cured with the use of bright lamps that simulate daylight, which can be used to artificially lengthen the sufferer's winter days. Shortening the day does not cure the summer SAD, however; some speculate that summer SAD might be more related to temperature than length of day (Wehr, Sack, & Rosenthal, 1987).

SCHIZOPHRENIC DISORDERS

Schizophrenia is a serious psychosis. It affects as many as 2 million people in the United States and many millions more throughout the world. The treatment of schizophrenia is estimated to cost the United States about $48 billion per year (Holden, 1987d). Although it is typically a disorder of young adults, it can occur at any age and it tends to run a slightly more severe course in men than in women (Goldstein, 1988).

Contrary to common belief, schizophrenia does not mean having more than one personality. As you recall, multiple personality is a dissociative disorder. The "schizo" in schizophrenia historically referred to a split between emotion and thought, a complete breakdown of integrated personality functioning. In instances of schizophrenia, emotions become flat and distorted. Thought, language, and behavior become bizarre and disturbed. These bizarre behaviors are commonly accompanied by delusions and hallucinations.

A **delusion** is a strong unrealistic belief that is maintained even though there is ample evidence of its falseness. Schizophrenics who believe that they are Jesus Christ or that the telephone company has wired their brain and is controlling their every movement are exhibiting delusions. Schizophrenics may also have **hallucinations,** which are sensory perceptions in the absence of appropriate external stimuli. In other words, schizophrenics often see objects or hear voices that are not there, and react to them, although schizophrenia may occur without hallucinations (Asaad & Shapiro, 1986).

SCHIZOPHRENIA
A term used to describe a number of psychotic disorders characterized by serious emotional disturbances, withdrawal, lack of or inappropriate emotional responses, hallucinations, and delusions.

DELUSION
A strong belief opposed to reality, which is maintained in spite of logical persuasion and evidence to the contrary; delusions are a symptom of psychosis. There are three main types: delusions of grandeur (the belief that one is an exalted personage), delusions of persecution (the belief that one is being plotted against), and delusions of reference (the belief that chance happenings and conversations concern oneself).

HALLUCINATION
A false sense perception for which there is no appropriate external stimulus.

Schizophrenia is a serious mental disorder and is classified as a psychosis.

The onset of schizophrenia can be gradual or rapid. Gradual onset is usually a worse sign, because it is associated with a poorer likelihood of recovery. Approximately 25 percent of schizophrenics who are treated undergo remission, during which symptoms abate. A cure is rarely claimed, because schizophrenia in remission can recur. Over the course of time, a schizophrenic may experience symptoms in varying degrees of severity (Harrow, Carone, & Westermeyer, 1985). Sometimes the behavioral disruption is relatively mild; at other times, it is extremely severe.

Figures 15.4 and 15.5 are paintings drawn by schizophrenics that illustrate the disintegration and reintegration of personality and sensation that often accompany a schizophrenic episode. Note the distortions of perception. Distortions in thought also are common to schizophrenia, as is apparent in the diary entry of a college-age schizophrenic, which is reproduced in the following case study.

FIGURE 15.4

Louis Wain (1860–1939) was a famous artist best known for his witty depictions of cats in human situations, such as giving a tea party. Fifteen years before his death, Wain suffered a schizophrenic breakdown. The changes in his cat paintings show a fascinating and frightening transition from his former style to one that highlights sensory distortion and turmoil. (Derik Bayles/ Courtesy Guttman-Maclay Collection. Life Picture Service.)

SCHIZOPHRENIA: THE CASE OF DAVID F.

David F. was a young college student who became more and more apprehensive about his future as he neared graduation. He also was concerned about his relationship with his girlfriend, and he had feelings of sexual inadequacy. David began to stay in his room and stopped attending classes almost entirely. He recorded many of his feelings in a diary. The following excerpts were written shortly before he was hospitalized:

Thursday, March 12, 11 A.M. I'm out! I'm through . . . boomed out of the tunnel sometime last night and it's raining stars . . . whooey . . . it's nice out there's time for everything . . . I can do it I did it and if it happens again I'll do it again twice as hard

I got a dexamyl high going and I'm not on dexamyl and I've been up for forty eight or more hours and I'm giddygiddygiddy and I took a test this morning and it was on Voltaire and I kicked him a couple of good ones for being down on Pascal that poor bastard with his shrivelled body and bottomless abysses they're not bottomless!! You get down far enough and it gets thick enough and black enough and then you claw claw claw your way out and pretty soon you're on top again. And I licked it by myself, all alone . . . I just sat in on one of those weddings of the soul and I tooted tooted . . . I don't care I can use it I can run on it it will be my psychic gasoline now I don't have to sleep sleep all the time to get away with it . . . but if I lose my typewriter? (Bowers, 1965, p. 351)

In DSM-III-R, schizophrenia is classified according to subtypes. There are five major subtypes, each marked by a somewhat different clustering of behaviors or symptoms (see Table 15.4). Although these subtypes are fairly stable, it is not uncommon for the same individual to show symptoms of different subtypes from time to time (Kendler, Gruenberg, & Tsuang, 1985).

Causes of Schizophrenia

During the last 100 years, just about every conceivable biological and environmental cause for schizophrenia has been proposed. For instance, during the 1920s, it was common to pull teeth in an attempt to alleviate schizophrenia, since at the time it was thought that a localized infection might be a possible cause. Needless to say, pulling teeth didn't work. During the 1940s and 1950s, interest in possible

497

biological causes decreased as environmental theories became more popular. Although scientists now believe that the environment can play a role in the onset of schizophrenia, the most intriguing new research into the origin of schizophrenia has once again focused on the biological, owing to recent discoveries in genetics, biochemistry, and neurology.

GENETIC AND ENVIRONMENTAL FACTORS. Studies of the incidence of schizophrenia among identical and fraternal twins have indicated an hereditary component to schizophrenia. For instance, a study in the United States found that if one identical twin had schizophrenia, there was a 42 percent chance that the other would, whereas there was only a 9 percent chance for a similar result among fraternal twins (Gottesman & Shields, 1972). (Fraternal twins, although born at the same time, do not share exactly the same genetic makeup.) Children of schizophrenics who were adopted by nonschizophrenics also have been found to have a higher incidence of schizophrenia than control populations (Barnes, 1987b). Another study indicated that close relatives of schizophrenics are almost 13 times more likely to suffer from schizophrenia (3.8 percent chance) than are individuals who have no such relatives (0.3 percent chance) (Baron, Gruen, Kane, & Asnis, 1985). In fact, data indicate that schizophrenia has a heritability that exceeds that for diabetes, ulcers, or high blood pressure (Loehlin, Willerman, & Horn, 1988), all disorders in which heredity is known to play an important role.

Curiously, though, the subtypes of schizophrenia shown in Table 15.4 do not run in families (Kendler, Gruenberg, & Tsuang, 1988). While the predisposition

FIGURE 15.5

A patient diagnosed as a paranoid schizophrenic was unable to make even a simple original drawing when asked to do so. A painting from a magazine (a) was provided as an aid. The patient's first attempt to copy (b) revealed visual distractions, confusions about language and letters, and lack of color. As therapy progressed, the patient's recovery was dramatically demonstrated by his improved ability to copy the original art, as shown in (c) and then (d). (Al Yercoutere—Malibu, California.)

(a)

(b)

498

TABLE 15.4 DSM-III-R Classifications of Schizophrenia Subtypes

SUBTYPE	CHARACTERISTICS
Disorganized	Earlier age of onset than most of the other types. Emotions are extremely distorted. The person may display grossly inappropriate silliness and laughter, unusual and bizarre mannerisms, and obscene behavior.
Catatonic	Alternating periods of intense excitement or extreme withdrawal. During extreme withdrawal, the person may hold his body very still, sometimes for hours. The positions assumed are often odd. During intense excitement, the person often walks about rapidly and carries on incoherent conversations. Behavior is uninhibited, wild, and impulsive.
Paranoid	The person has bizarre delusions. Feelings of persecution are common. Judgment is impaired and unpredictable; hallucinations are common.
Undifferentiated	No one subtype of schizophrenia dominates. The person shows rapidly changing mixtures of schizophrenic behaviors, delusions, hallucinations, bizarre thoughts, and emotions.
Residual	Subtle indications of schizophrenia that are occasionally observed in those who are recovering from a schizophrenic episode.

(c)

(d)

AL YERCOUTERE—MALIBU, CALIFORNIA

499

to become schizophrenic does appear to have a genetic component, the subtype of schizophrenia that eventually manifests itself may be the result of environmental influences or perhaps due to the severity of the schizophrenia, but does not itself seem to be part of the genetic picture.

Some studies have indicated that the environment may also have a pronounced influence on the onset of schizophrenia. In the UCLA high-risk study, 54 families with troubled teenagers who had no history of psychosis were studied for 15 years. Patterns of family interactions were also observed. Teenagers who developed schizophrenia were more likely to come from families who showed the most unusual or pathological patterns of communication, such as often saying one thing while really meaning another (Wynne, Singer, Bartko, & Toohey, 1977). This may indicate that among those predisposed to schizophrenia, additional stresses may bring on the disorder. Of course, it might also be that the families with the most pathological communication patterns demonstrate schizophrenic-like interaction, implying that they might have some biological problem that they pass on to their children.

Perhaps the best evidence that exists for both genetic and environmental factors in schizophrenia comes from the case of the Genain quadruplets (Rosenthal & Quinn, 1977). In 1930, these identical quadruplets caused something of a sensation. Quadruplets aren't that rare, but *identical* quadruplets (all stemming from one fertilized egg) are. The four girls are called, Nora, Iris, Myra, and Hester.* The fascinating thing was that by the time the girls had reached late adolescence, all four were schizophrenic. The odds of this happening by random chance were one in 2 billion, so it appears that genetics was an important factor—because they all share the same genes.

The severity of schizophrenia, however, was not at all the same for the 4 sisters, indicating also an environmental component. Of the four, Nora and Hester showed the most severe symptoms, but Iris was less affected, and Myra, less still. In fact, at last report, Myra was living with her husband and appeared to be leading a relatively normal life (Hamer, 1982).

Researcher Kenneth Kendler has examined these data and other similar studies and expressed the general consensus of professionals in this field when he said: "It is not fair to say that schizophrenia is a genetic disease . . . But the evidence is strong that schizophrenia, like coronary heart disease and early-onset hearing loss, tends to run in families (Barnes, 1987b, p. 430)."

BIOCHEMICAL FACTORS.   Research into the biochemistry of schizophrenia underwent a revolution in the late 1950s, when scientists discovered that small amounts of certain chemical agents, once in the body, could produce a number of mental changes (Huxley, 1954). Such hallucinogenic substances as LSD and mescaline were found to cause a temporary breakdown of the thought process, mental disorganization, and sensory experiences similar to the symptoms of psychosis. Some investigators wondered whether, in the case of schizophrenia, the body wasn't producing its own hallucinogenic substances. My father was a research psychiatrist, and in the late 1950s he began experiments with LSD to identify similarities between LSD intoxication and schizophrenia. My mother volunteered to be one of his subjects. Years before the general public had ever heard of LSD, my mother was "dropping acid" every Thursday under supervised conditions in a laboratory. Like

*These names are not the girls' real ones; they are fictional names corresponding to the initials of the National Institute of Mental Health (NIMH). In this way, data obtained about any one of the quadruplets cannot be directly identified with a given individual except by the medical researchers who have the original files and the correct names.

most schizophrenia research conducted at that time, the efforts, unfortunately, turned out not to be fruitful. Thursday night dinners, however, were unique (often including my mom's favorite—blue mashed potatoes).

To date, no internal hallucinogen similar to LSD has been found to be the cause of schizophrenia. Since the late 1950s, our understanding of schizophrenia has grown, and few researchers now think that its mysteries will ever be solved in a simple way.

In the past few years, the possibility that some physical or biochemical causes of schizophrenia may be uncovered has grown, however. Researchers now believe that if schizophrenia is caused by a biochemical agent or agents, these substances must be related to the neurotransmitters that send nerve impulses across synapses from neuron to neuron in the brain (see Chapter 2). In the 1970s, the neurotransmitter dopamine began to attract special interest (Lucins, 1975) because many of the antipsychotic drugs (drugs used to treat schizophrenia) are known to block dopamine action at the site of the dopamine receptor cell (Farde, Hall, Ehrin, & Sedvall, 1986). This possible explanation of schizophrenia became known as the **dopamine hypothesis.**

By late 1986, it was discovered through the use of the PET scan that although schizophrenics don't produce excess dopamine, they do have an unusually greater density of dopamine receptors in the portion of the brain known as the limbic system (see Chapter 2). PET scans of schizophrenics have also shown a decrease in frontal brain activity known as *hypofrontality*. One exciting idea currently under investigation is that too many dopamine receptors in the limbic system might account for the *positive* symptoms of schizophrenia (behaviors *added* on top of what is normal, such as bizarre actions, thoughts, or verbal statements), while hypofrontality might account for the *negative* symptoms of schizophrenia (behaviors that are *missing* from what is normal, such as the lack of spontaneity and emotionality or the inability to focus attention) (Andreasen, 1988).

STRUCTURAL AND ANATOMICAL FACTORS. Biochemical hypotheses concerning psychosis are only about 3 decades old. Before that time, most research centered on the possibility of structural abnormalities in the brains of psychotics. These older studies, some conducted more than 50 years ago, reported that the cerebral ventricles (the butterfly-shaped fluid-filled cavities found between the lobes of the brain) were abnormally enlarged in the brains of schizophrenics. At that time, the process used for studying brain structure was *pneumoencephalography*, which required that gas or air be injected into the ventricles of the brain so that they could be visualized on X-ray film and measured. The examination was an extremely painful experience to undergo, and, although enlarged ventricles were reported in some schizophrenics, these findings were dismissed by later researchers as erroneous. It was believed that the injection of gas or air could have artificially enlarged the ventricles and made them appear bigger on the X-ray images.

Modern researchers, however, using computed axial tomography (CAT) scans and magnetic resonance imaging (MRI) (see Chapter 2) to take more sophisticated pictures of the brain, have obtained findings that have confirmed the older research. In fact, some of these confirming brain scans were of John Hinckley, the man who shot President Reagan in 1981 and who was diagnosed as a schizophrenic. The scans showed him to have abnormally enlarged cerebral ventricles. Over the past 15 years, many researchers have presented data confirming that schizophrenics do, in fact, have abnormally enlarged cerebral ventricles as well as other consistent abnormalities of the central nervous system, such as less gray matter in the brain (see Chapter 2) (Andreasen, 1988; Shelton et al., 1988; Suddath et al., 1989; Raz & Raz, 1990). Studies also indicate that these structural changes are not the result

DOPAMINE HYPOTHESIS
The argument that abnormalities associated with the neurotransmitter dopamine are related to the onset and maintenance of schizophrenic episodes. Either an overabundance of dopamine or the existence of too many dopamine receptors in the brain is deemed responsible.

of medical treatments or of drug or alcohol use and that they are not related to how long a person has been in an institution. The structural changes seem to correlate only with schizophrenia. Perhaps the most telling study concerning enlarged cerebral ventricles in schizophrenics was conducted by Daniel Weinberger and his colleagues who examined the brain scans of 15 pairs of identical twins, in which one of each pair had been diagnosed as schizophrenic (Suddath, Christison, Torrey, Casanova & Weinberger, 1990). They noted that in 14 out of 15, the cerebral ventricles of the schizophrenic twin were abnormally enlarged when compared with the nonschizophrenic twin (see Figure 15.6). No abnormalities were noted among 7 normal twins who were used as controls.

The possibility that schizophrenia might be caused by a virus also has received attention. Virus infections in the brain are a known cause of enlarged ventricles, and some virus specific to schizophrenia might possibly be the cause of the enlargements observed in schizophrenics (Mirsky & Duncan, 1986). It also is not uncommon for an entire family to be exposed to the same virus, which might account for some of the data showing the disorder to run in families. Schizophrenics also are slightly more likely to have been born during the winter "flu" months, which also might imply a viral connection (Torrey & Peterson, 1976). It remains to be seen whether researchers will find strong evidence supporting this hypothesis.

Schizophrenia remains one of the great mysteries. Although we are beginning to make some headway, when all the current knowledge about the disorder is collected, it must be said that we still know precious little. In the words of Kenneth Kendler:

> If you put everything that is known about schizophrenia into a pot and boiled it down you would come up with three things—it seems to run in families, neuroleptics [drugs that interact in some way with the brain's dopamine system] make it better, and there may be something abnormal in the brains of schizophrenics. (Barnes, 1987b, p. 430)

DELUSIONAL (PARANOID) DISORDER

Delusional disorders are fairly uncommon, affecting about 0.05 to 0.1 percent of all individuals sometime during their lives. It is slightly more common in females than it is in males.

FIGURE 15.6

Brain scans of forty-four-year-old male identical twins. The brain on the left is normal. The brain on the right, however, clearly shows the enlarged cerebral ventricles that are associated with this individual's schizophrenia. SOURCE: *Suddath, Christison, Torrey, Casanova, & Weinberger, 1990.*

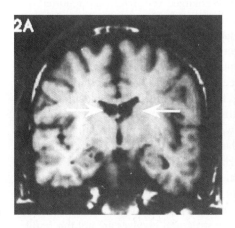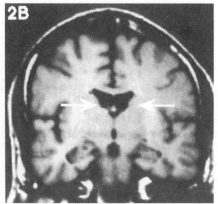

Delusional (Paranoid) Disorder

Paranoia is a system of delusions that the psychotic individual firmly believes or accepts. The difference between paranoia and paranoid schizophrenia is that in paranoia, hallucinations rarely occur and there is no serious disorganization of the personality. The delusional system usually develops slowly. Delusional (paranoid) disorder is categorized according to subtype depending on the particular kind of delusion that predominates (see Table 15.5).

The delusions are not simply misbeliefs; they are severe mental distortions. For example, paranoid people may feel that aliens are trying to take over their minds, or they may believe themselves to be Abraham Lincoln or Joan of Arc. Interestingly, the delusions are usually logical, in the sense that if you accept the basic premise (for example, that the patient's mind is being controlled by aliens), the rest of his ideas may seem perfectly reasonable (in that context). One of the most memorable depictions of paranoia in the history of motion pictures was Humphrey Bogart's portrayal of Fred C. Dobbs in the film *Treasure of the Sierra Madre*. Dobbs, a gold prospector, becomes more and more convinced that other people are after his share of gold, and he eventually attempts murder in "self-defense."

Induced Psychotic Disorder

Induced psychotic disorder is extremely rare. In this disorder, one person mimics or takes as her own the delusional system of another, who is usually a family member. Shared psychotic delusions are most common among husbands and wives, which eliminates heredity as the prime cause. Instead, the major factor may be that one partner takes a submissive role to the other's dominant role and in so doing accepts the dominant person's delusional system (Soni & Rockley, 1974). The following is a description of one such case:

Induced Psychotic Disorder: The Case of the Vietnam Vet

Mr. A, a 37-year-old . . . Vietnam veteran previously treated at several Veterans Administration hospitals . . . came to the emergency room stating, "My life is in danger." His wife accompanied him, and both wore combat fatigues. Mr. A told a semicoherent story of international spy intrigue that was built around the release of soldiers still missing in action or held as prisoners of war in Vietnam. He believed he was hunted by Vietnamese agents. He was unable to sleep without the protection of a shotgun propped against the door and a loaded revolver under his pillow. . . . Mrs. A visited

PARANOIA
A psychosis characterized by delusions and extreme suspiciousness. Hallucinations rarely occur, and the personality does not undergo the serious disorganization associated with schizophrenia.

INDUCED PSYCHOTIC DISORDER
A rare psychotic disorder in which one individual's paranoid delusional system is adopted by another, most commonly a spouse.

TABLE 15.5 Delusional (Paranoid) Disorder—Subtypes

SUBTYPE	DELUSION
Erotomanic	A person, usually of high status, is in love with the subject.
Grandiose	Inflated worth, power, knowledge, identity, or special relationship to a deity or famous person.
Jealous	One's sexual partner is unfaithful.
Persecutory	Someone or some group is treating the subject in a malevolent way.
Somatic	Physical defect, disorder, or disease.
Unspecified	Any delusion that does not fit one of the other categories.

her husband daily from the beginning of her husband's hospitalization, often accompanied by their children—two boys, age 14 and 12, and a girl, age 15. . . . [Mrs. A] would focus only on the very complicated and involved conspiracies involving the prisoners of war. She tended to speak in a disorganized and vague manner. . . . [I]t became clear that Mrs. A and the children shared Mr. A's paranoic viewpoint. Most problematic was the family's belief that they were in danger. The older son had been trained by Mr. A in karate and the use of shotguns to defend the household against "any Oriental who comes near." (Glassman, Magulac, & Darko, 1987, pp. 658–659)

Causes of Delusional (Paranoid) Disorder

Because delusional (paranoid) disorder is less common than psychotic mood disorders or schizophrenia, less is known about its possible causes. Some researchers believe that it is not accurate to consider delusional disorder as separate from schizophrenia, because paranoia is not always readily distinguishable from paranoid schizophrenia (Meissner, 1978). As a result, many of the potential causal factors that are associated with schizophrenia are being investigated as possible causes of delusional disorder as well. However, because delusional disorder doesn't appear to run in families in the way that schizophrenia does (Watt, 1985), and because the personality isn't nearly as shattered as it is in the case of schizophrenia, other researchers consider the two categories as distinct, which is the way they are presented in DSM-III-R.

PERSONALITY DISORDERS (AXIS II)

There are many types of **personality disorders.** The current list from DSM-III-R is shown in Table 15.6. This table may yet change in DSM-IV because many practitioners believe that too many of the personality disorders overlap and that a shorter list could still cover all of what are considered to be personality disorders (Blashfield & Breen, 1989). All personality disorders share certain qualities. People who have a personality disorder are typically severely impaired in terms of how they feel about themselves and how they get along with others (Drake & Vaillant, 1985). In fact, the most definitive aspect of a personality disorder is that the individual engages in behavior that *disrupts social relationships.*

Individuals with personality disorders seldom feel responsible for the troubles they cause because they generally attribute any problems to bad luck or perceive that the fault is someone else's. Another marked feature of personality disorders is that the maladaptive behavior pattern will typically persist until those who must deal with the individual finally become exhausted and break off the relationship. In personality disorder, we see an all-encompassing problem that permeates every single social interaction that the person has. Perhaps one of the best examples of personality disorder ever performed on film was actor Robert DeNiro's portrayal of the character Rupert Pupkin in the movie *The King of Comedy,* a masterful depiction of narcissistic personality disorder.

Another example, in this case of antisocial personality, is that of Dan F., a disk jockey at a radio station, who told his story to his friend, a clinical psychologist; it is reproduced in the following case study.

ANTISOCIAL PERSONALITY DISORDER: THE CASE OF DAN F.

"I can remember the first time in my life when I began to suspect I was a little different from most people. When I was in high school my best friend got leukemia and died and I went to his funeral. Everybody else was crying and feeling sorry for themselves and as they were praying to get him into heaven I suddenly realized that I wasn't feeling anything at all. He was a nice guy but what the hell. That night I thought about it some more and found out that I wouldn't miss my mother and father if they died and that I wasn't too nuts about my brothers and sisters, for that matter. I figured there wasn't anybody I really cared for but, then, I didn't need any of them anyway so I rolled over and went to sleep." As we discussed his early life he told me he could not recall a time when he was not "doing everybody I could and the easy ones twice." He remembered that when he was 12 years old he had read a book about "con men." It was then he decided it would be his life's work. They were heroes to him and he "fell down laughing" when they took some "mark" for his "bundle." As he said, "There is a sucker born every minute, and I'm glad the birth rate is so high."

TABLE 15.6 Personality Disorders

DSM-III-R-Category*	Description
Paranoid	Harbors a continuous unjustifiable suspiciousness and mistrust of people. Often appears cold or unemotional. Takes offense easily (behavior not due to schizophrenia or paranoid disorder).
Schizoid	Is unable to form social relationships, lacks warm or sentimental feelings for others, and is indifferent to praise, criticism, or the feelings of others (behavior is not due to schizophrenia or paranoid disorder).
Schizotypal	Exhibits strangeness in thought, speech, perception, and behavior, but not severe enough to classify as schizophrenic. Often socially isolated, suspicious, and oversensitive to criticism.
Histrionic	Is overreactive, intense, and overdramatic to the point of disturbing interpersonal relationships. Often displays an overreaction to minor situations, crying, tantrums. Is seen by others as vain, shallow, dependent, or manipulative.
Narcissistic	Has an unwarranted sense of self-importance, is preoccupied with fantasies of success. Demands attention, often believes she is entitled to special treatment. Tends to idolize or devaluate others. Lacks empathy.
Antisocial	Continuously violates the rights of others. Was antisocial prior to age 15 years; often fails to hold a job or to perform adequately on the job. Often lies, fights, steals, and is truant. Usually shows disrespect for the law. Can be engaging for own purposes, manipulative, impulsive. Lacks feelings for others.
Borderline	Is unstable in mood, behavior, and self-image. Is impulsive and unpredictable in behavior. Has intense and unstable relationships with others, inappropriate and uncontrollable anger. Is unable to be alone, has long-lasting feelings of boredom or emptiness. Makes suicidal gestures.
Avoidant	Is oversensitive to rejection or possible humiliation. Avoids relationships unless guaranteed to be accepted uncritically. Has low self-esteem. Is devastated by the slightest disapproval. Remains isolated although wanting to be with others.
Dependent	Allows others to take over and run his life. Lacks self-confidence and cannot function independently. Avoids opportunities to be self-reliant.
Obsessive compulsive	Has restricted ability to express warmth and affection. Has a need for perfectionism at the expense of others or at the expense of enjoying life. Insists that others do his or her bidding. Devoted to work and productivity at the expense of enjoying life.
Passive aggressive	Passively refuses to perform adequately in social relationships at work even though adequate effort is possible. The name for the disorder comes from the belief that the person is passively expressing overt aggression. Often shows procrastination, stubbornness, and intentional inefficiency.

*This table includes descriptions of only the most general nature and is completely inadequate for diagnostic purposes. In DSM-III-R the categories are described in far more detail.

One night, a colleague of Dan's committed suicide. . . . My phone started ringing early the next morning with the inevitable question "Why?" The executives at the station called but Dan F. never did. When I talked to him, he did not mention the suicide. Later, when I brought it to his attention, all he could say was that it was "the way the ball bounces." At the station, however, he was the one who collected money for the deceased and presented it personally to the new widow. As Dan observed, she was really built and had possibilities. (McNeil, 1967, pp. 85, 87)

Generally, people with personality disorders do poorly in therapy, believing that it is other people who are in need of help.

■ THE ASSESSMENT OF MENTAL DISORDERS

One of the most difficult problems faced by clinicians is assessment. Errors in assessment can lead to serious misunderstandings and inappropriate treatment. The effectiveness of assessment in actual practice has been the focus of a number of investigations and controversies.

Assessment Bias

Psychologist David Rosenhan of Stanford University, conducted one of the most interesting studies dealing with the problems of assessment. Rosenhan (1973) wondered whether a perfectly sane individual who gained admission to a mental hospital as a patient would be recognized as normal by the staff and discharged. To test his idea, he obtained the cooperation of eight people, who agreed to be pseudopatients. Among these eight were a psychology graduate student, three psychologists, a pediatrician, a psychiatrist, a painter, and a housewife. Rosenhan, himself, was one of the pseudopatients. With the exception of the hospital administrator and chief psychologist, no one else in the hospital knew that he was checking in as a patient. Twelve hospitals were chosen in five states on the East and West coasts. Some were old and rundown, some were very new; some were research hospitals, some weren't; some were private hospitals, some public.

The pseudopatients' task was to call their hospitals for an appointment, arrive, and complain of hearing voices. When asked what the voices said, the patients were instructed to reply that they weren't sure but that they could tell that the voices had said "empty," "hollow," and "thud." Except for alleging the symptoms and using a pseudonym (and, in certain cases, claiming a different vocation), the patients answered every other question asked by the staff during patient intake honestly. All the pseudopatients behaved in the hospital as they would normally have behaved. When asked by the staff how they felt, they indicted that they no longer had symptoms and were feeling fine. They politely responded to attendants who requested that they take medication (spitting it out later, however).

Rosenhan had told the pseudopatients that they would have to get by as best they could in their efforts to convince the staff that they were sane and should be discharged. As Rosenhan said,

> The psychological stresses associated with hospitalization were considerable, and all but one of the pseudopatients desired to be discharged almost immediately after being admitted. They were, therefore, motivated not only to behave sanely, but to be paragons of cooperation. That their behavior was in no way disruptive is confirmed by nursing reports, which have been obtained on most of the patients. These reports uniformly

David Rosenhan.

indicated that the patients were "friendly," "cooperative," and "exhibited no abnormal indications." (p. 252)

In no case was the sanity of the pseudopatient detected. The condition of seven out of eight was diagnosed as schizophrenia in remission. The pseudopatients stayed in the hospital from 7 to 52 days, with an average of 19 days. During the first of the hospitalizations, when careful data were kept, 35 out of a total of 118 of the other patients in the same hospitals became aware that the pseudopatients were sane. These patients would argue, "You're not crazy. You're a journalist, or a professor. You're checking up on the hospital" (p. 252). These patients recognized normality while the hospital staff failed to.

After Rosenhan published his results, one teaching hospital questioned his findings. The staff there argued that such errors were unlikely. Consequently, Rosenhan informed the staff that sometime during the next 3 months one or perhaps more pseudopatients might attempt to be admitted to that hospital. After admission, the patients would act sanely. The staff members were asked to try to expose the pseudopatients. The staff carefully examined 193 patients who were admitted for treatment. One member of the staff believed with high confidence that 41 of these patients were pseudopatients. One psychiatrist thought that about 23 were pseudopatients, and another psychiatrist, with one staff member, agreed that 19 were probably pseudopatients. At that point, Rosenhan admitted that he had never sent anyone to their hospital! Rosenhan concluded that "any diagnostic process that lends itself so readily to massive errors of this sort cannot be a very reliable one" (p. 252).

The pseudopatients also noticed during their stays that the staff often misinterpreted behavior. Boredom was misinterpreted as nervousness. Anger at being mistreated by an attendant was misinterpreted as berserk behavior caused by pathology. Once a group of patients was sitting outside the cafeteria half an hour before it opened, and a psychiatrist was overheard telling his residents that this was indicative of the oral stage of the patients' syndrome. Apparently it hadn't occurred to the psychiatrist that there was nothing much to do inside a hospital besides eat or wait for lunch.

Rosenhan came to the following conclusion:

It is clear that we cannot distinguish the sane from the insane in psychiatric hospitals. The hospital itself imposes a special environment in which the meanings of behavior can easily be misunderstood. The consequences to patients hospitalized in such an environment—the powerlessness, depersonalization, segregation, mortification, and self-labeling—seem undoubtedly counter-therapeutic. (p. 257)

Rosenhan replicated his initial study, carried out in 1973, with follow-up studies in 1973, 1974, and 1975. The later studies involved more than 10 hospitals (Greenberg, 1981). Rosenhan found essentially the same results.

A number of researchers and clinicians have taken issue with Rosenhan because of his methods and conclusions. For instance, psychologist Max Lewis of the University of Western Washington has stated:

I have some trouble with Rosenhan's study. First of all, subjects did report auditory hallucinations and ask to enter the hospital. Secondly, it is standard operating procedure to keep any admission for a period of observation. Thirdly, I don't have confidence that all pseudopatients presented a "normal" pattern of behavior; they were there to make a point. Fourthly, is it not possible that some of the pseudopatients did exhibit problems worthy of treatment? Obviously we would all be more comfortable if all the pseudopatients were immediately discovered. But a nineteen day stay is much different from being locked away without a follow-up. I think Rosenhan has an important point, but the situation doesn't seem so horrible to me as Rosenhan's discussion portrays it. (Lewis, 1981)

AN ENDURING QUESTION: SHOULD MENTAL DISORDERS BE CLASSIFIED BEFORE THEIR UNDERLYING CAUSES ARE UNDERSTOOD?

Last century in the United States, Dr. Samuel Cartwright described a "disease of the mind" to the Louisiana Medical Association. He called the disease *drapetomania*, from the Greek *drapetes*, which means "to run away." He said that drapetomania was the "insane desire to wander away from home," and, he argued, this was why slaves ran away—they had this disease of the mind (Chorover, 1979).

As you can see, labeling diseases of the mind without considering social or cultural factors or learning and experience can lead someone to assume that pathology exists when all that really exists is different behavior. Sometimes, as in the case of drapetomania, the behavior is different for a good reason. Critics of DSM-III-R have likened it to a symphony written by a committee; the notes are all there, but the way they are put together reflects the biases inherent in such a process. They argue that the DSM system is a haven for people who think that their job is to find a label to fit every subjective observation imaginable (Eysenck, Wakefield, & Friedman, 1983).

Because the underlying causes of these "pathologies" are frequently lacking, the DSM-III-R diagnoses are based on gross descriptions of complex behaviors that often appear different to different people (Schacht & Nathan, 1977; Smith & Kraft, 1983). This leads to arguments of the kind we have touched on lightly, such as whether delusional disorder is distinctly different from schizophrenia or whether obsessive–compulsive disorder should be considered an anxiety disorder.

Some professionals have gone so far as to reject all *psychological* assessment as invalid. For example, Thomas Szasz, a psychiatrist, has written about what he calls psychiatric injustice. He states that psychiatry has been used as a political weapon and that it has eliminated the civil liberties of many people who simply behaved differently, because it labels them sick and incarcerates them in hospitals. Szasz argues that in the past those who exhibited abnormal behavior were labeled witches or warlocks, whereas today they are labeled with psychiatric terms that serve the same purpose; that is, to justify the community in eliminating these people from effective participation in society. In his book *The Myth of Mental Illness* (1961), Szasz writes:

> The term "mental illness" is a metaphor. More particularly as this term is used in mental health legislation, "mental illness" is not the name of a medical illness or disorder, but is a quasi-medical label whose purpose is to conceal conflict as illness and to justify coercion as treatment. (p. xviii)

This view has been further supported in the conscience of the public by such films as *One Flew over the Cuckoo's Nest*, in which a man is placed in a mental institution simply because he has been disruptive; is forced to take drugs against his will; is given shock therapy, supposedly for treatment but really as a clandestine form of discipline; and eventually is given a lobotomy because he has challenged the rule of the ward nurse.

And yet, to abandon our system of assessment because errors may occur would probably be an overreaction. Most researchers now feel confident that Szasz is in error when he claims that mental illness is a myth. One researcher said about schizophrenia that although it has been argued that this form of mental illness is a myth, it is a "myth with a genetic basis and a pharmacological treatment" (Valenstein, 1980a, p. 321).

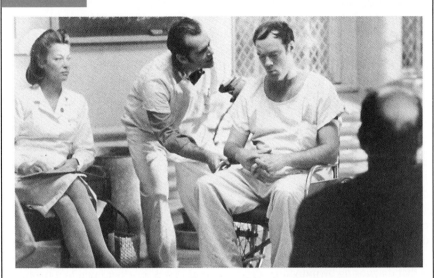

Films such as One Flew over the Cuckoo's Nest *helped underscore the growing concern people have about providing just and adequate care for the mentally ill.*

Supporters of DSM-III-R believe that competent clinicians are well aware of the limitations of the classification system. Professionals must be able to communicate with one another, and if DSM-III-R were not available, something less rigorous would take its place. Realistically, no one can expect to eliminate all terminology from psychiatry and psychology. Supporters argue that the DSM-III-R classifications are on the whole quite reliable; that is, different assessors tend to use the same descriptions when confronted with the same cases (Spitzer & Williams, 1987). They also argue that, by carefully describing behavior patterns that have aspects in common, they may be able to identify distinct groups that have a common underlying cause for their disorder. No doubt, this will not happen for every category, but it may lead to breakthroughs in certain areas.

Since DSM-III-R has been adopted—and it appears to be here to stay, at least until DSM-IV comes along—the general consensus is that it can be a valuable tool provided its limitations are clearly realized.

FOR CRITICAL ANALYSIS

1. Why is it that we often feel great sympathy and compassion for someone once a physical cause is discovered for their unwanted behavior?
2. Many of the people who are on death row for murder have very unusual electrical brain activity or other brain abnormalities. How would you feel if in the future we discover underlying physical disorders that cause people to become homicidal? How might we look back on the people whom we execute today?
3. Until the actual cause of schizophrenic behavior is known, why is it truly correct only to say that someone displays schizophrenic behavior, but not that she "has schizophrenia"?

Since the Rosenhan study, DSM-III and DSM-III-R have been published. The more reliable criteria of these advanced manuals should, we hope, make such misdiagnoses less likely. A survey of psychiatrists done 2 years after DSM-III was published, however, found that it had actually had little effect on diagnostic procedures. When asking their survey subjects how they would diagnose schizophrenia, the researchers observed that "a higher number of psychiatrists continued to approach the diagnosis of schizophrenia in an individualistic and unsystematic way" (Lipkowitz & Idupuganti, 1985, p. 634). In other words, they weren't using DSM-III.

Two years later, in a broader survey of physicians who were graduating from psychiatric training, 35 percent of these psychiatrists said that they were using DSM-III only because they had to during training and that, when given a choice, they wouldn't use it (Jampala, Sierles, & Taylor, 1986). The reasons respondents gave for not relying too much on the DSM system centered on the idea that a professional with the latest research and training should not be tied to textbook definitions. (Faust & Miner, 1986). After all, they argued, even DSM-III-R isn't written in stone—DSM-IV is already in the works. The counterargument, of course, is that diagnosing by individual determination leaves the door open to a haphazard use of labels. It also may make it more difficult to collect information about disorders, because professionals may not agree about whether an individual is, for example, a schizophrenic. The problems raised by the debate continue to plague the field.

Misdiagnosis

Sometimes patients are assessed inadequately, and important symptoms are overlooked or ignored. In such cases, it doesn't help much to have well-defined assessment categories, because the patient's difficulties are not being rigorously addressed. Researchers, wondering how often such misdiagnosis is likely to occur, have looked into the problem. One investigation examined 100 psychiatric patients. All the patients had originally been given an examination at a large psychiatric reception center, to which they had been brought by their families or by the police under mental health warrants. All were to be committed to state mental hospitals after the examination. When they volunteered to be part of the investigation, they were taken to a special clinical research ward instead. There they were given intensive physical and psychological tests. The physicians found that 46 of the 100 patients had medical illnesses that had gone undiagnosed and that probably either were the cause of their psychiatric symptoms or had exacerbated them considerably. Another 34 had previously undiagnosed physical illnesses that were not directly related to their psychiatric symptoms.

Once the underlying medical problem was treated, 61 percent recovered rapidly and their abnormal behavior disappeared. Among the medical problems that had been missed by those who had initially examined the patients were Addison's disease (an insufficiency of adrenaline, which can result in irritability, depression, and emotional instability); arsenic poisoning (from dust and paint chips in old houses); Wilson's disease (an inability to metabolize copper properly, which can lead to irritability, depression, emotional instability, high-pitched voice, and trembling); lead intoxication (from water running through old pipes and from paint dust); vitamin deficiency; and other dietary deficiencies. The number of physical illnesses discovered wasn't surprising, since the patients were mainly from the poorer areas of the city and had not received adequate routine medical care (Hall, Stickney, LeCann, & Popkin, 1980). The researchers believed that these 100 patients were generally representative of the population typically committed to a state mental hospital. They concluded that there was a serious failure to test incoming psychiatric patients properly for physical disorders and that the legal implication of this failure was profound. The medical tests given each patient by the researchers cost an average of only $400. A follow-up study at Baylor College of Medicine uncovered similar diagnostic oversights (Muecke & Krueger, 1981).

These kinds of oversights are, unfortunately, all too common when assessing elderly patients, because signs of mental deterioration often are greeted by physicians with the response, "Well, what do you expect, they're old." In fact, the difficulty might be treatable if only care were taken to do a proper and full medical workup (Kolata, 1987d).

Sometimes, the overlooked problem might even have a simple solution. For instance, some patients' mental disorders are made much worse by severe visual disorders that can often be treated with glasses or special ophthalmological intervention. Once treated, their symptoms often lessen significantly or even go away (Flach & Kaplan, 1983).

The following case study illustrates the problem of misdiagnosis.

THE ASSESSMENT OF PSYCHOPATHOLOGY: THE CASE OF CAROL T.

Carol T. was born in 1946; her troubles began in the summer of 1971. One day, she felt shaky and her mouth felt a little tight. Then, without warning, she fainted while at work. When she went to see her family doctor, he said she was overtired and gave her Valium (diazepam), a tranquilizer. One morning, at the end of July, Carol T. felt a strange compulsion for no apparent reason. She went into the bathroom, took a razor, and slashed her wrists. She survived. Two days later, she was given a psychiatric consultation. She spent 1 month in a psychiatric hospital and was given Thorazine (chlorpromazine), an antipsychotic drug. Carol then entered psychotherapy. For the next few years, she was in and out of mental hospitals and saw many different psychiatrists. She was given electroshock therapy, more antipsychotic drugs, and L-dopa, a drug to control Parkinson's disease. Still her symptoms got worse. She couldn't tie her shoes, open a jar, comb her hair, or write. She could hardly chew or swallow. She began to limp, she lost her balance, and she occasionally fell. Then she had trouble speaking, her voice became higher, and her speech became slurred. At that point, she was diagnosed as suffering from conversion disorder and was transferred to a community mental health center. There, one of the staff doctors just happened to stop in to see her. He took one look at Carol's eyes and recognized the copper-colored rings around her corneas as Kayser-Fleischer rings. These rings are an unmistakable sign of Wilson's disease. They are evidence of the actual buildup of copper in the body. The doctor said, "She was practically a textbook presentation. I think my secretaries could have made the diagnosis" (Roueche, 1980, p. 357). Carol was immediately placed on drugs to help leach the excess copper from her body. She is now fully recovered from the disease that would have cost her life had the doctor not spotted it.

One of the most difficult disorders to assess is schizophrenia. Although the DSM-III-R diagnostic criteria are fairly clear, these criteria can sometimes be satisfied by the early onset of disorders other than schizophrenia. For example, disordered and bizarre thinking is not unique to schizophrenia (Harrow & Quinlan, 1977), and hallucinations can occur in other disorders (Fitzgerald & Wells, 1977) and can even be experienced by otherwise normal individuals (Bentall, 1990). Adding to the problem is the fact that over half of those diagnosed as schizophrenic have learned to fake some or all of their symptoms and to mask others in order to be admitted to hospitals or to help lengthen or shorten their hospital stay (Martin, Hunter, & Moore, 1977; Pope, Jonas & Jones, 1982). As you can see, diagnostic assessment takes skill, knowledge, and experience. It is anything but simple.

EPILOGUE: THE TRICHOTILLOMANIAC

It began when Beth was 13 years old. She would sit before the mirror and look at her hair. One by one, she would take each strand of hair and pull it out by the root. Then she would bite off the root and lay the strand of hair down. She continued this ritualistic routine hair after hair, making a neat little pile of rootless strands that she placed before her.

After a few weeks of doing this each night, bald spots began to appear. She knew that what she was doing was crazy, but she couldn't bring herself to stop. In a desperate effort to save her hair, she sliced her fingertips with a razor blade hoping to make it too painful to grip hairs firmly enough to pull them out. She pulled her hair out anyway.

Afraid to tell her parents the truth, Beth was sent to a dermatologist (a physician specializing in disorders of the skin). She went for many treatments and was given different creams and ointments. By the time she was 16, she was bald. She finally told her parents what had been happening.

They sent her to a psychotherapist who diagnosed trichotillomania, *a $20 word meaning compulsive hair pulling. Her only comfort was that she found out she had company, over 2 million compulsive hair pullers in the United States alone, 90 percent of whom are women. She was considered a moderate case, not severe like those who also pulled out their pubic hairs and eyelashes. Unfortunately, psychotherapy did not help. Then one day in 1987, while watching TV, Beth heard about a drug that was being used to treat obsessive–compulsive disorder called clomipramine. She thought that what she was doing to herself sounded like a compulsion, so she contacted the researchers at the National Institute of Mental Health who had been mentioned in the news report and asked for help (Trotter, 1990).*

Up to that time, trichotillomania had not been classified as an obsessive–compulsive disorder. However, the researchers were curious about it, and a study was organized with a number of compulsive hair pullers, who were divided into an experimental and a control group (Rapoport, 1989). The experimental group received clomipramine and the control group a placebo. In the experimental group, 12 of the 13 women improved dramatically, including Beth. The placebo worked no better than chance would have predicted. In January 1990, based on these and other studies, the Food and Drug Administration approved the use of clomipramine for treating obsessive–compulsive disorder, in addition to depression for which it had been originally formulated.

Other clinical trials are examining the possibility of expanding the drug's usefulness for treating such disorders as compulsive nail biting or kleptomania (compulsive stealing). Thanks to this research, for the many people like Beth whose brain would fail to give a stop signal once a routine had begun, there is now a chance for a normal life free of compulsion.

SUMMARY

■ The distinction between normal and abnormal behavior is not always a clear one. For this reason, professionals must be careful when assessing behavior. For a behavior to be considered abnormal in the clinical sense, it must be not only different from the norm but also maladaptive or self-defeating.

■ In evaluating the abnormal behavior of another person, different models may be used to arrive at a better understanding of the underlying mechanisms that may contribute to the disorder. Some models may be more applicable in some circumstances than in others.

■ The medical model assumes that the underlying cause of a mental disorder is a biological dysfunction. According to the learning model, abnormal behaviors are acquired through conditioning. In the psychoanalytic model, the abnormal behaviors are viewed as evidence of unresolved unconscious conflicts. In the humanistic model, abnormal behaviors are considered the result of failure to fulfill self-potential.

■ *Insanity* is a legal term. There are different legal standards for determining whether a defendant in a criminal case is not guilty by reason of insanity.

■ In 1987 a new classification scheme, the revised third edition of the *Diagnostic and Statistical Manual* (DSM-III-R), was adopted. It provides assessment according to five dimensions or axes. The first three axes assess the immediate condition of the individual, while the fourth and fifth axes classify and assess the individual's past situation and overall ability to function.

■ Organic disorders are those in which the cause is physical or strongly suspected to be physical.

■ Anxiety disorders include simple phobia, in which an individual suffers from a specific unrealistic fear; generalized anxiety disorder, a relatively continuous state of tension, worry, and dread; panic disorder, in which a person may suddenly be overwhelmed by panic even though there is no apparent reason to be frightened; and obsessive–compulsive disorder, in which a person is obsessed by an unwanted thought or compulsively engages in actions and repetitive behaviors, perhaps as a way of coping with anxiety.

■ Somatoform disorders are patterns of behavior in which an individual has physical symptoms when, in fact, no illness can be found. Somatoform disorders include conversion disorder and hypochondriasis.

■ Dissociative disorders are those in which the person separates from the core of her personality. Included under dissociative disorders are psychogenic amnesia, which is a loss of memory; psychogenic fugue, in which the sufferer leaves home while in a state of amnesia; and multiple personality, in which more than one personality develops.

■ Some mood disorders, schizophrenic disorders, and delusional disorders are classified as psychoses. The psychotic person has lost contact with reality, and his personality becomes grossly distorted. In many cases, hospitalization is required.

■ Mood disorders are disorders of emotion. They include bipolar disorder, in which there may be extreme mood swings from depression to mania, and major depression, a state of severe and utter sadness bordering on suicide. Seasonal affective disorder is a form of depression that responds to the seasons, becoming more likely in the winter or summer months.

■ Recent evidence has indicated that mood disorder may have a genetic and biological component. The inherited form of depression is called endogenous depression, as opposed to environmentally induced depression.

■ Schizophrenic disorders involve a complete breakdown of integrated personality functioning. Emotions become flat and distorted. Thought, language, and behavior become bizarre and disturbed. Delusions and hallucinations often occur. Schizophrenic disorders include the disorganized type, the catatonic type, the paranoid type, the undifferentiated type, and the residual type.

■ Many causes of schizophrenia have been postulated, among them genetic and environmental factors, and biochemical, structural, and anatomical factors. There is evidence to support all these views, indicating that schizophrenia may have many causes.

■ One kind of schizophrenia may be the result of dopamine receptor abnormalities. A large percentage of the schizophrenics tested were found to have significantly more receptors for dopamine than normal people do.

■ Delusional (paranoid) disorders comprise a system of delusions that the psychotic individual firmly believes or accepts. Paranoia is different from paranoid schizophrenia because in paranoia, hallucinations rarely occur and there is no serious disorganization of the personality. Delusional disorders include paranoia and induced psychotic disorder.

■ Personality disorders are a separate axis in DSM-III-R. Although there are many different types of personality disorders, they all share certain qualities. Sufferers are essentially normal and do not exhibit the problems associated with psychosis. The most definitive aspect of a personality disorder is that the individual engages in behavior that disrupts social relationships.

■ One of the most difficult problems faced by clinicians is assessment. Errors in assessment can lead to serious misunderstandings and inappropriate treatment. Psychologist David Rosenhan has shown that relatively normal individuals may be assessed in a biased fashion once they have been labeled as suffering from a psychiatric disorder, such as schizophrenia.

■ Physical diseases may exacerbate behavioral problems, and many behavioral problems may be the result of misdiagnosed or undiagnosed physical ailments.

■ Like physical disorders, mental disorders are subject to misdiagnosis. Diagnostic assessment takes skill, knowledge, and experience. It is anything but simple.

Suggestions for Further Reading

1. Andreasen, N. C. (1984). *The broken brain*. New York: Harper & Row. A fascinating discussion of innovations in the field of psychiatry, including the future of psychiatric research. For the student or general reader.

2. Baur, S. (1988). *Hypochondria: Woeful imaginations*. Berkeley: University of California Press. A book for the layperson about hypochondria and how it affects our culture. Some famous hypochondriacs are discussed, including Charles Darwin and Leo Tolstoy. The final chapter covers treatment.

3. Coleman, J. C., Butcher, J. N., & Carson, R. C. (1988). *Abnormal psychology and modern life* (8th ed.). Glenview, IL: Scott Foresman. A college-level introduction to the field of abnormal psychology. A classic in the field

4. Goodwin, D. W. (1983). *Phobia: The facts*. New York: Oxford University Press. An introduction for the general reader to the subject of phobias, including their definitions, prevalence, and place in history. Treatments for common phobias are also discussed.

5. Kaplan, H. I., & Sadock, B. J. (Eds.) (1989). *Comprehensive textbook of psychiatry/V, Vols. 1 & 2*. Baltimore: Williams & Wilkins. An extremely comprehensive, high-level compendium of what is known about mental disorders. Hundreds of topics include phobic disorders, panic disorders, dissociative disorders, somatoform disorders, depressive disorders, schizophrenias, personality disorders, and many others.

6. Mondimore, F. M. (1990). *Depression: The mood disease*. Baltimore: Johns Hopkins University Press. Written for the general reader. The author describes the causes of and treatments for depression. Also addressed is why so many people who are afflicted refuse to seek help.

7. Rapoport, J. L. (1989). *The boy who couldn't stop washing: The experience and treatment of obsessive–compulsive disorder*. New York: E. P. Dutton. The first popular book on obsessive–compulsive disorder by one of the leading researchers in the field. Very interesting reading.

8. Rosenthal, N. E. (1989). *Seasons of the mind: Why you get the winter blues and what you can do about it*. New York: Bantam Books. A psychobiologist describes the winter variety of seasonal affective disorder, how to know if it is affecting you, and, if so, what you can do about it. Support groups are also listed.

9. Torrey, E. F. (1988). *Surviving schizophrenia: A family manual* (rev. ed.). New York: Harper & Row. A psychiatrist discusses the nature of schizophrenia and describes how it is diagnosed and treated. For the student or general reader.

CHAPTER 16 | Therapy

Prologue

Why Psychologists Study Therapies

The History of Therapy
  The Greek and Roman Era
  The Middle Ages
  The Renaissance
  After the Renaissance

Somatic Therapies
  Psychopharmacological Therapy
  Electroconvulsive Therapy
  Psychosurgery

Psychotherapy
  Psychoanalysis
  Humanistic–Existential Therapies
  Rational–Emotive Therapy
  Gestalt Therapy
  Group Therapies
  Behavior Therapy
  Hypnotherapy
  Brief Therapy

Epilogue: A Bird in the Hand

PROLOGUE

The year is 1803, and you are a journalist. You are visiting Dr. Johann Christian Reil in Germany, and he is taking you on a tour of a mad-house. He wants you to stay a day or two, observe the improvements, and write about them. Reil, a great believer in the Pinel system, is bringing this humanitarian French reform to Germany. "I have done more than reform the hospital," he says. "I have instituted therapies!"

"What kind of therapies?" you ask.

He replies, "Therapies to shock the patients back to reality," and he agrees to show you some of the therapies in practice.

The two of you step through a door into an alleyway leading to a garden on the grounds. Reil continues, "You see, most of these patients have left reality. They prefer their own worlds. It is our job to bring them back to reality, and sometimes we need to shock them to do it. Watch and I'll show you."

At the end of the alley you see an attendant. Next to him is a small cannon of the kind that is loaded with blank charges and used in ceremonies to fire off salutes. The attendant is peeking around the corner into the garden. Suddenly, he pulls back. "Here comes a patient now," he says.

"Good," whispers Reil. "Prepare." As the unsuspecting patient steps into view, the attendant fires the cannon. It explodes with a terrific boom. The patient leaps into the air, screams, turns, and looks in horror. He gasps for breath and runs away. "You see," says Reil. "His reaction was normal. For a moment he was normal. Any one of us might

515

TREPHINING
An ancient procedure in which the skull
was punctured by a sharp instrument so
that evil spirits might escape.

have reacted in the same way. Our hope is that he will stay normal for a while. At best, he will not return to his former disease state."

That night you watch more shock therapy. A sleeping patient is grabbed by two attendants, carried out to the garden, and thrown into an icy pond. Another attendant, dressed in a ghost outfit, makes strange sounds while standing on a table at the foot of a patient's bed. The patients awakes, screaming, horrified to see a ghost hovering over him.

The next evening the entire hospital staff participates in an elaborate tableau. Dressed in costumes and horribly made up, they gather behind a large curtain, props in hand, and freeze in assigned positions. The patients are seated before the curtain, which is abruptly drawn aside. "Tonight," explains Dr. Reil, "they are depicting the resurrection of the dead." One of the staff is being lifted from a coffin, his eyes rolled back. The patients gasp in horror. "A week ago, Reil says, "we did the Last Judgment. Next week we'll do the yawning gates of hell. We go to such lengths for only the most troublesome cases, though. We want to teach them that it's better to be healthy than to stay here and be sick. I like to call this method noninjurious torture" (Roueche, 1980).

As you leave the madhouse, you think that your readers will be pleased to know that Dr. Reil and his staff have things well in hand and are working hard to help the patients recover from their illness.

In this chapter, we will examine different ways to treat mental illness. We'll look at somatic therapies, including modern drug treatments, electroshock therapy, and psychosurgery. We'll also look at psychotherapies, such as Freudian psychoanalysis, behavior therapy, and hypnotherapy.

FIGURE 16.1

In the primitive procedure of trephining, a hole was cut in the skull, ostensibly to allow evil spirits or devils to escape. The procedure was dangerous, and the chance of herorrhage and infection was high. Still, trephining occasionally may have relieved pressure on the brain, caused by bleeding or a tumor, and brought about improvement.

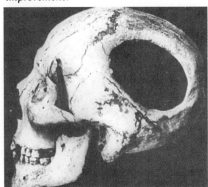

WHY PSYCHOLOGISTS STUDY THERAPIES

When people suffer from behavioral disorders, it's only reasonable that members of society should want to help. As you may have gathered from the Prologue, however, good intentions are not always sufficient. Any help or therapy that is provided should be beneficial. Unproved therapies, despite all the reasoning behind them, may do more harm than good. Psychologists study therapies because rigorous investigation is needed to determine the effectiveness of different therapeutic measures. Once an effective therapy is found, it often furnishes clues to the underlying cause of the disorder. On the other hand, once a therapy has proved ineffective, it can be eliminated so that patients no longer need be subjected to it.

THE HISTORY OF THERAPY

Therapeutic attempts to alleviate mental disorders are perhaps as old as humankind. Half a million years ago, Stone Age people applied "medical" techniques to open the skulls of patients in distress. The procedure was called **trephining** (see Figure 16.1). An opening was cut in the skull by chipping away at it with a sharp stone tool. Mad thoughts or evil spirits were supposed to escape through this opening.

Some trephined skulls show signs of healing around the opening, indicating that the individuals may have survived the procedure and lived to tell the tale.

Before the development and extensive use of the scientific method, it was widely believed that emotional disorders were due to the supernatural—to possessions by spirits, to witchcraft, and to the causes of ancestors. Even in the twentieth century, most primitive societies believe that mental disorders are brought on by supernatural forces (Gillin, 1948).

The Greek and Roman Era (Approximately 400 B.C. to A.D. 476)

From the time of the Greek physician Hippocrates (circa 460 to 377 B.C.) to the time of another Greek physician, Galen (circa A.D. 131 to 201), the Greeks and Romans, more often than not, argued for humane treatment of people who had mental disorders. As the Roman Empire expanded, the Greek and Roman countryside was dotted with hundreds of temples dedicated to the Roman god of medicine and healing, Aesculapius, where people who were troubled could go for rest, sleep, and gentle consultation. At these temples, the belief in supernatural causes persisted, but the priests also considered rational explanations for mental illness such as stress, and their attempts at magical cures did not preclude human treatment and consultation.

Although these cures weren't particularly effective, the ancient Greeks and Romans did document many disorders and separate them into categories that are still, to some degree, considered valid. For example, the ancients differentiated between acute and chronic disorders and between mania and depression, and they distinguished among illusions, delusions, and hallucinations. Some of the temple priests even relied on dream interpretation to draw conclusions about their patients (Mora, 1967).

The Middle Ages (A.D. 476 to 1453)

When the Roman Empire fell, rational efforts to understand mental disorders were largely displaced by reliance on religious demonology. People who suffered from mental disorders often were suspected of having been invaded by a spirit or a devil. Madness was sometimes thought to be the will of God, and therapy for madness was a religious ritual.

Psychotics often became targets of religious persecution. This reached its peak following the shock and horror of the bubonic plague that swept Europe during the fourteenth century. During that time, many people whose behavior was abnormal were burned as witches. These "witches" were convenient scapegoats on whom frightened and ignorant society could blame its troubles. Because the plague had killed half the population in Europe, their "troubles," it should be noted, were worse than anything seen before or since.

One of the major Christian treatises of the Middle Ages was the *Malleus Maleficarum*, the "witch's hammer." This was a book that described the kinds of signs by which a witch could be identified. The signs closely parallel many of the symptoms of behavioral disorders that are known today. The *Malleus Maleficarum* went through 29 editions, the last published in 1669. By then the Renaissance had established a more humane view of mental disorders.

The Renaissance (Approximately 1400 to 1600)

In 1453, Constantinople (now Istanbul) fell to the Turks. This marked the collapse of the Byzantine Empire, which, for 1000 years, had been the repository of Greek and Roman writing and civilization. Byzantine scholars fled to the West, especially

Crude restraining devices were commonly employed in early mental asylums.

to Italy, to escape from the Turks. They brought with them Greek and Roman scientific writings. Slowly, over the next few centuries, Western European scientists, investigators, and explorers built on this wealth of material and information. The understanding that nature was governed by physical laws encouraged a belief that the world could be shaped and controlled.

During the Renaissance, the writings of the early Greeks and Romans reemerged as a powerful force. Invention of the printing press made it possible to distribute these writings widely. Reading the ancient Greek and Latin texts quickly became the mark of the well educated. In fact, early in the twentieth century, it was a rare college that did not offer ancient Greek and Latin as part of its curriculum. Gradually, because of the new knowledge of the physical world, the demonology of the Middle Ages was abandoned in favor of a more rational and scientific approach to mental disorders.

After the Renaissance

The last several centuries have witnessed gradual reform in mental institutions and in mental-health care. Scientists have become aware of possible organic causes of mental disorder as well as of unconscious factors and environmental influences that may affect its course.

MENTAL INSTITUTIONS.   Asylums during the Middle Ages had been used to hold "suspects" and to protect society from the suspects' evil power. During the Renaissance, treatment became more "humane," if only in the sense that people were chained and shackled and treated like animals rather than being systematically tortured or killed. Reform of mental institutions did not really begin until the end of the 1700s.

In 1792, following the onset of the French Revolution, Philippe Pinel was placed in charge of an asylum for the mad in Paris. After repeated requests, Pinel received permission to try an experiment. Had he failed, he might well have been executed by the new revolutionary government. Believing strongly in the revolution, he argued that the inmates were citizens and brothers, not beasts or criminals. Pinel removed their chains and shackles and treated them with kindness and consideration. He placed them in sunny rooms and allowed them to exercise. The noise, the squalor, and the abuse gave way to a more peaceful atmosphere. The reforms were successful.

Pinel's reforms were adopted in many countries, helping to end the nightmare of torture and abuse that had been common practice. As the years passed, more enlightened treatment of patients progressed in piecemeal fashion, often depending on the country in question, with occasional lapses into the old horrors. In general, however, mental institutions in western nations continued to undergo reform throughout the eighteenth and nineteenth centuries. Still, there was little in the way of therapy, and many mental institutions remained barely more than holding pens where even basic care was often wanting.

THE ERA OF PSYCHOLOGY.   The last alleged witch to be publicly murdered by a sanctioned institution died in Switzerland in 1782. As enlightenment spread, the scientific method became the accepted way to advance knowledge, and a new understanding of behavior started to emerge.

By the mid-1800s, physicians and anatomists had begun to realize that abnormal behavior could result from damage to the brain or nervous system. They discovered, for instance, that syphilis bacteria were the cause of an organic psychosis known as **general paresis.**

Proponents of organic theory made a sharp break with demonologists in arguing that abnormal behavior was due to underlying physical causes. By implication, appeal to spirits was unnecessary; rectifying the underlying physical cause was what would lead to a cure. In many people who demonstrated abnormal behavior, however, problems with the brain or nervous system were still not evident. Consequently, additional avenues of interpretation were sought to supplement the organic view.

By the late 1800s, a psychological revolution was beginning. Psychiatrists argued that abnormal behavior might be the result of certain experiences such as stress or unresolved unconscious conflicts. Sigmund Freud, more than anyone else, championed these ideas.

In the United States, too, interest in understanding mental disorders was growing, owing in part to the publication of Clifford Beers's book *A Mind that Found Itself* (1908). Beers described his own emotional breakdown and recovery in a way that made it seem that it could happen to anyone. Even today, the book makes for fascinating reading, but in 1908 it was a shock, and it spurred a number of influential Americans to support financial and political projects aimed at developing therapies for people suffering from mental disorders.

The first half of the twentieth century saw advances in learning theory and humanistic therapies, both of which attempted to explain and treat mental disorders. Then, in the 1950s, medical and biological therapies advanced by great leaps, as scientists found certain drugs that helped to control psychotic disturbances and to alter mood. Our expanding knowledge of drug and brain chemistry and our new techniques for examining the brain indicate that the 1990s may herald another important scientific leap in medical and biological understanding of abnormal behavior and its treatment.

Today, many people are still treated in hospitals or special institutions for the mentally ill. In some of these institutions, the quality of care is excellent. Unfortunately, even in this day and age, too many institutions are places where drugs are misused or overused, and physical violence, rape, unexplained death, and filthy living conditions are commonplace (Weicker, 1987). This is especially the case in nonindustrialized nations.

Furthermore, many people who are in need of help are left to fend for themselves. It is estimated that somewhere between 10 and 40 percent of the homeless

GENERAL PARESIS
Tertiary (third-stage) syphilis (a sexually transmitted disease), which involves an invasion of and severe irreversible damage to the brain caused by the syphilis spirochete (a bacterium). The central nervous system damage often becomes noticeable 15 to 30 years after infection. The clinical picture includes tremors, loss of contact with reality, extreme personality deterioration, increasing paralysis, and delirium. The patient may survive many additional years in this condition. If the illness is diagnosed in time, through the use of a simple blood test (the Wassermann test), the administration of penicillin almost guarantees a cure.

in America are severely mentally ill and in need of psychological help, and between 20 and 30 percent are alcohol or drug abusers also in need of assistance ("Mental Illness," 1990). These percentages are broad because the true size of the problem is difficult to assess. The homeless are not easily counted or studied; many either refuse to be interviewed or deny that they are homeless.

Although institutions that treat the mentally ill vary widely, the best of them typically offer a large number of therapeutic techniques in response to the needs of individual patients. In the next few pages, we'll investigate some of these modern therapies.

SOMATIC THERAPIES

In 1956, I was 9 years old. My father was a physician, a staff resident in psychiatry at Brooklyn State Hospital, and we lived on the fourth floor of the staff house on the hospital grounds. From my window, I could look out across a narrow road to a large, ugly, four-story brick building. The windows of the building were barred, but I could still see into the large rooms. These were the wards for psychotics. My parents explained to me that the building was a hospital and that the people inside it were sick. I soon became accustomed to their bizarre behavior. One woman stood by the window most of the day directing an orchestra that didn't exist. Other patients threw themselves on the floor and got into fights. Others stayed in one place and stared straight ahead for hours on end. The only thing I didn't get used to was the screaming. From sunrise to sunset and all through the night, there was screaming. I heard screaming laughter, screaming crying, screaming curses, screaming poems, screaming fights. It never ended.

That year my father was drafted into the army, and we left the hospital for a 2-year tour of duty in California. In 1959, when we returned, something was very different. The building was still there, the patients were still there, but the screaming was gone. Days would pass by without a single scream from anyone. Attendants seemed to be busier making beds and serving food than rushing to break up fights. The patients took better care of themselves. They seemed to dress better and to be more sociable with one another. More of them had grounds privileges and were out walking about and sitting on the benches.

I didn't know it at the time, but during those 2 years the first of a series of new antipsychotic drugs had arrived; it was called *chlorpromazine*. The changes I was noticing were due to the effects of this drug.

Drug treatment, also known as psychopharmacological therapy, is one kind of **somatic therapy,** meaning a therapy that directly interacts with the body and its chemistry. Other somatic therapies are electroshock and psychosurgery.

Psychopharmacological Therapy

We will look at four classes of drugs that are used therapeutically: antipsychotic drugs, antidepressants, antimanic drugs, and antianxiety drugs. It is important to note that today, federal and state courts have affirmed that involuntary medication violates the rights of individuals who are able to decide for themselves whether they wish treatment. In other words, if you are legally competent, no one can force you to take medication, even if you have been involuntarily committed to a hospital. An exception to this rule is made for jailed offenders who have been found guilty of a crime and are believed to be dangerous to themselves or others. Among people who have been deemed by the courts to be mentally incompetent, the process of involuntary medication often follows what is known as the Jamison – Farabee consent decree, which is based on a legal case in California. The decree requires that outside psychiatrists, not associated with the committing hospital, must review and consent to the medication prescribed by the hospital. Approximately 1 percent of the time, prescriptions made by the hospital are overruled (Hargreaves, Shumway, Knutsen, Weinstein, & Senter, 1987).

NEUROLEPTICS (ANTI-PSYCHOTIC DRUGS).   Today, the most widely used agents to combat psychosis are the **phenothiazines.** They include such drugs as Thorazine, Stelazine, Compazine, and Mellaril. When these drugs first appeared, they were often referred to as the major tranquilizers. Although they do tend to quiet people, the term *tranquilizer* is not as descriptive as *antipsychotic agent* (Denber, 1967), since these drugs, unlike some tranquilizers, also have antipsychotic effects. Also important is the drug Haldol, which is classified separately as an antipsychotic agent. To prevent confusion, it is common to refer to all drugs that have an antipsychotic effect by the general term **neuroleptic.**

Neuroleptics vary in their effectiveness. Sometimes they fail to suppress psychotic symptoms, and sometimes their effects last only a short time. Their use often is accompanied by side effects such as a dry mouth or an uncomfortable feeling. They also can cause dizziness, which has been especially dangerous for elderly patients and has resulted in a number of hip-fracturing falls (Ray, Griffin, Schaffner, Baugh, & Melton, 1987).

Often, especially among people with acute psychoses, the drugs help to alleviate symptoms, to reduce the number of hallucinations, to control the severity of delusions, and to reduce violent or aggressive behavior. The phenothiazines usually have little effect, however, on other psychotic behaviors, such as severe emotional withdrawal or bizarre speech and affect. Haldol may be somewhat more effective in these instances. Medications rarely eliminate problems totally, and they are not considered cures.

To date, the only drug to show dramatic improvements among chronic schizophrenics is Clozapine. It is a fairly recent development and was approved by the Food and Drug Administration in 1989. Clozapine is only given to patients, however, after at least two attempts with other neuroleptics have failed because it can be dangerous, resulting in a potentially fatal blood disease in about 1 percent of those using it.

Because neuroleptics tend to calm patients and make the patients easier to handle, hospital staff sometimes administer them too freely. Overmedication has become a serious problem in many hospitals and institutions (Weicker, 1987). On some wards, all patients are medicated, regardless of their condition. This kind of institutional abuse of medication is not therapy; it is a chemical form of crowd control. Critics have contended that drugs are too often used indiscriminately; that psychiatrists, too busy being administrators, scribble out prescriptions without knowing their patients; and that pharmaceutical companies sometimes act as "pushers," providing massive numbers of free samples and consultations that advocate drugs as the primary mode of therapy. In a sense, these critics argue, chemical shackles have taken the place of the old iron ones.

These kinds of abuses are becoming less common, however. For one thing, it has been found that long-term use of antipsychotic medication can produce a condition called **tardive dyskinesia,** in which body and facial muscles twitch involuntarily. Tardive dyskinesia occurs in about 10 to 20 percent of people taking antipsychotic medication, many of whom might not have needed it (Culliton, 1985). The effects of tardive dyskinesia usually are permanent, and far too often the early symptoms are misdiagnosed as part of the mental disorder or simply go

PHENOTHIAZINES
Antipsychotic drugs, often called the major tranquilizers. These drugs help control and alleviate the symptoms of psychosis.

NEUROLEPTIC
Any of a collection of drugs that are known to have antipsychotic properties.

TARDIVE DYSKINESIA
A severe and relatively permanent neuromuscular reaction, following long-term use of, or a sudden withdrawal from, antipsychotic drugs. The disorder is manifested in involuntary twitching of body and facial muscles.

An often deadly reaction to neuroleptic drugs which occurs in 1–2 percent of patients receiving these drugs. The syndrome often comes quickly and the fatality rate is about 20 percent, owing to kidney or brain damage. The cause of the syndrome is unknown.

ANTIDEPRESSANTS
Drugs used to relieve the symptoms of extreme sadness and withdrawal from life that characterize severe depression. MAO inhibitors and tricyclic drugs are the two main classes of antidepressants.

unrecognized (Weiden, Mann, Haas, Mattson, & Frances, 1987). Tardive dyskinesia may occur because antipsychotic agents somehow affect the dopamine system in the brain (Snyder, 1984). Patients who are treated over a long period with blocking drugs such as the phenothiazines, and then are withdrawn from the drugs, show an extreme hypersensitivity to dopamine.

Due to the dangers of permanent damage from use of the phenothiazines, many professionals are now using these drugs for only short-term intervention to stop sudden flare-ups of psychotic symptoms (Herz, Szymanski, & Simon, 1982). Psychosis, especially schizophrenia, is a condition that tends to vary greatly over time. If the patient and professional staff are aware of the early signs of trouble, the latter can quickly administer neuroleptics for a brief time before things get really bad. The four major signs that a psychosis is about to become worse are (1) hallucinations, (2) increased suspiciousness, (3) sleep disturbances, and (4) excessive anxiety. When these signs appear, immediate short-term use of neuroleptics can be beneficial (Carpenter & Heinrichs, 1983). Some researchers have cautioned, however, that schizophrenia among people who are given low neuroleptic dosages often is more severe than it is among those who have had a full course of neuroleptic treatment (Marder et al., 1987). There appears to be no simple formula for selecting the proper neuroleptic dosage for individual schizophrenics.

Adding to the dangers of neuroleptics is the threat of **neuroleptic malignant syndrome.** The dangerous syndrome develops in roughly 1 percent of individuals treated with neuroleptics, often very quickly, and about 20 percent of those individuals who manifest the syndrome die from brain damage or kidney failure (Pope, Keck, & McElroy, 1986; Sternberg, 1986). The cause of the syndrome is unknown, and it is currently not possible to predict which people will react so adversely to neuroleptics.

ANTIDEPRESSANTS.   **Antidepressants** have sometimes been called mood elevators. At first, there were two main kinds, the tricyclics and the monoamine-oxidase (MAO) inhibitors. Among the tricyclics, the best known probably is Elavil; among the MAO inhibitors, the best known probably is Marplan. These drugs are given for depressions that are relatively severe. Their effectiveness in alleviating depression is somewhat variable, and it often takes 2 to 3 weeks of continuous use before any helpful effects are achieved. Antidepressants usually are more effective against endogenous depression (depression without apparent environmental cause) than against depression that is environmentally induced. Some of these drugs must be monitored carefully, because they can be dangerous. For example, MAO inhibitors must be used in conjunction with strict dietary restrictions; the person must avoid tyramine, a common substance found in many foods such as red wine, sour cream, bananas, liver, eggplant and soy sauce. Consuming tyramine with an MAO inhibitor can cause a deadly rise in blood pressure.

About 30 percent of depressed individuals do not respond to either tricyclics or MAO inhibitors, both of which have been on the market for over 20 years. A considerable number of these individuals and others have been helped by a new, second generation of antidepressants, such as the drug *fluoxetine*, better known by the brand name Prozac. In fact, Prozac may be one of the most successful drugs yet developed to treat a mental disorder. Since its introduction in December 1987, psychiatrists and psychologists have been having so much success with it, and so many fewer side effects have been reported than with previous antidepressants, that Prozac is now the nation's most prescribed antidepressant.

All antidepressants work by bolstering the action of two important neurotransmitters in the brain, serotonin and norepinephrine (Schatzberg, 1987). The tricyclics block reabsorption of these neurotransmitters by the neurons that release them, forcing the neurotransmitter to stay longer in the synapse (see Chapter 2), which increases its effect. The MAO inhibitors interfere with the enzymes that break the neurotransmitter down, which also causes the transmitter to linger in the synapse. Prozac works like the tricyclics, but exclusively on serotonin, which is suspected to play an important role in emotion. Serotonin is also believed to play an important role in the wake–sleep cycle. Interestingly, depressed individuals will often recover from their depressions for a time if they are deprived of sleep, while frequent naps often exacerbate depression (Wu & Bunney, 1990).

Although there have been a very few isolated cases of suicide among those using Prozac, it does appear to offer millions of people a relatively safe way to obtain relief from the misery of depression.

ANTIMANIC DRUGS. Perhaps the number-one drug success story in the history of psychopharmacology is the use of **litium carbonate** to treat bipolar disorder. Lithium carbonate, sold under a number of trade names, such as Lithonate and Lithotabs, often is very effective in resolving manic episodes. It is less effective against swings toward depression, perhaps because depression is a more heterogeneous entity. The following case study discusses how the drug helped Ruth H. to resume a normal life.

PSYCHOPHARMACOLOGICAL THERAPY: THE CASE OF RUTH H.

For nearly 20 years, Ruth H. suffered from bipolar disorder, reaching manic highs and then descending into deep depressions. She had been given antidepressants; she had had psychotherapy and electroshock therapy. Nothing seemed to help. In 1969, she was on the verge of committing suicide when she was given lithium carbonate. She has been able to live normally ever since.

Her bipolar disorder began when she was a child. After college she became an elementary school teacher, but her condition worsened, and she had to quit her job. After the birth of her first child she entered a deep depression. The depression was followed by a manic high and thus the pattern began. It was to characterize a major portion of her life for the next 20 years.

By 1968, her condition had deteriorated; her stable periods came less often. In 1969, she came to the attention of Dr. Ronald Fieve, a psychiatrist who was then developing the new lithium treatment for manic depression. Within a few months after beginning this treatment, Ruth was able to remain stable day after day. She now looks back on those times as bad years. She remembers, "Before I began taking the lithium I'd send out invitations to a party during a manic period and Bob (her husband) would have to cancel it later because I'd be in bed depressed. Now, if I plan a party it will go ahead as scheduled. I know I will be able to function" (Seligmann & Shapiro, 1979, p. 102).

Lithium administration must be monitored very carefully because it is a dangerous drug. The drug is highly toxic, and blood tests must be taken to measure the level of toxicity. Without close monitoring, lithium may promote kidney damage (Samiy & Rosnick, 1987). Monitoring the heart often is advisable as well, since lithium is suspected of causing fatal cardiovascular blockage in some cases (Jaffe, 1977). The probability of someone with bipolar disorder remaining free of a depressive episode after 2 years of lithium treatment is 40–50 percent (Peselow, Dunner, Fieve, & Lautin, 1982).

ANTIANXIETY DRUGS. The antianxiety drugs, collectively known as **benzodiazepines,** often are referred to as minor tranquilizers. Valium, Librium, and Xanax

LITHIUM CARBONATE
A chemical compound that has been found to be effective in controlling the severe mood swings associated with bipolar affective psychosis.

BENZODIAZEPINES
Antianxiety drugs, such as Valium and Librium, that help alleviate anxiety by directly interacting with the neurochemistry of the brain. They are often referred to as minor tranquilizers.

are among the most commonly known. The minor tranquilizers are not used to treat psychotics; they are used to help individuals with problems in which tension or anxiety is a central feature. Among their side effects are drowsiness and lethargy. The minor tranquilizers are toxic and can lead to dependence. For many years Valium was particularly abused and resulted in instances of Valium addiction, in which users experienced convulsions on sudden withdrawal of the drug. Many critics argue that antianxiety drugs are too often dispensed like Band-Aids and that our society is too quick to turn to drugs. Drugs, they say, should be treated with more respect, and should be used more judiciously.

Recently, there has been growing concern about the fact that many patients, perhaps a majority, who use benzodiazepines for a significant length of time experience *rebound anxiety*, in which their anxiety returns with an even greater severity when they stop taking the drug (Chouinard, Labonte, Fontaine, & Annable, 1983). The reason for this rebound is not clear, but it may result from a mechanism similar to the one that causes tardive dyskinesia.

Interestingly, scientists have discovered that antidepressive drugs, such as the tricyclics, often work better against *anxiety* than do the antianxiety drugs (Kahn et al., 1986). No one knows why this is the case, but it most likely has something to do with brain neurotransmitters which probably play a role in anxiety much as they have been found to do in depression. Supporting this idea is the finding that all the drugs known to have an effect against panic disorder augment the action of the neurotransmitter GABA (Breslow et al., 1989).

As neurologists and psychologists gain a deeper understanding of the brain and its neurotransmitters, and as pharmacologists further their knowledge of the interactions between chemistry and biology, we may find answers to such questions and develop new and more effective drug treatments.

Electroconvulsive Therapy

In the 1930s, in a crude practice in common use, schizophrenic patients were given substances that induced full-blown seizures. This treatment was based on a rather flawed theory that epilepsy was a counterforce to schizophrenia (Weiner,

In modern electroconvulsive therapy, muscle relaxants are administered beforehand to prevent the convulsions from tearing ligaments or breaking bones.

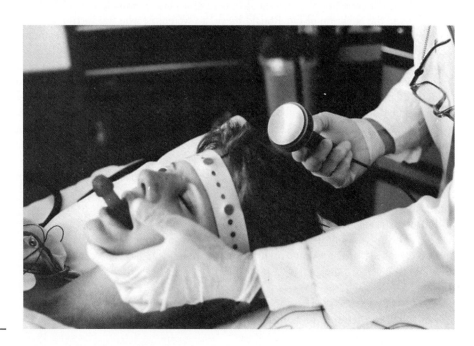

1989). Also in use were some of the "shocking" therapies like the one mentioned in the Prologue, where you met Johann Christian Reil, the German anatomist and neurologist who is credited with the first use of such therapy. In 1938, two Italian clinicians, Ugo Cerletti and Lucio Bini, developed what they believed to be an improvement. They called their new treatment *electroshock*. It consisted of administering an electric shock to the brain, which caused a convulsion, a kind of epileptic seizure. Cerletti and Bini used their treatment for schizophrenia and reported encouraging results.

Modern researchers refer to the treatment as **electroconvulsive therapy,** or **ECT,** and have found it to be most effective against depression and the depressive lows encountered in bipolar disorder (Thompson & Blaine, 1987). Approximately 2 to 3 percent of hospitalized psychiatric patients are treated with ECT (Thompson & Blaine, 1987). In the modern procedure, the patient is injected with a muscle-relaxing drug that prevents the convulsions that used to accompany electroshock therapy and that often resulted in broken bones and torn ligaments. An electrode is placed on each temple and, typically, between 80 and 90 volts are passed through the brain for a fraction of a second. During that time, cerebral functioning is halted—short-circuited. About 5 minutes of unconsciousness usually follow. The beneficial results derived are believed to occur because of that brief halting of cerebral functioning. How or why ECT works has never been clearly understood.

Many clinicians think that ECT is at least harmless, and is beneficial if used in the appropriate circumstances (Janicak et al., 1985; Markowitz, Brown, Sweeney, & Mann, 1987). Its use has not gone unchallenged, however. Memory for recent events is temporarily disrupted by ECT (Squire & Zouzounis, 1986), and some researchers have argued that memories for events in the more distant past may be permanently impaired after multiple ECT treatments (Costello, 1976; Roueche, 1980). Scientists have used sophisticated MRI scans (see Chapter 2) to look for structural damage following the administration of ECT, but no post-treatment structural changes have been observed (Coffey et al., 1988). This, of course, does not prove that ECT is harmless, only that any damage would probably be subtle, perhaps occurring at the biochemical or synaptic level.

The effectiveness of ECT is also hotly debated. ECT is currently accepted as good practice by most clinicians (Weiner, 1989) if the number of treatments are limited, if it is not used as the first choice of treatment, and if it is conducted under medical supervision and with proper care. ECT can even be a life-saver, because some suicidal depressions appear to respond to nothing else.

Psychosurgery

Psychosurgery is "a destruction of some region of the brain in order to alleviate severe, and otherwise intractable, psychiatric disorders" (Valenstein, 1980b, p. 12). Brain surgery undertaken to repair damage resulting from strokes or accidents or to treat tumors or spastic disorders is not considered psychosurgery. Similarly, brain surgery performed to prevent epilepsy is not considered psychosurgery because the problem is neurological.

FRONTAL LOBOTOMIES. In 1935, the Portuguese neurologist Antonio de Egas Moniz developed the technique that was the real beginning of psychosurgery. He had heard that the destruction of prefrontal areas in the brain of monkeys had had a calming effect on some of the more excitable animals, and he decided that destroying the prefrontal lobes in humans might be a way of controlling dangerous or manic patients. Moniz and his colleague Almidia Lima first performed a procedure in which they drilled holes over the portion of the cortex that they wished

ELECTROCONVULSIVE THERAPY (ECT)
Treatment of mental disorders by passing an electric current through the brain for a certain amount of time, which causes a convulsion, a temporary suspension of breathing, and a coma lasting from 5 to 30 minutes. ECT has been found to be most effective against depression and the depressive lows encountered in bipolar disorder.

PSYCHOSURGERY
Brain surgery for the purpose of altering behavior or alleviating mental disorders.

Every Wednesday and Friday for more than a year, a van from the Texas state psychiatric hospital at Austin cruised into downtown Houston, paused in front of the Greyhound bus station and dumped its cargo—about a dozen mental patients just discharged from the hospital. A few on each trip had somebody waiting for them at the terminal. The rest were left with no money and nowhere to go—just an appointment with a mental-health counselor in the next three months. So every Wednesday and Friday, bus-station security guard Ricky Cameron led a group to the Star of Hope mission two blocks away. Three times he called the state hospital to complain; three times he was rebuffed. (Karlen & Burgower, 1985, p. 17).

Figure 16.2 shows a graph of the inpatient population of state and county mental hospitals in the United States over the years. The number of inpatients reached a high in 1955, at a little over 550,000, and then decreased dramatically. By 1975, the inpatient population was below 200,000, a decrease of two-thirds in 20 years; by 1988 it was about 175,000.

The downward trend beginning in about 1956 was due in part to the availability of the new neuroleptic drugs that helped to control psychotic reactions and enabled patients to be released from the institutions and, in theory, rehabilitated in their own communities. This emphasis on **deinstitutionalization** increased at the beginning of the Johnson administration in 1964, when the country undertook a massive effort to reform mental-health systems. Instead of maintaining large state and county institutions, governments intended to deliver services at community mental-health centers

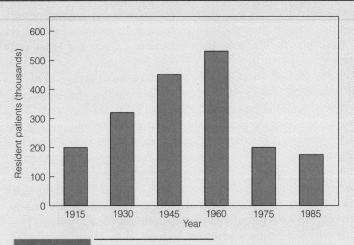

FIGURE 16.2

The inpatient population of state and county mental hospitals from 1900 through 1985. In the last 35 years, the policies of deinstitutionalization and *improved treatment have reduced the inpatient population by more than two-thirds. (Sources: Bassuk & Gerson, 1978; Kiesler, 1982a, 1982b).*

where patients would be close to their families and homes.

The idea behind the change was a good one. Data showed that patients who could live at home and see psychologists or psychiatrists as outpatients were faring much better (Kiesler, 1982a). Deinstitutionalization also helped to improve the institutions for patients who had to remain. In the late 1950s, it had not been uncommon for psychiatrists or psychologists to see each patient for only 15 minutes per month! Patients were crammed into rooms, many of them lying on floors with no place to go and not enough staff to attend to them. When the drastic overcrowding was reduced, psychiatrists and staff could spend more time with individual patients. Many institutions were carpeted and made more attractive, and they offered their patients better services. Unfortunately, the Vietnam war and the inflation that followed ate away at the financial support required by many community mental-health

centers which were supposed to support the deinstitutionalized. These centers were unable to maintain the staff necessary to assist the deinstitutionalized patients in their neighborhoods. Many centers either folded or saved money by staffing with paraprofessionals instead of professionals, and the quality of care declined (Lewis, 1981).

Because of these unfortunate events, as the quote at the beginning of this focus clearly shows, deinstitutionalization often has amounted to no more than "dumping." There also is a great lack of local support to do anything about the problem. As Texas County Judge Jim Scanlan said, when asked why citizens hadn't done something about the dumping of patients at the bus terminal by Austin State Hospital, "The public is more interested in mosquito control" (Karlen & Burgower, 1985, p. 17).

Oddly, although the number of patients hospitalized in state and county hospitals has decreased by more than two-thirds since 1955, the rate of hospital admissions for treatment of mental disorders has increased by 129 percent. This increase is not being handled by state or county mental hospitals, which are the ones counted in Figure 16.2. In fact, 60 percent of all hospital admissions for mental disorders are now being handled by general hospitals—and the majority of these hospitals do not have special psychiatric facilities. The average length of stay for mental disorders in a general hospital is 11.6 days, as opposed to an average 6-month stay in a state or county hospital. The patients who go to general hospitals usually are covered by Medicare, Medicaid, or private insurance plans that generally will not pay unless the patient is hospitalized. The deinstitutionalized patient who needs long-term care and may not directly qualify for insurance or government aid often is left to cope alone in a boardinghouse or on the street. In fact, one researcher has estimated

Even today, many patients lead lonely, isolated lives in institutions where care is inadequate.

that of the 250,000 homeless people in the United States, as many as 50 percent may have psychotic disorders (Bassuk, 1987). In addition, even

though the mentally ill are no more likely to commit crimes than is anyone else (Teplin, 1985), some deinstitutionalized mentally ill do run afoul of law, and are placed in prisons. In this sense, some patients have been *reinstitutionalized,* taken from the mental hospital and put in prison (Teplin, 1984). Furthermore, some communities, most notably New York City, are attempting to reinstitutionalize the mentally ill. This can lead to tricky problems in a free country such as the United States. As you might imagine, it is a little scary that vans can roam the city, pick up people who are acting "strangely," and hold these people against their will on no more than a psychiatrist's say-so. Although many homeless need our help, and some may need to be taken to a hospital, there is a great potential for abuse. In the wrong hands, such efforts could amount to the suspension of civil liberties for anyone deemed "undesirable" by people who have local power.

to destroy, and then poured alcohol into the holes. Moniz first performed this operation on a 63-year-old former prostitute who was suffering from brain syphilis. Two months after the surgery, he reported that she was cured. Obviously, from our modern understanding of medicine, we know that such a surgical procedure could not possibly have cured syphilis (Valenstein, 1980b). Moniz then dispensed with alcohol and refined his procedure by using wire loops to hook onto and sever parts of the brain that he wished to disconnect from the prefrontal cortex. His operation became known as a **frontal lobotomy.** Moniz was a highly respected neurologist and his results gained widespread attention, especially in 1944, when he was partially paralyzed after being shot by one of his lobotomized patients (Valenstein, 1973).

His technique was accepted for a number of reasons. First, it was practiced by surgeons, a highly respected group. Second, alternatives were lacking or limited. Before the discovery of psychopharmacological treatments, most care for psychotics was custodial. Third, in 1949, the Nobel Prize was given to Dr. Moniz for his development of the frontal lobotomy. Approximately 35,000 such operations have been performed in the United States since 1936 when American surgeons W. Freeman and J. Watts refined Moniz's procedure into a rather dramatic and, to some people, horrific operation. It made use of a surgical device shaped somewhat

DEINSTITUTIONALIZATION
The practice, begun in the early 1960s, of releasing mental patients from hospitals and assigning them to community health centers or treating them on an outpatient basis.

FRONTAL LOBOTOMY
A psychosurgical procedure, rarely performed today, in which a sharp instrument is inserted through the orbit of the eye and then slashed back and forth to separate specific nerve fibers connecting one part of the brain to another.

CHAPTER 16
THERAPY

like an ice pick, called a leukotome, which is inserted behind the eyeball and pushed or hammered beyond the orbit of the eye until the point punctures the brain. It is then slashed back and forth, destroying many of the white nerve fibers connecting one part of the brain with the other.

By 1970, however, interest in psychosurgery was beginning to wane. Effective drug treatments had become available for calming the uncontrollable and for treating mania. Moreover, the overall results from most lobotomy procedures had been disappointing. The majority of the patients either were unchanged or seemed to degenerate. Finally, a new attention to human rights and patient rights began to be paid, emphasizing that the patient must be properly informed before consenting to such a procedure. Yet, in the last few years, psychosurgery has once again attracted attention. Part of the renewed interest stems from the fact that modern psychosurgical techniques are safer and result in less gross physical and intellectual impairment than did the older lobotomy procedures. Also, the area of the brain that is destroyed in modern operations is much smaller and more localized (Henn, 1989).

THE EFFECTIVENESS OF MODERN PSYCHOSURGERY. A few years ago, the National Commission for the Protection of Human Subjects of Biomedical and Behavioral Research and the National Institute of Mental Health conducted a pilot study and a follow-up to investigate the current effectiveness of psychosurgery. The study found that a large majority of patients had received adequate preparation beforehand. They had discussed the risks and benefits with their physician and understood what was likely to happen. The investigators judged that the majority had improved markedly. They noted no neurological damage or deficit in any of the cases. However, almost half showed less improvement, from slight benefit to definite worsening (in three cases). Although it had been assumed that psychosurgery was most successful in treating depression, the follow-up studies showed that a favorable or unfavorable outcome was not associated with a particular mental disorder. Based on similar findings, Elliot Valenstein who helped prepare the report for the national commission said,

> The outcome of psychosurgery indicates that between 60 and 90 percent of the patients experience a significant reduction of their most troublesome symptoms. The risk of permanent adverse intellectual, emotional, and physical side effects is reported as minimal. The latter finding stands in sharp contrast to the results from older lobotomy operations (Henn, 1989, p. 1680).

A broad survey of modern psychosurgical outcomes is shown in Table 16.3. As Valenstein noted, the portrayal of post-surgical patients as semianimated veg-

FIGURE 16.3

Survey of psychosurgical outcomes, based on data from four studies. SOURCE: After Henn, 1989.

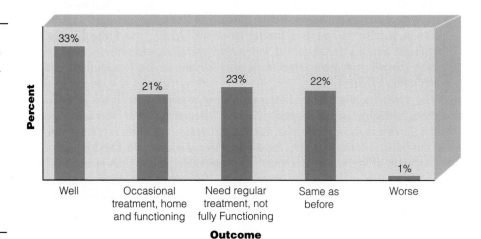

etables, such as commonly depicted in popular novels or films like *One Flew over the Cuckoo's Nest*, was not found to have a parallel in any of the patients studied, although this had sometimes been the fate of psychosurgery patients in the 1930s and 1940s, owing to the more extensive tissue damage inflicted then. The creation of semianimated vegetables is not considered likely to happen with modern psychosurgical techniques (Mirsky & Orzack, 1980).

▌ PSYCHOTHERAPY

Psychotherapy is any noninvasive psychological technique designed to bring about a positive change in someone's behavior, personality, or adjustment. *Noninvasive* means not directly interacting with the body or its chemistry, as somatic therapies do. Psychotherapies can often be just as effective as somatic therapies (Robinson, Berman, & Neimeyer, 1990). Although there are many kinds of psychotherapy, they have certain things in common.

In individual psychotherapy, the patient or client interacts directly with the therapist in a personal and trust-inspiring atmosphere. Concerns are discussed, and problems can be freely aired. Through interaction and the use of psychotherapeutic techniques, the person comes to have a better self-understanding. With this understanding, and supported by the psychotherapeutic encounter, the person may be better able to adjust to the stress and demands of his situation.

The focus varies with the type of psychotherapy. There are two sets of dimensions. In **insight therapy,** the therapist attempts to help the client or patient develop a better understanding of a situation or problem; **action therapy** usually focuses directly on changing a habit or problem that has been troublesome. In **directive therapy,** the therapist actually guides the client, giving instructions and advice; in **nondirective therapy,** primary responsibility for direction of the therapy is placed on the client's shoulders, and the therapist only helps the client to find personal solutions. The dimensions emphasized by different therapies are shown in Figure 16.4.

PSYCHOTHERAPY
A category of methods for treating psychological disorders. The primary technique is conversation between the patient and the therapist.

INSIGHT THERAPY
Psychotherapy that attempts to uncover the deep causes of the patient's or client's difficulty. The therapist tries to guide the individual to self-understanding.

ACTION THERAPY
Psychotherapy in which the therapist helps the patient or client take direct and immediate action to overcome problems through the use of special techniques.

DIRECTIVE THERAPY
Any approach in which the therapist takes an active role and directs the client or patient to confront problems and life situations.

NONDIRECTIVE THERAPY
A therapeutic technique based on humanistic psychology in which the therapist creates a supportive atmosphere so that clients can work out their own problems.

Psychotherapies rely on words to bring about a positive change in behavior, personality, or adjustment.

All the psychotherapies share some common ground. Researcher Jerome Frank (1986) has given perhaps the best description:

> All psychotherapies attempt to combat demoralization by replacing confusion with clarity . . . All schools of psychotherapy [attempt to replace] despair with hope, feelings of incompetence with self-confidence, and isolation with rewarding personal relationships. To bring about these transformations, psychotherapies rely on words . . . (p. 4)

Psychoanalysis

Psychoanalysis is an insight therapy based on the theory and work of Sigmund Freud. Many variations of psychoanalysis have been developed by both Freud's contemporaries and later practitioners.

In psychoanalysis, abnormal behavior is assumed to be the result of unconscious conflicts. By using special techniques, the psychoanalyst hopes to uncover these unconscious conflicts and repressed memories and hence to explain and deal with the motivation behind the abnormal behavior.

The techniques Freud devised for uncovering unconscious conflicts include free association and dream interpretation, which we touched on in earlier chapters. In free association, the patient is asked to say whatever comes to mind, no matter how ridiculous. Freud believed that unconscious desires were always brewing just below the surface; he argued, therefore, that apparently random thoughts might be closely related to the conflict. In dream interpretation, the patient describes the manifest (apparent) content of a dream and works with the analyst to uncover the latent (hidden) meaning. The idea is that unconscious thoughts and conflicts will come to the person during sleep, but that a psychic censor disguises the conflict in the dream so that it appears in symbolic form; the dream must be analyzed before its real content can be understood.

Freud also looked for points of resistance and analyzed those. By **resistance** he meant the patient's tendency to balk at the analyst's attempts to probe certain areas. Freud believed this reaction was a defense of the unconscious against giving up its secrets; resistance was therefore a sign that the therapist was getting close to the problem.

Analysis of **transference** is another important aspect of Freudian psychoanalysis. The patient often transfers feelings she has toward other people onto the analyst and then behaves, for example, as though the analyst were the "rejecting father" or "overbearing mother." In fact, Freud liked to have his patients recline on a couch so that he could sit behind them, removing his physical presence far enough so that transference became easier. He believed that the analyst could gain insight into patients' thought processes by observing how they began to transfer their feelings from their parent or lover to their analyst.

In its original form, Freudian psychoanalysis took a very long time. Freud thought that his therapy sessions should include three to five meetings per week for as long as 6 years.* At the current cost of $100 to $150 an hour, very few people can afford such intensive therapy.

To reduce the expense and the amount of time involved, modern psychoanalysts have developed techniques for shortening the therapy, to perhaps 1 hour per week for a few years. They have modified Freud's theories and procedures in other ways as well. Neo-Freudians, as these modern analysts often are called, sometimes attach as much importance to cultural, social, and interpersonal factors as to the psy-

FIGURE 16.4

Dimensions of psychotherapy. The term insight therapy *generally is reserved for therapies whose goal is an in-depth understanding of the individual's self. Although action therapies sometimes help individuals to develop insight into their problems, the term* action therapy *refers in general to therapeutic attempts to deal directly and immediately with specific difficulties or current problems.*

	DIRECTIVE	NONDIRECTIVE
INSIGHT	Psychoanalysis Gestalt therapy Transactional analysis	Client-centered Existential
ACTION	Rational-emotive therapy Behavior therapy Cognitive restructuring Hypnotherapy	Self-hypnosis Meditation

---

*In Woody Allen's movie *Sleeper*, Woody is placed in suspended animation for 2000 years. When he comes to and finds out how long he's been asleep he remarks, "My analyst was a strict Freudian. If I'd been going to him all this time, I'd almost be cured now."

chosexual aspects of development that Freud emphasized (see Chapter 13). Many of these psychoanalysts have dispensed with the Freudian couch and instead sit face to face with their clients, and they may explore conscious thoughts and desires as much as unconscious motives. Like Freud, however, neo-Freudians believe that insight into the unconscious is the key to resolving mental disorders.

Humanistic–Existential Therapies

Freud believed that people are motivated by instinctive urges toward aggression and death. His view of human beings, shaped by the carnage of the First World War, was essentially pessimistic. The humanistic–existential view, on the other hand, is optimistic; it regards human beings as capable of living rich, fulfilling lives, relatively free of urges toward unhappiness and destruction. The emphasis of therapy is on fulfilling potential, or self-actualizing. Having a sense of belonging, a feeling that one has an important role to play within the society, is also of great importance. Humanistic–existential therapies are considered insight therapies.

CLIENT-CENTERED THERAPY.   Carl Rogers, the humanistic psychologist, was the founder of **client-centered therapy.** Unlike psychoanalysts, who believe that unconscious motives and drives are the crucial aspects of an individual's personality, Rogers argued that conscious thoughts, feelings, and self-concept were primary. Client-centered therapy is a form of nondirective therapy; the therapist refrains from guiding the therapy in any particular direction. The client is considered responsible for his therapy and decides the direction in which the therapy will proceed. (Humanists shun the word *patient* because they do not view their clients as sick.)

The client-centered therapist relies on special techniques. First, the therapist must have an unconditional positive regard for each client. The client is accepted totally. Second, the therapist attempts to make the therapeutic atmosphere personal and forthright; the therapist doesn't hide behind her professional role. Third, the therapist tries to develop genuine empathy for the client.

In nondirective therapy, as we mentioned, the therapist never advises the client or tells him what to do. Instead, the therapist often reflects the thoughts of the client and the client's feelings by repeating or stating in different words what the client has said or by noting the client's emotional state. The following conversation between a client-centered therapist and a client will give you an impression of this technique.

CLIENT: Sometimes, even when there's no good reason to, I tell lies. I don't know why I do.
THERAPIST: (*Remains silent*)
CLIENT: I don't know why; it's as though there was some kind of drive or force that makes me do it.
THERAPIST: And how does this make you feel?
CLIENT: It makes me feel bad. I don't like to think of myself as a liar.
THERAPIST: When you tell lies, then, it makes you uncomfortable.
CLIENT: Yes. I feel better when I don't tell lies, when I don't feel the need to.
THERAPIST: There are times when you don't tell lies, and when that happens it makes you feel better?
CLIENT: Yes, I really like it better when I don't, but I don't seem to have any control.
THERAPIST: Then you have no control?
CLIENT: Well, sometimes I can decide what I want to do, and then I feel better.

A type of psychotherapy developed by Carl Rogers and based on the belief that the client is responsible for his or her own growth and self-actualization. The therapist creates an atmosphere of acceptance, refrains from directing the client, and reflects back to the client what the client has said.

THERAPIST: So sometimes you can control yourself. You can control your life, and this makes you feel better.

CLIENT: Yes, I suppose that's the main thing, to learn to control my own life.

THERAPIST: (*Does not respond, remains silent*)

CLIENT: That's really what I need to do, to control things for myself.

THERAPIST: You want your life to be in your own hands.

The therapist in this exchange unconditionally accepted the client and avoided interjecting her own thoughts and feelings, such as what she thinks about the act of telling a lie. Instead, she helped the client to better understand *his* feelings and thoughts. This technique of active listening can be valuable in getting to know someone much more intimately.

EXISTENTIAL THERAPY.   **Existential therapy** is much like client-centered therapy, except that it emphasizes the idea of free will. Existential therapist Rollo May has argued that people have learned to subordinate their own responsibility and self-image to society's. They begin to feel like nonentities, lost in society. Existential therapists try to restore people's courage, so that they can make choices for themselves and feel in control of the environment rather than controlled by it.

Humanistic and existential therapies are so similar that they often are referred to under one heading, humanistic–existential therapy. Both aim at improving a person's self-concept, developing self-acceptance, and developing the person's belief in his own ability.

Rational–Emotive Therapy

Rational–emotive therapy is an action therapy developed by Albert Ellis. It is based on the assumption that people engage in self-defeating behaviors because they hold onto beliefs that are unrealistic or faulty (Ellis, 1962). Rational–emotive therapy focuses on changing these beliefs by getting clients to understand that the faulty beliefs are the problem. For example, a student who is turned down for medical school and becomes deeply depressed, on the verge of suicide, has obviously developed faulty beliefs about the world and his situation in it. The faulty belief is that getting into medical school is the only possible way to have a happy and fulfilling life and that without it there is no point in living. Rational–emotive therapy attacks the faulty belief, examining the emotional beliefs rationally.

Rational–emotive therapy also is a directive therapy. The therapist directly interacts with the client and points out irrational beliefs and values, noting how they influence the client's thinking. The therapist may even give the client homework to do to help change the belief system. The hope is that eventually the client will learn a new belief system that is rational. The following is an example of an exchange between a rational–emotive therapist and a client. The client is a college student who has never been out on a date. Although he wants to, he's too afraid.

CLIENT: She's really nice, and I'd like to ask her out, but I just don't dare.

THERAPIST: What do you think will happen if she turns you down?

CLIENT: Oh, no. I couldn't bear it. It would be awful.

THERAPIST: If she turned you down it would be awful, and you couldn't bear it. Isn't that a little strong?

CLIENT: But it *would* make me feel awful if she turned me down.

THERAPIST: Why? Does everybody in the world have to like you? If she turns you

Albert Ellis, the founder of rational–emotive therapy.

down, isn't there somebody else you could ask out who would be just as good? Even better? Do you expect everyone in the world to like you?

CLIENT: Well, suppose I asked her out and she turned me down, and I asked somebody else out and she turned me down, too?

THERAPIST: You've got two people turning you down and you haven't even asked anybody out yet. Suppose only one percent of the women in the world like you, and the other ninety-nine percent didn't like you. What would it be like then?

CLIENT: I suppose it would be pretty awful.

THERAPIST: Why? How long could it take you to ask one hundred women out? A couple of weeks? A couple of weeks, and you would have a date. You would finally find someone who liked you. If you liked her, you'd be happy. Who cares what the other ninety-nine think?

CLIENT: I don't know. You make it sound simple.

THERAPIST: Well, it's not that simple, but I think you can make a good beginning by asking her out. Why don't you do that as homework? Go up to her and ask her out.

CLIENT: I don't know.

THERAPIST: What do you have to lose?

CLIENT: Nothing, I guess.

THERAPIST: That's right, nothing. Everybody doesn't have to like you. As long as they're not throwing rocks at you, it's OK. I know a good politician who says he can tell when he reaches a just solution, because that's when everybody hates him. Think about that. Now, you'll ask her out for homework, and you'll record her reactions and how you felt about them, and how things went. Right?

CLIENT: OK, I'll try it, but it might not work.

THERAPIST: And what should you tell yourself if you think it might not work?

CLIENT: That it doesn't matter. That there are other fish in the sea, right?

THERAPIST: Right.

As you can see, this therapy is directive. The therapist is forcefully trying to get the client to see the illogic of his fear, which could lead to a life of isolation. The client needs to understand that the consequences of being rejected are minor, whereas the rewards of tolerating a few rejections for an eventual acceptance could be major.

Rational–emotive therapy follows a particular pattern of therapist–client interaction, as do other therapies. But the pattern isn't rigid. Different psychotherapies don't have sets of strict rules that each therapist must follow without deviating. Therapists are human beings, and they have their own personalities. Ellis's own personality comes through when he discusses his views about people and their ability to maintain good mental health:

> I am still haunted by the reality, however, that humans—and I mean practically all humans—have a strong biological tendency to needlessly and severely disturb themselves and that, to make matters much worse, they are also powerfully predisposed to unconsciously and habitually prolong their mental dysfunctioning and to fight like hell against giving it up. No, I do not think that they are masochistic . . . I think that they are almost always extremely hedonistic but that they continually indulge in short-range rather than long-range hedonism, that they are obsessed with the pleasures of the moment rather than of the future, and that this is the main (though hardly the only) source of their resistance to achieving and maintaining mental health. (Ellis, 1987, p. 365)

And yet, Ellis remains an optimist. As he has said, "I believe that, along with their powerful self-defeating and self-destructive tendencies, humans also have great self-changing and self-actualizing powers" (p. 374).

(a) In group therapy situations, a number of people join together and share experiences and feelings under the supervision of a therapist. (b) In traditional psychoanalysis, the patient rests on a couch out of direct view of the analyst. (c) Most modern therapists sit face to face with their clients.

(a)

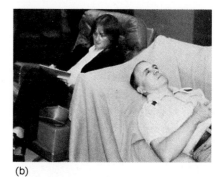

(b)

(c)

533

Gestalt Therapy

Frederick (Fritz) Perls (1893–1970) developed **Gestalt therapy,** an insight therapy. Gestalt therapy is not directly related to Gestalt psychology, which is concerned with perception (see Chapter 4). Instead, Gestalt therapy is based heavily on Freudian psychoanalytic ideas. As a technique, however, it differs from the Freudian approach to therapy.

Gestalt means "whole" in German. Fritz Perls believed that an adequate therapy must take into consideration all the different parts of a person's life. The ultimate goal is to balance and integrate emotion, thought, and action. Through awareness developed during therapy, clients can check imbalances in thoughts, actions, and feelings and can create a whole personality. The therapy is based on helping the client to leave behind unneeded defenses and to release pent-up emotions.

Gestalt therapy emphasizes what is happening here and now rather than what happened in the past or what may happen in the future. It focuses on what exists rather than on what is absent, and on what is real rather than on what is fantasy (Korchin, 1976).

This focus on the present brings the client into contact with his life, feelings, and thoughts as they really exist. The client is required to speak in the first person and to use the active voice. In this way, the client builds a personality centered on himself. For example, the client would be encouraged to say "I am unhappy" (statement from the self) instead of "Anybody could see that this would be upsetting" (referring to others).

Perls often conducted exercises in which clients played out different parts of their personalities. In this way, they developed awareness about their own feelings, actions, and thoughts. The goal of Gestalt therapy is to enable clients to take responsibility for their own actions and, starting with someone who is fragmented into many social roles and who feels helpless, to reintegrate all aspects of the personality into one whole, functioning person.

Group Therapies

One of the earliest group approaches to therapy was developed by J. L. Moreno, a Viennese psychiatrist who coined the term *group psychotherapy*. Moreno's ap-

An encounter group must be managed carefully and only by trained professionals, so it does not get out of hand and turn into a group assault on one individual.

proach, psychodrama, originated at Vienna's Theatre of Spontaneity in 1921. In **psychodrama,** an individual may take the role of a family member and portray or act out that person's behavior and feelings. Therapy comes from the release of pent-up emotions and from insights into the way other people feel and behave.

Group therapy was used infrequently before World War II. After World War II and again after the Korean war, the U.S. Army found that it did not have enough therapists to see all the soldiers who needed help. Consequently, it decided to try pairing more than one soldier with each therapist. The results were surprisingly beneficial. Under the direction of the therapist, members of the therapy group discovered that they often had experiences and insights to share with one another. They were relieved to find that other people had similar problems.

Most therapy groups have 7 to 10 members. Psychiatrists and psychologists frequently see clients individually once per week and also in a group once per week.

SENSITIVITY TRAINING AND ENCOUNTER GROUPS. During **sensitivity training,** participants learn to become sensitive to the needs and feelings of other people and to trust other people. For example, a person taking a "blind" walk is blindfolded and led about, having to trust the one who can see not to guide him into something that might be injurious. Or participants may extend their body awareness by touching one another in a platonic way. They may embrace one another as a way of communicating human affection and a bond. In this way, they achieve heightened sensitivity to others as human beings and a feeling of belonging to the group.

In **encounter groups,** individuals confront one another and attempt to break through defenses and false fronts. Sometimes, the discussions can be painfully honest and difficult to deal with. A qualified therapist should be present to keep things from getting out of hand, since tearing someone down is much easier than building someone up. The purpose of encounter groups is not to cause psychological injury but to help people encounter themselves by having others challenge their assertions and beliefs.

FAMILY THERAPY. In **family therapy,** the family is treated at the same time as a whole unit, the members interacting with one another and the therapist. This allows family relations and conflicts to be observed and examined by the therapist in a professional environment. Therapists who practice family therapy often see each family member in private one-on-one sessions as well.

TRANSACTIONAL ANALYSIS. **Transactional analysis,** originated by Eric Berne, is used with groups or couples. The idea behind transactional analysis is described in Berne's popular book *Games People Play* (1964). Berne argues that partners often create unwritten rules that may satisfy their own needs but get in the way of an honest and healthy relationship. Figure 16.5 shows several transactions. Horizontal transactions from A to A—that is, from adult to adult—indicate a more healthy interaction. In the diagonal transactions, P represents the parent role and C the child role (roles that anyone may adopt). These transactions, in which someone takes the parent role and someone takes the child role, may not be healthy interactions. If social interactions are analyzed to find out what kind of role a person is playing, the rules can be changed to promote mutual satisfaction, and unproductive games can be ended.

Behavior Therapy

Behavior therapy relies on learning theory and the principles of conditioning. Behavior therapy is a radical departure from the psychotherapies we have considered

PSYCHODRAMA
A specialized technique of psychotherapy developed to J. L. Moreno in which patients act out the roles, situations, and fantasies relevant to their personal problems. Psychodrama is usually conducted in front of a small audience of patients.

SENSITIVITY TRAINING
Group sessions conducted for the purpose of developing personal and interpersonal sensitivity to feelings and needs. The feelings among group members are channeled so that members' self-acceptance and growth are enhanced.

ENCOUNTER GROUPS
Therapeutic gatherings in which members of a group, under the guidance of a trained therapist, confront one another during a psychodynamic exchange that uncovers defenses and helps reveal hidden emotions.

FAMILY THERAPY
A general term for a number of therapies that treat the family as a whole. Family therapy is a theoretically neutral term, in that family therapy can be practiced as part of many different psychotherapeutic approaches.

TRANSACTIONAL ANALYSIS
A form of interpersonal therapy originated by Eric Berne based on the interactions of "child," "adult," and "parent" ego states.

BEHAVIOR THERAPY
A group of techniques based on learning principles and used to manipulate an individual's behavior directly to promote adaptive patterns while eliminating maladaptive ones.

FIGURE 16.5

Transactional analysis. Eric Berne describes the interactions shown here as crossed transactions. According to Berne, the personality can express itself as a child (C), adult (A), or parent (P) (roughly equivalent to Freud's concept of id, ego, and superego). Healthy transactions are from adult to adult. It's easy to see that the diagonal transactions are likely to create problems.

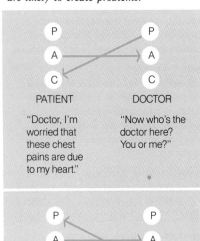

PATIENT   DOCTOR

"Doctor, I'm worried that these chest pains are due to my heart."

"Now who's the doctor here? You or me?"

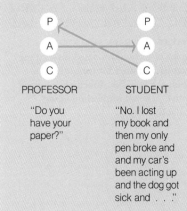

PROFESSOR   STUDENT

"Do you have your paper?"

"No. I lost my book and then my only pen broke and and my car's been acting up and the dog got sick and . . ."

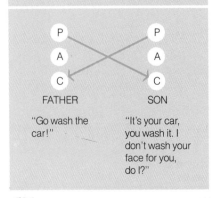

FATHER   SON

"Go wash the car!"

"It's your car, you wash it. I don't wash your face for you, do I?"

to this point. Behavior therapists are not interested in feelings or dreams for purposes of therapy; they concentrate only on observable behaviors and how these behaviors might be changed through conditioning or social learning.

Each therapeutic treatment deals with a specific problem, and terminology such as "passive–aggressive personality disorder" or "somatoform disorder" generally is not used, since behaviorists are concerned with observable behavior rather than with constructs such as personality or mental disorder. Behavior therapies rely on the principles of classical conditioning, operant conditioning, or social learning (described in Chapter 6), or on a combination of all three.

CLASSICAL CONDITIONING THERAPY. You may recall from Chapter 6 that Little Albert's fear of the rat was created through classical conditioning. Behavior therapists may make use of a paradigm of this experience called **aversive conditioning.** Aversive conditioning has been used in many situations; for instance, in attempts to help a person stop smoking or drinking.

To treat alcoholism in this fashion, the client may be taken to a laboratory where a bar, similar to a neighborhood bar, has been set up. The taste and smell of the alcohol and the feeling of the surroundings are all reminiscent of the place where the client usually drinks. However, an unconditioned stimulus, an electric shock, is given as the client is drinking. The favorite drink is continually paired with this painful stimulus. After enough pairings, the alcohol begins to elicit an aversive fear. In one large study using aversive conditioning to treat alcoholism, one-third of the alcoholics were found to be abstaining from drink 3 years after the conditioning (Wiens & Menustik, 1983).

Aversive conditioning can elicit a very strong response. You might think that a human being, well aware of being in a laboratory under special circumstances, would take up old habits at home, safe in the knowledge that a drink wouldn't be accompanied by an electric shock. Yet this kind of therapy often works. It happened to me once. I like pears. A couple of years ago, I was eating a pear and bit right through a large worm. Disgusting, isn't it? To this day I can't eat pears. It doesn't matter that the pears are canned or chopped thoroughly, so that I can tell that there's nothing in them. It doesn't matter that I can look carefully and see no worm holes. The aversive conditioning was very strong. I even hate writing about it.

Unfortunately, the desire to smoke or drink can be so strong that a person may be willing to risk the negative consequences of taking a puff or a sip even after aversive therapy. In this case, the conditioned response may be extinguished quickly, and the person will end up smoking or drinking once again. Aversive conditioning works frequently enough, however, to make the attempt worthwhile.

SYSTEMATIC DESENSITIZATION. Joseph Wolpe at Temple University has developed a therapy that he calls **systematic desensitization.** His therapy is based on the idea of associating a relaxed and tranquil feeling with stimuli that previously caused anxiety. Look at the following hierarchy of fear written by a person who has arachnophobia, an unrealistic fear of spiders. The higher in the hierarchy the item is, the more frightening it is to him.

Rating	Hierarchy Items
1	Planning a picnic.
10	Hearing about the possibility spiders may be nearby.
20	Hearing someone describe an encounter with a spider.
30	Trying to decide how to make sure there are no spiders in the house.
40	Having to do spring cleaning.

50	Thinking that a doctor will make me look at a spider during treatment.
60	Seeing a spider on a wall 20 feet away.
70	Crawling through a cobwebbed attic.
80	Seeing a spider crawl on my arm.
90	Having a large spider crawl on my face.
100	Falling into a dark pit where hundreds of spiders climb on me and try to crawl into my mouth and ears.

During systematic desensitization, the therapist leads the client through each of the steps in the hierarchy by having him lie down or relax in a chair and think carefully about his fear or even act it out. As he thinks about the first item in the hierarchy, he may experience mild anxiety. Eventually, he learns to relax while thinking of this item until, whenever he thinks of it, he feels calm and relaxed. Then the next step in the hierarchy is taken and this, too, is associated with relaxation and tranquility. After completing the hierarchy, fear of the object (in this case spiders) decreases, often dramatically.

OPERANT BEHAVIOR THERAPY.   Therapies based on operant conditioning attempt to end behavior that is inappropriate or to create appropriate behavior that is absent. Table 16.1 outlines the techniques used by operant conditioners in therapy. Because these techniques rely less on talking than do other forms of psychotherapy, they often can be useful with psychotics who have limited verbal ability. For instance, operant conditioning techniques have been used successfully to teach social skills to schizophrenics (Liberman, Mueser, & Wallace, 1986). Most of the time, however, these techniques are used to help alleviate less severe disorders. The following case study describes a typical instance of operant conditioning in therapy.

BEHAVIOR THERAPY: THE CASE OF JENNIFER

Jennifer, a 5-year-old girl, had run away from home three times. Each time, she was brought back by either a policeman or a neighbor and was treated kindly and affec-

AVERSIVE CONDITIONING
An element of behavior therapy in which unacceptable behavior becomes linked with painful stimuli and is thereafter avoided.

SYSTEMATIC DESENSITIZATION
A therapeutic procedure developed by Wolpe in which anxiety-producing stimuli are paired, in a graduated sequence or hierarchy, with a state of physical relaxation until the most difficult situation can be faced without anxiety.

TABLE 16.1 Operant Techniques Used in Behavior Modification

TECHNIQUE	DESCRIPTION
Positive reinforcement	Providing a reinforcer following an appropriate response.
Negative reinforcement	Removing an aversive stimulus following an appropriate response.
Punishment	Providing an aversive stimulus following an inappropriate response.
Extinction	Removing the reinforcer that is maintaining the inappropriate response.
Positive reinforcement of incompatible response	Reinforcing behavior that is incompatible with the inappropriate response (for example, reinforcing telling the truth, which is incompatible with lying).
Time-out from positive reinforcement	Essentially producing boredom following an inappropriate behavior by removing the opportunity to engage in any reinforcing activities for a brief time (usually a few minutes).
Altering response effort	Structuring the environment such that inappropriate responses are more difficult to make or appropriate responses are easier to make.
Token economy	Providing tokens (generalized secondary reinforcers) for appropriate behaviors. Tokens can be redeemed later for specific reinforcers unique to each person's taste.
Response cost	Imposing fines for inappropriate behavior (often used in conjunction with token economies).
Negative practice	Forcing repetition of an inappropriate behavior (for example, yelling) until it finally becomes aversive to engage in the behavior.

tionately. Once she was given candy. She had not been treated in any way at home that might make her want to run away. Instead, she seemed to run away for the attention and affection she found downtown. Downtown was approximately half a mile distant, down a sidewalk that ran along a park and did not cross streets. Jennifer was afraid to cross streets, but that long sidewalk made it easy for her to wander.

A behavior therapy program was set up in which a more important reinforcer, her mother's attention and affection, was provided to Jennifer for staying at home—a behavior that was incompatible with running away. At first, the reinforcement was given on a "rich" schedule. Jennifer was reinforced every 3 minutes by her mother's hugs and praise if she stayed home. Obviously, Jennifer wouldn't have had time to go far in 3 minutes.

This schedule of reinforcement could not be maintained indefinitely, however, because it was too difficult for Jennifer's mother. So, a slightly "leaner" schedule was begun, on which Jennifer was reinforced every 5 minutes; then every 10 minutes; later every 1/2 hour. It became almost a game with Jennifer, and every 1/2 hour she would come running in to let her mother know it was time to hug and kiss.

Eventually, the schedule was reduced even more, and the mother rewarded Jennifer only hourly. At that point, a variable schedule of reinforcement, rather than a fixed schedule, was put into effect, so that Jennifer would not realize that she could run away and still get back in time for her reward. Her mother reinforced her on the average every 2 hours, but the time of the reinforcement was unpredictable. Finally, the mother needed to reinforce Jennifer only once in the morning and once in the evening. Jennifer never ran away again.

Token economies are a popular means of modifying behavior. This technique uses tokens, such as poker chips, as currency. In institutions for delinquent children and in state hospitals, token economies have been found to be effective in controlling and developing behaviors. The tokens function as conditioned reinforcers. They can be given following appropriate behavior or withdrawn following inappropriate behavior. They can be useful both for initiating and for terminating behavior. The tokens can later be traded in for items that are of value. Once

Through modeling and counterconditioning, Albert Bandura was able to help those with snake phobia overcome their fears.

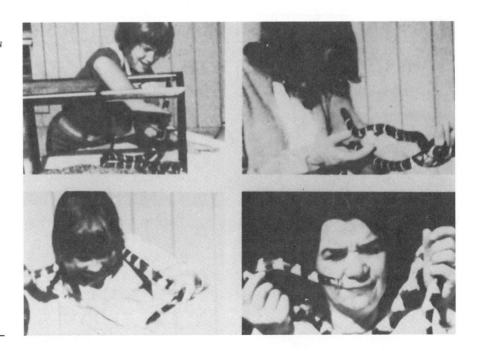

behaviors are established, praise and other social reinforcers can take the place of tokens.

Sometimes **behavior contracts** are set up between two parties, each one agreeing to a behavior desired by the other. A husband, for example, may promise to play tennis once a week with his wife if she in return promises to go bowling with him.

Behavior therapies also may be based on social learning principles. In social learning, models are used to demonstrate desired behaviors or responses. Modeling has been found to be a very effective way of producing behavior changes.

Considering John Watson's denial of the mind as an area of study, behaviorism represented a radical break from other forms of psychology. Nonetheless, many psychologists and psychiatrists recommend using behavior therapy in conjunction with other forms of psychotherapy (Goisman, 1985). In practice, behavior therapy isn't often used by itself (Farkas, 1980).

COGNITIVE BEHAVIOR THERAPY.   **Cognitive behavior therapy,** or cognitive restructuring, is a therapeutic treatment in which a client is helped to obtain information about himself through a series of unbiased encounters that can disprove false beliefs. The client is encouraged to explore, with the therapist, beliefs, attitudes, and expectations in order to form hypotheses that can be tested. In this way, the client can go out to test expectations experimentally and through the experiences can come to a new cognitive understanding of his world.

Less difficult tasks usually are assigned first, and more difficult ones later. Occasionally, the client's activities for the entire day will be planned moment by moment. These experiments help the client to disconfirm erroneous assumptions about the world by testing them.

Cognitive behavior therapy seems to be most effective with clients who selectively perceive their world as harmless or dangerous, ignoring any evidence to the contrary; who overgeneralize based on a few limited examples (for instance, because they fail at one thing, they decide they are totally worthless); who magnify unhappy events and blow them out of proportion (for instance, they believe that the loss of a job is the end of the world); and who engage in absolutist thinking (they always see things as black or white, good or bad, never as gray or mixed) (Hollon & Beck, 1978; Beck, Rush, Shaw, & Emery, 1979; Meichenbaum, 1977).

In Table 16.2 are a number of "coping statements" that the client can rehearse as a means of restructuring cognitive understanding and bolstering herself against

BEHAVIOR CONTRACTS
A technique often used in behavior, group, or family therapy, in which a contract or bargain is struck. The client promises to engage in a certain behavior in return for a particular behavior from another.

COGNITIVE BEHAVIOR THERAPY
A behavior therapy technique in which the client's beliefs, attitudes, and expectations are tested in reality in a formal and structured way.

TABLE 16.2 Coping Statements for Dealing with Stress

SITUATIONAL STAGE	COPING STATEMENTS
Preparing for stress	What is the task? You can work out a way to handle it.
Facing the stress	You can deal with your fear. Being tense is good; it makes you alert. Take a deep breath. Go one step at a time.
Dealing with being overwhelmed	Your fear will rise, but you can manage it. If you're too frightened, just pause. Keep in mind what to do this moment.
Reinforcing self	It's not as bad as you expected. You succeeded! You can control your thoughts.

SOURCE: After Meichenbaum, 1977.

HYPNOTHERAPY
Hypnosis used for therapeutic purposes in
cases of pain control or behavior pathology.
The method has been used in therapy,
dentistry, surgery, and childbirth.

stress or depression. These statements are not simply slogans; their validity has been demonstrated to the client during experimental explorations of each statement in real situations. In some forms of cognitive behavior therapy, the statements can even be organized and presented by a computer without the need of a therapist! Such computer programs can lead, say, depressed individuals through a series of explorations of their beliefs, and have been found to be as effective at reducing minor episodes of depression as are human therapists (Selmi, Klein, Greist, Sorrell, & Erdman, 1990).

Like the other therapies that we have discussed so far, cognitive behavior therapy is not a rigid system, but rather a general framework that has certain aspects or qualities that distinguishes it from other therapies. In fact, there are at least 22 popular variations of cognitive behavior therapy in current practice (Goldfried, Greenberg, & Marmar, 1990).

Hypnotherapy

Many modern psychotherapists rely on hypnosis for therapeutic intervention. They use **hypnotherapy** in a number of important ways, for instance, to make a recollection of a past emotion or memory seem more vivid (Nash, Johnson, & Tipton, 1979).

Hypnosis has been beneficial in conjunction with behavior therapy. Some behavior therapists have hypnotized clients during systematic desensitization to help the clients to relax more deeply and to imagine more vividly the feared object or situation in their hierarchy (Lazarus, 1976).

One of the oldest applications of hypnosis is in pain control. Hypnosis has been used successfully to control pain during major surgery and childbirth. Dentists and plastic surgeons have found it an effective substitute for drugs in carrying out procedures (Kroger, 1977). Hypnosis can even help to reduce and control chronic severe pain (Hilgard & Hilgard, 1975). EEG recordings (see Chapter 5) indicate that hypnotized subjects who are successful at managing pain actually alter their pain perception at the neurological level, rather than simply reporting that they have less pain because they know that they have been hypnotized (Spiegel, Bierre, & Rootenberg, 1989).

People with physical disorders, especially those associated with anxiety and stress, also may respond to hypnosis. This is especially true of people with disorders such as dermatitis, asthma, and rash, which can be made worse by stress and anxiety (DePiano & Salzberg, 1979).

Hypnosis has been effective in the treatment of dissociative disorders such as amnesia, fugue, and multiple personality. Under hypnosis, people sometimes can recall events more easily, which may help them to overcome the amnesia or fugue state or make multiple personalities more accessible.

Some researchers have suggested that hypnosis can affect dissociative disorders for two reasons. First, it can reduce the anxiety that interferes with recall. Second, mood-dependent and other memories become easier to retrieve through use of the vivid imagery and moods that hypnosis can create. Hypnosis also can be used to alter or reduce anxiety. In the following case study, hypnosis was used to alter a terrifying dream.

HYPNOTHERAPY: THE CASE OF MR. B

The chief complaint of Mr. B. [was] a recurring traumatic dream [dating from his time as a combat soldier]. . . . Mr. B dreamt of being shot by a Viet Cong sniper. He would hear the shot and see the bullet coming to kill him, awakening just before

In 1989, the American Psychiatric Association published the long-awaited 3000 page, four-volume *Treatments of Psychiatric Disorders.* It was meant to accompany DSM-III-R, and it outlined what experts suggest to be the best current therapeutic interventions for each of the mental disorders. The book discusses the characteristics of each mental condition, then notes which part of the problem is best treated by drugs, suggesting dosage, and which part is most amenable to psychotherapy, stating which psychotherapy is best, and how long the treatment should last. The book also lists alternative treatments and takes into consideration individual factors such as the patient's age and personality. In its conception, it seemed like a fine idea—a compendium of treatments telling how and when to apply them. Similar books dealing with physical diseases have been very successful. But was it too soon to try something like this for mental illness and its therapies? Was mental illness too poorly defined and were its therapies still too much of an art and too little of a science? Perhaps so, because the outcry was immediate.

Opponents straightaway expressed concerns that the manual would curb the development of new or alternative kinds of care, pointing out that if it had been written 30 years ago, it would have inhibited practitioners from trying anything on their patients other than ECT or psychosurgery. Psychologists, who are not M.D.s and therefore cannot write prescriptions, were especially concerned that there was so much reliance on psychopharmacology. They pointed out that much research has shown psychotherapy to be often as effective as somatic therapies.

Other fears were expressed. Among them were the worries that rigid instructors might treat the book as gospel or that reliance on the book might lead to problems in the courtroom. For example, if a therapist wanted to treat depression in a way *other* than those listed as "best" by the book, should she be concerned? If her client committed suicide, would she now be liable for malpractice because she had not followed the advice of the "experts"? Such a concern might keep a therapist who had considerable adeptness in, for instance, transactional analysis, from using her skill with that technique to treat depression simply because "the book" didn't list that as one of her choices. This problem was especially irksome for many practitioners be-

cause therapy is still so much of an art that it often appears to defy scientific analysis. In the words of one professional, "[The book makes] a rather arrogant presumption that a consensus opinion by psychiatrists is tantamount to what the 'experts say' and should be considered *the* standard for mental health treatment" ("Treatment Book," 1989, p. 19).

The treatment guide is currently used by many practitioners, but the controversy continues. The American Psychiatric Association has now included a disclaimer stating that the book was not officially endorsed by the association itself, but merely by the association's task force who had assembled it.

This controversy shows in the clearest way how therapy for the mentally ill is an evolving process, how little we really know about it, and how far we have to go. Once we have mastered the formidable challenge of mental illness, perhaps centuries from now, such a book will be on every practitioner's shelf, and there will be little controversy because we will finally know how best to treat such disorders. Until then, trained professionals—practicing artists, researchers, and experimenters—will be rewriting the book daily.

the bullet was going to strike his head. He had dreamt this nearly nightly for ten years. In the alteration of the dream, it was allowed to proceed in hypnotic trance until the bullet became visible about 50 yards away. At this point the bullet was transformed into a whipped cream pie, much in the manner of the old-time silent movies. The pie was then slowed and returned to the Viet Cong sniper. It struck the sniper in the face, so startling him that he fell from the tree. The event was so improbable that the Viet Cong and Mr. B broke into outrageous laughter and walked off together in disbelief. . . . Mr. B rehearsed the substituted dream at home with self-hypnosis. The revised dream was dreamt at night several times, replacing the traumatic dream. After this replacement the traumatic dream disappeared. It reappeared for two periods subsequently in the next 2 years but was again removed with a rehearsal of the altered dream (Eichelman, 1985, p. 113)

CHAPTER 16
THERAPY

Does psychotherapy work? In 1952, H. J. Eysenck assessed the effectiveness of psychoanalytic and nonpsychoanalytic psychotherapy. He did an exhaustive review of the literature and examined over 7000 cases; his conclusion was that the data failed to prove that psychotherapy of any kind facilitated recovery in patients with abnormal behavior. Eysenck argued that any apparent success was simply due to the fact that psychotherapy took so much time that spontaneous remission eventually occurred. He found that roughly two-thirds of any group of people with behavioral problems will recover or improve markedly within 2 years whether or not they receive psychotherapy. Eysenck has continued to present interesting arguments that psychotherapy is, in general, no better than no therapy (with the exception of behavior therapy, which, Eysenck argues, is often effective) (Eysenck, 1985).

Since Eysenck's findings were published, a number of studies have criticized his assumptions, especially his finding that two-thirds of people with behavioral problems will improve even without professional help (Bergin, 1971). Still, many researchers contend that the issue has not been settled and that no definite proof has been presented to show that psychotherapies are effective (Erwin, 1980).

Measuring the effectiveness of psychotherapy tends to be difficult, because the relationship between client and therapist is so complex that it's hard to observe what is or is not a beneficial change and whether any change that does take place is due to the therapy (Sacks, Carpenter, & Richmond, 1975). Researchers can make only a few unequivocal statements about psychotherapy. For example, the clients or patients who are most likely to improve are those who are the least maladjusted, have the shortest history of symptoms or of maladaptive behavior when they begin therapy (Shapiro, Struening, Shapiro, & Barten, 1976), are most motivated to change their behavior (Horowitz, Marmar, Weiss, DeWitt, & Rosenbaum, 1984), and come from the middle or upper class (Derogatis, Yevzeroff, & Wittelsberger, 1975). The therapists who are most likely to have successful results are the most experienced (Brenner & Howard, 1976). Studies of other characteristics of therapists, such as personal adjustment, warmth, empathy, genuineness, or professional status, do not show an obvious or clear relationship to effectiveness as therapists (Gomes-Schwartz, Hadley, & Strupp, 1978).

Eysenck's argument that psychotherapy and no therapy are equally effective depends on a particular definition of improvement and spontaneous remission. Using different criteria, other investigators have been able to argue that 83 percent of people who receive psychotherapy improve, while only 30 percent who receive no therapy improve (Bergin, 1971). On the other hand, a 30-year follow-up study of over 500 clients who began therapy in childhood found uniformly negative results when that group was compared with a comparable *untreated* group of children. The researcher suggested that the clients who received therapy had become too dependant on their therapists and saw themselves as people who always "need help" (McCord, 1977).

One of the most extensive analyses of the effectiveness of psychotherapy was conducted by Mary Smith and Gene Glass in 1977. They devised a statistical method that combined the results of 400 studies that had addressed the question of the effectiveness of psychotherapy. The 400 studies used may different criteria for assessing improvement. Smith and Glass found support for the effectiveness of psychotherapy (see Table 16.3). They concluded that all the psychotherapeutic treatments were more effective than was nontreatment, with small differences among the therapies; and group therapy was as effective as individual therapy.

Since the publication of Smith and Glass's findings, this research has been carefully scrutinized. Smith and Glass's complex statistical analysis has been supported (Landman & Dawes, 1982), but some have argued that the criterion for which studies to include (that is, which studies were well controlled and which were not) was not well defined (Orwin & Cordray, 1984). The fact that psychologists are continuing to debate whether psychotherapy works is a surprise to most students.

If psychotherapy did work optimally, there would be a specific remedy for each form of mental disorder. But this is not the case. Therapies are diverse, and sometimes they have limited success. Depending on the circumstances, some therapies may be more appropriate than others are (Pilkonis, Imber, Lewis, & Rubinsky, 1984). For instance, behavior modification has been found to be extremely useful in treating certain phobias. Often a psychologist uses a combination of therapies (say, drugs and behavioral therapy) and hopes for benefits from each. Such an interdisciplinary approach has raised hopes that psychotherapy will prove to be of greater benefit in the future.

Perhaps psychotherapy would be more effective if therapist and client always achieved rapport. Many therapists have noticed that they are personally more effective with one kind of client than with another. Good therapists often are viewed as artists more than as scientists. The exceptional ones frequently find it difficult to describe why they are successful or to teach other people to do as well as they. Supporting this assertion is the finding by researchers that *who* performs the therapy is often much more important than the *type* of therapy that is performed (Luborsky et al., 1986).

Research concerning the value of psychotherapy is growing, and scientific debate about whether it is *generally* effective continues.

FOR CRITICAL ANALYSIS

1. Observers once recorded Albert Ellis during therapy sessions to see whether he actually used the rational–emotive techniques of the therapy that he founded. The results indicated that he did use these techniques, but also that he varied his approach considerably from client to client based on his assessment of the client

---

TABLE 16.3 Effectiveness of Different Psychotherapies

TYPE OF THERAPY	MEDIAN TREATED PERSON'S PERCENTILE STATUS IN CONTROL GROUP*
Psychoanalytic	72
Transactional analysis	72
Rational—emotive	78
Gestalt	60
Client-centered	74
Systematic desensitization	82
Behavior modification	78

*The scores represent the median treated person's percentile status as measured against untreated control subjects. If there were no effect, the median treated person's percentile score would be 50. If there were a negative effect, the expected percentile score would be less than 50. In this study, the average treated person was better off than approximately 75 percent of the untreated controls.

SOURCE: Adapted from Smith & Glass, 1977, p. 756.

BRIEF INDIVIDUAL PSYCHOTHERAPIES
Any one-on-one psychotherapy usually
lasting no more than 30 sessions, which is
designed to provide limited support when
lack of time or money prevent regular
therapeutic intervention.

(Becker & Rosenfeld, 1976). Consider also that many therapists, while able to teach the basic principles behind what they do, are often not able to teach others how to obtain the same results that they themselves do. In what way do these data argue that much of therapy is an art and not a science? In this context, what are the differences between art and science?

2. As is the case with those who learn to play the violin, some people quickly learn how to be good therapists, while others never learn how even after much practice. Therapy and violin can both be taught as sciences. To master each, there are certain rules and procedures that must be followed. Why, then, are great therapists and great violinists considered to be artists? Why can't they teach others to be just as good as they are?

Brief Therapy

In recent years, a number of abbreviated versions of the major therapies have appeared and have gained in popularity (Goldfried, Greenberg, & Marmar, 1990). These versions go by the collective name of **brief individual psychotherapies.** Brief therapy usually lasts between one and 30 sessions. Generally, the goal of brief therapy is to provide support, to reduce a person's weaknesses while strengthening his defenses, and to do so with a minimum expenditure of money and time. This latter consideration has become especially important because many health insurance companies have recently changed their coverage by limiting the number of psychotherapy sessions for which they will pay (DeAngelis, 1987).

The development of brief therapy has led to considerable controversy. Some people believe that brief therapy is too short to be effective and therefore is an unethical practice, "while others worry if they don't hurry up and learn the techniques, they'll be forced out of business" (DeAngelis, 1987, p. 34). In general, more research will be required before the value of brief therapy can be well established (Ursano & Hales, 1986).

EPILOGUE: A BIRD IN THE HAND

Psychologists know that therapies sometimes can be effective in treating and eliminating certain kinds of behavior disorders. In the following account, a phobia is eliminated through behavior therapy.

In Chapter 15, you met Judy R., who had a bird phobia. She had come to the counseling center at a university because her unrealistic terror of birds was interfering with her life and her plans to become a teacher. The counselors at the center decided to use behavior therapy to help Judy unlearn her fear of birds.

First, the therapists set up a 35-step hierarchy for systematic desensitization, similar to the hierarchy described in this chapter. They decided that Judy would act out the hierarchy rather than just imagine it, since acting something out while learning to be calm is more effective.

A 27-year-old woman, the same age as Judy, served as a model. Judy watched as the model touched bird pictures, the first behavior that Judy was to imitate. The therapy proceeded slowly, with Judy first placing her hand on the model's hand and then touching the pictures by herself. A little later, the same procedure was used with feathers.

Then a stuffed bird from a museum was brought in. First the model and Judy looked at the stuffed bird from a distance of several feet, and then they slowly approached it. The model touched the bird first and then Judy touched it while wearing gloves. Later she removed the gloves. The therapy never moved fast enough to cause Judy much anxiety. Everything was done slowly and gently, and at each step Judy was allowed time to be sure she was calm and comfortable before the next step was taken.

Next, Judy took bird specimens home and kept them in a place where she would see them often. Then came a session in which she was trained to fight off birds, should any happen to fly at her, by waving her arms and shouting. These defensive measures were first modeled for Judy, and then Judy tried them on a group of live pigeons. She dispersed the birds without feeling afraid.

Following this success, Judy went to a live-poultry store and watched the model touch hundreds of small chicks. Next, Judy went to the zoo and spent time at the duck pond, the aviary, and the cages for large birds. Later, she was able to go with her model around a bird-populated city mall. Finally, Judy watched the model walk through a large closed aviary at the zoo where people could walk surrounded by hundreds of birds. Judy accompanied the model through the aviary, and then she was able to walk through on her own.

The therapists also employed cognitive restructuring. Judy was given many factual bits of information about birds that she was able to test on her own by experiencing birds firsthand. For example, Judy was informed that birds almost never fly at people except by accident, a hypothesis she was able to test firsthand on her walk through the aviary.

Before treatment, Judy was unable to get farther than about halfway up her hierarchy with a minimum amount of anxiety. After treatment, Judy no longer showed fear of birds (although she admitted that an uncaged eagle might still make her a little nervous). She did not go out of her way to avoid birds. She often drove with her car windows down. She went for walks on the beach and went sunbathing. She even wore a blouse imprinted with vivid pictures of birds. Eventually, Judy moved to a new apartment that was on a waterfront populated by seagulls. A follow-up 12 months later showed that her bird phobia had not returned (Lassen & McConnell, 1977).

SUMMARY

■ Therapeutic attempts to alleviate mental disorders are perhaps as old as humankind. Stone Age people resorted to trephining to help evil spirits escape the mind.

■ During the Greek and Roman eras, treatment of mental disorders often was combined with attempts to bring about magical cures.

- During the Middle Ages, a rational view of mental disorders was replaced by religious demonology.
- Early reforms of mental institutions followed the French Revolution and continued through the eighteenth and nineteenth centuries. Today, many people are still treated in hospitals or in special institutions for the mentally ill.
- By the mid-1800s, physicians began to realize that abnormal behavior could result from damage to the brain and nervous system.
- Somatic therapies directly interact with the body and its chemistry. They include psychopharmacological, electroconvulsive, and psychosurgical procedures.
- There are four major classes of drugs used in psychopharmacology: antipsychotic drugs, antidepressants, antimanic drugs, and antianxiety drugs.
- Tardive dyskinesia, an involuntary twitching of the body or facial muscles, can result from long-term use of antipsychotic drugs.
- Electroconvulsive therapy consists of an 80- to 90-volt electric shock administered to the brain, causing a convulsion. It has been used to treat depression and other disorders, but how it works is unknown, and its use is controversial.
- Psychosurgery is the destruction of a region of the brain for the purpose of alleviating severe psychiatric disorders. The frontal lobotomy, made popular in the 1930s and 1940s, has been criticized for causing irreparable injury to the brain and producing only mixed results. Modern psychosurgical techniques are less dangerous and destroy less tissue.
- Deinstitutionalization is the practice in which mental patients are assigned to community mental health centers or seen on an outpatient basis. Because of inadequate funding of the program, however, patients may not be given adequate care outside of the institution.
- Psychotherapy is a noninvasive psychological therapy designed to bring about a positive change in someone's behavior, personality, or adjustment. Psychotherapy can be divided into insight therapies, which emphasize developing awareness and understanding, and action therapies, which focus directly on changing a habit or problem. Psychotherapies can be further divided into directive therapies, in which the therapist guides the client, and nondirective therapies, in which the client is primarily responsible for direction of the therapy.
- Psychoanalysis is a therapy based on the work of Sigmund Freud. Psychoanalysts assume that abnormal behavior is the result of unconscious conflicts. They use various techniques, including free association and dream interpretation, to uncover these unconscious conflicts.
- In humanistic–existential therapies, people are considered capable of living rich and satisfying lives. The emphasis is on fulfilling their potential, or self-actualizing.
- Carl Rogers developed a client-centered therapy in which the therapist refrains from guiding the therapy but provides unconditional positive regard for the client. The client is responsible for the direction the therapy takes.
- Existential therapists argue that people must learn to accept responsibility, to make choices for themselves, and to control their environment rather than allowing it to control them.
- Rational–emotive therapy is an action therapy based on the assumption that people engage in self-defeating behaviors because they hang on to beliefs that are unrealistic or faulty.
- Gestalt therapy is an insight therapy based heavily on Freudian psychoanalytic ideas. The ultimate goal of Gestalt therapy is to balance and integrate emotion, thought, and action.
- One of the earliest group therapies was psychodrama. Following World War II, group therapy became more popular. Many therapists have found that group therapy is beneficial.
- During sensitivity training, participants learn to become sensitive to the needs and feelings of other people and to trust other people.
- In encounter groups, individuals confront one another in an attempt to break through defenses and false fronts.
- In family therapy, the family is treated together as a whole unit.
- Behavior therapy relies on learning theory and the principles of conditioning. Each therapeutic treatment deals with a specific problem. Important techniques include aversive conditioning, systematic desensitization, operant techniques, token economies, behavior contracts, and social modeling.
- Cognitive behavior therapy is a treatment in which the client is helped to obtain information about himself through a series of unbiased encounters that disprove false thoughts and beliefs.
- Modern clinicians use hypnotherapy in a number of important ways. Hypnotherapy can intensify the memory of past emotions and events, can be used in conjunction with behavior therapy, is useful in controlling pain, and is effective for the treatment of dissociative disorders.
- Researchers are divided on whether psychotherapy is effective. Most research indicates that it is effective to some degree.

SUGGESTIONS FOR FURTHER READING

1. Beers, C. (1908). *A mind that found itself.* New York: Longmans, Green. A classic account of one man's descent into psychosis and his rehabilitation early in this century. Contains one of the earliest descriptions of the mental institution as a place where occasional recovery is achieved despite inconsistent and in some cases inhumane treatment.
2. Gorman, J. M. (1990). *The essential guide to psychiatric drugs.* New York: St. Martin's Press. Dosages, uses, and side

effects of all psychiatric drugs. Includes advice on choosing a psychiatrist.

3. Kaplan, H. I., & Sadock, B. J. (Eds.). (1989). *Comprehensive textbook of psychiatry/V, Vols. 1 & 2*. Baltimore: Williams & Wilkins. An extremely comprehensive, high-level compendium of what is known about mental disorders and how to treat them. Hundreds of topics include psychosurgery, electroconvulsive therapy, psychopharmacology, psychotherapy, and many others.

4. Papolos, D. F., & Papolos, J., (1988). *Overcoming depression*. New York: Harper & Row. An exploration of depression and mania for the general reader. Includes a discussion of the medications used to treat mood disorders, their benefits and complications.

5. Valenstein, E. S. (1987). *Great and desperate cures: The rise and decline of psychosurgery and other radical treatments for mental illness*. New York: Basic Books. For the student, general reader, or professional, a discussion of the history of, current practices in, and controversies surrounding psychosurgery and other controversial therapies for mental illness.

6. Zilbergeld, B. (1983). *The shrinking of America: Myths of psychological change*. Boston: Little, Brown. A book that debunks many of the popular misconceptions people have about the nature of psychotherapy and its effectiveness. Written by a clinical psychologist who draws on his own years as a practicing therapist and on others' research in the area.

UNIT 5 | Relating to One Another

Chapter 17
Social Behavior

Prologue
Why Psychologists Study Social Behavior
Interpersonal Influence
Helping Others
Cooperation and Competition
The Influence of Groups
Prejudice and Discrimination
Social Attitudes and Changes in Attitudes
Epilogue: Brainwashed

Chapter 18
Sexuality, Attraction, and Intimacy

Prologue
Why Psychologists Study Sexuality, Attraction, and Intimacy
Biological Aspects of Human Sexuality
Gender-Role Acquisition
Attraction
Sexual Myths and Research
Epilogue: The Conquest of Spermatorrhea

Chapter 19
Applied Psychology

Prologue
Why Psychologists Are Interested in Applied Psychology
Industrial/Organizational Psychology
Sports Psychology
Environmental Psychology
Consumer Psychology
Educational Psychology
Epilogue: The Longest Throw

CHAPTER 17 | Social Behavior

Prologue

Why Psychologists Study Social Behavior

Interpersonal Influence
Conformity
Obedience
Conformity and Obedience

Helping Others

Cooperation and Competition

The Influence of Groups
Deindividuation
Polarization
Leadership

Prejudice and Discrimination
Personality and Prejudice
Overcoming Prejudice

Social Cognition and Attitude Change
Forming Social Attitudes
Changing Attitudes: Persuasive
Communication
Cognitive Dissonance and Attitude
Change
Attribution

Epilogue: Brainwashed

PROLOGUE

It is the early 1950s. You are a student working with Solomon Asch. Professor Asch is interested in studying conformity, and he has asked you to help him with an experiment. Your job is to collect the data and lead the subjects through the procedure.

After learning what you must do, you become worried. The kinds of results you will obtain are obvious to you already. You wish that Professor Asch had designed the experiment with more care. It's definitely not subtle enough.

You begin by having the subject enter a room along with eight other people. These eight people are secretly confederates of yours, but to the subject they're just other subjects.

Next, you show everyone three comparison lines. Each line is obviously of a different length, no doubt about that. Then you show a standard line and place it alongside the comparison lines (see Figure 17.1). You ask all the subjects which line in the comparison group is the same length as the standard line. The real subject is asked last. All of your confederates have been told to lie: They pick the medium-length line, a line that doesn't match the standard line.

Professor Asch wants to know how the real subject will respond. This is why you are worried about the experiment. The shorter comparison line that your confederates chose is so obviously different that nobody could expect it to be an honest mistake. The subject will either realize that the other eight people are confederates or think they're all crazy. Nobody could possibly agree that the standard line is the same length as the next shorter comparison line.

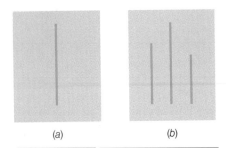

FIGURE 17.1

The stimulus cards used in Asch's experiment. The subjects were required to match the standard line on card (a) with the line of the same length on card (b) (After Asch, 1951).

One by one, subjects are led through this procedure, and, to your amazement, 75 percent of all subjects go along with the group's lies on at least one occasion (Asch, 1951).

Afterward, you explain the experiment to the subjects and question them. "Could you tell that everyone else was wrong when they said that one of the shorter lines equaled the standard line?"

"Yes," the subjects often reply. "I knew they were wrong."

"Then why did you agree with them?"

"I don't know," the subjects say. "I just didn't want to rock the boat. I just wanted to go along."

The more you think about the results of Asch's experiment, the more disturbed you are. You realize that many people would rather go against the evidence of their own eyes than openly disagree with the unanimous judgment of even a small group of people (Asch, 1951; Wheeler, Deci, Reis, & Zuckerman, 1978).

In this chapter, we'll examine many of the ways in which people influence one another. We'll take a look at the factors determining obedience, the effects that groups have on their members, and the ways in which our attitudes can be changed by those around us. We'll also study other areas of interest to social psychologists, such as competition and cooperation, conformity, negotiation and bargaining, helping others, moral behavior, and prejudice.

WHY PSYCHOLOGISTS STUDY SOCIAL BEHAVIOR

Except for extremely rare instances, no human being lives in total social isolation. Each of us interacts with other people. Social psychology is the study of how people affect the behavior, thoughts, and feelings of other people.

Social psychology is the study of the effects of groups and social interaction on behavior.

If you were told that you had to give up something in your life, probably the last thing you or anyone would choose to surrender would be the company of others. Most of us would rather live in a cave with other people than in a mansion with no hope of ever seeing another person. Other people are such a common element in our lives that we rarely consider what it would be like without them. They affect us, they shape us, they influence what we think and feel and do. We, in turn, influence them. Social psychologists study how groups behave and how being a member of a group or society affects individuals.

▐ INTERPERSONAL INFLUENCE

Groups can influence our behavior in important ways. Among the most important kinds of social influences are conformity and obedience.

Conformity

As you learned in the Prologue, the tendency to conform can be very strong. Asch demonstrated that we may conform even if it means disavowing the evidence of our own eyes. Still, a degree of **conformity** is important in any society. Without it, there would be chaos. The ways in which other people expect us to conform are known as **social norms.**

Some social norms are explicit and may even be spelled out: "No parking," "No smoking in this section," "Shirts and shoes must be worn in this establishment." Other social norms are unspoken and unwritten, but they still influence our behavior. For example, there is probably no functional reason for someone to attend a business meeting dressed in a suit rather than a sweatshirt, other than the fact that it is an unspoken social norm, and it is expected. There are many unspoken social rules, such as waiting your turn in line, shaking hands when you first meet someone, and not staring at strangers.

CONFORMITY
Action that results from social pressure to comply with social norms. When people conform, they act or behave in correspondence with current customs, rules, or styles.

SOCIAL NORMS
Shared standards of behavior accepted by and expected from group members.

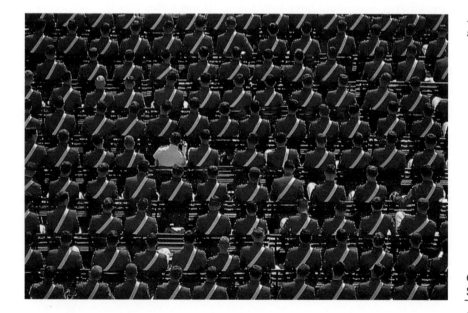

Although the pressure to conform may be strong, some struggle against it.

SOCIAL COMPARISON
Assessment of accuracy of our own attitudes, feelings, or beliefs by comparing them with those of others.

REFERENCE GROUP
A group with which we identify and that we use as our standard of behavior.

WHY PEOPLE CONFORM. Conformity is common, and people probably have two major reasons for conforming. First, they often are reinforced for conforming. Since childhood, we have been reinforced for adopting the "correct" beliefs and behaviors of our parents, guardians, and teachers. Even as adults, we often are reinforced for acting like other people. Because we are reinforced for conforming so often and under so many different circumstances, our conformity tends to generalize to new situations.

The second important force behind conformity may be the result of **social comparison.** We commonly compare ourselves with other people, especially those who are like us, as a way of assessing the accuracy of our attitudes, feelings, and beliefs. We like to view ourselves as rational and correct in our views. Consequently, people who rely heavily on social comparison may find it difficult not to change in the direction of conformity (Bleda & Castore, 1973; Fazio, 1979).

Someone who is very different from the other members of a group may make the group feel uncomfortable because he disrupts the group's stable basis for comparison. The group usually tries to force the individual to change. If it fails, the person who is viewed as deviant may be rejected.

REFERENCE GROUPS. Will a mathematician who hears that most sailors have tatoos want one also? If you read in an advertisement that all the "important people" of Norway vacation at a particular resort, will you want to go there, too? In both cases, the pressure to conform is small. Just because a particular group engages in a certain behavior does not necessarily mean that other people will want to do the same or will use that group for purposes of social comparison. Instead, we generally look to people we are like, or wish to be like, in making decisions about how we will conform. Social psychologists refer to such groups as **reference groups.** The norms of reference groups tend to be perpetuated because each new member who joins is under pressure to conform and to maintain the group's standards.

Much of the research on conformity grew out of a desire to understand the social forces that had been at work in Nazi Germany. Could you have been a member of the Nazi party? Could you have joined in the mass rallies and their persecutions? The students of Ron Jones's high school history class in California didn't think that they would have gone along with the Nazi movement had they lived in Germany at the time. They believed that they would have resisted. To help his class understand more fully the social forces that affected the Germans, Jones had the class simulate some of the German experience with Naziism for 5 days. To his horror, the pretend game became all too real, and a Nazi-like system of beliefs and control took root among his students and throughout the school (Jones, 1978).

What Jones had done to bring this about was quite simple. He began by limiting all answers in class to three words or less. Soon, new nonverbal leaders emerged. A Nazi-like salute was then incorporated, and slogans such as "strength through community" were shouted in unison. Banners were made, new recruits were enlisted from the rest of the school, and mandatory sitting postures were introduced. The group called itself the Third Wave. From Jones's small class, the group grew to over 100 members, and membership cards were issued. The better students often were thrown out of the class by the others. Once these "deviants" were purged, social comparison helped to strengthen conformity.

Jones decided to tell the Third Wave that they were part of a national organization of students who wanted a political change. He emphasized that they were a special group and that they had been selected to help the cause. In this way, he reinforced their conformity.

Jones announced that the next day a candidate for president of the United States would announce the formation of the Third Wave. The students were invited to view the occasion on the television monitor in the school auditorium. The following day, some 250 students filed into the auditorium wearing their special uniforms and homemade armbands. Muscular student guards stood at the door, while others, enlisted by Jones to help, pretended to be photographers and reporters and circulated among the students. This added charade helped the students to believe that they were about to become part of a nationwide movement. The students stood, rank upon rank, straight and proud. As they waited for the announcement, Jones began to show a movie of the Nazi rally at Nuremberg and the history of the Third Reich. The students just stood there, blankly watching what appeared to be an eerie reflection of themselves.

Afterward, Jones explained to the students what had been going on and how they had been manipulated. He predicted that they would never admit to having been part of this madness, to having been tricked into being followers of a "Nazi" movement. His prediction appears to be accurate, for few students wish to talk about that time. In 5 short days, seemingly healthy, normal students at Cubberley High School in California had banded together, purged their ranks of "intellectuals," and were ready to follow the orders of a national leader. They had even begun to take pride in relying on coercion and discrimination as means to an unknown end. They may never again have a lesson in history or social psychology of such importance and magnitude.

Look around you. Whom do you admire? What are your reference groups? How have you changed your behavior to conform to their standards? What are their goals, and are these goals that you desire? Of course, most conformity is innocuous. Conforming by wearing a shiny silk blazer when you're part of a bowling league is hardly the same as marching to the cadence of the Third Reich. And yet, as you may have begun to sense, there are similarities. In both cases, there is pressure to be part of the group and to demonstrate appropriate behaviors to new members.

Obedience

Although it's possible to get a group of high school students to conform to Nazi-like values and beliefs, it's still a long way from there to the death camps and the murder of millions of people. Or is it? During the Nuremberg trials, in which the Nazi war criminals were brought to account, one phrase was heard so often that it has come to be associated with the German underlings even by people who are not old enough to remember World War II. The phrase is, "I was just following orders." As the court records show, this excuse was not well received. The lowest-ranking officers, it was conceded, might possibly use such an excuse. But certainly the higher-ranking officers had a choice.

THE MILGRAM EXPERIMENT.   In the early 1960s, social psychologist Stanley Milgram investigated **obedience** in a study that is now considered a classic. Milgram began by using students from Yale University as subjects and later expanded his research to include a cross section of people of different ages, occupations, and educational levels.

Two subjects were ushered into an experimental room and were told that they were part of an investigation to test the effects of punishment, in the form of an electric shock, on memory. An experimenter, dressed in a white lab coat, would oversee the experiment. The subjects would draw lots to find out who would be the "learner" and who would be the "teacher." Unknown to the real subject, the other subject, "Mr. Wallace," a gentle-looking, friendly 50-year-old man, was really an actor working for Milgram. The lots were rigged so that the real subject would be assigned the role of teacher.

The teacher was given a sample shock of 45 volts to find out what it would feel like—it stung. The learner, Mr. Wallace, was then strapped into the electric chair as the subject chosen to be the teacher watched. The teacher-subject was

Nazis on trial in Nuremberg, November 25, 1945. Hermann Goering, Rudolf Hess, General Joachim von Ribbentrop, and General Wilhelm Keitel are shown in the front row.

then taken into an adjacent room and put in front of an array of switches ranging from "Slight shock, 15 volts," to "Danger: severe shock, 450 volts." The learner was instructed to repeat a list of words. Every time he made an error, the teacher was to administer a shock, starting with the lowest level and gradually increasing. The actor playing the role of learner had been given a script to follow for each voltage level, since the teacher would be able to hear him from the next room. As the shock level rose, the learner would begin to protest. The stronger the shock, the louder he was to protest. At 75 volts he would moan; at 150 volts he would demand to be released from the chair. At 180 volts he would yell that he could no longer stand the pain. At 300 volts he would protest that he had a heart condition and begin to scream. If the teacher complained at any time, the experimenter would say, "Teacher, you have no other choice; you must go on!" (Milgram, 1963, p. 374). After the 300-volt level, it was planned that there would be an ominous silence from the learner's room, as though he were unconscious or even dead. Unknown to the teacher, the learner received no real shocks.

Milgram's aim was to find out how much pressure to obey would be created by the experimenter in the lab coat when he said, "Teacher, you have no other choice; you must go on!" How far would subjects go under these circumstances? Before conducting the experiment, Milgram interviewed 40 psychiatrists, describing the procedure you have just read. He asked them to estimate the behavior of most subjects. The psychiatrists agreed that the majority would not go beyond 150 volts, and that perhaps only one in a thousand, those who were very deviant or sadistic, would go all the way to 450 volts. How far would you have gone?

To everyone's horror, when the experiment was conducted, 62 percent of the teacher-subjects went all the way to 450 volts! None of them seemed to enjoy it. For example, after delivering 180 volts, one subject said,

> He can't stand it! I'm not going to kill that man in there. You hear him hollering? He's hollering. He can't stand it. What if something happens to him? . . . I mean, who is going to take the responsibility if anything happens to that gentleman? (Milgram, 1965a, p. 67)

At that point, the experimenter said that he would take responsibility. The subject replied, "All right," and continued delivering shocks.

Of the 38 percent of the subjects who were not willing to go to 450 volts, many went to high levels (see Figure 17.2). All who refused to continue simply walked out of the experiment. Not one of them tried to see how Mr. Wallace was. Interestingly, the personality tests that were administered to the subjects failed to reveal any differences between the subjects who obeyed and those who refused.

Stanley Milgram (1933–1984).

VARIABLES INFLUENCING OBEDIENCE. Social psychologists have identified at least three variables in this experiment that may help to explain the high rate of obedience. First, a legitimate authority, the experimenter, was present and was willing to take responsibility. Second, the victim was in another room, and this distance may have lessened the teacher's stress by eliminating the need to see the learner's anguish. Third, the teacher-subject accepted the subordinate role, applying all the rules the subject had ever learned about being a good follower. Perhaps, as social psychologist Philip Zimbardo has suggested, such follower training in public situations begins on the first day of school, when the teacher says, "Stay in your seat no matter what" (Zimbardo, 1979).

It should be stressed that obedience does not happen only under these select conditions. Even if the learner is directly in front of the teacher-subject, the latter

In this variation of the Milgram experiment, a teacher-subject forces the learner's arm onto the electric plate. (Photos (c) 1965 by Stanley Milgram, from the film Obedience, *distributed by the New York University Film Library.)*

may still obey. In a variation of the Milgram experiment, the teacher-subject actually had to force the learner's hand down onto an electric shock plate. Obedience under these conditions, although less frequent, was still much higher than anyone had predicted.

By today's standards, the Milgram experiment may not be considered ethical because of the stress placed on the teacher-subject. Some of the subjects were shaking and weeping as they pressed the 450-volt lever. How do you debrief such a subject after the experiment? Do you say, "Don't feel bad—the learner is only an actor. I just wanted to see if you would electrocute a stranger just because I told you to." No serious aftereffects were observed among the teacher-subjects, but even after a careful debriefing many felt that they had discovered an evil side of themselves. Some of the volunteer experimenters who helped Milgram to conduct the research were called to account by university authorities, who asked why they had continued the experiment when they could plainly see that the teacher-subjects were under stress. Their frightening answer: "Milgram told us to!"

The Milgram findings are not specific to the United States. Similar results have been obtained in many other countries, including Germany and Australia (Kilham

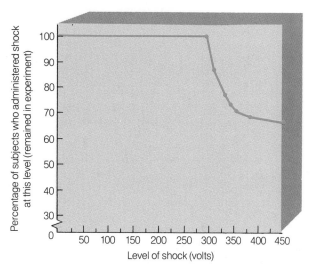

FIGURE 17.2

The percentage of subjects who delivered shock at different voltage levels in Milgram's experiment. Approximately two-thirds of the subjects continued to 450 volts despite the screaming protests of the learner. No subject discontinued shock before the 300-volt level. (SOURCE: *Adapted from Milgram, 1963.*)

& Mann, 1974; Mantell, 1971). The same results even were found among three groups of children, aged 7, 11, and 15 years, who were ordered to shock an innocent victim (Shanab & Yahya, 1977).

A further variation of the experiment was obtained, demonstrating that Milgram's results were due to the subjects' desire to be obedient rather than to any hidden sadistic pleasure they got from shocking the learner. In this study, 42 boys, aged 13 and 14 years, were asked to take part in an experiment in which they simultaneously were both the teacher and the learner. This was accomplished by giving the boys earphones to wear that would produce a high-pitched sound when they pressed buttons on the teacher's console. Whenever they made a mistake, they administered this sound to themselves. Although the tone was not actually dangerous, they were told they might suffer a 50-percent hearing loss. Using an experimental procedure similar to Milgram's, the researchers found that the subjects were willing to follow orders even though they believed they might cause self-injury (Martin, Lobb, Chapman, & Spillane, 1976).

Conformity and Obedience

As you might imagine, once social psychologists discovered variables that influenced conformity and variables that influenced obedience, they wanted to see how these variables interrelated.

As an example of research in this area, let's consider another variation of the Milgram experiment that makes use of one learner and three teacher-subjects. Only one of the teacher-subjects is a real subject, however. Unknown to that individual, the other two teacher subjects, as well as the learner, are actors. In this variation, the confederate teacher-subjects disobey. The first of the actors disobeys the experimenter at 150 volts and leaves. The second actor defies the experimenter at 225 volts and leaves. The real subject is then left alone to continue following orders. Under these circumstances, the real subject can use the other two "subjects" for social comparison. As it turned out, after the two actors defied the experimenter, only about 12 percent of the real subjects remained and went all the way to 450 volts (see Figure 17.3) (Milgram, 1965b). Conversely, if the two actors both argued for more shock, all the way to 450 volts, the real subject was more likely to obey than were the single teacher-subjects in the original experiment.

FIGURE 17.3

The percentage of subjects who delivered shock at different voltage levels in the repeat of Milgram's experiment when two other "subjects" disobeyed the researcher's request to shock the learner. The group pressure in this case allowed the subject to discontinue the shocks sooner. Only 12 percent went all the way to 450 volts. (SOURCE: Adapted from Milgram, 1965b.)

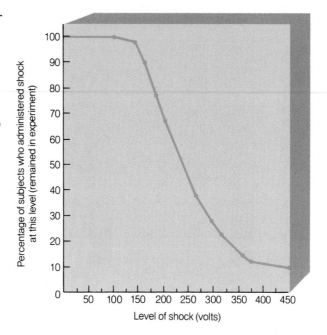

The Jonestown tragedy vividly demonstrated the potential consequences of conformity and blind obedience to authority. In 1978, almost 900 members of the California-based People's Temple died in a ritual mass suicide in Jonestown, Guyana, at the command of their leader, Reverend Jim Jones. Jones believed that his communal group was under attack from the outside by forces bent on destroying it. (This outside force was, in reality, nothing more than one congressman, Leo Ryan, who had come to the South American country to make sure that the people from his California district were all right and who was leaving with 14 of them who had asked to be taken home with him.) After Jones's men had murdered the congressman and several of his party, Jones ordered his followers to kill themselves by taking cyanide. The mass death shocked the world and left people wondering how such a thing could have happened.

Although a few members disobeyed Jones and ran into the jungle, most complied. The final tape recordings of Jonestown are horrifying to hear. The people went to their self-administered deaths crying and screaming for help. Most were not happy to die, which makes their deaths even more incomprehensible.

Now that you have learned something about conformity and obedience, you may begin to appreciate the powerful influences that were in force that day in Jonestown. The people in Jones's community were followers; they had learned through much practice and training to obey their leader, even carrying out mock suicides. Like Milgram's teacher-subjects, many of them cried and were under great stress at the end, but they obeyed. Social comparison certainly had an effect. We would predict that a person surrounded by hundreds of other people committing suicide would be much more likely to do the same than would a solitary person ordered to kill himself (Latane, 1981). By their actions, the people in Jonestown were also complying with reference group norms. Jones's followers had no other group to which they could refer. They were not only completely dependent on the group, but also isolated in a dense South American jungle, far from their homes.

Would you have been one of the few who escaped? It's easy to feel invulnerable to social forces when they aren't directly working on you. Most people believe that in all except extreme circumstances, such as a gun held to their head, their own internal values and belief systems would override external social forces. But social

Aftermath of the tragedy at Jonestown.

psychologists are finding that this is, in fact, a rarity. More often the opposite is true; the social forces turn out to be stronger than our personal values, beliefs, and feelings.

HELPING OTHERS

People do not always hurt each other or refuse to help someone in need in the way that the subjects in Milgram's experiment did. Sometimes people will go out of their way to help another or to prevent another from being hurt; at other times they will not. Social psychologists believe that the situational forces present at any given moment play a major role in determining whether people will help in an emergency. To test this theory, social psychologists have studied the factors at play during real and "arranged" emergencies. The following incident stimulated great interest in this area of investigation.

In 1964, on Austin Street in Queens, New York, a woman named Kitty Genovese was stabbed to death. It was nighttime when her killer attacked her on the street. She screamed and fought with him. Her screams were so loud that they alerted many people in apartments overlooking the street. Windows lighted up as the occupants awoke and looked outside to see what was happening; 38 presumably respectable and law-abiding citizens watched as she was stabbed. Their lights scared off the attacker. Kitty lay in the street, wounded but still alive. When the people turned off their lights and went back to bed, the attacker struck again. Once again,

People's tendency, especially pronounced under crowded conditions, to ignore others who need help or situations that call for action.

he was scared off by people looking out of their windows, and once again he returned when the lights went out. He stabbed her a third time, killing her. At no time during the entire attack did any of the 38 people call the police or an ambulance! The police were not called until after she had died. Why had these people not helped? They didn't have to fight with the killer. They were safe in their homes and needed only to pick up the telephone. According to the newspapers, this was one more example of unfeeling city people who have no concern for anyone but themselves. But was this the answer?

To shed a little light on what may have happened that night in Austin Street, let's examine an experiment by Darley and Latane conducted in 1968. The subjects were told that they would be taking part in a discussion about the kinds of problems students might face when they are away at college. On the pretext of maintaining anonymity, the students were isolated in separate cubicles; they could not see one another, and they could speak to one another only through an intercom. Each subject was led to believe that he or she would be participating in a discussion group in which there was either one other student, two other students, or five others. Actually, the subject was the only student in the experiment. The other subjects were voices on a tape recorder.

To begin, each student was requested to give a short introductory statement describing himself or herself. During the introduction, one of the pretend students said that he was embarrassed by the fact that he occasionally had epileptic seizures. As the "discussion" got underway, this particular participant began to have what sounded like an epileptic seizure (recorded on the tape beforehand). What would the real subject do? When the subject believed that there was only one other participant and that this other person was having a seizure, the subject was very likely to summon or provide help. However, the more participants the subject believed were taking part in this discussion, the *less* likely he or she was to do anything. This tendency is known as the **bystander effect.** The bystander effect may have been responsible for the fact that no one called for help when Kitty Genovese was being stabbed.

What gives rise to the bystander effect? Most people assume that help is more likely to be given when more people see that it is needed, rather than the other

Because of the bystander effect, this person may receive no help.

UNIT 5
RELATING TO ONE ANOTHER

562

way around. But social psychologists have found that the opposite is often true. There appear to be two reasons for the bystander effect: One is **diffusion of responsibility**, and the other is the fear of appearing foolish.

If you are the only one who sees a stranger in distress, and you know that you are the only one, then it is also apparent that if you take no action no help will be forthcoming. This perception places a burden of responsibility on you to act. However, if you know that many people besides yourself have seen the person in distress, then it becomes easy to assume that someone else will take action; it is no longer incumbent on you to do so. Many of the people who watched Kitty Genovese being stabbed also saw that others were watching. There may have been a great diffusion of responsibility, with everyone believing that someone else would do something. Or the witnesses may have thought that someone else should help and asked themselves, "Why me?" Ironically, had Kitty Genovese been in a more isolated place and been seen by a single witness, the witness might have been more likely to call the police or to take some other action. In fact, research has shown that the more populated a place is, the *less* likely people are to help those they see in need, which may partly explain the fact that rural people are generally more willing to offer assistance than are urban people (Steblay, 1987).

Have you ever arrived at a bad car accident where there was a large crowd and wondered why it was taking the ambulance so long to arrive? Perhaps you should have been wondering whether anyone had called an ambulance. Everyone may have assumed that someone must have called, or thought it was someone else's responsibility to call. Think of diffusion of responsibility the next time you see someone in need and there are many witnesses. It may still be incumbent on you to act, if only to summon help.

The second reason for the bystander effect may be the fear of appearing foolish. Some situations are clearly emergencies; other situations are more ambiguous. In ambiguous situations, people often are reluctant to act because they are afraid of looking foolish should it turn out that there was no emergency. To test this assertion, two researchers had students fill out a questionnaire in a small room. The researchers weren't really interested in the student's responses to the questionnaire; instead, they wanted to see how the students would react to something unusual that began to happen. The room had a small vent. As the students worked on the questionnaire, smoke began to pour through the vent. The smoke came from a smoke generator run by the researchers.

The subjects in this experiment were assigned to one of three conditions. They filled out the questionnaire alone, in the presence of two other subjects, or in the presence of two confederates posing as subjects. In the last case, the confederates were told to do nothing when the smoke began to fill the room.

The students who were in the room alone had no reason to fear embarrassment or to interpret the smoke as anything but an emergency. The great majority of subjects in this condition responded by telling the person in the outer room what was happening. When two other subjects were in the room, the amount of action taken was drastically lessened (see Figure 17.4). As smoke began to filter in, the subjects would look at one another, each examining the others' reactions. For each subject, the situation became ambiguous because the others weren't reacting (each of them, of course, was waiting to see wither someone else would react). Not wishing to appear foolish by misinterpreting something as an emergency, many subjects failed to act. In the condition with the two confederates, the real subject was even less likely to act because the confederates gave no hint of concern (unlike some participants in the condition that used three real subjects). The confederates made the situation even more ambiguous. Rather than appear foolish by acting in a situation that might not be an emergency, the real subject would sit in the room

DIFFUSION OF RESPONSIBILITY
One possible reason for the bystander effect. When someone is observed to be in need of help and there are many people around, individuals may believe that they need not act or give aid because they place responsibility to act on other people in the crowd. They may think, for instance, "Someone else will surely help" or "Why should I have to be the one to help?"

A measure of demand in terms of behavior required per unit of time. In conditions of high task load, there is much to do and little time to do it.

as it filled with smoke and would continue filling out the questionnaire (Latane & Darley, 1968).

In ambiguous situations, people are much less likely to help others than they are in obvious emergencies (Yakimovich & Saltz, 1971). For example, if an accident victim is seen to be bleeding, most people realize that the situation is not ambiguous and that help is absolutely required (Shotland & Huston, 1979). Researchers also have found that people are more likely to help if they are in familiar surroundings than if they are in an unfamiliar location, probably because unfamiliar surroundings heighten the ambiguity (Latane & Darley, 1970).

Latane and Darley (1970) have created a bystander intervention model that delineates five steps a person must complete before she is likely to give help.

1. The event must be observed.
2. The event must be interpreted as an emergency.
3. The person must accept responsibility for helping.
4. The person must decide how to help.
5. The person must take action.

Other factors may affect the chances that a bystander will lend aid. Researchers Shirlynn Spacapan and Sheldon Cohen (1977) conducted an experiment with female students in which **task load** (how busy the subject was) and diffusion of responsibility were measured simultaneously. The women were divided into two groups. Those in the first group were required to go into a shopping mall and buy 26 items specified on a list within half an hour. Since this requirement would be relatively easy to carry out and subjects would have time to spare, these subjects were considered the low-task group. The high-task group was required to buy 52 items within half an hour, a task that would take practically the whole time. Members of both groups were sent into the shopping mall during either crowded or uncrowded times.

The results demonstrated that how busy a person is and whether that person stands to lose something by helping may be as important a variable as is diffusion of responsibility. In each instance, a "victim" asked the subject to help look for a lost contact lens. In the uncrowded low-task situation, 80 percent of the subjects

FIGURE 17.4

Proportion of subjects who reported smoke in Latane and Darley's 1968 experiment. Subjects were much more likely to report the smoke if they were alone than if they were with two other subjects or two unresponsive confederates. (SOURCE: *Adapted from Latane & Darley, 1968, p. 218.*)

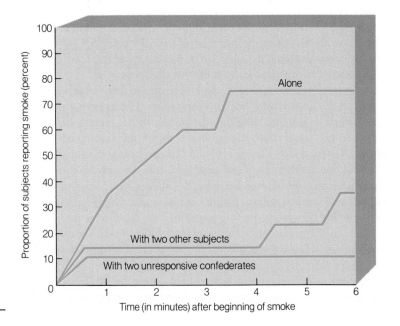

CONCEPT REVIEW: BYSTANDER INTERVENTION

The following example highlights Latane and Darley's five-step process of bystander intervention:

On January 13, 1982, a Boeing 737 took off in bad weather from National Airport in Washington, D.C. Unable to gain altitude, it crashed into the 14th Street bridge, flipped over, and smashed through the ice of the frozen Potomac River. Lenny Skutnik, a Washington office worker, was on his way home when he witnessed the disaster (step 1). As he reached the banks of the river, he observed a rescue helicopter attempting to save drowning victims of the crash (step 2). He noticed that one woman in the water apparently didn't have the strength to hold onto the life preserver dangling from the helicopter. At this point, Skutnik looked around and realized that "she was going to drown if I didn't get her, because nobody else was going to" (step 3).

The only way to reach her was to swim out to her and help her to safety (step 4). In a truly heroic action, Skutnik plunged into the freezing Potomac, amid ice chunks and potentially explosive jet fuel, and saved the woman's life (step 5). Empathy and compassion were also motivating forces for his action; as he stated in an interview with NBC news, "It was just in my heart. I just felt sorry for the girl."

Lenny Skutnik, a Washington, D.C., office worker, dove into the frozen Potomac River to save a victim of an airliner crash.

stopped to look; in the crowded high-task situation, none did! In the mixed situations—that is crowded low-task and uncrowded high-task—approximately one-third of the subjects complied with the request for help.

Researchers also have found that individuals who maintain their anonymity are less likely to help. In one study, students who wore hoods to hide their faces were found to be less likely to help a fellow student who appeared to have fainted (Solomon & Solomon, 1978). In another study, subjects were asked to administer shocks to a woman as part of an experiment. They were told either that the woman was a very nice person or that she was an extremely obnoxious person. In addition, the subjects either wore hoods and garments to disguise themselves or showed themselves and their faces to the woman. The results were that the subjects were only slightly more likely to shock the "obnoxious" woman than the "nice" woman. But if the subjects wore hoods and were able to disguise themselves, they gave the

As you have discovered, some people will conform to the standards of Nazi-like groups, obey orders to harm another person, or refuse to help someone in need. Other people will not conform or obey, and they will willingly give aid. The data presented in this chapter so far have indicated that situational factors determine a person's conformity, obedience, or desire to help. On the other hand, many psychologists believe that morality is not just situationally dependent, but is an integral part of an individual's personality. A moral person, they argue, will be less likely to harm another or to refuse to give aid than will an amoral person, regardless of the situational factors. During the last 2 decades, psychologists have examined the development of morals in an effort to learn how much people's morality is subject to situational factors.

Morals are the attitudes and beliefs a person holds that help him to determine what is right or wrong. Some researchers have come to believe that moral reasoning progresses through a series of stages as the individual is influenced by the reasoning of other people. Researcher Lawrence Kohlberg (1963, 1971) postulated six stages in the development of morality. According to Kohlberg, moral development begins in childhood with an orientation to obey in order to avoid punishment, and it may end with the emergence of concern for reciprocity among individuals and a sense of universal justice.

Kohlberg devised an assessment tool for determining the stage of moral development an individual has reached. Individuals are presented with a moral dilemma. The reasoning they use to resolve the dilemma indicates how advanced their moral

thinking is. Table 17.1 gives an example of one of these moral dilemmas. For each stage, actual answers have been provided that demonstrate the kinds of reasoning involved. The statements in the left column describe, in general terms, the quality of moral reasoning that defines each stage. As you can see, there are no right or wrong answers: Each stage is value-free. A person's position in the stages is determined not by the choice of right or wrong answers according to some value system, but rather by the kind of moral reasoning used to make the choice.

According to Kohlberg, each stage is built on the previous stage. More advanced stages of moral thinking reorganize the earlier stages in a way that furnishes the person with new criteria and perspectives for making moral judgments (Hoffman, 1979; Walker, de Vries, & Bichard, 1984). Kohlberg assumed that children begin at the first stage. As they interact with other people, they may progress through each stage, but they never skip a stage.

Kohlberg's most recent investigations, made just before his death, indicated that no clear distinction could be made between stages 5 and 6 (Colby, Kohlberg, Gibbs, & Lieberman, 1983). For this reason, stage 6 has been dropped from the current assessment procedures. Even so, Kohlberg believed that many people never reach the final stage. In fact, most people do not seem to develop much beyond stage 4 (Shaver & Strong, 1976). The third and fourth stages are therefore called the conventional stages, since they represent the stages reached by most adults.

In Kohlberg's view, people advance to a higher stage of moral develop-

ment by exposure to the moral reasoning of other people that is more advanced than their own. This social interaction places a person in a conflict that can be resolved only by accepting the more advanced stage of moral reasoning.

Psychologist David Rosenhan (1973) used Kohlberg's assessment techniques to measure different individuals' stages of moral thinking. Afterward, he placed these individuals in the role of the teacher-subject in a replication of Milgram's famous shock experiment, which you read about earlier. Even some subjects who scored at stage 6 when taking the moral dilemma tests went all the way to 450 volts when shocking the learner, and they were unable to give a reason for doing so that would accord with the universal principles supposedly possessed by someone at the sixth stage of moral development. The subjects at stage 6 were, however, less likely to continue up to 450 volts than were those subjects at Kohlberg's stage 1.

Although Kohlberg's theory presents a well-organized description of how moral development may occur, it has been strongly criticized for a number of reasons. Its most serious problem may be that it correlates poorly with moral behavior. Although teacher-subjects at stage 6 were less likely to shock learners than were those at stage 1, whether people will choose to behave in a moral way often is more dependent on the immediate situational and social forces than on their stage of moral reasoning. This indicates that fostering a high level of moral reasoning may not bring about more moral behavior (Kurtines & Greif, 1974). Researchers also have argued that Kohlberg's theory is culturally biased in favor of

Western ideas of what is morally "advanced" (Simpson, 1974; Hogan, 1975; Sampson, 1978), and is biased against women because all of Kohlberg's subjects were white, lower- and middle-class men, making it an inaccurate reflection of female moral reasoning (Gilligan, 1982). Still, Kohlberg's ideas have sparked an interest in how moral values emerge and how they may shape our behavior. Whether the sequential development of moral reasoning that Kohlberg discovered will eventually be considered an important part of development remains to be seen. For the moment, it certainly is intriguing.

TABLE 17.1 Presentation of a Moral Dilemma, with Answers Graded According to Kohlberg's Six Stages of Moral Development

In Europe, a woman was near death from cancer. One drug might save her, a form of radium that a druggist in the same town had recently discovered. The druggist was charging $2000, 10 times what the drug cost him to make. The sick woman's husband, Heinz, went to everyone he knew to borrow the money, but he could get together only about half of what the drug cost. He told the druggist that his wife was dying and asked him to sell the drug for less money or to let him pay later. But the druggist said, "No." The husband got desperate and broke into the man's store to steal the drug for his wife. Should the husband have done that? Why or why not?

STAGE	PRO	CON
Preconventional Stages *Stage 1:* Punishment and obedience orientation (physical consequences determine what is good or bad).	He should steal the drug. It isn't really bad to take it. It isn't like he didn't ask to pay for it first. The drug he'd take is only worth $200; he's not really taking a $2000 drug.	He shouldn't steal the drug. It's a big crime. He didn't get permission, he used force and broke and entered. He did a lot of damage, stealing a very expensive drug and breaking up the store, too.
Stage 2: Instrumental relativist orientation (what satisfies one's own needs is good).	It's all right to steal the drug because she needs it and he wants her to live. It isn't that he wants to steal; it's the way he has to use to get the drug to save her.	He shouldn't steal it. The druggist isn't wrong or bad, he just wants to make a profit. That's what you're in business for, to make money.
Conventional Stages *Stage 3:* Interpersonal concordance or "good boy—nice girl" orientation (what pleases or helps others is good).	He should steal the drug. He was only doing something that was natural for a good husband to do. You can't blame him for doing something out of love for his wife; you'd blame him if he didn't love his wife enough to save her.	He shouldn't steal. If his wife dies, he can't be blamed. It isn't because he's heartless or that he doesn't love her enough to do everything that he legally can. The druggist is the selfish or heartless one.
Stage 4: "Law and order" orientation (maintaining the social order, doing one's duty is good).	He should steal the drug. If he did nothing he'd be letting his wife die, and it's his responsibility if she dies. He should take the drug with the intent of paying the druggist later.	It is a natural thing for Heinz to want to save his wife, but it's still always wrong to steal. He still knows he's stealing and taking a valuable drug from the man who made it.
Postconventional Stages *Stage 5:* Social contact—legalistic orientation (values agreed on by society including individual rights and rules for consensus, determine what is right).	The law wasn't set up for these circumstances. Taking the drug in this situation isn't really right, but doing it is justified.	You can't completely blame someone for stealing, but extreme circumstances don't really justify taking the law into your own hands. You can't have everyone stealing whenever they get desperate. The end may be good, but the ends don't justify the means.
Stage 6: Universal ethical-principle orientation (what is right is a matter of conscience in accord with universal principles).	This is a situation that forces him to choose between stealing and letting his wife die. In a situation where the choice must be made, it is morally right to steal. He has to act in terms of the principles of preserving and respecting life.	Heinz is faced with the decision of whether to consider the other people who need the drug just as badly as his wife. Heinz ought to act not according to his particular feelings toward his wife, but considering the value of all the lives involved.

SOURCES: Description of Kohlberg's stages from Shaver & Strong, 1976. Dilemma and pro and con answers adapted from Rest, 1968.

MORALS
The attitudes and beliefs that people hold
that help them to determine what is right
or wrong.

former twice as much shock (Zimbardo, 1979). (The same woman played each role and was not really shocked.)

There are three important ways of encouraging people to help others. One, of course, is by studying social psychology. Now that you are aware of these studies, you are more likely to inquire whether your help is needed, even if it means attracting the attention of many people who are doing nothing. Helping others also can be fostered by teaching appropriate helping skills. People are more likely to help if they have some kind of training in what action to take (Shotland & Heinold, 1985). For instance, training seminars in cardiopulmonary resuscitation (CPR) have been successful in getting people to administer CPR quickly to heart attack victims, in order to keep the victim alive until help arrives. Training in what to do in case of an emergency prepares a person to take action. A third way of encouraging others to help is by reinforcing them for helping and by modeling helping behavior.

COOPERATION AND COMPETITION

When two or more people work together for their mutual benefit, they are cooperating. Cooperation is a valuable behavior, since societies would not be possible without it. Competition occurs when two or more people vie for a certain goal in which not all can be winners. Competition may be the best strategy in one circumstance, and cooperation in another.

Psychologists believe that competition and cooperation are taught by social interaction and that both strategies can be initiated at a very early age. Children often are spontaneously cooperative. But in our society, and in others, individual competition is so often modeled and reinforced that the desire to surpass others sometimes interferes with the need for cooperation. Irrational competition sometimes can spoil the success that cooperation might bring.

In one experiment, M. C. Madsen and his associates discovered that in certain cases cooperation declines as children grow older and that competition may become the most common mode of responding, even when it cannot possibly lead to success. Madsen had children of the same age sit across from each other at opposite ends of a small table (see Figure 17.5). Narrow gutters ran down the length of the table on both sides. The table surface was arched so that a marble placed anywhere on the table would immediately roll into the nearest gutter. A cup was imbedded in the tabletop in front of each child. At the start of the game, a marble was placed in a free-sliding marble holder in the center of the table. The marble holder prevented the marble from rolling into a gutter. Each child had a string attached to one end of the marble holder. To score, a child needed only to pull the string and cause the marble holder to pass over his cup. The marble would then drop into the cup and the child would have succeeded. However, if both children pulled their strings simultaneously, the marble holder would come apart and the marble would roll into the gutter.

Madsen found that cooperation was common among 4- and 5-year-old children playing this game. The children usually would negotiate to arrange that each received about half of the marbles. However, when Madsen tested school children in the second through fifth grades, he found their desire to compete so strong that a majority of them failed to obtain a single marble (Madsen, 1971). In a later study, some of the children were so competitive that they argued that it was impossible to get a marble! One child pointed out that success might be possible

FIGURE 17.5

Madsen's marble-pull game. (SOURCE: *Madsen, 1971, p. 367.)*

"if I could play alone" (Kagan & Madsen, 1971, p. 38). It never dawned on them to cooperate for their mutual benefit.

Older children appear to be much more competitive because of their experience and learning. Cross-cultural research supports this supposition. When Madsen examined children from different backgrounds, he obtained different results. His data indicate that a strong competitive outlook is more likely to develop among older children in urban surroundings. For instance, it was observed that city-dwelling Israeli children were more competitive than were Israeli children raised on a kibbutz (Madsen, 1971; Shapira & Madsen, 1974). American children generally were most competitive, regardless of their race, gender, or background, perhaps because competition is so emphasized in American society (Madsen & Shapira, 1970; Nelson & Madsen, 1969).

A more adult version of Madsen's game, known as the Acme–Bolt trucking game, was designed by researchers Deutsch and Krauss (1960). Figure 17.6 shows the layout of the trucking game. To begin, each player is given a trucking company, either the Acme Company or the Bolt Company. Each person's job is to move trucks along available routes until the goal is reached. Subjects are given 60 cents for each successful trip to the goal, minus 1 cent for each second it took to complete the trip. You can see that each company has two possible routes: an alternative route, which is long and time consuming, and the short route, which is a one-lane road. As you might imagine, the best way to play the game is for each person to cooperate with the other and to take turns. In this way, each can use the shortest route and use it quickly. In most cases, this was what happened. The players recognized that cooperation was the most logical and reasonable way to play the game.

In another variation of the trucking game, Deutsch and Krauss added gates at the positions shown in Figure 17.6. The gate on the left was controlled by Acme,

FIGURE 17.6

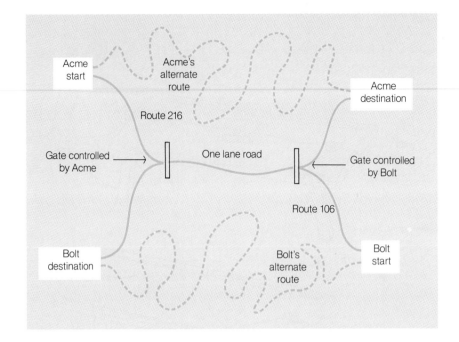

and the gate on the right by Bolt. The gates could be closed at any time by their respective owners to stop the other player from moving her truck along the one-land road. Two variations of this game were played. In one variation, the unilateral threat condition, only one of the players was given a gate. In the second condition, the bilateral threat condition, each of the players had a gate. Possessing a gate gave the owner a potential threat to use. The threat did not exist if the players were willing to trust each other, but if one person wanted to use the gate to accumulate more money than his opponent, he could do so. When both people possessed a gate, the danger that one might strike would prompt the other to strike first. Possession of one gate caused losses for both players, and possession of two gates caused the most losses (see Figure 17.7). Players would often slam their gates at the beginning of the session and leave them shut while each lost money. This research indicates that the chances of cooperation diminish as the ability to threaten

FIGURE 17.7

In the Acme—Bolt trucking game, Deutsch and Krauss discovered that cooperation decreased (costing both sides money) as the number of implied threats (the power to stop commerce by using a gate) increased. (SOURCE: *Deutsch & Krauss, 1960, p. 185.*)

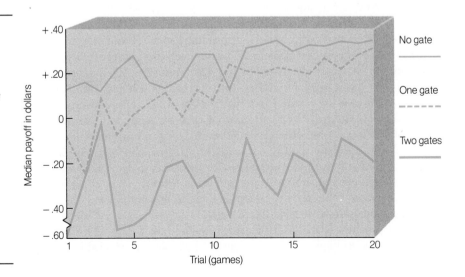

one another increases. We needn't travel too far from this simple game to draw parallels with the nuclear arms race. Indeed, if we discussed the game using phrases such as *first-strike capability, implicit threat, lack of cooperation, and mutual destruction*, you might well assume that we were weighing the prospects of a potential war between two world powers rather than considering the outcome of the Acme–Bolt trucking game.

▌THE INFLUENCE OF GROUPS

In social circumstances, we encounter groups as well as individuals. Psychologists have discovered that groups can affect a person's behavior in special ways. Not only do people rely on groups as a source of comparison and for social norms (Tajfel, 1982) but, depending on the situation, a group may occasionally deindividuate or polarize its members. Because deindividuation and polarization can strongly influence behavior, social psychologists have been drawn to study these processes.

Deindividuation

We are told from an early age that we are responsible for our actions. Almost no one is likely to walk up to a storefront, smash the window, and loot the store just because she sees something desirable. Similarly, few of us are likely to wait quietly until someone passes and then hit that person with a bottle. And not too many of us are likely to go over to the house of someone we don't like, drag that person out to a tree, and hold a lynching. Most of us would assume that anyone doing such things must be socially deviant. But these same behaviors, which few of us would ever dream of doing alone, are more likely to occur if we're part of a group. During blackouts, crowds often engage in looting. During raucous baseball games, people often throw things at the umpires or players. And during episodes of extreme racial hostility, mobs may engage in lynchings.

It seems that the social restraints that we normally accept can disappear once we become a member of a group that becomes aroused or angry. Why should a group have such a restraint-reducing influence? We have words for it—*mob mentality*, for instance. But mobs are made up of people. Why will people do things in a group that they'd never do when alone? It's not that groups change people in a permanent way. Individuals who've taken part in mob violence often feel ashamed of their behavior when they're alone again.

One reason may be the effects of modeling. When we see many other people engage in a behavior, we become more certain that that behavior is appropriate. A second reason may be that a diffusion of responsibility occurs; that is, we can distribute the blame for our actions. After all, "everyone else was doing it too." A third reason, **deindividuation,** has been suggested (Zimbardo, 1979; Diener, 1980). Deindividuation can occur when we become so caught up in events and in the feelings of the group that we lose our individuality. Once our individuality has been reduced, we lose track of who we are and what our values are. This, in turn, causes us to become more impulsive, more sensitive to our present emotional state, and, to some degree, less able to regulate our own behavior. Also, with such reduced individuality, we are less concerned about what other people think of us and what they might do to us. We are more concerned about responding as part of a group.

All of these social factors help to explain such incidences as the infamous Central Park jogger case that filled the headlines in 1989–90. A group of adolescents attacked a woman who was jogging in a New York City park. She was brutally beaten, raped, and almost killed. As an explanation, the boys said that they were "wilding," an expression not in most people's vocabulary at the time. It meant that they were roaming about *as a group* looking for victims or whatever action came along.

Wilding was heralded by the press as something new, a further example of our deteriorating moral values and decaying urban life. But these social forces aren't new. There have been endless examples throughout human history of similar group or mob behavior, probably dating back to the first time a group of aroused or aggressive humans ever went out together looking for something to do. And, lest you think that just the very existence of wilding says something about how our

Group attitudes may be altered if they are contradicted by the people in power.

Drawing by Booth; (c) 1977 The New Yorker Magazine, Inc.

cities have changed, consider that over 30 years ago the famous Olympic ice skater Dick Button was similarly attacked in Central Park by a gang of youths and almost beaten to death for no other reason than "kicks" (the term in vogue back then).

This is not to say that such incidences aren't on the increase in the United States or that urban crime isn't becoming worse, but only that regardless of the new names given to such behaviors, the *social forces* involved in these kinds of actions are not new in either our culture or our species, but have been with us from the dawn of civilization.

Reduced individuality is not an inevitable part of being a member of a group, but certain conditions can make it more likely to occur. One way to encourage reduced individuality is to camouflage the qualities that make us individuals. Taking away a person's individuality compels him to conform and blend into the group. Anything that fosters anonymity reduces individuality. Ku Klux Klan members wear hoods, supposedly to conceal their identity but undoubtedly also to reduce the individual sense of self and to make them more amenable to group desires. Concentration on events in the environment rather than on internal thoughts also helps to lessen individuality. Group unity and a high level of emotional arousal will reduce individuality even further.

Polarization

Very often, individuals who enter a group discussion with moderate views will change their views and eventually take a more polarized or extreme position; that is, they will become more conservative or more radical in their approach to a particular issue or decision. Consequently, a group may reach a more extreme position on an issue than its members might have chosen individually, had they decided the issue without group interaction.

In one study, researcher Jerald Greenberg (1979) asked 200 subjects individually how they would divide money between two people who had worked at a particular job. They were told that one of the people had done a better job than the other had, but that they could divide the money as they wished. On the average, subjects responded that 63.2 percent of the money should go to the one who had done the better job. Some time later, the subjects were again asked individually how they would divide the money. The average response the second time was that 64.3 percent should be given to the one who had done the better job, not much different from the first recommendation. In another group, the subjects were given the same information and were asked individually how they would divide the money. On the average, 64.4 percent of the money was awarded to the person who had done the better job. Then the subjects in this second group were allowed to discuss the situation with four other people. Afterward, they were again asked individually to make a recommendation, and this time the average response was that 76.5 percent of the money should be given to the person who had done the better job (see Figure 17.8).

The **polarization effect**—the tendency of members of a group to take a more extreme position than they would as individuals—has been demonstrated many times. The direction of the polarization may be strongly influenced by culture. In cases in which American groups were more likely to polarize in the direction of taking a risk, Chinese groups were more likely to polarize in the direction of caution (Hong, 1978).

There are a number of explanations for the polarization effect. First, when we are among other people who share our views, we may wish to gain their approval by exemplifying the beliefs and attitudes they hold. To show ourselves worthy of the group's esteem, we may want to be more extreme in ways that the group values.

POLARIZATION EFFECT
An effect in which members of a group tend to take a more extreme position (more conservative or more daring) than they would have as individuals. It is probably the result of social comparison or persuasive group arguments.

FIGURE 17.8

Subjects in all conditions were asked to divide money between two workers, when one was said to have done a better job. Subjects individually awarded more money to the better worker, but after group discussion the members shifted toward a more extreme position, which demonstrates the polarizing effect of the group on the judgments of its members. (SOURCE: After Greenberg, 1979.)

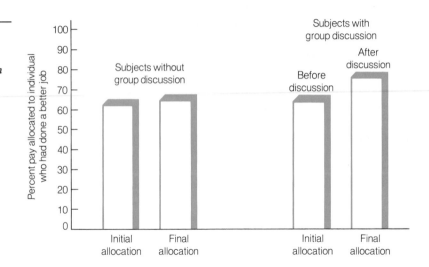

For example, jet fighter pilots admire coolheadedness and lack of emotion in a tough situation. Most other people who agree that coolheadedness is a fine attribute will try to demonstrate it to a degree and will express a certain admiration for this behavior. However, should they become fighter pilots and find themselves among many other people who admire the behavior, they may attempt to exemplify these attributes in the *extreme* to obtain the admiration of the group (Pruitt, 1971).

The second reason that groups may tend to polarize is a fairly obvious one. While exchanging information, individuals may make persuasive arguments, and the entire group may shift toward the most convincing of these arguments. A jury furnishes a good example of this kind of polarization effect. Jury members are selected because they are undecided to begin with; potential jurors with extreme views are weeded out. It is up to each side in the courtroom to give persuasive arguments. The jury is then expected to become more and more polarized during discussion in the jury room, until it reaches a verdict (Kaplan & Schwartz, 1977; MacCoun, 1989). We can only hope that juries become polarized because of the convincing arguments presented by the prosecution or the defense and not because of the wish of uncertain jurors to obtain the esteem of those who had already decided one way or the other. It is useful to keep the group polarization process in mind. As you recall from the chapter Prologue, it is easy to become convinced if many other people agree that something is true. Just because a group takes an extreme position does not necessarily mean that it's a more reasonable position than an individual might take.

The common view that groups tend to reach middle-of-the-road decisions is not altogether inaccurate, however. If all groups become polarized, all governments would become radical or reactionary, and all group plans would be extreme. In fact, much of the time, this does not happen. Whenever a group includes unified subgroups, each holding opposing views in the group discussion, a typical result is depolarization and compromise (Vinokur & Burnstein, 1978). A case in point is the United States Congress, made up of two subgroups, Democrats and Republicans.

Leadership

Individuals can affect groups, of course. Sometimes, an extremely influential group member will emerge as a leader. When a person becomes a leader, she is given the authority of a group and speaks for the group. Throughout history, people have wondered about the qualities of leadership and what makes leaders attractive to others. Psychologists who have studied leaders have arrived at two very different hypotheses to explain how a leader emerges.

The first, the **situational–environmental hypothesis,** argues that people are chosen as leaders because they happen to be in the right place at the right time. In other words, if they happen to have certain skills that meet a group's needs at a given moment, they may emerge as leaders (Hollander & Julian, 1970). The situational approach argues that an individual who may be a leader in one set of circumstances may be a follower in different circumstances. In other words, circumstances may arise in which any member of the group may emerge as a leader; it depends on the situation, not on the individual.

The other hypothesis, that leaders have particular traits that make them stand apart from other members of their group, is known as the **great-man, great-woman hypothesis.** This idea is not new. The special abilities of leaders have been heralded for centuries. However, these qualities have not been carefully examined until recently. Psychologists have found that one of the most important abilities—one shared by many leaders—is a high degree of verbal skill (Bavelas, Hastorf, Gross, & Kite, 1965). In addition, good leaders generally maintain the views of their group. Leaders who wander too far from their group's views tend to be discarded. Aside from these two characteristics, leaders are very different from one another. We have not yet uncovered specific personalities or important traits that are guaranteed to result in leadership.

Research has shown that both leadership hypotheses have merit and that they often work simultaneously. For example, whereas certain leaders may emerge owing to circumstances, some individuals, because of their personalities, are more likely than are other people to accept and capitalize on a situational call to leadership (Nydegger, 1975).

Leaders also have been classified according to their abilities to fill certain group needs. One researcher (Bales, 1970) has argued that groups need both *task leaders,* who are able to get certain jobs done, and *social-emotional leaders,* who can lift spirits and offer psychological comfort and a sense of well-being to group members. Bales has argued that great leaders combine the best of both task leaders and social-emotional leaders.

▌ PREJUDICE AND DISCRIMINATION

We have seen some of the effects of individuals on one another, and of groups on individuals, as well as the reasons why some individuals become leaders of groups. In addition, are the effects of attitudes and behaviors of members of one group on members of other groups. Social psychologists sometimes use the terms **in-group** and **out-group** when discussing the feelings that members of one group may have toward their own group and toward other groups. Whether someone considers a group to be an in-group or an out-group depends on his perspective. What is an in-group for you may be an out-group for someone else. By definition, a person has a positive regard for in-groups but views out-groups in a negative light. The way in which a person decides which are in-groups and which are out-groups has been of great interest to social psychologists studying prejudice and discrimination. After all, before prejudice can begin, it is necessary to identify the in-group and the out-group. A very prejudiced individual may perceive hundreds of out-groups, placing just about every person in existence into one or another of them.

Prejudice can be defined as learned values and beliefs that may lead an individual to be unfairly biased against members of particular groups. Because of

SITUATIONAL–ENVIRONMENTAL HYPOTHESIS
The hypothesis that individuals become leaders because of situational or circumstantial forces rather than because of their personality traits.

GREAT-MAN, GREAT-WOMAN HYPOTHESIS
The hypothesis that individuals become leaders primarily because of the personality or traits they possess.

IN-GROUP
Any group for whom an individual feels a positive regard. This is a subjective term, depending on the person's point of view.

OUT-GROUP
Any group that an individual views in a negative way. This is a subjective term, depending on the person's point of view.

PREJUDICE
Beliefs or judgments made without sufficient evidence and not easily changed by opposing facts or circumstances; preconceived hostile and irrational feelings, opinions, or attitudes about a group or an individual.

prejudice, people may behave differently toward other groups (out-groups) than they do toward their own (in-group). Differential behavior based on prejudice is called **discrimination.**

One of the classic demonstrations of prejudice was set up by teacher Jane Elliott in an experiment she conducted with her third-grade class in Riceville, Iowa. Elliott wanted her students to understand something about prejudice. All the students in her class were white, but their eye color differed. On the first day of the experiment, Elliott, who had blue eyes, announced to her class that it was a well-known fact that blue-eyed children were brighter and generally were superior to those with brown eyes. It was explained to the brown-eyed children in the classroom, who were fewer, that they were inferior and that the blue-eyed children should be deferred to because they were better people. To emphasize their inferiority, the brown-eyed children were forced to sit in the back of the room, to use paper cups instead of the drinking fountain, to stand at the end of the line, and to wear special collars that enabled the blue-eyed students to identify them immediately from a distance or from behind. The blue-eyed students, on the other hand, were given special privileges such as extra time at recess and second helpings at lunch.

Before the first hour had elapsed, the effects of discrimination had begun to show on the brown-eyed children. Their schoolwork deteriorated. They became angry and depressed. They described themselves as sad, stupid, or awful. (You may recall from Chapter 6 that this is not unlike the way in which the black children referred to the black doll in the experiment conducted by Clark and Clark.) In describing the effect on the blue-eyed children, the teacher stated, "What had been marvelously cooperative, thoughtful children became nasty, vicious, discriminating little third-graders . . . it was ghastly" (Zimbardo, 1979, p. 638).

The next day, Elliott informed the students that she had made a mistake and that it was really the blue-eyed children who were inferior. In short order, the behaviors of the children switched. The brown-eyed children began to do better at their schoolwork, while the blue-eyed children began to lose their self-confidence.

Feeling prejudice firsthand may be a valuable educational experience for those who, because of their cultural position, are not typically subjected to prejudice. The benefits that may be gained from the experience have been demonstrated in an experiment in which children in an all-white third-grade class were assigned

Before the civil rights movement in the United States, and resulting legislation, discrimination was openly practiced.

randomly to be either green or orange people. They wore colored armbands to show which group they belonged to. At first, the orange people were considered superior. They were told that they were cleaner and smarter. The green people were regarded as inferior and were denied many privileges given to the orange people. On the second day, the situation was reversed. The effects were similar to those produced in the Elliott study. Each time, the group discriminated against felt inferior, lost self-confidence, and did poorly in schoolwork. In this experiment, another all-white class served as a control group and was never exposed to the assignments of orange or green. On the third day, and again after 2 weeks, students in the control class and students who had gone through the orange and green experiment were asked whether they would like to go on a picnic with black children from a nearby school. On one occasion, only 62 percent of the children in the control group agreed to go, while 96 percent of the children in the group that had experienced prejudice firsthand agreed (Weiner & Wright, 1973).

Both the eye-color and the orange–green experiments show how easily prejudice can be learned. It can be taught by systematically associating other groups with unpleasant stimuli, by rewarding discriminatory behaviors, and by modeling discrimination.

Personality and Prejudice

Although individuals can learn to feel prejudice against a particular group, there is evidence that some people are prejudiced in a much more general way. These people place just about everyone in out-groups and treat them as **stereotypes.** In 1946, researcher Eugene Hartley, when measuring people's attitudes toward different minority groups, decided to list three minorities that didn't exist, Daneriens, Pirenians, and Walonians. He found that people who identified many out-groups were prejudiced against the made-up groups as well. One generally prejudiced person stated, "I don't know anything about them. Therefore, I would exclude them from my country" (Hartley, 1946).

Perhaps the best-known effort to explain prejudice was made by another team of researchers over 40 years ago (Adorno, Frenkel-Brunswik, Levinson, & Sanford, 1950). Adorno and his colleagues believed that people who were highly prejudiced were likely to have authoritarian personalities. Authoritarian people tend to be submissive and obedient to authority and to reject other groups in a punitive way. They usually see other people as either weak or strong: "Either you're with us or against us" (in-group or out-group). Adorno thought that individuals became authoritarian because of the harsh and punitive child-rearing practices of their parents (Stephan & Rosenfield, 1978).

To test this hypothesis, Adorno and his colleagues developed the California F scale to measure authoritarianism (see Chapter 13). Although the findings are not completely consistent, in general Adorno's hypothesis—that people who are extremely authoritarian are more likely to be prejudiced—has been supported (Cherry & Byrne, 1976).

Overcoming Prejudice

There are a number of ways in which to overcome prejudice. We might attempt to overcome it through contact—bringing antagonistic groups into contact with one another—but that may make matters worse. Groups also need a common goal. For example, racism is not likely to persist among members of a baseball team, because all the players have one goal. They must cooperate with one another to

STEREOTYPE
A set of simplistic and relatively fixed overgeneralizations concerning the physical or psychological characteristics of a class or group of people.

reach this goal; and, as a result, they come to think of one another as members of a common in-group.

Prejudice also can be combated by legislation. Although it is difficult to legislate values, prejudice can be encouraged or not by the structure of the laws in a society. The legal structure in South Africa, for example, makes racial prejudice more likely, since blacks and whites are segregated by law and the persistent economic and political inequalities between the groups are emphasized. In the United States in the past 25 years, laws such as the Voting Rights Act, which are designed to give minority members equal rights, have helped to change attitudes and beliefs among the population. In 1963 in the South, for example, 61 percent of the white parents said that they would not send their children to a school attended by even a few blacks. By 1975, this figure had decreased to 15 percent. Much of the difference was due to a new awareness brought about by legislation (Gallup, 1975).

Finally, through learning, self-esteem may be increased among people who are the victims of prejudice so as to lessen the adverse effects of the prejudice. Concepts such as "Black is beautiful" and "I am somebody" may protect potential victims from some of the detrimental effects of prejudice. Furthermore, all of us who are interested in eliminating prejudice can help by modeling nondiscriminatory behavior and by showing others that we are accepting of the members of potential out-groups. This holds true for sexual discrimination, which is discussed in Chapter 18, as well as for race, age, ethnic, and religious discrimination.

SOCIAL COGNITION AND ATTITUDE CHANGE

The attitudes that a person has about other people can be a powerful influence in social situations. Consequently, psychologists have been drawn to study how social attitudes are formed and how they change. A **social attitude** is a relatively enduring system of feelings, beliefs, and behaviors with respect to a social object. For example, the attitudes you have toward a family member would include your feelings and thoughts about that person and your behaviors toward that person that have been generated by the feelings and thoughts. Knowing how someone thinks about a particular issue makes it easier to predict the person's behavior (Cialdini, Petty, & Cacioppo, 1981). The interaction between social forces and thought processes has opened a relatively new area of social investigation known as **social cognition.**

Forming Social Attitudes

Research in social cognition has shown that experiences with social stimuli can affect our perceptions and evaluations of that stimuli. Recall from Chapter 6, for example, how the studies by Staats and Staats (1958) demonstrated through the process of associative learning how nationalities such as Swedish or Dutch and names such as Tom and Bill could be systematically paired with pleasant or unpleasant words to alter how people felt toward these nationalities and names.

Instrumental learning also can be important in the formation of attitudes. As children develop, parents typically reinforce or punish the behaviors that stem from the attitudes the children hold. We can all recall a childhood in which adults told us the attitudes that we should have about stealing other people's property or calling someone a name. Our attitudes and views were shaped as we were systematically rewarded for the "right" behaviors and punished for the "wrong" behaviors.

Social learning through modeling is another important source of attitude acquisition. We often based our attitudes on the behavior of other people, even if those others are not trying to transmit their attitudes to us directly. We look to others to help us decide which attitudes are best and appropriate.

MEASURING ATTITUDES.   Investigators often measure attitudes by means of questionnaires or scales. Such measurement devices must be used carefully, because subtle differences in the meanings of words that appear in them can bias responses. For an extreme example of such bias, examine Figure 17.9. Generally, however, if the questionnaire or scale is worded carefully and is used appropriately, it can provide much valuable information about attitudes.

Another problem that arises with questionnaires is that people often present attitudes different from their real ones, or alter their true beliefs, in an attempt to enhance their image in the eyes of the researcher (Braver, Linder, Corwin, & Cialdini, 1977; Schlenker, 1978). When this happens, it is difficult to make a true assessment of attitudes. To reduce the incidence of faked attitudes on questionnaires and scales, social psychologists have devised a unique arrangement known as the **bogus pipeline.** In this procedure, subjects are connected to a machine with impressive flashing lights. They are told that the machine will monitor their physiological responses and will reveal to the experimenter their true opinions whenever they supply an answer about their attitudes. A trick is used to help subjects believe in the bogus pipeline. The subject's views on certain questions have been subtly obtained by coworkers in the experiment, usually from his friends or family members days earlier. Now the subject is asked to respond to these questions first. Once the subjects are convinced that the machine can detect their real opinions, they are asked to respond to the questionnaire. It is assumed that they will no longer have a reason to fake when answering the attitude questionnaire if they believe that the machine will reveal their true feelings (Jones & Sigall, 1971).

There is evidence that real attitudes are tapped better by the bogus pipeline technique than by a questionnaire used alone. In one study, for instance, whites expressed a positive attitude toward blacks when asked to answer a standard questionnaire, but expressed more negative attitudes when connected to the bogus pipeline (Jones, Bell, & Aronson, 1972). In another experiment, students connected to the bogus pipeline were more likely to confess to having had the answers to a test beforehand than they were when asked the same question on a standardized questionnaire (Quigley-Fernandez & Tedeschi, 1978). The bogus pipeline technique has not always shown positive results, however (Cherry, Byrne, & Mitchell, 1976). It may even be possible that the bogus pipeline causes subjects to "confess" to attitudes more negative than those they really have (Gaes, Kalle, & Tedeschi, 1978).

Other approaches designed to reveal a person's real attitudes have been attempted. Real physiological monitors can be used to measure information about the intensity or direction of an emotional or attitudinal response (Mewborn & Rogers, 1979; White & Maltzman, 1978). Such monitors also have been used to measure physiological responses as attitudes undergo change (Cacioppo & Petty, 1979; Kroeber-Riel, 1979), but they are not always accurate, and they present the same problems encountered when lie detectors are used (see Chapter 10).

ATTITUDES AND SELF-AWARENESS.   Sometimes subjects aren't certain about their own attitudes, and they may respond to questions without carefully monitoring their feelings. The subjects in one experiment were asked about their attitudes toward working particular puzzles. In one condition, they described their feelings

BOGUS PIPELINE
A procedure for measuring a person's real attitudes and feelings rather than what the person wishes to present. Subjects are led to believe that a supposed physiological monitor is able to detect their real attitudes and feelings and that any attempt to hide them will be uncovered.

FIGURE 17.9

An example of how a questionnaire can be biased. Survey questions (a) and (b) appear to ask the same thing, but because of the connotations of the words used, survey (a) will report that people like to spend, while survey (b) will report that they like to save.

(a) How do you handle your money? Are you

☐ Generous, or ☐ Stingy

(b) How do you handle your money? Are you

☐ Extravagant, or ☐ Thrifty

PERSUASIVE COMMUNICATION
Arguments designed to alter attitudes by
appealing to reason by means of fact and
logic.

while seated before a mirror. In the control condition, the subjects saw no mirror. The hypothesis stated that people placed before a mirror will have more self-awareness and that this, in turn, will help them to concentrate on their feelings. The experimenters used the subjects' attitudes about how much fun the puzzles would be to predict how long they would play with the puzzles. The attitudes obtained from subjects seated before a mirror predicted much more accurately how long they would play with the puzzles than did the attitudes obtained from the other subjects (Pryor, Gibbons, Wicklund, Fazio, & Hood, 1977).

Changing Attitudes: Persuasive Communication

It seems that a day can't go by without someone trying to change our attitudes. All you need to do to find the attitude changers at work is to turn on a television set, to listen to a radio, or to look at a billboard.

Techniques for changing attitudes commonly rely on **persuasive communication.** In persuasive communication, we are provided with facts or logical arguments about why we should use a particular product or feel a particular way. These so-called facts or logical arguments often are self-serving, and biased. Sometimes the communications will influence our attitudes; sometimes they will not. The ability of messages from advertising agencies, political candidates, or even people we know to affect our attitudes depends on a number of complex interactions.

CHARACTERISTICS OF THE COMMUNICATOR. In general, we tend to trust information from experts (Eagly, 1983). Nonetheless, a communicator's intentions can affect our view of his credibility. We would normally consider a physician to be an expert on medical matters, but we might not believe a physician who tells us that cigarettes are good for our health once we find out that she owns a large share of a tobacco company. In such an instance, we might regard the communication as biased because of the obvious motives behind the expert's statement (Eagly & Himmelfarb, 1978).

Another important characteristic of the communicator is his perceived similarity with the audience. If members of the audience think that the speaker is similar to them (in socioeconomic class, occupation, appearance, and so on),

Techniques for changing attitudes commonly rely on persuasive communication.

they probably will find him to be more persuasive. Television commercials capitalize on this tendency, using actors or actresses who look like "someone off the street." In general, salespeople who are like their customers are even more successful at selling the product than are experts who are perceived to be unlike the customers (Brock, 1965).

During the past few years, researchers have gathered much evidence to show that the information people generate themselves is more powerful in determining attitudes than is information provided by other people (Cialdini, Petty, & Cacioppo, 1981). In other words, self-persuasion is most persuasive (Janis & King, 1954).

In one study, students were asked to write an essay about a particular issue using certain words that were associated with either a pro or an anti position. The students who used the most pro words became more favorable toward the position. Those who used the anti words became less favorable (Eiser & Ross, 1977; Eiser & Pancer, 1979). In a second study, subjects were given essays to read that contained either the pro words or the anti words; these essays did not affect the subjects' attitudes. In the first study, the subjects had used these words in their own essays (self-generated); in the second study, they had read essays in which the words had been used (generated) by other writers. These studies highlight the strong influence of self-generated arguments.

CHARACTERISTICS OF THE COMMUNICATION. Another important factor in producing attitude change is the form of the message or communication. One kind of communication may be more effective than another, depending on the initial view held by the recipient of the message. If the recipient initially opposes the idea that is to be presented, a two-sided argument (in which the speaker clearly presents both sides of the issue) will lower the recipient's resistance to persuasion more effectively than will a one-sided argument (in which the speaker presents only the side the recipient opposes). On the other hand, if the recipient initially agrees with the issue, a one-sided argument in favor of the issue will strengthen her attitude toward the issue more effectively than will a two-sided argument (Hovland, Lumsdaine, & Sheffield, 1949).

Some communications appeal to the emotions. Cigarette smokers are frightened by stories of lung cancer; a request for funds to feed the hungry is accompanied by photographs of malnourished children; and a message about driver safety is supplemented by an account of an automobile accident. **Emotional appeals** can be effective in changing attitudes and behavior, but only under certain conditions (Leventhal & Niles, 1965; Simonson & Lundy, 1966). For an emotional appeal to work, the viewers must believe that they can take action that will reduce the stress caused by the emotional appeal, such as giving to the hungry. If action is impossible, viewers tend to deny the emotional appeal or to try to ignore it. In addition, viewers who have high self-esteem are more likely to be influenced by emotional appeals (Leventhal, 1970). It may be that people with low self-esteem view themselves as helpless or as under too much stress to be worried about the problems of other people. If the recipients of the message think that they can do nothing, or if they have low self-esteem, a mild emotional appeal will have a greater effect than will a strong one (Janis & Feshbach, 1953).

There are also ways to help people resist attitude change. People who have been taught how to refute arguments that go against their beliefs are less likely to change their beliefs (McGuire, 1964). It's also possible to help people avoid attitude change by forewarning them that the speaker is intent on changing their beliefs (Petty & Cacioppo, 1979).

Simply being exposed to something can alter our attitude in favor of it (Zajonc, 1968). Advertisers, knowing this, attempt to show their products as often as possible.

EMOTIONAL APPEALS
Arguments designed to alter attitudes by appealing to the emotions through stirring visual and verbal messages.

This effect is known as the **mere exposure effect.** It does not hold true for things that have negative outcomes. For example, mere exposure to watching your car being damaged is not likely to make you feel better about it (Swap, 1977). In one clever experiment, researchers took photographs of subjects and of the subjects' friends or lovers. Then they made photographs from mirror images of the subjects and the subjects' friends and lovers. The photographs were mixed together and the subjects were asked which they felt most favorable toward. When subjects viewed themselves, they felt most favorable toward the photograph of the mirror image, which is the view of themselves with which they were most familiar, but when they viewed friends and lovers, they felt most favorable toward the direct photographs, which is the way they usually saw those people (Mita, Dermer, & Knight, 1977). Apparently, the stimulus doesn't even have to be observed consciously for the mere exposure effect to occur (Wilson, 1979). This may explain why people are more likely to vote for candidates they've seen or been exposed to than for candidates they've not seen. The effect persists even if voters are aware of the issues both candidates support and are not treating the election as a beauty contest (Grush, 1980).

CHARACTERISTICS OF THE LISTENER. Sometimes, people don't give much thought to a particular issue when it is presented, and yet their attitudes change anyway. For example, Miller and his colleagues discovered that listeners were more likely to change their attitudes in favor of a speaker who spoke quickly (Miller, Maruyama, Beaber, & Valone, 1976). Whether or not a listener has paid careful attention to a particular discussion, however, will affect the endurance of the attitude change. Researchers Petty and Cacioppo have argued that there are two basic routes of persuasion, **central route processing,** in which attitudes are changed while the person is motivated to think carefully about the issue, and **peripheral route processing,** in which attitudes are changed while motivation or ability to think about the issue is very low (Cooper & Croyle, 1984). An attitude change through the central route (for example, after carefully listening to a persuasive argument) is likely to be an enduring change. An attitude change through the peripheral route (for example, while noticing that a commercial has a pleasant jingle and nice-looking people) is more likely to be temporary (Cialdini, Levy, Herman, Kozlowski, & Petty, 1976).

One study clearly demonstrated the importance of these two routes of persuasion. Subjects were exposed to a message that contained either two or six arguments in favor of a particular positive position. The messages were given either by a likable or a dislikable person. One-half of the subjects was told that they would later be interviewed again concerning the issue, so they were motivated to pay attention and to think about it (central route). The other half was told that they would be interviewed later on an unrelated issue, and they therefore had little motivation to think about the message (peripheral route). The subjects who expected to be interviewed about the topic showed attitude change that was determined primarily by the number of arguments presented. The attitude change was greater when six rather than two arguments were given. Whether the speaker was likable or dislikable had no effect. Among the subjects who did not expect to be interviewed, the number of arguments (two or six) made little difference in attitude change. The important factor was whether the source, the speaker, was likable or dislikable. Furthermore, a measurement of attitudes taken 10 days later showed that the subjects who had expected to be interviewed about the topic (central route) had stable attitude changes, while those whose attitudes had been changed by the peripheral route had shifted back to their premessage attitudes (Chaiken, 1980).

The effect of the recipient's intelligence on his susceptibility to persuasion also has been examined. You might expect that it would be more difficult to change the attitudes of an intelligent person. In general, however, there is no reliable relationship between intelligence and ability to resist persuasion (Hovland, Lumsdaine, & Sheffield, 1949). The more intelligent a person is, however, the more likely it is that a two-sided argument will be effective in creating attitude change, compared with a one-sided argument (Miller & Buckhout, 1973).

A person's level of self-esteem has been shown to be an important predictor of her ability to resist persuasion (Linton & Graham, 1959). Nonetheless, a distinction must be drawn between long- and short-term self-esteem. Long-term self-esteem is the general feelings we have about ourselves over a long period of time, while short-term self-esteem can vary from moment to moment, depending on immediate events. For instance, although you may feel generally good about yourself (your long-term esteem is high) you may call yourself "stupid" if you drop a glass and break it (your short-term self-esteem is low). By giving subjects tasks in which they were destined to fail, researchers have manipulated short-term self-esteem. Interestingly, the level of short-term self-esteem seems to have a greater effect on the person's ability to resist persuasion than does his level of long-term self-esteem. As short-term self-esteem lowers, resistance to persuasion decreases (Gollob & Dittes, 1965; Zellner, 1970). Why this is so is not known.

Cognitive Dissonance and Attitude Change

In the late 1950s, Leon Festinger conducted what has become a classic experiment. Subjects were invited to participate in a study that was purposely made exceedingly dull. For 1 hour they were required to move spools on and off of a tray and to rotate pegs in a pegboard by quarter turns, always using only one hand. It's hard to imagine a task that could have been more boring. The subjects were unaware that they had been assigned to one of two groups. When they were finished, they were offered a monetary reward for participating in the experiment and were then asked to do something for the experimenter. Subjects in the first group were given only $1 and were asked to tell the next subject, who was waiting to participate in the experiment, that the experiment had been fun! After taking the dollar and complying with the request, the subjects were then asked by an interviewer about their *real* feelings about the experiment. Subjects in the second group were put through the same procedure but given $20 as a reward instead of $1. Interestingly, the subjects who had received the $20 reported really feeling that the experiment was horribly boring, while the subjects who had received only $1 said they really thought that the experiment had been interesting (Festinger & Carlsmith, 1959). Festinger argued that when a person acts in a manner that is *inconsistent with his real feelings or beliefs*, and can find no obvious reason for having done so, **cognitive dissonance** is created. Such dissonance, he argued, must be resolved, because it causes an uncomfortable feeling, and the best way to resolve it is to *change your attitude* so that the previous behavior will now appear to be consistent with your views. In other words, when subjects lied by telling another person that the dull task was really interesting, they behaved in a manner inconsistent with their feelings; those who had received only $1 for doing this were subjected to a high level of cognitive dissonance because they couldn't even look to the money as a reason for their lying. The real reason the subjects had lied, of course, was that they were being obedient to the experimenter. As we learned from the Milgram experiments, most people will be obedient. But, unable to find any obvious reason for telling a lie, the subjects resolved their dissonance by deciding that, in fact, they had not

COGNITIVE DISSONANCE
The condition in which one has beliefs or knowledge that are internally inconsistent or that disagree with one's behavior. When such cognitive dissonance arises, one is motivated to reduce the dissonance through changes in behavior or cognition.

FIGURE 17.10

Festinger and Carlsmith's experiment demonstrating the effects of cognitive dissonance. Subjects who lied (told the next subject that the experiment was fun) and received only $1 reduced their cognitive dissonance by claiming that they had, in fact, liked the experiment. Subjects who lied but received $20 experienced little or no dissonance and claimed to dislike the experiment. A control group, whose members moved spools and turned pegs but were not requested to lie and received no money, really disliked the experiment. (SOURCE: *Adapted from Festinger & Carlsmith, 1959, p. 207.*)

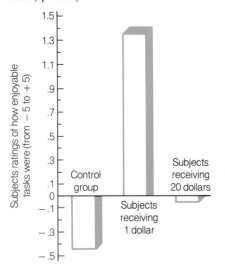

lied, that they had really enjoyed the experiment! By changing their attitudes, they did not have to face the unpleasant feelings of dissonance. Those subjects who received the $20, on the other hand, felt that they had a reason to lie, since they were being well paid to do so; therefore, they did not feel much dissonance. As a result, little attitude change occurred in this group (see Figure 17.10).

Cognitive dissonance theory had a great impact when it was introduced because it collided head-on with the two most popular psychological theories of its time, behaviorism and psychoanalytic (Freudian) theory. For example, no behaviorist would have predicted that the subjects who would be most likely to lie would have been the ones *least* reinforced for doing so. Freudian theory predicts that a catharsis (see Chapter 1) reduces anger you might have toward someone if you openly express that anger. Cognitive dissonance theory showed, however, that to justify their expressions of anger, people will denigrate the one at whom they are angry, making further anger even easier to express and, therefore, more likely to occur (DeAngelis, 1990).

Dissonance effects will not occur if people realize that they are being forced to make a choice inconsistent with their feelings or beliefs or if the actions they take that are inconsistent with their real views have no consequences (Schlenker & Schlenker, 1975). Most attempts to reduce cognitive dissonance, however, generally will cause attitudes to change. For instance, as a general rule attitudes about whether you will win a wager become more positive *after* you've placed a bet (Younger, Walker, & Arrowood, 1977). Dissonance theory helps to explain why most people perceive that they have made good decisions *after* they have made them. The amount of effort or money we have to expend to reach a goal or to acquire something may be more important in determining how we feel about it than is its actual value. For this reason, once a person, or even a nation, makes a commitment or invests in a particular action, it often becomes difficult to convince those responsible that the decision was not a good one and should not be pursued. They have changed their attitudes to agree with their decision in order to reduce their feelings of dissonance.

One of the best-known experiments that demonstrated this effect was conducted by Aronson and Mills in 1959. These researchers divided female college students into three different groups. In each group, the subjects were told that they would be listening to a supposedly exciting taped discussion about sex. The first group was admitted to hear the tape without passing any initiation test. The second group received a mild initiation in which they had to read five sex-related words such as *prostitute* or *virgin* to a male researcher. The third group was given a severe initiation in which subjects had to read a dozen obscene words and two very explicit sexual passages to a male researcher. After the initiations, the subjects did not listen to an exciting discussion concerning sexual behavior as they had been led to believe, but instead to a boring report about animal sexuality that made little sense. After listening to the tape, the subjects were asked to rate the value of the taped discussion. As expected, the more severe the initiation, the more the discussion was valued (Aronson & Mills, 1959). The investigators argued that those subjects who had gone through the stress of the severe initiation experienced cognitive dissonance when all they received for their efforts was a boring, senseless tape. Rather than feel upset, the subjects altered their perception of the tape and found listening to it to be a valuable experience.

In 1962, Elliot Aronson proposed a modification to Festinger's cognitive dissonance theory, which eventually became known as the **impression management hypothesis** (Tedeschi, 1981; Malkis, Kalle, & Tedeschi, 1982). This view argues that the results of dissonance theory could be explained by people's need to appear consistent to other people in their attitudes (Tedeschi, Schlenker, & Bonoma, 1971); that is, the subjects in the experiments on cognitive dissonance were not really changing their true attitudes but were reporting that their attitudes had changed so that they would appear consistent in the eyes of other people. For example, according to the impression-management hypothesis, the women who went through severe initiation in the experiment just discussed *truly* thought that the tape was boring but needed to appear consistent in the eyes of the investigators. They asserted that the tape was valuable so that they would not appear foolish for having gone through so much trouble to hear it. In other words, they needed to present attitudes that seemed consistent with their behaviors, although their *real* attitudes had not changed.

To examine this hypothesis, researchers conducted experiments on cognitive dissonance and obtained the subjects' reactions through the bogus pipeline procedure. The procedure indicated that the subjects' true attitudes often had *not* changed in situations in which the subjects in a typical dissonance experiment would normally demonstrate an attitude shift (Cialdini, Petty, & Cacioppo, 1981). Although the bogus pipeline procedure may be fallible, the idea of impression management must be considered as a possible explanation for the results of cognitive dissonance research (Leary & Kowalski, 1990).

Attribution

We often are curious about the personality or motivations of other people. We look for stable traits and underlying motives as a way of understanding others' behavior. We react to people's behavior differently depending on the motives or traits to which we attribute that behavior (Heider, 1958). We engage in **attribution** whenever we try to find the reasons for another's behavior or to understand his personality or motivation. In other words, we attribute a person's behavior to certain aspects of his personality or environment.

Social psychologists have found that one of the first tasks of attribution is to decide whether the individual's personality is determining the behavior (that is, whether the behavior is being shaped from within) or whether forces in the environment are controlling the behavior (that is, whether the behavior is being shaped from without). We assign blame or give credit depending, in part, on whether we attribute someone's behavior to internal or external factors. Consider what happened in 1957 when the Soviet Union launched the world's first artificial satellite, Sputnik. Stunned by this technological achievement, American scientists rushed to match it. Their early attempts to launch rockets failed utterly because they did not know much about how to build these machines. The only people in America who really knew how to build and fly rockets were Nazi scientists captured during World War II. The leading expert among them was Wernher von Braun, who had built the V-2 rocket that had been used against London with devastating effect. Many Americans were dismayed that the U.S. government had to turn to a former Nazi to get the rocket program literally off the ground. They argued that we should not entrust the program to a man who had developed missiles that killed civilians. These people attributed von Braun's behavior in working for the Nazis and being a Nazi to evil personality traits. Other people attributed von Braun's behavior to environmental causes. They argued that von Braun was not responsible, since the Nazis had forced him to build the V-2. People who attributed von Braun's behavior to internal motivations and personality traits held him accountable for what happened during the war and did not want him to head the missile program, while those who attributed his behavior to environmental forces believed that he had been forced to do what he had done and were not opposed to his appointment. In 1960, a film entitled *I Aim at the Stars* cast the German actor Curt Jurgens in the role of von Braun. Its basic premise was that von Braun was internally motivated

ATTRIBUTION
The psychosocial process through which we come to believe that certain events or dispositions are responsible for the behavior of ourselves or others.

only to explore rocketry and space flight and that his part in the Nazi war effort was attributable to the external forces brought to bear on him. One caustic movie reviewer, suspicious of this argument, entitled his review of the film "I Aim at the Stars, but I Hit London."

One of the most interesting aspects of the attribution process is that it can lead to a biased assessment of other people (Harvey & Weary, 1984). For instance, we tend to view our own behavior as stemming from situational or environmental forces, but we see the behavior of other people as stemming from internal forces (Eisen, 1979; Quattrone, 1982). Moreover, people usually find terms for traits to be better descriptions of other people than of themselves (Goldberg, 1978).

Psychologists have developed two hypotheses to explain this tendency. The **visual perspective hypothesis** argues that we attribute other people's behavior to internal forces and our own to external forces because of our visual perspective. Unless we're standing in front of a mirror, we rarely see ourselves as others see us. But we easily see the environmental forces that impinge on us from all directions. For this reason, we may be more aware of the environment than we are of ourselves. When dealing with other people, however, we tend to see whole people, the way we would see ourselves if we had a mirror. As a result, their "peopleness," with its accompanying traits and personality, may strike us more than the environmental circumstances affecting them. This theory may help to explain why therapists working with alcoholics have found that alcoholics are more willing to take the responsibility for controlling their drinking after they have viewed a videotape showing themselves intoxicated. By seeing themselves as they see other people, they may attribute more responsibility to internal traits and personality.

The second hypothesis argues that we tend to consider ourselves more than we do other people to be at the mercy of situational forces because we are more acutely aware of our own situation. This idea is known as the **information availability hypothesis.** The more information we obtain about another person, the more likely we are to attribute her behavior to environmental factors. Long before social psychologists found evidence for the information availability hypothesis, people in many cultures had demonstrated an understanding of this effect. As an American Indian saying puts it, if you want to know another person, walk a mile in his moccasins. Other cultures have similar sayings. Their import is that we can understand a person better once we really know the forces that impinge on her. Until then, we tend to attribute another's behavior to personality traits. In criminal trials, a defense lawyer will try to bring up as much information as possible about a client's hard life and difficult past. The more information the jury members hear about the person's situation, the more likely they are to attribute the person's action to environmental factors, rather than to personality. Both the visual perspective hypothesis and the information availability hypothesis have been supported by research (Eisen, 1979; Taylor & Fiske, 1978).

Another factor affecting attribution error is **self-serving bias.** This term describes the tendency to attribute behavior that results in a good outcome to internal forces and to attribute behavior that results in a bad outcome to environmental factors (Carver, DeGregorio, & Gillis, 1980; O'Malley & Becker, 1984). In other words, people tend to take responsibility for good results but to attribute bad results to factors beyond their control. Similarly, mothers view the positive personal characteristics of their children as stable and inborn, but see the negative characteristics as transitory (Gretarsson & Gelfand, 1988).

The self-serving bias probably occurs because people like to do "good" things and want their family to do good things, and are at a loss to explain why they occasionally do "bad" things. The bias probably stems from the belief that we should be in control of our behavior all of the time, in which case we must somehow deal with behavior that results in a bad outcome. The self-serving bias may be a form of rationalization, through which we deny that there are internal forces that lead us to behave in ways that we don't like or that we can't control.

EPILOGUE: BRAINWASHED

Psychologists know that behavior can be greatly influenced by social processes. The following is an account of how some of these processes influenced the behavior of the victim of a famous crime.

Attorney F. Lee Bailey had his hands full. He had to convince a jury that his client, Patricia Hearst, daughter of publisher William Randolph Hearst, was innocent of bank robbery.

In February 1974, Patricia Hearst, then 19 years old, was kidnapped from her apartment in Berkeley, California. Her kidnappers were members of the Symbionese Liberation Army (SLA), a group of radicals who argued that force was the only way to obtain justice for the poor. Patty was held for ransom. About two months after her kidnapping, the Hearst family received a tape in which Patty, who now called herself Tanya, stated that her father was a pig and that she had chosen to stay with the SLA. For almost 2 years, she avoided capture by the FBI. During this time, she was involved in at least one bank robbery.

After her capture (rescue?), when she was no longer under threat from the SLA, she continued to espouse the political beliefs of that organization and took credit for her actions. This, perhaps more than anything else, was damaging to her at her trial. Why, the jury wondered, would someone who had been freed from the threat of death by her captors continue to espouse the captors' views if they were really not her own views?

In her defense, Bailey argued that Patty had been brainwashed. He stated that she had gone along with the group's actions in order to reduce her fear. She was made to think up things to say that supported the group's position. She was rewarded by the group for agreeing with them. She may have felt that she could not justify her actions, and had therefore changed her attitudes to conform more to her behavior. She may have been polarized by the group to take a more extreme position. If you consider what you've learned about changing attitudes and group control of behavior, you may see that Patty was in a situation that could force her to change her attitudes and behavior drastically in a way that might continue even after she was freed. Bailey argued that Patty would have to be retrained socially, back to the person that everyone knew. He contended that she had been a victim.

But the jury members attributed Patty's behavior to the traits of her own personality rather than to situational forces, which is the way we commonly attribute behavior to others. As a result, they found her guilty.

Patricia "Tanya" Hearst posing as a member of the SLA. Was she "brainwashed"?

A short time later, the tragedy of Jonestown was in the news. Attorney Bailey, reflecting on the Hearst trial, said that if Jonestown had happened before the trial, Patty would never have been convicted. Perhaps he was right. Jonestown had taught a lesson in social psychology to everyone, a lesson in group compliance and obedience. And, with this lesson in mind, President Jimmy Carter granted Patty Hearst a full pardon.

SUMMARY

■ Social psychology is the study of how people affect the behavior, thoughts, and feelings of other people.

■ The ways in which other people expect us to conform are known as social norms.

■ People generally look to reference groups of similar individuals, or of individuals whom they would like to resemble, in order to make decisions about how to conform.

■ Researcher Stanley Milgram demonstrated the power of obedience when he found that a majority of people would administer shocks to a stranger when they were requested to, even though the stranger appeared to be in pain or in danger.

■ The tragedy of Jonestown demonstrated the dangers of blind obedience and conformity.

■ Situational factors at any given moment play a great role in whether people will help someone in an emergency. In some situations, people are less likely to help if there are more witnesses to the person's distress. This is known as the bystander effect. The bystander effect may be the result of diffusion of responsibility or of fear of appearing foolish by interpreting an ambiguous situation as an emergency when, in fact, it is not.

■ According to the bystander intervention model, for intervention to occur, the event must be observed and interpreted as an emergency, and the observer must take responsibility for helping and decide how to help. All these requirements must be met before action can be taken.

■ Morals are the attitudes and beliefs that help people to determine what is right or wrong. According to researcher Lawrence Kohlberg, moral development begins in childhood and progresses through six stages.

■ Both competition and cooperation are taught by social interaction. In certain instances, cooperation declines as children grow older, and competition becomes the common mode of responding, even when it cannot possibly lead to success. Cooperation between partners diminishes as their ability to threaten each other increases.

■ Individuals are influenced by groups in unique ways. Groups may deindividuate members, or they may lead members to be polarized and to take more extreme positions than they would as individuals.

■ Sometimes, an extremely effective group member will emerge as a leader. The situational–environmental hypothesis states that particular situations may arise in which a group member is fortuitously elevated to the position of leader because he or she happens to possess the skills needed at the moment. The great-man, great-woman hypothesis argues that certain people possess traits that make other group members likely to accept their leadership. Research has indicated that both hypotheses may be correct.

■ Prejudice consists of learned values and beliefs that may lead an individual to be unfairly biased against members of particular out-groups. Differential behavior based on prejudice is called discrimination.

■ Individuals with authoritarian personalities tend to be more prejudiced and are especially prone to categorize people as members of in-groups or out-groups.

■ Prejudice may be overcome by educating people, legislating nondiscriminatory behavior, increasing the self-esteem of the victims of prejudice, and creating contact between hostile groups as they work together to reach a common goal.

■ A social attitude is a relatively enduring system of feelings, beliefs, and behaviors toward a social object. Social attitudes can be formed through the processes of associative learning, instrumental learning, and social learning.

■ Social psychologists typically use questionnaires or scales to measure attitudes. The bogus pipeline procedure is designed to tap the real feelings and attitudes of subjects instead of the pretended feelings or attitudes subjects often report.

■ Individuals tend to assess their own attitudes more accurately and to express more self-awareness when placed in front of a mirror.

■ Techniques for changing attitudes commonly rely on persuasive communication. The characteristics of the communicator can affect the attitudes of the listener. Communicators who are similar to their audience in socioeconomic class, occupation, or appearance are more persuasive.

■ Self-generated persuasion is more effective than is persuasion generated by other people.

■ Two-sided arguments are more persuasive to individuals who initially oppose the idea that is presented. One-sided arguments are more persuasive if the recipient initially agrees with the idea.

■ Emotional appeals are effective in changing attitudes, and individuals with high self-esteem are more likely to be influenced by emotional appeals.

■ We can help people to resist persuasion by warning them that someone else is going to try to persuade them.

■ Simply being exposed to something that does not have a bad outcome can alter our attitude in favor of it. This is known as the mere exposure effect.

■ Central-route processing of a message generally leads to a permanent change in attitudes, while peripheral-route processing usually leads to a temporary change.

■ When subjects are made to state or do something that goes against their beliefs and they can see no valid reason for having made the statement, or taken the action, they are placed in cognitive dissonance.

■ Researchers argue that to resolve this dissonance, subjects tend to change their attitudes to bring them into line with the statements they have made or the actions they have taken.

■ The impression management hypothesis argues that cognitive dissonance results can be explained, not as real changes in attitudes and beliefs, but rather as professed changes for the purpose of maintaining an appearance of consistency in the eyes of other people.

■ We often look for stable traits in other people or for the motives behind their behaviors as a way of understanding them. Social psychologists call this attribution. People generally are held accountable for behavior that is attributed to personality or trait variables and are considered blameless for behavior that is attributed to environmental forces. People tend to attribute their own behavior more to environmental forces and to attribute the behavior of other people more to personality and trait forces.

■ The self-serving bias describes our tendency to attribute behavior that has a good outcome to our own personality traits and to attribute behavior that has a bad outcome to external forces that are beyond our control.

SUGGESTIONS FOR FURTHER READING

1. Aronson, E. (1987). *The social animal* (5th ed.). New York: W. H. Freeman. For the general reader or student of psychology, an examination of many areas in social psychology, including prejudice, political unrest, advertising, and sexual behavior.
2. Baron, R. A., & Byrne, D. (1987). *Social psychology: Understanding human interaction* (5th ed.). Boston: Allyn & Bacon. A college-level introductory textbook on social psychology.
3. Cialdini, R. B. (1985). *Influence: Science and practice.* New York: Random House. An interesting account of the ways human beings can influence each other. For the student or general reader.
4. Latane, B., & Darley, J. M. (1970). *The unresponsive bystander: Why doesn't he help?* New York: Appleton-Century-Crofts. The classic text on bystander intervention.
5. Lindzey, G., & Aronson, E. (Eds.). (1985). *Handbook of social psychology* (3rd ed.). Hillsdale, NJ: Erlbaum. A high-level comprehensive handbook on social psychology.
6. Milgram, S. (1974). *Obedience to authority.* New York: Harper & Row. Discusses Milgram's obedience research.
7. Paulus, P. B. (Ed.). (1980). *The psychology of group influence.* Hillsdale, NJ: Erlbaum. An advanced-level discussion of research in how groups influence each other.

CHAPTER 18 | Sexuality, Attraction, and Intimacy

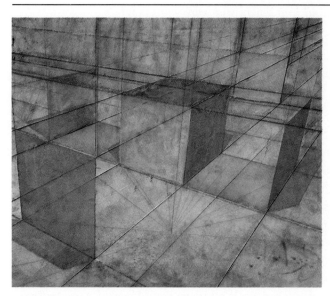

Prologue

Why Psychologists Study Sexuality, Attraction, and Intimacy

Biological Aspects of Human Sexuality
 Anatomical Characteristics
 The Effects of Hormones on Behavior

Gender-Role Acquisition
 Social Learning Theory
 The Cognitive View
 Gender Schema Theory
 Sexual Orientation

Attraction
 Liking
 Theories about Liking
 Love and Intimacy

Sexual Myths and Research
 Early "Research"
 Modern Research

Epilogue: The Conquest of Spermatorrhea

PROLOGUE

After a long ocean voyage, you've finally arrived at New Guinea, a South Pacific island not far from the equator. It is a land of thick jungles and towering green mountains. Although the year is 1935, you feel that modern civilization has barely touched this giant island.

As you arrive at your accommodations in the small town, the young anthropologist you've come so far to see is there to greet you. Her name is Margaret Mead. "I'm glad you're here," she says. "There's so much to show you."

"As you know from my telegram," you say, "my paper sent me here because they heard you were on to something. By the sound of it, it ought to shake up some people."

"Well, I don't know about that," Mead says, laughing. "But if we're to understand the power of culture and learning on our species, we have to see what's going on outside of Western civilization."

Later, you and Mead set off for a distant part of the island. You hadn't counted on the walking. The trails are narrow and slippery. They extend in a precise network into the precipitous mountains. After a time there are no more villages, only tiny settlements. This mountain land is barren and infertile. Skinny razor-backed pigs run wild. Shortly, you reach the village of Arapesh.

The Arapesh turn out to be an interesting tribe. It's almost immediately apparent that the Arapesh men are not aggressive. "They are taught to help other members of the tribe and to care deeply about others' needs and feelings," Mead tells you. "In temperament, the men of this village behave in ways that Westerners would consider feminine.

Among the Arapesh, both men and women are nurturing, caring, feeling, and unaggressive."

You leave the Arapesh and journey to the ocean, to the mouth of the Sepik River. You have been thinking about the old Arapesh man's comment when Mead told him where you were going next:

> You are going up the Sepik River, where the people are fierce, where they eat men. You are taking some of our boys with you. Go carefully. Do not be misled by your experience among us. We are another kind. They are another kind. So you will find it. (Mead, 1935/1963, p. 167)

A long boat ride brings you to the home of the Mundugumor tribe. Here you sense caution and tension among your party, as Mead enters the village and the Mundugumor recognize her and come to greet her. In short order you learn that the Mundugumor are a fierce tribe. They are headhunters and cannibals, although they have been under government control for the past 3 years and have promised not to kill or eat anybody. Both the men and the women are aggressive and dangerous. Both have highly sexed personalities, and both have no hesitation about engaging in forthright sexual behavior. "In this tribe," Mead points out, "the women behave in ways that Westerners would consider masculine. They are tough and strong, and they can be every bit as violent as the men." It's difficult for you to leave your Western ideas behind. It's as though the Arapesh were all feminine and the Mundugumor all masculine.

When you leave the Mundugumor, you travel down the Sepik River until you reach the lake, which is so full of vegetation that it looks like black enamel until the wind stirs it. Alongside the lake is the village of the Tchambuli. Here, sex and temperament roles appear to be reversed. The Tchambuli women are dominant and the men are passive. The men are artists; they paint, dance, and make music. The women fish and manufacture trade goods. As Mead notes,

> The women's attitude towards the men is one of kindly tolerance and appreciation. They enjoy the games that the men play, they particularly enjoy the theatricals that the men put on for their benefit. (Mead, 1935/1963, p. 255)

The men are emotional and easily embarrassed. The women are the leaders, and the men generally defer to their authority.

On your return trip to the coast, you think about the Arapesh, Mundugumor, and Tchambuli and wonder how they can be so different from the men and women of your culture. As Mead bids you good-bye, she says, "I think you can see now that what we consider natural behavior for men and women may be more a function of culture than of biology. Everyone in Western society should be aware of the people here and of the way in which we acquire our understanding of so-called natural sex roles."

In this chapter, we will examine the biological, cognitive, and social-cultural aspects of human sexuality. We will look at biological differences between the brains of men and women, the formation of sex roles and gender identity, and the pressure that society and culture bring to bear in shaping our sexual behavior. We'll also explore love and intimacy, the history of sexual research, and some sexual myths and misunderstandings.

WHY PSYCHOLOGISTS STUDY SEXUALITY, ATTRACTION, AND INTIMACY

Our sex greatly influences the relationships, pursuits, choices, and conflicts that we face in life. Because of this, psychologists are interested in every aspect of our sexuality. They want to know how the biological and hormonal aspects of sexuality may affect behavior, how our cognitive understanding of being either male or female shapes our relationships, and how social-cultural influences on sexuality can direct our futures and determine our roles in society. Psychologists also are interested in intimacy and love. The reason for their interest was probably best expressed by Harry Harlow in 1958, when he gave the presidential address to the American Psychological Association:

> Love is a wondrous state, deep, tender, and reassuring. Because of its intimate and personal nature it is regarded by some as an improper topic for experimental research. But, whatever our personal feelings may be, our assigned mission as psychologists is to analyze all facets of human and animal behavior into their component variables. So far as love or affection is concerned, psychologists have failed in their mission. The little we know about love does not transcend simple observation and the little we write about it has been written better by poets and novelists. (Harlow, 1958, p. 673)

BIOLOGICAL ASPECTS OF HUMAN SEXUALITY

Anatomical Characteristics

Anatomy is perhaps the most obvious aspect of a person's sexuality. The basic anatomical differences between males and females are quite apparent, in terms of both primary and secondary sexual characteristics. The penis, scrotum, and testes of the male and the vagina, uterus, and ovaries of the female are **primary sexual characteristics** (see Figure 18.1). **Secondary sexual characteristics** appear at puberty. In girls, these include the development of breasts and the widening of the hips; in boys, the deepening of the voice and the appearance of facial hair. In both sexes, underarm and pubic hair develops. The appearance of secondary characteristics signals that the body is preparing for the capacity to reproduce. This period is reached in males at the time when the ejaculation of sperm becomes possible and in females when **menarche** (the beginning of menstruation) occurs. These events usually take place between the ages of 11 and 14 years, with girls able to reproduce on the average slightly sooner than boys. Healthy males remain capable of reproduction throughout their lives, and healthy females are capable until menopause, which signals the end of the regular fertile cycles.

Both the primary and the secondary sexual characteristics are closely related to the actions of sex hormones. Hormones are body chemicals carried in the blood

PRIMARY SEXUAL CHARACTERISTICS
The penis, scrotum, and testes of the male; the vagina, ovaries, and uterus of the female.

SECONDARY SEXUAL CHARACTERISTICS
Physical characteristics that appear in humans around the age of puberty and are sex-differentiated but not necessary for sexual reproduction.

MENARCHE
The first occurrence of menstruation.

that can affect psychological and physiological development (see Chapter 2). The sex glands, called gonads, secrete hormones. The gonads in the female are the ovaries; in the male, they are the testes. The adrenal glands on the adrenal cortex of the kidney also are a source of sex hormones in both sexes. The female hormones are called **estrogens,** and the male hormones are called **androgens.*** Researchers, believe that the secretion of sexual hormones may be directed by the thymus gland (Rebar, Miyake, Low, & Goldstein, 1981), which is located behind the breastbone, and by the pituitary gland, which is located at the base of the forebrain. The pituitary itself is controlled by areas of the brain, especially the hypothalamus.

---

*All normal individuals produce both estrogens and androgens. It is the ratio of one substance to the other that affects sexual characteristics.

FIGURE 18.1

Primary sexual characteristics of the male (a) and the female (b).

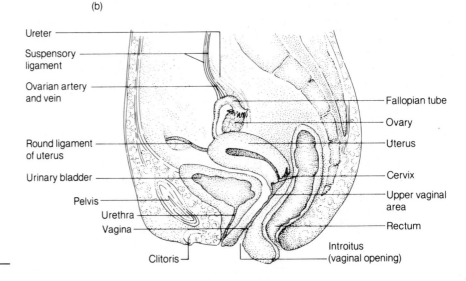

A child's genetic sex is determined at conception. The twenty-third pair of **chromosomes** (see Figure 18.2) determine the child's sex. The child will inherit an "X" shaped twenty-third chromosome from its mother, but may inherit either an "X" shaped or "Y" shaped twenty-third chromosome from its father. If the twenty-third pair of chromosomes consists of two Xs, then the child will be female; if the pair is XY, the child will be male. During the development of the embryo, if testosterone (one of the androgens) is present, as usually occurs under the direction of the genes on the Y chromosome, male genitals will develop in place of female ones (Money, 1965). In this way, the genes on the chromosomes determine sex indirectly through the action of hormones.

The Effects of Hormones on Behavior

In 1849, the German physiologist Arnold Berthold found that by castrating roosters he could stop them from fighting with one another. When the testicles were transplanted back into the castrated birds, the birds once again began to fight. The reimplanted testicles made connections, not with the rooster's nervous system, but rather with the circulatory system. This fact led Berthold and other scientists to assume that something was being carried in the blood that affected behavior. That "something" was later discovered to be a sex hormone.

In 1916, a Canadian physiologist named Frank Lillie presented a paper in which he explained why some genetically normal cows, called freemartins, acted and looked like bulls. Freemartins, he noted, always have a fraternal twin brother. Lillie speculated that the hormones from the testes of the male twin somehow masculinized the freemartins in the womb.

Researchers are interested in the effects of hormones on human beings because, as we have seen, hormones directly influence many behaviors in lower animals, such as aggression and sexual activity. Following Lillie's discovery about freemartins, researchers found that girls who had fraternal twin brothers were a little more

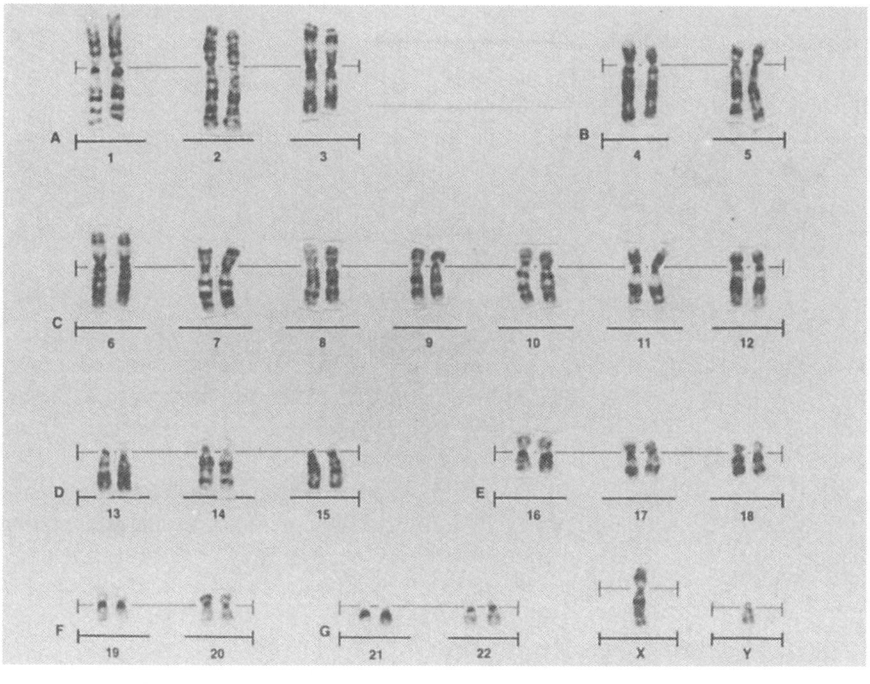

CHROMOSOME

A microscopic thread-shaped body contained within the nucleus of every cell, which determines the characteristics that will be passed on to the offspring of an organism. Chromosomes carry the genes. Humans have 23 pairs of chromosomes in each cell with the exception of the sperm and egg cells, which carry only 23 single chromosomes.

FIGURE 18.2

Humans have 23 pairs of chromosomes. In a photograph such as this, called a karyotype, the pairs are matched. One member from each pair is from the mother and one from the father. The 23rd pair are labeled either X or Y. This is a karyotype of a boy, because the 23rd pair is XY. If it had been a girl, the 23rd pair would have been XX.

CHAPTER 18
SEXUALITY, ATTRACTION, AND INTIMACY

GONADS
The sex glands that regulate sex drive and the physiological changes that accompany physical maturity; the ovaries in the female and the testes in the male.

likely to act tomboyish or to show a greater interest in what have been typically been considered "male" activities, such as contact sports. Because these girls were raised with brothers their own age with whom they played, it was not possible to isolate the effects of their environment from any possible hormonal effects. There is a way, however, to examine the effects of hormones on a human fetus.

Occasionally, a fetus may be exposed to levels of hormones that are higher than normal. Researchers have studied young girls who were exposed to abnormally large amounts of androgenic (male) hormones before birth. Such exposures may be caused by the administration of synthetic hormones for therapeutic reasons to the mother during pregnancy or by a disorder of the infant's own hormone secretions, known as congenital adrenal hyperplasia, or CAH. CAH occurs when the fetus secretes excessive androgen from the cortex of her kidneys. Sometimes female infants with this disorder are born with partially masculinized genitals, although their **gonads**, or sex glands, are female and normal.

During their preadolescence, these girls played in the rough-and-tumble way more commonly observed among boys, and they were characterized as less culturally feminine than most girls (Money & Ehrhardt, 1972; Baker, 1980; Eccles-Parsons, 1982; Hines, 1982). CAH girls also show a stronger preference for toys traditionally considered to be for boys than do matched female relatives without CAH (Adler, 1989).

Similarly, two populations of boys, aged 6 and 16 years, whose mothers received large doses of estrogens (female hormones) during pregnancy, were believed to be less athletic, less assertive, and less aggressive than most boys (Yalom, Green, & Fisk, 1973; Ehrhardt & Meyer-Bahlburg, 1981). It should be stressed, however, that studies of the effects of estrogen on males generally have been correlational or poorly controlled (Huston, 1983). Therefore, many researchers believe that no definite conclusions can yet be drawn concerning the effects of estrogen on males in the womb.

Although hormonal factors alone may account for some of the observed behavioral differences between males and females, the effects of androgynization, or exposure to male hormones, can't be all that strong. Once girls with CAH reach adolescence and adulthood, they no longer behave differentially from nonandrogynized females, and their sexual desires are just as likely to be heterosexual as are any woman's (Money & Mathews, 1982; Ehrhardt, & Meyer-Bahlburg, 1981). If androgynization in the womb had given these females strong "male" inclinations, we might assume that they would take a homosexual orientation in adulthood. The Soviets have also reported that androgynization of females in the womb in no way affects later sexual preference or orientation (Lev-Ran, 1974). Furthermore, male fetuses exposed to insufficient androgen levels in the womb are just as likely to have a heterosexual orientation as are other males (Ehrhardt & Meyer-Bahlburg, 1981).

Even so, the issue is a complex one, and answers are obviously not clearcut. For instance, just when most researchers were beginning to believe that although hormones may have a strong effect on the behavior of lower animals, they have only a weak effect on humans, researcher Julienne Imperato-McGinley of the Cornell University Medical College, presented data that suggested something different. She described 38 boys with a genetic disorder. All of them came from the city of Santo Domingo in the Dominican Republic, where this particular genetic disorder is relatively common. The genetic disorder keeps the male hormone testosterone from undergoing a chemical transition that would trigger the formation of male genitals during prenatal development. Boys who suffer from this disorder look like girls at birth. They are often given girls' names and raised as girls, because the parents are unaware that they are boys. However, owing to the further secretion of hormones at puberty, the penis, originally thought to be a clitoris, lengthens; the voice deepens; and the boy develops a muscular body. Even though the boys born with the genetic disorder have been socialized to be girls, after the physical change occurs, they easily adopt the culturally accepted male sex role in terms of identity, occupational desires, and sexual activity. The local Spanish slang terms for this disorder translate roughly to mean "penis-at-12" or "first woman, then man."

Imperato-McGinley concluded that the boys she studied in Santo Domingo could adjust to their sudden new male sex roles because their brains had *already* been masculinized in the womb by hormones. She argued that inside of each "girl's body," was the brain of a boy, made male, that is, *sensitized* by the testosterone that was present before birth and then, unlike the girls with CAH, *activated* by another surge of hormone (dihydrotestosterone) during the adolescent period (Imperato-McGinley, Peterson, Gautier, & Sturla, 1979). In this way, she believes, hormones are important in determining human behavior, because they sensitize the brain of the fetus in the womb to organize itself along certain lines in preparation for a later hit of hormone during puberty.

These data may indicate that the presence of male hormones predisposes individuals to adopt male roles. If this were the case, it would be expected that boys who were castrated at birth for medical reasons and were subsequently given estrogen treatment and raised as females would develop a male gender identity during adolescence. This does not appear to occur, however; such individuals are comfortable with their female identity (Wilson, Griffin, George, & Leshin, 1981). It is possible, therefore, that environmental forces were responsible for the ability of the children in Santo Domingo to change from a female to a male identity. As you know from reading about Mead's work in the Prologue, the environment can have a strong influence on sex roles. For instance, the "girls" in Santo Domingo who became men may have made the transition easily because their environment supported their new role (a couple of parents were even proud to discover that their daughter was really their son).

Currently, research concerning the ability of hormones or other biological forces to control directly or determine our behaviors is inconclusive. Part of the problem stems from the fact that it is very difficult to measure hormone levels in human beings. Hormone assays are very expensive and, in many instances, blood must be drawn from volunteers three or more times on the hour, leaving them with aching arms, a collapsed vein or two, and a fervent desire never again to volunteer for anything. Adding to this complication is the fact that in studies in which hormone levels were tracked over time, it has been shown that although absolute hormone levels in humans are a poor predictor of behavior, the *range of hormone fluctuation* throughout the day may be a valid predictor (Jacklin, 1989). Even so, if hormones do play an important role in our behavior, it is obviously not as strong as the one observed in lower species. If it were, we would have seen more conclusive research along the lines of Berthold's discovery that roosters completely stop fighting following castration. Actually, human males who have undergone castration for testicular cancer or other disorders are often unaffected in terms of sex drive or aggression, although this may be because their brains have already been hormone sensitized in the womb and activated at puberty, something that apparently isn't the major hormone mechanism in roosters.

To summarize, in our species hormones may, in a subtle way, play the greatest role in shaping behaviors related to gender, or culture and learning might. No one is certain.

GENDER ROLE
The behaviors associated with one sex or the other.

GENDER-ROLE IDENTIFICATION
The degree to which a child adopts the sex role of a particular model.

GENDER UNDERSTANDING
A person's comprehension that he or she is either a boy or a girl; usually develops in children by about the age of 3 years.

GENDER-ROLE ACQUISITION

As young children grow, certain behaviors come to be expected of them. Among these behaviors are the ones expected because of the child's gender. The acquisition of these behaviors is an example of the interaction between the child's cognitive development and his or her culture, which determines which behaviors are deemed appropriate for each gender. These behaviors constitute what is known as a **gender role.** *

The cultural shaping of gender roles may begin as early as birth. From the moment of an infant's birth, parents tend to treat boys and girls differently (Ban & Lewis, 1974; Will, Self, & Datan, 1976). Even though there are obvious anatomical differences, there are few behavioral differences between male and female babies. Nevertheless, most parents will describe their daughters as cuter, softer, and more delicate than they will their sons. Fathers tend to emphasize the beauty and delicacy of their newborn daughters and the strength and coordination of their newborn sons (Krieger, 1976). Later, fathers also are more likely to offer sons than daughters toys that are stereotypically male, such as trucks or footballs (Jacklin & Maccoby, 1983).

It is more difficult to determine how children acquire an understanding of gender roles than it is to discover when they do. To know *how* requires an explanation, whereas *when* can be determined from a description of behavior (see Chapter 1, p. 17). Even though it is a more difficult undertaking, let's try to examine the question of *how*.

Determining how children learn gender roles requires a theoretical understanding of **gender-role identification.** Psychoanalytic, social learning, and cognitive theories have all addressed this question. Each predicts that the parent's gender-role-related behavior should have a striking effect on the child's developing sexual identity, even though each theory views the development of gender-role identification differently.

According to the Freudian or psychoanalytic view, the identification of a boy with his father results from a drive to avoid retaliation for his initially desiring his mother because of the bond that he formed with her during feeding. This came to be known as the *Oedipus complex*, named after the mythical Greek king, Oedipus, who accidentally married his mother and killed his father without knowing who they really were. According to this view, once the boy child has identified with the father to avoid confronting him as a rival for the mother's affection, the boy adopts the father's ways as his own. Girls identify with their mothers in a more complex way known as the *Electra complex*. It is more complex because the girl also begins with an attachment to her mother via nursing, so a simple mirror image of the Oedipus complex can't be used as a sufficient explanation. Although psychologists find the Freudian view historically interesting and colorful, it is generally seen as scientifically limited (Jacklin, 1989), and few currently refer to it or consider it when examining this issue.

Some people have developed a more modern psychoanalytic approach to the question of gender-role identification, but they readily admit that their perspective is quite subjective (Stoller, 1985). Instead, most current researchers emphasize social learning theory or cognitive theory (Ruble, 1984).

*Some researchers prefer the term sex role. In practice, however, the two terms, *sex role* and *gender role* should be treated as synonymous (Maccoby, 1988).

Social Learning Theory

Social learning theory is based on the work of Albert Bandura, described in Chapter 6. In this view, children's behaviors are reinforced or punished according to what parents and society deem appropriate for the child's gender. We have already discussed how parents may differentially treat children based on gender. The toys parents provide for their daughters are different from those they give their sons, and parents encourage their children to develop gender-appropriate interests (Cairns, 1979; Rheingold & Cook, 1975).

In one entertaining experiment, the different reactions of mothers and fathers were clear. In this study, preschoolers were given toys commonly associated with one gender or the other, including kitchen play sets, a doll house, an army war game, or cowboy outfits. Both boys and girls were given "girls' toys" to play with on one occasion and "boys' toys" on another. The children were told to play with these toys *the way girls* (for girls' toys) *or boys* (for boys' toys) *would*. What the experimenters were interested in was the reaction of the mothers or fathers when they entered the room and saw which toys their children were playing with. Mothers showed little differential reaction to the toy sets. Fathers, on the other hand, showed far more negative reactions when their children were playing with the "inappropriate" toys. This was especially true if the fathers found their sons playing with "girls' toys" in the way that girls would. Fathers in these cases tended to interfere with play or show outward disgust (Langlois & Downs, 1980). Similarly, most research in this area has shown that mothers generally treat boy and girl infants less differently than do fathers. For this reason, fathers, in our culture, may have a greater effect on the early learning of gender roles (Power, 1981).

Modeling and observational learning are considered to be important aspects of social learning theory. Boys learn to observe men, and girls learn to observe women, to see how they are expected to behave. Boys observe that men are portrayed in books and the media more as the initiators of action. On television, for example, about 70 percent of the major characters who initiate actions in any kind of program are men (Huston, 1983). According to social learning theory, parents, television, peers, and society as a whole shape the acquisition of gender roles through modeling and observational learning.

The Cognitive View

Lawrence Kohlberg (1966) first proposed a cognitive conceptualization of gender-role acquisition. According to this view, after children realize that they have a self, they come to understand that they are either male or female, and this cognitive realization then guides the children to change their behavior to match what society deems appropriate for their gender. The time at which children first become aware of their gender and its meaning is an important consideration, because cognitive theory predicts that gender-role acquisition will not begin until the child has the concept that he is a boy or that she is a girl, and understands what it means to be a boy or a girl. This has led researchers to examine the development of a child's concept of gender as a way to test the theory's prediction that "gender-appropriate" behaviors will not precede the child's conceptual grasp of gender.

THE DEVELOPMENT OF GENDER UNDERSTANDING. Children appear to develop a **gender understanding**—that is, to comprehend that they are boys or girls—by about the age of 3 years (Thompson, 1975). Although a 2-year-old child may tell

From an early age, children engage in behavior that their culture considers appropriate for their gender.

GENDER CONSTANCY
The realization that one's sex is determined by unchanging criteria and is unaffected by one's activities or behavior; usually develops in children by the age of 6 or 7 years.

GENDER SCHEMA THEORY
The theory developed by Sandra Bem that explains how cognitive advances help the child to organize and integrate the information that he or she has learned about his or her sex.

you she is a girl, she may have trouble understanding who else is a girl or who is a boy or, for that matter, why she is called a girl. Also, 3-year-old children, whose cognitive processing is limited (see Chapter 11), generally fail to understand gender constancy.

Gender constancy is the understanding that your own sex will remain constant—once a boy, always a boy. A child is demonstrating a grasp of gender constancy when she understands that just because a girl puts on a jersey and plays football, she does not turn into a boy—she is still a girl. Surprising as it is to most adults to discover, the development of gender constancy isn't usually complete until a child reaches about the age of 6 years (Emmerich & Goldman, 1972; Wehren & De Lisi, 1983). Researchers have found that the progression from rudimentary gender understanding through the completion of gender constancy is similar in other cultures, although the final age at which gender constancy occurs may vary by a few years (Munroe, Shimmin, & Munroe, 1984).

GENDER CONSTANCY AND COGNITIVE THEORY. As we noted earlier, Kohlberg's cognitive theory predicts that children will not show gender-role acquisition to any significant degree until they have a cognitive grasp of what it means to be a boy or a girl; but this is not what happens. Children engage in stereotypical gender-role behaviors well *before* they are cognizant of their gender or its constancy. As early as 26 months of age, children are typically aware of the different things that constitute masculine and feminine dress and behavior—they already know that men often wear shirts and suits, and shave their chins, and that women often wear blouses and dresses and makeup. Some 26-month-old children already believe that if someone repairs cars, drives a truck, or is a firefighter, then he must be a man; but if someone washes dishes, irons clothes, cleans the house, or cooks a meal, that person must be a woman (Weinraub et al., 1984). It also is quite common for children as young as 3 or 4 years to prefer what are deemed by their culture as gender-appropriate toys and activities (Etaugh, Collins, & Gerson, 1975; Fein, Johnson, Kosson, Stork, & Wasserman, 1975). These data indicate that, contrary to the cognitive development view, children demonstrate the acquisition of gender roles *before* they have a complete understanding of which gender they are or that their gender remains constant.

Many researchers now believe that the two views—cognitive and social learning theory—should be intertwined to create a cognitive–social learning view (Serbin & Sprafkin, 1986). This is the current trend, one interesting version of which is, gender schema theory.

Gender Schema Theory

In 1981, researcher Sandra Bem suggested the **gender schema theory,** which is an amalgam of cognitive and social learning theories. In her view, as children develop, they reach a point when they are able to integrate cognitively all the different gender-specific behaviors they have acquired through social learning and conditioning. This cognitive integration helps to shape their attitudes and beliefs about gender roles, and guides them to their own decisions about what is gender-role-appropriate (Bem, 1981). Bem's view explains how children can show gender-specific behaviors long before they have gender constancy. The theory also explains how, bit by bit, cognitive advances can help the children to organize and integrate all the information they have acquired about gender roles, so that their attitudes and beliefs can be influenced by their changing cognitive development.

The great Greek philosopher Aristotle (384–322 B.C.) said that women were "more compassionate . . . more envious, more querulous, more slanderous, and more contentious . . ."; of men, he said they were "more disposed to give assistance in danger" and "more courageous" (Book IX of *The History of Animals*, Chapter 1; cited in Miles, 1935, p. 700). These he believed to be *natural* female and male traits. As recently as our own century, researchers made statements that equated the intelligence and abilities of women to those of primitive people or children; beliefs that we today find ridiculous. Even Sigmund Freud argued that females were psychologically inferior (Horney, 1939). But what do we really know about sex differences in skill or ability? Except for the obvious ones, such as the ability to give birth, what real sex differences are there? Over the last few years, there have been some heated discussions concerning this issue.

One part of the debate has even focused on the term *sex difference*. It is argued that a real sex difference exists when, for example, a rooster crows but a hen doesn't. What we observe in people, on the other hand, should be considered a *sex-related variation in ability*, because *on average* one sex may be slightly better than the other at certain skills (Caplan, MacPherson, & Tobin, 1985). However it is defined, "sex differences" is a hot issue. To get some of the flavor of the debate, let's look at a few select highlights from the history of research on sex differences:

1974

Research. Eleanor Maccoby and Carol Jacklin publish *The Psychology of Sex Differences* hoping to document thoroughly or to dismiss many of the beliefs concerning sex differences in behavior (Maccoby & Jacklin, 1974).
Conclusion. There are a few sex differences, but they are small. Among these differences are a superior verbal ability among girls and a superior spatial ability (the ability to understand how objects would appear at different angles and how they would relate to each other in a given space) among boys.
Effect. Researchers undertake to find out why these few differences exist; many biological theories to explain these sex differences are proposed (Kimura, 1985).

1979

Research. Researchers Camilla Benbow and Julian Stanley give the Scholastic Aptitude Test (SAT), which includes mathematical and verbal portions, to 9927 seventh and eighth graders who had had the same exposure to mathematics regardless of sex. The boys perform significantly better than do the girls on the mathematical portion. Among those students who score over 700 out of a possible 800, boys outnumber girls 13 to 1 (Benbow & Stanley, 1983). Using attitude questionnaires, the researchers find that the girls who were tested like math as much as the boys and believe that math will be valuable in their future careers (Benbow & Stanley, 1981).
Conclusion. Boys have a natural superiority in math.
Effect. Considering the importance of sexual equality in our conception of social justice, these data, as you can imagine, caused an uproar. In opposition, researchers argue that these kinds of tests alone do not demonstrate in any conclusive way that the superior mathematical ability of males is due to biological or brain differences. Furthermore, even if male mathematical superiority were traced

to sexually differentiated brain structures, such structures might still be the result of early childhood experience, because early experience might facilitate the development of specialized brain organization. Another possibility is that girls are socialized to be afraid of math or to believe that they can't master its apparent complexities (Licht & Dweck, 1984). Girls who are given special counseling to deal with math anxiety show significant improvement, whereas girls who are not counseled show no improvement (Genshaft & Hirt, 1980).

1982

Research. Eminent Harvard neurologist Norman Geschwind describes a possible hormonal basis to explain math excellence in boys. Geschwind recalls that an excess of testosterone during fetal development can change the brain anatomy of rats so that the right hemisphere of their brains becomes dominant; perhaps, he argues, the same occurs in humans. In his research, Geschwind finds, among humans with right-hemisphere dominance, certain kinds of giftedness, especially musical, mathematical, and artistic, as well as a greater proportion of left-handedness and immune-system disorders (Geschwind & Behan, 1982). Handedness is caused by the fact that hemispheres control the opposite side of the body—right-hemisphere dominance would be likely to lead to left-handedness. The immune-system disorders, Geschwind argues, may be due to a sensitivity reaction of the body to the excessive fetal testosterone levels that led to the right-hemisphere dominance in the first place.

To test Geschwind's view, Benbow and Stanley take a survey of 40,000 students for whom they had scores on the SAT mathematical portion. To their surprise, 20 percent of the mathematically gifted students are left-handed (more than twice the expected number) and 60 percent have immune-system disorders such as allergies and asthma (five times the expected level). In the same population of students, but among the ones whose scores are lower, left-handedness and immune-system disorders are found to occur at normal rates (Kolata, 1983c). Among those students who showed talent on the verbal portion of the SAT, boys and girls are found to be equally represented. Higher levels of left-handedness or immune-system disorders are not found in this group. Geschwind argues that this is because the testosterone sensitivity mechanism he proposed to explain mathematical giftedness does not function in verbal areas, which are more typically controlled by the brain's left hemisphere.

Conclusion. Hormonal influence appears to cause hemispheric changes responsible for superior math ability in boys.

Effect. There is increased interest in hormonal influences on the developing brain. There is also a growing fear among researchers that the public will misunderstand these subtle differences at the extreme end of the math talent spectrum, and will interpret them to mean that girls are somehow inferior. As researchers are quick to point out, finding that one sex may have inherently superior ability in a certain area in no way argues for the superiority of that sex and against the struggle for social equality. These differences, even if they exist, pertain to such an extreme end of the spectrum that the question is not whether boys are superior in mathematics because of their biology, but rather whether girls can learn math and whether girls can make fine scientists or engineers, and the answer is yes.

1983

Research. Researchers Roger Gorski at the University of California in Los Angeles transplants brain tissue found only in male rats into female rats. The tissue becomes incorporated into the female rats' brains. These females then act more like males in terms of their sexual receptivity (Silberner, 1984).

Conclusion. This is the proof of different brain structures distinguishing males from females by behavior.

Effect. Researchers try to find if something similar exists in humans. Human brains are collected for examination at autopsy. Of course, direct experimentation on humans, as was done with rats, would not be ethical and cannot be performed.

1985

Research. Danish scientists, following the work of Roger Gorski with rats, for the first time find proof from the autopsies of human brains that there are portions of male brains that are distinctly different from female brains (Swaab & Fliers, 1985). The differences appear in the hypothalamus, an area of the brain associated with sexual arousal, among other functions.

Conclusion. Real anatomical brain differences exist between the sexes.

Effect. Extensive debate concerning this discovery ensues. Debate ranges from belief that such structural differences are related to male and female thinking or abilities to arguments that they are merely reflections of the anatomical differences between males and females (for example, perhaps they are related to the parts of the brain necessary to control sperm production or ovulation).

1985

Research. In a detailed critique, years of research supporting male superiority in spatial ability is dismissed because of faulty methodology, debatable statistics, observer bias, and failure to define adequately what was meant by "spatial ability" (Caplan, MacPherson, & Tobin, 1985).

Conclusion. A great deal of research concerning sex differences in spatial ability is too poorly structured and biased to take seriously.

Effect. Many people agree and dismiss the previous conclusion that males have a superior spatial ability. Others tighten study protocols and definitions and continue to argue that research shows a difference in spatial ability. For example, one study has shown that males *and* females suffering from CAH (who were therefore exposed to testosterone in the womb) are superior at tasks that require that they find hidden patterns or make mental rotations, compared with unaffected females (Resnick, Berenbaum, Gottesman, & Bouchard, 1986).

1987

Research. Scientists continue to attempt to explain superior mathematical skills in boys. All studies designed to uncover possible environmental influences find nothing to explain the gender differences in scores (Raymond & Benbow, 1986). The possible explanation of greater math anxiety in girls also is found wanting (Holden, 1987e).

Conclusion. Boys probably do have some "natural" potential to excel in math over girls owing to organization of brain hemispheres in the womb under the direction of the hormone testosterone.

Effect. Many researchers, disturbed by the apparent inequity shown by these findings, increase their efforts to uncover solid environmental explanations that would indicate equality between the sexes. Others caution that researchers should always stress that these differences in math ability are fairly small because of the dangers that the public will misunderstand and expect less of women or will treat women as somehow inferior (Hogrebe, 1987).

1990

Research. A number of researchers point out that gender differences in spatial, mathematical, verbal, and intellectual abilities are not as great as they were 10 or 20 years ago (Feingold, 1988a; Hyde & Linn, 1988; Jacklin, 1989; Hyde, Fennema, & Lamon, 1990).

Conclusion. Some of the gender differences observed and recorded over the years must be the result of environment because there hasn't been enough time for evolutionary developments to account for the recent narrowing of gender differences. Some argue, however, that a recent bias toward equality is skewing the research. For instance, many of the tests used to measure gender differences have been altered to reduce the appearance of gender differences. The research, therefore, may be showing this effect rather than any change in real gender difference.

Effect. The belief is growing that studying gender differences has become far more complicated than anyone had originally envisioned and that much more will have to be discovered before we have a clear understanding of the nature–nurture aspect of gender difference.

As it stands now, the argument over whether one sex has superior skill or ability, or why such a difference might exist, remains more heated than ever. Perhaps future discoveries will help to resolve the issue.

FOR CRITICAL ANALYSIS

1. If you were a researcher, and you discovered beyond any reasonable doubt that men really were smarter than women, but the difference was so slight that it was of no practical significance, should you keep that knowledge to yourself? What harm might you cause if you announced your discovery? On the other hand, what value is there in sharing your finding with others?

2. As equality of the sexes became more politically popular, gender differences in scientific research were found to diminish. In this instance, how might politics be affecting scientific findings? When explaining behavior, the British have often emphasized nature as a cause, while Americans have often looked to nurture. How might the different historical backgrounds of these two nations account for such a bias? How can political biases in science be resolved?

Sexual Orientations

One dimension of a gender role is the orientation a person has toward a sexual partner. In our culture, the majority of people develop *heterosexual* orientations. Nonetheless, a large number of people express a *homosexual* orientation, and a still larger number develop a *bisexual* orientation in which they have, as adults, complete sexual experiences with members of both sexes. The most extensive survey among men conducted so far has shown that about one-fifth of adult males have had at least one homosexual experience, about 6 percent have homosexual contacts fairly often, and that most of these men are, or have been, married (Fay, Turner, Klassen, & Gagnon, 1989). Indications from other studies show that homosexuality among women is about 25 to 50 percent as common as it is among men.

No one yet knows what determines an individual's sexual orientation. Attempts to uncover hormonal differences between heterosexual and homosexual adults have not proved conclusive (Feder, 1984), although this approach toward understanding sexual orientation remains promising. For instance, in one study, three groups of volunteers were given the female sex hormone estrogen. The first group consisted of heterosexual women, the second of heterosexual men, and the third of primarily or exclusively homosexual men. The amount of LH (luteinizing hormone—a substance that triggers ovulation in women) was measured in each subject after she or he had taken the estrogen. The women showed a sharp increase in LH within 3 days of taking the estrogen. The heterosexual men, on the other hand, showed little or no increase. Interestingly, among the homosexual men, there was a significant elevation of LH to intermediate levels between those of heterosexual men and women (Gladue, Green, & Hellman, 1984). Of course, these findings show only that certain hormonal responses are related to sexual orientation, *not* that hormones control or direct that preference.

Richard Green (1987) also has conducted a long-term 15-year study in which he kept track of 66 boys who were described as extremely effeminate, who liked to dress as girls, and who played with girls or dolls. As adults, 44 of these boys were homosexual or bisexual, far more than would be expected among 66 boys who were chosen from a random population. This study, of course, doesn't tell us how such an orientation might begin, but it does indicate that it begins early in development.

A number of researchers have argued that the crucial time for the determination of sexual orientation occurs in the womb, sometime around or during the second trimester (middle third) of the pregnancy (Marmor, 1985). Researchers Lee Ellis and M. Ashley Ames (1987) have stated:

> The involvement of learning, by and large, only appears to alter how, when, and where the orientation is expressed. For humans, the crucial timing appears to be between the 2nd month of [pregnancy] and about the middle of the fifth month, during which time the hypothalamic-limbic regions of the male's nervous system are permanently diverted away from their otherwise-destined female [connections and organization]. (p. 251)

Ellis and Ames believe that biochemical changes that occur in the womb may change sexual orientation by altering the neural development of the fetus's brain

In our culture, a majority of people tend to express heterosexual orientations.

A surgical procedure for altering anatomy and appearance so that the individual resembles the opposite sex.

TRANSSEXUAL
An individual who exhibits the most extreme form of gender reversal, in which the individual feels that he or she is really a member of the opposite sex but has been trapped in the wrong-sexed body.

and that such changes might be brought on by stress experienced by the mother, drugs taken during the pregnancy, or other forces that might upset the environment of the womb (Ellis & Ames, 1987).

Evidence for the possible role of events in the womb as an explanation of sexual orientation is growing, but many researchers still believe that neural development in the womb may be only a small part of the explanation. During the last few years, the social learning and cognitive theories also have attempted to deal with this issue.

The social learning assumption is that, during childhood, individuals who are encouraged to display sexual attraction to members of the same sex, or who are encouraged to adopt the social-sexual role opposite to their own, may eventually express a homosexual orientation. Evidence for this assumption has come from other cultures, in which homosexuality has been clearly accepted and in which boys are sometimes specifically trained to grow up to be the lovers of other men. For instance, among the Sakalavas in Madagascar, boys who are considered pretty are raised as girls, and they readily adopt the woman's sex-appropriate role (Green, 1976). An even more striking example of the cultural influence on sexual orientation is provided by the Sambia tribe of New Guinea. Researcher John Money has observed that

> the Sambia believe that after being nourished on mothers' milk as young children, the youths must be nourished on the male equivalent—the semen of young, unmarried fellow tribesmen—before they can fully become men. When a bachelor reaches marrying age, he is paired up with a woman by his family and "embarks on the heterosexual phase of his career" . . . the Sambia view the omission of [homosexual] behavior during [adolescence] as abnormal and stigmatizing. (Bales, 1986, p. 18)

Considering the data that indicate that homosexual or heterosexual orientation might be strongly influenced by the environment, the question is then raised whether a parent whose sexual orientation and attitudes are known to his or her children would affect the sexual orientation of the child. To examine this issue, Richard Green conducted a study of 37 children being reared either by female homosexuals or by parents who had had sex-change operations (known as **sexual reassignments**) and who had adopted the social-sexual roles of their new (opposite) sex. The 18 males and 19 females studied by Green were between 3 and 20 years of age, with an average age of 11.3 years; 21 were being raised by homosexual parents and 16 by **transsexual** parents. (Most of the children in the latter group were aware that their parent had at one time been a member of the opposite sex.) The study was conducted over a 2-year period (Green, 1978). Green evaluated the sexual orientation of the younger children by the toys and games they preferred, by their peer preference, by the roles they chose during fantasy play, by their clothing preferences, and by their vocational desires. He also used the Draw-a-Person Test, in which children usually draw a person of their own sex before drawing a person of the opposite sex. For the adolescents in the study, Green gathered information about sexual desires and fantasies about sexual partners. He also took data on overt sexual behavior.

With the questionable exception of only one child, all 37 children in the study developed heterosexual orientations and a marked desire to conform to the social-sexual roles provided by their culture. Not one had homosexual or transsexual fantasies. The adolescents developed desires for the opposite sex. The young children all wanted to play with children of their own sex, which is typical of heterosexual children at ages 5 to 11 years. Boys expressed desires to be doctors, firefighters, police officers, engineers, or scientists, and girls wanted to be nurses, teachers, mothers, or homemakers (except for one girl who said that when she grew up she wanted to be the Popsicle lady). These findings led Green to surmise that influences other than the family may be critical in the formation of gender roles and sexual orientation. His view contradicts the positions held by psychoanalytic, behavioral, and cognitive theorists, but it does support the idea that orientation may develop very early, perhaps as the result of biological forces.

In a more comprehensive study, Alan Bell and his colleagues interviewed 979 homosexuals and 477 heterosexuals in the San Francisco area during 1969 and 1970. They organized their data into a model that included such possible social and familial variables as parental relationships, gender conformity, sibling identifications, and school influences. Once again, the data gathered supported the theory that homosexuality is a deeply ingrained trait that is manifested early and is relatively resistant to external influences (Bell, Weinberg, & Hammersmith, 1981). As you can see, it is still not apparent which factors actually determine sexual orientations.

ATTRACTION

It would be impossible to understand sexuality or intimacy fully without also investigating attraction between one person and another. Which factors determine who will be our lovers or intimate friends? Psychologists have examined many of the variables that affect our liking and loving of others. Let's look at some of these.

Liking

All of us know some people whom we especially like. These people have a special significance for us. We look forward to seeing them, we enjoy being with them, they make our lives happier. And one of the desires that most of us share is the hope that other people will like us.

In general, researchers have found that we tend to like people most who give us the most gratification for the least effort on our own part. If someone is nearby and is easy to get along with, if that person fills our needs and makes us laugh, the chances of "falling in like" are much greater than if the person is distant and difficult to get along with and meets only a few of our needs. Although this general assessment should hardly surprise you, it is interesting to examine each variable that may affect the probability of liking another person. You may find that some of the variables are more important and that some have a different effect than you imagined.

CLOSENESS.   Our relationships with other people depend a great deal on their physical proximity to us. There's a much greater chance that we will like those people who live nearby than those who live farther away. In a study in which marriage licenses were examined, one researcher found that half of the couples who applied for a license lived within 14 blocks of each other (Koller, 1953). Perhaps your one love in the world is really your one true love within 14 blocks! In another study, conducted in a college dormitory, students were asked to identify the other people in the dormitory whom they especially liked. The person next door was more often liked than was the person two doors down the hall. The person two doors away was more liked than was someone three doors away, and so on (Priest & Sawyer, 1967). Other studies have found that simply being someone's roommate will foster friendship more often than one might expect (Newcomb, 1961). One of the most striking demonstrations of this proximity effect came to light during research conducted among the students attending the state police training academy in Maryland. Students were asked to identify the members of the

class with whom they had become close friends. The researcher was surprised to find that over 44 percent of those identified came either immediately before or immediately after the trainee on the alphabetical list of names used at the academy (Segal, 1974). The explanation is that the trainees had been placed in dormitory rooms and assigned seats in the classroom based on alphabetical order. Consequently, those who were close to one another alphabetically were more likely to have contact.

It may have already occurred to you that proximity to another person sometimes leads to dislike as well. If people have dissimilar initial attitudes, then proximity generally will not lead to attraction. The same is true if one of the people involved is annoying. For instance, a stranger who sits close to you in the movie theater and talks incessantly throughout a film is not likely to become a close friend. If strangers stand too close, so that they invade your personal space, you are not likely to care for them. The people in proximity whom we dislike tend to be those who upset or disrupt our enjoyment of our immediate environment (Ebbesen, Kjos, & Konecni, 1976). As a rule, however, closeness leads to liking rather than to disliking.

SIMILARITY. Once we've had the chance to make the acquaintance of those in our immediate vicinity, whether we will like someone often depends on how similar to us that person appears to be in terms of shared values, attitudes, and beliefs. We also tend to prefer people who are similar to us in age, level of education, status of occupation, and political views (Laumann, 1969).

The fact that likes attract has been well documented. In one study, college students were paired by a computer according to similarity and dissimilarity of attitudes and beliefs. The couples were then sent on a half-hour date to the school cafeteria. When they returned, their attraction for each other was measured by how close they stood together and by a survey taken of their attitudes toward each other. Measures were taken immediately after the date and again several weeks later. Couples with similar attitudes and beliefs were more likely to want to have another date than were couples who were very dissimilar (Byrne, Ervin, & Lamberth, 1970).

A number of reasons have been put forth to help explain why people who are similar to each other are more likely to find each other attractive (Rubin, 1973). First, we feel good when people agree with us; agreement gives us confidence in our own opinions and boosts our self-esteem. Second, if other people share our views, we immediately think that we know more about them, and we may feel more comfortable bringing up new topics and less worried that we may start an argument. Third, we are more likely to share activities with people who share our views. We may find it easier to interact with them because they, too, want to go to the church meeting, the political rally, or the film festival. Finally, to maintain our self-concept, we like to believe that those who share our views are good people, people with whom we should associate.

Under certain circumstances, opposites may attract, too. At first, this observation may seem to contradict the research we've been discussing, but "opposite," in this case, doesn't refer to opposite attitudes and beliefs but rather to the fact that each person may be lacking something that the partner can provide. Psychologists refer to this as *sharing complementary needs*. For example, if you are a domineering and outgoing person, you may be more likely to find attractive someone who is reserved and submissive than you are someone who also is domineering and outgoing. Some researchers have argued that similarity is most important when a relationship is beginning, but that complementary needs begin to play a more important role as the relationship becomes a long-term one (Kerckhoff & Davis, 1962). Others believe that similarity remains the most important factor, especially among well-adjusted married couples (Meyer & Pepper, 1977).

COMPETENCE. We generally prefer someone who is competent. Very few of us appreciate incompetence, especially in those on whom we depend. In fact, demonstrating incompetence to people we have just met is a pretty sure way of making ourselves disliked. But sometimes people can seem too perfect, too superior. Such people can make us feel inferior; although we may have a grudging admiration for them, we may not like to be around them. Consequently, we may not like them. If a competent person is not too perfect and seems capable of mistakes, we are more likely to feel good about that person; she will seem more human and, therefore, more like ourselves.

In one experiment, subjects listened to one of four tapes that contained a recording made by a candidate for a quiz contest. The same person had made each tape. On two of the tapes, the contestant was described as extremely intelligent and very successful in college. On the other two tapes, the contestant was said to be of average intelligence and average ability in school. On one of the tapes in each condition, the contestant was overheard to have an accident.

REINFORCEMENT THEORY OF LIKING
A social theory of relationships that we like those whom we have been reinforced for liking or whom we associate with pleasurable events or circumstances.

EQUITY THEORY
A social theory of relationships that individuals attempt to strike a balance between what they give and what they receive; that they strive toward a collective reward system for equitably distributing costs and rewards.

He spilled coffee on himself. In the other two tapes, there was no accident. In this way, all four possibilities—superior–no accident, superior–accident, average–no accident, and average–accident—could be compared. None of the listeners heard more than one tape.

The groups of listeners rated how they felt about the contestant, and the results were compared. The best-liked contestant was the superior one who had the accident. Ranked next was the superior contestant who had no accident. Ranked third was the average contestant who had no accident, and ranked fourth, and last, was the average contestant who had the accident (Aronson, 1969). The accident had enhanced the likability of the superior contestant and had detracted from the likability of the average contestant. In terms of competence, then, the best-liked individuals appear to be those who are competent but who are also human and are likely to make occasional mistakes. Because they have proved their competence before, we are likely to forgive them their error—it makes them seem more like us. When a person whom we view as inferior makes a mistake, however, we often see the blunder as further evidence of inferiority, which is likely to detract from that individual's appeal.

Theories about Liking

As you have discovered, many variables can affect whether we will like someone. Researchers have attempted to integrate these findings into comprehensive theories. The four major theories about liking are reinforcement theory, equity theory, social exchange theory, and gain–loss theory.

REINFORCEMENT THEORY.   The **reinforcement theory of liking** argues that we come to like or dislike people as a result of our learning. As we discussed in Chapter 6, there are three major forms of learning: associative, instrumental, and social. According to the reinforcement theory, we come to like or dislike other people because of processes involved in these three modes of learning. Through associative learning, we come to like or dislike other people because of the experiences and stimuli we associate with them. We will like people whom we associate with pleasant experiences and attractive attributes more than we will those we associate with unpleasant experiences or unattractive attributes.

According to instrumental learning, we like the people who reward us, and we dislike the people who punish us. In this view, we are more likely to feel warmth toward someone who offers us important opportunities than we would had we interacted with the same person just as often but in a less rewarding situation (Clore & Byrne, 1974; Byrne & Clore, 1970).

According to social learning, we are more likely to like people whom we see are liked by others. Because others are modeling the liking of a particular individual, we may, especially if we admire the models, be more likely to imitate their behavior by also liking that person. Similarly, it becomes more probable that we will dislike someone whom we see disliked by others whom we admire.

EQUITY THEORY.   If simple reinforcement principles were totally in control of whether we liked someone, then it might be expected that we would like people who give us the most but take the least. In this kind of relationship, we could maximize our reinforcement. But psychologists have observed that in actual liking relationships, those we like most are often those with whom we share. People often say that they feel distressed when they are placed in a situation of social inequity; that is, when they are giving more than they receive or receiving more than they give. The **equity theory** modifies reinforcement theory by describing how people work toward a collective reward system for equitably distributing costs and rewards. According to the equity theory, people learn that what they receive from others should be in proportion to what they have placed in the relationship. Such a system of equity appears to be well established in most cultures. Most people will agree that if you expect a lot from a relationship, then you should expect to put a lot into it. Many of us feel that when someone does a favor for us, we are in one way or another obliged to return the favor. In this way, we can restore equity to the relationship. Even in relationships that other people may see as inequitable, the *participants* often feel that there is equity because they have psychologically distorted the exchanges that have been made through the use of defense mechanisms or other psychological means.

The equity theory argues that in romantic or liking relationships, the most successful arrangements are equitable ones. For this reason, a very attractive man might, perhaps unconsciously, attempt to match himself with a very attractive woman, so that he feels he is getting a fair return for his physical attractiveness. In fact, research does show that in romantic relationships, but not in platonic ones, the more attractive a person is, the more likely it is that he or she will pair up with a similarly attractive partner (Feingold, 1988b). The trade doesn't always have to be for a similar "commodity." For example, a wealthy woman might want to trade her money for an intelligent man. One interesting experiment demonstrated how intelligence might function as a commodity in the dating marketplace. In this experiment, researchers discovered that male subjects who were told that they had done poorly on a test were more likely to ask an unattractive women for a date, while male subjects who were told that they had scored well on a test were more likely to ask out an attractive woman (Kiesler & Baral, 1970). Presumably, the subjects' self-worth had been manipulated by the information that they had done either well or poorly, which left them with a greater or lesser amount of "social" currency that could be traded. If, after taking the test, the subject was led to believe that he was intelligent, he may have considered that he could trade his intelligence for beauty.

Equity theory can lead one to view the world of human relationships as cold, selfish, and materialistic. For this reason, it is sometimes unpopular among those who first encounter it because it highlights the more calculating side of human behavior. And yet, common everyday expressions such as "trophy wife" (the term used for a young, attractive woman who has just married a very successful older man who, in turn, has just divorced his wife of long-standing for her) show us that people clearly understand the trade "my success and money for your beauty." However callous an observation that may be, there is, sadly, much truth to it (see Focus on Research).

EXCHANGE THEORY.   The **exchange theory** argues that people will like each other only if, in the social exchange, they both end up with a net profit in terms of what they have put into the relationship. This theory helps to explain an attraction between people with opposite needs. In such a situation, each person fills the needs of the other, and each person feels that there has been a net gain in the exchange; that is, more has been obtained from the relationship than lost (Homans, 1961; Rubin, 1973). Although the exchange theory may clarify the formation and maintenance of liking relationships, it is difficult to apply because it is not easy to define loss or gain in a relationship; these terms are subjective. Furthermore, the exchange theory is hard-pressed to deal with acts of giving when no return for the action is expected. Such altruistic behavior, engaged in without hope of compensation, would not seem to have any value in the interpersonal marketplace that is described by the exchange theory.

EXCHANGE THEORY
A social theory of relationships that human interactions can best be understood by examining the costs and rewards to each person.

The Power of Good Looks

An old expression suggests that beauty is only skin deep. This is another way of saying that there is much more to a person than physical appearance and that to discriminate against those who are physically unattractive in favor of those who are attractive is a form of prejudice. Researchers have found, however, that people who are physically attractive are more often liked—not just sexually but also in most kinds of social situations. To a great degree, it seems that people think that beauty equals goodness.

In one study, psychologists deliberately left money in a telephone booth change return and then watched secretly as the next person came to use the telephone. The person in the telephone booth (both genders were tested) was then approached by either an attractive or an unattractive female confederate of the psychologists. This person would ask whether the subject in the telephone booth had found any money, because the confederate might have left some in the change return. Subjects were more likely to return the money to the attractive confederate (Sroufe, Chaikin, Cook, & Freeman, 1977). This outcome may have occurred because it's more reinforcing to get a smile and a thank you from a beautiful person or because the subject hoped that returning the change would begin a relationship. Alternatively, the confederate's good looks may simply have made the subject feel better and, therefore, more likely to give the money back.

In mock trials, psychologists have found that juries are more likely to give a less severe sentence to an attractive defendant (Leventhal & Krate, 1977). This is not always the case, however, If the defendant is said to

have used his or her good looks while committing the crime, the sentence is more likely to be harsh. Investigators also have found that attractive, better-dressed panhandlers make more money than do unattractive ones (Kleinke, 1977).

Children demonstrate at an early age that physical attractiveness is an important dimension. In one study, 3- to 6-year-old children were asked to illuminate a slide of either an attractive or an unattractive child. The children were significantly more likely to illuminate the slide of the attractive child (Dion, 1977). By the fifth or sixth grade, attractive children are more successful in influencing and changing the behavior of children of the opposite sex than are unattractive children (Dion & Stein, 1978). By college, attractive people are more likely to have dating experience and sexual experience than are unattractive people (Curran & Lippold, 1975).

The perception of attractiveness may even have a built-in component, that is, there may be an aesthetic prototype for attractiveness that we understand apart from what we are taught. Two studies highlight this possibility. In the first study, it was found that infants as young as 2 or 3 months of age show a preference (as measured by how long they looked) for attractive over unattractive faces (Langlois et al., 1987). Because these infants were probably too young to have been taught about what is or isn't attractive, it is assumed that their response showed an innate preference for symmetry or for some other aspects that we find common to attractive people. In the second study, psychologists asked themselves what makes a face attractive. Based on the idea that natural selection generally favors the average over the extreme,

Is this man attractive?

they took many different faces of women and had a computer make composites of 4, 8, 16, and 32 different faces. The more faces used, the more the composite face became an "averaged" face. When people were then asked to look at the composites and choose the most attractive, the most averaged face was the winner (see Figure 18.3). In fact, the more averaged a face was, the more beautiful it appeared to be (Langlois & Roggman, 1990)! It is known that infants are innately attracted to the human face (Dannemiller & Stephens, 1988). Perhaps, then, the most beautiful faces are the most prototypic faces. In other words, we generally find the most attractive faces to be the ones whose collection of individual features (eyes, nose, mouth, and so on) are closest to human averages.

Of course, the term *attractiveness* encompasses more than just physical features. Personality also plays a key role. And yet, knowing that you are

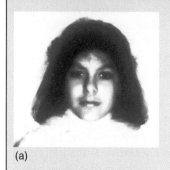
(a)

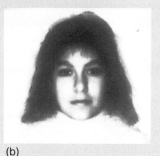
(b)

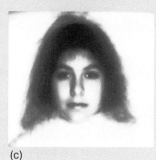
(c)

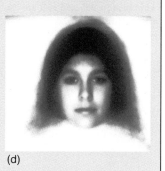
(d)

FIGURE 18.3

These are not photographs of real women, but rather are made from computer-blended images of faces. Images a–d represent composites of 4, 8, 16, and 32 faces, respectively. The pictures made from the most composites (c and d) were rated as the most attractive even when compared with the individual faces that made up the composites.

physically attractive or unattractive can directly affect your personality. One study demonstrated that social skill was positively correlated with physical attractiveness. In this study, individuals engaged in telephone conversations and were then rated by their telephone partners, who had not yet seen them, on dimensions of social skill, anxiety, liking, and desirability for future interaction. The more physically attractive an individual was, the higher his or her ratings tended to be. These results probably reflect the fact that unattractive individuals may lack the courage to initiate social interactions or that they have not been approached by other people and therefore have failed to obtain the social skills more often demonstrated by attractive individuals (Goldman & Lewis, 1977).

Physical beauty also can have a radiating effect. In one experiment, a film was made of a man walking arm in arm with either an attractive or an unattractive woman. Four different groups observed the films independently. Two groups saw the man with the attractive woman. The first group was told that she was a medical student and the second group that she

was a waitress. The third and fourth groups saw the man with an unattractive woman. The third group was told she was a medical student and the fourth group that she was a waitress. All groups were asked to rate the level of happiness and success they believed the *man* possessed. Whether the woman was a waitress or a medical student had some effect on the subjects' ratings of the man. However, in all cases, the man with an attractive woman was rated as significantly more successful and happy than was the same man with the unattractive woman (Meiners & Sheposh, 1977). It would be interesting to conduct the experiment once again, this time filming a woman with an attractive or unattractive man. Perhaps women would value the man's profession more, or perhaps not. What do you think?

Researchers also have demonstrated that attractive individuals are less likely to be affected by peer pressure. It may be that attractive individuals value their own opinion more than that of others because they have been told that they are themselves valuable. Unattractive individuals are more susceptible to peer

pressure because they appear to have a greater desire to be liked and are therefore more likely to comply with group demands (Adams, 1977).

Attractive individuals are not always assessed in a better light. Whether they are often depends on which aspect is being evaluated. For instance, people more often perceive attractive people as vain and egotistical and as more likely to have extramarital affairs (Dermer & Thiel, 1975). And, although it is true that physical beauty affects judgments of personality, the reverse is also true. In one experiment, photographs of female college students were rated attractive, average, or unattractive by a group of undergraduate subjects. Then another group of undergraduates were shown the photos with either favorable, average, or unfavorable personality descriptions attached to them. Photos accompanied by a favorable description of personality were rated as more attractive than were those without the description, and those accompanied by unfavorable descriptions were rated as less attractive than were those without the description (Gross & Crofton, 1977). In this case, what was good was beautiful.

613

GAIN–LOSS THEORY
A social theory of relationships that we are most attracted to those who have given us with greatest net gain and are least attracted to those who have caused the greatest net loss.

GAIN–LOSS THEORY. The **gain–loss theory** argues that if someone we come to know likes us more and more as time passes, we will generally like that person better than if he had liked us from the start. Similarly, we dislike people whose evaluations of us have become more and more negative with time more than we do people who have always held us in a negative light (Aronson, 1969). We do not know why the gain–loss effect occurs, but a number of explanations have been postulated. One may be that people tend to ignore things that don't change but pay particular attention to changes. For this reason, a loss or a gain may seem more important.

Another reason may be that we often attribute the gain or loss of someone's liking or affection to our own behavior; that is, we have either won someone over or have driven someone away. If, on the other hand, the person has always liked us or has always disliked us, we usually attribute this orientation to the individual's predispositions rather than to anything we have done. If this is true, then gaining someone's regard may enhance our self-esteem, and, because we associate the enhancement with that person, he or she appears more likable. The opposite would be true for someone who initially liked us but over time came to dislike us.

Finally, if someone comes to like us, it usually makes us less anxious about them. As we become less anxious, we like them more for reducing our anxiety. The opposite would be true for someone who began to dislike us more.

Love and Intimacy

To say that we love another is, perhaps, to give him or her the most positive evaluation of which we are capable. We talk a great deal about love, but researchers cannot always agree on what we mean by the word. In one sense, this is a semantic problem. Love can refer both to the heart-pounding excitement of a first sexual encounter and to the gentle affection between two elderly brothers.

Many people would just as soon not know why couples fall in love. Former senator William Proxmire once ridiculed two psychologists who were studying love and had requested an $84,000 federal grant. Proxmire stated, emphatically, "Right at the top of the things we don't want to know is why a man falls in love with a woman." At the same time, however, scientists are finding that, if anything, passionate love and interest in romantic feelings are growing. In the 1960s, when college students were asked whether they would marry someone who met all of their needs but whom they didn't love, 24 percent of the women and 60 percent of the men said that they wouldn't. When asked again in 1979, 80 percent of the women and 86 percent of the men said that they wouldn't. Love had apparently become more important than ever. *New York Times* columnist James Reston, responding to Senator Proxmire's statement, gave the following rationale for studying love:

> If the sociologists and psychologists can get even a suggestion of the answer to our patterns of romantic love, marriage, dissolution, divorce—and the children left behind— it could be the best investment of federal money since Mr. Jefferson made the Louisiana Purchase. (Reston, 1975)

H. H. Kelley (1983, p. 274) has outlined the behaviors of love as follows:

1. Verbal expression of affection
2. Self-disclosure: revealing intimate facts
3. Nonmaterial evidence of love: giving emotional and moral support, showing interest in another's activities and respect for his or her opinions
4. Feelings not expressed verbally: feeling happier, more secure, more relaxed when other is around

5. Material evidence of love: giving gifts, performing physical chores
6. Physical expression of love: hugging and kissing
7. Willingness to tolerate less pleasant aspects of other: tolerating demands in order to maintain the relationship

Love can be divided into two classifications: passionate love, which is a temporary but intense reaction to another, and conjugal love, which is a long-term relationship based on friendship and mutual respect.

PASSIONATE LOVE.   Passionate love is an intense emotional reaction, often based on strong sexual desire. An individual experiencing it thinks constantly about the person he wants to be with and thinks of that person in the context of love. Passionate love generally leads to an unrealistic evaluation of the love object.

Some researchers have noted three criteria that must be met before passionate love can occur (Berscheid & Walster, 1974). First, the person must be exposed by her culture to the idea of passionate love. In many cultures, the idea of love at first sight or passionate love is uncommon. Instead, marriages often are arranged, and love is viewed as something that may develop after many years of companionship. In modern Western culture, the idea of passionate love not only is common but also is expected. It is heralded in novels, songs, and theater and television dramas. Because of this, a person in our culture not only thinks more about spontaneous and passionate love but also expects to fall in love, even suddenly.

Second, for passionate love to occur, an appropriate person must be present. For most people, the person must be an attractive member of the opposite sex. Passionate love and sexual attraction are highly associated with each other.

The third important criterion is an emotional arousal that the individual interprets as love. This reaction may take the form of sexual arousal or even of anxiety at meeting the other person.

PASSIONATE LOVE
A strong sexual desire for another individual combined with the perception that one is in love. This perception is often the result of misattributing to love a heightened physiological arousal for any reason.

Passionate love is often the most exciting aspect of a new relationship, but it typically diminishes with time.

CONJUGAL LOVE
A deep and generally abiding love that develops between two people over long periods of time. It is associated with a desire to be together, share with one another, and sacrifice for one another. It is also called companionate love.

The onset of passionate love is relatively swift and sudden (Berscheid, 1983). Interestingly, a mild feeling such as liking, especially if it has continued over a long time, does not usually become something as intense as passionate love. This supports the idea that liking and passionate love are not simply different points along a single continuum of attraction, but rather are qualitatively different phenomena with different antecedents (Berscheid, 1983). Ironically, passionate love also is quite fragile, compared with something as stable as liking. Passionate love rarely lasts for long, and it is generally replaced by either a loss of interest or a more enduring conjugal love.

Unfortunately, a cultural expectation, an attractive person, and physical arousal don't give us much to go on if we plan to build a long-term relationship, such as a marriage. Countless couples have fallen in love and have married quickly, only to find later that they were not well suited to each other. A survey of over 200 college couples who were dating and who stated that they were in love, found that, by the end of 2 years, one-half of the couples had broken up. At the beginning of their love affairs, they had felt a strong physical attraction for each other and had believed that their futures would be shared. But by the time 2 years had passed, one-half of them stated that they were either bored with the relationship or had found that they did not share similar interests (Hill, Rubin, & Peplau, 1976).

These findings also may indicate that liking and loving are two different things (Sternberg, 1987). Consider the following, both of which are true stories, although the names have been changed.

> Tom sat right behind Jane in biology class. For Tom, it was love at first sight. From the very first day he saw Jane, he could think of little else: Thoughts of her preoccupied him constantly. Tom was therefore crushed when Jane found herself a boyfriend, Peter. Prior to that time, Tom had never really gotten to know Jane. His interactions with her all took place in his mind. Finally, Tom started having conversations with her and discovered that although he was still madly in love with her, he did not like her a whole lot.

> Mike and Louise had been dating for about 3 months. Both of them seemed happy in the relationship, but their friends saw trouble. Louise just seemed a whole lot more involved than Mike. One night, Louise confessed her love and let on to her plans for their future together. Mike was dumbfounded. He had not made any plans and did not want them. Mike told Louise that he liked her but did not love her and did not think he ever could. Mike broke off the relationship the next day. (Sternberg, 1987, p. 331)

These two examples highlight the problems of love without liking and liking without love. Perhaps the strongest relationships are the ones in which the two partners *both* like and love each other.

CONJUGAL LOVE. After we fall passionately in love with and are aroused by someone, our passion generally doesn't last long—at least not at the same level—even if we continue to love and stay with that person. Our diminishing emotional passion may be supplanted by a **conjugal love** relationship. People who have romantic expectations that their sexual passion will remain at a high level usually face disappointment. Psychologist Ellen Berscheid interviewed a large number of undergraduates and asked what their reaction would be if their passion disappeared from their marriage. More than one-half said that they would want a divorce (Berscheid, 1983). Yet psychologists have found that disappearance of passion is generally what happens. This may explain, at least to some degree, the high divorce rate in the United States.

Yet conjugal love often becomes deeper and more powerful than the initial passionate love was. Researchers have found that the most stressful experience the average person will ever face is the death of a spouse (Holmes & Rahe, 1967). Perhaps, more than any other factor, sharing experiences with each other develops conjugal love, or, as it is sometimes called, *companionate love*. Another aspect of conjugal love is the willingness to make sacrifices for each other.

MASTURBATION
Sexual self-stimulation.

SPERMATORRHEA
A term coined by the physician Claude l'Allemand based on the erroneous assumption that nocturnal emissions were related to the venereal disease gonorrhea.

SEXUAL MYTHS AND RESEARCH

Historically, there probably have been more myths and misunderstandings about human sexuality than there have been about any other subject. Many people think that sexual development and sexual behavior are very private matters. It's not uncommon for people to become embarrassed when discussing sex. Because of this, the study of sexuality often has lagged behind other areas of investigation or has been ignored. Before researchers began to study sexuality carefully, misunderstandings about sex were common.

Early "Research"

One of the first researchers to write in detail about human sexual behavior was Richard von Krafft-Ebing (1840–1902). He was a professor of psychiatry at the University of Strasbourg, Germany. *Psychopathia Sexualis*, his most powerful— and frightening—work, was first published in 1886 and was last reprinted in the 1960s. Krafft-Ebing did little real scientific research; rather, he collected a series of gruesome case histories that he used as evidence to support his feeling that human sexual behavior was an assortment of disgusting diseases. Krafft-Ebing even argued that **masturbation** was a loathsome disease, often the precursor to lust murder. It has been said that *Psychopathia Sexualis*, probably more than any other book, encouraged disgust and revulsion about sex (Brecher, 1976).

Predating von Krefft-Ebing was Samuel Tissot (1728–1797), a Swiss physician who predicted that masturbation would lead to blindness, impotence, acne, and insanity, ideas that are still common belief among the uneducated. Tissot's beliefs were unwavering, even though he never bothered to test his predictions to see whether they really came true in people who masturbated. In the early 1800s, Claude Francois l'Allemand, a French physician, equated nocturnal emissions of semen by a sleeping male with gonorrhea, believing that both had the same cause. As a result, he referred to harmless nocturnal emissions as **spermatorrhea** and considered them a serious disorder. Compounding the errors, Charles Drysdale, a physician, described spermatorrhea as a terminal disorder ending with death by a "kind of apoplexy . . . induced by the exhausted state of the brain" (Sussman, 1976, p. 23). These physicians weren't necessarily lying; they may have made some faulty assumptions and false deductions. For instance, Drysdale may have had a dying patient who also had nocturnal emissions of semen and, since Drysdale's training undoubtedly included nothing about the common nature of such emissions, and since no one ever discussed it, he may have erroneously linked the two as somehow showing cause and effect. At any rate, sex simply wasn't something that people of that time openly discussed. It was a forbidden subject, and few data about human sexual development existed. People didn't realize that the predictions were false because no one bothered to check.

Even as recently as 1900, physicians were so worried about the horrible consequences thought to result from the loss of semen through masturbation or from sexual stimulation that they openly advocated castration of male children who masturbated and clitoridectomy (removal of the clitoris) of female children who

Sexually transmitted diseases, or STDs, are diseases primarily passed through sexual contact. These diseases include chlamydia, gonorrhea, syphilis, venereal warts, genital herpes, and acquired immune deficiency syndrome (AIDS). Some of these diseases, such as chlamydia, gonorrhea, and syphilis, are treatable with antibiotics. Although if left untreated they can cause extensive damage to the reproductive system and, in the case of syphilis, even death. Lack of attention to these diseases is not uncommon, because chlamydia, gonorrhea, and syphilis often produce no immediate symptoms.

Venereal warts, genital herpes, and AIDS, because they are caused by viruses, are not susceptible to antibiotics. There are no cures for these disorders, and AIDS, is especially dangerous. In fact, in the United States in the year 1989, 21,771 people died of AIDS. Although it is not certain that infection with HIV (the virus that causes AIDS) will always lead to a full-blown case of AIDS, it has been found that the majority of those infected with HIV do, in fact, go on to develop it. To the best of our knowledge, AIDS, once it has developed, is 100% fatal. Because AIDS can take a long time to develop following infection with HIV, the number of people dying now indicate the rate of infection two to ten years ago, and not the larger number being infected today. By 1990, 1,000,000 Americans were estimated to have been infected with the HIV virus. AIDS is no longer a potential health crisis, but a very real health disaster.

Currently, on an alarming number of urban campuses throughout the United States, it is estimated that about 1 in every 300 students is in-

fected with HIV (CDC 1990). Campuses in the less densely populated areas of the nation, such as the mountain states, have lower rates of infection, but in all cases, the percentage of infected students is climbing.

Besides mode of transmission, STDs have something else in common. Each of them can be avoided by a change in *behavior*. In fact, there is no way currently to battle AIDS, or other incurable STDs, than through education and behavior change. And yet, in spite of the recent efforts to educate people to the dangers, many, including college students, remain woefully ignorant. And, many who are educated, still allow themselves to be exposed to the hazards of infection.

The role of psychology, therefore, is two-fold. First, psychologists must help educate people to the dangers of STDs by getting information to them. And, second, psychologists must illuminate the reasons for risk-taking among people even after they are aware of the dangers, and help them control their behavior.

Because psychology is at the forefront of the educational effort, it is important to provide information to those who may be lacking it. The need is definitely there. For example in a 1990 survey of Americans (Reinisch & Beasley, 1990), researchers found that a *majority* answered "yes" to the following: "Anal intercourse between uninfected people can cause AIDS." Because AIDS is caused by a virus, rather than by a particular sexual act, you cannot get AIDS from an uninfected partner. It is important to get this kind of factual information to the public.

Currently, researchers are going to great lengths to impress upon the

public that the AIDS virus is only transmitted by the exchange of bodily fluids, as occurs during sexual intercourse, oral sex (although it is difficult to show that this has ever been a mode of transmission), and by blood exchange (as occurred during blood transfusions before blood was screened for the virus, or during the sharing of unsterile needles as IV (intravenous) drug users often do). Casual contact such as might spread the common cold, has not been found to be a mode of transmission.

It is also important to know that a person may be infected with HIV for up to 6 months before a blood test will finally show positive because it can take a long time for the body to recognize the virus and begin to make the antibodies to which the test is sensitive (although it will usually register by 12 weeks after an infection has begun). For this reason, a negative HIV blood test is *not* proof that someone is uninfected, unless, for 6 months prior to the test, that person has been sexually abstinent and has not shared needles with someone who is infected. While use of condoms greatly reduces the chances of infection, they are not 100% effective. In fact, different brands of condoms have yielded different levels of safety. For this reason, abstinence remains the only completely "safe" approach to sex.

AIDS also continues to affect populations differently. The AIDS virus spread most rapidly among the homosexual population because of the greater number of sexual partners encountered by gay men, and because of the practice of anal intercourse (Shilts, 1987). Anal intercourse spreads the virus more easily than vaginal intercourse, because the bowel has a more fragile lining than

618

the vaginal canal and tears more easily giving the virus an entry point into the body proper. Similarly, AIDS is spreading rapidly through the heterosexual population in Africa, because so many people there have other STDs which leave sores or lesions allowing the virus entry. It is now so bad in some parts of Africa that in 1988–1989, for instance, AIDS was the most common cause of death among men, and the second leading cause among women, in the city of Abidjan, the capital of the Ivory Coast (De Cock, et al., 1990).

The reasons for people taking risks even though they are educated to the dangers are more complex than the excuse of simple ignorance. They center on the processes of denial and failure to delay gratification.

Denial is a powerful defense mechanism (see Chapter 13). It helps people to cope with stress. But it can also lead to danger if they allow their tendency to deny what they don't want to believe to affect their judgment. AIDS counselors hear the same phrase every day, "I never thought that it could happen to me."

Psychologists work to help people train themselves to believe that it can happen to them. For instance, people may be asked to think of circumstances in the past when they were either tempted to take a chance or did take a chance that might have exposed them to the AIDS virus. They are then encouraged to ask themselves how best to prepare for the next time they are tempted so as to reduce their chances of infection.

Another problem is that people don't like to delay gratification even for more important rewards later (Mischel, 1974). If someone is in a situation in which immediate sexual gratification is available, it can be very tempting for him or her to "chance it." Many denial processes may then come into play "he looks healthy; she's not 'that kind' of a person; he wouldn't lie to me; etc." For this reason, psychologists encourage people who choose to be sexually active to practice methods *beforehand* with which they can protect themselves, such as ways in which to insist on condom use without being awkward, and by always making sure to have a condom available.

Sex is exciting and, after all, is part of life. But by understanding the risks involved and by understanding human behavior, it needn't become a deadly experience.

If you have any questions or concerns about AIDS, or wish more information, contact the National AIDS Hotline (In the U.S. call 1-800-342-AIDS).

---

masturbated. Other physicians recommended severing the nerves to the penis or cauterization of the genitals with hot irons or glass rods dipped in caustic solutions. Special spermatorrhea rings were made for those who feared arousal or for male children who had erections. As Figure 18.4 shows, an erection would not have been in the best interest of the wearer of such devices (Sussman, 1976). Even Sigmund Freud believed, until the last years of his life, that the loss of 1 ounce of semen could cause the same fatigue as the loss of more than a quart of blood (Brecher, 1976) which, of course, is not only untrue, but ridiculous.

Psychologists now know that masturbation is a normal development in little boys and girls and that it continues to be a normal practice engaged in by a majority of adolescents and adults. Thanks to the efforts of modern sexual researchers, we have been able to break away from the prejudices of the past. We know, for instance,

SEXUALLY TRANSMITTED DISEASES (STDs)
Diseases that are primarily transmitted through sexual intercourse.

 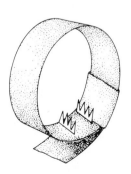

FIGURE 18.4

Spermatorrhea rings. (SOURCE: Sussman, 1976, p. 60.)

CHAPTER 18
SEXUALITY, ATTRACTION, AND INTIMACY

Alfred Kinsey (1894–1956). His pioneering research on the human sexual response helped dispel many myths and widened our understanding of human sexual behavior.

that it is normal for a sleeping male to have occasional nocturnal emissions of semen (sometimes called *wet dreams*) and for a male child to have erections before puberty. But this kind of information about human sexual development wasn't always available to the scientific community. It has come from careful data gathering.

Modern Research

At the end of World War II, Alfred Kinsey, a zoologist and an expert on wasps, published a compendium of human sexual behavior in two volumes, *Sexual Behavior in the Human Male* and *Sexual Behavior in the Human Female.* Included were sexual case histories of over 11,000 men and women. Kinsey was a professor at the University of Indiana. Occasionally, his students would confide in him and ask questions about human sexual behavior, often in response to his lectures on the sexual behavior of wasps. In an effort to help his students, Kinsey went to the library to search for answers. He found, to his surprise, that very little had been written about human sexual behavior. It was then that Kinsey decided to gather the data for himself.

The Kinsey reports came as a great relief to many people, who discovered that others had the same sexual feelings and behavior that they did. For instance, Kinsey found that more than one-half of the married women and over two-thirds of the married men in his sample had had premarital intercourse. Most of these people had no idea that they were in the majority. Kinsey also discovered that an overwhelming majority of men and women engaged in masturbation. He found that many heterosexual people had homosexual experiences, and vice versa.

Kinsey's data were generally of a survey type. Beginning in the 1960s, psychologists William Masters and Virginia Johnson began a detailed investigation of the human sexual response in the laboratory; their techniques, no doubt, would have shocked Krafft-Ebing and raised Sigmund Freud's eyebrows. Masters and Johnson's study of human sexuality was published in 1966. It contained detailed descriptions of volunteer subjects who had engaged in sexual behavior to the point of **orgasm.** Each subject had been monitored by sophisticated physiological devices.

William Masters and Virginia Johnson have conducted extensive research into human sexual responses.

Masters and Johnson discovered that male and female sexual responses were very similar. Both men and women proceed through four stages of sexual arousal. The first is an *excitement phase*, which can occur through sexual fantasizing or tactual stimulation. The second is a *plateau phase*, during which the genitals become prepared (erection in males, moisture of the vaginal walls in females) for orgasm. The *orgasmic phase* follows, in which, there are muscular contractions in the genitals of both sexes and ejaculation of semen in the male. Finally, there is a *resolution phase*, during which the body returns to its previous state. During the resolution phase, men have a *refractory period* lasting a few minutes; at this time a second ejaculation is impossible. Women, however, often are capable of having multiple orgasms with no waiting periods.

Masters and Johnson have found that orgasms are the same whether created by self-stimulation, fantasy, or intercourse. The fact that fantasy can cause the same arousal as physical stimulation emphasizes the cognitive nature of human sexuality. Both men and women react to erotic or sexual material. Physiological monitors suggest that men and women are equally aroused by explicit sexual literature (Heiman, 1977).

Masters and Johnson also developed sex therapy for people who suffer from sexual dysfunction of psychological origin (Masters & Johnson, 1970). Most of the therapeutic approaches concentrate on reducing people's worry about sex and encouraging people to center their attention on the pleasure of sex (Heiman, 1979).

Thanks to modern researchers such as Masters and Johnson, who have brought sexual research into the open, we are now better able to separate fact from myth and to gain a fuller understanding of ourselves and other people.

ORGASM
The climax of sexual excitement, normally marked by ejaculation of semen by the male and muscular spasms of the genitals in both sexes.

EPILOGUE: THE CONQUEST OF SPERMATORRHEA

Psychologists who study human intimacy and sexuality know that they must often overcome ignorance and superstition. The following account describes how a man was driven to find the truth about sexual behavior half a century before Masters and Johnson.

As a young man, Havelock Ellis (1859–1939) had read the works of Charles Drysdale, the eminent physician who had described the dread scourge spermatorrhea. Ellis was terrified. He would never masturbate, because he thought it was dangerous, but there was nothing he could do to prevent the nocturnal emissions that he had. He had spermatorrhea— he was a dead man! He wept and prayed, he searched desperately for a cure. Reading medical texts of the day, he was horrified at the gruesome measures suggested by physicians to control spermatorrhea. He planned suicide, but found himself too afraid to attempt it, so he decided to become a monk. After some thought, however, he felt unworthy to become a monk because his problem was sexual. Finally, in an attempt to give the short life remaining to him some meaning, he decided to keep a diary describing his deterioration and death due to spermatorrhea and to leave it as a gift to science.

Oddly, as the months came and went, his brain didn't turn to oatmeal. His eyes hadn't even lost their luster, an early symptom predicted by Dr. Drysdale. Slowly, anger overcame Ellis as he realized that the books were filled with lies. He had been put through a period of unneces-

sary fear. It was obvious that the loss of semen during nocturnal emissions did not result in deterioration and death. In that moment, Ellis knew he had a goal in life, to uncover the truth about sexuality. He decided to devote the rest of his days to careful and accurate sexual research.

Although Havelock Ellis is not as well known as Sigmund Freud, his investigation of human sexuality in the early part of this century marked the beginning of modern sexual research. In his books, Studies in the Psychology of Sex, *published between 1896 and 1928, Ellis pointed the way for later researchers such as Kinsey and Masters and Johnson. Ellis believed strongly that before people can label a sexual behavior deviant, they must document what normal sexual experiences are. Many of Ellis's findings are still valued. He noted, for instance, that sexual behavior was normal before puberty in both girls and boys, that masturbation was common in both sexes, that homosexuality and heterosexuality were not opposites but occurred in varying degrees, and that women had sexual desires, contrary to the myth advanced by the Victorians. He also found that orgasm is similar in men and women. Ellis stated that male impotence and female frigidity were in most cases caused by psychological problems and that, when it came to perversions, the range of variation within normal limits was so great that "unusual" sexual behavior was, in fact, commonplace.*

Largely as a result of Ellis's work, medical concerns about nocturnal emissions and masturbation came to an end early in this century (Brecher, 1976).

SUMMARY

■ The most obvious aspect of a person's sexuality is anatomical. The primary sexual characteristics are the penis, scrotum, and testes in the male and the vagina, uterus, and ovaries in the female. Secondary sexual characteristics appear at puberty and signal that the body is preparing for the capacity to reproduce.

■ The sex glands, called gonads, secrete hormones. Female hormones are called estrogens; male hormones are called androgens.

■ Exposure to excessive amounts of hormones prenatally may affect a person's later behavior, but most evidence indicates that the effect is transient and slight.

■ Men and women may have different natural traits or abilities. The differences associated with these traits or abilities are very slight, however.

■ Gender identity begins to develop at about the age of 2 years, and it becomes very strong once gender constancy is achieved at about age 6 years.

■ Through socialization, children learn what sex-role behaviors are deemed appropriate for them.

■ Gender identity appears to be shaped by both cognitive and social processes. Freudian, cognitive, and social learning theories all predict that gender identity is strongly affected by environmental, particularly parental, influences. Researcher Richard Green has demonstrated that gender identity may be strongly influenced by environmental forces beyond the immediate family and home.

■ Research has not uncovered conclusive evidence that there are hormonal differences between homosexual and heterosexual adults. Scientists believe that sexual preference may be strongly influenced by the environment in the womb. Culture and learning also may play important roles.

■ Researchers have found that we tend to like most those people who give us the most gratification in return for the least effort on our part.

■ Our relationships with other people depend a great deal on their physical proximity. Generally, we are more likely to become friends or lovers with those who are physically close to us. We also tend to prefer people who are similar to us in age, level of education, status of occupation, and political views.

■ Opposites may attract if the two persons have complementary needs.

■ We generally like people who are competent but who show that they are human and capable of mistakes, which makes them seem more like us.

■ Physically attractive people are generally better liked than are unattractive people.

■ Many theories have been developed to explain how people come to like or dislike others. Among the most influential of these theories are the reinforcement theory, the equity theory, the exchange theory, and the gain–loss theory.

■ Psychologists have not agreed on a definition of love. Generally, however, they divide love into two categories: passionate love and conjugal love. Passionate love may often be the result of sexual arousal. Conjugal love usually develops after people have spent much time together and have come to share things and to make sacrifices for each other.

■ Historically, there have probably been more myths and misunderstandings about human sexuality than about any other subject. Early researchers such as Krafft-Ebing believed that much sexual behavior was associated with disgusting diseases. Until the turn of this century, spermatorrhea (wet dreams) was considered to be a serious disease. It is now known to be a normal sexual occurrence.

■ Modern researchers such as Kinsey and Masters and Johnson have found normal sexual behavior to encompass a far greater range than earlier researchers had ever dreamed it did.

■ Masters and Johnson discovered that male and female sexual responses are very similar. Both men and women proceed through four stages of sexual arousal: the excitement phase, the plateau phase, the orgasmic phase, and the resolution phase. Masters and Johnson also developed sex therapy for people who suffer sexual dysfunction of psychological origin.

■ While some sexually transmitted diseases can be cured, the most deadly, AIDS, remains only preventable through education.

SUGGESTIONS FOR FURTHER READING

1. Bell, A. P., Weinberg, M. S., & Hammersmith, S. K. (1981). *Sexual preference: Its development in men and women.* Bloomington: Indiana University Press. Discusses the development of sexual orientations, including many of the variables found to correlate with the development of homosexual orientations.

2. Kelley, H. H., et al (Eds.). (1983). *Close relationships.* New York: W. H. Freeman. Analyzes the social aspects of human relationships, including love, commitment, power, emotion, and conflict. For the student or general reader.

3. Luria, Z., Friedman, S., & Rose, M. D. (1987). *Human sexuality.* New York: John Wiley. A college-level textbook on all aspects of human sexuality, including the social perspective.

4. Reinisch, J. M., & Beasley, R. (Eds.). (1990). *The Kinsey Institute new report on sex: What you must know to be sexually literate.* New York: St. Martin's Press. About 540 pages of the most up-to-date information about sexual matters, including topics such as love and commitment, contraception, STDs, fetishism, and exhibitionism. It also includes a survey of what Americans do and don't know about sex.

5. Sadock, B. J., Kaplan, H. I., & Freedman, A. M. (Eds.). (1976). *The sexual experience.* Baltimore: Williams & Wilkins. A college-level text that discusses sexual relationships, including the history of sexual research.

CHAPTER 19 | Applied Psychology

Prologue

Why Psychologists Are Interested in Applied Psychology

Industrial/Organizational Psychology
Organizational Behavior
Personnel Selection
Productivity and Personnel Behavior
Motivation and Performance

Sports Psychology
The History of Sports Psychology
The Physiology and Personality of the Athlete
The Peak Performance
Psychological Techniques for Achieving Peak Performance
Future Directions for Sports Psychology

Environmental Psychology
Illumination
Atmospheric Conditions and Toxic Hazards
The Structured Environment

Consumer Psychology
Consumer Research
The Psychological Approach
Consumer Protection

Educational Psychology
The School System
The Teacher
The Successful School

Epilogue: The Longest Throw

PROLOGUE

You have been working at the hospital for some time now, but you've never met anyone there quite like Roger Ulrich. You first became curious when he asked you to help him with an unusual study. Once you agreed, he started asking for what seemed like very odd information. He wanted to know about patients who had had gallbladder surgery during the last 8 years, but he was interested only if the surgery was performed between May and October when, as Roger said, the trees outside the windows were in bloom and the foliage was rich and green. Your curiosity drove you to find out more about what Roger was doing. When you asked him for details, he told you the following.

There are eight rooms for patients along each of the corridors on the three floors of the hospital—24 rooms in all. One-half of these rooms have lovely views; looking out these windows, you can see the trees and the sky. The other half of the rooms leave something to be desired, at least in terms of the view. All you can see from the windows of those rooms is a brick wall. For 8 years now, patients have been placed in one of the two kinds of rooms. By reviewing patients' records for many variables, such as smoking, obesity, and previous hospitalization, Ulrich carefully matched patients to create two fairly equal populations, so that only the views out the patients' windows differed (the independent variable). In other words, for each kind of patient who got a room with a view of the trees, Ulrich studied a similar patient who got a room with a view of the brick wall. All the patients were recovering from gallbladder surgery.

After his investigation, Roger Ulrich lets everyone know the results of his study. On the average, the patients who had rooms with windows looking out on the trees had a shorter postoperative stay in the hospital, elicited fewer negative comments in the nurse's evaluations, and asked for fewer painkillers than did those who had rooms facing the brick wall (Ulrich, 1984).

Curious about why this should happen, you ask Roger to explain. "Well," he says, "research shows that a view of vegetation will sustain interest and attention much more than a view of some urban site, such as a building or a brick wall. A natural view seems to elicit positive feelings, and it reduces the patient's fear and stress by holding his interest and blocking stressful thoughts that might normally make him anxious. It's interesting," he says, "how the environment can affect your health."

As a result of research like this, a number of hospitals are currently equipping sickrooms that had previously been windowless with simulated computerized windows (see Figure 19.1).

In this chapter, we'll briefly examine several areas in which psychology has been applied to aspects of daily life. Because of the limitations of space in a textbook such as this, it is impossible to examine each area in much detail, but this chapter will give you a general idea of specific applied areas. The areas include industrial/organizational psychology, sports psychology, environmental psychology, consumer psychology, and educational psychology.

WHY PSYCHOLOGISTS ARE INTERESTED IN APPLIED PSYCHOLOGY

Throughout this textbook, you have seen examples of the application of psychology to improve people's lives. Once basic research has been conducted and data gathered, and psychologists discover information that they believe might benefit people, their interests are likely to turn to applying this information to help build a technology of behavior and to advance and improve life. Whenever psychologists have sufficient information from which they believe the public can benefit, they begin to consider how they can apply it. Basic research is essential to the quest for knowledge; applying knowledge that we have gained to help other people often is a benefit of this quest.

INDUSTRIAL/ORGANIZATIONAL PSYCHOLOGY

Industrial/organizational psychologists, or I/O psychologists, as they are called, work for businesses, labor organizations, or governments, or teach at universities, where they may be allied with psychology or business departments. Traditionally, their main concern has been to improve the functioning of businesses and industries and to identify ways to make an organization efficient and effective. **I/O psychology** has grown along with American business and industry, and it is now a large and encompassing field of psychology. The roots of I/O psychology can be found in early time–motion studies, in which workers' movements were analyzed carefully for speed and efficiency. From there, the field expanded to consider the great range

FIGURE 19.1

This simulated window, showing pasture and billowing clouds, is in the cardiac intensive-care unit at the Stanford University Medical Center. A computer causes 650 separate light changes to occur in real time, starting with the soft pink hues of sunrise and ending with the vibrant colors and deeper shades of sunset. An updated version of the window includes a night view with twinkling stars and a moon.

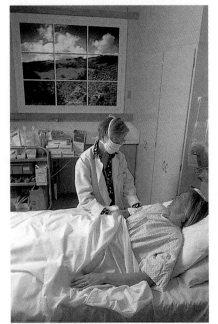

of variables that influence production and business success. The three major areas of concern among I/O psychologists are the creation and operation of organizations (typically business organizations), the selection and training of personnel and staff, and job performance and productivity.

Organizational Behavior

Organizational behavior includes the policies and procedures of managers, the way managers interact with workers, the tasks of jobs, and the structure of organizations. Studies of organizational behavior can range in scope from the study of a single employee to the study of an entire organization (Schneider, 1985). Research to date suggests that there is no one organizational arrangement, formula, management system, style of supervision, or type of employee that is suited for all jobs and all circumstances. The basic thrust of I/O psychology, therefore, is to find the criteria for what works in a given system or situation and to apply them.

LEADERSHIP AND SUPERVISION.   Among the best-studied organizational behaviors is leadership or supervisory capability. The Michigan and Ohio State studies conducted over 30 years ago provide the foundation of our modern understanding of leadership and supervision. In these studies, carried out in different industries, government agencies, hospitals, and volunteer organizations, leaders and supervisors were examined according to two dimensions: *employee-centered* and *job-centered*. Employee-centered supervisors or leaders were those who were most concerned with their workers' problems. They were supportive of workers and were friendly, and they helped to instill in the employees a sense of pride and personal value. They allowed workers considerable latitude and freedom in carrying out the job, and supervised the work in a general way. Job-centered supervisors or leaders, on the other hand, emphasized only production, watched the work closely, and made sure that the workers met their quotas. The studies indicated that employee-centered supervisors and leaders were more effective and were thus better able to increase production (Likert, 1961). Researchers also have shown that employee-centered and job-centered approaches aren't necessarily mutually exclusive; supervisors and leaders who are interested in their employees in a friendly and personal sense and who also emphasize job production also are likely to be successful (Cummins, 1971; Anastasi, 1979). Of course, studies of this kind are correlational, and it is difficult to establish a cause–effect relationship. For example, if production falls significantly, supervisors may become exceptionally concerned about productivity and therefore become job-centered. This, of course, is different from saying that job-centered supervisors cause lower production. On the whole, however, current research confirms the finding that employee-centered supervisors are more successful.

These findings have led some organizations to attempt to orient supervisors quickly to get along with people. High-pressure courses and 1-week manager-training sessions on interpersonal relations usually are not successful, however. Sudden changes in managers' or supervisors' behavior often are seen by employees as contrived. A sincerely employee-centered supervisor is spontaneous and honest. Such behavior is not easily taught. Most employee-centered managers are such because of the kind of personalities they have, and had before becoming managers (Anastasi, 1979).

Another area of concern among I/O psychologists is the "glass ceiling" (Morrison & Von Glinow, 1990), a gender-related problem. In many organizations, women who have proven their leadership ability are promoted to a level just below the top, but are allowed to go no farther. The "glass ceiling" refers to being close

I/O PSYCHOLOGY
Abbreviation for industrial/organizational psychology, the field of applied psychology concerned with the methods of training, counseling, selecting, and supervising personnel in business and industry. It also investigates ways to make organizations effective and efficient.

enough to see those who work on the top floor, while still being kept one floor down. Highlighting this problem is the fact that in the top 500 U.S. corporations, only 1.7 percent of the corporate officers are women (Offermann & Gowing, 1990). The circumstances for minorities are not much better (Morrison & Von Glinow, 1990). Discrimination of this kind is a major concern of I/O psychologists, not just for reasons of justice, but because they know that it denies organizations the talents and benefits of many potential leaders.

Currently, there are many theories concerning what it is that makes an effective leader and how that resource can be tapped (Ilgen & Klein, 1989). There is no consensus, however, about which factors are the most important or why some people seem so able to lead while others do not (House & Singh, 1987).

EMPLOYEE PARTICIPATION, FEEDBACK, AND CONFLICT RESOLUTION.   I/O psychologists also have found that employee participation in management decisions can be beneficial for an organization. This is especially true when a change occurs in the organization that requires the workers to learn new skills. In such a case, even if earnings are maintained, workers often resent having to learn new skills, and production suffers as grievances, absenteeism, and turnover increase. But if workers are given an opportunity to make suggestions and to help plan their new work, they often are more likely to accept the changes. Employee participation in management decisions is not always successful or even a good idea, however (Heller & Clark, 1976). For example, it may not be beneficial to an organization for employees to help in management decisions if the employees have no desire or wish for independence or work latitude or if the management decisions are unrelated to the kind of work the employees will be doing (for example, decisions pertaining to company finances or organizational structure).

Other important areas of organizational behavior that I/O psychologists are concerned with include feedback of results and resolution of organizational conflicts. Some kinds of feedback are fairly obvious and need little interpretation, such as monthly sales. Other kinds of feedback within an organization are subject to many psychological influences. For example, feedback concerning a worker's or manager's job performance can be influenced by beliefs among evaluators about locus of control (see Chapter 9) and attribution (see Chapter 17). A worker may be evaluated differently if the supervisor sees failure or success as a function of the worker versus a function of the system in which the worker was operating (internal or external locus of control). Skills or motives attributed to others, whether validly or not, often affect how those others are evaluated (Horn, 1985). Defense mechanisms (see Chapter 13) also can play a role. The supervisor who highly recommends a worker for a job is less likely to observe that worker's failures, because to do so would be to admit failure herself (Cummings, 1982). I/O psychologists try to make organizations aware of what these psychological influences are and how they may distort important feedback and communication.

I/O psychologists also are involved in helping to eliminate and resolve conflicts within an organization. Labor–management conflicts are the ones most widely publicized. Other important conflicts may occur, however, between different levels of management, sales, and production or between retailers and manufacturers, all of which can be disruptive to an organization (Brett, Goldberg, & Ury, 1990). By holding conflict-resolution workshops, by training the parties involved to develop skills of communication and to work out give-and-take solutions, I/O psychologists often help the parties to resolve problems more quickly, to the benefit of everyone. Sometimes, they provide training in interpersonal relations and mutual understanding. This training makes people more aware of psychological pitfalls—into which they may fall because of pride or face-saving—that would be detrimental to all parties to the conflict. Such workshops and conflict-resolution training have been helpful in many circumstances (Rubin & Brown, 1975; Brett, Goldberg, & Ury, 1990).

Personnel Selection

The personnel selected to run an organization may determine the organization's success or failure. I/O psychologists have been instrumental in developing valid personnel selection techniques and in devising the best ways for organizations to select a successful employee base (Hakel, 1986).

When a professional develops a personnel classification and selection system, the first important step he takes is **job analysis.** Before selecting someone for a job, an organization must know which tasks are required and what those tasks entail. In job analysis, the analyst details the tasks and outlines the traits and skills that a worker will need to perform the tasks. The analyst chooses predictors that help to identify the traits and skills required for the job. He then evaluates these predictors for reliability and validity.

JOB ANALYSIS
Analysis of the specific tasks required in a job and the training, physical abilities, educational level, vocational preparation, and temperament a person needs to perform the job.

CONCEPT REVIEW: PERSONNEL SELECTION

Perhaps the best way to review job analysis in personnel selection—to understand it in the way that an I/O psychologist would—is to have you do this kind of analysis yourself. Let's imagine that you are an I/O psychologist who has been called in by the Air Force to help select the best fighter pilots from hundreds of applicants.

It costs a tremendous amount of money to train a jet fighter pilot. It seems that everybody in the Air Force wants to be one, although few people actually have the necessary skills. Let's assume that you have 1000 applicants. Is there some way to choose the best 100?

After carefully analyzing the job requirements, you may delineate certain traits and skills that are needed: excellent eye–hand coordination, intelligence, courage, loyalty, good vision, rapid orientation, good physical condition, and a host of other abilities that are necessary to a good fighter pilot. To select your personnel, you want to develop assessment devices that will allow you to measure the personal characteristics you identified in the job analysis.

You can build many kinds of tests that might measure the traits you've selected. You may even try some tricky things. For instance, how about developing a test that cannot be passed, but that applicants believe they must pass to be admitted? As each applicant starts to fail at the impossible task, you may watch how frustration affects him or her. Good jet pilots need to stay cool and not panic. Maybe those people who become the most frustrated and upset should be eliminated. You can develop tests for good vision or use those already available. You can develop a chair in which applicants are spun around and then asked quickly where they are pointing—a test for orientation. You can devise many tests that are inexpensive and easy to administer. After you have devised them, all the applicants will take them. You should get a range of scores from very high to very low. You now have a personnel selection device and can take the top 100 applicants. But is the test valid?

As we noted in Chapters 12 and 13, the tests you have devised need to be both valid and reliable. They must measure the skill they purport to measure (they must accurately identify the best pilot candidates). Furthermore, if a candidate takes the tests several times, he should get the same or a close score each time. Assessment devices that meet these standards will help you to fit the job applicant to the job. You should eliminate any of the tests that fail to predict fairly well; retain those that are good predictors. In this way, you will eventually build a valid test battery for selection of fighter pilot trainees.

The Air Force pilots in the Concept Review may seem an exotic example, but there are hundreds of such personnel selection tests that show a certain amount of validity—that is, a high score on the test indicates that the applicant is likely to do well in a job that requires the skills measured by the test (see Figure 19.2) (Fleishman & Quaintance, 1984).

Of course, no test is perfect. Some people may be selected who shouldn't have been, and some may be turned away who should have been selected. Personnel selection remains a very inexact science (Schmitt & Robertson, 1990). The point is that a valid test will make an accurate selection most of the time. As you might imagine, such a selection device can be of great benefit to any organization.

Surprisingly, many organizations place too much stock in personnel assessment and selection devices of low validity. These include interviews, school grades, interest shown in a job, and letters of recommendation (Schmitt & Robertson, 1990). For instance, potential employees may gain excessively high ratings from interviewers simply by maintaining eye contact (Tessler & Sushelsky, 1978), speaking fluently, and maintaining composure (Hollandsworth, Kazelskis, Stevens, & Dressel, 1979). Letters of recommendation, especially if they are not confidential, typically include only favorable statements and often are general and vague because the recommender may have no idea what specific tasks are entailed in the job for which the letter eventually will be used.

Grades in high school or college give only a slight indication of occupational success (O'Leary, 1980). Even medical school graduates with the highest grades, once on the job, are no more or less likely to be rated as good physicians than are those who had the lowest grades. In fact, the correlation between grades and job performance as a physician is virtually zero (Albo, Taylor, & Page, 1982). Apparently, "book learning" and "on the job learning" are different from each other. This does not mean, of course, that schooling is unimportant; it indicates only that class ranking among physicians usually is not a good predictor of job success. People change on the job; they learn and they improve. Personnel selection tests, however, generally measure achievement rather than aptitude because aptitude is much more difficult to assess. After a few years on the job, employees are often found to be significantly more or less valuable to a company than their initial tests might have indicated they would be (Schmitt & Robertson, 1990). One of the best studies showing this effect was done by examining baseball players (Henry & Hulin, 1987). As any fan can recount, when baseball players are traded or acquired, even the best personnel selection tests (former averages, expert assessment, interviews, try-outs, and so on) can't tell the whole picture. Player trading is always a gamble;

FIGURE 19.2

Sample items from the Minnesota Clerical Test. This test measures one of the important clerical skills required for many jobs: The ability to recognize discrepancies in data from one set of books to another or from one column to another.

> **When the two numbers or names in a pair are *exactly the same*, make a check mark on the line between them.**
>
> 66273894_____66273984
>
> 527384578_____527384578
>
> New York World_____New York World
>
> Cargill Grain Co._____Cargil Grain Co.

some trades fall into the category of "brilliant," others "disastrous." The same is generally true with any company.

Finally, tests that measure a person's level of interest in a certain job, or that measure how well suited her personality might be for a certain job, usually have only marginal predictive ability (Borman, Rosse, & Abrahams, 1980). The best personnel selection devices often are tests that measure the highly specific skills required for a job. Educational level, interest in the job, personality variables, interviews, and letters of recommendation generally come in a poor second, although the information they provide is better than no information at all.

Productivity and Personnel Behavior

Productivity—a function of worker satisfaction, performance, and motivation—has long been an area of interest among I/O psychologists.

JOB SATISFACTION.   Most recent research concerning job satisfaction has been derived from surveys correlating different variables with attitudes expressed by workers. Perhaps it isn't surprising that, over and over, high levels of job satisfaction have been found to be associated with higher pay, greater chance for promotion, good supervisors, pleasant working conditions, and the chance for workers to use their skills and abilities to their fullest (Locke, 1976). In fact, these findings are so consistent that some researchers have become suspicious of them (Staw, 1984), noting that job satisfaction is almost always measured by questionnaire and wondering whether the questions are biased so that researchers often find what they expect to find. For example, questionnaires almost always ask for responses to such items as "I would prefer my job if the pay was good" or "if it was challenging." They don't tend to ask whether job satisfaction would be improved "if the job was easy" or "if the job didn't require any responsibility," or "if the job allowed me to get away from my family." What we have found may not really show all the possible variables associated with job satisfaction.

Job stress is another important area associated with job satisfaction, and more and more corporations are hiring I/O psychologists to help them to address this issue (Offermann & Gowing, 1990).

The kind of job the employee is required to do may strongly affect job satisfaction. Many people find this job of "keep the cans moving" very boring.

Job satisfaction is not easy to measure. In Chapter 9, the Prologue described how a task that Harlow's monkeys had enjoyed earlier became less satisfying after they received "pay" for it; soon they would no longer work at the task unless they were paid. Interestingly, some experiments have shown that increasing rewards for workers can actually *decrease* job satisfaction. It's as though the worker feels, at least at some level, "this job must really be lousy if you've got to pay me this much money to do it." Increasing a person's salary and reward doesn't always have this effect, however (Deci & Ryan, 1980).

ABSENTEEISM. I/O psychologists are especially concerned with absenteeism. Tens of billions of dollars are lost each year because employees don't come to work. Of course, health problems and injuries are causes of some absenteeism, but absenteeism also is related to job dissatisfaction. Many employees who are unhappy in their jobs withdraw from their work, taking days off when they have no health reason to do so (Johns & Nicholson, 1982). It's difficult to separate the influence of job satisfaction on absenteeism from that of all the other variables, but because of one interesting field study, we know that it probably makes a difference. The study measured absenteeism in relation to job satisfaction of salaried employees who were working for Sears Roebuck and Company in Chicago. As it happened, during the study there was a tremendous snowstorm that crippled the city. The Sears employees were told they didn't need to come to work unless they wanted to. As a result, only those who wanted to come to work did. It turned out that they were the ones who reported the highest job satisfaction. This study shows that in situations in which attendance is mostly voluntary, high job satisfaction is one of the greatest indicators of low absenteeism (Smith, 1977).

Other factors that may influence absenteeism are incentives to attend work, ease of transportation to work, flexibility of working hours, and family responsibilities of the worker. I/O psychologists address all these issues in an effort to make work attendance easier for employees. For example, some companies are now providing on-the-job day-care for children of employees. Although expensive, it often is effective enough in reducing absenteeism and increasing job satisfaction to make it worthwhile for the company.

I/O psychologists also have examined the other side of the absenteeism issue—the price a worker pays for *attending* work rather than what he obtains for being absent from it. In some jobs, this cost of attendance is recognized. Professional airline pilots are allowed to fly only a certain number of hours per week. The work hours per week also are limited for air traffic controllers and bus drivers. When jobs are dissatisfying, performance correlates positively with absenteeism. That is, workers who take off a few days now and then ("mental health" days) actually perform better, often enough to outweigh the costs of the time they have taken off (Staw & Oldham, 1978). Some industries have a double standard: They recognize that the top executives benefit from a few days off after a hard job, to "decompress," but any "mental health" days for the lower echelons are distinctly discouraged (Staw, 1984).

I/O psychologists have been instrumental in helping to introduce flexible working hours and 4-day work weeks to reduce absenteeism and increase production (Narayanan & Nath, 1982). They also have recently begun to investigate a new and growing phenomenon: the use of telecommunications and personal computers to allow people to work at home (see Focus on the Future).

TURNOVER. Job turnover is a serious problem for many industries and corporations. Whenever someone quits, another person must be trained to take that individual's place. As a result, I/O psychologists have been asked to find the causes

HOME WORK

Gregory is an actuarial analyst for a large insurance company. The company headquarters is in New York, and every day for the last 9 years he has boarded the Long Island Railroad, taken the 50-minute ride from his home into Manhattan, and battled the congestion and crowds to get to his small office on the nineteenth floor of an 80-story building. There he has worked with the information and the figures provided him, consulted his colleagues, and produced reports for the company. But he has dreamed about living elsewhere. He has always wanted a small home in the mountains in some rural upstate location far from the city, where his children could grow up surrounded by the forests and the hills.

Now, after 9 years, Gregory has his wish. He, his wife, and his children are living in a small rustic home in the Adirondack Mountains in a New York town of 1300 people. His children attend the local school, and Gregory no longer has to commute to his office in Manhattan. What's most amazing about this story is that Gregory never quit his job. He's still doing the same work for the same corporation, only he doesn't have to be in a company office to do it.

As factories in the United States are declining and industrial work is being replaced by administrative and service jobs—especially jobs dealing with information—a new kind of work organization is emerging. With the intervention of the computer, the picture is complete. Gregory wakes up each morning and goes to work by simply walking across his living room to a small office he has set aside. He flips on his computer, takes the telephone off the hook, and connects it to the computer modem, which puts him in direct contact with the main office in New York City. All the information he needs for that day—all the information he would have received in his office—is immediately sent to his home. Any books or literature he needs are delivered by mail or are available by computer access. Consultations with colleagues are accomplished by conference calls or using electronic mail. He sits at his computer, prepares his reports, makes his suggestions, and does all the work he would normally do in his little office in downtown Manhattan. Three times a year Gregory travels to New York City for major conferences, which he enjoys.

In the United States, the number of home-working professionals like Gregory now is about 13 million. By the twenty-first century, millions more in information service businesses may be operating at home in much the same way as Gregory.

This situation may sound ideal, but if you have a conversation with Gregory, you will discover that the emerging organizational structure creates new problems for employees. I/O psychologists are beginning to examine these problems and the stresses they impose. To begin with, Gregory reports touches of cabin fever. He doesn't leave the house as much as he used to. Because he doesn't need to get up at a certain hour, some days he sleeps late. There have been days when he never found the need to get dressed. "Basically," he says, "I just seem to be disorganized, though I get my work done."

He also reports that he misses socializing with his colleagues at work. Although he has made friends with neighbors and local residents, these relationships can't replace the camaraderie that he shared with others who are doing the same work. He feels a little lonely. Nonetheless, when asked whether he'd like to go back to the way he'd lived before, with the long commute, he says, "No way!"

Does he like the way things are now? "It's OK, I guess. The kids like it. But it's different from what my wife and I thought it would be." For example, Gregory is finding it difficult to separate work and family life (Becker, 1981). His wife and children have the same difficulty. Because he is always at home, he is accessible to them. His roles as husband and father become intermixed with his role as employee. It's very difficult for him to say, "I'm going to my office now; don't bother me no matter what," because when he's home he finds himself involved with his family.

Other things disrupt his work and influence his motivation. To begin with, no one is expecting him to "arrive" at work at a certain time. He has deadlines he must meet, but he can meet them in any way he wishes. He often gives himself a day off to be with the children, but the next day he has to do twice as much work. This practice is extremely common among people who work at home with fixed deadlines. Rather than work a steady 8 hours every day, they tend to take days off followed by 13- or 14-hour marathons of work. It's hard for Gregory to relax when he's not working, because he knows his work is building up. When he worked at the office in New York, he could leave his work behind him when he left for the day. Now it's somehow always there in the back of his mind. He knows he should organize his work more carefully, but he doesn't seem able to. He's never been one for making his own schedules and adhering to them. It was different before, when the structure was imposed from the outside. *(Continued on next page)*

I/O psychologists have a challenge. Workers like Gregory are obviously going to face new kinds of stresses and dilemmas while working at home on their own time. Psychologists are examining how to train workers to organize their time better, psychologically to separate family from work, and to socialize with other people who do not necessarily share their work interest but must now supplant the missing fellow workers. This kind of arrangement could offer a great deal of freedom to employees of many companies, and I/O psychologists are trying to find ways to prepare these workers to best use this freedom and to make the transition from office work to home work a smooth and comfortable one.

of turnover and the means by which it can best be eliminated. W. H. Mobley and other researchers have provided a theoretical model that explains the sequence that leads to turnover (see Figure 19.3).

Like absenteeism, turnover may be subjected to a double standard. Many organizations encourage turnover for their top executives, considering it to be a source of fresh ideas and invigoration (Brown, 1982), but discourage it among workers, even though it may be beneficial in some of these cases also. Similarly, some turnover in middle and lower management may be beneficial to companies (Katz, 1982), but it is rarely encouraged. As a compromise, some corporations are now looking at rotation of assignments within their companies to produce the beneficial effects of turnover without the adverse effects of losing valued employees (Staw, 1984).

Motivation and Performance

There are many valuable techniques for increasing the motivation to produce among employees (Katzell & Thompson, 1990). Behavior modification techniques (see Chapter 6) include the use of reinforcers for appropriate behavior. Workers who produce are given bonuses, promotions, better offices, more prestigious titles, or verbal praise in an effort to maintain and reinforce their successful behavior within the corporation (Komaki, Heinzmann, & Lawson, 1980; Hamner & Hamner, 1976; Komaki, Barwick, & Scott, 1978).

Goal setting is also a valuable technique (Staw, 1984). It is derived from cognitive psychology, and requires that specific goals be set for performance. Much research has shown that workers perform better if they have specific goals to aim for than they do if they are simply told, "Do your best." Knowing the exact goal required seems to help create within the worker an internal structure or organization for achieving that end; it gives her something to aim for. In some cases, the technique is no more complicated than posting a chart where every worker can see how well the company is progressing against a competitor. Goal setting is one of the most powerful ways to increase worker motivation.

Other valuable motivational aids include making sure that each worker is given a job that he or she can do well, that resources are made available to ensure the worker's performance (such as providing the right equipment, offering on-the-job coaching or training, or organizing problem-solving groups), that the leadership is trained to be sensitive to the needs of people, and that a certain air of dignity and quality in the workplace is maintained, which helps to instill pride (Katzell & Thompson, 1990).

I/O psychology is a growing area. For instance, many I/O psychologists are now working diligently to see whether the managerial techniques that have been so effective in Japan are culturally transferable to the United States. Such cultural applications are relatively new to American I/O psychology because, for the first time, we are seeing other nations with higher productivity. No doubt the field will continue to grow as psychology is further applied to business and industry.

SPORTS PSYCHOLOGY
The application of psychological techniques and principles to sports and other structured physical activities for the purpose of maintaining and maximizing performance and investigating applied clinical issues.

▌ SPORTS PSYCHOLOGY

Sports psychology is the application of psychological principles to physical activity and sports, either to maximize performance or to investigate applied clinical issues. Sports psychology in the United States has only recently attracted significant interest, but it has a long history in Europe, especially among the former Eastern bloc nations (Browne & Mahoney, 1984).

FIGURE 19.3

A typical decision process a worker might use to determine whether to leave a job. Many variables that may influence the person's willingness to search for new employment, such as the family's reaction *to moving, or the friends a worker must leave, are outside the company's control. Rather than addressing the variables that affect the utility of quitting, the company wishing to reduce turnover would do* *better to find ways to increase job satisfaction. By doing so, it may prevent the worker from considering quitting in the first place.*

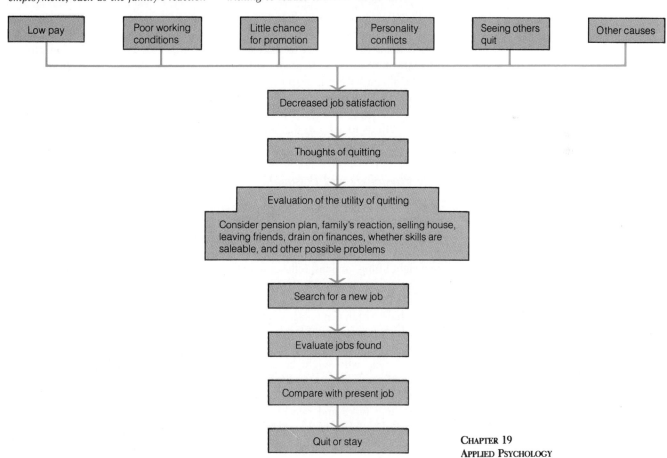

The History of Sports Psychology

Sports psychology has its roots in the work of experimental psychologists who were interested in motor learning and performance. Their early laboratory experiments measuring reaction time and other motor skills seem a far cry from modern sports psychology, but their work marked the first time that psychologists took an active interest in analyzing physical performance. Of course, modern sports psychology deals with the mental as well as the physical aspects of performance. Everyone knows the effects motivation and concentration can have on an athlete. In fact, the first sports psychology publication in the United States was an 1898 paper describing the enhancing effects of a cheering audience on competitive bicycling (Geron, 1982).

Serious work in American sports psychology did not begin until the 1920s when Coleman Griffith (1893–1966), known in the United States as the father of sports psychology, set up the first sports psychology laboratory. There he investigated the best ways to teach sports performance and to assess athletes' personalities in order to guide and develop these people. Even with Griffith's sports psychology laboratory, however, the United States and other Western countries lagged far behind the Soviet Union in sports psychology.

In 1965, the first International Congress of Sports Psychology was held in Rome, and there a network of information was organized, through which countries could exchange data on sports psychology. This was a landmark in Western work in this subject, and it heralded the rapid acceleration of sports psychology in the United States.

Today sports psychology has five major goals: (1) to take laboratory findings and apply them to the playing field to maximize athletic performance; (2) to discover what makes a successful athlete and which kinds of athletes are best suited for which kinds of sports; (3) to discover the best methods for preparing an athlete mentally for a major event or performance; (4) to investigate the effects, both beneficial and harmful, of sports on children; and (5) to find how best to use sports and exercise for leisure and mental and physical rehabilitation (Browne & Mahoney, 1984). The first three goals have attracted the most attention and research, but recently efforts to achieve the latter two goals have begun.

The Physiology and Personality of the Athlete

A great deal of what goes into making an athlete is inherited. Height, center of gravity, and muscle mass are, to a large extent, genetically determined and may limit the kind of sport in which a person might excel or athletic ability she might have. To state the obvious, height is an advantage in basketball, muscle mass helps in weight lifting, and fast reflexes help the boxer. There are other physical variables that are extremely important, if less obvious. The ratio of muscle fiber types is one example. Muscle fibers show either a fast or a slow twitch when stimulated. Some people have a high percentage of one kind of muscle fiber versus the other. Someone with a high percentage of fast-twitch muscle probably would be more successful at a sprint event, for instance, than would someone with a high percentage of slow-twitch muscle who might be far better at a marathon. The amount of oxygen consumed per minute per unit of body weight at a fixed amount of effort also is an important variable. In both men and women, these two variables—ratio of muscle fiber types and rate of oxygen consumption, are more than 90 percent determined by heredity (Fox & Mathews, 1981). Modern sports physiologists have the job of determining the kind of body a potential athlete possesses and which sports and skills are most likely to suit him.

Scientists also have attempted to determine the optimal personality for athletes in any given sport. Unfortunately, initial work in this area often was done by nonpsychologists who were unfamiliar with proper personality-testing procedures. They often used invalid or unreliable tests, and the results of their "experiments" often were flawed, misinterpreted, or biased (Mahoney, 1979; Morgan, 1980). Valid research in this area is hard to come by, and it appears that many variables go into making a great athlete. There are several findings, however, that have been supported by good research. For instance, persons who are good at contact sports tend to perceive pain as less aversive than do those who excel in noncontact sports (Ryan & Kovacic, 1966). Individuals with greater pain tolerance appear to seek out contact sports more often, rather than simply developing a pain tolerance from experience with such sports.

Optimal level of arousal is another variable that has some predictive validity. For example on an ice-hockey team, members who perform best when considerably aroused are more likely to be successful goalies (where action is most sudden and fast), while those players whose optimal performance occurs at a lower level of arousal might be more successful as a member of the forward line. By testing a person's ability to function at different levels of arousal, a sports psychologist can suggest which team position a player should be trained to fill or which kind of sport may offer a person the greatest likelihood of success. These are just a few of the areas in which a sports psychologist can be helpful in determining an athlete's performance, but much more research needs to be conducted before any psychologist can just walk up to a coach or sports director and lay out in detail which variables or constitutions are required for success in a given sporting activity (Browne & Mahoney, 1984). Sports psychology has this ability as one of its goals, but it still has a long way to go.

The Peak Performance

Nothing is more exciting to an athlete than to have a **peak performance,** in which she achieves a "personal best" or perhaps even sets a record. When peak performances occur, an athlete often has intense concentration and the feeling of being disassociated from her surroundings. Her body seems to be operating on its own and she has no awareness of pain or fatigue. Time seems to slow down, and the athlete has a sense of being in command and of having exceptional power (Unestahl, 1983). This kind of mental and physical "flow," which often leads to a peak performance, is a strange phenomenon. Athletes can't force it to happen. It's like trying to force yourself to fall asleep; the more you concentrate on it, the farther you get from it. Instead of making it happen, you just have to let it happen, which is an experience foreign to most athletes—they are used to trying hard.

Sports psychologists have found ways to help athletes find their flow, but the athletes' attempts to gain such control over their behavior, like the learning of any new skill, can disrupt their performance for a time, until the new ways are acquired. Because of this, a less experienced coach or athlete will sometimes give up prematurely on attempts to acquire these new control skills.

Psychological Techniques for Achieving Peak Performance

One of the most serious factors disrupting peak performance is the pressure of competition. If athletes become anxious during competition, they can become overaroused; that is, they go past the optimal zone of arousal required for a peak performance. One immediate problem of overarousal is muscle tension. Muscle tension interferes directly with muscle contraction; a muscle can contract only if

PEAK PERFORMANCE
The exceptional performance given by an athlete when physical and mental conditions are optimal.

For an athlete to achieve a peak performance, unwanted muscular tension must be kept to a minimum.

its antagonist muscle is relaxed. Proper muscle contraction is necessary for peak performance. Many athletes have talked about how well they did during practice only to blow it during competition because of excess muscle tension. Sports psychologists have devised a number of techniques to get around this problem.

The first technique is a fairly straightforward one. It is practice, practice, and practice, again and again, until the activity required of the athlete becomes so automatic that it is practically mindless. Soon the athlete has learned the procedures so well that he can act without thinking, and mental activity (which may include thoughts about failing or about what he is doing) is less likely to occur and to get in the way.

Monitoring arousal is another valuable technique for competitive performance. Most athletes don't like to pay attention to how nervous they are, fearing that they will only become even more jittery. But knowing how active his autonomic nervous system is can alert an athlete to take steps to avoid a problem. Sweating palms, upset stomach, intestinal problems, difficulty in breathing, trembling or tension, a heavy sensation in the legs, yawning, and fatigue are all signs of involvement of the autonomic nervous system. Mental signs include inability to pay attention to important information, lack of concentration, confusion, negative statements to oneself, excessive fear of failure, and loss of confidence. Athletes can be taught to control the muscle tension in major muscle groups when they feel their autonomic arousal becoming excessive. There are many ways to control muscle tension (see Chapter 14), such as medication, progressive relaxation, yoga, hypnosis, and biofeedback (Pressman, 1980). Once the muscles are relaxed, mental training can begin.

To help an athlete mentally prepare the muscles that will be used in the athletic event, having him carefully imagine the event is often helpful (Brown, 1980). This prepares his muscles to act in their appropriate sequence. The high jumper Dwight Stones made ample use of this technique before each jump. His mental imagery was a little more exaggerated than most, and people viewing him could actually watch how he prepared to jump in his mind's eye. He looked at each step he planned to take in his approach, and actually seemed to follow himself at a distance as he looked up and then dropped his gaze, imagining his leap over the high bar. As further mental preparation, athletes are taught not to say negative things to themselves and to establish realistic goals, such as a personal best rather than a world record (Meichenbaum, 1977; McClements & Botterill, 1980). These measures help to contain increasing anxiety and resulting loss of confidence.

When athletes practice constantly, monitor their arousal levels, find their optimal level, and control their arousal through relaxation and mental training, their skills often improve dramatically (Scott & Pelliccioni, 1982; Weinberg, 1981).

Future Directions for Sports Psychology

Most work in modern sports psychology has concentrated on helping athletes achieve peak performances. There is hardly a professional sports team or an Olympic athlete who hasn't had advice from sports psychologists. But the future of sports psychology is much broader than that. Psychologists are finding that people can benefit from participation in almost any sport and at almost any skill level (Sonstroem, 1981). Psychologists also have studied individuals who become "addicted" to exercise and sports (Glasser, 1976). Explanations for such incessant exercising often concern endorphins (see Chapter 2) (Moore, 1982) and brain neurotransmitters (Ransford, 1982). Much more research is needed before it is known how helpful sports can be for physical and mental rehabilitation and how sports affect children and their development, but these are growing areas of concern. Sports psychology is developing rapidly in the United States, and many scientists and psychologists are attracted to it. The future is wide open in this field, and researchers have just scratched the surface.

▌ ENVIRONMENTAL PSYCHOLOGY

ENVIRONMENTAL PSYCHOLOGY
The applied psychology concerned with the effects and influences of the environment on behavior.

Beginning in the 1960s, as public concern about environmental problems began to grow, a new area of psychology emerged, **environmental psychology.** It is concerned with the influences of the natural environment on behavior and vice versa (Holahan, 1986). The areas of interest to environmental psychologists are diverse, ranging from traditional topics, such as the effects of lighting in the workplace, to recent concerns, such as the influence on behavior of pollution and environmental toxic hazards. Environmental psychologists also are interested in developing and creating entire environments in accord with psychological principles in an effort to create harmony between individuals and their surroundings. Sometimes the work can even be a little exotic, such as figuring out how best to design the physical features of a bank so as to best deter bank robbers (Saegert & Winkel, 1990).

Illumination

One of the most studied areas in environmental psychology is illumination, or the amount of light necessary for optimal performance. This area is the wellspring from which the whole field of environmental psychology developed.

Years ago, industry used as little light as possible in the workplace, to save electricity or, even earlier, to save candles! Between 1910 and 1960, the recommended illumination levels for work and offices continually increased, as it was obvious that workers were performing better when they could see what they were doing and when they did not suffer from serious eye fatigue. At first reading, it may appear that this is stating the obvious and that there is little to this area of psychology. Actually, the applied psychology of illumination is really very complex (Meer, 1985). Environmental psychologists have studied and have helped to design the many new kinds of lighting available. For example, they were instrumental in developing the kinds of lighting necessary in surgical operating rooms where glare must be eliminated but a great amount of highly focused, high-intensity light must be available over the entire operating field.

Each job may require a different kind of lighting. Suppose you are a worker in the garment industry, and it's your job to examine clothing for loose threads. Look at Figure 19.4—you can see the amazing difference that proper lighting can make. Environmental psychologists have developed optimal illumination for many different environmental conditions. Optimal lighting can significantly increase performance (Faulkner & Murphy, 1973).

Another task of environmental psychologists working with illumination has been to eliminate glare. Glare, such as from bright metal surfaces or from glossy paper, can cause *phototropisms*. A phototropism is the natural inclination of the eye to look toward a light source or bright spot. Constantly fighting this tendency while trying to work at a task can lead to severe eye fatigue. Environmental psychologists have found optimal angles of lighting and levels of light distribution in situations where glare could be a problem. As you can imagine, environmental psychologists often work directly with commercial architects to develop the best work environment. Such an environment includes appropriate lighting for the work being done.

Atmospheric Conditions and Toxic Hazards

Environmental psychologists have studied the relation between different temperature conditions and behavior and, increasingly, the effects of environmental hazards on behavior.

HEAT. Regulation of heat is another important variable that affects body temperature, arousal, and attention. Individuals who are too warm are more likely to be aggressive and to work less efficiently (Calvert-Boyanowsky, Boyanowsky, Atkinson, Gaduto, & Reeves, 1976).

Violent crimes and riots are more likely to occur in hot summer months; suicides and depressions are more common in the winter; and admissions to psychiatric hospitals correlate well with increases in air pollution (Strahilevitz, Strahilevitz, & Miller, 1979). Because of these findings, environmental psychologists have been interested in weather and related conditions, and in their effects on human behavior.

POLLUTION AND ENVIRONMENTAL TOXINS. An initial concern about air pollution led environmental psychologists to examine pollution in general. They have now identified a number of toxic substances that they believe cause learning problems in children. These include heavy metals, such as cadium and lead. In poorer neighborhoods, whole buildings often have lead-based wall paint and plumbing. The water and dust in such buildings may contain excessive amounts of toxic heavy metals.

Air pollution is another source of lead contamination. A study conducted at the Case Western Reserve laboratory, using a mass spectrograph analysis of hair samples taken from children, showed that children who had serious learning difficulties also tended to have significantly higher levels of cadmium and lead in

FIGURE 19.4

For a worker in the garment industry whose job is to remove loose threads from cloth, a difference in lighting can be crucial. With 75 foot-candles of low angle grazing lighting (above) the thread is highly visible compared to its appearance under 650 foot-candles of general overhead diffuse illumination (below).

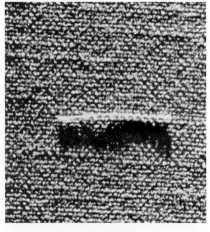

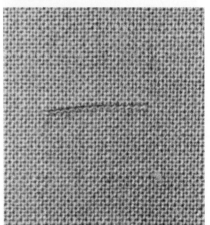

their bodies than did children from a well-matched control group (Pihl & Parkes, 1977).

Scientists believe that lead contamination in the air is a serious problem. They have estimated that one out of every five inner-city black children 5 years old or younger is carrying a sufficient amount of lead in her body to interfere with her ability to learn. The children of poor people (those with incomes below $6000 per year) showed eight to nine times the lead content found in children from high-income families (those with incomes exceeding $50,000 per year) (Raloff, 1982).

In more recent years, with the increasing use of unleaded gasoline, the amount of airborne lead has decreased significantly. The lower levels of airborne lead are especially noticeable in congested inner cities where the blood-lead levels in children have decreased in direct proportion to the decrease in the use of leaded gasoline. Environmental psychologists and members of the medical profession were directly responsible for bringing this information to the attention of appropriate government agencies. The effort is now underway to eliminate lead from all gasoline.

Environmental psychologists have discovered that subtle changes in human behavior sometimes can be an early sign of toxic exposure (Fein, Schwartz, Jacobson, & Jacobson, 1983; Weiss, 1983). They are now isolating the influence of these pollutants on behavior. Table 19.1 shows the kinds of behavioral changes associated with different metal toxins. **Behavioral toxicology** is a very new field, but the demand for it is growing. None of the 50 states escaped a significant amount of toxic hazard from untended or improperly stored toxic dump sites or contaminated water and air (Fein, Schwartz, Jacobson & Jacobson, 1983). For instance, after a fire retardant, polychlorinated biphenyl (PCB) was accidentally mixed with cattle grain feed and distributed throughout the state of Michigan, researchers found hardly a single person in that state who did not have PCB in his or her body.

NOISE.   Another environmental hazard that influences behavior is excessive noise—both abrupt and prolonged. Besides being a major distraction, excessive noise increases both blood pressure and the chance of hearing damage. Because of these findings, in many work conditions in which noise is excessive and prolonged, workers are now provided with sound-baffle earplugs or other equipment that helps to reduce noise while still enabling the workers to hear what is going on around them. Actually, most sources of extreme noise are not work-related; they are found in the home environment. Most cases of hearing damage have been found to occur through the inappropriate use of stereo headsets. Through habituation, the user finds higher and higher volume levels tolerable, leading to possible permanent ear damage. Working with environmental psychologists, the government has been quick to place noise standards and restrictions on the work environment, but the individual's attention to this problem is still wanting.

The Structured Environment

Environmental psychologists are well aware that the environment often determines the kinds of behaviors that will occur. In the Prologue, you saw how something as simple as a pleasant or unpleasant view from a hospital window could affect the length of a patient's postoperative recovery. Environmental psychologists use their skills to structure environments—both indoors and outdoors—to achieve particular results. Different environments affect behavior differently. The way people act in a church is different from the way they act in a classroom, an office lobby, or a baseball stadium. In each instance, behavior is influenced partly by the arrangement

BEHAVIORAL TOXICOLOGY
The classification and study of the behavioral effects of environmental toxins.

TABLE 19.1 Neurological and Psychological Signs and Symptoms Attributed to Metal Toxicity; Collected from Clinical and Experimental Sources

Signs and Symptoms	Aluminum	Antimony	Arsenic	Boron	Cadmium	Lead	Manganese	Mercury	Nickel	Selenium	Tellurium	Thallium	Tin	Vandium
Anosmia [loss of smell sense]			•		•									
Appetite loss		•						•			•		•	•
Convulsions						•		•						
Depression				•						•				•
Disorientation	•			•			•					•		
Dizziness		•	•						•	•			•	
Dysarthria [defective speech articulation]	•						•	•						
Fatigue, lethargy		•	•		•			•		•		•		
Headache		•	•	•				•	•				•	•
Incoordination	•					•	•	•				•		
Insomnia									•					
Jitteriness, irritability		•		•			•		•					•
Mental retardation						•		•						
Paralysis	•													
Paresthesias [unusual physical sensations]		•	•					•					•	
Peripheral neuropathy [peripheral nervous system disorders]	•		•		•	•		•						
Polyneuritis [multiple nerve inflammation]		•	•					•					•	
Psychiatric signs	•					•	•	•		•				•
Somnolence [sleepiness]										•	•			
Tremor	•					•	•	•						•
Visual disturbances			•			•	•	•		•			•	•
Weakness			•	•		•	•	•	•	•			•	

SOURCE: Adapted from Weiss, 1983, p. 1176.

of the physical properties of the environment, such as chairs and tables and room color.

Not too long ago, at the University of Texas in Austin, 108 clerical workers were hired, divided into three groups, and given various jobs to do. Their error rates, tardiness, and absenteeism were all evaluated by a supervisor, as one might expect them to be. No one ever thought to ask why the offices were all painted blue, or, in the case of another group, yellow, or even other colors. Although the workers were told they were participating in a study, they were unaware that the purpose of the study was to help NASA choose interior colors for space modules that would best facilitate human performance during a 30-month interval (Crawford, 1989).

Researchers have consistently found that they can predict a person's behavior by the environment that person is in more accurately than they can predict behavior through personality assessment tests (Barker, 1968). Behavioral and social learning psychologists refer to this influence of the environment as stimulus control (see Chapter 6). Conversely, some environmental psychologists argue that people are not directly controlled by their environment but rather form plans about how they wish to behave and then seek environments in which the behavior is accepted (Russell & Ward, 1982). In other words, you don't scream and cheer because the baseball park has cued you to do so, but instead you plan ahead to go someplace where you can enjoy yourself in a boisterous way, and so you choose the ballpark. Either way, the environment you're in is a good predictor of which behavior you will exhibit.

When developing environments that encourage particular behaviors, environmental psychologists often consider **proxemics.** Proxemics is the study of the behavioral effects of crowding, privacy, territory, and personal space. In a psychological sense, proxemics deals with what is perceived about these factors. For instance, when determining crowding, it's not possible simply to count how many people there are within a certain area. You may feel crowded in an office with 10 other people but not crowded in an elevator with 20, because in the office you expect more privacy, whereas in the elevator you expect to be packed in.

How crowding and lack of privacy affect behavior and work performance is an important issue in environmental psychology. The term *personal space* often is used to indicate how much room each person needs in order to feel sufficiently relaxed and comfortable. Personal space varies greatly from situation to situation. You may not feel your personal space invaded by a family member who touches you. On the other hand, if you were an inmate in a state prison, you might consider your personal space invaded if someone behind you got within 6 feet. Personal space is a perceived space. Researchers take proxemics into consideration when developing any environment.

Environmental psychology is a young and growing endeavor. Its future is wide open. In fact, environmental psychologists are currently busy planning and organizing the environment for the first permanent space station. By examining life in zero gravity, or in low levels of gravity, which might be attained in a rotating space station, they are arranging and organizing the environment to facilitate comfort, research, and social interaction. Wherever humankind needs to construct a beneficial environment, environmental psychologists, with their developing knowledge, are providing their expertise and skills.

Consumer Psychology

Consumer psychology began as the psychology of selling and advertising. Its objective was to get the manufacturer's message through to the consumer. Advertising goes back as far as human history. When the city of Pompeii was excavated centuries after it had been buried by the eruption of Mount Vesuvius, advertisements were found painted on the public walls of buildings. But it wasn't until the twentieth century that a systematic inquiry into the needs of the consumer and the desires of advertisers was developed.

Consumer Research

Modern consumer psychology is mainly concerned with conducting and applying consumer research. The major categories of consumer research are (1) advertising effectiveness, (2) consumer opinion, (3) assessment of consumer attitudes through

PROXEMICS
The study of nonverbal expression through the spatial distance people maintain when interacting, as well as their orientation toward each other as reflected by touch and eye contact.

CONSUMER PSYCHOLOGY
The field of applied psychology concerned with advertising and selling, whose object of study is effective communication from the manufacturer or distributor to the consumer.

rating scales and projective techniques, (4) psychological segmentation of markets, and (5) consumer behavior in natural environments.

To test advertising effectiveness, psychologists attempt to demonstrate the ability of a particular advertisement to influence the public. They also may test the power of the advertising medium. For example, a consumer psychologist might have designed the following study as a test of the effectiveness of billboards. A few years ago, when I was walking around in Salt Lake City, I noticed a number of large billboards at different locations that simply stated in great gold letters, "Calvin Coolidge was the 30th president of the United States." These billboards carried the message for a few weeks and then the messages were taken down. Before the billboards went up, a consumer psychologist probably went about surveying people at random and asking them who was the thirtieth president of the United States. She would then find out how many people, on the average, knew the answer. After 2 weeks of billboard exposure, the public would be surveyed again. Now many more people would probably know that Calvin Coolidge was the thirtieth president. This increase in knowledge would demonstrate the power of the billboard.

Consumer opinion surveys help businesses that market products to find out what consumers want and how they can provide it. Consumers' attitudes also can be assessed through rating scales and, if consumers are found to have different attitudes in different parts of the country or different countries, the market can be psychologically segmented to provide each area with what the people there desire (Lutz & Bettman, 1977). For example, Oil of Olay, a facial cream or lotion, is one of the 10 best-selling products of its type in the United States. Anyone with a television set has seen the advertisements for it. A couple of summers ago, I was in New Zealand and turned on a television set. On came an Oil of Olay commercial. It was exactly the same as the commercial that I had seen in the United States—only, when they displayed the product, it was called Oil of Ulam. No doubt, consumer psychologists had been at work again! As it turns out, in both Australia and New Zealand, there already was an "Olay Oil," used for cooking (Love, 1987). Something obviously had to be done, because leaving the name as it was would conjure up images of rubbing cooking oil all over one's face.

Probably, in a survey of consumer attitudes, New Zealanders and Australians were shown to like the word *Ulam* as well as, or better than, *Olay*. It's the consumer psychologist's job to find out which name sounds the most appealing. For example, some very tasty fish have atrocious names. You can't find them in your local supermarket, because no one wants to eat a hogsucker or a viperfish. With a little effort, however, a seller can find a nice name that people do like and rename the product. Call a hogsucker "rock salmon," for example, even though it has nothing to do with real salmon (or hogs, for that matter), and people are much more willing to eat it. Very few products are named simply by an owner or product manager who likes a particular name. In the modern consumer world, psychologists take many possible names and offer them to consumers in rating surveys to find which name not only sounds best but also sounds most like the product (see Figure 19.5).

Most advertisers rely on making sure that their message is perceived (Bettman, 1986). Modern consumer psychology uses information about cognitive processes such as perception, memory, and information processing and studies how advertisements affect the operation of these processes (Cohen & Chakravarti, 1990). Advertisers highlight their messages to gain and hold the audience's attention by using size, repetition, color, and so on. Making the product recognizable in a visual sense is important, but it's also important to make it recognizable verbally. If the product name is difficult to pronounce, it may need to be changed. The makers of Baume Bengue were dismayed because no one knew how to pronounce the name of their product. As a result, they placed the words "pronounced ben-

FIGURE 19.5

When developing names for products, it's important to consider that certain sounds seem to go with certain shapes or forms. Most everyone will choose (a) as Molana and (b) as Krakatok. M, N, and L have a gentle, flowing sound pattern, while T and K are sharp and short in sound, which translates into a visual perception of something angular and sharp.

Which of the two shapes is a Molana, and which is a Krakatok?

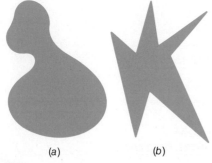

(a)   (b)

gay" on the label. Later, they dropped the original name altogether and just called it Ben-Gay.

In Chapter 17, we discussed the mere-exposure effect—the phenomenon that people tend to like something merely because they have been exposed to it repeatedly (assuming that the exposure has been in no way aversive). The mere-exposure effect is one of the most powerful influences in advertising (Bornstein, 1989). This is one of the reasons you may trust a brand name product even if you've never used it. Brand name products are often more expensive than are generic ones. Most consumers say that the higher price inspires confidence. They perceive the higher price to imply higher quality. In many cases, however, the product's higher price reflects only the expensive advertising necessary to make it a brand name!

To test products or advertisements successfully, consumer psychologists may investigate the ability of customers to identify brands or to state brand preferences. The effects of advertising can be measured by an increase in brand identification or a shift of brand preferences. Sometimes, advertising is so effective that brand names become words that stand for an entire class of products such as Kleenex, Q-tips, Band-Aids, or Xeroxes. Because of the power of continual exposure, one of the major thrusts of advertising is simply to get the product into the consumer's awareness, regardless of the message content. As long as the brand name is presented often enough that the consumer becomes familiar with it, it will have a certain amount of selling power. The most effective advertising technique, however, is to combine repeated exposure with persuasive communication (Petty, 1977; Day, 1976).

The Physiological Approach

Consumer psychologists have joined with physiologists in efforts to develop measuring devices that can record interest in products or advertisements. One device can track eye movements when a consumer watches an advertisement. In a laboratory setting, the investigators track eye movements by recording exactly which part of the advertisement the consumer is watching at any given time (Witt, 1977; Barton, 1980). Interestingly, people often watch the faces and hands of the actors in the ads more than they do the products. Faces and hands are just intrinsically interesting. This is frustrating to advertisers who want the product to stand out. One way around it is to link the product through a series of steps with the face and name of a person. This was done some years ago in an impressive series of advertisements by the Folger Coffee Company. An actress was given a name— Mrs. Olsen. Soon, when the advertisement came on and people looked at the face of the actress, they remembered she was Mrs. Olsen. And, of course, Mrs. Olsen was linked directly to Folger's coffee. After these very successful advertisements, Folger's coffee went from ninth to first place in the coffee market.

Researchers also have measured interest in advertisements by the relative amounts of alpha versus beta waves in subjects' EEGs or by arousal of the central nervous system while subjects were watching ads (Ryan, 1980; Kassarjian, 1982).

Consumer Protection

Because of the work they do, consumer psychologists often encounter ethical concerns of a special nature. Psychology should be used to benefit people, never to harm them. In some instances, however, advertisements may be designed to sell products that cost consumers their health or money without providing a reasonable benefit. Cigarettes are an example of a product that is deadly (and, unlike other dangerous products such as automobiles, is deadly *when used as intended*) and

The branch of applied psychology concerned with the psychological aspects of teaching and the formal learning process in school. Educational psychologists apply theories, methods, and test instruments for educational purposes.

which is sold through advertisements. Psychologists who offer their skills to help sell dangerous, worthless, or overpriced products at the expense of the consumer are doing the public a disservice.

We can ask a more general question, "Should psychologists be in the business of helping advertisers to push their products?" With this in mind, many consumer psychologists have concentrated their efforts on consumer protection and product safety. Their work involves studying ways to protect consumers from accidents and hazards while using a product or from dangerous misuse of a product. Childproof safety caps are an example. Consumer psychologists investigated the ability of children of different ages to think through the process of opening a complex cap. Soon they discovered that the opposing techniques of pressing down while turning were easily within the grasp of adults but were beyond the comprehension of almost all children young enough to be in danger. The techniques used for promoting products also have been used by consumer psychologists to point out the value of proper health care (such as performing breast examinations or giving up smoking). Other consumer psychologists have spent time developing ways to communicate effectively between professions and the consumer. Doctors, lawyers, and other professionals who deal with the public daily and who have difficulty communicating their information in ways the public can readily understand often consult consumer psychologists for the best methods to furnish information that will enable the public to make informed decisions. Whenever products or services of any kind are available and the public needs to be informed about them, consumer psychologists are able to provide a valuable service.

EDUCATIONAL PSYCHOLOGY

Practitioners of **educational psychology** are principally concerned with training teachers, improving student performance, and conducting educational research. Teacher-training programs generally focus on the teacher's need to be aware of what changes in behavior occur as children develop, how different ethnic and cultural backgrounds may influence students, how children learn attitudes and prejudices, what the social relations among groups are, what the effects of cooperation and competition are, and how conformity and the learning of social norms influence children (Johnson & Johnson, 1975). Educational psychologists often are instrumental in developing programs to give teachers the basic information they require about behavior. Modern teachers also must have considerable knowledge about psychological testing and test scores, especially aptitude and achievement tests, which educational psychologists often provide.

Many educational psychologists spend much of their time conducting research. Often this work is concerned with developing valid and reliable tests for measuring student aptitude and achievement or with developing techniques that help students to learn and teachers to teach. Educational psychologists also are concerned with the clinical aspects of behavior as they may relate to education—areas such as test anxiety and school phobia.

Educational psychologists have been especially interested in the effects of early education on disadvantaged children. As we mentioned in Chapter 12, Project Head Start and other early intervention projects have been successful in helping to redress the negative impact of a poor environment.

Educational psychology places special emphasis on the psychology of learning (Pintrich, Cross, Kozma, & McKeachie, 1986). In the literature of the field, different educational philosophies often are debated (see Focus on a Controversy).

Jeff was one of my closest friends in high school. When we were sophomores, we took geometry together. The geometry textbook was a little dull, the teacher was a little confusing. The way he liked to "teach" was to have students come up to the front of the room, do one of their homework problems on the board, and explain what they were doing. Looking back on it, I think that the teacher had found a way to make his students do his job, and they weren't very good at it. Frankly, it was pretty boring. I had to struggle to understand what we were doing. A few weeks into the class, I noticed that Jeff wasn't struggling with it any longer. He had given up. When we spent time together after class, I sort of knew not to mention geometry. He didn't mention it either. This went on for the entire semester—I never asked what grades he was receiving, and he never told me.

We took the final examination the next to the last day of class. We came back on the last day to receive our tests and to go over them. I had a bad feeling about Jeff's final. He showed it to me afterward: he scored 9 percent—that's 9 percent out of a possible 100! That would normally have been the end of it; he simply would have failed geometry—except that this was New York State, and something still could be done. New York has statewide Regents' examinations. Everyone in the high schools throughout the state must take these examinations, and they are given after each school has given its own finals. So 2 weeks after the day of our final, we all had to take the geometry Regents'. This was the state's way of measuring schools against one another. And there was an interesting rule: If you scored higher than 75 per-

cent on the examination, you had to be passed in the course, regardless of what you had scored in class during the year. Jeff didn't want to repeat geometry, so he said he'd try to get over 75 percent on the Regents', although he had only 2 weeks in which to study. He asked me whether I'd help him to learn the material.

After 2 days of working with Jeff, it was clear that he couldn't seem to understand what I was telling him. It wasn't that he was unintelligent—but how can anyone learn a semester of geometry in 2 weeks? With only 12 days to go before the test, I told him that I saw no hope and that I thought he'd have to take the course over. I didn't see Jeff again until the Regents' exam.

He sat two rows away as we took the test. He was the first one finished. But I just figured that if you only know 9 percent, it shouldn't take you very long to put it all on paper. I saw him afterward. He smiled strangely. "It was so boring doing all those easy problems. There wasn't a single one that could challenge me. Not even that last one. They tried to get tricky there, but, you know, there's more than one way to solve it. I figured out two other ways. I put all three down."

I was alarmed to see that he had finally snapped. He wouldn't say any more about the exam after that, but from time to time he'd laugh. I was sorry to see him that way; he had been such a nice guy.

Six days later, the Regents' grades were posted. I found my grade, then I found Jeff's—100 percent! I ran over to his house, pounded on the door, and insisted that he explain what had happened.

He said, "I discovered how to learn it on my own in just 12 days, that's all."

"And how did you do that?"

That's when he told me the story. He had found a book at the school bookstore that contained the last 15 years of Regents' geometry examinations. I knew about those books. You could buy them, but what good did they do? He told me that he went back to the earliest exam in the book and simply sat down and took it. It took him 2 1/2 hours. He scored 10 percent, which was about what he figured he'd get. Then he turned to the back of the book and studied the 90 percent that he had missed, seeing what he'd done wrong. Then he took the next Regents' examination. To his surprise, he scored 17 percent. Then he turned to the back of the book and studied the 83 percent that he had missed. He continued to do two tests each day in this way. Near the end, he was scoring 85 percent. That was good enough to ensure that he'd pass. But since there was only 15 percent left that he didn't know, he thought it was worthwhile to get that last bit, so he studied more. By the time he went to the actual Regents' exam, just 12 days after he had known practically no geometry, there wasn't anything about the subject that he couldn't answer. He knew geometry! It wasn't just that he could answer certain kinds of questions. He knew what he was talking about. He understood the principles, and he could integrate them. I was stunned.

What Jeff had accidentally discovered on his own was highlighted by the behaviorist B. F. Skinner many years ago. Teachers using such methods have elicited this kind of incredible learning. In 1960, an eighth-grade class in Roanoke, Virginia, was placed in an experiment in which the students were given algebra questions that they weren't due to study until the ninth grade. The questions were provided on simple teaching machines (crude by modern computer standards), in which a question would be presented, the students would try to answer it, and anything the students didn't know would be worked through until the students got the correct answer. Because the students received *immediate* feedback on each question, and because each one worked at his own pace, they rapidly gained information—it was reinforcing. The eighth graders learned *all* the ninth-grade algebra in one-half the time it usually took the ninth graders to do so (Rushton, 1965). Yet today, more than 30 years later and after hundreds of studies showing similar results, a behavioral

teaching technology is not widely developed or used in our school systems. B. F. Skinner believed that part of the problem is our fear that technology will invade our lives (Skinner, 1984).

Skinner disagreed with the National Commission's statement that educational foundations are being overloaded by a rising tide of mediocrity. He saw mediocrity as an *effect,* not a cause (Skinner, 1984). He believed that educational psychology, especially the behavioral sciences, can make the greatest contribution by giving students and teachers a better reason for learning and teaching. Instructional practices should be developed that are so effective and so attractive that no one will need to be

coerced to use them. Students would then proceed at their own speed, and programmed instruction would be available on almost every subject to provide immediate reinforcement for correct answers and to lead students through the educational experience (Skinner, 1984). In this way, like Jeff, students could master subjects with high speed and precision.

Perhaps such behavioral technology used on a wide basis would not be as effective as hoped. But isn't it worth a try? As Skinner said, "A culture that is not willing to accept scientific advances in the understanding of human behavior, together with the technology which emerges from these advances, will eventually be replaced by a culture that is" (p. 953).

One of the most prominent of these debates is the argument between the behaviorist and the cognitive philosophical orientations. Educational psychologists oriented toward the behaviorist view believe that children should be taught material in ways that make it easy to learn and acquire. In their view, teaching is mainly appropriate use of schedules of reinforcement and appropriate organization and presentation of material. Educational psychologists with a cognitive philosophy typically view the child as innately curious and believe that if the child is placed in an environment that stimulates this curiosity, the child will inevitably learn. Behaviorists respond that without appropriate schedules of reinforcement and contingencies for learning, simply placing the child in an environment that allows excessive freedom gives the child freedom not to learn. Cognitive theorists often counter that "programming" the child with prepackaged material inhibits creativity and spontaneity. The debate, which has been ongoing for about 40 years, has not been resolved.

In 1983, the National Commission on Excellence in Education concluded that the educational foundations of our society were being eroded by mediocrity. The commission argued that there was a crisis in American education, that students were learning less and less from teachers who were poorly trained. This challenge to American education has made the public increasingly aware of the many problems surrounding this great social task. Educational psychologists are at the forefront of efforts to develop more effective teacher-training methods and better ways for students to learn.

The School System

School serves the purpose of systematically passing on the wisdom (or prejudices) of a culture to its young. Educational psychologists have investigated schools to discover the variables that determine which schools are most successful and how that success can be generalized to schools that are less successful. Educational psychologists agree that huge differences exist among schools (Rutter, 1983). For instance, studies conducted in Great Britain found a great range in several measures of schools. In one school, 50 percent of the pupils went on to college; in another fewer than 9 percent did so. Delinquency rates varied from 1 percent to 19 percent, and absenteeism ranged from 6 percent to 26 percent (Rutter, Maughan, Mortimore, Ouston, & Smith, 1979). The range among American schools is even greater.

At first, it might seem that these differences are due only to the fact that schools may serve very different populations. Educational psychologists, however, have studied many pairs of schools that differ greatly in their delinquency, attendance, and college-acceptance rates but that serve similar student populations in terms of intellectual characteristics and socioeconomic status (Finlayson & Loughran, 1976; Reynolds & Murgatroyd, 1977). Furthermore, a number of schools have been found to turn out students consistently who attain high levels of scholastic achievement despite the fact that these students come from inner-city neighborhoods generally associated with low achievement (Weber, 1971). All these findings indicate that different schools may provide their students with very different educations despite the neighborhood from which the students come. Schools that show superior student achievement, whether the students come from poor neighborhoods or affluent ones, tend to maintain these high standards of excellence year after year. Schools with poor performance records, regardless of neighborhood, also tend to be consistent (Rutter, 1983).

To date, educational psychologists are unsure what it is that makes a school successful. There have been many speculations and debates about this issue. For example, although schools with good reputations consistently turn out more successful students than do schools with poor reputations, even if they draw from the same population, this is only a correlation, not a demonstrated cause–effect relationship. We don't know whether the school with the good reputation takes the students and changes their behavior, or whether the more motivated students in a particular neighborhood seek the "better" school, thereby maintaining its reputation for excellence, or what the process is.

The Teacher

Educational psychologists have discovered that only a handful of excellent, dedicated teachers may be an important factor in determining whether a particular school will be successful. In one study (Pedersen, Faucher, & Eaton, 1978), researchers found that the children in a particular elementary school who had achieved the highest grades and who later demonstrated superior status as adults all had one thing in common—the same first-grade teacher!

The academic material that the teacher taught obviously had little effect on the children once they had become adults. However, this teacher appeared to have made a lasting contribution to the students' attitudes toward learning and the desire to achieve, as well as to have helped students to set their sights on different life paths than they might ordinarily have considered. Think of the teachers you've had whom you greatly admired and respected. Did they teach you more than just the academic material? Did they teach you to do your best, to have confidence in yourself, to set high standards, and then to attain them? Did they make you want to stay in school and continue to learn? Perhaps such teachers, more than anything else, determine whether a school will be successful.

Educational psychologists know that one important factor in whether a school will be successful is the quality of the teaching staff.

The Successful School

Although it is a common assumption that the age of the school or the size of classrooms has an important effect on student achievement, educational psychologists have discovered that these two factors don't make much difference, assuming that reasonable minimal standards are met—that facilities are not completely dilapidated and that the school isn't out of funds for the most rudimentary equipment (Rutter, Maughan, Mortimore, Ouston, & Smith, 1979). Successful schools generally have an academic emphasis. Academic goals are clearly stated, there is a certain degree of structure, and there are high achievement expectations (Linney & Seidman, 1989). More specifically, effective schools are characterized by regularly assigned and graded homework and by a high proportion of time devoted to active teaching, instead of to miscellaneous activities such as calling roll, handing out papers, setting up equipment, and disciplining students. Effective schools also have a system of checks to make certain that teachers are following the intended practices of the school. This is especially important for inexperienced teachers, who tend to be the most inefficient in classroom management (Rutter, Maughan, Mortimore, Ouston, & Smith, 1979).

In this section, we have touched on only a few of the important issues addressed by educational psychologists, but we have examined other areas of interest to educational psychologists in other chapters. For instance, we examined test development in Chapters 12 and 13, learning and cognition in Chapters 6 and 8, and motivation in Chapter 9. All these areas, as well as others, are of concern to educational psychologists in the quest to understand how people become educated and how they apply their knowledge.

EPILOGUE: THE LONGEST THROW

Sports psychologists know that peak performance requires more than just will, determination, and muscle. There must be preparation, both physical and mental. The following is an example of such preparation.

Tom Petranoff is a world-class athlete. He throws the javelin. When he began, his drive and desire to win were exceptional, and they tended to make him want to try his very hardest at all the important competitions. But when his turn came to throw, he would become too tense, concerned about the crowd and his performance. The muscle tension caused muscles that should have been relaxed to conflict with the muscles he needed to use in the throw. His scores were good, but sports psychologist Robert Nideffer thought he could do better.

The uninitiated might think the best way to make a javelin throw would be to grab the javelin tightly in your hand, clench your teeth, hum the theme song from Rocky, *race down the runway, and fling the javelin as hard as you possibly can. Oddly, such a mental attitude, even if the body is in peak physical condition and training has been intensive, often can destroy an athlete's performance by creating too much physical tension.*

Tom Petranoff was an accomplished thrower, but he had not mastered mental concentration to overcome his tension. Nideffer began progressive relaxation training, and Petranoff slowly learned to "center"; that is, to calm himself just before attempting a peak performance, so that he felt comfortable and relaxed. After mastering the relaxation techniques, Petranoff went to his next athletic meet. As he stood on the runway holding the javelin in his hand, he relaxed, breathed deeply, and focused his eyes on a spot on the runway for about 20 seconds. He stood there, he said, "just feeling my heart beat and my shoulders low and then—boom—I took off" (Kiester, 1984, p. 24). As he ran down the runway, he didn't have to think about any of his movements. He had made them so many times before in practice that his mind was relaxed, he was on automatic. His muscles moved smoothly without tension. He released the javelin in one swift flowing action. The javelin sailed silently outward in a long high arc. The crowd in the stadium quieted as the javelin seemed to float magically far out over the event field, past where even the farthest judge was standing. It struck into the earth at 327 feet, 2 inches, a truly magnificent throw—a world record!

SUMMARY

■ Applied psychology is the use of basic psychological knowledge to enhance or develop behavioral technology.
■ Industrial/organizational (I/O) psychologists work for businesses, organizations, or governments, or teach at universities.

Their main concern has been to improve the functioning of business and industry and to investigate ways to make an organization efficient and effective.
■ The three major areas of concern among I/O psychologists

are the creation and operation of organizations, the selection and training of personnel and staff, and the improvement of job performance and productivity.

■ Organizational behavior includes the policies and procedures of managers, the ways managers interact with workers, the tasks of jobs, and the structure of organizations.

■ I/O psychologists have been instrumental in developing valid personnel selection techniques and in devising the best ways for organizations to select a successful employee base. The first important step in personnel selection is job analysis.

■ The development and construction of valid tests also are important concerns of I/O psychologists. Tests that measure the highly specific skills required for a particular job generally are more valid than are measures of other variables.

■ Job satisfaction is an important correlate of worker productivity.

■ The two most valuable techniques for increasing the motivation of workers to produce are behavior modification and goal setting.

■ Sports psychology is concerned with the application of psychological principles to physical activity and sports, either to maximize performance or to investigate applied clinical issues.

■ Techniques have been developed for improving peak performance. These include practicing, monitoring arousal, finding optimal arousal level, and training mentally.

■ Environmental psychology is concerned with the effects and influences of the environment on behavior.

■ Two of the most studied areas in environmental psychology are illumination and the effects of heat.

■ Environmental psychologists have identified a number of toxic substances that are believed to cause learning problems. These include cadmium and lead.

■ Excessive noise in the environment can be a major distraction, raise blood pressure, and increase the chance of hearing damage.

■ Environmental psychologists structure environments—both indoors and outdoors—to achieve particular behavioral results.

■ An important consideration in environmental psychology is proxemics, which is the study of conditions of crowding, privacy, territory, and personal space.

■ Consumer psychology is the psychology of selling and advertising. It is concerned with determining advertising effectiveness, surveying consumer opinion, assessing consumer attitudes, identifying the psychological market, and studying consumer behavior.

■ Consumer psychologists have helped to develop or incorporate devices that can record interest in products or advertisements. These include eye-movement tracking devices and the use of EEGs or other measures to monitor arousal of the central nervous system.

■ Educational psychologists are principally concerned with training teachers and conducting educational research.

■ A major focus of educational research is to develop valid and reliable tests for measuring student aptitude and achievement.

■ Educational psychologists place a special emphasis on the psychology of learning. One important ongoing debate is whether a behaviorist or a cognitive approach to teaching is most effective.

■ One important way of teaching students material is through self-paced programmed instruction that includes immediate feedback about correct and incorrect answers and instructions tailored to what the student needs to learn.

SUGGESTIONS FOR FURTHER READING

1. Anastasi, A. (1979). *Fields of applied psychology* (2nd ed.). New York: McGraw-Hill. A college-level text on applied psychology, including industrial/organizational, engineering/environmental, consumer, and community psychology.

2. Cox, R. H. (1985). *Sports psychology: Concepts and applications.* A college-level introductory text on sports psychology.

3. Glover, J., & Glover, R. B. (1987). *Educational psychology: Principles and applications.* Glenview, IL: Scott Foresman. A college-level textbook that covers all topics in educational psychology.

APPENDIX A | Statistics

Richard D. Rees

You are a student in introductory psychology who has developed a healthy respect for what psychology has to offer. You've been impressed with the research methods psychologists use and have decided to conduct a study of your own.

For a long time you have been concerned about television and its possible adverse effects on studies and grades. The children in your family and the children in your friends' families spend a lot of time watching TV. It seems obvious to you that, if they watched less, they would do better in school.

The hypothesis you want to test is that students who are heavy TV watchers do not perform as well in their academic studies as students who are light TV watchers.

With the cooperation of a friend, the principal of Tumbleweed Elementary School, and with the permission of the parents involved, you embark on a two-week research project with 50 fourth graders from Tumbleweed. Half of the students are assigned randomly to a group of heavy TV watchers and told to watch 35 hours or more of TV per week, and half are assigned to a group of light TV watchers and told to watch 6 or fewer hours of TV per week. At the end of two weeks, all students take the same unannounced spelling test consisting of 15 words from a current chapter of their spelling workbook. The results of the spelling test are given in Table A.1. You want to know whether the light watchers did better than the heavies.

At this point you can't tell for sure. Something must be done with the scores before you can make sense out of them. In this appendix we set out strategies and techniques that will help you interpret, understand, and make predictions from research data such as test scores. These strategies and techniques form a very valuable research tool, namely, statistics. So let's apply statistics to your TV watchers' spelling scores.

TABLE A.1 Spelling Scores of Heavy and Light TV Watchers

Heavy Watchers (35 Hours Or More Per Week)					Light Watchers (6 or Fewer Hours Per Week)				
11	1	7	4	13	13	10	13	11	13
7	5	2	10	6	15	11	9	14	7
0	15	6	1	7	8	15	14	12	13
9	2	7	0	7	14	11	11	5	8
6	5	8	2	9	13	14	13	5	3

TABLE A.2 Frequency Distribution of Spelling Scores of Heavy and Light TV Watchers

HEAVY TV WATCHERS		LIGHT TV WATCHERS	
Spelling Score	Number of Students (Frequency)	Spelling Score	Number of Students (Frequency)
15	1	15	2
14	0	14	4
13	1	13	6
12	0	12	1
11	1	11	4
10	1	10	1
9	2	9	1
8	1	8	2
7	5	7	1
6	3	6	0
5	2	5	2
4	1	4	0
3	0	3	1
2	3	2	0
1	2	1	0
0	2	0	0

DESCRIPTIVE STATISTICS

Descriptive statistics are used to summarize, organize, describe, boil down, and make sense out of large amounts of data. In Table A.1 you have an incoherent mass of test score data. The scores are disorganized and convey very little information.

Frequency Distributions and Graphs

One way of organizing the scores to make them more meaningful is to arrange them in a *frequency distribution*.

TABLE A.3 Grouped Frequency Distribution of Math Scores for 50 Students

MATH SCORES IN INTERVALS OF 5	NUMBER OF STUDENTS (FREQUENCY)
50–54	2
45–49	3
40–44	2
35–39	6
30–34	8
25–29	12
20–24	7
15–19	5
10–14	4
5–9	0
0–4	1

REGULAR FREQUENCY DISTRIBUTION. In a *regular frequency distribution*, each score value from highest to lowest is listed once; beside it, in the frequency column, the number of times that score occurs is written. In examining Table A.2 you can see, for example, that the score of 7 occurred 5 times among the heavy TV watchers.

GROUPED FREQUENCY DISTRIBUTION. If the spread of score values in a distribution is large (for example, a math test with 53 questions on it), then a *grouped frequency distribution* may be used. A grouped frequency distribution condenses the score values into intervals and then shows, in the frequency column, the number of people who received scores falling within each interval (see Table A.3).

To further clarify the arrangement of scores in a frequency distribution, so that you can see at a glance the visual pattern involved, the distribution can be graphed.

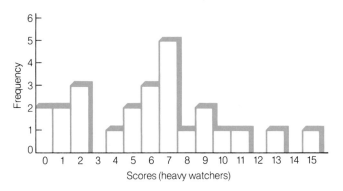

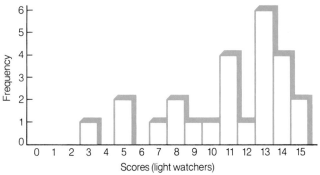

HISTOGRAM. A *histogram* (or *bar graph*) uses a series of vertical bars to show the pattern of scores (see Figure A.1). Notice that the sides of each bar are plotted midway between the scores so that each score falls in the center of the bar.

FREQUENCY POLYGON. A *frequency polygon* plots the frequencies of the scores as points that are then connected with a straight line. Figure A.2 shows you at a glance that the heavy TV watchers didn't do too well on the spelling test. It certainly conveys more information than the mass of scores in Table A.1.

When large amounts of data (thousands of scores) are plotted, the jagged edges tend to smooth out and the frequency polygon often takes on an identifiable shape. Some of the more commonly observed shapes are (1) a normal *bell-shaped curve* (where the majority of people scored in the middle of the distribution with very few at the extreme high and low ends), (2) a *positively skewed curve* (where most of the people got low scores, with fewer and fewer getting progressively higher ones),* (3) a *negatively skewed curve* (where nearly everyone aced the test), and (4) a *bimodal curve* (where very few people scored in the middle, most either acing the test or bombing it). The curves are shown in Figure A.3.

---

*A positively skewed curve often indicates poor performance, but not always. For example, reaction-time curves are usually positively skewed, indicating that most people have fast reaction times.

FIGURE A.2

Frequency polygon of spelling scores of heavy and light TV watchers.

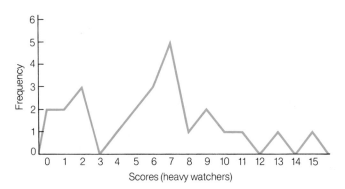

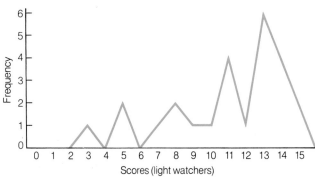

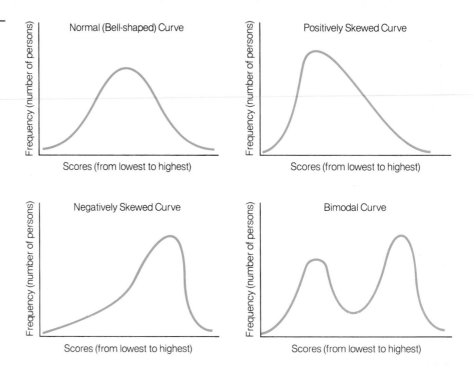

Central Tendency

Another useful descriptive statistic involves measuring the central tendency of a group of scores. *Central tendency* refers to a single number representing the middle or the average of a distribution. There are three measures of central tendency: the mean, the median, and the mode (see Table A.4).

MEAN. The *mean* is the arithmetic average and is obtained by adding up all the scores in the distribution and dividing that sum by the total number of scores. The heavy TV watchers' spelling scores add up to 150. Since there were 25 students in this group, we divide 150 by 25 to obtain a mean score of 6. The light TV watchers' scores total 275, which, divided by 25, gives a mean of 11. Out of 15 possible, the light watchers averaged 11 right, and the heavy watchers 6 right. Your hypothesis is looking more plausible all the time, isn't it?

MEDIAN. Although the mean is the most commonly used measure of central tendency in statistical analysis, there are times when it is not appropriate to use it (for instance with a highly skewed distribution containing extreme scores). Instead, the *median* is used. The median is the exact middle of a distribution of scores. Half the scores fall on one side of it and half on the other. There are precise methods for calculating the median, but for our purposes, a convenient way is to list each score from highest to lowest and then count in to the center.

MODE. The *mode* is a very crude measure of central tendency. It gives, at best, only a rough estimate of the middle area and is seldom used in statistical analysis. The mode is simply the score in a distribution that occurs more frequently than any other score. For the heavy watchers it is 7, and for the light watchers, 13.

HEAVY WATCHERS	LIGHT WATCHERS
Mean	
15 + 13 + 11 + 10 + 9 + 9 + 8 + 7 + 7 + 7 + 7 + 7 + 6 + 6 + 6 + 5 + 5 + 4 + 2 + 2 + 2 + 1 + 1 + 0 + 0 = 150	15 + 15 + 14 + 14 + 14 + 14 + 13 + 13 + 13 + 13 + 13 + 13 + 12 + 11 + 11 + 11 + 11 + 10 + 9 + 8 + 8 + 7 + 5 + 5 + 3 = 275
$\text{Mean} = \dfrac{\text{Sum of Scores}}{\text{Number of scores}} = \dfrac{150}{25} = 6$	$\text{Mean} = \dfrac{\text{Sum of Scores}}{\text{Number of Scores}} = \dfrac{275}{25} = 11$
Mean = 6	Mean = 11
Median	
15, 13, 11, 10, 9, 9, 8, 7, 7, 7, 7, 7, ⑥, 6, 6, 5, 5, 4, 2, 2, 2, 1, 1, 0, 0,	15, 15, 14, 14, 14, 14, 13, 13, 13, 13, 13, 13, ⑫, 11, 11, 11, 11, 10, 9, 8, 8, 7, 5, 5, 3,
Median = Exact middle score. There are exactly 12 scores on either side of the circled 6.	Median = Exact middle score. There are exactly 12 scores on either side of the circled 12.
Median = 6	Median = 12
Mode	
Mode = Most frequently occurring score. (There were 5 students who got a score of 7.)	Mode = Most frequent occurring score. (There were 6 students who got a score of 13.)
Mode = 7	Mode = 13

Variability

Variability refers to the dispersion or scatter of a group of scores. It is concerned with how spread out the scores are. High variability means that the scores are widely separated with much distance between them. Low variability indicates very little spread; the scores are tightly clustered together. Measures of variability include the range, the variance, and the standard deviation.

RANGE. The *range* is obtained by subtracting the lowest from the highest score. The range of spelling scores for the heavy TV watchers is 15 (the scores ranged from 0 to 15). For the light watchers, the range is 12 (from 3 to 15). Although easy to calculate, the range, like the mode, is a crude statistical measure. As you can see, it takes into account only two scores in the distribution, the highest and the lowest.

VARIANCE AND STANDARD DEVIATION. The *standard deviation* (SD) is the most useful measure of variability. It takes into account every score in the distribution. The standard deviation (which is the square root of the variance) can be thought of (generally speaking) as a number representing the average distance of the scores from the mean. The larger the standard deviation, the more spread out the scores. It is calculated by (1) finding the difference between the mean and each score, (2) squaring each of these differences, (3) adding up the squared differences, (4) dividing the sum of the squared differences by the total number of scores (N) minus

STATISTICS

one* (the average of the squared differences), and (5) taking the square root of the average of the squared differences. The calculations up through step 4 yield the variance. Taking the square root in step 5 (to return to the original units of measurement) gives the standard deviation.

As you can see in Table A.5, the heavy TV watchers had slightly greater variability on the spelling test than the light watchers. The heavies had a higher range and a larger variance and standard deviation.

Transformed Scores

Sometimes, for purposes of increased clarity or for making comparisons, it is desirable to change or transform scores into new units. Percentiles represent one type of transformed scores, and standard scores are another.

PERCENTILES.   Carol, a subject in the group of light TV watchers, scored 13 correct on the spelling test. Her friend Julie, in the heavy group, got 9 right.

To see how well each girl did in comparison with her own group, we need to transform the scores. A percentile shows the percentage of people in the reference group who scored at or below a certain score. In Carol's reference group (the light watchers), 19 children out of 25 got 13 or fewer words right. Dividing 19 by 25 gives us .76 or 76 percent. Thus, Carol's score of 13 places her at the 76th percentile. Julie's 9 represents the 84th percentile (21 students out of 25 got a score of 9 or less, $21/25 = .84$). So Julie with her 9 did better with respect to her group of heavy watchers than Carol with her 13 did with respect to the light watchers.

STANDARD SCORES (Z, T, SAT).   Z scores are transformed scores that have a mean of 0 and a standard deviation of 1. To obtain a Z score for any raw score in a distribution, simply subtract the mean from the score and divide the result by the standard deviation. Carol's Z score is 0.60 (her score of 13 minus the mean of 11 divided by the standard deviation 3.341 equals 0.60) in her light TV group. Julie's Z score is 9 minus 6 divided by 3.948 which equals 0.76. Again, you can see that Julie with her Z of 0.76 did better with respect to her group than Carol with her Z of 0.60 did with respect to hers, even though Carol's raw score of 13 was higher than Julie's raw score of 9.

Two other standard scores are T scores, which have a mean of 50 and a standard deviation of 10, and SAT scores, with a mean of 500 and an SD of 100. To obtain a T score, multiply the Z score by 10 and add 50. Carol's T (10 times 0.60 plus 50) equals 56.0, and Julie's T is 57.6 (10 times 0.76 plus 50). SAT scores are obtained by multiplying the T score by 10. Carol's SAT is 560, and Julie's is 576.

Table A.6 shows transformed scores for Carol with respect to the group of light TV watchers and Julie with respect to the heavy watchers.

Julie's boy friend, Ambitious Andy Angus, who lifts bulls for exercise, was also randomly assigned to the heavy watchers' group and got a score of 1 on the spelling test. His Z score is -1.27 (1 minus 6 divided by 3.948). His T score is 37.3 (-1.27 times 10 plus 50), and his SAT is 373.

T scores are easier to interpret for many people because, like Z scores, they avoid negative numbers (a Z of -1 is the same as a T of 40). Also, the results of some national exams, such as the Scholastic Aptitude Test and the Graduate Record Exam, are reported in SAT scores.

*Note: The divisor is N if you are merely describing a set of scores, and it is N minus 1 if you are making an inference about a population, as we will be doing with these data.

TABLE A.5 Measures of Variability of Spelling Scores for Heavy and Light TV Watchers

HEAVY WATCHERS		LIGHT WATCHERS		

Range

HEAVY WATCHERS	LIGHT WATCHERS
Range = Highest score minus lowest score	Range = Highest score minus lowest score
Range = 15–0	Range = 15–3
Range = 15	Range = 12

Variance and standard deviation (SD)

Scores	Scores minus mean of 6	Scores minus mean, squared	Scores	Scores minus mean of 11	Scores minus mean, squared
15	9	81	15	4	16
13	7	49	15	4	16
11	5	25	14	3	9
10	4	16	14	3	9
9	3	9	14	3	9
9	3	9	14	3	9
8	2	4	13	2	4
7	1	1	13	2	4
7	1	1	13	2	4
7	1	1	13	2	4
7	1	1	13	2	4
7	1	1	13	2	4
6	0	0	12	1	1
6	0	0	11	0	0
6	0	0	11	0	0
5	−1	1	11	0	0
5	−1	1	11	0	0
4	−2	4	10	−1	1
2	−4	16	9	−2	4
2	−4	16	8	−3	9
2	−4	16	8	−3	9
1	−5	25	7	−4	16
1	−5	25	5	−6	36
0	−6	36	5	−6	36
0	−6	36	3	−8	64

Heavy Watchers: Sum of scores minus mean, squared = 374

Light Watchers: Sum of scores minus mean, squared = 268

$$SD = \sqrt{\dfrac{\text{Sum of score minus mean, squared}}{\text{Number of scores minus one}}}$$

$$SD = \sqrt{\dfrac{374}{25-1}} = \sqrt{15.583} = 3.948$$

Variance = 15.583

Standard deviation = 3.948

$$SD = \sqrt{\dfrac{\text{Sum of scores minus mean, squared}}{\text{Number of scores minus one}}}$$

$$SD = \sqrt{\dfrac{268}{25-1}} = \sqrt{11.167} = 3.342$$

Variance = 11.167

Standard deviation = 3.342

TABLE A.6 Transformed Spelling Scores

	JULIE (IN HEAVY WATCHER'S GROUP)	CAROL (IN LIGHT WATCHER'S GROUP)
Actual score on spelling test	9	13
Percentile	84th	76th
Z score	+0.76	+0.60
T score	57.6	56.0
SAT score	576	560

The Normal Bell-Shaped Curve

Z scores and the standard deviation are related to the normal bell-shaped curve in a fixed and predictable manner. When a frequency polygon is drawn for large numbers of people on certain traits (for instance, intelligence, height, weight, extroversion), the resulting curve is bell-shaped. Because many traits in psychology take this bell shape, the normal curve is a very useful statistical tool. Since the percentages under the curve never change, by plugging in the standard deviation you can determine the percentage of the people falling above, below, or between certain scores. Look at Figure A.4. Assuming that the mean spelling score on a *25-item test* for a *large population* of light TV watchers is 11 with an SD of 3, you can see that about 68 percent of the subjects score between 8 and 14 on the test. Only 13/100 percent (0.13 percent) were above a score of 20.

A popular intelligence test (the Wechsler) has a mean IQ of 100 with an SD of 15. As you can see in Figure A.4, about 95 percent of the population have IQ scores between 70 and 130.

Z scores are expressed in standard deviation units, so that a person with a Z score of +3.00 would be standard deviations above the mean and would have outscored over 99 percent of those with scores on that variable. Remember, any score on any test can be converted to a Z score, and by examining the percentages under the curve, you can see at a glance how good that score is.*

INFERENTIAL STATISTICS

Whereas descriptive statistics merely describe, organize, and summarize data, inferential statistics are used to make predictions and draw conclusions about populations based on data from a sample.

Populations and Samples

The question you want to answer is: Do all fourth graders who are heavy TV watchers really obtain a lower spelling test average (mean) than all fourth graders who are light TV watchers? Your populations of interest, then, are *all* heavy and *all* light TV watchers who are in the fourth grade. However, you can't measure

---

*It must be assumed that the large population of test scores under consideration would form a frequency polygon that is shaped like the normal bell-shaped curve.

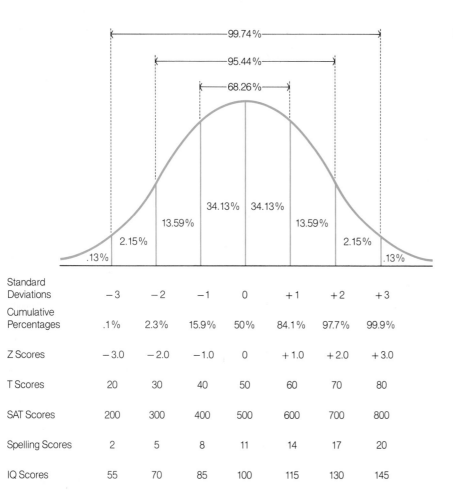

Standard Deviations	−3	−2	−1	0	+1	+2	+3
Cumulative Percentages	.1%	2.3%	15.9%	50%	84.1%	97.7%	99.9%
Z Scores	−3.0	−2.0	−1.0	0	+1.0	+2.0	+3.0
T Scores	20	30	40	50	60	70	80
SAT Scores	200	300	400	500	600	700	800
Spelling Scores	2	5	8	11	14	17	20
IQ Scores	55	70	85	100	115	130	145

FIGURE A.4

Normal bell-shaped curve showing various scores and percentages under the curve (total area equals 100 percent).

them all, so you obtain a sample of each, which is smaller and more manageable and which you *can* measure. If your samples are chosen at random (so that any member of the population has an equal chance of being selected), then they are likely to be representative of the population.

Probability

Inferential statistics are based on the laws of *probability* or chance. If heavy or light TV watching has no effect at all on spelling scores, then you would expect the mean scores for the two samples (heavy and light) to be about the same; that is, the probability is high that the means will be the same or nearly the same. The probability is very low that the heavy watchers' sample will average, say, a score of 2 and the light watchers sample will average, say, 14 if TV watching has no effect on spelling scores in the population. You wouldn't expect the averages to be so far apart from chance alone.

Null Hypothesis (Retain or Reject)

The procedure to follow in inferential statistics is (1) to state the *null hypothesis* (that there is *no* difference between the average scores in the two populations), (2) to draw a sample from each of the two populations of interest, (3) to find the two sample mean scores, (4) to determine how probable it is that the difference between the two means occurred by chance, and (5) to reject the null hypothesis if the probability is less than 5 percent that the difference could have occurred by chance (the choice of 5 percent is an arbitrary one that psychologists have generally found to be most useful).

In your present study, your null hypothesis is that heavy and light TV watchers will score the same on the spelling test (signifying that TV watching does not affect spelling scores). In your two samples, the heavy watchers and the light watchers scored a mean of 6 and 11, respectively, on the test. Could a mean of 6 in one group and 11 in the other have occurred just by chance if the null hypothesis is true? It could have, but it is not very likely. Using the normal curve and specific inferential statistical testing procedures, we find that the probability that means of 6 and 11 (a difference of 5 points) would occur by chance is less than 5 percent. This is so low that you reject the null hypothesis and conclude that, in the populations, fourth graders who are light TV watchers score better on the spelling test than those who are heavy TV watchers. You have found a significant difference between the means. *Significant* has a specific meaning in statistics. It means that the difference between the sample means could have occurred purely by chance less than five times in a hundred samplings (that is, in 5 percent) of the two populations if in fact the two population means are the same (that is, if the null hypothesis is true).

It was not chance that accounted for the heavy group's lower score, it was too much TV. Notice that in rejecting the null hypothesis you are supporting the research hypothesis that you formulated when you began the study. That is, students who are heavy TV watchers do not perform as well in their academic studies as students who are light TV watchers. You could have made an error in drawing this conclusion if that very slim probability (less than five chances in a hundred) actually happened in these samples. But the probability of your having made such an error (known as a *Type I error* in statistical terminology) is less than 5 percent.

CORRELATION

Showing that heavy TV watchers score lower on the spelling test than light watchers involved one major statistical procedure, namely, testing for differences between means.

Correlation, another major procedure in statistics, is designed to show relationships between variables. Correlation may be classified as descriptive or inferential depending on how it is used. Instead of getting up an experimental study with two groups of fourth graders assigned to two weeks of heavy or light TV viewing, we could simply select a group of fourth graders, ask them how much TV they watch per week, and give them a spelling test. The correlation or relationship between hours of TV and test scores could then be determined. A trend or tendency (a correlation) might show up. You might expect a strong negative correlation, but it is possible that it could be moderate, weak, or zero. It might even be positive.

Correlation Coefficient

The correlation between two variables is expressed as a number known as the *correlation coefficient*. It can range from 0 to 1 (usually expressed in hundredths, that is, .01, .09, .18, .45, .87, .93, etc.), with higher numbers showing stronger relationships, and it can be positive or negative. A correlation can also be perfect, although perfect correlations rarely occur with psychological data.

Positive, Negative, Perfect, and Zero Correlations

A *positive correlation* means that there is a tendency for the two variables to change together in the same direction. For instance, high school grade point average is positively correlated with college grade point average. That is to say, those who do well in high school tend to do well in college also, and vice versa. Of course, there are exceptions, but the tendency is nevertheless a strong one.

A *negative correlation* shows that, as one variable is increasing, the other is decreasing. The variables change in opposite directions. Absences and grades would probably be negatively correlated. As absences increase, grades decrease, and vice versa.

The strongest possible correlation is 1.00 (which can be either $+1.00$ or -1.00), and it is called a *perfect correlation*. A perfect positive correlation ($+1.00$) means that right down the line each person maintains his or her position from highest to lowest on both variables. The highest person on variable X is also the highest on variable Y, the next highest on X is next highest on Y, and so on, down to the person who is lowest on both variables. There are no exceptions to the pattern. For example, it costs 50¢ for an ice cream cone at the corner ice cream parlor. What is the correlation between money spent for ice cream cones and the number of cones purchased? It is perfect ($+1.00$), isn't it? The person who spends 50¢ gets one cone; whoever spends $1 gets two cones; $10, 20 cones; $50, 100 cones; and so on. You can *predict* exactly a person's "score" on one variable if you know the "score" on the other variable. (If someone spent $20 on ice cream cones, how many did he or she buy? Exactly 40, of course.)

Zero correlation means that there is no relationship between the two variables being studied. What would you expect the correlation to be between nose length and IQ for a group of 50 people? It would be zero, or very near to zero, since these two variables are not related.

Scatter Diagrams

A scatter diagram can show visually the direction and strength of a correlation. The correlation scatter diagrams in Figure A.5 were constructed by plotting a single dot for each person's score on both variables. The closer the dots approach a diagonal straight line, the higher the correlation; a diagonal straight line represents a perfect correlation of $+1.00$ or -1.00.

Table A.7 shows how different correlation coefficient values are interpreted. Remember, the size of the correlation coefficient shows how strong the relationship is, and the sign (plus or minus) indicates the direction of the relationship (positive meaning that the two variables change together and negative that they vary in opposite directions). A correlation coefficient of $-.83$, for example, indicates a stronger relationship than does one of $+.71$, since .83 is a larger value than .71.

Correlating Test Scores with TV Viewing

Let's take another look at the fourth-grade TV watchers. You want to know whether those who watch TV more tend to score lower on the spelling test. Select 10 fourth

Scatter diagrams showing positive, negative, perfect, and zero correlations (r = correlation coefficient).

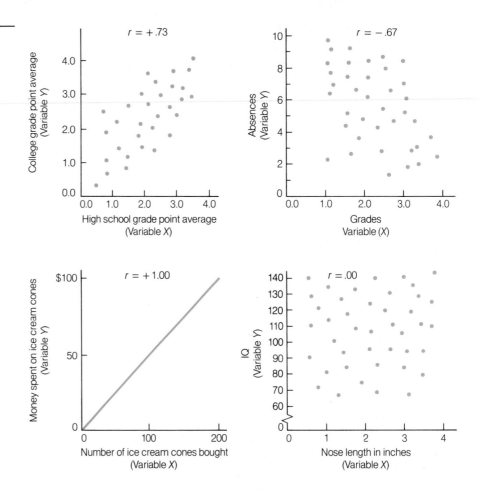

graders from Tumbleweed Elementary and find out how many hours per week each watches TV. Also obtain their scores on the spelling test. Table A.8 shows the TV hours and scores, and gives the calculations necessary to obtain the correlation coefficient.

The correlation coefficient of −.72 indicates a strong (almost a very strong) relationship between TV watching and spelling scores. The higher-scoring students watch less TV and vice versa. The correlation is not perfect (there are some exceptions to this trend), but the trend is nevertheless striking.

TABLE A.7 Interpreting Correlation Coefficients

CORRELATION COEFFICIENT (PLUS OR MINUS)	INTERPRETATION
1.00	Perfect relationship
.73 to .99	Very strong relationship
.60 to .72	Strong relationship
.31 to .59	Fairly strong (or moderate) relationship
.16 to .30	Weak relationship
.01 to .15	Very weak relationship
0.00	No relationship

Note that the data in this appendix were made up and exaggerated to illustrate the statistical concepts. You may not wixh to run your own study with real data in order to check your understanding of statistics and to indulge your curiosity about behavior.

Correlation and Causation

Experimental studies, which test the differences between means, help you to draw conclusions about case-and-effect relationships, but correlational studies do not establish causation. Just because two variables are correlated does not mean that one causes the other. It may be that when two variables are highly correlated, variable X causes variable Y, or variable Y causes variable X, or X causes Z which in turn causes Y, or W simultaneously causes both X and Y. The correlation coefficient gives us no information about causation. Much TV watching may cause low grades; low grades may cause more TV watching; or some other variable (such as increased study time, procrastination, depression, self-concept, intelligence, or social pressure) may be causing both higher grades and less TV or lower grades and more TV.

When birth statistics were examined for a number of European cities several years ago, a high positive correlation was supposedly found between the number

TABLE A.8 Calculation of Correlation Between Hours of TV Watching and Spelling Test Scores for 10 Fourth Graders

SUBJECT	HOURS OF TV PER WEEK (VARIABLE X)	VARIABLE X SQUARED (X^2)	SCORE ON 10-WORD SPELLING TEST (VARIABLE Y)	VARIABLE Y SQUARED (Y^2)	VARIABLE X TIMES VARIABLE Y (XY)
1	0	0	10	100	0
2	5	25	8	64	40
3	10	100	9	81	90
4	13	169	2	4	26
5	18	324	6	36	108
6	23	529	5	25	115
7	27	729	3	9	81
8	30	900	0	0	0
9	31	961	7	49	217
10	36	1296	1	1	36
Totals:	193	5033	51	369	713
	Sum of X	Sum of X^2	Sum of Y	Sum of Y^2	Sum of XY
	193	5033	51	369	713

N = Number of subjects = 10

$$r = \frac{N(\text{Sum of } XY) - (\text{Sum of } X)(\text{Sum of } Y)}{\sqrt{[N(\text{Sum of } X^2) - (\text{Sum of } X)^2][N(\text{Sum of } Y^2) - (\text{Sum of } Y)^2]}}$$

$$r = \frac{(10)(713) - (193)(51)}{\sqrt{[(10)(5033) - (193)^2][(10)(369) - (51)^2]}}$$

$$r = \frac{7130 - 9843}{\sqrt{(50330 - 37249)(3690 - 2601)}}$$

$$r = \frac{-2713}{\sqrt{(13081)(1089)}} \qquad r = \frac{-2713}{3774.2825}$$

$r = -.7188$ or $-.72$

of babies born per year and the number of storks nesting in the chimneys. Obviously, a hasty assumption about *causation* will lead you to an outdated conclusion. Even your TV-watching fourth graders wouldn't buy that one.

SUMMARY

■ Psychologists give tests, conduct experiments, and carry out extensive research into many facets of human and animal behavior. The data resulting from all this research must be analyzed, interpreted, summarized, and reported in a meaningful way. By using statistics, researchers can make sense out of the data and can draw valid conclusions about the results of their tests and experiments.

■ Statistics fall into two main categories: descriptive and inferential. Descriptive statistics are used to summarize, organize, and describe a set of research data, and inferential statistics are used to draw conclusions about populations based on the results obtained from a sample.

■ Descriptive statistics include frequency distributions (both regular and grouped), graphs (including histograms and frequency polygons), measures of central tendency (mean, median, and mode), measures of variability (range, variance, and standard deviation), and transformed scores (including percentiles and standard scores).

■ Although frequency polygons take many shapes (including skewed and bimodal), the most important shape for use in statistical analysis is the normal bell-shaped curve.

■ The normal curve has a fixed and predictable association with the standard deviation and Z scores, permitting direct comparison of the results of many diverse tests and experimental data. The normal curve is also a probability curve, which has special applications in conjunction with inferential statistics.

■ Inferential statistics are based on the laws of probability. Researchers are interested in determining the chances that the results obtained from certain samples represent the true state of affairs in the population. To do this, a null hypothesis (that no difference exists or that observed differences are due only to chance) is stated, and then the null hypothesis is retained or rejected depending on the results of the statistical test employed.

■ Correlation, another statistical procedure, shows the strength of the relationship between two variables. Correlation coefficients range from 0 to +1.00, or from 0 to −1.00. The higher the correlation coefficient, the stronger the relationship.

■ A positive correlation means that the two variables are changing together in the same direction. A negative correlation shows an inverse relationship (as one variable is getting larger the other is getting smaller, and vice versa).

■ Correlation coefficients may be visually displayed in scatter diagrams.

■ Correlation does not imply causation.

APPENDIX B ▌ How to Locate and Read Research Articles in Psychology

An introductory psychology text usually contains hundreds of references to books, journal articles, dissertations, and papers. While it is not possible in this appendix to describe and explain all the different sources of information you might encounter, it is valuable for you to be able to locate and read articles in psychological journals if you wish to know how psychologists report their research findings or wish to do further research on a topic.

The first part of this appendix describes the sources you can use to find articles, abstracts and other research sources. The second part describes in detail the parts of a journal article. The third part lists some of the major journals used by psychologists and gives a brief summary of the kind of research each reports.

Even though psychologists publish in many different journals and use a multitude of formats, this appendix describes the article organization preferred by the American Psychological Association,* since many of the major journals are published by that association and a number of other journals also use its format.

▌ RESEARCH SOURCES

Psychologists and psychology students can use many sources to obtain information about a specific subject. The most commonly used is *Psychological Abstracts*, which is published monthly by the American Psychological Association (APA). Each volume contains abstracts (summaries) of articles that have appeared in journals important to psychologists. The abstracts are indexed by both subject and author. The APA also publishes (quarterly) the *PsycSCAN* series, which includes abstracts in one specific area, such as clinical, applied, or developmental psychology. In addition, the APA's *PsycINFO* service provides custom computer searches for data or information.

Other important sources of interest include: *ERIC*, a catalog of selected documents in the area of education, which is closely tied to psychology; *Dissertation Abstracts*, which lists dissertations published throughout the world, including dissertations in psychology; and the *Science Citation Index*, which includes psychological literature, as well as psychiatric and relevant medical literature. The *Science Citation Index* is a valuable adjunct to *Psychological Abstracts*, because it includes information related to psychology published by other science disciplines, such as chemistry, biology, and medicine. It also includes more indexes than *Psychological Abstracts*—subject, author, country, and even institutional affiliation indexes.

---

*These guidelines are printed in the *Publication Manual of the American Psychological Association* (3rd edition), which was published in 1983.

THE RESEARCH ARTICLE

There are three major kinds of research articles published by psychologists. The first is a presentation of an emphirical study in which original research is reported. The second is a review article, which critically evaluates past and present research on a topic and often suggests ways to clarify problems relating to the research. The third is a theoretical article, which is similar to a review article in organization, but differs in using previous research to support a particular theoretical position. Other kinds of articles, such as brief reports, comments, replies, and case histories are also published in journals.

Most research reports follow a consistent organization. They present a *title*, an *abstract*, an introduction to the *problem*, the *method* of doing the research, the *results* obtained from the research, a *discussion* of the research results, and *references* to other research articles.

The Abstract

The abstract of an article is a short (usually under 150 words), comprehensive summary of the contents of the article. It generally gives the major issues confronted by the researchers and summarizes the major findings.

Methodology

The next section of an article describes in detail how the study was conducted. It often contains descriptions of the research subjects, any apparatus or materials used in the research, and the procedure followed to test the subjects or apparatus. A detailed methodology section is necessary so that others can evaluate and replicate the research results.

Results

The results section gives a detailed description of the research findings. It often includes a statistical treatment of the raw research data. Tables and figures summarizing these data are commonly presented. This is often the most complex and difficult section for the beginning student of psychology. Appendix A may help you understand the results section.

Discussion

The discussion section evaluates and interprets the research results. It summarizes them and may relate them to a theoretical position.

References

Reference citations add support to statements made in the body of the research article. They are often a source of further information about a topic and can be a good starting point for more detailed research.

SELECTED JOURNALS IN PSYCHOLOGY

The following list of journals in psychology is only a partial one. It includes all journals published by the APA, plus other journals in science and psychology. Most selections are followed by a notation of the chapters in this textbook to which the journal mainly relates.

The *American Psychologist* is the official journal of the APA. It contains all archival documents of the association plus other articles, notes, comments, and letters that directly affect the APA or inform the public about issues and problems facing psychology.
Chapters 1-19.

Behavioral Neuroscience is published by the APA and contains original research papers on the biological bases of behavior. It includes articles on the biological and neurological sciences that directly relate to psychology.
Chapters 2, 3, 4, 5, 9.

Contemporary Psychology is published by the APA and contains critical reviews of textbooks, films, and other media used in psychology.

Developmental Psychology is published by the APA and contains articles about human behavior across the life span.
Chapter 11.

The *Journal of Abnormal Psychology* is published by the APA and contains articles concerning psychopathology and abnormality. It usually does not include works on treatment of these disorders; those are more often published in the *Journal of Consulting and Clinical Psychology.*
Chapters 14, 15.

The *Journal of Applied Psychology* is published by the APA and contains articles about how psychology can be applied in every field except clinical psychology.
Chapter 19.

The *Journal of Comparative Psychology* is published by the APA and contains articles on the behavior of various species, related to evolution, development, ecology, control, and functional significance.
Chapters 2, 6, 8, 11.

The *Journal of Consulting and Clinical Psychology* is published by the APA and contains articles on the diagnosis and treatment of psychopathology.
Chapters 14, 16.

The *Journal of Counseling Psychology* is published by the APA and contains articles of interest to counselors in the school system, counseling agencies, and other counseling settings.
Chapters 13, 19.

The *Journal of Educational Psychology* is published by the APA and contains articles concerning learning and cognition, especially as these subjects relate to instruction.
Chapters 6, 8, 12, 19.

The *Journal of Experimental Psychology: General* is published by the APA and contains articles of interest to experimental psychologists.
Chapter 1, Appendix A.

The *Journal of Experimental Psychology: Animal Behavior* is published by the APA and contains articles on learning, motivation, memory, and other processes in animals.
Chapters 4, 6, 7, 9.

The *Journal of Experimental Psychology: Human Perception and Performance* is published by the APA and contains articles on human perception, verbal and motor performance, and human cognition.
Chapters 3, 4, 8, 12.

The *Journal of Experimental Psychology: Learning, Memory, and Cognition* is published by the APA and contains articles concerning learning, memory, and cognition, in both humans and animals.
Chapters 6, 7, 8.

The *Journal of Personality and Social Psychology* is published by the APA and contains articles on personality and social processes, including attitude measurement and the relationship between attitudes and behavior.
Chapters 13, 17, 18.

Professional Psychology: Research and Practice is published by the APA and contains articles on the application of psychology, including its scientific underpinnings.
Chapters 1, 16, 19, Appendix A.

Psychological Bulletin is published by the APA and contains evaluative reviews of important issues in psychology. Original research is usually reported only to back up the reviews.
Chapters 1-19.

Psychological Review is published by the APA and contains theoretical articles on any area of scientific psychology.
Chapters 1–19.

Science is published weekly by the American Association for the Advancement of Science and often includes articles of interest in scientific psychology.
Chapters 2-19.

Science News is published weekly by Science Service, Inc., and often includes psychology articles. Students especially enjoy this publication, as it is written for educated laypeoples as well as for scientists. It reports important research that has come out of annual meetings of both the American Psychological Association and the American Psychiatric Association, as well as other scientific organizations and sources.
Chapters 1–19.

GLOSSARY

A

A-B-A SINGLE-SUBJECT EXPERIMENTAL DESIGN An experimental design in which time is used as a control and only one subject is monitored. The independent variable is given in condition A and withdrawn in condition B. The dependent variable is the subject's behavioral change over time as the independent variable is presented, withdrawn, and finally presented again.

ABNORMAL BEHAVIOR Behavior that is statistically unusual, considered maladaptive or undesirable by most people, and self-defeating to the person who displays it.

ABSOLUTE THRESHOLD The minimum intensity a stimulus must have in order to produce a sensation.

ACCOMMODATION In vision, the adjustment of the lens of the eye to bring into focus on the retina objects that are relatively near.

ACHIEVEMENT TEST A test designed to evaluate a person's current state of knowledge or skill. Most IQ tests are achievement tests, although they are often used as aptitude tests.

ACHIEVING SOCIETY THEORY McClelland's theory that nations whose members show the lowest need for achievement also tend to have the lowest gross national product, whereas nations whose members show the highest need for achievement have the highest gross national product.

ACQUISITION The time during the learning process when there is a consistent increase in responsiveness; a time when learning is occurring.

ACTION POTENTIAL A localized, rapid change in electrical state that travels across the cell membrane of a neuron at the moment of excitation.

ACTION THERAPY Psychotherapy in which the therapist helps the patient or client take direct and immediate action to overcome problems through the use of special techniques.

ACTIVATION-SYNTHESIS MODEL A physiological model of dreaming that contends that the brain synthesizes random neural activity generated during sleep and organizes this activity into a dream.

ACUPUNCTURE A traditional Chinese therapeutic technique in which the body is punctured with fine needles. It usually is used as an anesthetic or to relieve pain.

ADAPTIVE THEORY A theory about why we sleep. It states that for each species a certain amount of waking time is necessary in order to survive, and sleep is nature's way of protecting organisms from getting into trouble during their extra time.

ADOPTION DESIGN A research design used for sorting the influence of nurture from nature. Genetically related individuals who are reared apart from one another or genetically unrelated individuals who are reared together are studied.

ADRENAL GLANDS Endocrine glands located above the kidneys that secrete the hormones adrenaline, noradrenaline, and steroids. These hormones influence metabolism and the body's reaction to stressful situations.

ADRENALINE A hormone secreted by the adrenal glands that stimulates the sympathetic nervous system; also called epinephrine.

AERIAL PERSPECTIVE A monocular depth cue. Nearby objects are brighter and sharper than distant objects.

AFFERENT NERVES Nerves that carry messages inward from the sense organs to the central nervous system.

AFFORDANCE In J. J. Gibson's theory of perception, the particular properties of an object that offer an organism perceptual information, which often is of unique interest to the organism or which may benefit the organism's survival; for example, a hammer affords a human its graspability.

AFTEREFFECTS An effect brought on by fatigue in visual receptors at higher levels in the visual system. Aftereffects, unlike afterimages, transfer from one eye to the other. Also known as negative aftereffects.

AGONIST A drug that acts to facilitate or enhance the actions of other drugs or naturally occurring biochemical substances.

ALARM REACTION STAGE The first stage of the general adaptation syndrome, during which cortical hormone levels rise and emotional arousal and tension increase.

ALGORITHMS Mathematical premises. In computer usage, an algorithm is a program that will search for an answer by examining every possibility.

ALPHA WAVES A pattern of brain waves typical of the relaxed, waking state.

ALTRUISM Behavior that benefits someone other than the actor, with little or no apparent benefit for the actor.

ALZHEIMER'S DISEASE An incurable disease of unknown cause, more common among the aged, that results in severe brain degeneration and death; it is characterized by increasing distortion and disruption of intellectual and motor functions as the disease progresses.

AMACRINE CELLS Large retinal neurons that connect ganglion cells laterally. There are at least 30 different varieties of amacrine cell. Image rectification appears to be one of their many functions. The functions of most amacrine cells are unknown.

AMES ROOM A specially designed room that is perceived as rectangular, even though it is not. Objects of the same size seem to be totally different in size at different points in the room.

AMINO ACIDS Any of a collection of organic compounds that contain both an amino and a carboxyl group. All life is based on only 20 different amino acids. The neurotransmitter gamma-aminobutyric acid is an example of an amino acid.

AMPHETAMINES Drugs that excite the central nervous system and suppress appetite, increase heart rate and blood pressure, and alter sleep patterns. Amphetamines are classified as stimulants.

AMPLITUDE A measurement of the amount of energy carried by a wave, shown in the height of the oscillation.

AMYGDALA A small bulb at the front of the brain that is associated with emotion. It is part of the limbic system.

ANAL RETENTIVE PERSONALITY According to Freud, a personality type formed by fixation at the anal stage. Its characteristics include stinginess, selfishness, and withholding.

ANDROGENS The male hormones that regulate sexual development. Some androgens are produced by the testes and others by the adrenal cortex. Testosterone is an androgen.

ANGULAR GYRUS A portion of the brain in the parietal lobe adjacent to Wernicke's area. The angular gyrus is involved with reading and appears to "translate" visual word images received by the primary visual cortex into auditory form before passing the information on to Wernicke's area.

ANIMAL MAGNETISM   The term coined by Anton Mesmer to describe the supposed magnetic force that people could exert on one another.

ANTAGONIST   A drug that acts to block or inhibit the actions of the other drugs or naturally occurring biochemical substances.

ANTEROGRADE AMNESIA   The inability to recall experiences or events that occur after an amnesia-causing trauma.

ANTICIPATORY EATING   Nonhomeostatic consumption of food owing to an awareness that food will soon be scarce or unavailable.

ANTIDEPRESSANTS   Drugs used to relieve the symptoms of extreme sadness and withdrawal from life that characterize severe depression. MAO inhibitors and tricyclic drugs are the two main classes of antidepressants.

ANXIETY   A state of apprehension in which the source is usually not specific, as it is in fear. There is a vague but persistent feeling that some future danger is in store, such as punishment or threat to self-esteem. Anxiety typically leads to defensive reactions.

ANXIOUS/AVOIDANT ATTACHMENT   A form of attachment observed by Ainsworth in her research. Children who show anxious/avoidant attachment do not approach—and actively avoid—their returning mothers.

ANXIOUS/RESISTANT ATTACHMENT   A form of attachment observed by Ainsworth in her research. Children who show anxious/resistant attachment approach their returning mothers, cry to be picked up, and then struggle to be free. Their behavior is ambivalent; they appear to wish to approach and to avoid their mothers simultaneously.

APHASIA   Loss of the ability to understand or to use speech; usually the result of brain damage.

APPARENT MOTION   Any phenomenon through which a person perceives motion in an object when the object is, in fact, stationary.

APTITUDE TEST   A test designed to evaluate a person's potential for achievement. Ideally, it is independent of current knowledge. An example might be a test of the nervous system that could predict to a certain degree how likely someone was to succeed at a given task.

ARCUATE FASCICULUS   The bundle of nerve fibers in the brain that connects Wernicke's area with Broca's area.

ARTIFICIAL INTELLIGENCE   A computer simulation of human cognitive ability and performance.

ASSOCIATION AREA   The parts of the cerebral cortex, other than the sensory and motor areas, that appear to be linked with language, thinking, and memory.

ATONIA   Loss of muscle tone. During REM sleep, atonia occurs simultaneously with arousal of the sympathetic nervous system. The atonia creates a state of semiparalysis in the REM sleeper.

ATTACHMENT   An especially close affectional bond formed between a living creature and another living creature or object.

ATTENTION   Perceptual sensitivity such that a certain stimulus within a perceptual field is given precedence by the filtering out or reduction of all surrounding or competing stimuli.

ATTRIBUTION   The psychosocial process through which we come to believe that certain events or dispositions are responsible for the behavior of ourselves or others.

AUDITORY NERVE   The nerve leading from the cochlea, which transmits sound impulses to the brain.

AUTOMATIC STORAGE   The spontaneous placement of a sensation or experience into the long-term memory without effort or intent.

AUTOMATIC WRITING   Writing done by the subject during a dissociated hypnotic state; the subject is not aware of writing.

AUTOMATIZATION   A process that occurs after a mental procedure is practiced sufficiently so that the number of If-Then connections is reduced to the barest required minimum. Once automatization has occurred, the mental procedure can be called on with a minimum of thought or effort. The mental procedures used by skilled experts tend to be highly automatized.

AUTONOMIC NERVOUS SYSTEM   The portion of the peripheral nervous system that carries information to and from organs, glands, and smooth muscles within the body.

AVERSIVE CONDITIONING   An element of behavior therapy in which unacceptable behavior becomes linked with painful stimuli and is thereafter avoided.

AXON   The long process of a neuron that transmits impulses away from the cell body to the synapse.

B

BEHAVIOR CONTRACTS   A technique often used in behavior, group, or family therapy, in which a contract or bargain is struck. The client promises to engage in a certain behavior in return for a particular behavior from another.

BEHAVIOR MODIFICATION   A set of procedures for changing human behavior, especially by using behavior therapy and operant conditioning techniques.

BEHAVIOR THERAPY   A group of techniques based on learning principles and used to manipulate an individual's behavior directly to promote adaptive patterns while eliminating maladaptive ones.

BEHAVIORAL GENETICS   The interdisciplinary science that focuses on the relationship of nature and nurture, that is, on the interaction of what is inherited and what is acquired and how that interaction affects behavior.

BEHAVIORAL GEOGRAPHY   A statistical technique that enables map makers to generate actual representations of cognitive maps. Behavioral geography has as its goal the production of information that will aid developers and planners to create environments that are more compatible with people's perceptions.

BEHAVIORAL TOXICOLOGY   The classification and study of the behavioral effects of environmental toxins.

BEHAVIORISM   The school of psychology that views learning as the most important aspect of an organism's development. Behaviorists objectively measure behavior and the way in which stimulus-response relationships are formed.

BENZODIAZEPINES   An important class of minor tranquilizers that, since the mid-1950s, has come to replace the more dangerous barbiturates. Usually prescribed by physicians to control anxiety and tension.

BENZODIAZEPINES   Antianxiety drugs, such as Valium and Librium, that help alleviate anxiety by directly interacting with the neurochemistry of the brain. They are often referred to as minor tranquilizers.

BETA-ENDORPHIN   A powerful natural neuropeptide. It means "the morphine within" and is so named because it has properties similar to those of heroin and morphine. It is a powerful painkiller and mood elevator.

BINOCULAR CUES   Depth cues that arise only when both eyes are used. Examples include convergence and retinal disparity.

BIPOLAR CELLS   Nerve cells of the retina, which receive impulses from rods and cones in the retina and transmit these impulses to the ganglion cells.

BIPOLAR DISORDER   A mood disorder characterized by severe cyclical mood swings. Formerly called manic-depression psychosis, bipolar disorder can often be controlled with lithium-based drugs.

BLIND SPOT   The region of the retina where the optic nerve attaches and where there are no photoreceptors. The fovea also is a blind spot when something is viewed in very dim light.

BLOB PATHWAY   A distinct brain pathway for the transmission of color information. So named because color information is conveyed via a route that travels from the cones of the retina through the midbrain and then to areas of the occipital cortex known as "blobs."

BLOOD-BRAIN BARRIER   The semipermeable membrane and tissue surrounding most brain structures that allows only limited brain access to substances borne in the blood. Usually, only specific molecules are able to enter. Many drugs as well as the cells from the body's own immune system are typically unable to cross the blood-brain barrier.

BOGUS PIPELINE   A procedure for measuring a person's real attitudes and feelings rather than what the person wishes to present. Subjects are led to believe that a supposed physiological monitor is able to detect their real attitudes and feelings and that any attempt to hide them will be uncovered.

BRADYKININ   A blood-borne neuropeptide that is cleaved from a larger inert molecule by enzymes a fraction of a second following any injury. Bradykinin stimulates pain-associated neurons and is considered to be one of the major producers of pain.

BRAIN   The portion of the central nervous system located in the cranium and responsible for the interpretation of sensory impulses, the coordination and control of body activities, and the exercise of emotion and thought.

BRAIN MAPPING   A technique neurosurgeons use to pinpoint the functions of different areas in the brain so that they don't destroy something vital during brain surgery.

BRIEF INDIVIDUAL PSYCHOTHERAPIES   Any one-on-one psychotherapy usually lasting no more than 30 sessions, which is designed to provide limited support when lack of time or money prevent regular therapeutic intervention.

BRIGHTNESS   A property of color determined by the number of photons issuing forth per square unit area. Shifts in brightness are perceived by the observer as changes along a light-dark continuum.

BRIGHTNESS CONSTANCY   The perception that objects maintain their brightness independent of lighting.

BRITISH EMPIRICISM   A theory put forth by British philosophers during the seventeenth and eighteenth centuries (most notably, by Locke, Berkeley, and Hume) arguing that all knowledge and understanding comes from only learning and experience. It can be observed in its extreme form through the concept of tabula rasa (the mind is a blank slate on which experience writes our nature) put forward by John Locke. In light of modern genetic research, the idea of tabula rasa is no longer seriously defended.

BROCA'S APHASIA   A disorder caused by damage to Broca's area. Individuals with this disorder have impaired articulation, labored speech, and difficulty in forming a grammatical sentence, but the semantic content of their speech is usually clear.

BROCA'S AREA   An area in the lateral frontal lobe (in the left hemisphere in most cases) that is associated with language production.

BYSTANDER EFFECT   People's tendency, especially pronounced under crowded conditions, to ignore others who need help or situations that call for action.

C

CANALIZATION   The process by which behaviors, due to genetic predisposition, are learned extremely easily, almost inevitably. The more canalized a behavior is, the more difficult it is to change or alter.

CARDINAL TRAITS   In Allport's theory, an encompassing trait that seems to influence almost every act of a person who possesses the trait. Cardinal traits are uncommon, observed in only a few people.

CASE STUDY   An intensive study of a single case, with all available data, test results, and opinions about that individual. Usually done in more dept than are studies of groups of individuals.

CAUSE-EFFECT RELATIONSHIP   A relationship in which one act, of necessity, regularly brings about a particular result.

CENTRAL NERVOUS SYSTEM   The brain and spinal cord. All other nerves compose the peripheral nervous system.

CENTRAL ROUTE PROCESSING   From social-information processing theory, a route of persuasion and attitude change that may occur when a person pays careful attention to a persuasive discussion. Any resulting attitude change is relatively enduring.

CENTRAL SULCUS   A major fissure in the brain, also known as the fissure of Rolando, which separates the frontal from the parietal lobes.

CENTRAL TRAITS   In Allport's theory, behavioral or personality tendencies that are highly characteristic of a given individual and easy to infer. Allport argues that surprisingly few central traits, perhaps five or ten, can give a fairly accurate description of an individual's personality.

CENTRATION   The child's tendency to focus, or center, on only one aspect of a changing system at any given time; characteristic of the preoperational stage.

CEREBELLUM   A portion of the hindbrain situated just beneath the posterior portion of the cerebrum. Its function is to coordinate muscle tone and fine motor control.

CEREBRAL CORTEX   The extensive outer layer of convoluted gray tissue of the cerebral hemispheres, which is largely responsible for higher nervous functions, including intellectual processes. It is also called the neocortex.

CEREBRUM   The large rounded structure of the brain occupying most of the cranial cavity, divided into two cerebral hemispheres by a deep fissure and joined at the bottom by the corpus callosum.

CHEMICAL DEPENDENCE   The strong and compelling desire to continue taking a chemical substance because of its physical or psychological effects.

CHOLECYSTOKININ (CCK) Cholecystokinin is a neuropeptide that is secreted by the intestine and which can stimulate receptors for satiation in the brain.

CHROMOSOME   A microscopic thread-shaped body contained within the nucleus of every cell, which determines the characteristics that will be passed on to the offspring of an organism. Chromosomes carry the genes. Humans have 23 pairs of chromosomes in each cell with the exception of the sperm and egg cells, which carry only 23 single chromosomes.

CHRONOLOGICAL AGE (CA) A concept developed by Alfred Binet that was subsequently incorporated in the formula mental age divided by chronological age X 100 = IQ. The chronological age of a person is his or her actual age.

CHUNK A bit of information that can be held in short-term memory. Chunks are not defined by the number of items they contain, such as letters or syllables, but rather by their meaning and organization. One number can be a chunk, but so can an entire sentence if it has a single meaning.

CIRCADIAN RHYTHM A daily cycle. The sleep-wake cycle is considered to be a circadian rhythm.

CLASSICAL CONDITIONING A learning procedure in which a stimulus that normally evokes a given reflex is associated with a stimulus that does not usually evoke that reflex, with the result that the latter stimulus will eventually evoke the reflex when presented by itself.

CLIENT-CENTERED THERAPY A type of psychotherapy developed by Carl Rogers and based on the belief that the client is responsible for his or her own growth and self-actualization. The therapist creates an atmosphere of acceptance, refrains from directing the client, and reflects back to the client what the client has said.

COCAINE A habit-forming stimulant that typically is inhaled, and is occasionally swallowed, smoked, or injected. It is derived from the leaves of the coca plant, and is used in medicine as a local anesthetic.

COCHLEA A spiral tube in the inner ear, resembling a snail shell, which contains nerve endings essential for hearing.

COGNITION The process that occurs between the sensing of a stimulus and the emergence of an overt response. It involves the interplay of concepts, symbols, and mediating responses.

COGNITIVE-APPRAISAL THEORY OF EMOTION Stanley Schachter's theory that emotion stems from our cognitive interpretations of a general physiological arousal occurring under specific circumstances.

COGNITIVE BEHAVIOR THERAPY A behavior therapy technique in which the client's internal beliefs, attitudes, and expectations are tested in reality in a formal and structured way.

COGNITIVE DISSONANCE The condition in which one has beliefs or knowledge that are internally inconsistent or that disagree with one's behavior. When such cognitive dissonance arises, one is motivated to reduce the dissonance through changes in behavior or cognition.

COGNITIVE MAP A mental representation of the location of things in relation to each other in a given environment.

COGNITIVE PSYCHOLOGY The study of behavior as it relates to perceiving, thinking, remembering, or problem solving.

COLLECTIVE UNCONSCIOUS Jung's concept that a portion of the unconscious contains certain shared experiences, predispositions, and symbols that are inherited and found in all members of a given race or species.

COLOR BLINDNESS The inability to see one or more colors. The most common kind is green-cone color blindness.

COLOR CONSTANCY The tendency for a color to appear unchanged regardless of changes in lighting conditions.

COMMON FATE A Gestalt principle that states that aspects of a perceptual field that move or act in a similar manner tend to be perceived as a single entity.

COMPLEX CELLS Cells in the visual cortex that respond to various combinations of motion, orientation, or color. Complex cells usually are associated with large receptive fields.

COMPONENTIAL INTELLIGENCE From Sternberg's triarchic theory of intelligence; that aspect of intelligence encompassing the cognitive problem-solving and information-processing skills measured by most IQ tests.

COMPULSION A useless, stereotyped, and repetitive act that a person is unable to inhibit.

CONCEALED INFORMATION TEST In polygraph administration, a method of examining suspects by providing them with specific information to which only someone with guilty knowledge could consistently react.

CONCEPT An abstract idea based on grouping objects or qualities by common properties.

CONDITIONED RESPONSE (CR) A learned response elicited by a conditioned stimulus, owing to previous reinforcement of the conditioned stimulus through association with an unconditioned stimulus.

CONDITIONED STIMULUS (CS) In classical conditioning, a previously neutral stimulus that is reinforced by being paired with an unconditioned stimulus, so that it acquires the ability to produce a conditioned response.

CONES Specialized photoreceptor cells in the retina that are primarily responsive to different wavelengths of light and are therefore important in color vision; cones also are associated with high visual acuity.

CONFORMITY Action that results from social pressure to comply with social norms. When people conform, they act or behave in correspondence with current customs, rules, or styles.

CONJUGAL LOVE A deep and generally abiding love that develops between two people over long periods of time. It is associated with a desire to be together, share with one another, and sacrifice for one another. It is also called companionate love.

CONONICAL STAGE A stage of language acquisition that typically occurs between the ages of 7 and 10 months typified by an increase in babbling and the production of cononical syllables (syllables made of consonant and vowel sounds of certain intensities). Duplicated sequences such as "dadada" or "mamama" also mark this stage.

CONSCIOUSNESS A state of awareness of sensations, perceptions, or memories. The aspects of mental life of which one is momentarily aware.

CONSERVATION The principle that quantities such as mass, weight, and volume remain constant regardless of changes in the appearance of these quantities, so long as nothing has been added or taken away.

CONSERVING-ENERGY THEORY A theory about why we sleep. It states that sleep is a good way of conserving energy in the face of sparse food supplies. This theory agrees with the adaptive theory that sleep can be a protective device.

CONSOLIDATION The strengthening process through which memory traces, or engrams, must go before they can become a fixed part of the long-term memory.

CONSUMER PSYCHOLOGY The field of applied psychology concerned with advertising and selling, whose object of study is effective communication from the manufacturer or distributor to the consumer.

CONTEXTUAL INTELLIGENCE From Sternberg's triarchic theory of intelligence; that aspect of intelligence encompassing the ability of the individual to adapt to her environment or culture.

CONTIGUOUS ASSOCIATION The occurrence of two events close enough in time so that they are perceived by the organism as somehow related. Also called temporal association.

CONTINGENCY DETECTION The process by which an organism makes a discrimination between stimuli that are only present when the US is presented and other stimuli that not only happen to be present when the US is presented but also when the US is not presented. The result is that the organism can rely on the sensing of the stimulus that is only present when the US is presented to predict that the US will soon appear.

CONTINUOUS REINFORCEMENT Reinforcement of a particular response each time it occurs.

CONTRACTION STAGE A stage of language acquisition that typically occurs between the ages of 10 and 14 months. So named because during this time the infant will begin to narrow her production of language sounds until it includes mostly the sounds that are common to the language to which she has been exposed. During this stage, infants also acquire the pacing and rhythm of their language.

CONTROL Deliberate arrangement of experimental or research conditions so that observed effects can be directly traced to a known variable or variables.

CONVERGENCE A binocular depth cue. The eyes tend to turn toward each other when focusing on nearby objects and tend to focus at infinity when viewing objects farther away.

CONVERGENT PRODUCTION In J. P. Guilford's model of intelligence, a type of thinking in which an individual searches through his or her knowledge and uses all that can be found to converge upon one correct answer.

CONVERSION DISORDER A somatoform disorder characterized by physical symptoms such as paralysis, blindness, deafness, and loss of sensation. The assumption is that anxiety has been converted into a tangible symptom.

CORNEA The transparent outer bulge in the front of the eye through which light waves pass.

CORPUS CALLOSUM The structure that connects the two cerebral hemispheres to each other. When it is severed, the two hemispheres can no longer communicate with each other.

CORRELATION The relationship between two variables.

CORTICOSTEROID HORMONES Any of the steroid hormones of the cortex of the adrenal glands.

CORTISOL A hormone produced by the cortex of the adrenal glands found just above the kidneys. It is critical for the metabolism of fats, carbohydrates, and proteins. It is very similar to cortisone.

CREATIVITY The ability to originate something new and appropriate by transcending common thought constraints.

CRITICAL DECAY DURATION From the opponent-process theory of motivation, a time of sufficient length between the onset of an affective A process and its repetition so that no decrease in A process intensity or increase in B process intensity is noted.

CRYSTALLIZED INTELLIGENCE The intelligence that reflects one's ability to make use of current knowledge and stored facts. Formal education, reading, traveling, and being with intelligent, stimulating people are considered to be ways of increasing crystallized intelligence.

CULTURE-FAIR TEST A test that is supposed to be free of cultural biases, usually constructed so that language differences and other cultural effects are minimized.

D

DARK ADAPTATION The process by which the eyes become more sensitive to light in dim illumination.

DECLARATIVE MEMORY The memory associated with cognitive skills not directly attributable to muscular or glandular responses. The complete memory may be acquired through a single exposure, but practice is beneficial. Declarative memory is required to recall factual information, and it is sometimes called fact memory. The ability to recognize a face, recall a number, or recall any verbal or sensory information requires declarative memory.

DEFENSE MECHANISMS Reactions to the anxiety caused by conflict that serve to protect and improve the self-image. The mechanisms are not deliberately chosen. They are common to everyone and raise serious problems for adjustment only when they are used excessively and prevent the person from coping realistically with difficulties.

DEINDIVIDUATION The process in which social restraints are weakened and impulsive and aggressive tendencies released as the person loses individual identity, usually as the result of being part of a large group or having his or her identity concealed in some way, for example, by a mask.

DEINSTITUTIONALIZATION The practice, begun in the early 1960s, of releasing mental patients from hospitals and assigning them to community health centers or treating them on an outpatient basis.

DELIRIUM TREMENS A state of delirium resulting from prolonged alcoholism and marked by extreme confusion, vivid hallucinations, and body tremors.

DELTA WAVES A pattern of brain waves associated with the deepest stages of sleep, often called slow waves because of their relatively low frequency.

DELUSION A strong belief opposed to reality, which is maintained in spite of logical persuasion and evidence to the contrary; delusions are a symptom of psychosis. There are three main types: delusions of grandeur (the belief that one is an exalted personage), delusions of persecution (the belief that one is being plotted against), and delusions of reference (the belief that chance happenings and conversations concern oneself).

DENDRITES The short, branched processes of a neuron that receive impulses from other neurons and conduct them toward the cell body.

DENIAL A defense mechanism in which the individual simply denies the existence of the events that have produced the anxiety.

DEPENDENT VARIABLE In an experiment, the variable that may change as a result of changes in the independent variable.

DEPRESSANTS Drugs that can depress or slow the central nervous system. Alcohol and tranquilizers are examples.

DEPRESSION A feeling of sadness and sometimes total apathy. Guilt or inability to cope with problems, frustration, or conflict is often behind depression. It may be influenced by chemical imbalances in the brain as well.

DEPTH PERCEPTION   Perceptual interpretation of visual cues indicating how far away objects are.

DESIGNER DRUGS   Drugs designed in a laboratory by unscrupulous chemists with the intention of creating substances that mimic the effects of a drug while avoiding the federal laws that forbid that specific drug.

DEVELOPMENTAL PSYCHOLOGY   The study of age-related changes in human behavior during the lifespan.

DEXAMETHASONE SUPPRESSION TEST (DST) A blood test used to indicate the presence of endogenous depression. Dexamethasone is administered and the suppression of cortisol is measured. Failure to suppress cortisol is an indication of endogenous depression.

DICHROMATS   People with color blindness due to the defective functioning of one of the three cone systems.

DIFFERENCE THRESHOLD   The minimum change that a stimulus must undergo before the change can be reliably detected; it is also called the just noticeable difference (JND).

DIFFUSION OF RESPONSIBILITY   One possible reason for the bystander effect. When someone is observed to be in need of help and there are many people around, individuals may believe that they need not act or give aid because they place responsibility to act on other people in the crowd. They may think, for instance, "Someone else will surely help" or "Why should I have to be the one to help?"

DIRECT COPING STRATEGIES   Active rational strategies intended to alleviate stress either by eliminating the stressor or by reducing the psychological effects of stress.

DIRECT-PERCEPTION THEORY   The theory that perceptions are a function of biological organization and innate perceptual mechanisms.

DIRECTIVE THERAPY   Any approach in which the therapist takes an active role and directs the client or patient to confront problems and life situations.

DISCRIMINATION   Differentially responding to two or more stimuli. The responding occurs in such a way that it is obvious that the organism can tell that the stimuli have certain properties that distinguish them from one another.

DISCRIMINATION   In social psychology, differential treatment of people on the basis of their race, ethnic group, or class, rather than on their relevant traits. Acts of discrimination are typically premised on prejudice.

DISCRIMINATIVE STIMULI   Stimuli in whose presence a response is likely to occur. Discriminative stimuli function as cues enabling us to know when a response is likely to be reinforced.

DISPLACEMENT   The loss of an item of information from short-term memory because of the addition of a new item of information.

DISSOCIATION   A separation or splitting off of mental processes often associated with the hypnotic state. Subjects can then perform acts that do not register in their conscious memory or can engage in two behaviors while remembering only one of them.

DISSOCIATIVE DISORDERS   Mental disorders that are characterized by an attempt to overcome anxiety by dissociating oneself from the core of one's personality.

DIVERGENT PRODUCTION   In Guilford's model of intelligence, a type of thinking in which a person searches for multiple ideas or solutions to a problem. It is characteristic of the creative thought process.

DNA   Deoxyribonucleic acid. A chemical constituent of cell nuclei, consisting of two long chemical chains of alternating phosphate and deoxyribose units twisted into a double helix and joined by bonds between the complementary chemical bases adenine, thymine, cytosine, and guanine. It is the substance that enables cells to copy themselves; it is the essence of all life.

DOPAMINE HYPOTHESIS   The argument that abnormalities associated with the neurotransmitter dopamine are related to the onset and maintenance of schizophrenic episodes. Either an overabundance of dopamine or the existence of too many dopamine receptors in the brain is deemed responsible.

DOUBLE-BLIND CONTROLLED EXPERIMENT   A research technique in which neither the subjects nor the experimenters know which subject shave been exposed to the independent variable. It is used for controlling biases that may be introduced by either the subjects or the experimenters.

DOUBLE DEPRESSION   Severe depression brought about by a combination of endogenous and environmental causes, either of which would have been sufficient in and by itself to create a serious depressive state.

DOWN SYNDROME   A chromosomal abnormality that manifests itself in such features as a thick tongue, extra eyelid folds, and heart deformities, as well as deficient intelligence. It is most often caused by the development of a third chromosome on the 21st chromosome pair.

DRIVE   The psychological representation of a need; a complex of internal conditions, resulting from the loss of homeostasis, that impels an organism to seek a goal.

DSM-III-R The third edition of the Diagnostic and Statistical Manual, revised, published by the American Psychiatric Association in 1987. The manual provides clinicians with the most current diagnostic and classification criteria for mental disorders.

DUAL-CODE THEORY   A theory of memory holding that memories contain both sensory and verbal information and that this information is stored directly, without being transformed.

DUALIST HYPOTHESIS   The philosophical position that the mind is like a disembodied spirit, that it functions independently from the body, and that the mind and body are separate entities functioning parallel to one another.

DYSLEXIA   An impairment of reading ability, in which little sense can be made of what is read and letters or words often appear transposed.

DYSTHEMIA   A common form of depression defined by a depressed mood for more days than not, lasting for at least 2 years with no respite from depression for more than 2 months at a time, and associated with some disruption or loss of sleep, appetite, energy, self-esteem, or concentration. Often accompanied by feelings of hopelessness.

E

ECTOMORPH   One of Sheldon's three body types. An ectomorph is relatively thin and physically weak. The corresponding temperament is cerebrotonic.

EDUCATIONAL PSYCHOLOGY   The branch of applied psychology concerned with the psychological aspects of teaching and the formal learning process in school. Educational psychologists apply theories, methods, and test instruments for educational purposes.

EFFERENT NERVES   Nerves that carry messages outward from the central nervous system to glands or muscles.

EGO In psychoanalytic theory, the part of the personality that regulates the impulses of the id in order to meet the demands of reality and maintain social approval and self-esteem.

EGOCENTRISM A thought process characteristic of children in Piaget's preoperational stage; they view themselves as the reference point in their dealings with the external world.

EIDETIC IMAGE The formation and reproduction of accurate mental images of objects not currently present. Possessors of these images are said to have photographic memories.

ELABORATION The process of building upon one memory by making many associations with it. Elaborated memories are easier to recall because items in the memory can be reached by many different routes.

ELECTROCONVULSIVE THERAPY (ECT) Treatment of mental disorders by passing an electric current through the brain for a certain amount of time, which causes a convulsion, a temporary suspension of breathing, and a coma lasting from 5 to 30 minutes. ECT has been found to be most effective against depression and the depressive lows encountered in bipolar disorder.

ELECTROENCEPHALOGRAPH (EEG) An instrument that records the electrical activity of the brain.

ELECTROMAGNETIC SPECTRUM The entire range of possible wavelengths for light, both visible and invisible (such as X rays and radio waves).

EMOTION A complex feeling-state involving conscious experience and internal and overt physical responses that tend to facilitate or inhibit motivated behavior.

EMOTIONAL APPEALS Arguments designed to alter attitudes by appealing to the emotions through stirring visual and verbal messages.

EMOTIONAL CONTRAST An emotional effect that plays an important part in Solomon's opponent-process theory of motivation. Following any emotional arousal (pleasant or aversive), there is often an opposite emotional state. This contrasting emotional state will last for a time and then diminish or end.

EMPTY NEST SYNDROME Depression, generally in women, brought on at the time their grown children leave home.

ENCODING VARIABILITY Acquisition of the same information in different moods, states, or circumstances. Greater encoding variability tends to improve test performance by increasing the chances that the test situation will resemble the learning environment.

ENCOUNTER GROUPS Therapeutic gatherings in which members of a group, under the guidance of a trained therapist, confront one another during a psychodynamic exchange that uncovers defenses and helps reveal hidden emotions.

ENDOCRINE GLANDS Ductless glands that pour their secretions directly into the bloodstream. The hormones secreted by the endocrine glands are important regulators of many body activities.

ENDOGENOUS DEPRESSION The suspected inherited form of major depression. Endogenous depression occurs without any apparent external cause. It is marked by long-term despair, dejection, and feelings of apprehension, gloom, and worthlessness.

ENDOMORPH One of Sheldon's three body types. An endomorph is broad or thick in proportion to height, is round, and has fairly weak muscles and bones. The corresponding temperament is viscerotonic.

ENGRAM A lasting trace or impression formed in living tissue responsible for memory.

ENVIRONMENTAL PSYCHOLOGY The applied psychology concerned with the effects and influences of the environment on behavior.

EPILEPSY A neural disorder characterized by recurring attacks of motor, sensory, or psychic malfunction with or without unconsciousness or convulsive movements.

EPISODIC MEMORY Memories stored with mental "tags" about where, when, and how you acquired the information. It mostly contains personal information, but also includes "flashbulb memories."

EQUIPOTENTIALITY Karl Lashley's concept that memory and learning are not localized in one particular area of the brain, but rather the entire brain is responsible for handling these functions.

EQUITY THEORY A social theory of relationships that individuals attempt to strike a balance between what they give and what they receive; that they strive toward a collective reward system for equitably distributing costs and rewards.

ESTROGENS The female sex hormones, produced by the ovaries. They are responsible for maturation of the female sex organs, secondary sex characteristics, and, in some species, sexual behavior.

ETHICS The study of the general nature of morals and of the specific moral choices to be made by the individual in professional relationships with others.

ETHOLOGY The study of human and animal behavior from a biological point of view; it is characterized by the study of animals in their natural environments.

ETIOLOGY The cause of a disease or disorder as determined by psychological or medical diagnosis.

EUGENICS Term coined by Sir Francis Galton referring to the science of improving the genetic characteristics of humans through breeding.

EXCHANGE THEORY A social theory of relationships that human interactions can best be understood by examining the costs and rewards to each person.

EXCITATORY SYNAPSES Synapses associated with depolarization of the receiving cell once neurotransmitter is secreted. If the receiving cell is a neuron, it will become more likely to fire or even to reach action potential.

EXECUTIVE HORMONES Hormones that order or control the secretion of other hormones.

EXHAUSTION STAGE The final stage of the general adaptation syndrome, during which resistance to the continuing stress begins to fail. Brain functioning may be hindered by metabolic changes; the immune system becomes much less efficient; and serious illness or disease becomes likely as the body begins to break down.

EXISTENTIAL THERAPY A form of psychotherapy, generally nondirective, that is derived from the existentialist philosophy that each individual has to choose values and decide on the meaning of his or her own life. The therapist tries to achieve an authentic, spontaneous relationship with the client in order to help the client discover free will and make his or her own choices.

EXOCRINE GLANDS Glands that secrete fluids through a duct to the outside of the body or to a specific organ.

EXPANSION STAGE A stage of language acquisition that typically occurs between the ages of 4 and 7 months. During this stage, infants produce many new sounds giving rise to babbling. The onset of the expansion stage does not appear to require feedback because deaf babies also babble. Toward the end of the stage, however, the effects of hearing experience begin to be discernible.

EXPERIENTIAL INTELLIGENCE From Sternberg's triarchic theory of intelligence; that aspect of intelligence encompassing the ability to take a newly learned skill and make it routine.

EXPLORATION-PLAY-APPLICATION SEQUENCE An ethological term describing the function of play as a bridge between the cautious exploration of the unfamiliar and its eventual application for useful purposes.

EXTINCTION In classical conditioning, the elimination of the power of the conditioned stimulus to elicit a conditioned response. Classical extinction will occur if the conditioned stimulus is repeatedly presented without being reinforced through further association with the unconditioned stimulus. In operant conditioning, the elimination of an operant response or its return to a prereinforcement rate of emission following discontinuation of the reinforcing consequence that had maintained it.

EXTROVERT One of Jung's personality types. An extrovert is gregarious, focuses on external events, is not introspective, and likes to be with others.

F

FACIAL-FEEDBACK THEORY A theory of emotion put forth by S. S. Tomkins stating that emotions are determined by feedback from our facial expressions, which are innate, universal responses to specific events.

FACTOR ANALYSIS A statistical procedure aimed at discovering the constituent traits within a complex system of personality or intelligence. The method enables the investigator to compute the minimum number of factors required to account for intercorrelations of the scores on the tests.

FACTOR LOAD The weight or emphasis given to any factor or ability.

FAMILY THERAPY A general term for a number of therapies that treat the family as a whole. Family therapy is a theoretically neutral term, in that family therapy can be practiced as part of many different psychotherapeutic approaches.

FEATURE DETECTORS Innate sensory mechanisms tuned specifically to respond to particular aspects of the environment.

FIGURE In perception, a perceptual experience that is characterized by contour, coherence, structure, and solidity. It is typically experienced against a ground (for example, it appears to be in the foreground).

FIXATION In psychoanalytic theory, inordinate persistence in a particular psychosexual stage of development because the id has received either too much or too little satisfaction.

FLASHBACK A sudden recurrence of a hallucination or sensory disturbance that occurs after the original effect of a hallucinogenic substance has worn off.

FLASHBULB MEMORY The vivid impression left on the memory by all of the stimuli associated with a shocking or surprising event.

FLUID INTELLIGENCE The intelligence that reflects one's ability to solve novel problems in creative ways. Tests of abstract thinking, reasoning, creativity, and problem solving are considered to be examples of fluid intelligence.

FOREBRAIN The top portion of the brain, which includes the thalamus, hypothalamus, corpus callosum, limbic system, and cerebrum.

FOVEA The area in the center of the retina characterized by a great density of cones and an absence of rods. Images focused on the fovea are seen with the highest acuity.

FREE ASSOCIATION A method used in psychoanalytic therapy in which the patient is asked to say whatever comes to mind, no matter how trivial, inconsequential, or unrelated to the matter being discussed. Freud believed that the first thing to come to mind was often a clue to what the unconscious was trying to conceal.

FREE-FLOATING ANXIETY A chronic state of foreboding that is unrelated to a specific situation or object but can be activated by any number of situations and activities.

FREE RUN The tendency for the sleep-wake cycle to break away from a 24-hour cycle. This is most likely to occur when day and night cues are reduced or eliminated. Most free running in humans involves a cycle of approximately 25 hours, but many other cycles are possible, most longer than 24 hours, some shorter.

FREQUENCY The number of cycles per unit of time in a periodic vibration. Frequency determines the pitch of a sound. Higher frequencies have shorter wavelengths.

FREQUENCY THEORY A theory of hearing designed to explain the reception of sound waves between 20 and 300 cycles per second. According to this theory, auditory neurons fire at rates well correlated with the frequency of the sound.

FRIENDSHIPS Close emotional ties formed with another person through mutual preference for interaction, skill at complementary and reciprocal peer play, and shared positive affect.

FRONTAL LOBES The portion of each hemisphere of the cerebrum extending from the very front of the cerebrum to the central sulcus. It includes the primary motor association areas, and it is known to be involved with emotion and language.

FRONTAL LOBOTOMY A psychosurgical procedure, rarely performed today, in which a sharp instrument is inserted through the orbit of the eye and then slashed back and forth to separate specific nerve fibers connecting one part of the brain to another.

FRUSTRATION-AGGRESSION HYPOTHESIS The idea that if one is blocked or prevented from reaching a desired goal, some form of aggression will be an inevitable result.

FUGUE A dissociative disorder in which the individual leaves his or her present situation and establishes a different existence in another place. Although the former life is blocked from memory, other abilities are unimpaired and the individual appears normal to others.

FUNCTIONAL FIXEDNESS A mental set in which you are unable to see beyond an object's customary function to its other possible uses because you have relied on too narrowly defined declarative information.

FUNCTIONALISM The school of psychological thought founded by William James, which proposed that the function, not the structure, of conscious experience should be studied.

G

GAIN-LOSS THEORY A social theory of relationships that we are most attracted to those who have given us with greatest net gain and are least attracted to those who have caused the greatest net loss.

GANGLION CELLS Nerve cells of the retina, which receive impulses from rods and cones via the bipolar cells and transmit these impulses to the brain.

GENDER CONSTANCY The realization that one's sex is determined by unchanging criteria and is unaffected by one's activities or behavior; usually develops in children by the age of 6 or 7 years.

GENDER ROLE The behaviors associated with one sex or the other.

GENDER-ROLE IDENTIFICATION The degree to which a child adopts the sex role of a particular model.

GENDER SCHEMA THEORY The theory developed by Sandra Bem that explains how cognitive advances help the child to organize and integrate the information that he or she has learned about his or her sex.

GENDER UNDERSTANDING A person's comprehension that he or she is either a boy or a girl; usually develops in children by about the age of 3 years.

GENERAL ADAPTATION SYNDROME Physiologist Hans Selye's description of the body's physiological-hormonal reaction to stressors. The reaction consists of three stages, the alarm reaction stage, the resistance stage, and the exhaustion stage.

GENERAL PARESIS Tertiary (third-stage) syphilis (a sexually transmitted disease), which involves an invasion of and severe irreversible damage to the brain caused by the syphilis spirochete (a bacterium). The central nervous system damage often becomes noticeable 15 to 30 years after infection. The clinical picture includes tremors, loss of contact with reality, extreme personality deterioration, increasing paralysis, and delirium. The patient may survive many additional years in this condition. If the illness is diagnosed in time, through the use of a simple blood test (the Wassermann test), the administration of penicillin almost guarantees a cure.

GENERALIZATION Responding to a stimulus other than the training stimulus as though it were the training stimulus. In classical conditioning, the response tends to diminish the more the other stimulus differs from the training stimulus, thereby creating a "gradient of generalization."

GENERALIZED ANXIETY DISORDER An anxiety state characterized by a relatively constant feeling of dread and tension, without apparent or reasonable cause. Free-floating anxiety is a common complaint.

GESTALT PSYCHOLOGY The school of psychological thought that emphasizes that wholes are more than the sum of their parts. Gestalt psychologists study forms and patterns and contend that stimuli are perceived as whole images rather than as parts built into images.

GESTALT THERAPY A form of psychotherapy originated by Fritz Perls, who adapted the fundamental concepts of traditional psychoanalysis but placed greater emphasis on the immediacy and importance of the here and now in breaking down the influence of the past. The patient-therapist relationship is more active and democratic than in traditional psychoanalysis.

GLIAL CELL Support cells in the central nervous system that provide neurons with physical and nutritional support. Glial cells outnumber neurons in the brain and recently have been suspected to be, like neurons, directly involved in information transmission.

GONADS The sex glands that regulate sex drive and the physiological changes that accompany physical maturity. These glands are the ovaries in the female and the testes in the male.

GOODNESS OF FIT From temperament theory; referring to how well suited a certain temperament is to a particular environment. Temperaments well matched with their environments are said to show "goodness of fit."

GOOING STAGE A stage of language acquisition that typically occurs between the ages of 2 and 4 months. During this stage, infants combine the vowel-like comfort sounds made earlier with harder sounds that are the precursors of consonants. An example, is "goo."

GRADIENT OF TEXTURE A depth cue. Closer objects show greater detail.

GRAMMAR A set of rules that determines how sounds may be put together to make words and how words may be put together to make sentences.

GRAMMATICAL MORPHEMES Words or parts of words that help add meaning to a sentence and that are acquired by children generally between the ages of 2 1/2 and 5 years of age. Conjunctions, prepositions, suffixes, and prefixes are examples of grammatical morphemes. Morphemes are the smallest language units to have meaning and cannot be broken down into smaller meaningful units.

GREAT-MAN, GREAT-WOMAN HYPOTHESIS The hypothesis that individuals become leaders primarily because of the personality or traits they possess.

GROUND In perception, all that is perceived to be background.

GROWTH SPURT The time during puberty in which an adolescent's growth undergoes a marked acceleration.

GYRI The prominent rounded and elevated convolutions at the surfaces of the cerebral hemispheres.

H

HABIT A series of cues, responses, and reinforcers linked together in such a way that each stimulus consequence reinforces the person's previous response and cues the next response.

HABITUATION A process in which an organism ceases to respond reflexively to an unconditioned stimulus that has been presented repeatedly.

HALLUCINATION A false sense perception for which there is no appropriate external stimulus.

HALLUCINOGENS Drugs that cause excitation at synapses associated with sense perception. A person taking these drugs may perceive sensations when there is nothing "real" to see, hear, or feel. LSD and mescaline are examples.

HEALTH PSYCHOLOGY Any aspect of psychology that bears on the experience of health and illness and the behavior that affects health status.

HEALTHY INSOMNIACS People who function well with only 3 hours of sleep per night or less, and who do not seem to need more sleep than this.

HEIGHT ON A PLANE A monocular depth cue. Objects higher on a plane are perceived as being farther away.

HEROIN A highly addictive narcotic drug derived from morphine.

HEURISTICS Methods for discovering the correct solution to a problem by exploring the possibilities that seem to offer the most reasonable approach to the goal, rather than all possibilities. Heuristics also involve obtaining successive approximations to the correct answer by means of analogies and other search techniques.

HIERARCHY OF MOTIVES A theory of motivation developed by Abraham Maslow in which more basic needs must be met before needs of a higher order can come into play.

HIGH-THRESHOLD FIBERS Stereocilia in the inner ear that are difficult to bend and thus respond only to loud noises or sounds.

HIGHWAY HYPNOSIS A hypnotic state experienced by a person operating a vehicle—often the result of relaxing too much during a long and boring drive.

HINDBRAIN The posterior section of the brain, which includes the cerebellum, pons, and medulla.

HIPPOCAMPUS A small area at the back of the forebrain that is known to be important in the memory process. It is part of the limbic system.

HOMEOSTASIS An internal environment in which such body components as blood pressure, blood chemistry, breathing, digestion, and temperature are kept at levels optimal for the survival of the organism through the creation of drives in the presence of needs.

HORIZONTAL CELLS Retinal cells with short dendrites and long axons that extend horizontally, linking rods with other rods and cones with other cones. These cells appear to be responsible, in part, for the effects described by the opponent-process theory of color vision.

HORMONE A blood-borne secretion of the endocrine glands that specifically affects metabolism and behavior.

HUE Specifically, the color of a visible light. Hue is determined by the wavelength of the visible light and, depending on the particular wavelength in question, may be called red, yellow, blue, and so on. Perceived hue may also be affected slightly by extreme changes in brightness.

HUMANISTIC PSYCHOLOGY A school of psychology that emphasizes the uniqueness of the individual and the search for self-actualization.

HYPERCOMPLEX CELLS Cells in the cerebral cortex that respond to complex combinations of visual stimuli, including width, length, edges, and certain forms.

HYPERMNESIC Having an unusually exact or vivid memory.

HYPNOSIS A state of consciousness characterized by relaxation and suggestibility.

HYPNOTHERAPY Hypnosis used for therapeutic purposes in cases of pain control or behavior pathology. The method has been used in therapy, dentistry, surgery, and childbirth.

HYPOCHONDRIASIS A somatoform disorder in which there is a persistent and exaggerated concern about diminished health and energy in the absence of demonstrable organic pathology.

HYPOTHALAMIC-PITUITARY-ADRENAL AXIS The glands and neural-hormonal complexes of the hypothalamus, the pituitary gland, and the adrenal glands of the kidneys, which together comprise an important stress reaction system.

HYPOTHALAMOCENTRIC HYPOTHESIS Stellar's hypothesis that a hunger center responsible for the homeostasis of food intake exists in the hypothalamus.

HYPOTHALAMUS An elongated structure in the forebrain that appears to control an entire range of autonomic functions, including sleep, body temperature, hunger, and thirst.

I

I/O PSYCHOLOGY Abbreviation for industrial/organizational psychology, the field of applied psychology concerned with the methods of training, counseling, selecting, and supervising personnel in business and industry. It also investigates ways to make organizations effective and efficient.

ID In psychoanalytic theory, the reservoir of instinctive drives; the most inaccessible and primitive portion of the mind.

IDEATIONAL FLUENCY A term used by Michael Wallach to describe an individual's ability to produce many ideas. Ideational fluency is sometimes used as a measure of creativity. It correlates poorly with average or above average IQ.

ILLUSION A significant and consistent interpretation of sensory information by a given population that is not in agreement with precise and objective measurement.

IMAGE AND CUE THEORY The theory that perceptions are learned by acquiring an understanding of the cues contained within the image that falls on the retina. A cue in this instance refers to any part of an image that is distinct from any other part and from which we may acquire information about our surroundings.

IMPRESSION-MANAGEMENT HYPOTHESIS The hypothesis that the results of cognitive dissonance experiments can be explained, not by changes in real attitudes made to reduce dissonance, but rather by a need to appear consistent in the eyes of others.

IMPRINTING As used by ethologists, a species-specific bonding that occurs within a limited period early in the life of the organism and that is relatively unmodifiable thereafter.

IN-GROUP Any group for whom an individual feels a positive regard. This is a subjective term, depending on the person's point of view.

INCUBATION EFFECT An effect associated with taking a break during creative problem solving. The individual often returns to the problem with a fresh approach and finds the solution.

INCUS One of the three small bones in the middle ear; it is also called the anvil.

INDEPENDENT VARIABLE In an experiment, the variable that is manipulated or treated to see what effect differences in it will have on the variables considered to be dependent on it.

INDUCED PSYCHOTIC DISORDER A rare psychotic disorder in which one individual's paranoid delusional system is adopted by another, most commonly a spouse.

INFORMATION AVAILABILITY HYPOTHESIS The hypothesis that explains people's tendency to attribute their own behavior to environmental causes rather than to personality traits as a function of the fact that they have more information about their personal situation, their environment, and the obvious forces in it than they have about others'.

INHIBITORY SYNAPSES A synapse associated with hyperpolarization of the receiving cell once neurotransmitter is secreted. If the receiving cell is a neuron, it will become harder to fire, or more difficult to reach action potential.

INNATE Inborn; arising as a hereditary component of a physiological or behavioral trait.

INSANE A legal term for those with a mental disorder, implying that they lack responsibility for their acts and are unable to manage their behavior.

INSIGHT In problem solving, the sudden perception of relationships leading to a solution. A solution arrived at in this way can be repeated promptly when the same or a similar problem is confronted.

INSIGHT THERAPY Psychotherapy that attempts to uncover the deep causes of the patient's or client's difficulty. The therapist tries to guide the individual to self-understanding.

INSOMNIA Difficulty in initiating or maintaining sleep for the necessary amount of time.

INSTRUMENTAL LEARNING The process by which an organism learns to behave because of the consequences that follow the behavior.

INTELLECTUAL DEGENERATION   A permanent and serious loss of intellectual functioning because of illness or trauma, often referred to as senility. It is not the normal result of the aging process.

INTELLIGENCE   A general term for a person's abilities in a wide range of tasks, including vocabulary, numbers, problem solving, and concepts. It may also include the ability to profit from experience, to learn new information, and to adjust to new situations.

INTELLIGENCE QUOTIENT (IQ) A quotient derived from the formula MA/CA X 100, where MA is mental age and CA is chronological age. The intelligence quotient was devised by the German psychologist L. William Stern and introduced in the United States by Lewis Terman.

INTERFERENCE EFFECTS   In memory, a conflict between information contained in the memory so that: (1) previously learned information makes it more difficult to learn new information—see proactive interference, or (2) recently learned information makes it more difficult to recall old information—see retroactive interference.

INTERMITTENT SCHEDULE   Reinforcement of a particular response, but not each time the response occurs.

INTEROBSERVER RELIABILITY   The degree of disagreement or agreement between two or more observers who simultaneously observe a single event.

INTRAORGANISMIC PERSPECTIVE   The view of attachment asserting that the infant has innate mechanisms that foster and promote the development of attachment. Such mechanisms are believed to have been naturally selected because they have survival value.

INTRINSIC MOTIVATION   A drive to engage in a behavior for its own sake in the absence of any obvious external reward or reinforcer.

INTROSPECTION   The method introduced by structural psychologists, in which the subject reports on his or her own conscious experiences.

INTROVERT   One of Jung's personality types. An introvert is socially withdrawn, emotionally reserved, and self-absorbed.

INVARIANTS   In J. J. Gibson's direct-perception theory, stimulus features that are unchanging or have proportions that are relatively fixed or constant.

ION CHANNELS   Gates or selective openings imbedded within the neuron's membrane that allow charged atoms (called ions) to enter or exit. Such ion exchanges are responsible for neural transmission and communication.

IRIS   The pigmented muscular membrane that controls the aperture in the center of the pupil, which determines the amount of light that enters the eye.

J

JAMES-LANGE THEORY OF EMOTION   A classical theory of emotion named for William James and Carl Lange, who independently proposed it. The theory posits that a stimulus first leads to visceral and motor responses and that the following awareness of these responses constitutes the experience of the emotion. According to this theory, for instance, we are sad because we cry, rather than we cry because we are sad.

JET LAG   An uncomfortable feeling caused by disruption of the sleep-wake cycle that follows an attempt to adjust to a new time zone too quickly. It is called jet lag because long- distance travelers often suffer from it.

JOB ANALYSIS   Analysis of the specific tasks required in a job and the training, physical abilities, educational level, vocational preparation, and temperament a person needs to perform the job.

K

KIBBUTZ   An Israeli farm or collective where children are often reared in groups and receive nurturance and guidance from many different adults and older children.

KINESTHESIS   An inclusive term for the muscle, tendon, and joint senses that yield information about the position and movement of various parts of the body.

L

LANGUAGE   Any means of communication that uses signs, symbols, or gestures within a grammar and through which novel constructions can be created.

LANGUAGE ACQUISITION DEVICE (LAD) Developed by Noam Chomsky: An hypothesized neural structure inborn in every healthy individual that is preprogrammed with the underlying rules of a universal form of grammar. Once the child is exposed to a particular language, he will select from the complete set of rules with which he was born, the ones required by the language he is speaking. Most psychologists and linguists currently find the idea to be interesting but agree that a proof is doubtful because it is so difficult to find ways to demonstrate the existence of such an hypothesized device.

LATENT CONTENT   In psychoanalytic theory, the hidden true meaning of a dream. The latent content of a dream, with all of its symbols and concealed meanings, can only be understood, according to this view, through the process of psychoanalysis.

LATENT LEARNING   Learning that occurs in the absence of any obvious reinforcement, apparently as a result of just being exposed to stimuli.

LAW OF EFFECT   Thorndike's principle that responses associated with pleasant consequences tend to be repeated, while those associated with discomforting consequences tend to be eliminated.

LEARNED HELPLESSNESS   Giving up, even though success is possible, because of previous experience with situations in which success was impossible.

LEARNING   A relatively permanent change in behavior as a result of experience.

LENS   The transparent biconvex structure of the eye behind the iris and pupil that focuses light rays entering through the pupil to form an image on the retina.

LIBIDO   According to Freud, the psychological energy driving the individual to seek gratification—principally sexual gratification, but also food, comfort, and happiness.

LIGHT ADAPTATION   The process by which the eyes become less sensitive to light in bright illumination.

LIMBIC SYSTEM   An aggregate of brain structures, the two major components of which are the amygdala and the hippocampus. Some of its major functions include attention, memory, emotion, and motivation.

LINEAR PERSPECTIVE   A monocular depth cue. Parallel lines appear to converge in the distance.

LINEAR PROGRESSION   Development that progresses steadily and continuously (as would a straight line). In this process, each development is dependent on those that came before.

LINGUISTIC RELATIVITY   Whorf's hypothesis that thought is structured according to the language spoken, so that those who speak different languages have different thinking patterns.

LINKS   In the propositional network theory of memory, the pathways between the nodes of the proposition. If two nodes are not directly linked, then recalling the information at one of the nodes will not lead directly to recalling the information at the other node.

LITHIUM CARBONATE   A chemical compound that has been found to be effective in controlling the severe mood swings associated with bipolar affective psychosis.

LOCAL EFFECT   The rapid depolarization of a section of the axon in response to the propagation of a neural transmission following the onset of neural firing. It is induced by the rapid depolarization of the soma, or of a nearby section of the axon. The local effect results in the rapid depolarization of the next section of axon, thereby maintaining the propagation of the neural transmission.

LOCUS-DEPENDENT MEMORY   A memory that has been associated with a particular location so that it is easier to recall when you are in that location.

LONG-TERM MEMORY   Memory with virtually unlimited storage capacity, in which short-term memories may be stored for long periods, even a lifetime.

LONGITUDINAL STUDIES   Research studies that are designed to investigate an individual over time, taking measurements at periodic intervals.

LOUDNESS   A measurement of sound intensity that corresponds to the amplitude of the sound waves.

LUCID DREAMING   The realization by a dreamer that he or she is, in fact, dreaming.

M

MAGNETIC RESONANCE IMAGING (MRI) A technique that makes internal body structures clearly visible. It uses radio waves to excite atoms in the body, and the excitations, monitored by a huge magnet, are interpreted by a computer to produce a composite picture.

MAGNO PATHWAY   A distinct brain pathway for the transmission of motion and stereoscopic depth perception. These messages begin in the retina with the stimulation of large ganglion cells and continue on to the midbrain where more large cells are stimulated. From there, the messages are sent to the occipital cortex.

MAINSTREAMING   The philosophy of keeping as many exceptional children within the regular classroom as possible.

MAJOR DEPRESSION   A lasting and continuous state of depression without any apparent cause. It is also known as unipolar depression. Major depression may include psychotic features such as hallucinations, delusions, or a depressive stupor.

MALLEUS   The largest of the three small bones in the middle ear; it is also called the hammer.

MANIFEST CONTENT In psychoanalytic theory, the overt, literal, dream content. Usually what is first described or reported by the dreamer.

MARIJUANA   A hallucinogenic drug derived from the dried flowers and leaves of the cannabis variety of hemp.

MASSED PRACTICE   A study method that does not create a spacing effect and is therefore not likely to lead to long-term retention. Material is studied in a single session without any interruption. The method is also known as cramming.

MASTERY   In motivation, the opposite of learned helplessness, the acquisition of skills or attitudes that enable one to persist in adversity and that help to "psychologically inoculate" one against giving up or feeling helpless.

MASTURBATION   Sexual self-stimulation.

MATERIALIST HYPOTHESIS   The philosophical position that the mind is part of the body and functions according to the laws of the physical world.

MATURATION   A genetically programmed biological plan of development that is relatively independent of experience.

MEANS-END ANALYSIS   A problem-solving process in which the difference between the current situation and the desired situation is defined and then a series of steps is taken to reduce, and finally eliminate, the difference. This process is applicable whenever there is a clearly specifiable problem and a clearly specifiable solution.

MEDITATION   Deep relaxation brought on by focusing one's attention on a particular sound or image, breathing deeply, and relaxing.

MEDULLA   The oblong structure at the top of the spinal cord that is responsible for many vital life-support functions, including breathing and heartbeat.

MELIORATION   In psychology, the tendency of organisms to shift behavioral allocations toward more lucrative alternatives.

MEMORY   The complex mental function of recalling what has been learned or experienced.

MENARCHE   The first occurrence of menstruation.

MENTAL AGE (MA) A concept developed by Alfred Binet that was subsequently incorporated in the formula mental age divided by chronological age X 100 = IQ. The mental age of a person is derived by comparing his or her score with the average scores of others within specific age groups.

MENTAL SET   A tendency to continue to use a particular approach or type of solution to a problem based on previously learned mental procedures.

MERE EXPOSURE EFFECT   The effect in which attitudes become more favorable toward something merely by being exposed to it.

MESMERISM   An early term for hypnosis, named after Anton Mesmer, who claimed he could cure the ill with magnetism. In mesmerism, "magnetic" forces were called on to relieve pain.

MESOMORPH   One of Sheldon's three body types. A mesomorph is characterized by a predominance of muscle and bone, as in an athlete. The corresponding temperament is somatotonic.

META-ANALYSIS   An examination of many studies that focus on one topic, in order to discover an overall consensus. Careful attention is paid to eliminate faulty studies.

METHOD OF LOCI   A mnemonic technique in which items are associated with positions or things along a familiar route in order to make them more easily remembered.

MICROELECTRODE   An extremely small electric probe capable of monitoring a single cell.

MIDBRAIN   The middle section of the brain, which contains the structures responsible for processing and relaying auditory and visual information.

MIDLIFE CRISIS   A sense of panic that strikes some individuals during middle age when they realize that the time left to them is limited; this panic in turn may cause a crisis in which rash behavior becomes more likely, as the person attempts to gain what has been missed or to regain lost youth.

THE MIND-BODY PROBLEM   A philosophical issue as yet unresolved centering on the question of whether conscious awareness is a function of the brain, and therefore the body, or whether it is a function of a spirit that is separate from the body.

MNEMONIC   Any device or technique for improving memory.

MODEL   A mathematical, logical, or mechanical replica of a relationship or a system of events so designed that a study of the model can yield some understanding of the real thing. In social learning theory, anyone who demonstrates a behavior that others observe.

MOLECULE   A electrically bound grouping of two or more atoms that comprise a chemically distinct entity.

MONOCHROMATS   People who have color blindness due to the defective functioning of two of their three cone systems. Most monochromats can see no color at all. Interestingly, all monochromats so far tested have functioning blue cones. This appears to occur because the genes for the red and green cones are located closely together, making it possible for a single error or trauma to knock out both red and green cone systems.

MONOCULAR DEPTH CUES   Cues seen with the use of only one eye that give rise to a perception of depth. These cues include an object's height on a plane, linear perspective, overlap, relative size, gradient of texture, aerial perspective, shadowing, and relative motion. On a flat movie screen (with the exception of 3-D movies), only monocular cues give the sensation of depth.

MOOD DISORDERS   A group of disorders characterized by extremes of mood and emotion.

MOON ILLUSION   A perceptual illusion created by the presence of the monocular cues of relative size and overlap, which make the moon appear 25 percent larger when rising than when overhead.

MORALS   The attitudes and beliefs that people hold that help them to determine what is right or wrong.

MOTIVATED FORGETTING   Purposeful forgetting in which memories are suppressed or repressed in order to fulfill unconscious desires to avoid the memories.

MOTIVATION   Any state or condition that causes an organism to produce, maintain, or inhibit a motor response or action.

MOTOR AREA   An area of the cerebrum that controls body movement. It is located in front of the brain's central sulcus.

MULTIPLE PERSONALITY   A dissociative disorder in which one person develops two or more distinct personalities, which often vie with each other for consciousness. One personality's memories are not usually accessible to another personality.

MULTIPLEXING   The act of simultaneously sending two or more distinct messages by way of a single transmission carrier.

MUTATION   Any heritable alteration of the genes or chromosomes of an organism.

MYELIN   A white, fatty covering on neural fibers that serves to channel impulses along the fibers and increase their speed.

N

NALOXONE   A heroin antagonist. Naloxone blocks and essentially neutralizes heroin. Naloxone has the same effect on morphine and beta-endorphin.

NARCOLEPSY   An inherited pathological condition character-

ized by sudden and uncontrollable lapses into deep sleep.

NATURAL SELECTION   The process, first suggested by Charles Darwin, by which the individuals of a species who are best adapted to their environment have a better chance of passing their genes on to the next generation than do those who are less well adapted.

NATURALISTIC OBSERVATIONS   Observations in which researchers refrain from interacting directly with the variables being observed.

NATURE   In developmental research, the hereditary component of an organism's development.

NEED   A condition whose satisfaction is necessary for the maintenance of homeostasis.

NEED FOR ACHIEVEMENT (n-Ach) A learned motivation described by researcher David McClelland. Those who score high in n-Ach often behave in different ways from those who score low in n-Ach.

NEGATIVE AFTERIMAGE   An opposite color image that persists briefly after the originally viewed object is removed. It is the result of fatigued color receptors in the retina.

NEGATIVE REINFORCEMENT   The process of removing or escaping from an aversive stimulus (following a response) that has the effect of increasing the probability that the response will be emitted again.

NEONATES   Newborn infants.

NERVE IMPULSE   The propagation of an electrical impulse down the length of a neural axon once a neuron has fired.

NERVES   Bundles of neural fibers that carry impulses from one point in the body to another.

NEURAL NETWORK   In computer science, computer hardware or circuits that alter their composition or connections in response to experience.

NEUROLEPTIC   Any of a collection of drugs that are known to have antipsychotic properties.

NEUROLEPTIC MALIGNANT SYNDROME   An often deadly reaction to neuroleptic drugs which occurs in 1-2 percent of patients receiving these drugs. The syndrome often comes quickly and the fatality rate is about 20 percent, owing to kidney or brain damage. The cause of the syndrome is unknown.

NEURONS   Specialized cells that transmit electrical impulses from one part of the body to another.

NEUROPEPTIDES   Extremely small chemical messengers made from short chains of amino acids. Beta-endorphin is a neuropeptide.

NEUROTRANSMITTERS   Chemicals secreted by neurons that have an effect on adjacent neurons, muscles, or glands.

NODES   In the propositional network theory of memory, the individual parts of the proposition. Nodes serve as junctions and access points in the memory.

NONDIRECTIVE THERAPY   A therapeutic technique based on humanistic psychology in which the therapist creates a supportive atmosphere so that clients can work out their own problems.

NONHOMEOSTATIC MECHANISMS   In motivation, a motivating system that regulates a drive or an impetus to act, but that is not counterbalanced by an opposing regulatory process that would reestablish the initial condition.

NORADRENALINE   A hormone secreted by the adrenal glands that brings about a number of body changes, including constriction of the blood vessels near the body's surface. It causes the adrenal glands to secrete steroids, which in turn release sugar so that energy is available for emergency action. It is also called norepinephrine.

NREM SLEEP (ORTHODOX SLEEP) Non-REM sleep, during which no rapid eye movement takes place. Also called orthodox or quiet sleep because the EEG pattern is markedly different from the waking state.

NUCLEUS A central body within a living cell that contains the cell's hereditary material and controls its metabolism, growth, and reproduction.

NURTURE In developmental research, the environmental component of an organism's development.

O

OBEDIENCE The willingness to follow commands or instructions.

OBJECT PERMANENCE Piaget's term for the individual's realization that objects continue to exist even though they are no longer visible.

OBSERVER BIAS An error in observation caused by the expectations of the observer.

OBSESSION A persistent idea or thought that the individual recognizes as irrational but feels compelled to dwell on.

OBSESSIVE-COMPULSIVE DISORDER An abnormal reaction characterized by anxiety, persistent unwanted thoughts, or the compulsion to repeat ritualistic acts over and over.

OCCIPITAL LOBES The hind portion of each hemisphere of the cerebrum. The primary visual areas are contained within the occipital lobes.

OEDIPUS COMPLEX A Freudian term representing the sexual attachment of a boy to his mother. This desire is repressed and disguised in various ways. The child expresses jealousy and hatred of his father because the father can have relations with the mother that the son is denied.

OFF-LINE TIME In computer science, the time when data are no longer being input, but rather are being analyzed, correlated, stored, or treated in some processing fashion. In dream theory, the time when the brain shuts down, or sleeps, to prevent continued input and engages in REM to process data already received—presumably to make room for further input when it awakens.

OLFACTORY BULB A mass of cells in the forebrain associated with the sense of smell. The olfactory nerve fibers enter and form a tract leading farther into the brain.

OLFACTORY EPITHELIUM Nasal membranes containing receptor cells sensitive to odors.

ONE-WORD STAGE The universal stage in language development in which children's speech is limited to single words.

OPERANT CONDITIONING Skinner's term for changes in behavior that occur as a result of consequences that reinforce or punish emitted responses. These responses are classified according to how they operate on the environment. They are, in turn, shaped by further environmental experiences. Also known as instrumental learning.

OPERANTS Skinner's term for any emitted responses that affect the environment. Operants are classified or grouped not according to the particular muscular combinations involved in creating the response but according to their effect on the environment, that is, how they "operate" on the environment. Therefore, Thorndike's cats used the same operant when they pressed the treadle that opened their cage regardless of which paw or muscles they used.

OPERATIONAL DEFINITION A definition derived from a set of operations that will produce what is being defined; for example, human strength = the amount of weight that can be lifted by a person from the floor to a height of 1 foot in 5 seconds. Although such definitions are exact, and work well in scientific studies, they are sometimes considered limited. For example, not everyone would necessarily agree that the definition of human strength is inclusive enough to cover all actions that might be considered to comprise this measure.

OPPONENT-PROCESS THEORY Hering's theory of color vision in which he argued that photoreceptors function along red-green, blue-yellow, and light-dark continuums and are in opposition to each other.

OPPONENT-PROCESS THEORY A theory of motivation by Richard Solomon proposing that many acquired motives, such as drug addiction, love, affection, social attachment, cravings for sensory and aesthetic experiences, skydiving, jogging, sauna bathing, and even self-administered aversive stimuli, seem to follow the laws of addiction.

OPTIC NERVE The bundle of nerve fibers connecting the retina and the brain.

ORGAN OF CORTI The organ located on the basilar membrane in the cochlea, which contains the hearing receptors.

ORGANIC MENTAL DISORDER A severe behavioral disturbance usually requiring hospitalization and resulting from some organic malfunctioning of the body.

ORGASM The climax of sexual excitement, normally marked by ejaculation of semen by the male and muscular spasms of the genitals in both sexes.

OSMOSIS The diffusion of fluid through a semipermeable membrane, such as that surrounding a living cell, until the concentrations of fluid on either side of the membrane are equal.

OUT-GROUP Any group that an individual views in a negative way. This is a subjective term, depending on the person's point of view.

OVERLAP A monocular depth cue. Objects that are behind (overlapped by) other objects are perceived as being farther away.

P

PAIN-ELICITED AGGRESSION The desire to harm or defeat another, brought on by pain or anguish. It is common to many species, including humans. Cognitive interpretations can often control or mediate the aggression in spite of the pain or anguish.

PANIC ATTACK A sudden overwhelming and debilitating onset of fear characteristic of panic disorder. There is no realistic reason or cause.

PARADOXICAL SLEEP REM sleep. The EEG pattern closely resembles that of a person who is awake, even though the person is still asleep. Most dreaming occurs during this kind of sleep. The sympathetic nervous system shows heightened activity.

PARALLEL PROCESSING In computer science or neuroanatomy, the handling of information in a manner so that many aspects of a particular problem are manipulated simultaneously, thereby saving time over serial methods in which each aspect of a problem is examined in sequence.

PARANOIA A psychosis characterized by delusions and extreme suspiciousness. Hallucinations rarely occur, and the personality does not undergo the serious disorganization associated with schizophrenia.

PARASYMPATHETIC NERVOUS SYSTEM The portion of the

autonomic nervous system that is most active during the body's quiescent states.

PARIETAL LOBES The top portion of each hemisphere of the cerebrum extending from the central sulcus to the beginning of the occipital lobes. The parietal lobes contain the primary somatosensory area as well as association areas, including language areas.

PARKINSON'S DISEASE A progressive nervous disease of the brain characterized by muscle tremor, slowing of movement, peculiarity of gait and posture, and weakness. It is a direct result of dopamine deficiency and can be temporarily treated with a dopamine-like drug, levodopa. The progress of the disease can also be slowed by use of the drug deprenyl.

PARVO-INTERBLOB PATHWAY A distinct brain pathway for the transmission of high-resolution perception of stationary shapes and forms. These messages begin in the retina with the stimulation of small ganglion cells and continue on to the midbrain where more small cells are stimulated. From there, the messages travel to areas that surround the blobs in the occipital cortex.

PASSIONATE LOVE A strong sexual desire for another individual combined with the perception that one is in love. This perception is often the result of misattributing to love a heightened physiological arousal for any reason.

PEAK PERFORMANCE The exceptional performance given by an athlete when physical and mental conditions are optimal.

PEERS Equals; developmentally, those persons who interact at about the same behavioral level regardless of age.

PERCEPTION The brain's interpretation of the information processed by the senses.

PERCEPTUAL CONSTANCIES The tendency to perceive objects as yielding the same or similar experiences, even though the viewing conditions may vary widely.

PERIPHERAL NERVOUS SYSTEM The motor and sensory nerves that carry impulses from the sense organs to the central nervous system and from the central nervous system to the muscles and glands of the body.

PERIPHERAL ROUTE PROCESSING From social-information processing theory, a route of persuasion and attitude change that may occur even when a person pays little attention to the persuasive message. Any resulting attitude change is usually temporary.

PERIPHERAL VISION All visual experiences outside the immediate line of sight; that is, experiences other than those derived from light focused on the fovea. The photoreceptor field on the retina surrounding the fovea gives rise to peripheral vision. Peripheral vision is especially important for determining motion.

PERSON-SITUATION DEBATE From personality theory, the argument concerning whether the primary drive behind a person's behavior is due to enduring internal qualities or environmental influences.

PERSONALITY The organization of relatively enduring characteristics unique to an individual, as revealed by the individual's interaction with his or her environment.

PERSONALITY DISORDER Deeply ingrained, habitual, and rigid patterns of behavior or character that severely limit the adaptive potential of the individual but that are often not seen by him or her to create problems or be maladaptive. They are sometimes called character disorders.

PERSUASIVE COMMUNICATION Arguments designed to alter attitudes by appealing to reason by means of fact and logic.

PHENCYCLIDINE HYDROCHLORIDE (PCP) A dangerous hallucinogenic drug that can lead to aggressive or psychotic behavior. It is also known as angel dust.

PHENOTHIAZINES Antipsychotic drugs, often called the major tranquilizers. These drugs help control and alleviate the symptoms of psychosis.

PHEROMONES Substances that, when secreted, are sexual attractants to receptive organisms via olfactory perception.

PHI PHENOMENON Specifically, a perceptual illusion brought about by observing two lights placed side by side in a darkened room and flashed alternately. The resulting perception is of one light moving back and forth. Also, often applied to any circumstance in which stationary objects presented in succession appear to be moving, such as occurs when we view a motion picture.

PHILOSOPHY In most general terms, philosophy is "the search for the truth." It encompasses two major branches: epistemology, which includes efforts to comprehend the origins, limits, and nature of knowledge; and metaphysics, in which the reality of existence is examined. Minor branches include esthetics, logic, and ethics.

PHONEMES The most basic distinctive sounds in any given language. Phonemes are combined into words.

PHONETICS The study and classification of speech sounds and their production, transmission, and perception.

PHOTONS Massless particles of light that carry energy. The energy carried is indirectly proportional to the wavelength of the particle: The shorter the wavelength, the greater the energy. Common names for photons depend on the wavelength and include, among others, radio waves, microwaves, visible light, and X rays.

PHOTORECEPTOR CELLS Light sensitive cells, called rods and cones, that comprise the third layer of the retina.

PHRENOLOGY A system developed by Franz Joseph Gall for identifying types of people by examining their physical features, especially the configuration of the skull.

PHYSICAL ADDICTION An overwhelming desire for a particular substance due to the mechanisms of tolerance and physical reaction to withdrawal.

PHYSIOLOGY The biological discipline that examines the functions of cells, tissues, and organs within the living organism.

PINEAL GLAND The pineal gland is located in the brain and it resembles a crude retina. It secretes melatonin, is sensitive to light, and secretes hormones in response to the length of day. The pineal gland is believed to regulate the 24-hour circadian rhythm.

PINNA The clearly visible outer portion of the ear. It serves to gather sound.

PITCH The perception of a tone's frequency. In general, shorter wavelengths (higher frequencies) are perceived as having a higher pitch, while longer wavlengths (lower frequencies) are perceived as having a lower pitch.

PITUITARY GLAND A gland located beneath the hypothalamus that controls many hormonal secretions. It often is called the master gland because it appears to control other glands throughout the body.

PLACE LEARNING Acquiring an understanding of the location of things relative to each other in an environment through experience with the environment.

PLACE THEORY A theory of hearing that attempts to explain the reception of sound waves between 5000 and 20,000 cycles per second. It asserts that different frequencies stimulate stereocilia at different places within the cochlea. High frequencies stimulate stereocilia near the oval window, while intermediate frequencies stimulate stereocilia away from the oval window.

PLACEBO   An inert substance often given to subjects in a control group in place of the treatment given to subjects in the experimental group.

PLASTICITY   The ability of brain tissue to subsume the functions that would have normally been carried out by other tissue that has been damaged or disrupted.

PLAY   Pleasurable activity engaged in for its own sake, with means emphasized rather than ends. Play is not usually engaged in as a serious activity and is flexible, in that it varies in form or context.

PLEASURE PRINCIPLE   The psychoanalytic postulate that an organism seeks immediate pleasure and avoids pain. The id functions according to the pleasure principle.

POLARIZATION EFFECT   An effect in which members of a group tend to take a more extreme position (more conservative or more daring) than they would have as individuals. It is probably the result of social comparison or persuasive group arguments.

POLARIZED   In reference to the neuron, to have been placed in a state of potential energy release by the resulting electrical forces created by ions on either side of the cell membrane. In the neuron, the polarization results in a resting potential of -70 millivolts across the membrane.

POLYGRAPH   A lie detector. This device measures physiological changes regulated by the autonomic nervous system (heartbeat, blood pressure, galvanic skin response, and breathing rate). The assumption is that deliberate lying will produce detectable physical reactions.

PONS   Part of the brain stem lying just above the medulla and regulating motor messages traveling from the higher brain downward through the pons to the cerebellum. It also regulates sensory information.

POSITIVE REINFORCEMENT   The process by which an organism encounters a stimulus (following a response) that has the effect of increasing the probability that the response will be emitted again.

POSITRON EMISSION TOMOGRAPHY (PET) A technique by which organ functions, especially brain function, can be directly observed. A scanning device monitors the emission of radiation following the injection of a positron-emitting substance that gathers in specific locations determined by ongoing organ functions.

POST-TRAUMATIC STRESS DISORDER   A disorder characterized by the recurrence of a particular traumatic event in the mind of the individual who experienced it, a numbness or lack of responsiveness to external stimuli, and two or more symptoms associated with depression and anxiety, such as sleep disturbances, low threshold for startling, impairment of memory, and guilt about having participated in the event.

POSTHYPNOTIC SUGGESTION   A suggestion made to a hypnotized subject to perform some task in response to a particular cue after the hypnotic session is over.

POSTSYNAPTIC SURFACE   The cell surface receiving neurotransmitter secreted into the synapse.

PREDICTIVE VALIDITY   The degree to which a score or assessment correlates with a specific outcome. A test with high predictive validity allows fairly accurate predictions to be made about certain future behaviors.

PREJUDICE   Beliefs or judgments made without sufficient evidence and not easily changed by opposing facts or circumstances; preconceived hostile and irrational feelings, opinions, or attitudes about a group or an individual.

PREMACK PRINCIPLE   The concept developed by David Premack that reinforcement is relative, not absolute, so that if two behaviors differ in their probability of occurrence at any given time, the chance to engage in the probable will serve to reinforce engaging in the less probable.

PRESYNAPTIC SURFACE   The cell surface from which neurotransmitter is secreted into the synapse.

PRIMARY COLORS   The three colors from which all other colors can be made, usually considered to be red, green, and blue.

PRIMARY PREVENTION   Efforts aimed at preventing an illness or pathological condition, mental or physical, from occurring. The focus is on optimizing health. As opposed to secondary prevention in which a pathological condition is treated after it has appeared in hopes of preventing it from becoming worse.

PRIMARY REINFORCER   A stimulus that can be innately reinforcing, such as food or sleep.

PRIMARY SEXUAL CHARACTERISTICS   The penis, scrotum, and testes of the male; the vagina, ovaries, and uterus of the female.

PRIMING MEMORY   A hypothetical memory thought possibly to exist as a distinct entity because in certain cases of amnesia, a form of declarative memory appears to yield access via small prompts. thereby giving it its name, "priming" memory.

PRIVILEGED SITE   A location (typically in the brain) in which foreign tissue is safe from attack by the body's immune system. Sites in the brain are generally privileged because cells from the body's immune system cannot penetrate the blood-brain barrier that surrounds and protects the brain.

PROACTIVE INTERFERENCE   The process by which previously learned material interferes with the ability to learn something new.

PROBABILISTIC EPIGENESIS   Literally, the direction in which growth will probably go. In cognitive development theory, the term is used to describe the stages of cognitive development as representing only what typically occurs during the development of most individuals, but not necessarily in the development of all individuals

PROCEDURAL MEMORY   The memory associated with recall of muscular or glandular responses that have been conditioned. Procedural memories are acquired slowly with practice. This memory is required to recall the skills necessary for object manipulation and learned physical activity. It is sometimes called skill or motor memory. Such skills as playing billiards, reading mirror writing, and playing the piano require procedural memory.

PROGRESSIVE RELAXATION   A technique in which deep relaxation is achieved through the progressive relaxation of one muscle group at a time, usually beginning with the feet and legs. The subject breathes deeply and focuses attention on each muscle group as it is relaxed.

PROJECTION   A defense mechanism in which the individual attributes his or her own motives or thoughts to others, especially when these motives or thoughts are considered undesirable.

PROPOSITIONAL NETWORK THEORY   The memory theory holding that sensory information and words are transformed into propositions in order to be stored in memory.

PROPOSITIONS   The smallest units of information about which it makes sense to render a judgment of true or false. For example, "red apple" is not a proposition. However, "The apple is red" is a proposition, since the statement is either true or false.

PROSOPAGNOSIA A disorder in which the subject can no longer recognize faces. It is rarely accompanied by other neurological or physiological symptoms.

PROTOCONCEPT A primary concept of the simplest form usually related directly to a tangible object and exemplifying a general category, (such as dog, house, boat)

PROXEMICS The study of nonverbal expression through the spatial distance people maintain when interacting, as well as their orientation toward each other as reflected by touch and eye contact.

PSYCHOACTIVE DRUGS Drugs that alter conscious awareness or perception.

PSYCHOANALYSIS A therapy that seeks to bring unconscious desires into consciousness and make it possible to resolve conflicts, which usually date back to early childhood experiences. Psychoanalysis is also the school of psychological thought founded by Sigmund Freud, which emphasizes the study of unconscious mental processes.

PSYCHOANALYST A practitioner who generally adheres to the school of psychological thought founded by Sigmund Freud that emphasizes the study of unconscious processes.

PSYCHODRAMA A specialized technique of psychotherapy developed to J. L. Moreno in which patients act out the roles, situations, and fantasies relevant to their personal problems. Psychodrama is usually conducted in front of a small audience of patients.

PSYCHOEVOLUTIONARY SYNTHESIS OF EMOTION- Robert Plutchik's theory that emotions evolved because they help a species to survive. In his theory, cognitive assessments of stimulus-events may give rise to innate emotional patterns, which in turn motivate behaviors that ultimately have survival value.

PSYCHOGENIC AMNESIA A dissociative disorder involving selective memory loss. The individual forgets, partially or totally, his or her past identity but remembers nonthreatening aspects of life.

PSYCHOLINGUISTS Those who specialize in the psychology of language.

PSYCHOLOGICAL ADDICTION An overwhelming desire for a particular substance due to the immediate sense of pleasure or fear reduction it provides. Psychological addiction often occurs in conjunction with physical addiction. The word dependence is often used to characterize either type of addiction and often is specific (for example, drug dependence).

PSYCHOLOGICAL RETICENCE A common reaction to initial failure, in which an individual tries to discover what is wrong and looks for ways in which to improve performance. After continued failure, psychological reticence may break down, and learned helplessness may begin.

PSYCHOLOGY The discipline that attempts to describe, explain, and predict the behavior of organisms.

PSYCHOSIS Any of a group of disorders involving extensive and severe psychological disintegration, disruption of all forms of adaptive behavior, and loss of contact with reality. Psychotic individuals may show bizarre motor behavior, extreme emotional states, absence of emotional responsiveness, withdrawal, delusions, hallucinations, and cognitive distortions. Psychosis often requires institutionalization.

PSYCHOSOCIAL STAGES The eight stages of ego development

as postulated by Erik Erikson. The stages incorporate both sexual and social aspects and include the entire lifespan.

PSYCHOSURGERY Brain surgery for the purpose of altering behavior or alleviating mental disorders.

PSYCHOTHERAPY A category of methods for treating psychological disorders. The primary technique is conversation between the patient and the therapist.

PUBERTY The stage of maturation in which the individual becomes physiologically capable of sexual reproduction.

PUNISHMENT An aversive stimulus consequence that has the effect of decreasing the strength of an emitted response.

PUPIL The dark circular aperture in the center of the iris of the eye that admits light.

Q

Q SORT A personality assessment technique based on a series of statements and traits that the test subject is required to sort into categories from "most like me" to "least like me."

R

RANDOMIZED RESPONSE A data-gathering technique designed to provide anonymity for the respondent by making it impossible to discern the truth from individual answers. In a simple version, subjects are asked to respond "yes" or "no" to a question after privately flipping a coin. If heads resulted, they must answer "yes"; if tails, they must tell the truth. The number of truthful responses may then be deduced by analyzing group data.

RAPID EYE MOVEMENT (REM) The rapid back-and-forth movement of the eyes during sleep. Dreaming is often associated with REM.

RASPBERRY In foodstuffs: a rather tasty fruit; a type of berry. In social discourse: an explosive sound owing to the rapid expulsion of air from the mouth that vigorously vibrates the lips (especially the lower lip), which, as required for the effect, have been deliberately placed in a configuration so as to make contact with, and surround, the protruded tongue. Considered unrequired in most social circumstances. (For an exception to this rule, see "Sporting events.")

RATIONAL-EMOTIVE THERAPY A form of directive therapy associated with Albert Ellis in which the therapeutic goal is modification of the client's inappropriate ideas about self-concept and relations with others.

RATIONALIZATION A defense mechanism in which irrational, impulsive action, or even failure, is justified to others and to oneself by substituting acceptable explanations for the real, but unacceptable, reasons.

REACTION FORMATION A defense mechanism in which the individual exhibits, and at the conscious level believes he or she possesses, feelings opposite to those possessed at the unconscious level.

REALITY PRINCIPLE According to Freud, the principle on which the conscious ego operates as it tries to mediate between the demands of the unconscious id and the realities of the environment.

RECEPTIVE FIELD The grouping of information from many neurons so that a single neuron may readily respond to the information as a single input. For example, a ganglion cell may be responsive to a receptive field created by many photoreceptors, or a complex cell may be responsive to a receptive field created by many simple cells.

RECONSTRUCTION In memory, the placement into memory of an unconscious deduction or assumption of what one believes must have happened. Such created memories are often recalled as though they were recollections of actual events.

REFERENCE GROUP A group with which we identify and that we use as our standard of behavior.

REFLEX ARC The pathway a sensory message travels from an afferent receptor to the spinal cord and back to an effector (the body organ that responds to the stimulation) in order to produce a reflex.

REHEARSAL A process by which memories can be held in the short-term memory for relatively long periods. In rehearsal, an item is repeated over and over so that it is not lost. This technique may eventually result in storage of the item in the long-term memory.

REINFORCEMENT In classical conditioning, any increase in the ability of a conditioned stimulus to elicit a conditioned response owing to the association of the conditioned stimulus with another stimulus (typically an unconditioned stimulus). The response is reinforced. In operant conditioning, an event that strengthens the response that preceded it. Operant (instrumental) conditioning is a process in which a response is reinforced.

REINFORCEMENT THEORY OF LIKING A social theory of relationships that we like those whom we have been reinforced for liking or whom we associate with pleasurable events or circumstances.

RELATIVE MOTION A monocular depth cue. Objects that are closer appear to move more than distant objects when the viewer's head is moved from side to side.

RELATIVE SIZE A monocular depth cue. Familiar objects appear larger than identical objects that are more distant.

RELIABILITY The extent to which a test, rating scale, classification system, or other measure is consistent, that is, produces the same results each time it is applied to the same thing in the same way.

REM REBOUND An increase in REM sleep demonstrated by a person who has been deprived of it.

REPRESSION A psychological process in which memories and motives are not permitted to enter consciousness but are operative at an unconscious level.

RESISTANCE In psychoanalytic therapy, a patient's opposition to attempts to bring repressed thoughts into the conscious mind.

RESISTANCE STAGE The second stage of the general adaptation syndrome, during which cortical hormones maintain high levels, physiological efforts to deal with stress reach full capacity, and resistance by means of defense mechanisms and coping strategies intensifies.

RESTING POTENTIAL The difference in electrical potential maintained between the outside and the inside of a resting nerve cell, usually about -70 millivolts.

RETICULAR ACTIVATING SYSTEM A complex network of neurons that monitors the general level of activity in the hindbrain, maintaining a state of arousal.

RETINA The delicate multilayer, light-sensitive membrane lining the inner eyeball. It consists of layers of ganglion and bipolar cells and photoreceptor cells called rods and cones.

RETINAL DISPARITY A binocular depth cue. Because the eyes are set apart, objects closer than 25 feet are sensed on significantly different locations on the left and right retinas. At close distances, retinal disparity, more than any other cue, gives a strong perception of depth.

RETRIEVAL CUE Any stimulus that can help you gain access to a memory.

RETRIEVE To bring material from the long-term memory to the working memory so that it can be examined.

RETROACTIVE INTERFERENCE The process by which learning something new interferes with the ability to recall previously learned information.

RETROGRADE AMNESIA An amnesia brought on by a sudden shock or trauma that causes events to be forgotten.

REVERSIBLE FIGURES Any of a class of figures that appear suddenly to change perspective or figure-ground relationship when looked at carefully and steadily.

RODS Specialized photoreceptor cells in the retina that are primarily responsive to changes in the intensity of light waves and are therefore important in peripheral vision and night vision.

ROLE CONFUSION An individual's confusion about his or her role in society as a consequence, according to Erikson, of the failure to establish a sense of identity during the fifth psychosocial stage. Without a sense of identity, a person has difficulty forming a life philosophy or creating a stable basis on which to build a career or have a family.

ROUTINE PROBLEM SOLVING Problem solving that requires concepts, thoughts, actions, and understandings that are already in your repertoire.

S

SATURATION The purity or richness of a color. Highly saturated colors are vivid and striking, while poorly saturated colors appear faded or washed out.

SCHEDULE-INDUCED POLYDIPSIA (SIP) Polydipsia means excessive drinking. Schedule-induced polydipsia refers to an increase in the drive to drink as a result of receiving little bits of food on an intermittent schedule.

SCHIZOPHRENIA A term used to describe a number of psychotic disorders characterized by serious emotional disturbances, withdrawal, lack of or inappropriate emotional responses, hallucinations, and delusions.

SCIENTIFIC METHOD The principles and processes used to conduct scientific investigations, including formation of hypotheses, observation, and experimentation.

SCLERA The white, elastic outer covering of the eye.

SCRIPT In cognitive study, one's knowledge of the appropriate events that should occur in a particular social setting and of how one might carry them out. This comprises knowledge of who is expected to do what to whom as well as when, where, and why. A script would include such typical behaviors as those expected of a person visiting a restaurant or going to a movie.

SEASONAL AFFECTIVE DISORDER (SAD) Depression associated with either a longer or shorter day. It commonly affects individuals in either the winter or summer months and typically passes once the season is over.

SECONDARY REINFORCER A reinforcer whose value is learned through its association with primary reinforcers or other secondary reinforcers. It is also called an acquired reinforcer.

SECONDARY SEXUAL CHARACTERISTICS Physical characteristics that appear in humans around the age of puberty and are sex-differentiated but not necessary for sexual reproduction.

SECONDARY TRAITS In Allport's theory, traits that are not as crucial as central traits for describing personality. Secondary traits are not demonstrated often because they are related to only a few stimuli and a few responses.

SECURE ATTACHMENT The most common form of attachment observed by Ainsworth in her research. Securely attached children respond happily to their mothers' return, greet them, and stay near them for a while.

SELF-ACTUALIZATION Abraham Maslow's term for the process in which an individual constantly strives to realize full potential.

SELF-EFFICACY How effective a person is in a particular situation. Perceived self-efficacy can be a powerful cognitive motivator.

SELF-HYPNOSIS A hypnotic state induced by the subject without the aid of a hypnotist.

SELF-SERVING BIAS An attribution bias describing the fact that people tend to attribute behavior that results in a good outcome to their own personality or traits and attribute behavior that results in a bad outcome to the forces or circumstances of the environment.

SEMANTIC MEMORY Memory of meanings, including all factual information of a general nature such as knowledge that the English alphabet contains twenty-six letters.

SEMANTICS The study of meaning in language.

SEMICIRCULAR CANALS Three small, liquid-filled canals located in the inner ear containing receptors sensitive to changes in spatial orientation.

SENSATION Any fundamental experience of events from within or without the body as the result of stimulation of some receptor system. Distinguished from perception in that perception requires the interpretation of a sensation. This distinction is somewhat arbitrary, however, because some perception of a sensation must occur before awareness is possible.

SENSITIVITY TRAINING Group sessions conducted for the purpose of developing personal and interpersonal sensitivity to feelings and needs. The feelings among group members are channeled so that members' self-acceptance and growth are enhanced.

SENSITIZATION The process by which a reflexive response is made stronger and more sensitive to stimuli by pairing the eliciting stimulus with a painful or unpleasant stimulus.

SENSORY ISOLATION Lack of a stimulus input needed for maintaining homeostasis. Prolonged reduction of external stimulation, in either intensity or variety, may produce boredom or restlessness, but is often experienced as profoundly relaxing.

SENSORY MEMORY The first stage in the declarative memory process. New information is held in the sensory memory for less than one second and will decay unless it is attended to, that is, encoded and placed in the short-term memory. Sensory memory is also called the sensory register.

SERIAL POSITION EFFECT A phenomenon in verbal learning. Items at the beginning or at the end of a long series are more easily remembered; items in the middle are the hardest to recall.

SET POINT A particular weight that the body seems to demand; it is maintained by a hypothetical homeostatic mechanism that monitors levels of fat in the body.

SEXUAL REASSIGNMENT A surgical procedure for altering anatomy and appearance so that the individual resembles the opposite sex.

SEXUALLY TRANSMITTED DISEASES (STDs) Diseases that are primarily transmitted through sexual intercourse.

SHADOWING A monocular depth cue. The distribution of light on a curved or angled surface conveys that some parts are closer and some farther away.

SHAPE CONSTANCY The learned perception that an object remains the same shape, although the image it casts on the retina may vary in shape depending on the viewing angle.

SHAPING A method of creating a goal behavior by reinforcing successive approximations toward the goal behavior.

SHORT-TERM MEMORY Declarative memory that has a limited storage capacity and a short duration. It is often called working memory because it must call up items from long-term memory so that the items can be examined. Information encoded from the sensory memory is held in the short-term memory and will decay unless the information is rehearsed or stored in the long-term memory.

SIMPLE CELLS Cells in the cerebral cortex that respond to lines of a particular orientation.

SIMPLE PHOBIA A person's pathological fear of an object or situation. The individual may realize that the fear is irrational but, being unable to control it, avoids the object or situation. Relatively easy to treat.

SITUATIONAL-ENVIRONMENTAL HYPOTHESIS The hypothesis that individuals become leaders because of situational or circumstantial forces rather than because of their personality traits.

SIZE CONSTANCY The learned perception that an object remains the same size, although the size of the image it casts on the retina varies with its distance from the viewer.

SLEEP APNEA A cessation of breathing during sleep. It may be brief or protracted. Brain damage can result if the apnea lasts long enough to create a significant oxygen deficiency.

SLOW-WAVE SLEEP The deepest stages of sleep, characterized by an EEG pattern of delta waves.

SOCIAL ATTITUDE An enduring system of positive or negative evaluations, feelings, and tendencies toward action with respect to a social object.

SOCIAL COGNITION An area of social psychology that is concerned with how social influences affect cognitive process such as thought, memory, or perception.

SOCIAL COMPARISON Assessment of accuracy of our own attitudes, feelings, or beliefs by comparing them with those of others.

SOCIAL LEARNING Learning by observing the actions of others. It is also called vicarious conditioning or observational learning.

SOCIAL MOTIVATION Learned motivational states that result from the individual's interaction with his or her social environment or culture.

SOCIAL NORMS Shared standards of behavior accepted by and expected from group members.

SOCIAL REFERENCING The use of emotional signals or cues from others as a guide for one's own behavior in ambiguous situations.

SOCIOBIOLOGY A theory of motivation and behavior stating that all human behavior is a function of an inherited biological drive to pass on the individual's genes. In this view, morality, love, kindness, aggression, anger, hatred, and all other aspects of human behavior are understood in terms of their functional value for ensuring the survival of a person's genes.

SOMA The cell body.

SOMATIC NERVOUS SYSTEM The portion of the peripheral nervous system that carries messages inward from the sense organs and outward to the muscles of the skeleton.

SOMATIC THERAPY Invasive therapeutic intervention that acts directly on the body and its chemistry. Included in this classification are psychopharmacological, electroconvulsive, and psychosurgical procedures.

SOMATOFORM DISORDERS Patterns of behavior characterized by complaints of physical symptoms in the absence of any real physical illness.

SOMATOGENIC AMNESIA Disorders involving selective memory loss for physical reasons such as brain trauma, disease, or toxic exposure. The kind of memory loss depends upon the type of injury or illness.

SOMATOSENSORY AREA An area in the cerebrum that controls sensation. It is located behind the central sulcus at the start of the parietal lobe.

SOURCE TRAITS From Cattell's theory of personality, traits that can be identified only through factor analysis and that are more important than surface traits. Cattell argues that personality can be reduced to 16 source traits and that, although surface traits may appear to be more valid to the common-sense observer, source traits have greater utility in accounting for behavior.

SPACED PRACTICE A study method that creates the spacing effect. Studying is accomplished over time with gaps between study sessions. The method is also known as distributed practice.

SPACING EFFECT The fact that repeated items are learned better and are more easily recalled the greater the amount of time between the first and the second exposure to the items.

SPERMATORRHEA A term coined by the physician Claude l'Allemand based on the erroneous assumption that nocturnal emissions were related to the venereal disease gonorrhea.

SPIKE A nerve impulse generated by the neuron reaching action potential.

SPINAL CORD The portion of the central nervous system encased in the backbone and serving as a pathway for the conduction of sensory and motor impulses to and from the brain.

SPONTANEOUS RECOVERY In operant conditioning, the brief recurrence of a response following extinction. In classical conditioning, the brief recurrence of eliciting power of a CS after extinction.

SPOONERISMS Unintentional transpositions of sounds in a sentence, as in "people in glass houses shouldn't stow thrones." The phenomenon is named for an English clergyman, William A. Spooner, who was well known for such errors.

SPORTS PSYCHOLOGY The application of psychological techniques and principles to sports and other structured physical activities for the purpose of maintaining and maximizing performance and investigating applied clinical issues.

STANDARDIZED INSTRUMENT In psychological testing, a test or measure that has been administered to a wide sample of the population for which it is intended, so that the range and probabilities of responses from that population to the test or measure are known.

STAPES One of the three small bones in the middle ear; it is also called the stirrup.

STATE-DEPENDENT LEARNING The phenomenon that memories are recalled with greater ease when you are in the same or similar mood or physical state as when you first acquired the memory.

STEREOCILIA Extremely short hairs extending from the surface of the cells in the inner ear.

STEREOTYPE A set of simplistic and relatively fixed overgeneralizations concerning the physical or psychological characteristics of a class or group of people.

STEROIDS Any of a number of organic compounds that have a 17-atom carbon ring, including some hormones. Cortical steroids (secreted from the adrenal glands) help to control the release of sugar stored for use in emergencies.

STIMULANTS Drugs that can stimulate or excite the central nervous system. Cocaine and amphetamines are examples.

STIMULUS Any energy or change in energy condition that is sensed.

STIMULUS CONTROL From learning theory, the idea that discriminative stimuli come to control the behavior they cue.

STIMULUS MOTIVES Drives or motives that appear to satisfy a need for certain amounts of sensory stimulation.

STRANGE SITUATION A laboratory test designed by Mary Ainsworth to demonstrate individual differences in the quality of attachment.

STREAM OF CONSCIOUSNESS A term coined by William James to describe the idea that conscious experience is like a river, always changing and flowing, rather than a permanent fixture.

STRESS A psychological state associated with physiological and hormonal changes caused by conflict, trauma, or other disquieting or disruptive influences.

STRUCTURALISM The school of psychological thought founded by Edward Titchener that is concerned with reducing experience to its basic parts, determining the laws by which the parts are synthesized, and investigating the structure and content of mental states by introspection.

SUBJECT BIAS Unwanted changes in a subject's behavior owing to her knowledge about the experiment or awareness of being observed.

SUBVOCAL SPEECH In learning theory, Watson's concept of thinking as a series of muscular responses.

SULCI The narrow fissures separating adjacent cerebral convolutions.

SUPERCHIASMATIC NUCLEI (SCN) Dense clusters of neurons located in the central nervous system close to the hypothalamus just above the optic chiasm where the optic nerves from both eyes intersect. The SCN is known to control the pacing and activation of many circadian rhythms.

SUPEREGO In psychoanalytic theory, the part of the personality that incorporates parental and social standards of morality.

SUPERSTITIOUS LEARNING Behavior learned simply by virtue of the fact that it happened to be followed by a reinforcer or punisher, even though this behavior was not the cause of the stimulus that followed the response.

SURFACE TRAITS From Cattell's theory of personality, a cluster or group of behaviors that are overt and appear to go together. Inferring the existence of a surface trait makes it possible to classify similar behaviors under one term; for example, constant fighting, yelling, and making angry facial expressions can be categorized under the surface trait term aggressive.

SURVEY A method of collecting data through the use of interviews and questionnaires.

SYMPATHETIC NERVOUS SYSTEM The portion of the autonomic nervous system that is primarily concerned with emergencies and emotional states.

SYNAPSE The small space between neurons into which neurotransmitter is secreted.

SYNAPTIC KNOBS The extreme ends of an axon in which neurotransmitter is stored.

SYNDROME A number of features, characteristics, events, or behaviors that appear to go with each other, or which are thought to be coordinated or interrelated in some way.

SYNTAX The body of linguistic rules that makes it possible to relate a series of words in a sentence to the underlying meaning of that sentence, that is, the rules governing word order in a language (sentence structure).

SYSTEMATIC DESENSITIZATION A therapeutic procedure developed by Wolpe in which anxiety-producing stimuli are paired, in a graduated sequence or hierarchy, with a state of physical relaxation until the most difficult situation can be faced without anxiety.

T

TACTILE SENSORY REPLACEMENT (TSR) A device to aid the blind. A television camera is connected to a vest worn by the subject. An image is then formed on the viewer's back or chest by means of tactile stimulation. Through practice, the wearer can obtain a perceptual understanding of the visual world.

TARDIVE DYSKINESIA A severe and relatively permanent neuromuscular reaction, following long-term use of, or a sudden withdrawal from, antipsychotic drugs. The disorder is manifested in involuntary twitching of body and facial muscles.

TASK LOAD A measure of demand in terms of behavior required per unit of time. In conditions of high task load, there is much to do and little time to do it.

TASTE BUDS Groups of cells distributed over the tongue that constitute the receptors of the sense of taste.

TELEGRAPHIC SPEECH The pattern of speech, including and following the two-word stage, in which children rely on a grammar of strict word order to convey their meaning and do not use conjunctions, prepositions, or other function words.

TEMPERAMENT THEORIES Theories of human development that place an emphasis on the enduring and stable aspects of personality, which are generally considered to be constitutional in nature, that is, due to the biogenetics of the individual.

TEMPORAL LOBES The portion of each hemisphere of the cerebrum on either side of the head near the temples. The temporal lobes contain the primary auditory areas, as well as association areas. They have to do with emotion, vision, and language.

TESTOSTERONE The male sex hormone produced by the testes. It controls the development of secondary sex characteristics, such as the growth of a beard, and may influence the sexual activity of the individual.

TETRAHYDROCANNABINOL (THC) The active ingredient in marijuana, which in high doses can cause hallucinations.

THALAMUS Part of the forebrain that relays sensory information and is involved in wakefulness and sleep.

TIP OF THE TONGUE PHENOMENON The experience of being almost able to recall a certain bit of information. You sense that the information is there, you can almost "feel" it, and yet you cannot grasp it.

TOKEN ECONOMIES Training, based on operant conditioning, that uses tokens as rewards for certain behaviors. The tokens can be redeemed for special privileges, or other reinforcers.

TOLERANCE In pharmacology, the ability to tolerate larger and larger doses of a drug after each exposure to it. A common tolerance mechanism, which occurs during opiate use, is for the body to create natural antidrug substances or antagonists in ever larger amounts following each exposure to the drug.

TRAITS Distinguishing qualities, properties, or attributes of a person that are consistently displayed. According to Allport, a trait is a predisposition to respond to many types of stimuli in the same manner.

TRANQUILIZERS Any of various drugs that are used to pacify.

TRANSACTIONAL ANALYSIS A form of interpersonal therapy originated by Eric Berne based on the interactions of "child," "adult," and "parent" ego states.

TRANSFERENCE A concept developed by Freud that refers to the tendency of a person in therapy to transfer to the therapist perceptions and feelings about other people rather than seeing the therapist as he or she really is.

TRANSSEXUAL An individual who exhibits the most extreme form of gender reversal, in which the individual feels that he or she is really a member of the opposite sex but has been trapped in the wrong-sexed body.

TREPHINING An ancient procedure in which the skull was punctured by a sharp instrument so that evil spirits might escape.

TRICHROMATS People with normal color vision, who have all three cone systems functioning correctly.

TWIN DESIGN A research design used for sorting the influence of nurture from nature. A characteristic or behavior is compared between identical twins; then the same characteristic or behavior is compared between fraternal twins.

TWO-WORD STAGE The universal stage of language development in which children's expressions are limited to two-word sentences.

TYMPANIC MEMBRANE The thin, semitransparent membrane separating the middle ear from the external ear; it is also called the eardrum.

U

UNCONDITIONED RESPONSE (UR) The response made to an unconditioned stimulus, such as salivation in response to food.

UNCONDITIONED STIMULUS (US) The stimulus that normally elicits an unconditioned response, such as the food that caused Pavlov's dog to respond with salivation.

V

VALIDITY The capacity of an instrument to measure what it purports to measure.

VASOPRESSIN A neuropeptide known to affect memory. Vasopressin nasal spray has been used clinically to improve memory.

VESTIBULAR SACS Two baglike structures at the base of the semicircular canals containing receptors for the sense of balance.

VESTIBULAR SENSE The sense that keeps an organism in proper balance.

VISIBLE SPECTRUM The range of wavelengths of light visible to the unaided eye.

VISUAL CLIFF An apparatus constructed to study depth perception in animals and human beings. It consists of a center board resting on a glass table. On one side of the board, a checkered surface is visible directly beneath the glass; on the other side, the surface is several feet below the glass, giving the impression of a dropoff.

VISUAL CORTEX   An area in the brain through which most visual information is processed. It is located in the occipital lobes.

VISUAL PERSPECTIVE HYPOTHESIS   The hypothesis that explains people's tendency to attribute their own behavior to environmental causes rather than to personality traits as a function of their visual perspective, because they view their surroundings more often than they view their own body.

VOLLEY THEORY   A theory of hearing designed to explain the reception of sound waves between 300 and 5000 cycles per second. According to this theory, auditory neurons fire in volleys that are well correlated with the frequency of the sound.

W

WAVELENGTH   The linear distance from a point on one oscillation of a wave to the corresponding point on the next oscillation of that wave.

WEBER'S LAW   The rule that the larger or stronger a stimulus, the larger the change required for an observer to notice a difference.

The smallest difference in intensity between two stimuli that can be reliably detected is a constant fraction of the original stimulus.

WERNICKE'S APHASIA   The inability to understand spoken language because of damage to Wernicke's area. Individuals with this disorder generally speak normally in terms of phonetics and grammar content, but their speech is semantically bizarre.

WERNICKE'S AREA   An area in the temporal and parietal lobes of the brain associated with speech control.

Y

YOGI   One who practices yoga, a Hindu discipline, the aim of which is to train consciousness to attain a state of perfect spiritual insight and tranquility. Control of body functions and mental states is practiced.

YOUNG-HELMHOLTZ THEORY   A theory of color vision stating that there are three basic colors (red, green, and blue) and three types of receptors, each of which is receptive to the wavelengths of one of the colors.

REFERENCES

Abelson, R. P. (1981). Psychological status of the script concept. *American Psychologist*, 36, 715-729.

Abraham, H. D. (1983). Visual phenomenology of the LSD flashback. *Archives of General Psychiatry*, 40, 884-889.

Abramovitch, R., Pepler, D., & Corter, C. (1982). Patterns of sibling interaction among preschool-age children. In M. E. Lamb & B. Sutton-Smith (Eds.), *Sibling relationships: Their nature and significance across the lifespan* (pp. 61-86). Hillsdale, NJ: Erlbaum.

Abramson, L. Y., Seligman, M. E. P., & Teasdale, J. D. (1978). Learned helplessness in humans: Critique and reformulation. *Journal of Abnormal Psychology*, 87, 49-74.

Adams, G. R. (1977). Physical attractiveness, personality, and social reactions to peer pressure. *Journal of Psychology*, 96, 287-296.

Adams, J. A. (1977). Feedback theory of how joint receptors regulate the timing and positioning of a limb. *Psychological Review*, 84, 503-523.

Adams, P. R., & Adams, G. R. (1984). Mount Saint Helens's ashfall. *American Psychologist*, 39, 252-260.

Adelmann, P. K., & Zajonc, R. B. (1989). Facial reference and the experience of emotion. *Annual Review of Psychology*, 40, 249-280.

Adler, A. (1927). *Practice and theory of individual psychology*. New York: Harcourt, Brace & World.

Adler, H. E., & Adler, L. L. (1978). What can dolphins (Tursiops Truncatus) learn by observation? *Cetology*, 30, 1-10.

Adler, J., & Carey, J. (1980, February 25). The science of love. *Newsweek*, pp. 89-90.

Adler, L. L., & Adler, H. E. (1977). Ontogeny of observational learning in the dog. *Developmental Psychobiology*, 10, 267-271.

Adler, L. L., & Adler, H. E. (1977). Observational learning in the California sea lion (Zalophus Californianus). *Aquatic Mammals*, 5(3), 72-77.

Adler, T. (1989, June). Early sex hormone exposure studied. *APA Monitor*, p. 9.

Adler, T. (1990, April). Does the "new" MMPI beat the "classic?" *APA Monitor*, pp. 18-19.

Adorno, T. W., Frenkel-Brunswik, E., Levinson, D. J., & Sanford, R. N. (1950). *The authoritarian personality*. New York: Harper.

Aho, A. C., Donner, K., Hyden, C., Larsen, L. O., & Reuter, T. (1988). Low retinal noise in animals with low body temperature allows high visual sensitivity. *Nature*, 334, 348-350.

Ainsworth, M. D. S. (1973). The development of infant-mother attachment. In B. Caldwell & H. Ricciuti (Eds.), *Review of child development research* (Vol. 3). Chicago: Univ. of Chicago Press.

Albo, D., Jr., Taylor, C. W., & Page, B. (1982). Evaluating residents against excellent physicians in practice. In J. S. Lloyd (Ed.), *Evaluation of noncognitive skills and clinical performance* (pp. 113-125). Chicago: American Board of Medical Spec.

Alexander, F. (1950). *Psychosomatic medicine*. New York: Norton.

Alker, H. A., & Owen, D. W. (1977). Biographical, trait, and behavioral-sampling predictions of performance in a stressful life setting. *Journal of Personality & Social Psychology*, 35, 717-723.

Alkon, D. L. (1989). Memory storage and neural systems. *Scientific American*, 261(1), 42-50.

Alley, T. R. (1981). Head shape and the perception of cuteness. *Developmental Psychology*, 17, 650–654.

Allison, T., & Cicchetti, D. V. (1976). Sleep in mammals: Ecological and constitutional correlates. *Science*, 194, 732-734.

Allman, W. F. (1985, October). Staying alive in the 20th century. *Science 85*, pp. 30-41.

Allman, W. F. (1986, May). Mindworks. *Science 86*, pp. 23-31.

Allport, G. W. (1937). *Personality: A psychological interpretation*. New York: Holt, Rinehart & Winston.

Allport, G. W. (1961). *Pattern and growth in personality*. New York: Holt, Rinehart & Winston.

Allport, G. W., & Odbert, H. S. (1936). Trait-names: A psycho-lexical study. *Psychological Monographs: General and Applied*. 47(1, Whole No. 211).

Alper, J. (1986, July/August). Our dual memory. *Science 86*, pp. 44-49.

Altus, W. D. (1967). Birth order and its sequelae. *International Journal of Psychiatry*, 3, 23-36.

Amarilio, J. D. (1979). Insanity—Guilty but mentally ill—Diminished capacity: An aggregate approach to madness. *John Marshall Journal of Practice and Procedure*, 12, 351-381.

Amsterdam, B. (1972). Mirror self-image reactions before age two. *Developmental Psychology*, 5, 297-305.

Anastasi, A. (1979). *Fields of applied psychology* (2nd ed.). New York: McGraw-Hill.

Ancoli-Israel, S., Kripke, D. F., Mason, W., & Kaplan, O. J. (1985). Sleep apnea and periodic movements in an aging sample. *Journal of Gerontology*, 40, 419-425.

Anderson, D. R., Lorch, E. P., Field, D. E., Collins, P. A., & Nathan, J. G. (1986). Television viewing at home: Age trends in visual attention and time with TV. *Child Development*, 57, 1024-1033.

Anderson, J. R. (1980). *Cognitive psychology and its implications*. New York: W. H. Freeman.

Anderson, J. R. (1983). Retrieval of information from long-term memory. *Science*, 220, 25-30.

Anderson, J. R. (1983). *The architecture of cognition*. Cambridge, Mass.: Harvard University Press.

Anderson, J. R., & Bower, G. H. (1973). *Human associative memory*. Washington, D.C.: Winston.

Anderson, L. D. (1939). The predictive value of infant tests in relation to intelligence at 5 years. *Child Development*, 10, 203-212.

Andersson, B. (1971). Thirst—and brain control of water balance. *American Scientist*, 59, 408-415.

Andreasen, N. C. (1988). Brain imaging: Applications in psychiatry. *Science*, 239, 1381-1388.

APA Task Force on Laboratory Tests in Psychiatry. (1987). The dexamethasone suppression test: An overview of its current status in psychiatry. *American Journal of Psychiatry*, 144, 1253-1262.

Arehart-Treichel, J. (1977, March 26). The science of sleep. *Science News*, p. 203.

Arendt, T., Allen, Y., Sinden, J., & Schugens, M. M. (1988). Cholinergic-rich brain transplants reverse alcohol-induced memory deficits. *Nature*, 332, 448-450.

Aronson, E. (1969). Some antecedents of interpersonal attraction. In W. J. Arnold & D. Levine (Eds.), *Nebraska symposium on motivation*. Lincoln, Nebraska: Univ. of Nebraska Press.

Aronson, E., & Mills, J. (1959). The effect of severity of initiation on liking for a group. *Journal of Abnormal and Social Psychology*, 59, 177-181.

Arvidson, K., & Friberg, U. (1980). Human taste—response and taste bud number in fugiform papillae. *Science*, 209, 807-808.

Asaad, G., & Shapiro, B. (1986). Hallucinations: theoretical and clinical overview. *American Journal of Psychiatry*, 143, 1088-1089.

Asch, S. E. (1951). Effects of group pressure upon the modification and distortion of judgment. In H. Guetzkow (Ed.), *Groups, leadership, and men*. Pittsburg, PA: Carnegie.

Assael, H. (1973). Constructive role of interorganizational conflict. In H. J. Leavitt & L. R. Pondy (Eds.), *Readings in managerial psychology* (2nd ed.) (pp. 542-556). Chicago: Univ. of Chicago Press.

Atkinson, J. W., & Raynor, J. O. (1974). *Motivation and achievement*. New York: Wiley.

Atkinson, R., & Shiffrin, R. (1968). Human memory: A proposed system and its control processes. In K. Spence and J. Spence (Eds.), *The psychology of learning and motivation* (vol. 2). New York: Academic Press.

Averill, J. R. (1983). Studies on anger and aggression: Implications for theories of emotion. *American Psychologist*, 38, 1145-1160.

Azrin, N. H., & Foxx, R. M. (1974). *Toilet training in less than a day*. New York: Simon & Schuster.

Azrin, N. H., & Holz, W. C. (1966). Punishment. In W. K. Honig (Ed.), *Operant behavior*. New York: Appleton-Century-Crofts.

Babbitt, B. C. (1982). Effect of task demands on dual coding of pictorial stimuli. *Journal of Experimental Psychology: Learning, Memory, and Cognition*, 8, 73-80.

Bach-Y-Rita, P., Collins, C. C., Saunders, F. A., White, B., & Scadden, L. (1969). Vision substitution by tactile image projection. *Nature*, 221, 963-964.

Bachman, J. G., O'Malley, P. M., & Johnston, J. (1978). *Adolescence to adulthood: Change and stability in the lives of young men.* Ann Arbor, MI: Institute for Social Research.

Bahrick, H. P. (1984). Semantic memory content in permastore: Fifty years of memory for Spanish learned in school. *Journal of Experimental Psychology: General, 113,* 1-29.

Bahrick, H. P., & Phelps, E. (1987). Retention of Spanish vocabulary over 8 years. *Journal of Experimental Psychology: Learning, Memory, & Cognition, 13,* 344-349.

Baillargeon, R. (1987). Object permanence in 3 1/2- and 4 1/2-month-old infants. *Developmental Psychology, 23,* 655-664.

Baker, S. W. (1980). Biological influences on human sex and gender. *Signs: Journal of Women in Culture and Society, 6,* 80-96.

Bales, J. (1986, November). Explaining sexuality? Consider the Sambia. *APA Monitor,* p. 18.

Bales, J. (1987, October). Northwest Airlines sets up walk-in counseling centers. *APA Monitor,* p. 26.

Bales, J. (1988, August). High court: Subjective tests can be validated. *APA Monitor,* p. 5.

Bales, R. F. (1970). *Personality and interpersonal behavior.* New York: Holt, Rinehart & Winston.

Ballenger, J. C. (1986). Biological aspects of panic disorder. *American Journal of Psychiatry, 143,* 516-518.

Balon, R., Jordan, M., Pohl, R., & Yeragani, V. K. (1989). Family history of anxiety disorders in control subjects with lactate-induced panic attacks. *American Journal of Psychiatry, 146,* 1304-1306.

Balster, R. L., & Chait, L. D. (1976). The behavioral pharmacology of phencyclidine. *Clinical Toxicology, 9,* 513-528.

Ban, P. L., & Lewis, M. (1974). Mothers and fathers, girls and boys: Attachment behavior in the one-year-old. *Merrill-Palmer Quarterly, 20,* 195-204.

Bandura, A. (1962). Social learning through imitation. In M. R. Jones (Ed.), *Nebraska symposium on motivation: 1962* (pp. 211-269). Lincoln, Nebraska: Univ. of Nebraska Press.

Bandura, A. (1965). Influence of models' reinforcement contingencies on the acquisition of imitative responses. *Journal of Personality & Social Psychology, 1,* 589-595.

Bandura, A. (1969). *Principles of behavior modification.* New York: Holt, Rinehart, & Winston.

Bandura, A. (1977). *Social learning theory.* Englewood Cliffs NJ: Prentice-Hall.

Bandura, A. (1978). The self system in reciprocal determinism. *American Psychologist, 33,* 344-358.

Bandura, A. (1982). Self-efficacy mechanism in human agency. *American Psychologist, 37,* 122-147.

Bandura, A. (1986). Fearful expectations and avoidant actions as coeffects of perceived self-inefficacy. *American Psychologist, 41,* 1389-1391.

Bandura, A., Ross, D., & Ross, S. A. (1963). Imitation of file-mediated aggressive models. *Journal of Abnormal and Social Psychology, 66,* 3-11.

Bandura, A., Ross, D., & Ross, S. A. (1963). A comparative test of the status envy, social power, and secondary reinforcement theories of identificatory learning. *Journal of Abnormal and Social Psychology, 67,* 527-534.

Barber, T. X. (1969). *Hypnosis: A scientific approach.* New York: Van Nostrand Reinhold.

Barglow, P., Vaughn, B. E., & Molitor, N. (1987). Effects of maternal absence due to employment on the quality of infant-mother attachment in a low-risk sample. *Child Development, 58,* 945-954.

Barinaga, M. (1990). Neuroscience models the brain. *Science, 247,* 524-526.

Barker, R. G. (1968). *Ecological psychology: Concepts and methods for studying the environment of human behavior.* Stanford, Calif.: Stanford Univ. Press.

Barlow, D. H., Blanchard, E. B., Vermilyea, J. A., Vermilyea, B. B., & DiNardo, P. A. (1986). Generalized anxiety and generalized anxiety disorder: Description and reconceptualization. *American Journal of Psychiatry, 143,* 40-44.

Barnes, D. M. (1986). Steroids may influence changes in mood. *Science, 232,* 1344-1345.

Barnes, D. M. (1987a). Neural models yield data on learning. *Science, 236,* 1628-1629.

Barnes, D. M. (1987b). Biological issues in schizophrenia. *Science, 235,* 430-433.

Baron, M., Gruen, R., Kane, J., & Asnis, L. (1985). Modern research criteria and the genetics of schizophrenia. *American Journal of Psychiatry, 142,* 697-701.

Baron, R. A., & Bell, P. A. (1975). Aggression and heat: Mediating effects of prior provocation and exposure to an aggressive model. *Journal of Personality & Social Psychology, 31,* 825-832.

Baron, R. A., & Ransberger, V. M. (1978). Ambient temperature and the occurrence of collective violence: The "long, hot summer" revisited. *Journal of Personality & Social Psychology, 36,* 351-360.

Barsky, A. J., & Klerman, G. L. (1985, December). Hypochondriasis. *Harvard Medical School Mental Health Letter,* pp. 4-6.

Barton, B. (1980). *Eye movements and advertising effectiveness.* Paper presented at the Annual Colloquium of European Economic Psychology, Leuven, Belgium.

Bartusiak, M. (1980), November). Beeper man. *Discover,* p. 57.

Bassuk, E. (1987, January). Mental health needs of homeless persons. *Harvard Medical School Mental Health Letter,* pp. 4-6.

Bassuk, E. L., & Gerson, S. (1978). Deinstitutionalization and mental health services. *Scientific American, 238*(2), 46-53.

Baum, A., Gatchel, R. J., & Schaeffer, M. A. (1983). Emotional, behavioral, and physiological effects of chronic stress at Three Mile Island. *Journal of Consulting and Clinical Psychology, 51,* 565-572.

Bavelas, A., Hastorf, A. H., Gross, A. E., & Kite, W. R. (1965). Experiments on the alteration of group structure. *Journal of Experimental Social Psychology, 1,* 55-70.

Bayer, A. E. (1966). Birth order and college attendance. *Journal of Marriage and the Family, 28,* 480-484.

Beach, B. H. (1980, September 8). Blood, sweat and fears. *Time,* p. 44.

Bear, M. F., Cooper, L. N., & Ebner, F. F. (1987). A physiological basis for a theory of synapse modification. *Science, 237,* 42-48.

Beauchamp, G. K., Yamazaki, K., & Boyse, E. A. (1985). The chemosensory recognition of genetic individuality. *Scientific American, 253*(1), 86-92.

Beck, A. T. (1972). *Depression: Causes and treatment.* Philadelphia, PA: Univ. of Penn. Press.

Beck, A. T., Rush, A. J., Shaw, B., & Emery, G. (1979). *Cognitive therapy of depression: A treatment manual.* New York: Guilford Press.

Becker, F. D. (1981). *Workspace: Creating environments in organizations.* New York: Praeger.

Becker, I. M., & Rosenfeld, J. G. (1976). Rational emotive therapy—A study of initial therapy sessions of Albert Ellis. *Journal of Clinical Psychology, 32,* 872-876.

Becker, W. C. (1960). The matching of behavior rating and questionnaire personality factors. *Psychological Bulletin, 57,* 201-212.

Beers, C. (1908). *A mind that found itself.* New York: Longmans, Green & Co.

Begley, S., & Carey, J. (1981, March 16). Can aging be controlled? *Newsweek,* p. 68.

Begley, S., Springen, K., Katz, S., Hager, M., & Jones, E. (1986, September 29). Memory. *Newsweek,* pp. 48-54.

Belbin, R. M. (1967). Middle-age: What happens to ability. In R. Owen (Ed.), *Middle age* (pp. 98-106). London: Cox and Wyman.

Bell, A. P., Weinberg, M. S., & Hammersmith, S. K. (1981). *Sexual preference: Its development in men and women.* Bloomington, Ind.: Indiana University Press.

Belmont, L., & Marolla, F. A. (1973). Birth order, family size, and intelligence. *Science, 182,* 1096-1101.

Belsky, J. (1986). Infant day care: A cause for concern. *Zero to Three, 7*(1), 1-7.

Belsky, J., & Most, R. K. (1981). From exploration to play: A cross-sectional study of infant free play behavior. *Developmental Psychology, 17,* 630-639.

Bem, D. J., & Allen, A. (1974). On predicting some of the people some of the time: The search for cross-situational consistencies in behavior. *Psychological Review, 81,* **506-520.**

Bem, D. J., & Funder, D. C. (1978). Predicting more of the people more of the time: Assessing the personality of situations. *Psychological Review, 85,* 485-501.

Bem, S. L. (1981). Gender schema theory: A cognitive account of sex typing. *Psychological Review, 88,* 354-364.

Benbow, C. P., & Stanley, J. C. (1981). Mathematical ability—is sex a factor? *Science, 212,* 118.

Benbow, C. P., & Stanley, J. C. (1983). Sex differences in mathematical reasoning ability: More facts. *Science, 222,* 1028-1031.

Bennett, W., & Gurin, J. (1982). *The dieter's dilemma.* New York: Basic Books.

Benson, H. (1975). *The relaxation response.* New York: Morrow.

Bentall, R. P. (1990). The illusion of reality: A review and integration of psychological research on hallucinations. *Psychological Bulletin, 107,* 82-95.

Berbaum, M. L., Markus, G. B., & Zajonc, R. B. (1982). A closer look at Galbraith's "closer look". *Developmental Psychology, 18,* 181-191.

Berbaum, M. L., & Moreland, R. L. (1985). Intellectual development within transracial adoptive families: Retesting the confluence model. *Child Development, 56,* 207-216.

Bergin, A. E. (1971). The evaluation of therapeutic outcomes. In A. E. Bergin & S. L. Garfield (Eds.), *Handbook of psychotherapy and behavior change: An empirical analysis.* New York: Wiley.

Berk, L. S. (1981, August 21). Personal communication.

Berko, J. (1958). The child's learning of English morphology. *Word, 14,* 150-177.

Berkowitz, L. (1965). The concept of aggressive drive: Some additional considerations. In L. Berkowitz (Ed.), *Advances in experimental social psychology* (Vol. 2). New York: Academic Press.

Berkowitz, L. (1983). Aversively stimulated aggression: Some parallels and differences in research with animals and humans. *American Psychologist, 38,* 1135-1144.

Berkowitz, L. (1990). On the formation and regulation of anger and aggression: A cognitive- neoassociationistic analysis. *American Psychologist, 45,* 494-503.

Berkowitz, L., Cochran, S. T., & Embree, M. C. (1981). Physical pain and the goal of aversively stimulated aggression. *Journal of Personality & Social Psychology, 40,* 687-700.

Bernard, H. W., & Fullmer, D. W. (1977). *Principles of guidance* (2nd ed.). New York: Thomas Y. Crowell.

Berndt, T. J., Hawkins, J. A., & Hoyle, S. G. (1986). Changes in friendship during a school year: Effects on children's and adolescents' impressions of friendship and sharing with friends. *Child Development, 57,* 1284-1297.

Berndt, T. J., & Perry, T. B. (1986). Children's perceptions of friendships as supportive relationships. *Developmental Psychology, 22,* 640-648.

Berne, E. (1964). *Games people play.* New York: Grove Press.

Berridge, K. C., & Fentress, J. C. (1985). Trigeminal-taste interaction in palatability processing. *Science, 228,* 747-750.

Berscheid, E. (1983). Emotion. In H. H. Kelley (Ed.), *Close relationships* (pp. 110-168). New York: W. H. Freeman.

Berscheid, E., & Walster, E. (1974). A little bit about love. In T. L. Huston (Ed.), *Foundations of interpersonal attraction.* New York: Academic Press.

Best, J. B. (1989). *Cognitive psychology* (2nd ed.). St. Paul: West Publishing Company.

Bettman, J. R. (1986). Consumer psychology. *Annual Review of Psychology, 37,* 257-289.

Biddle, W. (1986, March). The deception of detection. *Discover,* pp. 24-33.

Birch, H. G. (1945). The role of motivational factors in insightful problem-solving. *Journal of Comparative Psychology, 38,* 295-317.

Bischof, L. J. (1976). *Adult psychology* (2nd ed.). New York: Harper & Row.

Bitterman, M. E. (1969). Thorndike and the problem of animal intelligence. *American Psychologist, 24,* 444-453.

Blake, J. (1989). Number of siblings and educational attainment. *Science, 245,* 32-36.

Blashfield, R. K., & Breen, M. J. (1989). Face validity of the *DSM-III-R* personality disorders. *American Journal of Psychiatry, 146,* 1575-1579.

Blazer, D., Hughes, D., & George, L. K. (1987). Stressful life events and the onset of a generalized anxiety syndrome. *American Journal of Psychiatry, 144,* 1178-1183.

Bleda, P. R., & Castore, C. H. (1973). Social comparison, attraction, and choice of a comparison other. *Memory and Cognition, 1,* 420-424.

Bliss, E. L., & Jeppsen, E. A. (1985). Prevalence of multiple personality among inpatients and outpatients. *American Journal of Psychiatry, 142,* 250-251.

Block, J. (1961). *The Q-sort method in personality assessment and psychiatric research.* Springfield, Ill.: Charles C. Thomas.

Block, J. (1982). Assimilation accommodation, and the dynamics of personality development. *Child Development, 53,* 281-295.

Blood, R. O. (1972). *The family.* New York: Free Press.

Bloom, B. S. (1964). *Stability and change in human characteristics.* New York: Wiley.

Bloom, L. (1983). Tensions in psycholinguistics. *Science, 220,* 843-845.

Bloom, L., & Capatides, J. B. (1987). *Child Development, 58,* 1513-1522.

Blum, K., Briggs, A. H., Feinglass, S. J., Domey, R., & Wallace, J. E. (1977). Effects of Delta9 tetrahydrocannabinol on amphetamine-aggregate toxicity in mice. *Current Therapeutic Research, 21,* 241-244.

Blumenthal, A. L. (1980). Wilhelm Wundt and early American psychology: A class of cultures. In R. W. Reiber & K. Salzinger (Eds.), *Psychology: Theoretical-historical perspectives* (pp. 25-42). New York: Academic Press

Bogen, J. E., Fisher, E. D., & Vogel, P. J. (1965). Cerebral commissurotomy. *Journal of the American Medical Association, 194,* 1328-1329.

Boggiano, A. K., Klinger, C. A., & Main, D. S. (1986). Enhancing interest in peer interaction: A developmental analysis. *Child Development, 57,* 852-861.

Bohus, B., Conti, L., Kovacs, G. L., & Versteeg, D. H. G. (1982). Modulation of memory processes by neuropeptides: Interaction with neurotransmitter systems. In C. Ajmone Marsan, & H. Matthies (Eds.), *Neuronal plasticity and memory formation.* New York: Raven Books.

Bolles, R. C., & Fanselow, M. S. (1982). Endorphins and behavior. *Annual Review of Psychology, 33,* 87-101.

Bolter, A., Heminger, A., Martin, G., & Fry, M. (1976). Outpatient clinical experience in a community drug abuse program with phencyclidine abuse. *Clinical Toxicology, 9,* 593-600.

Booth, D. A. (1977). Satiety and appetite are conditioned reactions. *Psychosomatic Medicine, 39,* 76-81.

Borbely, A. (1986). *Secrets of sleep.* New York: Basic Books.

Borg, E., & Counter, S. A. (1989). The middle-ear muscles. *Scientific American, 261*(2), 74- 80.

Borman, W. C., Rosse, R. L., & Abrahams, N. M. (1980). An empirical construct validity approach to studying predictor-job performance links. *Journal of Applied Psychology, 65,* 662-671.

Bornstein, R. F. (1989). Exposure and affect: Overview and meta-analysis of research, 1968-1987. *Psychological Bulletin, 106,* 265-289.

Bouchard, T. J., Jr., & McGue, M. (1981). Familial studies of intelligence: A review. *Science, 212,* 1055-1059.

Boucher, J. D. (1973). *Facial behavior and the perception of emotion: Studies of Malays and Temuan Orang Asli.* Paper presented at the Conference of Psychology and Related Disciplines, Kuala Lumpur.

Bower, B. (1984, October 6). Not popular by reason of insanity. *Science News,* pp. 218-219.

Bower, B. (1986, November 15). Million-cell memories. *Science News,* pp. 313-315.

Bower, B. (1987, February 21). Deadly aftermath for Vietnam veterans. *Science News,* p. 117.

Bower, B. (1988, August 27). Retardation: The eyes have it. *Science News,* p. 140.

Bower, G. H., Karlin, M. B., & Dueck, A. (1975). Comprehension and memory for pictures. *Memory and Cognition, 3,* 216-220.

Bowers, M. (1965). The onset of psychosis—a diary account. *Psychiatry, 28,* 346-358.

Bowlby, J. (1958). The nature of the child's tie to his mother. *International Journal of Psycho-Analysis, 39,* 350-373.

Bowlby, J. (1982a). Attachment and loss: Retrospect and prospect. *American Journal of Orthopsychiatry, 52,* 664-678.

Bowlby, J. (1982b). *Attachment and loss: Vol. 1 Attachment* (2nd ed.). New York: Basic Books.

Boyd, J. H. (1986). Use of mental health services for the treatment of panic disorder. *American Journal of Psychiatry, 143,* 1569-1574.

Bozarth, M. A., & Wise, R. A. (1984). Anatomically distinct opiate receptor fields mediate reward and physical dependence. *Science, 224,* 516-517.

Brackbill, Y. (1958). Extinction of the smiling response in infants as a function of reinforcement schedule. *Child Development, 29,* 115-124.

Braine, M. D. S. (1963). The ontogeny of English phrase structure: The first phase. *Language, 39*(1), 1-13.

Brand, C. (1987). Intelligence testing: Bryter still and bryter? *Nature, 328,* 110.

Brandt, T., Wist, E. R, & Dichgans, J. (1975). Foreground and background in dynamic spacial orientation. *Perception and Psychophysics,* Vol. 17, 497-503.

Braver, S. L., Linder, D. E., Corwin, T. T., & Cialdini, R. B. (1977). Some conditions that affect admissions of attitude change. *Journal of Experimental Social Psychology, 13,* 565-576.

Bray, G. A., & York, D. A. (1971). Genetically transmitted obesity in rodents. *Physiological Reviews, 51,* 598-646.

Brazelton, T. B., Koslowski, B., & Main, H. (1974). The origins of reciprocity: The early infant-mother interaction. In M. Lewis, & L. A. Rosenblum (Eds.) *The effect of the infant on its caregiver* (pp. 49-76). New York: Wiley-Interscience.

Brecher, E. M. (1976). History of human sexual research and study. In B. J. Sadock, H. I. Kaplan, & A. M. Freedman, *The sexual experience* (pp. 71-78). Baltimore MD: Williams & Wilkins.

Breier, A., Albus, M., Pickar, D., Zahn, T. P., Wolkowitz, O. M., & Paul, S. M. (1987). Controllable and uncontrollable stress in humans: Alterations in mood and neuroendocrine and psychophysiolgical function. *American Journal of Psychiatry, 144,* 1419-1425.

Brenner, D., & Howard K. (1976). Clinical judgment as a function of experience and information. *Journal of Clinical Psychology, 32,* 721-728.

Breslau, N., & Davis, G. C. (1987). Posttraumatic stress disorder: the etiologic specificity of wartime stressors. *American Journal of Psychiatry, 144,* 578-583.

Breslow, M. F., Fankhauser, M. P., Potter, R. L., Meredith, K. E., Misiaszek, J., & Hope, D. G., Jr. (1989). Role of gamma-aminobutyric acid in antipanic drug efficacy. *American Journal of Psychiatry, 146,* 353-356.

Bretherton, I. (1985). Attachment theory: Retrospect and prospect. Monographs of the Society for Research in *Child Development, 50*(1-2, Serial No. 209), 3-35.

Brett, J. M., Goldberg, S. B., & Ury, W. L. (1990). Designing systems for resolving disputes in organizations. *American Psychologist, 45,* 162-170.

Brinkman, C., Porter, R., & Norman, J. (1983). Plasticity of motor behavior in monkeys with crossed forelimb nerves. *Science, 220,* 438-440.

Brobeck, J. R., Tepperman, J., & Long, C. N. H. (1943). Experimental hypothalamic hyperphagia in the albino rat. *Yale Journal of Biology and Medicine, 15,* 831-853.

Brock, T. C. (1965). Communicator-recipient similarity and decision change. *Journal of Personality & Social Psychology, 1,* 650-654.

Bronson, W. C. (1985). Growth in the organization of behavior over the second year of life. *Developmental Psychology, 21,* 108-117.

Brooks, J. (1985). Polygraph testing. *American Psychologist, 40,* 348-354.

Brou, P., Sciascia, T. R., Linden, L., & Lettvin, J. Y. (1986). The colors of things. *Scientific American, 255*(3), 84-91.

Brown, B. B. (1980). *Supermind: The ultimate energy.* New York: Harper & Row.

Brown, B. B., Clasen, D. R., & Eicher, S. A. (1986). Perceptions of peer pressure, peer conformity dispositions, and self-reported behavior among adolescents. *Developmental Psychology, 22,* 521-530.

Brown, B. B., Eicher, S. A., & Petrie, S. (1986). The importance of peer group ("crowd") affiliation in adolescence. *Journal of Adolescence, 9,* 73-96.

Brown, B. B., Lohr, M. J., & McClenahan, E. L. (1986). Early adolescents' perceptions of peer pressure. *Journal of Early Adolescence, 6,* 139-154.

Brown, J. B. (1984). Examination of grammatical morphemes in the language of hard-of-hearing children. *Volta Review, 86,* 229-238.

Brown, M. C. (1982). Administrative succession and organizational performance: The succession effect. *Administrative Science Quarterly, 27,* 1-16.

Brown, R. (1973). *A first language: The early stages.* Cambridge, Mass: Harvard Univ. Press.

Brown, R., & Kulik, J. (1977). Flashbulb memories. *Cognition, 5,* 73-99.

Brown, R. J., & Donderi, D. C. (1986). Dream content and self-reported well-being among recurrent dreamers, past-recurrent dreamers, and nonrecurrent dreamers. *Journal of Personality & Social Psychology, 50,* 612-623.

Browne, M. A., & Mahoney, M. J. (1984). Sport psychology. *Annual Review of Psychology, 35,* 605-625.

Buckhout, R. (1974). Eyewitness testimony. *Scientific American, 231*(6), 23-31.

Buhrmester, D., & Furman, W. (1987). The development of companionship and intimacy. *Child Development, 58,* 1101-1113.

Burbach, J. P. H., Kovacs, G. L., de Wied, D., van Nispen, J. W., & Greven, H. M. (1983). A major metabolite of arginine vasopressin in the brain is a highly potent neuropeptide. *Science, 221,* 1310-1312.

Burchinal, M., Lee, M., & Ramey, C. (1989). Type of day-care and preschool intellectual development in disadvantaged children. *Child Development, 60,* 128-137.

Burns, K. L., & Beier, E. G. (1973). Significance of vocal and visual channels in the decoding of emotional meaning. *Journal of Communication, 23,* 118-130.

Burns, T. L., Moll, P. P., & Lauer, R. M. (1989). The relation between ponderosity and coronary risk factors in children and their relatives. *American Journal of Epidemiology, 129,* 973-987.

Buss, A. H. (1989). Personality as traits. *American Psychologist, 44,* 1378-1388.

Buxton, C. E. (1985). *Points of view in the modern history of psychology.* Orlando, FL: Academic Press.

Byrne, D., & Clore, G. L. (1970). A reinforcement model of evaluative responses. *Personality: An International Journal, 1,* 103-128.

Byrne, D., Ervin, C. R., & Lamberth, J. (1970). Continuity between the experimental study of attraction and real-life computer dating. *Journal of Personality & Social Psychology, 16,* 157-165.

Cacioppo, J. T., & Petty, R. E. (1979). Attitudes and cognitive response: An electrophysiological approach. *Journal of Personality & Social Psychology, 37,* 2181-2199.

Cadoret, R. J., Cain, C. A., & Grove, W. M. (1980). Development of alcoholism in adoptees raised apart from alcoholic biologic relatives. *Archives of General Psychiatry, 37,* 561-563.

Cairns, R. B. (1979). *Social development: The origins and plasticity of interchanges.* San Francisco: W. H. Freeman.

Calabrese, J. R., Kling, M. A., & Gold, P. W. (1987). Alterations in immunocompetence during stress, bereavement, and depression: Focus on neuroendocrine regulation. *American Journal of Psychiatry, 144,* 1123-1134.

Calvert-Boyanowsky, J., Boyanowsky, E. O., Atkinson, M., Gaduto, D., & Reeves, J. (1976). Patterns of passion: Temperature and human emotion. In D. Krebs (Ed.), *Readings in social psychology: Contemporary perspectives* (pp. 96-99). New York: Harper & Row.

Campbell, T. (1982). *Formal cues and content difficulty as determinants of children's cognitive processing of televised educational messages.* Unpublished doctoral dissertation, University of Kansas.

Campos, J. J., Barrett, K. G., Lamb, M. E., Stenberg, C., & Goldsmith, H. H. (1983). Socioemotional development. In M. M. Haith & J. J. Campos (Eds.), *Infancy and developmental psychology.* In P. H. Mussen (Gen. Ed.), *Handbook of child psychology.* New York: Wiley.

Campos, J. J., Hiatt, S., Ramsay, D., Henderson, C., & Svejda, M. (1978). The emergence of fear on the visual cliff. In M. Lewis & L. A. Rosenblum (Eds.), *The development of affect* (pp. 149-182). New York: Plenum Press.

Cannon, W. B. (1927). The James-Lange theory of emotions: A critical examination and an alternative theory. *American Journal of Psychology, 39,* 106-124.

Cannon, W. B. (1939). *The wisdom of the body.* New York: Norton.

Cantin, M., & Genest, J. (1986). The heart as an endocrine gland. *Scientific American, 254*(2), 76-81.

Caplan, P. J., MacPherson, G. M., & Tobin, P. (1985). Do sex-related differences in spatial abilities exist? A multilevel critique with new data. *American Psychologist, 40,* 786-799.

Carey, G., Goldsmith, H. H., Tellegen, A., & Gottesman, I. I. (1978). Genetics and personality inventories: The limits of replication with twin data. *Behavior Genetics, 8,* 299-313.

Carlson, M. (1990, June 4). Daddy's little girl: Did eight-year-old Eileen Franklin see her father kill her friend? Or is 29-year-old Eileen Franklin-Lipsker looking for revenge. *Time,* p. 56.

Carlson, N. K., Drury, C. G., & Webber, J. A. (1977). Discriminability of large weights. *Ergonomics, 20,* 87-90.

Carlson, N. R. (1977). *Physiology of behavior.* Boston: Allyn and Bacon.

Carpenter, W. T., & Heinrichs, D. W. (1983). Early intervention, time-limited, targeted pharmacotherapy of schizophrenia. *Schizophrenia Bulletin, 9*(4), 533-542.

Carson, R. C. (1989). Personality. *Annual Review of Psychology, 40,* 227-248.

Carver, C. S., DeGregorio, E., & Gillis, R. (1980). Ego-defensive bias in attribution among two categories of observers. *Personality and Social Psychology Bulletin, 6,* 44-50.

Case, R. B., Heller, S. S., Case, N. B., & Moss, A. J. (1985). Type A behavior and survival after acute myocardial infarction. *New England Journal of Medicine, 312,* 737-741.

Casto, G., & Mastropieri, M. A. (1986). The efficacy of early intervention programs: A meta-analysis. *Exceptional Children, 52,* 417-424.

Cattell, R. B. (1950). *Personality: A systematic theoretical and factual study.* New York: McGraw-Hill.

Cattell, R. B. (1973, July). Personality pinned down. *Psychology Today,* pp. 40-46.

Cattell, R. B., Saunders, D. R., & Stice, G. F. (1950). *The 16 personality factor questionnaire.* Champaign, Illinois: Institute for Personality and Ability Testing.

Centers for Disease Control, The. (1988). Health status of Vietnam veterans. II. Physical health. *Journal of the American Medical Association, 259,* 2708-2714.

Centers for Disease Control, The. (1990, August). Personal communication.

Chaiken, S. (1980). Heuristic versus systematic information processing and the use of source versus message cues in persuasion. *Journal of Personality & Social Psychology, 39,* 752-766.

Chance, P. (1986, September). The divided self. *Psychology Today,* p. 72.

Charlesworth, W. R., & Kreutzer, M. A. (1973). Facial expression of infants and children. In P. Ekman (Ed.), *Darwin and facial expression.* New York: Academic Press.

Charney, D. S., Heninger, G. R., & Jatlow, P. I. (1985). Increased anxiogenic effects of caffeine in panic disorders. *Archives of General Psychiatry, 42,* 233-243.

Chase, M. H., & Morales, F. R. (1983). Subthreshold excitatory activity and motoneuron discharge during REM periods of active sleep. *Science, 221,* 1195-1198.

Chase, M. H., & Morales, F. R. (1990). The atonia and myoclonia of active (REM) sleep. *Annual Review of Psychology, 41,* 557-584.

Cherry, F., & Byrne, D. (1976). Authoritarianism. In T. Blass (Ed.), *Personality variables in social behavior.* Hillsdale, NJ: Erlbaum.

Cherry, F., Byrne, D., & Mitchell, H. E. (1976). Clogs in the bogus pipeline: Demand characteristics and social desirability. *Journal of Research in Personality, 10,* 69-75.

Chess, S., & Thomas, A. (1982). Infant bonding: Mystique and reality. *American Journal of Orthopsychiatry, 52,* 213-222.

Chess, S., & Thomas, A. (Eds.). (1986a). Cross-cultural temperament studies. In S. Chess & A. Thomas (Eds.), *Annual progress in child psychiatry and child development* (pp. 353-354). New York: Brunner/Mazel.

Chess, S., & Thomas, A. (1986b). Developmental issues. In S. Chess & A. Thomas (Eds.), *Annual progress in child psychiatry and child development* (pp. 21-26). New York: Brunner Mazel.

Cheyne, J. A., & Rubin, K. H. (1983). Playful precursors of problem solving in preschoolers. *Developmental Psychology, 19,* 577-584.

Child, I. L. (1985). Psychology and anomalous observations: The question of ESP in dreams. *American Psychologist, 40,* 1219-1230.

Chomsky, N. (1957). *Syntactic structures.* The Hague: Mouton.

Chorover, S. L. (1979). *From genesis to genocide: The meaning of human nature and the power of behavior control.* Cambridge, Mass.: MIT Press.

Chouinard, G., Labonte, A., Fontaine, R., & Annable, L. (1983). New concepts in benzodiazepine therapy: Rebound anxiety and new indications for the more potent benzodiazepines. *Progress in Neuro-psychopharmacology and Biological Psychiatry,* 7, 669-673.

Chumlea, W. M. (1982). Physical growth in adolescence. In B. B. Wolman (Ed.), *Handbook of developmental psychology* (pp. 471-485). Englewood Cliffs NJ: Prentice-Hall.

Churchland, P. M., & Churchland, P. S. (1990). Could a machine think? *Scientific American,* 262(1), 32-37.

Cialdini, R. B., & Schroeder, D. A. (1976). Increasing compliance by legitimizing paltry contributions: When even a penny helps. *Journal of Personality & Social Psychology,* 34, 599-604.

Cialdini, R. B., Levy, A., Herman, C. P., Kozlowski, L. T., & Petty, R. E. (1976). Elastic shifts of opinion: Determinants of direction and durability. *Journal of Personality & Social Psychology,* 34, 663-672.

Cialdini, R. B., Petty, R. E., & Cacioppo, J. T. (1981). Attitude and attitude change. *Annual Review of Psychology,* 32, 357-404.

Cicirelli, V. G. (1982). Sibling influence throughout the lifespan. In M. E. Lamb & B. Sutton-Smith (Eds.), *Sibling relationships: Their nature and significance across the lifespan* (pp. 267-284). Hillsdale, NJ: Erlbaum.

Cimmerman, A. (1981). The Fay case. *Criminal Defense,* 8, 7.

Clark, H. H. (1974). Semantics and comprehension. In R. A. Sebeok (Ed.), *Current trends in linguistics* (Vol. 12). The Hague: Mouton.

Clark, K. B., & Clark, M. P. (1947). Racial identification and preference in Negro children. In T. M. Newcomb & E. J. Hartley (Eds.), *Readings in social psychology.* New York: Holt.

Clayton, R. R. (1975). *The family, marriage, and social change.* Lexington, Mass.: D. C. Heath.

Clements, R. D. (1981). Modern architecture's debt to creativity education: A case study. *Gifted Child Quarterly,* 25, 119-122.

Clifton, R. K., Gwiazda, J., Bauer, J. A., Clarkson, M. G., & Held, R. M. (1988). Growth in head size during infancy: Implications for sound localization. *Developmental Psychology,* 24, 477-483.

Cloninger, C. R., Martin, R. L., Guze, S. B., & Clayton, P. J. (1986). A prospective follow-up and family study of somatization in men and women. *American Journal of Psychiatry,* 143, 873-878.

Clore, G. L., & Byrne, D. (1974). A reinforcement-affect model of attraction. In T. L. Huston (Ed.), *Foundations of interpersonal attraction.* New York: Academic Press.

Clum, G. A. (1987). Abandon the suicidal? A reply to Szasz. *American Psychologist,* 42, 883-884.

Coffey, C. E., Figiel, G. S., Djang, W. T., Sullivan, D. C., Herfkens, R. J., & Weiner, R. D. (1988). Effects of ECT on brain structure: A pilot prospective magnetic resonance imaging study. *American Journal of Psychiatry,* 145, 701-706.

Cohen, J. B., & Chakravarti, D. (1990). Consumer psychology. *Annual Review of Psychology,* 41, 243-288.

Cohen, N. J., McCloskey, M., & Wible, C. G. (1988). There is still no case for a flashbulb- memory mechanism: Reply to Schmidt and Bohannon. *Journal of Experimental Psychology: General,* 117, 336-338.

Cohen, S., Lichtenstein, E., Prochaska, J. O., Rossi, J. S., Gritz, E. R., Carr, C. R., Orleans, C. T., Schoenbach, V. J., Biener, L., Abrams, D., DiClemente, C., Curry, S., Marlatt, G. A., Cummings, K. M., Emont, S. L., Giovino, G., & Ossip-Klein, D. (1989). Debunking myths about self-quitting: Evidence from 10 prospective studies of persons who attempt to quit smoking by themselves. *American Psychologist,* 44, 1355-1365.

Colby, A., Kohlberg, L., Gibbs, J., & Lieberman, M. (1983). A longitudinal study of moral judgment. Monographs of the Society for Research in *Child Development,* 48(1-2, Serial No. 200).

Coleman, J. S., Campbell, E. Q., Hobson, C. J., McPartland, J., Mood, A. M., Weinfeld, F. D., & York, R. L. (1966). *Equality of educational opportunity.* Report from Office of Education. Washington, DC: U.S. Govt Printing Office.

Coleman, L. M., & Antonucci, T. C. (1983). Impact of work on women at midlife. *Developmental Psychology,* 19, 290-294.

Coleman, R. M. (1986). *Wide awake at 3:00 a.m.: By choice or by chance?* New York: W. H. Freeman.

Colligan, R. C., Osborne, D., Swenson, W. M., & Offord, K. P. (1983). *The MMPI: A contemporary normative study.* New York: Praeger.

Collins, W. A. (1984). Introduction. In W. A. Collins (Ed.), *Development during middle childhood: The years from six to twelve* (pp. 1-23). Washington, DC: National Academy Press.

Condry, J. C., Siman, M. L., & Bronfenbrenner, U. (1968). *Characteristics of peers and adult-oriented children.* Unpublished manuscript, Cornell University.

Constantine-Paton, M., & Law, M. I. (1982). The development of maps and stripes in the brain. *Scientific American,* 247(6), 62-70.

Cooper, C. R. (1977, March). *Collaboration in children: Dyadic interaction skills in problem solving.* Paper presented at the meeting of the Society for Research in Child Development, New Orleans, Louisiana.

Cooper, J., & Croyle, R. T. (1984). Attitudes and attitude change. *Annual Review of Psychology,* 35, 395-426.

Cordes, C. (1985, September). Chemical cruise steers emotions. *APA Monitor,* p. 18.

Cornell-Bell, A. H., Finkbeiner, S. M., Cooper, M. S., & Smith, S. J. (1989). Glutamate induces calcium waves in cultured astrocytes: Long-range glial signaling. *Science,* 247, 470-473.

Coryell, W., Endicott, J., Keller, M., Andreasen, N., Grove, W., Hirschfeld, R. M. A., & Scheftner, W. (1989). Bipolar affective disorder and high achievement: A familial association. *American Journal of Psychiatry,* 146, 983-988.

Costanzo, R. M., & Gardner, E. P. (1981). Multiple-joint neurons in somatosensory cortex of awake monkeys. *Brain Research,* 214, 321-333.

Costello, C. G. (1976). Electroconvulsive therapy: Is further investigation necessary? *Canadian Psychiatric Association Journal,* 21, 61-67.

Cowen, R. (1990, April 14). Cocaine and the nervous system. *Science News,* p. 238.

Crash trauma. (1979, January 8). *Time,* p. 61.

Craske, B. (1977). Perception of impossible limb positions induced by tendon vibration. *Science,* 196, 71-73.

Crawford, M. H. (1989). How color affects people and work. *Science,* 246, 761.

Crick, F. H. C. (1979). Thinking about the brain. *Scientific American,* 241(3), 219-232.

Crick, F., & Mitchison, G. (1983). The function of dream sleep. *Nature,* 304, 111-114.

Critchlow, B. (1986). The powers of John Barleycorn: Beliefs about the effects of alcohol on social behavior. *American Psychologist,* 41, 751-764.

Cronbach, L. J. (1970). *Essentials of psychological testing.* New York: Harper.

Cronbach, L. J. (1975). Five decades of public controversy over mental testing. *American Psychologist,* 30, 1-14.

Crusco, A. H., & Wetzel, C. G. (1984). The Midas Touch: The effects of interpersonal touch on restaurant tipping. Social *Psychological Bulletin,* 10, 512-517

Culliton, B. J. (1985). APA issues warning on antipsychotic drugs. *Science,* 229, 1248.

Culliton, B. J. (1987). Take two pets and call me in the morning. *Science,* 237, 1560-1561.

Cummings, L. L. (1982). Organizational behavior. *Annual Review of Psychology,* 33, 541-579.

Cummins, R. C. (1971). Relationship of initiating structure and job performance as moderated by consideration. *Journal of Applied Psychology,* 55, 489-490.

Curcio, C. A., Sloan, K. R., Jr., Packer, O., Hendrickson, A. E., & Kalina, R. E. (1987). Distribution of cones in human and monkey retina: Individual variability and radial asymmetry. *Science,* 236, 579-582.

Curran, J. P., & Lippold, S. (1975). The effects of physical attractiveness and attitude similarity on attraction in dating dyads. *Journal of Personality,* 43, 528-539.

Czeisler, C. A., Allan, J. S., Strogatz, S. H., Ronda, J. M., Sanchez, R., Rios, C. D., Freitag, W. O., Richardson, G. S., & Kronauer, R. E. (1986). Bright light resets the human circadian pacemaker independent of the timing of the sleep-wake cycle. *Science,* 233, 667-671.

Czeisler, C. A., Kronauer, R. E., Allan, J. S., Duffy, J. F., Jewett, M. E., Brown, E. N., & Ronda, J. M. (1989). Bright light induction of strong (type o) resetting of the human circadian pacemaker. *Science,* 244, 1328-1333.

Czeisler, C. A., Moore-Ede, M. C., & Coleman, R. M. (1982). Rotating shift work schedules that disrupt sleep are improved by applying circadian principles. *Science,* 217, 460-463.

Dannemiller, J. L., & Stephens, B. R. (1988). A critical test of infant pattern preference models. *Child Development,* 59, 210-216.

Darwin C. (1967). *The expression of the emotions in man and animals.* Chicago: Univ. of Chicago Press. (Original work published 1872).

Davis, D. J., Cahan, S., & Bashi, J. (1977). Birth order and intellectual development: The confluence model in the light of cross-cultural evidence. *Science,* 196, 1470-1472.

Davis, E. A. (1937). *The development of linguistic skills in twins, single twins with siblings, and only children from age 5 to 10 years.* Minneapolis: University of Minnesota Press, Institute of Child Welfare Series, No. 14.

Davison, G. C., & Neale, J. M. (1978). *Abnormal psychology* (2nd ed.). New York: Wiley.

Day, G. S. (1976). Assessing the effects of information disclosure requirements. *Journal of Marketing, 40*, 42-52.

De Cock, K. M., Barrere, B., Diaby, L., Lafontaine, M., Gnaore, E., Porter, A., Pantobe, D., Lafontant, G. C., Dago-Akribi, A., Ette, M., Odehouri, K., Heyward, W. L. (1990). AIDS— The leading cause of adult death in the West African city of Abidjian, Ivory Coast. *Science, 249*, 793-796.

De Valois, R. L., & De Valois, K. K. (1980). Spatial vision. *Annual Review of Psychology, 31*, 309-341.

de Vries, M. W. (1984). Temperament and infant mortality among the Masai of East Africa. *The American Journal of Psychiatry, 141*, 1189-1194.

de Wied, D., van Wimersma Greidanus, T. B., Bohus, B., Urban, I., & Gispen, W. H. (1976). Vasopressin and memory consolidation. *Progress in Brain Research, 45*, 181. ,

DeAngelis, T. (1987, August). Short-term therapy is "magical" choice for many patients. APA *Monitor*, p. 34.

DeAngelis, T. (1990, August). Cognitive dissonance theory alive and well. APA *Monitor*, p. 10.

DeCasper, A. J., & Fifer, W. P. (1980). Of human bonding: Newborns prefer their mothers' voices. *Science, 208*, 1174-1176.

deCharms, R. (1968). *Personal causation*. New York: Academic Press.

deCharms, R., & Muir, M. S. (1978). Motivation: Social approaches. *Annual Review of Psychology, 29*, 91-113.

Deci, E. L., & Ryan, R. (1980). The empirical exploration of intrinsic motivational processes. *Advances in Experimental Social Psychology, 13*, 39-80.

Denber, H. C. B. (1967). Tranquilizers in psychiatry. In A. M. Freedman & H. I. Kaplan (Eds.), *Psychiatry*. Baltimore: Williams & Wilkins.

DePiano, F. A., & Salzberg, H. C. (1979). Clinical applications of hypnosis to three psychosomatic disorders. *Psychological Bulletin, 86*, 1223-1235.

Depue, R. A., & Iacono, W. G. (1989). Neurobehavioral aspects of affective disorders. *Annual Review of Psychology, 40*, 457-492.

Deregowski, J. B. (1972). Pictorial perception and culture. *Scientific American, 227*(5), 82-88.

Dermer, M, & Thiel, D. L. (1975). When beauty may fail. *Journal of Personality & Social Psychology, 31*, 1168-1176.

Derogatis, L. R., Yevzeroff, H., & Wittelsberger, B. (1975). Social class, psychological disorder, and the nature of the psychopathologic indicator. *Journal of Consulting & Clinical Psychology, 43*, 183-191.

Dershowitz, A. (1973). Abolishing the insanity defense: The most significant feature of the administration's proposed criminal code. *Criminal Law Bulletin, 9*, 435.

Deutsch, M., & Krauss, R. M. (1960). The effect of threat upon interpersonal bargaining. *Journal of Abnormal and Social Psychology, 61*, 181-189.

deVilliers, J. G., & deVilliers, P. A. (1973). A cross-sectional study of the acquisition of grammatical morphemes in child speech. *Journal of Psycholinguistic Research, 2*, 267-278.

Dew, M. A., Bromet, E. J., Schulberg, H. C., Dunn, L. O., & Parkinson, D. K. (1987). Mental health effects of the Three Mile Island nuclear reactor restart. *American Journal of Psychiatry, 144*, 1074-1077.

Dewey, J. (1910). *How we think*. Boston: D. C. Heath and Company.

Diamond, M. C., Scheibel, A. B., Murphy, G. M., Jr., & Harvey, T. (1985). On the brain of a scientist: Albert Einstein. *Experimental Neurology, 88*, 198-204.

Diamond, S. (1980). Wundt before Leipzig. In R. W. Reiber (Ed.), *Wilhelm Wundt and the making of a scientific psychology* (pp. 3-70). New York: Plenum Press.

Diaz, R. M., & Berndt, T. J. (1982). Children's knowledge of a best friend: Fact or fancy? *Developmental Psychology, 18*, 787-794.

Dichgans, J., & Brandt, T. (1978). Visual-vestibular interaction: Effects on self-motion perception and posture control. In R. Held, H. W. Leibowitz, & H. L. Teuber, (Eds.), *Handbook of sensory physiology* (pp. 755-804). Berlin: Springer.

Dickson, D. (1989). Watson floats a plan to carve up the genome. *Science, 244*, 521-522.

Diener, E. (1980). Deindividuation: The absence of self-awareness and self-regulation in group members. In P. B. Paulus (Ed.), *The psychology of group influence*. Hillsdale, NJ: Erlbaum.

Dion, K. K. (1977). The incentive value of physical attractiveness for young children. *Personality and Social Psychology Bulletin, 3*, 67-70.

Dion, K. K., & Stein, S. (1978). Physical attractiveness and interpersonal influence. *Journal of Experimental Social Psychology, 14*, 97-108.

Dobelle, W. H., Mladejovsky, M. G., & Girvin, J. P. (1974). Artificial vision for the blind: Electrical stimulation of visual cortex offers hope for a functional prosthesis. *Science, 183*, 440-444.

Dodd, J., & Jessell, T. M. (1988). Axon guidance and the patterning of neuronal projections in vertebrates. *Science, 242*, 692-699.

Doherty, W. J. & Jacobson, N. S. (1982). Marriage and the family. In B. B. Wolman

(Ed.), *Handbook of developmental psychology* (pp. 667-680). Englewood Cliffs NJ: Prentice-Hall.

Doi, L. T. (1962). Amae: A key concept for understanding Japanese personality structure. In R. Smith & R. Beardsley (Eds.), *Japanese culture: Its development and characteristics*. New York: Wenner Gren Foundation for Anthropological Research.

Dollard, J., Doob, L. W., Miller, N. E., Mowrer, D. H., & Sears, R. R. (1939). *Frustration and aggression*. New Haven, CT: Yale University Press.

Dorow, R., Horowski, G., Paschelke, M. A., & Braestrup, C. (1983). *Lancet, 2*, 98.

Doty, R. L., Ford, M., Preti, G., & Huggins, G. R. (1975). Changes in the intensity and pleasantness of human vaginal odors during the menstrual cycle. *Science, 190*, 1316-1318.

Dourish, C. T., Rycroft, W., & Iversen, S. D. (1989). Postponement of satiety by blockade of brain cholecystokinin (CCK-B) receptors. *Science, 245*, 1509-1511.

Douvan, E., & Adelson, J. (1966). *The adolescent experience*. New York: Wiley.

Drake, R. E., & Vaillant, G. E. (1985). A validity study of Axis II of DSM-III. *American Journal of Psychiatry, 142*, 553-558.

Dunbar, F. (1943). *Psychosomatic diagnosis*. New York: Hoeber.

Duncker, K. (1945). On problem-solving. *Psychological Monographs, 58*, no. 270.

Durham v. United States. (1954). *Federal 2nd, 214*, 862.

Dutton, D. G., & Aron, A. P. (1974). Some evidence for heightened sexual attraction under conditions of high anxiety. *Journal of Personality & Social Psychology, 30*, 510-517.

Dywan, J., & Bowers, K. (1983). The use of hypnosis to enhance recall. *Science, 222*, 184-185.

Eagly, A. H. (1983). *Who says so? The processing of communicator cues in persuasion*. Paper presented at the meeting of the Eastern Psychological Association, Philadelphia, Pennsylvania.

Eagly, A. H., & Himmelfarb, S. (1978). Attitudes and opinions. *Annual Review of Psychology, 29*, 517-554.

Eaton, W. O., Chipperfield, J. G., & Singbeil, C. E. (1989). Birth order and activity level in children. *Developmental Psychology, 25*, 668-672.

Ebbesen, E. B., Kjos, G. L., & Konecni, V. J. (1976). Spatial ecology: Its effects on the choice of friends and enemies. *Journal of Experimental Social Psychology, 12*, 505-518.

Ebbinghaus, H. (1913). *Memory: A contrivution to experimental psychology*. (Translated by H. A. Ruger & C. E. Bussenius.) New York: New York Teacher's College, Columbia University. (Originally published, 1885).

Eccles-Parsons, J. (1982). Biology, experience and sex dimorphic behaviors. In W. Gove & G. R. Carpenter (Eds.), *The fundamental connection between nature and nurture: A review of the evidence*. Lexington, Mass: Lexington Books.

Eckerman, C. O., Whatley, J. L., & Kutz, S. L. (1975). Growth of social play with peers during the second year of life. *Developmental Psychology, 11*, 42-49.

Edwards, A. L. (1961). Social desirability or acquiescence in the MMPI? A case study with the SD scale. *Journal of Abnormal & Social Psychology, 63*, 351-359.

Edwards, D. D. (1986, January 18). Nicotine: A drug of choice? *Science News*, pp. 44-45.

Ehrhardt, A. A., & Meyer-Bahlburg, H. F. L. (1981). Effects of prenatal sex hormones on gender-related behavior. *Science, 211*, 1312-1318.

Eibl-Eibesfeldt, I. (1972). Similarities and differences between cultures in expressive movements. In R. A. Hinde (Ed.), *Nonverbal communication*. Cambridge, England: Cambridge Univ. Press.

Eichelman, B. (1985). Hypnotic change in combat dreams of two veterans with posttraumatic stress disorder. *American Journal of Psychiatry, 142*, 112-114.

Eisen, S. V. (1979). Actor-observer differences in information inferences and causal attribution. *Journal of Personality & Social Psychology, 37*, 261-272.

Eisenberg, R. B., & Marmarou, A. (1981). Behavioral reactions of newborns to speech-like sounds and their implications for developmental studies. *Infant Mental Health Journal, 2*, 129-138.

Eiser, J. R., & Pancer, S. M. (1979). Attitudinal effects of the use of evaluative biased language. *European Journal of Social Psychology, 9*, 39-47.

Eiser, J. R., & Ross, M. (1977). Partisan language, immediacy, and attitude change. *European Journal of Social Psychology, 7*, 477-489.

Eisert, D. C., & Kahle, L. R. (1982). Self-evaluation and social comparison of physical and role change during adolescence: A longitudinal analysis. *Child Development, 53*, 98-104.

Ekman, P. (1973). Cross cultural studies of facial expression. In P. Ekman (Ed.), *Darwin and facial expression*. New York: Academic Press.

Ekman, P., & Friesen, M. V. (1974). Detecting deception from the body or face. *Journal of Personality & Social Psychology, 29*, 288-298.

Ekman, P., Friesen, W. V., & O'Sullivan, M. (1988). Smiles when lying. *Journal of Personality & Social Psychology, 54,* 414-420.

Ekman, P., Friesen, W. V., O'Sullivan, M., Chan, A., Diacoyanni-Tarlatzis, I., Heider, K., Krause, R., LeCompte, W. A., Pitcairn, T., & Ricci-Bitti, P. E. (1987). Universals and cultural differences in the judgments of facial expressions of emotion. *Journal of Personality & Social Psychology, 53,* 712-717.

Ekman, P., Levenson, R. W., & Friesen, W. V. (1983). Autonomic nervous system activity distinguishes among emotions. *Science, 221,* 1208-1210.

Ekman, P., & Oster, H. (1979). Facial expressions of emotion. *Annual Review of Psychology, 30,* 527-554.

Ekman, P., Sorenson, E. R., & Friesen, W. V. (1969). Pan-cultural elements in facial displays of emotion. *Science, 164,* 86-88.

Elephant calls that humans can't hear. *Science News,* p. 122.

Elkind, D. (1967). Egocentrism in adolescence. *Child Development, 38,* 1025-1034.

Elkind, D. (1971). *A sympathetic understanding of the child six to sixteen.* Boston: Allyn & Bacon.

Ellis, A. (1962). *Reason and emotion in psychotherapy.* New York: Lyle Stuart.

Ellis, A. (1987). The impossibility of achieving consistently good mental health. *American Psychologist, 42,* 364-375.

Ellis, L., & Ames, M. A. (1987). Neurohormonal functioning and sexual orientation: A theory of homosexuality-heterosexuality. *Psychological Bulletin, 101,* 233-258.

Emmerich, W., & Goldman, K. S. (1972). Boy-girl identity task (technical report). In V. Shipman (Ed.), *Disadvantaged children and their first school experiences* (Technical Report PR-72-20). Educational Testing Service.

Emrick, C. D., & Hansen, J. (1983). Assertions regarding effectiveness of treatment for alcoholism. *American Psychologist, 38,* 1078-1088.

Endler, N. S., & Magnusson, D. (1976). Toward an interactional psychology of personality. *Psychological Bulletin, 83,* 956-974.

Epstein, A. W. (1985). The waking event-dream interval. *American Journal of Psychiatry, 142,* 123-124.

Epstein, S., & Fenz, W. D. (1965). Steepness of approach and avoidance gradients in humans as a function of experience. *Journal of Experimental Psychology, 70,* 1-12.

Erikson, E. H. (1968). *Identity, youth, and crisis.* New York: Norton.

Ernst, C., & Angst, J. (1983). *Birth order: Its influence on personality.* New York: Springer-Verlag.

Eron, L. D. (1987). The development of aggressive behavior from the perspective of a developing behaviorism. *American Psychologist, 42,* 435-442.

Eron, L. D., & Peterson, R. A. (1982). Abnormal behavior: Social approaches. *Annual Review of Psychology, 33,* 231-264.

Erwin, E. (1980). Psychoanalytic therapy. *American Psychologist, 35,* 435-443.

Erwin, G., Plomin, R., & Wilson, J. (1984, March 17). Alcohol test may be inaccurate. *Science News,* p. 171.

Etaugh, C. (1980). Effects of nonmaternal care on children. *American Psychologist, 35,* 309-319.

Etaugh, C., Collins, G., & Gerson, A. (1975). Reinforcement of sex-typed behaviors of two-year-old children in a nursery school setting. *Developmental Psychology, 11,* 255.

Eysenck, H. J. (1952). The effects of psychotherapy: An evaluation. *Journal of Consulting Psychology, 16,* 319-324.

Eysenck, H. J. (1985). Psychotherapy effects: Real or imaginary? *American Psychologist, 40,* 239-240.

Eysenck, H. J., Wakefield, J. A., Jr., & Friedman, A. F. (1983). Diagnosis and clinical assessment: The DSM-III. *Annual Review of Psychology, 34,* 167-193.

Fairchild, L., & Erwin, W. M. (1977). Physical punishment by parent figures as a model of aggressive behavior in children. *Journal of Genetic Psychology, 130,* 279-284.

Falbo, T. (1981). Relationships between birth category, achievement, and interpersonal orientation. *Journal of Personality & Social Psychology, 41,* 121-131.

Falk, J. L. (1961). Production of polydipsia in normal rats by an intermittent food schedule. *Science, 133,* 195-196.

Falk, J. L. (1971). The nature and determinants of adjunctive behavior. *Physiology and Behavior, 6,* 577-588.

Fantz, R. L. (1961). The origin of form perception. *Scientific American, 204,* 66-72.

Faraone, S. (1982). Psychiatry and political repression in the Soviet Union. *American Psychologist, 37,* 1105-1112.

Faraone, S. V., Kremen, W. S., & Tsuang, M. T. (1990). Genetic transmission of major affective disorders: Quantitative models and linkage analyses. *Psychological Bulletin, 108,* 109-127.

Faravelli, C., & Pallanti, S. (1989). Recent life events and panic disorder. *American Journal of Psychiatry, 146,* 622-626.

Farde, L., Hall, H., Ehrin, E., & Sedvall, G. (1986). Quantitative analysis of D2 dopamine receptor binding in the living human brain by PET. *Science, 231,* 258-261.

Farkas, G. M. (1980). An ontological analysis of behavior therapy. *American Psychologist, 35,* 364-374.

Farley, J., Richards, W. G., Ling, L. J., Liman, E., & Alkon, D. L. (1983). Membrane changes in a single photoreceptor cause associative learning in Hermissenda. *Science, 221,* 1201-1202.

Farr, F. (1961). *Frank Lloyd Wright.* New York: Scribners.

Farran, D. C., & Ramey, C. T. (1977). Infant day care and attachment behaviors toward mothers and teachers. *Child Development, 48,* 1112-1116.

Faulkner, T. W., & Murphy, T. J. (1973). Lighting for difficult visual tasks. *Human Factors, 15,* 149-162.

Faust, D., & Miner, R. A. (1986). The empiricist and his new clothes: DSM-III in perspective. *American Journal of Psychiatry, 143,* 962-967.

Favreau, O. E., & Corballis, M. C. (1976). Negative aftereffects in visual perception. *Scientific American, 235*(6), 42-48.

Fay, R. E., Turner, C. F., Klassen, A. D., & Gagnon, J. H. (1989). Prevalence and patterns of same-gender sexual contact among men. *Science, 243,* 338-348.

Fazio, R. H. (1979). Motives for social comparison: The construction-validation distinction. *Journal of Personality & Social Psychology, 37,* 1683-1698.

Feder, H. H. (1984). Hormones and sexual behavior. *Annual Review of Psychology, 35,* 165-200.

Fein, G. G., Schwartz, P. M., Jacobson, S. W., & Jacobson, J. L. (1983). Environmental toxins and behavioral development. *American Psychologist, 38,* 1188-1197.

Fein, G., Johnson, D., Kosson, N., Stork, L., & Wasserman, L. (1975). Sex stereotypes and preferences in toy choices in 20-month-old-boys and girls. *Developmental Psychology, 11,* 527-528.

Feingold, A. (1988a). Cognitive gender differences are disappearing. *American Psychologist, 43,* 95-103.

Feingold, A. (1988b). Matching for attractiveness in romantic partners and same-sex friends: A meta-analysis and theoretical critique. *Psychological Bulletin, 104,* 226-235.

Festinger, L., & Carlsmith, J. M. (1959). Cognitive consequences of forced compliance. *Journal of Abnormal and Social Psychology, 58,* 203-210.

Filsinger, E. E., & Anderson, C. C. (1982). Social class and self-esteem in late adolescence: Dissonant context or self-efficacy? *Developmental Psychology, 18,* 380-384.

Fine, A. (1986). Transplantation in the central nervous system. *Scientific American, 255*(2), 52-58B.

Finkelstein, N. W., & Ramey, C. T. (1977). Learning to control the environment in infancy. *Child Development, 48,* 806-819.

Finlayson, D. F., & Loughran, J. L. (1976). Pupils' perceptions in high and low delinquency schools. *Educational Research, 18,* 138-145.

Finn, P. R., & Pihl, R. O. (1987). Men at high risk for alcoholism: The effect of alcohol on cardiovascular response to unavoidable shock. *Journal of Abnormal Psychology, 96,* 230-236.

Fischer, K. W., & Silvern, L. (1985). Stages and individual differences in cognitive development. *Annual Review of Psychology, 36,* 613-648.

Fisher, K. (1986, January). Scrutiny attends more public role. *APA Monitor,* pp. 20-21.

Fiske, D. W., Conley, J. J., & Goldberg, L. R. (1987). E. Lowell Kelly (1905-1986). *American Psychologist, 42,* 511-512.

Fitzgerald, B. A., & Wells, C. E. (1977). Hallucinations as a conversion reaction. *Diseases of the Nervous System, 38,* 381-383.

Fitzgerald, L. F., & Osipow, S. H. (1986). An occupational analysis of counseling psychology: How special is the specialty? *American Psychologist, 41,* 535-544.

Fitzsimons, J. T. (1973). Some historical perspectives in the physiology of thirst. In A. N. Epstein, H. R. Kissileff, & E. Stellar (Eds.), *The neuropsychology of thirst.* Washington, D.C.: V. H. Winston.

Flach, F. F., & Kaplan, M. (1983). Visual perceptual dysfunction in psychiatric patients. *Comprehensive Psychiatry, 24,* 304-311.

Flavell, J. H. (1977). *Cognitive development.* Englewood Cliffs NJ: Prentice-Hall.

Fleishman, E. A., & Quaintance, M. K. (1984). *Taxonomies of human performance: The description of human tasks.* Orlando, FL: Academic Press.

Flood, J. F., Smith, G. E., & Morley, J. E. (1987). Modulation of memory processing by cholecystokinin: Dependence on the vagus nerve. *Science, 236,* 832-834.

Flynn, J. R. (1987). Massive IQ gains in 14 nations: What IQ tests really measure. *Psychological Bulletin, 101,* 171-191.

Ford, D. E., & Kamerow, D. B. (1989). Epidemiologic study of sleep disturbances and psychiatric disorders. An opportunity for prevention? *Journal of the American Medical Association, 262,* 1479-1484.

Foulkes, D., & Fleisher, S. (1975). Mental activity in relaxed wakefulness. *Journal of Abnormal Psychology, 84,* 66-75.

Fox, B. H. (1981). In R. Ader (Ed.), *Psychoneuroimmunology.* New York: Academic Press.

Fox, E. L., & Mathews, D. K. (1981). *The physiological basis of physical education and athletics* (3rd ed.). Philadelphia: Saunders.

Fox, N. A. (1989). Psychophysiological correlates of emotional reactivity during the first year of life. *Developmental Psychology, 25,* 364-372.

Fox, N. A., & Davidson, R. J. (1988). Patterns of brain electrical activity during facial signs of emotion in 10-month-old infants. *Developmental Psychology, 24,* 230-236.

Frank, J. D. (1986, May). Psychotherapy: The transformation of meanings. *Harvard Medical School Mental Health Letter,* pp. 4-6.

Frankenburg, W. K., & Dodds, J. B. (1967). The Denver Developmental Screening Test. *Journal of Pediatrics, 71,* 181-191.

Franklin, N., & Tversky, B. (1990). Searching imagined environments. *Journal of Experimental Psychology: General, 119,* 63-76.

Fredericksen, C. H. (1975). Representing logical and semantic structure of knowledge acquired from discourse. *Cognitive Psychology, 7,* 371-458.

Freud, S. (1885). *Ueber coca.* Vienna: Mortiz Perles.

Freud, S. (1953). The interpretation of dreams. In J. Strachey (Ed.), *The standard edition of the complete psychological works* (Vols. 4 and 5). (Originally published, 1900). London: Hogarth Press.

Freud, S. (1953). Three essays on sexuality. In J. Strachey (Ed.), *The standard edition of the complete psychological works* (Vol. 7). (Originally published, 1905). London: Hogarth Press.

Freud S. (1963). Introductory lectures on psycho-analysis. In J. Strachey (Ed.), *The standard edition of the complete psychological works* (Vols. 15 and 16). (Originally published, 1917). London: Hogarth Press.

Freud, S. (1964). An outline of psychoanalysis. In J. Strachey (Ed.), *The standard edition of the complete psychological works* (Vol. 23). (Originally published, 1940). London: Hogarth Press.

Frezza, M., di Padova, C., Pozzato, G., Terpin, M., Baraona, E., & Lieber, C. S. High blood alcohol levels in women. The role of decreased gastric alcohol dehydrogenase activity and first-pass metabolism. *New England Journal of Medicine, 322,* 95-99.

Friedman, H. S., & Booth-Kewley, S. (1987). The "disease-prone personality": A meta-analytic view of the construct. *American Psychologist, 42,* 539-555.

Friedman, H. S., & Booth-Kewley, S. (1988). Validity of the type A construct: A reprise. *Psychological Bulletin, 104,* 381-384.

Friedman, M., & Rosenman, R. H. (1959). Association of specific overt behavior pattern with blood and cardiovascular findings. *Journal of the American Medical Association, 169,* 1286-1296.

Frijda, N. H. (1988). The laws of emotion. *American Psychologist, 43,* 349-358.

Frodi, A., Bridges, L., & Grolnick, W. (1985). Correlates of mastery-related behavior: A short-term longitudinal study of infants in their second year. *Child Development, 56,* 1291-1298.

Fromm, E. (1970). Age regression with unexpected reappearance of a repressed childhood language. *International Journal of Clinical and Experimental Hypnosis, 18,* 79-88.

Frost, B. J., & Nakayama, K. (1983). Single visual neurons code opposing motion independent of direction. *Science, 220,* 744-745.

Furchtgott, E. (1984). Replicate, again and again. *American Psychologist, 39,* 1315-1316.

Furman, W., & Bierman, K. L. (1983). Developmental changes in young children's conceptions of friendship. *Child Development, 54,* 549-556.

Gaes, G. G., Kalle, R. J., & Tedeschi, J. T. (1978). Impression management in the forced compliance situation. *Journal of Experimental Social Psychology, 14,* 493-510.

Gage, F. H., Bjorklund, A., Stenevi, U., Dunnett, S. B., & Kelly, P. A. T. (1984). Intrahippocampal septal grafts ameliorate learning impairments in aged rats. *Science, 225,* 533-536.

Gagne, R. M. (1984). Learning outcomes and their effects: useful categories of human performance. *American Psychologist, 39,* 377-385.

Galbraith, R. C. (1982). Sibling spacing and intellectual development: A closer look at the confluence models. *Developmental Psychology, 18,* 151-173.

Galin, D., Diamond, R., & Braff, D. (1977). Lateralization of conversion symptoms: More frequent on the left. *American Journal of Psychiatry, 134,* 578-580.

Gallup, G. (1975, October 13). The growing acceptance of racial integration. *San Francisco Chronicle.*

Garcia, J., & Koelling, R. A. (1966). Relation of cue to consequence in avoidance learning. *Psychonomic Science, 4,* 123-124.

Gardner, E. P., & Costanzo, R. M. (1981). Properties of kinesthetic neurons in somatosensory cortex of awake monkeys. *Brain Research, 214,* 301-319.

Gardner, H. (1983). *Frames of mind: The theory of multiple intelligences.* New York: Basic Books.

Gardner, M. (1983, August). Illusions of the third dimension. *Psychology Today,* pp. 62-67.

Gardner, R. A., & Gardner, B. T. (1969). Teaching sign language to a chimpanzee. *Science, 165,* 664-672.

Gartrell, N., Herman, J., Olarte, S., Feldstein, M., & Localio, R. (1986). Psychiatrist-patient sexual contact: Results of a national survey, I: Prevalence. *American Journal of Psychiatry, 143,* 1126-1137.

Garvey, M. J., Wesner, R., & Godes, M. (1988). Comparison of seasonal and non-seasonal affective disorders. *American Journal of Psychiatry, 145,* 100-102.

Gazzaniga, M. S. (1970). *The bisected brain.* New York: Academic Press.

Gazzaniga, M. S. (1983). Right hemisphere language following brain bisection: A 20-year perspective. *American Psychologist, 38,* 525-537.

Gazzaniga, M. S. (1985, November). The social brain. *Psychology Today,* pp. 29-38.

Gazzaniga, M. S. (1989). Organization of the human brain. *Science, 245,* 947-952.

Geldard, F. A., & Sherrick, C. E. (1986). Space, time and touch, *Scientific American, 255*(1), 92-95.

Genshaft, J. L., & Hirt, M. L. (1980). The effectiveness of self-instructional training to enhance math achievement in women. *Cognitive Therapy & Research, 4,* 91-97.

Gerbner, G., Gross, L., Morgan, M., & Signorielli, N. (1980). The "mainstreaming" of America: Violence profile No. 11. *Journal of Communication, 30*(3), 10-29.

Gerner, R. H., Catlin, D. H., Gorelick, D. A., Hui, K. K., & Li, C. H. (1980). Beta-endorphin intravenous infusion causes behavioral change in psychiatric inpatients. *Archives of General Psychiatry, 37,* 642-647.

Geron, E. (1982). History and recent position of sport psychology. In E. Geron (Ed.), *Handbook of sport psychology* (pp. 25-42). Tel Aviv: Wingate Inst.

Geschwind, N. (1979). Specializations of the human brain. *Scientific American, 241*(3), 180-199.

Geschwind, N., & Behan, P. (1982). Left-handedness: Association with immune disease, migraine, and developmental learning disorder. *Proceedings of the National Academy of Sciences of the United States of America—Biological Sciences, 79,* 5097-5100.

Ghiselli, E. E. (1966). *The validity of occupational aptitude tests.* New York: Wiley.

Gibson, E. J., & Walk, R. D. (1960). The "visual cliff." *Scientific American, 202*(4), 64-71.

Gibson, J. J. (1979). *The ecological approach to visual perception.* Boston: Houghton Mifflin.

Gillam, B. (1980). Geometrical illusions. *Scientific American, 242*(1), 102-111.

Gilligan, C. (1982). *In a different voice.* Cambridge, MA: Harvard University Press.

Gillin, J. (1948). Magical fright. *Psychiatry, 11,* 387-400.

Gladue, B. A., Green, R., & Hellman, R. E. (1984). Neuroendocrine response to estrogen and sexual orientation. *Science, 225,* 1496-1498.

Glasser, W. (1976). *Positive addiction.* New York: Harper & Row.

Glassman, J. N., Magulac, M., & Darko, D. F. (1987). Folie a famille: Shared paranoid disorder in a Vietnam veteran and his family. *American Journal of Psychiatry, 144,* 648-660.

Gleitman, L. R., & Wanner, E. (1984). Current issues in language learning. In M. H. Bornstein & M. E. Lamb (Eds.), *Developmental psychology: An advanced textbook* (pp. 181-240). Hillsdale, NJ: Erlbaum.

Glenberg, A. M. (1976). Monotonic and nonmonotonic lag effects in paired-associate and recognition memory paradigms. *Journal of Verbal Learning and Verbal Behavior, 15,* 1-16.

Glick, I. O., Weiss, R. S., & Parkes, C. M. (1974). *The first year of bereavement.* New York: Wiley-Interscience.

Glick, P. C. (1977). Updating the life cycle of the family. *Journal of Marriage and the Family, 39,* 5-13.

Glick, P. C. (1979). The future of the American family. *Current Population Reports* (Special Studies Series P-23, No. 78). Washington, DC: US Govt. Printing Office.

Glickstein, M. (1988). The discovery of the visual cortex. *Scientific American, 259*(3), 118-127.

Glickstein, M., & Gibson, A. R. (1976). Visual cells in the pons of the brain. *Scientific*

American, 235(5), 90-98.

Glucksberg, S., & Danks, J. H. (1968). Effects of discriminative labels and nonsense labels upon the availability of novel function. *Journal of Verbal Learning and Verbal Behavior, 7,* 72-76.

Godden, D. R., & Baddeley, A. D. (1975). Context-dependent memory in two natural environments: On land and underwater. *British Journal of Psychology, 66,* 325-331.

Goeders, N. E., & Smith, J. E. (1983). Cortical dopaminergic involvement in cocaine reinforcement. *Science, 221,* 773-775.

Goisman, R. M. (1985). The psychodynamics of prescribing in behavior therapy. American *Journal of Psychiatry, 142,* 675-679.

Gold, P. W., Goodwin, F. K., & Chrousos, G. P. (1988a). Clinical and biochemical manifestations of depression. Relation to the neurobiology of stress (1). *New England Journal of Medicine, 319,* 348-353.

Gold, P. W., Goodwin, F. K., & Chrousos, G. P. (1988b). Clinical and biochemical manifestations of depression. Relation to the neurobiology of stress (2). *New England Journal of Medicine, 319,* 413-420.

Goldberg, J., True, W. R., Eisen, S. A., & Henderson, W. G. (1990). A twin study of the effects of the Vietnam War on posttraumatic stress disorder. *Journal of the American Medical Association, 263,* 1227-1232.

Goldberg, L. R. & Werts, C. E. (1966). The reliability of clinicians' judgments: A multitrait-multimethod approach. *Journal of Consulting Psychology, 30,* 199-206.

Goldberg, L. W. (1978). Differential attribution of trait-descriptive terms to oneself as compared to well-liked, neutral, and disliked others: A psychometric analysis. *Journal of Personality & Social Psychology, 36,* 1012-1028.

Golden, M. (1964). Some effects of combining psychological tests on clinical inferences. *Journal of Consulting Psychology, 28,* 440-446.

Goldfried, M. R., Greenberg, L. S., & Marmar, C. (1990). Individual psychotherapy: Process and outcome. *Annual Review of Psychology, 41,* 659-688.

Goldman, W., & Lewis, P. (1977). Beautiful is good: Evidence that the physically attractive are more socially skillful. *Journal of Experimental Social Psychology, 13,* 125-130.

Goldsmith, H. H. (1983). Genetic influences on personality from infancy to adulthood. *Child Development, 54,* 331-355.

Goldsmith, H. H., Buss, A. H., Plomin, R., Rothbart, M. K., Thomas, A., Chess, S., Hinde, R. A., & McCall, R. B. (1987). Roundtable: What is temperament? Four approaches. *Child Development, 58,* 505-529.

Goldstein, A., & Hilgard, E. R. (1975). Lack of influence of the morphine antagonist naloxone on hypnotic analgesia. Proceedings of the National Academy of *Science, 72,* 2041-2043.

Goldstein, M. J. (1988). The family and psychopathology. *Annual Review of Psychology, 39,* 283-299.

Goleman, D. (1980, February). 1,528 little geniuses and how they grew. *Psychology Today,* pp. 28-53.

Gollob, H. F., & Dittes, J. E. (1965). Effects of manipulated self-esteem on persuasibility depending on threat and complexity of communication. *Journal of Personality & Social Psychology, 2,* 195-201.

Gomes-Schwartz, B., Hadley, S. W., & Strupp, H. H. (1978). Individual psychotherapy and behavior therapy. *Annual Review of Psychology, 29,* 435-471.

Gorenstein, E. E. (1984). Debating mental illness: Implications for science, medicine, and social policy. *American Psychologist, 39,* 50-56.

Gottesman, I. I., & Shields, J. (1972). *Schizophrenia and genetics.* New York: Academic Press.

Gottlieb, D. I. (1988). GABAergic neurons. *Scientific American, 258*(2), 82-89.

Gottlieb, G. (1983). The psychobiological approach to developmental issues. In M. M. Haith & J. J. Campos (Eds.), *Handbook of child psychology* (Vol. 2, pp. 1-26). New York: Wiley.

Gottman, J. M. (1983). How children become friends. Monographs of the Society for Research in *Child Development, 48*(3, Serial No. 201).

Gould, J. L. (1986) The locale map of honey bees: Do insects have cognitive maps? *Science, 232,* 861-863.

Gould, J. L., & Marler, P. (1987). Learning by instinct. *Scientific American, 256*(1), 74-85.

Gould, S. J. (1981). *The mismeasure of man.* New York: Norton.

Gracely, R. H., Dubner, R., Wolskee, P. J., & Deeter, W. R. (1983). Placebo and naloxone can alter post-surgical pain by separate mechanisms. *Nature, 306,* 264-265.

Graham, C. H., & Hsia, Y. (1958). Color defect and color theory. *Science, 127,* 675-682.

Gray, S. W., & Ruttle, K. (1980). The family-oriented home visiting program: A longitudinal study. *Genetic Psychology Monographs, 102,* 299-316.

Green, R. (1976). Atypical sex role behavior during childhood. In B. J. Sadock, H. I. Kaplan, & A. M. Freedman (Eds.), *The sexual experience* (pp. 196-205). Baltimore, MD: Williams & Wilkins.

Green, R. (1978). Sexual identity of 37 children raised by homosexual or transsexual parents. *American Journal of Psychiatry, 135,* 692-697.

Green, R. (1987). *The "sissy boy syndrome" and the development of homosexuality.* New Haven, CT: Yale University Press.

Greenberg, J. (1978a, November 11). Blind drawings: A new perspective. *Science News,* pp. 332-333.

Greenberg, J. (1978b, July 29). Adulthood comes of age. *Science News,* pp. 74-79.

Greenberg, J. (1980a, May 10). Ape talk: More than "pigeon" English? *Science News,* pp. 298-300.

Greenberg, J. (1980b, May 24). Stressing the immune system. *Science News,* p. 335.

Greenberg, J. (1981, June/July). An interview with David Rosenhan. *APA Monitor,* pp. 4-5.

Greenberg, Jerald. (1979). Group vs. individual equity judgments: Is there a polarization effect? *Journal of Experimental Social Psychology, 15,* 504-512.

Greene, D., Sternberg, B., & Lepper, M. R. (1976). Overjustification in a token economy. *Journal of Personality & Social Psychology, 34,* 1219-1234.

Greeno, J. G. (1978). Natures of problem-solving abilities. In W. K. Estes (Ed.), *Handbook of learning and cognitive processes: Vol. 5 Human information processing* (pp. 329-270). Hillsdale, NJ: Erlbaum.

Gregory, R. L. (1970). *The intelligent eye.* New York: McGraw-Hill.

Gretarsson, S. J., & Gelfand, D. M. (1988). Mothers' attributions regarding their children's social behavior and personality characteristics. *Developmental Psychology, 24,* 264-269.

Griffitt, W., & Veitch, R. (1971). Hot and crowded: Influence of population density and temperature on interpersonal affective behavior. *Journal of Personality & Social Psychology, 17,* 92-98.

Grinspoon, L. (1986, March). Suicide—Part II. *Harvard Medical School Mental Health Letter,* pp. 1-4.

Gross, A. E., & Crofton, C. (1977). What is good is beautiful. *Sociometry, 40,* 85-90.

Grossman, S. P. (1972). Neurophysiologic aspects: Extrahypothalamic factors in the regulation of food intake. *Advances in Psychosomatic Medicine, 7,* 49-72.

Grossman, S. P. (1975). Role of the hypothalamus in the regulation of food and water intake. *Psychological Review, 82,* 200-224.

Grotevant, M. D., Scarr, S., & Weinberg, R. A. (1975, March). *Intellectual development in family constellations with adopted and natural children: A test of the Zajonc and Markus model.* Paper presented at the meeting of the Society for Research in Child Development, New Orleans.

Grush, J. E. (1980). The impact of candidate expenditures, regionality, and prior outcomes on the 1976 Democratic Presidential primaries. *Journal of Personality & Social Psychology, 38,* 337-347.

Guharay, F., & Sachs, F. (1985). Mechanotransducer ion channels in chick skeletal muscle: The effects of extracellular pH. *Journal of Physiology, 363,* 119-134.

Guidotti, A., Baraldi, M., Schwartz, J. P., Toffano, G., & Costa, E. (1979). Molecular mechanism for the action of benzodiazepines on gabaergic transmission. In P. Krogsgaardlarsen, J. Scheelkruger, & H. Kofod (Eds.), *Gaba-neurotransmitters.* New York: Academic Press.

Guilford, J. P. (1982). Cognitive psychology's ambiguities: Some suggested remedies. *Psychological Review, 89,* 48-59.

Guilford, J. P. (1983). Transformation abilities or functions. *Journal of Creative Behavior, 17,* 75-83.

Gulevich, G., Dement, W., & Johnson, L. (1966). Psychiatric and EEG observations on a case of prolonged (264-hour) wakefulness. *Archives of General Psychiatry, 15,* 29-35.

Gzesh, S. M., & Surber, C. F. (1985). Visual perspective-taking skills in children. *Child Development, 56,* 1204-1213.

Haber, R. N. (1969). Eidetic images. *Scientific American, 220*(4), 36-44.

Haber, R. N. (1985). Perception: A one-hundred-year-perspective. In S. Koch & D. E. Leary, A *century of psychology as science* (pp. 250-281). New York: McGraw-Hill.

Hakel, M. D. (1986). Personnel selection and placement. *Annual Review of Psychology, 37,* 351-380.

Hall, E. (1983, June). A conversation with Erik Erikson. *Psychology Today,* pp. 22-30.

Hall, E. (1984, December). A sense of control. *Psychology Today,* pp. 38-45.

R-9

Hall, R. C. W., Stickney, S. K., LeCann, A. F., & Popkin, M. K. (1980). Physical illness manifesting as psychiatric disease. 2. Analysis of a state-hospital inpatient population. *Archives of General Psychiatry, 37,* 989-995.

Hall, S. S. (1985, May). Aplysia & hermissenda. *Science 85,* pp. 30-39.

Hamer, B. (1982, July/August). All in the family. *Science 82,* pp. 88-89.

Hammen, C., Gordon, D., Burge, D., Adrian, C., Jaenicke, C., & Hiroto, D. (1987). Maternal affective disorders, illness, and stress: Risk for children's psychopathology. *American Journal of Psychiatry, 144,* 736-741.

Hamner, W. C., & Hamner, E. P. (1976). Behavior modification on the bottom line. *Organizational Dynamics, 4*(4), 2-21.

Haney, W. (1981). Validity, vaudeville, and values: A short history of social concerns over standardized testing. *American Psychologist, 36,* 1021-1034.

Hanratty, M. A. (1969). *Imitation of film-mediated aggression against live and inanimate victims.* Unpublished MA thesis, Vanderbilt University, Nashville, Tennessee.

Hanratty, M. A., O'Neal, E., & Sulzer, J. L. (1972). Effect of frustration upon imitation of aggression. *Journal of Personality & Social Psychology, 21,* 30-34.

Hargreaves, W. A., Shumway, M., Knutsen, E. J., Weinstein, A., & Senter, N. (1987). Effects of the Jamison-Farabee consent decree: Due process protection for involuntary psychiatric patients treated with psychoactive medication. *American Journal of Psychiatry, 144,* 188-192.

Harkey, J., Miles, D. L., & Rushing, W. A. (1976). The relation between social class and functional status: A new look at the drift hypothesis. *Journal of Health and Social Behavior, 17,* 194-204.

Harlow, H. F. (1950). Learning and satiation of response in intrinsically motivated complex puzzle performance in monkeys. *Journal of Comparative and Physiological Psychology, 43,* 289-294. Harlow, H. F. (1958). The nature of love. *American Psychologist, 13,* 673-685.

Harlow, H. F., & Zimmerman, R. R. (1959). Affectional responses in the infant monkey. *Science, 130,* 421-432.

Harlow, J. M. (1868). Recovery from the passage of an iron bar through the head. *Publ. Mass. Med. Soc., 2,* 327.

Harris, B. (1979). Whatever happened to Little Albert? *American Psychologist, 34,* 151-160.

Harris, J. A., Jackson, C. M., Patterson, D. G., & Scammon, R. E. (Eds.). (1930). *The measurement of man.* Minneapolis: Univ. of Minnesota Press.

Harris, R. A., & Allan, A. M. (1985). Functional coupling of gamma-aminobutyric acid receptors to chloride channels in brain membranes. *Science, 228,* 1108-1110.

Harrow, M., Carone, B. J., & Westermeyer, J. F. (1985). The course of psychosis in early phases of schizophrenia. *American Journal of Psychiatry, 142,* 702-707.

Harrow, M., & Quinlan, D. (1977). Is disordered thinking unique to schizophrenia? *Archives of General Psychiatry, 34,* 15-21.

Harrower, M. (1976, July). Were Hitler's henchmen mad? *Psychology Today,* pp. 76-80.

Hart, J., Berndt, R. S., & Caramazza, A. (1987). Category-specific naming deficit following cerebral infarction. *Nature, 316,* 439-440.

Hart, L. M., & Goldin-Meadow, S. (1984). The child as a nonegocentric art critic. *Child Development, 55,* 2122-2129.

Hartley, E. L. (1946). *Problems in prejudice.* New York: Kings Crown.

Hartup, W. W. (1970). Peer interaction and social organization. In P. H. Mussen (Ed.), *Carmichael's manual of child psychology* (3rd ed., Vol. 1, pp. 361-456). New York: Wiley.

Hartup, W. W. (1983). Peer relations. In P. H. Mussen (Ed.), *Handbook of child psychology* (4th ed., Vol. IV, pp. 103-196). New York: Wiley.

Hartup, W. W. (1984). The peer context in middle childhood. In W. A. Collins (Ed.), *Development during middle childhood: The years from six to twelve* (pp. 240-282). Washington, DC: National Academy Press.

Harvey, J. H., & Weary, G. (1984). Current issues in attribution theory and research. *Annual Review of Psychology, 35,* 427-459.

Hathaway, S. R., & McKinley, J. C. (1940). A multiphasic personality schedule (Minnesota): I. Construction of the schedule. *Journal of Psychology, 10,* 249-254.

Havighurst, R. J. (1972). *Developmental tasks and education* (3rd ed.). New York: David McKay.

Haviland, J. M., & Lelwica, M. (1987). The induced affect response: 10-week-old infants' responses to three emotion expressions. *Developmental Psychology, 23,* 97-104.

Hawkins, D. R. (1986, March). The importance of dreams. *Harvard Medical School Mental Health Letter,* pp. 5-7.

Hayashi, S., & Kimura, T. (1976). Sexual behavior of the naive male mouse as affected by the presence of a male and female performing mating behavior. *Physiology & Behavior, 17,* 807-810.

Hayes, K. J., & Hayes, C. (1952). Imitation in a home-raised chimpanzee. *Journal of Comparative and Physiological Psychology, 45,* 450-459.

Hayes, S. C., Nelson, R. O., & Jarrett, R. B. (1987). The treatment utility of assessment: A functional approach to evaluating assessment quality. *American Psychologist, 42,* 963-974.

Hayflick, L. (1980). The cell biology of human aging. *Scientific American, 242*(1), 58-65.

Hebb, D. O. (1949). *The organization of behavior.* New York: Wiley.

Hechinger, N. (1981, March). Seeing without eyes. *Science 81,* pp. 38-43.

Hefez, A., Metz, L., & Lavie, P. (1987). Long-term effects of extreme situational stress on sleep and dreaming. *American Journal of Psychiatry, 144,* 344-347.

Heider, F. (1958). *The psychology of interpersonal relations.* New York: Wiley.

Heiman, J. R. (1977). A psychophysiological exploration of sexual arousal patterns in females and males. *Psychophysiology, 14,* 266-274.

Heiman, J. R. (1979). Continuing revolutions in sex research. In Z. Rubin & E. B. McNeil, *The psychology of being human* (brief update edition). New York: Harper & Row.

Heit, G., Smith, M. E., & Halgren, E. (1988). Neural encoding of individual words and faces by the human hippocampus and amygdala. *Nature, 333,* 773-775.

Heller, F. A., & Clark, A. W. (1976). Personnel and human resources development. *Annual Review of Psychology, 27,* 405-435.

Helmholtz, H. von (1924). *Treatise on physiological optics* (Vol. II) (J. P. Southall, Ed. and trans., from the 3rd German ed). Rochester, NY: Optical Society of America. (originally published, 1866).

Helson, R., & Crutchfield, R. S. (1970). Mathematicians: The creative researcher and average Ph.D. *Journal of Consulting and Clinical Psychology, 34,* 250-257.

Henle, M. (1985). Rediscovering Gestalt psychology. In S. Koch & D. E. Leary, *A century of psychology as science* (pp. 100-120). New York: McGraw-Hill.

Henn, F. A. (1989). Psychosurgery. In H. I. Kaplan & B. J. Sadock (Eds.), *Comprehensive textbook of psychiatry/v* (pp. 1679-1680). Baltimore, MD: Williams & Wilkins.

Henry, R. A., & Hulin, C. L. (1987). Stability of skilled performance across time: Some generalizations and limitations on utilities. *Journal of Applied Psychology, 72,* 457-462.

Herbert, W. (1982a, May 8). TMI: Uncertainty is causing chronic stress. *Science News,* p. 308.

Herbert, W. (1982b, May 29). The three brains of Eve: EEG data. *Science News,* p. 356.

Herbert, W. (1983a, December 10). Remembrance of things partly. *Science News,* pp. 378-381.

Herbert, W. (1983b, June 25). Schizophrenia clues in angel dust. *Science News,* p. 407.

Herbert, W. (1983c, October 8). MMPI: Redefining normality for modern times. *Science News,* p. 228.

Herbert, W. (1985, March). Cyranoids: Artificial selves. *Psychology Today,* pp. 6-7.

Herbert, W. (1987, April). Science at a snail's pace. *Psychology Today,* p. 80.

Herrnstein, R. J. (1990). Rational choice theory: Necessary but not sufficient. *American Psychologist, 45,* 356-367.

Herz, M. I., Szymanski, H. V., & Simon, J. C. (1982). Intermittent medication for stable schizophrenic outpatients: An alternative to maintenance medication. *American Journal of Psychiatry, 139,* 918-922.

Hess, E. H. (1970). Ethology and developmental psychology. In P. H. Mussen (Ed.), *Carmichael's manual of child psychology* (Vol. 1, 3rd ed.). New York: Wiley.

Hetherington, E. M. (1979). Divorce: A child's perspective. *American Psychologist, 34,* 851-858.

Hilgard, E. R. (1977). *Divided consciousness: Multiple controls in human thought and action.* New York: Wiley-Interscience.

Hilgard, E. R. (1980). Consciousness in contemporary psychology. *Annual Review of Psychology, 31,* 1-26.

Hilgard, E. R., & Hilgard, J. R. (1975). *Hypnosis in the relief of pain.* Los Altos, CA: William Kaufmann.

Hilgard, E. R., & Hilgard, J. R. (1983). *Hypnosis in the relief of pain.* Los Altos, CA: Kaufmann.

Hill, C. T., Rubin, Z., & Peplau, L. A. (1976). Breakups before marriage: The end of 103 affairs. *Journal of Social Issues, 32*(1), 147-168.

Hines, M. (1982). Prenatal gonadal hormones and sex differences in human behavior. *Psychological Bulletin, 92,* 56-80.

Hobson, J. A., & McCarley, R. W. (1977). The brain as a dream state generator: An activation-synthesis hypothesis of the dream process. *The American Journal of Psychiatry, 134,* 1335-1348.

Hodgkins, J. (1962). Influence of age on the speed of reaction and movement in females. *Journal of Gerontology, 17,* 385-389.

Hoffman, L. W. (1979). Maternal employment: 1979. *American Psychologist, 34,* 859-

865.

Hogan, R. (1975). Theoretical egocentrism and the problem of compliance. *American Psychologist*, 30, 533-540.

Hogrebe, M. C. (1987). Gender differences in mathematics. *American Psychologist*, 42, 265-266.

Holden, C. (1986a). Amazing Randi one of 25 MacArthur Genius winners. *Science*, 233, 517.

Holden, C. (1986b). Researchers grapple with problems of updating classic psychological test. *Science*, 233, 1249-1251.

Holden, C. (1986c). Giving mental illness its research due. *Science*, 232, 1084-1085.

Holden, C. (1987a). NIMH finds a case of "serious misconduct." *Science*, 235, 1566-1567.

Holden, C. (1987b). Is alcoholism treatment effective? *Science*, 236, 20-22.

Holden, C. (1987c). Alcohol consumption down, research up. *Science*, 236, 773.

Holden, C. (1987d). A top priority at NIMH. *Science*, 235, 431.

Holden, C. (1987e). Female math anxiety on the wane. *Science*, 236, 660-661.

Hollander, E. P., & Julian, J. W. (1970). Studies in leader legitimacy, influence, and innovation. In L. Berkowitz (Ed.), *Advances in experimental social psychology* (Vol. 5). New York: Academic Press.

Hollandsworth, J. G., Jr., Kazelskis, R., Stevens, J., & Dressel, M. E. (1979). Relative contributions of verbal, articulative, and nonverbal communication to employment decisions in the job interview setting. *Personnel psychology*, 32, 359-367.

Hollon, S., & Beck, A. T. (1978). Psychotherapy and drug therapy: Comparisons and combinations. In S. L. Garfield & A. E. Bergin (Eds.), *Handbook of psychotherapy and behavior change*. New York: Wiley.

Holmes, C. B. (1987). Comment on Szasz's view of suicide prevention. *American Psychologist*, 42, 881-882.

Holmes, D. S. (1984). Meditation and somatic arousal reduction: A review of the experimental evidence. *American Psychologist*, 39, 1-10.

Holmes, T. H., & Rahe, R. H. (1967). The social readjustment rating scale. *Journal of Psychosomatic Research*, 11, 213-218.

Homans, G. C. (1961). *Social behavior: Its elementary forms*. New York: Harcourt Brace & World.

Hong, L. K. (1978). Risky shift and cautious shift: Some direct evidence on the cultural-value theory. *Social Psychology*, 41, 342-346.

Honts, C. R., Hodes, R. L., & Raskin, D. C. (1985). Effects of physical countermeasures on the physiological detection of deception. *Journal of Applied Psychology*, 70, 177-187.

Hook, S. (Ed.). (1960). *Psychoanalysis, scientific method and philosophy*. New York: Grove.

Hopson, J. L. (1986, June). The unraveling of insomnia. *Psychology Today*, pp. 42-49.

Horn, J. (1986). Intellectual ability concepts. In R. J. Sternberg (Ed.), *Advances in the psychology of human intelligence* (Vol. 3, pp. 35-77). Hillsdale, NJ: Erlbaum.

Horn, J. C. (1985, November). All carrot, no stick. *Psychology Today*, p. 19.

Horn, J. L., & Donaldson, G. Y. (1980). Cognitive development in adulthood. In O. G. Brim, Jr. & J. Kagan (Eds.), *Constancy and change in human development* (pp. 445-529). Cambridge, MA: Harvard University Press.

Horney, K. (1939). *New ways in psychoanalysis*. New York: Norton.

Horowitz, M. J., Marmar, C., Weiss, D. S., DeWitt, K. N., & Rosenbaum, R. (1984). Brief psychotherapy of bereavement reactions. *Archives of General Psychiatry*, 41, 438-448.

Hosobuchi, Y., Rossier, J., Bloom, F. E., & Guillemin, R. (1979). Stimulation of human periaqueductal gray for pain relief increases immunoreactive beta-endorphin in ventricular fluid. *Science*, 203, 279-281.

House, J. S., Landis, K. R., & Umberson, D. (1988). Social relationships and health. *Science*, 241, 540-545.

House, R. J., & Singh, J. V. (1987). Organizational behavior: Some new directions for I/O psychology. *Annual Review of Psychology*, 38, 669-718.

Houston, J. P., Schneider, N. G., & Jarvik, M. E. (1978). Effects of smoking on free recall and organization. *American Journal of Psychiatry*, 135, 220-222.

Hovland, C. I., Lumsdaine, A. A., & Sheffield, F. D. (1949). *Experiments on mass communication*. Princeton, NJ: Princeton Univ. Press.

Howes, C., & Olenick, M. (1986). Family and child care influences on toddler's compliance. *Child Development*, 57, 202-216.

Hsu, F., Anantharaman, T., Campbell, M., & Nowatzyk, A. (1990). A grandmaster chess machine. *Scientific American*, 263(4), 44-50.

Hubel, D. H. (1979). The brain. *Scientific American*, 241(3), 44-53.

Hubel, D. H., & Wiesel, T. N. (1979). Brain mechanisms of vision. *Scientific American*, 241(3), 150-162.

Hudson, A., & Clunies-Ross, G. (1984). A study of the integration of children with

intellectual handicaps into regular schools. *Australia & New Zealand Journal of Developmental Disabilities*, 10(3), 165-177.

Hudspeth, A. J. (1985). The cellular basis of hearing: The biophysics of hair cells. *Science*, 230, 745-752.

Hughes, J. R., & Hatsukami, D. (1986). Signs and symptoms of tobacco withdrawal. *Archives of General Psychiatry*, 43, 289-294.

Hull, C. L. (1943). *Principles of behavior*. New York: Appleton-Century-Crofts.

Humphreys, L. G., Rich, S. A., & Davey, T. C. (1985). A Piagetian test of general intelligence. *Developmental Psychology*, 21, 872-877.

Huston, A. C. (1983). Sex-typing. In P. H. Mussen (Ed.), *Handbook of child psychology* (4th ed., Vol. 4, pp. 388-467). New York: Wiley.

Hutt, S. J., Hutt, C., Lenard, H. G., Bernuth, H. V., & Muntjewerff, W. J. (1968). Auditory responsivity in the human neonate. *Nature*, 218(5144), 888-890.

Huxley, A. (1954). *The doors of perception*. New York: Harper & Row.

Hyde, J. S., Fennema, E., & Lamon, S. J. (1990). Gender differences in mathematics performance: A meta-analysis. *Psychological Bulletin*, 107, 139-155.

Hyde, J. S., & Linn, M. C. (1988). Are there sex differences in verbal abilities? A meta-analysis. *Psychological Bulletin*, 104, 53-69.

Hyland, M. E. (1987). Control theory interpretation of psychological mechanisms of depression: Comparison and integration of several theories. *Psychological Bulletin*, 102, 109-121.

Ilgen, D. R., & Klein, H. J. (1989). Organizational behavior. *Annual Review of Psychology*, 40, 327-351.

Imperato-McGinley, J., Peterson, R. E., Gautier, T., & Sturla, E. (1979). Androgens and the evolution of male-gender identity among male pseudohermaphrodites with 5-reductase deficiency. *New England Journal of Medicine*, 300, 1233-1237.

Inhelder, B., & Piaget, J. (1958). *The growth of logical thinking from childhood to adolescence*. New York: Basic Books.

IQ myth, The (1975). New York: CBS News.

Irwin, M., Daniels, M., Bloom, E. T., Smith, T. L., & Weiner, H. (1987). Life events, depressive symptoms, and immune function. *American Journal of Psychiatry*, 144, 437-441.

Ito, M. (1984). *The cerebellum and neural control*. New York: Raven.

Izard, C. (1971). *The face of emotion*. New York: Appleton Century Crofts.

Jacklin, C. N. (1989). Female and male: Issues of gender. *American Psychologist*, 44, 127-133.

Jacklin, C. N., & Maccoby, E. E. (1983). Issues of gender differentiation in normal development. In M. D. Levine, W. B. Carey, A. C. Crocker, & R. T. Gross (Eds.), *Developmental-behavioral pediatrics*. Philadelphia: W. B. Saunders.

Jackson, C. M. (1929). Some aspects of form and growth. In W. J. Robbins, S. Brody, A. F. Hogan, C. M. Jackson, & C. W. Greed (Eds.), *Growth*. New Haven, CT: Yale University Press.

Jackson, D. N., & Paunonen, S. V. (1980). Personality structure and assessment. *Annual Review of Psychology*, 31, 503-551.

Jackson, P. W., & Messick, D. (1968). Creativity. In P. London & D. Rosenhan (Eds.), *Foundations of abnormal psychology*. New York: Holt.

Jacobs, J. (1971). *Adolescent suicide*. New York: Wiley.

Jacobson, E. (1938). *Progressive relaxation* (2nd ed.). Chicago: Univ. of Chicago Press.

Jacobson, J. L., & Wille, D. E. (1984). Influence of attachment and separation experience on separation distress at 18 months. *Developmental Psychology*, 20, 477-484.

Jaffe, C. M. (1977). First-degree atrioventricular block during lithium carbonate treatment. *American Journal of Psychiatry*, 134, 88-89.

James, W. (1890). *The principles of psychology*. New York: Henry Holt and Company.

Jameson, D., & Hurvich, L. M. (1989). Essay concerning color constancy. *Annual Review of Psychology*, 40, 1-22.

Jampala, V. C., Sierles, F. S., & Taylor, M. A. (1986). Consumers' views of DSM-III: Attitudes and practices of U. S. psychiatrists and 1984 graduating psychiatric residents. *American Journal of Psychiatry*, 143, 148-153.

Janicak, P. G., Davis, J. M., Gibbons, R. D., Ericksen, S., Chang, S., & Gallagher, P. (1985). Efficacy of ECT: A meta-analysis. *American Journal of Psychiatry*, 142, 297-302.

Janik, A., & Toulmin, S. (1973). *Wittgenstein's Vienna*. New York: Simon and Schuster.

Janis, I. L., & Feshbach, S. (1953). Effects of fear-arousing communications. *Journal of Abnormal and Social Psychology*, 48, 78-92.

Janis, I. L., & King, B. T. (1954). The influence of role playing on opinion change.

R-11

Journal of Abnormal and Social Psychology, 49, 211-218.

Janowitz, H. D., & Grossman, M. I. (1949). Some factors affecting the food intake of normal dogs and dogs with esophagostomy and gastric fistula. *American Journal of Physiology, 159,* 143-148.

Jeffery, R. W. (1989). Risk behaviors and health: Contrasting individual and population perspectives. *American Psychologist, 44,* 1194-1202.

Jemerin, J. M., & Boyce, W. T. (1990). Psychobiological differences in childhood stress response: II. Cardiovascular markers of vulnerability. *Journal of Developmental & Behavioral Pediatrics, 11,* 140-150.

Jensen, A. R. (1969). How much can we boost IQ and scholastic achievement? *Harvard Educational Review, 39,* 1-123.

Joffe, L. S. (1980). *The relation between mother-infant attachment and compliance with maternal commands and prohibitions.* Unpublished doctoral dissertation, University of Minnesota.

Johansson, G., von Hofsten, C., & Jansson, G. (1980). Event perception. *Annual Review of Psychology, 31,* 27-63.

John, E. R. (1967). Mechanisms of Memory. New York: Academic Press.

Johns, G., & Nicholson, N. (1982). The meaning of absence: New strategies for theory and research. In B. M. Staw & L. L. Cummings (Eds.), *Research in organizational behavior.* Greenwich, Conn.: JAI Press.

Johnson, D. W., & Johnson, R. T. (1975). *Learning together and alone: Cooperation, competition, and individualization.* Englewood Cliffs, NJ: Prentice-Hall.

Johnson, L. C., & MacLeod, W. L. (1973). Sleep and wake behavior during gradual sleep reduction. *Perceptual and Motor Skills, 36,* 87-97.

Jones, E. E., & Sigall, H. (1971). The bogus pipeline: A new paradigm for measuring affect and attitude. *Psychological Bulletin, 76,* 349-364.

Jones, E. E., Bell, L., & Aronson, E. (1972). The reciprocation of attraction from similar and dissimilar others. In C. McClintock (Ed.), *Experimental social psychology.* New York: Holt, Rinehart & Winston.

Jones, H. S., & Oswald, I. (1968). Two cases of healthy insomnia. *Electroencephalography & Clinical Neurophysiology, 24,* 378-380.

Jones, J. W., & Bogat, G. A. (1978). Air pollution and human aggression. *Psychological Reports, 43,* 721-722.

Jones, R. (1978). The third wave. In A. Pines & C. Maslach (Eds.), *Experiencing social psychology.* New York: Knopf.

Jones, S. L., Nation, J. R., & Massad, P. (1977). Immunization against learned helplessness in man. *Journal of Abnormal Psychology, 86,* 75-83.

Josse, D., Leonard, M., Lezine, I., Robinot, F., & Rouchouse, J. (1973). Evolution de la communication entre l'enfant de 4 a 9 mois et un adulte. *Enfance, 3*(4), 175-206.

Jourard, S. M. (1967). Experimenter-subject dialogue: A paradigm for a humanistic science of psychology. In J. Bugental (Ed.), *Challenges of humanistic psychology.* New York: McGraw-Hill.

Jung, C. G. (1933). *Psychological types.* New York: Harcourt Brace & World.

Jung, C. G. (1959). Mandalas. In *Collected works* (Vol. 14). Princeton: Princeton University Press. (Originally published in 1955).

Jung, C. G. (1959). The concept of the collective unconscious. In *Collected works* (Vol. 9, Part I). Princeton: Princeton University Press. (Originally published in 1936).

Kagan, J. (1966). Reflection-impulsivity: The generality and dynamics of conceptual tempo. *Journal of Abnormal Psychology, 71,* 17-24.

Kagan, J. (1973). What is intelligence? *Social Policy, 4*(1), 88-94.

Kagan, S., & Madsen, M. C. (1971). Cooperation and competition of Mexican, Mexican-American, and Anglo-American children of two ages and four instructional sets. *Developmental Psychology, 5,* 32-39.

Kahn, R. J., McNair, D. M., Lipman, R. S., Covi, L., Rickles, K., Downing, R., Fisher, S., & Frankenthaler, L. M. (1986). Imipramine and chlordiazepoxide in depressive and anxiety disorders: II. Efficacy in anxious outpatients. *Archives of General Psychiatry, 43,* 79-85.

Kales, A., Caldwell, A. B., Preston, T. A., Healey, S., & Kales, J. D. (1976). Personality patterns in insomnia: Theoretical implications. *Archives of General Psychiatry, 33,* 1128-1134.

Kales, A., Tan, T. L., Kollar, E. J., Naitoh, P., Preston, T. A., & Malmstrom, E. J. (1970). Sleep patterns following 205 hr of sleep deprivation. *Psychosomatic Medicine, 32,* 189-200.

Kalil, R. E. (1989). Synapse formation in the developing brain. *Scientific American, 261*(6), 76-85.

Kanner, A. D., Coyne, J. C., Schaefer, C., & Lazarus, R. S. (1981). Comparison of two modes of stress measurement: Daily hassles and uplifts versus major life events. *Journal of Behavioral Medicine, 4,* 1-39.

Kaplan, M. (1983). A woman's view of DSM-III. *American Psychologist, 38,* 786-792.

Kaplan, M. F., & Schwartz, S. (Eds.) (1977). *Judgment and decision processes in applied settings.* New York: Academic Press.

Karlen, N., & Burgower, B. (1985, January 7). Dumping the mentally ill. *Newsweek,* p. 17.

Karnovsky, M. L. (1986). Muramyl peptides in mammalian tissues and their effects at the cellular level. *Federation Proceedings, 45,* 2556-2560.

Kashani, J. H., & Carlson, G. A. (1987). Seriously depressed preschoolers. *American Journal of Psychiatry, 144,* 348-350.

Kassarjian, H. H. (1982). Consumer psychology. *Annual Review of Psychology, 33,* 619-649.

Kastenbaum, R., & Costa, P. T. (1977). Psychological perspectives on death. In M. R. Rosenzweig, & L. W. Porter (Eds.), *Annual review of psychology* (Vol. 28). Palo Alto, CA: Annual Reviews, Inc.

Kastenbaum, R., & Durkee, N. (1964). Young people view old age. In R. Kastenbaum (Ed.), *New thoughts on old age* (pp. 237-250. New York: Springer Publishing.

Katz, R. (1982). The effects of group longevity on project communication and performance. *Administrative Science Quarterly, 27,* 81-104.

Katzell, R. A., & Thompson, D. E. (1990). Work motivation: Theory and practice. *American Psychologist, 45,* 144-153.

Kaufman, L., & Rock, I. (1962). The moon illusion, I. *Science, 136,* 953-961.

Kaylor, J. A., King, D. W., & King, L. A. (1987). Psychological effects of military service in Vietnam: A meta-analysis. *Psychological Bulletin, 102,* 257-271.

Keller, H., & Scholmerich, A. (1987). Infant vocalizations and parental reactions during the first 4 months of life. *Developmental Psychology, 23,* 62-67.

Kellermann, A. L., & Reay, D. T. (1986). Protection or peril? An analysis of firearm-related deaths in the home. *New England Journal of Medicine, 314,* 1557-1560.

Kelley, H. H. (1983). Love and commitment. In H. H. Kelley (Ed.), *Close relationships* (pp. 265-314). New York: W. H. Freeman.

Kelso, S. R., & Brown, T. H. (1986). Differential conditioning of associative synaptic enhancement in hippocampal brain slices. *Science, 232,* 85-87.

Kendell, R. E. (1970). Relationship between aggression and depression. *Archives of General Psychiatry, 22,* 308-318.

Kendler, K. S., Gruenberg, A. M., & Tsuang, M. T. (1985). Subtype stability in schizophrenia. *American Journal of Psychiatry, 142,* 827-832.

Kendler, K. S., Gruenberg, A. M., & Tsuang, M. T. (1988). A family study of the subtypes of schizophrenia. *American Journal of Psychiatry, 145,* 57-62.

Kennell, J. H., Jerauld, R., Wolfe, H., Chesler, D., Kreger, N. C., McAlpine, W., Steffa, N., & Klaus, M. H. (1974). Maternal behavior one year after early and extended post-partum contact. *Developmental Medicine and Child Neurology, 16,* 172-179.

Kennell, J. H., & Klaus, M. H. (1984). Mother-infant bonding: Weighing the evidence. *Developmental Review, 4,* 275-282.

Kennell, J. H., Voos, D. K., & Klaus, M. H. (1979). Parent-infant bonding. In J. Osofsky (Ed.), *Handbook of infant development* (pp. 786-798). New York: Wiley Interscience.

Kenrick, D. T., & Funder, D. C. (1988). Profiting from controversy: Lessons from the person- situation debate. *American Psychologist, 43,* 23-34.

Kerckhoff, A. C., & Davis, K. E. (1962). Value consensus and need complementarity in mate selection. *American Sociological Review, 27,* 295-303.

Kety, S. S., Rosenthal, D., Wender, P. H., Schulsinger, F., & Jacobsen, B. (1978). The biologic and adoptive families of adopted individuals who become schizophrenic: Prevalence of mental illness and other characteristics. In L. C. Wynne, R. L. Cromwell, & S. Matthysse (Eds.), *The nature of schizophrenia: New approaches to research and treatment.* New York: Wiley.

Khan, L. M. L., & James, S. L. (1983). Grammatical morpheme development in three language disordered children. *Journal of Childhood Communication Disorders, 6,* 85-100.

Kiesler, C. A. (1982a). Mental hospitals and alternative care: Noninstitutionalization as potential public policy for mental patients. *American Psychologist, 37,* 349-360.

Kiesler, C. A. (1982b). Public and professional myths about mental hospitalization. *American Psychologist, 37,* 1323-1339.

Kiesler, S., & Baral, R. (1970). The search for a romantic partner: The effects of self-esteem and physical attractiveness on romantic behavior. In K. Gergen & D. Marlowe (Eds.), *Personality and social behavior.* Reading, Mass.: Addison-Wesley.

Kiester, E., Jr. (1984, July). The playing fields of the mind. *Psychology Today,* pp. 18-24.

Kihlstrom, J. F. (1985). Hypnosis. *Annual Review of Psychology, 36,* 385-418.

Kihlstrom, J. F. (1987). The cognitive unconscious. *Science, 237,* 1445-1452.

Kilham, W., & Mann, L. (1974). Level of destructive obedience as a function of transmitter and executant roles in the Milgram obedience paradigm. *Journal of*

Personality & Social Psychology, 29, 696-702.

Kimura, D. (1985, November). Male brain, female brain: The hidden difference. *Psychology Today,* pp. 50-58.

Kintsch, W. (1974). *The representation of meaning in memory.* Hillsdale, NJ: Lawrence Erlbaum.

Kirk-Smith, M., Booth, D. A., Carroll, D., & Davies, P. (1978). Human social attitudes affected by androstenol. *Research Communications in Psychology, Psychiatry and Behavior, 3,* 379-384.

Klaus, M. H., & Kennell, J. H. (1976). *Maternal-infant bonding.* St. Louis: Mosby.

Klaus, M. H., Jerauld, R., Kreger, N. C., McAlpine, W., Steffa, M., & Kennell, J. H. (1972). Maternal attachment: Importance of the first postpartum days. *New England Journal of Medicine, 286,* 460-463.

Klein, D. N., Taylor, E. B., Harding, K., & Dickstein, S. (1988). Double depression and episodic major depression: Demographic, clinical, familial, personality, and socioenvironmental characteristics and short-term outcome. *American Journal of Psychiatry, 145,* 1226-1231.

Klein, M., Coles, M. G. H., & Donchin, E. (1984). People with absolute pitch process tones without producing a P300. *Science, 223,* 1306-1309.

Kleinginna, P. R., Jr., & Kleinginna, A. M. (1981). A categorized list of motivation definitions, with a suggestion for a consensual definition. *Motivation and Emotion, 5,* 263-291.

Kleinginna, P. R., Jr., & Kleinginna, A. M. (1988). Current trends toward convergence of the behavioristic, functional, and cognitive perspectives in experimental psychology. *The Psychological Record, 38,* 369-392.

Kleinke, C. L. (1977). Effects of dress on compliance to requests in a field setting. *Journal of Social Psychology, 101,* 223-224.

Kleinmuntz, B., & Szucko, J. J. (1984). Lie detection in ancient and modern times: A call for contemporary scientific study. *American Psychologist, 39,* 766-776.

Klinger, E. (1987, October). The power of daydreams. *Psychology Today,* pp. 37-44.

Klinnert, M. D., Emde, R. N., Butterfield, P., & Campos, J. J. (1986). Social referencing: The infant's use of emotional signals from a friendly adult with mother present. *Developmental Psychology, 22,* 427-432.

Koch, H. L. (1955). The relation of certain family constellation characteristics and the attitudes of children toward adults. *Child Development, 26,* 13-40.

Kogan, N., & Pankove, E. (1972). Creative ability over a five-year span. *Child Development, 43,* 427-442.

Kogan, N., & Shelton, F. C. (1962). Beliefs about "old people": A comparative study of older and younger samples. *Journal of Genetic Psychology, 100,* 93-111.

Kohlberg, L. (1963). The development of children's orientations toward a moral order: I. Sequence in the development of moral thought. *Vita Humana, 6,* 11-33.

Kohlberg, L. (1966). A cognitive-developmental analysis of children's sex-role concepts and attitudes. In E. E. Maccoby (Ed.), *The development of sex differences* (pp. 81-173). Stanford, Calif.: Stanford Univ. Press.

Kohlberg, L. (1971). From is to ought: How to commit the naturalistic fallacy and get away with it in the study of moral development. In T. Mischel (Ed.), *Cognitive development and genetic epistemology.* New York: Academic Press.

Kohler, W. (1925). Gestaltprobleme und Anfange einer Gestalttheorie. Jahresbericht u. d. ges. Physiol., 3, 512-539. (Translated in Ellis, W. D., *A source book of gestalt psychology.* New York: Harcourt, Brace, & World, 1938).

Kohler, W. (1927). *The mentality of apes.* London: Routledge & Kegan Paul.

Kolata, G. (1983a). Cell surgery to reconnect nerves. *Science, 221,* 538-539.

Kolata, G. (1983b). Brain-grafting work shows promise. *Science, 221,* 1277.

Kolata, G. (1983c). Math genius may have hormonal basis. *Science, 222,* 1312.

Kolata, G. (1984). Studying learning in the womb. *Science, 225,* 302-303.

Kolata, G. (1987a). How to ask about sex and get honest answers. *Science, 236,* 382.

Kolata, G. (1987b). Associations or rules in learning language? *Science, 237,* 133-134.

Kolata, G. (1987c). Manic-depression gene tied to chromosome 11. *Science, 235,* 1139-1140.

Kolata, G. (1987d). Panel urges dementia be diagnosed with care. *Science, 237,* 725.

Kolb, B. (1989). Brain development, plasticity, and behavior. *American Psychologist, 44,* 1203-1212.

Kolb, H., Nelson, R., & Mariani, A. (1981). Amacrine cells, bipolar cells and ganglion cells of the cat retina: A Golgi study. *Vision Research, 21,* 1081-1114.

Kolb, L. C. (1973). *Modern clinical psychiatry* (8th ed.). Philadelphia: W. B. Saunders.

Koller, M. R. (1953). Residential and occupational propinquity. In R. F. Winch & R. McGinnis (Eds.), *Marriage and the family.* New York: Holt, Rinehart & Winston.

Komaki, J., Barwick, K. D., & Scott, L. R. (1978). A behavioral approach to occupational safety: Pinpointing and reinforcing safe performance in a food manufacturing plant. *Journal of Applied Psychology, 63,* 434-445.

Komaki, J., Heinzmann, A. T., & Lawson, L. (1980). Effect of training and feedback: Component analysis of a behavioral safety program. *Journal of Applied Psychology,*

65, 261-270.

Konopasky, R. J., & Telegdy, G. A. (1977). Conformity in the rat: A leader's selection of door color versus a learned door-color discrimination. *Perceptual & Motor Skills, 44,* 31-37.

Koob, G. F., LeMoal, M., & Bloom, F. E. (1981). Enkephalin and endorphin influences on appetitive and aversive conditioning. In J. L. Martinez, Jr., R. A. Jensen, R. B. Messing, H. Rigter, & J. L. McGaugh (Eds.), *Endogenous Peptides and learning and memory processes* (pp. 249-267). New York Academic Press.

Korchin, S. J. (1976). *Modern clinical psychology.* New York: Basic Books.

Korner, A. F., Hutchinson, C. A., Koperski, J. A., Kraemer, H. C., & Schneider, P. A. (1981). Stability of individual differences of neonatal motor and crying patterns. *Child Development, 52,* 83-90.

Krantz, D. S., Grunberg, N. E., & Baum, A. (1985). Health psychology. *Annual Review of Psychology, 36,* 349-383.

Krieger, D. T. (1983). Brain peptides: What, where, and why? *Science, 222,* 975-985.

Krieger, W. G. (1976). Infant influences and the parent sex by child sex interaction in the socialization process. *JSAS Catalogue of Selected Documents in Psychology, 6*(1), 36 (Ms. No. 1234).

Kroeber-Riel, W. (1979). Activation research: Psychobiological approaches in consumer research. *Journal of Consumer Research, 5,* 240-250.

Kroger, W. S. (1977). *Clinical and experimental hypnosis* (2nd ed.). Philadelphia: J. B. Lippincott.

Krueger, J. M., Pappenheimer, J. R., & Karnovsky, M. L. (1982). The composition of sleep- promoting factor isolated from human urine. *Journal of Biological Chemistry, 257,* 1664- 1669.

Kuczaj, S. A. (1983). "I mell a kunk!"—evidence that children have more complex representations of word pronunciations which they simplify. *Journal of Psycholinguistic Research, 12,* 69-73.

Kurtines, W., & Greif, E. B. (1974). The development of moral thought: Review and evaluation of Kohlberg's approach. *Psychological Bulletin, 81,* 453-470.

LaBerge, S. P. (1981, January). Lucid dreaming. *Psychology Today,* pp. 48-57.

Ladd, G. T. (1887). *Elements of physiological psychology.* New York: Scribner's.

Laird, J. D. (1974). Self-attribution of emotion: The effects of expressive behavior on the quality of emotional experience. *Journal of Personality & Social Psychology, 29,* 475-486.

Lakoff, G. (1987). *Women, fire, and dangerous things: What categories reveal about the mind.* Chicago: Univ. of Chicago Press.

Lamb, M. E. (1978). The father's role in the infant's social world. In J. H. Stevens & M. Mathews (Eds.), *Mother/child, father/child relationships.* Washington, D.C.: National Association for the Education of Young Children.

Lamb, M. E. (1979). Paternal influences and the father's role. *American Psychologist, 34,* 938-943.

Lamb, M. E. (1984). Social and emotional development in infancy. In M. H. Bornstein & M. E. Lamb (Eds.), *Developmental psychology: An advanced textbook* (241-277). Hillsdale, NJ: Erlbaum.

Lamb, M. E. (1988). Social and emotional development in infancy. In M. H. Bornstein & M. E. Lamb (Eds.), *Developmental psychology: An advanced textbook* (pp. 359-410). Hillsdale, NJ: Lawrence Erlbaum.

Lamper, C., & Eisdorfer, C. (1971). Prestimulus activity level and responsivity in the neonate. *Child Development, 42,* 465-473.

Land, E. H. (1977). The retinex theory of color vision. *Scientific American, 237*(6), 108-128.

Landers, S. (1986, December). Judge reiterates IQ test ban. *APA Monitor,* p. 18.

Landis, D. (1980, October). A scan for mental illness. *Discover,* pp. 26-28.

Landman, J. T., & Dawes, R. M. (1982). Psychotherapy outcome: Smith and Glass' conclusions stand up under scrutiny. *American Psychologist, 37,* 504-516.

Lange, C. G., & James, W. (1922). *The emotions.* Baltimore, MD: Williams & Wilkins.

Langlois, J. H., & Downs, A. C. (1980). Mothers, fathers, and peers as socialization agents of sex-typed play behaviors in young children. *Child Development, 51,* 1237-1247.

Langlois, J. H., & Roggman, L. A. (1990). Attractive faces are only average. *Psychological Science, 1,* 115-121.

Langlois, J. H., Roggman, L. A., Casey, R. J., Ritter, J. M., Rieser-Danner, L. A., & Jenkins, V. Y. (1987). Infant preferences for attractive faces: Rudiments of a stereotype? *Developmental Psychology, 23,* 363-369.

Lashley, K. S. (1950). In search of the engram. In *Symposium of the Society for Experimental Biology* (Vol. 4). New York: Cambridge Univ. Press.

Lassen, M. K., & McConnell, S. C. (1977). Treatment of a severe bird phobia by participant modeling. *Journal of Behavior Therapy and Experimental Psychiatry, 8,* 165-168.

Latane, B. (1981). The psychology of social impact. *American Psychologist, 36,* 343-356.

Latane, B., & Darley, J. M. (1968). Group inhibition of bystander intervention in emergencies. *Journal of Personality & Social Psychology, 10,* 215-221.

Latane, B., & Darley, J. M. (1970). *The unresponsive bystander: Why doesn't he help?* New York: Appleton-Century-Crofts.

Laumann, E. O. (1969). Friends of urban men: An assessment of accuracy in reporting their socioeconomic attributes, mutual choice, and attitude agreement. *Sociometry, 32,* 54-69.

Laurence, J., & Perry, C. (1983). Hypnotically created memory among highly hypnotizable subjects. *Science, 222,* 523-524.

Lazar, I., & Darlington, R. (1982). Lasting effects of early education: A report from the Consortium for Longitudinal Studies. *Monographs of the Society for Research in Child Development, 47*(2-3, Serial No. 195).

Lazarus, A. A. (1976). *Multimodal behavior therapy.* New York: Springer.

Lazarus, R. S. (1984). On the primacy of cognition. *American Psychologist, 39,* 124-129.

Lazarus, R. S., Delongis, A., Folkman, S., & Gruen, R. (1985). Stress and adaptational outcomes: The problem of confounded measures. *American Psychologist, 40,* 770-779.

Leary, M. R., & Kowalski, R. M. (1990). Impression management: A literature review and two-component model. *Psychological Bulletin, 107,* 34-47.

Leaton, R. N., & Supple, W. F., Jr. (1986). Cerebellar vermis: Essential for long-term habituation of the acoustic startle response. *Science, 232,* 513-515.

Leavitt, H. J., & Schlosberg, H. (1944). The retention of verbal and motor skills. *Journal of Experimental Psychology, 34,* 404-417.

Lebra, T. S. (1976). *Japanese patterns of behavior.* Honolulu: University of Hawaii Press.

Lee, K., Wells, R. G., & Reed, R. R. (1987). Isolation of an olfactory cDNA: Similarity to retinol-binding protein suggests a role in olfaction. *Science, 235,* 1053-1056.

Leff, D. N. (1978, June). Brain chemistry may influence feelings, behavior. *Smithsonian,* pp. 64-70.

Legros, J. J., Gilot, P., Seron, X., Claessens, J., Adam, A., Moeglen, J. M., Audibert, A., & Berchier, P. (1978). Influence of vasopressin on learning and memory. *The Lancet, I*(8054), 41-42.

Lehmann, D., & Koukkou, M. (1980). Psychophysiologie des traumens und der neurosentherapie: Das zustands-wechsel-modell, eine synopsis. *Fortschritte der neurologie, Psychiatrie und ihrer Grenzgebiete, 48,* 324-350.

Lempert, H. (1989). Animacy constraints on preschool children's acquisition of syntax. *Child Development, 60,* 237-245.

Lenneberg, E. H. (1966). The natural history of language. In F. Smith & G. A. Miller (Eds.), *The genesis of language.* Cambridge, Mass.: M.I.T. Press.

Lenneberg, E. H. (1967). *Biological foundations of language.* New York: Wiley.

Leo, J., & White, A. (1980, July 7). How to commit suicide. *Time,* p. 49.

Lepper, M. R., Greene, D., & Nisbett, R. E. (1973). Undermining children's intrinsic interest with extrinsic reward: A test of the "overjustification" hypothesis. *Journal of Personality & Social Psychology, 28,* 129-137.

Lev-Ran, A. (1974). Sexuality and educational levels of women with the late-treated adrenogenital syndrome. *Archives of Sexual Behavior, 3,* 27-32.

Leventhal, G., & Krate, R. (1977). Physical attractiveness and severity of sentencing. *Psychological Reports, 40,* 315-318.

Leventhal, H. (1970). Findings and theory in the study of fear communications. In L. Berkowitz (Ed.), *Advances in experimental social psychology* (Vol. 5). New York: Academic Press.

Leventhal, H., & Niles, P. (1965). Persistence of influence for varying durations of exposure to threat stimuli. *Psychological Reports, 16,* 223-233.

Leventhal, H., & Tomarken, A. J. (1986). Emotion: Today's problems. *Annual Review of Psychology, 37,* 565-610.

Levine, J. D., Gordon, N. C., & Fields, H. L. (1978). The mechanism of placebo analgesia. *The Lancet, 2,* 654-657.

Levine, L. E. (1983). Mine: Self-definition in 2-year-old-boys. *Developmental Psychology, 19,* 544-549.

Lewin, R. (1984). Practice catches theory in kin recognition. *Science, 223,* 1049-1051.

Lewin, R. (1988). Brain graft puzzles. *Science, 240,* 879.

Lewis, M., & Rosenblum, L. A. (Eds.). (1975). *Friendship and peer relations.* New York: Wiley.

Lewis, M., Stanger, C., & Sullivan, M. W. (1989). Deception in 3-year-olds. *Developmental Psychology, 25,* 439-443.

Lewis, Max. (1981, November). Personal communication.

Lewontin, R. C., Rose, S., & Kamin, L. J. (1984). *Not in our genes.* New York: Pantheon Books.

Liberman, R. P., Mueser, K. T., & Wallace, C. J. (1986). Social skills training for schizophrenic individuals at risk for relapse. *American Journal of Psychiatry, 143,* 523-526.

Licht, B. G., & Dweck, C. S. (1984). Determinants of academic achievement: The interaction of children's achievement orientations with skill area. *Developmental Psychology, 20,* 628-636.

Liebert, R. M., & Sprafkin, J. (1988). *The early window: Effects of television on children and youth* (3rd ed.). New York: Pergamon Press.

Liebowitz, M. R., Fyer, A. J., Gorman, J. M., Dillon, D., Davies, S., Stein, J. M., Cohen, B. S., & Klein, D. F. (1985). Specificity of lactate infusions in social phobia versus panic disorders. *American Journal of Psychiatry, 142,* 947-950.

Light, K. C., Koepke, J. P., Obrist, P. A., & Willis, P. W., IV. (1983). Psychological stress induces sodium and fluid retention in men at high risk for hypertension. *Science, 220,* 429-431.

Likert, R. (1961). *New patterns of management.* New York: McGraw-Hill.

Lindvall, O., Brudin, P., Widner, H., Rehncrona, S., Gustavii, B., Frackowiak, R., Leenders, K. L., Sawle, G., Rothwell, J. C., Marsden, C. D., & Bjorklund, A. (1990). Grafts of fetal dopamine neurons survive and improve motor function in Parkinson's disease. *Science, 247,* 574-577.

Ling, G. S. F., MacLeod, J. M., Lee, S., Lockhart, S. H., & Pasternak, G. W. (1984). Separation of morphine analgesia from physical dependence. *Science, 226,* 462-464.

Linney, J. A., & Seidman, E. (1989). The future of schooling. *American Psychologist, 44,* 336-340.

Linton, H., & Graham, E. (1959). Personality correlates of persuasibility. In C. I. Hovland & I. L. Janis (Eds.), *Personality and persuasibility.* New Haven, Conn.: Yale University Press.

Lipkowitz, M. H., & Idupuganti, S. (1985). Diagnosing schizophrenia in 1982: The effect of DSM-III. *American Journal of Psychiatry, 142,* 634-637.

Lipowski, Z. J. (1988). Somatization: The concept and its clinical application. *American Journal of Psychiatry, 145,* 1358-1368.

Lippitt, R., Polansky, N., & Rosen, S. (1952). The dynamics of power. *Human Relations, 5,* 37-64.

Livingstone, M. S. (1988). Art, illusion and the visual system. *Scientific American, 258*(1), 78-85.

Llinas, R. R. (1988). The intrinsic electrophysiological properties of mammalian neurons: Insights into central nervous system function. *Science, 242,* 1654-1664.

Locke, E. A. (1976). The nature and causes of job satisfaction. In M. Dunnette (Ed.), *Handbook of industrial and organizational psychology.* Chicago: Rand-McNally.

Locke, S. E., Furst, M. W., Heisel, J. S., & Williams, R. M. (1978, April). *The influences of stress on the immune response.* Paper presented at the annual meeting of the American Psychosomatic Society, Washington, D. C.

Locke, S. E., Krause, L., Leserman, J., Hurst, M. W., Heisel, J. S., & Williams, R. M. (1984). Life change stress, psychiatric symptoms, and natural killer cell activity. *Psychosomatic Medicine, 46,* 441-453.

Loeb, G. E. (1985). The functional replacement of the ear. *Scientific American, 252*(2), 104-111.

Loehlin, J. C., Willerman, L., & Horn, J. M. (1988). Human behavior genetics. *Annual Review of Psychology, 39,* 101-133.

Loevinger, J., & Knoll, E. (1983). Personality: Stages, traits, and the self. *Annual Review of Psychology, 34,* 195-222.

Loewenstein, R. J., Hamilton, J., Alagna, S., Reid, N., & deVries, M. (1987). Experiential sampling in the study of multiple personality disorder. *American Journal of Psychiatry, 144,* 19-24.

Loftus, E. F., & Loftus, G. R. (1980). On the permanence of stored information in the human brain. *American Psychologist, 35,* 409-420.

Logothetis, N. K., & Schall, J. D. (1989). Neuronal correlates of subjective visual perception. *Science, 245,* 761-763.

Logue, A. W. (1986). *The psychology of eating and drinking.* New York: W. H. Freeman.

Loizos, C. (1967). Play behavior in higher primates: A review. In D. Morris (Ed.), *Primate ethology.* London: Weidenfeld & Nicholson.

Lorenz, K. (1943). Die angeborenen Formen moglicher Erfahrung. *Z. Tierpsychologie, 5,* 235-409.

Love, D. (1987, November 14). Personal communication.

Lowe, M. G. (1982). The role of anticipated deprivation in overeating. *Addictive Behaviors, 7,* 103-112.

Lozoff, B. (1983). Birth and "bonding" in non-industrial societies. *Developmental Medicine and Child Neurology, 25,* 595-600.

Lubin, B., Larsen, R. M., Matarazzo, J. D., & Seever, M. (1985). Psychological test usage patterns in five professional settings. *American Psychologist, 40,* 857-861.

Luborsky, L., Crits-Cristoph, P., McLellan, A. T., Woody, G., Piper, W., Liberman, B., Imber, S., & Pilkonis, P. (1986). Do therapists vary much in their success? Findings from four outcome studies. *American Journal of Orthopsychiatry, 56,* 501-512.

Luchins, A. S. (1942). Mechanization in problem solving. *Psychological Monographs, 54,* No. 248.

Lugaresi, E., Medori, R., Montagna, P., Baruzzi, A., Corelli, P., Lugaresi, A., Tinuper, P., Zucconi, M., & Gambetti, P. (1986). Fatal familial insomnia and dysautonomia with selective degeneration of thalamic nuclei. *New England Journal of Medicine, 315,* 997-1003.

Luisada, P. V., & Brown, B. I. (1976). Clinical management of the phencyclidine psychosis. *Clinical Toxicology, 9,* 539-545.

Luria, A R. (1968). *The mind of a mnemonist.* New York: Basic Books.

Lutz, R. J., & Bettman, J. R. (1977). Multiattribute models in marketing: A bicentennial review. In A. G. Woodside, J. N. Sheth, & P. D. Bennett (Eds.), *Consumer and industrial buying behavior* (pp. 137-149). New York: Evsevier North Holland.

Luxenberg, J. S., Swedo, S. E., Flament, M. F., Friedland, R. P., Rapoport, J., & Rapoport, S. I. (1988). Neuroanatomical abnormalities in obsessive-compulsive disorder detected with quantitative X-ray computed tomography. *American Journal of Psychiatry, 145,* 1089-1093.

Lykken, D. T. (1981). *A tremor in the blood: Uses and abuses of the lie detector.* New York: McGraw-Hill, 1981.

Lykken, D. T. (1981). The lie detector and the law. *Criminal Defense, 8,* 19-27.

Lykken, D. T. (1987, August). Genes and the mind. *Harvard Medical School Mental Health Letter,* pp. 4-6.

Lyle, J. (1971). Television in daily life: Patterns of use (overview). In *Television and social behavior* (Vol. 4, pp. 1-33). Washington, D. C.: U. S. Government Printing Office.

Lynch, G. (1986). *Synapses, circuits, and the beginnings of memory.* Cambridge, MA: MIT Press.

Lynn, K. S. (1987). *Hemingway.* New York: Simon & Schuster.

Lynn, S. J., & Rhue, J. W. (1988). Fantasy proneness. *American Psychologist, 43,* 35-44.

Lytton, H., Conway, D., & Suave, R. (1977). The impact of twinship on parent-child interaction. *Journal of Personality & Social Psychology, 35,* 97-107.

M'Naghten's Case. (1843). *English Reports, 8,* 718.

Maccoby, E. E., & Jacklin, C. N. (1974). *The psychology of sex differences.* Stanford, Calif.: Stanford Univ. Press.

MacCoun, R. J. (1989). Experimental research on jury decision-making. *Science, 244,* 1046- 1050.

MacKain, K., Studdert-Kennedy, M., Spieker, S., & Stern, D. (1983). Infant intermodal speech perception is a left-hemisphere function. *Science, 219,* 1347-1349.

MacKay, D. M. (1973). Lateral interaction between neural channels sensitive to texture density? *Nature, 245,* 159-161.

MacKay, D. M. (1985). Central processing of vision information. In R. Jung (Ed.), *Handbook of sensory physiology* (Vol. 7, part 3). Berlin: Springer-Verlag.

MacLeod, D. I. A. (1978). Visual sensitivity. *Annual Review of Psychology, 29,* 613-645.

MacNichol, E. F. (1964). Three pigment color vision. *Scientific American, 211*(6), 48-64.

MacWhinney, B. (1978). The acquisition of morphophonology. *Monographs of the Society for Research in Child Development, 43*(1-2, Serial No. 174).

Madden, N. A., & Slavin, R. E. (1983). Mainstreaming students with mild handicaps: Academic and social outcomes. *Review of Educational Research, 53,* 519-569.

Madigan, S. A. (1969). Intraserial repetition and coding processes in free recall. *Journal of Verbal Learning and Verbal Behavior, 8,* 828-835.

Madrazo, I., Drucker-Colin, R., Diaz, V., Martinez-Mata, J., Torres, C., & Becerril, J. J. (1987). Open microsurgical autograft of adrenal medulla to the right caudate nucleus in two patients with intractable Parkinson's disease. *New England Journal of Medicine, 316,* 831-834.

Madrazo, I., Leon, V., Torres, C., Aguilera, M. C., Varela, G., Alvarez, F., Fraga, A., Drucker- Colin, R., Ostrosky, F., & Skurovich, M. (1988). Transplantation of fetal substantia nigra and adrenal medulla to the caudate nucleus in two patients with Parkinson's disease. *New England Journal of Medicine, 318,* 51.

Madsen, M. C. (1971). Developmental and cross-cultural differences in the cooperative and competitive behavior of young children. *Journal of Cross-Cultural Psychology, 2,* 365-371.

Madsen, M. C., & Shapira, A. (1970). Cooperative and competitive behavior of urban Afro-American, Anglo-American, Mexican-American, and Mexican village children. *Developmental Psychology, 3,* 16-20.

Magnusson, D., & Endler, N. S. (1977). Interactional psychology: Present status and future prospects. In D. Magnusson & N. S. Endler (Eds.), *Personality at the crossroads.* New York: Wiley-Erlbaum.

Mahoney, M. J. (1979). Cognitive skills and athletic performance. In P. C. Kendall & S. D. Hollon (Eds.), *Cognitive-behavioral interventions: Theory, research, and procedures* (pp. 423-443). New York: Academic Press.

Mahoney, M. J. (1989). Scientific psychology and radical behaviorism. *American Psychologist, 44,* 1372-1377.

Maier, N. R. F. (1931). Reasoning in humans: II. The solution of a problem and its appearance in consciousness. *Journal of Comparative Psychology, 12,* 181-194.

Maile, F. R., & Selzer, M. (1975). *The Nuremberg mind: The psychology of the Nazi leaders.* New York: New York Times Book Co.

Malkis, F. S., Kalle, R. J., & Tedeschi, J. T. (1982). Attitudinal politics in the forced compliance situation. *Journal of Social Psychology, 117,* 79-91.

Manchester, W. (1974). The glory and the dream. Boston: Little, Brown.

Mancillas, J. R., Siggins, G. R., & Bloom, F. E. (1986). Systemic ethanol: Selective enhancement of responses to acetylcholine and somatostatin in hippocampus. *Science, 231,* 161-163.

Manicas, P. T., & Secord, P. F. (1983). Implications for psychology of the new philosophy of science. *American Psychologist, 38,* 399-413.

Mantell, D. M. (1971). The potential for violence in Germany. *Journal of Social Issues, 27*(4), 101-112.

Maranto, G. (1984, November). Emotions: How they affect your body. *Discover,* pp. 35-38.

Marbach, W. D., Carroll, G., & Miller, M. (1987, April 27). America's big risk. *Newsweek,* pp. 58-60.

Marcus, E. A., Nolen, T. G., Rankin, C. H., & Carew, T. J. (1988). Behavioral dissociation of dishabituation, sensitization, and inhibition in *Aplysia. Science, 241,* 210-213.

Marder, S. R., Van Putten, T., Mintz, J., Lebell, M., McKenzie, J., & May, P. R. (1987). Low- and conventional-dose maintenance therapy with fluphenazine decanoate. Two-year outcome. *Archives of General Psychiatry, 44,* 518-521.

Markowitz, J., Brown, R., Sweeney, J., & Mann, J. J. (1987). Reduced length and cost of hospital stay for major depression in patients treated with ECT. *American Journal of Psychiatry, 144,* 1025-1029.

Marks, P. A., & Seeman, W. (1963). *Actuarial description of abnormal personality.* Baltimore: Williams & Wilkins.

Marmor, J. (1985, October). Homosexuality: Nature vs nurture. *Harvard Medical School Mental Health Letter,* pp. 5-6.

Marschark, M., Richman, C. L., Yuille, J. C., & Hunt, R. R. (1987). The role of imagery in memory: On shared and distinctive information. *Psychological Bulletin, 102,* 28-41.

Marshall, G. D., & Zimbardo, P. G. (1979). Affective consequences of inadequately explained physiological arousal. *Journal of Personality & Social Psychology, 37,* 970-988.

Marshall, W. A. (1973). The body. In R. R. Sears & S. S. Feldman (Eds.), *The seven ages of man.* Los Altos, CA: William Kaufmann, Inc.

Martin, J., Lobb, B., Chapman, G. C., & Spillane, R. (1976). Obedience under conditions demanding self-immolation. *Human Relations, 29,* 345-356.

Martin, P. J., Hunter, M. L., & Moore, J. E. (1977). Pulling the wool: Impression-management among hospitalized schizophrenics. *Research Communications in Psychology, Psychiatry and Behavior, 2,* 21-26.

Marx, J. L. (1985). The immune system "belongs in the body". *Science, 227,* 1190-1192.

Marx, J. L. (1986). Nerve activity alters neurotransmitter synthesis. *Science, 232,* 1500-1501.

Marx, M. H., & Hillix, W. (1963). *Systems and theories in psychology.* New York: McGraw-Hill.

Maslach, C. (1979). Negative emotional biasing of unexplained arousal. *Journal of Personality & Social Psychology, 37,* 953-969. Masland, R. H. (1986). THe functional architecture of the retina. *Scientific American, 255*(6), 102-111.

Maslow, A. H. (1954). *Motivation and personality.* New York: Harper & Row.

Maslow, A. H. (1968). *Toward a psychology of being* (2nd ed.). New York: Van Nostrand.

Maslow, A. H. (1970). *Motivation and personality*. New York: Harper & Row.

Mason, W. A. (1965). The social development of monkeys and apes. In I. DeVore (Ed.), *Primate behavior: Field studies of monkeys and apes*. New York: Holt.

Masters, W. H., & Johnson, V. E. (1970). *Human sexual inadequacy*. Boston: Little, Brown.

Matarazzo, J. D. (1983). Computerized psychological testing. *Science, 221*, 323.

Matarazzo, J. D. (1986). Computerized clinical psychological test interpretations. *American Psychologist, 41*, 14-24.

Mather, D. B. (1987). The case against preventing suicide prevention: Comments on Szasz. *American Psychologist, 42*, 882-883.

Matheson, J. (1986, February). What is narcolepsy? *Harvard Medical School Mental Health Letter*, p. 8.

Matthews, K. A. (1988). Coronary heart disease and type A behaviors: Update on and alternative to the Booth-Kewley and Friedman (1987) quantitative review. *Psychological Bulletin, 104*, 373-380.

Mayr, E. (1982). *The growth of biological thought*. Cambridge, MA: Belknap Press.

Maziade, M., Cote, R., Boutin, P., Bernier, H., & Thivierge, J. (1988). Temperament and intellectual development: A longitudinal study from infancy to four years. In S. Chess, A. Thomas, & M. E. Hertzig (Eds.), *Annual progress in child psychiatry and child development* (pp. 335-349). New York: Brunner/Mazel.

Mazur, A., & Rosa, E. (1977). An empirical test of McClelland's "achieving society" theory. *Social Forces, 55*, 769-774.

McCall, J. N., & Johnson, O. G. (1972). The independence of intelligence from family size and birth order. *Journal of Genetic Psychology, 121*, 207-213.

McCall, R. B., Hogarty, P. S., & Hurlburt, N. (1972). Transitions in infant sensorimotor development and the prediction of childhood IQ. *American Psychologist, 27*, 728-748.

McCarthy, P. (1986, July). Scent: The tie that binds? *Psychology Today*, pp. 6, 10.

McCartney, K., & Scarr, S. (1984). Day care as language intervention. *First Language, 5*(13, Pt 1), 75-77.

McCartney, K., Scarr, S., Phillips, D., & Grajek, S. (1985). Day care as intervention: Comparisons of varying quality programs. Journal of Applied *Developmental Psychology, 6*(2-3), 247-260.

McClelland, D. C. (1961). *The achieving society*. New York: Van Nostrand.

McClelland, D. C. (1973). Testing for competence rather than for "intelligence." *American Psychologist, 28*, 1-14.

McClelland, D. C., Atkinson, J. W., Clark, R. A., & Lowell, E. L. (1953). *The achievement motive*. New York: Appleton-Century-Crofts.

McClements, J. D., & Botterill, C. B. (1980). Goal-setting in shaping of future performance in athletes. In P. Klavora & J. Daniel (Eds.), *Coach, athlete, and the sport psychologist* (pp. 199-210). Toronto: Univ. of Toronto Press.

McCord, J. (1977, November 26). Thirty year followup: Counseling fails. *Science News*, p. 357.

McCormick, D. A., & Thompson, R. F. (1984). Cerebellum: Essential involvement in the classically conditioned eyelid response. *Science, 223*, 296-299.

McDonough, R. J., Madden, J. J., Falek, A., Shafer, D. A., Pine, M., Gordon, D., Bokos, P., Kuehnle, J. C., & Mendelson, J. (1980). Alteration of T and null lymphocyte frequencies in the peripheral blood of human opiate addicts: In vivo evidence for opiate receptor sites on T lymphocytes. *Journal of Immunology, 125*, 2539-2543.

McGaugh, J. L. (1983). Preserving the presence of the past: Hormonal influences on memory storage. *American Psychologist, 38*, 161-174. McGuire, W. J. (1964). Inducing resistance to persuasion: Some contemporary approaches. *Advances in Experimental Social Psychology, 1*, 192-229.

McGuire, W. J. (1969). The nature of attitudes and attitude change. In G. Lindzey & E. Aronson (Eds.), *Handbook of social psychology* (2nd ed., Vol. 3, pp. 136-314). Reading, Mass.: Addison-Wesley.

McHale, S. M., & Huston, T. L. (1984). Men and women as parents: Sex role orientations, employment, and parental roles with infants. *Child Development, 55*, 1349-1361.

McKean, K. (1984, February). New parts for damaged brains. *Discover*, pp. 68-72.

McKean, K. (1986, October). Pain. *Discover*, pp. 82-92.

McKinney, J. P., & Moore, D. (1982). Attitudes and values during adolescence. In B. B. Wolman (Ed.), *Handbook of developmental psychology* (pp. 549-558). Englewood Cliffs, NJ: Prentice-Hall.

McNeil, E. B. (1967). *The quiet furies*. Englewood Cliffs, NJ: Prentice-Hall.

McWhirter, N. (Ed.). (1986). *Guinness book of world records*. New York: Bantam Books.

Mead, M. (1963). *Sex and temperament in three primitive societies*. New York: William Morrow. (Original work published 1935).

Meddis, R. (1975). On the function of sleep. *Animal Behaviour, 23*, 676-691.

Meddis, R., Pearson, A. J. D., & Langford, G. (1973). An extreme ease of healthy insomnia. *Electroencephalography & Clinical Neurophysiology, 35*, 213-221.

Medin, D. L. (1989). Concepts and conceptual structure. *American Psychologist, 44*, 1469-1481.

Medin, D. L., & Shoben, E. J. (1988). Context and structure in conceptual combination. *Cognitive Psychology, 20*, 158-190.

Meehl, P. E. (1978). Theoretical risks and tabular asterisks: Sir Karl, Sir Ronald, and the slow progress of soft psychology. *Journal of Consulting & Clinical Psychology, 46*, 806-834.

Meer, J. (1985, September). The light torch. *Psychology Today*, pp. 60-67.

Mefford, I. N., Baker, T. L., Boehme, R., Foutz, A. S., Ciarnello, R. D., Barchas, J. D., & Dement, W. C. (1983). Narcolepsy: Biogenic amine deficits in an animal model. *Science, 220*, 629-632.

Meichenbaum, D. (1977). *Cognitive-behavior modification: An integrative approach*. New York: Plenum Press.

Meiners, M. L., & Sheposh, J. P. (1977). Beauty or brains: Which image for your mate? *Personality and Social Psychology Bulletin, 3*, 262-265.

Meissner, W. W. (1978). *The paranoid process*. New York: Jason Aronson.

Meltzoff, A. N. (1988). Infant imitation after a 1-week delay: Long-term memory for novel acts and multiple stimuli. *Developmental Psychology, 24*, 470-476.

Menninger, K. (1968). *The crime of punishment*. New York: Viking.

Mental illness and homelessness: Part I. (1990, July). *The Harvard Mental Health Letter*, pp. 1-4.

Meredith, M. A., & Stein, B. E. (1983). Interactions among converging sensory inputs in the superior colliculus. *Science, 221*, 389-391.

Mergner, T., Anastosopoulos, D., Becker, W., & Deecke, L. (1981). Discrimination between trunk and head rotation: A study comparing neuronal data from the cat with human psychophysics. *Acta Psychologica, 48*, 291-302.

Messer, D. J., McCarthy, M. E., McQuiston, S., MacTurk, R. H., Yarrow, L. J., & Vietze, P. M. (1986). Relation between mastery behavior in infancy and competence in early childhood. *Developmental Psychology, 22*, 366-372.

Mewborn, C. R., & Rogers, R. W. (1979). Effects of threatening and reassuring components of fear appeals on physiological and verbal measures of emotion and attitudes. *Journal of Experimental Social Psychology, 15*, 242-253.

Meyer, A. (1982, June). Do lie detectors lie? *Science 82*, pp. 24-27.

Meyer, J. P., & Pepper, S. (1977). Need compatibility and marital adjustment in young married couples. *Journal of Personality & Social Psychology, 35*, 331-342.

Michael, R. P., & Bonsall, R. W. (1977). Peri-ovulatory synchronisation of behaviour in male and female rhesus monkeys. *Nature, 265*, 463-465.

Michael, R. P., & Zumpe, D. (1978). Potency in male rhesus monkeys: Effects of continuously receptive females. *Science, 200*, 451-453.

Michael, W. B. (1977). Cognitive and affective components of creativity in mathematics and the physical sciences. In J. C. Stanley, W. C. George, & C. H. Solano (Eds.), *The gifted and creative: A fifty-year perspective*. Baltimore, MD: Johns Hopkins Univ. Press.

Middlemist, R. D., Knowles, E. S., & Matter, C. F. (1976). Personal space invasions in the lavatory: Suggestive evidence for arousal. *Journal of Personality and Social Psychology, 33*, 541-546.

Miles, C. (1935). Sex in social psychology. In C. Murchinson (Ed.), *Handbook of social psychology*. Worcester, Mass.: Clark Univ. Press.

Milgram, S. (1963). Behavioral study of obedience. *Journal of Abnormal and Social Psychology, 67*, 371-378.

Milgram, S. (1965a). Some conditions of obedience and disobedience to authority. *Human Relations, 18*, 57-76.

Milgram, S. (1965b). Liberating effects of group pressure. *Journal of Personality & Social Psychology, 1*, 127-134.

Miller, G. A. (1956). The magical number seven, plus or minus two: Some limits on our capacity for processing information. *Psychological Review, 63*, 81-97.

Miller, G. A., & Buckhout, R. (1973). *Psychology: The science of mental life*. New York: Harper & Row.

Miller, G. A., & Gildea, P. M. (1987). How children learn words. *Scientific American, 257*(3), 94-99.

Miller, I. W., & Norman, W. H. (1979). Learned helplessness in humans: A review and attribution theory model. *Psychological Bulletin, 86*, 93-118.

Miller, J. A. (1984a, August 18). Allergy mechanisms: Learning and itching. *Science News*, p. 102.

Miller, J. A. (1984b, January 28). Mind maps. *Science News*, pp. 62-63.

Miller, J. A. (1985a, November 9). Carving out the nervous system. *Science News*, p. 297.

Miller, J. A. (1985b, November 16). Brain selects among sights and sounds. *Science News*, p. 312.

Miller, J. A. (1985c, November 9). Eye to (third) eye. *Science News*, pp. 298-299.

Miller, K. D., Keller, J. B., & Stryker, M. P. (1989). Ocular dominance column development: Analysis and simulation. *Science, 245*, 605-615.

Miller, L. B., & Dyer, J. L. (1975). Four preschool programs: Their dimensions and effects. *Monographs of the Society for Research in Child Development, 40*(5-6, Serial No. 162).

Miller, N. E. (1980). Obituary, Walter R. Miles (1885-1978). *American Psychologist, 35*, 595-596.

Miller, N., Maruyama, G., Beaber, R. J., & Valone, K. (1976). Speed of speech and persuasion. *Journal of Personality & Social Psychology, 34*, 615-624.

Miller, R. L., Brickman, P., & Bolen, D. (1975). Attribution versus persuasion as a means for modifying behavior. *Journal of Personality & Social Psychology, 31*, 430-441.

Mineka, S., & Hendersen, R. W. (1985). Controllability and predictability in acquired motivation. *Annual Review of Psychology, 36*, 495-529.

Mirsky, A. F., & Duncan, C. C. (1986). Etiology and expression of schizophrenia: Neurobiological and psychosocial factors. *Annual Review of Psychology, 37*, 291-319.

Mirsky, A. F., & Orzack, M. H. (1980). Two retrospective studies of psychosurgery. In E. S. Valenstein (Ed.), *The psychosurgery debate*. San Francisco: W. H. Freeman.

Mischel, W. (1974). Process in delay of gratification. In L. Berkowitz (Ed.), *Advances in experimental social psychology* (Vol. 7). New York: Academic Press.

Mischel, W. (1977). On the future of personality assessment. *American Psychologist, 32*, 246-254.

Mishara, B. L. (1975). The extent of adolescent suicidality. *Psychiatric Opinion, 12*, 32-37.

Mishkin, M., & Appenzeller, T. (1987). The anatomy of memory. *Scientific American, 256*(6), 80-89.

Mita, T. H., Dermer, M., & Knight, J. (1977). Reversed facial images and the mere-exposure hypothesis. *Journal of Personality & Social Psychology, 35*, 597-601.

Mittleman, G., & Valenstein, E. S. (1984). Ingestive behavior evoked by hypothalamic stimulation and schedule-induced polydipsia are related. *Science, 224*, 415-417.

Mohs, M. (1982, September). I.Q. *Discover*, pp. 18-24.

Money, J. (1965). Influence of hormones on sexual behavior. *Annual Review of Medicine, 16*, 67-82.

Money, J., & Ehrhardt, A. A. (1972). *Man and woman, boy and girl*. Baltimore, MD: Johns Hopkins.

Money, J., & Mathews, D. (1982). Prenatal exposure to virilizing progestins: An adult follow-up study of twelve women. *Archives of Sexual Behavior, 11*, 73-83.

Money, J., Berlin, F. S., Falck, A., & Stein, M. (1983). *Antiandrogenic and counseling treatment of sex offenders*. Baltimore: Department of Psychiatry and Behavioral Sciences, Johns Hopkins University School of Medicine.

Monk, T. H., Weitzman, E. D., Fookson, J. E., Moline, M. L., Kronauer, R. E., & Gander, P. H. (1983). Task variable determine which biological clock controls circadian-rhythms in human performance. *Nature, 304*, 543-545.

Moore, M. (1982). Endorphins and exercise. *The Physician and Sportsmedicine, 10*, 111-119.

Moore, R. Y. (1987). Parkinson's disease—A new therapy? *New England Journal of Medicine, 316*, 872-873.

Mora, G. (1967). History of psychiatry. In A. M. Freedman & H. I. Kaplan (Eds.), *Psychiatry*. Baltimore: Williams & Wilkins.

Moran, J., & Desimone, R. (1985). Selective attention gates visual processing in the extrastriate cortex. *Science, 229*, 782-784.

Morgan, M., & Gross, L. (1982). Television and educational achievement. In D. Pearl, L. Bouthilet, & J. Lazar (Eds.), *Television and behavior: Ten years of scientific progress and implications for the eighties* (Vol. 2). Washington, DC: U.S. Govt. Printing Office.

Morgan, W. P. (1980). The trait psychology controversy. *Research Quarterly for Exercise and Sport, 51*, 50-76.

Morongiello, B. A. (1988). Infants' localization of sounds along the horizontal axis: Estimates of minimum audible angle. *Developmental Psychology, 24*, 8-13.

Morrison, A. M., & Von Glinow, M. A. (1990). Women and minorities in management. *American Psychologist, 45*, 200-208.

Morrison, A. R. (1983). A window on the sleeping brain. *Scientific American, 248*(4), 94-102.

Moskowitz, B. A. (1978). The acquisition of language. *Scientific American, 239*(5), 92-108.

Mossler, D. G., Marvin, R. S., & Greenberg, M. T. (1976). Conceptual perspective taking in 2- to 6-year-old children. *Developmental Psychology, 12*, 85-86.

Motley, M. T. (1985). Slips of the tongue. *Scientific American, 253*(3), 116-127.

Muecke, L. N., & Krueger, D. W. (1981). Physical findings in a psychiatric outpatient clinic. *American Journal of Psychiatry, 138*, 1241-1242.

Mueller, E., & Brenner, J. (1977). The origins of social skills and interaction among playgroup toddlers. *Child Development, 48*, 854-861.

Mukhametov, L. M. (1984). Sleep in marine mammals. In A. A. Borbely & J. L. Valatx (Eds.), *Sleep mechanisms: Experimental brain research*. Heidelberg, W. Ger.: Springer-Verlag.

Munroe, R. H., Shimmin, H. S., & Munroe, R. L. (1984). Gender understanding and sex role preference in four cultures. *Developmental Psychology, 20*, 673-682.

Murray, C. (1988). *In pursuit of happiness and good government*. New York: Simon & Schuster.

Murray, M. (1986, July 19). Math teachers question role of tests. *Science News*, p. 38.

Myers, J. J. (1984). Right hemisphere language: Science or fiction? *American Psychologist, 39*, 315-320.

Narayanan, V. K., & Nath, R. (1982). A field test of some attitudinal and behavioral consequences of flextime. *Journal of Applied Psychology, 67*, 214-218.

Nash, M. (1987). What, if anything, is regressed about hypnotic age regression? A review of the empirical literature. *Psychological Bulletin, 102*, 42-52.

Nash, M. R., Johnson, L. S., & Tipton, R. D. (1979). Hypnotic age regression and the occurrence of transitional object relationships. *Journal of Abnormal Psychology, 88*, 547-554.

Nathans, J. (1989). The genes for color vision. *Scientific American, 260*(2), 42-49.

National Council on Aging. (1981). *The myth and reality of aging in America*. Washington, D.C.: Author.

Nauta, W. J. H., & Feirtag, M. (1986). *Fundamental neuroanatomy*. New York: W. H. Freeman.

Nauta, W. J. H., & Feirtag, M. (1979). The organization of the brain. *Scientific American, 241*(3), 88-111.

Neiss, R. (1988). Reconceptualizing arousal: Psychobiological states in motor performance. *Psychological Bulletin, 103*, 345-366.

Nelson, L., & Madsen, M. C. (1969). Cooperation and competition in four-year-olds as a function of reward contingency and subculture. *Developmental Psychology, 1*, 340-344.

Neugarten, B. L. (1968). Adult personality: Toward a psychology of the life cycle. In B. L. Neugarten (Ed.), *Middle age and aging: A reader in social psychology*. Chicago: Univ. of Chicago Press.

Neugarten, B. L., & Peterson, W. A. (1957). A study of the American age-grade system. *Proceedings of the Fourth Congress of the International Association of Gerontology, 3*, 497-502.

Neugarten, B. L., Wood, V., Kraines, R. J., & Loomis, B. (1963). Women's attitudes toward the menopause. *Vita Humana, 6*, 140-151.

Nevin, J. A. (1988). Behavioral momentum and the partial reinforcement effect. *Psychological Bulletin*, 44-56.

Newcomb, T. M. (1961). *The acquaintance process*. New York: Holt, Rinehart & Winston.

Newell, A., & Simon, H. (1972). *Human problem solving*. Englewood Cliffs, NJ: Prentice-Hall.

Newman, B. M. (1982). Mid-life development. In B. B. Wolman (Ed.), *Handbook of developmental psychology* (pp. 617-635). Englewood Cliffs, NJ: Prentice-Hall.

Newman, P. R. (1982). The peer group. In B. B. Wolman (Ed.), *Handbook of developmental psychology* (pp. 526-536). Englewood Cliffs, NJ: Prentice-Hall.

Nickerson, R. S., & Adams, M. J. (1979). Long-term memory for a common object. *Cognitive Psychology, 11*, 287-307.

Nicoll, R. A. (1989). The coupling of neurotransmitter receptors to ion channels in the brain. *Science, 241*, 545-551.

Norman, D. A., & Rumelhart, D. E. (1975). *Explorations in cognition*. San Francisco: W. H. Freeman.

Normann, R. A., Perlman, I., Kolb, H., Jones, J., & Daly, S. J. (1984). Direct excitatory interactions between cones of different spectral types in the turtle retina. *Science, 224*, 625-627.

Nottebohm, F. (1989). From bird song to neurogenesis. *Scientific American, 260*(2), 74-79.

Novin, D. (1976). Visceral mechanisms in the control of food intake. In D. Novin, W. Wyrwicka, & G. A. Bray (Eds.), *Hunger: Basic mechanisms and clinical implications*. New York: Raven.

Nowak, C. A. (1977). Does youthfulness equal attractiveness? In L. E. Troll, J. Israel, & K. Israel (Eds.), *Looking ahead: A woman's guide to the problems and joys of growing older*. Englewood Cliffs, NJ: Prentice-Hall.

Noyes, R., Jr., Clarkson, C., Crowe, R. R., Yates, W. R., & McChesney, C. M. (1987). A family study of generalized anxiety disorder. *American Journal of Psychiatry, 144*, 1019-1024.

Nydegger, R. V. (1975). Information processing complexity and leadership status. *Journal of Experimental Social Psychology, 11*, 317-328.

O'Connor, M. J., Cohen, S., & Parmelee, A. H. (1984). Infant auditory discrimination in preterm and full-term infants as a predictor of 5-year intelligence. *Developmental Psychology, 20*, 159-165.

O'Leary, B. S. (1980). *College grade point average as an indicator of occupational success: An update*. Personnel Research Dev. Cent. Report PRR-80-23. Washington, DC: Office of Personn. Mgmt.

O'Malley, M. N., & Becker, L. A. (1984). Removing the egocentric bias: The relevance of distress cues to evaluation of fairness. *Personality and Social Psychology Bulletin, 10*, 235-242.

Oden, G. C. (1987). Concept, knowledge, and thought. *Annual Review of Psychology, 38*, 203-227.

Offer, D., Ostrov, E., & Howard, K. I. (1981). *The adolescent: A psychological self-portrait*. New York: Basic Books.

Offermann, L. R., & Gowing, M. K. (1990). Organizations of the future: Changes and challenges. *American Psychologist, 45*, 95-108.

Olds, J. (1956). Pleasure centers in the brain. *Scientific American, 195*(4), 105-116.

Olds, M. E., & Fobes, J. L. (1981). The central basis of motivation: Intracranial self-stimulation studies. *Annual Review of Psychology, 32*, 523-574.

Oliveros, J. C., Jandali, M. K., Timsit-Berthier, M., Remy, R., Benghezal, A., Audibert, A., & Moeglen, J. M. (1978). Vasopressin in amnesia. *The Lancet, I*(8054), 42.

Oller, D. K., & Eilers, R. E. (1988). The role of audition in infant babbling. Child *Development, 59*, 441-449.

Olney, J. W., Labruyere, J., & Price, M. T. (1989). Pathological changes induced in cerebrocortical neurons by phencyclidine and related drugs. *Science, 244*, 1360-1362.

Optican, L. M., & Richmond, B. J. (1987). Temporal encoding of two-dimensional patterns by single units in primate inferior temporal cortex. III. Information theoretic analysis. *Journal of Neurophysiology, 57*, 162-178.

Orne, M. T. (1982, January 16). Hypnosis: Guilty of fraud? *Science News*, p. 42.

Orne, M. T., & Evans, F. J. (1965). Social control in the psychological experiment: Antisocial behavior and hypnosis. *Journal of Personality & Social Psychology, 1*, 189-200.

Orwin, R. G., & Cordray, D. S. (1984). Smith and Glass's psychotherapy conclusions need further probing: On Landman and Dawes' reanalysis. *American Psychologist, 39*, 71-72.

Osherson, D. N., & Markman, E. (1974-75). Language and the ability to evaluate contradictions and tautologies. *Cognition, 3*(3), 213-226.

Ostberg, O. (1973). Circadian rhythms of food intake and oral temperature in "morning" and "evening" groups of individuals. *Ergonomics, 16*, 203-209.

Oster, H. (1978). Facial expression and affect development. In M. Lewis, & L. A. Rosenblum (Eds.), *The development of affect* (pp. 43-76). New York: Plenum.

Oster, H., & Ekman, P. (1978). Facial behavior in child development. *Minnesota Symposia on Child Psychology, 11*, 231-276.

Ostroff, R. B., Giller, E., Harkness, L., & Mason, J. (1985). The norepinephrine-to-epinephrine ratio in patients with a history of suicide attempts. *American Journal of Psychiatry, 142*, 224-225.

Overton, D. A. (1972). State-dependent learning produced by alcohol and its relevance to alcoholism. In B. Kissin & H. Begleiter (Eds.), *Physiology and behavior* (Vol. 2). New York: Plenum Press.

Owen, D. (1985). *None of the above: Behind the myth of scholastic aptitude*. Boston: Houghton Mifflin.

Paivio, A. (1971). *Imagery and verbal processes*. New York: Holt, Rinehart & Winston.

Paivio, A., & Desrochers, A. (1980). A dual-coding approach to bilingual memory. *Canadian Journal of Psychology, 34*, 388-399.

Paivio, A., & Lambert, W. (1981). Dual coding and bilingual memory. *Journal of Verbal Learning and Verbal Behavior, 20*, 532-539.

Palca, J. (1989). Sleep researchers awake to possibilities. *Science, 245*, 351-352.

Palisin, H. (1986). Preschool temperament and performance on achievement tests. *Developmental Psychology, 22*, 766-770.

Panksepp, J. (1986). The neurochemistry of behavior. *Annual Review of Psychology, 37*, 77-107.

Pantev, C., Hoke, M., Lutkenhoner, B., & Lehnertz, K. (1989). Tonotopic organization of the auditory cortex: Pitch versus frequency representation. *Science, 246*, 486-488.

Pappenheimer, J. R. (1976). The sleep factor. *Scientific American, 235*(2), 24-29.

Pardes, H. (1986). Neuroscience and psychiatry: marriage or coexistence? *American Journal of Psychiatry, 143*, 1205-1212.

Parfit, M. (1984, May). Mapmaker who charts our hidden mental demons. *Smithsonian*, pp. 123-131.

Parke, R. D. (1978). Children's home environments: Social and cognitive effects. In I. Altman, & J. F. Wohlwill (Eds.), *Children and the environment*. New York: Plenum.

Parke, R. D., & O'Leary, S. E. (1976). Father-mother-infant interaction in the newborn period: Some findings, some observations and some unresolved issues. In K. F. Riegel & J. A. Meacham (Eds.), *The developing individual in a changing world: Vol. 2. Social and environmental issues*. Chicago: Aldine.

Parkes, C. M. (1972). *Bereavement*. New York: Int'l Universities Press.

Pascual-Leone, A., Dhuna, A., Altafullah, I., & Anderson, D. C. (1990). Cocaine-induced seizures. *Neurology, 40*, 404-407.

Patrick, G. T. W., & Gilbert, J. A. (1896). On the effects of loss of sleep. *Psychological Review, 3*, 469-483.

Patterson, F. (1979, April). *Creative and abstract uses of language: A gorilla case study*. Paper presented at the meeting of the Western Psychological Association, San Diego, California.

Patterson, F. G., Patterson, C. H., & Brentari, D. K. (1987). Language in child, chimp, and gorilla. *American Psychologist, 42*, 270-272.

Pavlov, I. P. (1927). *Conditioned reflexes*. New York: Oxford University Press.

Pearl, D., Bouthilet, L., & Lazar, J. (Eds.). (1982). *Television and behavior: Ten years of scientific progress and implications for the eighties* (Vols. 1 & 2). Washington, DC: U.S. Govt. Printing Office.

Pedersen, E., Faucher, T. A., & Eaton, W. W. (1978). A new perspective on the effects of first grade teachers on children's subsequent adult status. *Harvard Educational Review, 48*, 1-31.

Peele, S. (1981). Reductionism in the psychology of the eighties. *American Psychologist, 36*, 807-818.

Penfield, W., & Roberts, L. (1959). *Speech and brain mechanisms*. Princeton: Princeton Univ. Press.

Penrose, R. (1989). *The emperor's new mind: Concerning computers, minds & the laws of physics*. New York: Oxford University Press.

Pepler, D. J., & Ross, H. S. (1981). The effects of play on convergent and divergent problem solving. *Child Development, 52*, 1202-1210.

Persky, V. W., Kempthorne-Rawson, J., & Shekelle, R. B. (1987). Personality and risk of cancer: 20-year followup of the Western Electric Study. *Psychosomatic Medicine, 49*, 435-449.

Pervin, L. A. (1985). Personality: Current controversies, issues, and directions. *Annual Review of Psychology, 36*, 83-114.

Peselow, E. D., Dunner, D. L., Fieve, R. R., & Lautin, A. (1982). Lithium prophylaxis of depression in unipolar, bipolar II, and cyclothymic patients. *American Journal of Psychiatry, 139*, 747-752.

Petersen, A. C. (1987, September). Those gangly years. *Psychology Today*, pp. 28-34.

Petersen, A. C., & Taylor, B. (1980). The biological approach to adolescence. In J. Adelson (Ed.), *Handbook of adolescent psychology*. New York: Wiley.

Peterson, C., Seligman, M. E., & Vaillant, G. E. (1988). Pessimistic explanatory style is a risk factor for physical illness: A thirty-five-year longitudinal study. *Journal of Personality & Social Psychology, 55*, 23-27.

Petty, R. E. (1977). The importance of cognitive responses in persuasion. *Advances in Consumer Research, 4*, 357-362.

Petty, R. E., & Cacioppo, J. T. (1979). Effects of forewarning of persuasive intent and involvement on cognitive responses and persuasion. *Personality and Social Psychology Bulletin, 5*, 173-176.

Phares, E. J., & Lamiell, J. T. (1977). Personality. *Annual Review of Psychology, 28*, 113-140.

Piaget, J. (1967). *Six psychological studies*. New York: Random House.

Piaget, J., & Inhelder, B. (1969). *The psychology of the child*. (H. Weaver, Trans.). New York: Basic Books. (Original work published 1967).

Piccione, C., Hilgard, E. R., & Zimbardo, P. G. (1989). On the degree of stability of measured hypnotizability over a 25-year period. *Journal of Personality & Social Psychology, 56*, 289-295.

Pieterse, M., & Center, Y. (1984). The integration of eight Down's Syndrome children into regular schools. *Australia & New Zealand Journal of Developmental Disabilities, 10*(1), 11-20.

Pihl, R. O., & Parkes, M. (1977). Hair element content in learning disabled children. *Science, 198,* 204-206.

Pilkonis, P. A., Imber, S. D., Lewis, P., & Rubinsky, P. (1984). A comparative outcome study of individual, group, and conjoint psychotherapy. *Archives of General Psychiatry, 41,* 431-437.

Pines, M. (1966). *Revolution in learning: The years from birth to six.* New York: Harper & Row.

Pines, M. (1983, October). Suicide signals. *Science 83,* pp. 55-58.

Pintrich, P. R., Cross, D. R., Kozma, R. B., & McKeachie, W. J. (1986). Instructional psychology. *Annual Review of Psychology, 37,* 611-651.

Pion, G. (1986, January). Job focus shifts to service, policy. *APA Monitor,* p. 25.

Pittman, T. S., & Heller, J. F. (1987). Social motivation. *Annual Review of Psychology, 38,* 461-489.

Plomin, R. (1989). Environment and genes. *American Psychologist, 44,* 105-111.

Plutchik, R. (1980, February). A language for the emotions. *Psychology Today,* pp. 68-78.

Poggio, T., & Koch, C. (1987). Synapses that compute motion. *Scientific American, 256*(5), 46-52.

Poizner, H., Klima, E., & Bellugi, U. (1987). *What the hands reveal about the brain.* Cambridge, MA: MIT Press.

Polansky, N., Lippitt, R., & Redl, F. (1950). An investigation of behavioral contagion in groups. *Human Relations, 3,* 319-348.

Pollock, D. A., Rhodes, P., Boyle, C. A., Decoufle, P., & McGee, D. L. (1990). Estimating the number of suicides among Vietnam veterans. *American Journal of Psychiatry, 147,* 772-776.

Pool, R. (1989). Chaos theory: How big an advance? *Science, 245,* 26-28.

Pope, H. G., Jr., Jonas, J. M., & Jones, B. (1982). Factitious psychosis: Phenomenology, family history, and long-term outcome of nine patients. *American Journal of Psychiatry, 139,* 1480-1483.

Pope, H. G., Jr., Keck, P. E., Jr., & McElroy, S. L. (1986). Frequency and presentation of neuroleptic malignant syndrome in a large psychiatric hospital. *American Journal of Psychiatry, 143,* 1227-1233.

Postman, L., & Rau, L. (1957). Retention as a function of the method of measurement. *University of California Publications in Psychology, 8*(3).

Power, T. G. (1981). Sex-typing in infancy: The role of the father. *Infant Mental Health Journal, 2,* 226-240.

Poznanski, E., & Zrull, J. P. (1970). Childhood depression: Clinical characteristics of overtly depressed children. *Archives of General Psychiatry, 23,* 8-15.

Premack, D. (1959). Toward empirical behavior laws: Pt. 1. Positive reinforcement. *Psychological Review, 66,* 219-233.

Pressman, M. D. (1980). Psychological techniques for the advancement of sports potential. In R. M. Suinn (Ed.), *Psychology in sports: Methods and applications* (pp. 291-296). Minneapolis, Minn.: Burgess.

Priest, R. F., & Sawyer, J. (1967). Proximity and peership: Bases of balance in interpersonal attraction. *American Journal of Sociology, 72,* 633-649.

Pritchett, D. B., Luddens, H., & Seeburg, P. H. (1989). Type I and Type II GABAAbenzodiazepine receptors produced in transfected cells. *Science, 245,* 1389-1392.

Pruitt, D. G. (1971). Conclusions: Toward an understanding of choice shifts in group discussion. *Journal of Personality & Social Psychology, 20,* 495-510.

Pryor, J. B., Gibbons, F. X., Wicklund, R. A., Fazio, R. H., & Hood, R. (1977). Self-focused attention and self-report validity. *Journal of Personality, 45,* 513-527.

Psychic Abscam. (1983, March). *Discover,* pp. 10-12.

Purves, D., Voyvodic, J. T., Magrassi, L., & Yawo, H. (1987). Nerve terminal remodeling visualized in living mice by repeated examination of the same neuron. *Science, 238,* 1122-1126.

Quattrochi, J.J., Mamelak, A. N., Madison, R. D., Macklis, J. D., & Hobson, J. A. (1989). Mapping neuronal inputs to REM sleep induction sites with carbachol-fluorescent microspheres. *Science, 245,* 984-986.

Quattrone, G. A. (1982). Overattribution and unit formation: When behavior engulfs the person. *Journal of Personality & Social Psychology, 42,* 593-607.

Quigley-Fernandez, B., & Tedeschi, J. T. (1978). The bogus pipeline as lie detector: Two validity studies. *Journal of Personality & Social Psychology, 36,* 247-256.

Rader, N. (1979, April). *The behavior of pre-crawling infants on the visual cliff with locomotor aids.* Paper presented at the meeting of the Western Psychological Association, San Diego, California.

Raloff, J. (1982, February 6). Childhood lead: Worrisome national levels. *Science News,* p. 88.

Ralph, M. R., & Menaker, M. (1988). A mutation of the circadian system in golden hamsters. *Science, 241,* 1225-1227.

Ralph, M. R., Foster, R. G., Davis, F. C., & Menaker, M. (1990). Transplanted suprachiasmatic nucleus determines circadian period. *Science, 247,* 975-978.

Ramachandran, V. S., & Anstis, S. M. (1986). The perception of apparent motion. *Scientific American, 254*(66), 102-109.

Ramey, C. (1982). Commentary by Craig T. Ramey. Monographs of the Society for Research in *Child Development, 47*(2-3, Serial No. 195), 142-151.

Ramsay, D. S. (1984). Onset of duplicated syllable babbling and unimanual handedness in infancy: Evidence for developmental change in hemispheric specialization? *Developmental Psychology, 20,* 64-71.

Ransford, C. P. (1982). A role for amines in the antidepressant effect of exercise: A review. *Medicine and Science in Sports and Exercise, 14,* 1-10.

Rapoport, J. L. (1989). The biology of obsessions and compulsions. *Scientific American, 260*(3), 83-89.

Rarick, E. (1990, July 29). Hemlock. *United Press International.*

Ray, W. A., Griffin, M. R., Schaffner, W., Baugh, D. K., & Melton, L. J. (1987). Psychotropic drug use and the risk of hip fracture. *New England Journal of Medicine, 316,* 363-369.

Raymond, C. L., & Benbow, C. P. (1986). Gender differences in mathematics: A function of parental support and student sex typing? *Developmental Psychology, 22,* 808-819.

Raz, S., & Raz, N. (1990). Structural brain abnormalities in the major psychoses: A quantiative review of the evidence from computerized imaging. *Psychological Bulletin, 108,* 93-108.

Razran, G. (1961). The observable unconscious and the inferable conscious in current Soviet psychophysiology. *Psychological Review, 68,* 81-147.

Rebar, R. W., Miyake, A., Low, T. L. K., & Goldstein, A. L. (1981). Thymosin stimulates secretion of Luteinizing hormone-releasing factor. *Science, 214,* 669-671.

Rechtschaffen, A., Gilliland, M. A., Bergmann, B. M., & Winter, J. B. (1983). Physiological correlates of prolonged sleep deprivation in rats. *Science, 221,* 182-184.

Redican, W. K. (1975). Facial expression in nonhuman primates. In L. A. Rosenblum (Ed.), *Primate behavior* (Vol. 4). New York: Academic Press.

Redlich, F., & Kellert, S. R. (1978). Trends in American mental health. *American Journal of Psychiatry, 135,* 22-28.

Reiman, E. M., Raichle, M. E., Robins, E., Butler, F. K., Herscovitch, P., Fox, P., & Perlmutter, J. (1986). The application of positron emission tomography to the study of panic disorder. *American Journal of Psychiatry, 143,* 4699-477.

Regier, D. A., Boyd, J. H., Burke, J. D., Jr., Rae, D. S., Myers, J. K., Kramer, M., Robins, L. N., George, L. K., Karno, M., Locke, B. Z. (1988). One-month prevalence of mental disorders in the United States. *Archives of General Psychiatry, 45,* 977-986.

Reinisch, J. M. (1981). Prenatal exposure to synthetic progestins increases potential for aggression in humans. *Science, 211,* 1171-1173.

Reinisch, J. M., & Beasley, R. (Eds.). (1990). *The Kinsey Institute new report on sex: What you must know to be sexually literate.* New York: St. Martin's Press.

Reppert, S. M., Weaver, D. R., Rivkees, S. A., & Stopa, E. G. (1988). Putative melatonin receptors in human biological clock. *Science, 242,* 78-81.

Rescorla, R. A. (1988). Pavlovian conditioning: It's not what you think it is. *American Psychologist, 43,* 151-160.

Resnick, S. M., Berenbaum, S. A., Gottesman, I. I., & Bouchard, T. J., Jr. (1986). Early hormonal influences on cognitive functioning in congenital adrenal hyperplasia. *Developmental Psychology, 22,* 191-198.

Rest, J. (1968). *Developmental hierarchy in preference and comprehension of moral judgment.* Unpublished doctoral dissertation, University of Chicago.

Restak, R. M. (1982, January/February). Newborn knowledge. *Science 82,* pp. 58-65.

Reston, J. (1975, March 14). Proxmire on love. *New York Times.*

Reynolds, D., & Murgatroyd, S. (1977). The sociology of schooling and the absent pupil: The school as a factor in the generation of truancy. In H. C. M. Carroll (Ed.), *Absenteeism in South Wales: Studies of pupils, their homes and their secondary schools.* Swansea: Univ. of Swansea, Faculty of Educ.

Rheingold, H. L., & Cook, K. V. (1975). The content of boys' and girls' rooms as an index of parents' behavior. *Child Development, 46,* 459-463.

Rheingold, H. L., Gewirtz, J. L., & Ross, H. W. (1959). Social conditioning of vocalizations in the infant. *Journal of Comparative and Physiological Psychology, 52,* 68-73.

Ricaurte, G., Bryan, G., Strauss, L., Seiden, L., & Schuster, C. (1985). Hallucinogenic amphetamine selectively destroys brain serotonin nerve terminals. *Science,*

229, 986-988.

Rich, C. L., Fowler, R. C., Fogarty, L. A., & Young, D. (1988). San Diego suicide study. III. Relationships between diagnoses and stressors. *Archives of General Psychiatry, 45*, 589-592.

Rich, C. L., Young, J. G., Fowler, R. C., Wagner, J., & Black, N. A. (1990). Guns and suicide: Possible effects of some specific legislation. *American Journal of Psychiatry, 147*, 342-352.

Richards, R., Kinney, D. K., Lunde, I., Benet, M., & Merzel, A. P. C. (1988). Creativity in manic-depressives, cyclothymes, their normal relatives, and control subjects. *Journal of Abnormal Psychology, 97*, 281-288.

Roberts, K. (1988). Retrieval of a basic-level category in prelinguistic infants. *Developmental Psychology, 24*, 21-27.

Roberts, L. (1989). Genome mapping goal now in reach. *Science, 244*, 424-425.

Robins, L. N., & Helzer, J. E. (1986). Diagnosis and clinical assessment: The current state of psychiatric diagnosis. *Annual Review of Psychology, 37*, 409-432.

Robinson, L. A., Berman, J. S., & Neimeyer, R. A. (1990). Psychotherapy for the treatment of depression: A comprehensive review of controlled outcome research. *Psychological Bulletin, 108*, 30-49.

Rock, I. (1984). *Perception.* New York: Scientific American Books. Rodin, J. (1981). Current status of the internal-external hypothesis for obesity: What went wrong? *American Psychologist, 36*, 361-372.

Rodin, J., & Salovey, P. (1989). Health psychology. *Annual Review of Psychology, 40*, 533- 579.

Rodin, J., & Stone, G. (1987). Historical highlights in the emergence of the field. In G. C. Stone et al. (Eds.), *Health psychology: A discipline and a profession* (pp. 15-26). Chicago: Univ. of Chicago Press.

Roehrs, T., Timms, V., Zwyghuizen-Doorenbos, A., & Roth, T. (1989). Sleep extension in sleepy and alert normals. *Sleep, 12*, 449-457.

Roff, M. (1963). Childhood social interactions and young adult psychosis. *Journal of Clinical Psychology, 19*, 152-157.

Rogel, M. J. (1978). A critical evaluation of the possibility of higher primate reproductive and sexual pheromones. *Psychological Bulletin, 85*, 810-830.

Rogers, C. R. (1951). *Client-centered therapy: Its current practice, implications, and theory.* Boston: Houghton Mifflin.

Rogers, C. R. (1961). *On becoming a person.* Boston: Houghton Mifflin.

Rogers, M. (1987, February 9). Now, "artificial reality." *Newsweek,* pp. 56-57.

Rogers, R. (1987). APA's position on the insanity defense: Empiricism versus emotionalism. *American Psychologist, 42*, 840-848.

Roopnarine, J. L. (1981). Peer play interaction in a mixed-age preschool setting. *Journal of General Psychology, 104*, 161-166.

Roopnarine, J. L., & Johnson, J. E. (1984). Socialization in a mixed-age experimental program. *Developmental Psychology, 20*, 828-832.

Roper, S. D. (1989). The cell biology of vertebrate taste receptors. *Annual Review of Neuroscience, 12*, 329-353.

Rorer, L. G., & Widiger, T. A. (1982). *Ascription rules for trait descriptive adjectives.* Paper presented at the annual conference of the Midwestern Psychological Association, Minneapolis, Minnesota.

Rorer, L. G., & Widiger, T. A. (1983). Personality structure and assessment. *Annual Review of Psychology, 34*, 431-463.

Rosch, E. (1973). On the internal structure of perceptual and semantic categories. In T. E. Moore (Ed.), *Cognitive development and the acquisition of language.* New York: Academic Press.

Rosch, E. (1977). Human categorization. In N. Warren (Ed.), *Advances in cross-cultural psychology* (Vol. I). London: Academic Press.

Rose, S. A., Feldman, J. F., & Wallace, I. F. (1988). Individual differences in infants' information processing: Reliability, stability, and prediction. *Child Development, 59*, 1177- 1197.

Rosen, D. H. (1976). Suicide survivors: psychotherapeutic implications of egocide. *Suicide: A Quarterly Journal of Life-Threatening Behavior, 6*, 209-215.

Rosenblum, L. A., & Harlow, H. F. (1963). Approach-avoidance conflict in the mother surrogate situation. *Psychological Reports, 12*, 83-85.

Rosenhan, D. L. (1973). *Moral development.* CRM McGraw-Hill Films.

Rosenhan, D. L. (1973). On being sane in insane places. *Science, 179*, 250-258.

Rosenkrantz, A. L. (1978). A note on adolescent suicide: Incidence, dynamics and some suggestions for treatment. *Adolescence, 13*, 109-214.

Rosenthal, D., & Quinn, O. W. (1977). Quadruplet hallucinations: Phenotypic variations of a schizophrenic genotype. *Archives of General Psychiatry, 34*, 817-827.

Rosenthal, M. K. (1982). Vocal dialogues in the neonatal period. *Developmental Psychology, 18*, 17-21.

Rosenzweig, M. R. (1984). Experience, memory, and the brain. *American Psychologist, 39*, 365-376.

Rosenzweig, S. (1985). Freud and experimental psychology: The emergence of idiodynamics. In S. Koch & D. E. Leary (Eds.), *A century of psychology as science* (pp. 135-207). New York: McGraw-Hill.

Rotter, J. B. (1972). Beliefs, social attitudes, and behavior: A social learning analysis. In J. B. Rotter, J. E. Chance, & E. J. Phares (Eds.), *Applications of a social learning theory of personality.* New York: Holt, Rinehart & Winston.

Roueche, B. (1980). *The medical detectives.* New York: Truman Talley Books.

Roy, A., De Jong, J., & Linnoila, M. (1989). Cerebrospinal fluid monoamine metabolites and suicidal behavior in depressed patients. A 5-year follow-up study. *Archives of General Psychiatry, 46*, 609-612.

Roy-Byrne, P. P., Geraci, M., & Uhde, T. W. (1986). Life events and the onset of panic disorder. *American Journal of Psychiatry, 143*, 1424-1427.

Rubin, J. Z., & Brown, B. R. (1975). *The social psychology of bargaining and negotiation.* New York: Academic Press.

Rubin, Z. (1973). *Liking and loving: An invitation to social psychology.* New York: Holt, Rinehart & Winston.

Rubinstein, E. A. (1983). Television and behavior: Research conclusions of the 1982 NIMH report and their policy implications. *American Psychologist, 38*, 820-825.

Ruble, D. N. (1984). Sex-role development. In M. H. Bornstein, & M. E. Lamb (Eds.), *Developmental psychology: An advanced textbook* (pp. 325-371). Hillsdale, NJ: Lawrence Erlbaum.

Ruch, J. C. (1975). Self-hypnosis: The result of heterohypnosis or vice versa? *International Journal of Clinical and Experimental Hypnosis, 23*, 282-304.

Rucker, R. (1981, July/August). Who makes math marvelous, turns magic satin smooth, tends the looking-glass garden, and can make a winner of anyone who plays his games? *Science 81,* pp. 33-37.

Ruff, M. R., Wahl, S. M., Mergenhagen, S., & Pert, C. B. (1985). Opiate receptor-mediated chemotaxis of human monocytes. *Neuropeptides, 5*, 363-366.

Rundus, D. (1971). Analysis of rehearsal processes in free recall. *Journal of Experimental Psychology, 89*, 63-77.

Rushton, E. W. (1965). *The Roanoke experiment.* Chicago: Encyc. Britannica Press.

Russell, J. A., & Ward, L. M. (1982). Environmental psychology. *Annual Review of Psychology, 33*, 651-688.

Rutter, M. (1983). School effects on pupil progress: Research findings and policy implications. *Child Development, 54*, 1-29.

Rutter, M., Maughan, B., Mortimore, P., Ouston, J., & Smith, A. (1979). *Fifteen thousand hours: Secondary schools and their effects on children.* Cambridge, MA: Harvard University Press.

Ryan, E. D., & Kovacic, C. R. (1966). Pain tolerance and athletic participation. *Perceptual and Motor Skills, 22*, 383-390.

Ryan, M. J. (1980). Psychobiology and consumer research: A problem of construct validity. *Journal of Consumer Research, 7*, 92-96.

Sacks, M., Carpenter, W. T., & Richmond, M. B. (1975). Psychotherapy in hospitalized research patients. *Archives of General Psychiatry, 32*, 581-585.

Sacks, O. (1985). *The man who mistook his wife for a hat.* New York: Summit Books.

Saegert, S., & Winkel, G. H. (1990). Environmental psychology. *Annual Review of Psychology, 41*, 441-477.

Samiy, A. H., & Rosnick, P. B. (1987). Early identification of renal problems in patients receiving chronic lithium treatment. *American Journal of Psychiatry, 144*, 670-672.

Sampson, E. E. (1962). Birth order, need achievement, and conformity. *Journal of Abnormal and Social Psychology, 64*, 155-159.

Sampson, E. E. (1978). Scientific paradigms and social values: Wanted—A scientific revolution. *Journal of Personality & Social Psychology, 36*, 1332-1343.

Sandblom, R. E., Matsumoto, A. M., Schoene, R. B., Lee, K. A., Giblin, E. C., Bremner, W. J., & Pierson, D. J. (1983). Sleep apnea induced by testosterone administration. *New England Journal of Medicine, 308*, 508-510.

Sandman, C. A., George, J. M., Nolan, J. D., Van Riezen, H., & Kastin, A. J. (1975). Enhancement of attention in man with ACTH/MSH 4-10. *Physiology and Behavior, 15*, 427-431.

Sapolsky, R. M. (1990). Stress in the wild. *Scientific American, 262*(1), 116-123.

Sarbin, T. R. (1950). Contributions to role-taking theory: I. Hypnotic behavior. *Psychological Review, 57*, 255-270.

Sarbin, T. R., & Coe, W. C. (1972). *Hypnosis: A social psychological analysis of influence communication.* New York: Holt, Rinehart & Winston.

Savage-Rumbaugh, E. S., Rumbaugh, D. M., & Boysen, S. (1978). Symbolic communication between two chimpanzees. *Science, 201*, 641-644.

Savitsky, J. C., Rogers, R. W., Izard, C. E., & Liebert, R. M. (1971). Role of frustration and anger in the imitation of filmed aggression against a human victim.

Psychological Reports, 29, 807-810.

Saxe, L., Dougherty, D., & Cross, T. (1985). The validity of polygraph testing: Scientific analysis and public controversy. *American Psychologist, 40,* 355-366.

Scarr, S., & McCartney, K. (1988). Far from home: An experimental evaluation of the mother-child home program in Bermuda. *Child Development, 59,* 531-543.

Scarr, S., & Weinberg, R. A. (1976). IQ test performance of black children adopted by white families. *American Psychologist, 31,* 726-739.

Schacht, T., & Nathan, P. E. (1977). But is it good for the psychologists? *American Psychologist, 21,* 1017-1025.

Schachter, S. (1977). Studies of the interaction of psychological and pharmacological determinants of smoking: 1. Nicotine regulation in heavy and light smokers. *Journal of Experimental Psychology: General, 106,* 5-12.

Schachter, S. (1982). Recidivism and self-cure of smoking and obesity. *American Psychologist, 37,* 436-444.

Schachter, S., Kozlowski, L. T., & Silverstein, B. (1977). Studies of the interaction of psychological and pharmacological determinants of smoking: 2. Effects of urinary pH on cigarette smoking. *Journal of Experimental Psychology: General, 106,* 13-19.

Schachter, S., Silverstein, B., & Perlick, D. (1977). Studies of the interaction of psychological and pharmacological determinants of smoking: 5. Psychological and pharmacological explanations of smoking under stress. *Journal of Experimental Psychology: General, 106,* 31-40.

Schachter, S., & Singer, J. E. (1962). Cognitive, social, and physiological determinants of emotional state. *Psychological Review, 69,* 379-399.

Schaffer, H. R., & Emerson, P. E. (1964). The development of social attachments in infancy. *Monographs of the Society for Research in Child Development, 29*(3, Serial No. 94).

Schatzberg, A. F. (1987, July). New antidepressants. *Harvard Medical School Mental Health Letter,* p. 8.

Scheller, R. H., & Axel, R. (1984). How genes control an innate behavior. *Scientific American, 250*(3), 54-62.

Schiff, M., Duyme, M., Dumaret, A., & Tomkiewicz, S. (1982). How much could we boost scholastic achievement and IQ scores? A direct answer from a French adoption study. *Cognition, 12,* 165-196.

Schiller, P. H. (1957). Innate motor action as a basis of learning. In S. H. Schiller (Ed.), *Instinctive behavior.* New York: Int'l Universities Press.

Schleifer, S. J., Keller, S. E., Camerino, M., Thornton, J. C., & Stein, M. (1983). Suppression of lymphocyte stimulation following bereavement. *Journal of the American Medical Association, 250,* 374-377.

Schlenker, B. R. (1978). Attitudes as actions: Social identity theory and consumer research. *Advances in Consumer Research, 5,* 352-359.

Schlenker, B. R., & Schlenker, P. A. (1975). Reactions following counterattitudinal behavior which produces positive consequences. *Journal of Personality & Social Psychology, 31,* 962-971.

Schmitt, N., & Robertson, I. (1990). Personnel selection. *Annual Review of Psychology, 41,* 289-319.

Schnapf, J. L., & Baylor, D. A. (1987). How photoreceptor cells respond to light. *Scientific American, 256*(4), 40-47.

Schneider, B. (1985). Organizational behavior. *Annual Review of Psychology, 36,* 573-611.

Schuckit, M. A., Gold, E., & Risch, C. (1987). Serum prolactin levels in sons of alcoholics and control subjects. *American Journal of Psychiatry, 144,* 854-859.

Schwartz, R. H., Gruenewald, P. J., Klitzner, M., & Fedio, P. (1989). Short-term memory impairment in cannabis-dependent adolescents. *American Journal of Diseases of Children, 143,* 1214-1219.

Schweinhart, L. J., & Weikart, D. P. (1986). What do we know so far? A review of the Head Start Synthesis Project. *Young Children, 41,* 49-55.

Schweinhart, L. J., & Weikart, D. P. (1985). Evidence that good early childhood programs work. *Phi Delta Kappan, 66,* 545-551.

Scott, D. H. (1983). Brain size and "intelligence." *British Journal of Developmental Psychology, 1,* 279-287.

Scott, M. D., & Pelliccioni, L., Jr. (1982). *Don't choke: How athletes can become winners.* Englewood Cliffs, NJ: Prentice-Hall.

Sechenov, I. M. (1965). *Reflexes of the brain.* (Reprint of a 1961 translation by S. Belsky, printed in Moscow, of a work published in Russian in 1863). Cambridge, MA: MIT Press.

Sechrest, L. (1976). Personality. *Annual Review of Psychology, 27,* 1-28.

Segal, M. W. (1974). Alphabet and attraction: An unobtrusive measure of the effect of propinquity in a field setting. *Journal of Personality & Social Psychology, 30,* 654-657.

Segal, N. L. (1985). Monozygotic and dizygotic twins: A comparative analysis of mental ability profiles. *Child Development, 56,* 1051-1058.

Seligman, M E. P., & Maier, S. F. (1967). Failure to escape traumatic shock. *Journal of Experimental Psychology, 74,* 1-9.

Seligman, M. E. P. (1970). On the generality of the laws of learning. *Psychological Review, 77,* 406-418.

Seligman, J., & Donosky, L. (1980, April 7). A manual on how to commit suicide. *Newsweek,* p. 77.

Seligman, J., & Gosnell, M. (1986, March 3). Now, the gastric bubble. *Newsweek,* p. 59.

Seligmann, J., & Shapiro, D. (1979, November 12). Saved by lithium. *Newsweek,* p. 102.

Selmi, P. M., Klein, M. H., Greist, J. H., Sorrell, S. P., & Erdman, H. P. (1990). Computer- administered cognitive-behavioral therapy for depression. *American Journal of Psychiatry, 147,* 51-56.

Selye, H. (1976). *The stress of life* (2nd ed.). New York: McGraw-Hill, 1976.

Semmel, M. I., Gottlieb, J., & Robinson, N. M. (1979). Mainstreaming: Perspectives on educating handicapped children in the public schools. In D. C. Berliner (Ed.), *Review of research in education* (Vol. 7, pp. 223-279). Washington, DC: Amer. Educ. Research Ass.

Serbin, L. A., & Sprafkin, C. (1986). The salience of gender and the process of sex typing in three- to seven-year-old children. *Child Development, 57,* 1188-1199.

Serock, K., Seefeldt, C., Jantz, R. K., & Galper, A. (1977). As children see old folks. *Today's Education, 66*(2), 70-73.

Shanab, M. E., & Yahya, K. A. (1977). A behavioral study of obedience in children. *Journal of Personality & Social Psychology, 35,* 530-536.

Shapira, A., & Madsen, M. C. (1974). Between- and within-group cooperation and competition among kibbutz and nonkibbutz children. *Developmental Psychology, 10,* 140-145.

Shapiro, A. K., Struening, E., Shapiro, E., & Barten, H. (1976). Prognostic correlates of psychotherapy in psychiatric outpatients. *American Journal of Psychiatry, 133,* 802-808.

Shapiro, D. H., Jr. (1985). Clinical use of meditation as a self-regulation strategy: Comments on Holmes's conclusions and implications. *American Psychologist, 40,* 719-722.

Shatz, M. (1973). *Preschooler's ability to take account of others in a toy selection task.* Unpublished MA thesis, University of Pennsylvania, Philadelphia, Pennsylvania.

Shaver, J. P., & Strong, W. (1976). *Facing value decisions: Rationale-building for teachers.* Belmont, CA: Wadsworth.

Shekelle, R. B., Hulley, S. B., Neaton, J. D., Billings, J. H., Borhani, N. O., Gerace, T. A., Jacobs, D. R., Lasser, N. L., Mittlemark, M. B., & Stamler, J. (1985). The MRFIT behavior pattern study. II. Type A behavior and incidence of coronary heart disease. *American Journal of Epidemiology, 122,* 559-570.

Sheldon, W. H. (1940). *The varieties of human physique: An introduction to constitutional psychology.* New York: Harper.

Sheldon, W. H. (1944). Constitutional factors in personality. In J. McV. Hunt (Ed.), *Personality and the behavior disorders.* New York: Ronald Press.

Shelton, R. C., Karson, C. N., Doran, A. R., Pickar, D., Bigelow, L. B., & Weinberger, D. R. (1988). Cerebral structural pathology in schizophrenia: Evidence for a selective prefrontal cortical defect. *American Journal of Psychiatry, 145,* 154-163.

Shertzer, B., & Stone, S. C. (1976). *Fundamentals of guidance* (3rd ed.). Boston: Houghton Mifflin.

Shilts, R. (1987). *And the band played on.* New York: St. Martin's Press.

Shock, N. W. (1962). The physiology of aging, *Scientific American, 206*(1), 100-110.

Shore, J. H., Tatum, E. L., & Vollmer, W. M. (1986). Psychiatric reactions to disaster: The Mount St. Helens experience. *American Journal of Psychiatry, 143,* 590-595.

Shotland, R. L. & Heinold, W. D. (1985). Bystander response to arterial bleeding: Helping skills, the decision-making process, and differentiating the helping response. *Journal of Personality & Social Psychology, 49,* 347-356.

Shotland, R. L. & Huston, T. L. (1979). Emergencies: What are they and do they influence bystanders to intervene? *Journal of Personality & Social Psychology, 37,* 1822-1834.

Shrauger, J. S. & Osberg, T M. (1981). The relative accuracy of self-predictions and judgments by others in psychological assessment. *Psychological Bulletin, 90,* 322-352.

Shuchter, S. R., Zisook, S., Kirkorowicz, C., & Risch, C. (1986). The dexamethasone suppression test in acute grief. *American Journal of Psychiatry, 143,* 879-881.

Shulman, R. G. (1983). NMR spectroscopy of living cells. *Scientific American, 248*(1), 86-93.

Siegel, S. (1975). Evidence from rats that morphine tolerance is a learned response. *Journal of Comparative and Physiological Psychology, 89,* 498-506.

Siegel, S., Hinson, R. E., Krank, M. D., & McCully, J. (1982). Heroin "overdose" death: Contribution of drug-associated environmental causes. *Science, 216*, 436-437.

Siffre, M. (1975). Six months alone in a cave. *National Geographic, 147*, 426-435.

Silberner, J. (1984, July 14). Sex differences in the brain: Coming out of the closet. *Science News*, p. 23.

Silveira, J. (1971). *Incubation: The effect of interruption timing and length on problem solution and quality of problem processing*. Unpublished doctoral dissertation, University of Oregon.

Silverstein, B., Kozlowski, L. T., & Schachter, S. (1977). Studies of the interaction of psychological and pharmacological determinants of smoking: 3. Social life, cigarette smoking, and urinary pH. *Journal of Experimental Psychology: General, 106*, 20-23.

Simonson, N. R., & Lundy, R. M. (1966). The effectiveness of persuasive communication presented under conditions of irrelevant fear. *Journal of Communication, 16*, 32-37.

Simpson, E. L. (1974). Moral development research: A case study of scientific cultural bias. *Human Development, 17*, 81-106.

Singer, J. L., & Kolligan, J., Jr. (1987). Personality: Developments in the study of private experience. *Annual Review of Psychology, 38*, 533-574.

Singer, J. L., & Singer, D. G. (1983a). Psychologists look at television: Cognitive, developmental, personality, and social policy implications. *American Psychologist, 38*, 826-834.

Singer, J. L., & Singer, D. G. (1983b). Implications of childhood television viewing for cognition, imagination, and emotion. In J. Bryant, & D. R. Anderson (Eds.), *Children's understanding of television: Research on attention and comprehension*. New York: Academic Press.

Singer, L. M., Brodzinsky, D. M., Ramsay, D., Steir, M., & Waters, E. (1985). Mother-infant attachment in adoptive families. *Child Development, 56*, 1543-1551.

Skinner, B. F. (1953). *Science and human behavior*. New York: Macmillan.

Skinner, B. F. (1969). *Contingencies of reinforcement: A theoretical analysis*. New York: Appleton-Century-Crofts.

Skinner, B. F. (1984). The shame of American education. *American Psychologist, 39*, 947-954.

Skinner, B. F. (1989). The origins of cognitive thought. *American Psychologist, 44*, 13-18.

Slobin, D. I. (1970). Universals of grammatical development in children. In G. B. Flores d'Arcams & W. J. M. Levelt (Eds.), *Advances in psycholinguistics*. New York: American Elsevier.

Sloviter, R. S., Valiquette, G., Abrams, G. M., Ronk, E. C., Sollas, A. L., Paul, L. A., & Neubort, S. (1989). Selective loss of hippocampal granule cells in the mature rat brain after adrenalectomy. *Science, 243*, 535-538.

Smith, C. G., Almirez, R. G., Berenberg, J., & Asch, R. H. (1983). Tolerance develops to the disruptive effects of delta9-tetrahydrocannabinol on primate menstrual cycle. *Science, 219*, 1453-1455.

Smith, D., & Kraft, W. A. (1983). DSM-III: Do psychologists really want an alternative? *American Psychologist, 38*, 777-792.

Smith, F. J. (1977). Work attitudes as predictors of attendance on a specific day. *Journal of Applied Psychology, 62*, 16-19.

Smith, J. (1989). *Senses and sensibilities*. New York: John Wiley & Sons.

Smith, M. B. (1950). The phenomenological approach in personality theory: Some critical remarks. *Journal of Abnormal and Social Psychology, 45*, 516-522.

Smith, M. L., & Glass, G. V. (1977). Meta-analysis of psychotherapy outcome studies. *American Psychologist, 32*, 752-760.

Smith, S. M. (1985). Background music and context-dependent memory. *American Journal of Psychology, 98*, 591-603.

Smith, S. M., Brown, H. O., Toman, J. E. P., & Goodman, L. S. (1947). The lack of cerebral effects of d-Tubercurarine. *Anesthesiology, 8*, 1-14.

Smith, S. M., Glenberg, A., & Bjork, R. A. (1978). Environmental context and human memory. *Memory and Cognition, 6*, 342-353.

Snyder, C. R., Shenkel, R. J., & Lowery, C. R. (1977). Acceptance of personality interpretations: The "Barnum effect" and beyond. *Journal of Consulting & Clinical Psychology, 45*, 104-114.

Snyder, S. H. (1973). Amphetamine psychosis: A "model" schizophrenia mediated by catecholamines. *American Journal of Psychiatry, 130*, 61-67.

Snyder, S. H. (1984). Cholinergic mechanisms in affective disorder. *New England Journal of Medicine, 311*, 254-255.

Snyder, S. H. (1984). Drug and neurotransmitter receptors in the brain. *Science, 224*, 22-31.

Snyderman, M., & Rothman, S. (1987). Survey of expert opinion on intelligence and aptitude testing. *American Psychologist, 42*, 137-144.

Solomon, H., & Solomon, L. Z. (1978, March). *Effects of anonymity on helping in emergency situations*. Paper presented at the meeting of the Eastern Psychological Association, Washington, D.C.

Solomon, R. L. (1980). The opponent-process theory of acquired motivation: The costs of pleasure and the benefits of pain. *American Psychologist, 35*, 691-712.

Soni, S. D., & Rockley, G. J. (1974). Socio-clinical substrates of folie a deux. *British Journal of Psychiatry, 125*, 230-235.

Sonstroem, R. J. (1981). Exercise and self-esteem: Recommendations for expository research. *Quest, 33*, 124-139.

Sorbera, L. A., & Morad, M. (1990). Atrionatriuretic peptide transforms cardiac sodium channels into calcium-conducting channels. *Science, 247*, 969-973.

Sorce, J. F., Emde, R. N., Campos, J., & Klinnert, M. D. (1985). Maternal emotional signaling: Its effect on the visual cliff behavior of 1-year-olds. *Developmental Psychology, 21*, 195-200.

Soskin, W. F. (1959). Influence of four types of data on diagnostic conceptualization in psychological testing. *Journal of Abnormal and Social Psychology, 58*, 69-78.

Spacapan, S., & Cohen, S. (1977, August). *Density, task load, and helping: Interpreting the aftereffects of stress*. Paper presented at the meeting of the American Psychological Association, San Francisco.

Spanos, N. P., Ansari, F., & Stam, H. J. (1979). Hypnotic age regression and eidetic imagery: A failure to replicate. *Journal of Abnormal Psychology, 88*, 88-91.

Spearman, C. (1927). *The abilities of man*. New York: Macmillan.

Spence, J. T. (1985). Achievement American style. *American Psychologist, 40*, 1285-1295.

Sperling, G. (1960). The information available in brief visual presentations. *Psychological Monographs, 74*(11, Whole No. 498).

Spiegel, D., Bierre, P., & Rootenberg, J. (1989). Hypnotic alteration of somatosensory perception. *American Journal of Psychiatry, 146*, 749-754.

Spitz, R. A. (1945). Hospitalism: An inquiry into the genesis of psychiatric conditions in early childhood. *Psychoanalytic Study of the Child, 1*, 53-74.

Spitzer, R. L., & Williams, J. B. W. (Eds.). (1987) *Diagnostic and statistical manual of mental disorders* (3rd rev. ed.). Washington, DC: Am. Psychiatric Assn.

Spring, R. L. (1979). The end of insanity. *Washburn Law Journal, 19*, 23-37.

Squire, L. R. (1986). Mechanisms of memory. *Science, 232*, 1612-1616.

Squire, L. R., & Zouzounis, J. A. (1986). ECT and memory: Brief pulse versus sine wave. *American Journal of Psychiatry, 143*, 596-601.

Sroufe, L. A. (1983). Individual patterns of adaptation from infancy to preschool. In M. Perlmutter (Ed.), *Minnesota Symposium in Child Psychology* (Vol. 16). Hillsdale, NJ: Erlbaum.

Sroufe, R., Chaikin, A., Cook, R., & Freeman, V. (1977). The effects of physical attractiveness on honesty: A socially desirable response. *Personality and Social Psychology Bulletin, 3*, 59-62.

Staats, A. W., & Staats, C. K. (1958). Attitudes established by classical conditioning. *Journal of Abnormal and Social Psychology, 57*, 37-40.

Stallings, J. (1975). Implementation and child effects of teaching practices in Follow Through Classrooms. *Monographs of the Society for Research in Child Development, 40*(5, Serial No. 163).

Stanfiel, J. D. (1981, Spring). The questionable sanity of the insanity defense. *Barrister*, pp. 19-20; 48-51.

Stapp, J., & Fulcher, R. (1983). The employment of APA members: 1982. *American Psychologist, 38*, 1298-1320.

Stark, E. (1981, September). Pigeon patrol. *Science 81*, pp. 85-86.

Stark, E. (1984, February). Hypnosis on trial. *Psychology Today*, pp. 34-36.

Starr, M. D. (1978). An opponent-process theory of motivation: VI. Time and intensity variables in the development of separation-induced distress calling in ducklings. *Journal of Experimental Psychology: Animal Behavior Processes, 4*, 338-355.

Staw, B. M. (1984). Organizational behavior: A review and reformulation of the field's outcome variables. *Annual Review of Psychology, 35*, 627-666.

Staw, B. M., & Oldham, G. R. (1978). Reconsidering our dependent variables: A critique and empirical study. *Academy of Management Journal, 21*, 539-559.

Steadman, H. J., Callahan, L. A., Robbins, P. C., & Morrissey, J. P. (1989). Maintenance of an insanity defense under Montana's "abolition" of the insanity defense. *American Journal of Psychiatry, 146*, 357-360.

Steblay, N. M. (1987). Helping behavior in rural and urban environments: A meta-analysis. *Psychological Bulletin, 102*, 346-356.

Steele, C. M. (1986, January). What happens when you drink too much? *Psychology Today*, pp. 48-52.

Stephan, W. G. & Rosenfield, D. (1978). Effects of desegregation on racial attitudes. *Journal of Personality & Social Psychology, 36*, 795-804.

Stern, D. B. (1977). Handedness and the lateral distribution of conversion reactions.

Journal of Nervous & Mental Disease, 164, 122-128.

Sternberg, D. E. (1986). Neuroleptic malignant syndrome: The pendulum swings. *American Journal of Psychiatry, 143*, 1273-1275.

Sternberg, R. J. (1984). *Beyond IQ: A triarchic theory of human intelligence*. New York: Cambridge Univ. Press.

Sternberg, R. J. (1985). Human intelligence: The model is the message. *Science, 230*, 1111-1118.

Sternberg, R. J. (1987). Liking versus loving: A comparative evaluation of theories. *American Psychologist, 102*, 331-345.

Stevens, C. F. (1979). The neuron. *Scientific American, 241*(3), 54-65.

Stith, S. M., & Davis, A. J. (1984). Employed mothers and family day-care substitute caregivers: A comparative analysis of infant care. *Child Development, 55*, 1340-1348.

Stoel-Gammon, C., & Otomo, K. (1986). Babbling development of hearing-impaired and normally hearing subjects. *Journal of Speech & Hearing Disorders, 51*, 33-41.

Stoller, R. J. (1985). *Presentations of gender*. New Haven: Yale Univ. Press.

Strahilevitz, M., Strahilevitz, A., & Miller, J. E. (1979). Air pollutants and the admission rate of psychiatric patients. *American Journal of Psychiatry, 136*, 205-207.

Stunkard, A. J. (1958). The management of obesity. *New York State Journal of Medicine, 58*, 79-87.

Suddath, R. L., Casanova, M. F., Goldberg, T. E., Daniel, D. G., Kelsoe, J. R., Jr., & Weinberger, D. R. (1989). Temporal lobe pathology in schizophrenia: A quantitative magnetic resonance imaging study. *American Journal of Psychiatry, 146*, 464-472.

Suddath, R. L., Christison, G. W., Torrey, E. F., Casanova, M. F., & Weinberger, D. R. (1990). Anatomical abnormalities in the brains of monozygotic twins discordant for schizophrenia. *New England Journal of Medicine, 322*, 789-794.

Suedfeld, P., & Coren, S. (1989). Perceptual isolation, sensory deprivation, and rest: Moving introductory psychology texts out of the 1950s. *Canadian Psychology, 30*, 17-29.

Suedfeld, P., Ballard, E. J., & Murphy, M. (1983). Water immersion and flotation: From stress experiment to stress treatment. *Journal of Environmental Psychology, 3*, 147-155.

Suedfeld, P., & Kristeller, J. L. (1982). Stimulus reduction as a technique in health psychology. *Health Psychology, 1*, 337-357.

Suinn, R. M. (1977). Type A behavior pattern. In R. B. Williams, Jr. & W. D. Gentry (Eds.), *Behavioral approaches to medical treatment* (pp. 55-56). Cambridge, Mass.: Ballinger.

Suler, J. R. (1985). Meditation and somatic arousal: A comment on Holmes's review. *American Psychologist, 40*, 717.

Sulloway, F. J. (1979). *Freud: Biologist of the mind*. New York: Basic Books.

Sussman, N. (1976). Sex and sexuality in history. In B. J. Sadock, H. I. Kaplan, & A. M. Freedman (Eds.), *The sexual experience*. Baltimore, MD: Williams & Wilkins.

Svaetichin, G. (1956). Spectral response curves from single cones. *Acta Physiologica Scandinavica, 39*(Supplementum No. 134), 17-46.

Swaab, D. F., & Fliers, E. (1985). A sexually dimorphic nucleus in the human brain. *Science, 228*, 1112-1115.

Swap, W. C. (1977). Interpersonal attraction and repeated exposure to rewarders and punishers. *Personality and Social Psychology Bulletin, 3*, 248-251.

Swartz, M., Blazer, D., George, L., & Landerman, R. (1986). Somatization disorder in a community population. *American Journal of Psychiatry, 143*, 1403-1408.

Sylva, K., Bruner, J., & Genova, P. (1976). The role of play in the problem solving of children 3-5 years old. In J. S. Bruner, A. Jolly, & K. Sylva (Eds.), *Play*. New York: Basic Books.

Szasz, T. (1986). The case against suicide prevention. *American Psychologist, 41*, 806-812.

Szasz, T. (1987). Response to Clum. *American Psychologist, 42*, 885-886.

Szasz, T. S. (1961). *The myth of mental illness: Foundations of a theory of personal conduct*. New York: Harper & Row.

Szucko, J. J., & Kleinmuntz, B. (1981). Statistical versus clinical lie detection. *American Psychologist, 36*, 488-496.

Tajfel, H. (1982). Social psychology of intergroup relations. *Annual Review of Psychology, 33*, 1-39.

Tanner, J. M. (1969). Growth and endocrinology in the adolescent. In L. I. Gardner (Ed.), *Endocrine and genetic diseases of childhood*. Philadelphia, PA: Saunders.

Taub, J. M., & Berger, R. J. (1976). Altered sleep duration and sleep period time displacements: Effects on performance in habitual long sleepers. *Physiology & Behavior, 16*, 177-184.

Tauber, E. S. (1974). Phylogeny of sleep. In E. D. Weitzman (Ed.), *Advances in sleep research I.* (pp. 133-172). New York: Spectrum.

Taussig, H. B. (1969). "Death" from lightning and the possibility of living again. *American Scientist, 57*, 306-316.

Taylor, J. R., & Combs-Orme, T. (1985). Alcohol and strokes in young adults. *American Journal of Psychiatry, 142*, 116-120.

Taylor, M., & Gelman, S. A. (1989). Incorporating new words into the lexicon: Preliminary evidence for language hierarchies in two-year-old children. *Child Development, 60*, 625-636.

Taylor, S. E. (1990). Health psychology: The science and the field. *American Psychologist, 45*, 40-50.

Taylor, S. E., & Fiske, S. T. (1978). Salience, attention, and attribution: Top of the head phenomena. In L. Berkowitz (Ed.), *Advances in experimental social psychology* (Vol. 11). New York: Academic Press.

Teborg, R. H. (1968). *Dissipation of functional fixedness by means of conceptual grouping tasks*. Unpublished doctoral dissertation, Michigan State University.

Tedeschi, J. T. (Ed.). (1981). *Impression management theory and social psychological research*. New York: Academic Press.

Tedeschi, J. T., Schlenker, B. R., & Bonoma, T. V. (1971). Cognitive dissonance: Private ratiocination or public spectacle? *American Psychologist, 26*, 685-695.

Teplin, L. A. (1984). Criminalizing mental disorder: The comparative arrest rate of the mentally ill. *American Psychologist, 39*, 794-803.

Teplin, L. A. (1985). The criminality of the mentally ill: A dangerous misconception. *American Journal of Psychiatry, 142*, 593-599.

Terman, L. M. (1925). Mental and physical traits of a thousand gifted children. In L. M. Terman (Ed.), *Genetic studies of genius*. Stanford: Stanford University Press.

Terman, L. M. (1954). Scientists and nonscientists in a group of 800 gifted men. *Psychological Monographs, 68*(7), 1-44.

Terrace, H. S. (1979). *Nim*. New York: Knopf.

Terrace, H. S. (1987). Chunking by a pigeon in a serial learning task. *Nature, 325*, 149-151.

Tessler, R., & Sushelsky, L. (1978). Effects of eye contact and social status on the perception of a job applicant in an employment interviewing situation. *Journal of Vocational Behavior, 13*, 338-347.

Tetrud, J. W., & Langston, J. W. (1989). The effect of deprenyl (selegiline) on the natural history of Parkinson's disease. *Science, 245*, 519-522.

Thomas, A., Chess, S., & Birch, H. (1968). *Temperament and behavior disorders in children*. New York: New York Univ. Press.

Thomas, A., Chess, S., & Birch, H. G. (1970). The origin of personality. *Scientific American, 223*(2), 102-109.

Thompson, J. W., & Blaine, J. D. (1987). Use of ECT in the United States in 1975 and 1980. *American Journal of Psychiatry, 144*, 557-562.

Thompson, R. F. (1986). The neurobiology of learning and memory. *Science, 233*, 941-947.

Thompson, S. K. (1975). Gender labels and early sex role development. *Child Development, 46*, 339-347.

Thorndike, E. L. (1905). *The elements of psychology*. New York: Seiler.

Thurstone, L. L. (1938). Primary mental abilities. *Psychometric Monographs, 1*.

Timberlake, W., & Allison, J. (1974). An empirical approach to instrumental performance. *Psychological Review, 81*, 146-164.

Tollefson, D. L. (1984). Personal communication.

Tolman, E. C., Ritchie, B. F., & Kalish, D. (1964). Studies in spatial learning. I. Orientation and the short-cut. *Journal of Experimental Psychology, 36*, 13-24.

Tomkins, S. S. (1962). *Affect, imagery, consciousness, the positive affects* (Vol. 1). New York: Springer.

Tomkins, S. S. (1963). *Affect, imagery, consciousness, the negative affects* (Vol. 2). New York: Springer.

Tong, Y. C., Dowell, R. C., Blamey, P. J., & Clark, G. M. (1983). Two component hearing sensations produced by two-electrode stimulation in the cochlea of a deaf patient. *Science, 219*, 993-994.

Tordoff, M. G., & Friedman, M. I. (1989). Drinking saccharin increases food intake and preference. *Appetite, 12*, 37-56.

Torrance, E. P., & Wu, T. (1981). A comparative longitudinal study of the adult creative achievements of elementary school children identified as high intelligent and as highly creative. *Creative Child and Adult Quarterly, 6*, 71-76.

Torrey, E. F., & Peterson, M. R. (1976). The viral hypothesis of schizophrenia. *Schizophrenia Bulletin, 2*, 136-146.

Tourangeau, T., & Rasinski, K. A. (1988). Cognitive processes underlying context effects in attitude measurement. *Psychological Bulletin, 103*, 299-314.

Tranel, D., & Damasio, A. R. (1985). Knowledge without awareness: An automatic index of facial recognition by prosopagnosics. *Science, 228,* 1453-1454.

Treatment book is born in controversy. (1989, August). *APA Monitor,* pp. 19-20.

Troll, L. E. (1975). *Early and middle adulthood.* Monterey, CA: Brooks/Cole.

Trotter, R. J. (1987, May). You've come a long way, baby. *Psychology Today,* pp. 34-45.

Trotter, R. J. (1990, June). Chemistry of compulsion. *Discover,* pp. 26-27.

Tseng, W., Ebata, K., Miguchi, M., Egawa, M., & McLaughlin, D. G. (1990). Transethnic adoption and personality traits: A lesson from Japanese orphans returned from China to Japan. *American Journal of Psychiatry, 147,* 330-335.

Tulving, E. (1985). How many memory systems are there? *American Psychologist, 40,* 385-398.

Tulving, E., & Schacter, D. L. (1990). Priming and human memory systems. *Science, 247,* 301-306.

Tune, G. S. (1969). Sleep and wakefulness in 509 normal human adults. *British Journal of Medical Psychology, 42,* 75-79.

Turkington, C. (1986, April). Dolphins: Responses to signs, sounds suggest they understand our orders. *APA Monitor,* pp. 32-33.

Turkington, C. (1987, January). Alzheimer's & aluminum. *APA Monitor,* pp. 13-14.

Turnbull, C. M. (1961). Some observations regarding the experiences and behavior of the Bambuti Pygmies. *American Journal of Psychology, 74,* 304-308.

Turvey, M. T., & Shaw, R. E. (1979). The primacy of perceiving: An ecological reformulation of perception for understanding memory. In L. G. Nilsson (Ed.), *Perspectives on memory research* (pp. 167-222). Hillsdale, NJ: Erlbaum.

Tyler, L. E. (1956). *The psychology of human differences.* New York: Appleton.

Ulrich, R. E., & Azrin, N. H. (1962). Reflexive fighting in response to aversive stimulation. *Journal of the Experimental Analysis of Behavior, 5,* 511-520.

Ulrich, R. S. (1984). View through a window may influence recovery from surgery. *Science, 224,* 420-421.

Unestahl, L. E. (1983). *The mental aspects of gymnastics.* Orebro, Sweden: Veje.

Ungar, G., Desiderio, D. M., & Parr, W. (1972). Isolation, identification and synthesis of a specific-behaviour-inducing brain peptide. *Nature, 238,* 198-202.

Ungar, G., Galvan, L., & Clark, R. H. (1968). Chemical transfer of learned fear. *Nature, 217,* 1259-1261.

Ursano, R. J., & Hales, R. E. (1986). A review of brief individual psychotherapies. *American Journal of Psychiatry, 143,* 1507-1517.

Vaillant, G. E. (1979). Natural history of male psychologic health: Effects of mental health on physical health. *New England Journal of Medicine, 301,* 1249-1254.

Vaillant, G. F., & Vaillant, C. O. (1990). Natural history of male psychological health, XII: 45-year study of predictors of successful aging at age 65. *American Journal of Psychiatry, 147,* 31-37.

Valenstein, E. S. (1973). *Brain control: A critical examination of brain stimulation and psychosurgery.* New York: Wiley.

Valenstein, E. S. (1980a). Causes and treatment of mental disorders. In E. S. Valenstein (Ed.), *The psychosurgery debate.* San Francisco: W. H. Freeman.

Valenstein, E. S. (1980b). Historical perspective. In E. S. Valenstien (Ed.), *The psychosurgery debate.* San Francisco: W. H. Freeman.

Valins, S. (1966). Cognitive effects of false heartrate feedback. *Journal of Personality & Social Psychology, 4,* 400-408.

van Doorninck, W. J., Caldwell, B. M., Wright, C., & Frankenburg, W. K. (1981). The relationship between twelve-month home stimulation and school achievement. *Child Development, 52,* 1080-1083.

Van Dyke, C., & Byck, R. (1982). Cocaine. *Scientific American, 246*(3), 128-141.

van Ilzendoorn, M. H., & Kroonenberg, P. M. (1988). Cross-cultural patterns of attachment: A meta-analysis of the strange situation. *Child Development, 59,* 147-156.

Vandenberg, B. (1978). Play and development from an ethological perspective. *American Psychologist, 33,* 724-738.

Vandenberg, B. (1984). Developmental features of exploration. *Developmental Psychology, 20,* 3-8.

Vanderweele, D. A., & Sanderson, J. D. (1976). Peripheral glucosensitive satiety in the rabbit and the rat. In D. Novin, W. Wyrwicka, & G. A. Bray (Eds.), *Hunger: Basic mechanisms and clinical implications.* New York: Raven.

Vernon, P. E. (1965). Ability factors and environmental influences. *American Psychologist, 20,* 723-733.

Vinokur, A., & Burnstein, E. (1978). Depolarization of attitudes in groups. *Journal of Personality & Social Psychology, 36,* 872-885.

Vondracek, F. W., & Lerner, R. M. (1982). Vocational role development in adolescence. In B. B. Wolman (Ed.), *Handbook of developmental psychology* (pp. 602-614). Englewood Cliffs NJ: Prentice-Hall.

Wafford, K. A., Burnett, D. M., Dunwiddie, T. V., & Harris, R. A. (1990). Genetic differences in the ethanol sensitivity of GABAA receptors expressed in *xenopus* oocytes. *Science, 249,* 291-293.

Wagner, H. N., Jr., Burns, H. D., Dannals, R. F., Wong, D. F., Langstrom, B., Duelfer, T., Frost, J. J., Ravert, H. T., Links, J. M., Rosenbloom, S. B., Lukas, S. E., Kramer, A. V., & Kuhar, M. J. (1983). Imaging dopamine receptors in the human brain by positron tomography. *Science, 221,* 1264-1266.

Waldhauser, F., Weiszenbacher, G., Frisch, H., Zeitlhuber, U., Waldhauser, M., & Wurtman, R. J. (1984). Fall in nocturnal serum melatonin during prepuberty and pubescence. *Lancet, 1*(8373), 362-365.

Waldrop, M. M. (1984). Natural language understanding. *Science, 224,* 372-374.

Walker, E., & Lewine, R. J. (1990). Prediction of adult-onset schizophrenia from childhood home movies of the patients. *American Journal of Psychiatry, 147,* 1052-1056.

Walker, J. (1982). "Floaters": Visual artifacts that result from blood cells in front of the retina. *Scientific American, 246*(4), 150-161.

Walker, L. J., de Vries, B., & Bichard, S. L. (1984). The hierarchical nature of stages of moral development. *Developmental Psychology, 20,* 960-966.

Wallace, I., Wallenchinsky, D., Wallace, A., & Wallace, S. (1980). *The book of lists #2.* New York: Bantam Books.

Wallach, M. A. (1970). Creativity. In P. H. Mussen (Ed.), *Carmichael's manual of child psychology* (3rd ed., pp. 1211-1272). New York: Wiley.

Wallach, M. A., & Kogan, N. (1965). *Modes of thinking in young children: A study of the creativity-intelligence distinction.* New York: Holt.

Wallach, M. A., & Wing, C. W. (1969). *The talented student: A validation of the creativity-intelligence distinction.* New York: Holt.

Wallis, C., & Ludtke, M. (1987, June 22). Is day care bad for babies? *Time,* p. 63.

Wallis, C., Hull, J. D., Ludtke, M., & Taylor, E. (1987, June 22). The child-care dilemma. *Time,* pp. 54-60.

Wanner, E., & Gleitman, L. R. (Eds.) (1982). *The state of the art.* New York: Cambridge Univ. Press.

Wanner, H. E. (1968). *On remembering, forgetting, and understanding sentences: A study of the deep structure hypothesis.* Unpublished doctoral dissertation, Harvard University.

Washburn, S. L., & Hamburg, D. A. (1965). The study of primate behavior. In I. DeVore (Ed.), *Primate behavior: Field studies of monkeys and apes.* New York: Holt.

Watson, J. B. (1913). Psychology as the behaviorist views it. *Psychological Review, 20,* 158-177.

Watson, J. B. (1929). *Psychology from the standpoint of a behaviorist* (3rd ed.). Philadelphia: Lippincott.

Watson, J. B. (1930). *Behaviorism.* New York: Norton.

Watson, J. B., & Rayner, R. (1920). Conditioned emotional responses. *Journal of Experimental Psychology, 3,* 1-14.

Watson, J. S., & Ramey, C. T. (1969, March). *Reactions to responsive contingent stimulation in early infancy.* Paper presented at the biennial meeting of the Society for Research in Child Development, Santa Monica, California.

Watson, J. S., & Ramey, C. T. (1972). Reactions to response-contingent stimulation in early infancy. *Merrill-Palmer Quarterly, 18,* 219-227.

Watt, J. A. G. (1985). The relationship of paranoid states to schizophrenia. *American Journal of Psychiatry, 142,* 1456-1458.

Wayner, M. J., Barone, F. C., & Loullis, C. C. (1981). The lateral hypothalamus and adjunctive behavior. In P. J. Morgane & J. Panksepp (Eds.), *Handbook of the hypothalamus* (Vol. 3, Part B, pp. 107-145). New York: Dekker.

Webb, W. B. (1974). Sleep as an adaptive response. *Perceptual & Motor Skills, 38,* 1023-1027.

Webb, W. B. (1975). *Sleep the gentle tyrant.* Englewood Cliffs, NJ: Prentice-Hall.

Webb, W. B., & Cartwright, R. D. (1978). Sleep and dreams. *Annual Review of Psychology, 29,* 223-252.

Weber, G. (1971). *Inner city children can be taught to read: Four successful schools.* Washington, D.C.: Council for Basic Education, Occasional Paper no. 18.

Weber, R. J., & Pert, A. (1989). The periaqueductal gray matter mediates opiate-induced immunosuppression. *Science, 245,* 188-190.

Wehr, T. A., & Rosenthal, N. E. (1989). Seasonality and affective illness. *American Journal of Psychiatry, 146,* 829-839.

Wehr, T. A., Sack, D. A., & Rosenthal, N. E. (1987). Seasonal affective disorder with summer depression and winter hypomania. *American Journal of Psychiatry, 144,* 1602-1603.

Wehren, A., & De Lisi, R. (1983). The development of gender understanding: Judgments and explanations. *Child Development, 54*, 1568-1578.

Weicker, L., Jr. (1987). Federal response to institutional abuse and neglect. *American Psychologist, 42*, 1027-1028.

Weiden, P. J., Mann, J. J., Haas, G., Mattson, M., & Frances, A. (1987). Clinical nonrecognition of neuroleptic-induced movement disorders: A cautionary study. *American Journal of Psychiatry, 144*, 1148-1153.

Weinberg, R. A. (1989). Intelligence and IQ. *American Psychologist, 44*, 98-104.

Weinberg, R. S. (1981). The relationship between mental preparation strategies and motor performance: A review and critique. *Quest, 33*, 195-213.

Weinberger, N. M., Gold, P. E., & Sternberg, D. B. (1984). Epinephrine enables Pavlovian fear conditioning under anesthesia. *Science, 223*, 605-607.

Weiner, M. J., & Wright, F. E. (1973). Effects of undergoing arbitrary discrimination upon subsequent attitudes toward a minority group. *Journal of Applied Social Psychology, 3*, 94-102.

Weiner, R. D. (1989). Electroconvulsive therapy. In H. I. Kaplan & B. J. Sadock (Eds.), *Comprehensive textbook of psychiatry/v* (pp. 1670-1678). Baltimore, MD: Williams & Wilkins.

Weingarten, H. P. (1983). Conditioned cues elicit feeding in sated rats: A role for learning in meal initiation. *Science, 220*, 431-433.

Weingartner, H., Gold, P., Bullenger, J. C., Smallberg, S. A., Summers, R., Rubinow, D. R., Post, R. M., & Goodwin, F. K. (1981). Effects of vasopressin on human memory functions. *Science, 211*, 601-603.

Weinraub, M., Clemens, L. P., Sockloff, A., Ethridge, T., Gracely, E., & Myers, B. (1984). The development of sex role stereotypes in the third year: Relationships to gender labeling, gender identity, sex-typed toy preference, and family characteristics. *Child Development, 55*, 1493-1503.

Weinstein, N. D. (1989). Optimistic biases about personal risks. *Science, 246*, 1232-1233.

Weintraub, P. (1980, December). Wired for sound. *Discover*, pp. 50-51.

Weisfeld, G. E. (1982). The nature-nurture issue and the integrating concept of function. In B. B. Wolman (Ed.), *Handbook of developmental psychology* (pp. 208-209). Englewood Cliffs, NJ: Prentice-Hall.

Weisler, A., & McCall, R. B. (1976). Exploration and play. *American Psychologist, 31*, 492-508.

Weiss, B. (1983). Behavioral toxicology and environmental health science: Opportunity and challenge for psychology. *American Psychologist, 38*, 1174-1187.

Weiss, R. (1988, August 20). Acupuncture: an old debate continues. *Science News*, p. 122.

Weiss, R. (1989, January 21). Predisposition and prejudice. *Science News*, pp. 40-42.

Weiss, R. (1989, January 21). Safety gets short shrift on long night shift. *Science News*, p. 37.

Weissman, M. M., Klerman, G. L., Markowitz, J. S., & Ouellette, R. (1989). Suicidal ideation and suicide attempts in panic disorder and attacks. *New England Journal of Medicine, 321*, 1209-1214.

Weissman, M. M., Wickramaratne, P., Merikangas, K. R., Leckman, J. F., Prusoff, B. A., Caruso, K. A., Kidd, K. K., & Gammon, G. D. (1984). Onset of major depression in early adulthood. Increased familial loading and specificity. *Archives of General Psychiatry, 41*, 1136-1143.

Weitzenhoffer, A. M., & Hilgard, E. R. (1962). *The Stanford Hypnotic Susceptibility Scale, Form C.* Palo Alto, CA: Consulting Psyc. Press.

Weller, A., Smith, G. P., & Gibbs, J. (1990). Endogenous cholecystokinin reduces feeding in young rats. *Science, 247*, 1589-1591.

Wertheimer, M. (1912). Experimentelle Stuidien uber das Sehen von Bewegungen. *Zsch. f. Psychol., 61*, 161-165.

West, M. A. (1985). Meditation and somatic arousal reduction. *American Psychologist, 40*, 717-719.

Westheimer, G. (1984). Spatial vision. *Annual Review of Psychology, 35*, 201-226.

Whalen, R. E., & Simon, N. G. (1984). Biological motivation. *Annual Review of Psychology, 35*, 257-276.

Wheeler, L., Deci, L., Reis, H., & Zuckerman, M. (1978). *Interpersonal influence* (2nd ed.). Boston: Allyn & Bacon.

White, B. W., Saunders, F. A., Scadden, L., Bach-Y-Rita, P., & Collins, C. C. (1970). Seeing with the skin. *Perception and Psychophysics, 7*, 23-27.

White, G. L., & Maltzman, I. (1978). Pupillary activity while listening to verbal passages. *Journal of Research in Personality, 12*, 361-369.

Whitehurst, G. J. (1982). Language development. In B. B. Wolman (Ed.), *Handbook of developmental psychology* (pp. 367-386). Englewood Cliffs, NJ: Prentice-Hall.

Whorf, B. L. (1956). *Language, thought, and reality.* Cambridge, Mass.: MIT Press.

Wiens, A. N., & Menustik, C. E. (1983). Treatment outcome and patient charac-

teristics in an aversion therapy program for alcoholism. *American Psychologist, 38*, 1089-1096.

Will, J. A., Self, P. A., & Datan, N. (1976). Maternal behavior and perceived sex of infant. *American Journal of Orthopsychiatry, 46*, 135-139.

Williams, D. A., & King, P. (1980a, December 22). It really is a head start. *Newsweek*, p. 54.

Williams, D. A., & King, P. (1980b, December 15). Do males have a math gene? *Newsweek*, p. 72.

Williams, T. M. (Ed.). (1986). *The impact of television: A natural experiment in three communities.* Orlando, FL: Academic Press, Inc.

Wills, T. A., & Langner, T. S. (1980). Socioeconomic status and stress. In I. L. Kutach, L. B. Schlesinger & Associates (Eds.), *Handbook on stress and anxiety* (pp. 159-173). San Francisco: Jossey Bass.

Wilson, E. O. (1975). *Sociobiology.* Cambridge, Mass.: Belknap Press.

Wilson, J. D., Griffin, J. E., George, F. W., & Leshin, M. (1981). The role of gonadal steroids in sexual differentiation. *Recent Progress in Hormone Research, 37*, 1-39.

Wilson, W. R. (1979). Feeling more than we can know: Exposure effects without learning. *Journal of Personality & Social Psychology, 37*, 811-821.

Winson, J. (1985). *Brain and psyche: The biology of the unconscious.* New York: Anchor Press.

Winson, J. (1990). The meaning of dreams. *Scientific American, 263*(5), 86-96.

Winton, W. M. (1987). Do introductory textbooks present the Yerkes-Dodson Law correctly? *American Psychologist, 42*, 202-203.

Wise, R. A., & Rompre, P. P. (1989). Brain dopamine and reward. *Annual Review of Psychology, 40*, 191-225.

Witt, D. (1977). *Emotional advertising: The relationship between eye-movement patterns and memory-empirical study with the eye-movement monitor.* Ph.D. thesis, University of Saarland, Saarbrucken, West Germany.

Wong, S. C. P., & Frost, B. J. (1978). Subjective motion and acceleration induced by the movement of the observer's entire visual field. *Perception and Psychophysics, 24*, 115-120.

Wood, J. M., & Bootzin, R. R. (1990). The prevalence of nightmares and their independence from anxiety. *Journal of Abnormal Psychology, 99*, 64-68.

Woodhead, M. (1988). When psychology informs public policy: The case of early childhood intervention. *American Psychologist, 43*, 443-454.

Woolfolk, R. L., & Lehrer, P. M. (1984). Clinical stress reduction: An overview. In R. L. Woolfolk & P. M. Lehrer (Eds.), *Principles and practice of stress management* (pp. 1-11). New York: Guilford Press.

Wright, A. A., Santiago, H. C., Sands, S. F., Kendrick, D. F., & Cook, R. G. (1985). Memory processing of serial lists by pigeons, monkeys, and people. *Science, 229*, 287-289.

Wright, F. L. (1957). *A testament.* New York: Horizon Press.

Wu, J. C., & Bunney, W. E. (1990). The biological basis of an antidepressant response to sleep deprivation and relapse: Review and hypothesis. *American Journal of Psychiatry, 147*, 14-21.

Wundt, W. (1862). Die Geschwindigkeit des Gedankens. *Gartenlaube*, 263-265.

Wurtz, R. H., Goldberg, M. E., & Robinson, D. L. (1982). Brain mechanisms of visual attention. *Scientific American, 246*(6), 124-135.

Wynne, L. C., Singer, M. T., Bartko, J., & Toohey, M. L. (1977). Schiaphrenics and their families: Research on parental communication. In J. Tanner (Ed.), *Developments in psychiatric research* (pp. 254-286). London: Hodder & Stoughton.

Yager, T., Laufer, R., & Gallops, M. (1984). Some problems associated with war experience in men of the Vietnam generation. *Archives of General Psychiatry, 41*, 327-333.

Yakimovich, D., & Saltz, E. (1971). Helping behavior: The cry for help. *Psychonomic Science, 23*, 427-428.

Yalom, I. D., Green, R., & Fisk, N. (1973). Prenatal exposure to female hormones: Effect on psychosexual development in boys. *Archives of General Psychiatry, 28*, 554-561.

Yang, K. S. (1986). Chinese personality and its change. In M. H. Bond (Ed.), *The psychology of the Chinese people.* Hong Kong; Oxford University Press.

Yang, R. K., & Douthitt, T. C. (1974). Newborn responses to threshold tactile stimulation. *Child Development, 45*, 237-242.

Yerkes, R. M., & Dodson, J. D. (1908). The relation of strength of stimulus to rapidity of habit formation. *Journal of Comparative Neurology and Psychology, 18*, 459-482.

Yesavage, J. A., & Leirer, V. O. (1986). Hangover effects on aircraft pilots 14 hours after alcohol ingestion: A preliminary report. *American Journal of Psychiatry, 143*, 1546-1550.

Yesavage, J. A., Leirer, V. O., Denari, M., & Hollister, L. E. (1985). Carry-over effects of marijuana intoxication on aircraft pilot performance: A preliminary report. *American Journal of Psychiatry, 142,* 1325-1329.

Yogman, M., Dixon, S., Tronick, E., & Brazelton, T. B. (1976, April). *Development of infant social interaction with fathers.* Paper presented at the meeting of the Eastern Psychological Association, New York.

Yonas, A., Pettersen, L., & Granrud, C. E. (1982). Infants' sensitivity to familiar size as information for distance. *Child Development, 53,* 1285-1290.

Young, P. (1989, January 28). The nature and nurture of emotions. *Science News,* p. 59.

Younger, J. C., Walker, L., & Arrowood, A. J. (1977). Postdecision dissonance at the fair. *Personality and Social Psychology Bulletin, 3,* 284-287.

Zaidel, E. (1983). A response to Gazzaniga. *American Psychologist, 38,* 542-546.

Zajonc, R. (1968). Attitudinal effects of mere exposure. *Journal of Personality & Social Psychology, 9,* 1-27.

Zajonc, R. B. (1980). Feeling and thinking: Preferences need no interferences. *American Psychologist, 35,* 151-175.

Zajonc, R. B. (1984). On the primacy of affect. *American Psychologist, 39,* 117-123.

Zajonc, R. B., & Markus, G. B. (1975). Birth order and intellectual development. *Psychological Review, 82,* 74-88.

Zellner, M. (1970). Self-esteem, reception, and influenceability. *Journal of Personality & Social Psychology, 15,* 87-93.

Zimbardo, P. G. (1979). *Psychology and life* (10th ed.). Glenview, IL: Scott Foresman.

Zimbardo, P. G., Haney, C., Banks, W. C., & Jaffe, D. (1973, April 8). A pirandellian prison. *The New York Times Magazine,* pp. 38-60.

Zucker, L. M., & Zucker, T. F. (1961). Fatty, a new mutation in the rat. *Journal of Heredity, 52,* 275-278.

Zylman, R. (1975). Drinking-driving and fatal crashes: A new perspective. *Journal of Alcohol & Drug Education, 21,* 1-10.

NAME INDEX

Abelson, R. P., 241
Abraham, H. D., 177
Abrahams, N. M., 631
Abramovitch, R., 361
Abramson, L. Y., 304
Adams, D., 258
Adams, G. R., 450, 613
Adams, J., 240
Adams, J. A., 109
Adams, M. J., 242
Adams, P. R., 450
Adelmann, P. K., 330
Adelson, J., 365
Adkins, J., 462
Adler, A., 425, 429, 431
Adler, H. E., 210
Adler, L. L., 210
Adler, T., 436, 596
Adorno, T. W., 577
Aho, A. C., 85
Ainsworth, M. D. S., 353
Alagna, S., 489
Albert, "L.", 194–195, 197, 481, 536
Albo, D., Jr., 630
Alexander, F., 459
Alker, H. A., 436
Alkon, D. L., 197, 225–226
Allan, A. M., 46
Allen, A., 420
Allen, W., 530
Allen, Y., 234
Alley, T. R., 349
Allison, J., 208
Allison, T., 156
Allman, W. F., 258, 447
Allport, G. W., 418–420, 430
Almirez, R. G., 178
Alper, J., 225, 243
Altafullah, I., 175
Altus, W. D., 396
Amarilio, J. D., 475–476
Ames, A., 131
Ames, M. A., 605–606
Amsterdam, B., 361
Anantharaman, T., 265
Anastasi, A., 627

Anastosopoulos, D., 109
Ancoli-Israel, S., 164
Anderson, C. C., 373
Anderson, D. C., 175
Anderson, D. R., 366
Anderson, J. R., 232, 237–238, 243–244,
    247–248, 256–257, 274
Anderson, L. D., 401–402
Anderson, S., 488
Andersson, B., 294
Andreasen, N. C., 64, 501
Angst, J., 396
Annable, L., 524
Ansari, F., 173
Anstis, S. M., 120
Antonucci, T. C., 377
Appenzeller, T., 225
Arc, J., 503
Arehart-Treichel, J., 165
Arendt, T., 234
Aristotle, 8, 107, 601
Armstrong, N., 240
Aron, A. P., 328
Aronson, E., 579, 584, 610, 614
Arrowood, A. J., 584
Arvidson, K., 104
Asaad, G., 495
Asberg, M., 464
Asch, R. H., 178
Asch, S. E., 551–552
Aserinsky, E., 152
Asnis, L., 498
Atkinson, J. W., 301–302
Atkinson, M., 640
Atkinson, R., 262
Averill, J. R., 330
Axel, R., 217
Azrin, N. H., 204, 211, 323
Babbitt, B. C., 238
Bach-Y-Rita, P., 118
Bachman, J. G., 368
Baddeley, A. D., 245
Bahrick, H. P., 248
Bailey, F. L., 587–588
Baillargeon, R., 371
Baker, S. W., 596

Bales, J., 319, 469, 606
Bales, R. F., 575
Ballard, E. J., 299
Ballenger, J. C., 483
Balon, R., 483
Balster, R. L., 177
Ban, P. L., 598
Bandura, A., 18, 22–23, 208–212, 304,
    426–428, 430, 538, 599
Baral, R., 611
Baraldi, M., 176
Barber, T. X., 167
Bard, P., 325
Barglow, P., 356
Barinaga, M., 97
Barker, R. G., 642
Barlow, D. H., 482
Barnes, D. M., 197, 454, 498, 500, 502
Barnum, P. T., 435
Baron, M., 498
Baron, R. A., 323
Barone, F. C., 295, 323
Barrett, K. G., 357
Barrymore, J., 330
Barsky, A. J., 487
Barten, H., 542
Bartko, J., 500
Barton, B., 645
Bartusiak, M., 166
Barwick, K. D., 634
Bassuk, E., 526–527
Bauer, J. A., 144
Baugh, D. K., 521
Baum, A., 445–446, 450
Bavelas, A., 575
Bayer, A. E., 396
Bayley, N., 401–402
Baylor, D. A., 85
Beaber, R. J., 582
Beach, B. H., 318–319
Beary, J. F., 319
Beasley, R., 618
Beauchamp, G. K., 106
Beck, A. T., 493, 539
Becker, F. D., 633

Becker, I. M., 544
Becker, L. A., 586
Becker, W., 109
Becker, W. C., 420
Beers, C., 519
Begley, S., 234, 380
Behan, P., 602
Belbin, R. M., 376
Bell, A. P., 607
Bell, L., 579
Bell, P. A., 323
Bellugi, U., 281
Belmont, L., 386
Belsky, J., 356, 362
Bem, D. J., 420, 439
Bem, S. L., 600
Benbow, C. P., 601–603
Benet, M., 493
Bennett, W., 296
Benson, H., 456
Bentall, R. P., 511
Beraldo, W., 108
Berbaum, M. L., 396
Berenbaum, S. A., 603
Berenberg, J., 178
Berger, H., 151
Bergin, A. E., 542
Bergmann, B. M., 158–159
Berk, L. S., 52
Berko, J., 278
Berkowitz, L., 323–324
Berlin, F. S., 295
Berman, J. S., 529
Bernard, H. W., 375
Berndt, R. S., 222
Berndt, T. J., 362, 364–365
Berne, E., 535–536
Bernuth, H. V., 349
Berra, Y., 102
Berridge, K. C., 105
Berscheid, E., 615–616
Berson, L. 145–146
Berthold, A., 595, 597
Best, J. B., 15
Bettman, J. R., 644
Bichard, S. L., 566
Biddle, W., 318
Bierman, K. L., 362
Bierre, P., 540
Binet, A., 387, 398
Bini, L., 525
Birch, H., 346, 350, 362, 426
Bischof, L. J., 374
Bitterman, M. E., 199
Bjork, R. A., 246
Bjorklund, A., 50–51
Black, I., 48
Black, N. A., 449
Blaine, J. D., 525
Blake, J., 396
Blamey, P. J., 102
Blanchard, E. B., 482
Blashfield, R. K., 504
Blazer, D., 482, 486

Bleda, P. R., 554
Bliss, E. L., 490
Block, J., 371, 439
Blood, R. O., 375
Bloom, B. S., 402
Bloom, E. T., 457
Bloom, F. E., 75, 175, 234
Bloom, L., 276, 280
Blum, K., 178
Blumenthal, A. L., 9
Bogart, H., 503
Bogat, G. A., 323
Bogen, J. E., 70
Boggiano, A. K., 364
Bohus, B., 234, 241
Bolen, D., 303
Bolles, R. C., 52
Bolter, A., 178
Bonatti, W., 312
Bonoma, T. V., 584
Bonsall, R. W., 297–298
Booth, D. A., 106, 300
Booth-Kewley, S., 460
Bootzin, R. R., 179
Borbely, A., 152, 155, 157–158, 163
Borg, E., 101
Borman, W. C., 631
Bornstein, R. F., 645
Botterill, C. B., 639
Bouchard, T. J., Jr., 394–395, 603
Boucher, J. D., 328
Bouthilet, L., 367
Boutin, P., 351
Bower, B., 403, 453, 475
Bower, G. H., 233, 236
Bowers, K., 170
Bowers, M., 497
Bowlby, J., 353
Boyanowsky, E. O., 640
Boyce, W. T., 461
Boyd, J. H., 482
Boyle, C. A., 453
Boyse, E. A., 106
Boysen, S., 283
Bozarth, M. A., 176
Brackbill, Y., 353
Braestrup, C., 49
Braff, D., 487
Brahms, J., 286
Braine, M. D. S., 277
Brand, C., 400
Brandt, T., 143
Braver, S. L., 579
Bray, G. A., 296
Brazelton, T. B., 353, 361
Brecher, E. M., 619, 622
Breen, M. J., 504
Breier, A., 454
Brenner, D., 542
Brenner, J., 361
Brentari, D. K., 283–284
Breslau, N., 453
Breslow, M. F., 524
Bretherton, I., 352

Brett, A. S., 319
Brett, J. M., 628–629
Brickman, P., 303
Bridges, L., 353
Briggs, A. H., 178
Brinkman, C., 42
Broadbent, D., 15
Brobeck, J. R., 292
Broca, P., 281
Brock, T. C., 581
Brodzinsky, D. M., 354
Bromet, E. J., 446
Bronfenbrenner, U., 365
Bronson, W. C., 360
Brooks, J., 319
Brou, P., 95
Brown, B. B., 373, 638
Brown, B. I., 178
Brown, B. R., 629
Brown, H. O., 256
Brown, J. B., 278
Brown, M. C., 634
Brown, R., 241, 278, 525
Brown, R. J., 166
Brown, T. H., 197
Browne, M. A., 635–637
Bruner, J., 362
Bryan, G., 177
Buckhout, R., 145–146, 583
Buckley, J., 319
Buhrmester, D., 364
Bunney, W. E., 523
Burbach, J. P. H., 234
Burchinal, M., 401
Burgower, B., 526
Burnett, D. M., 451
Burns, T. L., 296
Burnstein, E., 574
Buss, A. H., 421
Butcher, J., 468–469
Butterfield, P., 320
Button, D., 573
Buxton, C. E., 10
Byck, R., 175
Byrne, D., 577, 579, 609–610
Cacioppo, J. T., 578–579, 581–582, 585
Cadoret, R. J., 451
Cain, C. A., 451
Cairns, R. B., 599
Calabrese, J. R., 457
Caldwell, A. B., 163
Caldwell, B. M., 401
Callahan, L. A., 475
Calvert-Boyanowsky, J., 640
Camerino, M., 456
Cameron, R., 526
Campbell, M., 265
Campbell, T., 367
Campos, J. J., 142, 320, 357
Cannon, W. B., 291, 325, 331
Cantin, M., 53
Capatides, J. B., 276
Caplan, P. J., 601, 603
Caramazza, A., 222

Carbone, R., 145–146
Carew, T. J., 188
Carey, G., 461
Carey, J., 380
Carlsmith, J. M., 583–584
Carlson, G. A., 493
Carlson, M., 249
Carlson, N. K., 80
Carlson, N. R., 294
Carone, B. J., 496
Carpenter, W. T., 522, 542
Carroll, D., 106
Carroll, G., 161
Carson, R. C., 427, 431
Carter, J., 588
Cartwright, R. D., 152, 155, 167
Cartwright, S., 508
Carver, C. S., 586
Casanova, M. F., 502
Case, N. B., 460
Case, R. B., 460
Casto, G., 401
Castore, C. H., 554
Catlin, D. H., 52
Cattell, R. B., 420–421, 430
Center, Y., 408
Cerletti, U., 525
Chaiken, S., 582
Chaikin, A., 612
Chait, L. D., 177
Chakravarti, D., 644
Chance, P., 491
Chaplin, C., 246–247
Chapman, G. C., 559
Charlesworth, W. R., 329
Charney, D. S., 483
Chase, M. H., 153
Cherry, F., 577, 579
Chess, S., 346, 350, 354, 426
Cheyne, J. A., 362
Child, I. L., 110
Chipperfield, J. G., 396
Chomsky, N., 279
Chorover, S. L., 508
Chouinard, G., 524
Christie, A., 56
Christison, G. W., 502
Chrousos, G. P., 456
Chumlea, W. M., 368
Churchland, P. M., 224
Churchland, P. S., 224
Cialdini, R. B., 426, 578–579, 581–582, 585
Cicchetti, D. V., 156
Cicirelli, V. G., 361
Cimmerman, A., 336
Clark, A. W., 628
Clark, G. M., 102
Clark, H. H., 236
Clark, K. B., 192, 576
Clark, M. P., 192, 576
Clark, R. A., 301
Clark, R. H., 214
Clarkson, C., 482–483

Clarkson, M. G., 144
Clasen, D. R., 373
Clayton, P. J., 486
Clayton, R. R., 375
Clements, R. D., 411
Clifton, R. K., 144
Cloninger, C. R., 486
Clore, G. L., 610
Clum, G. A., 463
Clunies-Ross, G., 408
Cochran, S. T., 323
Coe, W. C., 171, 173
Coffey, C. E., 525
Cohen, J. B., 644
Cohen, N. J., 241
Cohen, S., 403, 452, 564
Colby, A., 566
Coleman, J. S., 303
Coleman, L. M., 377
Coleman, R. M., 161–164
Coles, M. G. H., 144
Colligan, R. C., 435
Collins, C. C., 118
Collins, G., 600
Collins, W. A., 365
Combs-Orme, T., 176
Condry, J. C., 365
Conley, J. J., 134
Constantine-Paton, M., 97
Conti, L., 241
Conway, D., 396
Cook, K. V., 599
Cook, R., 612
Cook, R. G., 231
Coolidge, C., 644
Cooper, C. R., 362
Cooper, J., 582
Cooper, L. N., 42, 47
Cooper, M. S., 48
Copernicus, 11
Corballis, M. C., 95
Cordes, C., 49
Cordray, D. S., 543
Coren, S., 299
Cornell-Bell, A. H., 48
Corter, C., 361
Corwin, T. T., 579
Coryell, W., 493
Costa, E., 176
Costa, P. T., 346, 381
Costanzo, R. M., 109
Costello, C. G., 525
Cote, R., 351
Counter, S. A., 101
Cowen, R., 175
Coyne, J. C., 461
Craske, B., 109
Crawford, M. H., 642
Crick, F., 165–166, 345
Critchlow, B., 175
Crofton, C., 613
Cronbach, L. J., 388, 398
Cross, D. R., 646
Cross, T., 319

Crowe, R. R., 482–483
Croyle, R. T., 582
Crusco, A. H., 108
Crusoe, R., 261
Crutcher, M., 407
Crutchfield, R. S., 388
Culliton, B. J., 467, 521
Cummings, L. L., 628
Cummins, R. C., 627
Curcio, C. A., 87
Curran, J. P., 612
Czeisler, C. A., 160–162
Daly, S. J., 92
Damasio, A. R., 69
Daniels, M., 457
Danks, J. H., 271
Dannemiller, J. L., 612
Darko, D. F., 504
Darley, J. M., 562, 564
Darlington, R., 401
Darwin C., 10–11, 333, 386, 400
Datan, N., 598
Davey, T. C., 392
Davidson, A., 453
Davidson, R. J., 317
Davies, P., 106
Davis, A. J., 357
Davis, E. A., 396
Davis, F. C., 160
Davis, G. C., 453
Davis, K. E., 609
Davison, G. C., 482
Dawes, R. M., 543
Day, G. S., 645
De Cock, K. M., 619
de Egas Moniz, A., 525, 527
De Jong, J., 464
De Lisi, R., 600
de Vries, B., 566
de Vries, M. W., 351
de Wied, D., 234
DeAngelis, T., 544, 584
de Bergerac, C., 428
DeCasper, A. J., 341–342
deCharms, R., 290, 292
Deci, E. L., 632
Deci, L., 552
Decoufle, P., 453
Deecke, L., 109
Deeter, W. R., 52
DeGregorio, E., 586
Delongis, A., 460
Dement, W., 158, 164
Denari, M., 178
Denber, H. C. B., 521
DeNiro, R., 504
DePiano, F. A., 540
Depue, R. A., 492
Deregowski, J. B., 128
Dermer, M., 582, 613
Derogatis, L. R., 542
Dershowitz, A., 475
Descartes, R., 74
Desiderio, D. M., 224

Desimone, R., 263–264
Desrochers, A., 235
Deutsch, M., 569–570
deVilliers, J. G., 278
deVilliers, P. A., 278
deVries, M., 351, 489
Dew, M. A., 446
Dewey, J., 11
DeWitt, K. N., 542
Dhuna, A., 175
Diamond, M. C., 48
Diamond, R., 487
Diamond, S., 9
Diaz, R. M., 362
Dichgans, J., 143
Dickson, D., 345
Dickstein, S., 494
Diener, E., 571
DiNardo, P. A., 482
Dion, K. K., 612
Dittes, J. E., 583
Dixon, S., 361
Dobbs, F. C., 503
Dobelle, W. H., 103
Dodd, J., 50
Dodds, J. B., 351
Dodson, J. D., 299
Doherty, W. J., 374
Doi, L. T., 416
Dollard, J., 323
Domey, R., 178
Donaldson, G. Y., 403–404
Donchin, E., 144
Donderi, D. C., 166
Donner, K., 85
Donosky, L., 462
Doob, L. W., 323
Dorow, R., 49
Dorsett, S., 489–490
Doty, R. L., 298
Dougherty, D., 319
Dourish, C. T., 293
Douthitt, T. C., 349
Douvan, E., 365
Dowell, R. C., 102
Downs, A. C., 599
Drake, R. E., 504
Dressel, M. E., 630
Drummond, E., 475
Drury, C. G., 80
Drysdale, C., 617, 621
Dubner, R., 52
Dueck, A., 233
Dumaret, A., 398
Dunbar, F., 459
Duncan, C. C., 502
Duncker, K., 271
Dunn, L. O., 446
Dunner, D. L., 523
Dunnett, S. B., 51
Dunwiddie, T. V., 451
Durkee, N., 377
Dutton, D. G., 328
Duyme, M., 398

Dweck, C. S., 602
Dyer, J. L., 401
Dywan, J., 170
Eagly, A. H., 580
Eaton, W. O., 396
Eaton, W. W., 649
Ebata, K., 415–416
Ebbesen, E. B., 608
Ebbinghaus, H., 238
Ebner, F. F., 42, 47
Eccles-Parsons, J., 596
Eckerman, C. O., 361
Eddington, D., 102
Edison, T. A., 385–386, 389, 391, 408
Edwards, A. L., 436
Edwards, D. D., 452
Egawa, M., 415–416
Ehrhardt, A. A., 596
Ehrin, E., 501
Eibl-Eibesfeldt, I., 329
Eichelman, B., 541
Eicher, S. A., 373
Eilers, R. E., 275
Einstein, A., 386
Eisen, S. A., 453
Eisen, S. V., 586
Eisenberg, R. B., 346
Eisendorfer, C., 349
Eiser, J. R., 581
Eisert, D. C., 373
Ekman, P., 328–331, 333, 335, 357
Elkind, D., 365
Elliott, J., 576
Ellis, A., 532–533, 543
Ellis, H., 621–622
Ellis, L., 605–606
Embree, M. C., 323
Emde, R. N., 320
Emerson, P. E., 353
Emery, G., 539
Emmerich, W., 600
Emrick, C. D., 452
Endler, N. S., 420–421
Epstein, A. W., 166
Epstein, S., 307
Erdman, H. P., 540
Erikson, E. H., 343, 370, 373
Ernst, C., 396
Eron, L. D., 322, 473
Ervin, C. R., 609
Erwin, E., 425, 542
Erwin, G., 176
Erwin, W. M., 205
Ery, F., 336
Etaugh, C., 356, 600
Evans, F. J., 171
Eysenck, H. J., 508, 542
Fagan, J., 403
Fairchild, L., 205
Falbo, T., 396
Falck, A., 295
Falk, J. L., 294–295
Fanselow, M. S., 52
Fantz, R. L., 349

Faraone, S., 473, 492
Faravelli, C., 483
Farde, L., 501
Farkas, G. M., 539
Farley, J., 197
Farr, F., 411
Farran, D. C., 356
Faucher, T. A., 649
Faulkner, T. W., 640
Faust, D., 510
Favreau, O. E., 95
Fay, F., 336
Fay, R. E., 604
Fazio, R. H., 554, 580
Feder, H. H., 604
Fedio, P., 178
Fein, G., 600, 641
Feinglass, S. J., 178
Feingold, A., 604, 611
Feirtag, M., 40, 42, 57–59
Feldman, J. F., 403
Feldstein, M., 25
Fennema, E., 604
Fentress, J. C., 105
Fenz, W. D., 307
Feshbach, S., 581
Festinger, L., 583–584
Fields, H. L., 52
Fieve, R. R., 523
Fifer, W. P., 342
Filsinger, E. E., 373
Fine, A., 50
Finkbeiner, S. M., 48
Finkelstein, N. W., 303
Finlayson, D. F., 649
Finn, P. R., 451
Fischer, K. W., 371–372
Fisher, E. D., 70
Fisher, K., 25, 447
Fisk, N., 596
Fiske, D. W., 134
Fiske, S. T., 586
Fitzgerald, B. A., 511
Fitzgerald, L. F., 7
Fitzsimons, J. T., 293
Flach, F. F., 511
Fleisher, S., 167
Fleishman, E. A., 630
Fliers, E., 603
Flood, J. F., 241
Flynn, J. R., 400
Fobes, J. L., 293
Fogarty, L. A., 462
Folkman, S., 460
Follini, S., 149–150
Fontaine, R., 524
Ford, D. E., 163
Ford, M., 298
Foster, R. G., 160
Foulkes, D., 167
Fowler, R. C., 449, 463
Fox, B. H., 408
Fox, E. L., 636
Fox, N. A., 317

Foxx, R. M., 211
Frances, A., 522
Frank, J. D., 530
Frankenburg, W. K., 351, 401
Franklin, B., 167
Franklin, G., 249
Franklin, N., 237
Franklin-Lipsker, E., 249–250
Fredericksen, C. H., 236
Freed, W., 51
Freeman, V., 612
Freeman, W., 527
Frenkel-Brusnwik, E., 577
Freud, S., 11–12, 18, 22–23, 74, 165,
    174, 343, 422–424, 429–431, 519,
    530–531, 536, 601, 620
Frezza, M., 175
Friberg, U., 104
Friedman, A. F., 508
Friedman, H. S., 460
Friedman, M., 459
Friedman, M. I., 293
Friesen, M. V., 328, 330–331, 335
Frijda, N. H., 320–321
Fritsch, G., 61
Frodi, A., 353
Froebel, F., 410–411
Fromm, E., 173
Frost, B. J., 143
Fry, M., 178
Fulcher, R., 6
Fullmer, D. W., 375
Funder, D. C., 427, 439
Furchtgott, E., 22
Furman, W., 362, 364
Furst, M. W., 457
Gaduto, D., 640
Gaes, G. G., 579
Gage, F. H., 51
Gage, P., 27, 66
Gagne, R. M., 257, 261, 274
Gagnon, J. H., 604
Galbraith, R. C., 396
Galileo, G., 386
Galin, D., 487
Gall, F. J., 387
Gallops, M., 453
Gallup, G., 578
Galper, A., 377
Galton, F., 386–387, 395
Galvan, L., 224
Garcia, J., 217
Gardner, B. T., 280
Gardner, E. P., 109
Gardner, H., 391
Gardner, M., 131
Gardner, R. A., 280
Gartrell, N., 25
Garvey, M. J., 494
Gatchel, R. J., 446
Gautier, T., 597
Gazzaniga, M. S., 70–72, 74, 282
Geldard, F. A., 144
Gelfand, D. M., 586

Geller, U., 110
Gelman, S. A., 277
Genest, J., 53
Genova, P., 362
Genovese, K., 561–563
Genshaft, J. L., 602
George, F. W., 597
George, J. M., 241
George, L., 486
George, L. K., 482
Geraci, M., 483
Gerbner, G., 367
Gerner, R. H., 52
Geron, E., 636
Gershon, E., 492
Gerson, A., 526, 600
Geschwind, N., 64, 68–69, 602
Gewirtz, J. L., 353
Ghiselli, E. E., 389
Gibbons, F. X., 580
Gibbs, J., 293, 566
Gibson, A. R., 59
Gibson, E. J., 142
Gibson, J. J., 123, 125–126, 142
Gilbert, G., 440
Gilbert, J. A., 155
Gildea, P. M., 276–277
Gillam, B., 128–129
Giller, E., 464
Gilligan, C., 567
Gilliland, M. A., 158–159
Gillin, J., 517
Gillis, R., 586
Girvin, J. P., 103
Gispen, W. H., 234
Gladue, B. A., 605
Glass, G. V., 542–543
Glasser, W., 639
Glassman, J. N., 504
Gleitman, L. R., 274, 277, 280
Glenberg, A., 246, 248
Glick, I. O., 457
Glick, P. C., 374
Glickstein, M., 59, 63
Glucksberg, S., 271
Goddard, H., 397
Godden, D. R., 245
Godes, M., 494
Goeders, N. E., 175
Goering, H., 440, 556
Goisman, R. M., 539
Gold, E., 451
Gold, P. E., 197
Gold, P. W., 456–457
Goldberg, J., 453
Goldberg, L. R., 134, 437
Goldberg, L. W., 586
Goldberg, M. E., 263
Goldberg, S. B., 628–629
Golden, M., 437
Goldfried, M. R., 540, 544
Goldin-Meadow, S., 370
Goldman, K. S., 600
Goldman, W., 613

Goldmark, J., 285
Goldmark, K., 285
Goldmark, P., 285–286
Goldsmith, H. H., 350, 352, 357, 461
Goldstein, A., 49, 51, 170
Goldstein, A. L., 594
Goldstein, M. J., 492, 495
Goleman, D., 405
Gollob, H. F., 583
Gomes-Schwartz, B., 542
Goodman, L. S., 256
Goodwin, F. K., 456
Gorbachev, M., 473
Gordon, N. C., 52
Gorelick, D. A., 52
Gorenstein, E. E., 474
Gorski, R., 602–603
Gosnell, M., 292
Gottesman, I. I., 461, 498, 603
Gottlieb, D. I., 47, 264
Gottlieb, G., 371
Gottlieb, J., 407
Gottman, J. M., 363
Gould, J. L., 214, 216–217
Gould, S. J., 398
Gowing, M. K., 628, 631
Gracely, R. H., 52
Graham, C. H., 90
Graham, E., 583
Grajek, S., 357
Granrud, C. E., 130
Gray, S. W., 401
Green, R., 596, 605–606
Greenberg, J., 284, 377, 507
Greenberg, Jerald., 573–574
Greenberg, L. S., 540, 544
Greenberg, M. T., 370
Greene, D., 305–306
Greeno, J. G., 262
Gregory, R. L., 130
Greif, E. B., 566
Greist, J. H., 540
Gretarsson, S. J., 586
Greven, H. M., 234
Griffin, J. E., 597
Griffin, M. R., 521
Griffith, C., 636
Griffitt, W., 323
Grinspoon, L., 463
Grolnick, W., 353
Gross, A. E., 575, 613
Gross, L., 367
Grossman, M. I., 292
Grossman, S. P., 292
Grotevant, M. D., 396
Grove, W. M., 451
Gruen, R., 460, 498
Gruenberg, A. M., 497–498
Gruenewald, P. J., 178
Grunberg, N. E., 450
Grush, J. E., 582
Guharay, F., 44
Guidotti, A., 176
Guilford, J. P., 391, 408–409

Guillemin, R., 75
Gulevich, G., 158
Gurin, J., 296
Guze, S. B., 486
Gwiazda, J., 144
Gzesh, S. M., 359
Haas, G., 522
Haber, R. N., 92, 235
Hadley, S. W., 542
Hager, M., 234
Hakel, M. D., 629
Haldane, J. B. S., 306
Hales, R. E., 544
Halgren, E., 225
Hall, E., 296, 343
Hall, G. S., 11, 368, 447
Hall, H., 501
Hall, R. C. W., 510
Hall, S. S., 226
Hamburg, D. A., 216
Hamer, B., 500
Hamilton, J., 489
Hammen, C., 494
Hammersmith, S. K., 607
Hamner, E. P., 634
Hamner, W. C., 634
Haney, W., 398
Hanratty, M. A., 22
Hansen, J., 452
Harding, K., 494
Hargreaves, W. A., 521
Harkey, J., 473
Harkness, L., 464
Harlow, H. F., 289–290, 305, 352–353,
    593
Harlow, J. M., 27
Harris, B., 195
Harris, J. A., 347
Harris, R. A., 46, 451
Harrow, M., 496, 511
Harrower, M., 440
Hart, J., 221–222
Hart, L. M., 370
Hartley, E. L., 577
Hartup, W. W., 361–362, 364–366
Harvey, J. H., 586
Harvey, T., 48
Hastorf, A. H., 575
Hathaway, S. R., 432, 435
Hatsukami, D., 452
Havighurst, R. J., 371
Haviland, J. M., 357
Hawkins, D. R., 166
Hawkins, J. A., 165, 364
Hayashi, S., 210
Hayes, C., 280
Hayes, K. J., 280
Hayes, S. C., 480
Hayflick, L., 380–381
Healey, S., 163
Hearst, P., 587–588
Hebb, D. O., 236
Hechinger, N., 118
Hefez, A., 453

Heider, F., 585
Heiman, J. R., 621
Heinold, W. D., 568
Heinrichs, D. W., 522
Heinzmann, A. T., 634
Heisel, J. S., 457
Heit, G., 225
Held, R. M., 144
Heller, F. A., 628
Heller, J. F., 300
Heller, S. S., 460
Hellman, R. E., 605
Helmholtz, H. von, 89, 92, 124–125
Helson, R., 388
Helzer, J. E., 477
Heminger, A., 178
Hendersen, R. W., 305
Henderson, C., 142
Henderson, W. G., 453
Hendrickson, A. E., 87
Heninger, G. R., 483
Henle, M., 14
Henn, F. A., 528
Henry, R. A., 630
Herbert, W., 47, 227, 428, 435, 446
Hering, E., 92
Herman, C. P., 582
Herman, J., 25
Herrnstein, R. J., 311–312
Herz, M. I., 522
Hess, E. H., 216
Hess, R., 440, 556
Hetherington, E. M., 466
Hiatt, S., 142
Hilgard, E. R., 150, 168, 170, 540
Hilgard, J. R., 170, 540
Hill, B., 276
Hill, C. T., 616
Hillix, W., 12
Himmelfarb, S., 580
Hinckley, J. W., 475, 501
Hines, M., 596
Hinson, R. E., 194
Hippocrates, 8, 417, 430, 517
Hirt, M. L., 602
Hitchcock, A., 481
Hitler, A., 111, 440
Hitzig, E., 61
Hobson, J. A., 153, 165
Hodes, R. L., 319
Hodgkins, J., 374
Hoffman, L. W., 566
Hogan, R., 567
Hogarty, P. S., 402
Hogrebe, M. C., 603
Hoke, M., 144
Holahan, C. J., 639
Holden, C., 25, 432–433, 451–452, 477,
    495, 603
Hollander, E. P., 575
Hollandsworth, J. G., Jr., 630
Hollister, L. E., 178
Hollon, S., 539
Holmes, C. B., 463

Holmes, D. S., 172
Holmes, T. H., 457–458, 617
Holz, W. C., 204
Homans, G. C., 611
Hong, L. K., 573
Honts, C. R., 319
Hood, R., 580
Hook, S., 425
Hopson, J. L., 163
Horn, J., 392
Horn, J. C., 628
Horn, J. L., 403–404
Horn, J. M., 498
Horney, K., 601
Horowitz, M. J., 542
Horowitz, V., 286
Horowski, G., 49
Horrower, M., 440
Hosobuchi, Y., 75
House, J. S., 466
House, R. J., 628
Houston, J. P., 242
Hovland, C. I., 581, 583
Howard K., 542
Howard, K. I., 368
Howes, C., 357
Hoyle, S. G., 364
Hsia, Y., 90
Hsu, F., 265
Hubel, D. H., 62, 96
Huberty, J., 323–324
Hudson, A., 408
Hudspeth, A. J., 100
Huggins, G. R., 298
Hughes, D., 482
Hughes, J. R., 452
Hui, K. K., 52
Hulin, C. L., 630
Hull, C. L., 32, 291
Hull, J. D., 356
Humphreys, L. G., 392
Hunt, R. R., 236
Hunter, M. L., 511
Hurlburt, N., 402
Hurvich, L. M., 93
Huston, A. C., 596, 599
Huston, T. L., 361, 564
Hutchinson, C. A., 346
Hutt, C., 349
Hutt, S. J., 349
Huxley, A., 500
Hyde, J. S., 604
Hyden, C., 85
Hyland, M. E., 493
Iacono, W. G., 492
Idupuganti, S., 510
Ilgen, D. R., 628
Imber, S. D., 543
Imperato-McGinley, J., 596–597
Inhelder, B., 370–371
Irwin, M., 457
Ito, M., 58
Iversen, S. D., 293
Izard, C., 328

Izard, C. E., 22
Jacklin, C. N., 597–598, 601, 604
Jackson, C. M., 347, 351
Jackson, D. N., 421, 440
Jackson, P. W., 408
Jacobs, J., 462
Jacobsen, B., 494
Jacobson, E., 466
Jacobson, J. L., 353, 641
Jacobson, N. S., 374
Jacobson, S. W., 641
Jaffe, C. M., 523
James, S. L., 278
James, W., 10–11, 14, 233, 239–240,
    324–325, 330, 447
Jameson, D., 93
Jampala, V. C., 510
Janicak, P. G., 525
Janik, A., 9
Janis, I. L., 581
Janowitz, H. D., 292
Jansson, G., 123, 143
Jantz, R. K., 377
Jarrett, R. B., 480
Jarvik, M. E., 242
Jatlow, P. I., 483
Jefferson, T., 614
Jeffery, R. W., 448
Jemerin, J. M., 461
Jensen, A. R., 396–397
Jeppsen, E. A., 490
Jerome, J., 78
Jessell, T. M., 50
Joffe, L. S., 353
Johansson, G., 123, 143
John, E. R., 241, 243
Johns, G., 632
Johnson, D., 600
Johnson, D. W., 646
Johnson, J. E., 364
Johnson, L., 158
Johnson, L. B., 526
Johnson, L. C., 155
Johnson, L. S., 540
Johnson, O. G., 396
Johnson, R. T., 646
Johnson, V. E., 379, 620, 622
Johnston, J., 368
Jonas, J. M., 511
Jones, B., 511
Jones, E., 234
Jones, E. E., 579
Jones, H. S., 155
Jones, J., 92
Jones, J. W., 323
Jones, Jim, 560
Jones, R., 554–555
Jones, S. L., 305
Jordan, M., 483
Josse, D., 357
Jourard, S. M., 439
Julian, J. W., 575
Jung, C. G., 418, 425, 430–431
Jurgens, C., 585

Kagan, J., 396, 398
Kagan, S., 569
Kahle, L. R., 373
Kahn, R. J., 524
Kales, A., 158, 163
Kales, J. D., 163
Kalil, R. E., 47
Kalina, R. E., 87
Kalish, D., 213
Kalle, R. J., 579, 584
Kamerow, D. B., 163
Kamin, L. J., 398
Kandal, E., 226
Kane, J., 498
Kanner, A. D., 461
Kaplan, M., 164, 480, 511
Kaplan, M. F., 574
Kaplan, O. J., 164
Karlen, N., 426
Karlin, M. B., 233
Karnovsky, M. L., 156
Kashani, J. H., 493
Kassarjian, H. H., 645
Kastenbaum, R., 377, 381
Kastin, A. J., 241
Katz, R., 634
Katz, S., 234
Katzell, R. A., 634
Kaufman, L., 137
Kaylor, J. A., 453
Kazelskis, R., 630
Keck, P. E., Jr., 522
Keitel, W., 556
Keller, H., 349
Keller, J. B., 98
Keller, S. E., 456
Kellermann, A. L., 449
Kellert, S. R., 473
Kelley, H. H., 614
Kelly, E. L., 133–134
Kelly, P. A. T., 51
Kelso, S. R., 197
Kempthorne-Rawson, J., 456
Kendell, R. E., 324
Kendler, K. S., 497–498, 500, 502
Kendrick, D. F., 231
Kenge, 115–116, 124
Kennedy, J. F., 240
Kennedy, J. M., 118
Kennell, J. H., 354
Kenrick, D. T., 427
Kerckhoff, A. C., 609
Kety, S. S., 494
Kevorkian, J., 462
Kiesler, C. A., 526
Kiesler, S., 611
Kiester, E., Jr., 651
Kihlstrom, J. F., 170, 267, 425
Kilham, W., 558
Kimura, D., 601
Kimura, T., 210
King, B. T., 581
King, D. W., 453
King, L. A., 453

King, P., 400
Kinney, D. K., 493
Kinsey, A., 379, 620, 622
Kintsch, W., 236
Kirk-Smith, M., 106
Kirkorowicz, C., 494
Kite, W. R., 575
Kjos, G. L., 608
Khan, L. M. L., 248
Klassen, A. D., 604
Klaus, M. H., 354
Klein, D. N., 494
Klein, H. J., 628
Klein, M., 144
Klein, M. H., 540
Kleinginna, A. M., 16, 290
Kleinginna, P. R., Jr., 16, 290
Kleinke, C. L., 426, 612
Kleinmuntz, B., 319, 336
Klerman, G. L., 482, 487
Klima, E., 281
Kling, M. A., 457
Klinger, C. A., 364
Klinger, E., 166–167
Klinnert, M. D., 320
Klitzner, M., 178
Knight, J., 582
Knoll, E., 431
Knowles, E. S., 25
Knutsen, E. J., 521
Koch, C., 96
Koch, H. L., 395
Koelling, R. A., 217
Koepke, J. P., 456
Koffka, K., 14
Kogan, N., 377, 410
Kohlberg, L., 566–567, 599–600
Kohler, W., 14, 253–255
Koko, 283, 402
Kolata, G., 28, 42, 50, 274, 342, 511, 602
Kolb, B., 70
Kolb, H., 92, 95
Kolb, L. C., 484, 492
Koller, M. R., 607
Kolligan, J., Jr., 431
Komaki, J., 634
Konecni, V. J., 608
Konopasky, R. J., 210
Koob, G. F., 234
Koperski, J. A., 346
Korchin, S. J., 534
Korner, A. F., 346
Koslowski, B., 353
Kosson, N., 600
Koukkou, M., 166
Kovacic, C. R., 637
Kovacs, G. L., 234, 241
Kowalski, R. M., 585
Kozlowski, L. T., 452, 582
Kozma, R. B., 646
Kraemer, H. C., 346
Kraft, W. A., 508
Kraines, R. J., 376
Krank, M. D., 194

Krantz, D. S., 450
Krate, R., 612
Krauss, R. M., 569–570
Kremen, W. S., 492
Kreutzer, M. A., 329
Krieger, D. T., 49
Krieger, W. G., 598
Kripke, D. F., 164
Kristeller, J. L., 299
Kroeber-Riel, W., 579
Kroger, W. S., 540
Kroonenberg, P. M., 355
Krueger, D. W., 511
Krueger, J. M., 156
Kulik, J., 241
Kurtines, W., 566
Kutz, S. L., 361
l'Allemand, C. F., 617
LaBerge, S. P., 179–180
Labonte, A., 524
Labruyere, J., 178
Ladd, G. T., 150
Laird, J. D., 330
Lakoff, G., 262
Lamb, M. E., 352, 355, 357, 361
Lambert, W., 235
Lamberth, J., 235, 609
Lamiell, J. T., 431
Lamon, S. J., 604
Land, E. H., 87, 92
Landerman, R., 486
Landers, S., 399
Landis, D., 65
Landis, K. R., 466
Landman, J. T., 543
Lange, C. G., 325, 330
Langford, G., 155
Langlois, J. H., 599, 612
Langner, T. S., 473
Langston, J. W., 177
Lamper, C., 349
Larsen, L. O., 85
Larsen, R. M., 430, 437
Lashley, K. S., 223, 225
Lassen, M. K., 481, 545
Latane, B., 560, 562, 564
Lauer, R. M., 296
Laufer, R., 453
Laumann, E. O., 609
Laurence, J., 170
Lautin, A., 523
Lavie, P., 453
Law, M. I., 97
Lawson, L., 634
Lazar, I., 367, 401
Lazarus, A. A., 540
Lazarus, R. S., 316, 331, 460–461
Leary, M. R., 585
Leaton, R. N., 188
Leavitt, H. J., 273
Lebra, T. S., 416
LeCann, A. F., 510
Lee, K., 105
Lee, M., 401

Lee, S., 176
Leeman, S., 49
Leff, D. N., 177
Legros, J. J., 234
Lehmann, D., 166
Lehnertz, K., 144
Lehrer, P. M., 466
Leirer, V. O., 176, 178
Lelwica, M., 357
LeMoal, M., 234
Lempert, H., 279–280
Lenard, H. G., 349
Lenneberg, E. H., 277
Lennon, J., 240
Leo, J., 462
Leonard, M., 357
Lepper, M. R., 305–306
Lerner, R. M., 373
Leshin, M., 597
Lettvin, J. Y., 95
Lev-Ran, A., 596
Levenson, R. W., 330–331, 335
Leventhal, G., 612
Leventhal, H., 328, 330, 581
Levine, J. D., 52
Levine, L. E., 361
Levinson, D. J., 577
Levy, A., 582
Lewin, R., 51, 306
Lewine, R. J., 471–472
Lewis, M., 329, 361, 598
Lewis, Max., 507, 526
Lewis, P., 543, 613
Lewontin, R. C., 398
Lezine, I., 357
Li, C. H., 52
Liberman, R. P., 537
Licht, B. G., 602
Lieberman, M., 566
Liebert, R. M., 22, 366
Liebowitz, M. R., 483
Light, K. C., 456
Likert, R., 627
Lillie, F., 595
Lima, A., 525
Liman, E., 197
Lincoln, A., 502
Linden, L., 95
Linder, D. E., 579
Lindvall, O., 51
Ling, G. S. F., 176
Ling, L. J., 197
Linn, M. C., 604
Linney, J. A., 650
Linnoila, M., 464
Linton, H., 583
Lipkowitz, M. H., 510
Lipowski, Z. J., 486
Lippitt, R., 212
Lippold, S., 612
Livingstone, M. S., 117, 119, 119–120
Llinas, R. R., 44
Lobb, B., 559
Localio, R., 25

Locke, E. A., 631
Locke, S. E., 457
Lockhart, S. H., 176
Loeb, G. E., 101–102
Loehlin, J. C., 498
Loevinger, J., 431
Loewenstein, R. J., 489
Loftus, E. F., 238, 241
Loftus, G. R., 238
Logothetis, N. K., 119
Logue, A. W., 291, 293, 296–297
Lohr, M. J., 373
Loizos, C., 362
Lombroso, C., 318
Long, C. N. H., 292
Loomis, B., 376
Lorenz, K., 216, 349, 352
Loughran, J. L., 649
Loulis, 280
Loullis, C. C., 295
Love, D., 644
Low, T. L. K., 594
Lowe, M. G., 296
Lowell, E. L., 301
Lowery, C. R., 29, 435
Lozoff, B., 354
Lubin, B., 430, 437
Luborsky, L., 543
Luchins, A. S., 268–269
Luddens, H., 47
Ludtke, M., 356
Lugaresi, E., 159
Luisada, P. V., 178
Lumsdaine, A. A., 581, 583
Lunde, I., 493
Lundy, R. M., 581
Luria, A. R., 230
Lutkenhoner, B., 144
Lutz, R. J., 644
Luxenberg, J. S., 485
Lykken, D. T., 319, 336, 395
Lyle, J., 366
Lynch, G., 226
Lynn, S. J., 168
Lytton, H., 396
M'Naghten, D., 475–476
Maccoby, E. E., 598, 601
MacCoun, R. J., 574
MacKain, K., 71
MacKay, D. M., 135
Macklis, J. D., 153
MacLeod, D. I. A., 155
MacLeod, J. M., 176
MacLeod, W. L., 155
MacNichol, E. F., 90, 92
MacPherson, G. M., 601, 603
MacWhinney, B., 278
Madden, N. A., 407
Madigan, S. A., 247
Madison, R. D., 153
Madrazo, I., 50–51
Madsen, M. C., 568–569
Magnusson, D., 420–421
Magrassi, L., 42

Magulac, M., 504
Mahoney, M. J., 16, 635–637
Maier, N. R. F., 271
Maier, S. F., 302
Maile, F. R., 440
Main, D. S., 364
Main, H., 353
Malkis, F. S., 584
Mallory, G., 310
Maltzman, I., 579
Mamelak, A. N., 153
Manchester, W., 285–286
Mancillas, J. R., 175
Manicas, P. T., 13, 30
Mann, J. J., 522, 525
Mann, L., 559
Mantell, D. M., 559
Mao, t. T., 415
Maranto, G., 455
Marbach, W. D., 161
Marcus, E. A., 188
Marder, S. R., 522
Mariani, A., 95
Markman, E., 370
Markowitz, J., 525
Markowitz, J. S., 482
Marks, P. A., 432
Markus, G. B., 396
Marler, P., 216–217
Marmar, C., 540, 542, 544
Marmarou, A., 346
Marmor, J., 605
Marolla, F. A., 396
Marschark, M., 236
Marshall, G. D., 330
Marshall, W. A., 374
Marston, W., 318
Martin, G., 178
Martin, J., 559
Martin, P. J., 511
Martin, R. L., 486
Maruyama, G., 582
Marvin, R. S., 370
Marx, J. L., 48, 457
Marx, M. H., 12
Maslach, C., 330
Masland, R. H., 82
Maslow, A. H., 14, 301, 425, 429–431
Mason, J., 464
Mason, W., 164
Mason, W. A., 362
Massad, P., 305
Masters, W. H., 379, 620, 622
Mastropieri, M. A., 401
Matarazzo, J. D., 430, 435, 437
Mather, D. B., 463
Matheson, J., 164
Mathews, D., 596
Mathews, D. K., 636
Matter, C. F., 25
Matthews, K. A., 460
Mattson, M., 522
Maughan, B., 649–650
May, R., 532

Mayr, E., 392
Maziade, M., 351
Mazur, A., 302
McCall, J. N., 396
McCall, R. B., 362, 402
McCarley, R. W., 165
McCarthy, J., 260
McCarthy, P., 106
McCartney, K., 357, 401
McChesney, C. M., 482–483
McClelland, D. C., 301–302, 389
McClements, J. D., 639
McClenahan, E. L., 373
McCloskey, M., 241
McConnell, S. C., 481, 545
McCord, J., 542
McCormick, D. A., 197
McCrae, R. R., 346
McCully, J., 194
McDonnell, J., 110
McDonough, R. J., 177
McElroy, S. L., 522
McGaugh, J. L., 241
McGee, D. L., 453
McGue, M., 394
McGuire, W. J., 274, 581
McHale, S. M., 361
McKeachie, W. J., 646
McKean, K., 50, 108
McKinley, J. C., 432, 435
McKinney, J. P., 368
McLaughlin, D. G., 415–416
McNeil, E. B., 488, 506
McWhirter, N., 381
Mead, M., 591–592, 597
Meddis, R., 155–156
Medin, D. L., 262
Meehl, P. E., 431
Meer, J., 640
Mefford, I. N., 164
Meichenbaum, D., 539, 639
Meiners, M. L., 613
Meissner, W. W., 504
Melton, L. J., 521
Meltzoff, A. N., 371
Menaker, M., 160
Menninger, K., 475
Menustik, C. E., 536
Menzel, E., 214
Meredith, M. A., 59
Mergenhagen, S., 456
Mergner, T., 109
Merzel, A. P. C., 493
Mesmer, A., 167
Messer, D. J., 353
Messick, D., 408
Metz, L., 453
Mewborn, C. R., 579
Meyer, A., 318
Meyer, J. P., 436, 609
Meyer-Bahlburg, H. F. L., 596
Michael, R. P., 297–298
Michael, W. B., 408
Michelangelo, 386

Middlemist, R. D., 25
Miguchi, M., 415–416
Miles, C., 601
Miles, D. L., 473
Miles, W. R., 111–112
Milgram, S., 428, 556–561, 583
Miller, G., 231
Miller, G. A., 276–277, 583
Miller, I. W., 304
Miller, J. A., 70, 160, 214
Miller, J. E., 640
Miller, K. D., 98
Miller, L. B., 401
Miller, M., 161
Miller, N., 582
Miller, N. E., 112, 323
Miller, R. L., 303
Mills, J., 584
Mineka, S., 305
Miner, R. A., 510
Mirsky, A. F., 502, 529
Mischel, W., 421, 619
Mishara, B. L., 463
Mishkin, M., 225
Mita, T. H., 582
Mitchell, H. E., 579
Mitchison, G., 165–166
Mittleman, G., 295
Miyake, A., 594
Mladejovsky, M. G., 103
Mobley, W. H., 634
Mohs, M., 398
Molitor, N., 356
Moll, P. P., 296
Money, J., 295, 595–596, 606
Monk, T. H., 161
Moore, D., 368
Moore, J. E., 511
Moore, M., 639
Moore, R. Y., 50
Moore-Ede, M. C., 162
Mora, G., 517
Morad, M., 53
Morales, F. R., 153
Morales, G., 145–146
Moran, J., 263–264
Moreland, R. L., 396
Moreno, J. L., 534–535
Morgan, M., 367
Morgan, W. P., 637
Morley, J. E., 241
Morongiello, B. A., 144
Morrison, A. M., 627–628
Morrison, A. R., 153
Morrissey, J. P., 475
Mortimore, P., 649–650
Moss, A. J., 460
Mossler, D. G., 370
Most, R. K., 362
Motley, M. T., 279
Muntjewerff, W. J., 349
Mowrer, D. H., 323
Mozart, W. A., 386
Muecke, L. N., 511

Mueller, E., 361
Mueser, K. T., 537
Muir, M. S., 292
Mukhametov, L. M., 155
Munroe, R. H., 600
Munroe, R. L., 600
Murgatroyd, S., 649
Murphy, G. M., Jr., 48
Murphy, M., 299
Murphy, T. J., 640
Murray, C., 312
Murray, M., 270
Myers, J. J., 71
Myers, R. E., 70
Nakayama, K., 143
Narayanan, V. K., 632
Nash, M., 173
Nash, M. R., 540
Nason, S., 249
Nath, R., 632
Nathan, P. E., 508
Nathans, J., 89–90
Nation, J. R., 305
Nauta, W. J. H., 40, 42, 57–59
Neale, J. M., 482
Neimeyer, R. A., 529
Neiss, R., 299
Nelson, L., 569
Nelson, R., 95
Nelson, R. O., 480
Neugarten, B. L., 376
Nevin, J. A., 205
Newcomb, T. M., 607
Newell, A., 257, 265
Newman, B. M., 373, 376
Newman, P. R., 373
Newton, I., 386
Nicholson, N., 632
Nickerson, R. S., 242
Nicoll, R. A., 48
Nideffer, R., 651
Niethold, C., 75
Niles, P., 581
Nimchimpsky, 284
Nisbett, R. E., 305
Nolan, J. D., 241
Nolen, T. G., 188
Norman, D. A., 236
Norman, J., 42
Norman, W. H., 304
Normann, R. A., 92
Nottebohm, F., 70
Novin, D., 292–293
Nowak, C. A., 376
Nowatzyk, A., 265
Noyes, R., Jr., 482–483
Nydegger, R. V., 575
O'Brian, W. H., 132–135, 137
O'Connor, M. J., 403
O'Leary, B. S., 630
O'Leary, S. E., 361
O'Malley, M. N., 586
O'Malley, P. M., 368
O'Neal, E., 22

O'Sullivan, M., 330
Obrist, P. A., 456
Ochoa, G., 398–399, 407
Odbert, H. S., 419
Oden, G. C., 236, 257, 262
Oedipus, R., 598
Offer, D., 368
Offermann, L. R., 628, 6341
Offord, K. P., 435
Olarte, S., 25
Oldham, G. R., 632
Olds, J., 35–37
Olds, M. E., 293
Olenick, M., 357
Oliveros, J. C., 234
Oller, D. K., 275
Olney, J. W., 178
Optican, L. M., 96, 98
Orne, M. T., 170–171
Orwin, R. G., 543
Orzack, M. H., 529
Osberg, T. M., 435
Osborne, D., 435
Osherson, D. N., 370
Osipow, S. H., 7
Oster, H., 328, 357
Ostroff, R. B., 464
Ostrov, E., 368
Oswald, I., 155
Otomo, K., 280
Ouellette, R., 482
Ouston, J., 649–650
Overton, D. A., 247
Owen, D., 398
Owen, D. W., 436
Packer, O., 87
Page, B., 630
Paivio, A., 235
Palca, J., 161
Palisin, H., 351
Pallanti, S., 483
Pancer, S. M., 581
Pankove, E., 410
Panksepp, J., 47, 49, 52
Pantev, C., 144
Pappenheimer, J. R., 156
Pardes, H., 474
Parfit, M., 215–216
Parke, R. D., 361, 366
Parkes, C. M., 457, 641
Parkinson, D. K., 446
Parmelee, A. H., 403
Parr, W., 224
Paschelke, M. A., 49
Pascual-Leone, A., 175
Pasternak, G. W., 176
Patrick, G. T. W., 155
Patterson, C. H., 283–284
Patterson, D. G., 347
Patterson, F. G., 283–284
Paunonen, S. V., 421, 440
Pavlov, I. P., 189–190, 196–198
Pearl, D., 367
Pearson, A. J. D., 155

Pedersen, E., 649
Peel, R., 475
Peele, S., 38
Pelliccioni, L., Jr., 639
Penfield, W., 223
Penrose, R., 260, 274
Peplau, L. A., 616
Pepler, D., 361
Pepler, D. J., 409
Pepper, S., 436, 609
Perlick, D., 452
Perlman, I., 92
Perls, F., 534
Perry, C., 170
Perry, T. B., 365
Persky, V. W., 456
Pert, A., 456
Pert, C. B., 456
Pervin, L. A., 420–422, 431
Peselow, E. D., 523
Petersen, A. C., 368, 373
Peterson, C., 467
Peterson, M. R., 502
Peterson, R. A., 473
Peterson, R. E., 597
Peterson, W. A., 376
Petranoff, T., 651
Petrie, S., 373
Pettersen, L., 130
Petty, R. E., 578–579, 581–582, 585, 645
Phares, E. J., 431
Phelps, E., 248
Phillips, D., 357
Phillips. M., 319
Piaget, J., 358–359, 370–372
Piccione, C., 168
Pieterse, M., 408
Pihl, R. O., 451, 641
Pilkonis, P. A., 543
Pinel, P., 518
Pines, M., 358, 464
Pinker, S., 274
Pintrich, P. R., 646
Pion, G., 6
Pittman, T. S., 300
Plomin, R., 176, 395
Plutchik, R., 332–335
Poggio, T., 96
Pohl, R., 483
Poirot, H., 56
Poizner, H., 281
Polansky, N., 212
Pollock, D. A., 453
Pool, R., 30
Pope, H. G., Jr., 511, 522
Popkin, M. K., 510
Porter, R., 42
Postman, L., 230
Power, T. G., 599
Poznanski, E., 324
Premack, D., 208
Pressman, M. D., 638
Preston, T. A., 163
Preti, G., 298

Price, M. T., 178
Priest, R. F., 607
Pritchett, D. B., 47
Proxmire, W., 614
Pruitt, D. G., 574
Pryor, J. B., 580
Pupkin, R., 504
Purves, D., 42
Quaintance, M. K., 630
Quattrochi, J. J., 153
Quattrone, G. A., 586
Quigley-Fernandez, B., 579
Quinlan, D., 511
Quinn, O. W., 500
Rader, N., 142
Raderscheidt, A., 263–264, 281
Rahe, R. H., 457–458, 617
Raloff, J., 641
Ralph, M. R., 160
Ramachandran, V. S., 120
Ramey, C., 401
Ramey, C. T., 302–303, 356
Ramsay, D., 142, 354
Ramsay, D. S., 276
Randi, A., 110–111
Rankin, C. H., 188
Ransberger, V. M., 323
Ransford, C. P., 639
Rapoport, J. L., 485, 512
Rarick, E., 462
Rasinski, K. A., 273
Raskin, D. C., 319
Rau, L., 230
Ray, W. A., 521
Raymond, C. L., 603
Rayner, R., 194–195
Raynor, J. O., 302
Raz, N., 501
Raz, S., 501
Razran, G., 279
Reagan, R. W., 319, 475, 501
Reay, D. T., 449
Rebar, R. W., 594
Rechtschaffen, A., 158–159
Redican, W. K., 329
Redl, F., 212
Redlich, F., 473
Reed, R. R., 105
Reeves, J., 640
Regier, D. A., 477
Reid, N., 489
Reigl, H., 256
Reil, J. C., 515–516, 525
Reiman, E. M., 483
Reinisch, J. M., 53, 618
Reis, H., 552
Reppert, S. M., 162
Rescorla, R. A., 196
Resnick, S. M., 603
Rest, J., 567
Restak, R. M., 348
Reston, J., 614
Reuter, T., 85
Reynolds, D., 649

Rheingold, H. L., 353, 599
Rhodes, P., 453
Rhue, J. W., 168
Ricaurte, G., 177
Rich, C. L., 449, 463
Rich, S. A., 392
Richards, R., 493
Richards, W. G., 197
Richman, C. L., 236
Richmond, B. J., 96, 98
Richmond, M. B., 542
Riles, W., 398
Risch, C., 451, 494
Ritchie, B. F., 213
Rivkees, S. A., 162
Robbins, P. C., 475
Roberts, K., 277
Roberts, L., 223, 345, 448
Robertson, I., 630
Robinot, F., 357
Robins, L. N., 477
Robinson, D. L., 263
Robinson, L. A., 529
Robinson, N. M., 407
Rocha e Silva, M., 108
Rock, I., 123, 137
Rockley, G. J., 503
Rodin, J., 296, 300, 447, 460
Roehrs, T., 155
Roff, M., 366
Rogel, M. J., 106
Rogers, C. R., 14, 429–431, 439, 531
Rogers, M., 141
Rogers, R., 475
Rogers, R. W., 22, 579
Roggman, L. A., 612
Rompre, P. P., 47, 175
Roopnarine, J. L., 361, 364
Rootenberg, J., 540
Roper, S. D., 104
Rorer, L. G., 420–421, 427, 435
Rosa, E., 302
Rosch, E., 262, 275
Rose, S., 398
Rose, S. A., 403
Rosen, D. H., 309
Rosen, S., 212
Rosenbaum, R., 542
Rosenblum, L. A., 353, 361
Rosenfeld, J. G., 544
Rosenfield, D., 577
Rosenhan, D. L., 506–507, 510, 566
Rosenkrantz, A. L., 463
Rosenman, R. H., 459
Rosenthal, D., 494, 500
Rosenthal, M. K., 349
Rosenthal, N. E., 494
Rosenzweig, M. R., 234
Rosenzweig, S., 12
Rosnick, P. B., 523
Ross, D., 208
Ross, H. S., 409
Ross, H. W., 353
Ross, M., 581

Ross, S. A., 208
Rosse, R. L., 631
Rossier, J., 75
Roth, T., 155
Rothman, S., 398–399
Rotter, J. B., 427
Rouchouse, J., 357
Roueche, B., 511, 516
Roy, A., 464
Roy-Byrne, P. P., 483
Rubin, J. Z., 629
Rubin, K. H., 362
Rubin, L., 377
Rubin, Z., 609, 611, 616
Rubinsky, P., 543
Rubinstein, E. A., 366–367
Ruble, D. N., 598
Ruch, J. C., 169
Rucker, R., 110
Ruff, M. R., 456
Rumbaugh, D. M., 283–284
Rumelhart, D. E., 236
Rundus, D., 247
Rush, A. J., 539
Rushing, W. A., 473
Rushton, E. W., 648
Russell, B., 277
Russell, J. A., 643
Rutter, M., 649–650
Ruttle, K., 401
Ryan, E. D., 637
Ryan, L., 560
Ryan, M. J., 645
Ryan, R., 632
Rycroft, W., 293
Rynders, J., 408
Sachs, F., 44
Sack, D. A., 494
Sacks, M., 542
Sacks, O., 68
Saegert, S., 639
Salovey, P., 460
Saltz, E., 564
Salzberg, H. C., 540
Samiy, A. H., 523
Sampson, E. E., 396, 567
Sandblom, R. E., 164
Sanderson, J. D., 293
Sandman, C. A., 241
Sands, S. F., 231
Sanford, R. N., 577
Santiago, H. C., 231
Sapolsky, R. M., 457
Sarbin, T. R., 170–171, 173
Saunders, D. R., 420
Saunders, F. A., 118
Savage-Rumbaugh, E. S., 283–284
Savitsky, J. C., 22
Sawyer, J., 607
Saxe, L., 319
Scadden, L., 118
Scammon, R. E., 347
Scanlan, J., 526
Scarr, S., 357, 396, 398, 401

Schacht, T., 508
Schachter, S., 297, 325–328, 330–331, 333–335, 452
Schacter, D. L., 229
Schaefer, C., 461
Schaeffer, M. A., 446
Schaffer, H. R., 353
Schaffner, W., 521
Schall, J. D., 119
Schatzberg, A. F., 522
Scheibel, A. B., 48
Scheller, R. H., 217
Schiff, M., 398
Schiller, P. H., 362
Schleifer, S. J., 456
Schlenker, B. R., 579, 584
Schlenker, P. A., 584
Schlosberg, H., 273
Schmitt, N., 630
Schnapf, J. L., 85
Schneider, B., 627
Schneider, N. G., 242
Schneider, P. A., 346
Scholmerich, A., 349
Schroeder, D. A., 426
Schuckit, M. A., 451
Schugens, M. M., 234
Schulberg, H. C., 446
Schulsinger, F., 494
Schultz, G., 319
Schuster, C., 177
Schwartz, J. P., 176
Schwartz, P. M., 641
Schwartz, R. H., 178
Schwartz, S., 574
Schweinhart, L. J., 400
Sciascia, T. R., 95
Scott, D. H., 393
Scott, L. R., 634
Scott, M. D., 639
Sears, P., 405
Sears, R. R., 323, 405
Sechenov, I. M., 13
Sechrest, L., 431
Secord, P. F., 13, 30
Sedvall, G., 501
Seeburg, P. H., 47
Seefeldt, C., 377
Seeman, W., 432
Seever, M., 430, 437
Segal, M. W., 608
Segal, N. L., 395
Seiden, L., 177
Seidman, E., 650
Self, P. A., 598
Seligman, M. E. P., 216, 302, 304
Seligman, M. E., 467
Seligmann, J., 292, 462, 523
Selmi, P. M., 540
Selye, H., 454
Selzer, M., 440
Semmel, M. I., 407
Senter, N., 521
Serbin, L. A., 600

Serock, K., 377
Seuss, Dr., 341–342
Shakespeare, W., 212
Shanab, M. E., 559
Shapira, A., 569
Shapiro, A. K., 542
Shapiro, B., 495
Shapiro, D., 523
Shapiro, D. H., Jr., 172
Shapiro, E., 542
Shatz, M., 370
Shaver, J. P., 566–567
Shaw, B., 539
Shaw, R. E., 122
Sheffield, F. D., 581, 583
Shekelle, R. B., 460
Sheldon, W. H., 418–419, 430
Shelley, M., 50
Shelton, F. C., 377
Shelton, R. C., 501
Shenkel, R. J., 29, 435
Sheposh, J. P., 613
Sherrick, C. E., 144
Shertzer, B., 375
Shields, J., 498
Shiffrin, R., 262
Shilts, R., 618
Shimmin, H. S., 600
Shoben, E. J., 262
Shock, N. W., 379
Shockley, W., 397
Shore, J. H., 453
Shotland, R. L., 564, 568
Shrauger, J. S., 435
Shuchter, S. R., 494
Shulman, R. G., 66
Shumway, M., 521
Siegel, S., 193–194
Sierles, F. S., 510
Siffre, M., 160
Sigall, H., 579
Siggins, G. R., 175
Signorielli, N., 367
Silberner, J., 603
Silveira, J., 267–268
Silvern, L., 371–372
Silverstein, B., 452
Siman, M. L., 365
Simon, H., 257, 265
Simon, J. C., 522
Simon, N. G., 290
Simon, T., 387
Simonson, N. R., 581
Simpson, E. L., 567
Sinden, J., 234
Singbeil, C. E., 396
Singer, D. G., 367
Singer, J. E., 327
Singer, J. L., 367, 431
Singer, L. M., 354
Singer, M. T., 500
Singh, J. V., 628

Sims, E., 296
Skinner, B. F., 187–188, 199, 216–217, 256, 284, 370, 426, 430, 647–648
Skutnik, L., 565
Slavin, R. E., 407
Sloan, K. R., Jr., 87
Slobin, D. I., 277
Sloviter, R. S., 53
Smith, A., 649–650
Smith, C. G., 178
Smith, D., 508
Smith, F. J., 632
Smith, G. E., 241
Smith, G. P., 293
Smith, J., 105
Smith, J. E., 175
Smith, M. B., 429
Smith, M. E., 225
Smith, M. L., 542–543
Smith, S. J., 48
Smith, S. M., 246, 256
Smith, T. L., 457
Snyder, C. R., 29, 435
Snyder, S. H., 48, 174, 193, 522
Snyderman, M., 398–399
Solomon, H., 565
Solomon, L. Z., 565
Solomon, R. L., 306–309, 316, 321
Soni, S. D., 503
Sonstroem, R. J., 639
Sorbera, L. A., 53
Sorce, J. F., 320
Sorenson, E. R., 328
Sorrell, S. P., 540
Soskin, W. F., 437
Spacapan, S., 564
Spanos, N. P., 173
Spearman, C., 391
Speer, A., 440
Spence, J. T., 301
Sperling, G., 229
Sperry, R. W., 70
Spiegel, D., 540
Spieker, S., 71
Spillane, R., 559
Spitz, R. A., 355
Spitzer, R. L., 480, 491, 493, 509
Spooner, W. A., 279
Sprafkin, C., 600
Sprafkin, J., 366, 600
Spring, R. L., 475
Springen, K., 234
Squire, L. R., 227, 242, 525
Sroufe, L. A., 353
Sroufe, R., 612
Staats, A. W., 193, 578
Staats, C. K., 193, 578
Stallings, J., 401
Stam, H. J., 173
Stanfiel, J. D., 475
Stanger, C., 329
Stanley, J. C., 601–602
Stapp, J., 6

Stark, E., 170, 186
Starr, M. D., 309
Staw, B. M., 631–632, 634
Steadman, H. J., 475
Steblay, N. M., 563
Steele, C. M., 175
Stein, B. E., 59
Stein, M., 295, 456
Stein, S., 612
Steiner, J. E., 357
Steir, M., 354
Stellar, E., 292
Stenberg, C., 357
Stenevi, U., 51
Stephan, W. G., 577
Stephens, B. R., 612
Stern, D., 71
Stern, D. B., 487
Stern, L. W., 387
Sternberg, B., 306
Sternberg, D. B., 197
Sternberg, D. E., 522
Sternberg, R. J., 392–393, 616
Stevens, C. F., 43
Stevens, J., 630
Stice, G. F., 420
Stickney, S. K., 510
Stith, S. M., 357
Stoel-Gammon, C., 280
Stoller, R. J., 598
Stone, G., 447
Stone, S. C., 375
Stopa, E. G., 162
Stork, L., 600
Strahilevitz, A., 640
Strahilevitz, M., 640
Strauss, L., 177
Stricker, E. M., 295
Strong, W., 566–567
Struening, E., 542
Strupp, H. H., 542
Stryker, M. P., 98
Studdert-Kennedy, M., 71
Stunkard, A. J., 297
Sturla, E., 597
Suave, R., 396
Suddath, R. L., 501–502
Suedfeld, P., 299
Suinn, R. M., 459
Suler, J. R., 172
Sullivan, H. S., 431
Sullivan, M. W., 329
Sulloway, F. J., 11
Sultan, 253–254, 268
Sulzer, J. L., 22
Supple, W. F., Jr., 188
Surber, C. F., 359
Sushelsky, L., 630
Sussman, N., 617, 619
Svaetichin, G., 92
Svejda, M., 142
Swaab, D. F., 603
Swap, W. C., 582

Swartz, M., 486
Sweeney, J., 525
Swenson, W. M., 435
Sylva, K., 362
Szasz, T., 462–463, 508
Szucko, J. J., 319, 336
Szymanski, H. V., 522
Tajfel, H., 571
Tanner, J. M., 369
Tatum, E. L., 453
Tauber, E. S., 152
Taussig, H. B., 312–313
Taylor, B., 373
Taylor, C. W., 630
Taylor, E., 356
Taylor, E. B., 494
Taylor, J. R., 176
Taylor, M., 277
Taylor, M. A., 510
Taylor, S. E., 447, 450, 459, 466, 586
Teasdale, J. D., 304
Teborg, R. H., 271
Tedeschi, J. T., 579, 584
Telegdy, G. A., 210
Tellegen, A., 461
Teplin, L. A., 527
Tepperman, J., 292
Terman, L. M., 387–388, 403, 405–406, 410
Terrace, H. S., 231, 284
Tessler, R., 630
Tetrud, J. W., 177
Thiel, D. L., 613
Thivierge, J., 351
Thomas, A., 346, 350, 354, 426
Thompson, D. E., 634
Thompson, J. W., 525
Thompson, R. F., 197, 226
Thompson, S. K., 599
Thorndike, E. L., 198–199
Thornton, J. C., 456
Thurstone, L. L., 385–386, 389, 391
Timberlake, W., 208
Timms, V., 155
Tipton, R. D., 540
Tissot, S., 617
Titchener, E. B., 9–10
Tobin, P., 601, 603
Toffano, G., 176
Tollefson, D. L., 84
Tolman, E. C., 213–214
Toman, J. E. P., 256
Tomarken, A. J., 328, 330
Tomkiewicz, S., 398
Tomkins, S. S., 330
Tong, Y. C., 102
Toohey, M. L., 500
Tordoff, M. G., 293
Torrance, E. P., 408
Torrey, E. F., 502
Toulmin, S., 9
Tourangeau, T., 273
Tranel, D., 69

Troll, L. E., 374
Tronick, E., 361
Trotter, R. J., 348, 485, 512
True, W. R., 453
Tseng, W., 415–416
Tsuang, M. T., 492, 497–498
Tulving, E., 229, 235
Tune, G. S., 155
Turkington, C., 284, 407–408, 461
Turnbull, C. M., 115–116
Turner, C. F., 604
Turvey, M. T., 122
Tversky, B., 237
Tyler, L. E., 418
Uhde, T. W., 483
Ulrich, R. E., 323
Ulrich, R. S., 625–626
Umberson, D., 466
Unestahl, L. E., 637
Ungar, G., 223–224
Urban, I., 234
Ursano, R. J., 544
Ury, W. L., 628–629
Vaillant, C. O., 459
Vaillant, G. E., 459, 467
Valenstein, E. S., 295, 508, 525, 527–528
Valins, S., 315–316, 324, 331
Valone, K., 582
van Doorninck, W. J., 401
Van Dyke, C., 175
van IJzendoorn, M. H., 355
van Nispen, J. W., 234
Van Riezen, H., 241
van Wimersma Greidanus, T. B., 234
Vandenberg, B., 362
Vanderweele, D. A., 293
Vaughn, B. E., 356
Veitch, R., 323
Vermilyea, B. B., 482
Vermilyea, J. A., 482
Vernon, P. E., 399
Versteeg, D. H. G., 241
Viki, 280
Vinokur, A., 574
Vogel, P. J., 70
Vollmer, W. M., 453
von Beethoven, L., 386
von Braun, W., 585
Von Glinow, M. A., 627–628
von Hofsten, C., 123, 143
von Krafft-Ebing, R., 617, 620
von Ribbentrop, J., 556
Vondracek, F. W., 373
Voos, D. K., 354
Voyvodic, J. T., 42
Wafford, K. A., 451
Wagner, H. N., Jr., 66
Wagner, J., 449
Wahl, S. M., 456
Wain, L., 496
Wakefield, J. A., Jr., 508
Waldhauser, F., 368
Waldrop, M. M., 259

Walk, R. D., 142
Walker, E., 471–472
Walker, J., 83
Walker, L., 584
Walker, L. J., 566
Wallace, A., 488
Wallace, C. J., 537
Wallace, I., 488
Wallace, I. F., 403
Wallace, J. E., 178
Wallace, S., 488
Wallach, M. A., 409–410
Wallenchinsky, D., 488
Wallis, C., 356
Walster, E., 615
Wanner, E., 274, 277, 280
Wanner, H. E., 236
Ward, L. M., 643
Warner, S., 28
Washburn, S. L., 216
Washington, G., 227–228, 240
Washoe, 280, 283
Wasserman, L., 600
Waters, E., 354
Watson, J., 345
Watson, J. B., 12–13, 16, 150, 194–195,
        197, 212, 256, 290, 370, 425–426,
        539
Watson, J. S., 302
Watt, J. A. G., 504
Watts, J., 527
Wayner, M. J., 295
Weary, G., 586
Weaver, D. R., 162
Webb, W. B., 152, 155–156, 167
Webber, J. A., 80
Weber, E., 80
Weber, G., 649
Weber, R. J., 456
Wehr, T. A., 494
Wehren, A., 600
Weicker, L., Jr., 519, 521
Weiden, P. J., 522
Weikart, D. P., 400
Weinberg, M. S., 607
Weinberg, R. A., 391–393, 396, 398
Weinberg, R. S., 639
Weinberger, D. R., 502
Weinberger, N. M., 197
Weiner, H., 457
Weiner, M. J., 577
Weiner, R. D., 524–525
Weingarten, H. P., 296
Weingartner, H., 234
Weinraub, M., 600
Weinstein, A., 521
Weinstein, N. D., 447–448
Weintraub, P., 102–103

Weisfeld, G. E., 344
Weisler, A., 362
Weismuller, J., 278
Weiss, B., 641–642
Weiss, D. S., 542
Weiss, R., 51, 161, 345
Weiss, R. S., 457
Weissman, M. M., 482, 494
Weitzenhoffer, A. M., 168
Weller, A., 293
Wells, C. E., 511
Wells, R. G., 105
Wender, P. H., 494
Wernicke, C., 282
Wertheimer, M., 13–14
Werts, C. E., 437
Wesner, R., 494
West, M. A., 172
Westermeyer, J. F., 496
Westheimer, G., 95
Wetzel, C. G., 108
Whalen, R. E., 290
Whatley, J. L., 361
Wheeler, L., 552
White, A., 462
White, B. W., 118
White, G. L., 579
Whitehurst, G. J., 277
Whitman, C., 67–68
Whorf, B. L., 275
Wible, C. G., 241
Wicklund, R. A., 580
Widiger, T. A., 420–421, 427, 435
Wiens, A. N., 536
Wiesel, T. N., 96
Wilbur, C. B., 489–490
Wilkins, M., 345
Will, J. A., 598
Wille, D. E., 353
Willerman, L., 498
Williams, D. A., 400
Williams, J. B. W., 480, 491, 493, 509
Williams, R., 276
Williams, R. M., 457
Williams, T. M., 367
Willis, P. W., IV., 456
Wills, T. A., 473
Wilson, E. O., 306, 362
Wilson, J., 176
Wilson, J. D., 597
Wilson, W. R., 582
Wing, C. W., 410
Winkel, G. H., 639
Winson, J., 166
Winter, J. B., 158–159
Winton, W. M., 299
Wise, R. A., 47, 175–176
Wist, E. R., 143

Witt, D., 645
Wittelsberger, B., 542
Wolpe, J., 536–537
Wolskee, P. J., 52
Wong, S. C. P., 143
Wood, J. M., 179
Wood, V., 376
Woodhead, M., 401
Woolfolk, R. L., 466
Wray, F., 135
Wright, A. A., 231
Wright, C., 401
Wright, F. E., 577
Wright, F. L., 410–411
Wu, J. C., 523
Wu, T., 408
Wundt, W., 7–9, 12, 15
Wurtz, R. H., 263
Wyatt, R., 51
Wynne, L. C., 500
Yager, T., 453
Yahya, K. A., 559
Yakimovich, D., 564
Yalom, I. D., 596
Yamazaki, K., 106
Yang, K. S., 416
Yang, R. K., 349
Yates, W. R., 482–483
Yawo, H., 42
Yeragani, V. K., 483
Yercoutere, A., 498
Yerkes, R. M., 299
Yesavage, J. A., 176, 178
Yevzeroff, H., 542
Yogman, M., 361
Yonas, A., 130
York, D. A., 296
Young, D., 463
Young, J. G., 449
Young, T., 89, 92,
Younger, J. C., 584
Yuille, J. C., 236
Zaidel, E., 71
Zajonc, R. B., 331, 396, 581
Zellner, M., 583
Zich, J., 5
Zimbardo, P. G., 168, 283, 330, 557, 568,
        571, 576
Zimmerman, R. R., 352
Zisook, S., 494
Zouzounis, J. A., 525
Zrull, J. P., 324
Zucker, L. M., 296
Zucker, T. F., 296
Zuckerman, M., 552
Zumpe, D., 298
Zwyghuizen-Doorenbos, A., 155
Zylman, R. 176

SUBJECT INDEX

Note: Italicized page numbers that appear in this index refer to pages on which a running glossary definition of the particular term can be found.

AA, *see* Alcoholics Anonymous
A-B-A single-subject experimental design, 23–24
ACTH, *see* adrenocorticotropic hormone
Abnormal behavior, 471–473, 474–512
  assessment of, 506–511
  prevalence of, 477
Absolute threshold, 79
Accommodation, (of the eye's lens) *134–135*
Acetylcholine, 47
Achievement test, *403*
Achieving society theory of motivation, 302–303
Acme-Bolt trucking game (cooperation and competition), 569–571
Acquired immune deficiency syndrome (AIDS), 28, 447–448, 618–619
  changing behavior to avoid, 618–619
  hotline phone number, 619
Acquisition (learning), *189–190*
Acralick dermatitis (in dogs), 485
Action potential of neuron, 44–45
Action therapy, 529–533, 535–540, 544–545
Activation synthesis model of dreams, *165*
Acupuncture, *51*
Adaptive theory of sleep, *156–157*
Addiction, 175, 309–310
  physical, 175
  psychological, 175, 309–310
Addison's disease, 510
Additive mixing, 89
Adolescence, 344, 367–373, 381–382, 461, 593
  career choice, 371–373
  cognitive development during, 370–372, 381–382
  developmental tasks of, 371–373
  identity crisis, 344, 373
  role confusion, 373
  peer group relationships, 373
  physical changes during, 368–370
   growth spurt, 370

  puberty, 368–369, 593
  rite of passage, 367
  storm and stress during, 368
  suicide and, 461
Adoption design, 394
Adrenal glands, 54, 594
  adrenaline, 54, 510
  noradrenaline, 54
  steroids, 54
Adrenaline, 54, 510, *see also,* Epinephrine
Adrenocorticotropic hormone (ACTH), 241, 454–455
Adulthood, 374–380
  early (18–40 years), 374–375
   career development, 375
   marriage and parenthood, 374–375
   physical changes during, 374
  later (over 65 years), 377–380
   aging, prevention of, 380–381
   physical changes, 378–379
   sexual relationships during, 378–379
  middle (40–65 years), 376–377
   empty nest syndrome, 377
   menopause, 376
   midlife crisis, 376–377
   physical changes during, 376
Aerial perspective (depth cue), *134, 136–137*
Afferent nerves, 38, 40
Affordance, *122–123*
Aftereffects, 95
Age regression and hypnosis, 173
Aging, 380
  causes of, 380–381
  prevention of, 380
Aggression, 18–19, 22, 323–324, 423, 464, 521
  causes of, 18, 323–324, 423, 464
  frustration-aggression hypothesis, 322–323
  instinctive, 423
  learning of, 18
  pain-elicited, 322–323
  sudden, 323–324
  suicide, 464
Agonist (drug), 48–49
Ahistorical research, 17
AIDS, *see* Acquired immune deficiency syndrome

Al-Anon, 451–452
Alarm reaction stage, *454–455*
Alcohol, 175–176, 536
  absorption of, 175
  effects of, 175–176
  delirium tremens and, 176
Alcoholics Anonymous, 451
Alcoholism, 451–452, 536
  causes of, 451
  treatment for, 451–452, 536
Algorithms, 264–265
Allport's theory of personality, 419–420
Alpha waves (EEG), *151,* 154
Altruism, 303, 306, 611
Alzheimer's disease, 378
Amacrine cells (eye), 82–83, 94
American Cancer Society (phone number), 452
American Psychological Association, 11, 25
American Sign Language (ASL), 280
Ames room, *131–132*
Amino acid, 49
Amnesia, 69, 221–222, 229, 234, 242–243, 249–250, 478, 488
  anterograde, 243
  psychogenic, 242, 478, 488
  retrograde, 221–222, 234, 242, 488
  somatogenic, 221–222, 242–243
  vasopressin's effects on, 234
Amphetamine, 164, *173–174*
  effects of, 173–174
Amplitude (sound), 99–*100*
Amygdala, 60, 67, 225
  memory and, 225
  violence and, 60, 67
Anal retentive personality, 424
Androgens, 594–597
Angular gyrus, 282–283
Animal magnetism, 167
Antabuse, 451
Antagonist (drug), 48–49
Anterograde amnesia, 243
Anticipatory eating, 297
Antidepressants, 522–523
Antisocial personality,
Anxiety, *461,* 524
  rebound, 524
Anxiety disorders, 478–486
  causes of, 481–486

generalized anxiety disorder, 482
obsessive-compulsive disorders, 483–486
panic disorder, 482–483
simple phobia, 478–482
Anxious/avoidant attachment, 353, 355–356
Anxious/resistant attachment, 353, 355
Apes and language acquisition, 280, 283–284
arguments against, 284
Koko, 283
Nimchimsky, 284
Washoe, 280, 283
Aphasia, 69, 281–283
Broca's, 69, 281–283
Wernicke's, 282–283
Apnea, sleep, *164–165*
Apparent motion, 13, *120*, 122–123, *see also* Phi phenomenon
Applied research, 17
Aptitude test, 400, *403*
Aristotle's illusion, 107
Arcuate fasciculus, 282–283
Arousal, physiological, 39–40, 153, 174–175, 317, 636–638
and athletes, 636–638
Artificial intelligence, 256–260
meaning and, 258–259
mode of processing and, 259–260
ASL, *see* American Sign Language
Assessment of psychopathology, 506–511
bias, 506–507
misdiagnosis, 510–511
Association areas of brain, 63
Athletes, 636–638, 651
and peak performance, 637–639, 651
and personality, 636–637
and physiology, 636–637
Atonia, *153*
Attachment, 352–353, 354–357
anxious/avoidant 353, 355–356
anxious/resistant 353, 355
bonding's effects on, 354
cultural differences in, 355
human, 353–357
intraorganismic perspective on, 353
rhesus monkey studies of, 352–353
secure, 353, 355
Attention, 59, 263–264
and midbrain, 59, 117
Attitude change, 580–588
central route processing, 582
cognitive dissonance and, 583–585, 587
emotional appeals, 581
mere exposure effect, 582
peripheral route processing, 582
persuasive communication, 580–583
Attitudes, 273–274, 419, 572, 578–588
as cognitive skill, 273–274
bogus pipeline, 579
changing, 274, 580–588
measuring, 579
secondary traits as, 419
self-awareness and, 579–580

social, 572, 578–588
formation of, 578–579
Attraction, 607–617
liking, 607–614
closeness and, 607–608
competence and, 609–610
similarity and, 609
theories of, 610–611, 614
love, 614–617
conjugal, 616–617
passionate, 615–616
theories of liking, 610–611, 614
equity, 610–611
exchange, 611
gain-loss, 614
reinforcement, 610
Attractiveness, 612–613
Attribution, 585–588, 628
information availability hypothesis, 586
self-serving bias, 586
visual perspective hypothesis, 586
Audition, *see* hearing
Auditory nerve, *101–102*
Automatization, *261*
Automatic gain control, in color vision, 93
Automatic storage (memory), 232–233
Automatic writing, *168*
Autonomic nervous system, 39–40
Aversive conditioning, 218, 536–537
Axon, 42–45

Babbling (language), 275
Bradykinin, *108*
Barnum effect (psychological testing), 435
Basic research, 17
Bayley Mental and Motor Scale, 401
Behavior contracts, *539*
The Behavior of Organisms (Skinner), 187
Behavior modification, 13, *210*–211, 439, 481, 537, 543
techniques, list of, 537
Behavior therapy, 211, 218, 535–540, 543–545
aversive conditioning, 218, 536–537
classical conditioning, 536
operant, 211, 218, 537–539, 543–545
systematic desensitization, 211, 536–537, 543–545
Behavioral contracts,
Behavioral genetics, 393–395
Behavioral geography, 214–216
Behavioral toxicology, 640–*641*
Behaviorism, *12*–13, 150, 187, 208, 256, 370, 425–426, 584
basic tenets of, 187
challenges to, 208, 584
history of, 12–13, 150, 256
personality theory of, 425–427
Bender-Gestalt Visual-Motor Test, 437
Benzedrine, 173
Benzodiazepines, 176, 461, 523–524
effects of, 176, 524
Beta-endorphin, 49, 51–52, 75, 170, 177
hypnosis and, 170

pain relief and, 51–52, 75
placebo effect and, 52
Bhopal (chemical accident), 161
Biases, 20–22
Binocular cues for depth perception, *138*–139
convergence, 138–139
retinal disparity, 138–139
Biofeedback, 465, 467
Bipolar cells (eye), 82, 94
Bipolar disorder, 478, 491–493, 523, 525
cyclicity and, 491–492, 523
lithium and, 492, 523
Birth order and intelligence, 395–396
Bisexuality, 604
Blind spot (eye), 83–85, 87
foveal vision and, 87
testing for, 84
Black-box psychology, 13
Blob pathway, *117*, 119
Blood brain barrier, 50–*51*
Bogus pipeline, 579
Bonding (with infant), 354, *see also* Attachment
Botulism, 46
Brain, 15, 36–38, 39–42, 47–52, 54–75, 107, 109, 117, 119, 175, 177, 276, 283, 601–605
auditory information processing, 63, 282
effects on behavior of, 66–74
left-brain interpreter, 74
mapping of, 54–55
memory in, location of, 60, 63
number of neurons in, 42
perceptual pathways, 117, 119
plasticity, 70
pleasure center in, 36–37, 47, 52, 175, 177
right/left hemispheric differences in, 61–63, 66, 70–72, 74, 276, 602–603
scanners, 63–66
sexual differences in, 601–605
specialized areas in, 64,
split-brain research, 70–72, 74
structure of, 54–63
touch reception in, processing, 107
transplanting cells, 50–51, 602–603
visual information processing, 63,
Brain mapping, 54–55
Brain waves, 151–154
alpha, 151, 154
delta, 152, 154
Brainwashing, 587–588
Brief individual psychotherapies, 544
Brightness, 85
Brightness constancy, *131*–132
British empiricism, *10*
Broca's Aphasia, 281–283
Broca's area, 69, 280–282
aphasia and, 69, 281–283
language and, 69, 281–282
Bug detectors, 122–123
Bystander effect, *562*–563, 565

Bystander intervention model, 564–565

CAH, *see* Congenital adrenal hyperplasia
Calpain, 226
Canalization, 216–217
Cannon-Bard theory of emotion, 325
Cardinal traits, *419*
Case study, 26–27
The Cat in the Hat (Seuss), 342
CAT scan, *see* Computed axial tomography
Catatonic schizophrenia, 478, 499
Catecholamines, 446
Catharsis, *18*
Cattell's theory of personality, 420–422
  16-PF, 420–421
Cause-effect relationship, 22
CCK, *see* Cholecystokinin
Central nervous system, 38–40, 501
Central Park jogger, 571–573
Central route processing, 582
Central sulcus (brain), *61*
Central traits, *419*
Centration in cognitive development, 359
Cerebellum (brain), 58, 197
  learning in, 197
Cerebral cortex (brain), 58, 61, 63, 66, 69,
  93, 107, 109, 143–144, 263, 281
  frontal lobes of, 61, 63
  occipital lobes, 61, 63, 66, 69, 93, 97,
    143
  parietal lobes of, 61, 63, 107, 263
  temporal lobes of, 61, 63, 66, 143
Cerebral hemispheres, 61, 63, 69–72, 74,
  276, 317, 602–603
Cerebral ventricles (and schizophrenia),
  501–502
Cerebrum (brain), 58–59, 61–63
  parts of, 61
  progressive increase in evolutionary size
    of, 62
Chaos theory, 30–31
Cheap-necklace problem, 267–268
Chemical dependence, *450–452*
Chernobyl (nuclear accident), 161
Childhood, development during, 358–367
  early, 358–362
    cognitive development, 358–360, 372
    family relationships, 360–361
    peer relationships, 360–362
    personality development, 360
    play, 362
    sibling relationships, 361
    working mothers, 356,
  middle, 362–367
    cognitive development, 362–364, 372
    peer relationships, 364–366
    television's influence during, 365–367
Chlorpromazine, 520
Cholecystokinin 241, *293*
Cholera, 294
Chromosome, 344–345, 595
Chronological age, 387–388
Chunk (memory), 231–232
Circadian rhythm, 149–150, *159–163*

caves and, 149–150
disrupted as explanation for insomnia,
  163
genetics and, 160
jet lag and, 160
resetting, 162
shift work and, 161–162
Clairvoyance, 110
Classical conditioning, *189–197*, 201, 204,
  273, 300, 536
  fear and, 194–195, 204
  hunger and, 300
  Little Albert and, 194–195
  Pavlov's experiments and, 189–191, 193
  single cells and, 197
  therapy, 536
Client-centered therapy, 530–531, 532, 543
Clinical psychologist, 5–7
Clomipramine, 485, 512
Closure, Gestalt principle of, 120–121
Clozapine, 521
Cobra venom, 46
Coca-Cola, 174
Cocaine, *174–175*
Cochlea (ear), *100*
Codeine, 176
Cognition, 212–215, 253–255, 256–286,
  419, 572, 578–588
  attitudes, 273–274, 419, 572, 578–588
  cognitive strategies, 262–274
    algorithms, 264–265
    attention, 263–264
    heuristics, 264–266, 273
    incubation effect, 268
    means-end analysis, 266–267, 273,
      285–286
    problem solving, 266–272
    routine problem solving, 267, 272
  declarative knowledge, 227–233,
    235–238, 262, 266, 270, 273–274
  intellectual skills, 257, 261–262, 266,
    272–274
    concept formation, 257, 261–262, 273
    mental procedures, 257, 261, 273
  language, 274–284
  motor skills, 272–274
  place learning, 213–215
  social, 419, 572, 578–588
Cognitive behavior modification, 539–540
Cognitive development, 358–360,
  362–364, 370–372, 599–600, 607
  concrete operations stage, 362–364
  conservation during, 363–364
  criticisms of Piaget's theory of, 370–371
  egocentrism and, 358–359, 370
  formal operations stage, 370, 381–382
  general consensus of, 372
  gender role acquisition and, 599–600,
    607
  object permanence, achievement of,
    358–359, 370–371
  preoperational stage, 359–360
  sensorimotor stage, 358–359
Cognitive dissonance, 583–585

Cognitive map, *213–215*
Cognitive psychology, 15–16, *213*
Cognitive Psychology and Its Implications
  (Anderson), 243
Cognitive skills, human, 213–215, 257,
  261–286
Cognitive strategies, 262–274
Cognitive therapy, 467
  stress reduction and, 467
Cognitive appraisal theory of emotion
  (Schachter), 325–327, 328
Collective unconscious, 425
Color blindness, 90–91
Color constancy theory (Land), 92–93
Color vision, 88–94
  animals and, 88–89
  automatic gain control and, 93
  color blindness, 90–91
  opponent-process theory of, 92
  Young-Helmholtz theory of, 89–90
Communication, persuasive, 580–583, *see
  also*, Language
Common fate, Gestalt principle of, 120
Competition, 568–571
Complex cells, 96
Componential intelligence, 392
Compulsion, 484
Computed axial tomography scan (CAT),
  501
Computers, 97–98, 256–261, 265, 274,
  276, 633
  artificial intelligence and, 256–260
  modeling and, 97–98
  translations and, 259
Concealed information test, *319*
Concepts and their formation, 257,
  261–262, 273, 276–277
  definition of, 261
  formation of, 276–277
  protoconcept, 276–277
Concrete operations, stage of, 362–364
Conditioning, 185–212, 218, 536–540,
  543–545
  classical, 189–197, 201, 204, 536
  extinction of, 190–191, 205
  operant, 198–208, 218, 537–539,
    543–545
Conditioned response, *189–194*, 197, 300
Conditioned stimulus, *189–197*, 300
Cones, 82, 85, 87–96
Confidence, the teaching of, 304–305
Conformity, *551–555*, 559–561
Congenital adrenal hyperplasia (CAH), 596
Conjugal love, *616–617*
Cononical stage (of language), 275
Consolidation (memory), 241–242
Consciousness, 150–151, 152–180
  states of, 151–180
Conservation (cognitive development),
  363–364
Conserving-energy theory for sleeping, *156*
Consumer psychology, *643–646*
  and advertising, 643–645
  opinion surveys, 644–645

protection, consumer, 645–646
Contextual intelligence, 392
Contiguous association (learning), 195–196
  types of, 196
Contingency detection (learning), 195–196
Continuity, Gestalt principle of, 120–121
Continuity vs. discontinuity, in human
  development, 346–347
Continuous reinforcement, 205–206
Contraction stage (of language), 275–276
Control, 19–20, 304–305
  group (experiment), 19–20
  perceived, in mastery, 304–305
Convergence, see linear perspective
Convergent productions, 408–409
Conversion disorder, 478, 486–487
Cooperation, 568–571
Coping with stress, 422–424, 465–469
  defense mechanisms, 422–424, 465
  direct coping strategies, 465–468
Cornea, 81
Corpus callosum, 61, 70–72
  severing in split-brain, 70–72
Correlation between variables, 24,
  394–395, 401–403
  cause-effect relationship and, 24
Corticosteroid hormones, 454–455
Corticotropin-releasing factor, 454
Cortisol, 151, 159, 455, 494
Counseling psychologists, 7
Crack, 175, see also cocaine
Cramming (memory), 248
Creative problem solving, 267, 272
Creativity, 388, 406–411
  convergent production, 408–409
  criteria of, 408
    appropriateness, 408
    coalescence of meaning, 408
    novelty, 408
    transcendence of constraints, 408
  divergent production, 408–410
  ideational fluency in, 410
  teaching, 409–411
Criterion validity, see Predictive validity
Critical decay duration, 309–310
Critical period (imprinting), 216
Crystal, see Amphetamines
Crystallized intelligence, 403–404
Culture-fair test, 399–400
Cyranoids, 428

Dani tribe (and linguistic relativity), 275
Dark adaptation, 88, 111–112
  red light and, 111–112
Day-blindness, 90
Day care, 356–357
Daydreaming, 166–167, 169
Death, 380–381, 447–449
  common causes of, 447
  odds of, 449
Death clock, 380
Decathlon (Olympic), 389
Decibel scale, 99

Declarative knowledge, 227–233, 235–238,
  262, 266, 270, 273–274
Declarative memory, 227–233, 235–238,
  273
Defense mechanisms, 422–424, 454, 465,
  611, 628
  denial, 423, 465
  projection, 423, 465
  rationalization, 423, 465
  reaction formation, 423, 465
Deindividuation, 571–573
Deinstitutionalization, 526–527
Delirium tremens, 176
Delta waves (EEG), 152, 154
Delusional (paranoid) disorders, 478,
  502–504
  causes of, 503–504
  induced psychotic disorder, 478, 503–504
  paranoia, 478, 503–504
  subtypes, 503–504
Delusion, 495
Dendrites, 42–43
Denial, 423, 465
Denver Developmental Screening Test, 351
Deoxyribonucleic acid (DNA), 344–345
Dependent variable, 20
Depressants, 173, 175–177
Depression, 155, 323–324, 493–494
  aggression and, 323–324
  children and, 493
  double, 494
  dysthymia, 493
  endogenous, 155, 494
  heredity and, 492–494
  major depression, 493–494
  seasonal affective disorder (SAD), 494
  treatment of, 492, 494
Depth perception, 132–142
  binocular cues for, 138–139
  monocular cues for, 132–138
  3-D movies and, 139
Descriptive research, 17, 598
Designer drugs, 177
Detoxification, 451–452
Developmental psychology, 11, 342–343,
  344–383, see also, Human
  development
Dexamethasone suppression test, 494
Dexedrine, 173
*Diagnostic and Statistical Manual of
  Mental Disorders, Third edition,
  revised* (DSM III-R) (American
  Psychiatric Association), 477–480,
  482, 490, 497, 499, 504–505,
  508–511, 541
  Axis I, 476–504
  Axis II, 478, 504–506
  Axis III-V, 478
  Strengths and weaknesses of, 480
Dichromats, 90
Difference threshold, 79
Diffusion of responsibility, 563
Direct coping strategies, 465–468

Directive therapy, 529–531, 534–541,
  544–545
Direct-perception theory, 124–126
Discrimination, 191, 202, 345, 575–578
  genetic, 345
  of stimuli, 191, 202
  social, 575–578, see also, Prejudice
Discriminative stimuli, 206–207
Disorganized schizophrenia, 478, 499
Displacement (memory), 230–231
Dissociation (during hypnosis), 168–169,
  172
Dissociative disorders, 242, 249–250, 478,
  488–491
  multiple personality, 478, 489–491
  psychogenic amnesia, 242, 249–250,
  478, 488
  psychogenic fugue, 478, 488
Disulfiram, see Antabuse
Divergent production, 408–410
DNA, see Deoxyribonucleic acid
Dopamine, 47, 66, 485, 501
  concentration in brain, 66
Dopamine hypothesis, 501
Double-blind controlled experiment, 22
Double depression, 494
Down syndrome, 406–408
Drapetomania, 508
Dreams, 12, 153, 165–167, 179–180, 530
  interpretation of, 12, 165–166, 530
  lucid, 179–180
  activation-synthesis model of, 165
  housekeeping hypothesis, 165–166
  off-line hypothesis, 166
  psychoanalytic theory of, 12, 165, 530
Drive, 291–292
Drugs, 48–49, 173–178
  classifications of, 173
  neural receptors and, 48–49, 173–178
  overdose, 193–194
Dual-code theory of memory, 235–238
Dualist hypothesis, 73
Dyslexia, 282–283
Dysthymia, 493

Early intervention (intelligence), 400–401
Ear, 99–104, 109, 143
  and balance, 109, 143
  artificial, 102–103
  structure of, 99–100, 103
Ectomorph, 418
Edge detectors (vision), 96
EDGE, Project, 408
Educational psychology, 11, 646–650
  beginnings of, 11
  behavioral versus cognitive approaches,
  647–648
  and school system, 648–649
  and successful schools, 650
  and teachers, 649
Efferent nerves, 38, 40
Ego, 422–423,

Egocentrism in cognitive development, 358–359, 370
Eidetic image, 235
Elaboration (memory), 243–244
Elavil, 522
Electra complex, 598
Electrical brain stimulation (ESB), 35–37
Electroconvulsive therapy (ECT), 524–525
Electroencephalograph (EEG), 150–152, 153–154, 167, 169, 540
Electromagnetic spectrum, 85–86
Electroshock, *see* Electroconvulsive therapy (ECT)
Emotion, 108, 246–248, 315–317, 318–336, 581
  aggression and violence as, 323–324
  assessing, 315–316, 321–322, 325–331, 335
  biology of, 317
  commonsense concept of, 322
  defining, 317
  Ekman's contribution, 330–331
  functional aspects of, 333–335
  infant development and, 357
  memory and, 246–248
  physiological changes during, 315–317
  primary, 333–335
  secondary, 333
  theories of, 322, 324–335
    Cannon-Bard, 325
    cognitive appraisal (Schachter), 325–328
    facial-feedback, 328–331
    James-Lange, 324–325, 330, 334
    psychoevolutionary synthesis (Plutchik), 332–335
  touch and, 108
  wheel of, 333
Emotional appeals (attitude change), 581
Emotional contrast, 307–309, 312–313
Emotional expressions, 328–330
Empiricism, British, 10
Empty nest syndrome, 377
Encoding variability, 247–248
Encounter groups, 535
Endocrine glands, 53
Endocrine system, 53
Endogenous depression, 155, 494
Endomorph, 418
Engram, 223
Environmental psychology, 625–626, 639–643
  atmospheric conditions and, 640–641
    heat, 640
    noise, 641
    pollution, 640–641
  developing structured, 641–643
  illumination and, 639–640
  sickrooms and, 625–626
  toxic hazards and, 640–642
Epilepsy, 70–72
  split-brain research for, 70–72
Epinephrine, 446, 455, 464

Episodic memory, 228–229
ESP, *see* Extra-sensory perception
Estrogen, 594, 596, 604
Equipotentiality (memory theory), 223
Equity theory of liking, 610–611
Ethics in psychological research, 24–26
Ethology, 216–217
Etiology, 474
Eugenics, 387
Exchange theory of liking, 611
Excitatory synapses, 46
Executive hormones, 53
Exhaustion stage (in stress), 454, 456
Existential therapy, 532
Exocrine glands, 53
Expansion of research, 22
Expansion stage (of language), 275
Experiential intelligence, 392
Experiment, scientific, 16–18, 19–24, 30–31
  designing, 18–24
  ethical guidelines for, 25–26
  double-blind controlled, 21–22
  limits of, 30–31
  replication of, 22
  selecting subjects, 18
  single-subject, 17, 23–24
Experimental psychology, 6
Explanatory research, 17, 598
Exploration-play-application sequence, 362
The Expression of the Emotions in Man and Animals (Darwin), 333
Extinction (in classical conditioning), 190–191
Extinction (in operant conditioning), 199, 205
Extrasensory perception, 110–111
Extrovert, 418
Eye, 80–95, 103–104
  artificial, 103–104
  blind spot in, 83–85, 87
  structures of, 81
Eyewitness testimony, 145–146, 170

Facial-feedback theory of emotion (Tomkins), 328–330, 331
Factor analysis of intelligence, 389, 391
Factor load, 389, 391
Factor S, 156
Family therapy, 535
Feature detectors (vision), 96
Figure, 119–120
5HIAA, 464
Fixation, 424
  anal retentive personality formed by, 424
Flashback, 177
Flashbulb memory, 241
Floaters, in the eye, 83
Fluid intelligence, 403–404
Fluoxetine, *see* Prozac
Fodrin, 226
Forebrain, 58–61, 63, 165
Forgetting, causes of, 238–243

decay and loss, 238
failure of consolidation, 241–242
motivated, 242, 249–250
retrieval failure, 238–241
Forgetting curve, 238
Form perception, 119–123
Formal operations (cognitive development), 370, 372, 381–382
  algebra and, 381–382
Foster care, 355
Fovea, 82–83, 87, 143
Fraser's spiral, 116–117
Free association, 12
Free-floating anxiety, 482
Freemartin, 595
Free-run (sleep cycle), 149–150, 160
Frequency (sound), 98–99
Frequency theory of hearing, 101
Friendships, 362–363
Frontal lobes of cerebral cortex, 61, 63, 281
  Broca's area in, 69, 281
Frontal lobotomy, 525, 527–528
  criticisms of, 528
  history of, 525, 527
Frustration-aggression hypothesis, 322–323
Fugue, psychogenic, 488
Functional fixedness, 270–272
Functionalism, 10–11

Gain-loss theory of liking, 614
GABA, *see* Gamma-aminobutyric acid
Games People Play (Berne), 535
Gamma-aminobutyric acid, 47, 49, 176, 524
Ganglion cells (eye), 81–82, 92, 94–96, 117
Gastrin (hormone), 455
Gender constancy, 600
Gender roles, 361, 591–592, 598–600, 604–607
  acquisition, 598–600
    cognitive theory, 599–600
    gender schema theory, 600
    social-learning theory, 599–600
  culture and, 591–592
Gender role identification, 598–600, 605–607
  sexual preferences and, 605–607
Gender schema theory, 600
Gender understanding, 598–600
Gene, 345
General adaptation syndrome (Selye), 454–456
  alarm reaction stage, 454–455
  exhaustion stage, 454, 456
  resistance stage, 454–455
General paresis, 519
General problem solver (GPS), 266
Generalized anxiety disorder, 478, 482
Generalization, 191, 202
Genetic discrimination, 345
Genome, *see* Human genome
Gestalt psychology, 13–14, 116, 119–121

history of, 13–14
perceptual organization, principles of, 119–121
 closure, 120–121
 common fate, 120
 continuity, 120–121
 nearness, 120–121
 similarity, 120–121
 simplicity, 120–121
Gestalt therapy, 530, 534, 543
Glass ceiling, 627–628
Glial cell, 48
Glove anesthesia, 486–487
Goal setting, 634
Golgi stain, 55
Gonads, 54, 594–596
 diagram of male and female, 594
 hormone secretions of, 54, 594–597
Goodness of fit (temperament), 350–353
Gooing stage (of language), 275
Gradient of texture (depth cue), 125–126, 133
Grammar, 274, 277–280
Grammatical morphemes, 278
Grand theories, 301
Great-man, great-woman hypothesis, 575
Ground, 119–120
Group research, 17
Group therapy, 530, 534–535
 encounter groups, 535
 psychodrama, 535
 sensitivity training, 535
 transactional analysis, 530, 535, 543
Groups, influence of, 571–575
 deindividuation and, 571–573
 leadership, 574–575
 polarization, 573–574
Growth spurt, 370
A Guide to Self-Deliverance (Exit), 462
Gyri, 56

Habit, 207
Habituation, 188, 348
Hair-pulling, compulsive, see Trichotillomania
Haldol, 521
Hallucination, 158, 176–177, 178, 495, 503, 511, 521–522
Hallucinogens, 48, 173, 177–178
 effects of, 48, 177–178
Hassles, 460–461
Hazard perception, 448–450
Head Start, Project, 400
Healthy insomniacs, 155
Health psychology, 445–446, 447–469
Hearing process, 98–104, 144, 341–342
 artificial, 102–103
 in animals, 99
 perception of sound, 144
 prenatal, 341–342
 theories of, 100–101
 frequency theory, 101
 place theory, 101
 volley theory, 101

Height on a plane (depth cue), 132, 136, 138
Helping, 561–565, 568
 bystander effect, 562–563, 565
 bystander intervention model, 564–565
 diffusion of responsibility, 563
 task load, effect of, 564–565
Heroin, 176–177, 193–194
Heterosexuality, 604–606
Heuristics, 264–265, 266, 273
Hierarchy of motives (Maslow), 301
High-threshold fibers (ear), 100–101
Higher order conditioning, 191–193, 273
Highway hypnosis, 169
Hindbrain, 58–59
Hippocampus, 60, 68, 175, 225
Historical research, 17
The History of Animals, Book IX, (Aristotle), 601
Hitchhiker's Guide to the Galaxy (Adams), 258
Homeless, the, 519–520, 526–527
Homeostasis, 291–293
Homosexuality, 604–607
Horizontal cells (eye), 82, 92, 94
Hormone, 49, 52–54, 151, 159, 241, 293–295, 297–298, 368, 376, 454–455, 593–597, 602–604
 adrenaline, 54, 510
 adrenocorticotropic hormone (ACTH), 241, 454–455
 androgens, 594–597
 behavior and, 595–597
 brain and, 454–455, 597, 602–603
 cholecystokinin, 241, 293
 corticosteroids, 454–455
 corticotropin-releasing factor, 454
 cortisol, 151, 159, 455, 494
 endocrine system and, 53
 estrogen, 594, 596, 604
 executive hormones, 53
 exocrine system and, 53
 estrogens, 594, 596, 604
 fluctuation, in individuals, 597
 gastrin, 455
 influence on sex drives, 295, 297–298, 595–597
 luteinizing hormone (LH), 605
 melatonin, 162, 368
 memory and, 241
 menopause, 376
 noradrenaline, 54
 renin, 455
 puberty and, 368
 stress and, 241, 454–455
 testosterone, 164, 295, 595–597, 602–603
Hot flashes, 376
Hue, 85
Human development, 341–382
 issues in, 343–344, 346
 continuity vs. discontinuity, 346–347
 nature vs. nurture, 343–344, 347
 stability vs. change, 346–347

Human genome, 345
Human Genome Project, 345
Humanistic psychology, 14–15, 428–430, 439–440, 531–532
 history of, 14–15
 personality assessment and, 439–440
 personality theory of, 428–430
Humanistic-existential therapy, 531–532
 client-centered therapy, 530–532, 543
 existential therapy, 532
Humors, bodily, 8
Hunger, biological motivation of, 292–295
 interaction with thirst, 294–295
Hypercomplex cells, 96
Hypermnesic, 234–235
Hyperpolarization, of neuron, 44–46
Hypertension, 456
Hypnosis, 167–173, 467, 540–541
 age regression and, 173
 behavior changes and, 168, 170–172
 definition of, 167
 disinhibition during, 171–172
 dissociation in, 168–169, 171
 automatic writing, 168
 highway hypnosis, 169
 self-, 168–169
 emotional changes and, 170, 172
 memory enhancement during, 169–170, 172
 pain relief and, 170, 172
 posthypnotic suggestion, 171–172
 susceptibility to, 167–168
 therapy and, 467, 540–541
Hypnotherapy, 467, 540–541
Hypofrontality (in schizophrenia), 501
Hypochondriasis, 478, 487–488
Hypothalamic-pituitary-adrenal axis, 53–54, 454–455, 494, 594
Hypothalamocentric hypothesis (hunger), 292–293
Hypothalamus, 60, 292–293, 325, 454–455, 494, 594, 603
Hypothesis, 18

I Aim at the Stars, 585–586
Ice, see Amphetamines
Id, 422–423
Ideational fluency, 410
Illumination, 639–640
Illusions, 116–117, 127–129, 137–138
 Delboeuf, 127
 Fraser's spiral, 116–117
 Judd, 127
 Lipps, 127
 Moon, 137–138
 Muller-Lyer, 127–129
 Poggendorff, 127–128
 Ponzo, 127–128
 Titchener, 127
 Zollner, 127–128
Image and cue theory of perception, 124–126
Imax (3-D), 139
Imitation, see Social learning

Immune system, 455–457, 602
  stress and, 455–457
Impression-management hypothesis,
  584–585
Imprinting, 216–217
Incubation effect (problem solving), 268
Incus (ear), 100
Independent variable, 20
Induced psychotic disorder, 478, 503–504
Industrial or organizational psychology, 7,
  11, 626–627, 628–635
  organizational behavior, 627–631
    conflict resolution, 628–629
    personnel selection, 629–631
    supervisors and, 627–628
Infant development, 320, 341–342,
  346–357
  emotional, 320, 357,
  habituation during, 348
  maturation during, 349
  personality and social, 350–355
  physical and motor, 347, 349–351
  temperament, 350–352
Information availability hypothesis, 586
In-group, 575–576
Inherited behavior, 216–217, 387
Inhibitory synapses, 46, 264
Innate, 142
Insanity (legal term), 474–475
Insanity defense, 475–476
Insight (problem solving), 254–255, 268
Insight therapy, 529–532, 534–535,
Insomnia, 159, 163
  circadian rhythms and, 163
  healthy insomniacs, 155
  jet lag and, 160
Instrumental learning, 198
  Law of effect and, 198
  reinforcement and, 198–199
Intellectual changes over time, 401–406
  difficulties in measuring, 402–403
  Terman's study, 403, 405–406
Intellectual degeneration, 378
Intellectual skills, 257, 261–262, 266,
  272–274
Intelligence, 385–386, 387–411, 583
  birth order and, 395–396
  categories of, 407
  common beliefs about, 406
  crystallized, 403–404
  defining, 386–387
  environmental stimulation on, effects of,
    400–401
  factor analysis of, 389, 391
  fluid, 403–404
  general vs. specific, 385–386, 389–390
  habituitation in infants and, 403
  heritability of, 393–395
  infants, measuring, 401–403
  persuaded, ability to be, and, 583
  race and, 396–399
  testing, 388–406
    court rulings and, 398–399
    cultural bias and, 397–400

  reliability, 402
  validity, 388–389
  theories of, 389–390, 392–393
    Gardner's, 389
    Guilford's, 389
    Spearman's, 389
    Sternberg's, 392–393
    Thurstone's, 385–386, 389
Intelligence Applied, Sternberg, 393
Intelligence quotient (IQ), 387–389,
  392–410
  by category, 407
  formula for, 387
Interference effects (memory), 238–240
  proactive, 238–239
  retroactive, 239
  tip of the tongue phenomenon, 239–240
Intermittent schedule (of reinforcement),
  205–206, 207
Interobserver reliability, 19
Interviews, 27–28, 439–440
Intraorganismic perspective (attachment),
  353
Intrinsic motivation, 289–290, 303,
  305–306
Introspection, 9–10
Introvert, 418
Invariants (perception), 125–126, 134, 142
Iris, 81
IQ test, see Intelligence testing

James-Lange theory of emotion, 324–325,
  330, 334
Jararaca snake, 108
Jet lag, 160
Job, 627–635
  absenteeism, 632
  analysis, 629–630
  satisfaction, 631–633
  turnover, 632, 634–635
  working at home, 633–634
Job analysis, 629–630
Jonestown, tragedy at, 559–561, 588
Just noticeable difference (JND), 79

Karyotype (of chromosomes), 595
Kibbutz, 401
The King, the Mice and the Cheese (Seuss),
  342
Kin recognition (olfaction), 106
Kinesthesis, 109
Kinesthetic sense, 108–109
The King of Comedy, 504

Laboratory, first psychological (Wundt),
  8–9
LAD, see Language acquisition device
Language, 274–284
  acquisition, 275–280, 283
  apes, teaching, 280, 283–284
  as cognitive ability, 274–275
  expression of meaning in, 258–259,
    278–280
  grammar in, 274, 277–280

  physiology of, 281–282
  thinking and, 274–275
Language acquisition, 275–280, 283, 359
  apes and, 280, 283–284
  cononical stage in, 275
  contraction stage in, 275–276
  expansion stage in, 275
  gooing stage in, 275
  one-word stage in, 276–277
  phonetic expansion and contraction,
    275–276
  protoconcept, 276–277
  rates of, 277
  telegraphic speech, 278
  topic and, 280
  two-word stage in, 277
Language acquisition device (LAD), 279
Latent content (of dreams), 165, 530
Latent learning, 212
Law of effect, 198
Leadership, 574–575, 627–628
  great-man, great-woman hypothesis, 575
  situational environmental hypothesis, 575
Learned helplessness, 302–303
Learned motivation, 300–310
Learning, 185–187, 188–218, 239,
  427–428, 599–600, 606–607
  cognitive, 212–215
  via habituation, 188
  importance of, 187–188
  as inherited tendency, 216–217
  instrumental, 198–199
  latent, 212
  negative transfer of, 239
  via sensitization, 188
  simple forms of, 188
  social, 18, 208–212, 427–428, 599–600,
    606–607
Left-brain interpreter, 74
Left-handedness and brain lateralization,
  276, 602
Lens of eye, 81
Leukemia cells, 457
Leukotome, 528
LH, see Luteinizing hormone
Libido, 422
Lie detector, see polygraph
Lifespan development, 341–382, see also,
  Human development
Light adaptation, 88
Liking, 607–614
  closeness and, 607–608
  competence and, 609–610
  similarity and, 609
  theories of, 610–611, 614
    equity, 610–611
    exchange, 611
    gain-loss, 614
    reinforcement, 610
Limbic system, 60, 106
Linear perspective (depth cue), 133–134,
  136–137
Linear progression (development), 346
Linguistic relativity, 274–275

Links (memory), 236–237
Lithium carbonate, 492, 523
Local effect (neural transmission), 44
Locus-dependent memory, 245–246
Longevity, causes and limits, 380–381
Longitudinal studies, 346, 360
Long-term memory, 229–230, 231–233, 236–242
  forgetting, 238–243
  interferences in, 238–240
  retrieval cues for, 233, 240–241
  storage and retrieval techniques, 233
Loudness, 99–100
Love, 614–617
  conjugal, 616–617
  passionate, 615–616
LSD, 48, 177, 500–501
Lucid dreaming, 179–180
Luchins' water-jug problems, 268–269
"Lumpers" (of intelligence), 391
Luteinizing hormone (LH), 605

M'Naghten rule (of insanity), 475–476
The Magic of Uri Geller, 110
Magnetic Resonance Imaging (MRI), 66, 501, 525
Magno pathway, 117, 119–120
Mainstreaming (the intellectually handicapped), 406–408
Major depression, 478, 493–494
Malleus (ear), 100
Manifest content (of dreams), 165, 530
Manipulative research, 17
MAO inhibitors, see Monoamine-oxidase inhibitors,
Marijuana, 178
  abuses of, 178
  effects of, 178
  THC in, 178
Marplan, 522
Massed practice (cramming), 247–248
Mastery, 304–305
Masturbation, 617, 619–622
Materialist hypothesis, 73
Maternal-Infant Bonding (Klaus & Kennell), 354
Mathematical ability, sex differences in, 601–604
Matterhorn, 312
Maturation, 349
Maulavi, 172
Means-end analysis, 266–267, 273, 285–286
  Peter Goldmark and, 285–286
Meditation, 171–172, 467
  stress and, 172, 467
  Yogis and, 172
Medulla, 58
Melatonin, 162, 368
Melioration, of responses, 311
Memory, 60, 68, 106, 169–170, 172, 221–222, 223–250, 490–491, 525
  amnesia, 221–222, 229, 234, 242–243, 249–250, 491, 525

biology of, 223–226
consolidation, 241–242
declarative, 227–233, 235–238
  onset of, 227
  operation of, 227–233
  theories on storage, 221–222, 235–238
electroconvulsive therapy and memory loss, 525
encoding effects on, 247–248
enhancement during hypnosis, 169–170, 172
episodic, 228–229
interferences in retrieval, 238–240
location in brain of, 60, 223–226
locus dependent, 245–246
long-term, 229, 231–233, 236–242
massed practice, 247–248
meaning and, 233, 236
multiple personality and, 490–491
model of declarative, 229
organization of, 221–222, 224
priming, 229
procedural, 227–228
recall, aids to, 233
reconstruction, 241
rehearsal, 229–230
retrieval cues for, 233, 240–241
scripts and, 241
semantic, 228
sensory, 229
short-term, 229–232
smell and, 106
spaced practice, 247
spacing effect on, 247–248
state dependent, 246–248
storage and retrieval techniques, 233
strengthening through elaboration, 243–244
theories of, 233–238
Menarche, 593
Menopause, 376
Mental age, 387–388, 402
Mental disorder, 471–512
  assessment of, 506–511
  prevalence of, 477
Mental institutions, 506–507, 515–520, 526–527
Mental procedures, 257, 261, 273
Mental set (problem solving), 268–269, 270, 272
  Luchins' water-jug and, 268–269
MPTP, 177
Mere exposure effect, 582
Mesmerism, 167
Mesomorph, 418
Meta-analysis, 460
Methedrine, 173
Method of loci, 233
Microelectrode, 35–36, 44
Micro-sleep, 158
Midbrain, 58–59, 117
Middle age, 376–377
  empty nest syndrome in, 377
  menopause, 376

midlife crisis during, 376–377
Midlife crisis, 376–377
Mind-body problem, the, 73–74
A Mind that Found Itself (Beers), 519
Minnesota Clerical Test, 630
Minnesota Multiphasic Personality Inventory (MMPI), 430, 432–436
  description of, 430, 432–433
  profile, 434
  scales, 433
  standardization group in, 432,
Minnesota Multiphasic Personality Inventory, revised (MMPI-2), 435–436
  description of, 435
  standardization group in, 435–436
Misdiagnosis, 510–511
Mnemonic, 233
  method of loci, 233
Model, 96–98, 208–212, 474–476
  scientific, 96–98
  social learning, 208–212
Models of psychopathology, 474–476, 484, 486
  humanistic-existential, 476, 484
  learning, 476, 484
  legal, 475–476
  medical, 474, 484, 486
  psychoanalytic, 476, 484
Modified progressive relaxation, 467
Molecule, 105
Monoamine-oxidase (MAO) inhibitors, 522–523
Monochromats, 90
Monocular cues for depth perception, 132–133, 134–138
  accommodation, 134–135
  aerial perspective, 134, 136–137
  gradient of texture, 125–126, 133
  height on a plane, 132, 136, 138
  linear perspective, 133–134, 136–137
  overlap, 134, 136–137
  relative motion, 134–136–137
  relative size, 134, 136–137
  shadowing, 134, 136–137
Mood disorders, 478, 491–494
  bipolar disorder, 478, 491–493
  major depression, 478, 493–494
Moon illusion, 137–138
Morality, development of, 566–567
Morals, 566–568
Morpheme, see Grammatical morphemes
Morphine, 176
Motion perception, 142–143
Motivated forgetting, 242, 249–250
Motivation, 289–291, 292–313, 318, 634
  biological, 291–299
    individual differences and, 295
  learned, 300–310
  nonhomeostatic, 296–297
  and performance, 299, 634
  sociobiological view of, 306–307
  for stimulation, 298–299
  and work, 634
Motor area of brain, 61, 64

Motor skills, 272–274
Mount Saint Helens (stress), 450, 453
MRI, *see* Magnetic resonance imaging
Muller-Lyer illusion, 127–129
Multiple personality, 478, 489–451
Multiplexing, 98
Mutation, 380–*381*
Myelin, 56
The Myth of Mental Illness (Szasz), 508

Naloxone, 51–52
Narcolepsy, *163–164*
Narcotic, 176
National Council on Alcoholism (phone number), 452
National Hemlock Society, 462
Natural selection, 10–11, 120, *400*
Naturalistic observations, 17, 26–27
The Nature of a Child's Tie to His Mother (Bowlby), 353
Nature-nurture questions, 124–126,
   142–143, 280, 284, 343–347,
   350–352, 387–395, 427, 451,
   482–483, 492–494, 498, 500–502
   of alcoholism, 451
   of human development, 343–344, 347
   of intelligence, 387, 393–395
   of language, 280, 284
   of mental disorder, 482–483, 492–494,
      498, 500–502
   of perception, 124–126, 142–143
   of personality, 427
   of temperament, 350–352
Nearness, Gestalt principle of, 120–121
Need, *291*
Need for achievement (n-Ach) as motivator,
   301–302
Negative afterimage, 93
Negative fixation, 424
Negative reinforcement, *202–204*
Negative transfer of learning, 239
Neonates, 346–348
Nerve gas, 46
Nerve impulse, *44*
Nerves, *38*
   afferent, 38
   efferent, 38
   impulses, 44–45
   ion channels, 44–45
Nervous system, 35–112
   divisions of, 39
Neural network (computers), *260*
Neural transmission, 43–48
   action potential and, 44–45
   resting potential and, 44
Neurobiological approach (to psychology),
   15, 35–75
Neurogenesis, 70
Neuroleptic malignant syndrome, 522
Neuroleptics, *521–522*
Neurons, structure and function of, 40–48,
   70, 82–96
   in children, 70
   long-term changes in, 47

photoreceptor, 82–96
   structure of, 42–43
   transmissions between, 43–45
Neuropeptides, *49*, 51–52, 293, 456
Neuropsychological and psychobiological
   psychologists, 6
Neurotransmitters, *44*–53, 155, 173–178,
   483, 485, 501, 522–524
   drugs' effect on, 48–49, 173–178
   nature and function of, 44–53
   mental disorder and, 483, 485, 501,
      522–524
      anxiety and, 483, 524
      depression and, 522–523
   synaptic transmissions and, 45–48
New York Longitudinal Study, 350
Newborn, *see* Neonate
Nicotine dependence, 452
Night vision, 85, 88, 111–112
Nightmare, 153, 179–180
Nodes (memory), 236–237, 239–240,
   243–244
Nondirective therapy, 529–532
Nonexperimental research methods, 24,
   26–29
   case studies, 26–27
   correlational, 24
   naturalistic observations, 26–27
   surveys, 26–29
   testing, 29
Nonhomeostatic mechanisms, 296–297
Nonparental care, 355–357
Noradrenaline, *54*, *see also*, Norepinephrine
NREM sleep, *153–155*
Norepinephrine, 446, 464, 522
Nucleus of neuron, 42–43
Nurture, *see* Nature-nurture questions
Nuremburg trials, 440, 556

Obedience, 556–561, 587
   Milgram's experiment, 556–559
   variables influencing, 557–559, 587
Obesity, 296–297
Object permanence, 358–359, 370–371
Observer bias, *20*–22
Obsession, 483–484
Obsessive-compulsive disorder (OCD), 478,
   483–486, 512
   biology of, 485,
Occipital lobes of cerebral cortex, *61*, 63,
   66, 69, 93, 97, 117, 143
   vision and, 63, 69, 93, 97, 117, 143
Ocular dominance columns, 97
Oedipus complex, 422, 598
Off-line time, *166*
Olfactory bulb, 59
Olfactory epithelium, 105–106
One Flew Over the Cuckoo's Nest, 508, 529
One-word stage (language acquisition),
   276–277
Operant behavioral therapy, 211, 218
Operant conditioning, *198*–208, 218
Operants, *198–199*
Operational definition, 18–*19*

Opiate, 51–52, 176–177
Opponent-process theory of color vision
   (Hering), 92
Opponent-process theory of motivation,
   306–307, 308–310
   critical decay duration of, 309–310
   emotional contrast in, 307–309, 312–313
Optic nerve, *81*–84, 95
Organic mental disorders, 478–479
Organ of Corti (ear), 100–*101*
Organizational behavior, 627–631
   conflict resolution, 628–629
   personnel selection, 629–631
   supervisors and, 627–628
Orgasm, *621*
Orthodox sleep, *see* NREM sleep
Osmosis, *294*
Out-group, 575–576
Overlap (depth cue), *134*, 136–137

Pain-elicited aggression, 322–323
Panic attack, 482–483
   caffeine and, 483
   sodium lactate and, 483
Panic disorder, 478, 482–483
Pain, 51–52, 75, 108, 323
Paradoxical sleep, *153*
Parallel processing (computers), 259–260
Paranoia, 503–504
Paranoid disorders, *see* delusional (paranoid)
   disorders
Paranoid schizophrenia, 478, 499
Parasympathetic nervous system, 39–40,
   175, 317
   emotional arousal and, 39–40, 317
Parietal lobes of cerebral cortex, *61*, 63,
   107, 263
Parkinson's disease, 49–51, 177
   designer drugs and, 177
   transplanting brain cells for, 50–51
Parvo-interblob Pathway, *117*, 119–120
Passionate love, *615–616*
PCP, *see* Phencyclidine hydrochloride
Peak performance, 637–639, 651
   techniques for achieving, 637–639
Peers, 360–*361*, 362, 364–366, 373
   during adolescence, 373
   during early childhood, 360–362
   during middle childhood, 364–366
Perception, 59, 114–*116*, 117–147,
   263–264, 496–497
   affordances and, 122–123
   attention and, 59, 263–264
   brain pathways of, 117, 119
   constancies of, 129–132
   definition of, 116
   depth, 132–139, 142
   extrasensory, 110–111
   form, 119–123
   Gestalt principles of, 120–121
   of illusions, 127–129
   invariants, 125–126, 134, 142
   motion, 142–143
   pitch, 144

schizophrenia, distortions owing to, 496–497
shape, 119–123
size, 114–115, 130
theories of, 124–126
Perceptual constancies, 115–116, 129–132
Ames room and, 131–132
brightness constancy, 131–132
shape constancy, 130–131
size constancy, 115–116, 130
Peripheral nervous system, 38–40
autonomic division of, 39–40
somatic division of, 38–40
Peripheral route processing, 582
Peripheral vision, 143
Person-situation debate, 437, 587–588
Personality, 360, 415–417, 418–440, 459–460, 577, 637
assessment of, 429–440
behavioral, 438–439
humanistic, 439–440
psychoanalytic, 437–439
trait, 430, 432–437
disease-prone, 459–460
prejudice and, 577
theories of, 417–429
Allport's, 419–420
behavioral, 425–427, 430
Cattell's, 420–422
comparing, 430
future, 431–432
Hippocrates, 417–418
humanistic, 428–430
Jung's, 425
psychoanalytic, 422–425, 430
Sheldon's, 418–419
social learning, 427–428
trait, 415–416, 419–422, 427–428, 430
type, categorizing individuals by, 417–418, 430, 459–460
type A, 459–460
type B, 459–460
Personality disorders, 504–506
types of, 505
Personnel, 629–635
classification and selection, 629–631
and productivity, 634–635
absenteeism, 632
job satisfaction, 631–633
turnover, 632, 634–635
testing, 629–631
Persuasive communication, 580–583
PET (position emission tomography) scan, 63–64, 65–66, 483, 501
Phencyclidine hydrochloride (PCP), 177–178
Phenothiazines, 521
Pheromones, 105–106, 295, 298
Phi phenomenon, 13, 120, 122–123, 144
Philosophy, 7–8
Phobia, 195, 211, 478–482, 536–537, 543–545

treatment of, 211, 481–482, 536–537, 543–545
Phonemes, 275–276
Photons, 85
Photoreceptor cells (eye), 82–96
Phototropism, 640
Phrenology, 387
Physical addiction, 175
Physiology, 7–8, 636–638, 645
of athlete, 636–638
consumer psychology and, 645
Pineal gland, 53, 160
Pinna, 100
Pitch, 98–99, 144
perception of, 144
Pituitary gland, 53–54, 454–455, 594
Place learning, 213–214, 215
Place theory of hearing, 101
Placebo, 52
Placebo reactors, 52
Plasticity (brain), 70
Play, 362
Pleasure center in brain, 36–37, 47, 52, 175, 177
Pleasure principle, 422
Pneumoencephalography, 501
Polarization effect, 573–574, 587
Polarization, neural, 44–45
Polygraph, 317–319, 336
concealed information test and, 319
Pons, 59, 153, 165
Proactive interference (memory), 238–239
Positive fixation, 424
Positive reinforcement, 202–204, 211
Postsynaptic surface, 45–47
Post-traumatic stress disorder, 453
Precognition, 110
Predictive validity, 388–389, 434–436, 437
Prejudice, 192–193, 575–578
overcoming, 577–578
personality and, 577
Premack principle, 208
Preoperational stage (cognitive development), 359–360, 372
Preparedness, see canalization
Presynaptic surface, 45–47
Primary colors, 89
Primary emotions, 333–335
Primary prevention, 446–447
Primary reinforcer, 205
Primary sexual characteristics, 593
Priming (memory), 229
Principles of Psychology (James), 10
Privileged site, 50–51
Probabilistic epigenesis, 371
Problem solving, 266–272
algorithms and, 264–265
cheap-necklace problem, 267–268
creative, 267, 272
heuristics and, 264–266, 285–286
incubation effect in, 268
impediments to, 268–272
routine, 267, 272

Procedural memory, 227–228, 273
Progressive relaxation, 466–467
Project EDGE, 408
Project Head Start, 400
Project Sea Hunt, 185–186
Projection, 423, 465
Projective tests, 437–438, 440
Rorschach ink blot test, 437, 440
Thematic apperception test (TAT), 301, 437
Propositions, 236–238, 243–244
Propositional network theory of memory, 236–238, 243–244, 490–491
links in, 236–237, 491
nodes in, 236–237, 239–240, 243–244, 491
multiple personality and, 490–491
propositions in, 236–238, 243–244
Prospective research, 459
Prosopagnosia, 69
Protoconcept, 276–277
Proxemics, 643
Prozac, 522–523
Pseudopatients (Rosenhan's study), 506–507
Psychiatrists, 6
Psychoactive drugs, 48, 173–178
depressants, effect as, 175–177
hallucinogens, effect as, 48, 177–178
stimulants, effect as, 173–175
Psychoanalysis, 11–12, 422–425, 481, 530–531, 584, 598
cognitive dissonance theory and, 584
gender acquisition and, 598, 607
history of, 11–12, 422–425
therapy, 481, 530–531
Psychoanalyst, 343, 531
Psychoanalytic theory of personality, 11–12, 418, 422–425
Adler's, 425
Freud's, 11–12, 422–424
instinctive drives, 423
Oedipus complex, 422
psychosexual stages of development, 424
three-part personality, 422–423
influence of, 425
Jung's, 418, 425
Psychodrama, 535
Psychoevolutionary synthesis of emotion (Plutchik), 332–335
Psychogenic amnesia, 242, 249–250, 478, 488
Psychogenic fugue, 478, 488
Psychokinesis, 110
Psycholinguists, 278–280
Psychological addiction, 175, 309–310
Psychologists (general types and training), 5–6
clinical, 5–7,
cognitive, 7,
counseling, 7
developmental, 7
educational, 7

experimental, 6
industrial/organizational, 7, 11
neuropsychological and psychobiological, 6
social, 7
training of, 5–6
where they work, 6
Psychology (general overview), 3–16
  definition of, 3–5,
  emergence of scientific, 16
  history of, 7–16
  research methods in, 16–29
  specializations in, 5–7
Psychology as the Behaviorist Views It (Watson), 150
The Psychology of Sex Differences (Maccoby and Jacklin), 601
Psychoneuroimmunology, 5, 457
Psychopathia Sexualis (Krafft-Ebing), 617
Psychopathology, 471–512
  assessment of, 506–511
  models of, 474–476, 484, 486
Psychopharmacological therapy, 467, 492, 520–524
  anti-anxiety agents, 523–524
  antidepressants, 522–523
  antimanic agents, 492, 523
  antipsychotic agents, 521–522
Psychosexual stages of development (Freud), 424
Psychosis, 478, 491–504
Psychosocial stages of development (Erikson), 343–344, 373
Psychosurgery, 525, 527–529
  effectiveness of, 528–529
  frontal lobotomy, 525, 527–528
  modern, 528–529
Psychotherapy, 11–12, 211, 218, 450–452, 515–516, 530–545
  behavior therapy, 211, 218, 530, 535–540, 543–545
    aversive conditioning, 218, 536–537
    classical conditioning, 536
    operant, 211, 218, 537–539, 543–545
    systematic desensitization, 211, 536–537, 543–545
  brief individual psychotherapies, 544
  chemical dependence and, 451–452
  cognitive behavior and modification, 539–540
  effectiveness of, 542–544
  family therapy, 535
  Gestalt therapy, 530, 534, 543
  group therapy, 534–535
    encounter groups, 535
    psychodrama, 535
    sensitivity training, 535
    transactional analysis, 530, 535, 543
  humanistic-existential therapy, 531–532
    client-centered, 530–532, 543
    existential, 532
  hypnotherapy, 540–541
  psychoanalysis, 11–12, 530–531, 543

rational-emotive, 530, 532–533, 543
sex therapy, 621
Puberty, 368–369
Public law 94–142, 407–408
Public law 99–457, 408
Punishment, 203–205, 218, *see also*, Aversive conditioning
Pupil, *81*
Puzzle box (Thorndike), 199

Q sorting, *439*
Quadruplets (identical schizophrenic), 500

Race, and IQ, 396–399
Randomized response technique, 28–29
Rapid eye movement (REM) sleep, *152–155*, 158, 165–166, 180
  NREM sleep, 153–155
  orthodox sleep, 153–155
  REM rebound, 153
Raspberry (sound), 275
Rational emotive therapy, 530, 532–533, 543
Rationalization, 423, *465*
Raven Progressive Matrices Test, 399–400
Reaction formation, 423, *465*
Reaction time, 9
Ready rooms, 111–112
Reality principle, 422
Rebound anxiety, 524
Receptive field, 95–96, 98, 107, 264
  in attention, 264
  in touch, 107
  in vision, 95–96, 98
Reconstruction (memory), *241*
Reference groups, 554–555
Reflex arc, 38–39
Rehearsal (memory), 229–230
Reinforcement (in classical conditioning), *189*, 192
Reinforcement (in operant conditioning), *199–212*, 538
  continuous, 205–206
  intermittent schedule of, 205–207, 538
  negative, 202–204
  positive, 202–204, 211, 538
  primary and secondary, 205
  schedules of, 205–207, 538
Reinforcement theory of liking, *610*
Relative motion (depth cue), *134–136*
Relative size (depth cue), *134*, 136–137
Reliability, 19, *437*
  interobserver, 19
  personality assessment and, 437
REM rebound, *153*
REM sleep, 152–155, 158, 165–166, 180
  atonia during, 153
  characteristics of, 152–155
  deprivation of and endogenous depression, 155
  lucid dreaming and, 180
Renin (hormone), 455

Replication of experiment, 22
Repression, 242, 249–250
Reptilian brain, 58
Research, psychological, 16–32
  dimensions of, 17
  ethical guidelines for, 25–26
  expansion of, 22
  limits of psychological, 30–31
  methods, 16–29
    experimental, 16–24
    nonexperimental, 24–29
Residual schizophrenia, 478, 499
Resistance stage (in stress), *454–455*
Resistance (in psychoanalysis), 530
Response, 189–194, 197, 300
  conditioned, 189–194, 197, 300
  unconditioned, 189–194, 197, 300
Resting potential of neuron, *44*
Reticular activating system, 59, 165
Retina, 80–96
  fovea of, 82–83, 87, 143
  layers of, 81–82
    amacrine cells, 82–83, 94
    bipolar cells, 82, 94
    horizontal cells, 82, 92, 94
    ganglion cells, 81–82, 92, 94–96, 117
    rods and cones, 82, 85, 87–96
  projection onto the, 80
Retinal disparity (depth cue), *138–139*
  3-D movies and, 139
Retrieve (memory), *231*
Retrieval cue (memory), 240–241
Retroactive interference (memory), 239
Retrograde amnesia, 221–222, 234, 242, 249–250
Reversible figures, *119–120*
Rhesus monkeys, 289–290, 305, 352–353
  attachment studies, 352–353
  and motivation, 289–290, 305
Risk assessment, 446–450
Rods and cones (eye), 82, 85, 87–96
  sensitivity of rods in cold-blooded creatures, 85
Rogers' self theory of personality, 429
Role confusion, 373
Rorschach ink blot test, 437, 440
Rotary-drum room, 143
Routine problem solving, 267, 272

Sample, *18*
SAT, *see* Scholastic Aptitude Test
Saturation, 85
Schachter's cognitive theory of emotion, 325–328
  compared to Plutchik's, 335
Schedule-induced polydipsia (SIP), 294–295
Schedules of reinforcement, 205–207, 538
  fixed interval, 207
  fixed ratio, 207
  variable interval, 207, 538
  variable ratio, 207

Schizophrenia, 48, 471–472, 478, 495–502, 509, 511, 524–525
  cerebral ventricles, enlarged, 501–502
  hypofrontality and, 501
  positive and negative symptoms of, 501
  prevalence, 477
Schizophrenic disorders, 471–472, 478, 495–502
  biochemical factors in, 500–501
  catatonic, 478, 499
  causes of, 497–498, 500–502
  disorganized, 478, 499
  dopamine hypothesis, 501
  environmental factors in, 497, 498, 500
  genetic factors in, 498, 500, 502
  infection and, 497, 502
  paranoid, 478, 499
  prediction of occurrence, 471–472
  residual, 478, 499
  structural and anatomical factors in, 501–502
  undifferentiated, 478, 499
Scholastic Aptitude Test, 601
Scientific method, 16
Scientific psychology, 16
Sclera, 81
Scotophobin, 223–224
Script, 241, 430
In Search of the Engram (Lashley), 223
Seasonal affective disorder, 494
Secondary reinforcer, 205
Secondary sexual characteristics, 368–369, 593
Secondary traits, 419
Secure attachment, 353, 355
Self-actualization, 14, 301, 424, 429, 531
  motivation to reach, 14, 301, 429
Self-awareness, 359, 361, 579–580
Self-efficacy as motivator, perceived, 304–305
Self-esteem, 583
Self-hypnosis, 168, 530
Self-interest, failure to demonstrate, 310–312
Self-serving bias, 586
Self, theory of, 428–429
Semantic memory, 228
Semantics, 278–280, 283
  physiology of, 283
  structure of, 278–280
Semicircular canals (ear), 109, 143
Sensation, 77–79–112
Senses, 80–112
  hearing, 98–104, 144
  kinesthetic, 108–109
  smell, 105–106
  taste, 104–105
  touch, 106–108, 144
  vestibular, 108–109
  vision, 80–98
Sensitivity training, 535
Sensitization, 188
Sensorimotor stage (cognitive development), 358–359, 372

Sensory isolation, 299
Sensory memory, 229
Sensory thresholds, 79–80
  absolute threshold, 79
  difference threshold, 79
  Weber's Law and, 80
Serendipitous research, 17
Serial position effect (memory), 230
Serotonin, 464, 485, 522–523
  aggression and, 464
  depression and, 522–523
  obsessive-compulsive disorder and, 485
  suicide and, 464
Set point (body weight), 292, 296
Sex, biological motivation for, 295, 297–298, 379
Sex differences, in behavior, 600–604
Sex drives, 295, 297–298, 423
  hormones and, 295, 455
  menstrual cycle and, 297–298, 455
  pheromones and, 295, 298
Sex-linked disorders, 90
  color blindness, 90
Sex role, see Gender role
Sex therapy, 621
Sexual Behavior in the Human Female (Kinsey), 620
Sexual Behavior in the Human Male (Kinsey), 620
Sexual communication, smell in, 105–106
Sexual myths, 379, 617, 621–622
Sexual orientations, 596, 604–607
  prenatal development and, 605–606
Sexual reassignment, 606
Sexual research, history of, 600–604, 617, 619–622
  early, 617, 619–622
  Ellis, 621–622
  Freud, 619
  Kinsey, 620
  Krafft-Ebing, 617
  Masters and Johnson, 621
  modern, 620–621
Sexual response (human), 621
  excitement phase, 621
  orgasmic phase, 621
  plateau phase, 621
  refractory period, 621
  resolution phase, 621
Sexually transmitted disease, 618–619
Shadowing (depth cue), 134
Shape constancy, 130–131
Shape perception, 119–123
Shaping, 200–201
Sheldon's theory of personality types, 418–419
Shock therapy, 515–516, 525, see also, Electroconvulsive therapy (ECT)
Short-term memory, 229–232
  chunking and, 231–232
  displacement in, 229–231
  rehearsal and, 229–230
Sibling rivalry, 361
Sign language, 280–281, 283–284

apes and, 280, 283–284
Similarity, Gestalt principle of, 120–121
Simple cells, 96
Simple phobia, 478–479–482
Simplicity, Gestalt principle of, 120–121
Single-subject experiment, 17, 23–24
SIP, see Schedule-induced polydipsia
Situational-environmental hypothesis, 575
Sixteen Personality Factor Test (Cattell's 16-PF), 420–421
Size constancy, 130
SLA, see Symbionese Liberation Army
Sleep, 59, 151–166
  abnormalities and pathology, 160, 163–165
  apnea, 164–165
  biochemical basis of, 156
  cycle, 152
  deprivation, 155, 158–159
  dreaming during, 153, 165–166, 179–180
  duration, 155
  factor S, 156
  insomnia, 159, 163
  NREM, 153–155
  oversleeping, 155
  paradoxical, 153
  patterns, 151–155
  promoting substance, 156–157
  purposes of, 156–157
  REM, 152–155, 158, 165–166, 180
    deprivation of, 155
  reticular activating system and, 59, 165
  sleeptalking, 153
  sleepwalking, 153
  spindles, 152, 154
  stages of, 152–155
  theories of, 156–157
    adaptive, 156–157
    conserving energy, 156
Sleep spindles (EEG), 152, 154
Sleeptalking, 153
Sleepwalking, 153
Slips of the tongue, 12
Slow-wave sleep, 152, 156, see also, Delta waves
Smell, sense of, 59, 105–106
  brain structures involved in, 59, 106
  lock and key system in, 105
  memory and, 106
Smoking, see nicotine dependence
Snake, jararaca, 108
Social attitudes, 419, 572, 578–588
Social cognition, 578–588
Social comparison, 554
Social learning, 18, 208–212, 427–428, 599–600, 606–607
  gender role acquisition and, 599–600, 606–607
  models and, 208–212
  performance versus acquisition in, 210, 212
  personality and, 427–428
  violence and, 18, 208–209

Social motivation, 301–310
   intrinsic motivation, 289–290, 303, 305–306
   learned helplessness, 302–303
   Maslow's hierarchy of, 301
   need for achievement, 301–302
   self-efficacy, 304–305
   Solomon's opponent-process theory of, 306–310
Social norms, 553
Social psychology, 192–193, 273–273, 419, 551–588
   attitudes, 273–274, 419, 572, 578–588
     as cognitive skill, 273–274
     bogus pipeline, 579
     changing, 274, 580–588
     measuring, 579
     secondary traits, as, 419
     self-awareness and, 579–580
     social, 572, 578–588
     formation of, 578–579
   attribution, 585–588
     informational availability hypothesis, 586
     self-serving bias, 586
     visual perspective hypothesis, 586
   cognitive dissonance, 583–585, 587
   conformity, 551–555, 559–561
   competition and cooperation, 568–571
   groups, influence of, 571–575
     deindividuation and, 571–573
     leadership, 574–575
     polarization, 573–574, 587
   helping, 561–565, 568
     bystander effect, 562–563, 565
     bystander intervention model, 564–565
     diffusion of responsibility, 563
     task load, effect of, 564–565
   prejudice, 192–193, 575–578
     overcoming, 577–578
     personality and, 577
   obedience, 556–561, 587
     Milgram's experiment, 556–559
     variables influencing, 557–559, 587
Social Readjustment Rating Scale, 457–458
Social referencing, 320
Sociobiology, 306–307
Sodium-potassium pumps, 44
Soma of neuron, 42–43
Somatic nervous system, 38–40
Somatic therapy, 467, 520–525, 527–529
   electroconvulsive, 524–525
   psychopharmacological, 520–524
   psychosurgery, 525, 527–529
Somatoform disorders, 478, 486–488
   conversion disorder, 478, 486–487, 511
   hypochondriasis, 478, 487–488
Somatogenic amnesia, 221–222, 234, 242–243
Somatosensory area of brain, 61, 64, 107
Sound, creation of, 98–99
Source traits, 420
Soviet Union (mental illness and), 473
Spaced practice, 247–248

Spacing effect on memory, 247–248
   encoding variability and, 247–248
     massed practice, 248
     spaced practice, 247–248
Spanking and behavior control, 204–205
Species specificity, 217
Speed, see Amphetamines
Spermatorrhea, 617, 619, 621–622
Spermatorrhea rings, 619
Spike in nerve impulse, 44–45
Spinal cord, 38–41
Split brain research, 70–72
"Splitters" (of intelligence), 391
Spontaneous recovery, 205
Spoonerisms, 279
Sports psychology, 635–639, 651
   future directions, 639
   history, 636
   and peak performance, 637–639, 651
   and personality, 636–637
   and physiology, 636–637
S-R psychology, 13
Stability vs. change, in human development, 346–347
Stanford-Binet intelligence test, 388–389, 401
Stanford Hypnotic Susceptibility Scale, Form C, 168
Standardized instrument, 432–433
Stapes (ear), 100
State-dependent learning, 246–248
Statistics, 22, also in Appendix A
STD, see Sexually transmitted disease
Stereocilia, 101–102, 109
Stereotype, 577
Steroids, 54
Stern's formula, for IQ, 387
Stimulants, 173–175
Stimulus, 188–197
   conditioned, 189–197, 300
   unconditioned, 189–197, 300
Stimulus control, 206–207
Stimulus motives, 298–299
Strange situation, 353, 355
Stream of consciousness, 10
Stress, 446, 450–451, 453–457, 468–469
   acute and chronic, 450, 453–454, 468–469
   coping with, 465–469
   definition of, 446
   hassles, 460–461
   illness and, 456–460
   immunosuppression in, 455–457
   management, 465–468
   personality and, 559–560
   reactions to, 445–446, 450–451, 453–457, 468–469
Striving for superiority (Adler), 425
Structuralism, 9–10
Subject bias, 20, 21, 22
Subtractive mixing, 89
Subvocal speech, 256
Success, teaching, 304–305
Suicide, 324, 449, 453, 461–464, 482,

491, 493, 523
   anxiety and, 482
   assisted, 462
   depression and, 324, 491, 493
   guns and, 449
   Prozac and, 523
   right to commit, 462–463
   and serotonin, 464
   Vietnam veterans and, 453
   warning signs of, 463
Sulci, 56
Superchiasmatic nuclei (SCN), 160, 162
Superego, 422–423
Superstitious learning, 203
Surface traits, 420
Surrogate mother (monkeys), 352–353
Survey, 26–29
Sybil (Wilbur), 489
Symbionese Liberation Army (SLA), 587
Sympathetic nervous system, 39–40, 153, 174–175, 317
   during sleep, 153
   emotional arousal and, 39–40, 317
Synapse, 45–48, 173–178, 264
   excitatory, 46
   inhibitory, 46, 264
   long-term changes in, 47
Synaptic knobs, 45–46
Synaptic transmission, 45–48
Syndrome, 479
Syntax, 279–280
Syphilis, 519
Systematic desensitization, 530, 536–537, 543

Tactile sensory replacement (TSR), 118–119
Tardive dyskinesia, 521–522
Task load, 564–565
Taste, sense of, 104–105
   evolution's role in, 105
Taste buds, 104–105
Telegraphic speech, 278
Telepathy, 110
Television, effects on child development, 18–23, 365–367
Television of tomorrow, 140–141
Temperament theories, 350–352
Temporal lobes of cerebral cortex, 61, 63, 66, 143–144
Terman's study, 403, 405–406
Tests, psychological, 29, 168, 301, 351, 388–391, 399–401, 420–421, 430, 432–439, 630
   Bender-Gestalt Visual-Motor Test, 437
   Denver Developmental Screening Test, 351
   Minnesota Clerical Test, 630
   Minnesota Multiphasic Personality Inventory (MMPI), 430, 432–436
   Minnesota Multiphasic Personality Inventory, revised (MMPI-2), 435–436
   Q sort, 439

Raven Progressive Matrices Test, 399–400
Rorschach ink blot test, 437, 440
Sixteen Personality Factor Test (Cattell's 16-PF), 420–421
Stanford-Binet intelligence test, 388–389, 401
Stanford Hypnotic Susceptibility Scale, Form C, 168
Thematic Apperception Test, 301, 437
Wechsler Adult Intelligence Scale, Revised (WAIS-R), 388–391, 437
Testosterone, 164, 295, 595–597, 602–603
  genital development and, 595–597
Tetrahydrocannabinol (THC), 178
Thalamus, 59, 159, 325
Thematic Apperception Test, 301, 437
Theoretical research, 17
Therapy, 467, 515–545
  Greek and Roman eras, 517
  Middle Ages, 517
  psychotherapy, 467, 529–545
  recipes for, 541
  Renaissance, 517–518
  Renaissance, after, 518–520
  somatic, 467, 520–525, 527–529
Thinking, see cognition
Thirst, biological motivation of, 293–295
  interaction with hunger, 294–295
Thought meter, 8–9
Thought, speed of, 9
Three-bears rule (language), 276–277
Three color theory (Young-Helmholtz), 89–90, 92
Three-D movies, 139
Three Faces of Eve, 489
Three-Mile Island, 161, 445–446
Three-part personality (Freud), 422–423
Thymus gland, 594
Tip of the tongue phenomenon, 239–240
Time-motion studies, 11
Time out (from positive reinforcement), 537
Toilet training, 211
Toilet Training in Less Than a Day (Azrin and Foxx), 211
Token economy, 289–290, 305, 538–539
  intrinsic motivation and, 289–290, 305
Tolerance (drug), 174, 193–194
Touch, 106–108, 144
  perception of, 144
  sense of, 106–108

Tracheotomy, 165
Trait theories of personality, 415–416, 418–422, 427–428, 430
  Allport's, 419–420
    cardinal, 419
    central, 419
    secondary, 419
  Cattell's, 420–422
    source, 420
    surface, 420
Tranquilizers, 176
Transactional analysis, 530, 535, 543
Transference, 530
Transsexualism, 606
Treasure of the Sierra Madre, 503
Treatments of Psychiatric Disorders (American Psychiatric Association), 541
Trephining, 516–517
Triarchic theory (of intelligence, Sternberg), 392–393
Trichotillomania (compulsive hair-pulling), 512
Trichromats, 90
Tricyclics, 522–523
Twin design, 393–395, 498, 500–502
Two-word stage (language acquisition), 277
Tympanic membrane, 100
Type A personality, 459–460
Type B personality, 459–460

Unconditioned response, 189–194, 197, 300
Unconditioned stimulus, 189–197, 300
Unconscious mind, 11–12, 74, 423, 425, 530–531
Undifferentiated schizophrenia, 478, 499
Validity of tests, 29, 388–389, 434–437, 629–631
  intelligence testing and, 388–389
  personality assessment and, 434–437
  personnel selection and, 629–631
Valium, 461
Variables, 20, 24
  dependent, 20
  independent, 20
  correlation between, 24
Vasopressin (memory), 234–235
Ventricles, see Cerebral ventricles
Verbal information, see Declarative knowledge

Vestibular sacs (ear), 109
Vestibular sense, 109
Violence, see Aggression
Virtual environments, 140–141
Visible spectrum, 85–86
Vision, 59, 80–98, 138–139
  peripheral, 59, 143
  aftereffects, 95
  afterimages, 93
  binocular, 138–139
  color, 88–94
  dark adaptation, 88
  light adaptation, 88
  for sightless persons, 103–104, 118
Visual cliff, 142
Visual cortex (brain), 63, 95–98
  aftereffects and processing in the, 95
Visual perspective hypothesis, 586
Volley theory of hearing, 101

Water-jug problems, see Luchin's water-jug problems
Wavelength, 85–86, 99
  of light, 85–86
  of sound, 99
Weber's law, 80
Wechsler Adult Intelligence Scale, Revised (WAIS-R), 388–391, 437
Wernicke's aphasia, 282–283
Wernicke's area, 281–283
  aphasia and, 282–283
  language and, 282
Whirling Dervish, 172
Whorf hypothesis, see Linguistic relativity
Wilson's disease, 510–511
Working at home, 633–634
Working memory, see Short-term memory
Wugs (language acquisition), 278

Xanax, 461

Yerkes-Dodson law, 299
Yogi, 172
Yogic therapy, 467
Young-Helmholtz theory of color vision, 89–90, 92
Ypsilanti Project, 400–401

Zulu tribe, 128–129

Photo Credits

3 Helen Fraukenthaler, *Tutti Fruitti*, Albright-Knox Art Gallery, Buffalo, New York, Gift of Seymour H. Knox, 1976; 8 Brown Brothers; 9 Brown Brothers; 10 Brown Brothers; 12 Brown Brothers; 14 © Ted Polumbaum; 21 © 1979 Joel Gordon; 29 Sepp Seitz, Woodfin Camp and Associates; 35 Roberto Echuarren Matta, *Inscape* 1939, oil on canvas, 28½ × 36″, Collection of Gordon Onslow Ford, San Francisco Museum of Art; 52 Paul Biddle & Tim Mal Yon/Science Photo Library; 55 Courtesy Carolina Biological Supply Company; 56 Lester V. Bergman and Associates; 60 Susan McCartney, Photo Researchers; 65 Courtesy of M.E. Phelps and J.C. Mazziotta, UCLA School of Medicine; 66 and 67 Dr. Dean F. Wong, Division of Nuclear Medicine, The Johns Hopkins Medical Institutions; 77 Joan Mitchell, *Rosebud*, Albright-Knox Art Gallery, Buffalo, New York, Gift of Mr. and Mrs. Armand J. Castellani, 1982; 84 From "The Functional Architecture of the Retina," by Richard H. Masland, *Scientific American*, December, 1986; 88 Harvey Eisner, Taurus; 89 Fritz Goro, Life Magazine; 94 Photo by author; 97 (left) Simon LeVay, Harvard Medical School; 97 (right) Courtesy of Michael Stryker and Kenneth Miller; 104 Frank Siteman, Stock, Boston; 107 Christopher Johnson, Stock Boston; 108 Paolo Fridman, Sygma; 109 Ellis Herwig, Stock, Boston; 112 Peter Menzel, Stock, Boston, 118 Black Star; 115 Al Held, *Pietro's Piazza*, Albright-Knox Art Gallery, Buffalo, New York, Gift of Seymour H. Knox, 1982; 120 Photography by Kaiser Porcelain Limited; 123 Bob Evans, Peter Arnold; 125 Nicholas Foster, The Image Bank; 126 Art Wolfe, The Image Bank; 129 Robert Capato, Stock, Boston; 132 (top) © Baron Wolman; 132 (bottom) R. Rowan, Photo Researchers; 135 The Museum of Modern Art Film Stills Archive; 137 Kazuhiko More, Taurus; 139 Shigeo Kogure/Time Magazine; 140 NASA Photo, Ames Research Center; 142 Martin Rogers, Stock, Boston; 149 Clyfford Still, *1957-D No. 1*, Albright-Knox Art Gallary, Buffalo, New York, Gift of Seymour H. Knox, 1959; 149 and 150 Tom Ives/Time Magazine; 153 Monte S. Buscsbaum, M.D., College of Medicine, University of California, Irvine, 154 Photos by author; 157 Culver Pictures; 161 Blair Seitz, Photo Researchers; 169 Ken Robert Buck, Stock, Boston; 172 Joel Gordon; 174 Courtesy of Peter Wih, M.D.; 185 Michael Goldenberg, Le Grotte Vecchie I, Albright-Knox Art Gallery, Buffalo, New York, George B. & Jenny R. Mathews Fund, 1981; 186 U.S. Navy Photos; 187 Christopher S. Johnson, Stock, Boston: 189 The Bettmann Archive; 192 AP/Wide World; 194 Courtesy of Dr. Ben Harris, from J.B. Watson's *Experimental Investigation of Babies*; 198 Brown Brothers; 200 Michael Murphy, Photo Researchers; 203 Baron Wolman, Woodfin Camp & Associates; 206 Leif Skoogfors, Woodfin Camp & Associates; 209 Courtesy of Albert Bandura, Standford University; 210 John Renning, Stock, Boston; 215 Hank Morgan, Photo Researchers; 221 Morris Louis, *No. 1*, Albright-Knox Art Gallery, Buffalo, New York, Gift of the Martha Jackson Collection, 1974; 238 Bettmann Archive; 246 (left) Chip Henderson, Woodfin Camp & Associates; 246 (right) Joseph Nettis, Photo Researchers; 248 Culver Pictures; 253 Hans Hofmann, *Summer Night's Dream*, Albright-Knox Art Gallery, Buffalo, New York, Gift of Seymour H. Knox, 1978; 254 from *The Mentality of Apes* by Wolfgang Kohler; 258 Ron James; 261 Junebug Clark, Photo Researchers; 265 Richard Hutchings, Photo Researchers; 272 David R. Frazier, Photo Researchers; 276 © Joel Gordon; 280 Roger Fouts, Central Washington University; 285 Wide World; 289 Wassily Kandinsky, *Fragment 2 for Composition VII*, Albright-Knox Art Gallery, Buffalo, New York, Room of Contemporary Art Fund, 1947; 292 Courtesy Dr. Neal E. Miller; 294 (left) Ira Kirschenbaum, Stock, Boston; 294 (right) Mike Mazzaschi, Stock, Boston; 300 Peter Menzel, Stock, Boston, 302 Harvard University News Office; 303 Billy E. Barnes, Stock, Boston; 306 (top) University of Wisconsin Primate Laboratory; 306 (bottom) Ellis Herwig, Stock, Boston; 310 Paolo Koch, Photo Researchers; 315 Willem de Kooning, *Gotham News*, Albright-Knox Art Gallery, Buffalo, New York, Gift of Seymour H. Knox; 318 Bruce Roberts, Photo Researchers; 320 Michal Heron, Woodfin Camp & Associates; 322 Mary Ellen Mark, Archive Pictures; 326 Mary Ellen Mark, Archive Pictures; 327 Courtesy of the Capilano Suspension Bridge; 329 Reproduced by special permission from *Pictures of Facial Affect* by Dr. Wallace Friesen and Dr. Paul Ekman, Copyright 1976, published by Consulting Psychologists Press, Inc., Palo Alto, CA 94306; 332 (top left) Ylla, Photo Researchers; 332 (top right) Barbara Rios, Photo Researchers; 332 (bottom left) Peter Menzel, Stock, Boston; 332 (bottom right) Ellis Herwig, Stock, Boston; 341 Frank Stella, Lac Laronge III, Albright-Knox Art Gallery, Buffalo, New York, Gift of Seymour H. Knox, 1970; 342 Photo courtesy of Anthony DeCasper, Photographer Walter Salinger; 343 UPI; 348 Herb Snitzer, Stock, Boston; 352 (top) Jon Feingersh, Stock, Boston; 352 (bottom) University of Wisconsin Primate Laboratory; 358 Wide World; 359 Doug Goodman, Monkmeyer Press; 360 Owen Franken, Stock, Boston; 362 Mike Mazzaschi, Stock, Boston; 364 Donald Dietz, Stock, Boston; 366 Cary Wolinsky, Stock, Boston; 371 J. Berndt, Stock, Boston; 375 Herb Snitzer, Stock, Boston; 379 Steve Hansen, Stock, Boston; 385 Richard Diebenkorn, *Berkley #54*, Albright-Knox Art Gallery, Buffalo, New York, Gift of the Martha Jackson Collection, 1977; 395 Jean Boughton, Stock, Boston; 397 National Archives, Photo Researchers; 401 Daemmrich, Stock, Boston; 403 Courtesy Marc Bornstein, New York University; 405 News and Publications Service, Stanford University; 409 Tom Bross, Stock, Boston; 415 Kupka, *Disks of Newton*, Georges Pompidau National Art and Culture Center; 419 UPI; 424 Wide World; 427 Culver Pictures; 429 Bettmann Archive; 445 Philip Guston, Voyage, Albright-Knox Art Gallery, Buffalo, New York, Gift of Seymour H. Knox, 1957; 449 Barbara Alper, Stock, Boston; 450 Collier, Stock, Boston; 454

UPI; **456** Laima Druskis, Stock, Boston; **462** Amy E. Powers, Gamma-Liaison; **465** Owen Franken, Stock, Boston; **471** Alberto Magnelli, *Peinture No. 0528*, Albright-Knox Art Gallery, Buffalo, New York, by exchange, Room of Contemporary Art Fund, 1982; **483** Courtesy of Marcus Raichle, Washington University School of Medicine in St. Louis; **489** Culver Pictures; **493** Mike Mazzaschi, Stock, Boston; **495** Michael Weisbrot, Stock, Boston; **502** Copyright Paul Ekman, 1988; **506** News and Publications Service, Stanford University; **509** Culver Pictures; **515** Frantisek Kupka, *Lines, Planes, Depth*, Albright-Knox Art Gallery, Buffalo, New York, George B. and Jenny R. Mathews Fund, 1977; **516** Bettmann Archive; **518** Bettmann Archive; **524** Will McIntyre, Photo Researchers; **527** Peter Southwick, Stock, Boston; **529** Richard Pasley, Stock Boston; **532** UPI; **534** Catherine Ursillo, Photo Researchers; **538** Courtesy of Albert Bandura, Standard University; **551** Arshile Gorky, *The Liver is the Cock's Comb*, Albright-Knox Art Gallery, Buffalo, New York, Gift of Seymour H. Knox, 1956; **552** Steve Hansen, Stock, Boston; **553** James Holland, Stock, Boston; **555** Paul Mozell, Stock, Boston; **556** UPI; **557** Courtesy of Stanley Milgram; **558** Courtesy of Stanley Milgram; **561** Wide World Photos, Inc.; **562** Jan Lukas Photo Researchers; **565** WJLA TV Washington D.C.; **576** Bob Hammond, Stock, Boston; **580** Arthur Grace, Stock, Boston; **587** D. B. Owen, Black Star; **591** Ron Davis, *Cube and Four Panels*, Albright-Knox Art Gallery, Buffalo, New York, by exchange, National Endowment for the Arts Purchase Grant and Matching Funds, 1976; **599** (top) Jeff Persons, Stock, Boston; **599** (bottom) Bob Daemmrich, Stock, Boston; **605** Lincoln Russell, Stock, Boston; **608** (top left) Stern, Black Star; **608** (top right) Ed Lettau, Photo Researchers; **608** (bottom) Rene Burri, Magnum; **612** Bettmann Archive; **615** Mike Mazzaschi, Stock, Boston; **620** (top) AP/Wide World; **620** (bottom) Robert J. Levin, Black Star; **625** Robert Delaunay, *Sun, Tower, Airplane*, Albright-Knox Art Gallery, Buffalo, New York, A. Conger Goodyear Fund, 1964; **626** Rick Browne Photoreporters; **631** Martin Rogers, Stock, Boston; **638** Bill Gallery, Stock, Boston; **640** Courtesy of Eastman Kodak Company; **650** Donald Dietz, Stock, Boston.

Acknowledgements

Page 5, cartoon. © Jane Zich, 1986. This cartoon was originally published in the January 1986 edition of the APA *Monitor*; page 43, Fig. 2.5. From "The Neuron," by Charles F. Stevens. Copyright © 1979 by Scientific American, Inc. All rights reserved; page 57-58, Figs. 2.11-2.12. From "The Organization of the Brain," by Walle J. H. Nauta and Michael Feirtag. Copyright © 1979 by Scientific American, Inc. All rights reserved; page 62, Fig. 2.13. From "The Brain," by David H. Hubel. Copyright © 1979 by Scientific American, Inc. All rights reserved; page 64, Fig. 2.15. From "Specializations of the Human Brain," by Norman Geschwind. Copyright © 1979 by Scientific American, inc. All rights reserved; page 72, Fig. 2.20. REPRINTED FROM PSYCHOLOGY TODAY MAGAZINE. Copyright © 1985. Reprinted by permission of Psychology Today, Inc. page 83, Fig. 3.4; From "floaters" by Jearl Walker. Copyright © 1982 by Scientific American, Inc. All rights reserved; page 103, Fig. 3.20. George Nicholson © DISCOVER Magazine, December 1980, Family Media, Inc.; page 123, Fig. 4.9. From "Asking the What for Question in Auditory Perception," by A. S. Bregman, 1981, in M. Q. Kubovy & J. Pomeranz (Eds.), *Perceptual Organization*. Copyright 1981 by Lawrence Erlbaum and Associates. Reprinted by permission; page 131, Fig. 4.17. REPRINTED FROM PSYCHOLOGY TODAY MAGAZINE. Copyright © 1983. Reprinted by permission of Psychology Today, Inc.; page 158, Fig. 5.4. From "Physiological Correlates of Prolonged Sleep Deprivation in Rats," by A. Rechtschaffen, M. A. Gilliland, B. M. Bergmann, & J. B. Winter. In *Science*, 1983, 221, pp. 182-184. Copyright 1983 by the American Association for the Advancement of Science; page 162, Fig. 5.6. From WIDE AWAKE AT 3:00 A.M. by Richard M. Coleman. Richard M. Coleman, Ph.D., psychologist, is a former co-director of the Stanford University Sleep Disorders Clinic; serves on the Clinical Faculty of the Stanford University Medical School; and is president of Coleman & Associates (since 1980)—an international corporate work/shirt scheduling firm in Ross, California; page 168, Table 5.2. Copyrighted, Stanford University, 1962, and used by permission; page 199, Fig. 6.8. From "Thorndike and the Problem of Animal Intelligence," by M. E. Bitterman. In *American Psychologist*, 1969, 24, 444-453. Copyright 1969 by the American Psychological Association. Reprinted by permission of the publisher and author; page 199, Fig. 6.9. From "Thorndike and the Problem of Animal Intelligence," by M. E. Bitterman. In *American Psychologist*, 1969, 24, 444-453. Copyright 1969 by the American Psychological Association. Reprinted by permission of the publisher and author; pages 209-210, quotation. Reprinted from 1962 NEBRASKA SYMPOSIUM ON MOTIVATION, by permission of University of Nebraska Press. Copyright © 1962 by the University of Nebraska Press; page 212, cartoon. Drawing by S. Gross. © 1978 The New Yorker Magazine, Inc.; page 216, Fig. 6.13. Used with the permission of Stansbury, Ronsaville, Wood, Inc.; page 224, Fig. 7.2. From "Could a Machine Think?" by Paul M. Churchland and Patricia Smith Churchland. Copyright © 1990 by Scientific American, Inc. All rights reserved; page 230, Fig. 7.5. From "Retention as a Function of the Method of Measurement," by L. Postman & L. Rau. In *University of California Publications in Psychology*, 1957, 8(3). Reprinted by permission of the University of California Press; page 242, Fig. 7.13. From "Long-term Memory for a Common